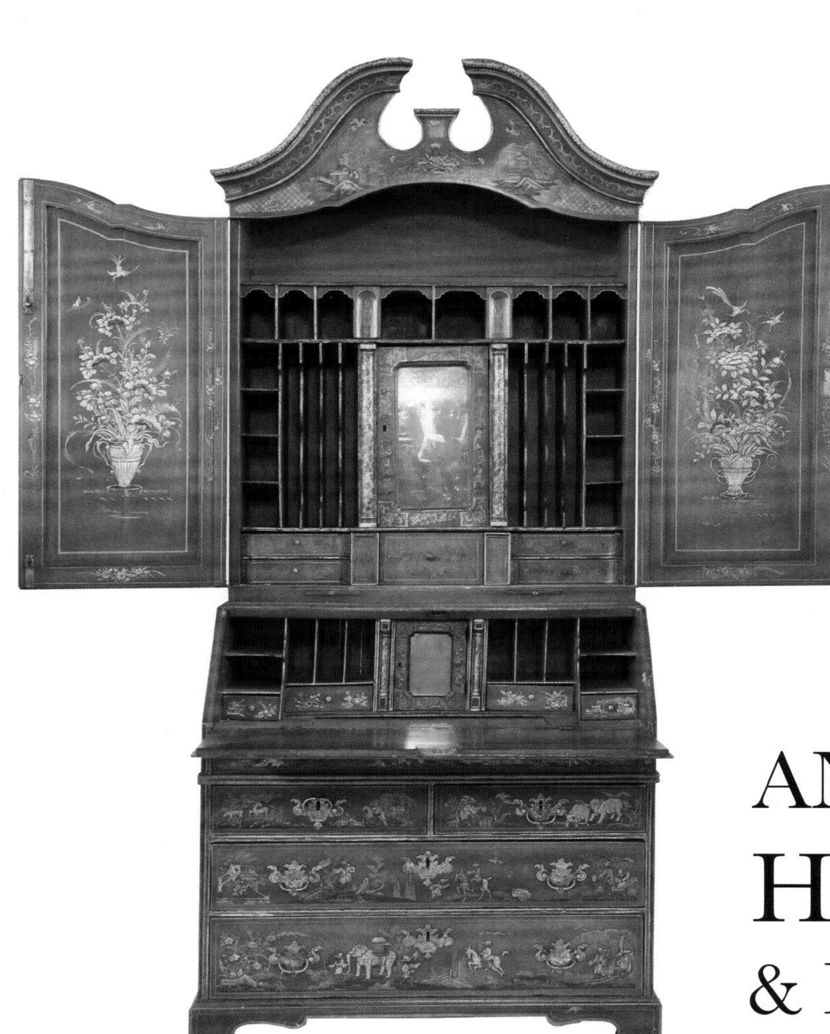

ANTIQUES Handbook & Price Guide 2020~2021

Miller's Antiques Handbook & Price Guide 2020–2021
By Judith Miller

First published in Great Britain in 2019 by Miller's, a division of Mitchell Beazley,
imprints of Octopus Publishing Group Ltd., Carmelite House,
50 Victoria Embankment, London, EC4Y 0DZ
www.octopusbooks.co.uk

An Hachette UK Company
www.hachette.co.uk

Distributed in the US by Hachette Book Group
1290 Avenue of the Americas, 4th and 5th Floors, New York, NY 10104

Distributed in Canada by Canadian Manda Group
664 Annette St., Toronoto, Ontario, Canada, M6S 2C8

ISBN: 978 1 78472 526 6

A CIP record for this book is available from the British Library

Set in Frutiger

Printed and bound in China

1 3 5 7 9 10 8 6 4 2

Publisher Alison Starling
Assistant Editor Katie Lumsden
Proofreader John Wainwright
Advertising Sales Julie Brooke
Indexer Hilary Bird
Art Director Juliette Norsworthy
Designer Ali Scrivens, T J Graphics
Senior Production Manager Peter Hunt

Photographs of Judith Miller page 7, by Chris Terry

Page 1: A George II and later red lacquered and gilt chinoiserie bureau bookcase. 91in (231cm) high £12,000-15,000 SWO
Page 3: A 1930s Lenci figure, 'Nella' by Helen Konig Scavini, date mark 11-XI-33. 9in (23cm) high £5,000-6,000 FLD
Page 4 from left to right: A Chinese Ming-style vase, with star motifs between formal bands. 8¾in (22.5cm) high £23,000-27,000 WW;
A Regency mahogany double-sided stool, in the manner of William Trotter. c1815 51½in (131cm) wide £25,000-30,000 DN;
A Wedgwood Fairyland lustre Malfrey vase and cover, 'Ghostly Wood' pattern. c1926 13in (33cm) high £26,000-30,000 SWO;
A George II Channel Islands silver hot milk jug, by Guillaume Henry, Guernsey. c1727 4½in (11.5cm) high £23,000-28,000 MART;
A Tiffany Studios Favrile ruffled compote, etched '1529-1259M L.C. Tiffany-Favrile'. c1918 6in (15cm) wide £1,500-2,000 DRA;
A Clarice Cliff 'Conical' teapot, 'Blue Autumn' pattern. c1930 5½in (14cm) high £1,400-1,800 FLD;
A George III Blue John campana urn, on a black marble plinth. 8¾in (22.5cm) high £5,000-5,500 WW;
A late 17thC bracket clock, by Thomas Tompion, London, with double-fusee bell-striking movement. c1690 14¼in (36cm) high £250,000-300,000 HAN
Page 7 from left to right: A Meissen teapot and cover, with Böttger lustre glaze, 'M.P.M.' mark. c1722 6½in (16.5cm) wide £18,000-22,000 REEM;
A Chinese Republic Period fan. 20¾in (52.5cm) wide £11,000-15,000 L&T
A late 19thC Black Forest bench, the bears with glass eyes. 31½in (80cm) wide £3,500-4,000 L&T

ANTIQUES Handbook & Price Guide

2020~2021

Judith Miller

MILLER'S

Contents

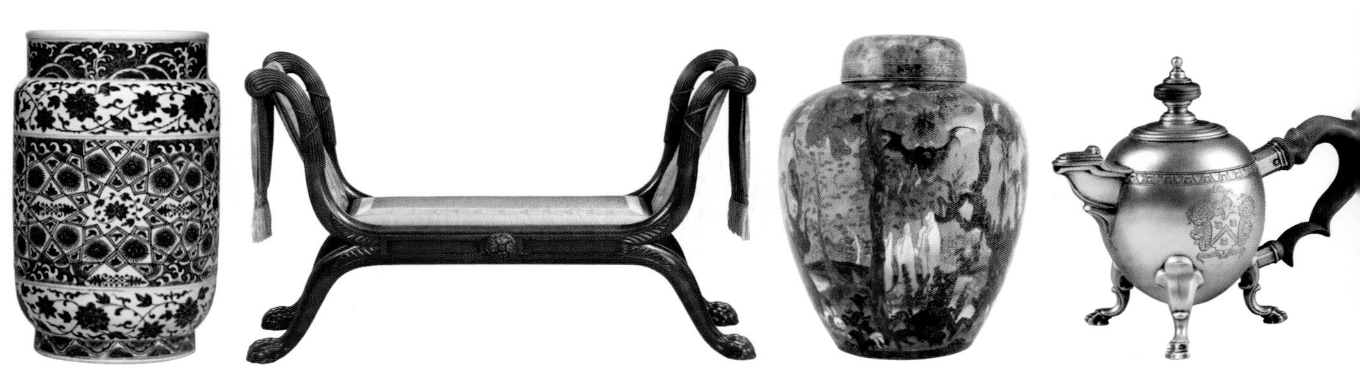

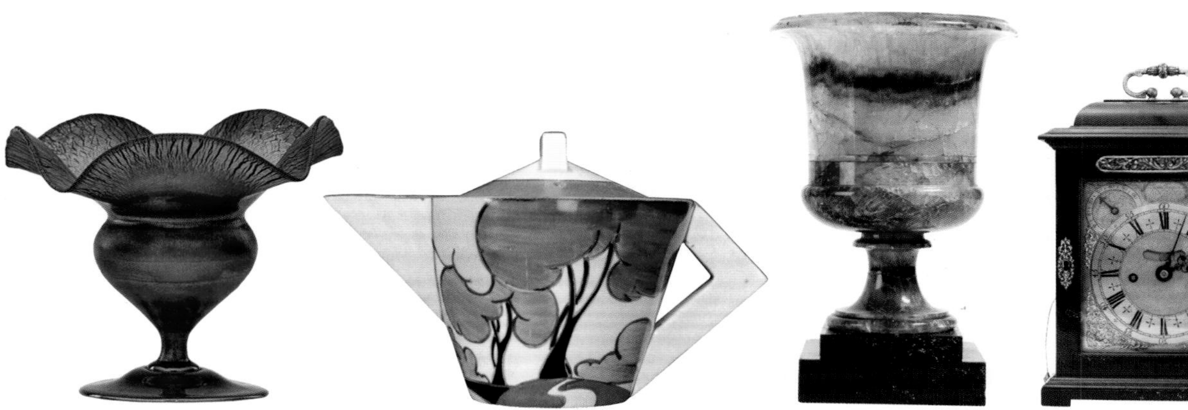

LIST OF CONSULTANTS

At Miller's we are extremely lucky to be able to call on a large number of specialists for advice. My colleagues and friends on the BBC Antiques Roadshow have a wealth of knowledge and their advice on the state of the market is invaluable. It is also important to keep in touch with dealers as they are really at the coalface dealing directly with collectors. Certain parts of the market have been extremely volatile over the past year, so up-to-date information is critical.

ASIAN

John Axford & Jeremy Morgan
Woolley & Wallis
51-61 Castle Street
Salisbury SP1 3SU

Dan Bray
Gorringes
15 North Street
Lewes
East Sussex BN7 2PE

Adrian Rathbone
Hansons
Heage Lane
Derbyshire DE65 6LS

Lee Young
Duke's
Brewery Square
Dorchester DT1 1GA

Ling Zhu
Lyon & Turnbull
33 Broughton Place
Edinburgh EH1 3RR

CERAMICS

John Axford
Woolley & Wallis
51-61 Castle Street
Salisbury SP1 3SU

Ed Crichton
Lacy Scott & Knight
10 Risbygate St
Suffolk IP33 3AA

Fergus Gambon
Bonhams
101 New Bond Street
London W1S 1SR

Nic Saintey
Bearnes Hampton & Littlewood
St Edmund's Court
Okehampton Street
Exeter EX4 1DU

CLOCKS

Paul Archard
Derek Roberts
25 Shipbourne Road
Tonbridge TN10 3DN

DECORATIVE ARTS

Wayne Chapman
Lynways
www.lynways.com

Will Farmer
Fieldings
Mill Race Lane
Stourbridge DY8 1JN

Michael Jeffrey
Woolley & Wallis
51-61 Castle Street
Salisbury, SP1 3SU

John Mackie
Lyon & Turnbull
33 Broughton Place
Edinburgh EH1 3RR

Mike Moir
www.manddmoir.co.uk

Steven Moore
Burleigh Pottery
Middleport Pottery, Port Street,
Burslem ST6 3PE

David Rago
Rago Arts
333 North Main Street,
Lambertville, NJ 08530 USA

FURNITURE

Lennox Cato
1 The Square, Edenbridge
Kent TN8 5BD

Guy Schooling
Sworders
Cambridge Road
Stansted Mountfitchet
Essex CM24 8GE

JEWELLERY

Trevor Kyle
Lyon & Turnbull
33 Broughton Place
Edinburgh EH1 3RR

Gemma Redmond
5 Roby Mill, Wigan,
Skelmersdale WN8 0QF

MODERN DESIGN

John Mackie
Lyon & Turnbull
33 Broughton Place
Edinburgh EH1 3RR

SILVER

Duncan Campbell
Beau Nash
31 Brock Street
Bath BA1 2LN

Alastair Dickenson
90 Jermyn Street
London SW1 6JD

SPORTING

Graham Budd
Graham Budd
PO Box 47519
N14 6XD

TRIBAL

Alex Tweedy
Lyon & Turnbull
33 Broughton Place
Edinburgh EH1 3RR

Waddington's
275 King Street East,
Toronto, Ontario
Canada M5A 1K2

HOW TO USE THIS BOOK

Running head Indicates the sub-category of the main heading.

Page tab This appears on every page and identifies the main category heading as identified in the Contents List on pages 4-5.

Essential reference Gives key facts about the factory, maker or style, along with stylistic identification points, value tips and advice on fakes.

Closer look Does exactly that. We show identifying aspects of a factory or maker, point out rare colours or shapes, and explain why a particular piece is so desirable.

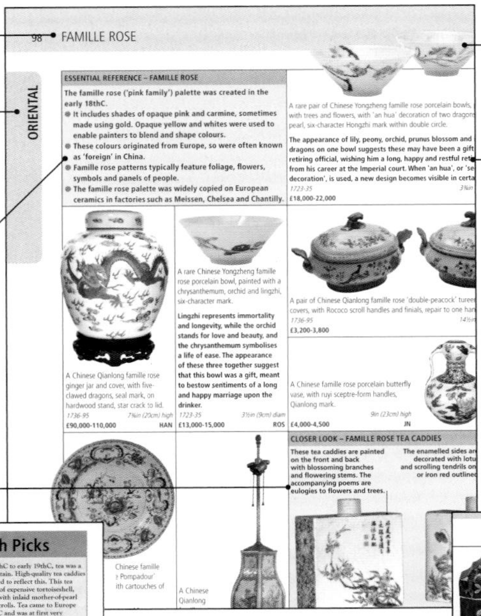

The object The antiques are shown in full colour. This is a vital aid to identification and valuation. With many objects, a slight colour variation can signify a large price differential.

Caption The description of the item illustrated, including when relevant, the period, the maker or factory, medium, the year it was made, dimensions and condition. Many captions have **footnotes** which explain terminology or give identification or valuation information.

The price guide These price ranges give a ball park figure of what you should pay for a similar item. The great joy of antiques is that there is not a recommended retail price. The price ranges in this book are based on actual prices, either what a dealer will take or the full auction price.

Source code Every item has been specially photographed at an auction house, a dealer, an antiques market or a private collection. These are credited by code at the end of the caption, and can be checked against the Key to Illustrations on pages 588-589.

Judith Picks Items chosen specially by Judith, either because they are important or interesting, or because they're good investments.

INTRODUCTION

Welcome to the 2020–2021 edition of *Miller's Antiques Handbook and Price Guide* – it is an unbelievable 40 years since we published the first black and white edition in 1979. The BBC commissioned 'Antiques Roadshow' in that same year when antiques were still considered elitist, but how the antiques world has changed since those heady days! In the early 1970s there were many more antiques shops in every high street, and more general auction sales where potential 'sleepers' (unidentified treasures) could be found. There was no internet. Collectors scoured the country and abroad to find that hidden gem. The recession and changing tastes have hit the antiques market hard. Many shops have closed, and many traditional areas of the market are struggling to survive. However, there are indications of an up-turn. Many dealers have joined together in antiques centres, many display their antiques at fairs, and many now deal primarily online.

A Chinese Republic Period fan. 20¾in (52.5cm) wide £11,000-15,000 L&T

Across the board there is a certain cautious optimism about the future of the antiques trade. Some areas are very strong, such as the Asian, Russian and Indian markets. Any good-quality, top-end antique in original condition that is fresh to the market will excite collectors' interest.

This guide is, as always, packed with more than 8,000 images of antiques and fine decorative objects that are completely new to this edition. I am often asked if we update the prices in each edition – we don't: when we publish a new edition we start from scratch to properly reflect changes and developments in the market.

I am also often asked, 'Do antiques have a future?'

A Meissen teapot and cover, with Böttger lustre glaze, underglazed blue 'M.P.M.' mark. c1722 6½in (16.5cm) wide £18,000-22,000 REEM

It's an interesting question. Some people say young people seem less interested in collecting, favouring a more minimal look within their homes. Largely true, the consequence of this is in fact a transition from more traditional collecting fields to Mid-century and Modern. Indeed, there is a shortage of good antiques – the dealers' lament today is that having made a sale, the hardest part is finding good-quality antiques to replace it.

There is also the eco argument. Buying solid mahogany furniture is more ethical than buying disposable MDF pieces, and in many cases, buying second-hand is cheaper than brand new alternatives: no one is going to convince me MDF will prove a good investment. That solid, plain mahogany early- to mid-19th century chest of drawers will still be a practical storage piece in 200 years' time, and if your taste is for Gastavian, then paint it.

The internet has meant that antiques are now more accessible than ever – we can easily browse large numbers of pieces of different styles and periods. Due to the power of the internet, auction houses outside the big cities are getting record prices for rare pieces.

I am constantly asked, 'What is your advice on buying antiques? What is the next "big" thing?' My answer is always the same. Buy what you like. Buy something that will bring you pleasure – if it increases in value that's a bonus. I have included images of a few personal likes – a Meissen teapot, a 19th century Chinese fan and a Black Forest bench on this page – and note, Meissen, when early, rare and exquisite quality, will always fetch record prices!

A late 19thC Black Forest bench, the bears with glass eyes. 31½in (80cm) wide £3,500-4,000 L&T

We live in uncertain times. With all the political upheaval in America, and Brexit in Europe, who knows what the future will hold? However, in times of economic uncertainty, top-quality antiques are often seen as a good investment, and you have the added benefit of enjoying them.

Indeed, now is a great time to be buying antiques. So please use this guide to increase your knowledge, your commercial acumen and your enjoyment. Those hidden treasures are still out there just waiting to be discovered!

Judith Miller.

THE PORCELAIN MARKET

Although there is a feeling that the market is improving, there has been continued nervousness fuelled by porcelain collectors' very real concern that the ceramic market is 'soft'. Private collectors are, however, prepared to buy when items are rare and of excellent quality. As mentioned by Steven Moore, ceramics specialist on the BBC's 'Antiques Roadshow', '2019 was the year that saw some ceramic pieces come out of the china cabinet and into the trophy cabinet. I'm thinking of pieces like the previously unrecorded teapot attributed to the John Bartlam factory in Cain Hoy, South Carolina [above], sold by Woolley and Wallis, and the Rothschild ceramics at Sotheby's.'

There has been very little change to the market over the last few years. The market leaders Sèvres and Meissen have remained in demand, particularly for early 18th century examples. The 'golden age' of Meissen, from the early years of the factory to the end of the Seven Years War (1710–59) is still very strong, and in this area collectors are even prepared to accept some damage. However, really high-quality figures from the late 19th century, if of superb quality, are still in demand. Dresden, Vienna and Limoges pieces have to be particularly impressive to sell well. The Paris factories have also struggled, and buyers are still suspicious of many so-called 'Samson' pieces that do not have the quality of the true Samson copies.

Another area that is still struggling is British blue and white from both the 18th and 19th centuries. Buyers will pay for pieces in exceptional condition and with a rare early pattern. Large platters are also in demand, but not if they have a transfer-printed common pattern. Some Worcester has also been in demand, but only really early pieces with rare hand-painted patterns. Later transfer-printed pieces have struggled to find pre-recession prices, with many auctioneers combining pieces in job lots. If someone is considering starting a collection of 18th century English porcelain, this could be a good time to start. Many pieces fail to find the price levels that I was paying 30 years ago.

Pieces that have continued to excite collectors are the 'Girl-in-a-Swing' groups from a London factory, possibly run by Charles Gouyn (also known as the St James' factory). These have that magical combination of superb quality and rarity. There has also been a great deal of research done on these groups, much by the English Ceramic Circle, which has again stimulated the market.

Lowestoft continues to have a loyal group of collectors and prices remain strong – again this is particularly true when rare shapes and patterns are on offer. Nantgarw and Swansea are also still in demand due in part to rarity and superb quality. Unrecorded early Derby figures always excite the market. Royal Worcester ewers and vases painted by such artists as Charles Baldwin, Harry Davis and the Stintons still have their collectors and prices have remained steady, but the pieces have to be of a good size and preferably fresh to the market.

Top Left: An important American porcelain teapot, attributed to John Bartlam, Cain Hoy, South Carolina, USA, damaged.

c1765-69 *7in (17.5cm) wide*

£600,000+ **WW**

Above: A late 19thC Meissen figure of Count Bruhl's Tailor, after the model by J.J. Kändler.

16½in (42cm) high

£10,000-12,000 **BRI**

ESSENTIAL REFERENCE – BERLIN

The first Berlin porcelain factory was founded in 1752 by Wilhelm Kaspar Wegely. It produced Meissen-style decorative wares, typically floral vases, and copies of Meissen figures. The factory closed in 1757.

- **In 1761 Johann Ernst Gotzkowsky purchased Wegely's old stock and, with support from Prussian King Frederick II, founded the Königliche Porzellan-Manufaktur Berlin (Royal Porcelain Manufactory Berlin), or KPM Berlin.**
- **Under Gotzkowsky, the factory developed its own late Rococo style. Gotzkowsky worked with Friedrich and William Meyer to create Classical figures, often painted in black, puce and salmon pink. The factory also used porcelain as a vehicle for miniature painting. KPM Berlin is still active today.**
- **Wegely porcelain was marked with an underglaze blue 'W'. Gotzkowsky's pieces were marked with a sceptre. From 1832, 'KPM' was added. In the years 1849-70, pieces were marked with a Prussian eagle holding an orb and sceptre.**

A 19thC Berlin group, the infant Bacchus drinking wine, with a female attendant, underglaze blue mark, impressed '634', minor gilt rubbing.

7¾in (19.5cm) high

£220-280 FELL

A KPM Berlin group, of a putto with a chariot drawn by a ram.

£160-200 HALL

A late 19thC Berlin plaque, painted with a praying lady, impressed 'KPM. SZ', incised '407-269', framed.

16in (40.5cm) high

£5,000-5,500 HT

A KPM Berlin plaque, with a classically-draped maiden, impressed marks, scratches to enamel.

9in (23cm) high

£1,400-1,800 CHOR

A late 19thC KPM Berlin plaque, painted with 'The Immaculate Conception', after Bartolomé Esteban Murillo, impressed 'KPM', sceptre mark, within a gilt frame.

plaque 10¾in (27.5cm) high

£1,500-2,000 TOV

A late 19thC KPM Berlin plaque, painted by R. Dittrich, impressed factory marks, titled 'Heimathlos Nach Kray', framed.

9¾in (24.5cm) high

£1,400-1,800 TOV

A late 19thC Berlin plaque, after Ludwig Sturm (1844-1926), inscribed 'Kinder Lust v. Lasch 4, Sturm, Wien', incised 'K.P.M.', in later gilt frame.

plaque 19¼in (49cm) high

£13,000-16,000 CA

A late 19thC Berlin plaque, with a portrait of a young lady, signed 'Wagner', impressed factory marks, within a gilt frame.

3¼in (8.5cm) high

£180-220 TOV

BERLIN MARKS

KPM Berlin

Mark used from 1832

ESSENTIAL REFERENCE – BOW

The Bow factory was founded in London c1744 by Thomas Frye and Edward Heylyn. Its porcelain wares were inexpensive and at first very popular, but the factory declined in the 1760s and closed in 1776.

- **Bow porcelain was white and chalky, with an irregular surface and granular texture. Its glassy glaze was of a grey-green hue. Its wares were usually painted in blues, yellows and purples.**
- **Inspired by oriental designs, most early Bow wares were plain blanc-de-Chine or decorated in underglaze blue. Later enamelled wares were based on the famille rose palette or Kakiemon designs.**
- **Bow figures were press-moulded rather than slip-cast, making them heavy and less fine than those made by Chelsea or Derby.**
- **Early Bow is generally unmarked. From c1765 an anchor and dagger mark was painted in red enamel.**

A Bow white-glazed figure of a pedlar, the stick broken off and repaired.
c1754 *6½in (16.5cm) high*
£1,800-2,200 **WW**

A Bow white-glazed figure of a female hunter and dog, beside a water fountain, minor damages.
c1752 *5in (13cm) high*
£550-650 **WW**

A Bow blue and white tea bowl, painted with a boat, islands with pagodas, 'Q' mark to base.
c1752-54 *3¾in (9.5cm) diam*
£300-350 **WW**

A Bow white-glazed footed gravy boat, of silver shape, small chips to feet.
c1754 *7in (18cm) wide*
£550-650 **WW**

A small Bow blue and white fluted cream boat, painted with the 'Desirable Residence' pattern.
c1755-60 *4¼in (11cm) long*
£250-300 **BELL**

A rare Bow blue and white dish, painted with islands, pagodas, trees and a figure on a sampan.
c1755-58 *10¾in (27.5cm) long*
£500-600 **WW**

A rare Bow famille rose plate, with a chinoiserie figure, micro-fritting to rim.
c1756-58 *9¼in (23.5cm) diam*
£850-950 **HAN**

A rare Bow teapot stand, with a landscape by Jefferys Hammet O'Neal, wear to enamels, hairline crack.
c1758 *4¾in (12cm) wide*
£1,000-1,400 **HAN**

CLOSER LOOK – BLUE AND WHITE PINT MUG

The reverse is decorated with a Classical architectural ornament and a man holding a trowel.

This side depicts a man with a hunting flintlock rifle.

The mug is decorated in underglaze blue with the armorial of the Worshipful Company of Tylers and Bricklayers and the inscription 'in God is all our trust'.

It was probably made at the Bow factory. The base is marked 'M W, E Jan, 1757', dating it to the factory's high point, when it employed roughly 3,000 people.

A rare English soft-paste porcelain pint mug, some chips to the rim, cracked handle.
1757 *5¾in (14.5cm) high*
£22,000-26,000 **STA**

PORCELAIN

A rare Bow duck tureen base, the plumage finely painted.

This form derives from George Edwards, 'Natural History of Uncommon Birds' (1743-47), volume III, plate 157.

c1755-58 *4¾in (12cm) wide*

£1,800-2,200 WW

A rare Bow model of a pug, in polychrome enamels, some small chips.

c1755 *4¼in (11cm) high*

£3,200-3,600 WW

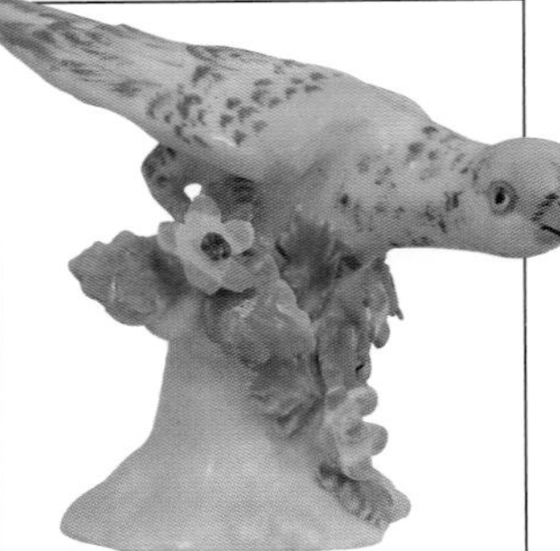

A Bow model of a canary, restoration to tail, wing and flowers.

c1758 *9½in (24cm) wide*

£400-450 HAN

A rare Bow figure of Il Capitano, from the Commedia dell'Arte series, some restoration.

c1755 *7¼in (18.5cm) high*

£3,500-4,000 WW

A rare Bow figure of Pedrolino or Pierrot, from the Commedia dell'Arte series.

This figure was first modelled by Reinicke at Meissen, using an engraving by Francois Joullain in Louis Riccobini, 'Histoire du Theatre Italien' (1731), and was faithfully copied by Bow.

c1755 *6in (15cm) high*

£2,000-2,500 WW

A Bow figure of Fame as a winged angel, on a cloud base, restoration to fingers.

c1756-58 *7in (18cm) high*

£1,600-2,000 BE

A Bow figure of a salt box player, some restoration.

c1758 *4¾in (12cm) high*

£1,200-1,500 WW

A set of Bow figures of the Adolescent Seasons, some restoration.

c1765 *7in (17.5cm) high*

£2,000-2,500 WW

ESSENTIAL REFERENCE – CAUGHLEY

Caughley was founded in the 1750s by Ambrose Gallimore in Caughley, Shropshire, UK, as the Salopian China Manufactory. It continued production until it was purchased by John Rose of the Coalport factory in 1799.

- **Gallimore worked closely with Thomas Turner and later Robert Hancock, both previously employees of the Worcester factory. Together they produced and decorated soft-paste porcelain, made with soapstone and clay imported from Devon and Cornwall.**
- **Caughley wares included a range of tableware, homeware and miniature 'toy' items. These were decorated in blue and white, with occasional gilded or enamelled details.**
- **Caughley designs emulated Chinese porcelain, with a French influence in later decades. The best-known Caughley patterns include 'Fisherman' and 'Willow', both later adopted by other factories, including Worcester.**
- **Wares were usually marked 'S' for Salopian or 'C' for Caughley.**

A Caughley teapot, painted with the rare 'Bird in the Ring' pattern, lacking cover, 'S' mark.

This is a copy of the Worcester version of this pattern, and is the only Caughley example known.

c1776-79 *4¼in (10.5cm) high*

£550-650 **HALL**

A Caughley coffee cup and saucer, transfer-printed with the 'Bridge and Windmill' pattern, 'S' mark, minor chip to saucer.

c1780

£500-550 **PW**

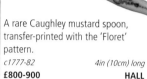

A rare Caughley mustard spoon, transfer-printed with the 'Floret' pattern.

c1777-82 *4in (10cm) long*

£800-900 **HALL**

A Caughley mask-head jug, transfer-printed with the 'Fisherman' or 'Pleasure Boat' pattern, inscribed 'God Speed the Plough'.

c1780-90 *9in (23cm) high*

£1,000-1,400 **HALL**

A Caughley butter pot and cover, transfer-printed with the'Gillyflower II' pattern, 'S' mark.

c1776-79 *4¼in (10.5cm) wide*

£550-650 **HALL**

A Caughley toy cider jug, painted with the 'Island' pattern, reversed 'S' mark.

c1780-90 *2in (5cm) high*

£700-800 **HALL**

A rare Caughley rice spoon, painted with the 'Maltese Cross' pattern, 'C' mark.

5¼in (13.5cm) long

£1,200-1,600 **HALL**

A Caughley chestnut basket, cover and stand, transfer-printed with the 'Ripe Pomegranate' pattern.

The chestnuts in this basket would have been roasted and peeled, then eaten. The piercing to the basket is functional, allowing the escape of steam from the hot chestnuts.

c1780-90 *basket 8¼in (21cm) wide*

£1,200-1,600 **HALL**

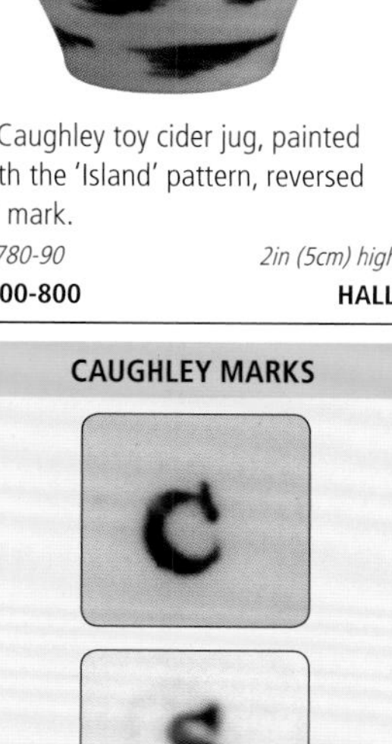

CAUGHLEY MARKS

C

S

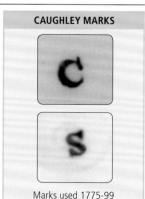

Marks used 1775-99

A Caughley punch bowl, transfer-printed with the 'Punch Bowl Sprays' pattern, with monogrammed initials 'E.H REA', glaze craze to foot rim.
10¼in (26cm) diam
£550-650 **HALL**

A deep Caughley bowl, painted with the rare 'Rock and Willow' pattern, 'C' mark, chip.
c1778-85 *4in (10cm) diam*
£600-700 **HALL**

A Caughley mug, transfer-printed with the 'Thorny Rose' pattern, 'S' mark.
c1776-80 *4¾in (12cm) high*
£900-1,100 **HALL**

A Caughley vase, transfer-printed with the 'Sliced Apple' pattern, originally one of a pair.
c1778-86 *5in (12.5cm) high*
£700-800 **HALL**

A Caughley mask-head jug, painted with the 'Salopian Rose Sprays' pattern, initialled, 'S' mark, firing crack, dated.

The monogram reads 'J', 'I' or 'T H' and '1790'. This may possibly refer to a member of the Hill family of Hawkstone who turned 21 that year.

1790 *7½in (19cm) high*
£1,000-1,400 **HALL**

A Caughley pounce pot, transfer-printed with sprigs, 'C' mark.

Pounce is a fine powder, made predominantly from cuttlefish bone, which was used to dry ink and make rough surfaces suitable for writing on. After sprinkling the paper, ink would generally take around ten seconds to dry before the paper could safely be folded without the risk of blotting.

c1776-85 *3¼in (8cm) high*
£2,200-2,800 **HALL**

A rare Caughley eye bath, painted with the 'Locre Sprigs' pattern, hairline crack and filled chip.

These eye baths were used to wash out people's eyes with boric acid when they became infected. Initially, in the 16thC, the wealthy had eye baths made of silver. It was not until the 18thC that they were made of earthenware or porcelain and came into more general use.

c1785-93 *2¼in (5.5cm) high*
£800-900 **HALL**

A Caughley chocolate cup and saucer, painted with the 'Salopian Sprig' pattern, 'S' mark.
c1785-92 *saucer 6in (15.5cm) diam*
£350-400 **HALL**

A Caughley dry mustard pot, transfer-printed with the 'Travellers' pattern, 'S' mark, chip to rim.

After 1720, the processing of mustard seeds in a mill resulted in a fine flour which came to be commercially known as 'Durham mustard'. Mustard pots would contain either dry or prepared mustard and were common in 18thC kitchens.

c1778-85 *3½in (9cm) high*
£1,200-1,500 **HALL**

A Caughley dessert plate, with a blue-painted scene with a gilt spangled border, from the 'Star and Spangles' service, impressed 'Salopian' mark, gilding rubbed.
c1785-93 *8¼in (21cm) diam*
£500-600 **HALL**

ESSENTIAL REFERENCE – CHELSEA

The Chelsea factory was founded in London c1744 by Flemish silversmith Nicholas Sprimont. Sprimont focused on luxury porcelain goods, aiming his products at 'the Quality and Gentry'. Chelsea's phases can be defined by its changing marks.

- **Early pieces, chiefly small-scale tableware, such as jugs, beakers, teapots and salts, were marked with an incised triangle. These were influenced by French Rococo style and by Sprimont's past as a silversmith.**
- **Pieces from the Raised Anchor Period (c1749-52) were in part inspired by oriental Kakiemon shapes and by Meissen designs.**
- **In the Red Anchor Period (c1752-56), Chelsea changed its porcelain formula. The new wares were finished with a clear bluish glaze. Chelsea began to produce its famous Rococo tureens in the shapes of fruit, vegetables and animals.**
- **In the Gold Anchor Period (c1756-69), inspired by Sèvres, Chelsea wares became more elaborate in form and design. A new thick blush glaze was introduced. Wares were painted in a brighter palette and often gilded.**
- **In c1769, the Chelsea factory was purchased by William Duesbury, owner of the Derby porcelain factory.**

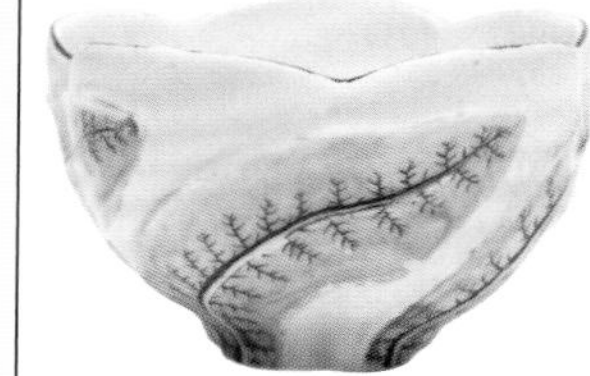

A Chelsea 'Scolopendrium' moulded large tea bowl, raised anchor mark, short firing crack to lower body.

Scolopendrium is a variety of fern, sometimes known as 'hart's-tongue' fern.

c1750-52 *3¾in (9.5cm) diam*
£1,500-2,000 **BE**

A Chelsea beaker, in the Kakiemon style, raised anchor mark.

c1750-52 *2¼in (5.5cm) high*
£2,000-2,500 **BE**

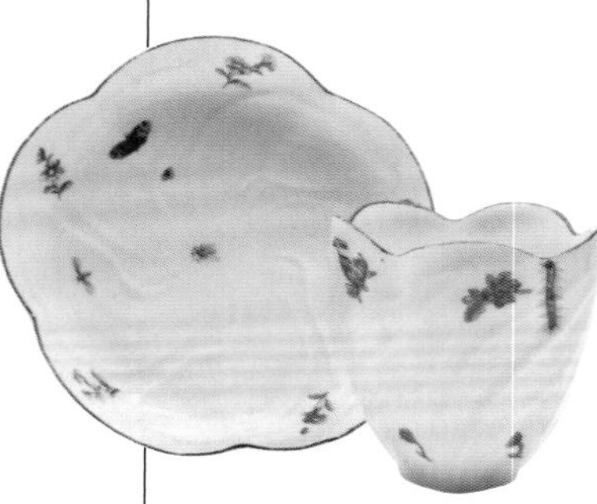

A Chelsea 'Scolopendrium' beaker and saucer, painted with insects and floral sprays, raised anchor marks, firing cracks to beaker, restored chip to saucer.

c1750-52 *saucer 5in (13cm) diam*
£4,000-5,000 **BE**

A Chelsea plate, after Meissen, in the Kakiemon style, red anchor mark.

c1752-54 *9½in (24cm) wide*
£600-700 **WW**

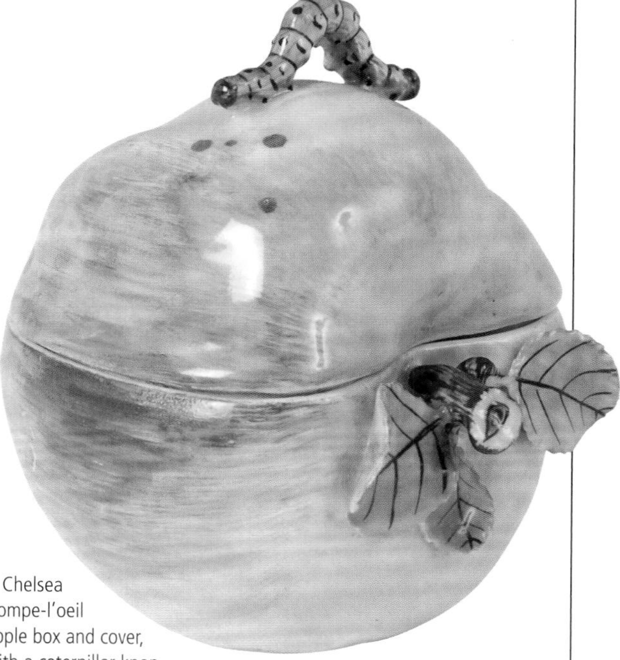

A Chelsea trompe-l'oeil apple box and cover, with a caterpillar knop, red anchor mark, '48' in iron red.

c1755 *4in (10cm) high*
£18,000-22,000 **LSK**

A Chelsea coffee cup and saucer, with crabstock handle, painted with Meissen-style flowers, red anchor marks, red '21' to saucer, minor glaze cracks.

c1755
£600-700 **PW**

A Chelsea mug, painted with a Meissen-style bouquet, red anchor mark, minor wear to rim.

c1756-58 *3½in (9cm) high*
£550-650 **BE**

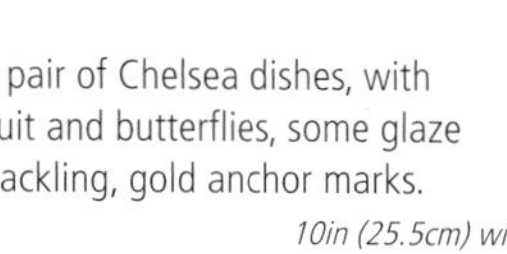

A pair of Chelsea dishes, with fruit and butterflies, some glaze crackling, gold anchor marks.

10in (25.5cm) wide
£350-450 **CHEF**

CHELSEA PORCELAIN MARKS

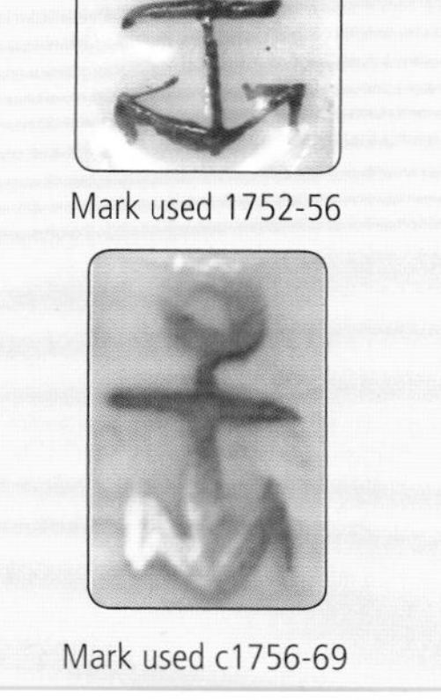

Mark used 1752-56

Mark used c1756-69

A Chelsea botanical Hans Sloane-type plate, gold anchor mark, two pieces re-attached.

c1758 *9¼in (23.5cm) diam*

£1,000-1,400 **HAN**

A Chelsea silver-form dish, painted with two birds in a landscape, gold anchor mark.

c1765 *9¾in (24.5cm) wide*

£1,300-1,600 **BE**

A gilt-metal-mounted Chelsea vase and cover, painted with Classical figures, some repairs and losses.

The scene is from an engraving of 'Aeneas Bearing Anchises from Troy'. The original painting, by Carle van Loo in 1729, is now in the Louvre.

c1765 *10¾in (27cm) high*

£10,000-14,000 **TEN**

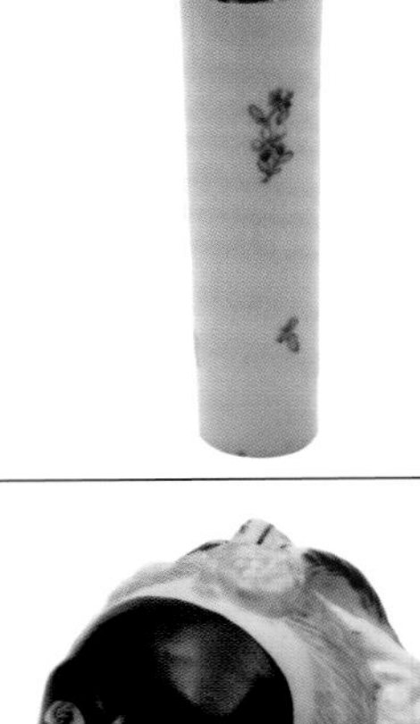

A Chelsea gilt-metal-mounted étui or bodkin case, the top as the head of Columbine.

c1760 *4¾in (12cm) high*

£2,500-3,000 **BE**

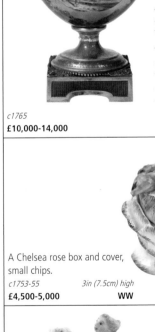

A Chelsea rose box and cover, small chips.

c1753-55 *3in (7.5cm) high*

£4,500-5,000 **WW**

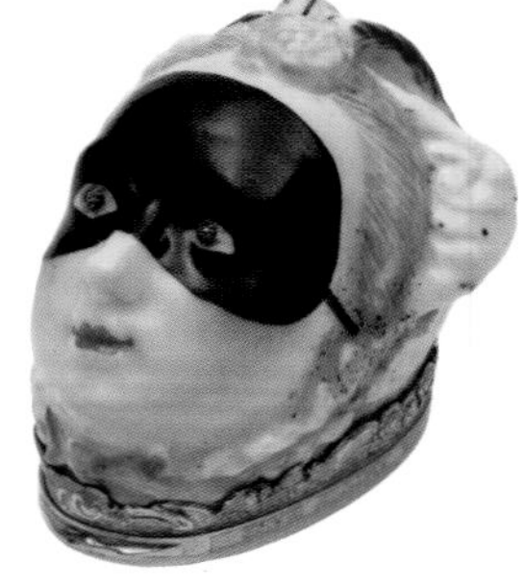

A Chelsea bonbonnière, the gold mount inscribed 'Votre Amitie Fait/ Mon Bonheur' ('Your friendship makes my happiness').

c1755-60 *1¾in (4.5cm) long*

£5,500-6,500 **BE**

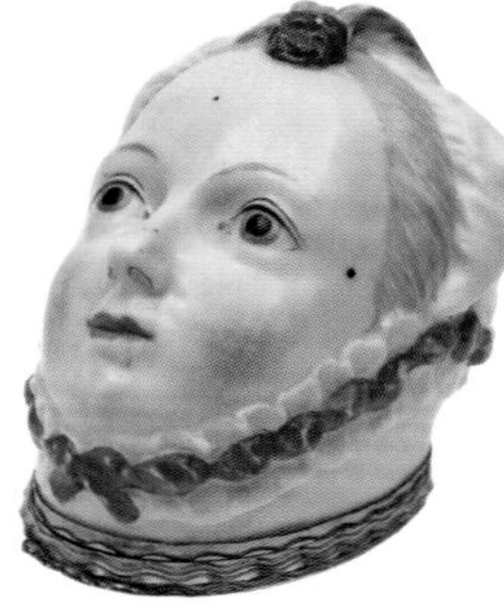

A Chelsea bonbonnière, with gilt-metal mounts and enamel cover, minor stress cracks, crazing to enamel.

c1760 *2½in (6.5cm) long*

£2,000-2,500 **BE**

A Chelsea bonbonnière, a maiden blindfolding Cupid, titled 'Aimant Aveuglement', gilt-metal mounts, hardstone base.

c1760 *2in (5cm) high*

£2,000-2,500 **WW**

A Chelsea gold-mounted bonbonnière, with three children and a dog, the boy wearing a sash inscribed 'La Curiousité Des Belles'.

c1760 *5½in (14cm) high*

£6,000-7,000 **WW**

A Chelsea figure of Autumn, from the Rustic Seasons, red anchor mark, some restoration.

The figures in this series were copied from Meissen, and also copied by Longton Hall.

c1755 *5¼in (13.5cm) high*

£1,500-2,000 WW

A Chelsea figure of a Levantine lady, modelled by Joseph Willems after Meissen, red anchor mark, some restoration.

c1755 *6in (15cm) high*

£1,700-2,000 WW

A Chelsea figure, 'The Night-Watchman's Companion', gold anchor mark, some restoration.

This figure derives from Meissen's 'Cris de Paris' series.

c1760 *6in (15cm) high*

£1,500-2,000 WW

A Chelsea figure of one of the Nine Muses, probably Thalia, on an associated stand for Erato, with gold anchor and impressed 'R' marks, the figure numbered '1', some restoration.

c1760-65 *15¾in (40cm) high*

£4,500-5,000 WW

A Chelsea figure of a gardener, gold anchor mark, some restoration.

c1760-65 *9in (23cm) high*

£1,800-2,200 WW

A Chelsea figure of a musician, gold anchor mark, minor restoration.

c1762 *6in (15cm) high*

£1,500-2,000 WW

A Chelsea flower-holder 'Chinaman' figure, gold anchor mark, some restoration.

c1762 *7¾in (20cm) high*

£800-1,000 WW

A pair of Chelsea figures of Imperial Shepherds, gold anchor marks, small damages.

c1765 *12½in (32cm) high*

£7,000-8,000 WW

A Chelsea candlestick group, modelled in the Fable manner, gold anchor mark, one ear restored, some chips.

c1760 *8¾in (22cm) high*

£3,000-3,500 WW

A Chelsea 18ct gold-mounted scent bottle, modelled as Harlequin, with chained head stopper, some firing cracks, some restoration.

Harlequin was one of the principle stock characters of the Italia Commedia dell'Arte – a comic Italian theatrical form that flourished throughout Europe from the 16thC to 18thC. Harlequin was a comic figure of a valet or servant, characterised by his checkered costume.

c1950 *3¼in (8.5cm) high*
£10,000-12,000 SWO

A Chelsea 18ct gold-mounted scent bottle, of a lady playing a hurdy-gurdy, stopper mount in poor condition, some chips and staining, chain missing.

c1950 *3¼in (8.5cm) high*
£10,000-12,000 SWO

A Chelsea 9ct gold-mounted scent bottle, of a shepherdess tending lambs, inscribed 'Votre Douceur Fait Mon Bonheur', chain broken, some chips and restoration, in a shagreen case.

3¼in (8.5cm) high
£7,000-8,000 SWO

A Chelsea scent bottle, modelled as a boy and his dog, now with dragonfly stopper.

c1950 *3in (7.5cm) high*
£1,200-1,600 SWO

A Chelsea gold-mounted scent bottle, with flower stopper, some losses and chips, stopper repaired.

c1950 *3¼in (8cm) high*
£4,500-5,000 SWO

A Chelsea scent bottle, modelled as a lady cradling her baby, some restoration.

c1950 *3¼in (8.5cm) high*
£5,000-5,500 SWO

A Chelsea 15ct gold-mounted scent bottle, modelled as a flower seller with dog, cracked in half and restored, some damages.

c1950 *3¼in (8.5cm) high*
£4,000-4,500 SWO

A Chelsea gold-mounted scent bottle, of a flower-encrusted vase, some losses and restoration, stopper stuck in.

3in (7.5cm) high

£7,000-8,000 SWO

A Chelsea 18ct gold-mounted double scent bottle, of a monkey with a baby monkey on its back, some restoration.

This monkey is holding a basketwork flask. The more usual form has no flagon.

c1950 *3in (7.5cm) high*
£4,000-4,500 SWO

ESSENTIAL REFERENCE – COALPORT

The Coalport factory was founded by John Rose in the 1790s in Shropshire. After John Rose's death in 1841, the company continued under the name John Rose & Co.

- **Rose had previously trained at Caughley, and purchased the Caughley factory in 1799. He bought the Nantgarw factory in 1819 and took on former Nantgarw employees William Billingsley and Samuel Walker as his chief painter and chemist respectively.**
- **Coalport concentrated on table and decorative wares. In the second half of the 19thC, it also began to produce flower-encrusted Rococo pieces and Sèvres-style vases.**
- **Its varied decorative patterns included Neo-classical designs, Imari decoration, landscape scenes and bouquets of summer flowers. These were often set against a solid dark blue ground. Green and beige grounds were also common.**

A rare Coalport commemorative beaker, painted with military motifs, inscribed 'Wenlock Loyal Volunteers'.

The Wenlock Loyal Volunteers were formed in 1799 in response to the threat of invasion from France. Thomas Turner, proprietor of the Caughley factory, was a captain. Only a handful of commemorative pieces are recorded. Most are in museum collections.

c1800 *3¼in (8.5cm) high*
£1,800-2,200 **WW**

A Coalport câchepot and stand, painted with birds, with lion masks, on paw feet, the base broken and re-glued.
c1815-20 *7½in (19cm) high*
£140-180 **WW**

A Coalport tea kettle and cover, applied with flowers and leaves, with swan knop, painted 'CD' mark.
c1825 *6in (15.5cm) high*
£350-400 **SWO**

A pair of Coalport vases and covers, pattern no.A1412, printed mark.
c1875-81 *7in (17.5cm) high*
£800-900 **HALL**

A late 19thC Coalport jewelled cabinet cup and saucer, pattern no.T309, retailers' mark for Ovington Brothers, printed green factory mark.
saucer 4in (10cm) diam
£250-300 **HALL**

A Coalport cabinet plate, with a handpainted woman, by J. Keeling.
8¾in (22.5cm) diam
£350-400 **PSA**

A Coalport cabinet plate, by Frederick Chiver (1881-1965), signed, printed green factory mark and gilt pattern number.
8¾in (22.5cm) diam
£200-250 **HALL**

A Coalport vase, with a handpainted woman, by E.N. Sutton, heavily gilded.
10¾in (27.5cm) high
£2,000-2,500 **PSA**

ESSENTIAL REFERENCE – DERBY

A porcelain factory was founded in Derby, UK, in c1748 by Frenchman André Planché. In 1756 it was bought by John Heath and William Duesbury, previously decorators for Chelsea. In 1770 they bought out the Chelsea factory, and operated together as Chelsea-Derby until 1784. In 1811, the company was acquired by Robert Bloor, who managed the factory until its closure in 1848.

- **Early Derby soft-paste porcelain is fine-grained, glazed in greyish white or greyish green. Its early wares were mostly figures. These were pastoral and allegorical subjects, often left in white. In the 1750s-60s, Derby figures were typically Rococo in style, standing on scrolled bases.**
- **After 1756, Derby's range expanded to include tureens, baskets and other tableware. Tea wares often cracked during use, so examples are rare.**
- **After the acquisition of Chelsea, the paste became a pure white and the glaze a clear blush. New designs included landscapes, detailed flowers and exotic birds. Many patterns were loose copies of Chelsea or Sèvres designs.**

A pair of Derby sweetmeat figures of a gallant and companion, attributed to Andrew Planché, some restoration.

c1753-55 *6¼in (16cm) high*

£2,500-3,000 **WW**

A Derby 'pale family' figure of a lady, one finger lacking, minor chips.

The design was adapted from a Meissen figure by J.J. Kandler. The 'Pale Family' refers to the figures of c1755-56, which were lightly decorated beneath a white glaze.

c1755-58 *5½in (14cm) high*

£3,000-3,500 **BE**

A Derby figure, 'The Farmer's Wife', some chips.

c1757 *6in (15cm) high*

£500-600 **WW**

A pair of Derby figures of vintners, some chips, the man's hat restored.

c1758 *5in (13cm) high*

£1,000-1,400 **WW**

A rare set of Derby figures from the Four Quarters of the Globe series, emblematic of Asia, Africa, America and Europe, some damages and restoration.

This series was first created by Kändler at Meissen around 1745, and adapted a few years later by Meyer using children instead. Meyer's series was copied at Chelsea, and it is likely that this Derby series derives from Chelsea rather than the German originals.

c1760 *9¾in (25cm) high*

£3,500-4,500 **WW**

DERBY PORCELAIN MARKS

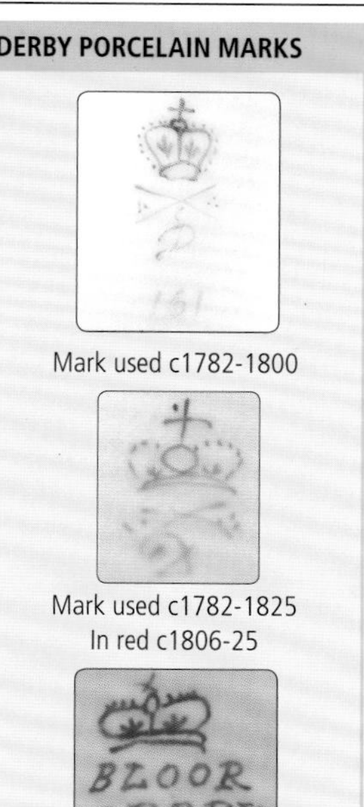

Mark used c1782-1800

Mark used c1782-1825
In red c1806-25

Mark used c1820-40

A Derby figure of Jupiter, paper label for the R. Parker collection.

c1760-65 *9¾in (24.5cm) high*

£1,400-1,800 **WW**

A Derby sweetmeat figure of a kneeling man.

c1765 *8½in (21.5cm) high*

£1,500-2,000 **WW**

A Derby mythological figure of Leda and the Swan, some restoration.
c1765 *10¼in (26cm) high*
£1,300-1,600 WW

A Derby mythological figure of Europa and the Bull, chip to horn.
c1765 *11¼in (28.5cm) high*
£1,800-2,200 WW

A Derby figure of a map seller, restoration to hat, minor chips.
c1765 *6¼in (16cm) high*
£850-950 TEN

A Derby group of children playing Hazard, incised '95', some damages.
This group is copied from a 1736 painting by François Boucher, entitled 'Country Fair'. A similar version was produced at Sèvres, modelled by Falconet.
c1780 *6in (15cm) high*
£400-500 WW

A pair of Derby figures of dancers, each incised 'No. 317', some restoration.
c1790 *8in (20.5cm) high*
£600-700 WW

A Derby bisque figure of a shepherd, sheep and dog, modelled by William Coffee, incised '396'.

William Coffee (1773-c1846) was a modeller at the Derby China Manufactory in the 1790s. He worked for other local factories, both as a modeller and a travelling salesman, before establishing his own business as a sculptor in 1803. In c1816-17 he moved to America, where he continued to work as a sculptor, later with the patronage of Thomas Jefferson.
14¼in (36cm) high
£5,000-5,500 HAN

A Derby bisque figure of a shepherdess at gate, possibly modelled by William Coffee, incised '395'.
£2,500-3,000 HAN

An early 19thC Derby group, of two maidens awakening Cupid, incised '195'.
13in (33cm) high
£350-400 FLD

A Bloor Derby figure of John Liston in the role of Paul Pry, hands restored.
c1820 *6¼in (16cm) high*
£100-150 CHOR

A Derby coffee cup, painted with birds, possibly Bitterns, hairline to handle.
c1758-60 *2¼in (5.5cm) high*
£450-500 **BE**

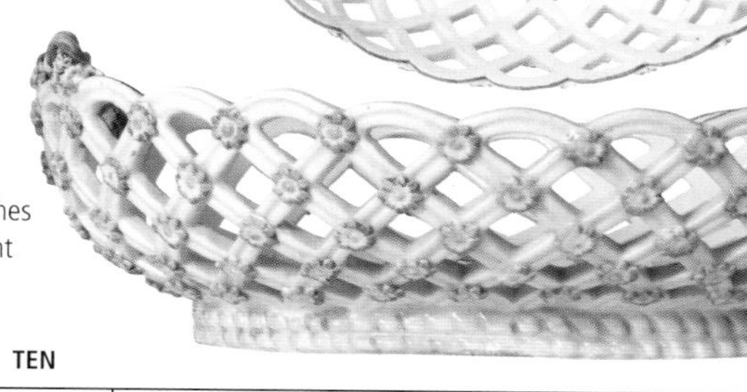

A pair of Derby baskets, painted with fruiting branches and moths, one replacement handle, hairline cracks.
c1760
£1,800-2,200 **TEN**

A Derby inkstand.
c1760 *8¾in (22cm) wide*
£1,200-1,500 **WW**

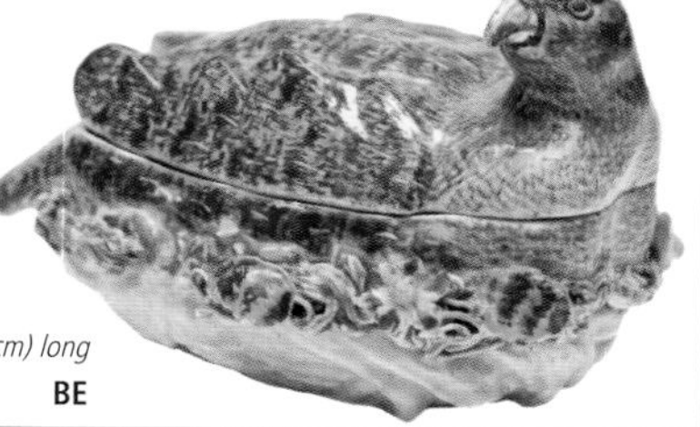

A Derby partridge tureen and cover, minor chips to flowers.
c1760 *5in (13cm) long*
£1,000-1,400 **BE**

A Derby basket and cover, with applied flowers and bird finial, small chips.
c1765 *6in (15.5cm) high*
£1,500-2,000 **WW**

A pair of Chelsea-Derby custard cups and covers, minor damages.
c1770 *3¾in (9.5cm) high*
£2,200-2,600 **WW**

A Derby wine taster.

Derby wine tasters in polychrome enamels are uncommon.
c1765-70 *3¼in (8cm) wide*
£350-400 **WW**

A Derby trout head stirrup cup, crack and chip restored.
c1800 *¾in (2cm) long*
£550-650 **HAN**

A Derby vase, painted with a child, spaniel and lady, marks in red, chip to base.
c1805 *12¾in (32.5cm) high*
£650-700 **CHEF**

An English porcelain plaque, probably Derby, by James Rouse Senior (1802-88), signed, framed and glazed.

James Rouse Senior was apprenticed to Robert Bloor at the Nottingham Road Works, Derby. He left Derby in c1826 and worked for John Rose at Coalport. In 1871 he left Coalport and worked for Ridgway before heading back to Derby in 1875 to work for Sampson Hancock in King Street. In 1882 he moved again to work at the factory on Osmaston Road.

plaque 7½in (19cm) wide
£550-600 **DN**

A Richard Chaffers Liverpool mug, printed with the arms of the Ancient and Honourable Society of Bucks, signed 'Sadler Liverpool', chip to inside rim.

The print is after an engraving by H. Copeland, dated 1748, and is attributed to Jeremiah Evans. It can be found on Worcester and Longton Hall porcelain.

c1760 *4¾in (12cm) high*

£350-400 WW

A Chaffers Liverpool famille verte coffee pot and cover, minor nibbles to cover.

8in (20.5cm) high

£1,500-2,000 HAN

A Christian's Liverpool famille rose gravy boat, painted with Chinese figures, small chips.

c1765 *6in (15.5cm) wide*

£400-500 BELL

A William Reid Liverpool Rococo cream jug, stress crack to front.

c1755-58 *4¼in (11cm) high*

£1,500-2,000 HAN

A Philip Christian Liverpool tea canister and cover, painted with the arms of Brougham impaling Lamplugh.

A tea and coffee service was made for Peter Brougham, possibly on the occasion of a proposed marriage to his cousin, Elizabeth Falconer, prior to her death in May 1769.

c1768 *4¼in (11cm) high*

£1,000-1,400 WW

A William Reid Liverpool tankard, painted with an oriental figure and a dog.

c1756-58 *3½in (9cm) high*

£2,200-2,800 HAN

A William Reid Liverpool shell salt.

c1756-61 *4½in (11.5cm) wide*

£2,500-3,000 WW

A William Reid Liverpool famille verte teapot stand.

c1758 *4¼in (11cm) wide*

£1,500-2,000 HAN

A William Reid Liverpool teapot, marked '6', cover lacking, the spout chipped.

c1756-60 *7in (17.5cm) wide*

£400-500 WW

ESSENTIAL REFERENCE – LOWESTOFT

The Lowestoft factory was founded in 1757 by Robert Browne and three partners in Suffolk.

- **It made phosphate porcelain, similar to Bow, with a tendency to discolouration. The glaze is of a greenish or greyish tone.**
- **In the factory's first ten years, it made wares decorated in underglaze blue, influenced by Worcester and by Chinese blue and white ceramics.**
- **From the mid-1760s, overglaze colours and underglaze blue printing were introduced. The factory also began to produce figures, often of dogs, cats and sheep.**
- **The factory closed in 1800.**

A Lowestoft miniature teapot and cover, decorator's mark '17', two chips to lid.
c1765 *3¼in (8cm) high*
£1,500-2,000 **LOW**

A Lowestoft miniature sucrier and cover, decorator's mark, chip inside lid.
c1765 *2in (5cm) high*
£1,800-2,200 **LOW**

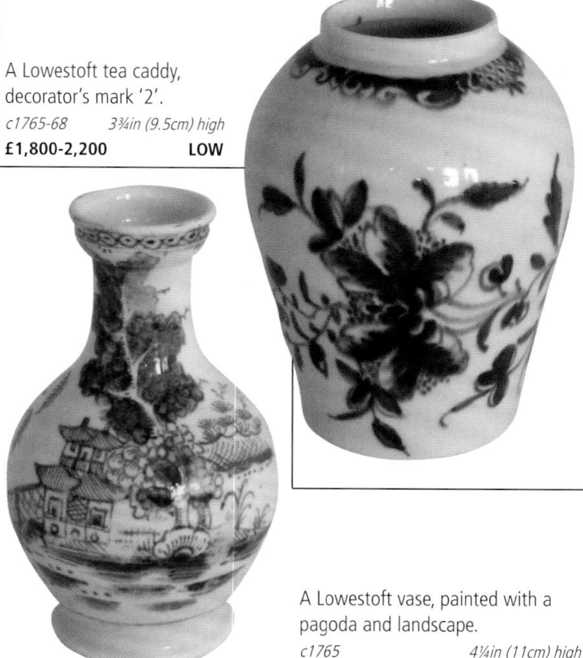

A Lowestoft tea caddy, decorator's mark '2'.
c1765-68 *3¾in (9.5cm) high*
£1,800-2,200 **LOW**

A Lowestoft vase, painted with a pagoda and landscape.
c1765 *4¼in (11cm) high*
£1,800-2,200 **LOW**

A Lowestoft feeding cup, decorator's mark '5'.

This is a rare shape for 18thC English porcelain. Lowestoft was the only factory to produce feeding cups in any quantity.
c1768 *3½in (9cm) high*
£1,500-2,000 **KEY**

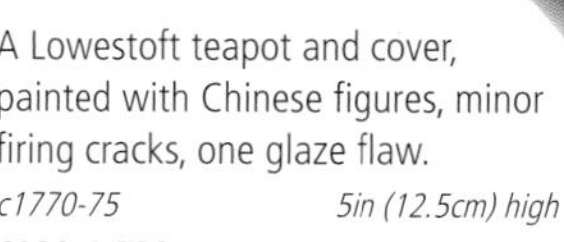

A Lowestoft teapot and cover, painted with Chinese figures, minor firing cracks, one glaze flaw.
c1770-75 *5in (12.5cm) high*
£800-1,200 **BE**

A 1780s Lowestoft milk jug and cover, with flower knop, crescent mark.
£750-850 **LOW**

A Lowestoft coffee cup and saucer, painted with Chinese figures, minor glaze flaws.
c1770-80 *saucer 4¾in (12cm) diam*
£1,000-1,500 **BE**

LOWESTOFT MARKS

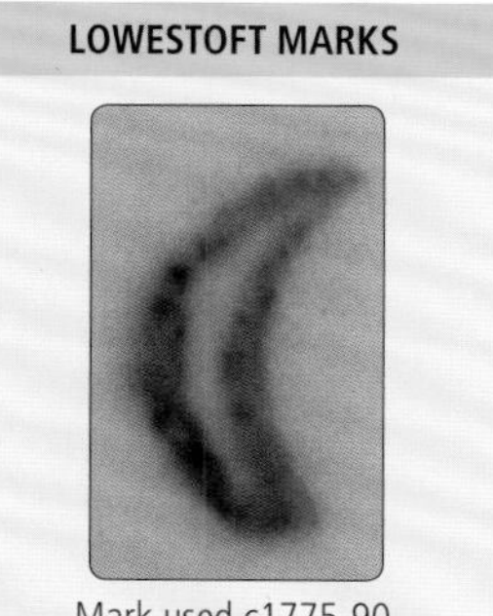

Mark used c1775-90

PORCELAIN

A Lowestoft vase and cover, painted with oriental figures.
c1770-80 *5½in (14cm) high*
£1,500-2,000 **BE**

A Lowestoft tea canister and silver cover, painted in the 'Curtis' pattern, the cover hallmarked 'R.P', London 1773, decorated by 'T. Rose'.
c1770-80 *4in (10cm) high*
£650-750 **BE**

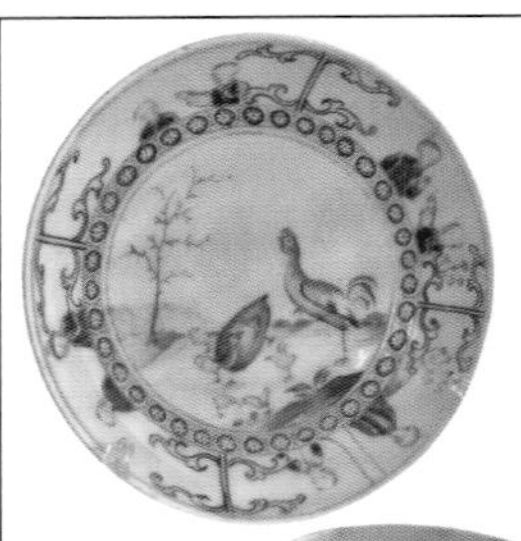

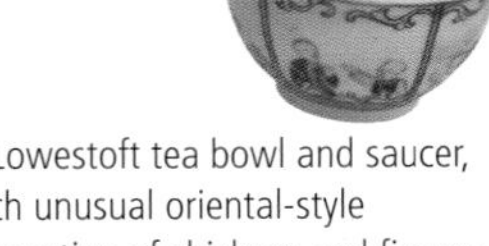

A Lowestoft tea bowl and saucer, with unusual oriental-style decoration of chickens and figures, some hairline cracks.
c1775
£2,500-3,000 **LOW**

A Lowestoft enamelled mug, painted with a bridge scene.
c1775-80 *3½in (9cm) high*
£3,000-4,000 **LOW**

A Lowestoft coffee cup and saucer, 'Tobacco Leaf' pattern, decorator's mark '2', minor staining.
c1780
£900-1,100 **LOW**

A Lowestoft mug, painted with oriental figures.
c1775-80 *3½in (9cm) high*
£1,200-1,600 **BE**

A Lowestoft polychrome coffee cup.
c1780
£350-400 **LOW**

A Lowestoft sparrowbeak jug, with an oriental woman and child.
c1780-85
£500-600 **LOW**

A Lowestoft teapot and lid, small crack, chip to lid.
c1780-85
£600-700 **LOW**

A Lowestoft garniture vase, chips to rim, small stress cracks from base.

c1785 *6in (15cm) high*

£2,500-3,000 **LOW**

A Lowestoft vase, painted with the 'Curtis' pattern, small chip to rim.

c1785 *4¼in (11cm) high*

£1,800-2,200 **LOW**

A Lowestoft 'Royal Commemorative' mug, with scroll handle, inscribed 'Long Live The King', with paper label.

In 1788-89 George III suffered his first episode of serious ill health. However, from March 1789 he was in remission for 12 years and reigned as a much loved monarch and a symbol of security in the era of France's revolutionary chaos. This rare decoration and inscription is thought to celebrate the King's return to health in the 1790s and is apparently unrecorded.

c1790-95 *3¼in (8.5cm) high*

£6,500-7,000 **BE**

A Lowestoft inkpot, inscribed 'HL'.

Hewling Luson was the owner of the Gunton Estate, near Lowestoft, where clay deposits were found by one of his tenants, Lowestoft founder Philip Walker. This inkpot was likely a presentation piece to Hewling Luson's son and the distinctive script of the initials are the work of Robert Allen.

c1790-95 *2¾in (7cm) diam*

£4,500-5,000 **BE**

A 1790s Lowestoft tea bowl and saucer, with cornflower sprays.

£550-650 **LOW**

A rare Lowestoft swan, in the white.

c1770-80 *2¾in (7cm) long*

£5,500-6,000 **BE**

A Lowestoft cat, some chips, lacking part of its tail.

Although badly damaged, this cat commands a high price due to its rarity.

c1780 *2½in (6.5cm) high*

£4,500-5,500 **JN**

A Lowestoft ram, on a pad base with glazed vent hole, small chips to extremities.

During its final two decades of production, the factory made some unsophisticated animal models: a pair of pugs, a cat, three bird groups, a ram and ewe. All are considered rarities.

c1785-90 *2in (5cm) high*

£3,000-3,500 **PBE**

CLOSER LOOK – LOWESTOFT FIGURES

These Lowestoft figures are modelled as musicians, in contemporary dress and dancing poses, the male holding a triangle, the female with a mandolin or lute.

Despite restoration to both figures, their rarity ensures their value. This pair was the first to come onto the market in the last thirty years.

Each is mounted on a four-scroll base decorated with flowers.

Lowestoft's white-glazed figures are thought to be the forerunners of enamelled figures produced a decade or so later.

A pair of Lowestoft musicians.

c1770 *larger 7½in (19cm) high*

£5,000-6,000 **KEY**

PORCELAIN

ESSENTIAL REFERENCE – MEISSEN

True hard-paste porcelain was first developed in Europe in 1708 by Johann Friedrich Böttger and Walther von Tschirnhausen. Böttger, an alchemist famed for his claims that he could create gold, had been ordered by Augustus the Strong, Elector Prince of Saxony and King of Poland, to assist the scientist von Tschirnhausen in his porcelain experiments. In 1710, Augustus the Strong set up the Meissen factory near Dresden. It was Europe's first hard-paste porcelain factory.

- **The factory prospered under J.G. Höroldt, who was appointed as chief painter in 1720. Johann Joachim Kändler joined as chief modeller from 1733, and helped produce some of Meissen's most striking figures.**
- **Early decoration was highly influenced by oriental design. Copies of Japanese Kakiemon wares were produced, and many pieces were inspired by Chinese famille verte.**
- **From the 1730s, European themes became more popular, and pieces were decorated with harbour scenes, landscapes or naturalistic flowers, known as 'Deutsche Blumen' (German flowers).**
- **From the 1750s, wares were made in the newly popular Rococo style, embellished with scrolled bases and painted in pastel colours.**
- **Meissen's shapes, decoration and crossed swords mark were widely copied by other European porcelain makers.**
- **In the 19thC, Meissen produced pieces in the popular Neo-classical, Biedermeier, Empire and Gothic Revival styles. Meissen continued into the 20thC, where new designs were produced by Paul Scheurich and Max Esser. The factory is still active today.**

A rare Meissen teapot and cover, with Böttger lustre glaze, painted with landscape vignettes, underglazed blue 'M.P.M.' mark, some gilding wear and chips.

The underglaze blue 'M.P.M.' (Meissener Porzellan Manufaktur) mark is believed to have only been used for one year before the factory introduced the blue crossed swords mark in 1723. This teapot may have been decorated by young Johann Gregorius Höroldt (1696-1775), who worked as a porcelain painter for Meissen for over fifty years.

c1722 *6½in (16.5cm) wide*
£18,000-22,000 **REEM**

A Meissen Hausmaler teapot and cover, blue crossed swords mark, some wear.

c1720-25 *6¼in (16cm) high*
£1,800-2,200 **WW**

A Meissen chinoiserie tea bowl and saucer, numbered '50', minor wear to gilding.

c1723-25 *saucer 5in (12.5cm) diam*
£2,000-2,500 **HAN**

A Meissen plate, attributed to Christian Friedrich Herold, with maritime scenes and Chinese figures, blue crossed swords mark, some restoration.

c1725 *9½in (24cm) diam*
£4,000-5,000 **SOU**

A Meissen Kakiemon beaker and trembleuse saucer, blue crossed swords marks, small filled rim chip.

c1730 *5in (12.5cm) high*
£900-1,200 **WW**

A Meissen cabinet plate, with courting couples, blue crossed swords mark.

c1735-40 *9¼in (23.5cm) diam*
£2,500-3,000 **WW**

A Meissen jug, with a harbour scene, a Rococo shield and amorini, blue crossed swords mark and gilt dot, lacking lid, some scratches and rubbing.

c1735 *6¾in (17cm) high*
£3,500-4,000 **MOR**

MEISSEN MARKS

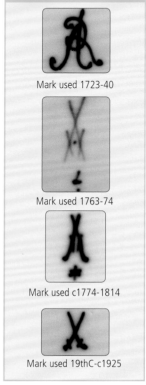

Mark used 1723-40

Mark used 1763-74

Mark used c1774-1814

Mark used 19thC-c1925

CLOSER LOOK – 'SWAN' SERVICE PLATE

This plate is from the 'Schwanenservice' or 'Swan' service, created by J.J. Kändler and Johann Friedrich Eberlein for Count von Brühl, in c1737-42. The service consisted of 2,200 individual parts, one of the largest ever made.

The plate is moulded in the form of a shallow sea shell, decorated with swans in relief and painted with flowers to the rim.

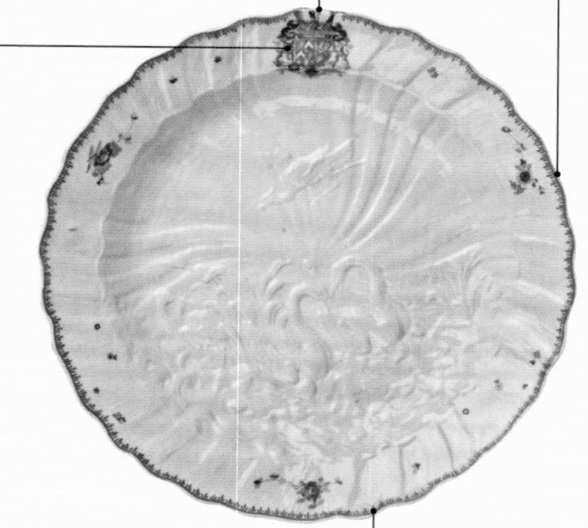

It is further decorated with the crest of the Count von Brühl and his wife, Countess Franziska Kolowrat-Krakowsky. Count von Brühl was First Minister of the Electorate of Saxony from 1746 and director of the Meissen factory 1733-63.

More than half the 'Swan' service is thought to have been destroyed in World War II, so pieces are rare. The high quality of the porcelain and the ties to Count von Brühl further increase the value.

A Meissen plate, underglaze blue sword mark.

1738 *16½in (42cm) diam*

£20,000-25,000 MTZ

A Meissen cup and saucer, blue crossed swords mark, gilt number '1', impressed '23' to saucer, small chip to saucer.

c1740 *saucer 5in (13cm) diam*

£1,800-2,200 HAN

A Meissen gold-mounted snuff box, painted with courting couples, discharge mark.

c1740 *3in (7.5cm) long*

£1,800-2,200 WW

A rare Meissen gold-mounted snuff box, with courting couples and Commedia dell'Arte figures.

c1750 *3¼in (8cm) long*

£12,000-15,000 WW

A Meissen figure of Harlequin, later decorated in bright enamels, some damages.

c1745 *5¾in (14.5cm) high*

£400-500 MOR

A Meissen snuff box, with osier-type moulding, painted with 'Deutsche Blumen', the interior lid with a spaniel, gilt-metal mounts, paper Hasse Collection label.

c1760 *3¼in (8cm) long*

£3,500-4,000 WW

A Meissen figure of a woman playing a hurdy-gurdy, blue crossed swords mark.

c1750 *figure 6in (15cm) high*

£900-1,200 JN

A miniature Meissen bottle, blue crossed swords mark, painted 'k.H.C'.

This is from the 'Red Dragon' service, made for the Saxon Royal Court Pantry, Dresden.

c1740-50 *3in (7.5cm) high*

£2,000-2,500 HAN

A mid-18thC Meissen monkey band figure, modelled by Peter Reinicke, blue crossed swords mark, some restoration.

6in (15cm) high

£1,200-1,500 WW

A mid-18thC Meissen Harlequin scent bottle, faint blue crossed swords mark, some damages.

3¼in (8cm) high

£1,400-1,800 WW

A pair of Meissen figures of a blacksmith and woodcutter, the blacksmith incised '50', small blue crossed swords mark, minor chips and hairlines.

The puce scrolls on the bases and the very small blue marks are more commonly found on English copies of Meissen pieces than on Meissen originals, but there are some comparable examples. This pair is extremely rare.

c1750 *8¾in (22cm) high*

£6,500-7,500 FELL

A Meissen figure of a fox, blue crossed swords mark, some restoration.

c1760 *4in (10cm) wide*

£400-500 WW

A Meissen group, 'The Good Mother', blue crossed swords mark, incised 'E69', some damages.

c1860 *8¾in (22cm) high*

£500-600 CHOR

A pair of 19thC Meissen groups, blue crossed swords marks, incised 'H81' and '82'.

5¾in (14.5cm) high

£1,500-2,000 JN

A 19thC Meissen figure of a gardener, numbered '59' and '692', minor losses to extremities.

7½in (19cm) high

£300-350 APAR

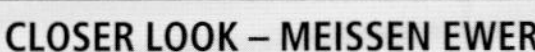

A Meissen group, after the original by Michel Victor Acier and Johann Carl Schönheit, blue crossed swords mark, marked 'G32', '57' and '10', some losses and chips.

c1875-80 *10¾in (27cm) high*

£850-950 SWO

A pair of Meissen figures, after the originals by Johann Carl Schönheit, impressed 'B65', cancelled and ground out crossed swords mark, some damages.

c1875-80 *19¼in (49cm) high*

£3,500-4,500 SWO

CLOSER LOOK – MEISSEN EWER

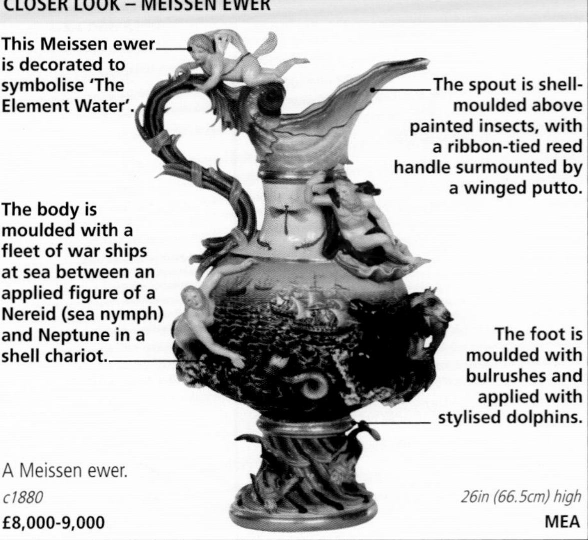

This Meissen ewer is decorated to symbolise 'The Element Water'.

The spout is shell-moulded above painted insects, with a ribbon-tied reed handle surmounted by a winged putto.

The body is moulded with a fleet of war ships at sea between an applied figure of a Nereid (sea nymph) and Neptune in a shell chariot.

The foot is moulded with bulrushes and applied with stylised dolphins.

A Meissen ewer.

c1880 *26in (66.5cm) high*

£8,000-9,000 MEA

A late 19thC Meissen centrepiece bowl-on-stand, blue crossed swords marks, some damages and losses.

22¾in (58cm) wide

£12,000-15,000 **BELL**

A Meissen model of Zemira, after the original by J.J. Kändler, blue crossed swords mark, rubbed inscription, 'Chien favorit de feu SM l'Imperatrice Catherine de Russie', losses to tassels.

Catherine II of Russia, better known as Catherine the Great, loved greyhounds. Her most treasured companion was Zemira, named after the heroine from a Beauty and the Beast opera, Zemira and Azor. Zemira joined Catherine for daily walks and slept on a silk cushion in her chambers. After Zemira's death, Catherine is said to have been so upset that she shut herself in her room for several days. Catherine had Zemira's tombstone engraved with an epitaph written by the French Ambassador, Count Ségur: 'Here lies Zemira and the mourning graces ought to throw flowers on her grave... The gods, witnesses of her faithfulness, should have rewarded her for her loyalty with immortality.'

c1850-70 *17in (43cm) long*

£8,000-9,000 **BE**

A Meissen group, by Gustav Deloy, blue crossed swords mark, incised 'No. P114'.

c1890

£1,000-1,400 **JN**

A late 19thC Meissen parrot, blue crossed swords mark, incised model 'No 53X' and '89'.

13in (33cm) high

£800-900 **BELL**

A late 19thC Meissen parrot, blue crossed swords mark, incised, some restoration.

10¾in (27.5cm) high

£450-550 **BELL**

A Meissen parrot, blue crossed swords mark.

12in (30.5cm) high

£1,200-1,500 **JN**

An early 20thC Meissen 'Onion' part dinner service, with 48 plates, a tureen and cover, 2 gravy boats, a fish dish, 5 serving dishes, blue crossed swords marks, one dish with cancellation marks.

£10,000-14,000 **DN**

A late 19thC Meissen Bolognese hound, after the original by J.J. Kändler, underscored blue crossed swords mark, tail detached.

9in (23cm) high

£600-700 **BELL**

A Meissen goat, modelled by Eric Hoesel, blue crossed swords mark, incised 'No. V107'.

c1925 *12½in (32cm) high*

£1,000-1,400 JN

A rare Meissen Japanese chin, modelled by Eric Hoesel, blue crossed swords mark, incised 'N148'.

c1915 *4½in (11.5cm) high*

£1,200-1,600 JN

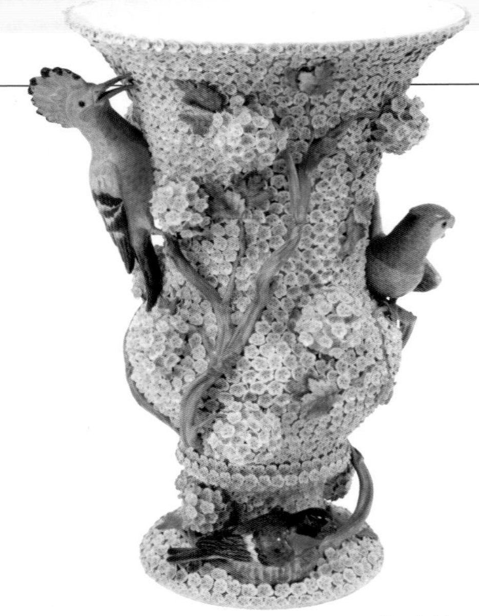

An early 20thC Meissen Schneeballen vase, encrusted with blossom, branches and birds, minor restoration, the parrot previously broken off.

19¼in (49cm) high

£11,000-15,000 CHOR

A pair of Meissen figures of the Senses, blue crossed swords mark, impressed 'No.122', incised 'E2', firing crack to base of one.

5in (12.5cm) high

£1,400-1,800 CHOR

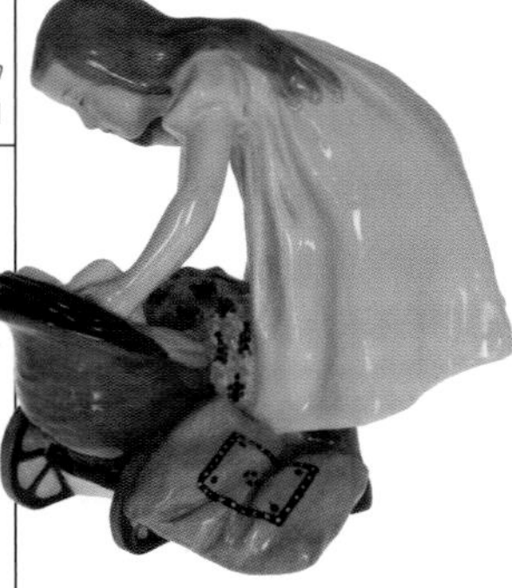

A Meissen figure of a girl, doll and pram, by Konrad Hentschel, incised 'W124', blue crossed swords.

Konrad Hentschel (1872-1907) designed a series of figures for Meissen in the Art Nouveau style c1905. They were seen as a refreshing change from the earlier 'old' figures produced by Meissen and became an instant success.

c1905 *5in (12.5cm) high*

£1,400-1,800 TW

A Meissen group of lovers, modelled by Alfred König, blue crossed swords mark, incised '4257'.

c1912 *9in (23cm) high*

£2,000-2,500 JN

A Meissen figure of two girls, modelled after the original by Alfred König, blue crossed swords mark, impressed 'Y.181' and '34'.

7¾in (20cm) high

£2,000-2,500 BE

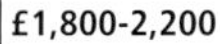

An Art Nouveau Meissen figure of a girl, attributed to Alfred König, model H.157, impressed marks, crossed swords mark.

8in (20.5cm) high

£1,800-2,200 WW

A Meissen porcelain figure group, modelled by Paul Scheurich (1883-1945), no.A1226, blue crossed swords mark, incised and impressed '1186', incised 'Scheurich'.

14¼in (36cm) high

£2,500-3,000 CAN

ESSENTIAL REFERENCE – NANTGARW

In 1813, William Weston Young and William Billingsley, previously a decorator at Derby, set up a factory at Nantgarw, Wales.

- **In 1814, the company moved to Swansea and merged with Lewis Weston Dillwyn's Cambrian Pottery. In 1817, Dillwyn left the business and Billingsley and Young returned to Nantgarw and reopened the factory. It was purchased by Coalport in 1819 and remained open until 1823.**
- **The porcelain was so fine that it was exceptionally difficult to fire, and a large proportion was lost in the kiln. Nantgarw chiefly made teawares and flatwares. Large hollowwares are very rare.**
- **Nantgarw porcelain is usually very translucent and almost pure white when held to the light. The glaze tends to be thick and smooth.**
- **Billingsley was particularly known for his flower painting. Decorating was done either at Nantgarw or in London.**
- **Nantgarw wares tend to be impressed 'NANTGARW CW' (CW for China Works).**

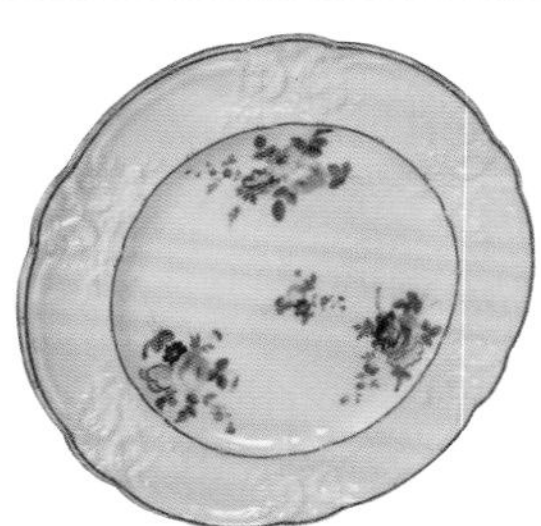

A Nantgarw plate, decorated by Mortlock's, London, impressed 'NANT GARW CW', inscribed 'Mortlock's' in gold.

It is unusual for pieces made at Nantgarw and painted in London to be marked with their London decorator.

9in (23cm) diam

£500-600 **JON**

A Nantgarw tureen, cover and stand, from the Brace service, with pineapple knop.

c1818-20 *5in (13cm) high*

£4,000-5,000 **JON**

A Nantgarw cup and saucer.

£400-500 **JON**

A Nantgarw dessert dish, decorated in London, impressed 'NANT GARW CW' to base.

c1818-20 *9½in (24cm) diam*

£1,500-2,000 **JON**

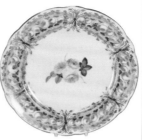

A Nantgarw plate, impressed 'NANT GARW CW'.

9½in (24cm) diam

£600-700 **JON**

A Nantgarw dish, painted in the manner of William Pollard, impressed 'Nantgarw CW', incised 'B'.

Impressed letters and incised numerals are occasionally found in conjunction with the usual Nantgarw mark; their significance is discussed by David M. Phillips in 'Swansea Nantgarw Review No 2'.

c1818-20 *11¾in (30cm) wide*

£750-850 **WW**

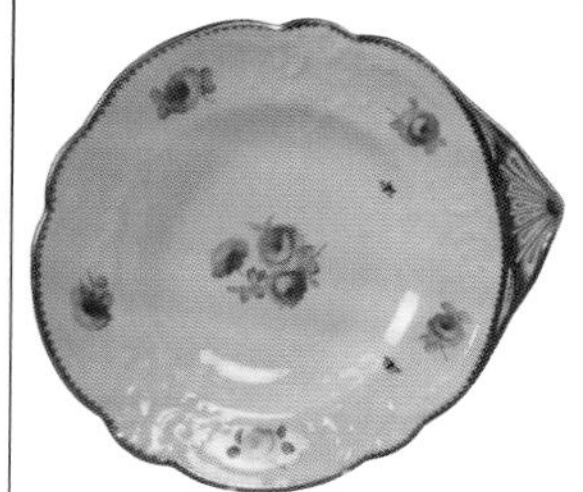

A Nantgarw fan-handled dish, impressed 'NANT GARW CW'.

9in (23cm) wide

£600-700 **JON**

CLOSER LOOK – MASONIC TUMBLER

This tumbler is gilt-decorated with Masonic symbols, with a set square and compass to the obverse.

The reverse is intricately decorated with the sun as a deity.

The tapered body has gilt bands to the top and bottom.

It is probably one of only six ever made, originally sold in 1821 by Nantgarw founder William Billingsley to a Mr Hopkin-Jones, at 4/6 each.

A rare Nantgarw Masonic tumbler.

1819 *3¼in (8cm) high*

£5,000-6,000 **JON**

A mid-to-late 18thC Sèvres biscuit figure of a girl, 'La Petite Fille a la Cage', incised 'F' to base, some chips and firing cracks.

8½in (21.5cm) high

£300-350 **BELL**

A Sèvres biscuit figure, possibly modelled by Josse-François-Joseph Leriche, titled 'M'elle LAFOREST (l'ainé) role de Jeanette', incised marks.

This figure depicts Mademoiselle La Forrest in her role as Jeanette in A.L. De Beaunoir's play 'Jeanette ou Les Battus ne payent pas toujours l'amende', a one-act comedy.

c1780 *11in (29cm) high*

£500-600 **WW**

A pair of Sèvres stands, painted by Pierre Antoine Merault (fl.1754-91) and François Binet (fl.1750-75), painted marks, glazed-over rim chip, minor wear.

1756/59 *10¾in (27.5cm) wide*

£450-500 **TEN**

Two Sèvres cups and saucers, painted by François Aloncle, date codes to one.

c1760 *saucer 5¼in (13.5cm) diam*

£2,000-2,500 **WW**

A pair of Sèvres serving dishes, interlaced 'LL' mark to one, some wear.

c1760 *13¾in (35cm) wide*

£1,800-2,200 **WW**

A Sèvres jug and basin, crowned interlaced 'LL' marks, some wear to enamel.

c1760-70 *10¼in (26cm) high*

£2,200-2,600 **WW**

A Sèvres coffee cup and saucer, probably London-decorated, with an oeil-de-perdrix ground, blue interlaced 'LL' marks.

c1760-70 *saucer 5¼in (13.5cm) diam*

£450-550 **WW**

A Sèvres pot and cover, blue interlaced 'LL' marks, date code 'L'.

c1764 *2¾in (7cm) high*

£350-400 **WW**

SÈVRES MARKS

Mark used 1769-93

A pair of Sèvres orange-tubs, blue interlaced 'LL' marks, date code 'M' above S', hairline cracks, one finial re-stuck.

c1765 *5¾in (14.5cm) high*
£450-500 **BELL**

A Sèvres cup and saucer, the saucer incised 'pate no. 43', blue interlaced 'LL' mark, painter's initials 'SC', date code.
1768 *saucer 4¼in (11cm) diam*
£500-600 **WW**

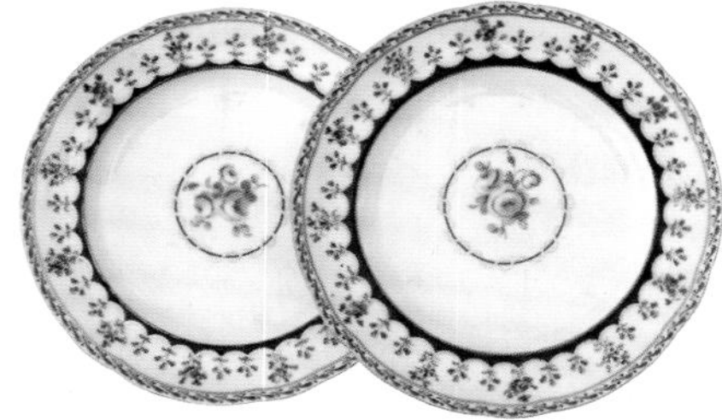

A pair of Sèvres dessert plates, in the 'Jardin' design, stacking wear, some rubbing, dated.

These plates are almost certainly from a service of 48 delivered to MM Boyd Kerr et Compagnie, Paris-based British bankers, acting as intermediaries for Jacques Gordon, possibly James Gordon MP.
1789 *9½in (24cm) diam*
£1,200-1,600 **CHOR**

A Sèvres bowl, moulded with feuilles-de-choux, blue interlaced 'LL' mark, painter's mark 'a', script 'G', date code 'Q'.
1796 *10¼in (26cm) diam*
£350-450 **MOR**

A 19thC Sèvres porcelain tea for two set.
tray 13in (34cm) wide
£20,000-25,000 **HANN**

A pair of Sèvres pots and covers, painted by Claude Antoine Tardy, blue interlaced 'LL' marks, painter's mark, date code.
1766 *4in (10cm) diam*
£1,800-2,200 **WW**

A Sèvres saucer dish, grey interlaced 'LL' mark, gilder's mark, date code 'Z'.
1777 *8½in (21.5cm) diam*
£1,500-2,000 **LC**

A pair of French Empire porcelain and ormolu-mounted faux tortoiseshell urns, possibly Sèvres or Dihl & Guerhard, the mounts attributed to Pierre-Philippe Thomire (1751-1843).
19in (48.5cm) high
£30,000-35,000 **WW**

A Sèvres cabinet plate, depicting 'Le Mort de Gaston de Foix en 1512', from 'Bataille de Ravenies', the border with portrait medallions including Louis XIV and Marie Antoinette.
12½in (34cm) long
£2,000-2,500 **HAN**

A Sèvres Imperial teapot, with monkey decoration, dated.

Having been made for Royalty, this teapot is highly desirable, despite restoration to the handle, which has previously been broken and repaired.

1833 *6¼in (16cm) high*

£15,000-20,000 K&O

A Sèvres plate, painted with Raoul de Beaumont, incised marks, printed date, painted inscription, minor glaze scratches and gilt rubbing.

The Beaumont and later Beaumont-Brienne family were the Viscounts of Maine, France from the 10thC to the 14thC.

1835 *9½in (24cm) diam*

£4,000-4,500 PW

A Sèvres chocolate cup and saucer, incised fabrication marks, the saucer with stencilled mark for Louis XVIII, minor wear.

c1814-24 *saucer 6¼in (16cm) diam*

£2,000-2,500 BE

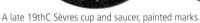

A late 19thC Sèvres cup and saucer, painted marks.

saucer 5in (12.5cm) diam

£1,500-2,000 DUK

A Sèvres reticulated teacup and saucer, with bamboo-style handle.

c1884

£1,200-1,600 HAN

A pair of late 19thC to early 20thC Sèvres 'Summer' and 'Winter' plates, overglaze blue painted factory mark.

9¾in (25cm) diam

£300-400 HALL

A late 19thC to early 20thC Sèvres-style parcel-gilt biscuit jardinière, with ram's mask handles, moulded with putti, blue interlaced 'LL' mark, some loss and wear.

18in (46cm) diam

£1,800-2,200 BELL

A Sèvres Art Nouveau-style floor vase, designed by A. Gumery, inscribed 'A. GUMERY', printed factory marks to interior, dated.

1913 *23¼in (59cm) high*

£7,500-8,500 DN

A Vauxhall teapot, with a Chinese cover, restoration to spout, star crack to base, chips to rim.
c1755
£550-650 **PW**

A Vauxhall milk jug, metal replacement handle, some faults.
c1758-60 *3¼in (8cm) high*
£250-300 **WW**

A Vauxhall cream boat, with interior cailloute panel, restoration to rim.
c1760-65 *5½in (14cm) long*
£500-600 **WW**

A Vauxhall tea bowl and saucer, painted in the Imari palette, minor faults to foot rims.
c1755
£750-850 **PW**

A Vauxhall porcelain group, of two putti and a dolphin.
c1755 *6¾in (17cm) high*
£1,100-1,500 **BELL**

A pair of Vauxhall porcelain figures of a gardener and his companion.
c1755 *6in (15cm) high*
£1,000-1,400 **DN**

A pair of Vauxhall porcelain figures.
c1755 *5in (13cm) high*
£650-750 **DN**

A rare Vauxhall figure of a man, reclining on a scrolled base, restoration to right arm.
c1760 *6in (15.5cm) high*
£2,000-2,500 **WW**

A pair of late 19thC Vienna tea caddies and covers, blue beehive marks, some rubbing and scratches.

8¾in (22.5cm) high

£300-350 MOR

A 19thC Vienna tureen, cover and stand, with drinking and gambling scenes, underglaze blue marks, broken and re-glued.

10¼in (26cm) high

£400-500 SWO

A gilt-metal-mounted Vienna tankard and cover, titled 'Darius', blue shield mark, minor surface scratches.

c1900 *6¼in (16cm) high*

£1,200-1,600 TEN

A 19thC Vienna dish, depicting Aeneas saving Anchises, blue beehive mark.

13½in (34.5cm) wide

£900-1,200 BELL

A late 19thC Vienna charger, depicting Neptune, signed 'Rob Pilz', painted mark and title to base, minor surface wear.

14in (35.5cm) diam

£1,000-1,400 DRA

A 19thC Vienna-style tray, painted with 'The Spirit of the Alps', after Konrad Dielitz, signed 'P Hoffmann', titled to the reverse, blue shield mark.

20in (50.5cm) diam

£1,800-2,200 WW

A pair of Vienna plaques, one titled 'Reflection', the other 'Erbluht', both signed 'Wagner'.

The Wagners were a family of artists working for KPM and other German porcelain makers in the 19thC. The signature 'Wagner' also appears on Vienna wares. Pieces signed 'Wagner', especially portraits, tend to be of very high quality.

7¼in (18.5cm) high

£500-600 GWA

A 19thC Vienna cabinet plate, depicting Ruth, marked and titled to base, minor wear.

9½in (24cm) diam

£550-600 APAR

VIENNA MARK

Mark used 1784 onwards

ESSENTIAL REFERENCE – WORCESTER

The first Worcester factory was established in 1751 by a team of fifteen men, headed by Dr John Wall. It produced tableware, tea and coffee services, inkwells and more, made from soft-paste porcelain with a greenish or bluish glaze, often with Chinese-style decoration.

- **After Dr Wall's retirement in 1783, the Worcester factory was purchased by Thomas Flight. It was managed by the family for nearly sixty years, known variously as Flight (1783-92), Flight & Barr (1792-1804), Barr, Flight & Barr (1804-13) and Flight, Barr & Barr (1813-40). Thomas Flight introduced hard-paste porcelain. In the early 19thC, the factory continued to produce tableware and mantel-shelf pieces, increasingly in Neo-classical and Rococo designs.**
- **At the same time, two further Worcester factories were operating: that of Humphrey Chamberlain, founded c1786; and that of Thomas Grainger, founded c1806. Chamberlain's and Flight's merged in 1840 to form Chamberlain & Co. Henry Kerr and Richard William Binns took over the management of the Chamberlain & Co. works 1852-62.**
- **In 1862, Kerr left the company and Binns continued to manage the factory alone. It became known as Royal Worcester, and focused on the production of figures and vases. It is especially known for its Japonaise wares and its individually decorated vases and pot pourris in Classical shapes.**

A Worcester pickle dish, painted with a 'Long Eliza' figure, small rim chips.

'Long Eliza' is the term for elongated female figures often found on Chinese porcelain, and later imitated by English factories. This design derives from Limehouse and is seen on Lund's Bristol and very early Worcester porcelain. Lund's examples tend to be slightly narrower than Worcester ones (see page 47).

c1751-52 *4in (10cm) high*
£1,200-1,500 **WW**

A Worcester tea bowl and saucer, painted with the 'Romantic Rocks' pattern, workman's marks, some rim chips.

c1755 *5in (12.5cm) high*
£750-850 **WW**

A Worcester cream jug, painted with the 'Indian Fisherman' pattern, workman's mark, minor damages.

c1755-56 *4in (10cm) high*
£900-1,100 **WW**

A Worcester mug, painted with the 'The Walk In The Garden' pattern.

1755-65 *5¾in (14.5cm) high*
£400-500 **JN**

A Worcester tea bowl and saucer, printed with the 'Two Swan Precipice' pattern.

c1757-60 *saucer 4½in (11.5cm) wide*
£1,000-1,400 **WW**

A Worcester coffee cup, painted in the 'Solid Fence Pavilion' pattern, workman's mark.

c1760 *3in (7.5cm) high*
£450-500 **TEN**

A Worcester water bottle or guglet and basin, painted with the 'Willow Bridge Fisherman' pattern, open crescent mark, script 'W', the bowl broken and repaired.

The term 'guglet' is believed to derive from the sound made by liquid pouring out of the wide neck of such shaped bottles. The flared neck of this bottle is less common at Worcester than the narrow truncated opening on similar bottles.

c1760-65 *11in (28cm) high*
£1,000-1,400 **WW**

WORCESTER MARKS

Mark used c1755-75

Mark used c1755-90

A Worcester dish, by Robert Hancock, printed in black with the King of Prussia, after a portrait by Antoine Pesne, signed 'RH Worcester', dated.

Robert Hancock was an engraver and painter who joined the Worcester Porcelain Company in 1756. He later became a partner of the firm. At Worcester, he engraved copper plates for transfer-printing on porcelain, adapting many designs from contemporary engravings and paintings.

1757 *7in (17.5cm) diam*

£1,600-2,000 WW

A Worcester slop bowl, printed in black with Britannia and figures, one with a banner reading 'Marine Society', the interior with a portrait of George II, chip to rim.

The source for this print is an engraving by Thomas Major after a drawing by Samuel Wale from Motives for the Establishment of the Marine Society, London 1757. The society, the world's first maritime charity, had been set up the previous year to support the navy at the start of the Seven Year's War.

c1760 *6½in (16.5cm) wide*

£600-700 WW

A Worcester 'Pitt the Elder' mug.

c1760 *3¼in (8.5cm) high*

£2,200-2,600 H&C

A Worcester mug, printed with the 'Tree Grafters' and 'Whitton Anglers' patterns, slight glaze flaw.

c1765 *3¼in (8.5cm) high*

£500-600 HAN

A Worcester coffee pot and cover, printed with the 'Milkmaids' pattern, later coloured with polychrome enamels, overglaze blue crossed swords mark.

c1770 *8in (20cm) high*

£450-550 WW

A Worcester cream boat, painted in famille verte enamels, restoration to handle, glaze frit to lip.

c1752-53 *4¼in (11cm) wide*

£950-1,200 BE

A Worcester coffee can, painted with flowers and insects, some factory faults, chip to rim.

c1753 *2¼in (5.5cm) high*

£1,100-1,400 PW

A Worcester coffee cup, painted with the 'Snake in a Basket' pattern, glaze flaw to rim.

c1753-54 *2¼in (6cm) high*

£1,100-1,400 BE

A Worcester coffee cup, with grooved loop handle, printed with the 'The Fortune Teller, no. 2' pattern, after Robert Hancock.

c1754-55 *2¼in (6cm) high*

£1,100-1,400 BE

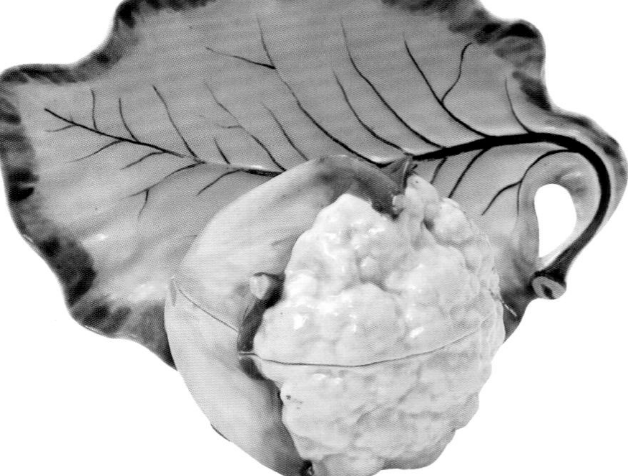

A Worcester cauliflower tureen, cover and stand.

c1757-60 *stand 8½in (21.5cm) long*

£1,600-2,000 WW

A Worcester coffee cup, painted in the Kakiemon palette with the 'Two Quails' pattern, with scrolled wishbone handle.

c1758 *2¼in (6cm) high*

£550-650 **WW**

A Worcester cabbage leaf-shaped dish, painted in the Kakiemon palette with the 'Banded Hedge' pattern.

c1760 *8½in (21.5cm) wide*

£1,100-1,500 **BE**

A Worcester teacup, probably painted in the workshops of James Giles, underglaze blue crossed swords mark, numeral '9' and dot.

This pattern is apparently unrecorded and could possibly be the work of the painter Jefferyes Hamett O'Neale.

c1765 *3¾in (9.5cm) wide*

£1,000-1,500 **BE**

A Worcester cream boat, of 'Dolphin Ewer' form, moulded with shells and dolphins.

c1765-68 *3½in (9cm) long*

£900-1,200 **BE**

A Worcester tea bowl and saucer, painted in famille verte colours with the 'Chequered Tent' pattern, square mark.

c1768-70 *saucer 4¾in (12cm) diam*

£800-900 **BE**

A Worcester garniture, decorated in the Kakiemon palette with the 'Jabberwocky' pattern, one vase restored.

c1768-72 *vase 10½in (26.5cm) high*

£1,500-2,000 **WW**

A Worcester plate, of 'Grubbe' type, painted in the workshops of James Giles, restored.

The Worcester 'Grubbe' plates were four dessert plates donated to the Victoria and Albert Museum in the 1930s by Mrs Dora Edgell Grubbe, the widow of an ancestor of James Giles.

c1770 *8¾in (22.5cm) wide*

£1,800-2,200 **WW**

A Worcester coffee can, decorated in the workshops of James Giles, with a bullfinch, a butterfly to the reverse.

James Giles of London was an independent firm who sometimes decorated pieces for Worcester. Giles employed several painters from the Chelsea factory following its closure in 1768. The workshop decorated Worcester blanks, along with glassware, Derby and Bow porcelain, and pieces from China. One of the specialities of Giles's workshop was exotic or imaginary birds in unusual landscapes. Pieces from the workshop of James Giles are highly valuable.

c1770-72 *2¼in (6cm) high*

£7,500-8,500 **BE**

A pair of Worcester coffee cans and saucers, painted with the 'Royal Lily' pattern, blue open crescent marks, solid gold crown and crescent marks.

The 'Lily' pattern was allegedly renamed 'Royal Lily' after George III and Queen Charlotte visited Worcester in 1788, and ordered a 'Lily' pattern service.

c1788-90 *saucers 5¼in (13.5cm) diam*

£1,000-1,500 **BE**

A rare pair of early 19thC Chamberlain's vases, one with Stafford's of New Bond Street label, one with restoration.

6¼in (16cm) high

£6,000-6,500 **LSK**

A pair of Flight soup bowls, from 'The Celebrated Hope' service ordered by The Duke of Clarence, decorated by John Pennington, blue Flight mark.

c1790 *9¾in (24.5cm) diam*

£1,000-1,500 **DUK**

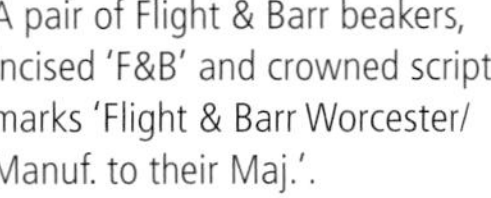

A pair of Flight & Barr beakers, incised 'F&B' and crowned script marks 'Flight & Barr Worcester/ Manuf. to their Maj.'.

c1800 *4in (10cm) high*

£1,800-2,200 **BE**

A Flight & Barr triple-spill vase, painted by Thomas Baxter, incised 'B' mark, minor wear to gilding.

The rare orange ground, combined with the quality of Thomas Baxter's shell painting makes this vase very desirable.

c1800-05 *5¾in (14.5cm) high*

£22,000-26,000 **BE**

A Flight & Barr jug, painted with a portrait of George III, probably by John Pennington (1773-1841), script crown mark to base.

The use of the painted Flight & Barr mark is recorded c1792-1807, although the company was chiefly known as Barr, Flight & Barr from 1804.

c1807 *6¾in (17cm) high*

£3,000-3,500 **H&C**

A Barr, Flight & Barr vase, with dolphin handles, painted with Tintern Abbey, Monmouthshire, crown mark, script title and marks.

c1805-10 *13in (33cm) high*

£9,000-10,000 **BE**

A Barr, Flight & Barr dessert service, by William Billingsley, with 2 tureens and covers, 2 dishes and 24 plates, impressed and printed marks, one plate chipped, restoration to finials, some gilt rubbing.

William Billingsley (1758-1828) was born in Derby and apprenticed at the William Duesbury Derby China Works. He left Derby in 1795 and later worked for Barr, Flight & Barr, Nantgarw, Swansea, Coalport and the Torksey Porcelain Manufactory, Lincolnshire. He was a highly talented painter, particularly known for his depictions of flowers.

c1810 *plates 8¼in (21cm) diam*

£15,000-20,000 for the set **H&C**

A pair of Flight, Barr & Barr urns, of Neo-classical design, impressed and script marks.

c1815-20 *7¾in (20cm) high*

£5,500-6,000 **BE**

A Flight, Barr & Barr 'King Fisher' vase and cover, possibly painted by William Doe, titled to reverse, script marks, chip to flambé finial.

c1815-20 *7¼in (18.5cm) high*

£6,500-7,000 **BE**

WORCESTER MARKS

Mark used c1807-13

Mark used c1813-40

A Flight, Barr & Barr pastille burner and stand, impressed and script marks, cracked.
c1825-30 *6¾in (17cm) high*
£650-750 **BE**

A Royal Worcester fruit-painted vase and cover, by Harry Ayrton, signed.
Harry Ayrton (1905-76) started at the Royal Worcester factory in 1920 and worked there until his retirement in 1970.
£3,500-4,000 **HAN**

A pair of framed Royal Worcester plaques, by Harry Davis, with puce factory marks, signed, date code.
1920 *4in (10cm) diam*
£4,500-5,000 **LC**

CLOSER LOOK – 'HUNTING' VASE

This vase is of campana form, with a pineapple finial and rope-twist fox-head handles.

Each side is painted with a hunting scene, 'Swishing at a rasper' and 'Going in and out clever' on a claret ground.

It would have been the centre vase of a 'Hunting' garniture.

The vase is marked in script, 'Flight, Barr & Barr/Royal Porcelain Works, Worcester/ London House 1, Coventry Street'.

A Flight, Barr & Barr 'Hunting' vase and cover.
c1830 *20in (51cm) high*
£11,000-15,000 **BE**

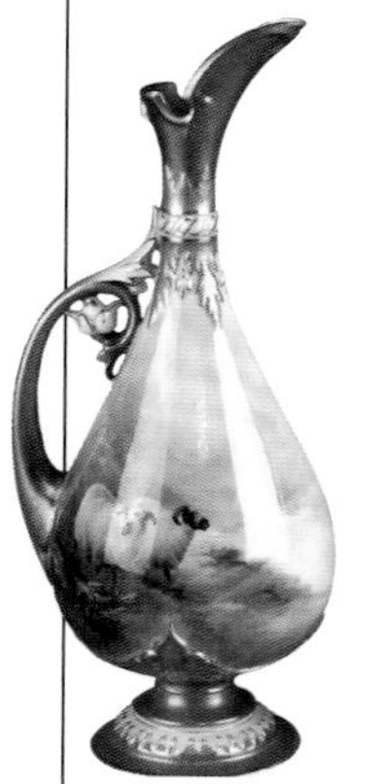

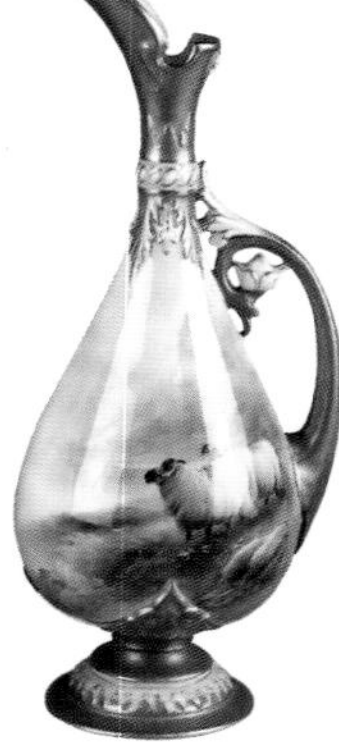

A pair of Royal Worcester ewers, by Harry Davis, signed, with printed factory marks.
Harry Davis (1885-1970), the son of a Royal Worcester china figure maker, was apprenticed at Royal Worcester at the age of fourteen. He is known for his landscapes and depictions of nature.
11½in (29cm) high
£9,000-11,000 **HALL**

An Aesthetic Movement Royal Worcester vase, in the style of Christopher Dresser, with puce and moulded marks.

Besides the typically Aesthetic Japonaise bird and foliage design, the grotesque handles are reminiscent of one of Dresser's most famous designs for Ault Pottery, known as the 'Tongue Vase'.
1877 *13½in (34cm) high*
£450-500 **HAN**

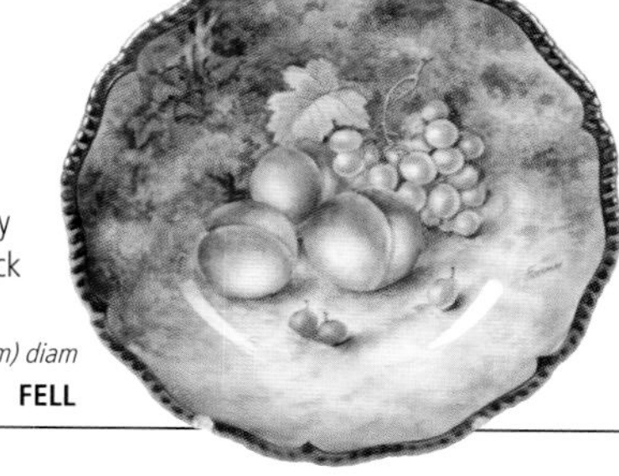

A Royal Worcester plate, by John Freeman, signed, black printed mark.
9½in (24cm) diam
£550-600 **FELL**

A Royal Worcester vase, decorated by William Jarman, signed, green printed mark with date code.
1910 *14¼in (36cm) high*
£450-500 **FLD**

WORCESTER PORCELAIN MARKS

Mark used 1852-62

Mark used 1891-

A Royal Worcester vase, by Arthur Lewis, signed, with puce marks, marked '1410'.

1909 *11in (28cm) high*

£2,000-2,500 **HAN**

A Royal Worcester reticulated goblet, attributed to George Owen, printed green mark, date code.

George Owen (1845-1917) began working for Royal Worcester in 1859. He is especially known for his pierced or reticulated porcelain, where an inner wall of porcelain is left intact inside an outer wall with piercings, emulating the style of many Chinese ivory carvings. This technique required a very high level of skill.

1878 *7¾in (19.5cm) high*

£4,000-4,500 **LSK**

A Royal Worcester reticulated cup and saucer, attributed to George Owen, green backstamp, indistinct date code and gilder's mark.

c1882

£6,000-6,500 **BE**

A Royal Worcester reticulated vase and cover, by George Owen, with incised signature, gilt marks and '169'.

1912 *6½in (16.5cm) high*

£12,000-15,000 **HAN**

An early 20thC Royal Worcester reticulated ewer vase, by George Owen, signed, gilt mark and '1581'.

6¼in (16cm) high

£10,000-14,000 **HAN**

A pair of Royal Worcester plaques, 'Off Hastings' and 'The Port of Havre', painted by Raymond Rushton, signed and titled, puce marks and date code, framed.

1919 *6in (15cm) wide*

£1,300-1,600 **BE**

A pair of Royal Worcester vases and covers, by John Stinton, puce marks.

John Stinton was born in 1854. His father worked for Royal Worcester, but he himself did not discover porcelain painting until the age of 35. He was a talented painter, best known for his depictions of British cattle and castles. He lived to be 102 years old.

11½in (29.5cm) high

£1,800-2,200 **HAN**

A Royal Worcester vase, painted by D. Shinnie, signed.

D. Shinnie was a painter and decorator at Royal Worcester, active in the second half of the 20thC.

£1,100-1,400 **HAN**

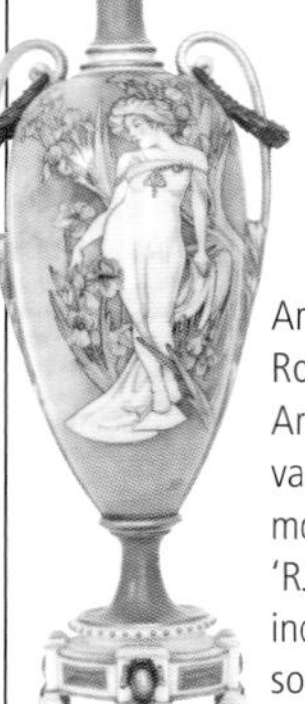

An early 20thC Royal Worcester Art Nouveau vase, shape 1686, monogrammed 'RJD', puce mark, indistinct date code, some damages.

18¾in (47.5cm) high

£550-650 **FLD**

A framed Royal Worcester plaque, by John Stinton, signed, puce mark to reverse.

plaque 4¼in (10.5cm) diam

£1,500-2,000 **GWA**

A Baddeley-Littler jug, glaze blemish to rim.

c1780-85 *3¼in (8.5cm) high*

£500-600 **PW**

A Calcut Jackfield blue and white cabbage leaf jug, transfer-printed with the 'Elephant' pattern.

The Calcut China Manufactory operated in the Jackfield area of Shropshire, UK. Very little documentation survives regarding the factory, but it is likely that was operational by late 1794, and had been subsumed into John Rose's Coalport factory by the end of 1796. See Roger S. Edmundson, 'Northern Ceramic Society Journal' (2011), 27, 75.

c1794-96 *7¾in (20cm) high*

£1,200-1,600 **HALL**

Judith Picks

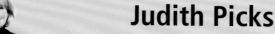

This teapot was purchased at a Lincolnshire sale for £15 and, two years on, sold at auction for £460,000 plus premium. It is now in the Metropolitan Museum, New York. It is probably America's oldest porcelain teapot, only identified very recently. It is the seventh recorded piece of John Bartlam's porcelain and bears significant similarities to his other designs, and to fragments excavated from the site of his factory in Cain Hoy, South Carolina.

John Bartlam was born in England and apprenticed to a potter in Staffordshire. He left England c1763, and travelled to South Carolina, where he established himself as a potter in Cain Hoy. South Carolina was then one of the wealthiest areas of America, and residents were eager for the latest and finest ceramics from England. The area also had easy access to kaolin clay.

Bartlam therefore endeavoured to make porcelain to rival that being imported from England, probably with the help of someone with experience in the British porcelain industry. By 1768, Bartlam was having financial difficulties. His factory relocated to Charleston in 1770. By 1772, his financial situation was again precarious, and he moved further north to Camden, New Jersey, where he produced pottery until 1776. He died c1781.

An important American porcelain teapot, attributed to John Bartlam, Cain Hoy, South Carolina, printed in underglaze blue with two cranes, the reverse with a version of the 'Man on the Bridge' pattern, the cover lacking, the handle broken off and re-stuck.

c1765-69 *7in (17.5cm) wide*

£600,000+ **WW**

A Chantilly saucer, painted in the Kakiemon pallette with the 'Two Quails' pattern, red hunting horn mark.

Chantilly was a French factory that produced soft-paste porcelain wares from c1725, including figures, jardinières, teapots, beakers, plates, jugs and coffee pots. Pieces were often decorated in the typical Japanese Kakiemon colours of iron red, turquoise, blue, yellow, gold and black. The factory closed c1789.

c1730-35 *5in (12.5cm) wide*

£1,300-1,600 **WW**

A Chantilly beaker, painted in the Kakiemon pallette with the 'Two Quails' pattern, red hunting horn mark.

c1730-40 *2¼in (6cm) high*

£1,800-2,200 **WW**

A Davenport tray, decorated with a 'Japan' pattern, highlighted in gilding.

18½in (47cm) long

£400-450 **TRI**

A pair of 20thC Dresden jardinières, with gilt ram-head handles, blue printed marks.

8¾in (22cm) high

£500-600 **BELL**

A Frankenthal figure of Venus, probably modelled by Adam Bauer, blue crowned 'CT' monogram, some restoration, dated.

1775 *9¾in (24.5cm) wide*

£1,000-1,400 WW

A Frankenthal figure of a fruit vendor, blue crowned 'CT' monogram, workmans' marks 'AB' and 'GHM'.

c1760 *5½in (14cm) high*

£850-950 WW

A late 18thC Furstenberg group of Europe and America, by Anton Carl Luplau, incised 'f' mark, some restoration.

7in (18cm) high

£400-500 WW

A 'Girl-in-a-Swing'-type gold-mounted scent bottle, modelled as a lady holding a basket, some chips and losses.

The 'Girl-in-a-Swing' group of small porcelain figures, scent bottles and other wares were originally attributed to Chelsea. A specific figure, of a girl in a swing, shed doubt on this, and many wares are now thought to have been made elsewhere, at the so-called 'Girl-in-a-Swing' factory, possibly run by Charles Gouyn (d.1785).

c1950 *3¾in (9.5cm) high*

£3,000-3,500 SWO

A 'Girl-in-a-Swing'-type gold-mounted scent bottle, some restoration, some incomplete leaves.

c1950 *3¾in (9.5cm) high*

£4,500-5,500 SWO

A Continental étui, possibly Kelsterbach, modelled as a crying swaddled baby.

c1765 *4¼in (11cm) high*

£800-900 WW

A rare Limehouse gravy boat, crack to rim.

Although relatively little known today, Limehouse was probably the first English factory to make blue and white porcelain.

c1746-48 *6½in (16.5cm) wide*

£3,000-3,500 WW

A pair of Longton Hall figures of a nun and her novice, the nun's book titled 'Of Absolution', the novice's 'Of Purgatory', some restoration.

Longton Hall was one of the earliest of the famous Staffordshire factories. It was founded at Longton Hall by salt-glaze manufacturer William Littler in 1749 and continued production until 1760.

c1755 *5in (12.5cm) high*

£1,200-1,600 WW

A pair of Longton Hall figures of a sportsman and companion, the man's head and wrist broken and re-glued.

c1755 *7in (18cm) high*

£1,300-1,600 DN

A Longton Hall figure of Summer, minor losses to flowers.

c1758 *5in (13cm) high*

£1,000-1,400 **WW**

A Lund's Bristol pickle dish, painted with a 'Long Eliza' figure, some repairs.

See page 39 for a similar pickle dish made by Worcester.

c1750 *4in (10cm) long*

£1,500-2,000 **WW**

A Lund's Bristol pickle dish,painted with a 'Long Eliza' figure, one clean crack.

Analysis of similar dishes has shown the inclusion of soaprock in the body, indicating an attribution to Lund's Bristol, rather than Worcester.

c1750 *3in (7.5cm) long*

£1,000-1,400 **WW**

A Mennecy silver-mounted snuff box and cover, with Kakiemon flowers, Paris discharge mark.

c1740 *3¼in (8cm) long*

£2,000-2,500 **WW**

A Mintons part dinner service, retailed by Thomas Goode & Co., London, with 24 plates, 4 coffee cups and saucers, 3 tureens and covers, 7 serving dishes, printed and impressed marks, date code, a saucer cracked.

1882

£4,000-5,000 **DN**

A German porcelain snuff box, perhaps Nymphenburg.

c1770 *3in (7.5cm) wide*

£650-750 **WW**

A pair of Paris Empire-style Locre Russinger Pouyat vases, underglaze blue crossed torches marks, minor wear to gilt.

c1820 *13in (33cm) high*

£2,300-2,600 **BE**

A Paris part coffee service, with a milk jug, a sucrier and cover, 6 cups and saucers, 2 surplus lids, wear to gilding, chip to sucrier.

c1830

£400-500 **DN**

A garniture of Pinxton bough pots, painted en camaïeu, one titled 'Butterley Hall', two signed 'Sarah or S Jessop', cracks and chips to larger pot, minor wear to all gilding.

As well as being a talented decorator, Sarah Jessop was the wife of William Jessop, the noted civil engineer, best known for his work on canals, harbours and as the co-founder of the Butterley Iron Works, Derbyshire.

c1800 *largest 9¾in (24.5cm) wide*

£8,500-9,500 CHOR

A Plymouth figure of Autumn, as a putto squeezing grapes into a goblet.

c1768 *6in (15cm) high*

£650-750 WW

A Plymouth shell salt, some restoration.

c1768-70 *5in (13cm) long*

£750-850 WW

A pair of Potschappel urns and covers, by Carl Thieme, after Antoine Watteau, blue 'T' marks, some chips.

1900 *22¾in (58cm) high*

£800-900 DN

A Ridgway 'Rococo revival' part tea and coffee service, with teapot, cover and stand, a milk jug, a slop bowl, a dish, 13 teacups, 11 coffee cups and 12 saucers, iron red fractional mark, '2/1008', some damages.

c1835

£400-500 DN

A Saint Cloud white-glazed tea bowl and saucer, applied with prunus blossom.

Saint Cloud was the first major porcelain factory in France. The business enjoyed the patronage of Philippe, duc d'Orléans, King Louis XIV's brother. It was initially established as a faience earthenware factory in 1666, but by the 1690s was producing soft-paste porcelain. Saint Cloud closed in 1766.

c1730-40 *saucer 4¾in (12cm) wide*

£500-600 WW

A Saint Cloud cup and trembleuse saucer, painted with tied gourds and auspicious objects in the Chinese manner.

Trembleuse cups and saucers were first developed in Paris in the 1690s. The saucer would be made with central well in which the cup could snugly sit, ensuring that people with unsteady hands were able to safely drink hot chocolate and later tea and coffee.

c1730-40 *saucer 5in (13cm) diam*

£500-600 WW

A St James's Charles Gouyn étui, some restoration.

c1755-59 *4in (10cm) high*

£2,000-2,500 BE

A Staffordshire porcelain porter mug, painted with the 'Independent Taliho' stagecoach, inscribed 'Henry Truslove', some faults and wear.

Dunchurch, near Rugby, UK, was an important staging post for stagecoaches and the mail coach. The 'Independent Tally-Ho' was one of the London-to-Birmingham coaches which passed through regularly. There were several coaching inns at Dunchurch, including The Bell, which was under the management of Henry Truslove in 1828.

c1825-30 *5in (12.5cm) high*

£500-600 WW

A rare Swansea taperstick, red 'SWANSEA' script mark to base.

2¾in (7cm) diam

£2,500-3,000 **JON**

A Swansea sauce tureen, stand and a cover, possibly painted by William Pollard, the tureen with puce script mark, the saucer impressed 'SWANSEA', slight rubbing to gilding, cover possibly a replacement.

1814-22 *saucer 7½in (19cm) diam*

£1,500-2,000 **DN**

A pair of Swansea tureens, covers and stands, iron red script marks.

c1815-17 *7½in (19cm) diam*

£1,600-2,000 **WW**

A Swansea pen tray, some wear to gilding.

c1815-17 *10in (25.5cm) wide*

£1,300-1,600 **GORL**

An 18thC probably German porcelain model of a seated bull mastiff, probably once part of a fireside pair, lacking tail.

15in (38cm) high

£5,500-6,000 **DUK**

CLOSER LOOK – SWANSEA CABINET CUP AND SAUCER

This cup and saucer were decorated by William Pollard (1803-54) one of Swansea's best-known decorators. He was active in the 1820s and is known for his 'romantic' and expansive style.

Both cup and saucer are exquisitely decorated with an array of garden fruit and colourful wildflowers, embellished with continuous beading, and gilding in bands to some areas.

The rarity of and superb quality of Swansea porcelain adds to the price.

The cup is raised on three claw feet, with a gryphon handle.

A Swansea cabinet cup and saucer, script mark to base.

saucer 6in (15cm) diam

£12,000-16,000 **JON**

A Swansea cabinet cup, with a titled view of the Old Bridge at Hawick, iron red mark, chip to one foot.

c1815-17 *5in (12.5cm) high*

£1,000-1,400 **WW**

A Victorian porcelain fairing, 'To Epsom'.

Fairings are small ornaments made to be cheaply sold or given out as prizes at country fairs during the Victorian and Edwardian periods. Many were made in Germany.

£1,600-2,000 **H&C**

A pair of late 19thC French Louis XVI-style ormolu and turquoise porcelain mounted tazza.

9½in (24cm) high

£4,000-4,500 **WW**

THE POTTERY MARKET

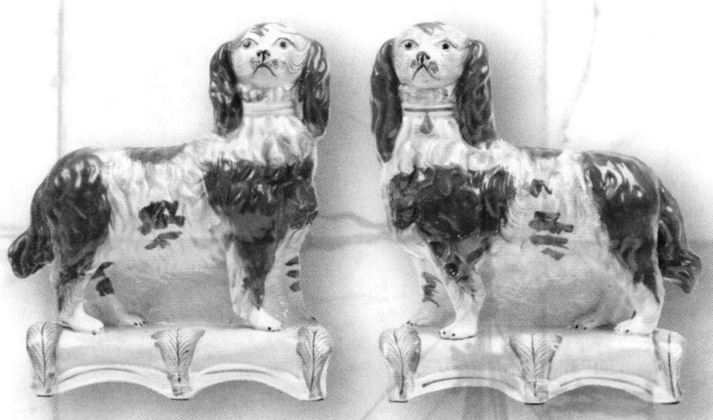

As with most areas, pottery collectors have been affected by the economic climate. As always, when good, rare, early and, especially, dated pieces come fresh to the market, top prices are paid. Mid-priced and low-end pieces have struggled, particularly if they were produced in large quantities, such as some of the more common transfer-printed Staffordshire patterns. However, the best meat platters have weathered the dip in fortune of Staffordshire pearlware; the Durham Ox series remains a favourite with collectors. Delftware again has to be early and of a rare shape and decoration to achieve strong prices – the tile tableau (opposite) is a good example. For the more modest collector who is interested in delft and slipware it is an excellent time to buy. At many sales there is strong competition for the top-end pieces, but the market is generally sluggish for the more common pottery.

As in the previous edition of *The Miller's Antiques Handbook and Price Guide*, the American market for pottery is generally stronger than the UK market. Good quality pre-1830 pottery is still in demand. Business is mainly through the internet, as we are still not seeing the number of American buyers travelling around the country as in the past, although there are indications that the collectors are returning.

Victorian pottery and Staffordshire figures have to be exceptionally rare to attract any interest. The Staffordshire dogs (above) are good quality, early, in excellent condition and with the added embellishment of delicate cushions. There is still the problem of fake 'Staffordshire' coming from the Far East – I have seen examples on both sides of the Atlantic. They are really quite easy to spot, as they don't have the same quality of period examples. If you are in any doubt you should buy from a reputable dealer or auction house. Again, it is worth taking a look at good, original 'right' pieces to 'get your eye in'.

It is around the time when we published the first *Miller's Antiques Handbook and Price Guide* that 19th century pot lids were in great demand. As with many areas, rarity drives the prices. At Andrew Hilton's Historical & Collectable Auctions, rare lids showing the Bay of Naples, 'How I love to laugh' and 'Pet rabbits' all sold for in excess of £2,000. But as Andrew Hilton said, 'At the other end of the market, lids selling at £20 were making £40 in the 1970s (the equivalent of about £220 today). 'As in most markets there is a limited number of top-end collectors and when they have got all they want, the market sinks until newcomers arrive.' This rings true for the pottery market in general.

There have been some dramatic prices paid for some early pottery, particularly the Italian *maiolica istoriato* ware plates, dishes and apothecary jars created in the 16th century. Interest in good and early (16th century) Hispano Moresque pottery remains strong, but little comes to the market. Mason's ironstone has to be an interesting shape with good strong colours to make any money. Good quality early Wedgwood, particularly if the piece has unusual colour combinations, seems to be selling better in the US sale rooms. American stoneware also continues to have a strong collectors' market, particularly for rare shapes and makers, and the more unusual designs. Redware has seen a sluggish period where only the most unusual pieces fetch high prices.

Top Left: A pair of Staffordshire pottery spaniels.
c1850 *9¾in (25cm) high*
£2,200-2,600 **BELL**

Above: An unusual 18thC manganese tiled tableau, probably Dutch, several tiles cracked.
35¾in (91cm) wide
£5,000-6,000 **CHOR**

An English delft plate, probably Bristol, with a portrait of George I, initialled 'GR', cracked.
c1714 *8¾in (22cm) diam*
£5,500-6,500 **H&C**

A Bristol delft plate, depicting a smouldering bottle kiln.

This is a rare and interesting subject.
c1720 *8¾in (22.5cm) diam*
£3,500-4,500 **WW**

A Bristol delft 'Farmhouse' plate, painted with a cockerel, between sponged trees.
c1720-30 *9in (23cm) diam*
£2,500-3,000 **WW**

A Bristol delft bowl, with 'pie-crust' rim, painted with a lake landscape and Chinese figures, large star crack, some chips.
c1740-50 *13½in (34cm) diam*
£6,000-6,500 **BE**

A mid-18thC delft charger, possibly Bristol, filled glaze chips to the rim.
11½in (29cm) diam
£1,000-1,400 **PW**

A Bristol delft 'King of Prussia' plate, with a portrait of Frederick the Great below the letters 'K P', minor rim chips.

During the Seven Years War (1756-63), Frederick II of Prussia was an ally and a popular figure in Great Britain.
c1760 *8¾in (22cm) diam*
£1,500-2,000 **BE**

A documentary Liverpool delft plate, the reverse inscribed 'Richard Bury of Royley in the Township of Wrighton, 1750'.

Several other named and dated delft pieces have been recorded, including several plates featuring the names of landowners in the Oldham and Bury areas of Lancashire, possibly those associated with the coal-mining industry. Richard Bury (c1715-90) is mentioned in the Quarter Sessions at Rochdale on 3 October 1757 for non-repair of a stretch of the Kings Highway, leading to the sluice carrying water to the coal pits.
1750 *8¾in (22cm) diam*
£800-900 **WW**

A delft plate, Liverpool or Dublin, painted with the 'La Pêche' pattern, chip to rim.

This design, commonly seen on Caughley and Worcester porcelain, is copied from a design by Jean Pillement, engraved by P.C. Canot and published in 1759.
c1770 *9in (23cm) wide*
£450-550 **WW**

A London delft Royal portrait blue-dash charger, painted with William III, inscribed 'WR', fine hairline crack, some glaze flaking.

There were several London factories producing delft pieces in the 17thC and 18thC, most notably at Aldgate, Bermondsey, Lambeth, Southwark and Vauxhall.

c1690 *13½in (34cm) diam*

£10,000-14,000 **DN**

A delft dish, probably London, painted with portraits of William and Mary, initialled 'WMR', minor glaze loss to rim, one small chip.

c1690 *8¼in (21cm) diam*

£4,500-5,000 **H&C**

A delft dish, possibly London, painted with a portrait medallion of Queen Anne, initialled 'AR', glaze loss to rim.

c1702 *9in (23cm) diam*

£5,000-6,000 **H&C**

A London delft plate, attributed to Vauxhall, depicting a working pot kiln.

c1750 *8¾in (22.5cm) diam*

£3,500-4,500 **HALL**

An English delft dish, depicting William III, initialled 'KW', restored.

c1690 *13½in (34cm) diam*

£2,500-3,000 **H&C**

CLOSER LOOK – DELFT PILL SLAB

This delft pottery slab would have been used for rolling out pills.

It is painted in blue with the arms of the Worshipful Company of Apothecaries, a London livery company founded in 1617.

The arms feature Apollo, two unicorns and a rhinoceros.

Beneath is painted the motto 'OPIFER QUE PER ORBEM DICOR' ('Throughout the world they speak of me as a bringer of help') and the arms of the City of London.

A London delft pill slab, hairline crack, flat glaze chips, minor wear.

c1740 *10¾in (27cm) high*

£7,500-8,500 **TEN**

A rare Vauxhall delft teapot and cover, minor chip to cover rim, typical fritting.

c1720 *4in (10cm) high*

£6,500-7,500 **HAN**

An early 18thC dated delft marriage plate, painted with a 'merryman'-style cartouche of winged griffons, a crown and cherub's head, inscribed 'TGD 1705', hairline crack, minor glaze losses.

1705 *10in (25.5cm) diam*

£550-650 **BE**

An early 18thC delft posset pot, painted with Chinese figures, the cover lacking, some faults.

12½in (31.5cm) wide

£2,000-2,500 **WW**

ESSENTIAL REFERENCE – DUTCH DELFT

Tin-glazed pottery was made in the Netherlands from the late 15thC. While potteries were established in Haarlem, Rotterdam and Amsterdam, the town of Delft rose to prominence in the mid-17thC, hence the term Dutch Delft.

- **From the mid-16thC, pottery was painted in high-fired colours, such as copper green, yellow and ochre, and boldly outlined in cobalt blue. Early wares included household objects such as dishes, plates, syrup-jugs and pots. Early patterns tended to be inspired by Italian designs.**
- **From the late 16thC, tiles were made in large quantities, for both floors and walls. These were often decorated in simple patterns and repeated motifs.**
- **In the 17thC, when blue and white Chinese porcelain was imported to the Netherlands, Dutch pottery began to emulate its patterns. Pottery was produced in blue and white. When imports from China ceased in the mid-17thC, due to China's invasion from Manchuria, the demand for blue and white pottery in the Netherlands became even greater. Repeated floral patterns, Dutch landscape and biblical subjects were common.**
- **The increasing popularity of English creamware throughout Europe led to the decline of the tin-glazed industry in the Netherlands from the early 19thC.**

A mid-to-late 17thC Dutch Delft pewter-mounted jug, by De Metaale Pot, marked 'LVE' to base, some chips.

12½in (32cm) high

£9,000-11,000 RMA

A Dutch Delft dish, with a portrait of Queen Mary, initialled 'KM', hairline crack.

c1690 13½in (34cm) diam

£1,500-2,000 H&C

An early 18thC Dutch Delft teapot and cover, red 'LF' monogram mark for Lambertus van Eenhoorn, the handle broken off and re-glued, some chipping.

Lambertus van Eenhoorn was the son of Wouter van Eenhoorn and brother of Samuel van Eenhoorn, both of whom ran De Grieksche A factory. Lambertus ran De Metaale Pot (The Metal Pot) factory from the death of its previous owner in 1691 until his own death in 1721.

6in (15cm) high

£850-950 WW

An 18thC Dutch Delft tobacco jar, painted 'Duinkerker' and '5', painted marks, with associated brass cover.

15in (38cm) high

£2,500-3,000 DUK

A pair of 18thC Dutch Delft 'kraak' chargers, by De Metaale Pot.

13½in (34.5cm) diam

£1,000-1,400 L&T

An early to mid-18thC Dutch Delft cuspidor, with tobacco harvesting scenes, some small rim chips.

5in (13cm) diam

£8,000-9,000 RMA

A rare 18thC Dutch Delft yellow ground 'Sample' or 'Hundred Antiquities' plate.

8¾in (22.5cm) diam

£16,000-18,000 RMA

A pair of early 19thC Dutch Delft six-tile panels of Roman soldiers.

The source material for these tile panels could be a series of Virtue and Vices (these emblematic of War) by Jacques de Gheyn II. Soldiers, especially Dutch soldiers, were a popular subject for Delft tiles in the 17thC.

15in (38cm) high

£700-800 DN

ESSENTIAL REFERENCE – FAIENCE

The term faience, otherwise spelt faïence or fayence, refers to tin-glazed pottery made in France, Germany, Spain and Scandinavia. It is distinguished from tin-glazed pottery made in Italy, called maiolica, or made in the Netherlands, called Dutch Delft, or in England, called delft.

- **The name faience came from the similarity in design between early 16thC French earthenware and the maiolica made in Faenza, Italy. French faience soon took on its own style, influenced by Baroque styles and Chinese blue and white ceramics.**
- **The majority of German faience dates from the late 17thC to early 19thC. Early German faience pieces often resemble Dutch Delft. Such patterns were later replaced by a more native style, featuring birds, foliage, buildings, landscapes, double-headed eagles and coats of arms.**
- **In Spain, production of faience wear was led by a factory in Alcora, north of Valencia, where high-quality 'loza fina' faience ware was made. Painted designs often included landscapes, figures and animals.**
- **Many faience factories across Continental Europe struggled and ultimately closed in the late 18thC due to competition with porcelain and with English creamware.**

A pair of 18thC French faience 'Chinaman' figures, attributed to the Charles Hannong workshop, Strasbourg.

12¼in (31cm) high

£4,000-6,000 **RMA**

A rare 18thC French faience playing cards dish, possibly by Ferrat, Moustiers or Nevers, minor surface chips and glaze loss.

This piece has a tag to the back for the collection of G. Papillon, former conservator of the Sèvres ceramics museum.

9½in (24cm) diam

£3,000-4,000 **RMA**

A French faience tureen and cover, with associated stand.

c1770-80 *13½in (34cm) wide*

£300-400 **WW**

A late 18thC French faience albarello, Paris or Rouen, inscribed 'Ung. de Styrace', some restoration.

Unguent de Styrace is recorded as being used as a form of poultice to help clean infected wounds.

7in (18cm) high

£250-300 **WW**

An early 18thC Frankfurt faience vase, blue circle mark to base, cover lacking.

10¾in (27.5cm) high

£600-700 **WW**

A Höchst faience figure, possibly from the Commedia dell'Arte series.

c1760 *6in (15cm) high*

£550-650 **WW**

A set of four Antonibon faience plates, blue star marks.

Tin-glazed earthenware made at Antonibon, Nove, in Northern Italy, is typically closer to the French style, and so is generally referred to as faience rather than maiolica.

c1775 *9¼in (23.5cm) diam*

£800-900 **WW**

A large mid-18thC Spanish faience syrup jar, initialled 'SP', a banner reading 'A:Di:Boragne', some glaze chipping.

13½in (34cm) high

£550-650 **WW**

A Spanish faience albarello and cover, probably Talavera, inscribed with 'IHS', and 'C. Ammon', the base inscribed 'JHC', some glaze chipping, dated.

1773 *12in (30.5cm) high*

£500-600 **WW**

A 15thC Montelupo maiolica jug, painted in enamels with an owl, some glaze wear and chipping.

6½in (16.5cm) high

£4,000-4,500 **WW**

An early 16thC Montelupo maiolica armorial albarello, inscribed 'Pill Cotie' beneath the arms of Luigi di Antonio Aldobrandini of Florence, handles inscribed 'Bo', cracked.

5in (13cm) high

£1,500-2,000 **WW**

A mid-16thC Italian maiolica albarello, attributed to Pesaro, inscribed 'Confet o cingul orum', inscribed 'RB', some restoration.

Previously attributed to Faenza or Castel Durante, similar jars inscribed 'RB' (probably for a pharmacy) are now believed to have been made at Pesaro.

10½in (26.5cm) high

£6,500-7,000 **WW**

A Montelupo maiolica dish, broken and cleanly repaired.

c1500 *14¼in (36.5cm) diam*

£2,000-2,500 **WW**

A Montelupo maiolica albarello, decorated with Persian palmettes, some restoration.

c1520 *8¾in (22cm) high*

£2,200-2,600 **WW**

A Venetian maiolica albarello.

c1560-80 *6in (15cm) high*

£1,500-2,000 **WW**

A pair of 16thC Antwerp maiolica 'A foglie' albarelli, one inscribed 'MITRIDATUM', the other 'CERASA-COND', some chips and hairlines, minor glaze loss.

As Antwerp became an important European hub, Italian maiolica artists moved from Venice and other areas in Italy to Antwerp, Guido di Savino being the most famous. Antwerp maiolica was only made during a short time span, as artisans moved north to Dutch cities such as Delft and Haarlem during the Inquisition and Spanish rule in the late 1570s and early 1580s.

9¾in (24.5cm) high

£14,000-16,000 **RMA**

A pair of mid-16thC Faenza maiolica albarelli, with portraits inscribed 'Vargel' and 'Fabio', and 'Sy. De onphafu' and 'Dia. Fribuf', some restoration.

12½in (32cm) high

£7,500-8,500 **WW**

A rare 'Faenza' maiolica vessel, with a siren handle, a grimacing grotesque mask forming the aperture.

One comparable boot is in the Ashmolean Museum, Oxford, and another at Waddesdon Manor, the latter with the mark of the Faenza potter Don Pino Bettisi. It is unclear whether these vessels had a celebratory purpose, comparable to the tradition of drinking from a bride's shoe at a wedding, or were merely novelty objects.

c1580 *9¼in (23.5cm) high*

£6,000-7,000 **DUK**

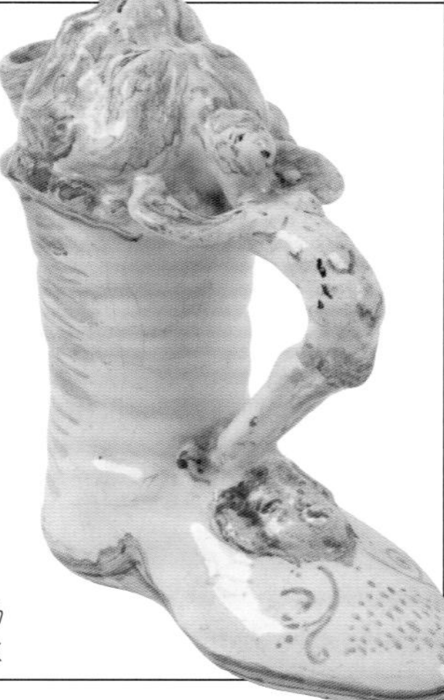

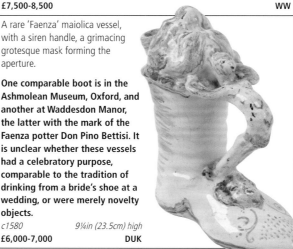

An Italian maiolica albarello, probably Siena, inscribed 'F Di Cappi', surface chip, dated.

Caper flowers were used as a culinary spice and an anti-inflammatory.

1613 *6in (15cm) high*

£1,800-2,200 WW

A Castelli maiolica charger, from the workshop of Francesco Grue, with Alexander the Great accepting the keys to Nysa, hairline cracks and chips, some repairs.

c1650 *18½in (47cm) diam*

£3,500-4,000 TEN

An Italian maiolica syrup or wet drug jar, possibly Deruta, inscribed 'Sy. di Lupoli', restored, dated.

The label refers to Syrup of Hops, which has a sedative effect used to treat bouts of delirium and sleeplessness.

1676 *11½in (29cm) high*

£2,000-3,000 WW

A pair of early 18thC Laterza maiolica albarelli, marked 'GE'.

10¾in (27cm) high

£1,200-1,500 WW

An 18thC Castelli maiolica basin and cover, the base broken and re-glued.

18½in (47cm) diam

£2,000-2,500 TEN

A 18thC Sicilian maiolica jar.

8¾in (22cm) high

£400-500 WW

An 18thC Italian maiolica syrup jar, inscribed 'PLANTAGINIS', small chip to foot.

Plantain has a variety of medicinal uses, including as an expectorant and diuretic when taken internally, or for fistulae and ulcers as an external lotion.

8½in (21.5cm) high

£500-600 WW

A mid-18thC Castelli maiolica plaque.

12½in (32.5cm) long

£600-700 WW

A Castelli maiolica plaque, painted with a lady and attendants.

c1730 *7¼in (18.5cm) high*

£1,800-2,200 WW

POTTERY

ESSENTIAL REFERENCE – ENGLISH REDWARE

English Redware was inspired by Chinese Yixing stoneware.

- **It was first made in the Netherlands, and probably introduced to the Staffordshire area by migrant potters in the late 17thC or early 18thC. English Redware is sometimes described as 'Elers ware', after Dutch brothers John and David Elers, who settled in Staffordshire in 1686.**
- **It fell out of fashion in England in the mid-to-late 18thC, as white stoneware and creamware grew in popularity.**

A Staffordshire glazed redware jug and cover, decorated in cream slip, some chipping.
c1745 *5½in (14cm) high*
£350-400 **WW**

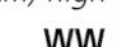

A Staffordshire redware punch pot and cover, some chipping.
c1760 *7¾in (19.5cm) high*
£220-260 **TEN**

A Staffordshire redware milk jug.
c1760 *3¼in (8cm) high*
£400-450 **WW**

An early 19thC Spode redware teapot and cover, impressed mark, some chips, glued break to handle.
8in (20.5cm) long
£1,000-1,400 **SK**

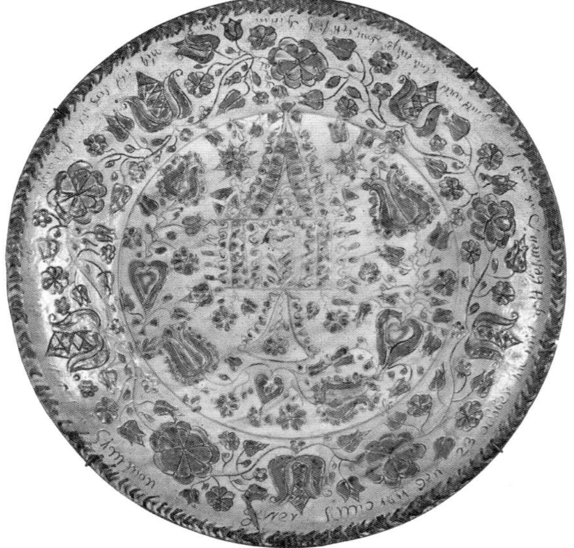

A German redware charger, with sgraffito decoration and an inscribed verse.
c1800 *21in (53.5cm) diam*
£1,800-2,200 **POOK**

ESSENTIAL REFERENCE – AMERICAN REDWARE

Redware was brought to America by German and Dutch settlers in the 17thC. After it fell out of fashion in England, it remained popular in the American colonies, where clay was abundant, making redware pieces affordable.

- **Redware was often decorated with simple patterns in liquid clay slip, or with the more complex sgraffito technique.**
- **Pieces were finished with a lead-based glaze to ensure they were waterproofed for cooking and food storage.**
- **Whiteware and stoneware began to take over in the 19thC, but redware production continued in areas of Pennsylvania, North Carolina and Virginia into the 20thC.**

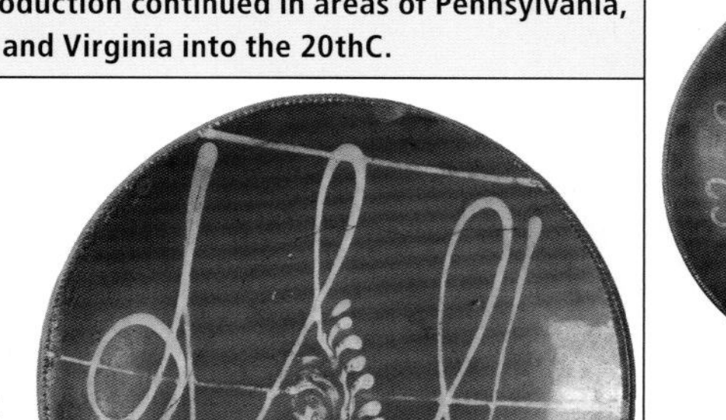

A 19thC Connecticut redware charger, large re-glued break.
12½in (32cm) diam
£250-300 **POOK**

A 19thC Long Island redware charger, old rim chip.
12in (30.5cm) diam
£550-600 **POOK**

An early 19thC New England redware jar, attributed to Hartford, Connecticut.
8in (20.5cm) high
£600-650 **POOK**

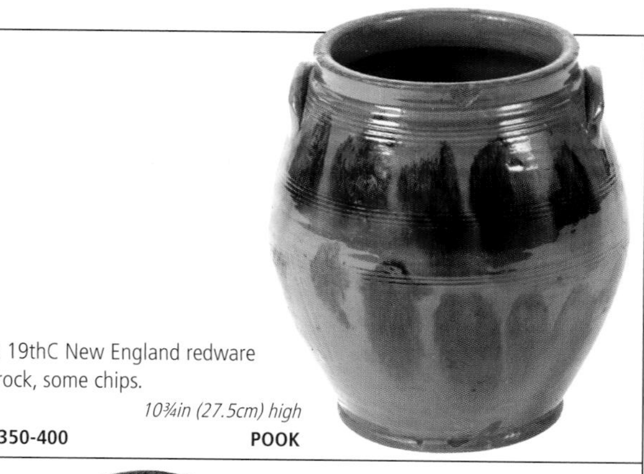

A 19thC New England redware crock, some chips.

10¾in (27.5cm) high

£350-400 **POOK**

A 19thC New England slip-decorated redware charger, with coggled rim.

12in (30.5cm) high

£500-600 **SK**

A Pennsylvania Bucks County sgraffito redware charger, attributed to Conrad Mumbauer, dated.

1810 *11¾in (30cm) diam*

£3,000-3,500 **POOK**

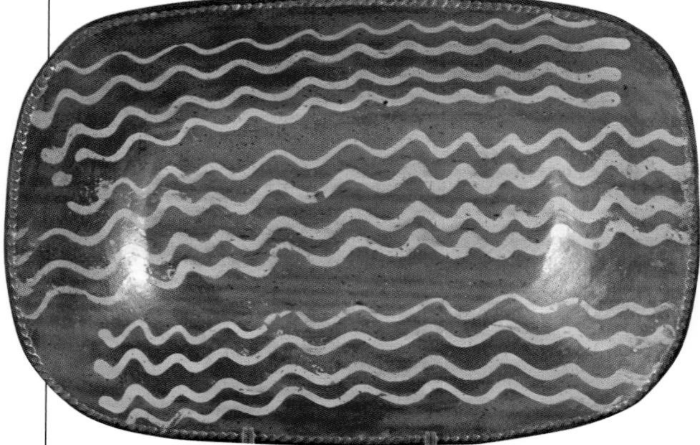

A 19thC Pennsylvania redware loaf dish.

15¾in (40cm) wide

£950-1,100 **POOK**

A 19thC Pennsylvania redware charger, old rim chip.

14½in (37cm) diam

£1,000-1,400 **POOK**

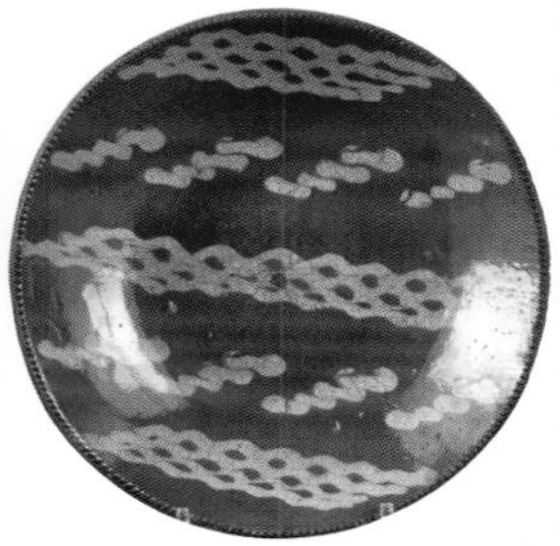

A 19thC Pennsylvania redware plate, glaze loss to centre.

11¼in (28.5cm) diam

£400-450 **POOK**

A 19thC Pennsylvania slip-decorated redware toddy plate, some cracks and chip.

5¾in (14.5cm) diam

£350-450 **SK**

A 19thC Pennsylvania redware bird rattle, chip to base.

3in (7.5cm) high

£800-850 **POOK**

A large 19thC American redware jar, some cracks and repairs.

13½in (34.5cm) high

£1,200-1,600 **SK**

Three 18thC creamware pedestal dishes, crack to one.
max 11in (28cm) wide
£600-700 **MOR**

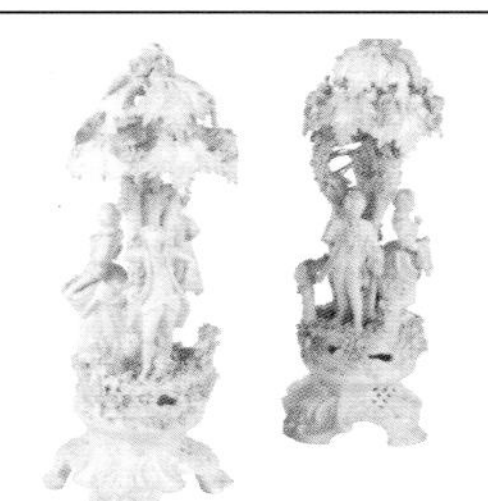

A pair of 18thC Continental creamware groups, probably Italian.
15½in (39.5cm) high
£1,000-1,400 **DUK**

A creamware teapot, transfer-printed with a portrait of John Wesley, the reverse with verse.

John Wesley (1703-91) was one of the founders of Methodism, along with his brother Charles Wesley, Robert Kirkham and William Morgan. He was ordained as a deacon of the Church of England in 1725, and in 1726 became a fellow of Lincoln College, Oxford, where he helped establish the Holy Club, known as 'Methodist' due to its prescribed method of studying the Bible. Concerned that the poor felt excluded from the church, Wesley began to address the public in open areas, something which became a key feature of Methodism.

c1750
£1,600-2,000 **HAN**

A transfer-printed creamware teapot, depicting John Wesley within a ring of 15 preachers, some hairline and crazing.
c1760
£1,500-2,000 **HAN**

A Staffordshire Whieldon-type creamware puzzle jug, the neck incised 'IL' within the date, some restoration.
1752 *7in (18cm) high*
£650-750 **WW**

A Whieldon-type creamware plate.
c1760 *9¼in (23.5cm) diam*
£500-600 **WW**

A Whieldon creamware pug, some restoration.

Thomas Whieldon (fl.1740-80) was a leading Staffordshire potter, briefly the partner of Josiah Wedgwood and later High Sheriff of Staffordshire.

c1760 *3¼in (8cm) high*
£800-900 **TEN**

A miniature creamware Whieldon-type teapot and cover, cracked.
c1770 *5½in (14cm) wide*
£350-400 **WW**

A William Greatbatch creamware teapot and cover, printed and overpainted with 'The Prodigal Son Receives His Patrimony', the reverse with 'The Prodigal Son Taking Leave', some chips and staining, minor cracks.

William Greatbatch (1735-1813) was an important Staffordshire potter, active from the mid-18thC to the early 19thC. He ran his own pottery, and was also employed by Josiah Wedgwood to supply block-moulds for the Wedgwood factory.

c1770-82 *5in (12.5cm) high*
£700-800 **TEN**

A creamware coffee pot and cover, hairline crack.
c1770 *11½in (29cm) high*
£300-400 **TEN**

A creamware mug, painted with a piper, some restoration.
c1770 *6½in (16.5cm) high*
£550-650 **TEN**

A Wedgwood creamware jelly mould cone, impressed mark to base, small chip to top.
c1780 *8¼in (21cm) high*
£800-900 **WW**

A Neale & Co. creamware figure of Apollo, some chipping.
c1795-1800 *6in (15cm) high*
£350-400 **WW**

A late 18thC Wilson creamware jelly mould cone, the base pierced with eight holes, impressed mark.

Robert Wilson was part of Neale & Co., a partnership which dissolved in 1792. The factory continued under Robert and David Wilson into the 19thC, and continued to use earlier moulds and styles.

8in (20.5cm) high
£1,100-1,400 **WW**

A Bovey Tracey documentary creamware tea canister, inscribed 'Mary Coombs, Exeter', one cherub restored, dated.
1796 *5in (13cm) high*
£1,200-1,500 **BE**

An Italian creamware cardinal on a horse, probably Naples, some restoration, horse's leg detached, some glaze flakes.
c1800 *18in (46cm) high*
£2,000-2,500 **TEN**

A pair of early 19thC Herculaneum creamware plates, with printed portraits of Nelson, impressed marks.
9¾in (25cm) diam
£650-750 **WW**

A Staffordshire creamware cat, some chipping.
c1800 *3¼in (8.5cm) high*
£550-650 **WW**

A creamware slip-decorated creamer, some chips.

c1800 *4in (10cm) high*

£2,500-3,000 **SK**

A pair of early 19thC Leeds Pottery creamware plates, painted with a Chinese man, impressed marks.

9½in (24cm) diam

£250-300 **WW**

A Wedgwood creamware part service, printed with the 'Waterlily' pattern, with 2 chargers, a tureen and cover, 2 plates, a mug, an oval stand and a sauce ladle.

This design derives from prints in the Botanist's Repository and the Botanical Magazine, from 1803-06. The design was probably inspired by the interests of Josiah Wedgwood's eldest son John, who was a founding member of the Royal Horticultural Society.

c1810

£1,800-2,200 **WW**

A creamware cow creamer and cover, with mottled manganese and green glaze.

c1800 *6¾in (17cm) long*

£450-550 **TEN**

A creamware model of a horse, minor restoration.

c1800-20 *6in (15cm) high*

£1,000-1,400 **BE**

An early 19thC creamware jug, printed with Masonic designs, glaze chips to spout, prints retouched.

10½in (26.5cm) high

£200-300 **PW**

A 19thC Liverpool creamware mug, transfer-printed with the 'Success to the Duke of York & His Brave Army', restored.

6in (15cm) high

£300-400 **POOK**

A Wedgwood creamware charger, painted with Meissen-style songbirds, impressed mark.

c1820 *14¼in (36cm) diam*

£350-400 **WW**

ESSENTIAL REFERENCE – PEARLWARE

Pearlware was introduced by Wedgwood c1779, in an attempt to improve creamware.

- **Pearlware included more white clay and flint in the body than creamware and thus was of a whiter colour. Cobalt oxide was added to the glaze, giving it a bluish-white tint.**
- **Pearlware included dishes, plates, teapots, coffee pots, jugs and figural groups.**
- **Pearlware was often decorated in underglaze blue by painting or transfer-printing. Designs included the chinoiserie 'Willow' pattern, and many varieties of Classical designs and English landscapes.**

A rare pearlware bonbonnière, modelled as the head of a lady.
c1780 *3¼in (8cm) long*
£2,000-2,500 **WW**

A slip-marbled pearlware jug, repaired spout, some scratches and chips.
c1800 *9in (23cm) high*
£7,000-7,500 **SK**

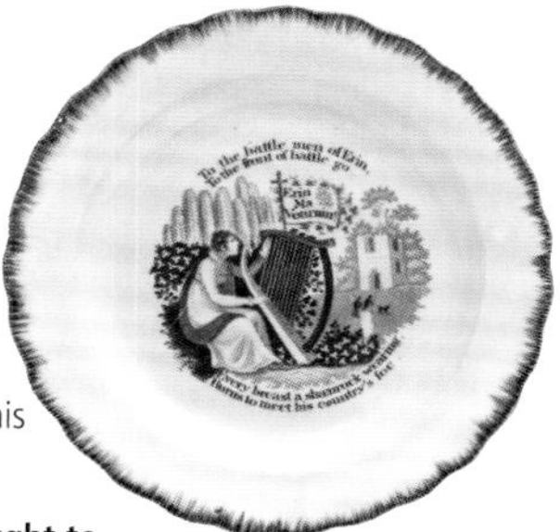

An early 19thC pearlware plate, transfer-printed with a woman playing a harp, inscribed 'Erin Ma Vournin!' (My Beloved Ireland, or Ireland Vien of My Heart), and 'To the battle men of Erin,/To the front of battle go,/Every breast a shamrock wearing,/Burns to meet his country's foe', hairline to rim.

This piece is undated, but is thought to be associated with the Irish Republican movement. It was possibly produced to commemorate an uprising.

7in (18cm) diam
£550-650 **BE**

A pearlware transfer-printed jug, with Masonic decoration, chipping to rim, star hairline to base.
12½in (32cm) high
£350-400 **HAN**

A rare pearlware pug dog bonbonnière or snuff box, decorated in Portobello-type colours, the interior inscribed 'Rose', with a pewter hinged lid and mount.
c1800 *2¾in (7cm) long*
£1,500-2,000 **WW**

A pearlware quart mug and cover, crack to base and rim, repair to lid.
c1790 *7in (18cm) high*
£2,500-3,000 **SK**

A pearlware jug, painted with a barge inscribed 'J Yates Colton 18 tons' and 'Victoria', inscribed 'Joseph Tomlinson Little Haywood', the handle restored, dated.

The 1841 census lists Joseph Tomlinson as a publican in the village of Little Haywood, while William White, 'History, Gazetteer and Directory of Staffordshire of 1834' mentions John Yates of Colton, 'an extensive maltster and corn merchant'. Possibly the latter commissioned this jug as a gift for the former.

1839 *10¼in (26cm) high*
£350-400 **WW**

A copper lustre banded pearlware mug, printed with an unusual named portrait of George IV, restored.
1821 *3¼in (8cm) high*
£600-700 **H&C**

CLOSER LOOK – BOXING TANKARD

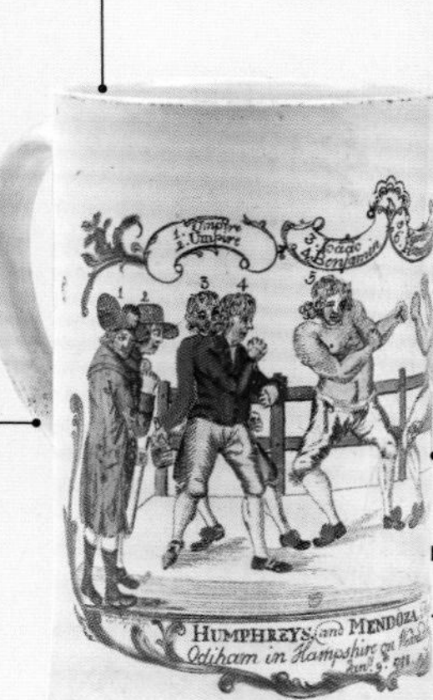

This tankard depicts a boxing match between rivals Richard Humphreys and Daniel Mendoza, fought at Odiham, Hampshire, on Wednesday 9 January 1788, with a key naming the eight attendants.

The rivalry between Humphreys and Mendoza was arguably one of the reasons for boxing's surge in popularity in the late 18thC.

The tankard is signed 'Jno Aynsley, Lane End' for John Aynsley, a Staffordshire pottery company founded in 1775. Today Aynsley continues as part of Belleek Pottery in Ireland.

Despite some repairs to surface scratches, the tankard keeps its value due to the interest of the subject matter.

A John Aynsley pearlware tankard, minor damages.
c1788 *5in (12.5cm) high*
£5,000-5,500 **BELL**

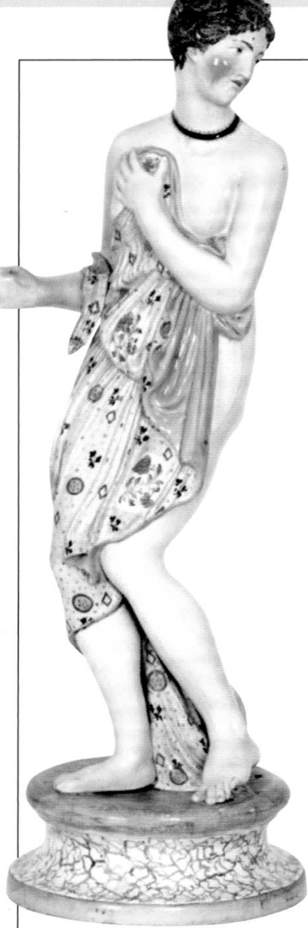

A large late 18thC Staffordshire Enoch Wood pearlware statue, possibly depicting Salmacis.

Salmacis is a naiad, or nymph, in Greek mythology.

28¾in (73cm) high

£3,000-3,500 FLD

A Staffordshire Pratt-type pearlware group of St George and the Dragon, some restoration.

c1800 *11¾in (30cm) high*

£750-850 DN

A Staffordshire pearlware figure group, 'Savoyard with Dancing Bear'.

8½in (21.5cm) high

£550-650 SWO

An early 19thC Staffordshire pearlware group, 'The Dandies' or 'Dandy and Dandizette', some restoration.

7¼in (18.5cm) high

£1,800-2,200 BELL

An Obadiah Sherratt pearlware bust, of Reverend John Wesley.

c1820 *12¼in (31cm) high*

£2,500-3,000 WW

A pair of Walton pearlware groups, 'Flight into Egypt' and 'Return from Egypt', depicting Mary, Joseph, baby Jesus and a donkey, some restoration.

John Walton was a Staffordshire figure potter active c1805-30s.

c1820 *7½in (19cm) high*

£2,000-2,500 BELL

A Staffordshire pearlware group, 'Gretna Green', in the manner of Obadiah Sherratt, some restoration.

c1830 *8¼in (21cm) wide*

£1,000-1,400 BELL

A pair of Staffordshire pearlware figures of Geoffrey Chaucer and Sir Isaac Newton, on square marbled bases, some restoration and minor damages.

12in (31cm) high

£1,500-2,000 CHIL

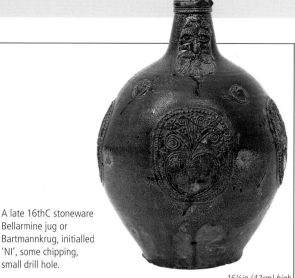

A late 16thC stoneware Bellarmine jug or Bartmannkrug, initialled 'NI', some chipping, small drill hole.

16½in (42cm) high

£4,500-5,000 **WW**

A late 17thC German Westerwald salt-glazed stoneware jug, with a crowned 'WR' medallion.

7¾in (20cm) high

£3,200-3,600 **BE**

A Staffordshire salt-glazed stoneware bear jug and cover.

c1750 *8¾in (22cm) high*

£1,800-2,200 **TEN**

CLOSER LOOK – STONEWARE JUG

This early buff stoneware jug is of a type commonly associated with the potteries of Fulham and Vauxhall.

It is unusual in form. Mugs are more common than jugs with spouts.

It is applied with a relief moulded fouled anchor, probably denoting the name of a tavern.

It is marked 'WR', signalling the William III period, but might date from afterwards, as this mark was used throughout the 18thC.

A William III stoneware jug.

5in (13cm) high

£4,000-5,000 **SWO**

An early to mid-18thC stoneware tankard, London, with applied moulded portraits of William and Mary and Charles.

This mug was probably produced shortly after the Jacobite rising of the Old Pretender (James Stuart, son of James II) in 1715, in support of a Protestant Monarchy. It could have been produced in reference to the Young Pretender (Charles Stuart, 'Bonnie Prince Charlie', grandson of James II) in 1745, but the reference to William and Mary makes this unlikely. Mugs with similar handles and mouldings often date from the 1720s and are attributed to Vauxhall, Southwark or Fulham Potteries.

7¾in (20cm) high

£3,000-3,500 **H&C**

A Staffordshire salt-glazed stoneware teapot and cover, some chips and firing flaws.

c1750 *4¼in (10.5cm) high*

£600-700 **TEN**

A salt-glazed stoneware teapot and cover, some restoration.

The full blown roses on the teapot represent The Old Pretender; the buds represent The Young Pretender.

c1755 *6in (15cm) high*

£1,200-1,600 **TEN**

A Staffordshire salt-glazed stoneware teapot and cover, painted with a garden scene, restoration to spout, some hairlines and chips.

c1760 *7½in (19cm) long*

£650-750 **TEN**

A Staffordshire salt-glazed stoneware coffee pot and cover, one hairline crack, minor wear.

c1760 *9½in (24cm) high*

£1,400-1,800 **TEN**

A 19thC salt-glazed stoneware pub dispensing jug, with relief-moulded hunting scenes, profile portraits and a Royal coat of arms, tap hole to bottom.

23in (58.5cm) high

£2,200-2,600 **MART**

A 19thC stoneware bottle, 'Irish Reform Cordial, Daniel O'Connell Esq.', by Denby and Codnor Park, Bournes Potteries Derbyshire.

Daniel O'Connell (1775-1847) was a lawyer and one of the first Irish nationalist leaders. He campaigned for Catholic emancipation in Ireland and was the first Catholic MP.

8in (20.5cm) high

£300-350 **AST**

An early 19thC salt-glazed stoneware bottle, inscribed 'Warrens Liquid Blacking Wholesale & for Exportation 14 St Martins Lane'.

Warren's Blacking was a leading manufacturer of shoe-black, or shoe-polish, in the 19thC. The polish was sold as a liquid in bottles or as a paste in pots. Charles Dickens famously worked at Warren's Blacking Factory as a child while his father was in debtor's prison.

7in (18cm) high

£600-700 **MART**

A Doulton & Watts Lambeth Pottery stoneware Nelson flagon, impressed 'TRAFALGAR 1805 ENGLAND EXPECTS EVERY MAN TO DO HIS DUTY', some faults.

This half-length model is particularly rare in bottle form, although it is sometimes seen as a jug.

c1840-50 *16¼in (41.5cm) high*

£1,800-2,200 **WW**

A salt-glazed stoneware Sir Robert Peel spirit flask, holding corn and a scroll reading 'Bread for the Millions', the base embossed 'Sir R. Peel', chips to base.

c1846 *9¾in (24.5cm) high*

£300-400 **BE**

A 19thC Western Pennsylvania three-gallon stoneware crock, inscribed 'Hamilton & Jones 3'.

13½in (34.5cm) high

£4,000-4,500 **POOK**

A large 19thC Pennsylvania stoneware lidded crock, some flakes and chips, sprayed hairlines.

11½in (29cm) diam

£350-400 **POOK**

A two-gallon stoneware pitcher, probably Maryland or Virginia, old chips, small hairline, dated.

1843 *13¾in (35cm) high*

£750-850 **POOK**

ESSENTIAL REFERENCE – TRANSFER-PRINTING

Transfer-printing was developed in the mid-18thC as a quicker and cheaper alternative to painting ceramics by hand.

- **The design would be engraved onto a copper plate. The plate was then covered in ink, and the design transferred to the ceramic surface using paper, then sealed under a clear glaze.**
- **Transfer-printed pieces were usually blue and white, as underglaze cobalt blue was most suited to withstanding the heat of a kiln.**
- **The technique was used by Worcester, Spode, Davenport and many other factories.**
- **Transfer-printed ware featuring American landscapes and buildings was made in Staffordshire and exported to North America.**

A mid-19thC Davenport earthenware punch bowl, printed and impressed marks, surface scratches and glaze loss.
17¾in (45cm) diam
£650-750 BELL

A Jones & Son tazza, from the 'British History' series, the well transfer-printed with 'The Death of Nelson', the sides with 'Charles I Ordering the Speaker to Give up the Five Members', crack to foot.
c1826-28 11¼in (28.5cm) wide
£1,200-1,500 WW

A Spode 'Indian Sporting Series' platter, transfer-printed with 'Battle Between a Buffalo and a Tiger', printed marks.
9in (23cm) long
£650-750 HAN

A 19thC Staffordshire meat platter, transfer-printed with the 'Bee Keeping' pattern.
21¾in (55.5cm) long
£1,500-2,000 HAN

Judith Picks

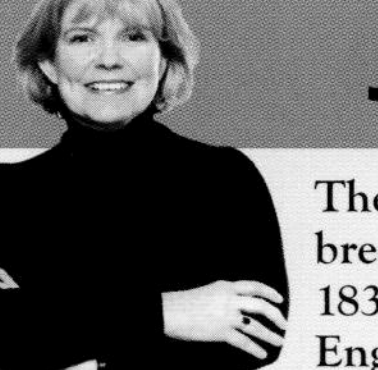

The Durham Ox was a shorthorn bull, bred in 1796 by Charles Colling (1751-1836) of Ketton Hall, near Darlington, England. It was famous for its shape, size and massive weight, with contemporary estimates ranging from 171 to 270 stone. In 1801 it was bought by John Day for £250. Day and his wife travelled the country for several years, transporting the Durham Ox in a specially built four-horse cart, and displaying it to paying customers. The Durham Ox proved such a spectacle that it could bring its owners up to £100 a day. Dozens of inn and pubs at which it had stopped changed their original names to 'The Durham Ox'.

An early 19thC Staffordshire meat platter, transfer-printed with the 'Durham Ox' pattern, some restoration.
19¾in (50cm) long
£600-700 HAN

A 19thC Staffordshire plate, transfer-printed with a portrait medallion of King George III.
9in (23cm) diam
£550-600 POOK

A 19thC Staffordshire plate, transfer-printed with 'Sacred to the Memory of George III', two rim repairs.
10in (25.5cm) diam
£500-600 POOK

A Victorian foot bath, transfer-printed with children and animals, an Asian landscape to the interior, some crazing, staining and cracks.
21¼in (54cm) wide
£700-800 BELL

CLOSER LOOK – ARMS OF PENNSYLVANIA PLATTER

This platter is widely considered one of the most desirable pieces of Historical Staffordshire to collectors.

It is transfer-printed with the 'Arms of Pennsylvania' design, with a border of flowers and foliage.

It is impressed 'T. Mayer', for Thomas Mayer, a skilled potter based in Staffordshire, born c1800.

The quality of the transfer-printing is incredibly clear.

A 19thC Historical Staffordshire 'Arms of Pennsylvania' platter, some small knife marks.

21in (53.5cm) wide

£30,000-35,000 POOK

An early 19thC Historical Staffordshire anti-slavery/ constitution plate, transfer-decorated with 'CONGRESS SHALL MAKE NO LAW...' inscription.

9½in (24cm) diam

£350-400 SK

A 19thC Staffordshire coffeepot, transfer-printed with a spread eagle, some chips.

11in (28cm) high

£900-1,200 SK

An early 19thC Historical Staffordshire pitcher, transfer-printed with the 'Views of the Erie Canal' pattern, small chip to handle.

7¾in (20cm) high

£750-850 SK

A 19thC Historical Staffordshire fruit bowl, the interior transfer-printed with 'Commodore MacDonnough's Victory', the exterior with 'Dixcove on the Gold Coast of Africa'.

10½in (26.5cm) diam

£7,000-8,000 POOK

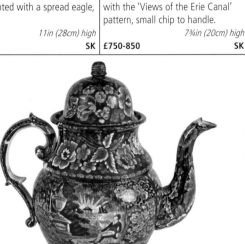

A Historical Staffordshire coffee pot, transfer-printed with the 'Lafayette at Franklin's Tomb' pattern, flake to spout, chip to lid.

12¼in (31cm) high

£950-1,100 POOK

A Historical Staffordshire fruit bowl and undertray, transfer-printed with the 'Landing of Lafayette' pattern, by James and Ralph Clewes, Cobridge, England.

c1824-36 *12in (30.5cm) wide*

£1,200-1,600 SK

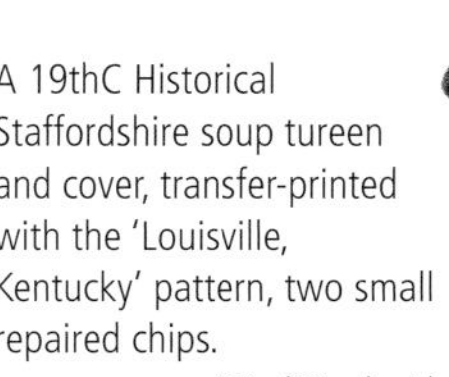

A 19thC Historical Staffordshire soup tureen and cover, transfer-printed with the 'Louisville, Kentucky' pattern, two small repaired chips.

15in (38cm) wide

£9,500-11,500 POOK

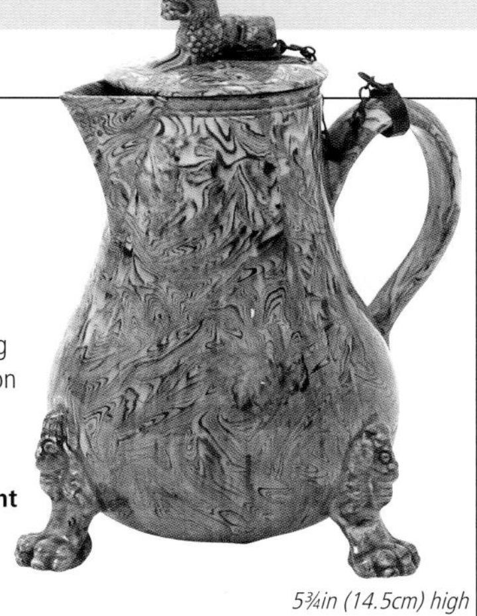

A Staffordshire agateware jug and cover, with recumbent lion dog finial, small damages.

Agateware is made from the combination of different coloured clays, giving an overall marbled effect.

c1755 *5¾in (14.5cm) high*

£3,000-3,500 **WW**

A Staffordshire pottery 'Porter' mug, transfer-printed with 'Porter/Super Fine/Peace and Roast Beef to the Friends of Liberty', hairline to base.

c1805-10 *3¼in (8cm) high*

£400-450 **BE**

A Staffordshire Prattware Wesleyan Chapel moneybox.

£1,000-1,400 **HAN**

A Staffordshire treacle-glaze bear jug and cover, holding a dog, with monkey handle.

c1830 *11in (27.5cm) high*

£500-600 **TEN**

CLOSER LOOK – PIPE-SMOKING SPANIELS

While common Staffordshire dogs are not particularly desirable, rare models such as these pipe-smoking spaniels can fetch higher prices.

Staffordshire pottery pipe-smoking dogs were inspired by the painting 'A Quiet Pipe', by Edwin Henry Landseer (1802-73).

Both spaniels have characterful faces and detailed fur, with enamel details.

Their front legs are separately moulded on an unusual foliate scroll base.

A pair of 19thC Staffordshire pottery pipe-smoking spaniels, flaking to black enamel.

8¼in (21cm) high

£1,800-2,200 **BELL**

A 19thC Staffordshire pottery leopard, cracks and chips, flaking to enamel.

7½in (19cm) high

£600-700 **CHOR**

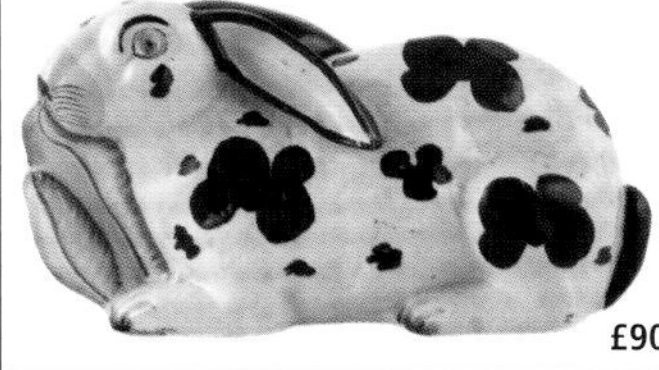

A mid-19thC Staffordshire pottery rabbit.

9in (23cm) wide

£900-1,200 **PW**

A pair of 19thC Staffordshire pottery 'Disraeli' greyhounds, one with a hare in its mouth, minor chips, losses to enamel.

These 'Disraeli' Staffordshire dogs are painted with a similar haircut to Benjamin Disraeli (1804-81), Prime Minister 1868 and 1874-80.

27½in (70cm) high

£400-500 **BELL**

A Staffordshire pottery elephant, 'Jumbo', scratches to enamel.

Jumbo was an African elephant obtained by London Zoo in 1865. In 1881 he became dangerous and the American showman P.T. Barnum agreed to purchase him. His stay in the Americas was short-lived, as he was killed by a locomotive in Ontario, Canada, in 1885, aged 24.

c1885 *10¾in (27.5cm) high*

£1,800-2,200 BELL

A 19thC Staffordshire figure of Daniel O'Connell, flaking to enamels.

16in (40.5cm) high

£600-700 BELL

A 19thC Staffordshire figure, modelled as Mr Barton and Miss Rosa Henry as Selim (or Giaffier) and Zuleika from 'The Bride of Abydos'.

13in (33cm) high

£300-400 FLD

A Staffordshire group, 'The Alphington Ponies', titled 'A Present from Torquay'.

The Misses Durnford moved from Alphington to Torquay with their mother, and became locally notorious for promenading around the town identically dressed in outlandish costume and heavily made up. They became known as 'The Alphington Ponies' because they often rode out in a carriage with ponies. Their brother was so irritated by their habits and clothing that he offered to increase their allowance if they stopped. They refused.

c1845 *4¾in (12cm) high*

£250-300 WW

A 19thC Staffordshire figure of Louis Napoleon, some minor wear.

This is a rare large figure, decorated in excellent polychrome enamels and in good condition.

23½in (60cm) high

£3,500-4,000 BELL

A pair of Staffordshire pottery figures of Emily Stanford and James Blomfield Rush, some chips.

The Rush and Stanford figures were produced immediately after the 1849 trial of the notorious murders at Stanfield Hall. Norfolk tenant farmer and fraudster Rush shot and killed his landlord and the landlord's son. Stanford, who refused to give him an alibi, was found not guilty.

c1849 *10in (25cm) high*

£1,500-2,000 CHIL

A 19thC Staffordshire figure of Field Marshal Lord Raglan, on a gilt titled base.

Lord Raglan (1788-1855) served in the British army in the Napoleonic wars and later in the Crimean war. He lost part of his right arm in the Battle of Waterloo, hence the figure's missing right hand. He is best known today, alongside the Earl of Lucan and the Earl of Cardigan, for his part in instigating the disastrous charge of the Light Cavalry Brigade in 1854.

13in (33cm) high

£350-400 BELL

An early 20thC Staffordshire bust of General William Booth (1829-1912), founder of the Salvation Army, with 'Blood and Fire' shield to his chest.

13½in (34.5cm) high

£900-1,000 FLD

An early Whitaker & Co. 'Bear in a Ravine' pot lid, attributed to Ridgway, minor glaze defect.

3in (7.5cm) diam

£2,500-3,000 **H&C**

An early 'Bears with Valentines' pot lid, attributed to Ridgway.

This design comes from an engraving featured in Alfred Elwes's children's book, 'The Adventures of a Bear'.

2¾in (7cm) diam

£2,000-2,500 **H&C**

A 'Performing Bear' pot lid, attributed to Ridgway, small rim chip.

2¾in (7cm) diam

£1,300-1,800 **H&C**

A 'Bears Reading Newspapers' pot lid, attributed to Ridgway.

2¾in (7cm) diam

£1,800-2,200 **H&C**

A 'Spanish Lady' pot lid, attributed to the Pratt factory, from a painting by G. Herbert.

3¼in (8cm) diam

£2,000-2,500 **H&C**

An early 'Belle Vue Tavern with Cart' pot lid, attributed to the Pratt factory.

5in (12.5cm) diam

£600-800 **H&C**

An early 'Pegwell Bay' pot lid, attributed to T.J. & J. Mayer.

3½in (9cm) high

£1,200-1,600 **H&C**

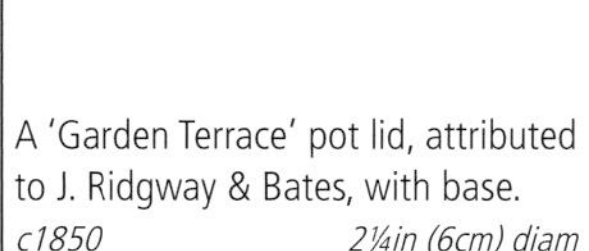

A 'Garden Terrace' pot lid, attributed to J. Ridgway & Bates, with base.

c1850 *2¼in (6cm) diam*

£1,800-2,200 **H&C**

A Bates, Brown-Westhead & Moore 'Pet Rabbits' pot lid, after the Le Blond print.

c1850 *4in (10cm) diam*

£3,500-4,000 **H&C**

A T.J. & J. Mayer 'Great Exhibition Closing Ceremony' pot lid.

This design comes from W. Simpson's painting 'The Transept looking towards the Grand Entrance'.

4¾in (12cm) diam

£750-850 H&C

A 'Jenny Lind' pot lid, attributed to Ridgway.

Born in Stockholm in 1820, Jenny Lind travelled to England in 1847, where she became a famous singer.

3in (7.5cm) diam

£1,800-2,200 H&C

A 'Royal Arms and Allied Flags of Crimea' pot lid, with flags of Turkey, Britain and France.

3¼in (8.5cm) diam

£2,800-3,200 H&C

ESSENTIAL REFERENCE – JOHN WILKES

John Wilkes (1725-98) was an English radical, journalist and politician. He was elected Member of Parliament in 1757, but was repeatedly expelled for his radical views.

- **He founded his political radical newspaper, 'The North Briton', in 1862. The inscription on this mug refers to its 45th issue, in which Wilkes attacked George III's 1763 speech endorsing the Paris Peace Treaty. A warrant was put out for his arrest for libel, but Wilkes was cleared.**
- **Wilkes was a hero to American Founding Fathers Samuel Adams and John Hancock, as he criticised the British government's taxation policy in the colonies and was a supporter of the rebels in 1776.**
- **The few surviving objects that bear Wilkes' name carry a premium among political memorabilia collectors.**

A rare mid-to-late 18thC creamware mug, painted with John Wilkes, titled 'Wilkes & Liberty No.45'.

c1763 5in (12.5cm) high

£13,000-16,000 WW

A George III Prattware tea caddy, inscribed 'God Save the King' and 'Super Fine Tea', the silver cover inset with a coin, chip to one corner.

4¼in (11cm) high

£1,500-2,000 CHEF

An early 19thC Staffordshire 'Long Live Queen Caroline' commemorative jug, printed with a portrait and hunting scenes, restored chips.

Caroline of Brunswick (1768-1821) married George, Prince of Wales, in 1795. Their marriage was an unhappy one. Following the birth of their daughter Princess Charlotte, the couple separated, and Caroline later left the country. When Prince George became King in 1820, Charlotte travelled back to England to claim her title. The new King attempted to pass a bill to divorce her, but the bill was so unpopular it was dropped. Queen Charlotte was refused entry to the coronation service and died in London three weeks after her husband had been crowned.

8¾in (22cm) high

£400-450 PW

A creamware mug, commemorating the betrothal of Princess Charlotte, with a caricature of the Princess and three figures from Punch, one holding a placard inscribed 'A Prize of 30,000£ Huzza'.

This is seemingly the only commemorative ever produced to take against the otherwise adored Princess. This scene derides her Civil List allocation.

1816 4½in (11.5cm) high

£3,500-4,000 H&C

A pearlware mourning cup and saucer, printed with Princess Charlotte and 'HRH Princess Charlotte Died Nov 6 1817 at 21'.

c1818 saucer 5½in (14cm) diam

£130-180 WW

A Meyer Prattware commemorative Crimea War paste pot, 'Landing of the British Army'.

Prattware has recently had a considerable boost from new collectors from Australia and New Zealand.

c1842-55

£4,000-4,500 H&C

ESSENTIAL REFERENCE – NELSON

Admiral Lord Horatio Nelson (1758-1805) was a British naval commander, famous for his victories against the French during the Napoleonic Wars.

- **Nelson was the sixth son of a clergyman. He grew up in Norfolk, joined the navy at the age of 12 and was a captain by 20.**
- **When Britain entered the French Revolutionary Wars in 1793, Nelson was given command of the Agamemnon. He won victories against the Spanish off Cape Vincent in 1797 and against Napoleon's fleet at the Battle of the Nile in 1798. He was promoted to vice-admiral in 1801.**
- **Before the battle at Cape Trafalgar in October 1805, which ultimately saved Britain from threat of French invasion, Nelson famously sent off the signal to his fleet: 'England expects that every man will do his duty'. He was killed by a French sniper a few hours later.**
- **Nelson's status as a national hero ensured that many commemorative pieces were made to celebrate his victories and to mourn his death. He remains one of Britain's most important national figures, and Nelson commemoratives are very popular with collectors today.**

A mug, transfer-printed with Britannia holding a portrait of Nelson before a monument, star crack to base.

c1805 *8in (20.5cm) high*

£400-450 **WW**

A creamware Nelson Battle of the Nile jug, marked 'Silk', some restoration and crazing, dated.

1805 *9¾in (25cm) high*

£700-750 **PW**

A Prattware jug, with Nelson driving Neptune's chariot, inscribed 'JW', some restoration, dated.

1809 *6in (15.5cm) high*

£600-700 **WW**

An early 19thC creamware mug, printed with Nelson, the interior modelled with a frog, star crack to base.

5½in (14cm) high

£500-600 **WW**

An early to mid-19thC Liverpool creamware jug, printed with Nelson, the reverse with a ship, painted with 'William Baker born September 12th 1806', chipping to foot, crack to spout.

8¾in (22.5cm) high

£650-750 **WW**

A 19thC Nelson teapot and cover, possibly Leeds, some restoration.

8½in (21.5cm) high

£250-300 **WW**

An early to mid-19thC pearlware jug, printed with Nelson, inscribed 'England Expects that Every Man Will do His Duty', the reverse with Britannia weeping at a tomb.

6in (15cm) high

£250-300 **WW**

A Copeland subscriber's issue tyg, printed with a naval battle, Nelson, and Britannia, the inside rim inscribed 'England Expects That Every Man Will Do His Duty', printed mark.

1905 was the 100th anniversary of Nelson's death.

c1905 *5¾in (14.5cm) high*

£600-700 **WW**

A Staffordshire pearlware Toby jug, an upright barrel between his feet.

Toby jugs emerged in the early 18thC. There are several theories as to where the name 'Toby' came from; it may be a reference to Sir Toby Belch in Shakespeare's Twelfth Night, or to Toby Fillpot, an infamous drinker from the popular 18thC song 'The Brown Jug'.

c1780 *9¾in (25cm) high*

£850-950 WW

A creamware Wood-type 'Long Face' Toby jug, restoration to hat.

While the market for Toby jugs is deflated in comparison to the market twenty years ago, a niche market for them still exists and shows some signs of picking up. Condition and age play an enormous part in the value of a Toby jug, and rare or early examples in very good condition can reach four figures.

c1780-90 *10¾in (27cm) high*

£1,500-2,000 WW

A late 18thC Ralph Wood-type 'Ordinary' Toby jug.

9in (23cm) high

£1,500-2,000 FLD

A late 18thC Ralph Wood-type 'Ordinary' Toby jug, restored.

10¼in (26cm) high

£250-300 FLD

A late 18thC Ralph Wood-type 'Ordinary' Toby jug, some damages.

9¾in (25cm) high

£900-1,100 FLD

A creamware Ralph Wood-type Toby jug.

c1785-90 *9¾in (25cm) high*

£1,300-1,600 WW

A creamware Toby jug, in Whieldon-type running glazes, hat restored.

c1790 *9½in (24cm) high*

£1,000-1,400 WW

A 19thC Staffordshire Wood-type 'The Sailor Toby' jug, some damages.

12in (30.5cm) high

£1,100-1,500 FLD

A 19thC Squire Toby jug, brown painted mark to base, some damages.

12½in (32cm) high

£350-400 FLD

A rare early 19thC Mexborough (Yorkshire) Toby jug, holding a miniature Toby jug, a dog between his feet, impressed crown mark, some good restoration.

10¼in (26cm) high

£2,500-3,000 WW

An early 19thC pearlware pottery Toby jug, probably Scottish.

9¾in (24.5cm) high

£600-700 BE

A pearlware Toby jug, with some marbled decoration.

c1810 10in (25.5cm) high

£500-600 H&C

A 'Hearty Good Fellow' Toby jug, holding a pipe and jug of ale, restoration to hat.

c1810 11½in (29.5cm) high

£300-350 WW

A 'Squire' Toby jug, some chipping, replacement pipe.

c1810-20 11½in (29.5cm) high

£700-800 WW

A pearlware 'Hearty Good Fellow' Toby jug, restored.

c1820 9¼in (23.5cm) high

£500-600 H&C

A 19thC Staffordshire 'Thin Man' Toby jug, seated, holding a jug and a pipe.

9¾in (25cm) high

£1,400-1,800 FLD

A Prattware 'Martha Gunn' Toby jug, holding a gin bottle and glass, restoration to hat.

Martha Gunn (1726-1815) was a famous dipper. A dipper was the operator of a bathing machine used by women bathers. She worked as an attendant at Brighton from her youth until her late eighties, and was a favourite with George, Prince of Wales, later Prince Regent and King George IV.

c1800 10¼in (26cm) high

£1,000-1,400 WW

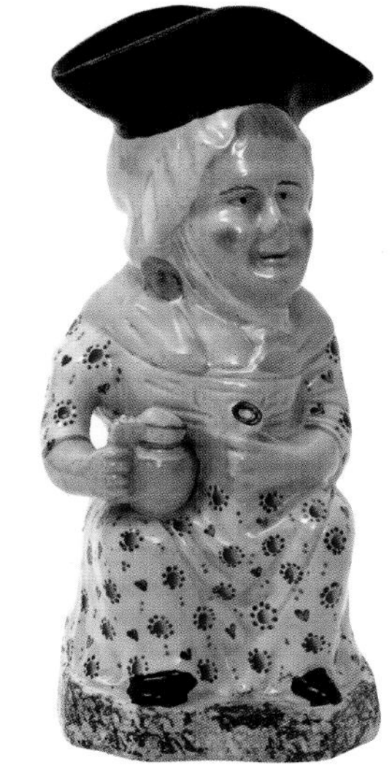

A 'Martha Gunn' Toby jug.

c1820-40 10¼in (26cm) high

£550-650 WW

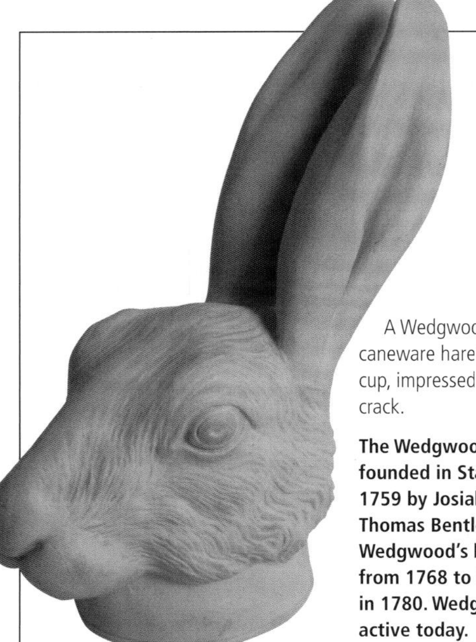

A Wedgwood & Bentley caneware hare's head stirrup cup, impressed mark, firing crack.

The Wedgwood pottery was founded in Staffordshire in 1759 by Josiah Wedgwood. Thomas Bentley was his Wedgwood's business partner from 1768 to Bentley's death in 1780. Wedgwood is still active today.

c1770 *7in (18cm) high*
£3,500-4,000 BRI

A Wedgwood & Bentley agateware vase, labelled medallion mark, adapted to be a lamp.

c1770 *10¾in (27.5cm) high*
£600-700 CHEF

A Prestige Wedgwood & Bentley black basalt candlestick, 'Minerva Goddess of Wisdom', from a limited edition of 200, boxed with certificate.

1775 *13¾in (35cm) high*
£500-600 PSA

A 19thC Wedgwood Jasperware 'Portland' vase.

9¾in (25cm) high
£900-1,200 PSA

A mid-to-late 19thC near pair of Wedgwood Jasperware ormolu-mounted Zodiac vases and covers, top covers lacking.

13in (33cm) high
£1,000-1,400 WW

A pair of Wedgwood black basalt portrait plaques, impressed 'WEDGWOOD'.

c1865 *4in (10cm) high*
£450-550 JN

A pair of late 19thC Wedgwood basalt 'wine' and 'water' ewers, impressed marks, some damages.

15in (38cm) high
£1,000-1,400 BELL

A Wedgwood Jasperware 'Trafalgar' vase, with sphinx handles, impressed 'Wedgwood' to base, small chips.

This vase commemorates the centenary of the Battle of Trafalgar in 1805.

c1905 *9¾in (25cm) high*
£650-750 BELL

A Cockpit Hill Derby 'pineapple' teapot, with strawberry pattern spout.
c1765 *48in (122cm) high*
£2,000-2,500 **MOR**

A 19thC Mason's Ironstone Imari dole/bread bin and cover, printed mark in blue.
c1820
£1,200-1,600 **CHEF**

A Prattware cow, calf and attendant, chip to cow's ear, minor chips to udders.
c1815 *5¾in (14.5cm) high*
£750-850 **BELL**

A Pratt-type horse, possibly St Anthony, Newcastle, ears lacking.
c1810 *6in (15.5cm) high*
£2,500-3,000 **TEN**

A Prattware horse, with sponge decoration, tail restored.
6½in (16.5cm) long
£1,500-2,000 **BRI**

A Rockingham pottery spirit flask, with a man astride a barrel, impressed 'J Smith The Mormon Prophet', dated.

Joseph Smith (1805-44) was the founder of the Mormon movement and author of the Book of Mormon. The movement is famously teetotal and flasks of this type were produced to mock the non-drinkers.

1830 *8¾in (22.5cm) high*
£400-500 **WW**

A marbled and combed slipware jug, with chinoiserie embellishments, some chips.
c1775 *6½in (16.5cm) high*
£3,000-3,500 **SK**

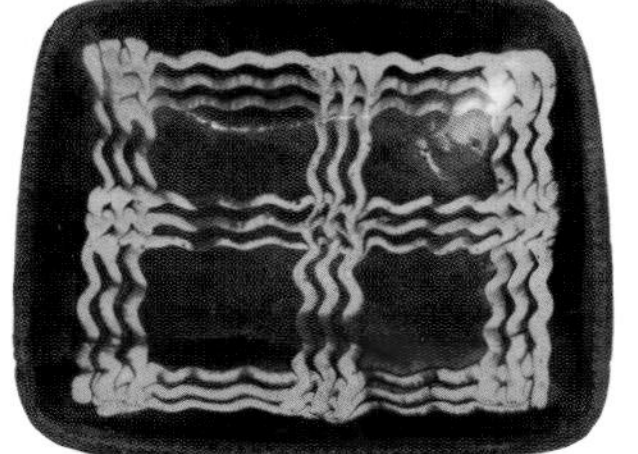

A late 18thC slipware baking dish.
14in (35.5cm) wide
£4,000-5,000 **LSK**

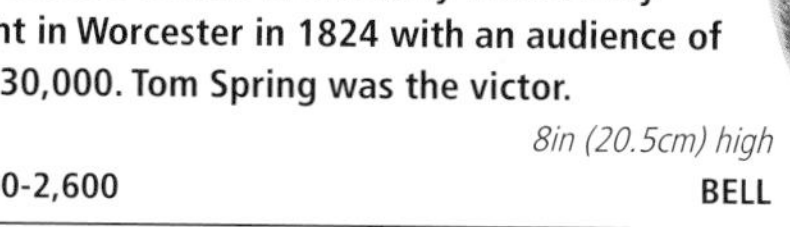

A 19thC Sunderland pink lustre jug, printed and overpainted with Spring and Langan, blue 'T.W', light surface scratches.

Tom Spring and Jack Langan were well-known bare-knuckle boxers in the early 19thC. They fought in Worcester in 1824 with an audience of over 30,000. Tom Spring was the victor.

8in (20.5cm) high
£2,300-2,600 **BELL**

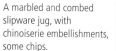

THE ASIAN MARKET

Over the past few years Asian works of art, whether jade or ceramic, have bucked the trend in a depressed economic climate and it seems that not a week passes by without some record price being achieved. However, the market is getting a lot more discerning, with top prices being reserved for rare pieces with Imperial provenance. Also, prices have been fluctuating; a lot may fetch a record price in Hong Kong, but a similar piece may fail to meet its much lower reserve in London, or the reverse.

The Chinese collectors are particularly discerning and are looking for excellent quality, rare Imperial pieces. As in many areas it helps if they are 'fresh to market'.

There was considerable excitement at the Drouot sale in Paris in December 2018 when a bronze dragon head estimated at €20,000, sold for €3million (£2.2million). This was fuelled by speculation that this was one of the five missing heads from the zodiac fountain in the Haiyantang area of the Yuanmingyuan (the Old Summer Palace in Beijing), designed by Jesuit Giuseppe Castiglione for the Qianlong emperor. The heads were removed by the French and British forces who looted the palace in the Second Opium War in 1860, and they have since become symbolic of China's humiliation by the Imperial west.

On the market for Japanese antiques, Lee Young, Managing Director and Head of Asian Art at Duke's Auctions in Dorchester said, 'We have, over the last few years, seen a noticeable increase in the number of buyers for Japanese items, resulting in higher prices in key areas such as cloisonné and mixed metal wares. However, the regained vigour of the Japanese market is still considerably overshadowed by the incredible strength of the Chinese market. With European and American collectors now often unable to compete with new and extremely affluent Chinese purchasers intent on buying back their heritage.'

However, the strength in the Japanese market is increasing. There is a strong demand for rare and unusual Chinese snuff bottles, but they must be top quality. Good-quality jade continues to excite buyers. The problem with ivory continues. Just before Christmas 2018, the UK government passed through a Bill confirming the ban on the sale of all ivory (with exceptions). There are various exemptions from the Ivory Act, as follows:

- Items which contain only a small amount of ivory. Such items must be comprised of less than 10 per cent ivory by volume and made prior to 1947.
- Musical instruments. These must have an ivory content of less than 20 per cent and made prior to 1975.
- Portrait miniatures. A specific exemption for portrait miniatures – which were often painted on thin slivers of ivory – made before 1918.
- Sales to and between accredited museums. This applies to museums accredited by Arts Council England, the Welsh Government, The Scottish Government or the Northern Ireland Museums Council in the UK, or, for museums outside the UK, The International Council of Museums.
- The rarest and most important items of their type. Items of outstanding artistic, cultural or historic significance, and made prior to 1918. Such items will be subject to the advice of specialists at institutions such as the UK's most prestigious museums.

Because of the ongoing uncertainty, we have decided to exclude ivory items from this chapter since they are extremely difficult to value.

Left: A Chinese Tang painted pottery horse.
618-906 *20½in (52cm) high*
£5,000-5,500 **TEN**

Below: A Chinese Jiajing 'peony' yuhuchunping vase, six-character mark, neck restored.
1522-66 *12¼in (31cm) high*
£85,000-95,000 **WW**

CHINESE REIGN PERIODS AND MARKS

Imperial reign marks were adopted during the Ming dynasty, and some of the most common are illustrated here. Certain emperors forbade the use of their own reign mark, lest they should suffer the disrespect of a broken vessel bearing their name being thrown away. This is where the convention of using earlier reign marks comes from – a custom that was enthusiastically adopted by potters as a way of showing their respect for their predecessors.

It is worth remembering that a great deal of Imperial porcelain is marked misleadingly, and pieces bearing the reign mark for the period in which they were made are, therefore, especially sought after.

EARLY PERIODS AND DATES

Xia Dynasty	*c2000-1500 BC*	Three Kingdoms	*221-280*	The Five Dynasties	*907-960*
Shang Dynasty	*1500-1028 BC*	Jin Dynasty	*265-420*	Song Dynasty	*960-1279*
Zhou Dynasty	*1028-221 BC*	Northern and Southern Dynasties	*420-581*	Jin Dynasty	*1115-1234*
Qin Dynasty	*221-206 BC*	Sui Dynasty	*581-618*	Yuan Dynasty	*1260-1368*
Han Dynasty	*206 BC-220 AD*	Tang Dynasty	*618-906*		

EARLY MING DYNASTY REIGNS

Hongwu	*1368-98*	Zhengtong	*1436-49*
Jianwen	*1399-1402*	Jingtai	*1450-57*
Yongle	*1403-24*	Tianshun	*1457-64*
Hongxi	*1425*	Chenghua	*1465-87*
Xuande	*1426-35*		

MING DYNASTY MARKS

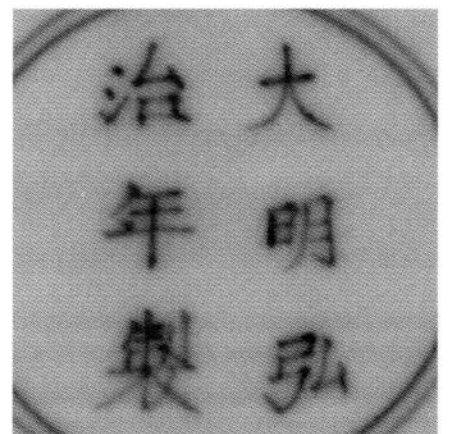

Hongzhi
1488-1505

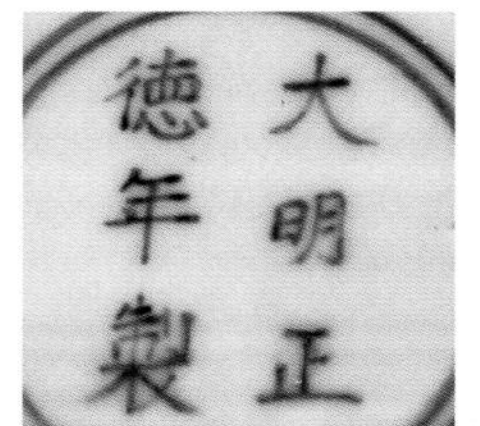

Zhengde
1506-21

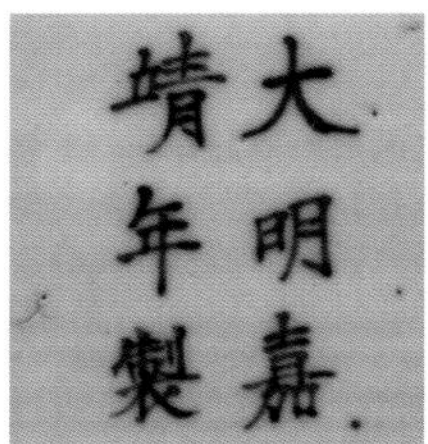

Jiajing
1522-66

Wanli
1573-1619

Chongzhen
1628-44

QING DYNASTY MARKS

Kangxi
1662-1722

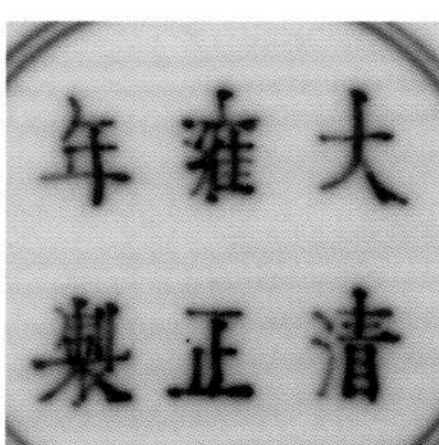

Yongzheng
1723-35

Qianlong
1736-95

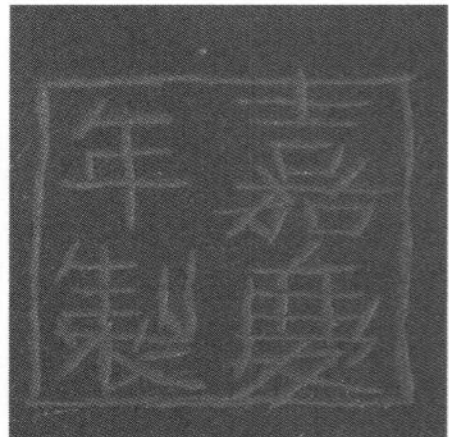
Jiaqing
1796-1820

Daoguang
1821-50

Xianfeng
1851-61

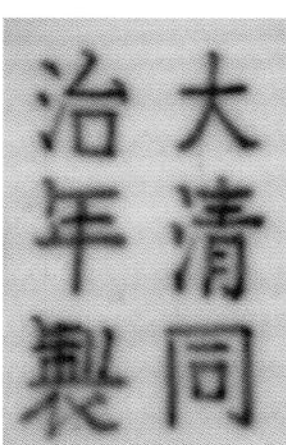

Tongzhi
1862-74

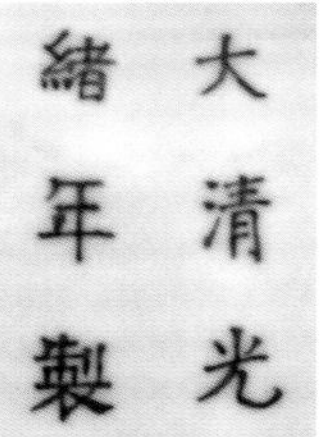

Guangxu
1875-1908

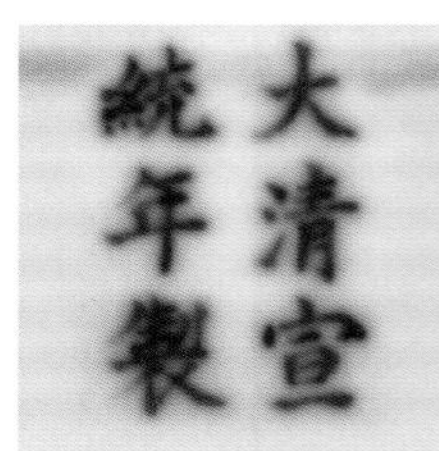

Xuantong
1909-11

Hongxian
1915-16

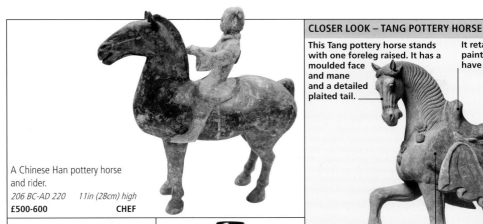

A Chinese Han pottery horse and rider.
206 BC-AD 220 *11in (28cm) high*
£500-600 **CHEF**

CLOSER LOOK – TANG POTTERY HORSE

This Tang pottery horse stands with one foreleg raised. It has a moulded face and mane and a detailed plaited tail.

It retains the remains of cold-painted decoration and would have once been fully painted.

It is fitted with a saddle with fan-type guards, with rosettes and conch shells moulded on its chest, and rosettes and tassels moulded either side of its rump.

The horse is in restored excavated condition, with authentication certificate, sample no.C112b25, dated 20 February 2012.

A Chinese Tang painted pottery horse.
618-906 *20½in (52cm) high*
£5,000-5,500 **TEN**

A Chinese Tang chestnut-glazed pottery horse, traces of pigment to saddle.
618-906 *18in (45.5cm) high*
£4,500-5,000 **JN**

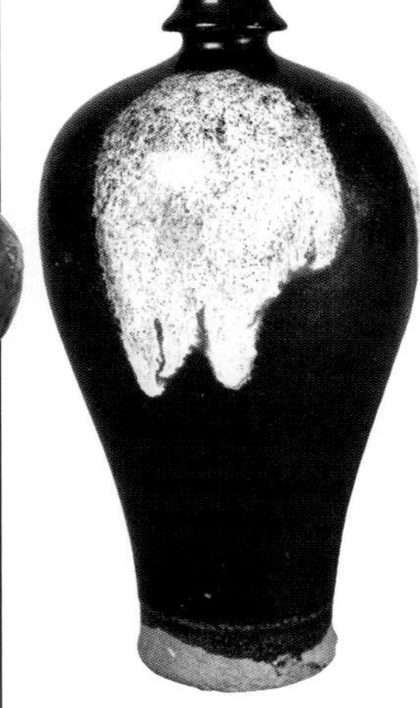

A Chinese Tang phosphatic-splashed meiping.
618-906 *10¾in (27cm) high*
£2,000-2,500 **ROS**

A Chinese Song Cizhou brown-splashed black-glazed jar.

This pottery was produced in Handan (formerly Cizhou), Hebei province, primarily during the Song dynasty. Most vessels were simply decorated, often in brown, grey, cream and sometimes turquoise. Pale backgrounds were often achieved by applying a coat of slip to the vessel before firing.
960-1279 *7¼in (18.5cm) high*
£13,000-16,000 **WW**

A Chinese Tang or later phosphatic-splashed ewer.
618-c906 *7¾in (19.5cm) high*
£4,000-4,500 **WW**

A Chinese Song ding bowl, the interior incised with stylised flowerheads, the exterior with concentric bands.
960-1279 *3¾in (9.5cm) wide*
£7,500-8,000 **WW**

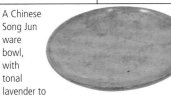

A Chinese Song Jun ware bowl, with tonal lavender to celadon glaze.

Jun ware is a type of pottery from one of the five kilns of the Song dynasty – Ru, Guan, Ge, Ding and Jun. Jun ware is mostly of opalescent blue, sometimes splashed or mottled in purple or crimson. The Jun kiln produced its wares for the Imperial household.
960-1279 *6in (15.5cm) wide*
£2,000-2,500 **FLD**

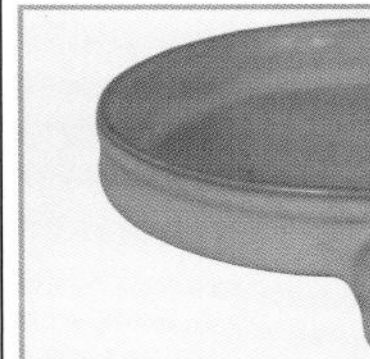

A reproduction Chinese Jun ware ceramic tripod censer, the base with spur marks.

This censer is a reproduction of a Song dynasty Jun ware piece, made within the last few years. Despite not being original, its high quality means that it is still a desirable item.
5½in (14cm) diam
£3,000-3,500 **JN**

A Chinese Southern Song celadon-glazed Longquan-type tripod censer, with wood cover and stand, some crazing and chips, finial re-stuck.
c1127-1279 *4¼in (11cm) wide*
£11,000-14,000 **DN**

A Chinese Guan-type vase, with a greyish crackled celadon glaze, raised on a short foot.

Guan was one of the five kilns of the Song dynasty, characterised by a wash of brown slip and pale green, blue or purple glazes. Guan ware was later replicated in the Ming and Qing dynasties.
6in (15cm) high
£80,000-90,000 **WW**

A Chinese Yuan celadon dish, with a dragon chasing a pearl.

In Chinese mythology, the dragon is a symbol of strength and good fortune, often portrayed in art, textiles and ceramics as chasing a luminous or flaming pearl, against a sky of clouds and flames. The five-clawed dragon in particular was used as a symbol of the Chinese Emperors. The pearl is a symbol of wisdom, related to yang energy in early Taoism.
1260-1368 *12in (30.5cm) diam*
£3,500-4,000 **CHEF**

A Chinese Yuan/Ming Longquan celadon stoneware dish.

This dish was recovered from a shipwreck near Mergui in Burma. Longquan celadon stoneware was produced in the town of Longquan from the Song to the mid-Qing dynasties. Decoration was typically incised or moulded, with a transparent green glaze.
13¾in (35cm) diam
£700-800 **JN**

A Chinese Yuan/Ming Longquan celadon bottle vase, on wood stand.
8¾in (22cm) high
£1,000-1,400 **JN**

A Chinese Ming Longquan celadon bowl.
11½in (29.5cm) diam
£6,500-7,500 **WW**

A Chinese Ming Longquan celadon dish, carved with a spray of camelia.
14in (35.5cm) diam
£5,500-6,000 **WW**

A 17thC to 18thC Chinese celadon-glazed porcelain kendi, with ribbed sides and spout.

A kendi is a type of pouring vessel with no handle and a spout on the side.
6in (15cm) high
£500-600 **JN**

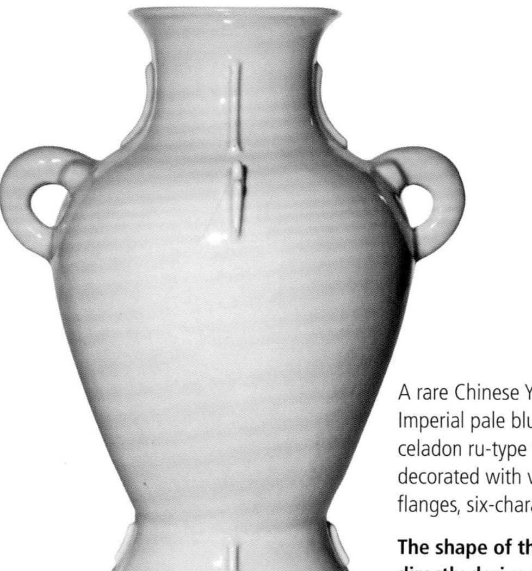

A rare Chinese Yongzheng Imperial pale blue-ground celadon ru-type vase, decorated with vertical flanges, six-character mark.

The shape of this vase is directly derived from a Shang dynasty bronze lei.
1723-35 *13in (33cm) high*
£160,000-200,000 **WW**

A 19thC Chinese celadon-ground porcelain bottle vase, slip-decorated with dragons chasing pearls.
23in (58.5cm) high
£4,500-5,000 **JN**

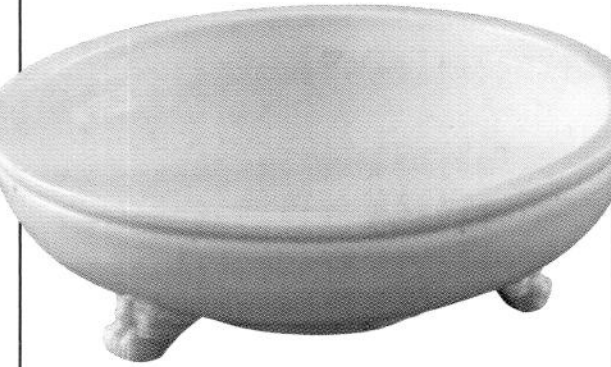

A 16thC to 17thC Chinese Dehua blanc-de-Chine censer, minor glaze imperfections and scratches.

Blanc-de-Chine ('White from China') is the European term for a type of monochrome white Chinese porcelain, made at Dehua, Fujian province, produced from the Ming dynasty onwards. Large quantities were exported to Europe in the early 18thC and it was copied at Meissen and elsewhere.

6in (15cm) diam

£600-700 GORL

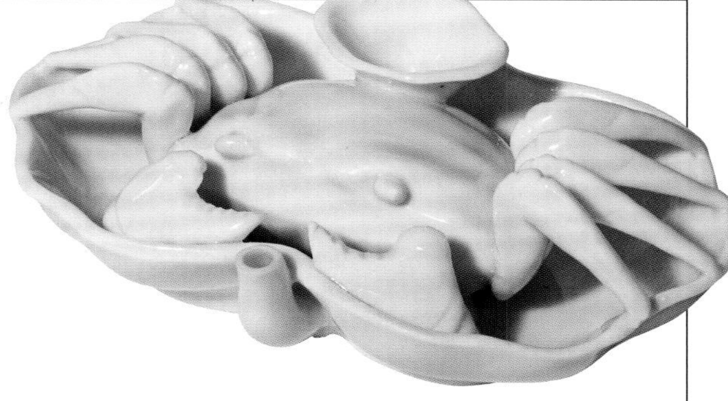

A 17thC Chinese blanc-de-Chine water dropper, formed as a crab.

5¼in (13.5cm) long

£3,500-4,000 WW

A Chinese early Qing blanc-de-Chine 'rhinoceros horn' libation cup, moulded with a deer, two dragons to reverse.

6in (15.5cm) high

£750-850 WW

An 17thC to 18thC Chinese blanc-de-Chine bombé censer, with lion mask handles, impressed seal mark, with wood cover, nick to foot rim.

4¼in (11cm) wide

£2,200-2,600 BELL

A bronze-mounted 18thC Chinese blanc-de-Chine gu vase, incised with leaves, dragon mask and tongue handles.

15¼in (39cm) high

£2,200-2,800 CHEF

A Chinese early Qing blanc-de-Chine model of Guanyin, on a wave and lotus stand, her head broken off, marked 'He Chaozong'.

Guanyin is the bodhisattva (Buddha-to-be) of compassion and mercy.

Provenance: from the Annette Worsley-Taylor family collection, acquired no later than the early 20thC. That this item has been off the market for 100 years increases its desirability. It is badly damaged, with the head broken off and restuck with a wooden stump, and the neck badly ground down. However, interest has recently increased in the artist He Chaozong, and undamaged pieces by him can fetch over £1,000,000.

14¾in (37.5cm) high

£45,000-50,000 WW

A 19thC Chinese blanc-de-Chine Guanyin riding a Buddhistic lion, possibly by Su Xuejin (1869-1919), impressed Boji Yuren seal mark.

11in (28cm) high

£5,500-6,000 JN

A Chinese late Qing Dehua blanc-de-Chine qilin, on a plinth, decorated with Taoist emblems, impressed Boji Yuren seal mark.

The Boji Yuren seal mark approximates to 'virtue extends to all, including fishermen'. A qilin, or kylin, is a mythical beast with the hooves of a horse, the body of a deer, the tail of an ox and the horn of a unicorn.

12in (30.5cm) high

£220-280 BRI

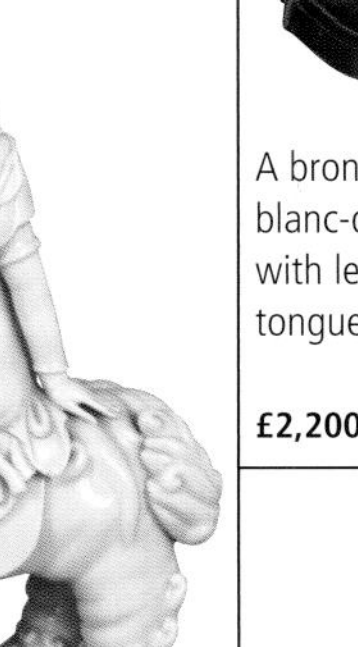

A 20thC Chinese blanc-de-Chine standing figure of Guanyin, holding a lotus spray.

22½in (57cm) high

£1,100-1,400 L&T

A Chinese Yuan or early Ming guan-type mallet vase, minor surface scratches, some glaze cracks.

9½in (24cm) high

£45,000-50,000 TEN

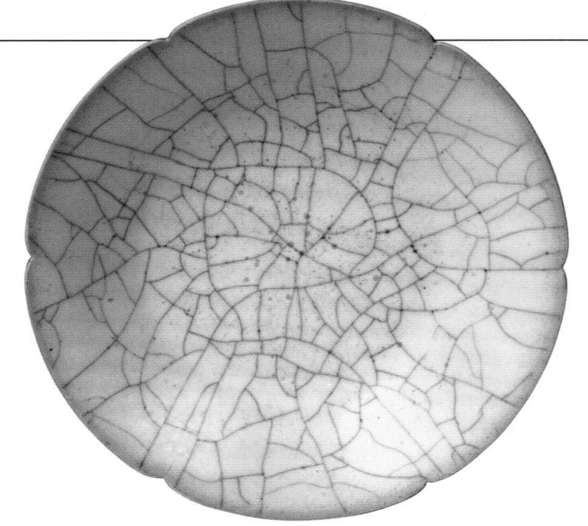

A Chinese Ming Guan-type hexafoil dish, allover crackle to glaze.

6¼in (16cm) diam

£60,000-70,000 TEN

A Chinese porcelain bottle vase, carved with stylised foliage, six-character Xuande reign mark, some spotting.

15¼in (39cm) high

£4,500-5,500 TEN

An 18thC Chinese Claire-de-Lune glazed scribe's box and cover.

8¾in (22cm) long

£40,000-45,000 GORL

A Chinese white-glazed soft-paste porcelain vase, carved with archaic designs and borders, elephant-head handles, incised Qianlong mark.

1736-95 9½in (24cm) high

£30,000-35,000 JN

An early 19thC Chinese white crackled glaze moulded porcelain vase, with dragon panels.

This piece was bought in Rangoon in 1928 from the collection of a Tuchan Warlord.

17¾in (45cm) high

£6,000-7,000 JN

One of a pair of 18thC to 19thC Chinese bowls, six-character Kangxi mark, on hardwood stands.

These bowls are engraved with the bajixiang, which are the Eight Buddhist Emblems.

bowls 5½in (14cm) wide

£40,000-45,000 the pair JN

A Chinese porcelain bowl and cover, of archaic bronze form, the cover with four flanges, Qianlong seal mark.

10¾in (27.5cm) wide

£5,000-6,000 JN

A Chinese vase, with dragon roundels and Buddhist emblems, on a 19thC spinach jade and ivory-mounted stand, Qianlong mark to vase, chips to extremities.

4¼in (11cm) high

£3,500-4,000 BELL

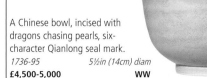

A Chinese bowl, incised with dragons chasing pearls, six-character Qianlong seal mark.

1736-95 5½in (14cm) diam

£4,500-5,000 WW

A Chinese Daoguang archaistic ritual food 'fu' vessel, with elephant-head handles, six-character mark.

1821-50 9in (23cm) high

£3,500-4,000 WW

A pair of Chinese Kangxi hounds.
1662-1772 *6in (15.5cm) high*
£2,500-3,000 **L&T**

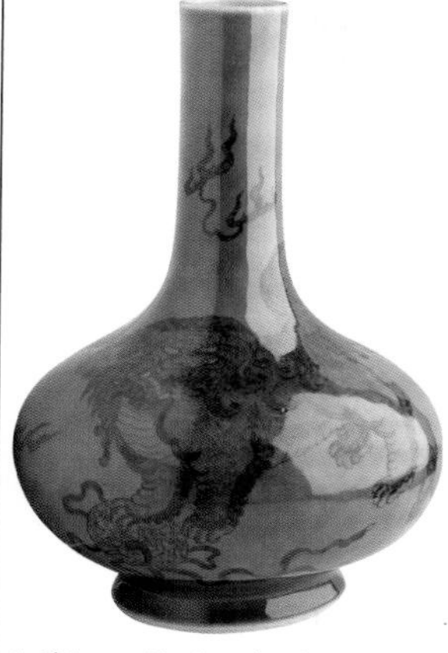

A Chinese Qianlong bottle vase, painted with a Buddhist lion.
1736-95 *12¼in (31cm) high*
£1,000-1,500 **L&T**

A 18thC to 19thC Chinese 'lu tou zun' vase, decorated in gilt with deer in a mountainous landscape, with stag-head handles, six-character Qianlong mark.
18½in (47cm) high
£6,000-7,000 **L&T**

A 19thC Chinese 'yuhuchun' vase, with white rim and foot rim, apocryphal six-character Yongzheng mark.

Chinese makers in the Qing dynasty and later often added apocryphal marks (reign marks of former Emperors) to their pieces. This was sometimes done in order to pass a piece off as older than it was to buyers. However, it was also done as a sign of respect and reverence for earlier periods in history. For example, Qing pieces in Ming style often carry a Ming Emperor's reign mark. Some pieces with apocryphal marks may also be direct copies of earlier pieces.
14¼in (36cm) high
£3,000-3,500 **L&T**

A mid-20thC Chinese bottle vase, with pâte-sur-pâte-style decoration of a fisherman before a mountain, blue four-character seal mark.

The very fine translucent body and the high-quality workmanship of the decoration makes this a valuable piece.
8¼in (21cm) high
£5,000-6,000 **LC**

A Chinese Southern Song Longquan stoneware jar and cover, the shoulders moulded with a cat and a kitten, with bird finial.
1127-1279 *8¾in (22cm) high*
£4,000-5,000 **JN**

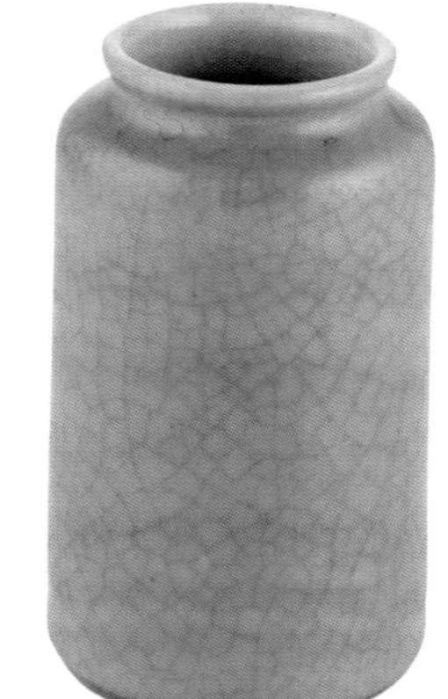

An 18thC Chinese Qing green crackled glaze vase.
4½in (11.5cm) high
£750-850 **L&T**

An 18thC Chinese porcelain rouleau vase, with turquoise-green glaze.
17¾in (45cm) high
£3,500-4,000 **JN**

A 19thC Chinese imitation bronze porcelain bottle vase, with panels of dragons amidst cloud scrolls, reserved on a linked wan swastika ground, moulded Qianlong mark.

This vase was bought in Rangoon in 1927 from the collection of a Tuchan Warlord.
15¼in (38.5cm) high
£3,000-4,000 **JN**

A Chinese Qing sang-de-boeuf vase, on wood stand, some crazing.

Sang-de-boeuf ('oxblood'), also known as flambé or langyao, refers to a rich glossy red glaze, often streaked in purple or turquoise. The effect is produced by a method of firing which incorporates copper. It was used to decorate Chinese ceramics from the Ming dynasty onwards. It was difficult to control, but had been mastered by the early Qing dynasty.

7¾in (20cm) high

£3,500-4,000 DN

An 18thC Chinese Kangxi sang-de-boeuf porcelain vase, with a streaked and crackled glaze.

16¾in (42.5cm) high

£5,000-6,000 JN

An 18thC Chinese iron rust glazed porcelain vase, with iridescent black speckling, on wood stand.

12¾in (32.5cm) high

£2,500-3,000 JN

An 18thC Chinese sang-de-boeuf porcelain bottle vase, with bronze neck fitting, the glaze thinning to green above the unglazed base.

14½in (37cm) high

£2,000-2,500 JN

An 18thC Chinese vase, with stylised bats, glazed in tonal lilac to red sang-de-boeuf.

6¼in (16cm) high

£1,200-1,600 FLD

An 18thC Chinese sang-de-bouef teardrop-form porcelain vase, archaic three-character mark, base drilled, on wood stand, some chips and hairlines.

11in (28cm) high

£3,500-4,000 MART

A Chinese copper red porcelain saucer dish, underglaze blue Qianlong mark.

1736-95 *8¼in (21cm) diam*

£6,000-7,000 JN

An 18thC to 19thC Chinese sang-de-boeuf vase, glaze thinning at neck, on wood stand.

16¼in (41cm) high

£3,200-3,800 BE

A 19thC Chinese copper red vase, apocryphal Qianlong mark, glaze fault.

8¼in (21cm) high

£4,500-5,500 DN

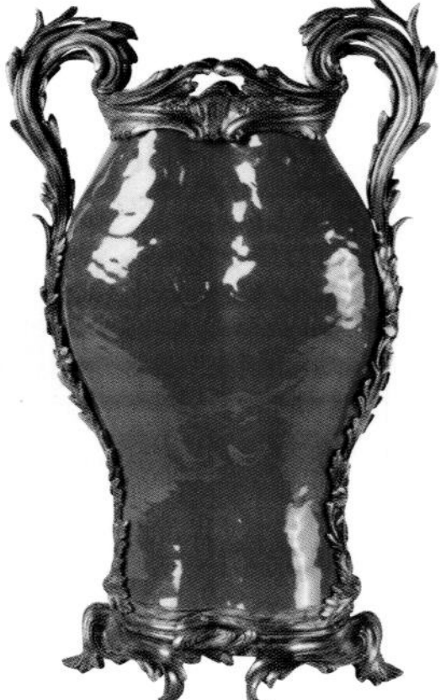

A 19thC Chinese porcelain sang-de-boeuf glazed double-fish vase, with 19thC French ormolu mounts.

18½in (47cm) high

£2,000-3,000 ROS

A 19thC Chinese sang-de-boeuf vase, underglaze blue apocryphal Qianlong six-character mark.

7in (18cm) high

£3,000-3,500 LC

ESSENTIAL REFERENCE – YIXING TEAPOTS

From the early 16thC, clay teapots and other red stonewares were produced in Yixing, in the Eastern province of Jiangsu.

- **They were very popular with the upper classes, especially amongst scholars.**
- **As Yixing teapots were only washed out with water, the clay would absorb the aroma and flavour of tea over time. After many years of use, a scholar would be able to brew tea simply by pouring boiling water into the empty pot.**
- **Yixing wares were exported to Europe from the mid-17thC to the late 18thC, and influenced Dutch and Staffordshire redware (see pages 58-59).**

A Chinese early Qing Yixing teapot and cover, by Chen Bo Fang, the handle as a geranium stem, the spout as a leaf, the cover as an upturned flower, signed to lid.

7¼in (18.5cm) high

£20,000-25,000 **WW**

A Chinese enamelled Yixing teapot and cover, with sprays of chrysanthemum and bamboo, six-character Qianlong mark.

1736-95 *7in (17.5cm) wide*

£5,000-6,000 **WW**

A 17thC to 18thC Chinese Yixing teapot and associated cover, with metal mounts to handle, oval seal and five-character mark to base, 'jing xi hui meng chen'.

The mark refers to Hui Mengchen, a Yixing potter active in the late Ming and early Qing dynasties.

7in (17.5cm) high

£10,000-12,000 **WW**

A Chinese Qing Yixing teapot and cover, moulded with chrysanthemums and clouds, surmounted with a buffalo.

5½in (14cm) high

£3,500-4,000 **WW**

An 18thC Chinese Yixing teapot and cover, with a dragon's head spout and dragon's tail handle, with a Buddhist lion dog finial.

6¼in (16cm) high

£7,000-8,000 **WW**

An 18thC Chinese Yixing teapot and cover, with moulded vine leaves and squirrels, the handle, spout and cover formed as vine branches.

8¾in (22cm) high

£5,500-6,000 **WW**

A Chinese Qing pewter-encased Yixing teapot and cover, by Yang Peng Nian, with a jade handle and glass replacement knop, incised by Wang Qia with poems about tea, four-character seal mark.

6¼in (16cm) high

£6,500-7,000 **WW**

A Chinese Qing turquoise-glazed Yixing teapot, seal marks to cover reading 'zhi yuan', four-character seal to base.

7½in (19cm) high

£1,500-2,000 **WW**

A Chinese Qing Yixing duan ni vase, with a figure amongst bamboo, inscribed with a poem, impressed mark to base 'li yong gogn so chui pin'.

Duan ni is a rare clay, typically of a yellowish white colour.

9¼in (23.5cm) high

£4,500-5,000 **WW**

A Chinese Qing Yixing jar and cover, with enamelled coloured bands, marked 'shou' to lid.

'Shou' is the Chinese character for longevity.

8¾in (22cm) high

£3,000-3,500 **WW**

ESSENTIAL REFERENCE – BLUE AND WHITE CERAMICS

- **The use of underglaze blue decoration in China dates from the Tang dynasty, and rose to prominence under the Mongol Yuan dynasty in the late 13thC and 14thC.**
- **Jingdezhen, Jiangxi province, became the centre of the Chinese porcelain industry, producing blue and white ceramics, from Imperial wares to export pieces.**
- **Blue and white ceramics made in the Ming dynasty, especially those from the Chenghau period or before, are generally considered to be of the highest quality.**
- **The shade of blue varied considerably over time. Cobalt imported from Persia produced a dark blue-black colour, while blues derived from local ores were often lighter.**
- **Chinese blue and white porcelain was very popular with the export market in the late 16thC and 17thC. Pieces were imported in vast quantities to Europe, and imitated in many European factories.**

A Chinese Jiajing 'peony' yuhuchunping vase, six-character mark, neck restored.

Provenance: purchased from Sotheby's London, 8 March 1954. That it has been off the market for sixty years very much increased the desirability of this piece. Jeremy Morgan, Senior Specialist of Asian Art at Woolley & Wallis, has said that finely painted 16thC Ming pieces are currently on the rise, and have increased in value in the last twelve to eighteen months.

1522-66 *12¼in (31cm) high*
£85,000-95,000 WW

A Chinese Transitional porcelain double-gourd vase, minor surface wear.

The Transitional period in Chinese ceramics refers to the years when the Ming dynasty had lost control of the Imperial porcelain factories in Jingdezhen, Jiangxi province, and the Qing dynasty was yet to gain control of them. It is usually dated from the death of the Wanli emperor in 1620 to the arrival of Zang Yingxuan as Director of the Imperial factories in 1683.

11¼in (28.5cm) high
£4,500-5,000 TEN

A Chinese Jiajing porcelain box and cover, painted with birds in flight, six-character mark, some cracks.

1521-67 *11¾in (30cm) wide*
£12,000-16,000 JN

A Chinese Wanli porcelain vase, with two five-clawed dragons, six-character mark.

1573-1620 *20½in (52cm) high*
£25,000-30,000 JN

A Chinese Wanli or later elephant kendi, some glaze fritting.

1573-c1620 *9in (23cm) high*
£8,500-9,500 DN

A Chinese late Ming or Kangxi 'scholar's table' bowl, painted with mythical sea creatures, minor firing blemishes.

5¼in (13.5cm) diam
£10,000-14,000 DN

A 17thC Chinese ewer, zoomorphic handle and three further mask handles, painted with mythical animals and some of the 'Eight Treasures', some firing faults.

The 'Eight Treasures', or 'Eight Precious Things', are Chinese symbols of good fortune, often featuring in ceramic decoration from the Yuan dynasty onwards. The symbols are a jewel (symbolising the granting of wishes), a coin (symbolising wealth), a lozenge (victory), a pair of books (learning), a mirror (counteracting evil), a jade gong (celebration), a pair of rhinoceros horns (happiness) and an artemisia leaf (good luck and health).

7½in (19cm) high
£3,000-3,500 DN

A Chinese Transitional 'sleeve' vase, with a scene from the 'Water Margin', long crack to body.

c1640 *19in (48cm) high*
£25,000-30,000 WW

A Chinese Transitional bombé-shaped incense burner, painted with six figures of Immortals.

c1640 *7¾in (20cm) diam*

£6,500-7,500 **WW**

A pair of mid-17thC Chinese 'Eight Horses of Mu Wang' bowls, apocryphal Jiajing marks, some hairlines and chips.

In Chinese legend, the chariot of Emperor Mu, the fifth emperor of the Zhou dynasty, was pulled by eight horses. Each horse had a different power, such as galloping without touching the ground or possessing wings.

7in (17.5cm) diam

£1,200-1,800 **HAN**

A mid-17thC Chinese Transitional gu vase or brush pot, painted with insects and birds, firing crack to unglazed base.

Dan Bray, Valuer at Gorringes Auctioneers, has said that 'larger pieces of blue and white porcelain from the Transitional and Kangxi period are particularly popular with mainland Chinese buyers at the moment'.

9¾in (24.5cm) high

£5,000-6,000 **GORL**

A Chinese Kangxi jar, painted with courtiers on a terrace, with a reticulated wood cover carved with the bajixiang (Eight Buddhist Emblems).

1662-1722 *8¼in (21cm) high*

£7,500-8,500 **WW**

A Chinese probably Kangxi vase, painted with mountainous landscapes and flowers, with replacement hardwood and metal cover and ebonised stand.

19¼in (49cm) high

£4,500-5,000 **LC**

A Chinese Kangxi rouleau vase, painted with two sages and a xianren, some hairlines and glaze fritting.

1662-1722 *18¼in (46.5cm) diam*

£5,000-6,000 **GORL**

A Chinese Kangxi flask, painted with figurative scenes, the neck with Buddhist emblems, four-character Xuande mark, cover missing, some fritting.

1662-1722 *11¼in (28.5cm) high*

£2,200-2,800 **BELL**

A pair of Chinese Kangxi jars, painted with phoenix amongst flowers, with pierced wood covers, one section re-glued.

1662-1722 *9¼in (23.5cm) high*

£3,000-3,500 **CHEF**

A pair of Chinese Kangxi 'yen yen' vases, painted with deer and cranes.

1662-1722 *18in (45.5cm) high*

£20,000-30,000 **WW**

A Chinese Kangxi porcelain vase, painted with a village landscape, with mountains and fisherman.
1662-1722 *31½in (80cm) high*
£9,000-11,000 **ROS**

A Chinese Kangxi vase, painted with ladies and boys in a garden, with wood cover and stand.
1662-1722 *8in (20.5cm) high*
£3,500-4,000 **WW**

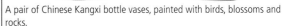

A pair of Chinese Kangxi bottle vases, painted with birds, blossoms and rocks.
1662-1722 *7¾in (20cm) high*
£4,000-5,000 **WW**

A Chinese Kangxi vase, painted with peony scrolls, with a pierced hardwood cover.
1662-1722 *vase 18½in (47cm) high*
£3,400-3,800 **DUK**

A Chinese Kangxi porcelain bowl, painted with figures in a landscape and a waterside shrine, minor stain, lacking cover.
1662-1722 *9½in (24cm) diam*
£4,000-5,000 **BE**

A Chinese Kangxi bowl, painted with foliage, Chenghua six-character mark, minor firing blemishes.
1662-1722 *6in (15.5cm) diam*
£2,000-2,500 **DN**

A pair of Chinese Kangxi gilt-metal-mounted porcelain jars and covers, painted with prunus blossom, with a crackled-ice ground.
1662-1722 *6½in (16.5cm) high*
£1,100-1,400 **JN**

A Chinese Kangxi porcelain vase, painted with foliage and vases, the base unglazed.
c1700 *19in (48.5cm) high*
£5,500-6,000 **JN**

A Chinese Kangxi porcelain vase and cover, painted with lotus, peony and other flowers, with a stepped lotus bud finial.
c1700 *24in (61cm) high*
£3,500-4,000 **JN**

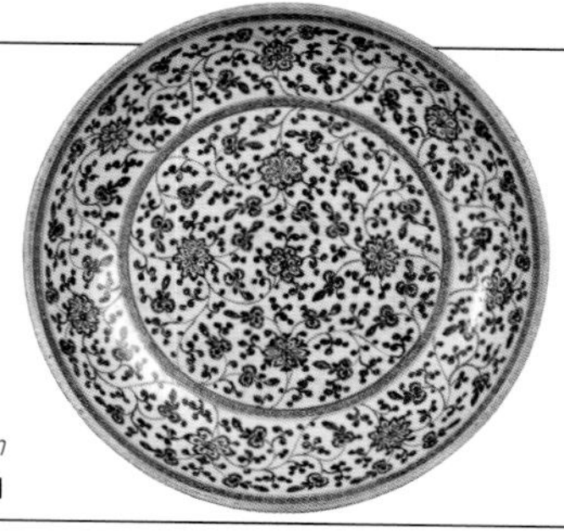

A Chinese Yongzheng Ming-style porcelain dish, painted with scrolling lotus, the base unglazed.

1723-35 *14½in (37cm) diam*

£3,000-4,000 **JN**

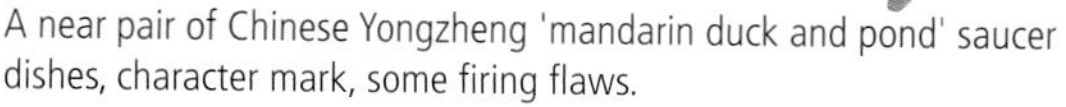

A near pair of Chinese Yongzheng 'mandarin duck and pond' saucer dishes, character mark, some firing flaws.

1723-35 *6in (15.5cm) diam*

£3,500-4,000 **GORL**

CLOSER LOOK – YONGZHENG DISH

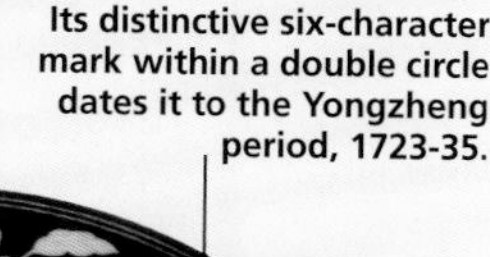

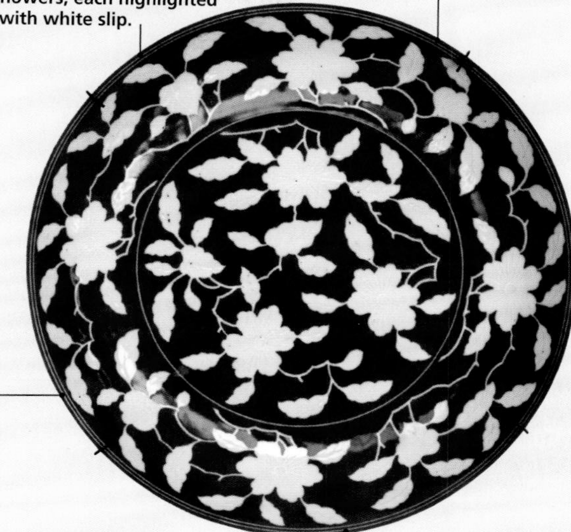

The dish is decorated with three gardenia flowers on leafy branches to the centre, within a border of four further flowers, each highlighted with white slip.

Its distinctive six-character mark within a double circle dates it to the Yongzheng period, 1723-35.

The rare unusual and striking reverse decoration with raised slip detailing is inspired by Ming and Yuan ceramics.

It is in very good condition, with only minor surface scratches and some rim fritting.

A Chinese Yongzheng dish.

Provenance: Formerly the property of Alexander Robertson Esquire, who purchased the dish in Chicago in 1911.

13in (33cm) diam

£280,000-320,000 **HAN**

A Chinese porcelain bottle vase, painted with peony and the bajixiang, Qianlong mark, on carved hardwood stand.

The bajixiang, the 'Eight Buddhist Emblems' or 'Eight Auspicious Symbols', were introduced to China with Buddhism in the Yuan dynasty. The symbols are the dharma (symbolising knowledge), conch shell (symbolising the thoughts of Buddha), victory banner (victory of Buddha's teaching), parasol (protection and spiritual power), lotus flower (purity and enlightenment), treasure vase (treasure and wealth), fish pair (happiness and freedom from restraint) and the endless knot (harmony).

vase 13in (33cm) high

£2,000-2,500 **JN**

A Chinese Ming-style porcelain vase, six-character Yongzheng mark.

8in (20.5cm) high

£1,000-1,400 **JN**

A Chinese Ming-style yuhuchunping porcelain vase, decorated with a garden scene, Qianlong mark.

A yuhuchunping is a distinctive kind of Chinese bottle or pear-form vase.

11½in (29cm) high

£2,000-2,500 **JN**

A Chinese Ming-style porcelain vase, decorated with archaic bands of dragons and key-fret, Qianlong mark.

7¾in (20cm) high

£2,000-3,000 **JN**

A Chinese Qianlong bottle vase, with Ming-style lotus flowers within foliate scroll ground, six-character mark.

1736-95 *14½in (37cm) high*

£7,000-8,000 **HAN**

A Chinese Qianlong 'dragon' dish, with five-clawed dragons chasing pearls, six-character mark.

From the Ming dynasty onwards, the five-clawed dragon was a symbol of Imperial power. It was only used on wares for the Emperor.

1736-95 *10in (25.5cm) diam*

£10,000-15,000 L&T

A Chinese porcelain hu vase, decorated with scrolling lotus, Qianlong mark.

14in (35.5cm) high

£2,000-2,500 JN

A Chinese porcelain bottle vase, decorated with scrolling flowerheads, Qianlong mark.

19in (48.5cm) high

£4,500-5,500 JN

A Chinese Qianlong Imperial wine cup, decorated with the bajixiang (Eight Buddhist Emblems), six-character mark.

1736-95 *2¾in (7cm) high*

£7,500-8,500 WW

A Chinese porcelain stem bowl, with Ming-style 'heaped and piled' scrolling lotus, extended Qianlong mark.

1736-95 *6¼in (16cm) diam*

£1,400-1,800 JN

A Chinese Ming-style porcelain vase, with moulded horse-head handles, with bands of formal decoration, Qianlong mark.

16in (40.5cm) high

£1,000-1,400 JN

A Chinese Ming-style porcelain moon flask, with scrolling lotus and flowerheads, Qianlong mark.

The moon flask, also 'bianhu' or 'baoyueping' is characterised by a circular body, representing the moon, a flat base, narrow cylindrical neck and two arched side handles. 'Baoyue' literally means 'embracing the moon'.

16in (40.5cm) high

£1,500-2,000 JN

An 18thC Chinese kendi, with panels of plants, hairline to rim, some losses to glaze.

7½in (19cm) high

£850-950 CHOR

A Chinese Ming-style vase, with star motifs between formal bands.

Vases of this shape typically date from the Qianlong period (1736-95). This was catalogued as Ming-style, not genuine Ming, but several bidders on the day believed it to be a true Qianlong example.

8¾in (22.5cm) high

£23,000-27,000 WW

QIANLONG MARK

Qianlong mark, 1736-95

An 18thC Chinese vase, with lotus blossoms and foliage, with elephant-head handles.

13½in (34cm) high

£12,000-15,000 **WW**

An 18thC Chinese saucer dish, ten-character horizontal mark, some kiln dust to glaze, initialled 'N.Y.' to foot rim.

14½in (37cm) diam

£4,500-5,000 **MART**

A 18thC Chinese Ming-style dish, with a central lotus bouquet within floral border, broken and repaired.

20½in (52cm) diam

£12,000-15,000 **BELL**

A pair of Chinese late Qing triple-gourd vases, adapted as lamps, one with star crack to base, some firming blemishes.

17¾in (45cm) high

£4,500-5,000 **DN**

A mid-19thC Chinese porcelain bottle vase, painted with children presenting gifts to an official.

12¼in (31cm) high

£1,500-2,000 **ROS**

A Chinese probably Tongzhi 'Phoenix' plate, apocryphal six-character Kangxi mark, one hairline crack.

6½in (16.5cm) diam

£5,000-6,000 **DN**

One of a pair of 19thC Chinese footed bowls, painted with lotus, four-character mark for 'well-shaded hall', the second bowl broken through bottom of the stem.

Despite extensive damage to the lower half of the second bowl, this pair is still desirable.

5¼in (13.5cm) high

£14,000-18,000 the pair **BELL**

A 19thC Chinese tripod censer jar and cover, decorated with lotus and Buddhist emblem, with fu lion finial, handles re-stuck, some chips.

14¼in (36cm) high

£3,200-3,800 **PSA**

A 19thC Chinese saucer dish, painted with pomegranates, blue eight-character mark.

13in (33cm) diam

£850-950 **LC**

A Chinese Ming-style Guangxu porcelain bottle vase, with 'heaped and piled' bands of flowerheads, six-character mark.
1875-1908 *15¼in (38.5cm) high*
£30,000-35,000 **JN**

A Chinese Guangxu truncated bowl, decorated with chrysanthemums, marked, some scratches, firing crack to foot.
1875-1908 *9in (23cm) diam*
£2,000-2,500 **DRA**

A Chinese Guangxu 'hundred deer' snuff bottle, 'shou' characters to the neck, single deer and five-character 'su yun dao ren zhi' mark to base.

Suyun Daoren (1839-95), also known by his monk's name Liu Cheng Yin, or Liu Duo Shen, was one of the most powerful eunuchs in the court of the Empress Dowager Ci Xi, and one of her most trusted political advisors.
1875-1908 *4¼in (11cm) high*
£2,500-3,000 **WW**

A 20thC Chinese porcelain bottle vase, painted with dragons, with lion mask handles, apocryphal Qianlong mark.
19¼in (49cm) high
£3,500-4,000 **ROS**

An early 20thC Chinese crackled glaze rouleau vase, with mounted warriors and foot soldiers, signed within battle standard, impressed character mark.
24in (61cm) high
£1,100-1,400 **MART**

A Chinese Yuan-style meiping porcelain vase, decorated with a dragon and phoenix, the base unglazed.
13¾in (35cm) high
£2,500-3,000 **JN**

A Chinese moon flask, painted with flowers, vines and plantain leaves.
9¾in (25cm) high
£6,500-7,500 **L&T**

A Chinese Ming-style porcelain moon flask, decorated with lotus.
12½in (32cm) high
£4,000-5,000 **JN**

A Chinese bottle vase, with animals and vases, apocryphal six-character Kangxi mark, firing flaw to base.
15½in (39.5cm) high
£1,500-2,000 **CHOR**

A pair of 17thC Chinese Transitional famille verte porcelain jars, painted with squirrels and vines, bases unglazed.

The famille verte ('green family') palette is characterised by the use of green, yellow, blue, red and purple overglaze enamels. This palette was favoured in the reign of the emperor Kangxi (1661-1722).

12½in (34cm) high

£3,000-4,000 JN

A Chinese famille verte 'month' cup, painted with prunus blossom, the reverse with a poem and seal mark, six-character Kangxi mark.

This would have been one from a set of twelve cups, each depicting a different month of the year. The prunus blossom here represents the first month of the year.

2½in (6.5cm) diam

£750-850 JN

A Chinese Kangxi famille verte bowl, painted with warriors, officials and figures, the rim with auspicious objects, some minor frits, with stand and case.

1662-1722 *15¼in (39cm) diam*

£15,000-20,000 BE

A Chinese probably Kangxi famille verte vase and cover with lion finial, with a tiger hunting scene.

23¼in (59cm) high

£8,500-9,500 LC

A Chinese Kangxi famille verte bottle vase, painted with magpies and the 'three friends of winter'.

The 'three friends of winter' refer to the pine, bamboo and plum trees. This vase has a paper label for the BADA Art Treasures Exhibition 1932 to base.

1662-1722 *7¾in (19.5cm) high*

£1,800-2,200 WW

A Chinese Kangxi famille verte tea bowl and saucer, with Buddhist emblems, a hare to base of tea bowl.

From the collection of John Snelgrove, a captain of the East India Company.

1622-1722 *saucer 4¼in (11cm) diam*

£1,500-2,000 WW

A Chinese Kangxi famille verte rouleau vase, with a battle scene, with chrysanthemums to the shoulder, a river landscape to the neck.

1662-1722 *17¾in (45cm) high*

£18,000-22,000 WW

A Chinese Kangxi famille verte porcelain dish, with floral panels, the interior rim with insect vignettes.

c1700 *12in (30.5cm) wide*

£1,200-1,800 JN

A garniture of three Chinese Kangxi famille verte vases, with panels of animals and flowers, some chips, the jar with hairline cracks.
1662-1722 *max 15¾in (40cm) high*
£9,000-10,000 **CHOR**

A Chinese Kangxi famille verte 'yen yen' vase, painted with warriors and beasts in battle.
c1685-1710 *17¾in (45cm) high*
£2,200-2,600 **PW**

A Chinese Yongzheng porcelain famille verte vase, with scholars and butterflies, with 'shou' characters, some restoration, minor scratching.
1723-35 *14½in (37cm) high*
£2,500-3,000 **TEN**

A mid-19thC Chinese famille verte porcelain hu vase, with warring soldiers, with Buddhist lion mask handles.
20in (51cm) high
£2,600-3,000 **ROS**

A pair of 19thC Chinese famille verte stoneware floor vases, enamelled with exotic objects, one rim chip, one body crack.
35¾in (91cm) high
£1,800-2,200 **LSK**

A pair of 19thC Chinese famille verte porcelain saucer dishes, with scholars and attendants, some scratches and chips.
15¾in (40cm) diam
£2,200-2,800 **DN**

A 19thC Chinese famille verte porcelain bowl, with figural panels, iron red lingzhi mark to base.
11in (28cm) diam
£550-650 **JN**

A probably 19thC Chinese porcelain famille verte 'yen yen' vase, depicting five lion dogs and a brocade ball, blue concentric rings.
17in (43cm) high
£1,200-1,500 **BE**

A 19thC to 20thC Chinese famille verte porcelain rouleau vase, with a terrace scene, four-character Kangxi mark.

17¾in (45cm) high

£1,000-1,400 JN

A Chinese late Qing or Republic hardwood table screen with famille verte plaque, with five scholars on a veranda within a landscape.

The quality of decoration suggests that this plaque may be an unsigned piece by the famous Republic porcelain painter He Xuren.

15¼in (39cm) high

£5,500-6,000 L&T

A pair of Chinese famille verte vases, with warriors, officials and landscapes, gilded with auspicious objects, insects and foliage.

13½in (34cm) high

£900-1,200 BE

A pair of Chinese famille verte garden seats, with vignettes of birds and flowers.

18in (46cm) high

£3,000-3,500 GKID

A Chinese famille verte vase, with birds and flowers, on hardwood stand.

vase 13½in (34.5cm) high

£1,200-1,600 MOR

A Chinese famille verte porcelain brush pot, with figures and mythical beasts in landscape with inscription, minor wear.

5¾in (14.5cm) high

£7,500-8,500 TEN

A Chinese famille verte porcelain brushpot, the base unglazed.

5½in (14cm) high

£1,200-1,600 JN

A 19thC Chinese famille rose-verte porcelain jardinière, painted with ducks, the base unglazed.

15¾in (40cm) diam

£2,200-2,600 JN

A Chinese famille rose-verte porcelain model of a seated Buddha, his robes with 'shou' characters, the base unglazed.

8¾in (22cm) high

£1,200-1,600 JN

ESSENTIAL REFERENCE – FAMILLE ROSE

The famille rose ('pink family') palette was created in the early 18thC.

- **It includes shades of opaque pink and carmine, sometimes made using gold. Opaque yellow and whites were used to enable painters to blend and shape colours.**
- **These colours originated from Europe, so were often known as 'foreign' in China.**
- **Famille rose patterns typically feature foliage, flowers, symbols and panels of people.**
- **The famille rose palette was widely copied on European ceramics in factories such as Meissen, Chelsea and Chantilly.**

A rare pair of Chinese Yongzheng famille rose porcelain bowls, painted with trees and flowers, with 'an hua' decoration of two dragons chasing a pearl, six-character Hongzhi mark within double circle.

The appearance of lily, peony, orchid, prunus blossom and incised dragons on one bowl suggests these may have been a gift to a retiring official, wishing him a long, happy and restful retirement from his career at the Imperial court. When 'an hua', or 'secret decoration', is used a new design becomes visible in certain light.

1723-35 *3¾in (9.5cm) diam*

£18,000-22,000 ROS

A Chinese Qianlong famille rose ginger jar and cover, with five-clawed dragons, seal mark, on hardwood stand, star crack to lid.

1736-95 *7¾in (20cm) high*

£90,000-110,000 HAN

A rare Chinese Yongzheng famille rose porcelain bowl, painted with a chrysanthemum, orchid and lingzhi, six-character mark.

Lingzhi represents immortality and longevity, while the orchid stands for love and beauty, and the chrysanthemum symbolises a life of ease. The appearance of these three together suggest that this bowl was a gift, meant to bestow sentiments of a long and happy marriage upon the drinker.

1723-35 *3½in (9cm) diam*

£13,000-15,000 ROS

A pair of Chinese Qianlong famille rose 'double-peacock' tureens and covers, with Rococo scroll handles and finials, repair to one handle.

1736-95 *14½in (37cm) wide*

£3,200-3,800 BE

A Chinese famille rose porcelain butterfly vase, with ruyi sceptre-form handles, Qianlong mark.

9in (23cm) high

£4,000-4,500 JN

One of a pair of Chinese famille rose 'Madame de Pompadour' plates, the rim with cartouches of fish and eagles.

It has been suggested by art historians that this design was commissioned by Madame de Pompadour, the famous mistress of King Louis XV. The eagles symbolise King Louis XV. The fish represent Madame de Pompadour, whose surname was Poisson.

c1745 *9in (23cm) diam*

£2,500-3,000 the pair WW

A Chinese Qianlong famille rose porcelain vase, painted with figural riverside terrace scenes, converted to a lamp.

1736-95 *37in (94cm) high*

£2,500-3,000 JN

CLOSER LOOK – FAMILLE ROSE TEA CADDIES

These tea caddies are painted on the front and back with blossoming branches and flowering stems. The accompanying poems are eulogies to flowers and trees.

The enamelled sides are densely decorated with lotus flowers and scrolling tendrils on a yellow or iron red outlined ground.

The two red seals suggest the caddies were produced under the supervision of the celebrated ceramicist Tan Ying (1682-1756).

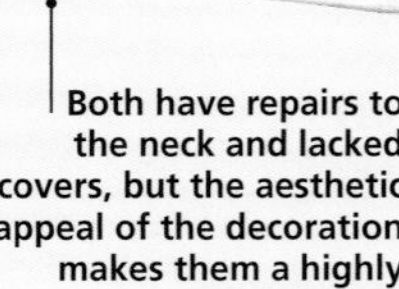

Both have repairs to the neck and lacked covers, but the aesthetic appeal of the decoration makes them a highly desirable pair.

A pair of Chinese Qing famille rose porcelain tea caddies.

6½in (16.5cm) high

£180,000-220,000 TOV

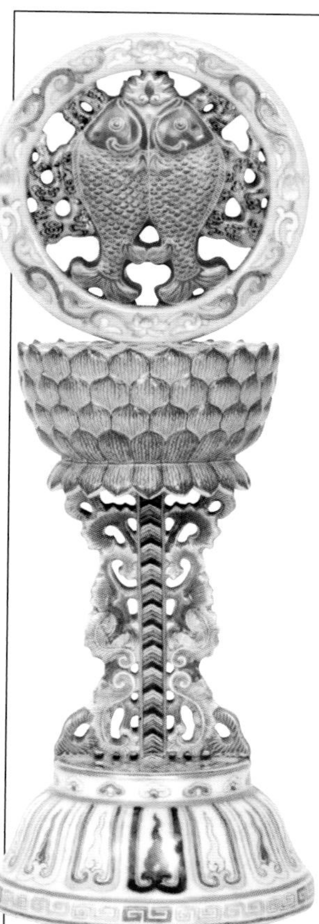

A Chinese Qianlong famille rose Buddhist Emblem altar vessel, with twin carp within a ring, on a lotus pedestal, seal mark.

Sets of eight Buddhist Emblems were produced to ornament altars.

1736-95 *11½in (29cm) high*
£70,000-80,000 FLD

A rare Chinese export Qianlong famille rose 'cornucopia' wall vase, the base with a Chinese landscape.

Ling Zhu, Asian Art Specialist at Lyon & Turnbull, said that 'the quality of the painting matches that of Imperial famille rose pieces', and that therefore 'some of the bidders believe this was done by an artist working in the Imperial court.'

1736-95 *9½in (24cm) high*
£24,000-28,000 L&T

A Chinese Qianlong famille rose 'tobacco-leaf' trumpet vase.

1736-95 *16¼in (41cm) high*
£5,500-6,000 MAL

ESSENTIAL REFERENCE – TOBACCO-LEAF

'Tobacco-leaf' pieces are among the most luxurious of all 18thC China trade porcelain. The complex floral pattern, picked out in famille rose over-glaze enamels, often combined with underglaze blue and gold, was highly popular, and the design was often used on export porcelain created for the European and American market. The name is something of a misnomer. The pattern was once thought to depict the flowering nicotiana plant – hence the name – but it actually depicts the wide serrated leaves of hibiscus, peony and passion flowers. It was probably based on an 18thC textile pattern.

A set of six Chinese Qianlong famille rose 'tobacco-leaf' meat plates.

1736-95 *max 18in (46cm) long*
£32,000-36,000 MAL

A Chinese Qianlong famille rose 'tobacco-leaf' tureen, with lotus bud handles, the cover with a fruit finial.

1736-95 *7½in (19cm) wide*
£14,000-18,000 MAL

CLOSER LOOK – 'HONG' PUNCH BOWL

This punch bowl is intricately decorated with a panoramic view of the 'hongs' – the offices, factories, warehouses and living spaces for foreign merchants in Canton, China.

The buildings are embellished with their national flags, including those of Great Britain, France, Spain and the USA, amongst others. The flag of the USA was only added in the late 1780s, dating this bowl to c1790.

The interior is decorated with foliate swags hung from a gilt lattice border.

'Hong' punch bowls, created specifically for the export market, were made in the Southern Chinese town of Jingdezhen, then carried to Canton to be decorated.

A Chinese famille rose porcelain 'Hong' punch bowl.

c1790 *14¼in (36.5cm) diam*
£85,000-95,000 TEN

A Chinese Qianlong famille rose 'tobacco-leaf' tankard.

1736-95 *6in (15cm) high*
£2,500-3,000 MAL

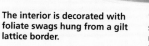

An 18thC Chinese Qing famille rose meiping vase, painted with a scholar on horseback, and a boy carrying books and supplies.

It is possible that the scholar depicted is on his way to Beijing to take the Imperial Civil Service Examination.

7½in (19cm) high
£3,500-4,000 L&T

A pair of Chinese Jiaqing famille rose yellow-ground porcelain gu vases, enamelled with the bajixiang (Eight Buddhist Emblems), six-character mark.

1796-1820 *10¾in (27.5cm) high*

£35,000-40,000 **FELL**

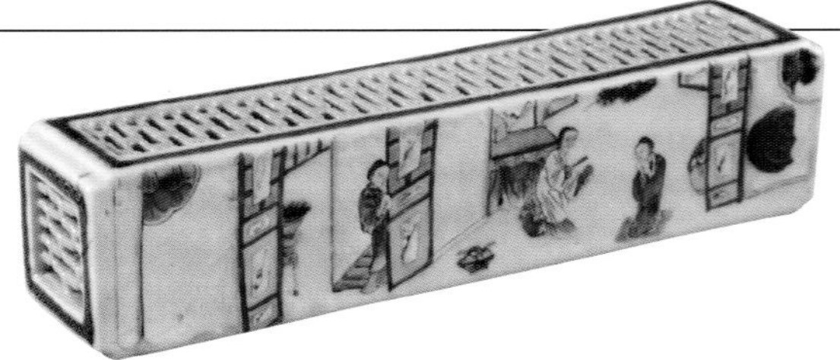

A Chinese Jiaqing famille rose cricket cage, pierced with trellis work, one end with a bayonet fitting and cover, with spike finial, slight wear, firing crack to edge.

1796-1820 *8¾in (22cm) long*

£4,000-4,500 **GORL**

A late 18thC to early 19thC Chinese famille rose porcelain Guanyin and child.

20in (51cm) high

£8,000-9,000 **ROS**

A Chinese Daoguang famille rose sgraffito yellow-ground medallion bowl, six-character mark, hairline cracks.

1821-50 *5½in (14cm) diam*

£9,000-11,000 **GORL**

A Chinese Daoguang famille rose 'cats' snuff bottle, four-character mark.

1821-50 *2¼in (6cm) high*

£7,500-8,500 **WW**

A Chinese Daoguang famille rose porcelain pebble-form 'butterflies' snuff bottle.

1821-50 *2½in (6.5cm) high*

£3,000-4,000 **WW**

A Chinese Daoguang famille rose porcelain snuff bottle, with a scholar, a poem to the reverse, four-character mark.

The scholar depicted is based on Qiu Sheng Fu, a Confucian scholar of the Qin and Western Han dynasties of ancient China.

1821-50 *2¼in (6cm) high*

£3,000-4,000 **WW**

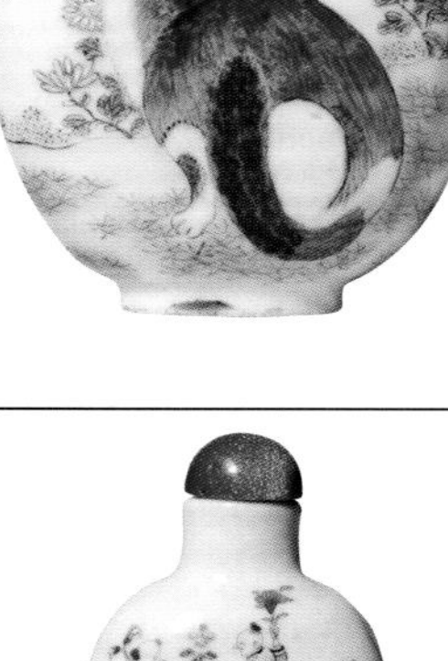

A Chinese Daoguang famille rose 'sixteen boys' snuff bottle, four-character mark.

1821-50 *2¼in (6cm) high*

£4,500-5,000 **WW**

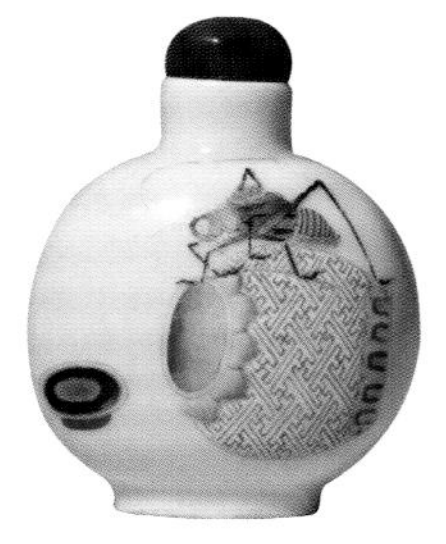

A Chinese Daoguang famille rose 'crickets' snuff bottle, four-character mark.

1821-50 *2¼in (5.5cm) high*

£4,500-5,000 **WW**

A Chinese Daoguang famille rose porcelain 'three rams' snuff bottle, four-character mark.

1821-50 *2¾in (7cm) high*

£3,500-4,000 **WW**

A Chinese Daoguang famille rose 'European subject' vase, with two medallions of Roman figures, four-character Qianlong mark, on ivory stand.
1821-50 without stand 3½in (9cm) high
£12,000-16,000 **L&T**

A Chinese Daoguang famille rose bowl, painted with the bajixiang (Eight Buddhist Emblems), seal mark, minor scratches.

This bowl is very finely painted, which makes it more desirable.
1821-50 4¼in (10.5cm) diam
£7,500-8,500 **GORL**

A Chinese famille rose porcelain bowl, decorated with chrysanthemum, peony and prunus, red Daoguang mark.
6¼in (16cm) diam
£1,600-2,000 **BE**

A mid-19thC Chinese famille rose 'bats and peaches' porcelain charger.
19in (48cm) diam
£4,000-5,000 **ROS**

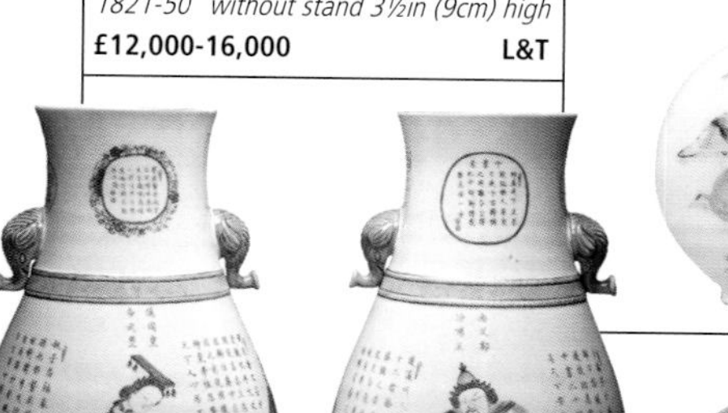

A pair of Chinese famille rose porcelain vases, with elephant mask handles, enamelled with four figures from the 'Wu Shuang Pu', with poetic texts, Xianfeng mark.
15in (38cm) high
£3,000-3,500 **BE**

A Chinese Xianfeng famille rose 'monkeys' snuff bottle, the rim gilded, four-character mark.
1851-61 2¼in (6cm) high
£1,300-1,600 **WW**

A Chinese Tongzhi famille rose 'marriage' basin, painted with butterflies, fruit and 'shuangxi' characters, with a gilt 'fu' character, six-character mark.

The Chinese character 'fu' means fortune or good luck.
1862-74 16½in (42cm) diam
£15,000-20,000 **WW**

A 19thC Chinese famille rose vase, with folk heroes from the 'Wu Shuang Pu'.

The 'Wu Shuang Pu' ('Table of Peerless Heroes'), published in the late 17thC by Jin Guilang, illustrates forty imagined portraits of Chinese folk heroes, warriors and poets.
24¾in (63cm) high
£6,000-7,000 **WW**

A Chinese Guangxu famille rose yellow-ground part service, comprising 5 dishes, 7 bowls and 6 covers, 5 saucer dishes, 7 cup stands, 6 bowls and a replica spoon, each piece with characters for 'longevity without limit', six-character marks, some chips and cracks, some dishes re-glued, wear to gilding.
1875-1908 dishes 7¼in (18.5cm) diam
£15,000-20,000 **DN**

A late 19thC Chinese famille rose vase, painted with scholars, iron red Qianlong mark.

16¼in (41.5cm) high

£2,500-3,000 **BELL**

A 19thC to 20thC Chinese famille rose porcelain jardinière, with birds and foliage, the base unglazed.

16in (40.5cm) diam

£1,600-2,000 **JN**

A Chinese Republic famille rose 'nine peaches' tianqiuping bottle vase, six-character Qianlong mark.

In Chinese mythology, peaches symbolise immortality. The number nine represents perfection and the eternal. Ling Zhu, Asian Art Specialist at Lyon & Turnbull, said that this item was a good example of the 'surging prices paid for fine quality Republic period porcelain in recent years'.

1912-49 *12½in (31.5cm) high*

£20,000-25,000 **L&T**

A Chinese Republic famille rose revolving vase, constructed in three sections, with panels of dragons, the internal section with flowers, clouds and bats, six-character Qianlong mark.

From the collection of Hugh Malcolm (1886-1961), Managing Director of the Rising Sun Petroleum Company in Japan (today known as Shell) from 1924-36. He lived in Kobe and Yokohama between 1913-36.

1912-49 *9¼in (23.5cm) high*

£18,000-22,000 **WW**

A Chinese Republic famille rose vase, with a figure in a pavilion, six-character mark, on wood stand, some wear to gilt rim.

1912-49 *11in (28cm) high*

£30,000-35,000 **DN**

A pair of Chinese Republic or later famille rose vases, painted with Zhong Kui and a lady, four-character Qianlong mark.

Zhong Kui is a figure in Chinese mythology, often depicted performing an exorcist's dance or subduing demons. His image was thought to ward off evil, especially at the Chinese New Year or the time of Double Five, the fifth day of the fifth lunar month.

c1912-49 *7½in (19cm) high*

£18,000-22,000 **WW**

A Chinese Republic famille rose figure of Wang Xi Zhi, a goose to his left side, four-character marks, 'ruan jin kai zao', and 'fu jian hui guan', on a stand.

Wang Xi Zhi (303-361), a Chinese official from the Jin dynasty (265-420), was a celebrated calligrapher. He is said to have reared geese and supposedly learned the technique of twisting his wrist whilst writing from observing the birds turning their necks.

1912-49 *6½in (16.5cm) high*

£4,000-4,500 **WW**

A 20thC Chinese famille rose teapot and cover, with a bird amongst wisteria in the Dowager Empress style, six-character Tongzhi mark.

6in (15.5cm) high

£750-800 **WW**

A 20thC Chinese famille rose Cantonese-style fish bowl or jardinière.

22¼in (56.5cm) high

£1,400-1,800 **DN**

A pair of mid-20thC Chinese famille rose vases, with flowers and birds, six-character Qianlong mark, on wood stands.

8¼in (21cm) high

£4,000-4,500 **WW**

A mid-19thC Chinese Canton famille rose porcelain vase, with warriors, on a ground of peony and pomegranate, with dragon handles.

Until 1842, all European trade with China was confined to the port of Guangzhou (Canton). Most pieces were made elsewhere in China and transported across long distances to reach the port.

24in (61cm) high

£6,000-7,000 **ROS**

A pair of mid-19thC Chinese Canton famille rose vases, with gilt lion dog and puppy handles, painted with figures and mythical beasts, one with re-stuck rim section.

17¾in (45cm) high

£1,500-2,000 **BE**

A pair of mid-19thC Chinese Canton famille rose porcelain vases, with mythical beast handles, one repair, wear to gilding.

23in (58.5cm) high

£1,800-2,200 **TEN**

A pair of mid-19thC Chinese Canton famille rose porcelain garden seats, with panels of figural scenes, one cracked.

19in (48cm) high

£3,000-4,000 **TOV**

A 19thC Chinese Canton famille rose punch bowl, enamelled with figural panels, on a gilt floral scroll ground.

15¾in (40cm) high

£500-700 **L&T**

A 19thC Chinese Canton famille rose vase, with panels of scholars and beauties in a garden, with four lion-mask handles.

17¼in (44cm) high

£500-600 **L&T**

A pair of 19thC Chinese Canton porcelain vases and covers, with vases, butterflies, fruit and foliage, with elephant-head handles.

15¾in (40cm) high

£2,000-2,500 **JN**

A pair of 19thC Chinese Canton famille rose porcelain vases, with figural and landscape panels.

24¼in (61.5cm) high

£2,000-2,500 **JN**

A 19thC Chinese Canton famille rose porcelain moon flask and cover, with figures, butterflies and foliage, with bat-form handles.

17¼in (44cm) high

£700-800 **JN**

A 19thC Chinese Canton famille rose punch bowl, the interior painted with Bijin in a landscape, the exterior with horsemen, warriors, boatmen and dignitaries, on hardwood stand, hairline crack.

Bijin, or Bijin-ga, is a term for beautiful women, used in several Asian languages including Japanese, Chinese and Korean.

15¾in (40cm) diam

£2,200-2,800 **MOR**

A Chinese Qianlong armorial porcelain famille rose punch bowl, with the arms of Cooke quartering Warren and Twysden in pretence, long crack, minor wear.
1736-95 *11¼in (28.5cm) diam*
£1,600-2,000 **TEN**

A Chinese Qianlong armorial porcelain famille rose punch bowl, with the arms of Lewin with Pollard in pretence, chip to rim, minor wear.
1736-95 *11¾in (30cm) diam*
£1,100-1,400 **TEN**

A Chinese Qianlong armorial porcelain famille rose tea bowl and saucer, with the arms of Marshall, small flake to saucer.
1736-95
£400-500 **TEN**

A Chinese Qianlong armorial porcelain famille rose tea bowl and saucer, with the arms of Browne, minor surface wear.
1736-95
£400-500 **TEN**

A Chinese Qianlong armorial famille rose porcelain platter, with the arms of Hutchinson impaling Calthrop, surface wear, restored rim chip and crack.
1736-95 *15in (38cm) wide*
£500-600 **TEN**

A mid-18thC Chinese armorial plate, with the arms of Taswell.
9in (23cm) diam
£350-400 **WW**

A pair of 18thC Chinese export rose mandarin armorial shrimp dishes, with the arms of Seton of Tough (Scotland) with the motto 'Forward ours'.
9½in (24cm) long
£1,000-1,400 **FRE**

An 18thC Chinese porcelain armorial charger, for the Dutch market.
17½in (44.5cm) diam
£1,000-1,400 **CAN**

A Chinese famille rose armorial plate, painted with shields and gilt foliage.
10¾in (27cm) diam
£220-280 **HANN**

A Chinese probably Kangxi doucai 'Phoenix and Bamboo' conical cup, painted with a phoenix and bamboo shoots, six-character Chenghua mark, minor scratches.

Doucai can be translated as 'colours which fit together' or 'contrasting colours'. Invented during the Xuande period (1426-35), and mostly associated with Chenghua's reign (1465-87), Doucai pieces are decorated in underglaze cobalt blue outlines, with coloured enamels added over the fired glaze. The technique was revived in the 18thC.

3¾in (9.5cm) diam

£7,500-8,500 **DN**

A Chinese Qing doucai bowl, with scholars in a landscape, the interior centred with a four-character Yongle mark, two rim chips.

4¼in (11cm) diam

£2,500-3,000 **DN**

A Chinese doucai porcelain saucer dish, decorated with formal scrolling lotus, Qianlong mark.

8¼in (21cm) diam

£900-1,100 **JN**

A Chinese doucai porcelain dish, with a horse above waves, six-character Yongzheng mark.

7¾in (20cm) diam

£600-700 **JN**

A Chinese doucai porcelain jue stand, with a peach amongst wave scrolls, surrounded by peonies and 'shou' characters, four-character Qianlong mark.

A jue is a type of Chinese ritual bronze vessel or goblet.

6¾in (17cm) diam

£2,500-3,000 **BE**

A 20thC Chinese doucai sectional calendar vase, Qianlong mark.

9in (23cm) high

£2,500-3,000 **JN**

An early 19thC Chinese doucai dish, painted with precious objects, heightened in gilt.

8in (20.5cm) wide

£300-350 **PW**

A Chinese doucai 'Bamboo' wine cup, enamelled with bamboo, apocryphal six-character Yongzheng mark, hairline to rim.

2¼in (6cm) diam

£1,400-1,600 **DN**

A Chinese Wanli Imperial wucai 'dragon' dish, painted with a five-clawed red dragon chasing a pearl, the rim with four phoenix, six-character mark.

Wucai means 'five enamels'. Decoration is chiefly in red, green and yellow, with outlines in dark cobalt blue. With the white porcelain body, this makes five colours. Wucai decoration originated in the Ming period, especially during the reign of Jiajing (1522-66), Longqing (1567-72) and Wanli (1573-1620). It was revived in the Qing dynasty.

1573-1620 *6¼in (16cm) diam*

£5,000-6,000 WW

A Chinese Transitional wucai vase, painted with elderly scholars examining a scroll, accompanied by attendants.

19½in (49.5cm) high

£5,500-6,000 L&T

A Chinese Transitional wucai vase, with an official and two attendants, inscribed with 'jia guan jin jue' characters.

c1640 *7¾in (19.5cm) high*

£2,000-2,500 WW

A Chinese Shunzhi wucai vase, with floral roundels, the neck with scroll and cracked-ice motifs, some firing faults and wear.

1644-61 *10¼in (26cm) high*

£3,000-3,500 DN

A Chinese Transitional wucai porcelain vase, painted with squirrels amidst vines, the base unglazed.

c1650 *15½in (39.5cm) high*

£3,500-4,000 JN

A mid-17thC Chinese wucai vase and cover, painted with ladies and boys in a garden, a cracked-ice band to the shoulder.

12½in (31.5cm) high

£4,000-5,000 WW

A 19thC Chinese wucai meiping, with a dragon and phoenix with a flaming pearl, on wood stand, six-character Kangxi mark.

17½in (44.5cm) high

£3,000-4,000 CHEF

A 19thC Chinese wucai porcelain jar and cover, with boys and court figures on a terrace.

13¾in (35cm) high

£3,000-3,500 L&T

A 19thC Chinese Kangxi-style wucai jar and cover, with figures in a landscape, including an Emperor, some damages and wear.

19¾in (50cm) high

£3,500-4,000 GORL

A Chinese Kangxi rouleau 'carp' vase, with carp and gilt plants, 'shou' characters and flyfots to the neck.

1662-1722 *18in (46cm) high*

£22,000-26,000 **WW**

A Chinese Qing susancai dish, painted pomegranates, the reverse with camellia blossoms, with incised dragons chasing pearls, six-character Kangxi mark.

14¼in (36cm) diam

£5,500-6,000 **WW**

A Chinese Ming fahua meiping stoneware vase, base unglazed.

Fahua is a type of Chinese decoration, typically in bold blue, turquoise, purple, green and yellow, with motifs outlined by raised trails of white slip.

8¼in (21cm) high

£7,000-8,000 **JN**

A Chinese Kangxi iron red and gilt vase, metal collar to rim.

1662-1722 *17¼in (44cm) high*

£4,000-5,000 **CHEF**

A Chinese Qing moulded porcelain double-gourd 'wu fu' snuff bottle and stopper, with bats amidst vines, restoration to rim.

Bats are symbols of happiness and fortune in China. 'Fu' in Chinese means both 'fortune' and 'bat', so that 'wu fu' can be translated as 'five blessings' or 'five bats'.

4½in (11.5cm) high

£10,000-14,000 **DN**

CLOSER LOOK – KANGXI IMPERIAL WATERPOT

Apple-shaped waterpots such as this belong to a class of wares produced during the Kangxi period for scholars' tables, known as badama or 'The Eight Great Numbers'.

The in-curved rim is encircled with scrolling leaves and lotus flowerheads between concentric blue bands.

It is decorated in underglaze copper red, with four stylised flower sprays of lotus, chrysanthemum, peony and hibiscus.

The base holds a six-character Kangxi Imperial mark.

A Chinese Kangxi Imperial waterpot.

1662-1722 *3¾in (9.5cm) diam*

£50,000-60,000 **WW**

A Chinese Kangxi enamelled biscuit susancai 'nine horses' dish, painted with horses amid auspicious objects, hairline cracks and rim chips.

Susancai can be translated as 'plain three-coloured', and is the name given to a style of decoration originating in the Kangxi period, featuring green, brown and yellow hues, on a black, yellow or white ground.

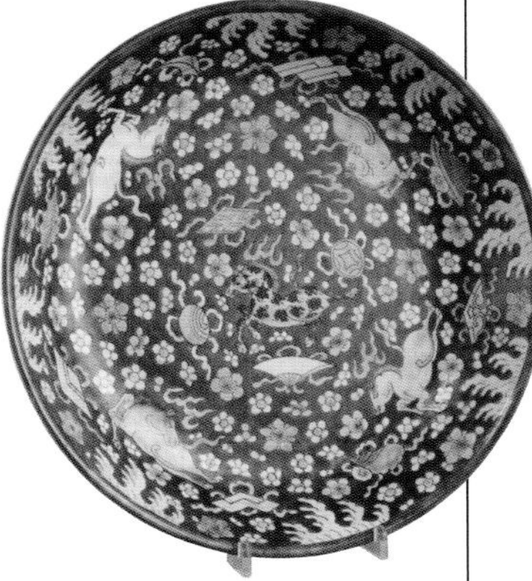

1662-1722 *12¾in (32.5cm) diam*

£2,000-2,500 **GORL**

A Chinese Ming-style porcelain vase, with scrolling lotus and ribboned emblems, Qianlong mark.

14¾in (37.5cm) high

£1,800-2,200 **JN**

A Chinese Qianlong bowl, with incised and green painted birds amongst peach branches, six-character zhuanshu script marks and mark.

4¾in (12cm) diam

£7,000-8,000 **LC**

A pair of Chinese Qianlong Imperial yellow and blue-ground 'dragon' dishes, with five-clawed dragons chasing pearls, six-character marks.

Dishes of this colour and pattern were produced for the use of a fifth-rank Imperial concubine.

1736-95 *10in (25.5cm) diam*

£40,000-45,000 **WW**

A pair of Chinese Qianlong dogs, with iron red patched coats.

1736-95 *9in (23cm) long*

£15,000-20,000 **DUK**

A Chinese porcelain vase, with dragons amongst scrolling lotus, six-character Qianlong mark, minor surface wear.

10¼in (26cm) high

£1,100-1,400 **TEN**

An 18thC Chinese Ming-style moon flask, with geometric patterns enclosing a central hexagonal star with a stylised lotus head.

This moon flask would originally have had two handles, but these have been broken off. However, its fine painting and aesthetic appeal means it is still a desirable piece. Copper red porcelain is popular in the present market.

7in (18cm) high

£50,000-60,000 **WW**

An 18thC Chinese export 'Hongs of Canton' punchbowl, with the Canton waterfront, the Western 'hongs' identified by their flags, the interior with a ship, restored.

14¼in (36.5cm) diam

£35,000-40,000 **HALL**

A probably 18thC Chinese porcelain vase, with a five-clawed dragon and phoenix amongst flowers, part of neck missing.

The depiction of the Imperial five-clawed dragon makes this a desirable vase, despite severe damage to the neck.

16¼in (41cm) high

£12,000-15,000 **TEN**

An 18thC to 19thC Chinese porcelain vase, with birds amongst flowering prunus, some hairline cracks.

18in (46cm) high

£10,000-12,000 **BELL**

A pair of Chinese mid-Qing fish bowls, with fish, shrimps and crabs, with a border of ruyiheads.

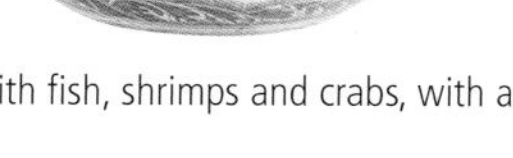

15¼in (39cm) wide

£6,000-7,000 **L&T**

An 18thC or 19thC Chinese 'Eight Immortals' saucer dish, the exterior with the Eight Taoist Immortals, the interior with Shoulao beside a deer, four-character Caihua Tangshi mark, crack and chips to rim.

Shoulao, or Shouxing, is the god of longevity in Chinese mythology. He is usually depicted as a bearded old man with a high brow and crooked staff.

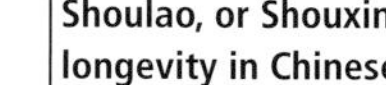
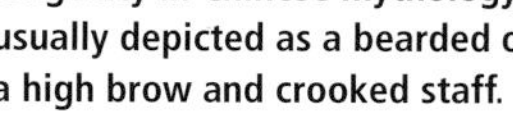

5¾in (14.5cm) diam

£12,000-15,000 **DN**

A Chinese Daoguang Imperial porcelain dish, with flowerheads and foliage, six-character mark, losses to rim.

1821-50 *5¾in (14.5cm) wide*

£24,000-28,000 **T&F**

A Chinese yellow-ground bowl, with goats, the interior with three goats within a border of lucky charms, Daoguang mark.

This was purchased in the 1950s for less than £1.

6in (15cm) diam

£30,000-35,000 **HAN**

A Chinese Daoguang 'dragon' cup, with two dragons chasing pearls, six-character mark.

1821-50 *1¾in (4.5cm) high*

£5,500-6,000 **WW**

A 19thC Chinese famille jaune finger bowl, decorated with cranes, six-character mark.

4¼in (10.5cm) diam

£450-500 **WHP**

A 19thC Chinese Qing sancai glaze joss stick holder, modelled as a figure on a qilin, with 'Chinese Porcelain Company' paper label.

6¾in (17cm) high

£1,300-1,600 **DUK**

A Chinese Ming-style porcelain tripod censer, six-character Tongzhi mark, on wood stand.

12½in (32cm) wide

£6,000-7,000 **JN**

A Chinese porcelain plaque, by Liu Yin Chang, in the Qianjiang palette, with the Yangtze river, inscribed 'Wide river reaches to the sky' 'Painted for the Mayor of Jingdezhen, Mr Lin Sun', framed, wear and chips.

c1880 10¾in (27.5cm) diam

£4,000-5,000 **CHOR**

A late 19thC Chinese porcelain vase, decorated with figures.

23¾in (60.5cm) high

£5,000-6,000 **POOK**

A Chinese Republic-style porcelain vase, with a carp leaping from water weeds, seal mark to base.

6in (15cm) high

£550-650 **JN**

A pair of Chinese Republic porcelain vases, with cockerels in a yard to one side, artist colophon to the other side, Liu Yucen seal mark to base.

Liu Yucen (1904-69) was the youngest of the 'Eight Friends of Zhushan', a group of porcelain painters active in late 19thC to mid-20thC China. The group, led by Wang Yi, played a key role in revitalising the Chinese porcelain industry after the fall of the Qing dynasty.

13¼in (33.5cm) high

£350-400 APAR

A pair of Chinese Republic porcelain Meiping vases, decorated with prunus blossom in the Yongzheng Imperial style, with a poem referring to immortality, 'One Thousand Autumns', Yongzheng mark.

c1920 *7½in (19cm) high*

£7,500-8,000 CHOR

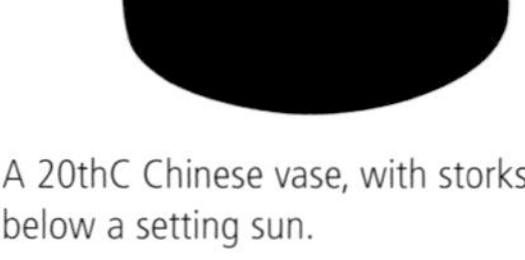

A 20thC Chinese vase, with storks below a setting sun.

72in (183cm) high

£2,000-2,500 SWO

A pair of 20thC Chinese Daya Zhai-style grisaille-decorated vases and covers, after Guangxu originals, Yong Qng Chang Chun four-character marks, some scratches.

These vases are based on 1870s originals, which had been intended to furnish a restored Yuanming Yuan (Old Summer Palace) after its destruction in 1860. The restoration never happened, and the original porcelain was stockpiled in the Forbidden City. The mark Daya Zhai refers to 'Studio of the Greater Odes', which has never been identified.

24½in (62cm) high

£4,000-5,000 DN

A Chinese porcelain vase, with elephant mask handles, mounted as a lamp, six-character mark, broken and re-glued.

vase 9½in (24cm) high

£4,000-5,000 CHT

A pair of Chinese porcelain famille noire vases, with figures in landscapes, apocryphal six-character Kangxi marks, some wear.

19¾in (50cm) high

£1,500-2,000 BE

A Chinese porcelain 'dragon' bowl, with dragons chasing pearls, red six-character mark.

6in (15.5cm) diam

£550-650 BE

A Chinese Wang Bingrong-style porcelain moon flask, with moulded dragon panels, moulded seal mark.

Wang Bingrong was a notable potter and porcelain carver, active in the Tongzhi to Guangxu periods (1862-1908).

14in (35.5cm) high

£250-300 JN

A Chinese, painted in gilt with bats and the long life character, apocryphal Daoguang mark, repair to handle, wear to gilding.

10½in (26.5cm) high

£750-850 DN

ESSENTIAL REFERENCE – SATSUMA

Satsuma porcelain was produced in the towns of Satsuma and Kyoto from the mid-19thC.

- **Satsuma designs are distinctive: a cream ground, with a finely crackled glaze, and enamelled and gilded decoration.**
- **They often feature panels depicting miniature scenes and landscapes, surrounded by ornate borders.**
- **The demand for Satsuma porcelain in the West grew rapidly after it was shown at international exhibitions.**
- **Later Satsuma pieces can therefore vary in quality, from items of very high craftsmanship to those made more cheaply for foreign department stores.**

A Japanese Meiji Imperial Satsuma earthenware vase, painted with a collection of porcelain vases and koros, the base with description of the decoration, with Keihou artist's mark and Shimazu mark.

14½in (37cm) high

£7,000-8,000 **JN**

A Japanese Meiji Satsuma jar and cover, with figural panels and smaller floral panels, Shozan mark, signed in gilt.

5in (13cm) high

£1,500-2,000 **L&T**

A Japanese Meiji Satsuma vase, painted with four panels, of an Imperial procession, birds and flowers, a hunting party and a rooster, chicken and chick, Kinkozan Tsukuru seal mark.

The Kinkozan family were potters active c1645-1927, when their factory closed.

12½in (32cm) high

£13,000-16,000 **LC**

A 19thC Japanese porcelain Satsuma vase, with overlapping framed panels.

15in (38cm) high

£5,000-6,000 **WHYT**

A 19thC Japanese Satsuma three-footed porcelain box, the lid with a figural scene, marked, some crazing and wear.

7½in (19cm) diam

£3,500-4,000 **DRA**

A Japanese Meiji Satsuma earthenware vase, with figural and floral panels, maker's marks to base.

11¾in (30cm) high

£2,200-2,800 **JN**

A Japanese Satsuma Meiji earthenware jar and cover, painted with immortals, signed, minor surface wear.

14½in (37cm) high

£1,500-2,000 **TEN**

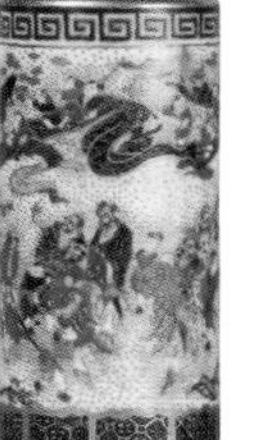

A pair of miniature Japanese Meiji Satsuma vases, painted with a celestial scene, signed.

2¼in (6cm) high

£1,500-2,000 **ROS**

A Japanese Meiji Satsuma pottery pot pourri, with gilt-metal strapwork cover, Kinkozan mark.

4¾in (12cm) high

£1,500-2,000 **HW**

A late 19thC Japanese Satsuma coffee pot and cover, decorated with robed figures, the handle and spout formed as a dragon, gilt ten-character mark.

11½in (29cm) high

£600-700 **FLD**

A Japanese Imari porcelain jar, with panels of flowering branches, lacking cover, minor wear.

Imari porcelain was traditionally made in the town of Arita. It was extensively exported to Europe in the 17thC and 18thC, shipped from the port of Imari. Designs were influenced by Japanese textiles, with imagery featuring landscapes, birds and women in detailed kimonos, often in a palette of cobalt blue, reddish-orange and gold.

c1700 *20½in (52cm) high*

£3,000-4,000 **TEN**

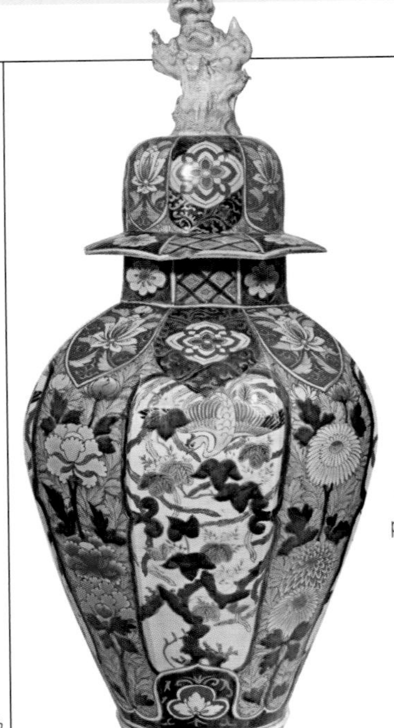

An early 18thC Japanese Imari vase and cover, with phoenix flying over paulownia, with shishi finial.

36¼in (92cm) high

£3,500-4,000 **WW**

A 18thC Japanese Imari bowl and cover, with panels of hawks, flowers and butterflies, restored.

19in (48.5cm) high

£700-800 **WW**

An early 18thC Japanese Imari vase and cover.

23in (58.5cm) high

£2,500-3,000 **DUK**

A pair of 18thC Japanese Edo Imari jars and covers, the covers with silver finials.

12½in (32cm) high

£550-650 **L&T**

A 19thC Japanese Imari charger, with a deer and boys playing mahjong, the sides with peacocks, the base marked 'fuki choshun' (wealth and everlasting spring), on wood stand.

22½in (57cm) high

£350-400 **WW**

A pair of Japanese Meiji Imari vases and covers.

16in (40.5cm) high

£400-500 **TRI**

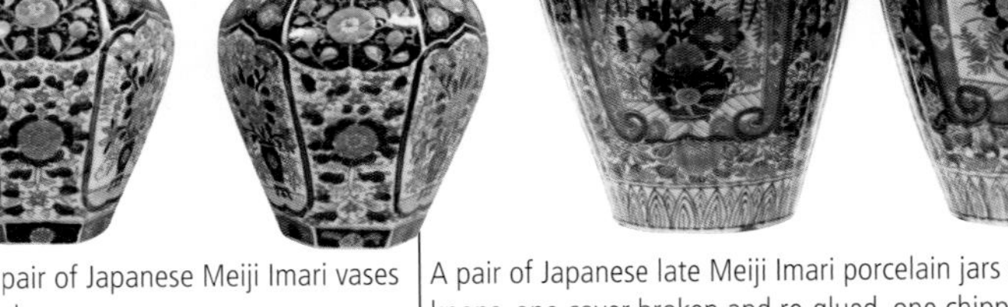

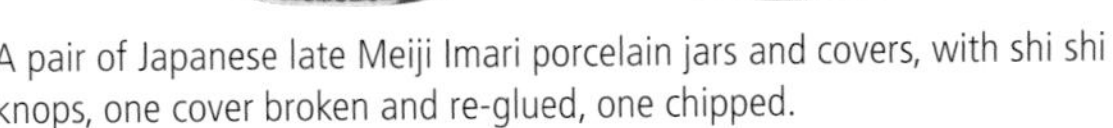

A pair of Japanese late Meiji Imari porcelain jars and covers, with shi shi knops, one cover broken and re-glued, one chipped.

21¾in (55cm) high

£350-400 **BE**

A Japanese late Meiji Imari porcelain bottle vase, embossed with dragons.

19¾in (50cm) high

£250-300 **BE**

A rare Japanese Edo Nabeshima-style celadon shaku-zara dish, incised with three books and two paint brushes, the ground with kikko (hexagonal cells).

Nabeshima ware refers to the porcelain plates, bowls and dishes made at the kilns directly operated by the Nabeshima clan, a Japanese samurai kin group who ruled the Saga Domain between the 1640s and 1871.

12in (30.5cm) diam

£4,000-5,000 **WW**

An 18thC Japanese Arita Nabeshima plate, some rim chips, one section re-glued.

8in (20cm) diam

£5,000-5,500 **CHEF**

A 17thC Japanese Arita kraak dish, chip to rim.

12½in (32cm) diam

£300-350 **CHEF**

A late 17thC Japanese Arita vase, painted with flowers, trees and geese, some cracking to foot, brass support.

16in (40.5cm) high

£1,200-1,600 **CHEF**

An early 18thC Japanese Kakiemon beaker.

Kakiemon is a delicate porcelain with a distinctive palette of iron red, blue, turquoise, yellow, gold and black. The name comes from a family of potters working in Arita, who are believed to have introduced overglaze enamelling on porcelain in the 1640s. It was a style regularly copied in Europe.

3in (7.5cm) diam

£650-750 **BE**

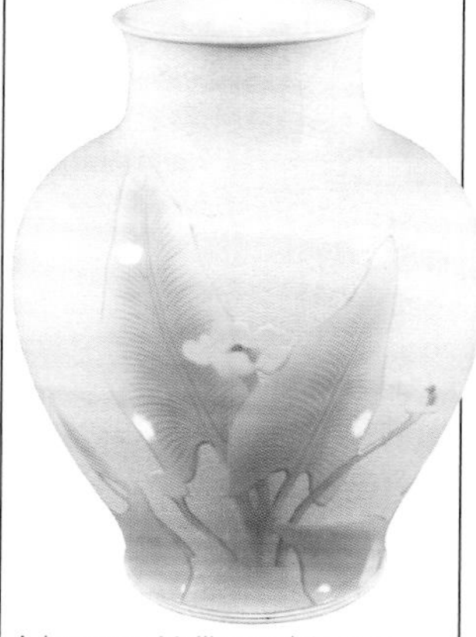

A Japanese Meiji porcelain vase, by Makuzu Kozan, decorated with Omodaka leaves and flowers in relief, seal mark 'makuzu gama kozan sei'.

10¾in (27cm) high

£4,000-4,500 **DN**

A Japanese Meiji Kutani porcelain jar, with decorated reserves of fish, birds and flowers, some surface dimples.

Kutani pottery originated in the 17thC in the village of Kutani and enjoyed great popularity in the 19thC. It was typically decorated with overglaze painting in vivid blues, greens, yellows, purples and reds. In the Meiji era, much Kutani pottery was exported to Europe.

17¾in (45cm) high

£550-600 **CHOR**

A late 19thC Japanese Arita porcelain bottle, painted with birds perched on branches, minor rim chips.

10in (25.5cm) high

£2,000-2,500 **TOV**

A 19thC Japanese Hirado cockerel and hen.

max 19in (48cm) high

£2,000-2,500 **CHEF**

A Chinese Canton enamel bowl, painted with flowers and 'shou' character roundels, the interior with roundel surrounded by the bajixiang (Eight Buddhist Emblems), Qianlong mark, some restoration, some stress cracks.

7¼in (18.5cm) diam

£5,500-6,000 **DN**

An 18thC Chinese Canton enamel box and cover.

4½in (11.5cm) long

£850-950 **L&T**

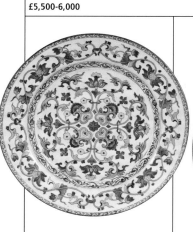

An 18thC to 19thC Chinese Canton enamel dish, with a scrolling lotus and ruyi design.

7¼in (18.5cm) diam

£1,500-2,000 **JN**

A Chinese late Qing enamel 'carps' dish, the exterior with phoenix and flowerheads, raised on foot.

22¾in (57.5cm) diam

£6,500-7,500 **WW**

A 19thC Chinese Canton enamel vase, with bronze neck rim.

14¾in (37.5cm) high

£1,200-1,600 **JN**

One of a pair of 19thC Chinese Canton enamel ewers, of Middle Eastern form, with painted bat, bird, fish and floral decoration, some losses.

12½in (32cm) high

£500-600 the pair **REEM**

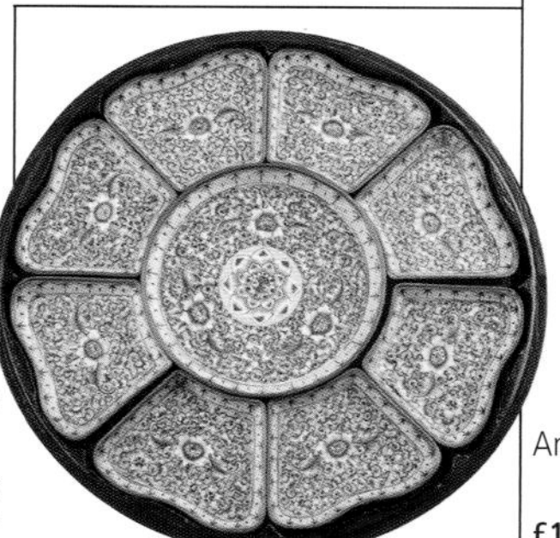

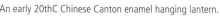

A late 19thC to early 20thC Chinese Canton enamel sweetmeat set.

12½in (32cm) diam

£500-600 **L&T**

An early 20thC Chinese Canton enamel hanging lantern.

9½in (24cm) high

£14,000-18,000 **DUK**

ESSENTIAL REFERENCE – CLOISONNÉ

Cloisonné is an ancient technique for decorating metal objects.

- **The technique was known in the Byzantine Empire, and had spread to China by the 14thC.**
- **It involves firing enamel powder in compartments, 'cloisons' in French, formed by metal wires soldered to the main surface.**
- **Early cloisonné pieces used dark green, cobalt blue, red, yellow and white, often on a turquoise background. Rose pink was added in the 18thC.**

A 16thC Chinese Ming cloisonné bowl, decorated with Buddhistic lions, the copper interior undecorated.

8½in (21.5cm) diam

£3,500-4,500 **JN**

A 17thC to 18thC Chinese cloisonné seal paste box and cover, some corrosion to inside, minor losses.

2¾in (7cm) wide 4oz

£5,000-6,000 **DN**

A pair of Chinese Qianlong cloisonné cups, with stylised lotus flowerheads, four-character marks.

1736-95 *2¾in (7cm) high*

£15,000-20,000 **WW**

A Chinese Qianlong cloisonné enamel bottle vase, four-character Qianlong mark and further mark, minor surface wear and enamel loss.

1736-95 *5¾in (14.5cm) high*

£12,000-15,000 **TEN**

A Chinese Qianlong Imperial cloisonné tripod censer, with Ming-style lotus scrolls, four-character mark and further character.

The further character can be read as 'cheng' (pure/clear water) or 'deng' (allowing articles in the water to fall to the bottom). This character is also found below the Qianlong reign mark on some Imperial glass wares and is believed by some scholars to be a serial number from the Chinese classic poem, 'Qianziwen' ('The One Thousand Word Essay'), with a strong connection to the Imperial workshops.

1736-95 *3½in (9cm) diam*

£45,000-50,000 **CAN**

A Chinese cloisonné bottle, with dragons flanking a red 'shou' character, with gilt copper eagle mask handles, four-character Qianlong mark.

4½in (11.5cm) high

£1,800-2,200 **CHEF**

A Chinese Qing cloisonné 'lotus' vase, gilt rim, foot rim and inner neck, four-character Qianlong mark, small damages.

13in (33cm) high

£1,500-2,000 **DN**

A pair of 19thC Chinese cloisonné magpies, some wear.

11in (28cm) high 18oz each

£7,500-8,500 **DN**

A pair of 19thC Chinese Qing cloisonné magpies.

7in (17.5cm) long

£1,200-1,500 **L&T**

A pair of early to mid-20thC Chinese cloisonné cranes.

30¼in (77cm) high

£2,500-3,000 **JN**

A pair of Japanese Meiji cloisonné vases, with koi fish.

12½in (31.5cm) high

£11,500-13,500 **L&T**

A Japanese Meiji cloisonné vase and cover, with phoenix and dragons, with a kiku finial.

11¾in (30cm) high

£900-1,200 **BELL**

A Japanese Meiji silver and cloisonné millefleur censer and cover, the legs issuing from lion masks, with two elephant-head handles.

7in (18cm) high 17.9oz

£8,500-9,000 **L&T**

A pair of Japanese Meiji cloisonné enamel chargers, with magpies on maple trees, raised on a short circular foot.

23¾in (60.5cm) wide

£3,500-4,000 **L&T**

A pair of Japanese Meiji or Taisho cloisonné ground vases, from the studio of Hayashi Kodenji, impressed lozenge marks to bases, star crack to one, some pitting to enamels, tarnishing to silver wire.

These are a particularly unusual shape for the maker, and in excellent condition considering that they are top heavy and liable to fall over.

12½in (31.5cm) high

£15,000-20,000 **GORL**

A Japanese Meiji cloisonné vase, in the style of Hayashi Kodenji (1831-1915), the mouth and foot with silver mount.

7½in (19cm) high

£3,000-3,500 **L&T**

A Japanese Meiji cloisonné vase, the rims with silver mount.

8¾in (22.5cm) high

£650-750 **L&T**

A late 19thC Japanese cloisonné box, by Hayashi Kodenji (1831-1915), marked, some wear.

5¼in (13.5cm) wide

£1,000-1,400 **DRA**

A pair of Japanese cloisonné vases, with birds of prey on a pine tree.

12¼in (31cm) high

£2,500-3,000 **GWA**

A Japanese cloisonné censor and cover, possibly by Sato, marked.

6in (15cm) high

£600-700 **HT**

A Chinese Ming gilt-bronze incense burner, modelled as a luduan, the base with a later applied Japanese nine-character mark.

Luduan are mythical beasts with rounded bodies and clawed feet. They are believed to have the ability to detect the truth, travel over great distances in a very short time and speak all the languages of the world.

17¾in (45cm) high 494oz

£20,000-25,000 WW

CLOSER LOOK – BRONZE DING

This bronze ding, in the form of a cauldron, is incised in gold and silver with dragons and scrolling designs.

The carved wooden cover is topped with a jade mandarin duck finial.

It is raised on three tapered legs and placed on a carved wood stand.

The stand and cover are probably 18thC or 19thC, but the vessel itself is attributed to the early Ming period, which substantially increases the value.

A Chinese Ming bronze ding, on a later wood stand, some cracks, chips and hairlines, losses to metalwork.

11¾in (30cm) high

£25,000-30,000 CHOR

A Chinese late Ming bronze bodhisattva of Ksitigarbha, standing on a double lotus platform with a dog.

Ksitigarbha, the Essence of the Earth, is one of the eight principal Mahayana students, or 'heart sons', of the Buddha, Shakyamuni. Ksitigarbha is known for his vow to take responsibility for the instruction of all beings in the six worlds between the death of Gautama Buddha and the rise of Maitreya, as well as his vow not to achieve Buddhahood until all hells are emptied. He is therefore often regarded as the bodhisattva who brings help and comfort to those in the underworld realm of hell beings.

31¾in (80.5cm) high

£15,000-20,000 SWO

A Chinese late Ming bronze incense burner, decorated with dragons chasing jewels, the handles shaped as chilong dragons, four-character seal mark to base reading 'hu wen ming zh'.

5¼in (13.5cm) wide 27oz

£12,000-15,000 WW

A Chinese late Ming or early Qing gilt-bronze figure of Guanyin, seated in dhyanasana with hands in dhyanamudra, traces of red lacquer, wear to gilding.

14¼in (36cm) high

£45,000-50,000 DN

A Chinese early Qing bronze incense burner, with mythical creatures, with lion mask handles, six-character Xuande mark.

5¼in (13.5cm) high 41¾oz

£6,500-7,500 WW

A rare 17thC to 18thC Chinese bronze Islamic market vase, cast with two panels of Arabic script, 'Glory be to God'.

This vase would have formed an incense set, including a censer, box and cover.

5¾in (14.5cm) high 28.6oz

£12,000-15,000 ROS

A 17thC to 18thC Chinese bronze vase, cast with flowers and fruit, with elephant-head handles.

9in (23cm) high 48¼oz

£5,500-6,000 WW

A 17thC to 18thC Chinese bronze 'qian qing gong' tripod censer and stand, Zhengde mark.

8¾in (22cm) wide 137.4oz

£4,000-5,000 ROS

A 18thC Chinese bronze fang ding form censer, archaistic four-character seal mark, on hongmu wood stand with silver wire inlay, polished.

Just 15 years ago there was little market for bronze censers which had been polished and had their patina removed. Yet the current fashion in China is for plain polished bronze censers dating from the 16thC to 18thC, almost always with apocryphal Xuande marks. The vast majority seen are circular on a tripod base (ding) or a circular foot (gui). It is rare to find a plain example of a rectangular-form (fang-ding) censer such as this.

6in (15cm) wide 67½oz

£20,000-25,000 GORL

An 18thC Chinese bronze gold-splash censer, with lion mask handles, six-character Xuande mark.

5½in (14cm) wide 18.6oz

£7,500-8,500 ROS

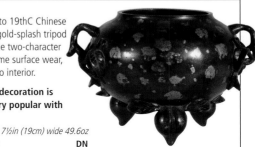

A late 18thC to 19thC Chinese Qing bronze gold-splash tripod censer, Xuande two-character seal mark, some surface wear, casting hole to interior.

Gold-splash decoration is generally very popular with collectors.

7½in (19cm) wide 49.6oz

£7,000-8,000 DN

A Chinese Tang-style bronze mirror, cast in relief with dragons and Chinese characters, on carved hardwood stand.

14in (35.5cm) high

£3,200-3,800 WW

A Chinese late Qing bronze tripod censor, six-character Xuande mark.

11in (28cm) wide

£2,200-2,600 HAN

A Chinese bronze p'ou form wine vessel, decorated with taotie, phoenix and geometric bands, with four-character mark within a three-clawed dragon.

The taotie is a demonic beast in Chinese mythology.

8½in (21.5cm) high

£1,300-1,600 MART

A 19thC Chinese archaistic gold-splashed bronze fang ding censer, in Western Zhou-style, cast with mythical beasts on zoomorphic feet, pierced wood cover, lacking finial, some scratches.

7¾in (20cm) high

£6,000-6,500 GORL

A Chinese Qing tiehua iron picture, in a wooden frame.

49¼in (125cm) high

£1,800-2,200 WW

A Chinese cast iron water cistern, the sides cast with Taoist panels, with inscription reading, 'Dated to the sixth year of Qianlong in the fifth month on an auspicious day the world enjoyed peace, the nine regions shared their joy, this is recorded in this inscription', some rusting.

Such cisterns were used to store water in case of fires. They would have been found in temples and larger buildings. Super sized gilded examples can be seen in the Imperial Palace, Beijing.

1741 24in (61cm) diam

£1,100-1,500 CHEF

A Chinese silver tea set and kettle-on-stand, by Hung Chong, Shanghai, decorated with snarling dragons, character marks, kettle, stand and burner marked 'HC'.
c1860-1930 *68oz*
£3,000-4,000 **BRI**

A Chinese Qing gold and silver inlaid tripod incense burner, decorated with taotie masks and other mythical beasts.
19½in (49.5cm) high 578¾oz
£2,500-3,000 **WW**

A late 19thC to early 20thC Chinese silver tray, maker's mark 'WO'.
21½in (54.5cm) high 67.6oz
£3,000-3,500 **BE**

A Chinese silver teapot, with embossed and chased decoration, maker's mark 'N.M'.
c1900 *7¼in (18.5cm) high 15¼oz*
£1,100-1,500 **PSA**

A pair of late 19thC to early 20thC Chinese enamelled silver beakers, decorated with characters, maker's marks to bases.
3½in (9cm) high 16¾oz
£400-500 **JN**

A Chinese silver bowl, by Luen Wo, Shanghai, applied with a dragon.
c1920 *7¾in (19.5cm) diam 26¾oz*
£1,500-2,000 **WW**

A 1920s-30s Chinese silver and enamel trinket box, the lid centred with a carved tiger's eye, base stamped 'Silver made in China', some scratches.
4¼in (11cm) long 8.6oz
£450-500 **APAR**

A Chinese silver cocktail shaker, by Wing Nam and Co., Hong Kong, inscribed 'Presented to Mrs E.R.C. MacVicker by the Crew of H.M.S Otus, as a token of esteem 1933-35'.
c1935 *9in (23cm) high 11oz*
£600-700 **WW**

A Chinese three-piece tea set, comprising a teapot, sugar bowl and milk jug, with dragon handles, with Chinese character marks, with unmarked claw-ended sugar tongs, decorated with dragons, some dents, teapot lid loose.
32¼oz
£3,500-4,500 **BELL**

A pair of 19thC Japanese Meiji bronze vases and stands, in the manner of Otake Norikuno, decorated with raised carp.

18½in (47cm) high

£20,000-25,000 **HANN**

A Japanese Meiji bronze elephant, with ivory inset tusks, signed 'Seiya saku', cast three-character mark, tail broken and re-glued.

24¾in (63cm) long

£1,500-2,000 **GORL**

A Japanese Meiji bronze group of an elephant being attacked by two tigers, signed 'Morimitsu', lacking tusks.

34¼in (87cm) long

£5,000-6,000 **BE**

A Japanese Meiji bronze tiger, signed with seal mark verso.

20¾in (53cm) wide

£1,100-1,500 **LSK**

A Japanese Meiji patinated bronze stork standing on a turtle, base signed.

15½in (39.5cm) high

£220-280 **TRI**

A pair of Japanese Meiji bronze rats, signed to base.

larger 3¾in (9.5cm) long

£450-550 **APAR**

A Japanese Meiji bronze figure of a peasant smoking a pipe, on a rootwood base, bronze signed to base, the pipe replaced, surface wear.

15¼in (39cm) high

£1,000-1,400 **APAR**

A Japanese Meiji bronze fisherman, on wood stand, fishing rod loose, surface wear.

36¼in (92cm) high

£2,000-2,500 **TEN**

A Japanese probably Meiji bronze fuchi, with gold inlay, three-character signature, '?-kane-tomo?'.

A fuchi is part of a katana, a Japanese sword. It is the metal bordering piece or collar between the sword's guard and handle.

1½in (4cm) long

£200-250 **FELL**

A late 19thC to early 20thC Japanese inlaid bronze vase and cover, surmounted by a warrior riding an eagle, the body with dragon handles and a warrior scene, signed to lid, some losses, re-glued quiver.

20in (51cm) high

£1,300-1,600 **CHEF**

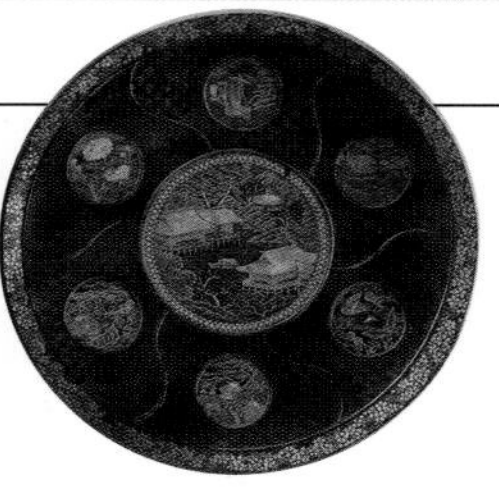

A near pair of Japanese Meiji iron dishes, inlaid with nunome zogan panels, one signed 'Made by Komai living Kyoto Japan', the other 'Made by Komai'.

Nunome zogan is a traditional Japanese decoration technique of silver or gold inlay, probably imported to Japan from Syria in the 12thC. The technique is closely associated with the Komai family, prominent metalsmiths operating in Kyoto in the 19thC, who widely used and developed the technique.

6in (15cm) diam

£2,500-3,000 L&T

A pair of Japanese iron vases, decorated in nunome zogan with landscape panels, both signed 'Kyoto no ju Komai sei' (made by Komai of Kyoto).

The landscapes depicted may be inspired by the Omi Hakkei, the traditional eight views of Omi Province where Japan's largest lake is located, a few miles east of Kyoto.

c1880 *8½in (21.5cm) high*

£25,000-30,000 WW

A Japanese iron plate, with nunome zogan panels of dragons, landscapes and flowers, the base signed 'Kyoto no ju Komai sei' (made by Komai of Kyoto).

c1880 *10¾in (27.5cm) diam*

£3,500-4,000 WW

A 20thC Japanese iron plate, decorated in nunome zogan with a dressed rat and Daikoku carrying a sack, with Komai Seibei/Otojiro II seal mark and inscription for Kinzan.

In Japanese mythology, Daikoku is the god of wealth and the guardian of farmers. Kinzan was a gold mine in the Izu Peninsula, Japan; this mark possibly relates to the riches in the god's sack.

10¼in (26cm) diam

£650-750 WW

A Japanese Komai-style iron model of a pagoda, decorated in gold and silver nunome zogan, with opening doors and drawers, bells hung at the corners.

The panels include decoration of the Kiyomizu-dera temple and of Mount Fuji.

c1910-15 *14½in (37cm) high*

£20,000-25,000 WW

A Japanese Meiji silver warming bowl, by the Miyamoto company, fitted with removable grill, marked for Miyamoto and sterling silver.

22½in (57cm) wide

£9,000-11,000 L&T

A Japanese Meiji silver and enamel koro incense burner, signed 'Baiosen', with box.

4¼in (11cm) high

£3,500-4,000 DUK

A Japanese Meiji or Taisho silver elephant, with a cartouche with gilt seal of Koreyoshi.

18½in (47cm) long 187.9oz

£20,000-25,000 L&T

A Japanese silver tea caddy, embossed with pond scenes, maker's mark 'S' in a circle within a fan-shaped punch.

4¼in (11cm) high 9¾oz

£800-900 WW

A Chinese Qing rhino horn libation cup, carved in high relief with a pagoda, figures, flowers and blossom.

Collectors ought to bear in mind that CITES Export licences are unlikely to be granted for items made of horn. CITES is the Convention on International Trade in Endangered Species of Wild Fauna and Flora, an international agreement between governments that came into force in 1975, requiring a permit for import and export of certain species or materials. Pieces such as this rhino horn libation cup will most likely have to remain in the country of purchase.

4in (10cm) high 5.9oz

£20,000-24,000 HAN

A Chinese Qing rhinoceros horn 'loquat' libation cup.

3in (7.5cm) wide 6¼oz

£30,000-35,000 WW

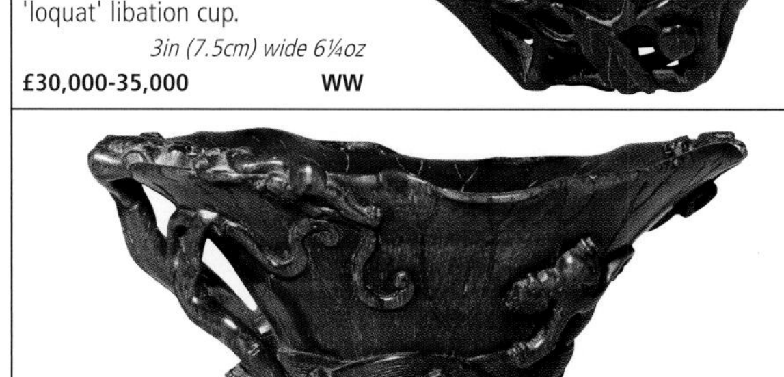

A 17thC Chinese rhinoceros horn 'nine dragon' libation cup, with nine chilong dragons.

Provenance: from the collection of William Cleverley Alexander. William Cleverley Alexander (1840-1916) was one of the most noted connoisseurs of his day, renowned for his taste in Western paintings and Asian works of art. The collection was started in 1867 and included items from the Tang, Song, Ming and Qing dynasties.

6in (15.5cm) wide 9oz

£50,000-55,000 WW

A Chinese early Qing bamboo 'prunus' libation cup.

5½in (14cm) wide

£8,000-9,000 WW

A 19thC Chinese Qing bamboo brushpot, carved with figures.

5½in (14cm) high

£1,100-1,500 L&T

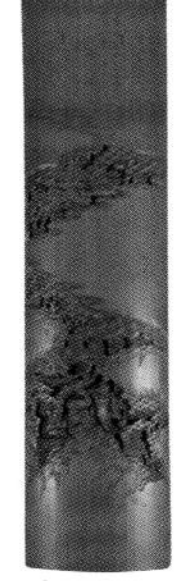

A Chinese bamboo wrist rest, carved with a landscape, inscribed 'Blessings from the Three Fortune Gods', stain to reverse, dated.

1875 11½in (29cm) high

£1,800-2,200 DN

A 19thC or early 20thC Chinese 'Seven Sages' bamboo brush pot.

The Seven Sages of the Bamboo Grove, were a group of Chinese scholars, writers and musicians in the mid-3rdC AD who gathered together in a bamboo grove to enjoy their respective talents and reject the outside world.

8¼in (21cm) high

£350-400 DN

A Chinese bamboo brushpot, signed 'Lao Tong', carved with the essay 'Valediction to Dong Shaonan' by Han Yu, dated Spring, wuchen year.

6¾in (17cm) high

£2,500-3,000 L&T

A Chinese bamboo group of Shoulao and five attendants, some worm damage and losses.

12¾in (32.5cm) high

£3,000-3,500 GORL

An 18thC Chinese Qing bamboo figure of Zhongli Quan.

Zhongli Quan, also known as Han Zhongli, is one of the Baxian, Eight Immortals of Taoism. His fan supposedly had the power to revive the dead.

3¼in (8.5cm) high

£3,000-4,000 L&T

A Chinese Kangxi hardwood bitong, probably zitan, carved with nine scholars and an acolyte preparing tea, the rim inlaid in mother-of-pearl and silver wire.

6¼in (16cm) high

£65,000-70,000 **WW**

A Chinese Qing aloeswood section, carved with Shoulao holding a ruyi sceptre, with further Immortals and the characters 'zhi ri'.

14in (35.5cm) high

£7,500-8,500 **WW**

A Chinese Qing carved wood elephant pole stand, painted with polychrome and gilt lacquer.

20¾in (52.5cm) high

£7,500-8,500 **WW**

A 17thC to 18thC Chinese wood figure of a Wenchang, old cracks to wood.

Wenchang, or Wendi, is the Chinese god of literature.

5in (13cm) high

£1,500-2,000 **DN**

An 18thC to 19thC Chinese giltwood carving of Amitayus, traces of gilt painted moulded gesso, inscription to reverse.

16½in (42cm) high

£8,500-9,500 **ROS**

A 18thC to 19thC Chinese carved sandalwood casket and cover, by Sung Sing Gung.

This casket was exhibited at the International Exhibition or Great London Exposition in 1862.

15¼in (39cm) long

£2,000-2,500 **HANN**

A 19thC Chinese rosewood stand, carved with stylised chi-dragons and tight scrolls, joints re-stuck, some chips.

9in (23cm) wide

£1,500-2,000 **GORL**

A Chinese wood carving of Guanyin holding a child, probably Huangyang wood, minor nicks and knocks.

9¾in (24.5cm) high

£2,400-2,800 **DN**

A late 18thC to early 19thC Japanese Edo carved hardwood Hozuki fruit, by Toyomasa, signed.

1¾in (4.5cm) long

£2,500-3,000 **PW**

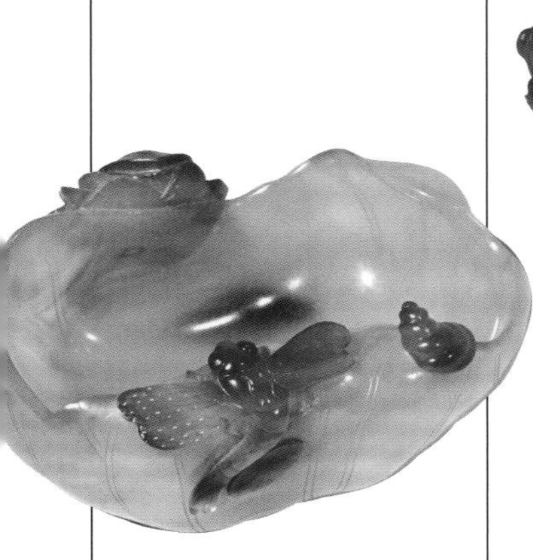

A Chinese Qing or later agate 'dragonfly and lotus' brush washer.

3¼in (8.5cm) long

£4,000-4,500 WW

A 20thC Chinese two-tone carved agate 'tree trunk' libation cup, on green-stained carved ivory and hardwood stand.

6in (15cm) high

£6,500-7,000 TOV

A Chinese Qing or later carnelian-agate pendant, carved as a goldfish, two snails and a leafy spray.

2in (5cm) high

£2,500-3,000 WW

A 18thC to 19thC Chinese carnelian-agate vase, carved as a tree trunk overgrown with fungus, with four bats.

5¾in (14.5cm) high

£4,000-5,000 WW

A set of four Qianlong soapstone inlaid 'Story of the Western Wing' panels, each panel inlaid with the couple Zhang Sheng and Cui Yingying, the top panels showing traditional courting, the bottom panels showing them in amorous embrace.

The 'Story of the Western Wing', also translated as 'Romance of the Western Chamber', is one of the most famous Chinese dramatic works. Written by the Yuan dynasty playwright Wang Shifu and set in the Tang dynasty, it tells the story of the young couple Zhang Sheng and Cui Yingying consummating their love without parental approval and outside of the bond of marriage. Hailed as the 'Chinese lover's bible', the story has inspired Chinese public imagination for centuries, and has been adapted across a broad range of artistic media, from paintings to woodblock prints, from porcelain to ivory carvings. Soapstone inlaid panels from the Qianlong period are extremely rare, increasing the value of this set.

1736-95 *9¾in (24.5cm) high*

£25,000-30,000 L&T

A 19thC to 20thC Chinese red coral carving, of Guanyin.

5¾in (14.5cm) wide

£500-600 JN

A Chinese Qing soapstone fang hu vase, carved with a horned beast, the reverse with inscription, with animal mask handles, some chips.

6¾in (17cm) high

£550-650 GORL

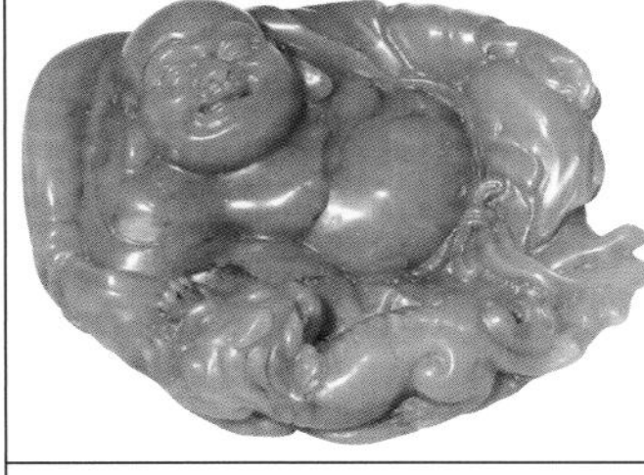

A Chinese Qing or later soapstone carving of Budai Heshang, a mythical beast at his side, signed 'Yuan Kang'.

2¼in (6cm) high

£650-750 WW

A 20thC Chinese carved soapstone figure of a seated man, minor repair to one hand.

4¼in (10.5cm) high

£800-900 TOV

ESSENTIAL REFERENCE – JADE

Jade has a long history in China, and traditionally has been prized almost as much as gold. It has long been carved into jewellery and ritual, ceremonial or decorative items, with pieces of worked Chinese jade found dating from c4000BC.

- **Jade technically refers to two separate minerals, nephrite and jadeite, although items carved from other stones are sometimes also referred to as jades.**
- **Most Chinese jades are fashioned from nephrite, which was mined in eastern central Asia. Its colour can vary from creams and whites to greens and blacks. Jadeite can contain green, white and red within a single piece.**
- **Ming dynasty jades tend to be carved from different coloured stones and have a soft polish, while Qing dynasty jades are often white, almost translucent.**
- **Heavier, more elaborate pieces are likely to be more recent, but in general jade is very difficult to date.**
- **Jade is a very hard material, so must be worked on with saws, discs and drills. It is also brittle and easily scratched, so condition is important.**
- **The small size of Chinese jades, and the intricacy of their carvings, ensure their popularity today.**
- **The jade market is fairly unpredictable; it is not uncommon for Chinese jades to go to auction undated, with low estimates, and sell for much more than expected.**

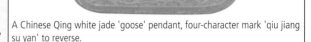

A Chinese Qing white jade 'goose' pendant, four-character mark 'qiu jiang su yan' to reverse.

2in (5cm) high

£20,000-25,000 **WW**

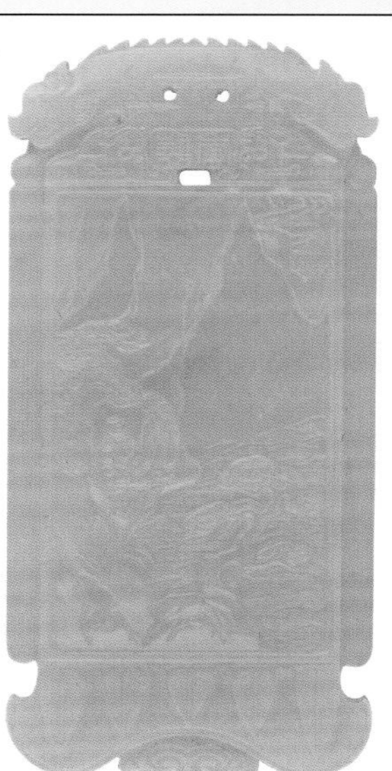

A carved Chinese Qinglong white jade 'landscape' pendant, surmounted by a pair of dragons, carved with a sage and attendant, signed 'San Qiao', marked.

3¼in (8cm) high

£30,000-35,000 **L&T**

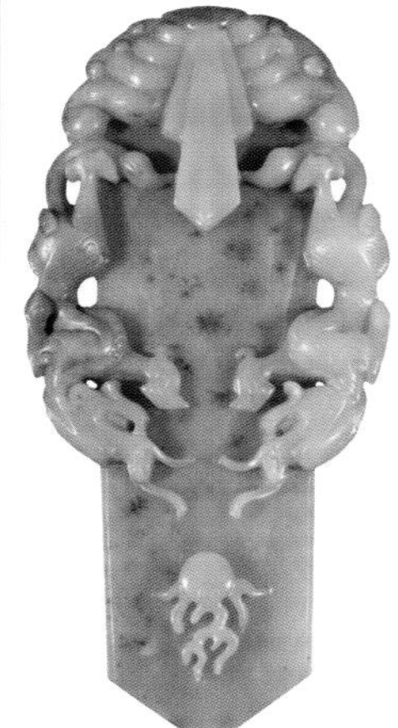

A Chinese celadon jade ceremonial tablet, carved Gui rising from waves, dragons chasing a pearl, with russet, brown and white inclusions.

7in (17.5cm) high

£3,000-4,000 **DN**

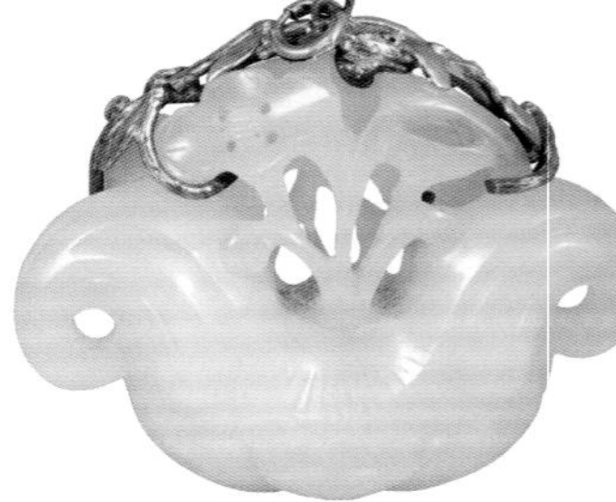

A Chinese white carved jade pendant, with gilt-metal clasp.

2in (5cm) wide

£1,800-2,200 **JN**

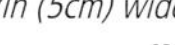

A white jade pendant, surmounted by ruyihead clouds, carved with a boy on a water buffalo, the reverse inscribed 'yu fu' (jade amulet).

2¼in (6cm) high

£4,500-5,500 **L&T**

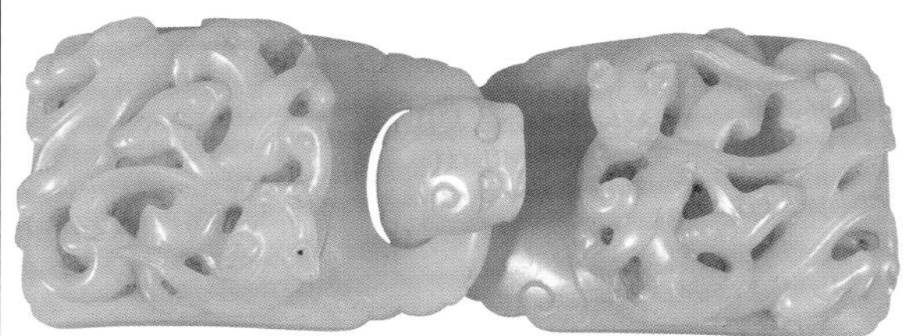

A Chinese white jade double belt buckle, carved with a chilong grasping a sprig of lingzhi, the hook a dragon's head, some old repairs.

4½in (11.5cm) long

£4,000-5,000 **DN**

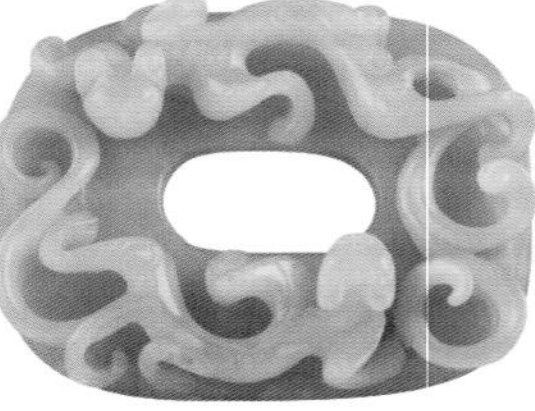

A Chinese probably Ming celadon jade 'chilong' disc, with light russet inclusions.

2¾in (7cm) long

£6,500-7,000 **L&T**

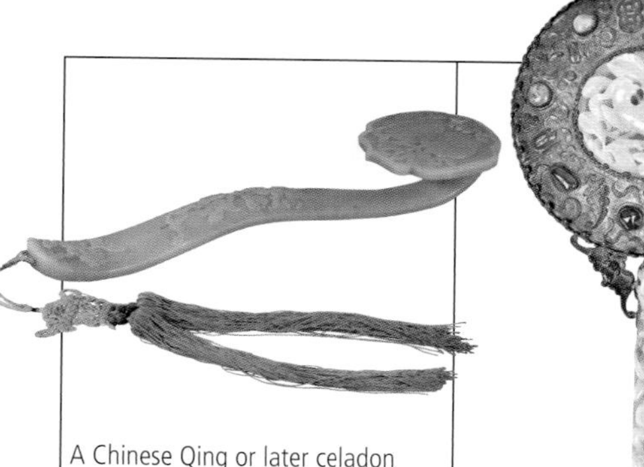

A Chinese Qing or later celadon jade ruyi sceptre, carved with peaches, a bat, and a finger citron, the reverse with Zen Buddhism from 'the Diamond Sutra', the seal itself reading 'getting great freedom of mind', with tassle, minor blemishes.

15¼in (38.5cm) long

£12,500-15,000 **DN**

A 19thC Chinese silver-plate-mounted jade hand mirror, decorated with Buddhist emblems and inset with semi-precious stones and hardstones, some wear.

7¾in (19.5cm) long

£3,000-3,500 **BELL**

A 17thC Chinese pale celadon jade beaker Gu vase, carved with nine dragons amid clouds, with later wood stand.

Whilst the number nine is auspicious in Chinese folk beliefs, the depiction here probably refers to the nine sons of the Dragon King, who was an important figure in Chinese mythology, and regarded as the dispenser of rain.

9¾in (24.5cm) high

£60,000-70,000 **ROS**

A Chinese Qianlong pale celadon jade 'prunus' vase.

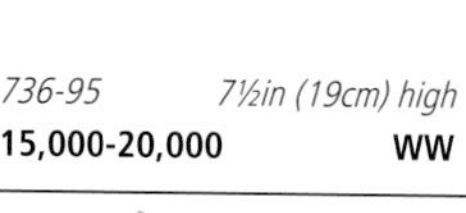

1736-95 *7½in (19cm) high*

£15,000-20,000 **WW**

A Chinese Qianlong jade box and cover, carved as a peach, with four bats, on wood stand.

2in (5cm) wide

£4,000-5,000 **L&T**

An 18thC Chinese celadon jade rhyton, carved with a chilong dragon, phoenix, vase and archaistic motifs, on stand.

6¾in (17cm) high

£10,000-14,000 **ROS**

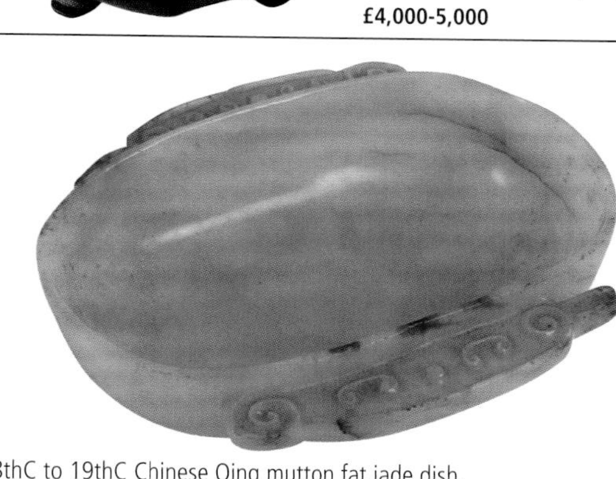

A 18thC to 19thC Chinese Qing mutton fat jade dish.

This form is extremely rare for jade and is more often seen in lacquer.

4in (10cm) long

£14,000-18,000 **BATE**

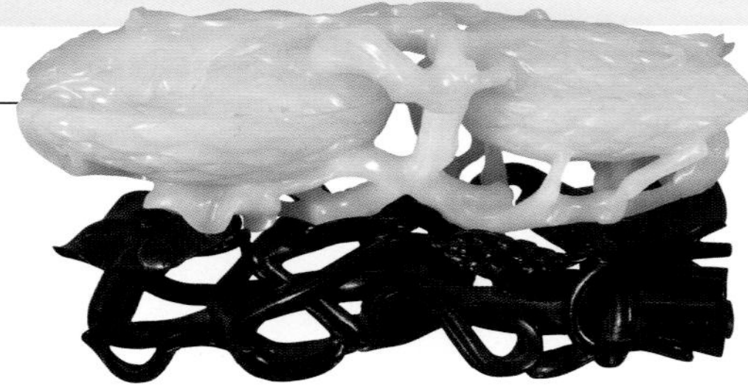

A 19thC or 20thC Chinese white jade double 'fruit' box and cover, on wood stand, the cover broken and re-attached.

5in (13cm) long

£7,000-8,000 **DN**

An archaistic jade tripod censer and cover, carved with archaistic scrolls forming taotie masks, with four-petal finial, of a greyish tone with dark patches.

9½in (24cm) high

£15,000-20,000 **L&T**

A celadon jade vase and cover, with dragons in pursuit of a pearl.

4¾in (12cm) wide

£9,000-11,000 **L&T**

A Chinese Qing pale celadon jade carving of a luohan, with a small Buddhist lion.

Luohan is the Chinese word for an arhat, a person within Buddhism who has achieved nirvana (enlightenment).

5in (12.5cm) wide

£7,500-8,500 **WW**

A Chinese jadeite carved celadon and russet vase, carved with cranes, a stag, a bat, lunzhi fungus, prunus and a pine tree, some damages.

7in (18cm) wide

£3,500-4,000 **DN**

A Chinese Qing white jade carving of a boy.

3in (7.5cm) long

£5,000-5,500 **WW**

A Chinese celedon jade crouching scholar figure.

3¾in (9.5cm) high

£6,000-7,000 **BAM**

A celadon jade carving of fishermen on a boat, with russet veins.

7in (18cm) long

£8,500-9,500 **L&T**

A Chinese Qing pale celadon jade carving of a mountain, with five scholars and an attendant boy.

4½in (11.5cm) high

£8,500-9,500 **WW**

An 18thC Chinese Qing pale green nephrite jade boulder carving, with four children and an elephant in a mountain landscape, on later wood stand.

6in (15cm) high

£20,000-25,000 **CHEF**

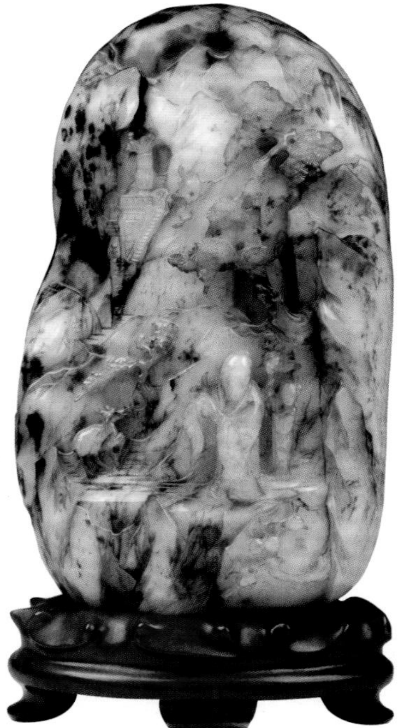

A Chinese celadon and dark brown mottled jade mountain carving, carved with a gentleman and boy, on wood stand.

10¾in (27.5cm) high

£11,000-14,000 **MART**

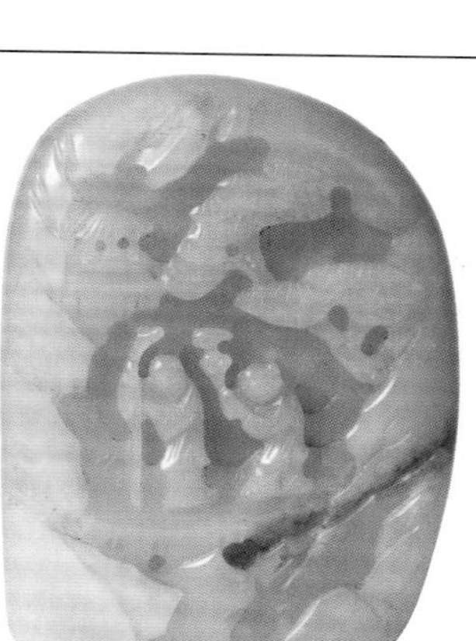

A Chinese jade boulder, with two figures in landscape, the reverse with a deer, minor surface abrasions, some russet inclusions.

3½in (9cm) high

£3,500-4,000 **TEN**

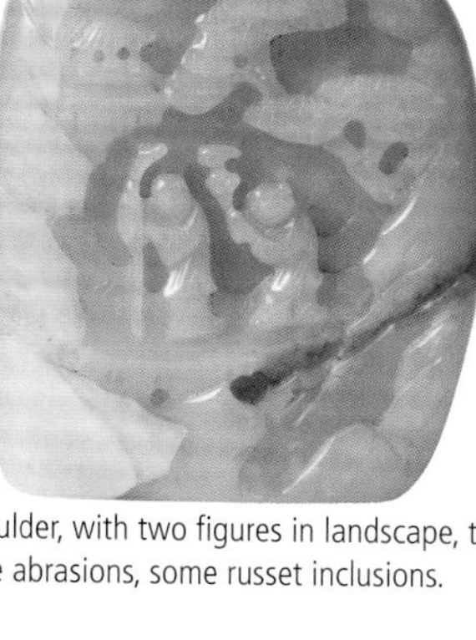

A Chinese Qing white jade carving of a finger citron and a bat, with russet markings.

The finger citron, also known as Buddha's hand is a fruit segmented into finger-like sections.

4¾in (12cm) long

£23,000-28,000 **WW**

A Chinese Qing white jade carving of two mandarin ducks, on wood stand.
2in (5cm) long
£4,500-5,000 **WW**

A Chinese Qing white and grey jade carving of two hounds.
2¾in (7cm) long
£15,000-20,000 **WW**

A Chinese Qing yellow-green jade carving of a hound.
2¾in (7cm) long
£2,500-3,000 **WW**

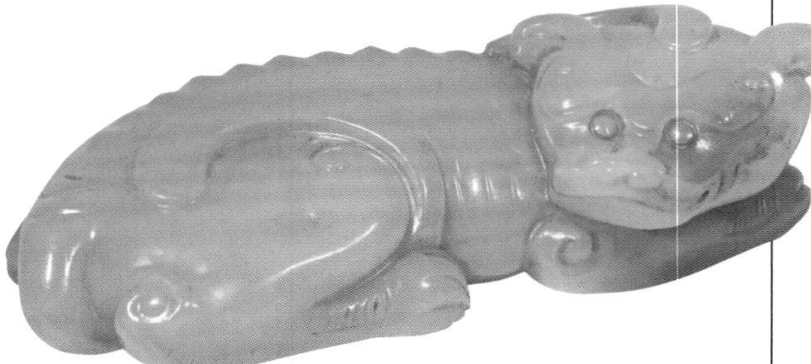

An 18thC Chinese pale celadon jade carving of a qilin.
4¼in (10.5cm) long
£8,000-9,000 **WW**

A late Chinese Qing pale celadon jade carving of a boy on a water buffalo, on wood stand.
3½in (9cm) wide
£2,000-2,500 **BE**

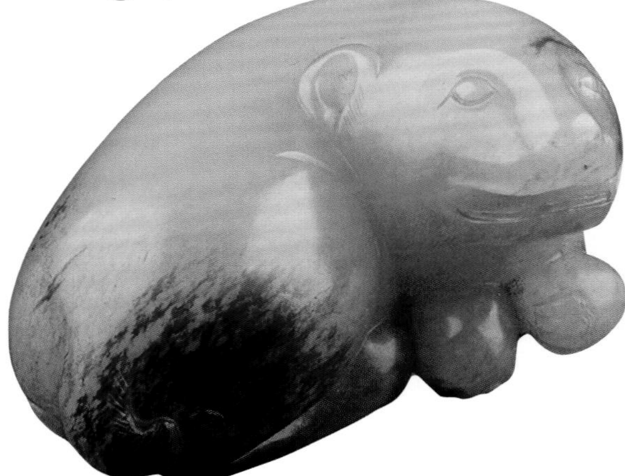

A Chinese late Qing pale celadon jade model of a bear.
2½in (6.5cm) long
£14,000-18,000 **L&T**

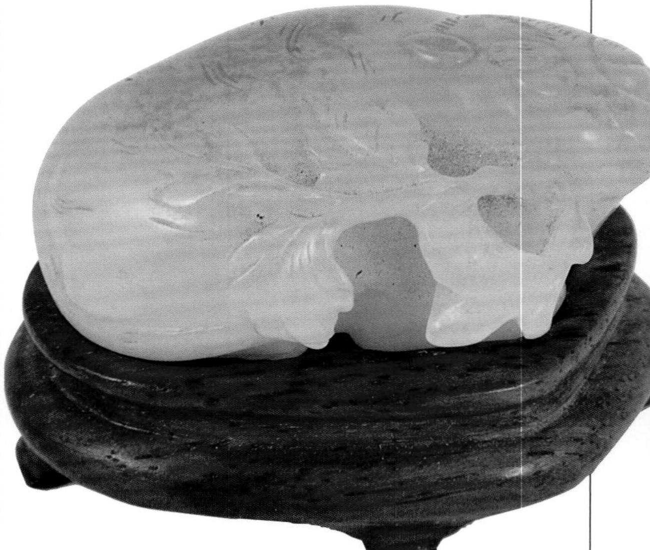

A Chinese white-grey and russet jade carving of a cat.
2in (5cm) long
£5,000-6,000 **SOU**

A Chinese Ming or Qing laque burgauté and tixi lacquer dish, decorated with figures in a garden, inlaid with mother-of-pearl.

Laque Burgauté is a technique of decorating lacquer ware with shell inlay, made from the shell of the sea-ear (Haliotis).

13½in (34cm) wide

£3,500-4,000 WW

A Chinese Qianlong cinnabar lacquer 'Eight Immortals' box and cover.

The Eight Immortals, or the Baxian, are a group of holy Taoists, consisting of He Xiangu, Lü Dongbin, Lan Caihe, Han Xiangzi, Zhang Guolao, Li Tieguai, Han Zhongli and Cao Guojiu.

1736-95 5in (13cm) diam

£3,500-4,500 L&T

An 18thC Chinese Qing cinnabar lacquer 'peach' box and cover, possibly depicting Zhang Guolao with an attendant, some cracks.

6¼in (16cm) wide

£4,000-4,500 DN

A Chinese Tianqi lacquer necklace box and cover, with five-clawed dragons chasing pearls, later Qianlong mark.

10¼in (26cm) diam

£5,000-6,000 L&T

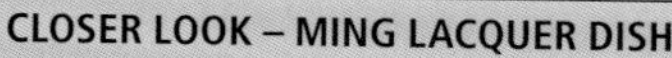

CLOSER LOOK – MING LACQUER DISH

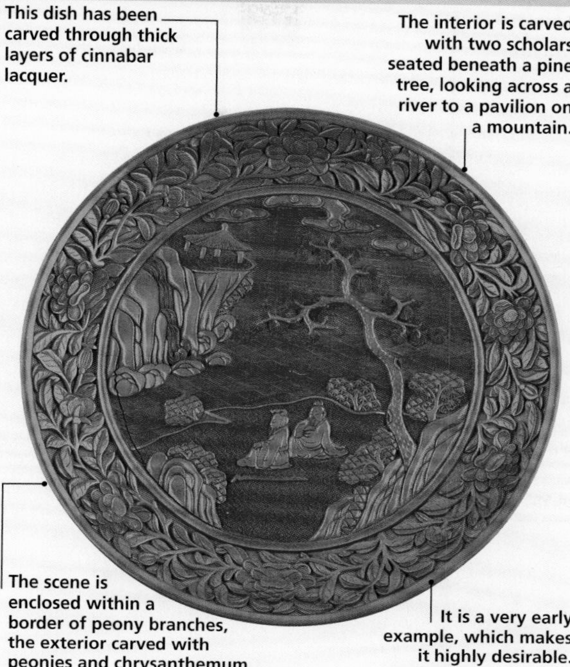

This dish has been carved through thick layers of cinnabar lacquer.

The interior is carved with two scholars seated beneath a pine tree, looking across a river to a pavilion on a mountain.

The scene is enclosed within a border of peony branches, the exterior carved with peonies and chrysanthemum.

It is a very early example, which makes it highly desirable.

A 16thC Chinese Ming cinnabar lacquer dish.

10in (25.5cm) diam

£12,000-15,000 L&T

A rare 17thC Chinese marbled xipi lacquer vase.

Xipi translates literally as 'rhinoceros hide'. The technique involved applying layers of different coloured lacquers over an uneven surface. It is then polished so that the layers appear as different colours, in an abstract pattern.

3¾in (9.5cm) high

£4,000-5,000 ROS

A 19thC Chinese export lacquer panel, decorated in gilt with figures, pavilions and landscapes, splits and wear.

35¾in (91cm) high

£2,000-2,500 DN

An 18thC Chinese lacquered painted wood panel, with Guanyin and an attendant in a landscape.

69in (175.5cm) high

£4,000-5,000 BELL

A Chinese Qing lacquered 'dragon' robe box, with a five-clawed dragon and a flaming ball.

25½in (65cm) wide

£1,500-2,000 L&T

ESSENTIAL REFERENCE – NAMBAN CASKET

In the late 16thC, Europeans began to arrive in Japan to establish Christian missions and to trade. To furnish the new churches, and to contribute to export trade, Japanese lacquer workers began to make items in traditional European forms, such as chests, boxes, coffers, cabinets or caskets, but using traditional Japanese decorative designs. These items were named 'Namban' or 'Nanban', translating literally as 'southern barbarians', after the foreign settlers who had promoted their creation. Namban lacquer pieces are similar in design to the Kodaiji lacquer pieces made in Kyoto in the late Momoyama and early Edo period; both feature gold hiramakie on a roironuri, or black ground. However, Namban pieces are typically further decorated with mother-of-pearl panels and shell inlay, and often combine Japanese designs with Western geometric borders.

A rare Japanese Momoyama Namban lacquer casket, decorated in gold hiramakie and inlaid in mother-of-pearl on a black ground.

c1574-1600 *9in (23cm) wide*

£6,000-7,000 BRI

A pair of Japanese Meiji lacquer and Shibayama bottle vases, on three elephant-head feet, some losses, minor surface wear.

Shibayama is a type of Japanese inlay, popular during the Meiji period on both objets d'art and furniture. It was created from a variety of materials, including mother-of-pearl, ivory, glass, horn, tortoiseshell and jade. The pieces would be individually carved, then set into a wood, lacquer or ivory ground.

8¾in (22cm) high

£7,000-8,000 TEN

A Japanese Meiji Shibayama lacquered 'kankodori' box and cover, signed 'Masahisa'.

9¾in (24.5cm) long

£2,000-2,500 L&T

A Japanese Meiji lacquer box, decorated with landscape and floral panels and fans on a millefleur ground, multi-artist signatures.

This item may have been a diplomatic gift.

4¼in (11cm) wide

£1,500-2,000 GORL

A Japanese Meiji black and gilt lacquer box.

8¼in (21cm) high

£750-850 DUK

A Japanese Edo lacquer kettle and cover.

Nashiji is a technique within lacquerwork. Gold or silver flakes are sprinkled onto a lacquered surface. A layer of Nashiji lacquer is then applied and burnished with charcoal, so that the gold or silver can be seen through the top layer of lacquer.

12in (30.5cm) long

£350-450 JN

A pair of Japanese Meiji Shibayama and lacquer vases, with birds and foliage in mother-of-pearl, ivory and tortoiseshell, each neck and foot with a silver-metal rim.

6in (15cm) high

£2,000-2,500 JN

A Japanese Meiji gold lacquer tray, with mother-of-pearl and coral decoration.

11¾in (30cm) wide

£900-1,100 DUK

A Japanese late Meiji silver-mounted Shibayama gold lacquer tsuba, depicting a courtesan entertaining Daruma, signed 'Ryogetsu', with original silk pouch.

A tsuba is a traditional Japanese sword guard.

4in (10cm) wide

£4,500-5,000 BE

A Chinese Qing white jade 'cats' snuff bottle.

Tobacco was introduced to China by the Portuguese in the mid-to-late 16thC. It was originally smoked in pipes, but by the late 17thC, the use of snuff and snuff bottles had become a regular part of the social rituals of the upper classes. Snuff bottles became objects of beauty, ways to display social status and wealth.

2¼in (6cm) high

£10,000-12,000 **WW**

A Chinese Qing celadon jade snuff bottle, with four-character seal mark 'chang yi zi sun' to base.

2½in (6.5cm) high

£5,500-6,000 **WW**

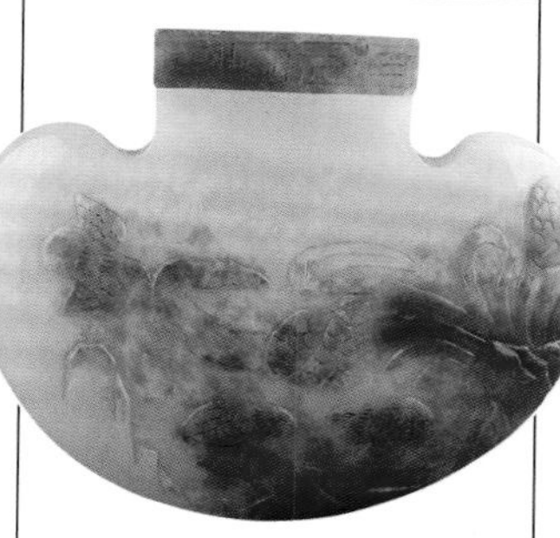

A Chinese white and russet jade snuff bottle, carved with chicks and a poem, the stopper with an apocryphal Qianlong mark.

2½in (6.5cm) wide

£2,500-3,000 **L&T**

A Chinese Qianlong pewter 'chilong dragon' snuff bottle.

1736-95 *2in (5cm) high*

£400-500 **WW**

An 18thC to 19thC Chinese gilt-decorated soapstone snuff bottle.

1¾in (4.5cm) high

£1,300-1,600 **WW**

A Chinese Tongzhi copper snuff bottle, cast with a scholar in a landscape, stopper with mother-of-pearl inset, four-character mark.

1862-74 *2¼in (6cm) high*

£800-900 **WW**

A 19thC Chinese coconut shell snuff bottle, incised with a scholar courting a young lady, the reverse with a poetic stanza, ivory stopper.

3¼in (8cm) high

£2,000-2,500 **L&T**

A Chinese Guangxu parcel-gilt and glass snuff bottle, with a European glass micromosaic, marked.

1875-1908 *1¾in (4.5cm) high*

£500-600 **WW**

A late 19thC Chinese interior-painted rock crystal snuff bottle, some damages.

4¼in (11cm) high

£200-250 **FLD**

A Chinese interior-painted glass snuff bottle, signed 'Yu Tian' and dated.

1895 *2½in (6.5cm) high*

£650-750 **WW**

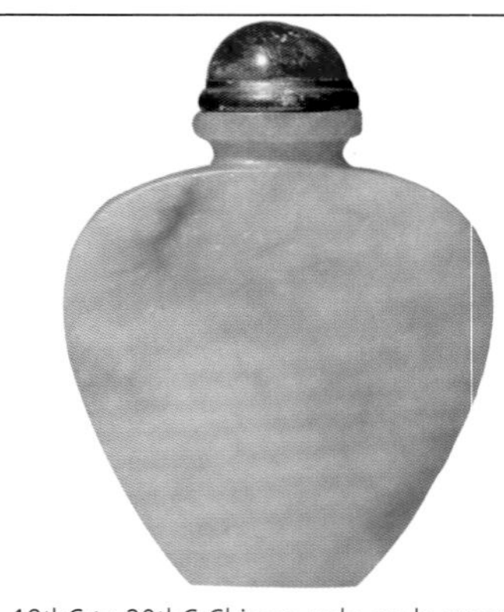

A 19thC to 20thC Chinese pale apple-green jadeite snuff bottle.

2¼in (5.5cm) high

£1,800-2,200 **WW**

A Chinese interior-painted rock crystal snuff bottle, painted with a cockerel and small birds, signed 'Ye Zhong Shan', dated.

1912 *2½in (6.5cm) high*

£1,000-1,400 **WW**

A coral table snuff bottle, carved as a vase amongst flowers, with bird stopper.

3½in (9cm) high

£600-700 **L&T**

A Chinese pale celadon jade snuff bottle, with carved dragons forming the flanges.

3in (7.5cm) high

£600-800 **L&T**

A Chinese pale jade snuff bottle and cornelian stopper.

2¼in (6cm) high

£1,500-2,000 **LC**

A Chinese white jade snuff bottle and stopper, with a coral stopper.

2¼in (6cm) high

£1,200-1,500 **LC**

ESSENTIAL REFERENCE – OPIUM

Opium is a very powerful drug, which had been used in China for medicinal purposes as early as the 7thC. After the arrival of tobacco in the 17thC, small amounts of opium were often added to tobacco when it was smoked. Opium was eventually smoked on its own.

- **Eager for goods to trade with China in exchange for the vast quantities of tea it purchased, Britain began cultivating opium in India and shipping it to China for sale. This resulted in the widespread recreational use of opium in China.**
- **In 1729, the smoking of opium was banned in China. In 1800 its cultivation and importation were also banned. However, opium continued to be illegally smuggled into China.**
- **In 1839, the Chinese authorities ordered 20,000 chests of foreign opium to be destroyed. The British demanded compensation, triggering the First Opium War (1839-42).**
- **After its defeat, China was forced to hand over Hong Kong Island to the British, and allow the British to trade in more ports. After the Second Opium War (1856-60), the sale of opium was legalised. It is thought that by 1900, several million people in China were addicted to opium.**
- **Opium played an important role in Chinese social life, and opium pipes were often objects of great beauty. They were exquisitely crafted from bamboo, sugarcane, ivory or porcelain, sometimes covered in enamel or tortoiseshell, often elaborately decorated and finished with silver.**
- **A typical pipe has a metal fitting or 'saddle' towards one end, to which a detachable bowl is connected, designed to vaporise the opium when held over a lamp.**

A Chinese porcelain opium pipe, with redware pottery bowl with a monk, some restoration.

19¾in (50cm) long

£5,000-5,500 **FLD**

A Chinese opium pipe, with bamboo stem and brass saddle, with three cabochon stones in copper collars with green hardstone ends.

22½in (57cm) long

£500-600 **FLD**

A Chinese opium pipe, with tortoiseshell overlaid bamboo stem, brass saddle, black terracotta bowl and enamelled collars to ends.

22¾in (58cm) long

£1,000-1,400 **FLD**

A Chinese opium pipe, with bamboo stem and ivory tips, green glazed pottery bowl and silver saddle.

21¾in (55cm) long

£600-700 **FLD**

An early 19thC bamboo, ivory and white metal opium pipe.

24in (61cm) long

£400-500 **BE**

A Chinese ribbed wood opium pipe, with toad-form silver saddle and green hardstone mouth piece.

24¾in (63cm) long

£150-200 **FLD**

An early 19thC bamboo, ivory and white metal opium pipe, decorated with a butterfly.

21½in (54.5cm) long

£400-500 **BE**

A Chinese opium pipe, with lacquered stem, embossed silver saddle and cloisonné enamelled ends, with signed floral pottery bowl.

21¼in (54cm) long

£600-700 **FLD**

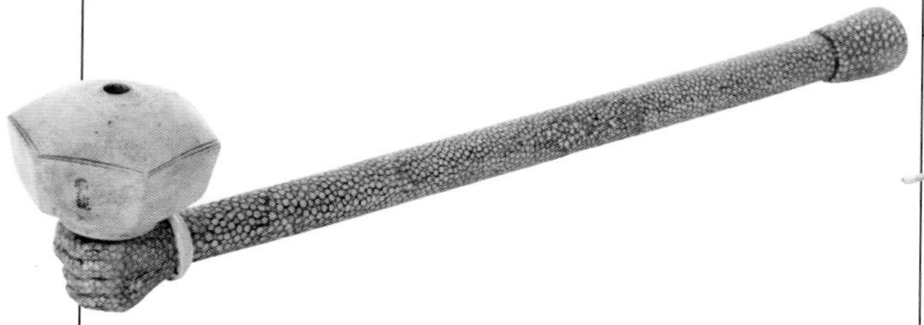

A Chinese shagreen opium pipe, in the form of a fist, with greyware bowl.

12¼in (31cm) long

£650-750 **FLD**

A Chinese bone opium pipe, with figures in landscapes, with embossed plated saddle and grey pottery bowl, stamped with symbols and characters.

20in (51cm) long

£150-200 **FLD**

A Chinese bone opium pipe, with panels of immortals, mounted with a silver saddle, with redware pottery bowl, some damages.

20in (51cm) long

£300-350 **FLD**

A Chinese Qianlong mottled yellow glass facetted bottle vase, swirled with orange, four-character mark.

6in (15cm) high

£6,500-7,000 **L&T**

An 18thC Chinese Peking glass yellow and red overlay bottle vase, a chilong dragon around the neck.

5¼in (13.5cm) high

£1,300-1,600 **WW**

A glass yellow and red overlay brushpot, with chilong dragons, the tails framing a taotie mask.

4¼in (10.5cm) high

£300-350 **L&T**

A Chinese Peking glass vase, depicting dragons chasing pearls, on wood stand, slither chips to base.

10½in (26.5cm) high

£250-300 **APAR**

A 19thC Chinese Peking glass ermine red bowl, carved with dragons contesting a pearl, small bubble in glass, rim chip ground out.

X-ray fluorescence tests show unusual amounts of lead, arsenic and iron in this piece.

7¾in (19.5cm) wide

£500-600 **DN**

A Chinese Qing Peking glass vase, carved with bifid-tailed dragons, Qianlong four-character mark, some surface blemishes.

6½in (16.5cm) high

£3,000-3,500 **DN**

A probably 18thC Chinese Peking glass jar, with double mask handles, in overlaid metal with two chilong, one crack, small flake to rim.

3¼in (8cm) high

£850-950 **DN**

A Chinese Jiaqing Peking glass vase, remnants of gilding to the engraved mark, four-character Jiaqing mark, some nicks and scratches.

1796-1820 *7in (18cm) high*

£5,000-5,500 **GORL**

A Japanese Meiji gilt-silver filigree and champlevé enamel glass vase, the glass mounted with gilt-silver scrolls with enamelled lily, lotus and wisteria blossoms, signed 'Somei', stamped 'C.T. Marsh & Co'.

11½in (29.5cm) high 39.9oz

£6,500-7,500 **L&T**

A Japanese Edo gold-lacquer four-case inro, with a takamakie ground and nashiji interiors, signed 'Koho'.

An inro, literally 'seal-basket', is a small container hung from the waist in traditional Japanese clothing, consisting of several small sections held together by a chord.

4in (10cm) long

£2,500-3,000 DUK

A Japanese Edo gold-lacquer four-case inro, decorated in hiramakie and takamakie with a sage on horseback, a scholar-official on a dragon to the reverse, signed 'Koma Kyuhaku'.

Hiramakie is a form of decoration in low relief. Takamakie is a form of decoration in bold relief. Both are typically used on lacquer in gold or silver.

3¼in (8.5cm) long

£2,500-3,000 L&T

A Japanese Edo five-case lacquer inro, decorated in gold hiramakie on a roiro ground with three cranes.

3¼in (8cm) long

£750-850 L&T

A mid-19thC Japanese four-case inro, with a crayfish, with a silver pierced dragon ojime and a red lacquer manju chrysanthemum flower netsuke, some damages.

3¼in (8.5cm) long

£2,500-3,000 FLD

A Japanese four-case lacquer inro, by Jitokusai Gyokuzan, with a mountain cat amongst foliage, the reverse with a waterfall, signed and with seal.

3¼in (8.5cm) high

£4,000-4,500 BE

An early 19thC Japanese five-case inro, decorated in takamakie and hiramakie, with a lacquered iron ojime and late 18thC stag antler teahouse netsuke.

4in (10cm) long

£2,500-3,000 FLD

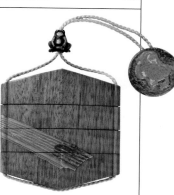

A Japanese Meiji gold-lacquer four-case inro, the kinji ground decorated in gold takamakie, hiramakie and kirikane.

Kirikane is a decorative technique where small pieces of gold and silver-plate or foil are arranged on lacquer to create a design.

3¾in (9.5cm) high

£900-1,200 L&T

A 19thC Japanese Meiji four-case gold lacquer inro, decorated with Mount Fuji, with nashiji interiors.

3¼in (8cm) long

£450-550 JN

A late 19thC Japanese three-case wooden inro, probably Keyaki, with a koto in gold takamakie and silver, signed 'Jokasai', with a pressed brass toad ojime and manju probably Kyoto late 18thC netsuke.

3¼in (8.5cm) long

£1,200-1,500 FLD

A Japanese Edo hardwood netsuke of a mother tiger and cub, possibly by Kokei of Kuwana, faintly signed.

Netsuke are small sculptural objects, typically made of wood or ivory. In traditional Japanese dress, they were attached to the top of the chord of an inro (see page 137) to keep it in place.

1¼in (3cm) high

£2,500-3,000 PW

A Japanese Edo wood netsuke of a nursing mermaid.

c1790 *2¼in (5.5cm) long*

£2,500-3,000 MAB

A Japanese late Edo wood netsuke of Ashinaga and Tenaga, signed 'Minzan'.

c1820 *1¾in (4.5cm) high*

£3,000-3,500 MAB

A Japanese Meiji wood netsuke of Ashinaga and Tenaga, signed 'Tomin'.

4in (10cm) high

£900-1,200 MAB

Ashinaga and Tenaga are a pair of Yōkai, or spirits, in Japanese mythology. Ashinaga ('long legs') and Tenaga ('long arms') are often shown working together, with Tenaga on the back of Ashinaga, enabling them to catch fish.

A Japanese Meiji carved wood netsuke of a pug, the eyes inlaid with translucent horn, signed 'Toyomasa', some wear.

1½in (3.5cm) high

£450-550 L&T

A Japanese Meiji carved wood netsuke of two playful puppies.

1½in (4cm) high

£550-650 TOV

A Japanese early Meiji boxwood netsuke of Fukusuke, typically carved with exaggerated head, the eyes inlaid in horn, signed 'Shuzan'.

c1870 *2in (5cm) high*

£1,300-1,600 MAB

A 19thC Japanese wood netsuke of a tanuki, by Masanaga, signed.

A Tanuki is a Japanese raccoon dog.

1¼in (3cm) high

£500-600 BRI

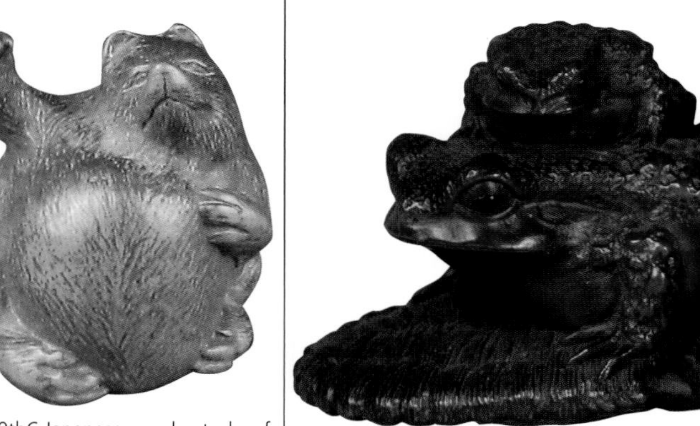

An early 20thC Japanese boxwood netsuke of three toads on a discarded sandal, signed.

2½in (6.5cm) long

£2,500-3,000 ROS

An early 20thC Japanese boxwood netsuke of a toad on a straw sandal, signed.

2in (5cm) long

£1,500-2,000 ROS

A Chinese Qing ground silk suit of ceremonial armour and helmet of a General, the helmet with gold dragons.

Provenance: formerly the collection of Diana Kearny Powell, Washington, who inherited the suit from her father Colonel William Glasgow Powell, USMC (1871-1955), who participated in the relief of Peking in 1900.

jacket and skirt 59in (150cm) high

£55,000-60,000 WW

A late Chinese Qing Imperial Manchu noblewoman's embroidered silk court chao gua outer vest, embroidered with five-clawed dragons chasing a pearl, gold braid on edges loose, minor wear.

54¼in (138cm) high

£2,500-3,000 DN

An early to mid-19thC Chinese Qing embroidered 'dragon' robe/jifu, with bats, 'shou' characters and dragons chasing pearls, some splits, wear and stains.

The robe would have originally been worn by a Mandarin of the Imperial court. It is possible this robe was never intended to be lined as the embroidery is of such high quality and is almost double-sided.

87¾in (223cm) wide

£18,000-22,000 DN

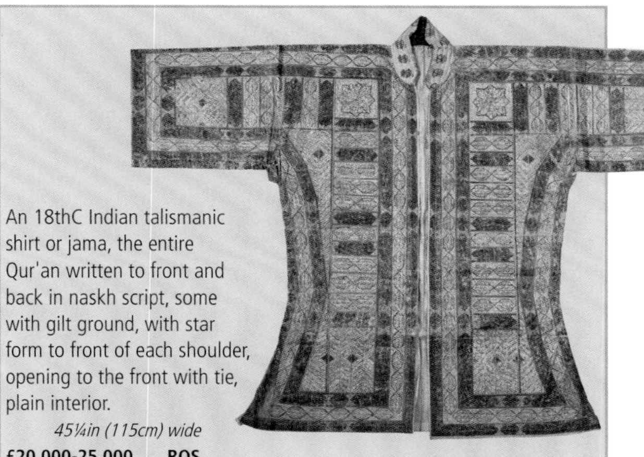

An 18thC Indian talismanic shirt or jama, the entire Qur'an written to front and back in naskh script, some with gilt ground, with star form to front of each shoulder, opening to the front with tie, plain interior.

45¼in (115cm) wide

£20,000-25,000 ROS

A 19thC Chinese silk 'nine dragon' robe/jifu, embroidered with silk and gold thread with cranes, dragons chasing pearls, and other auspicious objects.

82in (208cm) wide

£10,000-14,000 WW

An early 19thC Indian youth's cotton talismanic shirt, inscribed with the entire text of the Qur'an, written in naskh and thuluth script, reverse with foliate motif on a green ground, foliate motifs containing script to chest.

39¼in (99.5cm) high

£25,000-30,000 ROS

The earliest surviving Qur'an jama date from the middle of the Delhi Sultanate (1206-1626), although the tradition of a shirt with protective powers might be much older. They were fashioned from three pieces of cotton cloth stiffened to provide a smooth surface for scribes and illuminators to work. They were covered with the entire text of the Qur'an, plus the asma-al-husna (99 names of God), and the Shahadah (the profession of faith). Jama may have been worn under battle armour, or used to protect the Muslim elite against such dangers as disease and difficult childbirth.

Judith Picks

While the market for English 'brown' furniture is slow, Chinese furniture is currently very popular. This is partly because of its timeless quality. The simplicity of design means that Chinese furniture looks and feels at home in modern interiors. Many 19thC or 20thC items bare strong similarities to Ming designs. For example, a closely related stool to this pair has been identified as huanghuali and dated to the Ming dynasty. Huanghuali (literally 'yellow flowering pear' wood) is a member of the rosewood family. It is a slow growing tree of relatively small size and therefore extremely rare. The use of huanghuali wood in Chinese furniture is another reason for the market's strength.

A pair of 19thC Chinese hardwood corner-leg stools, the legs terminating in hoof feet and with humpback stretchers.

19¼in (49cm) wide

£35,000-40,000 WW

CLOSER LOOK – PADOUK THRONE CHAIR

The back of this chair is pierced and carved with prunus blossom and a central qilin roundel.

It is of a large and unusual size, implying that it was made for a Chinese gentleman of importance, which appeals to the Chinese market today.

The carving throughout is of extremely high quality.

It has square-section legs joined by an elaborate pierced interwoven splat.

A Chinese padouk throne chair.

c1900 *44½in (113cm) wide*

£12,000-15,000 HT

A Chinese huanhuali yoke-back armchair, with cane seat.

45¾in (116cm) high

£1,600-1,800 DUK

A Chinese Qing huanghuali, huamu and jichimu 'official's hat' or yoke-back guanmaoyi armchair, with woven cane seat.

37in (94cm) high

£5,000-5,500 BRI

An early 20thC Chinese hardwood folding horseshoe-back jiaoyi armchair, partly Huanghuali wood, with cash roundel and geometric pattern, the backsplat carved with a ruyihead cartouche.

Provenance: Collected by a Scottish businessman whilst working in Hong Kong in the 1950s-60s.

43¼in (110cm) high

£8,500-9,500 L&T

An early 20thC Chinese red lacquer corner chair with dragon carved arms.

43¼in (110cm) high

£300-400 BELL

A pair of early to mid-20thC Chinese hardwood horseshoe-back jiaoyi armchairs, partly Huanghuali wood, the backsplat with a qilin below a cartouche of a dragon.

44½in (113cm) high

£12,500-14,500 L&T

A 20thC Chinese huali low-back armchair, the backsplat pierced with an openwork ruyihead.

37in (94cm) high

£9,500-11,500 L&T

A rare 17thC Chinese huanghuali and huamu-inset recessed leg pingtou'an table, the burr wood top set within a mitred mortice-and-tenon frame.

Woodblock prints depict similar tables used in everyday life, for writing, displaying objects and dining. Burlwood inserted table tops were highly prized by scholars for the dynamic contrast in the colour and grain. Such tables were particularly intended to enhance the display of antiques.

46½in (118cm) high

£25,000-30,000 **BRI**

A 18thC to 19thC Chinese Qing hardwood corner-leg tiao zhuo table, carved with keyfret, flowers and kuilong dragons.

66½in (169cm) high

£40,000-50,000 **L&T**

A 18thC to 19thC Chinese hongmu wood altar table.

49½in (125.5cm) wide

£1,300-1,600 **JN**

A Chinese late Qing hardwood scroll table.

49½in (126cm) long

£3,000-3,500 **ROS**

A Chinese late Qing hardwood kang table, the apron carved with auspicious objects.

42¼in (107cm) long

£900-1,200 **L&T**

A Chinese late Qing hardwood table, the frieze carved with archaic ruyi C- and S-scrolls and bead motifs.

46¾in (119cm) long

£9,000-11,000 **TOV**

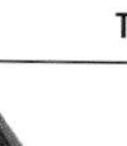

A 19thC Chinese 'rosewood' hall table.

100in (254cm) wide

£2,800-3,200 **LSK**

A 19thC Chinese export lacquer table, decorated with figures and pavilions in a landscape, with later stand, some craquelure and shrinkage.

The panel was probably adapted from a screen.

69¾in (177cm) long

£4,000-4,500 **DN**

A 19thC Chinese elm faux bamboo altar table.

112in (284.5cm) long

£1,500-2,000 **WW**

A mid-19thC Chinese Qing huali wood and pink marble tripod table.
31in (79cm) high
£400-500 **L&T**

A Chinese Guangxu huanghuali folding tray-top table, Guangxu marks to hinges, some shrinkage, some repairs.
1875-1908 *31¼in (79.5cm) wide*
£1,400-1,800 **GORL**

A Chinese late Qing hardwood writing desk, with two drawers and galleried upper section, loss to gallery, some shrinkage.
46¾in (119cm) high
£2,200-2,800 **DN**

A Chinese nanmu-inset huanghuali wine table.
39in (99cm) wide
£10,000-14,000 **MOR**

A late 19thC to early 20thC Chinese padouk twin-pedestal desk.
54½in (138.5cm) wide
£600-700 **WW**

A Chinese carved wood altar table, the apron pierced with scrollwork and bats.
74¼in (188.5cm) long
£2,500-3,000 **BE**

A Chinese hardwood table, with white metal leafy brackets.
71¼in (181cm) wide
£6,000-7,000 **MOR**

A Chinese marble-top console table, with a carved and pierced 'dragon and carp' frieze, the legs decorated with blossoming branches.
32¼in (82cm) high
£2,500-3,000 **L&T**

A Chinese Qing hardwood display cabinet, carved with dragons, clouds, birds, flowers and fruiting branches.

70¾in (180cm) high

£15,000-20,000 **WW**

A probably 18thC Chinese lacquered cabinet-on-stand, engraved metal mounts and gilt warriors, on a later ebonised base.

18in (45.5cm) wide

£3,500-4,000 **LC**

A 19thC Chinese softwood display cabinet, carved with figures and warriors in a landscape.

106¾in (271cm) high

£1,200-1,500 **TEN**

A late 19thC Chinese Qing red lacquer gilt-decorated cabinet.

76in (193cm) high

£300-400 **L&T**

A late 19thC Chinese hardwood stepped display cabinet, some losses to moulding.

32¼in (82cm) wide

£2,200-2,800 **APAR**

A late 19thC to early 20thC Chinese red lacquer parcel gilt press cupboard.

72½in (184cm) high

£700-800 **DN**

A pair of Chinese Qing huali Ming-style openwork book shelves, carved with stylised dragons.

75¼in (191cm) high

£2,500-3,000 **WW**

A Chinese rosewood sideboard, carved with dragons and cloud motifs.

74in (188cm) wide

£3,500-4,000 **CAN**

A Chinese hardwood side cabinet, inlaid with mother-of-pearl floral sprays and figures amongst pavilions.

43in (109cm) wide

£750-850 **DUK**

A Japanese Meiji Shibayama wood cabinet, the doors inlaid with figures, mythical beasts, birds and flowers, on matching stand.

76in (193cm) high

£8,500-9,500 **L&T**

A Japanese Meiji lacquer display cabinet, Shodana, decorated in gold hiramakie on a roiro ground.

41in (104cm) high

£850-950 **L&T**

A Japanese Meiji lacquered wood chest, with metal strappings, handles and lockplates.

44½in (113cm) high

£2,000-2,500 **L&T**

A Japanese Meiji carved softwood shidana.

63¾in (162cm) high

£1,000-1,500 **LSK**

An early to mid-20thC Japanese lacquer cabinet-on-stand, with gilt figures and temples, several drawers within, on later carved stand.

67in (170cm) high

£4,500-5,500 **L&T**

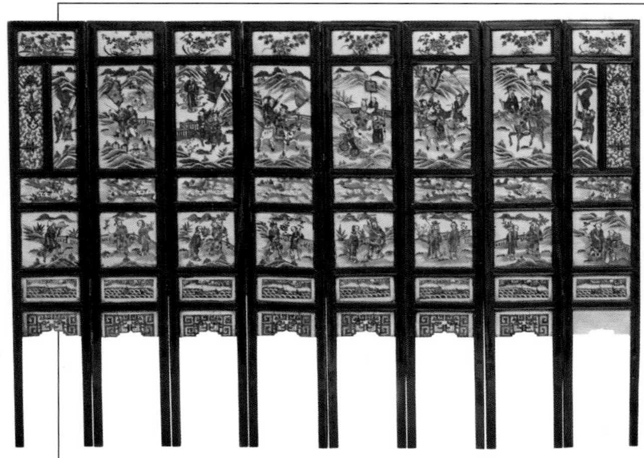

A 19thC Chinese porcelain and ebonised wood eight-leaf screen, painted with figures in landscapes, flowers, fish and taotie masks, one panel missing.

53½in (136cm) high

£1,800-2,200 BELL

A late 18thC to early 19thC Chinese wallpaper four-leaf screen, handpainted with exotic birds and butterflies.

110¼in (280cm) wide

£7,000-8,000 L&T

A Chinese Qing kingfisher feather table screen, depicting a river and village landscape, with poems and seals, on wood stand.

The technique of inlaying feathers is called diancui, meaning 'dotting the kingfishers', whereby the feather is cut into shape and attached with glue onto the base. The most expensive and highest quality works traditionally used feathers imported from Cambodia and it is said that Chinese Imperial demand for kingfisher feathers may have contributed to the wealth of the Khmer Empire.

24¾in (63cm) high

£6,000-6,500 WW

A 19thC Chinese late Qing inlaid hardstone four-leaf screen, some losses and cracks.

68in (173cm) high

£4,000-5,000 DN

A 19thC Chinese slate table screen panel, carved with a prunus tree, on later legs, hairline crack and scratches.

9¾in (25cm) wide

£4,000-4,500 GORL

A pair of 20thC Chinese jade and hardwood screens, carved with a dignitary and attendants arriving at a pavilion, the reverses with inscriptions in zhuanshu script.

panels 25½in (65cm) high

£2,000-3,000 CHEF

A Chinese painted marble and wood screen, depicting a Taoist myth, the reverse with a poem.

In the myth depicted here, during the Yellow Emperor's battle with Chiyou, another mythical tribal leader, Xuan Nv, a disciple of the Queen Mother of the West, was sent by Heaven, leading the Troop of Thunder, to assist the Yellow Emperor, and bestowed various legendary artefacts, books and maps. With her help, Chiyou and his army could not hold out and were hence defeated by the Yellow Emperor.

marble 11½in (29cm) high

£1,500-2,000 DN

A 20thC Chinese dinner gong and beater.

41in (104cm) high

£220-280 FLD

THE FURNITURE MARKET

To be perfectly honest, the furniture market has remained virtually unchanged since the last edition of *Miller's Antiques Handbook and Price Guide*. The market has continued to be very polarized; 'brown furniture' has continued to fall. Most auctioneers are reporting that the plain utilitarian 18th century and 19th century mahogany is proving difficult, if not impossible, to sell. Some dealers are quoting a substantial drop in prices and a general lack of interest. At the other end of the spectrum, furniture that is really top quality, fresh to the market and 'honest', continues to rise in value. It is not just age that determines the value of a piece of furniture – quality, condition and 'eye appeal' are all important factors, too.

The reasons for the decline in value of average, mid-range furniture is complex, most of it is down to fashion – this is true for all antiques. I often say when valuing an item to apply my CARD principle: Condition, Age, Rarity and Desirability – and the most important of those is desirability. Younger buyers believe that old mahogany furniture is just not 'cool' and does not fit into today's interiors. There is also a lack of really good-quality examples on the market. Another problem is that vendors are reluctant to enter good antique furniture to auction while prices are depressed.

Pieces that are too bulky for modern interiors need to be of exceptional quality to attract buyers. There is no doubt that Georgian, and especially Regency, pieces sell better than their heavy Victorian counterparts. Also, pieces like the davenport, Canterbury and bureau do not have any real function in today's homes. However, while ordinary 'Georgian-Victorian brown' furniture has nose-dived in value, 20th century, especially Mid-Century Modern, furniture has continued its renaissance. Many dealers also record that American buyers are still not visiting in their previous numbers and this has had a dramatic effect on export sales. However, good-quality American furniture is doing very well.

So, has the low- to mid-range furniture market reached its nadir? Some of the prices achieved at auction are ridiculously low. These pieces are made of solid wood by skilled craftsmen, and not merely fashioned out of MDF (medium-density fibreboard which is, quite simply, wood fibres, combined with wax and a resin binder). There are some indicators that prices may be beginning to climb slightly. People are coming round to the idea that 'antiques are green' and that recycling or upcycling old furniture is more responsible than destroying more of the Amazon jungle. Also, with some prices so low, younger buyers are looking at auctions when furnishing their first flat or house. With the interest in Scandinavian furniture growing, young buyers are often sourcing mahogany furniture and painting it. I still find it amusing when I see Gustavian furniture described as with 'original' paint – very unlikely – it was made to be repainted.

Sturdy, good-quality, highly-functional pieces are excellent value for money. These pieces could well provide good investment potential, as prices should increase when (and if!) the economy improves.

Above: A 19thC Italian ebony pietra dura and gilt metal cabinet-on-stand, opening to a shelved interior.

c1840 *62¼in (158cm) high*

£80,000-100,000 **DUK**

Top Left: A satinwood cream-painted and parcel-gilt console table, in the manner of Robert Adam.

41¾in (106cm) wide

£3,000-3,500 **DUK**

<table>
<tr><th>UK PERIOD</th><th>USA PERIOD</th><th>FRENCH PERIOD</th><th>GERMAN PERIOD</th></tr>
<tr><td>Elizabethan
Elizabeth I (1558-1603)</td><td rowspan="2"></td><td rowspan="2">Renaissance
(to c1610)</td><td rowspan="3">Renaissance
(to c1650)</td></tr>
<tr><td>Jacobean
James I (1603-25)</td></tr>
<tr><td>Carolean
Charles I (1625-49)</td><td rowspan="3">Early Colonial
(1620s-1700)</td><td>Louis XIII
(1610-43)</td></tr>
<tr><td>Cromwellian
Commonwealth (1649-60)</td><td rowspan="6">Louis XIV
(1643-1715)</td><td rowspan="4">Renaissance/ Baroque
(c1650-1700)</td></tr>
<tr><td>Restoration
Charles II (1660-85)
James II (1685-88)</td></tr>
<tr><td>William and Mary
(1689-94)</td><td rowspan="3">William and Mary
(1690-1720)</td></tr>
<tr><td>William III
(1694-1702)</td></tr>
<tr><td rowspan="2">Queen Anne
(1702-14)</td><td rowspan="3">Baroque
(c1700-30)</td></tr>
<tr><td rowspan="3">Queen Anne
(1720-50)</td></tr>
<tr><td rowspan="4">Early Georgian
George I (1714-27)
George II (1727-60)</td><td>Régence
(1715-23)</td></tr>
<tr><td rowspan="2">Louis XV
(1723-74)</td><td rowspan="2">Rococo
(c1730-60)</td></tr>
<tr><td rowspan="2">Chippendale
(1750-90)</td></tr>
<tr><td rowspan="2">Louis XVI
(1774-92)</td><td rowspan="2">Neo-classicism
(c1760-1800)</td></tr>
<tr><td rowspan="3">Late Georgian
George III (1760-1811)</td><td rowspan="3">Early Federal
(1790-1810)
American Directoire (1798-1804)
American Empire (1804-15)</td></tr>
<tr><td>Directoire
(1792-99)</td><td rowspan="2">Empire
(c1800-15)</td></tr>
<tr><td>Empire
(1799-1815)</td></tr>
<tr><td>Regency
George III (1812-20)</td><td rowspan="3">Later Federal
(1810-30)</td><td rowspan="2">Restauration
(1815-30)
Louis XVIII (1814-24)
Charles X (1824-30)</td><td rowspan="2">Biedermeier
(c1815-48)</td></tr>
<tr><td>George IV
(1820-30)</td></tr>
<tr><td>William IV
(1830-37)</td><td>Louis Phillipe
(1830-48)</td><td rowspan="2">Revivale
(c1830-80)</td></tr>
<tr><td>Victorian
Victoria (1837-1901)</td><td rowspan="2">Victorian
(1840-1900)</td><td>2nd Empire
(1848-70)</td></tr>
<tr><td>Edwardian
Edward VII (1901-10)</td><td>3rd Republic
(1871-1940)</td><td>Jugendstil
(c1880-1920)</td></tr>
</table>

A Charles II oak armchair, the arched scroll top carved with flowers and leaves above strapwork panels.
£2,500-3,000 **WW**

A Charles II carved oak wainscot chair.
44½in (113cm) high
£1,000-1,400 **LC**

A 17thC carved oak joint armchair, with shaped cresting rail above a decorative panel, some replacements.
43in (109cm) high
£850-950 **PW**

A 17thC oak panel-back armchair, with chevron carved top rail.
£1,200-1,600 **CHOR**

A 17thC carved oak wainscot armchair, with scrollwork top rail over a floral panel.
£1,100-1,600 **SWO**

A 17thC wainscot armchair, with leafage carved and pierced top rail, and floral carved panel back.
£1,100-1,600 **BRI**

A pair of William and Mary carved walnut armchairs, with lion finials, serpent arms and a pierced scroll stretcher carved with mythical creatures.
c1690 *50½in (128cm) high*
£3,000-3,500 **DN**

A late 17thC carved oak armchair, with strapwork panelled back.
42¼in (107cm) deep
£1,200-1,600 **SWO**

An 18thC oak lambing chair.
£1,400-1,800 **BRI**

ESSENTIAL REFERENCE – COUNTRY CHAIRS

Country furniture is furniture made by rural craftsmen.

- **The Windsor is a well-known type of country chair, common in Britain from the 17thC, and later made by European settlers in North America.**
- **Windsor chairs are characterised by their solid saddle seats, into which are dowelled the bow and the turned or rounded spindles and legs.**
- **In Britain they were commonly made of ash, beech, elm or yew.**
- **In North America, they were commonly made of ash, hickory, oak, pine or poplar. American examples were often painted.**

A mid-18thC ash, elm and fruitwood spindle-back Windsor armchair, later caps, some woodworm.

38¼in (97cm) high

£1,200-1,600 **DN**

A mid-18thC fruitwood and ash Windsor armchair, attributed to John Pitt.

John Pitt (1714-59) was a chair maker and wheelwright based in Slough, England. Windsor chairs attributed to him are typically of comb-back form with four cabriole legs. Surviving English Windsor chairs with cabriole legs are not common and those with four cabriole legs, considered to be the earlier type, are especially rare.

£1,100-1,500 **WW**

An 18thC yew stick-back Windsor armchair, seat repaired.

£550-600 **SWO**

A late 18thC elm stick-back Windsor armchair.

42¼in (107cm) high

£1,400-1,800 **L&T**

A Philadelphia fan-back Windsor armchair, with carved ears, knuckle band rests, repaired break to one arm, small blowout to crest on leg.

c1790

£1,500-2,000 **POOK**

A New England continuous-arm Windsor armchair, some worm holes.

c1790

£1,500-2,000 **POOK**

A set of six New England sack-back Windsor armchairs, minor repairs.

c1790

£2,200-2,800 **POOK**

A late 18thC black-painted comb-back Windsor armchair, possibly New Hampshire, some wear.

42in (106.5cm) high

£3,500-4,000 **SK**

A pair of Philadelphia hoop-back Windsor armchairs, with early written owner's label for 'John Broomall', metal bracket securing one leg, one arm support replaced.

c1800

£850-950 **POOK**

An early 19thC Scottish Windsor armchair.

46½in (118cm) high

£1,000-1,400 L&T

A mid-19thC Nottinghamshire elm and yew Windsor armchair, stamped 'F Walker Rockley'.

The Rockley workshop was opened in 1823 in the village of Rockley, Nottinghamshire, England, by William Wheatland. Frederick Walker (fl.1823-71) was a long-serving chair maker for Rockley and later took over the workshop.

£500-600 WHP

A 19thC yew high-back Windsor armchair, elm saddle seat.

£350-450 PW

A matched set of four ash and elm Windsor elbow chairs.

£600-700 BRI

A New England painted rod-back Windsor settee, with original floral stencilled crest and red and black graining.

c1820 *77in (195.5cm) wide*

£1,300-1,600 POOK

A mid-18thC New England slat-back armchair, painted red with yellow pinstripes and floral patterns to the slats.

43¾in (111cm) high

£3,000-3,500 SK

A mid-18thC Philadelphia William and Mary ladder-back armchair, with a later blue surface by Peter Deen, some wear.

£1,200-1,600 POOK

A set of six 19thC painted plank seat dining chairs, Lancaster County, Pennsylvania, minor wear.

£1,500-2,000 POOK

An early 19thC elm comb-back armchair.

36½in (93cm) high

£1,000-1,400 L&T

A 19thC fruitwood and elm Mendlesham chair.

£350-400 LSK

A set of six mahogany dining chairs, Portsmouth, New Hampshire.
c1770 *37¾in (96cm) high*
£4,000-4,500 **SK**

A Pennsylvania Chippendale walnut dining chair, some replacements and repairs.
c1770
£3,000-3,500 **POOK**

A set of six 18thC Anglo-Dutch carved walnut and marquetry dining chairs.

Provenance: The Kent Gallery, London, purchased on 1 April 1925 for £420.
£3,500-4,000 **WW**

Six of a set of twelve George III mahogany dining chairs, including two carvers, replacement seat rails.
c1790
£12,000-16,000 the set **DN**

Two of a set of eight Regency brass-strung mahogany dining chairs, with two carvers.
35in (89cm) high
£2,500-3,000 the set **GORL**

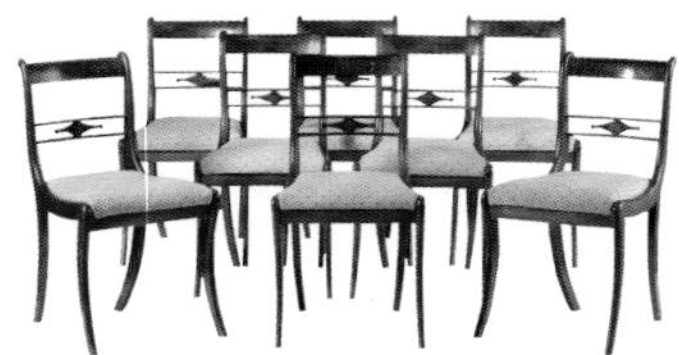

A set of eight Regency rosewood and brass inlaid dining chairs, the frames stamped 'WILKINSON LUDGATE HILL', maker's initials 'JM' and model '2801', with later upholstery.

Joshua Wilkinson established a cabinet, upholstery, carpet and looking-glass warehouse in 1766 in Moorfields, London. The company produced well-made pieces conforming to Regency fashions and marked their furniture, usually with the impressed stamp 'WILKINSON LUDGATE HILL'. The firm continued to trade under different names into the 20thC.
33in (84cm) high
£2,500-3,000 **L&T**

A set of six Regency mahogany dining chairs.
32in (81cm) high
£1,000-1,500 **L&T**

A set of six Regency mahogany dining chairs, with two carvers.
c1820 *19in (48cm) high*
£550-600 **DN**

Three of a set of six late Regency mahogany dining chairs, each with anthemion to bar back, with two carvers.
c1820
£600-700 the set DN

A set of twelve late Regency rosewood dining chairs, attributed to Gillows, with scroll carved horizontal splats, some rails stamped with workmen's initials 'W', 'TB' and 'GG'.
£6,000-7,000 WW

Six of a set of eight William IV mahogany dining chairs, with two carvers.
36¼in (92cm) high
£800-900 the set CHEF

A set of sixteen William IV mahogany dining chairs, the back rails carved with flowers, with two carvers.
carvers 34¼in (87cm) high
£15,000-20,000 L&T

Six of a set of eight Irish mahogany dining chairs, stamped and labelled 'John Dooly & Son Ltd., Dublin', with two carvers.
c1840
£2,500-3,000 the set SWO

A set of eight early Victorian mahogany dining chairs, the legs ending in brass caps and porcelain casters.
37in (94cm) high
£5,000-6,000 L&T

Six of a set of fourteen carved Victorian mahogany dining chairs, by Eadon and Sons, Sheffield, all stamped.

George Eadon was a cabinetmaker, upholsterer, carver and gilder, working at 23 Newchurch Street, Sheffield in the mid-19thC.
£5,500-6,500 the set MEA

A set of six Victorian mahogany balloon-back dining chairs.
£400-500 LSK

Two of a set of eighteen Victorian oak dining chairs, with padded scroll backs and serpentine stuffover seats, on tapered, turned and fluted legs with porcelain casters.
35½in (90cm) high
£3,000-4,000 the set L&T

A set of ten Victorian mahogany dining chairs, on tapered reeded legs with porcelain casters.

35in (89cm) high

£1,800-2,200 L&T

Three of a set of twelve 19thC Regency-style hardwood dining chairs, on sabre legs.

£1,500-2,000 the set DN

Four of a set of eight Victorian mahogany balloon-back dining chairs, with two carvers.

c1870

£850-950 the set DN

A set of six 19thC North Italian parcel gilt polychrome-painted dining chairs.

49¼in (125cm) high

£2,500-3,000 BELL

A set of twelve 19thC oak and leather dining chairs, in the manner of A.W.N. Pugin.

Augustus Welby Northmore Pugin (1812-52) was an architect, designer and writer, and a key figure in the Gothic Revival movement. He worked in mediums including metalwork, wallpaper, stained glass, ceramics and furniture.

£3,000-4,000 WW

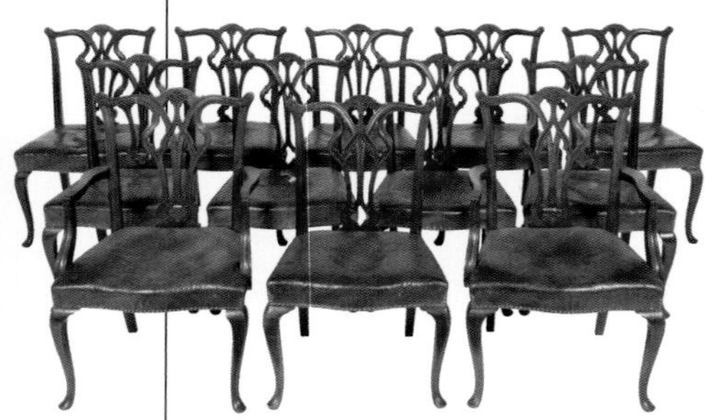

A set of twelve late 19thC George II-style carved mahogany dining chairs, attributed to R. Strahan of Dublin.

37in (94cm) high

£2,200-2,800 TEN

A set of eight late 19thC George III-style mahogany dining chairs, possibly Scottish, in the Hepplewhite style, the splats carved with Prince of Wales plumes and shells, with two carvers.

37¼in (94.5cm) high

£2,500-3,000 L&T

Three of a set of twelve Gothic-style oak framed dining chairs.

43in (109cm) high

£2,000-2,500 the set CHEF

A pair of George I giltwood side chairs, in the manner of James Moore.

£12,000-15,000 WW

A pair of George II walnut side chairs, on cabriole legs ending in claw-and-ball feet, stamped with a coronet and initial 'D'.

39in (99cm) high

£1,100-1,500 L&T

A walnut side chair, probably Massachusetts.

c1740-60 *40½in (103cm) high*

£4,200-4,600 SK

A carved tiger maple side chair, attributed to William Savery, Philadelphia, Pennsylvania.

c1760-85 *40¾in (103.5cm) high*

£3,000-3,500 SK

A carved mahogany side chair, Newport, Rhode Island, the crest centring a carved shell above a vasiform splat, refinished.

An identical chair, with original finish, is in Henry Du Pont's bedroom at Winterthur.

c1760 *40in (101.5cm) high*

£4,000-4,500 SK

A pair of mahogany side chairs, some wear, repairs and replacements.

c1750 *38½in (98cm) high*

£1,000-1,500 DN

An 18thC Chippendale carved mahogany side chair, some imperfections.

37in (94cm) high

£550-650 SK

An early 19thC German giltwood gilt side chair, by Johann Valentin Raab, with anthemion decorated cresting, on carved lion monopodia front legs, with stamp.

Johann Valentin Raab (1777-1839) was a Frankfurt-based chair-maker. His principal commissions included furniture supplied for the Schloss in Würzburg c1807-09.

£900-1,200 DN

A set of six 19thC Italian ebonised and specimen marble inlaid side chairs, Florence, in late 17thC style.

c1860

£6,500-7,500 DN

A set of five George II mahogany sgabello hall chairs, each with a dished seat.

The sgabello chair originated in Renaissance Italy. Typically the seat is a small wooden slab, supported at front and back by solid boards cut into an ornamental shape. A solid piece of wood then forms the back.

£3,000-3,500 **WW**

A pair of George II mahogany hall chairs, the backs with pierced Gothic motifs, some woodworm and wear.

c1750 *38½in (98cm) high*

£2,500-3,000 **DN**

A late George II mahogany hall chair, the scallop-shell-back carved with an armorial, probably a Drummond widow or possibly Bassett of Cornwall.

38½in (98cm) high

£2,500-3,000 **DUK**

A pair of late George III mahogany hall chairs, old repairs to backs.

35½in (90cm) high

£2,000-2,500 **BELL**

A pair of mahogany hall chairs, the backs with painted leopard's head heraldic panel.

c1825

£1,000-1,400 **DN**

A pair of late George III mahogany hall chairs, the backs carved with a double-headed eagle.

£4,500-5,500 **WW**

A pair of William IV Gothic Revival oak hall chairs.

c1830 *36¼in (92cm) high*

£6,500-7,000 **DN**

A mid-to-late 18thC walnut corner chair, Massachusetts.

31½in (80cm) high

£1,800-2,200 **SK**

A 19thC George III corner chair.

29½in (75cm) high

£900-1,200 **DRA**

A 17thC oak box stool with hinged top, worm, structure loose, burn marks.

17in (43cm) wide

£2,200-2,800 **CHEF**

A late 18thC to early 19thC turned birch Windsor stool, possibly northern New England.

According to expert Nancy Goyne Evans, the appearance of birch in this stool more likely places it in northern New England, perhaps Maine, than in Pennsylvania.

25½in (65cm) high

£2,500-3,000 **SK**

CLOSER LOOK – REGENCY STOOL

This stool is double-sided, with an X-shaped frame.

Its rope-twist arms and paw feet are intricately carved, as is the rossette to the centre of the frame.

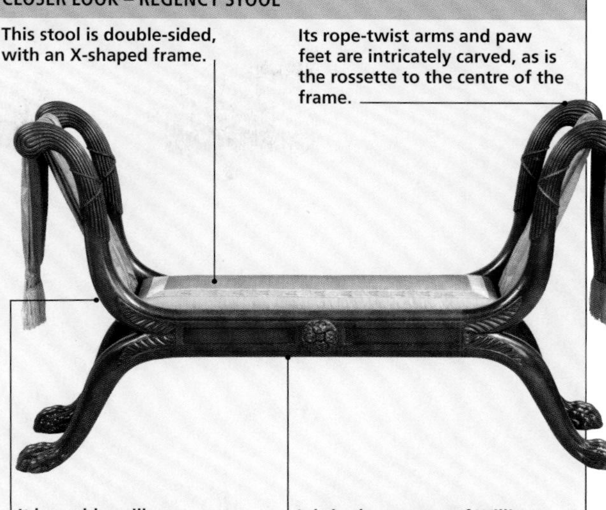

It has a blue silk-covered drop-in seat.

It is in the manner of William Trotter (d.1834), a Scottish cabinetmaker based in Princes Street, Edinburgh, who was highly influenced by Classical Revival style.

A Regency mahogany double-sided stool, in the manner of William Trotter, some wear, iron reinforcing braces.

c1815 *51½in (131cm) wide*

£25,000-30,000 **DN**

A George III mahogany footstool, with carved eagle head and lion paw supports, with original needlework upholstery.

19in (48.5cm) long

£4,000-4,500 **MART**

A near pair of Regency rosewood footstools, attributed to William Trotter.

19¼in (49cm) wide

£1,800-2,200 **BELL**

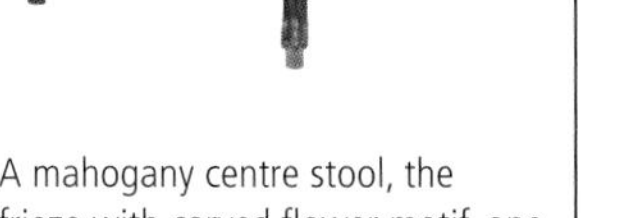

A mahogany centre stool, the frieze with carved flower motif, one stretcher stamped 'C. MUNRO'.

c1860 *45in (114cm) wide*

£1,800-2,200 **DN**

A Victorian mahogany centre stool.

49½in (126cm) long

£3,500-4,000 **L&T**

A French 19thC giltwood dressing stool.

£750-850 **BLEA**

A mahogany stool, possibly Irish, with trade label inscribed 'FRANK PARTRIDGE WORKS OF ART 26, KING ST., ST. JAMES'S AND NEW YORK'.

19in (48cm) wide

£1,500-2,000 **WW**

A pair of late 17thC to early 18thC Louis XIV carved walnut armchairs.

47¼in (120cm) high

£4,500-5,500 **DN**

A pair of Louis XV walnut armchairs, carved with stylised shell work and foliate elements.

c1730 *41¼in (105cm) high*

£7,000-8,000 **DN**

A Louis XV carved walnut armchair, by Deshayes, carved with stylised shells and anthemion motifs, stamped 'SHAYES' and 'JME', some restoration.

Louis Deshayes was made a master craftsman in 1756. Established on the Rue des Vieux-Augustins, Paris, he was still active at the beginning of the Revolution.

c1750 *43in (109cm) high*

£1,300-1,600 **DN**

A mid-18thC George III mahogany Gainsborough armchair.

A Gainsborough armchair was a type of chair popular in England in the 18thC. It was wide in form, with a high back, open sides, upholstered back and seat, and short upholstered arms. These were sometimes known as 'French chairs', as designs were often inspired by French Rococo style.

41in (104cm) high

£3,500-4,000 **L&T**

A George III mahogany Gainsborough or library chair.

39in (99cm) high

£5,500-6,000 **SWO**

A George III mahogany Gainsborough armchair.

£3,500-4,000 **WW**

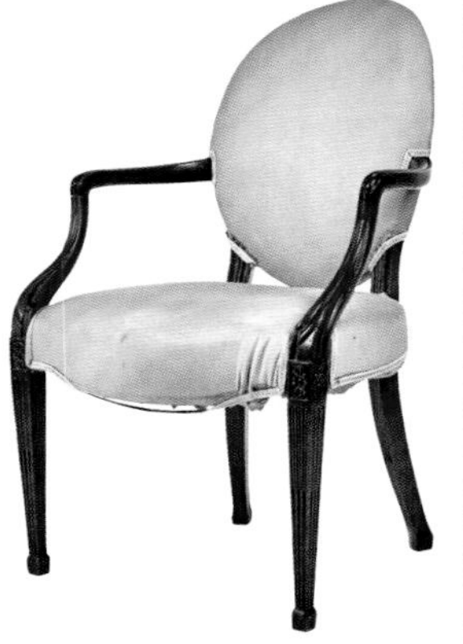

A George III mahogany open armchair, some repairs.

37in (94cm) high

£1,000-1,400 **BELL**

One of a set of four George III ebonised and painted open armchairs, later cane work, rubbing to ebonising.

35½in (90cm) high

£3,000-3,500 the set **BELL**

A pair of late 18thC George III mahogany wheel-back open armchairs, in the Sheraton manner.

37in (94cm) high

£900-1,200 **WAD**

An inlaid lolling chair, probably North Shore, Massachusetts.
c1800 *46¼in (117.5cm) high*
£8,500-9,500 **SK**

A George III mahogany metamorphic library armchair, attributed to Gillows, after the design by Morgan & Sanders, some wear and repairs.
c1810 *36¼in (92cm) high*
£3,500-4,000 **DN**

A pair of Regency Pavilion-style bamboo armchairs, in the manner of William Chambers, some losses.

The fashion for bamboo furniture started with the designs of Sir William Chambers in 1757. The design of these chairs show the influence of Chambers, as well as the designs of Brighton Pavilion by Crace & Co. There was a resurgence of the chinoiserie style with the creation of Brighton Pavilion by the Prince Regent (later George IV) from 1815-22.

35½in (90cm) high
£2,000-2,500 **CHEF**

A pair of George III mahogany shield-back armchairs, attributed to Gillows, some professional restoration.

This pair of armchairs relates very closely in design to a Gillows drawing of 1786, for one of a set of ten 'Êbriole Armchair' made for the Conservative statesman Sir Robert Peel.
c1790 *28¾in (73cm) high*
£4,500-5,000 **DN**

A late 18thC to early 19thC Russian mahogany and brass inlaid Neo-classical open armchair, with carved eagle's head arm supports.
£1,000-1,500 **WW**

A pair of Regency mahogany bergères, some wear and restoration.
c1810 *37in (94cm) high*
£8,000-9,000 **DN**

A pair of Regency ebonised parcel-gilt lattice-back open armchairs.
33in (84cm) high
£1,300-1,600 **BELL**

A pair of Empire carved mahogany fauteuils, in the manner of Jacob Frères.
c1815 *17in (43cm) high*
£4,000-5,000 **DN**

A George IV beechwood bobbin-turned armchair, on brass casters.
£700-800 **WW**

A George IV oak leather armchair, attributed to Gillows.

42½in (108cm) high

£2,000-2,500 **L&T**

A pair of George IV mahogany open armchairs.

£750-850 **WW**

ESSENTIAL REFERENCE – GOTHIC REVIVAL

- **The Gothic Revival movement emerged in Britain in the mid-18thC and reached its height in the late 19thC. It reflected contemporary interest in the medieval period, particularly in the Gothic style of the 12thC.**
- **Gothic Revival furniture took inspiration from Gothic Revival architecture, using pointed arches, heraldic motifs and trefoil and quatrefoil shapes.**
- **Rosewood, oak or walnut would often be decorated with heavy, intricate carving and finished with dark staining.**
- **Upholstery was generally in heavy fabrics such as velvet, leather or brocade.**
- **Although primarily associated with English taste, the Gothic Revival style also appeared in France during the reign of Louis Philippe. It is possible that these chairs may be French, as their design closely relates to a chair attributed to Joseph Pierre Francois Jeanselme, an early to mid-19thC French cabinetmaker.**

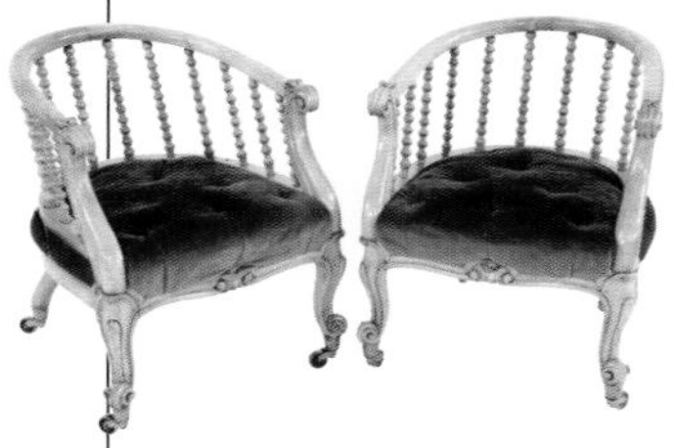

A pair of Victorian satin walnut tub chairs, stamped 'J Kerr & Co. 59399'.

£750-850 **SWO**

A pair of 19thC Italian Baroque iron and brass curule armchairs.

39in (99cm) high

£2,200-2,800 **L&T**

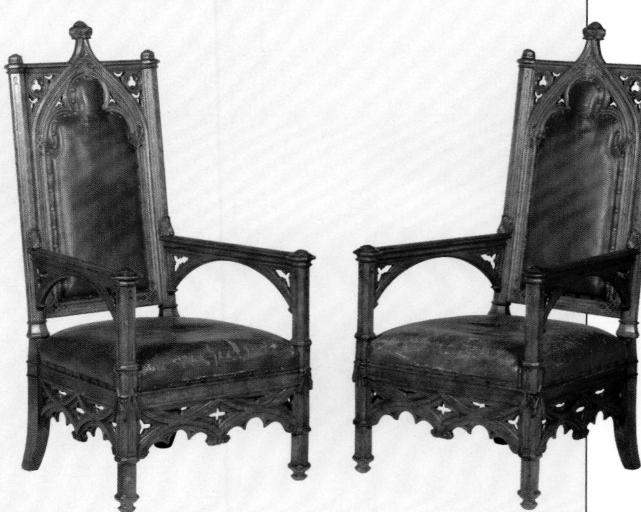

A pair of Victorian Gothic Revival oak armchairs, with lancet, trefoil and quatrefoil motifs, each with a paper label marked 'Great Hall'.

c1850 *51¼in (130cm) high*

£5,000-6,000 **DN**

Two of a set of four early 19thC mahogany shield-back open armchairs, in the Hepplewhite taste.

£4,000-4,500 the set **BE**

Three of a set of five late 19thC Black Forest open armchairs.

39in (99cm) high

£1,000-1,400 the set **BELL**

A pair of late 19thC to early 20thC French beech and needlework upholstered armchairs.

35in (89cm) high

£1,800-2,200 **L&T**

A George II and later walnut wing armchair, on cabochon leaf and husk carved cabriole legs and paw feet.

£6,000-7,000 **WW**

A mid-18thC mahogany framed tub-back armchair, 'NORMAN ADAMS' trade label to underside, later upholstery, some repairs.

36¼in (92cm) high

£3,000-3,500 **BELL**

A George III mahogany wing armchair.

c1770 *43in (109cm) high*

£4,000-4,500 **DN**

A Philadelphia Chippendale mahogany easy chair, with Marlborough feet, some upholstery removed.

c1780

£4,500-5,000 **POOK**

A Regency ebonised and brass-mounted bergère, one rear leg replaced.

c1810 *43¼in (110cm) high*

£3,000-3,500 **DN**

A George IV rosewood library armchair, in the manner of Gillows, with leaf carved scroll arm fronts, above quarter rosettes.

£5,000-6,000 **WW**

A William IV oak library armchair, carved with acanthus leaves and rope-twist and lappet borders.

£3,500-4,000 **WW**

A William IV mahogany and buttoned leather upholstered adjustable armchair, in the manner of Robert Daws, some wear, filler plugs to joints.

c1835 *45in (114cm) high*

£1,800-2,200 **DN**

An early Victorian mahogany library armchair.

£1,800-2,200 **WW**

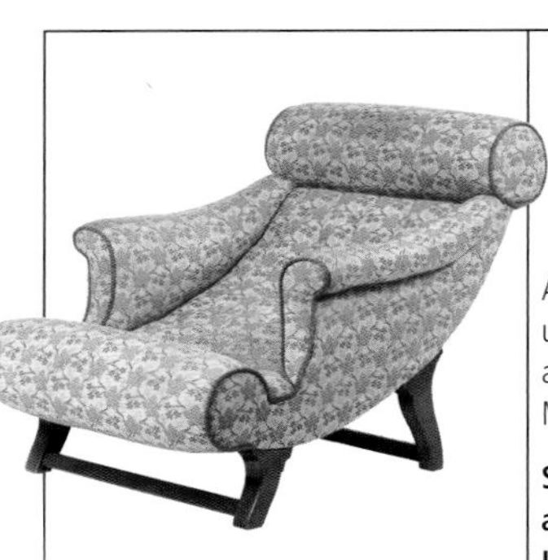

A Victorian scroll-back easy armchair, by William Birch, stamped 'WB 81(?)', tatty upholstery, re-tipping to back legs.

43¼in (110cm) long

£2,500-3,000 **BELL**

A Gothic Revival oak and leather-upholstered reclining armchair, attributed to Charles Bevan for Marsh & Jones.

See Jeremy Cooper, 'Victorian and Edwardian Furniture and Interiors', Thames & Hudson, 1987, figure 267, where a related chair designed by Charles Bevan, and manufactured on licence by Marsh & Jones is illustrated.

c1870 *39¼in (100cm) high*

£2,500-3,000 **L&T**

ESSENTIAL REFERENCE – HOWARD & SONS

Howard & Sons began in 1820 when John Howard started trading on Lemon Street, London as a cabinetmaker.

- **Howard & Sons pieces are of very high quality and received much acclaim at the time, winning prizes at the 1862 and 1878 International Exhibitions and the 1900 Paris Exhibition.**
- **In 1866 George Howard patented the 'elastic seat', which radically re-designed the interior working of traditional upholstery.**
- **Howard & Sons chairs and sofas typically have a name or number stamped on the back foot, a paper label on the hessian, or a name stamp on the caster.**
- **Howard and Sons ceased trading in 1947. Today, chairs which follow George Howard's patent are sold by Howard Chairs Limited of London.**

A late Victorian walnut and upholstered armchair, by Howard & Sons, one rear leg stamped '7410 6539' and 'HOWARD & SONS BERNERS ST'.

33in (84cm) high

£4,000-4,500 **DN**

A 19thC satinwood brass-mounted bergère.

35¾in (91cm) high

£1,500-2,000 **L&T**

A pair of early 20thC Howard & Sons leather club armchairs, the rear legs stamped 'HOWARD & SONS LTD/BERNERS ST' and numbered '12667/9010' and '13050/9897'.

31in (79cm) high

£3,000-4,000 **L&T**

A pair of French Louis XVI-style mahogany and ormolu-mounted bergères, attributed to François Linke.

The chairs were originally part of a suite of furniture that came from a château in the Loire valley. François Linke (1855-1946) was an important Parisian cabinetmaker of the late 19thC and early 20thC.

c1900

£4,000-4,500 **WW**

An early 20thC pair of leather upholstered barrel-back wing armchairs.

43in (109cm) high

£3,500-4,000 **L&T**

An early 20thC George II-style walnut framed wing armchair.

42½in (108cm) high

£2,000-2,500 **L&T**

A pair of 20thC 18thC-style high wing-back armchairs.

52in (132cm) high

£1,500-2,000 **BELL**

An 18thC Louis XIV walnut sofa, upholstered with 17thC tapestry panels and cushions.

71¾in (182cm) wide

£3,500-4,000 **SWO**

An early 18thC and later walnut settee.

44¼in (112.5cm) wide

£4,000-5,000 **WW**

A George II walnut chair-back settee, with tapered cabriole legs with carved claw-and-ball feet, some repairs to needlework.

c1735 *46in (117cm) wide*

£6,500-7,000 **DN**

ESSENTIAL REFERENCE – GEORGE HEPPLEWHITE

George Hepplewhite (d.1786) was an English cabinetmaker and furniture designer.

- **He was originally apprenticed to Robert Gillow of Lancaster and later moved to London, where he opened his own shop on Redcross Street.**
- **His furniture was simple and elegant, typically in Neo-classical style. He often added inlaid and painted decoration to his work.**
- **He is known for his pattern-book, 'The Cabinet-maker and Upholsterer's Guide', published posthumously in 1788. It was highly influential both in Europe and North America, and cabinetmakers often used the guide as a trade catalogue. It featured many of his designs, and many simpler versions of designs by Robert Adam, making them more accessible to the wider marker.**
- **No piece is unequivocally attributed to Hepplewhite or his firm.**

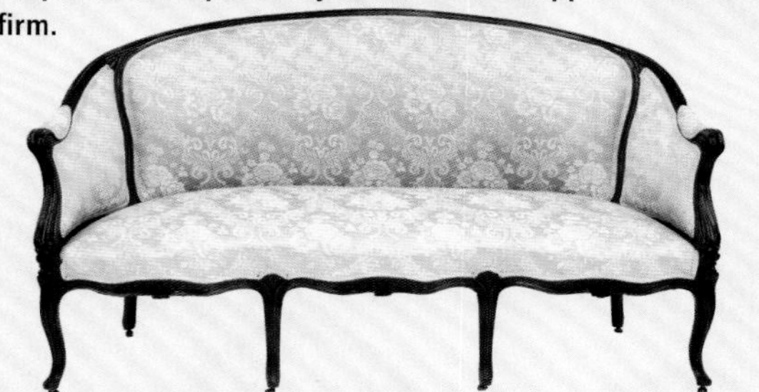

A George III Hepplewhite-style mahogany settee.

c1780 *69in (175cm) wide*

£1,800-2,200 **SWO**

A late 18thC giltwood settee, possibly English, in Louis XV style.

57in (144.5cm) wide

£1,000-1,400 **WW**

A George III mahogany and upholstered sofa, some scratches, hairline cracks to one leg.

c1790 *75½in (192cm) wide*

£3,500-4,000 **DN**

A George III mahogany settee.

78¼in (199cm) wide

£4,000-4,500 **SWO**

An 18thC gilt-framed sofa.

63¾in (162cm) wide

£1,200-1,500 **CHEF**

A 19thC American Empire revival sofa, the mahogany frame carved with cornucopias, restored.

79in (200.5cm) wide

£1,000-1,400 **DRA**

A Regency ebonised and parcel gilt sofa.

89½in (227cm) long

£2,500-3,000 **L&T**

A George IV carved mahogany sofa.

93¼in (237cm) wide

£1,100-1,500 **L&T**

A late Regency mahogany scroll-end settee, one rear leg with moulding loss, one leg repaired.

67in (170cm) wide

£1,200-1,600 **CHEF**

An early 19thC mahogany framed sofa.

76in (193cm) wide

£1,500-2,000 **PW**

An early Victorian rosewood framed sofa.

75½in (192cm) long

£1,500-2,000 **L&T**

An early Victorian carved mahogany sofa, in modern silk upholstery.

83½in (212cm) long

£850-950 **L&T**

A mid-19thC Victorian double-spoon-back mahogany sofa.

67¾in (172cm) wide

£650-750 **L&T**

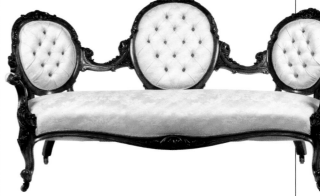

A Victorian triple-chair-back sofa, restored.

67¾in (172cm) wide

£1,400-1,800 **BELL**

A Victorian leather button-upholstered Chesterfield sofa.

85¾in (218cm) long

£4,500-5,000 **L&T**

A Victorian walnut and upholstered sofa, the two front casters stamped 'HOWARD & SONS, LONDON', some looseness to frame.

c1870 *72¾in (185cm) wide*

£8,500-9,000 **DN**

A 19thC curved gilt-framed sofa, with opposing C-scroll crest and carved floral chased frame.

104¼in (265cm) wide

£1,800-2,200 **BELL**

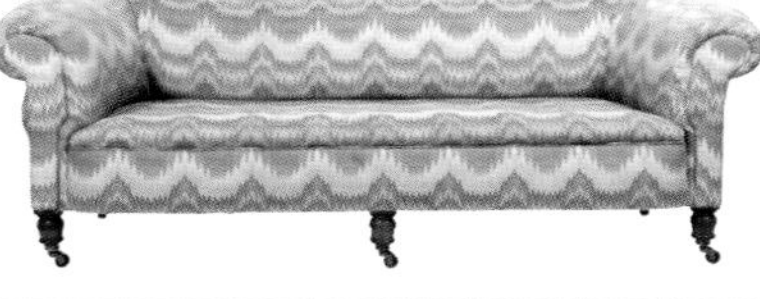

A late Victorian walnut Chesterfield sofa.

82in (208.5cm) long

£1,000-1,400 **WW**

A late 19thC Victorian Chesterfield sofa, the rear leg stamped '13075 9954 HOWARD & SONS LTD/BERNERS ST'.

75½in (192cm) wide

£2,500-3,000 **L&T**

A late 19thC George III-style mahogany sofa.

65¾in (167cm) wide

£2,500-3,000 **L&T**

A late 19thC to early 20thC mahogany settee, in Chippendale style.

66¼in (168cm) long

£350-450 **WW**

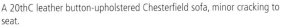

A 20thC leather button-upholstered Chesterfield sofa, minor cracking to seat.

82¾in (210cm) wide

£700-800 **BELL**

A late Regency rosewood chaise longue.

82in (208cm) long

£650-750 **L&T**

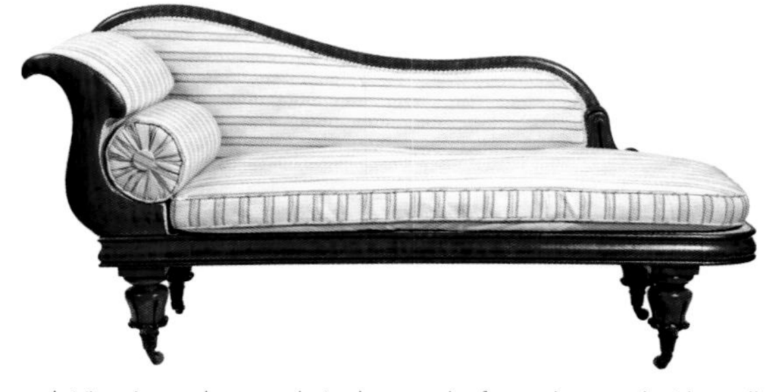

An early Victorian mahogany chaise longue, the frame decorated with scrolls.

67¾in (172cm) wide

£550-650 **WW**

A mid-18thC panelled elm bacon settle, door and cupboards to the reverse, with armrests and small cupboards to the box seat base, some shrinkage and wear.

Bacon settles were a feature of the farmhouse kitchen throughout the 18thC and 19thC. They have always been associated with the hanging of cured sides of bacon, but it seems more likely that the use of these high back settles was as a hanging space for outdoor clothing, as a display shelf, and as a room divider. The principal living room in a West Country farmhouse was the kitchen, with the entrance directly from the outside and an open fire creating cold draughts. The use of a high back settle could avert the draught, creating warmth around the hearth.

72in (183cm) high

£2,500-3,000 **CHEF**

An 18thC Dutch Renaissance oak hall bench, the back reinforced.

66¼in (168cm) wide

£2,500-3,000 **CHEF**

A George III oak 'Gothick' settle, the back and sides with trefoil shaped X-form pierced panels.

70in (178cm) long

£10,000-14,000 **L&T**

A pair of Regency or later mahogany window seats, in the manner of Marsh & Tatham.

31½in (80cm) high

£1,600-2,000 **CHEF**

One of a pair of William IV rosewood window seats.

c1835 *52in (132cm) wide*

£1,500-2,000 the pair **DN**

A late 19thC Black Forest bench, the carved plank seat supported by twin carved bears with glass eyes.

'Black Forest' carvings and furniture were once thought to have been made in the Black Forest reigion of Bavaria, Germany, but were in fact mostly produced in Brienz, Switzerland. The craftsman of Brienz carved boxes, clock cases, figures and furniture from tree trunks. Bears were popular subjects. **See page 251.**

31½in (80cm) wide

£3,500-4,000 **L&T**

An early 17thC and later oak refectory table, the frieze carved with lunettes.

A refectory table is a long narrow dining table. They were first used in monasteries in Medieval Europe, in the refectory, or communal dining room.

103in (216.5cm) long

£2,500-3,000 **WW**

A 17thC oak refectory table, on gun barrel ring-turned legs and block feet.

82¾in (210cm) wide

£3,000-3,500 **SWO**

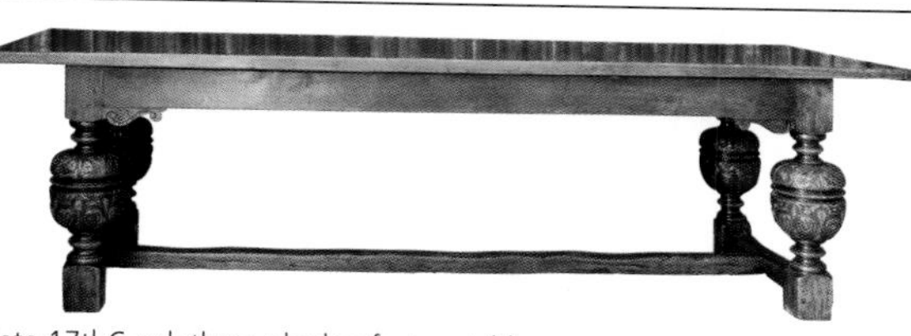

A late 17thC oak three-plank refectory table.

110¼in (280cm) wide

£2,000-3,000 **SWO**

A 17thC and later oak refectory table, the plank top with cleated ends.

109in (277cm) long

£4,500-5,000 **L&T**

An oak refectory table, with associated cleated top.

c1700 *84in (213.5cm) long*

£1,200-1,600 **HT**

An early 18thC Continental joined oak refectory dining table, with a single frieze drawer.

89¼in (227cm) long

£1,200-1,600 **TEN**

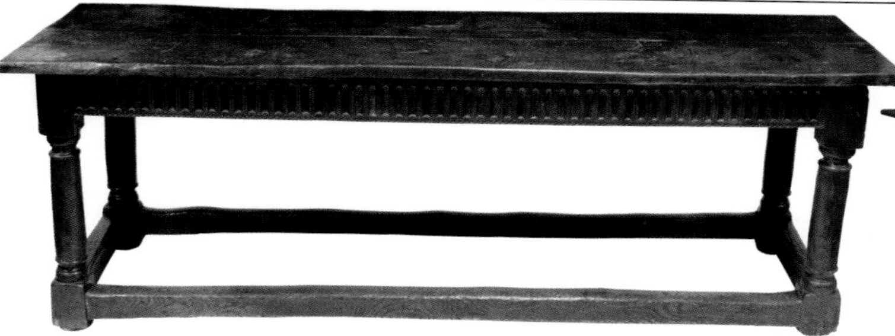

An 18thC elm two-plank refectory table, on four gun-barrel legs.

91in (231cm) wide

£1,100-1,500 **CHOR**

An 18thC Georgian oak refectory table, the five-board cleated top above a scroll carved frieze.

81½in (207cm) long

£1,000-1,500 **L&T**

A William and Mary oak one-drawer gateleg table.
45¼in (115cm) long
£4,500-5,000 **SK**

A Pennsylvania William and Mary walnut gateleg table, top and brasses replaced.
c1740 *45¾in (116cm) long*
£900-1,200 **POOK**

A George II Irish mahogany drop-leaf table, with plain frieze and cabriole legs with hoof feet.
c1750 *43¼in (110cm) wide*
£900-1,200 **DN**

A George II mahogany drop-leaf dining table, some mildew to underside.
c1760 *48in (122cm) long*
£500-600 **POOK**

A George II mahogany drop-leaf dining table, possibly Irish.
42¼in (107.5cm) long
£500-600 **WW**

A George II oak double drop-leaf table, with two frieze drawers.
open 71¼in (181cm) wide
£600-700 **SWO**

A late 18thC George III oak gateleg table, with a single drawer and opposing dummy drawer.
open 66½in (169cm) long
£900-1,200 **L&T**

A 19thC elm gateleg table on turned supports and stretchered base.
56¾in (144cm) long
£600-700 **ECGW**

A George III mahogany two-pedestal Cumberland action extending dining table, in the manner of Wilkinson & Sons, some wear.
c1810 *extended 129¼in (328cm) long*
£7,500-8,500 **DN**

A mahogany triple-pedestal dining table, with rosewood crossbanding, some restoration.
c1820 *extended 216½in (550cm) long*
£10,000-12,000 **DN**

An early 19thC Regency mahogany pedestal dining table, the crossbanded tilt top with ebony banding.
71¾in (182cm) diam
£7,000-8,000 **L&T**

A Regency mahogany and brass inlaid twin-pedestal dining table, the frieze with carved rosettes, with two additional leaves.
extended 50½in (128cm) long
£4,500-5,000 **BE**

A George IV mahogany twin-pedestal dining table, with one leaf extension.
111in (282cm) long
£3,500-4,000 **L&T**

An early 19thC three-part mahogany extending dining table, the centre section with swivelling top over an ebony inlaid frieze and pull-out ends to support the additional leaves, raised on eight legs, with two pedestal D-ends, with four additional leaves.
extended 149½in (380cm) long
£4,000-4,500 **MART**

An early 19thC and later mahogany D-end dining table, with end pedestals and six ring-turned legs, opening with a gateleg action to support final two sections.
155¾in (395.5cm) long
£2,500-3,000 **SWO**

A mid-Victorian mahogany triple-pedestal dining table, with three additional leaves, some restoration and wear.
154¾in (393cm) long
£7,000-8,000 **TEN**

A George III mahogany extending dining table, with kingwood crossbanding, with two D-ends, a central section and four extra leaves.

151½in (385cm) long

£2,200-2,800 **LC**

An early 19thC mahogany extending dining table, with five extra leaves.

190½in (484cm) wide

£14,000-18,000 **SWO**

A Regency mahogany telescopic extending dining table, with three additional leaves and two rounded drop flaps, some scratches and bruising.

86½in (220cm) long

£1,400-1,800 **TEN**

CLOSER LOOK – REGENCY EXTENDING DINING TABLE

This table is in the style of George Bullock (c1778-1818), a sculptor and furniture-maker based in Liverpool, celebrated for his impressive craftsmanship and use of exotic woods.

It has four semi-elliptical additional leaves, each decorated with foliate ebony marquetry, attached with pull-out supports.

The turned feet and shaped plinth and embellished with further floral carving and motifs.

The quality of the craftsmanship is very fine and the condition excellent.

A Regency mahogany circular extending dining table, in the manner of George Bullock.

91¼in (232cm) diam

£60,000-70,000 **DN**

An early 19thC mahogany extending dining table, with concertina action, four additional leaves, restored, some wear.

136¼in (346cm) long

£4,000-5,000 **CHEF**

An early Victorian mahogany extending dining table, with eight leaves.

171¼in (435cm) long

£6,000-6,500 **SWO**

A Victorian Lambs of Manchester figured and bog oak extending dining table, with five extra leaves, stamped to the runner.

Lambs of Manchester was a renowned cabinet-making firm founded by James Lamb (1816-1903). It won medals at London 1862 Exhibition and the Paris 1867 Exhibition.

extended 169¼in (430cm) long

£3,000-4,000 **BELL**

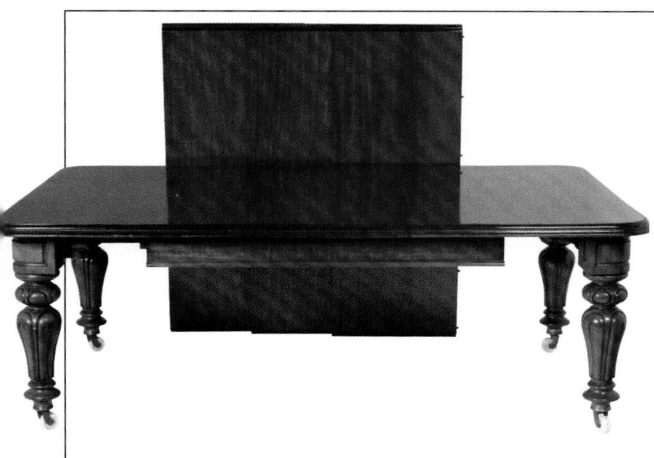

A Victorian mahogany wind-out dining table, with four leaves, on baluster tapered legs and casters, restored and re-polished.
c1850 *143¼in (364cm) long*
£3,000-3,500 **TEN**

A late Victorian mahogany extending dining table, with two extra leaves and wind-out action.
90½in (230cm) long
£1,000-1,400 **LSK**

A Regency mahogany dining table, in the manner of Gillows, in four sections with three additional leaves, some cracks and wear.
68in (173cm) wide
£70,000-80,000 **CHEF**

An early 19thC late George III mahogany tilt-top breakfast table.
61¾in (157cm) long
£2,500-3,500 **L&T**

ESSENTIAL REFERENCE – IRISH FURNITURE

Throughout much of the 18thC, Irish furniture was stylistically very different from English furniture.

- **Low relief carvings on the aprons of tables included festoons, winged birds and rosettes. Goblin heads, scallop shells and lion masks also depicted.**
- **Many pieces were decorated with animalistic additions, with muscle or fetlock being carved above the paw or claw feet.**
- **Antique Irish furniture is highly desirable today, due to its high quality, and can often fetch more than similar English pieces. Despite being in need of restoration, this table is very valuable.**

A George II Irish mahogany table, on carved lion mask and foliate carved cabriole legs and hairy paw feet, some damages, in need of restoration.
68in (173cm) long
£65,000-75,000 **CHEF**

A George III mahogany breakfast table, with rosewood banding, on a turned pillar and outswept reeded legs, with lion casters.
c1810 *54¼in (138cm) wide*
£1,000-1,500 **DN**

A Regency rosewood flip-top breakfast table, in the manner of George Bullock, on ring-turned stem with brass-inlaid pod and splayed legs, with cast brass lion paw feet.
61¾in (157cm) long
£10,000-15,000 **MEA**

FURNITURE

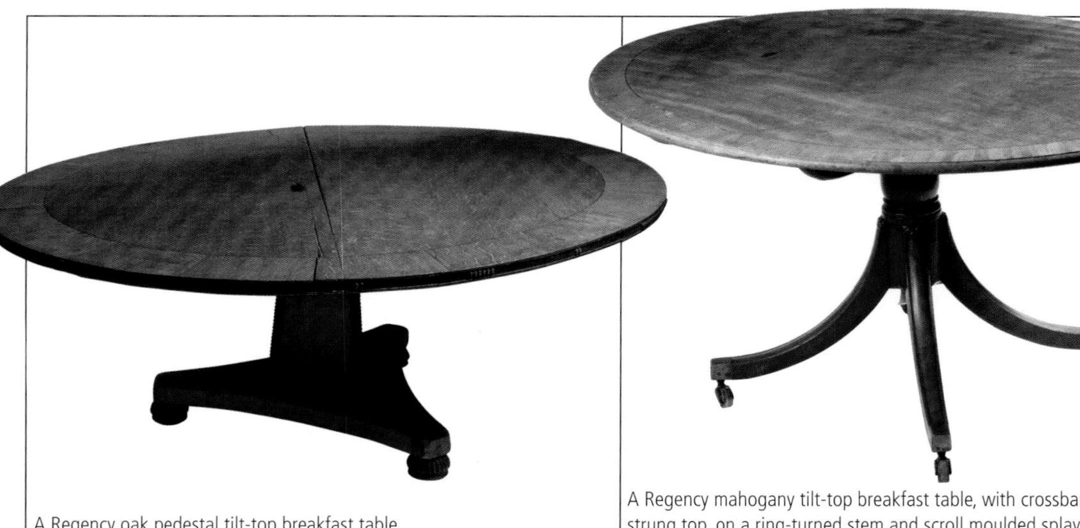

A Regency oak pedestal tilt-top breakfast table.

70¾in (180cm) diam

£8,500-9,000 **LSK**

A Regency mahogany tilt-top breakfast table, with crossbanded and ebony strung top, on a ring-turned stem and scroll moulded splay legs.

56in (142cm) wide

£7,000-7,500 **WW**

A Regency mahogany pedestal tilt-top breakfast table, with crossbanded and ebony strung top.

c1825 *61in (155cm) long*

£500-600 **HAN**

A William IV mahogany tilt-top breakfast table, on a ring-turned column to four hipped swept supports.

49½in (125.5cm) diam

£750-850 **MART**

A William IV rosewood snap-top breakfast table.

52½in (133cm) wide

£300-400 **BELL**

A William IV rosewood tilt-top breakfast table.

51½in (131cm) diam

£450-550 **LSK**

A William IV rosewood breakfast table.

c1840 *29in (73.5cm) high*

£1,500-2,000 **WAD**

A Victorian oak tilt-top breakfast table, with crossbanded and ebonised strung top, on a triform stem with applied strapwork decoration and three spiral twist columns.

50in (127cm) diam

£2,500-3,000 **WW**

A Victorian flame mahogany tilt-top breakfast table, raised on triangular plinth base.

53¼in (135cm) diam

£1,100-1,500 **WM**

A Regency rosewood and parcel-gilt centre table, with grey marble top.

28¼in (72cm) diam

£950-1,100 **BLEA**

A Regency rosewood centre table, on a faux rosewood turned column, some minor repairs.

49¼in (125cm) diam

£1,500-2,000 **SWO**

CLOSER LOOK – GRAND TOUR TABLE

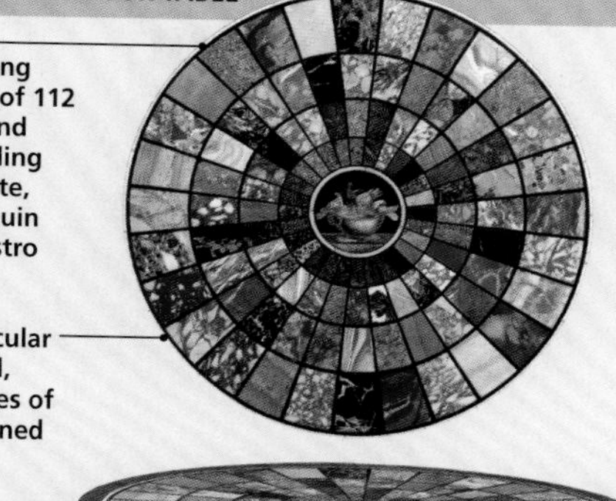

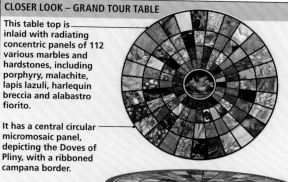

This table top is inlaid with radiating concentric panels of 112 various marbles and hardstones, including porphyry, malachite, lapis lazuli, harlequin breccia and alabastro fiorito.

It has a central circular micromosaic panel, depicting the Doves of Pliny, with a ribboned campana border.

Specimen marble tops were the ultimate souvenir from the Grand Tour; many were purchased in Italy by young elite travellers and brought back to England.

The Regency base is in the manner of Gillows, with lobed and nulled decoration, a triform base, leaf carved scroll feet and brass casters.

An early 19thC Italian Roman specimen marble-topped Grand Tour table.

34¾in (88.5cm) diam

£35,000-40,000 **WW**

A Regency ormolu-mounted rosewood centre table, some restoration.

c1815 *45½in (115.5cm) diam*

£4,000-5,000 **DRA**

A George IV specimen marble and mahogany centre table, inset with a marble fan motif and black slate border.

30in (76cm) diam

£9,000-11,000 **L&T**

An early 19thC Charles X maplewood table-de-milieu, with Egyptian red porphyry top within a ormolu surround, some damages and losses.

42¼in (107cm) wide

£35,000-40,000 **TEN**

An early Victorian rosewood, satinwood and mahogany parquetry centre table, the tilt-top centred by a fan medallion and radiating 'tumbling block' veneer panels.

31½in (80cm) diam

£2,500-3,000 **L&T**

A mid-19thC Anglo-Indian rosewood snap-top centre table, some losses to fretwork.

53¼in (135cm) wide

£850-950 **SHAP**

A mid-19thC Anglo-Indian padouk centre table, with a foliate carved frieze.

30¾in (78cm) wide

£2,000-2,500 **L&T**

A Sèvres centre table, with gilt-metal mounts, the top inset with porcelain panels, the central panel of Louis XVI.

42in (106.5cm) diam

£7,000-8,000 **JN**

A Napoleon III mahogany, kingwood, burr walnut and marquetry table-de-milieu, in the Louis XVI style, the drawer applied with mounts in the Weisweiler style.

49½in (126cm) wide

£8,500-9,500 **BE**

A Victorian carved walnut and marble-mounted centre table, the pierced frieze decorated with fruiting branches and armorial shields, one titled 'CHABLAIS', some chips and losses.

c1860 *59in (150cm) wide*

£7,500-8,500 **DN**

A Victorian walnut snap-top centre table.

59in (150cm) long

£2,000-2,500 **BELL**

A 19thC French boullework marquetry centre table, with cut brass inlay on a tortoiseshell ground, with strapwork, leaves, scrolls and winged cherubs.

Boullework is a type of marquetry or inlay developed by the French cabinetmaker André Charles Boulle (1642-1732). It involves veneering furniture with a marquetry of silver, brass, pewter or tortoiseshell.

58¼in (148cm) wide

£1,800-2,200 **WW**

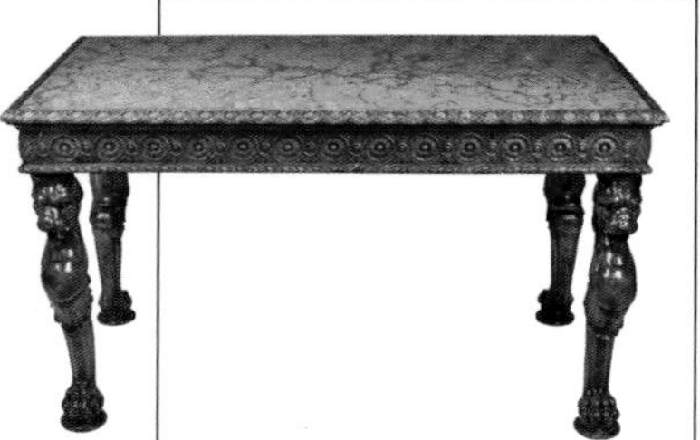

A 19thC centre table, in 17thC Italian style, the inset marble top within a carved rosette frieze, filled crack to top.

70in (178cm) wide

£2,500-3,000 **BELL**

A Victorian Gothic revival oak centre table, designed by Collier & Plucknett, Warwick, the base designed by John Henry Chamberlain, table top possibly a later replacement.

60in (152.5cm) diam

£1,600-2,000 **GORL**

A 19thC Irish mahogany and marble centre table, with four lion monopodia supports, united by platform undertier.

23½in (60cm) diam

£900-1,000 **BELL**

An early 20thC Dresden porcelain centre table, the top with panels of figures in 18thC dress, in a gilt-metal and wood frame, the feet joined by a shaped X-stretcher surmounted by a putto.

30¼in (77cm) diam

£9,000-11,000 **L&T**

An 18thC mahogany drum table, with leather inset top, above four real and four dummy drawers, one handle missing, replaced crossbanding.

35¾in (91cm) diam

£6,500-7,500 SWO

A late George III mahogany library table, with later inset writing surface, above four real and four dummy drawers, drawer linings restored, some scratches.

37½in (95cm) wide

£1,400-1,800 TEN

A Regency mahogany crossbanded and inlaid revolving drum library table, bordered with ebony lines, with alternate frieze and dummy drawers.

36in (91.5cm) diam

£2,200-2,600 BE

A Regency rosewood library table, in the manner of Gillows, with painted inset Grand Tour marble tablet.

53½in (136cm) wide

£10,000-14,000 CHEF

A Regency rosewood library table.

101½in (258cm) wide

£3,500-4,500 L&T

An early 19thC Regency mahogany drum table, in the manner of Gillows, with a frieze fitted with four real and four dummy drawers, raised on lotus carved paw feet with brass casters.

50½in (128.5cm) diam

£9,000-11,000 L&T

A Regency mahogany library table, in the manner of Gillows.

53in (100cm) long

£1,300-1,800 CHEF

An early Victorian oak and ebony library table, in the Baroque style.

65¾in (167cm) wide

£5,000-6,000 L&T

An early Victorian mahogany drum library table, with six drawers, on a chamfered tapered support and ogee bracket feet.

48¾in (124cm) diam

£650-750 HAN

A George II giltwood console table, with a marble top over a carved frieze, on twisted dolphin supports.

This distinctive table is reminiscent of William Kent's oeuvre. It also relates closely to the designs of Batty Langley and William Jones, published in 1740. The table may originally have had a rectangular plinth base.

49in (124.5cm) wide

£35,000-40,000 DUK

A cream-painted and parcel-gilt console table, in the manner of Robert Adam, the satinwood top painted with a mythological medallion amongst foliage.

Robert Adam (1728-92) was an influential Neo-classical architect and designer active in the 18thC. He worked alongside his brother James Adam (1730-94).

41¾in (106cm) wide

£3,000-3,500 DUK

A William IV 'plum pudding' mahogany marble-topped console table.

70½in (179cm) wide

£2,000-2,500 DUK

A Louis Phillipe mahogany gilt-metal and marble-mounted console table, with serpentine marble top.

c1840 *38½in (98cm) wide*

£650-750 DN

A Victorian mahogany console table, with acanthus leaf carved cabriole front supports with claw feet, with a mirrored back.

63¾in (162cm) long

£1,800-2,200 BE

One of a pair of late 18thC Italian grey painted and parcel-gilt pier tables, with breche violette marble tops above fluted and leaf sprigged frieze, some wear.

46in (117cm) wide

£8,000-9,000 the pair DN

A late 18thC carved silvered wood marble-topped console table, the frieze as two cherubs and a bird of prey, amidst flowers and foliage, the hipped cabriole supports with fruit and flowers.

Reputedly, this table originally stood in the 'silver room' of Château de Fontainebleau, the favoured residence and hunting lodge of the kings of France from the Middle Ages through to Napoleon III. The 'silver room' may refer to the Boudoir de la Reine, which was Marie Antoinette's bedroom and lavishly decorated with silvered panels and furniture by the Rousseau brothers in 1786.

39¼in (100cm) wide

£25,000-30,000 LSK

A 19thC carved giltwood console table, of 18thC design, lacking marble top, some replacements and repairs.

63½in (161cm) wide

£2,000-2,500 BELL

An Irish George III mahogany side or serving table, the top with a 'plum pudding' central reserve outlined with boxwood stringing and oblique crossbanding, some repairs to joints.
c1760 *60¼in (153cm) wide*
£7,500-8,500 **DN**

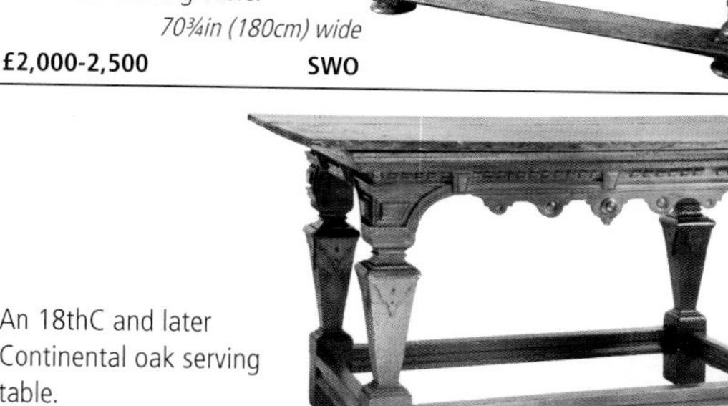

A 17thC to 18thC Flemish oak draw-leaf serving table.
70¾in (180cm) wide
£2,000-2,500 **SWO**

An 18thC and later Continental oak serving table.
56¼in (143cm) wide
£1,200-1,500 **SWO**

A late 18thC George III mahogany and ebony serpentine serving table.
67¼in (171cm) wide
£2,000-2,500 **L&T**

A mahogany and inlaid serving table, of serpentine outline.
c1790 *72½in (184cm) wide*
£2,500-3,000 **DN**

A Regency mahogany serving table, in the manner of Gillows, the top carved with leaves, with three blind frieze drawers.
102¼in (260cm) wide
£5,500-6,500 **CHEF**

An Irish Regency mahogany serving table, by Gillingtons of Dublin, stamped 'GILLINGTONS/34251'.
61¾in (157cm) wide
£2,000-2,500 **L&T**

A Regency mahogany inverted breakfront serving table.
93in (236cm) long
£2,200-2,800 **L&T**

A George IV rosewood marble-topped decanting table, in the manner of Gillows, on ring-turned and lozenge carved tapered legs.
36in (91.5cm) wide
£5,000-6,000 **WW**

A Charles II carved giltwood side table, the top inset with later yellow marble.

This side table was formerly the base of a cabinet-on-stand.

33¾in (86cm) wide

£3,500-4,500 **WW**

An early 18thC walnut and cocus wood side table, on bobbin and disc-turned legs.

29¾in (75.5cm) wide

£2,500-3,000 **WW**

A Sheraton period mahogany, satinwood banded and polychrome decorated demi-lune side table, probably Irish.

52in (132cm) wide

£1,300-1,800 **LSK**

A Scottish Regency rosewood side table, attributed to William Trotter, Edinburgh.

William Trotter was born into a family of merchants in 1772. He became a member of The Merchant Company in 1797 and by 1809 was sole proprietor of the firm Young & Trotter. In 1819 he was elected Master of The Merchant Company and from 1825-27 he was Lord Provost of Edinburgh. Trotter continued to trade from 9 Princes Street until his death in 1833.

35½in (90cm) wide

£3,000-3,500 **L&T**

A Regency mahogany side table, in the manner of Gillows.

c1820 *35¾in (91cm) wide*

£900-1,100 **DN**

A French kingwood, ormolu and marquetry side table.

30in (76cm) wide

£1,800-2,200 **JN**

An early 19thC Dutch walnut marquetry and bone inlaid side table.

29¼in (74cm) wide

£700-800 **L&T**

A 19thC Italian carved wood and silvered side table, in the Rococo style, with a faux-marble top, the pierced apron with scrolling acanthus leaves centred by a female mask.

51¼in (130cm) wide

£1,500-2,000 **BE**

A late Regency specimen wood tilt-top occasional table, possibly Isle of Man.

21¼in (54cm) diam

£850-950 **L&T**

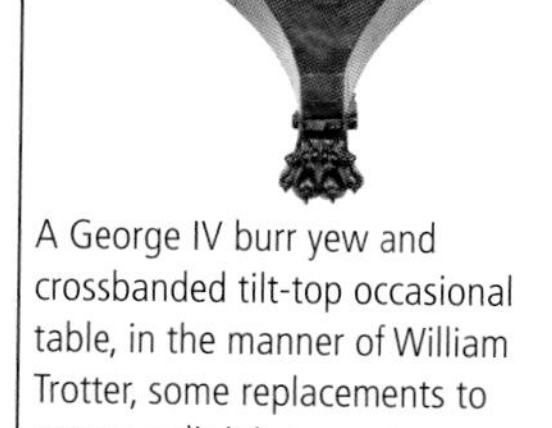

A George IV burr yew and crossbanded tilt-top occasional table, in the manner of William Trotter, some replacements to veneer, split join to centre.

c1825 *29in (73.5cm) diam*

£1,500-2,000 **DN**

A Regency septarian nodule inset rosewood occasional table.

c1825 *21¾in (55cm) diam*

£1,000-1,400 **WAD**

A pair of Victorian black lacquer and parcel-gilt occasional tables, with mother-of-pearl inlay.

c1860 *17¼in (44cm) diam*

£525-600 **DN**

One of a pair of 19thC Continental Empire-style ash occasional tables, the tops with oak marquetry inlay.

31½in (80cm) diam

£4,000-5,000 the pair **DN**

A Scottish slate and ebonised wood occasional table, the top painted with a Highland hunt scene, probably after Landseer, on faux bamboo supports.

20in (51cm) diam

£1,500-2,000 **WW**

A late Victorian walnut and specimen marble-top table.

22¾in (58cm) wide

£2,500-3,000 **CHEF**

An Edwardian two-tier oval satinwood occasional table, in the manner of Waring and Gillows, with mirror inset panels.

26½in (67cm) wide

£300-350 **FLD**

An Edwardian nest of four occasional tables, each with whitewood stringing, on spider leg supports and sledge feet, damaged stretcher on smallest table.

max 15in (38cm) wide

£500-600 **PW**

ESSENTIAL REFERENCE – SOFA & PEMBROKE TABLES

- **The term Pembroke table originated with the Countess of Pembroke, who is said to have ordered the first example of its time.**
- **Pembroke tables were lightweight, easily movable drop-leaf tables, with one or two drawers, which could be used as a bedside table, or for dining, writing and serving tea. They were usually on casters for ease of use.**
- **Sofa tables evolved from the Pembroke table during the later 18thC. They were narrower and longer than Pembroke tables, and were primarily designed to stand behind sofas. Candlesticks or table-lamps might be placed upon them.**

A George III rosewood and marquetry inlaid Pembroke table, with tulipwood crossbanding, centred with a satinwood fan patera, on faux fluted square tapered legs and spade feet.

36½in (92.5cm) wide

£2,000-2,500 **WW**

A George III mahogany Pembroke table, with satinwood and tulipwood crossbanding, over a single end drawer and opposing faux drawer.

31in (78.5cm) long

£550-650 **MART**

ESSENTIAL REFERENCE – GILLOWS OF LANCASTER

Gillows of Lancaster was established c1730 by Robert Gillow.

- **The firm rapidly established a reputation for supplying high-quality furniture to the richest families in the country.**
- **It is best known for its restrained mahogany furniture, made with superb technical craftsmanship. The mahogany was often imported from the West Indies and Jamaica.**
- **In 1897, Gillows merged with Waring of Liverpool to become Waring and Gillow. In 1980 Waring and Gillow joined with the cabinet making firm Maple & Co., to become Maple, Waring and Gillow, subsequently part of Allied Maples Group Ltd.**
- **Some Gillows furniture is stamped, but as a large proportion is not, pieces are often attributed to Gillows based on their style and design.**

A Regency mahogany Pembroke table, by Gillows of Lancaster, the frieze drawers stamped 'GILLOWS LANCASTER'.

44½in (113cm) wide

£1,000-1,500 **L&T**

A late 18thC George III painted satinwood, rosewood, mahogany harlequin Pembroke table, the top with a spring-released superstructure with drawers and pigeonholes.

42¼in (107cm) wide

£5,500-6,000 **L&T**

A George III satinwood Pembroke table, with kingwood banding, later painted with Venus and two cherubs, on brass caps and leather roller casters, stamped with workman's initials 'IC'.

The initials 'IC' might relate to Isaac Greenwood, a cabinetmaker for Gillows. In August 1780 he was noted as making 'satten wood' Pembroke tables.

open 37¼in (94.5cm) wide

£1,000-1,400 **WW**

A George III mahogany 'butterfly' pembroke table, with boxwood stringing and mahogany crossbanded decoration.

30in (76cm) long

£1,000-1,400 **JN**

A Regency japanned Pembroke table, the top decorated with three figures flying a kite, replacement piece to hinge, casters broken.

£550-650 **SWO**

A 19thC satinwood Pembroke table, painted with stylised floral and foliate motifs, some ring marks, losses and scratches.

35in (89cm) wide

£900-1,000 **ECGW**

A Regency mahogany and coromandel sofa table, with ebony line inlay.

38½in (98cm) wide

£2,000-2,500 **L&T**

A Regency mahogany and satinwood crossbanded sofa table, some damages.

48in (122cm) wide

£550-650 **CHOR**

A late Regency rosewood and brass marquetry sofa table, crossbanded and inlaid with flowers and leaves.

57¼in (145.5cm) wide

£1,500-2,000 **WW**

A George IV rosewood and satinwood crossbanded sofa table, some repairs, split across top.

closed 40½in (103cm) wide

£1,200-1,500 **DN**

A mahogany sofa 'dressing' table, with lifting section enclosing a fitted interior, some later replacements.

c1825 *57in (145cm) wide*

£400-500 **DN**

A Regency mahogany satinwood crossbanded and strung sofa table.

c1825 *35½in (90cm) wide*

£650-750 **HAN**

An early 19thC rosewood and inlaid sofa table, bordered with sycamore, ebonised and brass lines.

extended 48½in (123cm) wide

£700-800 **BE**

An 18thC George III mahogany writing table, with gilt tooled leather insert, two frieze drawers to one side, dummy drawers to the others.

50in (127cm) wide

£3,000-3,500 **L&T**

A George III harewood and marquetry lady's writing table, in the manner of John Cobb, with satinwood panels.

27½in (70cm) wide

£1,100-1,500 **WW**

A late George III mahogany writing table, with a leather effect writing surface.

c1810 *53½in (136cm) square*

£1,600-2,000 **MOR**

A Regency mahogany specimen marble-topped writing table.

31½in (80cm) wide

£4,000-5,000 **CHEF**

A George IV mahogany writing table, attributed to Gillows, the top inset with gilt tooled leather.

42¼in (107cm) wide

£1,500-2,000 **WW**

A Charles X mahogany writing table, with replaced tooled leather inset writing surface, on columnar-turned legs, flat 'H'-shaped stretchers, with concealed casters.

c1830 *38in (96.5cm) wide*

£4,000-4,500 **DN**

An early to mid-19thC bird's eye maple writing table, by Gillows, signed 'John Mason Jnr', leather top replaced, some slight wear.

42¼in (107cm) wide

£1,800-2,200 **TEN**

An English walnut writing table, the top inset with gilt tooled leather, the single drawer and front applied with ormolu rose and scroll mounts, the knees with foliate pendants and sides with bearded masks.

c1860 *51½in (131cm) wide*

£3,500-4,500 **MOR**

A Victorian satinwood writing table, with a pierced brass gallery with roundel ornament, with a tooled leather inset writing surface.

40¼in (102cm) wide

£1,500-2,000 **BE**

A late 19thC French tulipwood and ormolu-mounted writing table, in the Louis XV style, possibly by François Linke, with vernis Martin-style decoration, one foot mount detached, wear to one leg.

52¼in (133cm) high

£22,000-28,000 **DN**

A Louis XV-style ebony and red boullework bureau plat, the scrolled angled legs with applied ormolu mounts, with masks to each side, scrolling sabots and brass casters.

c1900 *69in (175.5cm) wide*

£10,000-14,000 **SWO**

An early 18thC Queen Anne burr walnut fold-over card table, opening to a gros - and petit-point panel of a courtly scene, with candle stands and guinea wells.

36¼in (92cm) wide

£11,000-14,000 **L&T**

A pair of George III 'D' shaped mahogany and inlaid card tables, with satinwood and rosewood crossbanding and boxwood stringing, re-polished finish, bowing to top of both, minor restoration, baize replaced.

c1800 *36¼in (92cm) wide*

£7,500-8,500 **DN**

A pair of George III French Hepplewhite mahogany fold-over card tables, with urn-carved friezes, on anthemion carved and cabriole legs, some scuffing and sun-bleaching, one crack.

36in (91.5cm) wide

£35,000-40,000 **GORL**

A mahogany and mahogany veneer inlaid card table, probably Langley Boardman (1774-1833), Portsmouth, New Hampshire, inlaid with stringing, bellflowers and panels.

c1807 *35¼in (89.5cm) wide*

£8,000-9,000 **SK**

An early to mid-Victorian rosewood and Tunbridgeware fold-over games table, attributed to Edmund Nye.

Edmund Nye worked in Tunbridge Wells from 1809 until his death in 1863. He was renowned for the high quality of his work, earning Royal patronage from 1836 and exhibiting at the Great Exhibition of 1851.

35¾in (91cm) wide

£3,500-4,000 **L&T**

A pair of Victorian walnut and marquetry inlaid hinged-top card tables, with labels for 'W&A Chapman Ltd. 20-26 North Street Taunton', and 'Trevor Page Nos. G20719/G20720'.

35in (89cm) wide

£2,000-3,000 **LSK**

A late Victorian amaranth, kingwood, parquetry and marquetry fold-over games table.

34in (86.5cm) wide

£3,500-4,500 **L&T**

A French ormolu-mounted mahogany concertina action card table, by Henry Dasson, repolish starting to split.

1881 *33¾in (85.5cm) wide*

£2,000-2,500 **BELL**

An Edwardian mahogany and satinwood crossbanded hinged-top games table, with a roulette wheel flanked by four games counter sections, with baize table opposite.

37in (94cm) wide

£2,000-2,500 **GWA**

A late 17thC William and Mary oak lowboy.

33in (84cm) wide

£850-950 **L&T**

A George I walnut lowboy, with veneered and crossbanded top.

26¾in (68cm) wide

£6,000-7,000 **L&T**

A Philadelphia Queen Anne walnut dressing table, on cabriole legs with shell carved knees ending in trifid feet.

c1760 *32in (81.5cm) wide*

£23,000-26,000 **POOK**

An early 18thC featherbanded walnut lowboy, with quarter-veneered top and concave starburst central drawer, on later cabriole legs.

30in (76cm) wide

£9,000-10,000 **GORL**

An 18thC walnut lowboy, fitted three small drawers, later handles, some scratches.

30in (76cm) wide

£700-800 **CHEF**

A Chippendale walnut dressing table, Lancaster, Pennsylvania, the thumb-moulded top overhanging a case with shell and spandrel carved drawer.

c1770 *38¼in (97cm) wide*

£43,000-48,000 **POOK**

A Regency mahogany and gilt-metal-mounted marble-topped dressing table, the frieze with revolving drawers, maker's stamp 'WILKINSON LUDGATE HILL', minor discolouration.

c1820 *61in (155cm) high*

£1,100-1,400 **DN**

A late Regency mahogany dressing table.

44in (112cm) wide

£2,000-2,500 **L&T**

A George IV mahogany dressing table, attributed to Gillows, with reeded edged three-quarter gallery.

47¾in (121cm) wide

£3,500-4,000 **WW**

A George III mahogany piecrust tea table.
c1765 *30½in (77.5cm) diam*
£750-850 **POOK**

A Chippendale walnut tea table, Pennsylvania, some wear to top.
c1770 *32¾in (83cm) wide*
£2,500-3,000 **POOK**

A Chippendale mahogany tea table, Lancaster or Reading, Pennsylvania.
c1775 *33in (84cm) wide*
£13,000-16,000 **POOK**

A 19thC rosewood wine table, by Gillows of Lancaster, stamped 'GILLOWS', some old repairs.
19¾in (50cm) wide
£2,000-2,500 **PFR**

A pair of George III mahogany and marquetry fold-over tea tables, inlaid with chequer stringing and kingwood banding.
42¼in (107cm) wide
£5,500-6,000 **WW**

An early Victorian mahogany teapoy, in the manner of Gillows, the interior fitted lidded compartments and mixing bowls, one glass bowl broken.
c1840 *29¼in (74cm) high*
£500-600 **DN**

A late Victorian walnut teapoy, the interior fitted with mixing bowls, labelled 'ROBERT ROUGH', hinge top loose, lifting and losses to veneer.
28½in (72.5cm) high
£400-500 **DRA**

A late 19thC French Second Empire giltwood, patinated metal and porcelain-mounted guéridon, the top depicting Napoleon, signed 'Seller', enclosed in a border of twelve portrait plaques.
23½in (60cm) diam
£4,000-5,000 **L&T**

An Irish exhibition yew wood carved fold-over tea-table, the frieze carved with a harp and shamrock sprays, on an ornate baluster stem, the quadruple pod adorned with shamrock, thistle and rose, on scroll legs.

This table was an exhibition piece displayed at the Irish International Exhibition, a world fair held in Dublin in 1907. The decision to hold the exhibition was taken at the Irish Industrial Conference in April 1903 and was inspired by a small exhibition in Cork (The Cork International Exhibition) five years earlier, which was intended to improve the trade of Irish goods.

38in (97cm) long
£14,000-18,000 **MEA**

A Federal mahogany, birch and rosewood veneer work table, attributed to Judkins and Senter, Portsmouth, New Hampshire, left rear leg broken and repaired.

c1810-20 *30¾in (78cm) high*

£5,500-6,000 **SK**

A Regency lacquer chinoiserie work table.

24½in (62cm) wide

£400-500 **BELL**

A Louis Philippe burr walnut sewing table.

16½in (42cm) diam

£450-500 **BLEA**

A George III mahogany architect's table, with a baize-lined sliding panel and compartments including a pivoted quadrant pen drawer, some wear, small crack to top.

c1760 *35¾in (91cm) wide*

£4,000-5,000 **DN**

A 17thC monk's oak tilt-top table, folding back to create a chair, later supports, seat split, later carving.

A monk's table is a dual piece of furniture, designed to save space. When the table is not in use, the top folds back to create a chair or settle. Tables of this type were made in Europe from the 16thC, although it is unclear whether they were actually used by monks.

37in (94cm) wide

£3,000-3,500 **CHOR**

A Regency mahogany horseshoe hunt table, attributed to Gillows, some wear, gouge to front right.

A hunt table is semi-circular drinking table, often with grooves for coasters and a well for decanters or unopened bottles. It was used for drinks and refreshments before and after a fox hunt.

67¾in (172cm) wide

£20,000-30,000 **CHOR**

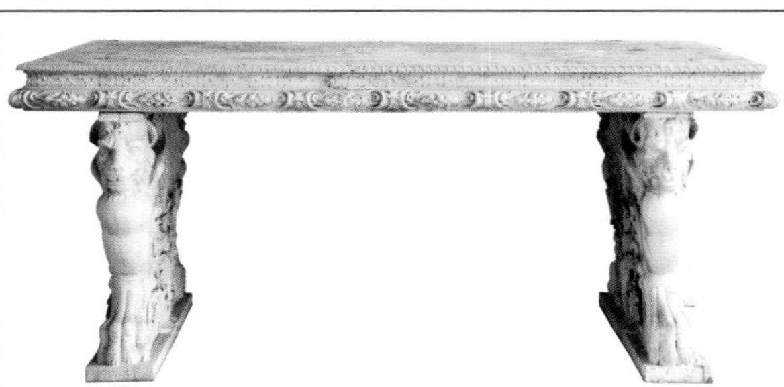

A 19thC Italian Istrian marble table, carved with a top panel of a griffin, the supports carved with winged lion monopedia and acanthus.

78¾in (200cm) wide

£25,000-30,000 **SWO**

A 19thC coromandel lacquer-topped low table, on a later stand, minor chips to stand, decorated refreshed.

59¾in (152cm) wide

£6,000-7,000 **DN**

A late 17thC oak dresser base, section missing from top, replacement escutcheons and handles.
68in (172.5cm) wide
£600-700 **PW**

A late 17thC oak dresser, on block and turned spiral twist cup and cover supports.
63¼in (160.5cm) wide
£3,500-4,000 **WW**

A joined ash open dresser.
c1700 *82¾in (210cm) long*
£1,800-2,200 **TEN**

A George II oak dresser, with three mahogany banded frieze drawers and an arc d'arbelète apron.
80½in (204.5cm) wide
£2,000-2,500 **WW**

A late 18thC oak dresser, some shrinkage and veneer losses.
91¾in (233cm) wide
£800-1,000 **CHEF**

A George III oak dresser base.
c1780 *65¾in (167cm) wide*
£1,100-1,500 **DN**

A 17thC oak dresser.
75½in (192cm) high
£900-1,200 **PW**

An early 18thC oak dresser, the plate rack with flared ogee pediment over a pierced arcaded frieze.
76in (193cm) wide
£4,000-4,500 **MART**

A George II oak dresser, the base with a central fretwork arch and planked pot shelf, later support for shelf, replacement brass handles.

80in (203cm) wide

£2,000-2,500 **PW**

A mid-18thC oak potboard dresser.

72¼in (183.5cm) high

£800-1,000 **WW**

An 18thC oak dresser, loose cornice section to the right hand side, stains to the top surface.

89¾in (228cm) wide

£4,000-4,500 **CHEF**

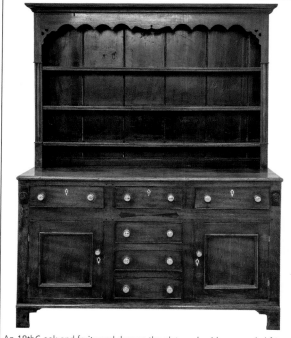

An 18thC oak and fruitwood dresser, the plate rack with an arcaded frieze, on later bracket feet.

80in (203cm) high

£3,000-3,500 **MART**

An 18thC Welsh Swansea Valley potboard dresser, some minor spots, minor undulation.

Dressers flourished from the 17thC, especially in Wales. Those made in South Wales were typically low dressers, with an open rack below a potboard, while North Wales dressers were tall, closed, with boards behind the upper shelves. Some mid-Wales dressers combined the northern and southern forms. Welsh dressers were made to be great showpieces, handed down from generation to generation, and were often embellished with decorative motifs.

82in (208cm) high

£1,200-1,600 **PFR**

An 18thC and later oak potboard dresser.

71¼in (181cm) wide

£1,500-2,000 **FLD**

An 18thC and later oak Welsh Conway Valley dresser.

58¾in (149cm) wide

£700-900 **WHP**

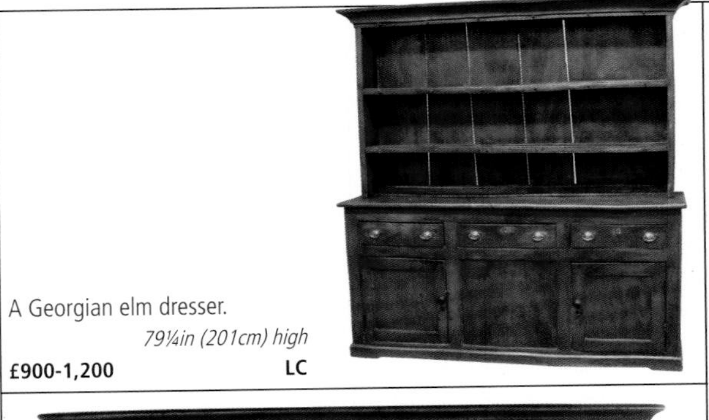

A Georgian elm dresser.
79¼in (201cm) high
£900-1,200 **LC**

A late 18thC George III oak potboard dresser base and associated plate rack canopy, some wear, drawers re-lined, split to frieze.
74in (188cm) high
£1,400-2,000 **DN**

A late 18thC George III oak open potboard dresser, some restoration.
77¼in (196cm) high
£1,400-2,000 **TEN**

A 18thC to 19thC George II-style oak Welsh dresser, possibly composed of earlier elements, backboard replaced.
83in (211cm) high
£800-1,200 **DRA**

A late 18thC to early 19thC oak Swansea Valley potboard dresser, some repairs, replacements, losses and cracks.
71¾in (182cm) high
£1,100-1,500 **PFR**

A George III enclosed dresser, some staining, rack possibly associated, base slightly bowed, some repairs.
c1800 *81¼in (206cm) high*
£700-900 **TEN**

A mid-19thC George II-style oak Welsh dresser, some repairs and replacements, braces to legs.
78in (198cm) wide
£800-1,000 **DRA**

A late 16thC Tuscan walnut side cupboard.

26¾in (68cm) wide

£1,800-2,200 **ROS**

A 17thC joined oak Westmorland Court cupboard, with lunette and guilloché carving, with initials 'ID', some decay and splits, repairs to hinges, one later shelf, later locks, dated.

1696 *70¾in (180cm) high*

£1,200-1,600 **TEN**

A George I black lacquer and gilt japanned hanging bowfront corner cupboard, attributed to John Belchier, some marks and scratches.

The design bears close relation to an example bearing John Belchier's trade label, and the quality of the decoration supports the attribution. John Belchier (fl.1717-53) owes his high reputation to a distinguished series of bureau cabinets decorated in green or scarlet japanning or veneered with fine cuts of burr walnut.

c1720 41¾in (106cm) high

£5,500-6,000 **DN**

A late 18thC painted poplar hanging cupboard, Pennsylvania, front surface worn down.

40in (101.5cm) high

£3,000-3,500 **POOK**

A late 17thC to early 18thC South German walnut and marquetry cupboard, some wear, some timber lacking to back boards, fabric lining distressed.

87¾in (223cm) high

£4,000-5,000 **DN**

A late 17thC to early 18thC panelled oak tridarn.

74¾in (190cm) high

£3,000-4,000 **SWO**

A pair of 18thC French crossbanded kingwood corner cupboards, with shaped Breche d'Alep marble tops, with gilt-metal mounts, marble cracked, bases restored.

32¾in (83cm) wide

£5,500-6,000 **BELL**

A late 18thC poplar two-part Dutch cupboard, Pennsylvania, with matchstick cornice, panels and spice drawers, some shrinkage, chips and cracks, brasses replaced.

83¾in (212.5cm) high

£7,500-8,000 **POOK**

A George III mahogany floor corner cupboard, swan-neck pediment with key pattern and rosette moulding.
87in (221cm) high
£3,500-4,000 **PW**

A George III oak hanging cupboard, on bracket feet.
78¾in (200cm) high
£1,800-2,200 **CHEF**

A painted pine and poplar two-part Dutch cupboard, Lancaster County, Pennsylvania, with faux tiger and crotch grain decoration, with smoke decorated doors.
c1830 *84¼in (214cm) high*
£38,000-42,000 **POOK**

An early 19thC Canadian painted pine Dutch cupboard.
85½in (217cm) high
£3,000-4,000 **POOK**

An early 19thC oak housekeeper's cupboard.
74in (188cm) wide
£2,000-2,500 **BRI**

An early to mid-19thC North European painted pine press cupboard.
81½in (207cm) wide
£750-850 **DN**

A 19thC Northern European painted pine cupboard, locked shut with no key, some wear.
70in (178cm) high
£500-600 **DN**

A 19thC oak and fruitwood marquetry court cupboard, with some late 16thC to early 17thC marquetry panels, some probably German.
63¾in (162cm) high
£2,000-3,000 **WW**

A George II mahogany clothes press, the panelled doors incorporating four false drawer fronts.
c1750 *83in (211cm) high*
£2,500-3,000 **DN**

An 18thC French oak armoire, with 'love-bird' carved cresting, stripped and limed, some warping, some timber loss.
90½in (230cm) high
£1,800-2,200 **CHEF**

An 18thC Dutch walnut and marquetry kas or armoire, inlaid with fruitwoods, mother-of-pearl and ivory.
95¼in (242cm) high
£7,000-8,000 **WW**

A New Jersey Chippendale highly figured walnut linen press.
c1780 *83½in (212cm) high*
£2,800-3,400 **POOK**

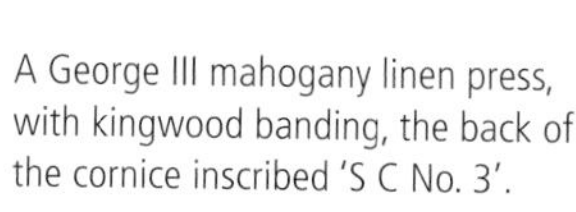

A George III mahogany linen press, with kingwood banding, the back of the cornice inscribed 'S C No. 3'.
82¾in (210cm) high
£3,000-4,000 **WW**

A Regency mahogany clothes press, in the manner of George Bullock.
c1815 *73¼in (186cm) high*
£1,500-2,000 **DN**

A George IV Channel Islands mahogany and satinwood strung clothes press, locks stamped 'Threshers, London', warping to inset panels, some replacement stringing, one section of moulding detached.
c1825 *85¾in (218cm) high*
£2,200-3,000 **DN**

A pair of 19thC japanned wardrobes, with chinoiserie decoration, the brass hinges stamped 'HORNE PATENT'.
72¼in (183.5cm) high
£5,000-6,000 **WW**

FURNITURE

A mid-to-late 15thC French oak chest.

81in (206cm) wide

£4,500-5,500 **SWO**

A 16thC Italian walnut cassone, carved with grotesques, birds and foliate scrolls centred by a profile portrait, with iron handles.

43¾in (111cm) wide

£3,000-3,500 **L&T**

A late 16thC to early 17thC Anglo-German oak and parquetry Nonsuch chest, inlaid with buildings and geometric borders, with iron handles.

Nonsuch chests are thought to have been made in Southwark by émigré German and Dutch cabinetmakers. Their decoration of parquetry spired buildings derive from prints by Hans Vredeman de Vries (1527-1604). They became to be known as 'Nonsuch' chests after Henry VIII's palace of Nonsuch because their decoration was thought, wrongly, to represent that building.

48½in (123cm) wide

£2,000-3,000 **WW**

A walnut cassone, dated.

1644 *58¼in (148cm) wide*

£2,200-2,800 **SWO**

A 17thC Italian walnut cassone.

69¼in (176cm) long

£3,500-4,000 **ECGW**

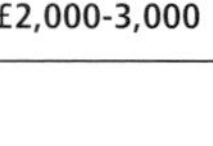

A late 17thC oak coffer, with bird carved frieze.

50in (127cm) wide

£500-600 **BRI**

An 18thC and later Welsh oak coffer bach.

69in (175.5cm) wide

£600-700 **WW**

An early 18thC North Italian painted cassone.

57in (145cm) long

£1,400-1,800 **BE**

A 19thC black lacquer chest, with chinoiserie decoration, the interior with a later lift-out metal liner.

Provenance: Castletown, Co. Kildare purchased c1910 for £9.

47¾in (121cm) wide

£4,000-5,000 **WW**

A painted dower chest, Pennsylvania, sponge-decoration with star panels, initialled 'IHC', dated.
1773 *50in (127cm) wide*
£2,800-3,400 **POOK**

A late 18thC painted pine dower chest, Pennsylvania, with panels of hearts and flowers.
48½in (123cm) wide
£3,000-4,000 **POOK**

A late 18thC paint-decorated blanket chest, New England, some moulding replaced.
48in (122cm) wide
£6,000-7,000 **SK**

A late 18thC Chippendale walnut blanket chest, Pennsylvania, with wrought iron hardware and brasses, newer blocking to feet.
46in (117cm) long
£2,800-3,400 **POOK**

A painted pine dower chest, Berks County, Pennsylvania, inscribed 'Cadarina Schefern', feet and brasses replaced, dated.
1816 *47¾in (121.5cm) wide*
£4,000-5,000 **POOK**

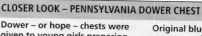

CLOSER LOOK – PENNSYLVANIA DOWER CHEST

Dower – or hope – chests were given to young girls preparing for marriage, and used to store household items, such as embroidery and linens.

Original blue painted grounds are rare and especially sought after, particularly when in excellent condition.

The chest is painted with unicorns, birds, horses and tulips, with a central ivory star medallion to the top.

The painted soldiers holding tulips on the lower drawers are rare on a chest like this.

A painted pine dower chest, Berks County, Pennsylvania.
c1775 *49in (124.5cm) wide*
£230,000-280,000 **POOK**

A painted pine dower chest, Lebanon County, Pennsylvania, minor wear.
c1815 *41½in (105.5cm) wide*
£9,000-10,000 **POOK**

A painted pine dower chest, Centre County, Pennsylvania, with trees, love birds and flowers, inscribed 'Daniel Houser', repaired breaks to foot facings, hardware replaced, dated.
1817 *47½in (120.5cm) wide*
£16,000-20,000 **POOK**

A Charles II oak chest-of-drawers, the top drawer not staying closed, minor losses.
c1660 *30in (76cm) wide*
£1,400-1,800 **DN**

A late 18thC William and Mary oak chest-of-drawers.
40¼in (102cm) wide
£1,500-2,000 **L&T**

A William and Mary oyster veneered chest-of-drawers, with sycamore crossbanding.
37½in (95cm) wide
£6,000-7,000 **LC**

A late 17thC to early 18thC oyster veneered chest-of-drawers, with holly banding and stringing.
35in (89cm) wide
£3,000-4,000 **HT**

CLOSER LOOK – STUDDED LEATHER CHEST

This chest is entirely covered in leather, with the exception of the pine back. English leather-covered trunks and chests were produced by coffer-makers, primarily intended for travelling.

The domed top has a coronet and initials 'C.R.'. This may relate to James Brydges, 8th Baron Chandos (1642-1714) or his son, also James Brydges and later 1st Duke of Chandos (1674-1744).

There is extensive studwork decoration to the front, top and sides, with scrolls, flowers and borders of hearts.

This piece may have been by William Johnson, who succeeded Richard Pigg Junior as Royal coffer-maker in 1707. The nailing patterns are similar to pieces made for the Royal household.

An early 18thC George I studded leather muniment or travelling chest, with one long and eight short drawers.

There are two notes attached to the interior, one reads: 'This chest with drawers is covered in horse-hide: it is possible, but not probable that it was a travelling chest: Mr Percy Macquoid inclines to the opinion it was not: the frame work of the stand and the upper part of the legs indicate that it was not so used: English: about 1640 A:D: Purchased: 1917: cost £65'. The second references a similar chest, sold by Sotheby's 6 December 1918, now on a later low stand.
40¼in (102.5cm) wide
£12,000-15,000 **SWO**

A Queen Anne olivewood oyster veneered chest-of-drawers, inlaid with holly banding, on later bracket feet.
40in (101.5cm) wide
£2,500-3,000 **WW**

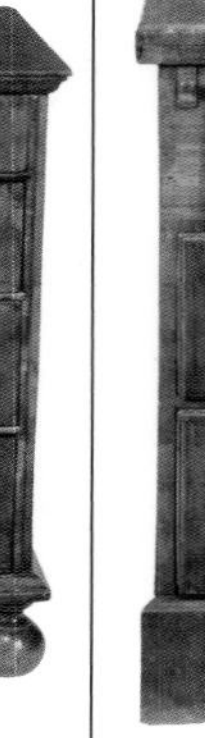

A Queen Anne walnut chest-of-drawers, inlaid with stringing, with quarter veneered and crossbanded top.
c1710 *38¼in (97cm) wide*
£4,500-5,000 **DN**

An early 18thC walnut bachelor's chest, the quarter-veneered hinged fold-over top with cross and feather banding.
30in (76cm) wide
£5,000-6,000 **WW**

ESSENTIAL REFERENCE – GILES GRENDY

Giles Grendy was an important furniture maker of the 18thC.

- **He was apprenticed in 1709, and by 1716 was established and taking on his own apprentices.**
- **He had a workshop in St John's Square, Clerkenwell, from where he ran a successful, largely export business.**
- **He made a large selection of furniture, including tables, chairs, mirrors and case furniture.**
- **Although it is known that he had a thriving workshop, firm attributions are rare, with little evidence of bills in country house records and few pieces still in existence bearing one of his two trade labels. However, a virtually identical chest to this, bearing the trade label of Giles Grendy, has been previously recorded.**

A George II walnut and featherbanded chest-of-drawers, attributed to Giles Grendey, with moulded quarter-veneered top, some old repairs, feet rollers lacking, handles and locks replaced.
c1740 *31½in (80cm) wide*
£25,000-30,000 **DN**

A George II mahogany harlequin bachelor's chest, the fold-over top with a baize surface and a rising secrétaire compartment, the front with three sham drawers, above two real drawers.
28in (71cm) wide
£2,000-2,500 **WW**

A George III mahogany serpentine chest-of-drawers.
c1760 *37½in (95cm) wide*
£5,500-6,500 **L&T**

A Pennsylvania Queen Anne walnut semi-tall chest-of-drawers, with herringbone inlays.
c1760 *38¾in (98.5cm) wide*
£3,000-3,500 **POOK**

A cherry chest-of-drawers, possibly Litchfield County, Connecticut, with fluted quarter-columns and a scalloped skirt, replacement brasses, refinished.
c1770 *39¼in (99.5cm) wide*
£5,000-6,000 **POOK**

A Queen Anne cherry chest-of-drawers, Pennsylvania, some repairs.
c1770 *34½in (87.5cm) wide*
£4,000-5,000 **POOK**

An 18thC Dutch floral marquetry inlaid walnut serpentine chest-of-drawers.
32¼in (82cm) wide
£1,500-2,000 **BELL**

A late 18thC Dutch floral marquetry inlaid chest-of-drawers, with later handles, some splits.
35¾in (91cm) wide
£1,500-2,000 **BELL**

A late 18thC birch chest-of-drawers, by Joseph Short, Newburyport, Massachusetts, shrinkage crack to left side.

36in (91.5cm) wide

£3,500-4,000 **SK**

An 18thC George III mahogany serpentine chest-of-drawers, the drawers with banded inlay.

43¼in (110cm) wide

£2,500-3,000 **L&T**

An 18thC George III oak and walnut double chest-of-drawers.

59¾in (152cm) wide

£2,500-3,000 **L&T**

A George III mahogany gentleman's dressing chest, in the manner of Gillows, inlaid with satinwood banding.

43in (109cm) wide

£5,000-6,000 **HAN**

A George III figured mahogany bachelor's chest, with a brushing slide, previously refinished, replacement brass fittings, filled shrinkage split.

29¾in (75.5cm) wide

£2,000-2,500 **MART**

A George III mahogany and crossbanded chest-of-drawers, the top drawer opening to a sliding panel.

c1800 *36¼in (92cm) wide*

£1,300-1,800 **DN**

A George III satinwood serpentine chest-of-drawers, with rosewood banding to top, some damage to veneers, water splash marks.

39in (99cm) wide

£3,000-3,500 **CHEF**

A George III serpentine mahogany chest-of-drawers, the top drawer with baize-covered slide with further compartments.

36¼in (92cm) wide

£3,000-4,000 **ECGW**

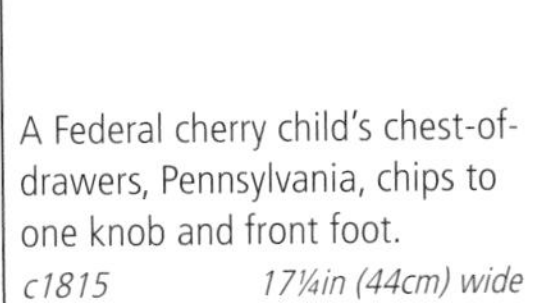

A Federal cherry child's chest-of-drawers, Pennsylvania, chips to one knob and front foot.

c1815 *17¼in (44cm) wide*

£2,500-3,000 **POOK**

A Sheraton tiger maple chest-of-drawers, Pennsylvania, with mahogany inlaid stiles, stains to top.
c1820 *42in (106.5cm) wide*
£3,000-4,000 **POOK**

A late Regency Channel Islands mahogany and tulipwood chequer-banded chest-of-drawers, some wear, some replacements to veneers.
c1820 *43¾in (111cm) wide*
£2,000-2,500 **DN**

A late Regency mahogany campaign washstand chest-of-drawers, the hinged top opening to a mirror and recesses, with tin wash basins.
32¾in (83cm) wide
£2,000-3,000 **L&T**

A painted pine child's chest-of-drawers, possibly by Lehn, Pennsylvania, minor wear.
c1830 *19in (48.5cm) wide*
£2,500-3,000 **POOK**

An early 19thC Anglo-Chinese teak campaign chest, in two halves, the top incised 'H.A.'.
Campaign chests were chests-of-drawers designed to be easy to break up or fold for ease for travelling, such as when on military campaigns.
29½in (75cm) wide
£3,000-3,500 **WW**

An early 19thC putty-painted pine blanket chest, New England, the top opening to a well, loose panel, minor paint wear.
38½in (98cm) wide
£3,000-3,500 **SK**

An early 19thC satinwood and mahogany chest-of-drawers, with crossbanded top, some wear, oak-lined.
46¾in (119cm) wide
£1,800-2,200 **DN**

A poplar chest-of-drawers, by John Sala, Soap Hollow, Pennsylvania, painted red with stencilled highlights, the sides with black-painted panels with date and initials 'LC', 'Manufactured By John Sala', minor wear, one scallop repaired to backsplash.
1871 *38in (96.5cm) wide*
£25,000-30,000 **POOK**

A 19thC mahogany serpentine chest-of-drawers, with brushing slide.
45¾in (116cm) wide
£4,500-5,000 **DUK**

A Louis XV to Louis XVI transitional kingwood marquetry block-front marble-topped commode.
37¾in (96cm) wide
£2,800-3,400 **BE**

A Louis XV kingwood and parquetry bombé commode, with breche violette marble top, the corners and feet mounted with ormolu mounts.
c1730 *52¾in (134cm) wide*
£10,000-14,000 **L&T**

An early 18thC Maltese olivewood and parquetry serpentine commode, with brass swan-neck handles supported by Maltese lions, cracks to veneer.
46in (117cm) wide
£2,500-3,000 **CHOR**

A Louis XV kingwood, tulip and ormolu-mounted bombé marble-topped commode, by Leonard Boudin.
c1750
£5,000-6,000 **JN**

A mid-18thC Austrian walnut parquetry petite commode, with gilt-metal mounts.
21¾in (55cm) wide
£500-600 **L&T**

A Louis XV kingwood and amaranth marble-topped marquetry commode, with gilt-metal mounts.
31½in (80cm) wide
£1,500-2,000 **L&T**

A Louis XV kingwood, inlaid and gilt-metal-mounted serpentine bombé marble-topped commode.
51½in (130.5cm) wide
£3,500-4,000 **BE**

A Louis XV serpentine kingwood marble-topped commode.
52in (132cm) wide
£3,500-4,000 **SWO**

An 18thC Sicilian painted and lacquered serpentine commode.
55½in (141cm) wide
£3,500-4,000 **BELL**

An 18thC Italian Neo-classical marquetry inlaid walnut commode, in the manner of Giuseppe Maggiolini, minor warp and losses of veneer, shrinkage splits, woodworm damage.

Giuseppe Maggiolini (1738-1814) was an important cabinet-maker from Milan, Italy. His work is characterised by superb Neo-classical and arabesque marquetry in walnut, olivewood, tulipwood and sometimes rosewood.

49¼in (125cm) wide

£4,000-4,500 **BELL**

An 18thC French marquetry marble-topped breakfront commode, ormolu mounts.

37in (94cm) wide

£4,000-4,500 **JN**

An 18thC French kingwood and ormolu marble-topped commode.

47in (119.5cm) wide

£3,500-4,000 **JN**

CLOSER LOOK – NORTH ITALIAN COMMODE

This commode has a pair of short drawers to the top, with a pair of long drawers beneath.

It is decorated with marquetry reserves depicting Neo-classical motifs, such as flowering urns, cornucopia and scrolling acanthus.

The style resembles that of influential Milanese Neo-classical cabinetmaker Giuseppe Maggiolini.

The detail is exquisite throughout.

One of a pair of North Italian walnut, tulipwood and marquetry commodes.

c1790

48¾in (124cm) wide

£20,000-25,000 the pair **DN**

An 18thC Italian marquetry inlaid walnut commode, with mythological figural and foliate scrolling decoration.

46¼in (117.5cm) wide

£5,000-6,000 **WAD**

A Dutch rosewood and marquetry serpentine commode, some warping to top, losses to veneer, shrinkage gaps.

c1780

39¾in (101cm) wide

£2,500-3,000 **DN**

A late 18thC George III satinwood and tulipwood commode, with crossbanding and painted floral panels, on trompe-l'oeil square legs, some scratches and splits, losses to veneer.

52¾in (134cm) wide

£4,500-5,000 **TEN**

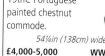

A French Directoire mahogany marble-topped commode.

50in (127cm) wide

£1,500-2,000 **WW**

A late 18thC to early 19thC Portuguese painted chestnut commode.

54¼in (138cm) wide

£4,000-5,000 **WW**

A late George III crossbanded satinwood and mahogany bow-front commode.

44½in (113cm) wide

£2,200-2,800 MOR

A 19thC Continental painted serpentine commode, some woodworm, splits to joins.

56¼in (143cm) wide

£3,500-4,000 DN

A pair of 19thC Italian marquetry inlaid walnut commodes, after Giuseppe Maggiolini, later suede lining, minor warping to veneer.

48¾in (124cm) wide

£7,000-8,000 BELL

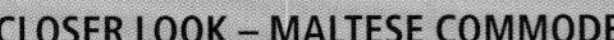

CLOSER LOOK – MALTESE COMMODE

This commode is inlaid with intricate seaweed marquetry panels.

There is a cartouche of a stag and hound to the top and panels of putti to the sides.

It was originally one of a pair owned by William Parnis, an eminent 19thC Maltese lawyer. It was inherited by his younger son and passed down by descent.

Despite some damage and wear, the aesthetic appeal of this piece ensures its value.

A Maltese marquetry commode, on ebonised bun feet, general wear, losses to veneer and inlay, splits to drawer bases.

62½in (159cm) wide

£35,000-40,000 CHOR

A 19thC French mahogany, parquetry and ormolu marble-topped petit commode.

35in (89cm) wide

£1,500-2,000 JN

A 19thC Italian walnut and marquetry commode.

34in (86.5cm) wide

£1,500-2,000 DUK

A late 19thC Italian-style marble-topped commode, stamped 'Gillows Lancaster'.

50¾in (129cm) wide

£1,500-2,000 LC

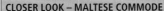

A late 19thC Louis XVI-style marble-topped commode, after Jean-Henri Riesener.

46¾in (119cm) wide

£5,000-6,000 WW

A French ormolu-mounted marble-topped kingwood and vernis Martin decorated bombé commode, with a paper label printed 'FOREST/ TAPISSERIE/EBENISTERIE/33, rue de Provence/PAR', light scratches.

Maison Forest was a renowned manufacturer and retailer in Paris in the late 19thC.

c1900 *35¾in (91cm) wide*

£5,000-6,000 BELL

A Jacobean geometric moulded and joined oak chest-on-stand, with some later additions and restoration.

50¾in (129cm) high

£1,500-2,000 **LSK**

A 17thC Continental moulded and panelled oak chest-on-stand, twenty-two drawers within.

54¼in (138cm) high

£4,000-5,000 **SWO**

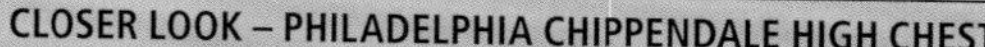

CLOSER LOOK – PHILADELPHIA CHIPPENDALE HIGH CHEST

While chests-on-stands were supplanted by chests-on-chests in late 18thC England, chests-on-stands, or high chests, remained fashionable in America, and were often influenced by Thomas Chippendale's designs.

This high chest has a broken-arch bonnet with applied floral carving.

The central drawer of the lower section is carved with Rococo shell and grasses.

In the USA today, high chests are amongst the most sought-after pieces of furniture on the collecting market.

A Philadelphia Chippendale walnut high chest, on cabriole legs with claw-and-ball feet.

c1770 *95in (241.5cm) high*

£18,000-22,000 **POOK**

A Queen Anne walnut crossbanded chest-on-stand.

60¼in (153cm) high

£1,200-1,600 **L&T**

A George I walnut chest-on-stand, inlaid with stringing, the back with an ivorine inventory label, inscribed 'J.G.L.105'.

55½in (141cm) high

£4,000-5,000 **WW**

A mid-18thC red-painted carved cherry high chest, by Elijah Booth, Woodbury, Connecticut, some replacements, some scratches, losses to thumb-moulding.

£9,000-11,000 **SK**

A Queen Anne tiger maple high chest, possibly New Jersey, minor repairs and replacements, lacking drops.

c1765 *73in (185.5cm) high*

£11,000-14,000 **POOK**

A Queen Anne Octorara tall chest, Chester County, Pennsylvania, with removable cabriole legs with lambrequin knees, some lip repairs.

Octorara chests typically stand on short detachable cabriole legs or have ogee feet with bracket cusps. This chest has a combination of both. The name derives from the Octoraro Creek in Pennsylvania.

c1780 *66in (167.5cm) high*

£8,500-9,500 **POOK**

A George I walnut chest-on-chest, with cross and feather-banded burr veneered drawers, the lowest drawer with a parquetry inlaid sunburst concave panel.

71½in (181.5cm) high

£9,000-11,000 **WW**

A George I walnut chest-on-chest, the lowest drawer with 'sunburst' marquetry panel, one handle off.

70in (178cm) high

£5,000-6,000 **CHEF**

An early 18thC walnut and crossbanded chest-on-chest, with a moulded dentil cornice.

67¾in (172cm) high

£3,000-4,000 **BE**

A mid-18thC elm chest-on-chest.

77¼in (196cm) high

£650-750 **BELL**

A mid-18thC George III mahogany chest-on-chest, with a blind fret carved frieze.

73½in (187cm) high

£2,200-2,800 **L&T**

A New England Chippendale maple chest-on-chest, with a bonnet top and fan-carved drawer.

c1770 *86½in (219.5cm) high*

£4,000-5,000 **POOK**

An 18thC walnut secrétaire chest-on-chest, with feather and crossbanding, sunburst inlay to bottom drawer.

42in (106.5cm) high

£1,000-1,300 **BRI**

A George III oak chest-on-chest, with pine-lined drawers, some wear and splits, replacement handles.
c1780 *69in (175cm) high*
£700-800 **DN**

A late 18thC George III mahogany chest-on-chest, minor faults to drawers.
70½in (179cm) high
£1,500-2,000 **TEN**

A George III mahogany chest-on-chest, with a Greek key frieze, the base with brushing slide.
c1790 *73¾in (187cm) high*
£1,800-2,200 **DN**

A George III mahogany chest-on-chest.
44in (112cm) high
£2,000-2,500 **BRI**

A George III mahogany chest-on-chest, with applied carved frieze and dentil cornice, on bracket feet.
48in (122cm) wide
£1,500-2,000 **FLD**

A George III mahogany bowfront chest-on-chest.
c1800 *61½in (156cm) high*
£600-700 **DN**

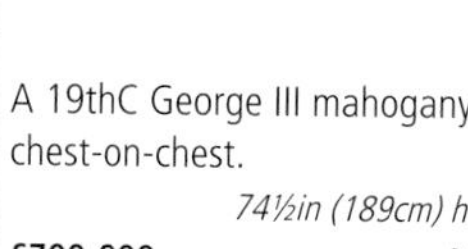

A 19thC George III mahogany chest-on-chest.
74½in (189cm) high
£700-800 **L&T**

A 19thC figured walnut chest-on-chest, with brass handles.
66¼in (168cm) high
£1,500-2,000 **ECGW**

A George II burr walnut secrétaire cabinet, the interior with twelve drawers, above a secrétaire drawer fitted with pigeonholes and further drawers.

76½in (194.5cm) high

£5,000-6,000 **WW**

A mid-18thC early George III mahogany secrétaire cabinet, brass handles to the sides.

79½in (202cm) high

£3,500-4,000 **L&T**

An 18thC and later secrétaire-on-chest, with feather and crossbanding, the fall enclosing pigeonholes and marquetry drawers, with a later leather writing surface.

49in (124.5cm) high

£3,000-4,000 **WW**

A late 18thC painted walnut two-part secrétaire, probably Lancaster County, Pennsylvania.

83½in (212cm) high

£8,000-9,000 **POOK**

A George III mahogany secrétaire cabinet, the interior with sixteen satinwood and rosewood crossbanded drawers, the base with a secrétaire above six short drawers.

78¾in (200cm) high

£4,000-5,000 **SWO**

A Regency fiddleback mahogany and gilt-metal-mounted secrétaire cabinet, in the manner of George Bullock, the fall opening to a leather inset, small drawers and pigeonholes, some marks and wear, some shelves lacking.

A related cabinet design is published in Richard Brown, 'The Rudiments of Drawing Cabinet and Upholstery Furniture' (1822), plate XVIII. Brown appears to have copied an unpublished design of George Bullock, who supplied a pair of bookcases of this form for New Longwood, the residence-in-exile of Napoleon.

c1815 *78¾in (200cm) high*

£5,000-6,000 **DN**

A 19thC Louis XVI-style mahogany, satinwood and parquetry secrétaire à abbatant, in the manner of Jean Henri Riesener, opening to an interior fitted for writing.

Jean-Henri Riesener (1734-1806) was one of the best-known cabinetmakers in France during the reign of Louis XVI.

55½in (141cm) high

£3,500-4,500 **L&T**

A Victorian pollard oak Wellington secrétaire chest, the second and third drawers fitted as a secrétaire.

51¼in (130cm) high

£3,500-4,000 **L&T**

An early George III mahogany secrétaire bookcase, with unusual pagoda moulding to base, some moulding and beading losses.

90½in (230cm) high

£20,000-25,000 **CHEF**

A Boston Massachusetts Chippendale mahogany secrétaire desk and bookcase, with flame carved finials, rosettes and centre pediment, on an oxbow form base with fan-carved interior.

c1770 *95in (241.5cm) high*

£10,000-14,000 **POOK**

A late 18thC George III mahogany secrétaire bookcase, with a secrétaire drawer fitted with drawers and pigeonholes.

43¼in (110cm) wide

£1,800-2,200 **L&T**

A late 18thC George III mahogany and inlay secrétaire bookcase, with a secrétaire drawer fitted with pigeonholes and drawers.

92½in (235cm) high

£2,500-3,000 **L&T**

A George III mahogany secrétaire bookcase, the secrétaire drawer enclosing an arrangement of drawers and pigeonholes.

c1800 *86½in (220cm) high*

£700-800 **DN**

A 19thC George III mahogany secrétaire bookcase, with a secrétaire drawer opening to pigeonholes and drawers.

91¾in (233cm) high

£1,200-1,800 **L&T**

A Pennsylvania or Southern Federal walnut secrétaire bookcase, the broken-arch bonnet with star inlaid rosettes, some losses, repairs and replacements.

c1810 *98½in (250cm) high*

£15,000-20,000 **POOK**

A Queen Anne walnut bureau bookcase, the interior with drawers and a central cupboard, the fall enclosing drawers and a well compartment, lacking original feet, door mirrors replaced by silk-backed glass.

81¼in (206cm) high

£4,000-5,000 **CHEF**

A George I walnut and burr walnut bureau bookcase, feather and crossbanded, with three adjustable shelves, a pair of candle slides, the stepped interior with pigeonholes and doors, with a sliding well cover and a later leather lined writing surface.

88in (223.5cm) high

£13,000-16,000 **WW**

A George I walnut bureau bookcase, with mirror doors and a featherbanded fall, the interior with pigeonholes and drawers, later mirror doors, some repairs.

83½in (212cm) high

£2,200-2,800 **TEN**

An early 18thC slope-front walnut bureau cabinet, the arch top door panels inlaid with boxwood and ebony string, the interior, with two concave cupboard doors, two secret compartments and pigeonholed compartment and drawers.

79in (201cm) high

£6,000-7,000 **MEA**

A pair of early 18thC black lacquer bureau bookcases-on-stands, the base with fall front.

60in (152.5cm) high

£9,000-12,000 **JN**

An early 18thC Italian walnut and marquetry bureau bookcase, possibly Genova, the fall revealing a later baize writing surface and eight drawers, with a sliding well cover and two secret drawers.

Provenance: Count Redmond Toler Clayton-Browne Clayton (1863-1937) of the Villa La Punta, Cervara, Santa Margherita, Liguria, Italy.

80in (203cm) high

£2,500-3,000 **WW**

An 18thC Dutch feather-banded figured walnut bureau cabinet, the fall enclosing a stepped and welled interior, restored, hole cut in back section of top.

92½in (235cm) high

£2,000-2,500 **BELL**

A George I walnut and burr walnut bureau cabinet, cross and feather banded, the hinged fall opening to pigeonholes and drawers, on later bracket feet.

76¾in (195cm) high

£4,000-5,000 **WW**

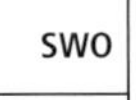

A George II walnut bureau bookcase, shelves and drawers within, losses and wear, replacement feet, back shelves missing.

£2,000-2,500 **SWO**

An 18thC Portuguese painted bureau cabinet, with faux marble and floral decoration, the doors enclosing shelves, the hinged fall revealing pigeonholes and drawers.

80in (203.5cm) high

£7,500-8,500 **WW**

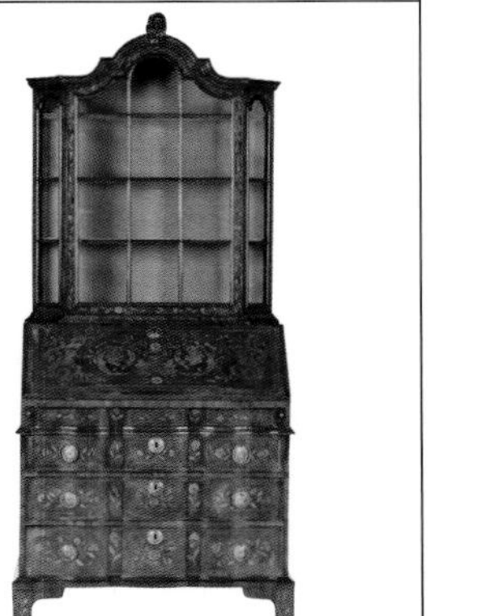

A 19thC Dutch walnut and marquetry bureau bookcase, with all over floral and bird marquetry, in three parts, with associated top.

87¾in (223cm) high

£4,500-5,500 **L&T**

A George II mahogany breakfront library bookcase, with a triangular arched pediment and diamond-shaped glazing bars, the base with panelled cupboards.

97in (246.5cm) high

£25,000-30,000 **DUK**

A 18thC George III mahogany breakfront bookcase, with a broken-arch pediment.

106¾in (271cm) high

£2,500-3,000 **L&T**

A George III and later mahogany secrétaire breakfront library bookcase, the doors with Prince of Wales plumes of feathers, with a sécretaire drawer fitted with pigeonholes and drawers, with satinwood faux-fluted secret pilaster compartments, with a leather-lined writing surface.

130in (330cm) wide

£4,000-5,000 **WW**

A George III mahogany breakfront bookcase.

85½in (217cm) wide

£3,500-4,000 **SWO**

A George III mahogany breakfront library bookcase, in the manner of Thomas Chippendale, some wear and replacements, previously cut in half.

This bookcase relates in design and scale to a pair of bookcases supplied by Thomas Chippendale to Sir Lawrence Dundas (1712-81) for his library at 19 Arlington Street, Piccadilly, London and for his country seat in Yorkshire Aske Hall in 1764. The Arlington and Aske bookcases, invoiced at £80 and £73 respectively, were the most expensive items of furniture on Chippendale's invoice to Sir Lawrence Dundas.

c1780 *149½in (380cm) wide*

£12,000-15,000 **DN**

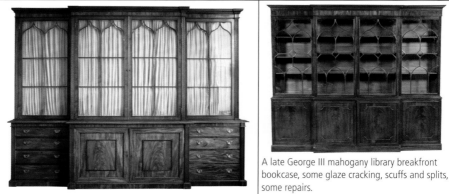

A late 18thC George III mahogany breakfront library bookcase, after a design by Thomas Sheraton, with moulded cornice and tassel moulded frieze.

The designs for the astragal moulding on the doors of the present bookcase are taken directly from Thomas Sheraton's 'Cabinet-Maker and Upholsterer's Drawing Book', 1791.

124in (315cm) wide

£11,500-13,500 **L&T**

A George III mahogany breakfront bookcase, with four glazed doors with arched astragals and fabric linings within fluted columns, the base with two panelled doors flanked by two banks of drawers.

137¾in (350cm) wide

£6,500-7,500 **SWO**

A late George III mahogany library breakfront bookcase, some glaze cracking, scuffs and splits, some repairs.

96¾in (246cm) wide

£4,000-5,000 **TEN**

An Irish Regency mahogany and ebony breakfront bookcase, with ebony line inlay, one door stamped '1083'.

89in (226cm) high

£9,500-11,500 **L&T**

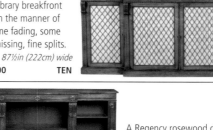

An early 19thC Regency rosewood library breakfront bookcase, in the manner of Gillows, some fading, some moulding missing, fine splits.

87½in (222cm) wide

£4,000-5,000 **TEN**

A Regency rosewood dwarf breakfront bookcase.

72½in (184cm) wide

£3,500-4,000 **L&T**

A Victorian mahogany breakfront library bookcase, with reeded foliate scroll corbels flanking the cupboards.

86in (218.5cm) long

£1,500-2,000 **BE**

A Victorian oak breakfront bookcase, in the Gothic Revival taste, the stepped castellated cornice with pine cone finials, some replacement locks, general wear and fading.

c1880 *120in (305cm) wide*

£4,000-5,000 **DN**

CLOSER LOOK – BREAKFRONT BOOKCASE

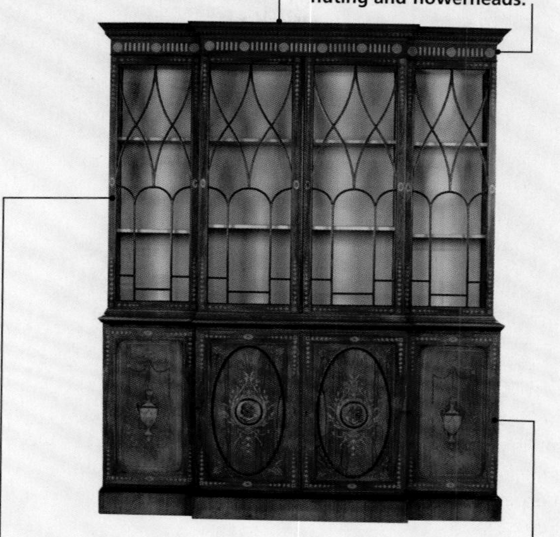

This bookcase is of exhibition quality in the Sheraton taste.

The dentil moulded cornice sits above a frieze inlaid with fluting and flowerheads.

The astragal glazed doors are inlaid with husk trails.

The base has four panel doors, two painted with en grisaille roundels of Classical busts, two inlaid with ribbon-tied garlands and urns.

A late 19thC rosewood, satinwood, mahogany, marquetry ebonised and polychromed breakfront bookcase.

91¾in (233cm) high

£15,000-20,000 **L&T**

A Regency mahogany 'Gothick' bookcase on stand, the astragal and arch moulded glazed doors opening to shelves, the stand with a fret moulded apron.

81in (206cm) high

£1,200-1,600 **L&T**

An early 19thC red-painted 'Harvard' stacking bookcase, probably Massachusetts, some losses and cracks.

102in (259cm) high

£7,000-8,000 **SK**

An early 19thC satinwood bookcase cabinet, inlaid with ebonised stringing, with detachable Classical pediment.

82in (208.5cm) high

£2,500-3,000 **WW**

A Victorian burr oak bookcase.

98½in (250cm) high

£1,000-1,400 **MOR**

A late Victorian oak bookcase, in the manner of A.W.N. Pugin, the frieze decorated with courtly musicians in a landscape.

101¼in (257cm) high

£5,000-6,000 **BE**

A Regency green painted pine bookcase cabinet.

45¾in (116cm) high

£1,000-1,400 **L&T**

A Regency mahogany double-sided bookcase, on a writhen turned pedestal and four moulded cabriole legs, carved leaf caps and brass casters.

27½in (70cm) wide

£1,300-1,600 **MOR**

One of a pair of Regency mahogany waterfall bookcases, on turned feet with brass caps and casters.

c1815 *33in (84cm) wide*

£7,000-8,000 the pair **DN**

A Regency lacquered, painted and parcel gilt waterfall bookcase, the lower cupboard with a reverse-painted glass panel, some wear, chips to paint, gilt rubbed.

c1815 *54in (137cm) high*

£1,000-1,400 **DN**

A Regency simulated rosewood waterfall bookcase cabinet.

c1815 *47¼in (120cm) high*

£650-750 **DN**

An early Victorian marble-topped mahogany glazed bookcase cabinet.

c1840 *52¼in (133cm) wide*

£950-1,100 **HAN**

A Victorian marble-topped mahogany and ebonised beaded low bookcase, stamped 'Holland & Sons'.

64½in (164cm) wide

£4,000-5,000 **BE**

A 19thC Louis XIV-style ormolu-mounted figured walnut ebony and ebonised open bookcase, with winding mechanism for retractable silk cover, slight fading.

66½in (169cm) wide

£2,800-3,200 **BELL**

A late 16thC Flemish oak cabinet, carved with strapwork panels and fluted pilasters, the lower section with Romayne head panels, split to one panel.

66½in (169cm) high

£2,500-3,000 **SWO**

A late 18thC to early 19thC Dutch walnut and floral marquetry domed display cabinet, of canted outline.

85in (216cm) high

£1,800-2,200 **BE**

A William IV rosewood collector's cabinet, with thirty small drawers behind arched panel doors, flanked by Classical columns.

52¾in (134cm) high

£1,500-2,200 **CHEF**

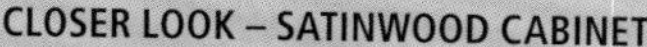

CLOSER LOOK – SATINWOOD CABINET

This cabinet of is exhibition quality and in excellent condition.

It may have been made by Holland and Sons, manufacturers to Queen Victoria.

There is inlaid, strung and crossbanded decoration throughout, and ormolu mounts with intricate foliate details.

The single panelled door is beautifully inlaid in bone and various woods with ribbon-tied musical instruments, scrolling foliage and geometric motifs.

A mid-18thC satinwood cabinet.

59½in (151cm) high

£25,000-30,000 **SWO**

A 19thC walnut and floral marquetry bombé cabinet.

79in (200.5cm) high

£2,200-2,600 **BRI**

An early 19thC dovetail-constructed painted spice cabinet, New England, with twenty-four named drawers, one drawer replaced, bracket base replaced.

48½in (123cm) high

£5,500-6,500 **SK**

A 19thC rosewood, tulipwood and ormolu-mounted breakfront cabinet, in the Louis XV style, with inset porcelain panels depicting 18thC figures, some scuffs and veneer losses, one split.

62¼in (158cm) wide

£15,000-20,000 **TEN**

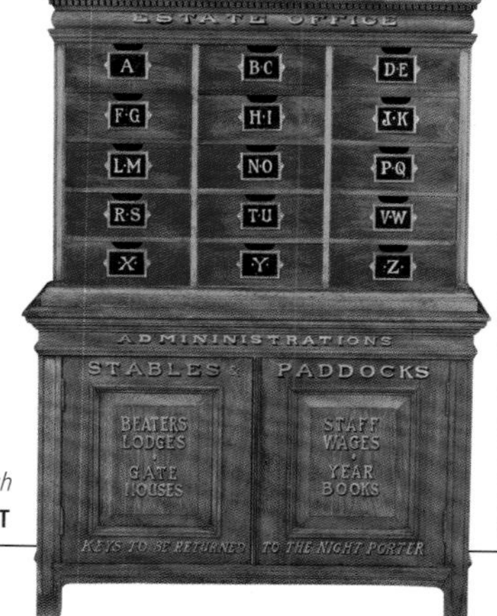

A late Victorian oak estate cabinet, the top with fifteen short drawers with painted labels, the base with labelled cupboard doors opening to a shelved interior.

61in (155cm) high

£1,600-2,000 **L&T**

A late 19thC Italian ebonised and tortoiseshell display cabinet, with ivory marquetry panels of grotesques, applied with lapis lazuli and hardstone cabouchons.

67¼in (170.5cm) high

£2,500-3,000 **WW**

A late 19thC French kingwood, parquetry, marquetry and gilt-metal-mounted breakfront vitrine, the sides with shaped projecting angles headed with sculptured Classical masks.

70¾in (180cm) high

£13,000-15,000 **BE**

A late 19thC Louis XV-style vernis Martin bombé display cabinet, veneered in kingwood, with five painted panels, with brass mounts.

Vernis Martin was developed by the Martin family, an 18thC French family of artists. The Martins included four brothers, Guillaume, Julien, Robert and Étienne-Simon, and Robert's son Jean-Alexandre. Vernis Martin was a japanning or lacquer technique designed to imitate East Asian lacquer, used widely in 18thC and early 19thC France.

76in (193cm) high

£5,500-6,500 **PW**

An early 20thC French kingwood and vernis Martin marble-top display cabinet, the frieze with gilt-metal rams' masks, laurel garlands, and musical trophies.

56¼in (143cm) high

£5,000-6,000 **L&T**

An Edwardian satinwood standing corner cabinet, with Howard & Sons label.

74¾in (190cm) high

£1,500-2,000 **MOR**

ESSENTIAL REFERENCE – FRANÇOIS LINKE

François Linke (1855-1946) was an important Parisian cabinetmaker of the late 19thC and early 20thC and one of the key figures of the Louis XVI Revival movement.

- **He was born in Pankraz, in what is now the Czech Republic, and moved to Paris at the age of twenty.**
- **By 1881 he had established a workshop in Paris in the Faubourg St Antoine.**
- **He was soon known for the exceedingly high quality of his craftsmanship, and his impressive ability to work in wood carving, bronze and marquetry.**
- **He won the gold medal at the Paris Exposition Universelle in 1900.**
- **He took inspiration from Louis XV and XVI furniture, and his work typically includes fine lavish mounts applied to comparatively plain structures of quarter-veneered kingwood or tulipwood.**
- **Pieces by or attributed to François Linke often fetch higher prices than work by earlier cabinetmakers.**

A late 19thC to early 20thC French kingwood vitrine cabinet, in the manner of François Linke.

77¼in (196cm) high

£9,000-11,000 **L&T**

A 17thC Flemish tortoiseshell and ebony cabinet-on-stand, possibly Antwerp, with painted scenes from the Life of Christ, the inlaid interior with mirror back, some restoration.

70¾in (180cm) high

£8,000-9,000 **CHOR**

A William and Mary black japanned cabinet-on-stand, decorated with chinoiserie pavilions and figures, the interior with twelve drawers, on a later silvered carved stand.

65½in (166.5cm) high

£3,500-4,500 **DUK**

A William and Mary collector's cabinet-on-stand, of oyster veneered laburnum wood, on a later inlaid stand.

45¾in (116cm) high

£3,500-4,000 SWO

A William III walnut and crossbanded cabinet-on-stand, the interior with eleven drawers and a cupboard with three further drawers, on later stand, some wear, splits to doors, later handles and hinges.

c1695 *59in (150cm) high*

£2,000-2,500 DN

CLOSER LOOK – ITALIAN CABINET-ON-STAND

This cabinet has a central pietra dura panel of a parrot amongst fruit and foliage. Pietra dura is an inlay technique, where semi-precious stones are used in mosaic form to create a picture.

This panel is flanked by metal capped columns and pietra dura simulated drawers within ripple moulding.

The lower section has a further panel of parrots, above tapered fluted legs joined by an X-form stretcher.

The quality and condition of the piece are superb.

A 19thC Italian ebony pietra dura and gilt-metal cabinet-on-stand, opening to reveal a shelved interior.

c1840 *62¼in (158cm) high*

£80,000-100,000 DUK

A late 17thC to early 18thC Continental walnut, rosewood, tortoiseshell and ivory cabinet-on-stand, Dutch or Flemish, some possible restoration.

47¼in (120cm) wide

£2,500-3,000 DN

An 18thC Dutch rosewood and ebony Baroque cabinet-on-stand or luiermanskastje, with ripple mouldings, floral carving and three Corinthian capital pilasters.

79¼in (201.5cm) high

£5,000-6,000 WW

An 18thC mahogany Chippendale-style display cabinet, interior worn, some glass cracked.

70½in (179cm) high

£3,000-3,500 SWO

A late 18thC Continental walnut side cabinet, inlaid with marquetry baskets of flowers, interior with five short drawers and single shelf, base with long frieze drawer, on square-section tapered legs with wavy stretchers.

7in (195.5cm) high

£4,000-5,000 PW

A mid-19thC walnut and marquetry inlaid credenza, the top and frieze inlaid with satinwood marquetry, the door with marquetry depicting a musical theme.

A credenza is a long side cabinet with shelves at either end. They were popular in the mid-to-late 19thC.

£4,000-4,500 **HAN**

A Victorian walnut credenza, the central panel door with satinwood inlay, fronted by turned and fluted pilasters with gilt-metal Corinthian capitals.

78in (198cm) wide

£1,500-2,000 **BRI**

A Victorian gilt-metal-mounted marquetry inlaid figured walnut credenza.

59½in (151cm) wide

£1,600-2,000 **BELL**

A Victorian gilt-metal-mounted figured walnut credenza, with ceramic-mounted central panel door.

72in (183cm) wide

£1,200-1,500 **BELL**

A Victorian figured walnut, marquetry inlaid and gilt-metal-mounted breakfront credenza, the centre panelled door with proud pilasters.

67in (170cm) wide

£1,600-2,000 **LSK**

A Regency mahogany and marble-topped fitted chiffonier, enclosing three flights of eight drawers.

49¼in (125cm) wide

£2,000-2,500 **LSK**

An early 19thC Regency rosewood chiffonier, crack to central mirror, small losses to the carved decoration.

48½in (123cm) high

£1,800-2,200 **TEN**

A William IV mahogany chiffonier.

77¼in (196cm) high

£750-850 **SWO**

A late 17thC to early 18thC Flemish ebony and kingwood cabinet, inlaid with ivory stringing, with geometric panelled decoration, on an associated later ebonised stand.

40½in (103cm) wide

£3,000-3,500 **WW**

A Regency rosewood and brass-mounted secrétaire side cabinet, in the manner of Gillows, with a later leather writing surface.

33½in (85cm) wide

£3,500-4,500 **WW**

A Regency rosewood marble-topped side cabinet, with reeded column angles, on turned toupie feet.

37in (94cm) wide

£5,000-6,000 **L&T**

CLOSER LOOK – SIDE CABINET

This sideboard has a shaped Carrara marble top, above a frieze decorated with stars and roundels.

It has a hinged lattice door with faux leather book spines, flanked by columns with Egyptian Revival sphinx heads and concave mirrored shelves.

It stands on high-quality carved lion's paw feet.

It is in the manner of James Newton (1773-1821), a prominent Regency cabinetmaker.

One of a pair of Regency rosewood and giltwood side cabinets.

51½in (131cm) wide

£45,000-50,000 the pair **WW**

A Regency rosewood and brass inlaid marble-topped side cabinet, the frieze inlaid with cut brass panels, on ebonised turned feet.

50in (127cm) wide

£1,100-1,500 **L&T**

A Regency rosewood and brass inlaid side cabinet, in the manner of John McLean, the frieze with a gilt-metal mount depicting a male mask, the shaped outset corners with female mask mounts, some wear, internal shelf lacking.

c1815 *47¼in (120cm) wide*

£8,000-10,000 **DN**

A Regency rosewood and brass inlaid low breakfront side cabinet, with brass inlaid doors and grille inserts lined with silk.

100in (254cm) long

£1,200-1,600 **L&T**

A William IV marble-topped side cabinet, in the manner of Marsh & Tatham, repaired split to marble, chipping to gilt scrolls, one rosette detached.

73½in (187cm) wide

£3,500-4,000 **BELL**

An early 19thC Anglo-Indian rosewood side cabinet, the doors carved and centred by leaf carved roundels, on carved paw feet.

60¾in (154cm) wide

£5,000-6,000 **L&T**

A pair of mid-19thC kingwood, crossbanded and gilt-metal-mounted pier cabinets, with applied scagliola panels, the canted angles headed with palmette, foliate and scroll ornament.

31in (79cm) wide

£7,500-8,500 **BE**

A pair of Napoleon III gilt-metal-mounted premier and contra-partie boullework side cabinets, the protective glass tops scratched and chipped, minor rubbing to ebonising.

31½in (80cm) wide

£3,500-4,500 **BELL**

A 19thC French rosewood, harewood and ormolu-mounted glazed standing side cabinet.

53in (134.5cm) wide

£1,100-1,400 **TRI**

A pair of 19thC specimen wood floral marquetry inlaid bowfront corner cabinets.

27½in (70cm) wide

£1,800-2,200 **BELL**

A Victorian walnut and tulipwood banded display/side cabinet, with vitrine top above two drawers, some wear.

c1880 *31in (79cm) wide*

£1,000-1,500 **DN**

An early 20thC satinwood vitrine or bijouterie cabinet, on square tapered legs, lacking cross-stretcher.

19in (48cm) wide

£950-1,100 **FLD**

An early 18thC Queen Anne burr walnut miniature apothecary's cabinet, with a fitted interior, some marks and shrinkage, minor restoration.

20½in (52cm) wide

£5,000-6,000 **DN**

A George II walnut side cabinet, the fold-over top above a frieze drawer, with a fitted interior.

31in (78.5cm) wide

£1,100-1,600 **CHOR**

An early 19thC late George III mahogany and satinwood crossbanded breakfront sideboard, with two inlaid shell medallions, outlined with plain and chequer stringing.

94½in (240cm) wide

£1,000-1,500 **L&T**

A Regency mahogany three-piece sideboard, with ebonised beaded frieze with applied cast bronze leaf and fruit wreaths, raised on a pair of carved, painted, bronze-effect 'panther' monopodia, flanked by matching pedestals.

96in (244cm) wide

£6,500-7,500 **SWO**

A 19thC Sheraton-style mahogany and inlaid sideboard, with satinwood crossbanding and marquetry inlays.

66¼in (168cm) wide

£1,800-2,200 **LSK**

A Scottish Regency mahogany sideboard, by James Mein, Kelso, with ebonised decoration, maker's label inside drawer 'JAMES MEIN/ CABINET MAKER/KELSO'.

The Mein family were cabinetmakers in Kelso, Scotland, c1784-1851. After James Mein the Elder died in 1830, his nephew, also called James Mein, took over the business until it went bankrupt in 1851. Their patrons included the 5th and 6th Dukes of Roxburghe for Floors Castle and the Earl of Haddington for Mellerstain.

c1830 *70in (178cm) wide*

£4,000-5,000 **L&T**

A Mid-Atlantic Sheraton mahogany and tiger maple sideboard, some veneer/inlay repairs.

The Mid-Atlantic region of the USA sits roughly in the middle of the East Coast, located between New England and the South Atlantic states. The region includes Delaware, Maryland, New York, New Jersey, Pennsylvania, Washington D.C., Virginia and West Virginia.

c1830 *78in (198cm) wide*

£3,000-3,500 **POOK**

A Gothic Revival Marsh & Jones inlaid oak sideboard, attributed to Charles Bevan.

c1870 *96in (244cm) wide*

£9,000-10,000 **L&T**

A late Victorian oak sideboard, the raised back with a dentil and carved frieze over five leaded glass doors and turned Ionic columns, the base with two panelled doors, one enclosing a cellaret.

106¾in (271cm) wide

£2,500-3,000 **SWO**

A George III mahogany partner's desk, the locks signed 'Joseph Brammah', replacement handles, splits to leather top.
c1770 *47¾in (121cm) wide*
£2,200-2,800 **DN**

A George III mahogany pedestal desk.
c1780 *67¾in (172cm) wide*
£750-850 **DN**

A George III mahogany four-pedestal partner's desk, inset with a later tooled suede writing surface, with outline mouldings, on casters.
43¼in (110cm) wide
£4,000-4,500 **WW**

A George III mahogany pedestal desk.
49¼in (125cm) wide
£2,000-2,500 **HAN**

A Charles X birch and ebonised partner's desk, with later gilt-tooled leather inset, on moulded block feet, one small section lacking.
c1830 *61in (155cm) wide*
£1,000-1,500 **DN**

A mid-19thC camphorwood and ebony campaign desk, with fitted inset brass sunken handles, lacking feet, top worn, some losses and splits.
47in (119.5cm) wide
£1,800-2,200 **SWO**

A Victorian brass-bound pollard oak partner's desk, with replacement green skiver, one side sun-bleached, fine cracks to veneers.
63in (160cm) wide
£4,500-5,000 **GORL**

A Victorian oak pedestal desk, by Edwards & Roberts, with later leather top, chips to handles, key missing.

Edwards & Roberts was founded in 1845 and became one of the leading London cabinetmakers of the 19thC, producing high-quality new furniture and also restoring, adapting and making replicas of earlier English and French pieces. The firm's pieces were typically of Georgian design, often with satinwood marquetry.

54in (137cm) wide
£800-900 **BELL**

A Victorian mahogany partner's desk.
71¾in (182cm) wide
£1,800-2,200 **L&T**

An early Georgian walnut kneehole desk, veneered with feather banding, with brass drop handles.

31in (78.5cm) wide

£4,000-5,000 **HT**

A George II mahogany kneehole desk.

35¾in (91.5cm) wide

£1,000-1,500 **WW**

An 18thC walnut kneehole pedestal desk.

29¼in (74cm) wide

£1,500-2,000 **APAR**

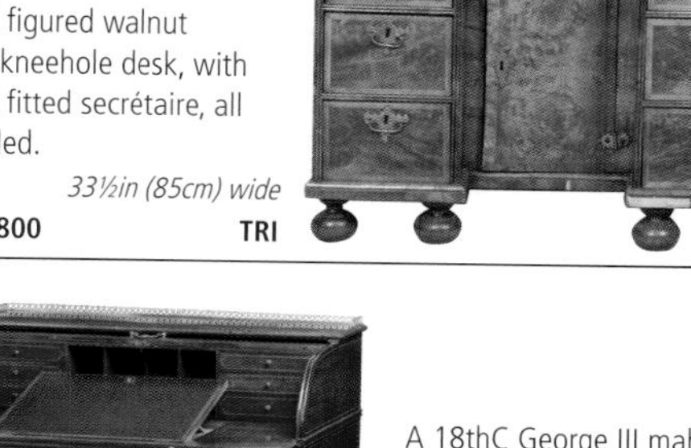

An 18thC figured walnut veneered kneehole desk, with a pull-out fitted secrétaire, all crossbanded.

33½in (85cm) wide

£1,300-1,800 **TRI**

A late 19thC lacquer chinoiserie kneehole writing desk, two handles lacking backing screws, central drawer damaged.

51¼in (130cm) wide

£1,800-2,200 **BELL**

A 18thC George III mahogany and inlay roll-top desk, the top enclosing drawers and pigeonholes, with a pull-out ratchet adjusted leather writing surface.

43in (109cm) wide

£2,500-3,000 **L&T**

A mid-Victorian mahogany Carlton House desk, polished and restored, drawer linings replaced.

Carlton House desks were developed during the Regency period, and named after the London home of the Prince of Wales (later George IV).They were typically made from mahogany and satinwood, and characterised by a superstructure of drawers and pigeonholes running along the back and sides of the desk.

47¾in (121cm) wide

£3,000-3,500 **TEN**

A Sheraton revival desk, painted with cherubs, replacement leather top.

40¼in (102cm) wide

£1,500-2,000 **CHOR**

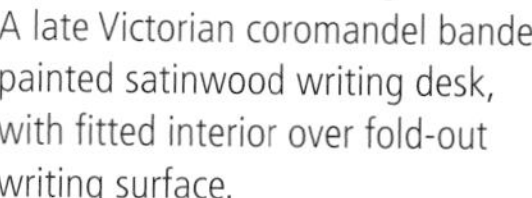

A late Victorian coromandel banded painted satinwood writing desk, with fitted interior over fold-out writing surface.

24¾in (63cm) wide

£1,500-2,000 **BELL**

A George III satinwood, mahogany and ebony bonheur-du-jour.

28¼in (72cm) wide

£1,800-2,200 **L&T**

A Regency rosewood bonheur-du-jour, inlaid with boxwood and brass, with a lidded pen tray and inkwell compartment, the right side with a pull-out sewing frame.

23in (58.5cm) wide

£1,800-2,200 **WW**

A Victorian walnut bonheur-du-jour, on cabriole supports with ormolu mounts.

42in (106.5cm) high

£1,000-1,500 **BRI**

A 19thC French marquetry inlaid gilt-metal-mounted rosewood bonheur-du-jour, restored.

34¾in (88cm) wide

£2,200-2,800 **BELL**

A late Victorian ebonised amboyna, gilt-metal-mounted and porcelain plaque adorned bonheur-du-jour, lacking feet.

53¼in (135cm) wide

£3,000-4,000 **APAR**

A late 19thC Louis XVI-style tulipwood, satinwood and purple heart bonheur-du-jour, with Sèvres-style porcelain mounts.

48in (122cm) wide

£2,000-2,500 **TEN**

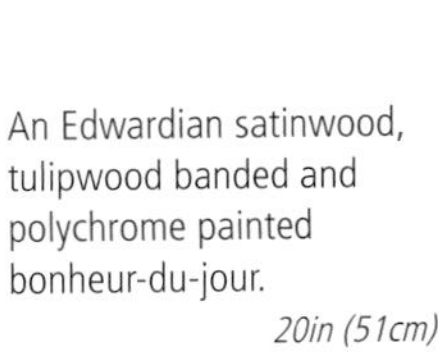

An Edwardian satinwood, tulipwood banded and polychrome painted bonheur-du-jour.

20in (51cm) wide

£2,000-2,500 **TEN**

A French kingwood brass-mounted bonheur-du-jour, inset with painted porcelain ovals, with a pull-out writing surface.

28in (71cm) wide

£2,500-3,000 **MEA**

An early 18thC oak bureau, on bracket feet.

25in (63.5cm) high

£1,200-1,600 **BRI**

A Chippendale-style carved mahogany block-front slant-lid desk, scratches to left side, replacement feet, some repairs and damages.

39¾in (101cm) wide

£2,200-2,800 **SK**

CLOSER LOOK – JAPANNED BUREAU

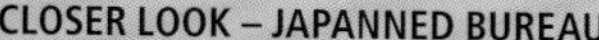

Japanning was a technique developed in Britain in the 17thC to 19thC in order to imitate imported Asian lacquer.

This bureau is intricately decorated, with floral and figural motifs, and a scene of figures and temples to the slanting front panel.

Beneath are two long drawers, on a separate stand with a pierced frieze, raised on cabriole legs.

The panel opens to an interior with pigeonholes and drawers, all with further decoration.

An early 18thC George I japanned bureau.

27¼in (69cm) wide

£8,500-9,500 **L&T**

A mid-18thC George III mahogany slant-front bureau, opening to drawers and pigeonholes.

43in (109cm) wide

£2,000-3,000 **L&T**

A late 18thC George III rosewood and padouk bureau.

49¼in (125cm) wide

£800-900 **DN**

A George III mahogany campaign bureau, in two sections, with pull-out writing surface, fitted with pigeonholes and drawers.

c1770

34¼in (87cm) wide

£3,000-4,000 **HAN**

A late 18thC Continental south German or Italian fruitwood and marquetry bureau, with ebonised carved decoration, inlaid with figures with ivory details.

48½in (123.5cm) wide

£1,300-1,800 **WW**

A George III walnut writing bureau, the crossbanded fall opening to a fitted interior with boxwood stringing, replacement brass batwing escutcheons.

35½in (90cm) wide

£500-600 LSK

An early 19thC Dutch mahogany and marquetry cylinder bureau, the fall with drawers and pigeonholes, some wear and repairs.

46in (117cm) wide

£1,500-2,000 DN

A Regency campaign cylinder-top bureau, with a writing slide and pigeonholes and drawers, brass handles to the sides.

42½in (108cm) high

£1,800-2,200 L&T

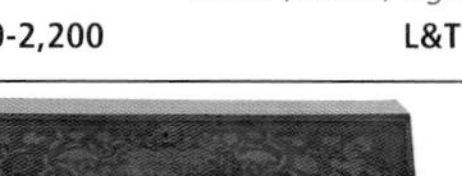

A 19thC Dutch walnut and marquetry inlaid writing bureau, with a fitted interior with a well.

44in (112cm) wide

£2,000-2,500 LSK

A late 19thC Italian cylinder bureau, by Luigi Pasquale (1822-94), with inlaid decoration, with Luigi Pasquale paper label, inscribed 'Ricordo sagliano 1880 Pietro Micca'.

Pietro Micca was a hero of the city of Turin when in 1706 he sacrificed his own life for the good of the city in blowing up a tunnel with French soldiers about to attack.

1880 *34¼in (87cm) wide*

£3,000-4,000 APAR

A 19thC Dutch mahogany and marquetry inlaid cylinder bureau, some shrinkage, small veneer losses.

47¼in (120cm) wide

£1,200-1,600 TEN

A late 19thC Louis XV-style kingwood bureau-de-dame, the roll-top with a vernis Martin panel.

33in (84cm) wide

£650-750 L&T

A late 19thC to early 20thC Louis XVI-style mahogany, parquetry and ormolu-mounted bureau-à-cylindre, Paris, after a model by Jean-Henri Riesener, possibly by François Linke, some interior drawers lacking, wear to writing surface.

42½in (108cm) wide

£7,000-9,000 DN

ESSENTIAL REFERENCE – DAVENPORTS

The Davenport developed in the late 18thC. It is a type of desk or small writing cabinet.

- **Gillows made a desk of this type for a Captain Davenport in the 1790s – hence the name.**
- **The basic form consisted of a small chest-of-drawers, with a desk compartment on top, sometimes with pull-out slides to hold papers or finished letters.**
- **Davenports are typically symmetrical, with dummy drawers on one side to match the real ones. The finest examples often have secret drawers.**
- **For most of the 19thC, Davenports were used by women.**
- **Mahogany was the most popular wood for Davenports, but rosewood and burr walnut were also used.**

An early Victorian mahogany Davenport, stamped 'Miles & Edward, 134 Oxford Street London', numbered '40570', some fading and shrinkage.
c1840 *19in (48cm) wide*
£750-850 **TEN**

A Victorian walnut piano-top Davenport, with brass grill.
24in (61cm) wide
£1,200-1,800 **JN**

A 19thC figured walnut piano-top Davenport, with fitted interior.
12in (30.5cm) wide
£900-1,000 **JN**

A George IV rosewood Davenport, by Gillows of Lancaster, opening to reveal four short drawers and a secret dummy drawer, stamped.
20¾in (53cm) wide
£800-900 **LSK**

A William IV amboyna and rosewood Davenport, the interior with two drawers, two false drawers and a secret stationary drawer, replacement locks.
c1835 *22in (56cm) wide*
£1,400-1,800 **DN**

A Victorian figured walnut Davenport, inlaid in satinwood with stringing, with a pop-up stationery compartment.
23in (58.5cm) wide
£600-700 **MOR**

A Victorian walnut Davenport, with jack-in-the-box stationery cabinet.
22in (56cm) wide
£650-750 **LC**

A Victorian mahogany Davenport desk.
c1880 *19¾in (50cm) wide*
£450-550 **K&O**

A Regency rosewood Canterbury.

There are two kinds of Canterbury. The first is an open-topped rack, with partitions for storing sheet music or music books. The second kind is designed to stand by a table at supper and has partitions to hold cutlery and plates. It is thought that the Canterbury was named after the Archbishop of Canterbury, who commissioned the first example.

18in (46cm) wide

£650-750 **L&T**

A Regency mahogany Canterbury.

17in (43cm) wide

£700-800 **CHEF**

A Regency rosewood Canterbury.

17¾in (45cm) wide

£650-750 **BE**

A Regency mahogany Canterbury, the drawer with brass handles.

20¾in (53cm) wide

£750-850 **DN**

A Regency mahogany Canterbury, with ebonised stringing.

c1815 *20in (51cm) wide*

£450-550 **DN**

A Regency mahogany Canterbury.

c1820 *20in (51cm) wide*

£600-700 **DN**

A Regency mahogany Canterbury.

22in (56cm) wide

£1,000-1,500 **L&T**

A Victorian burr walnut Canterbury, with a brass gallery.

35¾in (91cm) high

£550-600 **SWO**

A Victorian rosewood Canterbury.

61in (155cm) wide

£350-400 **PW**

A mid-Victorian walnut Canterbury.

c1870 *22in (56cm) wide*

£700-800 **DN**

Judith Picks

This needlework mirror is an exquisite piece. Its designs are worked in coloured silks and metal thread. There is a country house to the arch, beneath which are animals, insects, flowers and trees. The central mirror is flanked with full-length depictions of Charles II and his wife Catherine of Braganz. To the bottom are a lion and unicorn, with further flowers and insects and a central fish pond.

A Charles II silk and walnut needlework mirror, with a central mirror in a moulded frame.
26in (66cm) high
£4,000-5,000 WW

A Charles II silver mirror, embossed with foliate decoration and putti, the pediment with a female mask.
c1680 *27½in (70cm) high*
£7,000-8,000 WW

A Queen Anne and later giltwood pier mirror.
64¾in (164.5cm) high
£4,000-5,000 WW

CLOSER LOOK – GEORGE II WALL MIRROR

This mirror has a rocaille and column frame, with exquisitely detailed pierced and carved chinoiserie decoration.

The top is carved with a Chinese man seated under a leaf canopy hung with bells and flanked with exotic birds.

The edges are carved with leaf branches, supporting brackets for porcelain vases or figures, with rockwork and trellis decoration.

Chinoiserie decoration was popular with some of the most celebrated mid-18thC mirror designers, including Matthias Lock, Thomas Johnson and John Linnell.

A George II giltwood and carton-pierre wall mirror.
c1755-60 *74½in (189cm) high*
£100,000-140,000 WW

One of pair of George III carved giltwood mirrors, in the manner of Matthias Lock, some wear.
c1770 *50½in (128cm) high*
£15,000-20,000 the pair DN

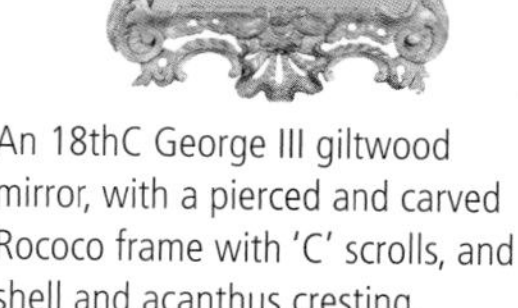

An 18thC George III giltwood mirror, with a pierced and carved Rococo frame with 'C' scrolls, and shell and acanthus cresting.
56¼in (143cm) high
£2,000-2,500 L&T

One of a pair of George III giltwood wall mirrors, some wear and restoration.
c1790 *53¼in (135cm) high*
£16,000-20,000 the pair DN

A George III carved giltwood convex wall mirror, with eagle surmount.
c1800 *48½in (123cm) high*
£1,600-2,000 DN

A Regency convex mirror, with an eagle finial, the base with fish or serpents.

59¾in (152cm) high

£6,500-7,500 **LC**

An early to mid-19thC Continental carved giltwood, composition and cream painted wall mirror, possibly Scandinavian, some wear.

86¼in (219cm) high

£2,500-3,000 **DN**

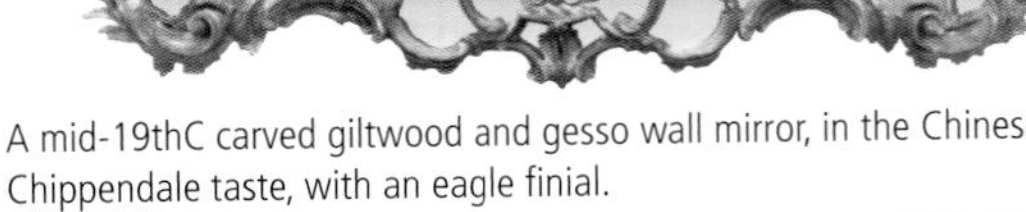

A mid-19thC carved giltwood and gesso wall mirror, in the Chinese Chippendale taste, with an eagle finial.

86½in (220cm) high

£13,000-16,000 **WHP**

A Victorian Rococo-style carved giltwood mirror.

49¼in (125cm) high

£3,500-4,500 **L&T**

A 19thC Italian Baroque gilt framed wall mirror, with floral baskets and cornucopia amongst acanthus sprays, flanked by winged beasts.

Provenance: Formerly the property of Cecil Chubb, the one-time owner of Stonehenge, who gifted the monument to the nation.

145in (368cm) high

£7,000-8,000 **BELL**

A 19thC George II-style walnut and painted mirror.

58¾in (149cm) high

£500-700 **L&T**

A 19thC George III-style giltwood wall mirror, in the manner of John Linnell, some wear, losses to silvering

33¾in (86cm) high

£2,500-3,000 **DN**

A 19thC Italian Venetian blue glass and giltwood wall mirror.

41¾in (106cm) high

£3,000-3,500 **WW**

A late 19thC George III-style carved giltwood and composition wall mirror.

76in (193cm) high

£3,000-3,500 **DN**

A Regency giltwood and painted overmantel mirror, the frieze depicting 'Love Disarmed'.

58¾in (149cm) long

£550-650 **L&T**

A Regency gilt triple overmantel mirror, the frieze depicting Mars in a Chariot, flanked by lyres.

57½in (146cm) wide

£1,300-1,800 **L&T**

An early 19thC rosewood overmantel mirror.

50½in (128.5cm) wide

£750-850 **WW**

A Victorian gilt framed overmantel wall mirror, minor chips to gilding, some losses.

86½in (220cm) high

£1,000-1,400 **BELL**

A Victorian giltwood overmantel mirror, in Rococo style, by J. & W. Vokins, the back with a stencil mark inscribed 'J & W VOKINS, Carvers & Gilders, To the Royal Family 14 & 16 GREAT PORTLAND, ST. W., LATE 5, JOHN ST., OXFORD ST. & 3 GREAT CASTLE STREET'.

50in (127cm) high

£3,000-3,500 **WW**

A Victorian giltwood and gesso overmantel mirror, in Rococo style, with cherubs holding swags of flowers.

60¾in (154.5cm) wide

£600-700 **WW**

A Victorian giltwood and stucco overmantel mirror.

50in (127cm) wide

£400-500 **TRI**

A George III carved giltwood girandole mirror, in the manner of John Bradburn and William France, re-gilded, some losses, restored break to leaf.

Two almost identical mirrors hang in the gallery of Aske Hall, the Yorkshire estate purchased by Sir Lawrence Dundas, 1st Baronet (1712-81) in 1763 and the present seat of the 4th Marquess of Zetland. These were made for Sir Lawrence in c1764-65 by John Bradburn and William France.

c1765 *59in (150cm) high*

£35,000-40,000 **DN**

A pair of carved giltwood two-branch girandoles, surmounted by a ho ho bird, some repairs, some small losses, mirror plates tarnished.

47¼in (120cm) high

£7,500-8,500 **TEN**

A Regency mahogany and ebonised cheval mirror.

'Cheval' is French for horse. Mirrors of this type were called 'cheval' because of their four supporting legs.

65½in (166.5cm) high

£3,000-3,500 **WW**

A Regency mahogany, brass strung and gilt-metal-mounted cheval mirror, with lion mask handles, re-polished, some discolouration to plate.

c1815 *63¾in (162cm) high*

£3,000-3,500 **DN**

A William IV mahogany cheval mirror.

78¾in (200cm) high

£3,000-3,500 **L&T**

A late 19thC Georgian-style mahogany and satinwood cheval mirror.

91¼in (232cm) high

£1,500-2,000 **L&T**

An Edwardian mahogany cheval mirror, with Classical blind fret and broken swan-neck pediment, some discolouration.

65in (164cm) high

£600-700 **PW**

A George IV mahogany and brass inlaid dressing mirror, probably Irish, minor chips and replacements to veneers and mouldings, some discolouration.

c1825 *20¾in (53cm) high*

£1,500-2,000 **DN**

A late 19thC rosewood and ivory-mounted 'skeleton' dressing mirror, with a later oval plate, with label for 'HARRIS & SONS, Plymouth/14-9-93'.

1893 *20¾in (53cm) high*

£1,000-1,500 **DN**

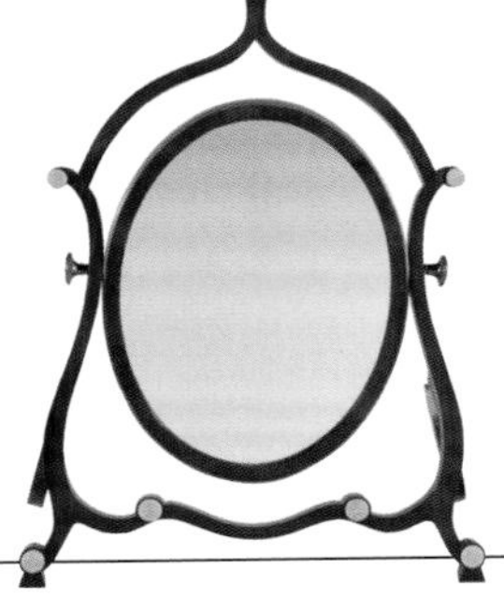

An Edwardian silver-mounted dressing table mirror, by Henry Matthews, Birmingham.

1903 *11¼in (28.5cm) high*

£1,800-2,200 **DN**

An 18thC mahogany brass bound wine cooler.

25¼in (64cm) high

£400-500 **HAN**

A George III mahogany and brass bound wine cooler, the lid with axe-head handle, with zinc-lined interior.

c1780 *28¼in (72cm) high*

£1,100-1,500 **DN**

A 18thC George III brass banded mahogany wine cooler, with a metal-lined interior.

21¼in (54cm) high

£1,500-2,000 **L&T**

A 18thC George III mahogany wine cooler, with a lead-lined interior.

27½in (70cm) high

£1,000-1,400 **L&T**

A George III mahogany wine cooler, with brass banding.

24½in (62cm) high

£650-750 **LC**

A George IV mahogany sarcophagus-form cellaret, with associated gilt-metal lion's paw feet, some damage to hinge.

28¾in (73cm) wide

£1,000-1,400 **BELL**

A George IV mahogany sarcophagus-form wine cooler, some chips, old paper label.

c1825 *35in (89cm) wide*

£1,400-1,800 **DN**

An early 19thC and later mahogany and brass bound wine cooler, with Gillows-style cast brass lion's mask ring handles.

25¼in (64cm) wide

£700-800 **WW**

A late Victorian ebonised and bone étagère, by Howard & Sons, with bone spindles, stamped 'HOWARD & SONS BERNERS STREET'.

31in (79cm) high

£3,500-4,000 **L&T**

An early George III mahogany kettle stand, with piecrust top.

20½in (52cm) high

£6,500-7,000 **L&T**

A late 18thC and later matched pair of elm and mahogany dumb waiters, possibly Scottish or Isle of Man.

39¼in (100cm) high

£1,300-1,600 **DN**

A George III mahogany kettle stand, on a turned and wrythen column and tripod base with claw-and-ball feet.

c1790 *22in (56cm) high*

£2,500-3,000 **LC**

A Regency mahogany dumb waiter.

41½in (105.5cm) high

£650-750 **WW**

ESSENTIAL REFERENCE – GERRIT JENSEN

Gerrit Jensen (fl.1680-1715) was of Dutch or Flemish origin. He was known to be working in St Martin's Lane, London, by 1680, and was known as a pre-eminent 'Cabbinet maker and Glasse seller'. He was the only cabinetmaker working in England during this period known to have used metal inlays and elaborate 'seaweed' or 'arabesque' marquetry. His furniture reflects the fashionable French court styles of Pierre Golle, André Charles Boulle and Daniel Marot.

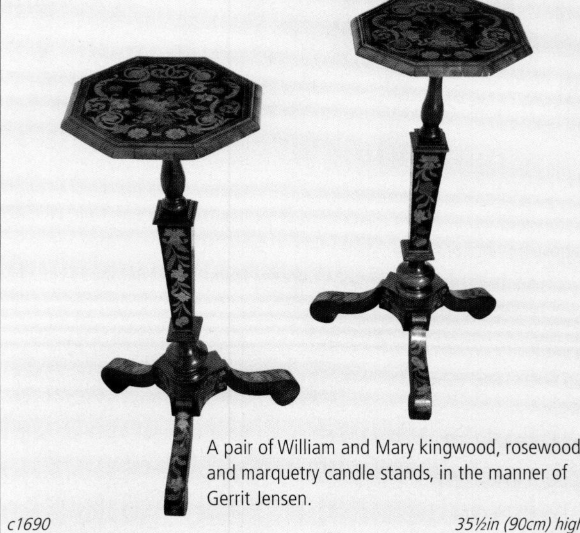

A pair of William and Mary kingwood, rosewood and marquetry candle stands, in the manner of Gerrit Jensen.

c1690 *35½in (90cm) high*

£15,000-20,000 **DN**

A late 18thC black-painted cherry candle stand, attributed to Nathaniel Dominy V, East Hampton, Long Island, New York.

26in (66cm) high

£1,000-1,500 **SK**

A Regency mahogany folding dumb waiter, by Gillows, on tapered reeded and turned supports, on four reeded legs with brass caps and casters.

45¼in (115cm) high

£4,500-5,000 **L&T**

A Regency mahogany whatnot, with four tiers above a Canterbury base, splits and losses to central divider, handles misshapen, drawer-lining with glued repairs.

c1815 *65¼in (166cm) high*

£700-800 **DN**

A 19thC Irish Killarney yew and marquetry four-tier whatnot.

39¾in (101cm) high

£1,300-1,600 **WW**

A late 18thC Dutch Neo-classical satinwood and coromandel vase stand, with a pierced brass gallery.

19in (48cm) high

£600-700 **L&T**

A George III mahogany dished tray, with central ivory plaque inscribed 'Mary Dolby February the 14th 1766'.

Presumably, given the date, this tray was given as a Valentine's present.

18½in (47cm) diam

£400-500 **WW**

A Georgian mahogany butler's tray, on a later stand.

35in (89cm) wide

£750-850 **CHEF**

A late 18thC George III mahogany butler's tray, on a later turned stand.

tray 24in (61cm) wide

£1,100-1,500 **L&T**

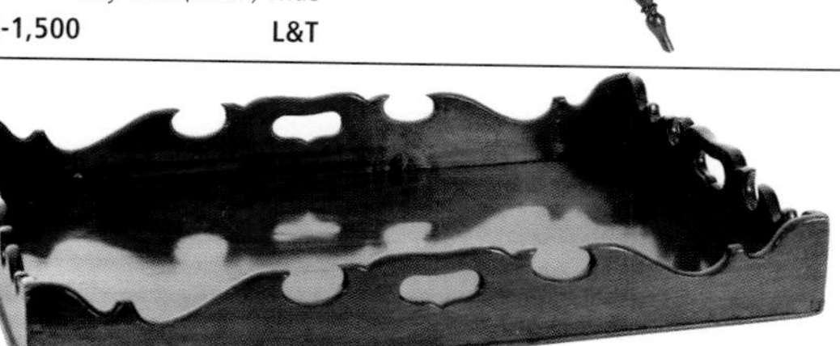

A George III Scottish tray.

22¾in (58cm) wide

£300-400 **CHOR**

A George III mahogany tray, previously mounted.

23in (58.5cm) wide

£450-550 **WW**

A mid-to-late Victorian lacquer and parcel gilt papier mâché tray, in the manner of Jennens and Bettridge.

32¾in (83cm) wide

£700-800 **DN**

A 17thC oak tester bed, the canopy with a gouged cornice and fluted apron, with later incised foliate lozenge panels.

78¾in (200cm) long

£5,000-6,000 **BE**

A Regency mahogany and brass campaign four-poster bed, by Morgan and Sanders, London, with brass trade plaque, 'Patent/Morgan & Sanders Manufacturers/16 & 17 Catherine Street, Strand, London', with modern hangings.

Established in 1800, Thomas Morgan and Joseph Sanders' cabinetmaking firm was one of London's most successful of the early 19thC. Their designs were highly sought after by wealthy patrons, including several members of the Royal Family and Lord Nelson. Today their pieces are particularly desirable.

95¼in (242cm) high

£7,000-8,000 **L&T**

An early Victorian mahogany tester bed frame, with later headboard, one carved leaf knocked upright, footboard missing, canopy with old splits and cracks.

c1840 *87¾in (223cm) long*

£850-950 **DN**

A late 19thC to early 20thC Louis XVI-style fruitwood marquetry and parquetry mahogany bedframe, the mounts by Jean Rabiant.

This piece is made after a design by Jean-Henri Riesener (1734-1806) for the commode for La Chambre de Louis XVI à Versailles.

72¾in (185cm) long

£8,000-10,000 **FRE**

An 18thC Dutch polychrome painted and parcel gilt leather six-leaf screen, in the style of Hondecoeter, some damages.

130in (330cm) wide

£2,500-3,000 **MOR**

An 18thC and later four-leaf room screen, each panel inset with a tapestry panel, with later damask covers to rear of screen.

69in (175cm) high

£2,800-3,200 **DN**

A Victorian and later oak four-leaf room divider, inset with oil landscapes.

52¼in (133cm) high

£600-700 **WHP**

Judith Picks

This screen has an interesting origin. Its velvet panels depict the rose, thistle and shamrock, national flowers of England, Scotland and Ireland, and these were in fact removed from the dais at Delhi from which Queen Victoria was proclaimed Empress of India in 1877 by the Viceroy of India, Lord Lytton (1831-99). The Dehli Durbar of 1877 was the culmination of transfer of control of much of India from the British East India Company to The Crown.

An ebonised three-leaf screen, with 19thC embroidered velvet panels, hinges discoloured.

66¼in (168cm) high

£2,200-2,800 **DN**

A Regency tortoiseshell and ivory tea caddy, with single lidded interior, minor chips.

Tortoiseshell is a material produced from the shells of certain species of tortoise or sea turtle. It was used decoratively on luxury furniture, jewellery, boxes, clocks and more. Tortoiseshell antiques are controlled by trade rules under the CITIES act.

4¾in (12cm) wide

£600-700 BELL

A Regency mother-of-pearl inlaid tortoiseshell tea caddy, with a twin lidded interior, on gilt-metal ball feet.

7½in (19cm) wide

£550-650 BELL

A Regency blonde tortoiseshell and white metal inlaid tea caddy, with an initialled cartouche.

7in (18cm) wide

£500-600 LSK

A 19thC green tortoiseshell two-division tea caddy, with ivory and pewter stringing, with a monogrammed plaque.

7¼in (18.5cm) wide

£2,500-3,000 FLD

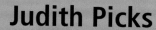

Judith Picks

From the 17thC to early 19thC, tea was a luxury in Britain. High-quality tea caddies were produced to reflect this. This tea caddy, made of expensive tortoiseshell, is decorated with inlaid mother-of-pearl floral borders and acanthus scrolls. Tea came to Europe from China in the early 17thC and was at first very expensive. Drinking tea became an important social pastime in fashionable circles, in part to give hosts the opportunity to display their wealth. Tea was kept in small locked caddies to protect theft or spillage by servants. The mistress of the house would have kept the key.

A Regency inlaid tortoiseshell sarcophagus-form tea caddy.

8in (20.5cm) wide

£1,500-2,000 L&T

CLOSER LOOK – TORTOISESHELL TEA CADDY

This tortoiseshell tea caddy is embellished with ivory banding and foliate mother-of-pearl marquetry.

The top has graduated cavetto mouldings.

The front is gadrooned. Tortoiseshell can be difficult to manipulate, making this kind of detail hard to achieve.

The interior has twin lidded compartments, with fabric and metal lining.

A George IV or William IV tortoiseshell veneered tea caddy.

c1830 *7in (17.5cm) wide*

£1,200-1,600 DN

A late Regency tortoiseshell tea caddy, inlaid with pewter and ivory stringing, the lid with a gold metal plaque initialled 'G.P.', the sides with lion masks, ring handles.

9¾in (25cm) wide

£600-700 WW

A 19thC tortoiseshell tea caddy, with ivory stringing, with twin lidded compartments, some damages.

6¼in (16cm) long

£500-600 FLD

An Edwardian blonde tortoiseshell tea caddy, by Martin Hall & Co., Sheffield, with stylised foliate and scrollwork silver mounts.

1903 *4¼in (11cm) wide*

£1,500-2,000 BE

A Regency penwork sarcophagus-form tea caddy, with chinoiserie decoration, later gilt-metal handles and claw-and-ball feet.

9in (23cm) wide

£950-1,100 **BRI**

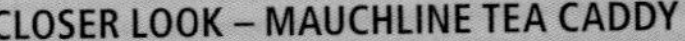

CLOSER LOOK – MAUCHLINE TEA CADDY

This tea caddy is in excellent condition and comes from the collection of the late John Wright, who was a member of The Mauchline Collectors Club.

Mauchline ware was produced in Mauchline and its surrounding towns in South West Scotland over the 19thC and early 20thC.

The lid, all four sides, and the three interior lidded caddies are decorated in detailed penwork with images of Scottish country houses: Keithock, Stracathro, Burn, Langley Park, Edzell, Findhaven Castle, Dunellar Castle, and the Abbey of Aberbrathwick.

Larger pieces of Mauchline ware tend to fetch good prices, especially if, as here, the subject matter is rare.

A Victorian Mauchline ware sycamore and penwork tea caddy, by C. Stiven, Laurencekirk.

12in (30.5cm) wide

£6,500-7,500 **CAN**

A Regency penwork sarcophagus-form tea caddy, with chinoiserie decoration, the interior with two lidded compartments.

8in (20.5cm) wide

£950-1,100 **WW**

A Regency penwork sarcophagus-form tea caddy, the interior lid painted with a country house.

7¾in (19.5cm) wide

£650-750 **SWO**

A Regency penwork sarcophagus-form tea caddy, decorated with exotic figures with a camel and elephant.

9¾in (25cm) wide

£600-700 **WW**

A George III mahogany and quillwork tea caddy, with lidded interior.

5in (13cm) wide

£450-550 **BE**

A George III curled paper tea caddy, each panel with stylised flowers.

4¾in (12cm) wide

£1,000-1,400 **FLD**

A pear-shaped fruitwood tea caddy.

7in (18cm) high

£900-1,100 **K&O**

A melon-shaped fruitwood tea caddy.

6in (15cm) high

£1,600-2,000 **K&O**

A Georgian painted wood inn two-division tea caddy, with two dormer roof windows, inn sign missing.

10¼in (26cm) high

£1,200-1,800 **JN**

A 19thC painted house tea caddy, with twin lidded compartments with ivory handles, decorated with trellis glazed windows and a verandah, the back with a stable door.

7¾in (19.5cm) wide

£4,000-5,000 **WW**

A novelty 19thC painted wood Gothic castle tea chest, with lancet windows, painted with shields, with a clock tower compartment for a pocket watch, the interior with two mahogany lidded lift-out canisters and a sugar bowl.

9¾in (24.5cm) high

£1,500-2,000 **WW**

A Georgian painted wood tea caddy, the roof lifting to reveal two tea canisters.

7½in (19cm) long

£1,000-1,500 **JN**

A Georgian painted wood two-division tea caddy, with door, five windows and creepers growing up the side.

8½in (21.5cm) long

£1,000-1,500 **JN**

A 19thC painted cottage tea caddy, with trellis glazed windows, the foiled interior lacking lid.

6¾in (17cm) high

£1,400-1,800 **WW**

A George III mahogany tea caddy, inlaid with a ribbon and swag, the top with a shell.

5¾in (14.5cm) wide

£400-500 **SWO**

A George III mahogany inlaid tea caddy.

6in (15cm) wide

£500-600 **SWO**

A 18thC two-division tea caddy, inlaid with mother-of-pearl ovals depicting 'FIDES' (faith), 'SPES' (hope), and 'CHARITAS' (charity).

8in (20.5cm) high

£4,500-5,000 JN

A George III tea caddy, attributed to Henry Clay, with ground Nashiji mother-of-pearl and lacquer finish.

Nashiji is a form of Japanese lacquer-work (see page 132). Henry Clay (d.1812) was an 18thC artist and inventor, known for his Classical-style tea caddies. He was a key figure in Birmingham's jappaning industry and later became the 'Japanner in Ordinary to His Majesty and His Royal Highness the Prince of Wales'.

4¾in (12cm) wide

£1,500-2,000 BELL

A George III yew wood inlaid tea caddy, with boxwood and chequer strung.

7¾in (19.5cm) wide

£400-500 SWO

A late 18thC to early 19thC burr elm tea caddy, opening to a single covered compartment and glass bowl, inlaid with the coat of arms for the Coke family.

6¾in (17cm) wide

£600-700 L&T

A Regency rosewood tea caddy, of lyre form, with brass inlaid 'strings', hidden drawer to one side.

8¼in (21cm) high

£500-600 LC

An early 19thC cube parquetry tea caddy, inlaid with rosewood, birch and mahogany, with twin lidded interior.

9¾in (24.5cm) wide

£600-700 WW

A Victorian gilt-brass-mounted walnut tea caddy, the lidded compartments with brass plaques inscribed 'BLACK' and 'GREEN'.

8¾in (22.5cm) wide

£550-650 L&T

A 19thC Irish tea caddy, with figures and deer in landscape, with hunter and dog surmount, with two lidded compartments and mixing bowl.

14½in (37cm) wide

£600-700 BRI

A 19thC Irish Killarney yew and fruitwood marquetry tea chest, the interior with two lift-out lidded canisters and a sugar bowl.

13½in (34.5cm) wide

£350-400 WW

A painted and découpage decorated dresser box, by Joseph Lehn (1798-1892), Lancaster, Pennsylvania, minor wear.

13¼in (33.5cm) wide

£750-850 **POOK**

A mid-19thC painted pine dresser box, by Jacob or Jonas Weber, Lancaster County, Pennsylvania, inscribed on underside 'Made in 1850', some wear.

7½in (19cm) wide

£40,000-50,000 **POOK**

A mid-19thC painted pine dresser box, by Jacob or Jonas Weber, Lancaster County, Pennsylvania.

4¼in (11cm) wide

£30,000-40,000 **POOK**

A Victorian rosewood brass-bound travelling toiletry box, fitted with twelve silver-gilt jars and boxes, by Thomas Diller, London, the lock stamped 'J. Bramah of 124 Piccadilly', with leather outer case.

1847 *14¼in (36cm) wide*

£650-750 **LSK**

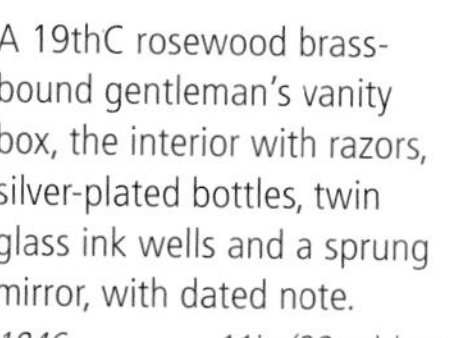

A 19thC rosewood brass-bound gentleman's vanity box, the interior with razors, silver-plated bottles, twin glass ink wells and a sprung mirror, with dated note.

1846 *11in (28cm) long*

£350-400 **FLD**

A Victorian walnut dressing case, fitted with silver-gilt-mounted cut-glass bottles and boxes, the lids engraved 'ED', with a mirror, blotter and lift-out tray with accessories, with marks for 'W. & J. MILNE, MAKERS, 126 PRINCES ST./ EDINBURGH'.

1860 *13½in (34.5cm) wide*

£1,500-2,000 **L&T**

A Victorian silver travelling dressing table set, by Thomas Johnson, London, retailed by H. Tooke, Liverpool, initialled, hob-nail cut-glass bodies, in a brass-bound walnut case, the cover with a brass cartouche 'F.E. Edwards 28 November 1866'.

1865 *13¼in (33.5cm) long 9⅞oz*

£2,000-2,500 **WW**

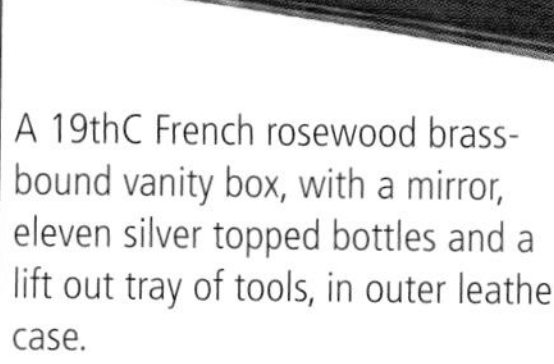

A 19thC French rosewood brass-bound vanity box, with a mirror, eleven silver topped bottles and a lift out tray of tools, in outer leather case.

11¾in (30cm) long

£850-950 **FLD**

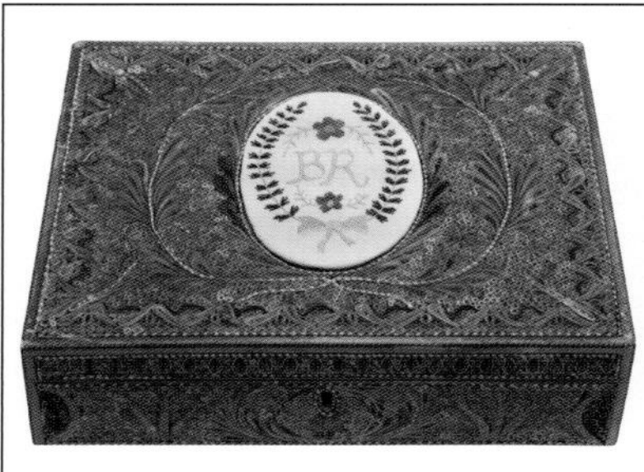

A George III quillwork decorated sewing box, with later oval embroidered panel with initials 'BR', fitted compartments to the interior.

11in (28cm) wide

£350-400 **BE**

A Napoleonic prisoner-of-war straw work box, the interior fitted with boxes and drawers.

15in (38cm) wide

£250-300 **ECGW**

A Regency blond tortoiseshell sewing box, the domed lid divided by pewter lines to an ivory boss.

7¾in (20cm) wide

£300-400 **BLEA**

A Regency penwork work box, with ivory handles and feet, handwritten label to underside.

11½in (29cm) wide

£1,000-1,500 **L&T**

A burr ash and steel-studded Palais Royal sewing box, the interior with fitted tray of mother-of-pearl tools, some wear to edges.

The Palais Royal was the area of Paris surrounding the Royal Palace, which in the 18thC and 19thC was known for producing and selling small and elaborate objets d'art, including sewing boxes and tools. Palais Royal pieces are typically of very high quality.

c1830 *7½in (19cm) wide*

£800-900 **BLEA**

A 19thC specimen wood inlaid sewing box, the metal inscribed 'Presented to Mrs Lawrence by the Scholars attending the Sabbath School of Crossmichael as a token of their gratitude and regard July 1842'.

12¼in (31cm) wide

£250-300 **WHP**

An ebony sewing box, inlaid in cut mother-of-pearl and abalone shell, the interior with letter compartment and tray of sewing tools.

c1860 *14in (35.5cm) wide*

£550-650 **BLEA**

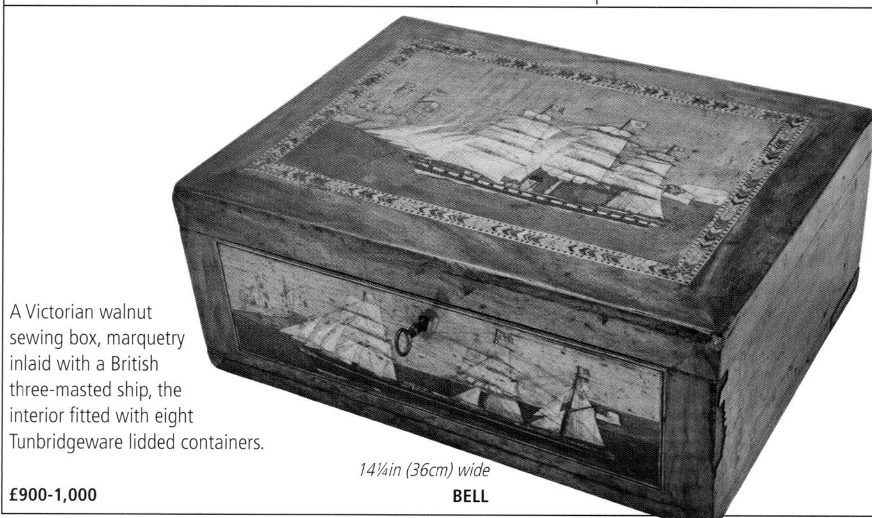

A Victorian walnut sewing box, marquetry inlaid with a British three-masted ship, the interior fitted with eight Tunbridgeware lidded containers.

14¼in (36cm) wide

£900-1,000 **BELL**

A late 19thC Italian rosewood sewing box, by Luigi Pasquale (1822-94), with ivory, copper, pewter and specimen wood inlay, enclosing lift out trays, lacking mirror.

9¾in (25cm) wide

£400-500 **APAR**

A late 17thC to early 18thC Chinese hardwood and engraved paktong mounted writing box, possibly Huanghuali, some losses, staining and splits.

This box is of the style and form made for the Dutch East India Company.

18½in (47cm) long

£2,500-3,000 **BELL**

A late 18thC George III tortoiseshell and silver-mounted travelling writing nécessaire, with silver plaque engraved 'EM', the interior with two silver-topped glass inkwells, four nibs and a propelling pencil, some cracks, feet slightly bent.

3¼in (8cm) wide

£2,000-2,500 **CHEF**

An early 19thC fiddleback mahogany and satinwood drum or keg shape stationery box, the lid with a leather note and pen holder.

10¾in (27.5cm) high

£600-700 **WW**

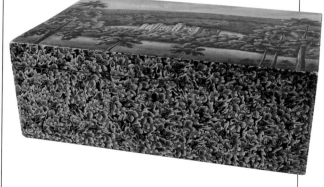

A mid-Victorian coromandel writing box, decorated with an Indian tiger hunt in gilt-metal, abalone shell and mother-of-pearl, fitted with letter and pen and ink compartments.

16in (40.5cm) wide

£1,300-1,800 **TRI**

A Victorian Mauchline ware sycamore and penwork writing box, decorated with a castle within woodland, the interior with seven lidded compartments.

12in (30.5cm) wide

£4,000-4,500 **CAN**

A Victorian walnut and brass-mounted writing box, with a Jasperware plaque, with a fitted interior with stationery compartments, mother-of-pearl tools and fold-out slope.

17¾in (45cm) wide

£1,800-2,200 **LC**

An Edwardian mahogany and satinwood writing box, the interior with a leather-lined fold-out writing surface, small drawers and stationery divisions.

14½in (37cm) wide

£250-300 **MOR**

A Regency rosewood letter box, possibly Irish, with brass plates inscribed 'Answer'd, Unanswer'd' and Antrim beneath a coronet.

7½in (19cm) wide

£1,800-2,200 **LC**

A mid-Victorian red boullework letter box, with fitted interior, bearing a label 'Falstaff & Hannaford, Regents Street'.

7½in (19cm) wide

£600-650 **TRI**

A 16thC South German domed-top box, with 273 inlaid pieces, depicting dogs, falcons, rabbits, hares, birds, lions, tortoises and snails.

The engraved animals are based on designs by Virgil Solis (1514-62).

18½in (47cm) wide

£15,000-20,000 **SWO**

A needlework raised stumpwork casket, with animals, flowers and figures, possibly with Charles II and Catherine of Braganza, some sun-bleaching, minor staining, some losses.

c1670 *12¼in (31cm) wide*

£11,000-15,000 **TEN**

A 17thC Indo-Portuguese bone inlaid table cabinet, decorated with micromosaic panels, with fitted drawers, heavy wear throughout, handles missing.

Despite the damage, the intricacy of this table cabinet assures its value.

10¾in (27cm) wide

£5,500-6,000 **APAR**

A late 17thC to early 18thC kingwood strong box or coffre fort, with strapwork brass mounts, with secret drawers to lid.

15¼in (39cm) wide

£3,000-3,500 **WW**

An 18thC Georgian shagreen decanter box, fitted with six cut-glass decanters and stoppers, a wine funnel and a wine glass.

10¼in (26cm) wide

£1,200-1,600 **L&T**

A late George III mahogany box, with rosewood crossbanding, set with Chinese pith paintings of birds.

10in (25.5cm) wide

£1,500-2,000 **DUK**

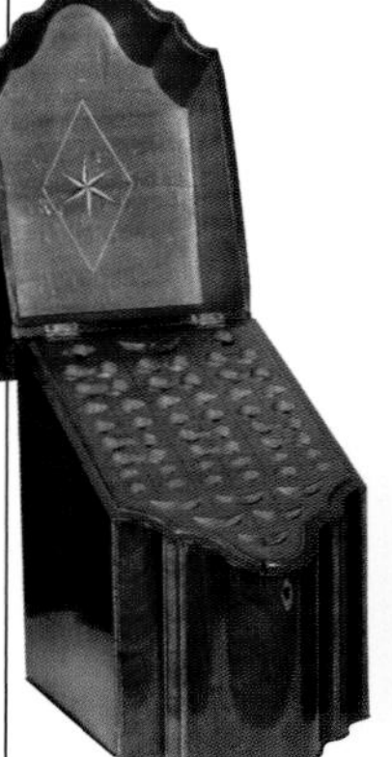

A pair of George III mahogany cutlery boxes, banded in tulip wood, and with fitted interiors, some splits, scratches and blemishes.

£1,100-1,400 **CHOR**

A George III Neo-classical inlaid mahogany urn-shaped knife or cutlery stand, the later pop-up mechanism damaged.

24½in (62cm) high

£1,800-2,200 **BELL**

An early 19thC painted poplar dome lid box, by the 'Compass Artist', Lancaster County, Pennsylvania, leather handles added and removed from sides, hinges replaced.

16¾in (42.5cm) wide

£22,000-26,000 **POOK**

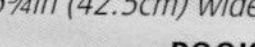

A 19thC painted poplar dome lid box, by the 'Compass Artist', Lancaster County, Pennsylvania, repaired blowout to one hinge.

7½in (19cm) wide

£30,000-35,000 **POOK**

These boxes are part of a group of over 60 objects that have been attributed to the 'Compass Artist'. They are attributed to the same artist due to his use of very distinctive compass work and freehand decoration.

A painted pine slide lid box, made for Peter Nehs, by John Drissell (1762-1846), Bucks County, Pennsylvania, inscribed 'Ich kam in ein Land da stund geschrieben an der Wand/Sei fromm und ver schwiegen was nicht dein ist das lass liegen'.

The inscription translates as 'I came to a land where it was written on the wall,/Be pious and never hide anything that is not yours, let it lie'.

10¾in (27.5cm) long

£15,000-20,000 **POOK**

A mid-19thC painted pine slide-lid box, by Jacob or Jonas Weber, Lancaster County, Pennsylvania, with floral decoration on a dark blue ground, lacking interior dividers.

7in (18cm) wide

£9,000-11,000 **POOK**

A Victorian Howell James & Co. coromandel table casket, pierced Gothic silver mounts, the hinged cover releasing five leather-bound household books.

8¾in (22cm) wide

£800-900 **HAN**

A Victorian Mauchline ware sycamore and penwork gaming box, decorated with stately homes, the interior with gaming counter compartments and card division packs.

11½in (29cm) wide

£6,500-7,000 **CAN**

A 19thC Italian marquetry box, with interlacing foliate scrolls.

14¼in (36cm) wide

£2,000-2,600 **CHOR**

A late 19thC shagreen jewellery box, with silver mounts, with inset miniature, the silver feet engraved 'TW' and 'TM' and the date '9.9.91'.

1891 *5¾in (14.5cm) wide*

£2,000-2,500 **DN**

An Indian hardwood and bone inlaid casket.

9¾in (25cm) wide

£1,400-1,800 **SWO**

A 19thC American tôleware tray.

8¾in (22cm) wide

£4,000-5,000 **POOK**

A 19thC American black tôleware coffee pot, some wear.

10¼in (26cm) high

£350-400 **POOK**

A 19thC American black tôleware box, some wear.

9¼in (23.5cm) wide

£220-280 **POOK**

A 19thC tôleware chinoiserie tea canister, later converted into a table lamp.

19½in (49.5cm) high

£1,400-1,800 **WW**

A Victorian Tunbridgeware tea caddy, with a view of Battle Abbey Gatehouse, enclosing a glass mixing bowl and two lidded canisters.

Tunbridgeware is a form of decorative woodware, created by gluing strips of wood together to form a pattern. Various types of wood were used to create colours, including oak, sycamore, maple and holly. Pieces became popular souvenirs for visitors to Tunbridge in the 18thC and 19thC.

14½in (37cm) long

£1,500-2,000 **TEN**

CLOSER LOOK – AMERICAN TÔLEWARE TRAY

Tôleware refers to items made of tinplated sheet iron or steel, covered in black asphaltum and then painted; the name comes from the French tôle peinte, meaning 'painted sheet'.

This tray is in very good condition, with the original decoration still vibrant and in tact.

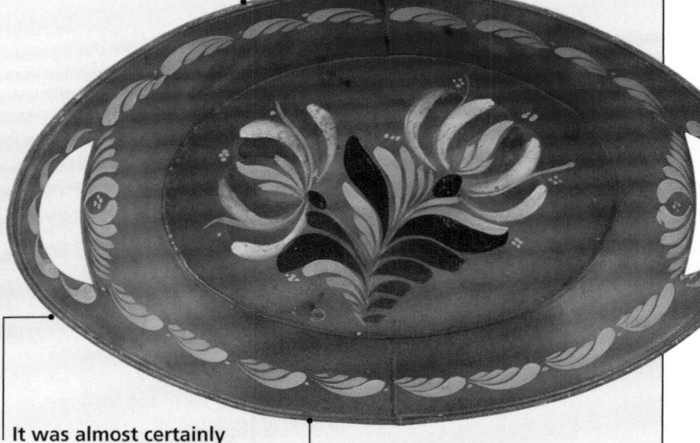

It was almost certainly made in Pennsylvania.

It is painted red, which is an uncommon and therefore valuable colour in American tôleware.

A 19thC American red tôleware bread tray.

10½in (26.5cm) wide

£9,000-11,000 **POOK**

A pair of late Victorian tôleware tea canisters, with Chinese figures and gilt and mother-of-pearl highlights.

29in (73.5cm) high

£3,000-3,500 **WW**

A 19thC Tunbridgeware tea caddy, depicting a church, some cracks and chips, one small repair.

9¾in (25cm) wide

£750-850 **ECGW**

A 19thC Tunbridgeware box, the cover with a country house, label verso 'W. Childs of Brighton', some scratches, losses, and warping.

9½in (24cm) wide

£600-700 **ECGW**

An 18thC miniature oak chest-on-chest.

28in (71cm) high

£2,000-2,500 **SWO**

An early 19thC Continental miniature walnut and line-inlaid bowfront chest-of-drawers, with bone handles and bun feet.

6¼in (16cm) wide

£1,200-1,600 **REEM**

An early 19thC miniature mahogany chest-of-drawers, the top with burr wood veneers.

12½in (32cm) wide

£500-600 **L&T**

A George III miniature mahogany and crossbanded chest-of-drawers.

c1820 *16½in (42cm) wide*

£400-500 **HAN**

A Classical miniature carved mahogany chest-of-drawers, Ossining, New York, inscribed in graphite on backboard, 'To Mifs. Sarah Jane Brewster Presented to her By Her Grand-Father Wm. G. Burr, March 20, 1843 Made at the Sing Sing State Prison.'

Sarah Jane Brewster (1839-91) was the daughter of Mary Burr Brewster (1815-59) and W.H. Brewster of Cazenovia, New York. Sarah lived with her grandparents for most of her life. Her grandfather William G. Burr (1790-1860), a cooper by trade, worked at the New York State Auburn Prison and later the Sing Sing Prison as keeper of the cooperage department. He remained in Ossining as an agent for prison-made goods for several years.

1843 *13½in (34.5cm) wide*

£11,000-14,000 **FRE**

A miniature mahogany chest-of-drawers, with inlaid stringing.

8¾in (22cm) high

£250-300 **SWO**

A 19thC miniature painted pine and poplar chest-of-drawers, Pennsylvania, one knob replaced.

12in (30.5cm) high

£900-1,100 **POOK**

A 19thC miniature painted pine drysink.

21¾in (55cm) wide

£600-700 **POOK**

A George III mahogany tilt-top apprentice table, on tripod legs.

10½in (26.5cm) high

£1,000-1,500 **JN**

A mid-19thC miniature fruitwood and parquetry table.

17in (43cm) wide

£300-400 **L&T**

A Classical miniature carved mahogany sofa, probably Philadelphia, Pennsylvania, retaining early, possibly original upholstery.

c1825 *17½in (44.5cm) long*

£2,000-2,500 **FRE**

A Federal miniature painted and stencilled Windsor settee.

c1830 *15in (38cm) long*

£800-900 **FRE**

A mid-19thC miniature Pennsylvania painted plank seat chair, minor wear.

12½in (32cm) high

£700-800 **POOK**

A 17thC boxwood shoe-form snuff box, with armorial and floral decoration, the sole with a two-masted ship, the sliding lid with a bull's head, dated.
1639 *4in (10cm) long*
£2,000-2,500 **TOV**

A late 18thC Scandinavian maple snuff box, relief-carved with an urn and lion.
5in (13cm) long
£750-850 **WW**

A late 18thC to early 19thC mahogany frog snuff box, with a pull button opening the spring-loaded head.
3¼in (8cm) long
£2,200-2,800 **TOV**

An early 19thC Stobwasser-type lidded snuff box, painted with bearded figure with Masonic regalia.
3½in (9cm) diam
£400-500 **HAN**

A 19thC wooden fish snuff box, probably Scandinavian.
4¼in (11cm) long
£280-320 **BLEA**

A 19thC treen snuff shoe, with tack, mother-of-pearl and bone inlay.
5½in (14cm) long
£400-500 **WW**

CLOSER LOOK – NAPOLEONIC SNUFF BOX

This rare snuff box is carved in the form of warship, with gun ports to port and starboard, and cannons and cannon balls to the sides.

The top is carved with a figure of Napoleon, below Napoleon's crest with 'N' in a laurel wreath with flags.

The figurehead depicts the Merovingian King Childeric I, whom Napoleon believed he was descended from.

It is mounted on a later stained wood plinth, with a gilt plaque inscribed 'SNUFF BOX, CARVED BY ONE OF NAPOLEON'S STAFF, AT LONGWOOD, ST. HELENA, 1819'. Longwood House was the residence of Napoleon from his exile in 1815 until his death in 1821.

A Napoleonic carved coquilla nut table snuff box.
1819 *6¼in (16cm) long*
£8,000-9,000 **WW**

An early 19thC French carved coquilla nut snuff box, the lid with a coach and horses.
3in (7.5cm) wide
£180-220 **WW**

A 19thC pressed treen snuff box, with Masonic Temple and emblems, tortoiseshell simulated interior.
3¼in (8.5cm) diam
£400-500 **HAN**

A 19thC French pressed burr snuff box, inscribed 'Fideite-Amour-Amitie-Pont Les De La Vie', tortoiseshell liner, cracked.
3½in (9cm) diam
£450-500 **BLEA**

A mid-17thC lignum vitae wassail bowl, with a single reeded girdle moulding.

The word 'wassail' originates from the Anglo-Saxon phrase 'waes hael', which means 'be in good health'. Wassail, a kind of hot mulled punch, was drank in celebration, typically on the Twelfth Night, 5 January.

8in (20.5cm) high

£2,000-2,500 **WW**

A Charles II lignum vitae wassail bowl, with a later silver rim above reeded bands.

14¼in (36cm) high

£4,000-5,000 **WW**

CLOSER LOOK – WASSAIL BOWL

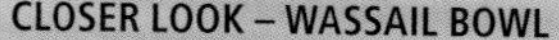

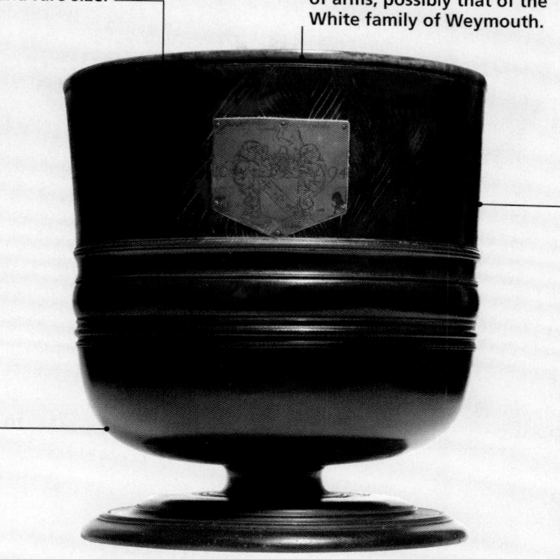

This wassail bowl is of a large and rare size.

The brass plaque bears a coat of arms, possibly that of the White family of Weymouth.

It is dated '1694'. It is very unusual for wassail bowls to be dated, which adds to the value.

It is inscribed 'Thomas White' and 'Bibi Potum et non Defundo', roughly translating as 'Drink and do not spill'.

A William and Mary lignum vitae wassail bowl, on a ring-turned foot.

15¼in (38.5cm) high

£17,000-20,000 **WW**

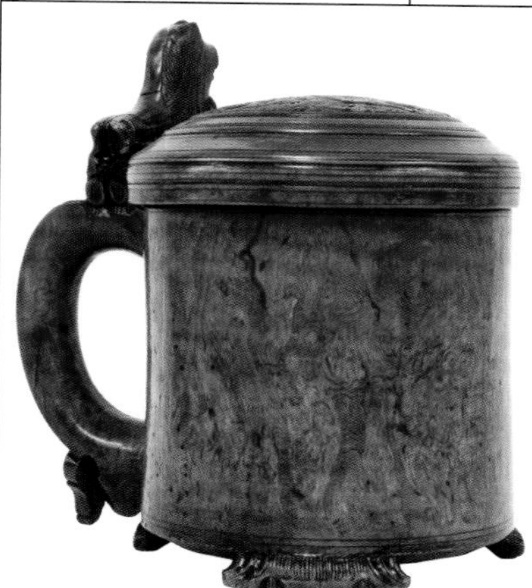

An 18thC Norwegian Karelian birch peg tankard, with lion thumbpiece and carved rampant lion to lid.

Karelian birch is a distinctive tree growing only in Karelia, a historic region covering parts of Finland, Sweden and Russia.

9¾in (25cm) high

£750-850 **SWO**

A Norwegian birch and pine peg tankard, bound in leather strips, with scrolling handle.

6¾in (17cm) high

£250-300 **LC**

A 19thC German carved and turned rhinoceros horn goblet, the faceted bowl on a spreading foot and a conforming plinth.

7½in (19cm) high 29⅞oz

£11,000-13,000 **WW**

A 19thC treen turned lignum vitae flask, with stopper.

8¾in (22.5cm) high

£230-280 **WW**

A treen carved lignum vitae castellated turret spill vase.

6¼in (16cm) high

£160-200 **BE**

A carved pine lollipop butter stamp, decorated with tulips, initialled 'FC', some wear, dated.
1816 *8¾in (22cm) high*
£2,500-3,000 **POOK**

A 19thC Scottish treen sycamore butter stamp, carved with thistles, a flowerhead and hearts, the handle inscribed 'HAYFARM' and 'WE FEAR NAE FOE'.
9¾in (24.5cm) long
£400-500 **WW**

A 19thC turned and carved eagle butter stamp, some surface loss to centre.
4½in (11.5cm) diam
£150-200 **POOK**

An early 19thC carved coquilla nut nutmeg grater, lacking grater.
2¼in (6cm) high
£120-160 **WW**

An 18thC fruitwood knitting stick, carved with St George slaying the dragon, with a bone-mounted aperture.

Knitting sticks were commonly found in the households of the British working classes from the 17thC to the 19thC. They were used to mend or make clothes, and were usually carved by hand.

5½in (14cm) long
£2,000-2,500 **BLEA**

A 19thC treen sailor's nutmeg grater, of whale form, the base with a steel grater.
2¼in (5.5cm) long
£2,200-2,800 **WW**

A Regency treen spoon, possibly Welsh, the handle punch decorated with a heart, inscribed 'MADE for MJ', dated.
1816 *7½in (19cm) long*
£1,000-1,400 **WW**

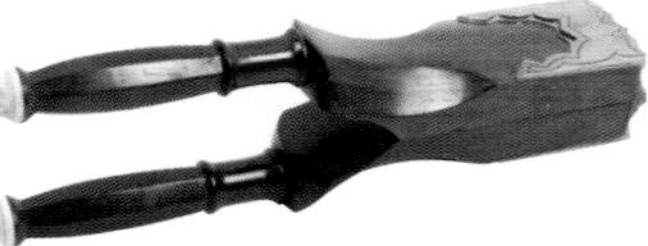

A 19thC hardwood juice press, the brass hinge stamped 'Will and Finck S.F. Cal', with bone terminals.
9¾in (25cm) long
£350-400 **BLEA**

A fruitwood knitting stick, of exaggerated scroll form, initialled 'JB', mount with brass plate.
9in (23cm) long
£400-450 **BLEA**

A late 18thC boxwood knitting sheath, initialled 'R.M.F.B. 1785 19 Sepr A.P'.
1785 *8in (20.5cm) long*
£1,200-1,600 **TOV**

A treen 'goose wing' sheath, with female figure to one side and geometric and heart decoration to the other, dated.
1714 *8¾in (22.5cm) long*
£250-300 **BE**

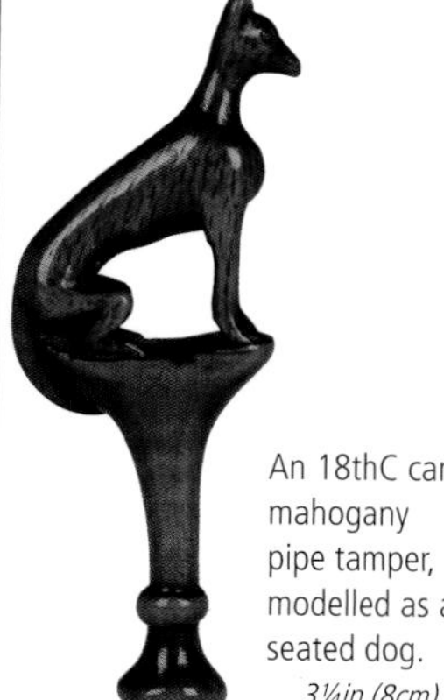

An 18thC carved mahogany pipe tamper, modelled as a seated dog.
3¼in (8cm) high
£400-450 **TOV**

A late 18thC to early 19thC hand-held fruitwood braid loom, probably Welsh.
6½in (16.5cm) long
£450-500 **BLEA**

ESSENTIAL REFERENCE – SHAKESPEARE MEDALLION

This medallion is supposedly carved from the mulberry tree that William Shakespeare planted in his garden at New Place in Stratford-on-Avon, and was possibly worn by 18thC actor David Garrick when performing in Shakespeare's plays. The owner of New Place in the mid-18thC, Reverand Francis Gastrell, grew annoyed with the quantity of tourists, and in the 1750s felled the tree and later demolished New Place. Objects carved from the mulberry tree first started to appear around 1760-70, after Gastrell sold the wood to local carvers and turners such as Thomas Sharp and George Cooper, who were eager to make souvenirs.

An 18thC carved treen Shakespeare bust medallion, probably of mulberry wood, with a silver mount.
3¼in (8.5cm) diam
£2,500-3,000 **WW**

A 19thC treen candle box, in the form a north-eastern fisherman's house, on brass ball feet, some splitting.
7in (18cm) wide
£2,800-3,200 **TEN**

A 19thC pair of walnut bellows, relief-carved with a horse and rider, with fitted bronze spout.
36½in (93cm) long
£900-1,100 **MOR**

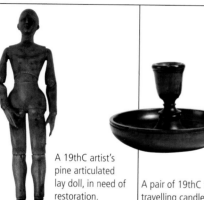

A 19thC artist's pine articulated lay doll, in need of restoration.
12½in (31.5cm) high
£950-1,100 **LOCK**

A pair of 19thC treen Brighton bun travelling candlesticks, with snuffer.
5in (12.5cm) diam
£300-400 **WW**

A 19thC treen child's rocking chair money box.
6¼in (16cm) high
£140-180 **BE**

A late 19thC to early 20thC treen pen tray, of two pigs feeding at a trough.
15½in (39.5cm) long
£500-600 **WW**

An early 18thC yew wood lever nutcracker, probably English, scratch-carved with vases of flowers and hearts.

4½in (11.5cm) long

£1,000-1,400 **TOV**

A George II boxwood treen nutcracker, initialled 'SL' with geometric carved decoration, dated.

It is rare to find an authentic date on this kind of boxwood nutcracker.

1739 *3in (7.5cm) high*

£4,000-5,000 **MAB**

A 19thC carved treen nutcracker, in the form of Mr Punch.

7¾in (19.5cm) long

£120-160 **FLD**

A 19thC carved oak nutcracker of a bearded figure, stamped 'Cop of original now 1874 rotten with age pray preserve this'.

7¾in (20cm) high

£1,500-2,000 **FLD**

A 19thC carved wooden novelty nutcracker, modelled as a monkey's head, some surface wear and rubbing.

7¾in (19.5cm) high

£80-100 **FELL**

A late 19thC Swiss Black Forest-style carved walnut figural nutcracker, in the form of a laughing gnome.

10¼in (26cm) high

£140-180 **WW**

A Swiss Black Forest-style carved wood nutcracker, modelled a bear's head, the grip inscribed 'Grindelwald', surface wear and rubbing.

7¾in (19.5cm) high

£150-200 **FELL**

A late 19thC to early 20thC Black Forest carved wood nutcracker, playing music when handle is lifted.

1½in (4cm) high

£600-700 **WW**

A 19thC Black Forest carved bear stick stand, with glass eyes.

43¼in (110cm) high

£2,500-3,000 **L&T**

A late 19thC Black Forest carved wood group of two bears, the adult about to spank the younger with a golf club.

14¼in (36cm) high

£2,200-2,800 **WW**

A late 19thC Black Forest coat hook, the bear holding a hat, skis and pole, with horn hooks.

15¾in (40cm) high

£2,500-3,000 **WW**

A rare Bavarian Black Forest tobacco jar and cover, modelled as a hound holding a pipe, his head and back pouch opening to reveal interiors for tobacco.

This is thought to be one of only two known examples of this figure.

19¼in (49cm) high

£11,000-14,000 **HANN**

A pair of late 19thC Bavarian Black Forest seated bear wall brackets.

8¾in (22cm) high

£750-850 **HANN**

A late 19thC to early 20thC Black Forest carved wood bear stick stand, with removable metal drip tray, some damages.

25in (63.5cm) high

£800-900 **FLD**

A 19thC Bavarian Black Forest St Bernard dog.

15¾in (40cm) long

£2,200-2,800 **HANN**

A late 19thC Black Forest carved wood wall plaque, depicting dead game, two fish, a heron and a game bird.

24¾in (63cm) high

£650-750 **WW**

A late 19thC Black Forest carved wood model of a mountain dog, possibly a St Bernard, with glass eyes.

9½in (24cm) long

£900-1,100 **WW**

A late 19thC Black Forest chamois group, with distributor's label, 'C.D. Schirrmann, 7 Rue Royale Paris'.

43¼in (110cm) high

£5,000-6,000 **MEA**

ESSENTIAL REFERENCE – NOTTINGHAM ALABASTER

Nottingham alabaster was mainly quarried in Tutbury and Chellaston near Nottingham. During the 14thC to 16thC altarpieces and devotional images were incredibly popular at home and abroad, with high demand for carvings from the merchant classes and religious institutions. Many hundreds of English alabasters were exported to the continent with some discovered at Santiago de Compostela in Spain and as far north as Iceland.

A 15thC Nottingham alabaster and polychrome decorated fragment, depicting the Coronation of the Virgin, with gilt highlights.

11¼in (28.5cm) wide

£11,000-14,000 WW

A 16thC South Netherlands oak carving of St Martin and the beggar.

22in (56cm) high

£2,500-3,000 GORL

A 17thC carved and painted pine and limed wood carving of the Madonna, standing on cherubs' heads.

12in (30.5cm) high

£650-750 SWO

A 17thC Flemish carved oak Entombment group, a small section broken away.

This piece was exhibited in 'Treasures from Sussex Houses', in 'Bronzino to Boy George', Brighton Museum, 1985.

22½in (57cm) high

£9,000-11,000 GORL

A late 17thC to early 18thC Spanish carved polychrome and parcel-gilt figure of saint, possibly Francis Xavier.

68¼in (173.5cm) high

£1,000-1,500 L&T

A pair of early 18thC Flemish sculpted limewood models of putti, some cracks, chips and knocks.

28½in (72.5cm) high

£3,500-4,000 DN

An 18thC and later, possibly Flemish, carved oak figure of St George and the dragon.

22¾in (58cm) high

£1,800-2,200 LC

A late 18thC Continental carved wood Corpus Christi, the figure of Christ mounted on a fruitwood crucifix above a skull, some faults and repairs.

26¾in (68cm) high

£1,500-2,000 TOV

A late 18thC Italian carved and polychromed wood cherub.

22in (56cm) high

£1,200-1,600 L&T

An early 20thC carved and painted carousel chariot side panel, by Gustav Dentzel.

31½in (80cm) wide

£1,000-1,400 **POOK**

A carved and painted bird tree with hanging cherries, by David Guilmet.

20½in (52cm) high

£2,200-2,800 **POOK**

A late 19thC carved and painted carousel figure of a giraffe, attributed to Daniel Muller at the Dentzel Company, Philadelphia.

66in (167.5cm) high

£75,000-85,000 **SK**

A Pennsylvania carved and painted rooster, signed 'W. Kinstler', minor wear.

c1900 *23½in (59.5cm) high*

£10,000-14,000 **POOK**

A turned and painted saffron cup, by Joseph Lehn (1798-1892), Lancaster, Pennsylvania.

3in (7.5cm) high

£5,500-6,000 **POOK**

A carved and painted bird on stump, by Schtockschnitzler Simmons (fl.1885-1910), south-eastern Pennsylvania.

7in (18cm) high

£7,000-8,000 **POOK**

A carved and painted pine eaglet, by Wilhelm Schimmel (1817-90), Cumberland Valley, Pennsylvania, some flakes to talons.

4in (10cm) high

£11,000-14,000 **POOK**

An early 20thC folk art carved and painted seated dog, found in Zanesville, Ohio.

19½in (49.5cm) high

£2,500-3,000 **POOK**

A 19thC carved and painted carnival target bust, as the head of a woman with black cloth headband, metal plate at base reads 'MIETTE'.

19¾in (50cm) high

£1,000-1,400 **SK**

A late 17thC walnut and seaweed marquetry inlaid longcase clock, by John Shaw, Holborn, with brass eight-day five-pillar bell-striking movement, the dial engraved with the Doves of Pliny.

86½in (220cm) high

£9,000-10,000 LSK

A late 17thC walnut and beech marquetry inlaid longcase clock, with eight-day two-train movement, the dial signed 'Rich: Fennel Kinsington'.

86½in (220.5cm) high

£7,500-8,500 PW

ESSENTIAL REFERENCE – WILLIAM CLEMENT

William Clement was one of the leading London clockmakers of the late 17thC.

- **He was born in Rotherhithe and spent his early career as an anchorsmith and blacksmith.**
- **He turned to clockmaking when he moved to Southwark in 1677, and later became Master of the London Clockmakers' Company in 1694.**
- **Clement was one of the earliest makers to apply the anchor escapement to clockwork, making a long pendulum practicable.**

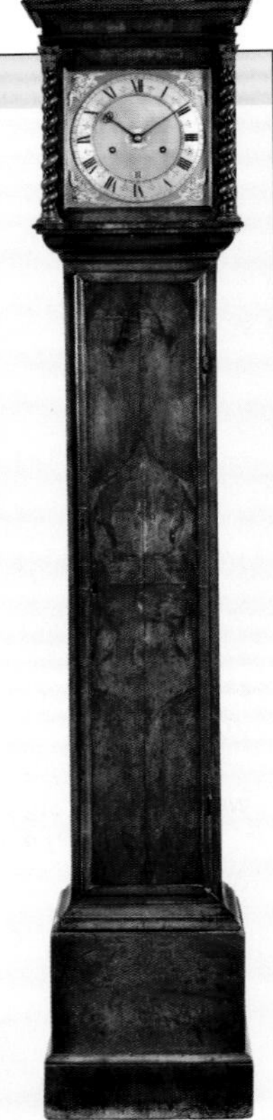

A William and Mary walnut longcase clock, by William Clement, with one-month five-pillar bell-striking movement with anchor escapement, the dial, signed 'Gulielmus Clement Londini Fecit'.

79¾in (202.5cm) high

£50,000-60,000 WW

A William and Mary longcase clock, by Samuel Watson, signed to dial, the case inlaid with floral and foliate marquetry and ebonised trim.

Samuel Watson (fl.1687-1710) was as an important Coventry and later London clock and watchmaker, known for his timekeeping innovations, including the five-minute repeater watch. Over his career, Watson was commissioned by Charles II and by Sir Isaac Newton.

82in (208cm) high

£15,000-18,000 L&T

A William and Mary longcase clock, by John Knibb, Oxford, with eight-day bell-striking movement with recoil anchor escapement and outside countwheel, signed to dial, in a walnut and ebony case with marquetry panels.

John Knibb was born c1650 and was apprenticed c1664 to Joseph Knibb, his older brother, in St Clement. Joseph moved to London in 1670, John took over the Oxford business. He was Mayor of Oxford 1698-99 and 1710-11 and continued making clocks until 1722.

82¾in (210cm) high

£15,000-20,000 WW

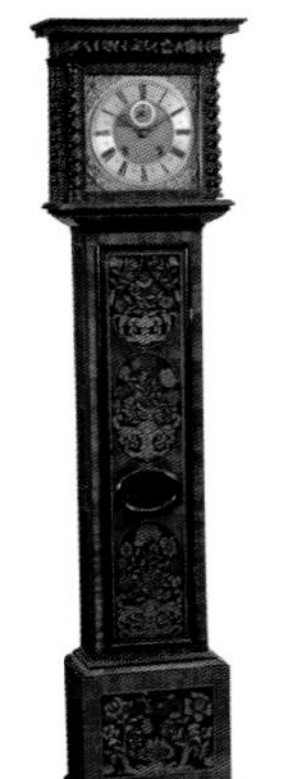

A William and Mary walnut, olive wood and floral marquetry longcase clock, by James Clowes, London, with one-month five-pillar bell-striking movement with outside countwheel and anchor escapement, signed to dial, some restoration to case.

James Clowes (c1643-1705) was born in Astbury, Cheshire, older brother of John (b.1751) and son to James Clowes senior, a nail maker of Odd Rode. James Clowes junior became a Free Brother of The Clockmakers' Company in 1671.

c1690 78½in (199.5cm) high

£15,000-20,000 DN

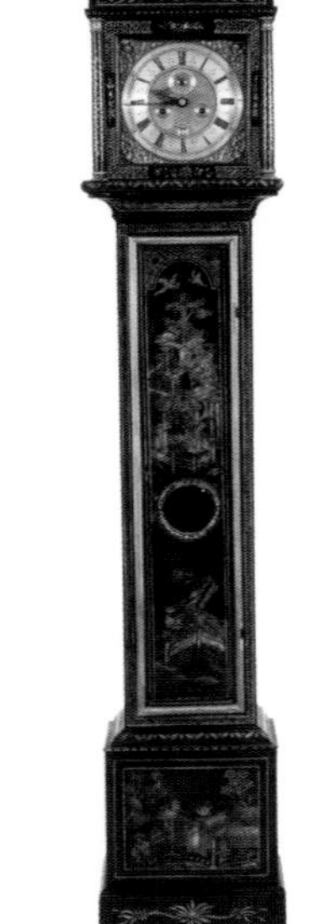

A longcase clock, by Samuel Barrow, London, with eight-day bell-striking movement, in a black lacquered case with chinoiserie decoration.

Samuel Barrow was apprenticed in 1688 to John Barrow, and became a Freeman of the Clockmakers' Company in 1696, working until c1704.

84¼in (214cm) high

£2,200-2,600 BE

ESSENTIAL REFERENCE – JOSEPH WINDMILLS

Joseph Windmills was one of the finest clockmakers of late 17thC London.

- **He was born c1640-50, and joined the Clockmakers' Company as a Free Brother on 29 September 1671.**
- **In 1699, he was elected as the youngest Warden of Clockmakers' Company, and in 1702 became Master.**
- **His son Thomas Windmills later went into business with him, and the firm lasted until Thomas's death in 1737.**
- **Clocks made by the firm were typically signed 'Windmills' or 'J & T Windmills'.**

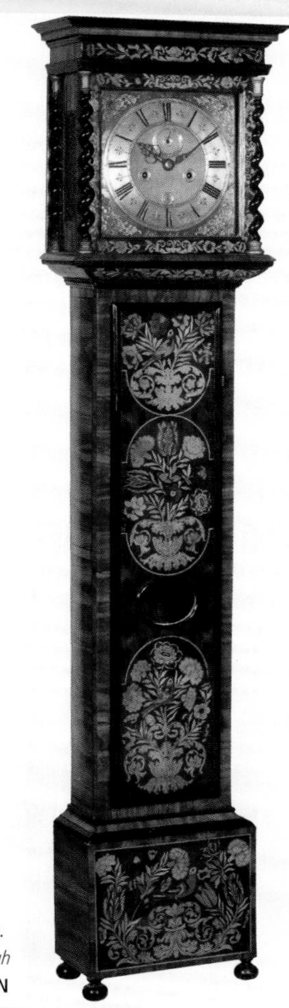

A William III burr walnut and marquetry longcase clock, by Joseph Windmills, London, with one-month bell-striking movement with countwheel and anchor escapement, some replacements to case.
c1695 *81in (206cm) high*
£22,000-26,000 **DN**

A burr walnut longcase clock, by Joseph Windmills, London, with one-month six-pillar bell-striking movement with anchor escapement and outside countwheel, signed to dial, re-built caddy top, later finials, plinth restored.
c1695 *89in (226cm) high*
£14,000-18,000 **TEN**

An early 18thC walnut marquetry inlaid longcase clock, by Joseph Windmills, London, with one-month bell-striking movement, the dial signed.
87¾in (223cm) high
£10,000-14,000 **L&T**

A William III walnut and foliate marquetry longcase clock, by John Williamson, Leeds, with twin-train bell-striking movement with internal countwheel, the signed dial.

John Williamson (c1651-1748) was born in Guisley, near Leeds. He trained in London, and gained his freedom of the Worshipful Company of Clockmakers in 1682, before returning the following year to Leeds. The workmanship and quality of his clocks are considered equal to the main London makers of the time.
c1700 *82in (208cm) high*
£20,000-24,000 **BELL**

An early 18thC Queen Anne seaweed marquetry longcase clock, by Robert Pike, London, with eight-day twin-fusee bell-striking movement, the dial signed.
85in (216cm) high
£6,000-7,000 **L&T**

A Queen Anne walnut eight-day longcase clock, by Lewis Beavan, Bristol, with four-pillar bell-striking movement with anchor escapement, signed to dial, columns missing from hood.
c1705 *89½in (227.5cm) high*
£3,000-3,500 **DN**

A walnut marquetry inlaid longcase clock, by Richard Rooker (fl.1694-1748), London, with eight-day six-pillar bell-striking movement, signed to dial, some restoration.
72¾in (185cm) high
£12,000-15,000 **BE**

A George I walnut eight-day longcase clock, by Henry Battercon, London, with five-finned pillar inside rack and bell-striking movement with anchor escapement, signed to dial, some replacements and restoration.

Henry Batterson was born in Waddesdon, Buckinghamshire in 1676 and apprenticed to William Davison in 1694, transferring to Jonathan Puller in 1696 and gaining his freedom of the Clockmakers' Company in 1701.

c1720 *90½in (230cm) high*

£5,500-6,000 DN

A burr walnut longcase clock, by John Jefferies, London, with ringed five-pillar eight-day bell-striking movement, signed to dial.

c1730 *94½in (240cm) high*

£3,500-4,000 SWO

An early to mid-18thC carved oak longcase clock, by Thomas Gorsuch, Salop, Shrewsbury, with eight-day two-train bell-striking movement, some damages.

82in (208cm) high

£1,600-2,000 PW

A mid-18thC George II mahogany longcase clock, by Miles Wedred (Wetherhead), Kirkby Lonsdale, the case attributed to Gillows, with eight-day bell-striking movement, the dial with revolving moon phases, engraved 'Tempus Fugit'.

93¼in (237cm) high

£5,500-6,500 L&T

An 18thC scarlet lacquer and gilt chinoiserie longcase clock, by William Jourdain, London.

96in (224cm) high

£3,000-3,500 BRI

A mahogany longcase clock, case possibly by Gillows, with eight-day four-pillar bell-striking movement with anchor escapement, the dial signed 'Finney, Liverpool' and inscribed 'The Man is Yet Unborn, Who duly Weighs an hour', some chips and scratches to case.

c1780 *101¼in (257cm) high*

£3,500-4,000 TEN

A mid-18thC eight-day longcase clock, by Robert Grinling, Yarmouth, in a black japanned chinoiserie case.

£1,500-2,000 CHOR

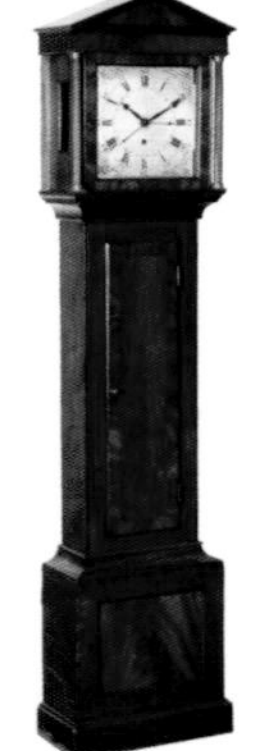

A late 18thC precision longcase timepiece, with four-finned-pillar eight-day movement with deadbeat duplex escapement regulated by seconds pendulum, in an architectural mahogany case, replacement hands, some wear.

81in (205.5cm) high

£2,000-2,500 DN

A George III mahogany musical longcase clock, by Samuel Deacon, Barton-in-the-Beans for Robotham, Leicester, with eight-day four-pillar triple-train bell-striking movement with anchor escapement, with music train playing seven tunes, the frontplate engraved 'S.D.B. 1788', the dial inscribed 'ROBOTHAM', the arch painted with an automaton scene of musicians, some wear.

Samuel Deacon (1746-1816) was born in Ratby, Leicestershire. After his apprenticeship, he was employed as a clockmaker's journeyman, later setting up on his own as a clockmaker in the small hamlet of Barton-in-the-Beans.

1788 *98in (249cm) high*
£9,000-11,000 **DN**

A Chippendale walnut tallcase clock, by George Fix, Reading, Pennsylvania, with eight-day movement, signed to dial, the case with a broken-arch bonnet, some losses and replacements.

This is one of the finest Reading clocks known and remains in remarkable condition.

c1795 *93in (236cm) high*
£20,000-25,000 **POOK**

A Federal walnut tallcase clock, by John Hoff, Lancaster, Pennsylvania, with eight-day movement, the case with line inlay.

c1805 *91½in (232.5cm) high*
£4,500-5,000 **POOK**

A Regency mahogany longcase clock, with eight-day striking deadbeat movement, the dial signed 'Wieland of Walworth', with brass fretwork decoration.

c1810 *81½in (207cm) high*
£6,000-7,000 **SWO**

An early 19thC American Federal mahogany tallcase clock, with painted dial, the case inlaid with an eagle.

90½in (230cm) high
£1,800-2,200 **DRA**

A Regency mahogany and marquetry inlaid longcase clock, by Davies, North Shields, with twin-train bell-striking movement with anchor escapement, signed to dial, with 'rocking ship' automaton to arch, some damages.

89¼in (227cm) high
£2,500-3,000 **BELL**

An early 19thC mahogany longcase regulator, by Edward Smith, Dublin, signed dial, with eight-day six-pillar single-train movement with deadbeat escapement and mercury jar pendulum, crack to plinth, losses to canopy.

Edward Smith worked as a clock manufacturer and brass founder at 34 Jervis Street in Dublin, c1801-58. In 1801 he was appointed Clock Manufacturer to the General Post Office.

92¼in (234cm) high
£4,000-4,500 **PW**

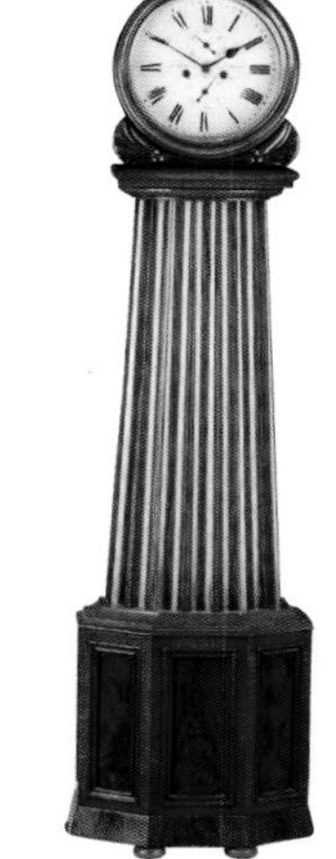

An early 19thC Scottish longcase clock, by John Donald, Glasgow, the painted dial in a drumhead case above a fluted column trunk and moulded panel base.

78in (198cm) high
£3,000-3,500 **L&T**

An early 19thC Portuguese painted chestnut longcase clock, with eight-day bell-striking birdcage movement, the dial signed 'Jeremie Girod Porto e Coruna'.

91¾in (233cm) high

£1,000-1,400 **WW**

A William IV mahogany three-train quarter-striking longcase clock, by Pryor, London, with three-train movement with anchor escapement and internal countwheel, signed to dial.

83in (211cm) high

£1,800-2,200 **BELL**

A William IV mahogany longcase regulator timepiece, by James McCabe, London, with brass eight-day five-pillar movement with deadbeat escapement, jewelled pallets and beat adjustment, with a mercury jar compensated pendulum, signed to dial, numbered '2476', in Gothic carved case.

In 1811, James McCabe inherited his father's clock, chronometer and watch making business, which had been founded in 1778. James McCabe had been previously apprenticed to Reid and Auld of Edinburgh.

76¾in (195cm) high

£8,000-9,000 **WW**

A mid-to-late Victorian carved oak longcase regulator timepiece, by James McCabe, London, with eight-day six-pillar movement with Harrison's maintaining power and deadbeat escapement, signed to dial and numbered '3330', some shrinkage and losses to veneers.

76½in (194.5cm) high

£10,000-14,000 **DN**

A mid-19thC French mahogany weight-driven long-duration longcase regulator, by Jean-Aimé Jacob, Paris, the case inset with a barometer and two thermometers.

Jean-Aimé Jacob (1793-1871) was apprenticed in 1813 to Pierre Louis Berthoud. By 1825, he had established his own workshop where he styled himself Élève de Breguet. Long-duration year-going regulators were a speciality.

72½in (184cm) high

£9,000-11,000 **ECGW**

A Victorian walnut longcase regulator, the movement attributed to Odber, Birmingham, with eight-day movement with deadbeat escapement with split anchor and jewelled pallets, with mercury jar pendulum, signed 'Bennett, Torquay' to dial.

Although unsigned, two identical movements have been noted with similar shaped plates and with split anchors, both signed for Odber, Birmingham, with a further floor-standing regulator signed for Reid & Sons, Newcastle-on-Tyne, also housing a near-identical movement. Bennett owned the retail jewellers premises situated in Lower Union Street, Torquay, from their opening in the mid-Victorian period until closing in 1985.

76¾in (195cm) high

£6,500-7,500 **BE**

A mid-Victorian Reformed Gothic carved oak longcase wall regulator timepiece, in the manner of A.W.N. Pugin, with eight-day five double-screwed baluster pillar frosted gilt movement, engraved 'ARNOLD & LEWIS, SUCCESSORS TO, I. SIMMONS, WATCH & CLOCK MANUFACTURERS', some wear to case.

Isaac Simmons was working in Manchester c1834-51, and was succeeded by Arnold and Lewis, who continued at the same address until c1905. The movement may have been supplied by James Condliff, Liverpool (fl.c1816-62). The quality of the movement suggests this clock was intended for an important location where great accuracy was required. It may have been the 'shop regulator', used to set the times of other clocks made by Simmons, or a clock made specifically for a wealthy private client or business.

85in (216cm) high

£8,500-9,500 **DN**

A late 17thC basket-top bracket clock, by Edmund Appley, London, with eight-day double-fusee five-pillar bell-striking movement with verge escapement, in an ebonised case with brass filigree work.

Edmund Appley (d.1688) was born in Westmoreland and moved to London, where he was apprenticed in 1670 to Jeffrey Bayley. He became a Freeman of the Clockmakers' Company in 1678.

13in (33cm) high

£6,500-7,500 BE

CLOSER LOOK – RÉGENCE BRACKET CLOCK

Parquetry of this sort is rare in clocks from the late Régence period, when boullework marquetry was more commonly used.

The matching bracket is decorated with an ormolu eagle and a pair of masques de comédie. The masques are identical to a pair found on a Régence bombé commode by Etienne Doirat (1675-1732), suggesting the case and bracket may have been made at Doirat's workshop in Paris.

The dial has a double ring of blue numerals against a white dial, assembled from twenty-five individual pieces. It was possibly made by Siméon de Ville, who was Roquelon's brother-in-law and l'Emailleur du Roi (the Royal Enameller).

The quality of the individual elements – parquetry, ormolu, enamel and movement – together make this an exceptional piece.

A Régence ormolu-mounted parquetry kingwood and amaranth bracket clock, by Etienne Roquelon (b.1718), Paris, with eight-day movement with silk suspension and verge escapement, signed to backplate.

c1730-40 *41in (104cm) high*

£7,500-8,500 FRE

A Charles II or William and Mary ormolu-mounted walnut calendar clock, by John Knibb, Oxford, with eight-day double-fusee movement with verge escapement, signed to backplate and dial.

See page 254 for another John Knibb clock.

c1690 *14½in (37cm) high*

£12,000-15,000 FRE

A mid-18thC ebonised bracket clock, by John Hampson, Wrexham, with single-fusee bell-striking movement, signed and numbered '1160'.

17¾in (45cm) high

£2,200-2,800 PW

An early to mid-18thC French boullework bracket clock, by Estienne, Paris, with signed bell-striking movement with verge escapement.

46in (117cm) high

£2,000-2,500 KEY

A George II ebonised bracket clock, by Samuel Whichcote, London, with twin-fusee movement with verge escapement, with signed backplate.

24in (61cm) high

£4,000-5,000 DUK

A bracket clock, by Samuel Toulmin, London, with eight-day double-fusee movement with verge escapement and pull quarter-repeat, in an ebonised bell-top case.

Samuel Toulmin worked in the Strand c1757-83. A number of watches and clocks are known signed by him, including a bracket clock in the Virginia Museum, a watch in the China Gelis collection and a watch in the Guildhall Museum.

21¼in (54cm) high

£3,500-4,500 BE

A George III ormolu-mounted ebonised balloon bracket clock, by Justin Vulliamy, London, with twin-train fusee bell-striking movement converted to anchor escapement, signed to dial, some restoration.

François-Justin Vulliamy (1712-97) was the son of a pastor at Gingins, in the Pays de Vaud region in Switzerland. He emigrated to England in 1730, and in 1743 went into partnership with Benjamin Gray (d.1764). Gray had received a Royal Warrant in 1742, which later passed to Vulliamy. François-Justin Vulliamy's son, Benjamin Vulliamy, was also a prominent clockmaker (see page 265).

c1770 *20¾in (53cm) high*

£4,500-5,000 BELL

An 18thC six-hour bracket clock, by Charles Goode (fl.1686-1730), London, with two-train fusee bell-striking movement, in olivewood case.

This is a six-hour clock made for the Italian market. The dial is numbered one to six, dividing the day into the quarters to regulate the prayer cycle of monks. Generally such clocks had a single hand, although this one has two. Six-hour clocks were common in 15thC to 17thC Tuscany.

18in (45.5cm) high

£16,000-20,000 DUK

An 18thC mahogany double-fusee repeating bracket clock, by Thomas Upjohn, Exon, with two-train bell-striking movement, recently refurbished.

19¾in (50cm) high

£4,500-5,000 **ECGW**

A late 18thC mahogany bracket clock, by John Hamilton, Glasgow, with double-fusee movement, in Chinese Chippendale-style case.

1780-84 *18in (46cm) high*

£4,000-4,500 **PW**

An ebonised chiming bracket clock, by James Tregent, London, with two-train repeater bell-striking movement, on ogee wall bracket.

clock 6½in (16.5cm) high

£9,000-10,000 **HT**

A George III ebony-cased bracket clock, by Clay, London, quarter-chiming, with verge escapement.

c1790

£6,500-7,500 **JN**

A George III mahogany bell-top bracket clock, by John Davidge, London, with twin-fusee bell-striking movement with anchor escapement, signed to dial.

19¾in (50cm) high

£3,500-4,500 **WW**

A George III ebonised bracket clock, by John Ward, London, with twin-fusee bell-striking movement with verge escapement, signed to dial.

19½in (49.5cm) high

£3,500-4,500 **WW**

A George III mahogany bracket clock, by Rolfe, Clerkenwell, with double-fusee bell-striking movement.

15in (38cm) high

£1,200-1,800 **HAN**

A late Regency mahogany bracket clock, in the manner of Thomas Hope, by James Gorham, Kensington, with twin-train bell-striking chain fusee movement with anchor escapement, the dial signed 'James Gorham/ KENSINGTON/Clock & Watch Maker/to The Royal Family', door hinges repaired.

c1820 *18½in (47cm) high*

£2,200-2,800 **BELL**

An early 19thC Irish bracket clock, by Milton & Sons, Dublin, with triple-fusee bell-striking movement with anchor escapement, in an ebonised case with brass and mother-of-pearl inlay.

19¾in (50cm) high

£4,500-5,500 **ECGW**

An early 19thC ebonised bracket clock, with three-train fusee movement striking ten chimes, losses to corner frieze.

24½in (62cm) high

£2,500-3,000 **ECGW**

A Victorian mahogany bracket clock, with eight-day triple-fusee bell-striking movement, some wear.

c1840 *20½in (52cm) high*

£2,000-2,500 **DN**

A mahogany musical bracket clock, by Parkinson and Frodsham, Change Alley, London, with eight-day five-pillar bell-striking double-fusee movement.

The Romano-Egyptian-style case to the design of Thomas Hope.

20in (51cm) high

£1,800-2,200 **BE**

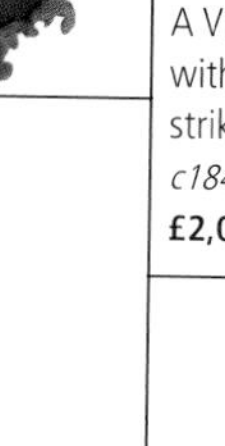

A 19thC French tortoiseshell and boullework bracket clock, with eight-day bell-striking movement, stamped 'LaGarde a Paris', serial no.3112.

31in (79cm) high

£3,500-4,000 **L&T**

A 19thC French Louis XV-style japanned bracket clock, with eight-day bell-striking movement, serial no.3747, on matching bracket.

26½in (67cm) high

£2,000-2,500 **L&T**

A 19thC mahogany and gilded Gothic bracket clock, with triple-fusee gong-striking movement.

28½in (72.5cm) high

£3,500-4,000 **PW**

A Victorian ormolu-mounted tortoiseshell bracket clock, by J.C. Jennens, London, with triple-train chain fusee bell-striking movement with anchor escapement, signed.

c1880 *22in (56cm) high*

£3,500-4,000 **BELL**

A late 19thC Louis XV boullework ormolu-mounted bracket clock, the movement stamped 'Bright, Paris', on matching bracket, some missing inlay, feet loose.

23¼in (59cm) high

£2,000-2,500 **SWO**

An Edwardian mahogany musical gong and bell-striking bracket clock, inscribed 'Syd F Stanley, Chancery Lane', with chime selector subsidiary dials.

24in (61cm) high

£2,500-3,000 **SWO**

A French Régence tortoiseshell and ormolu-mounted mantel clock, by Baltazar Martinot, Paris, with eight-day twin-train bell-striking movement.

Baltazar Martinot (1636-1716) came from an important dynasty of Rouen watchmakers. He received his master's degree in watchmaking in Paris in 1660 and became Valet de Chambre-Horloger Ordinaire of the Queen Mother in 1665.

24in (61cm) high

£2,500-3,000 **WW**

A late 18thC Viennese grande sonnerie mantel clock, with two-day gong-striking movement.

22¾in (58cm) high

£2,500-3,000 **BE**

A late 18thC Meissen Marcolini porcelain mantel clock, with Swiss four-pillar bell-striking fusee movement with watch-type verge escapement, underglaze blue crossed swords and asterisk mark, some repairs and restoration.

10½in (26.5cm) high

£3,000-3,500 **DN**

A Louis XVI ormolu and pietra dura mantel clock, with eight-day bell-striking movement.

14in (35.5cm) high

£1,100-1,400 **JN**

A Regency ormolu and patinated bronze mantel timepiece, with four-pillar eight-day single-chain fusee movement with anchor escapement, replacement hour hand, some wear.

12in (30.5cm) high

£2,500-3,000 **DN**

A Regency mahogany and brass line inlaid lancet-shaped mantel clock, retailed by John Grant, Fleet Street, London, movement by Handley & Moore, no.3781, with bell-striking twin-train gut fusee movement with anchor escapement.

John Grant (d.1810), an eminent maker, was a member of the Clockmakers' Company by 1781. Handley & Moore, apprenticed to Thwaites, supplied high-quality movements to the trade.

17¼in (44cm) high

£1,500-2,000 **BELL**

An Empire ormolu mantel clock, by L. Moinet, Paris, with twin-train bell-striking movement with external countwheel, lacking bell, dial chipped.

Louis Moinet (d.1853) was the secrétaire of Abraham-Louis Breguet (1747-1823), founder of Breguet, a watchmakers' company today owned by Swatch.

26¾in (68cm) high

£2,500-3,000 **BELL**

A late Regency brass-mounted ebonised mantel timepiece, by Finer & Nowland, London (fl.1805-25), with four-pillar chain fusee movement with anchor escapement, repair to the dial, some wear to ebonising.

c1820 *8¾in (22cm) high*

£4,500-5,000 **BELL**

An early 19thC French Empire gilt and patinated metal mantel clock, with eight-day bell-striking movement.

14½in (37cm) high

£1,500-2,000 **L&T**

An early 19thC French Empire gilt-metal mantel clock, by Blanc Fils, Palais Royal, with eight-day bell-striking movement.

17¾in (45cm) high

£2,500-3,000 **L&T**

A gilt bronze mantel clock, by Arnold & Dent, London, the movement numbered '524'.

The partnership of Edward J. Dent and John Roger Arnold began in 1830 and lasted ten years. The firm specialised in chronometers, precise clocks and other instruments. Its clocks are of extremely high quality.

c1835 *24¼in (61.5cm) high*

£5,000-6,000 **L&T**

A mid-19thC Louis Philippe ormolu striking portico mantel clock, by Destape, Paris, with two-train movement with countwheel.

18½in (47cm) high

£550-600 **BELL**

A mid-19thC French boullework portico mantel clock, with twin-train bell-striking movement, signed 'Laine Paris', numbered '424/72', with visible pendulum.

c1850 *20in (50.5cm) high*

£600-700 **MOR**

A mid-19thC French gilt bronze and porcelain mantel clock, by Lerolle, Paris, with eight-day bell-striking cylinder movement, numbered '814', with Sèvres-style porcelain dial.

25¼in (64cm) wide

£2,000-2,500 **LSK**

A carved mahogany pediment, wall or mantel clock, by Sir John Bennett, London, with eight-day chain-fusee movement, backplate stamped '5784', signed to dial.

Sir John Bennett (1814-97) was an eminent clockmaker and watchmaker, the son of watchmaker John Bennett. He was later knighted and became a politician.

21¼in (54cm) high

£1,400-1,800 **BE**

A mid-19thC Paris porcelain mantel clock, signed 'Rey â Paris'.

15¾in (40cm) wide

£1,000-1,400 **BE**

A 19thC Black Forest mantel clock, with brass movement.

24½in (62cm) high

£1,000-1,400 **WW**

A 19thC Bavarian Black Forest musical mantel clock.

26in (66cm) high

£4,500-5,000 **HANN**

A 19thC carved oak Black Forest cuckoo mantel clock, some damages.

25¼in (64cm) high

£650-750 **FLD**

A 19thC French patinated and gilt-bronze mantel clock, by Japy Frères, Paris, with eight-day bell-striking movement, signed, stamped 'E.P. LÉPOSÉ/5564'.

The firm of Japy Frères et Cie was founded in 1774 by Frederick Japy. The business rapidly expanded and by 1804 Japy employed 300 people at his factory in Beaucourt. From 1806, he took five of his sons into partnership and the firm expanded, eventually becoming one of the largest makers of clocks in Europe. The business continued into the 20thC but during the inter-war period went into decline and closed c1940.

21¼in (54cm) high

£2,500-3,000 L&T

A 19thC French marble mantel clock, by Raingo Frères, Paris, with eight-day bell-striking movement with brocket escapement.

Raingo Frères was founded in Paris in 1813 by Belgian Zacharie Joseph Raingo (1775-1847) along with his three brothers. Zacharie's speciality was astronomical clocks. The company also made a variety of clocks, including some for the home of Emperor Napoleon III.

18½in (47cm) high

£1,100-1,400 PW

A bronze and ormolu Gothic mantel clock, by Valogne à Paris, with eight-day bell-striking movement with outside countwheel, the backplate stamped '811'.

24½in (62cm) high

£1,100-1,400 BE

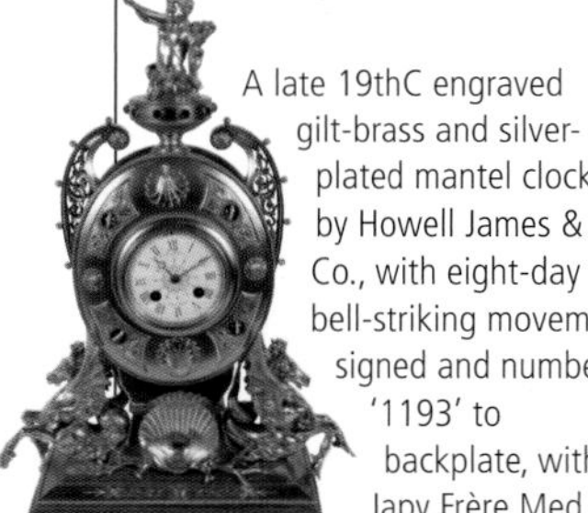

A late 19thC engraved gilt-brass and silver-plated mantel clock, by Howell James & Co., with eight-day bell-striking movement, signed and numbered '1193' to backplate, with Japy Frère Med D'Honn roundel.

19¾in (50cm) high

£1,500-2,000 DN

A marble, bronze and ormolul mantel clock, by Marti, Paris, with eight-day bell-striking movement, no.8288, the dial marked 'Fd. Viteau, 7 Rue Vivienne'.

Samuel Marti was a prolific 19thC French clockmaker, known to be working c1860 at Le Pays de Montbeliard, Paris, making roulant blancs. He joined forces with Japy Frères and Roux in 1863 in order to market their movements to firms such as L'Epée.

19in (48cm) high

£1,200-1,600 BE

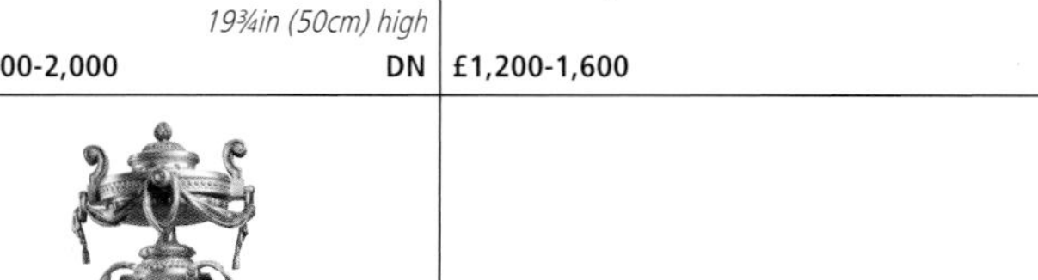

A French Louis XVI-style ormolu mantel clock, by S. Marti, with twin-train bell-striking movement, no.138.

c1885 *24½in (62cm) high*

£1,200-1,600 BELL

A late Victorian walnut Gothic Revival mantel clock, by Dent, London, no.41210, with three-train chain fusee striking movement with anchor escapement.

c1890 *24¾in (63cm) high*

£3,000-3,500 BELL

A gilt-metal-mounted ebonised mantel clock, retailed by Wilson, Penrith, with three-train chain fusee bell-striking movement with anchor escapement.

c1890 *29½in (75cm) high*

£2,800-3,200 BELL

A night-and-day spring table clock, attributed to Joseph Knibb, London, with twin-fusee bell-striking movement with verge escapement and revolving night hour disc set on a pivot, with later dial and ebonised case.

Joseph Knibb (1640-1711) was born in Oxford and apprenticed in Newport Pagnell. He later operated in both Oxford and London. He was elected as a Steward of the Clockmakers' Company in 1684 and Assistant in 1689. He retired in 1697. He was the elder brother of John Knibb (see page 254).

c1675 *16¼in (41.5cm) high*

£9,500-11,500 **DN**

A George III mahogany musical automata table clock with pull-repeat, by Thomas Hunter Junior, London, with five-pillar three-train fusee movement with verge escapement, some repairs and replacements.

Thomas Hunter Junior was apprenticed 1734 and became free of the Clockmakers' Company in 1742. He was appointed Warden of the Clockmakers' Company in 1762, and Master in 1765. He died in 1785.

c1760 *19¾in (50cm) high*

£9,000-11,000 **BELL**

ESSENTIAL REFERENCE – BENJAMIN VULLIAMY

Benjamin Vulliamy was born in 1747 and probably trained by his father, Justin Vulliamy (see page 259). He became the King's Clockmaker by Royal appointment in 1773.

- **He built a regulator for the King's Observatory at Kew, which served as the Prime Meridian until Greenwich Royal Observatory took over in 1884.**
- **He is best known for his decorative sculptural timepieces in the Neo-classical taste, created from white marble and Derby biscuit porcelain with fine cast and chased ormolu mounts. As Royal clockmaker, Vulliamy supplied several timepieces of this type to the Royal family, many of which still reside in the Royal collection.**
- **He was succeeded by his son, Benjamin Lewis, who worked from 52 Pall Mall, served as Warden 1821-25 and was appointed Master five times.**

A George III ebonised table clock, by Benjamin Vulliamy, London, no.272, the five-pillar twin-fusee rack and bell-striking movement with half deadbeat escapement and pull-quarter repeat, minor repairs and adjustments, with contemporary wall bracket.

c1796 *25½in (65cm) high*

£20,000-25,000 **DN**

CLOSER LOOK – JOSEPH WINDMILLS BRACKET CLOCK

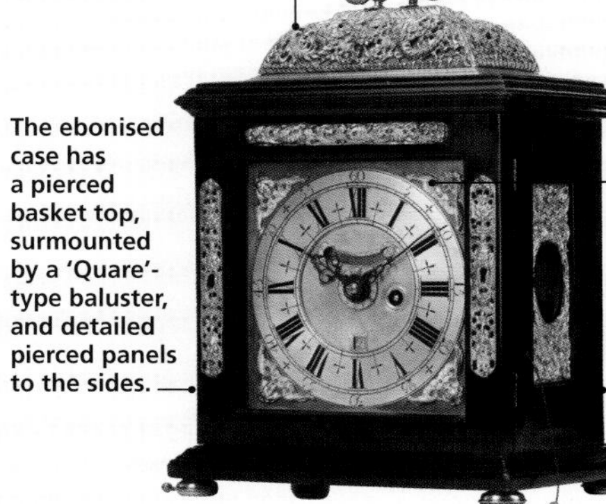

This bracket clock contains a four-pillared gut fusee movement with verge escapement, with a pull repeat chiming the hours and quarters on two bells, and a pull chord to chime the alarm.

The brass dial has a silvered chapter ring, with winged cherub spandrels to the corners.

The ebonised case has a pierced basket top, surmounted by a 'Quare'-type baluster, and detailed pierced panels to the sides.

It was made by Joseph Windmills, a prominent and highly skilled clockmaker of the late 17thC. See page 255 for his longcase clocks.

A late 17thC ebonised table or bracket clock, by Joseph Windmills, London.

15¼in (39cm) high

£24,000-28,000 **CA**

A George III table clock, by Robert Philp, London, with six-pillar triple-chain fusee movement with verge escapement, chiming a melody, in an ebonised case with Rococo brass mounts, some shrinkage.

Robert Philp worked in London c1740-81. He was a maker of musical and astronomical clocks and watches, known to have supplied clocks sent to China.

c1770 *22in (56cm) high*

£9,000-11,000 **DN**

A late 18thC George III gilt-brass-mounted mahogany musical table clock, by William Bull (fl.1770-1804), Stratford, with six-pillar triple-chain fusee movement with verge escapement, playing seven melodies, the curtain rising when music plays to reveal a festival scene, minor restoration.

25¼in (64cm) high

£6,500-7,500 **DN**

A late 18thC ebonised striking table clock, by Robert Dovers, Bath, with three-train fusee bell-striking movement with anchor escapement.

20in (51cm) high

£5,000-6,000 **HT**

A 19thC Victorian Gothic Revival rosewood regulator table clock, by Charles Frodsham, with balance-wheel fusee movement.

Charles Frodsham (1810-71) was maker of clocks, watches and chronometers. His company was known for making high-quality carriage clocks and time-precision regulator clocks.

18in (46cm) high

£4,000-5,000 **L&T**

An early to mid-19thC English carriage timepiece, in the manner of Thomas Cole, with eight-day three-pillar single-chain fusee movement with Harrison's maintaining power train with underslung English lever escapement, some wear, replacement foot.

4¼in (11cm) high

£1,500-2,000 **DN**

A 'Goliath' carriage clock, by John Moore & Sons, London, with twin-fusee gong-striking movement, the backplate signed and numbered '13480'.

John Moore & Sons of Clerkenwell was located at 38 Clerkenwell Close, c1801-75.

21½in (54.5cm) high

£8,000-9,000 **GTH**

An engraved bell-striking brass carriage clock, by Breguet à Paris, with repeat and alarm, in leather case.

5½in (14cm) high

£4,000-4,500 **JN**

A Regency Gothic Revival ormolu carriage timepiece, by Dwerrihouse and Fletcher, London, with eight-day four-pillar single-chain fusee movement with vertical English lever escapement, some wear.

John Fletcher was a chronometer maker to the Admiralty. He was a finisher and a springer, meaning he was highly skilled in his work. Later Fletcher bought out Dwerrihouse & Carter of 27 Davies St, Berkeley Square; timepieces signed 'Fletcher, late Dwerrihouse & Carter' are also known.

c1830 *7in (18cm) high*

£3,000-3,500 **DN**

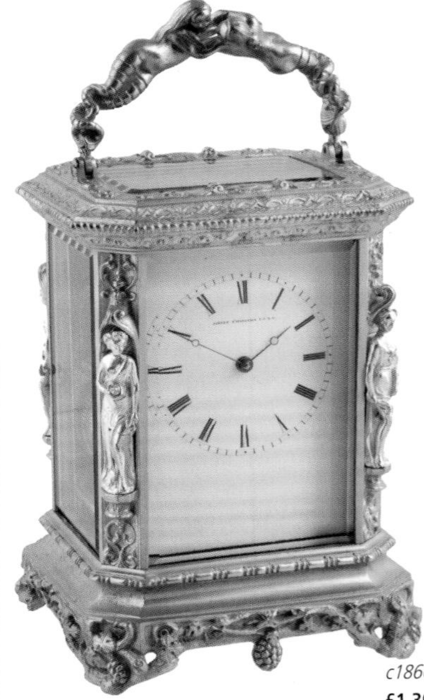

A French gilt-brass carriage clock, by Japy Frères, Beaucourt and Paris, with eight-day two-train bell-striking movement with gilt platform lever escapement, stamped to backplate.

c1860 *7¼in (18.5cm) high*

£1,300-1,800 **DN**

A mid-19thC French boullework 'pendule portative', Moser, Paris, no.8976, with two-train eight-day bell-striking movement with two-plane 'chaffcutter' escapement, some damages.

8¼in (21cm) high

£2,000-2,500 **DN**

A 19thC brass carriage clock, with two-train eight-day gong-striking movement with repeater.

6½in (16.5cm) high

£1,400-1,800 **PW**

A 19thC French brass Aesthetic Movement clock, inset with painted pottery panels.

7in (18cm) high

£2,500-3,000 **HANN**

A mid-to-late 19thC French engraved gilt-brass gorge cased petit sonnerie striking carriage clock, possibly by Drocourt, with eight-day two-train bell-striking movement with silvered platform lever escapement and push-button repeat and alarm, dial lacking alarm hand.

4½in (11.5cm) high

£4,000-5,000 **DN**

A miniature 'Japonesque' enamel carriage timepiece, retailed by Le Roy & Fils, Paris, with eight-day movement with vertical lever escapement, the backplate inscribed.

The firm of 'Le Roy & Fils' was founded in Palais Royal, Paris in 1785 by Basille Charles Le Roy. On his death, he left the business to his son, Charles-Louis, who continued producing clocks signed 'Le Roy & Fils' until 1845, when the firm was sold to Casimir Halley Desfontaines, later succeeded by his son. The firm continued trading in the hands of various successors well into the 20thC.

c1880 *2¾in (7cm) high*

£2,500-3,000 **DN**

A L'Epée brass repeating carriage clock, with two-train gong-striking movement with visible escapement, mild surface wear.

6in (15.5cm) high

£2,000-2,500 **BELL**

A late 19thC brass and champlevé carriage clock, by Sharman D. Neill, Belfast, with brass eight-day gong-striking movement with repeater, with leather case.

7in (18cm) high

£1,300-1,600 **LC**

A late 19thC French brass and chinoiserie repeating carriage clock, with eight-day gong-striking movement with a lever escapement, the backplate stamped 'PATENT SURETY POLLER' and 'G.L.', without handle

7in (17.5cm) high

£3,000-3,500 **WW**

A late 19thC brass repeating carriage clock, by Sharman D. Neill, Belfast, with gong-striking movement and visible escapement, with case.

8¼in (21cm) high

£2,500-3,000 **HAN**

A silver-mounted tortoiseshell carriage clock, London, with twin-train movement with push/repeat and lever escapement, the backplate stamped 'E G L' and 'PARIS No 2655'.

1893 *6in (15cm) high*

£800-900 **BELL**

A French gilt-brass gorge-cased grande and petite sonnerie carriage clock, by Drocourt, no.16290, with platform lever escapement, signed, with leather travelling box, some wear.

Pierre and Alfred Drocourt had a Paris-based business with a factory at Saint Nicolas d'Aliermont. Its carriage clocks are generally of the best quality, and the firm won numerous medals at International Exhibitions in the second half of the 19thC.

c1890 *7in (17.5cm) high*

£9,500-11,000 **BELL**

A French grande and petite sonnerie carriage clock, by Drocourt, no.30089, with twin-train movement with Chinese duplex platform escapement, stamped, with leather travelling case.

c1900 *8in (20.5cm) high*

£7,500-8,500 **BELL**

A French brass and champlevé enamel carriage clock, with twin-barrel gong-striking movement with repeated, with leather carrying case.

1900 *6½in (16.5cm) high*

£3,000-3,500 **HT**

A rare Charles I 'first period' brass lantern clock, with posted bell-striking movement, now with verge escapement, the dial later inscribed 'John Harford, Bath, 1658', some replacements and repairs, blackplate missing.

Comparisons with similar clocks suggest this may be the work of Richard Milborne, from the London 'first period' of lantern clockmaking. John Harford, active in Bath from c1654, may have acquired and overhauled the clock later, then sold it under his own name.

c1620-30 *15½in (39.5cm) high*
£14,000-18,000 **DN**

An early 17thC iron-framed lantern clock, with posted countwheel bell-striking movement with verge escapement, some restoration.

15in (38cm) high
£4,500-5,000 **DN**

A Charles II brass lantern clock, London, with posted countwheel bell-striking movement with verge escapement, some wears and repairs, movement converted.

c1670 *15in (38cm) high*
£4,500-5,000 **DN**

A Charles II brass lantern clock, by Edward Webb, Chew Stoke, with posted countwheel bell-striking movement with later anchor escapement, in typical 'Chew Valley' frame, some replacements and repairs, alarm lacking.

Edward Webb was a clockmaker active 1678-93 in Chew Stoke, Chew Valley, Somerset. He was probably the son of Charles Webb, who owned a foundry in Chew Stoke. After his death, he was succeeded by clockmaker Edward Bilbie.

c1680 *15¾in (40cm) high*
£5,000-6,000 **DN**

A Charles II brass miniature striking lantern clock, by Joseph Knibb, London, with converted verge escapement and alarm train, later handles and latches.

c1670 *9¼in (23.5cm) high*
£5,000-6,000 **BELL**

A William and Mary brass miniature lantern timepiece, by Daniel Parker, Fleet Street, London, the movement with verge escapement and alarm train, some replacements, one foot broken.

9½in (24cm) high
£1,600-2,000 **BELL**

A pyramidical brass skeleton timepiece, by John Pace, Bury St Edmunds, no.253, with eighteen-day movement with Graham's deadbeat escapement, under a glass dome.

John Pace (d.1867) lived and worked in Bury St Edmunds. His workshop was at 19 Abbeygate Street. He exhibited a virtually identical skeleton timepiece at the 1851 Great Exhibition.

c1855 *17in (43cm) high*
£4,000-5,000 **BELL**

A brass skeleton clock, with chain-driven movement, under a glass dome, on a walnut base.

19¾in (50cm) high
£1,200-1,600 **LC**

A Victorian brass skeleton clock, by W.E. Vale, Lichfield, with glass display case.

9¾in (24.5cm) high
£400-500 **LOCK**

A George III ormolu, Geneva enamel and paste set automaton timepiece, for the Chinese market, attributed to William Carpenter, with later musical movement, no.33702.

William Carpenter was a member of the Clockmakers' Company 1770-1817, gaining his freedom in 1781. During his working career, he produced many complex automata clocks, often for the Chinese market. The Chinese Emperor Qianlong (1735-95) collected clocks throughout his reign, as had his grandfather, Emperor Kangxi. This resulted in a substantial expansion for English merchants and makers. The missionary Valentine Chalier observed in 1736 that the Chinese Imperial palace contained more than 4000 clocks.

c1800 *11½in (29cm) high*

£45,000-50,000 BELL

A George III brass-cased travelling alarm timepiece, by Thomas Mudge and William Dutton, with thirty-hour movement with verge escapement, with later oak bracket.

5¼in (13.5cm) high

£13,000-16,000 WW

A mahogany and cherry dwarf clock, Lancaster County, Pennsylvania, with eight-day movement, the dial signed 'Geoe. Eby Manheim' above a reverse-painted panel.

Very few examples of this form are known.

c1830 *40½in (103cm) high*

£20,000-25,000 POOK

CLOSER LOOK – NIGHT CLOCK

This clock is modelled as a Classical vase with lion's head handles and ormolu ornamentation, on a bronze plinth with a large ormolu starburst.

The dial is signed 'Bofenschen à Paris', an expert clockmaker and inventor (fl.1780-1813), who worked alongside French horologist Abraham Louis Breguet (1747-1823).

It is an unusual piece, designed to be used both during the day and at night. The vase contains an oil reserve and wick that can be lit at night, which projects the time through an adjustable lens in the reverse.

Despite some wear and untested movement, the rarity of this night clock assures its value.

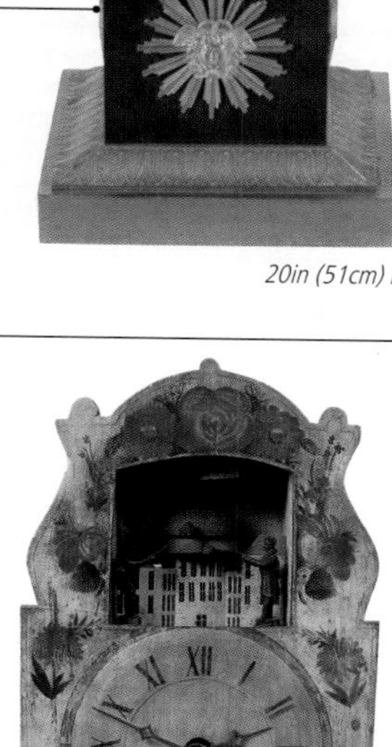

An early 19thC bronze and ormolu night clock, some scratches to lens, chips to enamel.

20in (51cm) high

£11,000-14,000 DN

A rare mid-19thC Black Forest Schild clock, with weight-driven movement, with triple automata and painted dial, with an architectural scene and three men with hammers for the bells.

12in (30.5cm) high

£3,000-3,500 LSK

A mid-19thC cast iron Turret clock, by Smith & Sons, St John's Square, Clerkenwell, with twin-winding barrels below eight cogs, some damages.

£1,200-1,500 FLD

A Black Forest carved wood clock, with Paris eight-day movement.

20in (51cm) wide

£3,500-4,000 JN

A Russian 'Fabergé' model enamel urn-shaped clock, with Classical enamel portraits below a band with silvered dial, key pattern and scrolled feet.

6in (15cm) high

£2,500-3,000 JN

A rare French silver beehive clock, movement by Saudrais A. Nantes, the sides with applied bees, on claw feet.

5in (12.5cm) high

£1,500-2,000 JN

A Louis XVI blue porcelain and gilt-metal clock garniture, with eight-day movement, with candelabra.

clock 21in (53.5cm) high

£1,800-2,200 **JN**

An early 19thC Charles X rouge marble and bronze clock garniture, with eight-day bell-striking movement, with a pair of urns.

clock 20in (50.5cm) high

£1,300-1,600 **L&T**

A mid-19thC French ormolu and silvered metal clock garniture, with eight-day bell-striking movement, the case in Gothic Revival or troubadour style, with a pair of urns.

clock 19¾in (50cm) high

£1,500-2,000 **DN**

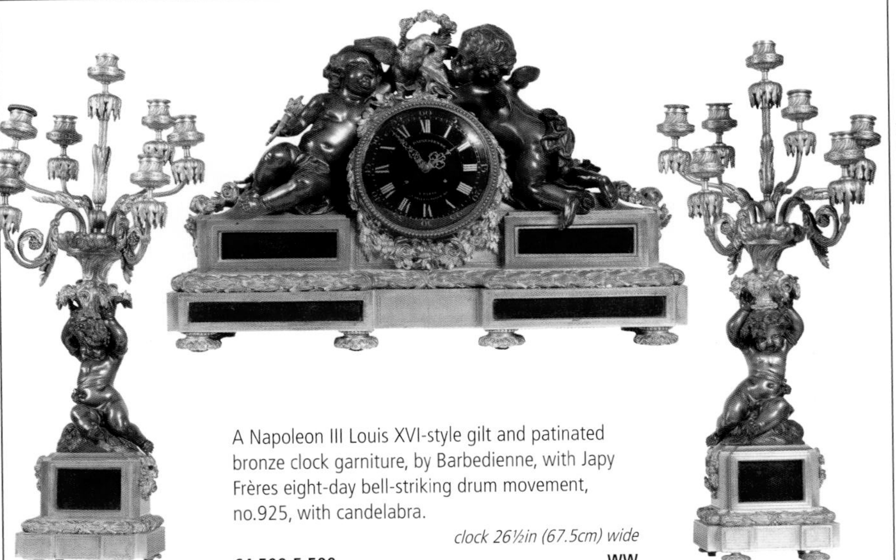

A Napoleon III Louis XVI-style gilt and patinated bronze clock garniture, by Barbedienne, with Japy Frères eight-day bell-striking drum movement, no.925, with candelabra.

clock 26½in (67.5cm) wide

£4,500-5,500 **WW**

A Napoleon III Louis XVI-style ormolu and patinated bronze figural clock garniture, by Brulfer, Paris, with eight-day bell-striking movement, with candlesticks.

clock 21¾in (55.5cm) high

£4,000-5,000 **WW**

A 19thC French ormolu and champlevé enamel mantel clock garniture, by Dufaud, Paris, with candlesticks.

clock 12in (30.5cm) high

£2,000-2,500 **GWA**

A 19thC French ormolu clock garniture, by Raingo Frères, Paris, with candelabra.

clock 17in (43cm) high

£2,500-3,000 **JN**

A 19thC French clock marble and ormolu garniture, signed 'DROUARD, CALAIS', with candelabra.

clock 32in (81.5cm) high

£3,000-4,000 **JN**

A mid-to-late 19thC French porcelain Sèvres-style gilt-metal-mounted clock garniture, with eight-day two-train movement, painted with Watteauesque and landscape panels.

clock 24½in (62cm) high

£12,000-15,000 **DN**

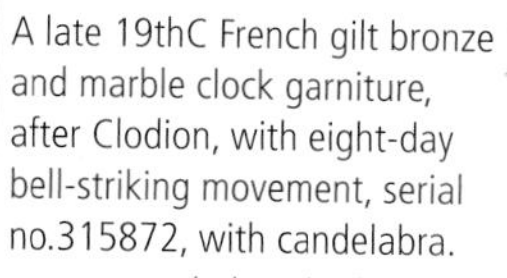

A late 19thC French gilt bronze and marble clock garniture, after Clodion, with eight-day bell-striking movement, serial no.315872, with candelabra.

clock 15¼in (39cm) high

£3,500-4,000 **L&T**

A late 19thC gilt bronze and rouge griotte marble four-glass clock garniture, by Julien Leroy, Paris, with twin-train bell-striking movement, with Cupid-form candelabra.

clock 18in (46cm) high

£2,500-3,000 **CA**

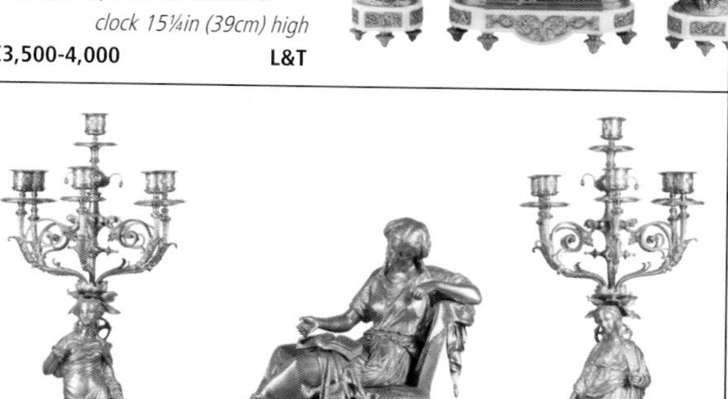

A late 19thC gilt bronze and malachite mantel clock garniture, by Moreau, Paris, with twin-train bell-striking movement with outside countwheel, with candelabra.

clock 22½in (57cm) high

£10,000-13,000 **CA**

A late 19thC German Dresden porcelain clock garniture, with brass eight-day striking drum movement, stamped '180248', with associated Berlin candelabra.

clock 23¾in (60.5cm) high

£2,200-2,800 **WW**

A late 19thC brass French mantel clock garniture, with twin-barrel gong-striking movement, with champlevé decoration and a porcelain panel in the style of Boucher, with two urns.

Champlevé is a decorative technique where hollows are made in a metal surface, then filled with coloured enamels.

clock 12¼in (31cm) high

£3,000-4,000 **PW**

A French 'Japonisme' ormolu, bronze and cloisonné enamel clock garniture, movement no.20176, with cylinder escapement, re-gilt, hand missing, with candleabra.

c1890

clock 15¾in (40cm) high

£3,000-4,000 **BELL**

A late 19thC to early 20thC French porcelain and gilt-brass clock garniture, with gong-striking movement, the dial marked 'R. STEWART/PARIS', with porcelain urns.

clock 13½in (34.5cm) high

£1,300-1,800 **L&T**

An 18thC thirty-hour striking wall clock, signed 'Henry Baker, Malling', with four-posted movement with anchor escapement, with a later wall bracket.

c1750 *11in (28cm) high*

£1,000-1,400 **TEN**

A late 18thC parcel-gilt and chinoiserie tavern timepiece, by William Buckland, Thame, with single-train movement with anchor escapement, some damages.

59in (150cm) high

£2,800-3,200 **BELL**

ESSENTIAL REFERENCE – ACT OF PARLIAMENT CLOCKS

Wall clocks for taverns, inns, assembly rooms and other public buildings were introduced in the 1720s.

- **These tavern clocks had large dials, as they were designed to be seen clearly from a distance.**
- **They are often called Act of Parliament clocks, although this is something of a misnomer.**
- **In 1797, the Prime Minister, William Pitt the Younger passed an act introducing a five-shilling duty on clocks.**
- **The act was repealed a year later due to its negative effect on the clock industry, but it gave rise to the popular misconception that these clocks were put up in taverns for customers who could not afford to own one. In fact, most tavern clocks predate the act.**

An Act of Parliament clock, by James Coates, Cirencester, with black japanned trunk, some splits to dial, dents and losses.

58in (147.5cm) high

£4,000-4,500 **GORL**

A George III red japanned tavern timepiece, by John Dwerryhouse, London, with recoil anchor escapement, signed.

John Dwerryhouse is recorded as working at 23 Charles Street, Berkeley Square from 1770-1805.

58¼in (148cm) high

£4,000-4,500 **WW**

A mahogany wall clock, with eight-day bell-striking movement, the painted dial signed 'Upjohn, Exeter'.

The Upjohn family were a well-known and prolific family of clockmakers working in both Exeter and London. The Exeter branch of the family included William Upjohn (b.c1754), John Upjohn (b.1771), and his son Robert Wittingham Upjohn (b.1807) who took over from his father as keeper of the Exeter Cathedral clock.

47¼in (120cm) high

£2,000-2,500 **BE**

A Massachusetts Federal lyre-form striking banjo timepiece, by Aaron Willard, Boston, with eight-day striking movement, neck panel replaced.

c1815 *38in (96.5cm) high*

£4,500-5,000 **POOK**

A Regency mahogany 'Norfolk' drop-dial wall timepiece, by Matthew Read (1756-1826), Aylsham, with four-pillar movement with anchor escapement, some replacements.

c1820 *49¼in (125cm) high*

£750-850 **BELL**

A Regency mahogany wall timepiece, by Handley and Moore, London, with four-pillar single-fusee movement, in a saltbox-type case, dial refinished, restoration to case.

George Handley and John Moore went into partnership after their former Master, John Thwaites, died in 1800. The business was continued as John Moore and Sons after the death of George Handley. The workshop was known for producing public clocks and supplying movements to other makers, and continued into the early years of the 20thC.

19in (48.5cm) high

£1,800-2,200 **DN**

A Viennese mahogany 'Lanterndlur' wall timepiece, by Andreas Alzinger, Vienna, with one-month four-pillar movement with deadbeat escapement, some wear.

c1825 *45¼in (115cm) high*

£3,500-4,000 **DN**

A late Regency to William IV parcel-gilt faux rosewood world-time tavern timepiece, possibly East Anglian School, with four-pillar movement with anchor escapement, loose central panel, crack to trunk, decoration worn.

57½in (146cm) high

£3,000-3,500 **BELL**

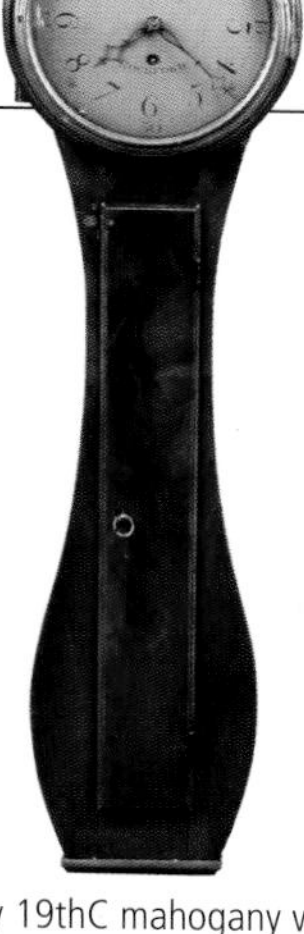

An early 19thC mahogany wall timepiece, by John Draper, Rochford, the brass movement with tapered plates and long pendulum.

45¼in (115cm) high

£1,800-2,200 **CHEF**

A Viennese inlaid mahogany grande sonnerie Biedermeier wall clock, with four-pillar triple-train gong-striking movement with lenticular bob pendulum, some wear.

c1840 *43¼in (110cm) high*

£1,400-1,800 **DN**

An early Victorian mahogany drop-dial wall timepiece, Vulliamy, London, with four-pillar single-fusee movement with half-deadbeat escapement, numbered '1378', the dial signed, with crowned Royal 'V.R.' cipher, inscribed 'POOR LAW COMMISSION', some wear.

This piece seems to have been supplied for use by The Poor Law Commission at Somerset House in c1837, shortly after Victoria had ascended the throne. The Poor Law Commission was a body established after the passing of the Poor Law Amendment Act 1834, to administer poor relief and tackle unemployment and homelessness, generally by placing those unable to provide for themselves in a workhouse.

c1836-37 *24in (61cm) high*

£8,500-9,500 **DN**

A Viennese mahogany and boxwood outlined wall regulator, 'Dachluhr', by Peter Peuker, Wien, the movement with deadbeat escapement and Harrison's maintaining power.

c1845 *34in (86.5cm) high*

£2,000-2,500 **BELL**

A late 19thC Black Forest cuckoo clock, with two-train movement, paper label for Camerer, Kuss & Co., half the door detached, chips and cracks.

15¾in (40cm) high

£700-800 **BELL**

A carved oak cuckoo clock, with eight-day double-fusee gong-striking movement, labelled 'Camerer Cuss of 186, Uxbridge Road'.

33½in (85cm) high

£1,800-2,200 **BE**

A late 19thC to early 20thC American perpetual calendar wall clock, by the William L. Gilbert Clock Company.

33½in (85cm) high

£600-700 **APAR**

A 20thC gold, diamond and enamel strut clock, by Asprey, London, the engine-turned enamel dial with diamond-inset hands, signed, hallmarked for London.

4¼in (11cm) high

£5,500-6,000 **BE**

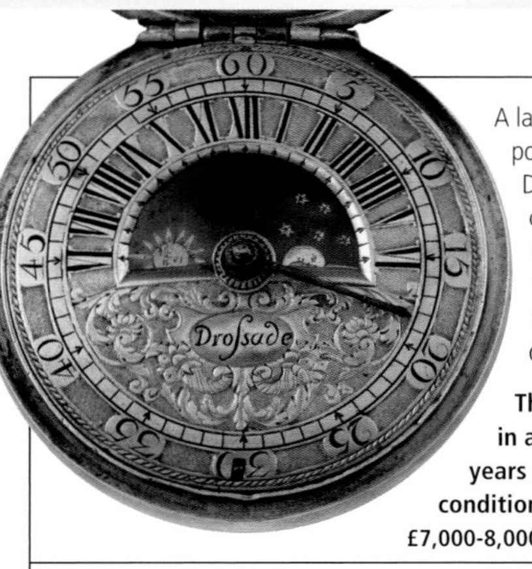

A late 17thC pair-cased pocket watch, by Sam Drossade, London, with crown wheel and verge escapement, with a rotating blue steel disc with moon and sun, some denting and scratching.

This watch has been in a safe for at least 50 years and so is in very good condition for its age.

£7,000-8,000 **ECGW**

A fusee pocket watch, by Thomas Tompion, London, signed, numbered '4360', in copper case.

1709-13 *2in (5cm) diam 4oz*

£3,000-3,500 **GWA**

A pair-case pocket watch, by C. Cabrier, London, with verge movement, no.5829, gilt-metal case, some wear.

c1730 *1½in (3.5cm) diam*

£950-1,100 **HAN**

A mid-18thC French yellow metal and rock crystal cased pocket watch, by J.J. Bourdillat, Paris, with chain-driven verge fusee movement, with silver regulator dial.

1¾in (4.5cm) diam 1¾oz

£4,000-5,000 **LSK**

A George II gold pair-cased pocket watch, by James Chater, London, with single-fusee verge movement, later converted to lever escapement, the case repoussé decorated with 'Roman Charity' scene, some dents.

James Chater senior was admitted to the Clockmakers' Company 1718, gaining his freedom in 1726. He died in 1762. The layout of the decoration to the outer case bears strong similarities to an example by Augustin Heckel, a German émigré working in London c1715-46.

c1739 *2in (5cm) diam*

£2,500-3,000 **DN**

A George II triple-cased verge pocket watch, for the Middle Eastern market, by Markwick, Markham, Perigal, London, with single-fusee verge movement with verge escapement and Tompion-type adjustment, marked 'R.D.' and '12988', in tortoiseshell outer case.

During the second half of the 18thC, the firm Markwick, Markham, Perigal specialised in producing clocks and watches for export to the Middle East. The firm was founded when James Marwick (junior) went into partnership with his son-in-law, Robert Markham. After Marwick's death in 1730, the business was continued by Markham and his successors, with Francis Perigal senior joining the business in c1750.

c1751 *2½in (6.5cm) diam*

£1,500-2,000 **DN**

A gold pair-cased open-faced pocket watch, with verge fusee movement, engraved 'Jn. Mansfield, London', the back cover chased with the Choice of Hercules, minute hand missing, with leather case.

1762 *2in (5cm) diam 3⅜oz*

£1,800-2,200 **DN**

A Regency silver cylinder pocket watch, by John Roger Arnold, London, with gilt full-plate single-fusee movement with cylinder escapement with jewelled escapewheel pivots, numbered '3438', the case hallmarked 'A.G.' over 'J.M.', some hairlines and dents.

John Roger Arnold (1769-1840) was the son of the renowned Chronometer maker John Arnold. He was apprenticed in 1792 and gained his freedom by 1796. He became Master of the Clockmakers' Company in 1817 and later went into partnership with E.J. Dent.

c1814 *2¼in (5.5cm) diam*

£2,500-3,000 **DN**

A gold Continental skeletonised quarter repeater Jacquemart automaton pocket watch, with verge movement, some wear, automata mechanism missing.

c1820 *2¼in (5.5cm) wide 4⅜oz*

£3,500-4,000 **TEN**

An early 19thC Swiss automaton repeater striking pocket watch, with blue enamel and gold crescent moon.

2¼in (5.5cm) diam

£2,000-2,500 **HANN**

An early 19thC Swiss gold- and enamel-cased fob watch, by G. Henry Valentin, with keywind chain-driven verge fusee movement, the back enamelled.

1½in (4cm) diam 1¾oz

£3,000-4,000 **LSK**

A pair-case silver pocket watch, with fusee and chain movement with verge escapement, hallmarked London, wear to movement, dent to case.

1847 *2¼in (5.5cm) diam*

£350-400 **FELL**

A Victorian lady's black enamelled key-wind open-faced fob watch, with gilt cylinder movement, the inner case with 'Pigot a Geneve, No 915', movement not working, some damage to case.

1½in (4cm) diam 1⅜oz

£400-450 **BELL**

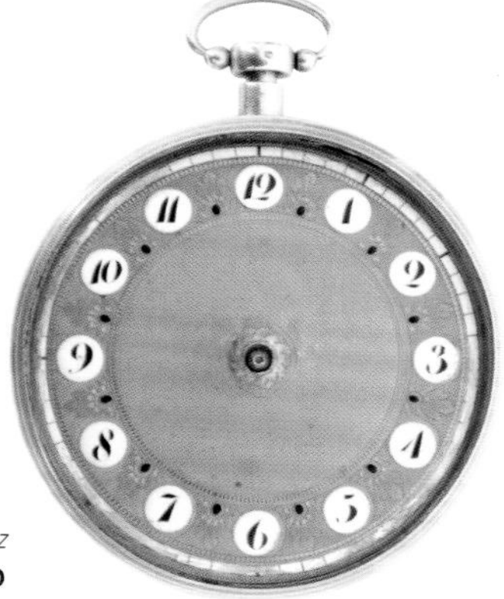

A 19thC Swiss gold open-faced key-wind musical/repeater pocket watch.

2¼in (6cm) diam 4⅛oz

£2,500-3,000 **FLD**

A 19thC 18ct gold top-wind fob watch, with enamelled case back, signed 'ALTENLOH A BRUXELLES', lacking suspensory loop.

1oz

£550-650 **AST**

A late 19thC Mensor double-sided open-faced chronograph tachymeter pocket watch.

2¼in (5.5cm) diam

£550-600 **LOCK**

An 18ct hallmarked half-hunter crown wing pocket watch, by W. Rogers, Liverpool and London.

1888 *4⅝oz*

£1,500-2,000 **FLD**

A late 19thC lapis lazuli cased watch, possibly by Hermann Böhm, with verge fusee movement and disc-type regulator, movement not functioning, some wear.

c1890 *1½in (3.5cm) wide*

£1,000-1,400 **DN**

An 18ct gold keyless wind half-hunter pocket watch, with three-quarter plate movement and lever escapement, no.30207, engraved 'R.C. Oldfield Liverpool', with presentation inscription, hallmarked London, some hairlines.

1891 *2in (5cm) diam 3⅞oz*

£1,200-1,600 **DN**

An 18ct gold full-hunter pocket watch, by Waltham Mass, with lever movement with bimetallic balance, blued overcoil hairspring, no. '6028383', with presentation inscription, stamped 'ROY 18k U.S Assay' and '147224', some scratches, loose glass.

This pocket watch was presented to Captain John Ramsay Gordon from the President of the United States of America for saving lives from a stricken ship of the American Schooner 'Frank O Dame' at sea 12 October 1896.

2in (5cm) diam 3½oz

£3,000-3,500 **TEN**

An 18ct hallmarked open-faced crown wing chronograph pocket watch, by Thomas Russell & Son, Liverpool and Chester.

1897 *5oz*

£1,400-1,800 **FLD**

A gentleman's 18ct gold-cased open-faced pocket watch, the movement signed 'John Bull & Co. 49 High Street Bedford no.28550', hallmarked London.

1897 *3⅞oz*

£1,200-1,600 **LOCK**

A Cartier diamond-set platinum and rock crystal pendant fob watch, with keyless-wind movement with club-tooth lever escapement, signed to dial, suspending from a bar brooch, the bezel initialled 'F.J.', French control mark, numbered '9020', with fitted case.

c1915 *1½in (4cm) wide*

£17,000-20,000 **WW**

An Art Deco lady's Cartier gold and enamel pendant watch, the movement signed 'European Clock and Watch Company', dial signed 'Cartier' and 'Bte S.G.D.E', the gold case with red and black enamel, with a fixed gold and enamel hoop with attached jade rings.

1in (2.5cm) diam

£7,000-8,000 **BOUR**

An 18ct gold top-wind half-hunter pocket watch, the balance cock with diamond end-stone, the backplate engraved 'The Field', the dial inscribed 'J.W. Benson', London.

1920

£1,200-1,600 **HT**

A George V gentleman's 9ct gold-cased half-hunter pocket watch, with 17-jewel keyless movement, the backplate numbered '240627', on a 18ct gold curblink watch chain, on a 9ct gold pendant.

5¾oz

£2,500-3,000 **LSK**

A 9ct gold Waltham USA pocket watch, with 15-jewel movement with damascened plates and lever escapement, numbered '24043334', signed, the case numbered '813385' hallmarked Birmingham, with 9ct Albert chain.

1925 *1⅝oz*

£1,000-1,400 **ECGW**

A gentleman's Rolex Prince wristwatch, reference no.1490, serial no.28184, with signed manual wind movement, yellow metal case stamped '14k', some wear.
c1926 *1in (2.5cm) high*
£3,200-3,800 **FELL**

A gentleman's Rolex Prince wristwatch, reference no.1490, serial no.07709, with signed manual wind movement, numbered '72210', silver case hallmarked Glasgow, some wear.
1930 *1in (2.5cm) high*
£3,200-4,000 **FELL**

CLOSER LOOK – ROLEX WRISTWATCH

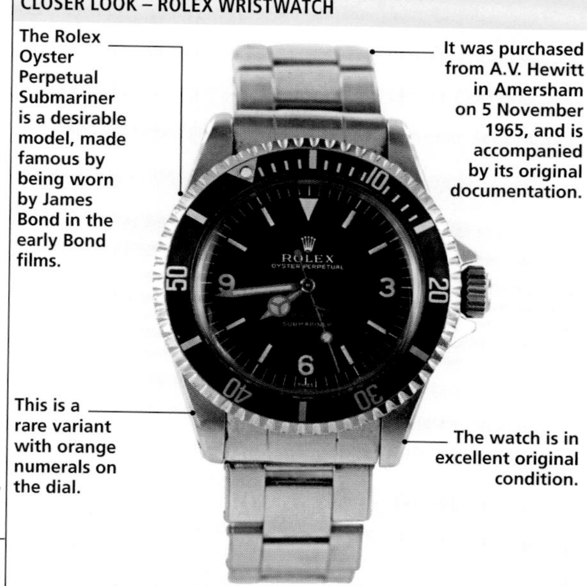
The Rolex Oyster Perpetual Submariner is a desirable model, made famous by being worn by James Bond in the early Bond films.

It was purchased from A.V. Hewitt in Amersham on 5 November 1965, and is accompanied by its original documentation.

This is a rare variant with orange numerals on the dial.

The watch is in excellent original condition.

A Rolex wristwatch, model no.1023420, serial no.1029/6636, with box.

The sale of this watch made the British auction record for a Rolex Submariner.

£300,000-350,000 **LOCK**

A 1950s gentleman's Rolex Shock Resisting 9ct gold wristwatch, on later 9ct bracelet.
1¼in (3cm) diam
£1,100-1,400 **HAN**

A Rolex Oyster Perpetual 18ct gold wristwatch, ref.6564, no.385054, with 25-jewel automatic movement, adjusted to five positions and temperature, cal.1030, no.N674293, on a crocodile strap, light wear.
c1958 *1½in (3.5cm) diam*
£2,500-3,000 **DN**

A 1970s gentleman's Rolex Oysterquartz Day-Date wristwatch, model no.19018, ref.6123446, with 18ct gold case and Rolex President bracelet.
1½in (3.5cm) wide
£4,500-5,000 **BRI**

A gentleman's Rolex Oyster Perpetual GMT-Master bracelet watch, reference no.1675, serial no.3386008, signed automatic calibre 1570, with a signed stainless steel Oyster bracelet with Oysterclasp, with box and papers.
c1973 *1½in (4cm) diam*
£13,000-18,000 **FELL**

A lady's Rolex Oyster Perpetual Datejust bracelet watch, ref.6927, serial no.7563936, signed automatic calibre 2030, with mother-of-pearl dial, with 18ct yellow gold case and President bracelet with folding Crownclasp, some scratches.
c1983 *1in (2.5cm) diam*
£3,500-4,000 **FELL**

A Rolex Oyster Perpetual Day-Date 18ct gold wristwatch, model no.16613, serial no.Z348177, the dial with diamond numerals, integral President 18ct gold bracelet, with two Rolex pouches, minor wear.
dial 1¼in (3cm) diam
£13,000-18,000 **HAN**

A gentleman's Girard-Perregaux Gyromatic wristwatch, numbered '12894 872054', with signed automatic movement, the 9ct yellow gold case hallmarked Birmingham, on lizard strap, some scratches.
1958 *1½in (4.5cm) high*
£450-550 **FELL**

A gentleman's Hublot 'Big Bang' chronograph wristwatch, no.029743, signed automatic calibre 4100 with quick date set, with factory diamond set bezel, on a signed rubber strap, with box and papers.
2in (5cm) diam
£7,000-8,000 **FELL**

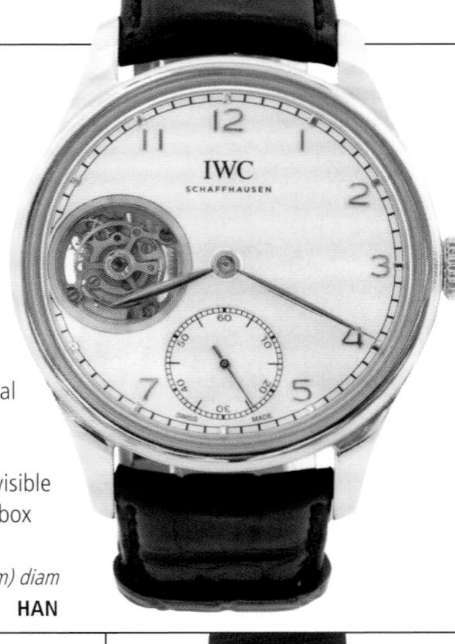

A gentleman's International Watch Co. 18ct rose gold Portugieser Tourbillon wristwatch, the dial with visible movement aperture, with box and paperwork.
c2014 *dial 1¾in (4.5cm) diam*
£15,000-20,000 **HAN**

A gentleman's Jacob & Co. limited edition Epic I chronograph wristwatch, no.488, with signed automatic movement, with subsidiary recorder dials, on a rubber strap, some wear.
1¾in (4.5cm) high
£5,000-6,000 **FELL**

A gentleman's Longines Greenlander British military issue stainless steel wristwatch, with luminous Cathederal hands, the case stamped 'WWW 23088 1810 F 5534', lacking glass.
c1944
£2,000-2,500 **LSK**

A gentleman's Omega Speedmaster stainless steel-cased wristwatch, serial no.19832636, original bracelet, missing pin.
c1962
£40,000-50,000 **LOCK**

A Patek Philippe 18ct yellow gold wristwatch, ref.590 no.900327, with bimetallic split balance, numbered '621563', convention mark '750', with leather watch pouch and documentation, later strap, some scratches.
1940 *1¼in (3cm) wide*
£5,500-6,500 **TEN**

An 18ct gold automatic calendar wristwatch, signed 'Universal, Geneve', the cloisonné dial depicting Saudi Arabia, signed and numbered '1666757 100105 3', with convention mark '18k0.750', some wear.

This watch was made to commemorate the forming of Saudi Arabia by King Abdul Al Aziz. Polychrome enamel dials are extremely rare and are usually made to commemorate events or special limited edition series.

c1953 *1½in (3.5cm) wide*
£6,000-7,000 **TEN**

A gentleman's Vacheron Constantin 18ct gold World Time wristwatch, with box and paperwork, light wear.
c2016 *dial 1½in (4cm) diam*
£12,000-15,000 **HAN**

A George III mahogany cistern tube stick barometer, by Benjamin Martin, London, with hygrometer, and Fahrenheit and Reaumur mercury thermometer, signed.

Benjamin Martin (fl.1756-82) was a prolific writer on the subjects of science, art and instruments, and launched the monthly 'General Magazine of the Arts and Sciences' in 1755. He is thought to have been the first maker to incorporate a hygrometer into a barometer with thermometer and marketed the instrument as a 'Triple Weather Glass'.

c1760 *36½in (93cm) high*
£4,000-5,000 **DN**

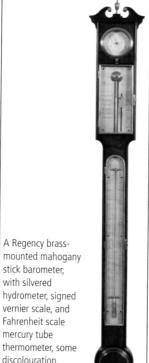

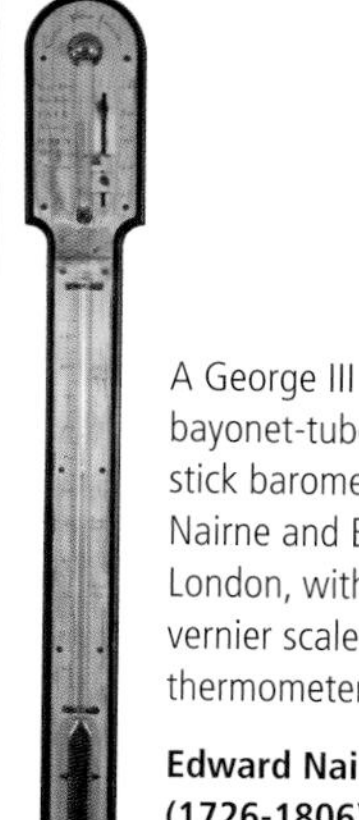

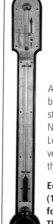

A George III mahogany bayonet-tube mercury stick barometer, by Nairne and Blunt, London, with signed vernier scale and spirit thermometer, some wear.

Edward Nairne (1726-1806) and his former apprentice Thomas Blunt (d.1822) collaborated from 1774 until 1793.

c1780 *38in (96.5cm) high*
£4,000-5,000 **DN**

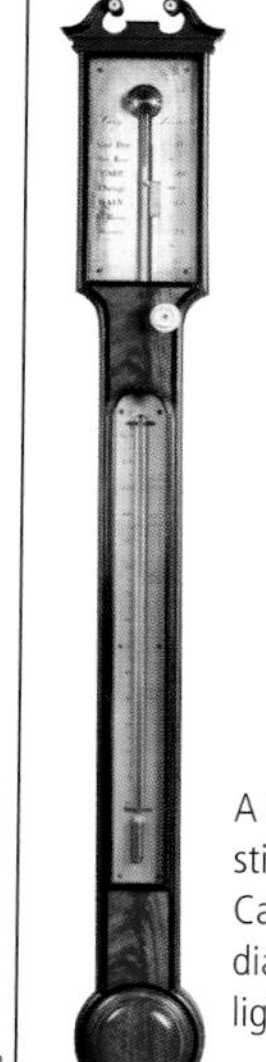

A George III mahogany stick barometer, by Cary, London, signed to dial, with vernier scale, light tarnishing.

38¼in (97cm) high
£1,200-1,600 **BELL**

A Regency mahogany mercury stick barometer, by Alexander Adie, Edinburgh, with brass vernier adjustment screw and signed vernier scale, probably for use in a lighthouse.

Alexander Adie (1774-1858) was apprenticed to his uncle, the eminent Scottish instrument maker John Miller, in 1789. In 1804, Miller and Adie went into partnership after Miller's death in 1815. Adie was particularly interested in meteorological instruments and is perhaps best known as the inventor of the Sympiesometer in 1818. He later took his son into partnership in 1835.

37¼in (94.5cm) high
£3,500-4,000 **DN**

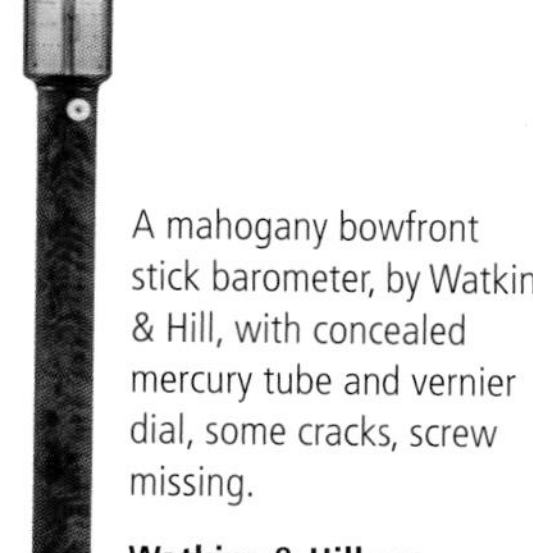

A mahogany bowfront stick barometer, by Watkins & Hill, with concealed mercury tube and vernier dial, some cracks, screw missing.

Watkins & Hill are recorded as working at Charing Cross London between 1819-57.

c1830 *38½in (98cm) high*
£2,500-3,000 **TEN**

A Regency brass-mounted mahogany stick barometer, with silvered hydrometer, signed vernier scale, and Fahrenheit scale mercury tube thermometer, some discolouration.

This barometer is almost certainly by Robert Brettell Bate, who operated in London c1808-47. Bate was celebrated for his nautical instruments including marine barometers and was appointed as 'Instrument-maker to Her Majesty's Honourable Boards of Excise and Customs'.

c1815 *43¾in (111cm) high*
£3,500-4,000 **DN**

A rosewood bowfront stick barometer, by Alexander Adie & Son, Edinburgh, with pressure vernier dial, signed, crack to pediment, finial loose, vernier knob missing.

c1835-45 *41¾in (106cm) high*
£4,500-5,500 **FELL**

A mahogany bowfront stick barometer, with mercury tube, vernier dial, and thermometer box, signed 'Dollond, London', some cracks to veneer.

The Dollond family of scientific instrument makers began with Peter Dollond in 1750 and continued until the firm's acquisition by Aitchison in 1913. This barometer would have been made by George Dollond (1774-1856), who continued the business after the death of his uncle, Peter, in 1820. George was instrument-maker to both William IV and Queen Victoria.

c1840 *38½in (98cm) high*
£2,200-2,800 **TEN**

A George III mahogany wheel barometer and timepiece, by James Gatty and George Jamison, London, with hydrometer, Fahrenheit scale mercury thermometer, spirit level and timepiece with eight-day four-pillar single-fusee movement, signed, in triple-strung rosewood crossbanded case.

James Gatty worked in London as a maker of barometers in the late 18thC to early 19thC. He is one of the most sought-after makers of early wheel barometers. George Jamison was a watchmaker and clockmaker working in London and Portsmouth 1786-1810, known for his chronometers and his complex spherical skeleton clocks.

46in (117cm) high

£3,500-4,500 **DN**

A George III inlaid mahogany mercury wheel barometer, by James Gatty, London, with hygrometer, mercury thermometer, spirit level, signed, some repairs and replacements.

c1800 *38¼in (97cm) high*

£1,500-2,000 **DN**

A Louis XV ormolu-mounted kingwood barometer, by Lange de Bourbon, with a wheel barometer and thermometer.

Lange de Bourbon (fl.1750-75) was a notable maker of clocks and barometers, awarded the title of 'Machiniste-Faiseur de Baromètre du Roi' before 1757. The form of this barometer, attributed to Claude-Joseph Desgodets, exists in a number of examples by important makers.

c1760 *45½in (115.5cm) high*

£17,000-20,000 **FRE**

A mahogany barometer, by John Hargraves and Thomas Tatham, with quadrant-form half-circular scale, concealed mercury tube, signed and dated.

Similar examples have been found signed 'Thomas Hargraves of Settle', possibly a relation of John Hargraves. They must have been working in Settle around the same time, and producing unusual barometers, possibly in the same workplace.

1830 *40¼in (102cm) high*

£2,800-3,200 **TEN**

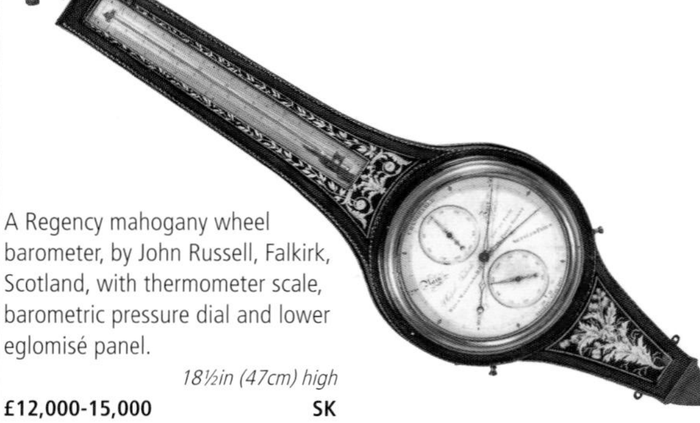

A Regency mahogany wheel barometer, by John Russell, Falkirk, Scotland, with thermometer scale, barometric pressure dial and lower eglomisé panel.

18½in (47cm) high

£12,000-15,000 **SK**

CLOSER LOOK – HENRY PYEFINCH BAROMETER

It consists of an angled mercury tube, a thermometer tube, a register dial and central hygrometer dial.

The centre shows a printed 'Perpetual Regulation of Time' dial, with apertures for the equation of days of the month, sun rises and sun sets, feast days, Zodiac signs and high water at London Bridge.

The instruments are housed within a mahogany case with an architectural pediment and turned brass finials.

It is in need of restoration, with a broken thermometer, a cracked mercury tube, and losses to the dial – but the rarity and unusual form of this barometer make it a valuable piece.

A mahogany angle barometer, by H. Pyefinch, in need of restoration.

Henry Pyefinch (fl.1763-90) was an instrument maker based in London. In 1765, in conjunction with Portuguese scientist J.H. de Magellan, he patented an instrument to measure the effect of the weight of the atmosphere and the variations caused by heat and cold.

c1765 *43in (109cm) high*

£11,000-15,000 **TEN**

An Edwardian 15ct gold-cased aneroid pocket barometer and altimeter scale, by Ross, London, inscribed 'ROB'T EMMET. MORETON MORRELL, WARWICK, ENG.', hallmarked Chester, some wear.

The inscription relates to Robert Emmet, a wealthy American-born banker of Irish heritage born in New York in 1872. He later moved to Warwickshire, England, where he built a substantial recreation of an Elizabethan manor house called Moreton Paddox at Moreton Morrell.

1907 *2in (5cm) diam*

£600-700 **DN**

A barograph, by Negretti & Zambra, London, the clockwork drum mounted on lacquered brass bedplate with signed maker's plate, the atmosphere drums acting on counterweighted pen arm.

A barograph is a barometer used for recording barometric pressure over time, by marking changes in atmospheric pressure on a paper chart.

c1920 *19in (48cm) wide*

£1,800-2,400 **CM**

A George III pocket globe, by J. Newton, London, applied with twelve hand-coloured printed gores and two polar calottes, in a fishskin case, some damages and losses.

1782 *3in (7.5cm) diam*

£12,000-15,000 **DN**

A George III pocket celestial globe, by John & William Cary, with twelve hand-coloured printed gores, marked 'NEW CELESTIAL GLOBE by J & W Cary, Strand', with a shagreen case.

3in (7.5cm) diam

£6,000-7,000 **TEN**

A Gilbert and Sons pocket globe, the case decorated with signs of the Zodiac, dated.

1807 *3in (7.5cm) diam*

£3,000-3,500 **PW**

A Regency library table globe, by G. & J. Cary, London, the sphere applied with twelve coloured printed gores, trade label 'CARY'S, NEW SIX INCH, TERRESTRIAL GLOBE, DRAWN, from the latest AUTHORITIES., London Published by G. & J.Cary, January I, 1824', stand re-glued.

1825 *10in (25.5cm) high*

£5,000-6,000 **DN**

A Newton's 'New and Improved Terrestrial Table Globe', on a wood stand, split to globe, some surface wear.

12in (30.5cm) diam

£2,000-2,500 **CHOR**

A pair of early Victorian terrestrial and celestial globe, on mahogany stands, labelled 'Newton's New and Improved Celestial/Terrestrial globe, manufactured by Newton & Son, Chancery Lane, London', stand engraved 'published 1st January 1844'.

Founded in 1780 by John Newton, the firm of Newton & Son went on to be among the leading manufacturers of fine globes in the 19thC.

c1844 *globes 12in (30.5cm) diam*

£22,000-26,000 **CHOR**

A Victorian terrestrial library globe, by Cruchley, with twelve gores, inscribed 'CRUCHLEY'S NEW TERRESTRIAL GLOBE From the most recent Authorities EXHIBITING THE DISCOVERIES IN EQUATORIAL AFRICA, NORTH POLE, And the new Settlements & Divisions of AUSTRALIA, NEW ZEALAND, CALIFORNIA, TEXAS & c. LONDON G.F. CRUCHLEY MAP SELLER, GLOBE MAKER & PUBLISHER, 81 FLEET STREET', on a mahogany stand, dated.

1869 *36½in (92.5cm) high*

£5,000-6,000 **WW**

A mid-19thC Terrestrial Globe, by J.G. Klinger, Nuremberg, with twelve coloured gores and brass pins at the pole, inscribed 'The Earth', in original case.

2¼in (6cm) diam

£1,800-2,200 **TEN**

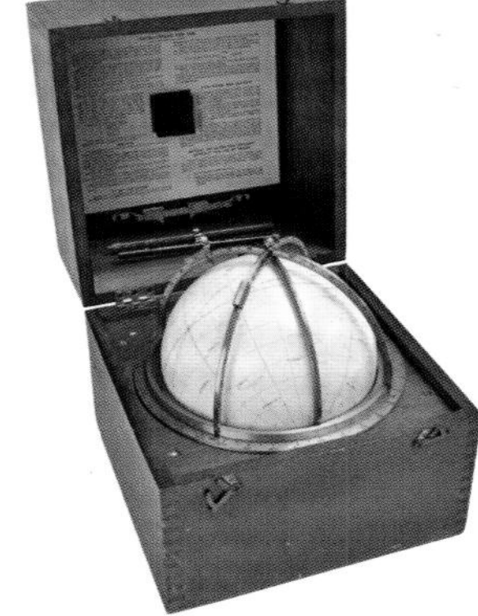

A Kelvin Hughes star globe, set within lacquered brass horizon and meridian rings, in a mahogany case.

1975 *10¾in (27cm) wide*

£450-550 **BELL**

CLOSER LOOK – VARIABLE MICROSCOPE

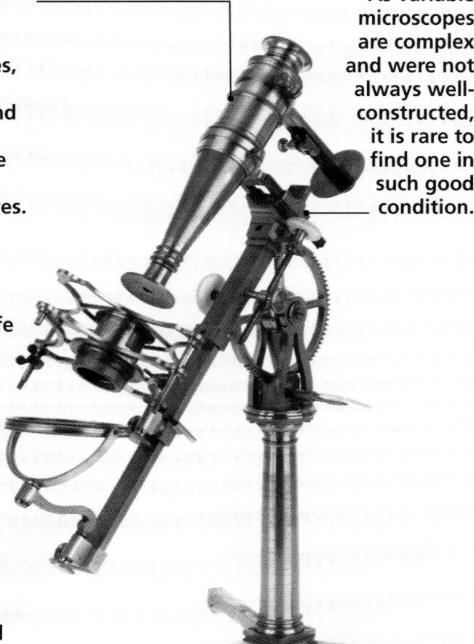

It comes with a Martin lens, five Lieberkuhn lenses, 2 high-power lenses, 5 button-type objective lenses, and a collar allowing the objectives to be combined to make compound objectives.

As variable microscopes are complex and were not always well-constructed, it is rare to find one in such good condition.

This microscope is signed 'Ann and George Adams', referring to the wife and son of George Adams Senior (c1709-73); Ann Adams and George Adams Junior (1750-95) traded under this name (1773-75), until George completed his apprenticeship. It is rare to for an instrument of this period to be signed by a woman.

A variable microscope can be used as a simple microscope using just one lens, or as a compound microscope, using many lenses. These were rare in the 18thC, due to their expense.

An Adams variable microscope.
c1773
£110,000-140,000 **FLIN**

A Cuff-type brass microscope, with plano mirror, screw focussing and brass tilting stand, some repairs, in mahogany case.
c1780
£2,500-3,000 **TEN**

A brass-cased astronomical telescope, by Broadhurst Clarkson & Co., the lens with a two draw eyepiece, stamped 'ADVANCED STARBOY, BROADHURST CLARKSON & CO.', in a wood box, with folding tripod stand.
50in (127cm) long
£800-900 **WW**

An astronomical refracting telescope, by T. Cooke & Sons Ltd., London and York, the main tube with star finder and eyepiece, signed, with original pine box, with performance statement, tripod and accessories.
84in (213.5cm) high
£2,500-3,000 **CM**

A mid-to-late 18thC ptolemaic armillary sphere, probably Italian, with an axis with sun and moon orbits within armillary universe, on a pinewood figure of Atlas, holding articulated models of Saturn and Jupiter, on a Corinthian column.

The number of moons depicted is interesting. Saturn was thought to have five moons between 1684 (when Cassini discovered the fifth) and 1789, when Herschel found two more. Jupiter's four moons were all discovered by Galileo in 1609-10, with no more being found until 1892.

63in (160cm) high
£10,000-14,000 **CM**

A mid-17thC English brass Gunter-pattern horary quadrant, with twin pinhole sight vanes, the apex pierced with a hole for plumb line and engraved with a shadow square annotated 1-10 in both directions and divided into fifths, with a sector arranged as a quarter of an astrolabe for a fixed latitude showing the sky projection between equator and tropics.

Edmund Gunter was born in Hertfordshire in 1581 and studied at Oxford 1600-03, during which time he developed his interest in mathematics and started designing his own instruments. In 1615 he took holy orders. In 1620 he became professor of astronomy at Gresham College. In 1623 he published his work 'De Sectore et Radio or The Description and Use of the Sector, the Cross-staffe and other instruments', which included the design of quadrant on which this piece is very closely based.

4in (10cm) wide
£2,000-3,000 **DN**

A noon-day cannon dial, probably French, the marble base incised with sun dial and latitude 46:50, with lacquered brass fittings.
c1880 *6in (15cm) high*
£1,300-1,800 **CM**

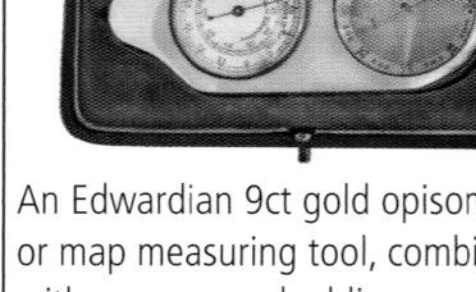

An Edwardian 9ct gold opisometer or map measuring tool, combined with a compass doubling as a magnifying glass, hallmarked for J.C. Vickery, London, in original case.
1908 *3½in (9cm) long 2¼oz*
£1,500-2,000 **MART**

A brass-bound mahogany-cased two-day marine chronometer, by Parkinson & Frodsham, London, no.456, with chain fusee movement with cylindrical ring-turned pillars, with Earnshaw spring detent escapement.

Parkinson & Frodsham was established in 1801 by William James Frodsham (1778-1850) and William Parkinson (d.1842). Their business continued throughout the 19thC at Change Alley, supplying chronometers to the Admiralty and to shipping lines.

c1825 *5in (13cm) long*

£4,500-5,000 **BELL**

An early 19thC mahogany-cased marine chronometer, by William Cozens, London, no.104, with chain-driven fusee movement, in gimbaled lacquered brass case.

6½in (16.5cm) wide

£3,200-4,000 **LSK**

A two-day brass marine chronometer, the movement with Earnshaw escapement, the dial inscribed 'Thomas Adams, Maker to H.R.H. PRINCE ALBERT, 36 Lombard St. London, 3132'.

c1860 *7in (18cm) wide*

£2,000-3,000 **CM**

A brass-bound rosewood two-day Royal Observatory Marine Chronometer, by Charles Frodsham, London, no.3169, with signed chain fusee movement with Earnshaw detent escapement, cut bi-metallic compensated balance with Airy's bar and Rokeby's side winding mechanism, engraved with Government arrow.

The Royal Observatory records show that this chronometer was issued to seven HM ships across the late 19thC and early 20thC, before being transferred to the Australian Government in 1921.

c1860-64 *7½in (19cm) square*

£10,000-14,000 **BELL**

A 19thC rosewood-cased marine chronometer, by Thomas Charles Tidmas, London, no.6576, with chain-driven fusee movement, the case with plaque 'Sold by A Baharie, Lawrence Street, Sunderland' and paper label for 'George Gowland, Liverpool'.

7in (17.5cm) wide

£4,000-5,000 **LSK**

A late 19thC brass-mounted mahogany 2½ days ship's marine chronometer, by John Fletcher, London, no.2130, with silvered metal plaque inscribed 'Cork', restored split to top.

7in (17.5cm) wide

£2,000-2,500 **GORL**

A late 19thC mahogany-cased two-day marine chronometer, by Negretti and Zambra, London, the circular four-pillar single-chain fusee movement with Harrison's maintaining power, Earnshaw-type spring detent escapement, fitted with electrical wiring posts.

The firm of Negretti & Zambra was established in 1850 by Enrico Negretti and Joseph Warren Zambra and became one of the most prolific makers of scientific instruments, continuing trading well into the 20thC. The design of the middle-error temperature compensation to the balance of the present timepiece was developed by Swedish Victor Kullberg, who set up in London c1851 and became one of the finest makers of marine chronometers of the later 19thC.

7in (18cm) wide

£2,000-2,500 **DN**

A two-day Kaisermarine chronometer, by W.G. Ehrlich, Bremerhaven, no.451, the movement with Earnshaw escapement, Uhrig-type balance, and helical balance spring with jewelled detent, with a bowl engraved with Kaisermaine crown and 'M', top lid of box missing.

c1886 *7½in (19cm) wide*

£2,000-3,000 **CM**

A George III mahogany and brass Hadley's navigational octant, possibly by George Adams senior, London, with inset engraved boxwood diagonal scale divided into 20 arcminutes, with pinhole sight, index arm and hinged filters.

In 1760 George Adams senior was appointed as Mathematical Instrument Maker to King George III, for whom he supplied a vast range of apparatus. A near identical instrument attributed to Adams is illustrated in J.A. Bennett, 'The Divided Circle', page 132.

c1770 *8¼in (21cm) long*

£1,400-2,000 **DN**

A vernier octant, by Christopher Johnson, the ivory scale divided to 95°, with brass index arm, pinhole sight, note plate and pin feet, missing shades, mirrors replaced, dated.

1796 *15½in (39.5cm) radius*

£1,000-1,500 **CM**

A whaling octant, probably by David White Laird, Leith, the ivory scale divided to 100° and stamped 'WH' by 50°, the index arm inscribed 'James Clark/First Mate Whaling Barque "North of Scotland"/of Peterhead; died at NORTH GREENLAND,/26th July, 1847' pinhole sights, three shades, mirrors and feet, some losses.

The 'North of Scotland' was a 297 ton whaling barque built at Sunderland in 1845. It seems James Clark died en route from Iceland on the 26 July 1847 aged 46. This octant, which has little sign of use, was probably presented to his widow by the owners. It is unknown who the scale divider 'WH' is. Only one other similar example exists, which is held by the National Museum of Scotland in Edinburgh, with a maker's label for David White Laird, Leith (fl.1834-51).

c1847 *10½in (26.5cm) radius*

£800-1,200 **CM**

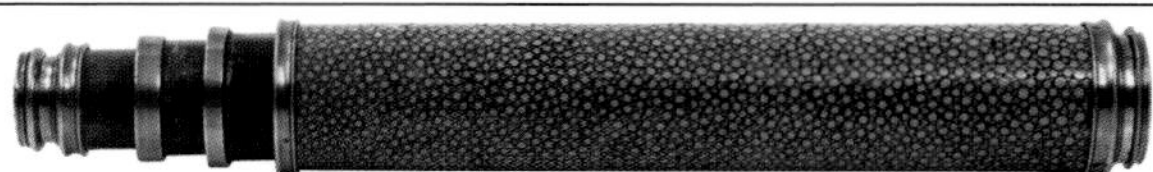

A shagreen and card three-draw telescope, by Dollond, London, with polished brass mounts, signed, with dust slides.

c1780 *closed 10½in (26.5cm) long*

£700-800 **CM**

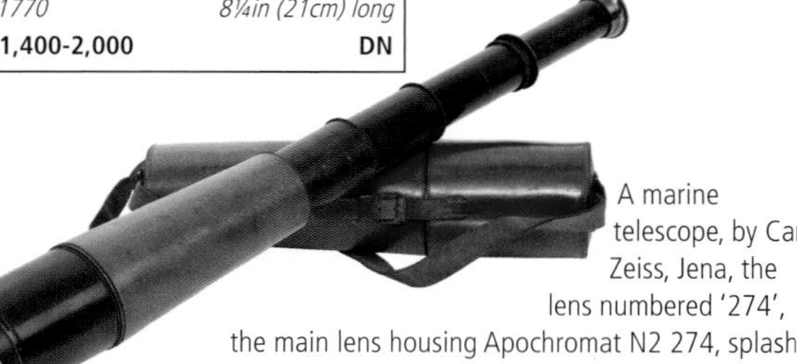

A marine telescope, by Carl Zeiss, Jena, the lens numbered '274', the main lens housing Apochromat N2 274, splash cuff, tapered leather-covered main tube and dust-slide, within lined leather tube.

The telescope is believed to have been owned by Grand Admiral Karl Dönitz (1891-1980), who succeeded Erich Raeder as Commander-in-Chief of the Kriegsmarine on 30 January 1943. He quickly developed the infamous 'wolfpacks' of submarines used to persecute allied convoys. After Hitler's suicide on 30 April 1945, Dönitz was, briefly, Chancellor of the crumbling Reich until the arrest of the Flensburg Government on 23 May. This telescope may have been given to Dönitz when he was commissioned as an acting sub-lieutenant in 1913.

c1900-06 *closed 13in (33cm) long*

£1,700-2,000 **CM**

A late 18thC Italian card and vellum eight-draw telescope, with turned ivory dividers, with original lenses, the main tube covered in shark skin.

closed 17in (43cm) long

£3,500-4,000 **CM**

ESSENTIAL REFERENCE – TRACTION TORPEDO

A. Légé & Co. were a firm of scientific instrument makers based in Hatton Garden, London. The idea behind the Traction Torpedo was that several would be hitched to an endless chain within the confines of a harbour or secure area. When not in use, they would settle harmlessly on the sea bed, but when needed, the chain was started and the torpedoes rose and 'patrolled' the harbour. The accompanying research refers to one other example made of 'Delta Metal' which was supposed to be resistant to sea water. As this one appears to be brass, it may be a working prototype used as a sales pitch to Governments. Their rarity suggests that this complicated and dangerous system was never deployed, perhaps unsurprisingly when the risk to the users' own ships was greater than that of their enemies.

A pair of 7 x 50 Kriegsmarine U-boat binoculars, by Leitz, stamped 'BEH' and '459822', with rubberised eye-piece caps, maker's code and Kriegsmarine mark, dated, in original case.

1944 *10in (25.5cm) high*

£1,400-2,000 **CM**

A Kriegsmarine U-boat brass clock, the dial marked and numbered '15953', with going-barrel movement, backstamped '16725'.

8in (20cm) wide

£4,500-5,000 **CM**

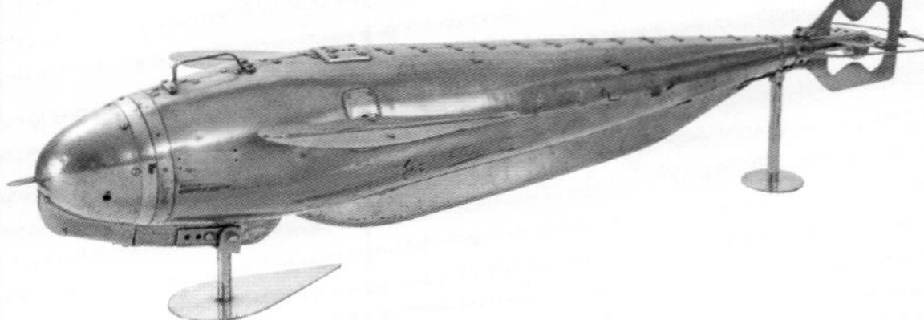

A rare A. Légé & Co. patent 'traction torpedo', London, constructed in brass panels with adjustable side planes and tail fins, split ballast keel and explosive plunger.

c1886 *60in (152.5cm) long*

£5,500-6,000 **CM**

Judith Picks

Scrimshaw pieces always need to be examined very carefully. There are a lot of fakes on the market, and only about 30% of those I see are actually genuine. Look out for later resin reproductions. Be wary of pieces that seem too perfect, that note the name of the ship and the date, as genuine examples with this information are very rare. If it seems too good to be true, it probably is!

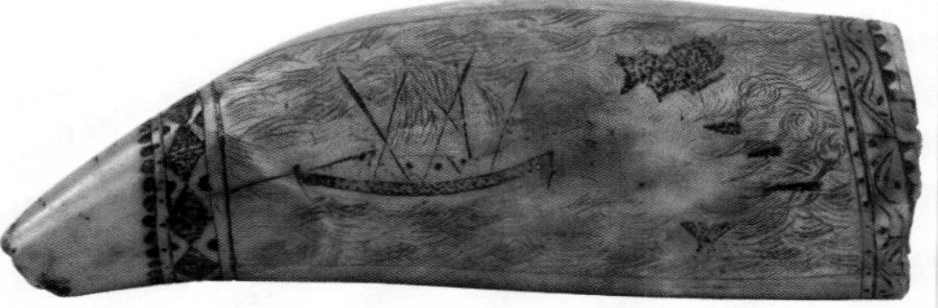

A sailorwork scrimshaw whale tooth, incised and carved with a whaleboat and school of whales.
c1840 *5¾in (14.5cm) high 8¾oz*
£500-600 **CM**

A scrimshaw whale's tooth depicting the S.S. Great Britain.
5in (13cm) high
£450-550 **CM**

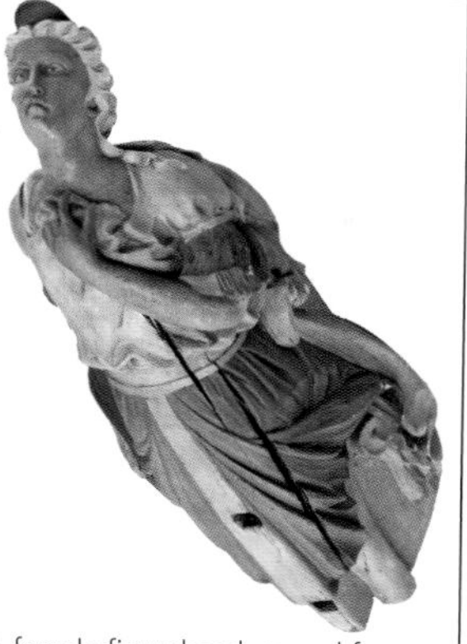

A female figurehead, carved from laminated wood with polychrome finish, on base with two thole pins.
c1860 *54in (137cm) high*
£11,000-15,000 **CM**

A 19thC carved laminated yellow pine figurehead, possibly of Amerigo Vespucci, on an ebonised plinth.
without plinth 59in (150cm) high
£1,500-2,000 **CM**

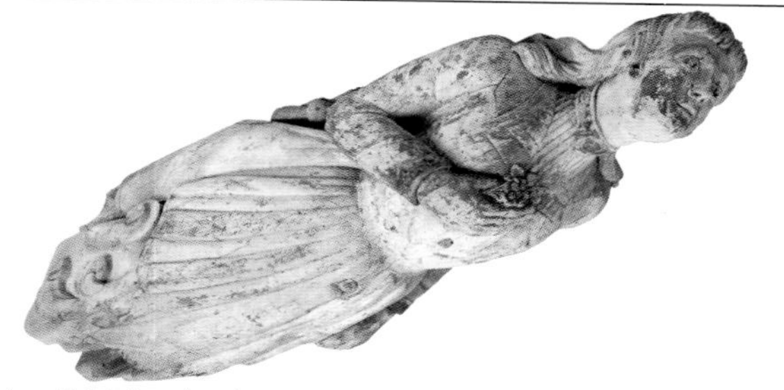

A late 19thC figurehead, probably from a private steam yacht, modelled as a young lady clutching a flower, restoration to terminus.
64in (162.5cm) high
£20,000-25,000 **CM**

A bell from the Cunard liner R.M.S. Lucania.

One of a famous pair of late Victorian Cunarders, Lucania was built by Fairfield's at Glasgow and launched in 1893. She took the Blue Riband for the fastest Atlantic crossing one month after her maiden voyage. Lucania's career was brought to an abrupt end when she caught fire in Liverpool in 1909.
1893 *10in (25.5cm) high*
£6,000-7,000 **CM**

A brass ship's bell from HMS 'Hurst', inscribed with the ship's name, with later threaded suspension loop.

The success of chartered pleasure steamers as mine sweepers and submarine hunters in WWI inspired the Admiralty to design and build their own. Hurst was a 'Racecourse' Class paddle minesweeper built under the Emergency War Programme by Dunlop, Bremner & Co. Also known as the 'Ascot' Class, 32 were built. They were lightly armed and manned by a crew of fifty. HMS 'Hurst' was broken up in 1922.
1916 *14in (35.5cm) high*
£850-950 **CM**

A brass and oak mounted model cannon, set on timber from HMS Victory, the hallmarked silver plaque detailed 'H.M.S Victory, piece of one of the planks on which Lord Nelson fell, given to M.L.G on board during repairs to quarter deck'.

It is not uncommon to find pieces that are reputedly from the HMS Victory. Most are worth very little because most are not in fact from the HMS Victory. This item, deemed genuine by trade and collectors alike, is much more valuable.
6in (15.5cm) wide
£4,000-5,000 **BELL**

A 12-bolt diving helmet, by Siebe Gorman & Co. Ltd., no.19342, with spring return valve telephone port, exhaust, fitted internally with chin buzzer and telephone speaker, finished with remnant tinning.
19in (48.5cm) high
£4,000-5,000 **CM**

A Union Flag, landed with the 3rd Canadian Division at Juno Beach, D-Day 6 June 1944, carried by 'P' Commando Sub-Lieutenant. Alan Dalton R.N., the canvas sleeve stencilled '3YD JACR[?]', some wear.

Sir Alan Dalton C.B.E. D.L. (1923-2006) joined the Royal Navy in April 1943. In September 1943 he was posted to 'P' Commando and trained with Force 'J' for operation Neptune (the naval element of the Normandy landings). On D-Day the unit was landed just before 07.30 and Dalton guided this division of 14,000 men across the beachhead carrying this flag.
68½in (174cm) wide
£38,000-45,000 **CM**

An early part overture musical box, by Henri Joseph Lecoultre, no.224, exposed controls, playing four airs, professional restoration, with walnut case.

c1826 *12¼in (31cm) wide*

£4,500-5,000 APAR

A mid-19thC rosewood key wind musical box, by Nicole Frères, the brass cylinder playing eight operatic airs with original tune sheet, no.32011.

Nicole Frères was established in Geneva in 1814. The firm made music boxes of an exceptionally high quality, which are highly sought after today.

20½in (52cm) wide

£1,000-1,400 CHOR

A Nicole Fréres walnut and inlaid cased polyphon, with original labels, with fourteen discs.

£1,000-1,400 APAR

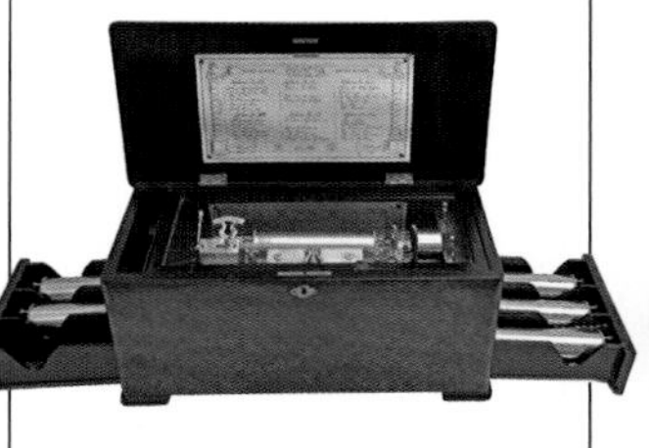

A late 19thC Swiss amboyna-cased cylinder music box, with change/ repeat and stop/start, with six cylinders.

21¼in (54cm) wide

£1,800-2,200 BELL

A late 19thC Swiss burr walnut cylinder music box, playing eight airs, with Asian figures drumming on six bells.

case 21¼in (54cm) wide

£2,200-2,800 BELL

A late 19thC Swiss marquetry rosewood cylinder music box, six bells with Chinaman drummer and dancing ballerina, imperfection to case.

32in (81.5cm) wide

£2,200-2,800 POOK

A 19thC rosewood musical box and matching stand, by Nicole Frères, Geneva, the movement with brass bedplate with twin combs playing six airs on seven cylinders, plus six cylinders and three tune sheets.

box 37in (94cm) wide

£12,000-15,000 CHOR

A 19thC German symphonium, in a walnut case, the cover depicting a dancing couple.

18in (46cm) wide

£850-950 WM

A Victorian penny-in-the-slot Sirion polyphon, with 30 discs each playing 2 tunes, some cracks and chips.

discs 22¾in (57.5cm) diam

£9,000-12,000 UNI

A 19thC Swiss rosewood musical box with clock, retailed by Keith Prowse & Co., London, playing ten airs with nine bells, the clock dial, with eight-day bell-striking movement.

28in (71cm) wide

£5,500-6,500 **WW**

A late 19thC Symphonion Rococo walnut disc musical box, with harmony comb arrangement, with 44 discs.

19in (48cm) wide

£2,000-2,500 **SWO**

A late 19thC Mermod Frères rosewood and inlaid twelve-air musical box, with cylinder and three pairs of bells, with a Mandarin striking them, with patent number plaque.

25½in (65cm) wide

£1,400-1,800 **APAR**

A bells-in-view musical box, playing ten airs with tune card, in crossbanded rosewood case inlaid with musical instruments to the top and front.

23½in (60cm) wide

£2,000-2,500 **FLD**

A late 19thC probably Swiss tortoiseshell-cased singing bird box, in fitted leather box, split to one corner.

4in (10cm) wide

£2,000-2,500 **APAR**

A late 19thC to early 20thC Swiss tortoiseshell musical singing bird box, retailed by Finnigans, New Bond Street, inscribed 'TO SARAH FROM Mary + Douglas', the back with a hinged compartment possibly for snuff.

4in (10cm) wide

£1,800-2,200 **WW**

A German silver singing bird box, by Karl Griesbaum, with key.

c1925 *4in (10cm) wide*

£1,500-2,000 **SWO**

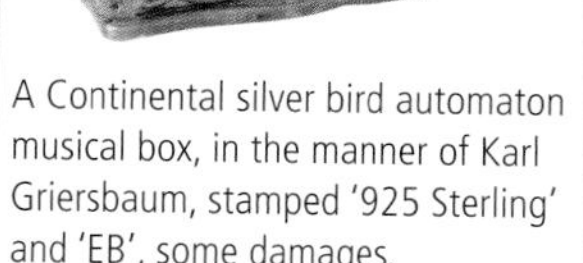

A Continental silver bird automaton musical box, in the manner of Karl Griersbaum, stamped '925 Sterling' and 'EB', some damages.

4in (10cm) long

£2,000-2,500 **FLD**

A Patek Philippe tortoiseshell, gold and enamel singing bird music box, several chips, lacking winder, case broken at hinges.

Patek Philippe was founded in Geneva in 1839. Today it remains an independent, family-owned watch manufacturer.

3¾in (9.5cm) wide

£16,000-20,000 **POOK**

CLOSER LOOK – JAMES II CANDLESTICKS

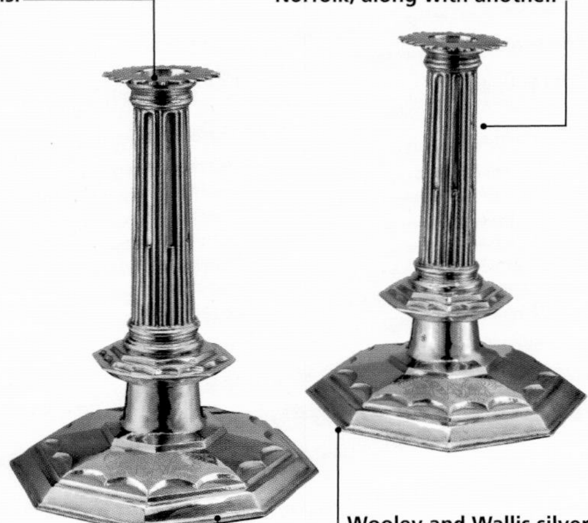

These candlesticks have octagonal bases, fluted columns and shaped drip pans.

They are engraved within feather mantling with the armorial of Burnell of Essex impaling Gybbons of Norfolk, along with another.

They are in exceptional condition for their age, having been stored in a bank vault.

Wooley and Wallis silver specialist Rupert Slingsby described them as 'amongst the best of the best in terms of condition, colour, form and marks.'

A pair of James II silver candlesticks, maker's mark 'TD', probably Thomas Dymock, London.

1685 *9¾in (24.5cm) high 3⅝oz*

£78,000-84,000 **WW**

A pair of George II silver candlesticks, engraved with a cipher, by Abraham Buteux, London.

1730 *6in (15cm) high 21oz*

£6,000-7,000 **WW**

A pair of George II silver candlesticks, with engraved armorials, by James Gould, London.

1737 *7½in (19cm) high 34⅜oz*

£2,500-3,000 **LSK**

A set of four George II cast silver candlesticks, by John White, London, two sticks wobbling.

1738 *8¼in (21cm) high 83oz*

£14,000-18,000 **CHEF**

An Irish George II silver candlestick, by Robert Calderwood, Dublin.

c1740 *9in (23cm) high 19oz*

£1,500-2,000 **ADA**

A pair of George II Channel Islands silver Rococo candlesticks, with engraved crest of the Carey family of Guernsey, by Guillaume Henry, Guernsey.

See Frederick Cohen and Nicholas Du Quesne Bird, 'Silver in the Channel Islands', Jersey Museums Service, page 43.

8in (20.5cm) high 28¼oz

£25,000-30,000 **MART**

A pair of mid-18thC Irish silver candlesticks, by Bartholomew Mosse, Dublin.

c1740 *8¼in (21cm) high 29oz*

£2,500-3,000 **WW**

A pair of George II silver candlesticks, each engraved with a crest, scratch weights to base: 'N:1 27=17' and 'N: 2 28', by John Cafe, London.

John Cafe was a silversmith based in London who specialised in candlesticks. He died in 1757.

1748 *9½in (24cm) high 54oz*

£3,500-4,000 **SWO**

A pair of George II cast silver candlesticks, with engraved crests, by William Grundy, London.

1754 *9½in (24cm) high 43oz*

£1,800-2,200 **FLD**

A pair of George II silver table candlesticks, the bases cast with stylised shells, by John Cafe, London.
1755 *8¾in (22.5cm) high 36½oz*
£4,000-4,500 **SWO**

A pair of George III silver candlesticks, by John Robinson II, London.
1763 *9in (23cm) high 34oz*
£2,500-3,000 **WW**

A pair of George III silver candlesticks, engraved with a crest, by Ebenezer Coker, London.
The crest is that of Beckford, Charlewood, Meade, Nichols, Lovat, Upton and other families.
1765 *10¼in (26cm) high 41¾oz*
£3,000-3,500 **WW**

A pair of George III silver candlesticks, crested to bases, by John Cox, London, general surface wear.
1767 *9in (23cm) high 32oz*
£2,800-3,200 **APAR**

A pair of George III silver candlesticks, with two vacant cartouches, maker's mark 'I.W', possibly John Welding or James Wiburd, London.
1772 *12½in (32cm) high*
£2,200-2,800 **WW**

A pair of George III Channel Islands silver Rococo candlesticks, decorated with shells and anthemion, maker's mark 'IA', Guernsey.
c1763-1807 *10in (25.5cm) high 42oz*
£25,000-30,000 **MART**

A set of four George III silver candlesticks, by John Schofield, London, some scratches and dents.
1783 *11¼in (28.5cm) high 67¾oz*
£7,500-8,500 **CHOR**

A pair of George IV silver five-light candelabra, with Royal arms, by Charles and John Fry II, London.
These candelabra were owned by one of George III's seven sons. However, they could not have been owned by his eldest son, George, who succeeded to the throne as King George IV in 1820, or by fourth son, Edward Duke of Kent, who died in the same year.
1824 *29¼in (74cm) high*
£45,000-50,000 **SWO**

A Victorian silver candelabrum centrepiece, the base depicting a fox-hunting scene, the stem decorated with oak leaves, inscribed to base 'Presented To John Stapylton Sutton Esq, of Elton Hall in the County of Durham by the Members of the Hurworth & Durham County Hunts and Other Friends in Consideration of His Disinterested Preservation of Foxes', some splits and scratches, Hennell house mark, by Robert Hennell, London.
1853 *22½in (57cm) high 197oz*
£9,000-11,000 **TEN**

A set of four Tiffany & Co. silver candlesticks, reproduced from a design by David Willaume in 1739, marked, minor wear.
c1914 *9¼in (23.5cm) high 83¼oz*
£3,500-4,000 **DRA**

A rare George II Channel Islands silver chamberstick, by Jean Gavey (fl.c1715-75), Jersey.

This is believed to be the only known example of a Channel Islands silver chamberstick in existence. It was probably a special commission from a client who had seen such pieces in England or on the Continent. Contrary to most English examples, it does not feature a fitting for a separate snuffer.

5½in (14cm) diam

£7,000-8,000 **MART**

ESSENTIAL REFERENCE – PAUL STORR

Paul Storr (1771-1844) was one of the greatest silversmiths of his time.

- **He was apprenticed c1785 to Andrew Fogelberg, and by 1796 had started his own shop.**
- **He began working with the firm Rundell and Bridge in 1807, and in 1822 went into partnership with John Mortimer.**
- **Although he held no official title, Storr enjoyed patronage from many important figures of the period, including George III, and carried out commissions from the Duke of Portland and Lord Nelson, among others.**
- **Storr's designs were influenced by Neo-classical decorative styles and ancient Roman silver. His work is known for its superior quality and its high level of craftsmanship.**

A George III silver chamberstick, engraved with an episcopal mitre and the badge of a Royal Duke, probably for Frederick, Duke of York and Albany and Bishop of Osnabruck, by Paul Storr, London.

1817 *6¼in (16cm) diam 14oz*

£1,400-1,800 **WW**

A George III silver chamberstick, initialled, by John Carter II, London.

1775 *8⅛oz*

£400-500 **BE**

A pair of George III silver chambersticks, one snuffing cone associated, by Henry Chawner, London.

1794 *16¼oz*

£850-950 **BELL**

A pair of George III silver chambersticks, probably by John Hutson, London, splits to sconces, repairs to handles.

1797 *25¾oz*

£850-950 **BELL**

A George III silver chamberstick and scissor snuffers, engraved with a monogram, by William Fountain, London, the scissors unmarked.

1798 *6¼in (16cm) long 9⅞oz*

£400-500 **WW**

A pair of Victorian silver chambersticks, crests of Boughton and Crabtree to the snuffers, by Robert Dicker, London.

1874 *4¾in (12cm) diam 15½oz*

£1,100-1,400 **WW**

A pair of Victorian travelling silver chambersticks, by Wright & Davies, London.

1885 *3¾in (9.5cm) long 6¼oz*

£600-700 **WW**

A Charles I silver wine cup, scratch initialled 'W' over 'E*A', maker's mark attributed to Barnabus Gregory, London.
1630 *5in (13cm) high 4oz*
£15,000-20,000 **WW**

A Charles II provincial silver chalice, marks worn, probably by Thomas Mangy, York.
c1675 *9¼in (23.5cm) high 13¾oz*
£4,000-4,500 **WW**

A pair of James II silver mugs, with chinoiserie decoration, by Francis Singleton, London.
1688 *3½in (9cm) high 8¾oz*
£5,500-6,000 **WW**

A William and Mary silver chinoiserie mug, the front with an armorial, the base scratch initialled '1695', 'A.H' over 'A.H', stamped 'W.T. ANDREW', maker's mark 'IA', probably by John Austin, London.

The shield is that of Hayne of Fryer Wadon, Dorset, granted in 1604.
1689 *3½in (9cm) high 6⅛oz*
£6,500-7,500 **WW**

A late 17thC Channel Islands silver wine cup or goblet, inscribed 'M.T', 'I.B' and 'G.O', by Robert Barbedor (fl.c1677-1704), Jersey and Guernsey.
c1690 *5½in (14.5cm) high 7⅛oz*
£8,000-9,000 **MART**

A William III silver cup and cover, the underside with scratch weight '36:3', by Pierre Harache, London.
1698 *7in (17.5cm) high 34½oz*
£5,000-6,000 **WW**

A Queen Anne silver mug, with later initials, by John Elston, Exeter.
1709 *3½in (9cm) high 3¾oz*
£1,500-2,000 **WW**

An early George I Britannia Standard silver tumbler cup, engraved with an 18thC cipher, detailed 'March 15th 1717', maker's mark indistinct, London, some dents.
1716 *1¾in (4.5cm) high 2oz*
£1,500-2,000 **BELL**

An early 18thC Scottish thistle tot cup, with reeded girdle and engraved armorial shield above, by John Seaton.
1½in (4cm) high 1⅛oz
£4,500-5,000 **L&T**

A George II mug, by Dougal Ged, Edinburgh, Assay Master Archibald Ure.

1734 *3in (7.5cm) high 5oz*

£2,000-2,500 **L&T**

An 18thC Channel Islands silver christening cup, inscribed 'a AB don de Son Parain & Mareine Isaac Le Lacheur & Jeanne Bevi 1771', by Guillaume Henry, Guernsey.

This cup was exhibited at the 1978 Channel Islands Silver Exhibition, Guernsey Museum & Art Gallery.

2½in (6cm) high 3⅜oz

£950-1,100 **MART**

A pair of George III silver wine goblets, maker's mark rubbed, London, some knocks.

1774 *7¼in (18.5cm) high 14⅜oz*

£600-700 **GORL**

A George III communion cup, engraved 'Relief Church Paisley 1785', engraved to opposing side 'Drink abundantly o beloved for my blood is drink indeed', by Alexander Gairdner, Edinburgh.

1784 *8¼in (21cm) high 16⅞oz*

£7,000-8,000 **L&T**

A pair of George III silver goblets, engraved with the Wynne crest, by John Wakelin and Robert Garrard, London.

1796 *6in (15cm) high 16oz*

£1,800-2,200 **WW**

A Canadian silver christening mug, inscribed 'Matilda G. Faribault, from her affectionate Godfather, Jno. Fraiser, 1st Jan/1832', by Laurent Amiot, Quebec City.

c1820 *2½in (6.5cm) high*

£5,500-6,000 **FRE**

An early Victorian fox-mask stirrup cup, gilt interior, by George Fox, London.

A stirrup cup is a cup of wine or other alcoholic drink offered to someone on horseback who is about to depart on a journey or hunt.

1845 *4¾in (12cm) long 6¾oz*

£5,000-6,000 **LC**

A French silver goblet, maker's mark obscured, export mark, light scratches, in a fitted case.

c1840-79 *4¾in (12cm) high 6¼oz*

£250-300 **DN**

A Victorian silver beaker, the underside stamped 'Hunt and Roskell, Late Storr and Mortimer 3183', by John Samuel Hunt, London.

1864 *3½in (9cm) high 5¼oz*

£1,200-1,500 **WW**

A Victorian silver goblet, presentation inscribed, London.

1865 *7¾in (20cm) high 10oz*

£450-500 **BELL**

An early 17thC German embossed and engraved silver-gilt tankard, possibly by Augsburg, some wear and repairs.

11½in (29cm) high 47⁵⁄₈oz

£15,000-20,000 **CHEF**

A Charles II silver tankard, with an armorial shield, maker's mark 'R.P', London.

1667 6¾in (17cm) high 27⁵⁄₈oz

£7,000-8,000 **WW**

A George I silver tankard, the front later initialled, by Richard Bayley, London, some repairs.

1724 7in (18cm) high 25oz

£1,000-1,400 **WW**

A Philadelphia silver tankard, by Jeremiah Elfreth.

c1750 8½in (21.5cm) high 40½oz

£4,000-5,000 **POOK**

A George II Channel Islands silver half pint baluster tankard, inscribed 'TD LH', by Jean Henry (fl.c1727-83), Guernsey.

c1750 3½in (9cm) high 5¾oz

£3,000-3,500 **MART**

A George II silver and parcel-gilt tankard, later decorated in the Rococo manner, by William Shaw and William Priest, London.

1756 7¼in (18.5cm) high 22oz

£1,300-1,600 **WHP**

An 18thC Scandinavian silver peg tankard, the cover with rampant lion and set with a coin, inscribed, maker's mark 'PC', dated.

1761 7in (17.5cm) high 19½oz

£2,000-3,000 **WW**

A George III silver tankard, crested and initialled, by William Turton, London.

1776 7¾in (20cm) high

£1,300-1,600 **BE**

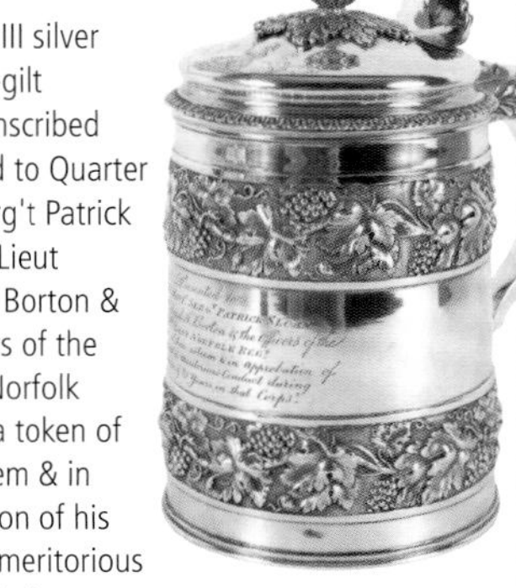

A George III silver and silver-gilt tankard, inscribed 'Presented to Quarter Mast'r Serg't Patrick Sloan, By Lieut Colonel A Borton & the officers of the 9th East Norfolk Reg't, as a token of their esteem & in appreciation of his gallant & meritorious Conduct during a service of 21 Years in the Corps', by Rebecca Emes & Edward Barnard, London.

1814 8¼in (21cm) high 32⁵⁄₈oz

£2,500-3,000 **CHOR**

An early George II silver miniature or toy bullet teapot, by Micou Melun, Falmouth, with broken wooden handle, some scratches and wear.

c1730 *4¾in (12cm) long 2⅜oz*

£1,200-1,600 **DN**

A George II Scottish silver teapot, ivory spacers to handle, by George Cooper, Aberdeen.

c1735 *6in (15cm) high 19½oz*

£4,000-5,000 **SWO**

A George II bullet teapot, the interior grill pierced, by James Ker, Edinburgh, Assay Master Edward Lothian.

James Ker was an important silver- and goldsmith working in Edinburgh. He entered into partnership with his son-in-law William Dempster as Ker & Dempster, and together they made some of the most important mid-18thC Scottish plate.

1742 *5¾in (14.5cm) high 19⅛oz*

£3,000-4,000 **L&T**

A George II Channel Islands silver teapot, with ebonised wooden handle, by Jean Gavey (fl.c1715-75), Jersey.

8½in (22cm) long 17⅛oz

£14,000-18,000 **MART**

A George III silver teapot and stand, with monograms, by Hester Bateman, London, some wear and splits.

Hester Bateman (1709-94), née Needham, was an important 18thC silversmith. After the death of her husband, a gold and silversmith, in 1760, she took over the family business. Her pieces are graceful and refined in shape, with restrained decoration, typically in the form of beaded edges. She was later joined by her sons Peter and Jonathan.

1786 *stand 6¼in (16cm) wide 16½oz*

£1,400-1,800 **GORL**

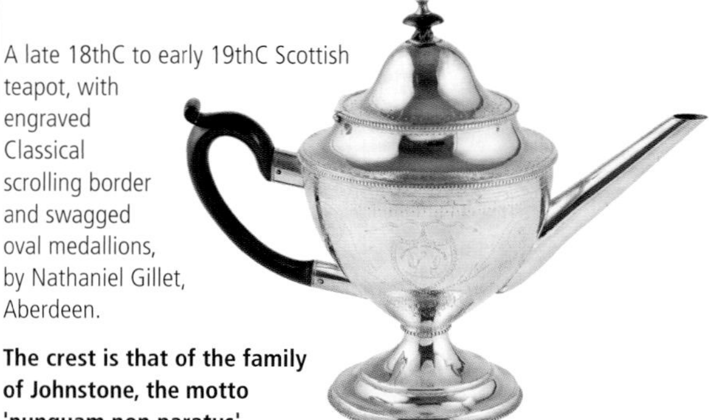

A late 18thC to early 19thC Scottish teapot, with engraved Classical scrolling border and swagged oval medallions, by Nathaniel Gillet, Aberdeen.

The crest is that of the family of Johnstone, the motto 'nunquam non paratus' (Never unprepared).

9½in (24cm) high 18½oz

£2,500-3,000 **L&T**

A George III silver teapot, with ivory finial and wooden handle, by Alice & George Burrows II, London, some hairlines, dent to spout.

1803 *11¼in (28.5cm) long 13⅝oz*

£250-300 **DN**

A George III silver teapot, by Crispin Fuller, London, some light scratches, splits to ivory bands.

1805 *11in (28cm) 18¾oz*

£400-500 **DN**

An American silver teapot, with carved ivory handle, monogrammed, by Gorham and Co., retailed by Mermoid and Jaccards.

c1900 *6in (15.5cm) high 10½oz*

£250-300 **WW**

A George II silver coffee pot, with wooden handle, by James Kirkup, Newcastle.

The crest is that recorded for Aurd, Bell, Hunt, Kerr, Frazer and other families.

1728 *9¾in (25cm) high 25⅜oz*

£2,000-2,500 **WW**

A George II coffee pot, by William Beilby, Newcastle.

1748 *10¼in (26cm) high 26¾oz*

£2,000-2,500 **L&T**

CLOSER LOOK – CHANNEL ISLANDS COFFEE POT

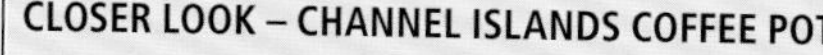

This coffee pot was made by Guillaume Henry, arguably the finest silver maker of the Channel Islands. He worked on Guernsey c1720-67.

Like many pieces of Channel Islands silver, the decoration is relatively plain and simple.

It has a curved spout with a bold anthemion mount and stiff leaf surmount.

The side is engraved with the arms of the Guernsey Dobree family impaling the Jersey Bonamy family on their joining through marriage.

A George II Channel Islands silver coffee pot, inscribed 'M.L.H' to base, by Guillaume Henry, Guernsey.

9½in (24cm) high 34½oz

£32,000-38,000 **MART**

A George II silver coffee pot, with fruitwood handle, by Ayme Videau, London.

1754 *7¾in (20cm) high 18¾oz*

£1,200-1,600 **SWO**

A George II coffee pot, by Lothian & Robertson, Edinburgh.

1759 *10in (25.5cm) high 35½oz*

£3,000-3,500 **L&T**

A George III Irish silver coffee pot, with timber C-scroll handle, by John Loughlin, Dublin.

1770 *11¾in (30cm) high 30oz*

£2,000-2,500 **ADA**

A George III silver coffee pot, crested, by James Young, London.

1772 *11in (28cm) high 26⅝oz*

£900-1,000 **BE**

A George III silver coffee pot, repoussé-decorated in the Rococo manner, maker 'IR', Newcastle.

1800 *12in (30.5cm) high 29oz*

£600-700 **WHP**

An American coin-silver coffee pot, with ram-headed handle, floral repoussé decoration, by S. Kirk & Son, Baltimore, MD.

1868-90 *8in (20.5cm) high 17¼oz*

£1,400-1,800 **FRE**

A Queen Anne Britannia standard silver chocolate pot, marks rubbed.

10¼in (26cm) high 27⅜oz

£2,500-3,000 CHOR

A Queen Anne silver hot milk pot, engraved with an armorial, the underside with scratch weight '11=14=0', by Thomas Parr I, London.

1713 7½in (19cm) high 11¼oz

£4,000-5,000 WW

A Queen Anne silver chocolate pot, by Gabriel Sleath, London.

1713 9½in (24cm) high 23⅞oz

£2,500-3,000 WW

A George II Channel Islands silver covered hot milk jug, with boxwood handle and finial, with engraved armorial, by Guillaume Henry, Guernsey.

This piece was inspired by an original design by Paul de Lamerie of London.

c1727 4½in (11.5cm) high 8⅞oz

£23,000-28,000 MART

A George II silver tea kettle-on-stand, with lamp, later chased with chinoiserie figures, later inscribed, with raffia covered swing handle, by Daniel Chartier, London, some repairs and losses.

The inscription records the presentation of the kettle in 1873 to Helen Mary 'May' (1853-1940), on the occasion of her marriage to Henry Brooks Gaskell (1846-1907) of Kiddington Hall, Oxford. May Gaskell was reputedly the last love of Pre-Raphaelite artist Edward Burne Jones and may possibly have served him tea from this pot.

1743 12in (30.5cm) high 56¾oz

£1,400-1,800 BELL

A repoussé silver kettle-on-stand, by J. Charles Edington, some dents.

1831-32 15¾in (40cm) high 129oz

£4,000-4,500 POOK

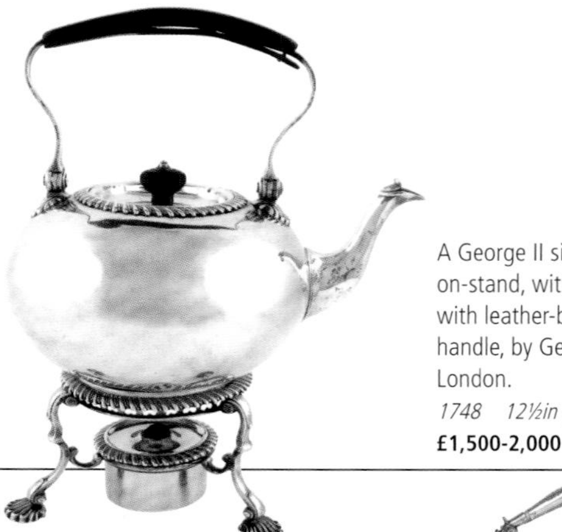

A George II silver kettle-on-stand, with burner, with leather-bound hinged handle, by George Methuen, London.

1748 12½in (32cm) high 60oz

£1,500-2,000 WW

A Victorian silver kettle-on-stand, with 18thC-style Rococo decoration, by Walter Morisse, London, burning lacking.

1849 without handle 12½in (31.5cm) high 71¼oz

£1,800-2,200 TEN

A matched 1820s tea service, London.
6½in (16.5cm) high 48⅜oz
£700-800 **L&T**

A William IV silver tea service, chased with forget-me-not flowers within acanthus panels, by Robert Hennell, London.
1834 *teapot 11in (28cm) wide 50⅜oz*
£1,800-2,200 **HT**

A Philadelphia coin-silver tea and coffee service, in Neo-classical style, inscribed to underside 'Julia C. Mayer, wife of the Hon. George May Keim of Reading Pennsylvania From her mother Mrs. Christopher Mayer of Lancaster 1826', by R. & W. Wilson.
c1826 *coffee pot 12in (30.5cm) high 118⅝oz*
£3,000-4,000 **POOK**

A Victorian silver tea set, engraved with a crest, by Walter Morrisse, London.

The crest is that of Dod of Edge, Cheshire.
1850 *11¼in (28.5cm) high 48¾oz*
£850-950 **WW**

A silver tea service, with gilt lining to sugar bowl and milk jug, by Edward & John Barnard, London.
1865 *8¼in (21cm) high 91¾oz*
£1,800-2,200 **L&T**

A silver tea service, with crest engraved cartouches, numbered '5650' and '5601', tea and coffee pots impressed 'Late Storr & Mortimer', by John Hunt & Robert Roskell, London, some tarnishing, cracking to spacers.
1870 *11in (28cm) long 82¼oz*
£4,000-4,500 **FELL**

A Victorian engraved tea and coffee service, the teapot handle detached but present, by John Ruddock, Sheffield.
1874 *coffee pot 9¾in (25cm) high 70¾oz*
£950-1,100 **LC**

A Victorian silver tea and coffee service, by Roberts & Belk, Sheffield.
1875 *82⅞oz*
£3,000-3,500 **WAD**

A late Victorian silver bachelor's tea set, by Mappin & Webb, London.
1890 *22oz*
£750-850 **FLD**

An early George I silver tea caddy, the base engraved with marriage initials, by John East, London.

1724 *4in (10cm) high 4⅞oz*

£1,200-1,600 **HT**

A George I silver tea caddy, the base inscribed 'The Gift of Mr. John Bristol to Madame Martha Carey Wife of Darell Carey J.M.S', by John Newton, London, date letter rubbed.

The inscription relates to the Carey family of Guernsey.

c1730 *5½in (14cm) high 8oz*

£1,800-2,200 **MART**

CLOSER LOOK – SCOTTISH TEA CADDY

Scottish silver tea caddies are exceedingly rare. While the use of tea caddies would have been as common in Scotland as elsewhere in Britain, it seems the fashion in Scotland was for wooden caddies, or that English makers generally supplied silver tea caddies to Scotland.

The lid is engraved with a foliate border, with a fruiting bud finial.

This caddy is decorated with an foliate engraved border and a keyhole pendant cartouche with crest and motto within.

The condition and quality are very high.

A rare George III drum tea caddy, by William Kerr, Edinburgh.

1772 *4¾in (12cm) high 1¼oz*

£4,500-5,500 **L&T**

A pair of George II silver tea caddies, with detachable lead liners, by Samuel Taylor, London.

1744 *5¾in (14.5cm) high 19¾oz*

£1,800-2,200 **WW**

A pair of George II silver tea caddies, by Samuel Taylor, London.

1750 *5½in (14cm) high 17½oz*

£2,000-2,500 **TEN**

A pair of George III silver tea caddies, engraved with the Wynne Finch crests, by Lewis Hearne and Francis Butty, London.

1760 *6½in (16.5cm) high 19oz*

£1,300-1,600 **WW**

A pair of early George III silver tea caddies, by Pierre Gillois, London.

1761 *4¾in (12cm) high 13⅝oz*

£2,200-2,800 **MART**

A George III silver tea caddy, by Hester Bateman, London.

1782 *4¼in (11cm) long 9¾oz*

£3,500-4,000 **WW**

A George III silver tea caddy, by Robert Hennell, London, some repairs.

1791 *5¾in (14.5cm) high 12¾oz*

£950-1,100 **BELL**

An unusual late 15thC silver-gilt seal-top spoon, probably French, later assayed in London, marked with a tent.

The leopard's head mark in the bowl was used in London 1528-34 and the date letter mark refers to 1530. However, the maker's mark, a tent, is not elsewhere recorded on English silver, suggesting that this spoon was probably made by a Continental craftsman. It was probably made in France, c1470 and later submitted for assay in London in 1530.

c1470 *6¼in (16cm) long 1¼oz*
£7,500-8,500 **WW**

A Henry VIII silver Apostle spoon, 'The Master', the reverse prick-dot initialled '1628' 'I.A' over 'R.P', with gilded Apostle finial, maker's mark of a device, possibly a basket, London.

1534 *7in (17.5cm) long 1¾oz*
£9,500-11,000 **WW**

An Elizabeth I provincial silver seal-top spoon, the reverse scratch initialled 'A.D', by John Gladwin and John Utting, Lichfield.

c1580 *6in (15.5cm) long 1⅛oz*
£6,000-7,000 **WW**

An Elizabeth I provincial lion sejant spoon, by John Avery, Exeter.

c1590 *6in (15cm) long ⅞oz*
£1,500-2,000 **LC**

A James I silver Apostle spoon, with gilded finial of St Mathias, the reverse prick-dot initialled, 'N.H' over 'H.B', over '1621', by William Cawdell, London.

1611 *7in (18cm) long 1⅞oz*
£5,000-5,500 **WW**

A Charles I silver Apostle spoon, with finial probably of St Paul, by Edward Hole, London.

1632 *7in (17.5cm) long 1⅝oz*
£1,500-2,000 **WW**

A Charles I seal-top spoon, initialled seal 'MN', by Benjamin Yates, London.

1637 *6in (15cm) long ⅞oz*
£650-750 **BE**

A Charles I silver Apostle spoon, with gilded finial of St Jude, the reverse prick-dot initialled, 'G.Y', probably by Thomas Paulson, London.

1637 *7in (18cm) long 1⅞oz*
£2,200-2,800 **WW**

A Charles II provincial silver Trefid spoon, with a rudimentary rat-tail, the reverse scratch initialled 'T*S', by Marmaduke Best, York.

This is an important York spoon as it was made to the new design outside of London, indicating the mobility of goldsmiths and journeyman and their wish to produce the latest fashions. The goldsmith had not quite shaken off the earlier style of spoon-making – he struck a mark in the bowl, unusually for a Trefid. You would expect to see a reeded rat-tail but this spoon has a rudimentary rat-tail.

1665 *7½in (19cm) long 1⅜oz*
£2,200-2,800 **WW**

A James II silver Trefid spoon, with a plain rat-tail, by John King, London.

Interestingly, this spoon has an additional punch which contains a crest. Crests are usually engraved on silver, not struck, so the owner must have commissioned this punch for their own silver.

1686 *10¼in (26cm) long 3¾oz*
£4,000-5,000 **WW**

A pair of late 17thC provincial silver Trefid spoons, with ribbed rat-tails, prick-dot initialled 'B' over 'I*I', by Thomas Havers, Norwich.

c1689 *7½in (19cm) long 3¼oz*
£6,000-7,000 **WW**

A William and Mary Sussex silver Trefid spoon, with a ribbed rat-tail, scratch initialled 'E' over 'IM' over 'WA', by Robert Colegate, Lewes.
c1690 *7¾in (20cm) long 1⅝oz*
£1,400-1,800 **WW**

A William III West Country silver lace-back Trefid spoon, prick-dot initialled 'T.W' over 'W.W' over '1700', by Richard Sweet II, Chard.
c1700 *7¾in (20cm) long 1½oz*
£3,000-4,000 **WW**

A William III silver lace-back Trefid spoon, with foliate scroll decoration, scroll rat-tail, prick-dot initialled 'A.N' over 'R.T' 'April 25 1701', by Richard Sweet III, Honiton.
c1701 *8in (20.5cm) long 1¾oz*
£3,500-4,000 **WW**

A Queen Anne Scottish provincial silver dog-nose spoon, scratch initialled 'RG' over 'HG' over 'Od' over '11 9', by David Dunlop, Canongate.
c1704 *7¾in (19.5cm) long 1¾oz*
£4,500-5,000 **WW**

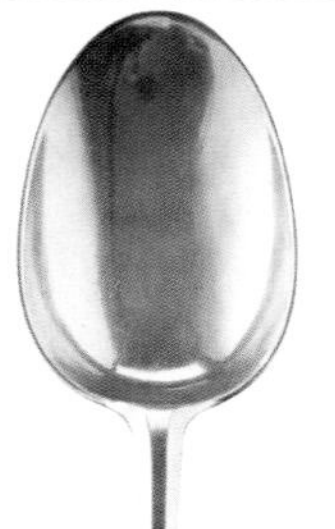

A Scottish provincial Hanoverian pattern tablespoon, the reverse engraved 'WF/SG', with engraved fleur-de-lis rat tail, with armorial shield, by John and Francis Brown, Perth.

The working careers of John and his son Francis Brown are somewhat confused. Although recorded in Perth as early as 1724, they appear to have worked in Edinburgh and possibly Elgin as well. No marks have been confidently ascribed to either of these periods and all their work is tied to Perth. The double drop and engraved rat tail is also a feature unique to these makers in Scottish silver and shows much closer comparison to Continental European work than British.
7¾in (20cm) 1⅞oz
£6,500-7,500 **L&T**

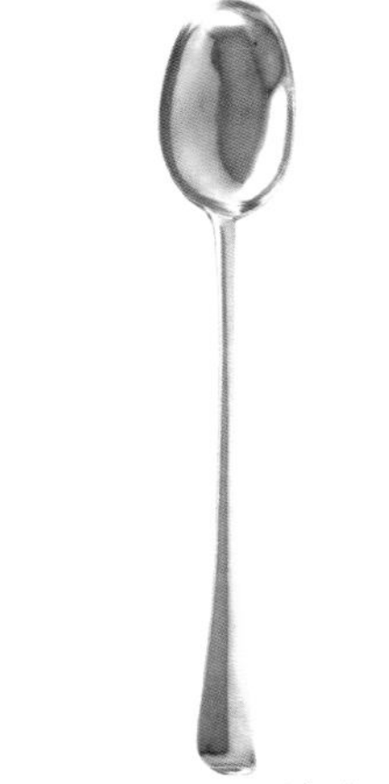

A Queen Anne provincial silver Hanoverian pattern basting spoon, by Thomas Robinson, Chester.
1711 *14¼in (36cm) long 5⅝oz*
£2,000-2,500 **WW**

A George II Channel Islands silver Hanoverian pattern soup ladle, marked 'PA' for Pierre Amiraux, I, II and III.
c1740 *12½in (32cm) long 5⅛oz*
£950-1,100 **MART**

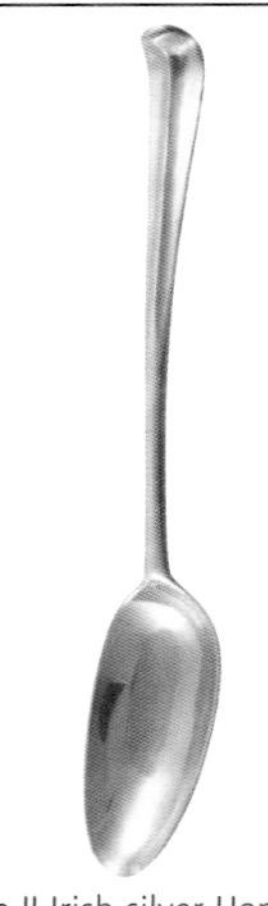

A George II Irish silver Hanoverian pattern dessert spoon, by George Hodder, Cork.
c1740 *6¾in (17cm) long*
£300-400 **ADA**

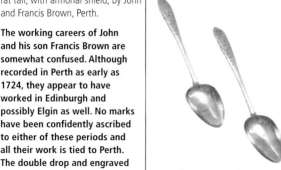

A pair of George III Irish provincial bright-cut silver table spoons, engraved with a crown and leopard's head crest, by William Fitzgerald, Limerick.
c1800 *9½in (24cm) long 4oz*
£2,500-3,000 **ADA**

A George III Irish provincial silver Celtic-point basting spoon, erased terminal, by Maurice Fitzgerald, Limerick.
c1800 *12½in (32cm) long 3⅝oz*
£1,800-2,200 **WW**

A Scottish provincial fiddle-pattern toddy ladle, initialled 'B', marks 'IPR' and castle turrets, by John and Patrick Riach, Forres.
1825-35 *6½in (16.5cm) long 1¼oz*
£2,800-3,200 **LC**

A George I Irish flagon, with a harp-shaped handle, engraved with a coat of arms, by Thomas Williamson, Dublin.

1718 *12in (30.5cm) high 35⅜oz*

£7,000-8,000 **LC**

A George II Irish silver cream jug, by John Hamilton, Dublin, some repairs and wear.

c1730-40 *4¾in (12cm) high 7⅜oz*

£8,000-9,000 **TEN**

A George II silver beer jug, by John Swift, London, engraved with an armorial, with traces of gilding.

The Arms are possibly that of the Duke of Hamilton.

1736 *12¾in (32.5cm) high 59oz*

£7,500-8,500 **WW**

A pair of George II provincial silver sauceboats, with flying dolphin handles, engraved with an armorial and a tiger crest for Dent, initialled 'D' over 'I.I', by James Kirkup, Newcastle, some wear.

1747 *7¾in (19.5cm) long 28¼oz*

£9,000-10,000 **TEN**

A George II Channel Islands silver cream jug, inscribed 'I.C.L', by Pierre Maingy (fl.c1739-76), Guernsey.

3½in (9cm) high 3⅛oz

£6,500-7,500 **MART**

A mid-to-late 18thC beer jug, probably Colonial, crested.

7¼in (18.5cm) high 26oz

£2,000-2,500 **LC**

An Irish provincial silver cream jug, stamped 'STERLING', by Michael McDermott and Daniel McCarthy, Cork.

c1780 *5in (12.5cm) high 5½oz*

£2,000-2,500 **ADA**

An American coin-silver repoussé water pitcher, by S. Kirk & Son, Baltimore, MD.

1868-90 *9in (23cm) high 31¼oz*

£1,500-2,000 **FRE**

A silver cow creamer, with import marks for London, some dents, lid loose.

c1897 *5½in (14cm) 6¼oz*

£1,300-1,600 **BELL**

A Dutch silver goat creamer, with red glass eyes.

1905 *5½in (14cm) long 4⅞oz*

£1,200-1,600 **WW**

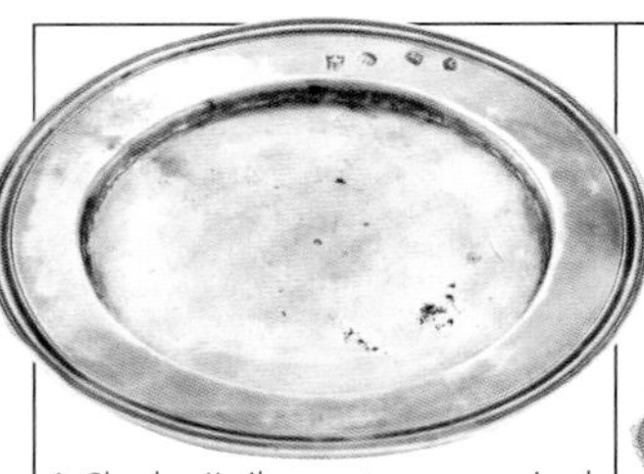

A Charles II silver paten, on a raised foot, maker's mark 'L.S' crowned, probably by Leonard Sutton, London.

A paten, or diskos, is a small plate, usually made of silver or gold, used to hold Eucharistic bread which is to be consecrated during Mass.

1680 *6½in (16.5cm) diam 9⅝oz*

£2,000-2,500 WW

A George II silver kettle stand, with an armorial, on three lion paw feet, by George Hindmarsh, London.

The marital arms of Sir Edmund Isham, 6th Baronet (1690-1772) Lamport Hall, Northants, impaling (Elizabeth) Wood.

1732 *9¾in (25cm) long 28oz*

£6,000-7,000 WW

A George II silver side dish, with an armorial, detailed underneath 'No 60 20 = 9', by Paul de Lamerie, London.

1737 *9½in (24cm) diam 20oz*

£4,000-5,000 BELL

A George II silver strawberry dish, engraved with an armorial, by Christian Hillan, London.

1739 *9in (23cm) diam 15oz*

£2,300-2,800 WW

A George II Channel Islands silver card waiter, inscribed 'M.L.H' to underside, by Guillaume Henry, Guernsey.

7in (18cm) diam 8¾oz

£4,000-4,500 MART

A George III salver, with armorial, by William and Patrick Cunningham, Edinburgh.

The motto reads 'leges juraque serva' (observe the laws).

1802 *18in (46cm) diam 84½oz*

£3,000-3,500 L&T

A Scottish silver salver, engraved with a coat of arms and motto, Edinburgh.

c1805 *20in (51cm) diam 93¾oz*

£1,800-2,200 BELL

A George III silver salver, engraved with an armorial, on four foliate shell feet, maker's mark 'WS', possibly by William Stroud, London.

1815 *24¾in (63cm) diam 223oz*

£8,500-9,500 TEN

A set of ten George IV silver-gilt plates, with chased and repoussé Rococo decoration, by Thomas Burwash, London.

1821 *9½in (24cm) diam total 186⅞oz*

£7,000-8,000 HT

A George IV silver meat dish, with engraved armorials, by William Eaton, London, small repair to rim, some scratches.

1824 *24in (61cm) long 108oz*

£1,500-2,000 **GORL**

A George IV silver salver, with presentation inscription, by John Carter II, London.

1825 *17in (43cm) diam 74oz*

£1,200-1,800 **LSK**

A pair of George IV silver soup plates, engraved with an armorial beneath a baron's coronet and motto 'Fax Mentis Honestae Gloria', by Paul Storr, London, some scratches.

1829 *9¾in (24.5cm) diam 38⅞oz*

£2,000-2,500 **TEN**

A Victorian silver salver, on scrolling acanthus feet, by William Ker Reid, London, some wear.

1837 *20½in (52cm) diam 100oz*

£1,800-2,200 **PW**

A Victorian silver gallery tray, Sheffield, base requiring repair.

1891 *27in (68.5cm) wide 173½oz*

£2,300-2,700 **BELL**

A Victorian silver salver, engraved with an armorial, on pierced scroll bracket feet, by Hawksworth, Eyre and Co., Sheffield.

The shield and crest are those of Andersen impaling Burgate/ Canbroke/Shambrooke/Williams. The motto is that of Michelson.

1839 *21¼in (54cm) diam 106oz*

£2,500-3,000 **WW**

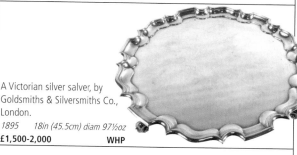

A Victorian silver salver, by Goldsmiths & Silversmiths Co., London.

1895 *18in (45.5cm) diam 97½oz*

£1,500-2,000 **WHP**

A Victorian silver tray, with presentation inscription to 'Mr Ermerson Crawford Herdman from Sion Mills on the occasion of his marriage, September 1895', by John Newton Mappin, Mappin & Webb, London, some wear.

1894 *29½in (75cm) wide 137⅞oz*

£5,000-6,000 **TEN**

An Edwardian silver tray, by Harry Brasted, London, maker's mark partially obscured, decoration rubbed.

1902 *24¼in (61.5cm) long 98¼oz*

£1,200-1,600 **DN**

A Charles II silver porringer and cover, engraved with an armorial, maker's mark 'WC', London.

The cover has a later spool-shaped finial with London Assay Office additions hallmarks for 2008 (case number 8566).

1662 *7¾in (19.5cm) high 31oz*

£7,000-8,000 **WW**

A James II Irish silver porringer and cover, with scroll handles with female heads, by John Phillips, Dublin.

1685-87 *7¾in (20cm) high 28½oz*

£10,000-12,000 **WW**

A William III silver monteith, the underside with scratch weight '56=0', by Robert Cooper, London.

1701 *11in (28cm) diam 55¼oz*

£15,000-20,000 **WW**

CLOSER LOOK – QUEEN ANNE MONTIETH

A montieth is a form of large punch bowl, with a notched rim for suspending punch cups.

This example is decorated with foliate strapwork and crests, with lion masque handles.

The collar is detachable, and has a scalloped rim applied with cherub heads flanked by rope-twist scrolls.

The foot is inscribed, 'Presented to H.J. Hines by the Directors of the Royal Exchange Assurance. 1919'. The Royal Exchange Assurance Corporation was a British insurance company operating 1720-1968.

A Queen Anne Britannia silver monteith, by Robert Timbrell and Joseph Bell, London.

1710 *11in (28cm) diam 64⅜oz*

£12,000-15,000 **FRE**

A rare George I sugar bowl and cover, with engraved crest, by Henry Bethune, Edinburgh.

When compared to the survival of early teapots, the rarity of early sugar bowls becomes much more apparent. Few surviving sugar bowls still have their original cover. This piece was probably part of a matching tea service.

1725 *4¾in (12cm) diam 12½oz*

£10,000-12,000 **L&T**

A George III soup tureen and cover, on lion's paw feet, engraved with the arms of Cholmeley and Harrison, by William Bennett, London.

1812 *17in (43cm) wide 171⅝oz*

£5,000-6,000 **HAN**

An early 19thC Maltese silver sugar bowl and cover, maker's mark 'GC', possibly for Gaetano Cauchi or Giuseppe Cousin, Captain Sir Alexander Ball period.

Captain Sir Alexander John Ball was a Rear Admiral and close friend of Lord Nelson. He directed the blockade of Malta 1798-1800 and served as Civil Commissioner of the island 1802-09.

1800-09 *5¼in (13.5cm) high 8¾oz*

£1,800-2,200 **WW**

An American silver tureen and cover, with female bust handles, by Samuel Kirk, Baltimore, Maryland, some dings.

c1828 *16¼in (41.5cm) wide 104⅝oz*

£7,000-8,000 **POOK**

A William IV graduated set of four silver meat dishes, each engraved with a coat of arms, with Old Sheffield Plate covers, the dishes by John Bridge, London.

The Arms on the dishes are slightly different to those on the covers, but they are both the Arms of Maitland.

1831 *max 24in (61cm) long 317oz*

£10,000-12,000 **LC**

A Victorian Irish silver soup tureen and cover, with poppy seed handle finial on a bed of poppy leaves, by Patrick Loughlin, Dublin, dent to interior rim.

1838 *14¼in (36cm) long 91¾oz*

£3,000-4,000 **GORL**

A James II silver lighthouse-form sugar caster, maker's mark 'CW', possibly for Caleb Westbrook, London.

1686 *7¾in (19.5cm) high 11oz*

£6,500-7,500 **WW**

A George III silver sugar vase and cover, engraved with the Macaulay crest, by Daniel Smith and Robert Sharp, London.

1787 *7¾in (19.5cm) high 17¾oz*

£2,000-2,500 **WW**

A William and Mary Channel Islands silver lighthouse pepper pot, of Huguenot influenced form, inscribed 'E.G' to base, by Abraham Hebert (fl.c1660-1700), Jersey.

4in (10cm) high 2⅞oz

£9,500-11,000 **MART**

A George II silver cake basket, the centre with an armorial, by Samuel Herbert & Co., London.

The shield is that of Fleetwood.

1751 *14¼in (36cm) long 53¾oz*

£3,000-4,000 **WW**

A George III Irish silver dish ring, later engraved crest and motto, probably by Michael Homer, Dublin.

The crest is associated with O'Duinne, Doyne and Dunn of Ireland.

c1785 *7½in (19cm) diam 15¼oz*

£1,300-1,600 **WW**

A late 19thC American silver dish ring, owned by 'Boss' Croker, pierced with shamrocks, harps, a round tower and a wolfhound, with the arms of the Croker family, stamped 'Sterling'.

Richard 'Boss' Welstead Croker (1843-1922), was an Irish-American politician and a leader of New York City's Tammany Hall, a political organisation founded in 1789 which later began a centre for Democratic politics.

9½oz

£950-1,1000 **WHYT**

A pair of Victorian silver fish servers, by Francis Higgins II, London, light scratches.

1865 *knife 13¼in (33.5cm) long 13½oz*

£1,500-2,000 **DN**

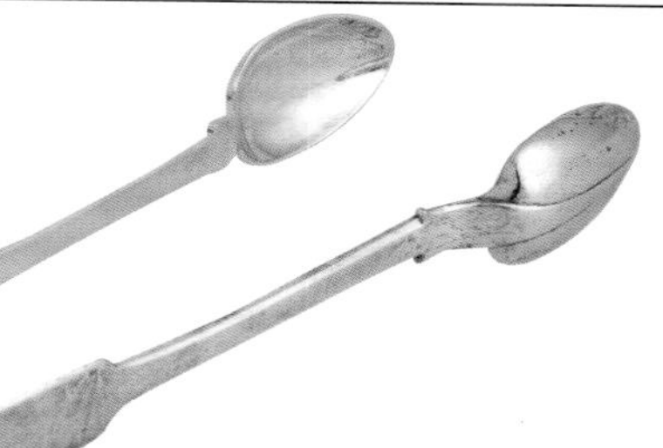

A William IV Irish silver fiddle pattern over-sized tongs with rat tail bowls, crested and inscribed with monogram, by Philip Weekes, Dublin.

1830 *11¼in (28.5cm) long 10oz*

£7,000-8,000 **ADA**

An set of eighteen early 20thC German silver crowned-cipher knife rests.

30¾oz

£1,500-2,000 **WAD**

A George III silver jockey cap caddy spoon, by Joseph Taylor, Birmingham.
1799 *2in (5cm) long ¼oz*
£450-550 **WW**

A George III silver-mounted shell caddy spoon, engraved with Markham crest, by Matthew Linwood, Birmingham.
c1810 *3in (7.5cm) long*
£550-650 **WW**

A mid-18thC Dutch silver table bell, by Cornelis De Haan, The Hague.
1768 *5¼in (13.5cm) high 10oz*
£7,500-8,500 **WW**

An Elkington & Co. silver-gilt, enamel and glass Graeco-Pompeian-style three-piece table garniture, with three later glass dishes.

The Graeco-Pompeian service was created for the 1862 International Exhibition in London. It comprised of thirteen pieces and was designed by W. Albert Willms (d.1899), who was awarded a medal of artistic merit for it. Willms trained as a modeller and engraver at Klagman, Dieterle and Constant in Paris, but later relocated to London. In 1857 he became head of Elkington's design studio.
1862 *largest 16in (40.5cm) high 149¾oz*
£11,000-14,000 **BELL**

A George III silver cream pail, with blue glass liner, by William Plummer, London.
1770 *4¼in (105cm) 2⅜oz*
£1,400-1,800 **WW**

CLOSER LOOK – VICTORIAN SILVER CENTREPIECE

This impressive Victorian centrepiece is modelled as a lady falconer seated on a horse, holding her falcon, about to let it fly.

Beside her stands a cadger, carrying a padded wooden cadge, which is a frame on which birds of preys are carried.

This prize was originally won by William Stuart Sterling Crawfurd (1819-87) who, having a reputation for hosting good horse races, was invited by King William of the Netherlands to bring his horses to Dorn, in the Netherlands, to race them at the King's own club, the Hawking Club.

This is mounted on a wooden base applied with the Dutch Royal Coat of arms, inscribed 'LOO CHALLENGE CUP 1851' and 'CHALLENGE CUP GIVEN BY HM THE KING OF THE NETHERLANDS TO BE WON TWO YEARS IN SUCCESSION BY THE SAME PERSON WON IN 1851 AND 1852, BY MR STIRLING CRAWFURD'S DARKIE'.

A Victorian presentation silver centrepiece, by John Samuel Hunt, overstamping another maker, London.
1851 *28in (71cm) high 176oz*
£45,000-50,000 **WW**

A William and Mary silver dog collar, inscribed 'Miss R Jenkins, Charlton Hill 1691', minor wear.
3¾in (9.5cm) diam
£3,000-3,500 **TEN**

A George III silver honey skep and stand, by John Emes, London.

A skep is a man-made beehive or basket, used for catching and transporting bees. First, the swarm is shaken off the branch so that they fall into the skep. The skep is then turned upside down, propped on a stone, and transported.
1802 *5½in (14cm) diam 14½oz*
£10,000-12,000 **WW**

A pair of Spanish silver snuffers, Madrid.
1841 *5⅛oz*
£300-400 **WAD**

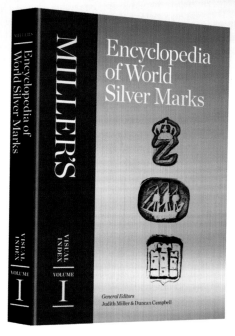

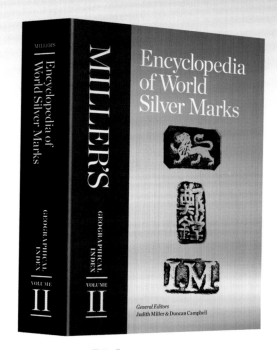

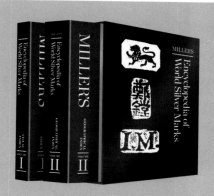

ESSENTIAL REFERENCE – WINE LABELS

Wine labels became popular in the mid-18thC.

- **They were generally made of silver or silver-plate, although enamel, pottery, porcelain and other materials were also used.**
- **More than 500 silversmiths are recorded as having made wine labels. Intricate examples from the great London makers, such as Paul Storr or Benjamin Smith, are sought after. Labels from the workshop of Hester Bateman are also popular.**
- **In the 1860s, new legislation allowed the sale of single bottles of wine with paper labels. Wine was increasingly served straight from the bottle in which it had been purchased, and wine labels fell largely out of use.**

A George III silver wine label, incised 'SHERRY', by Hester Bateman, London.
c1775 *2¼in (6cm) long ¼oz*
£700-800 **WW**

A George III Irish provincial silver armorial wine label, incised 'PORT', by John Warner, Cork.
c1790 *2¼in (5.5cm) long ¼oz*
£450-550 **WW**

A George III silver armorial wine label, incised 'SHERRY', maker's mark worn, London.
1791 *3½in (9cm) long 1¼oz*
£750-850 **WW**

A George III silver wine label, with mounted Prince of Wales feathers, incised and blackened 'FALERNUM', by Peter and Ann Bateman, London.

Peter Bateman was the son of Hester Bateman (see page 294). Ann Bateman was Hester's daughter-in-law, and the widow of another of her sons, Jonathan Bateman.
1792 *2in (5cm) long ¼oz*
£500-600 **WW**

A George III silver armorial wine label, incised 'SHERRY'.
c1795 *1½in (4cm) long ⅜oz*
£400-500 **WW**

A pair of George III silver wine labels, incised 'HERMITAGE' and 'RED CHAMPAGNE', by Paul Storr, London.
1814 *2in (5cm) long 2¼oz*
£1,500-2,000 **WW**

A set of six Irish George III silver wine labels, engraved 'BAR SAC', 'FRONTIGNAN', 'CALCAVELLA', 'HERMITAGE', 'CLARET' and 'HOCK', probably by John Townsend, Dublin.
c1809 *2¼in (6cm) wide 2⅛oz*
£1,500-2,000 **GORL**

A George III silver armorial elephant wine label, pierced 'LISBON', by Edward Farrell, London.
1815 *3¼in (8.5cm) long ¾oz*
£3,500-4,000 **WW**

A George III silver wine label, incised 'SIRCIAL', by William Bateman, London.

William Bateman was the son of Jonathan and Ann Bateman, and the grandson of Hester Bateman.
1815 *2in (5cm) long ¼oz*
£550-600 **WW**

A George III silver-gilt lion's pelt wine label, inscribed 'CHAMPAIGN', by Paul Storr, London.

1815 *2¾in (7cm) long 1⅝oz*

£1,000-1,500 **WW**

A George III Scottish rhodium-plated silver wine label, inscribed 'To Mrs M. Whytock for HOME MADE WINE from Cal: Hort: Soc 1816', by William Peat, Edinburgh.

1815 *2¾in (7cm) long 1⅛oz*

£300-400 **WW**

A George III silver-gilt armorial wine label, pierced 'CLARET', by John Reily, London.

The crest is that of the 6th Earl of Shaftsbury.

c1817 *2¼in (6cm) long ¾oz*

£550-600 **WW**

A pair of George IV silver wine labels, pierced 'DANTZIC' and 'EAU D'OR', by Philip Rundell, London.

1823 *2in (5cm) long 2oz*

£750-850 **WW**

An early 19thC Scottish provincial silver wine label, incised 'CURRANT', by William Ferguson, Peterhead.

c1825 *1¾in (4.5cm) long ¼oz*

£850-950 **WW**

A William IV cast wine label, pierced 'MADEIRA', by Paul Storr, London.

1835 *2¼in (5.5cm) long ¾oz*

£650-750 **LC**

A pair of Victorian silver fox wine labels, incised 'PORT' and 'MADEIRA', by Robert Garrard, London.

1849 *2½in (6.5cm) long 2oz*

£700-800 **WW**

A Victorian silver armorial wine label, pierced 'SHERRY', by Rawlings and Summers, London.

c1850 *2¼in (6cm) long 1oz*

£350-450 **WW**

A Victorian silver armorial wine label, pierced 'SHERRY'.

2½in (6.5cm) long

£700-800 **WW**

A George III silver wine funnel, initialled, by Peter, Ann and William Bateman, London.
1812 *5in (12.5cm) high 2½oz*
£400-500 **WW**

A William IV silver wine funnel, with detachable strainer, by Charles Fox, London.
1833 *5¾in (14.5cm) long 8⅜oz*
£3,000-3,500 **TEN**

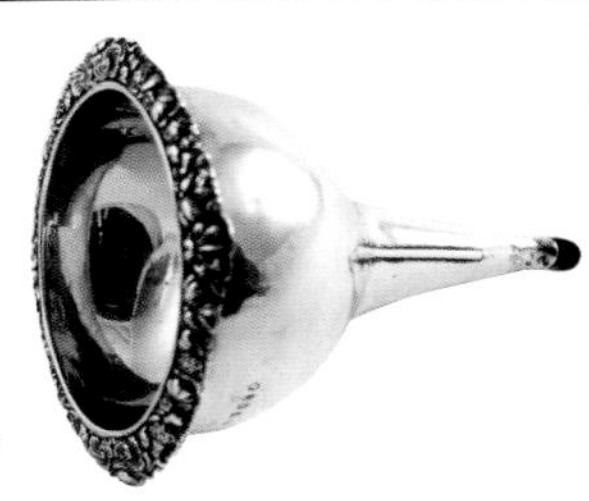

A George III wine funnel, with muslin ring, by Thomas Paine Dexter, London.
1818 *5½in (14cm) long 6½oz*
£550-600 **LC**

A pair of George III silver wine coasters, with turned wooden bases, by J.E. Terrey & Co., London, some nicks, marks rubbed.
1816 *5in (12.5cm) diam 11⅞oz*
£1,200-1,600 **GORL**

A pair of George III silver armorial wine coolers, the handles numbered '1' and '2', by Paul Storr, London.

The arms are those of Baring, Baron Ashburton.

1795 *8¾in (22.5cm) high 79⅜oz*
£13,000-16,000 **WW**

A pair of George IV tall silver coasters, engraved with a crest and motto, by Emes and Barnard, London.

The motto and crests are those for Carus-Wilson of Casterton Hall, Westmorland.

1828 *4in (10cm) high 19oz*
£3,500-4,000 **WW**

A rare early Charles II miniature or toy wine taster, maker's mark 'WG', London.
1665 *2in (5cm) diam ⅜oz*
£1,500-2,000 **LC**

A late 17thC Channel Islands silver wine taster, inscribed 'E.B' to side, by Robert Barbedor (c1677-1704), Jersey and Guernsey.
4¾in (12cm) long 3¼oz
£7,000-8,000 **MART**

A Canadian silver wine taster, by Paul Lambert, Quebec.
c1740 *5⅜oz*
£9,500-12,000 **FRE**

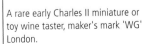

A George IV silver brandy pan, by William Sharp, London.
1820 *13in (33cm) long 23oz*
£1,300-1,600 **WW**

ESSENTIAL REFERENCE – SILVER PLATE

The invention of Sheffield plate in the mid-18thC was a key development in the production of silver objects. Silver plate was cheaper and more suitable for mass-produced objects.

- **Plating was developed in 1742 by Thomas Bolsover (1704-88) of Sheffield. The process involved fusing copper and silver together under heat, then rolling the fused metals under pressure to produce a sheet of workable metal. This technique was commonly used from the 1770s.**
- **In 1840 Elkington & Co. took out a patent for electroplating. A metal object (originally copper, later nickel) attached to a positive anode and a block of pure silver attached to a negative anode would both be immersed in a plating bath. An electric current would be passed from positive to negative, resulting in a fine sheet of silver being applied to the object. Electroplating is typically whiter and harsher in appearance than Old Sheffield plate.**
- **Electroplating ultimately came to replace Old Sheffield plate. The process was safer, and made complex structural ornament and decoration easier to achieve.**

A George III Old Sheffield Plate argyle, with a hinged water compartment.

An argyle is a pot used for keeping gravy or sauce warm, first used by the 5th Duke of Argyle. It has an outer liner that can be filled with boiling water via the spout, keeping the gravy within warm while on the table.

c1790 *6¼in (16cm) high*
£200-250 **WW**

A Sheffield silver-plated épergne, minor fleabites to glass.
c1810 *18in (45.5cm) high*
£950-1,100 **POOK**

A George III Old Sheffield Plate ewer, by Matthew Boutlon.
c1810 *10¾in (27.5cm) high*
£180-220 **WW**

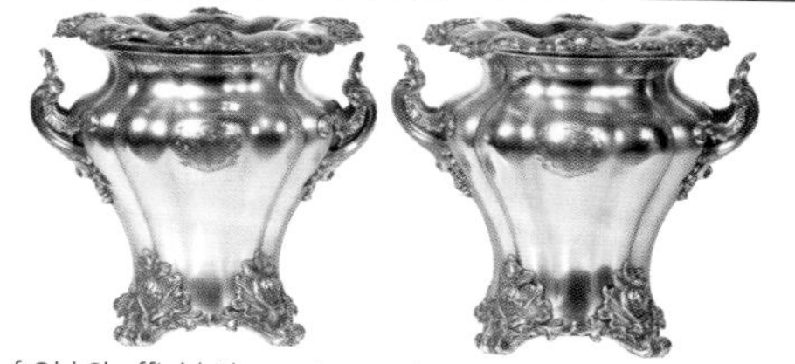

A pair of Old Sheffield Plate wine coolers, engraved with armorials and the motto 'Gloria Finis', for the Brooke family, liners present, some wear, copper showing under feet.
c1820/30 *10¼in (26cm) high*
£2,000-2,500 **TEN**

An Old Sheffield Plate wine cooler, by Matthew Boulton.
c1820 *9½in (24cm) high*
£300-400 **WAD**

A Victorian silver-plated whisky cask, modelled as a barrel on a cart, with attached bucket, inscribed 'Whisky' and 'From C R & R R to W W 1st November 1867', under glass dome on stand.
17in (43cm) long
£750-850 **GWA**

A pair of 19thC Sheffield silver-plated two-branch three-light candelabra, by Creswick & Co., Sheffield.
20in (51cm) high
£500-600 **MEA**

A New York Fireman's silver-plated speaking trumpet, for the Wandowonack Fire Co., Queens County, one dent, dated.
1890 *19in (48.5cm) high*
£1,300-1,600 **POOK**

A Victorian electroplated argyle, with interior water compartment, with Wynne Finch crests, by Martin, Hall and Co.
5½in (14cm) high
£220-280 **WW**

A pair of late 19thC George II-style electroplated candlesticks, probably by James Pinder & Co.
12½in (32cm) high
£300-350 **DN**

ESSENTIAL REFERENCE – VENETO-SARACENIC

Veneto-Saracenic ware is characterised by the technique of inlaying precious silver, gold or black compound onto brass within intricate decorative schemes of arabesques and other abstract motifs.

- **It was initially made in the Levant and Persia and subsequently manufactured in Northern Italy.**
- **The patterns are interpretations of Islamic compositions encompassing European motifs such as curling tendrils, flowers and knotwork.**
- **This type of metalwork was much sought after in Europe during the 15thC and 16thC.**

A Veneto-Saracenic brass salver, possibly 16thC Venetian, with silver-inlaid decoration.
19¼in (49cm) wide
£4,500-5,500 **CHEF**

A Dutch bronze mortar, cast with a band reading 'Wibrans Tot Amsterdam 1696'.
1696 *13¼in (33.5cm) high*
£8,000-9,000 **SWO**

A pair of pewter trumpet-base candlesticks, marked 'B B 1664', possibly for Beza Boston.
1664 *7in (18cm) high*
£1,400-1,800 **WW**

An 18thC Edinburgh pewter flagon.
13½in (34.5cm) high
£600-700 **HT**

An 18thC Italian copper wine cooler, with repoussé decoration, lion's mask ring handles and lift-out liner.
36¾in (93.5cm) wide
£3,500-4,000 **WW**

A 19thC copper and brass peat/log bin, with lion mask loop handles.
24¾in (63cm) high
£450-550 **L&T**

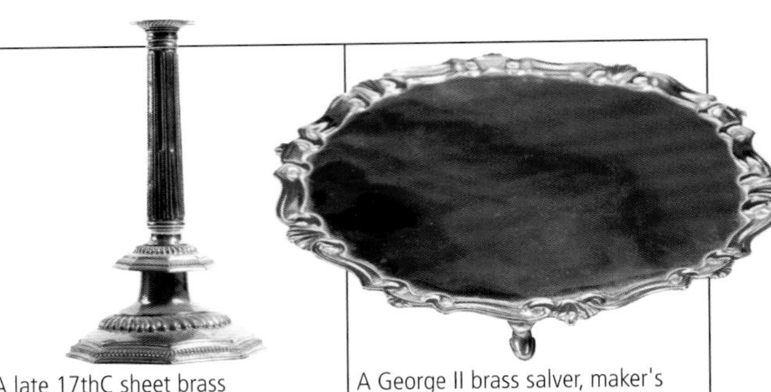

A late 17thC sheet brass candlestick, initialled 'SWM'.
17¾in (45cm) high
£4,000-4,500 **WW**

A George II brass salver, maker's mark 'TW'.
8¾in (22.5cm) diam
£2,500-3,000 **WW**

An Edwardian brass eagle floor-standing lectern, by Jones & Willis, with inscription to commemorate the coronation of King Edward VII and Queen Alexandra.
c1902 *70in (178cm) high*
£2,200-2,600 **FLD**

Judith Picks

This dog collar was worn by Boatswain, the beloved Newfoundland dog of Lord Byron, celebrated poet and leading figure in the Romantic movement. Byron was as much famed for his scandalous behaviour as for his literary talent. When told he could not bring a dog to Cambridge University, he brought a bear instead. Indeed, Byron's gamekeeper's widow reported that damage had been done to this very collar 'by a Bear which Lord Byron kept for his own amusement and with which Boatswain had many severe encounters'. Lord Byron adored Boatswain, for whom he constructed a monument at Newstead Abbey and wrote his 'Epitaph To a Dog' after his death in 1808. In this epitaph, Boatswain was said to possess, 'Beauty without Vanity,/Strength without Insolence,/Courage without Ferocity,/and all the virtues of Man without his Vices'.

A brass dog collar, engraved 'Rt. Honble LORD BYRON', ten teeth missing, minor splitting and wear, in later fitted mahogany display case with accompanying documentation.
17¼in (44cm) diam
£17,000-20,000 **TEN**

A Philadelphia pewter tankard, by Parks Boyd.

c1805 *7½in (19cm) high*

£5,500-6,000 **POOK**

A pewter dish, by Joseph Danforth, Middletown, Connecticut, some dents.

c1785 *13¼in (33.5cm) diam*

£550-600 **POOK**

A pewter basin, by Joseph Danforth Junior, Richmond, Virginia, marked with eagles above 'JD'.

1807-12 *12in (30.5cm) diam*

£950-1,100 **SK**

A pewter flagon, by Boardman & Co., New York.

c1835 *13¾in (35cm) high*

£400-500 **POOK**

A 19thC pewter ciborium, by George Richardson, Cranston, Rhode Island, repair to hinge, crack to body.

A ciborium is a vessel, usually of metal, used in the Christian Church to hold consecrated Eucharistic bread.

6¾in (17cm) wide

£450-500 **POOK**

A copper coffee pot, by Peter Derr (1793-1868), Berks County, Pennsylvania, impressed 'P. Derr', some wear.

10in (25.5cm) high

£5,500-6,500 **POOK**

A 19thC Pennsylvania punched tin coffee pot, with floral and heart decoration.

10in (25.5cm) high

£1,000-1,400 **POOK**

A 19thC Pennsylvania punched tin coffee pot, with a gooseneck spout, impressed 'Sands'.

11in (28cm) high

£2,200-2,800 **POOK**

A 19thC punched tin heart-form cheese strainer, some wear.

15½in (39.5cm) wide

£3,000-3,500 **POOK**

A George III silver vinaigrette, with silver-gilt interior and domed pierced grill, by Thomas Meriton, London.

Vinaigrettes are small boxes used to hold sponges soaked in smelling salts, pleasant smelling oils, perfume or aromatic vinegar. They were used by Georgian and Victorian ladies and gentlemen to revive faintness and ward off the unpleasant odours.

1800

£350-400 **FLD**

A George IV silver 'castle-top' vinaigrette, depicting Abbotsford, maker's mark 'T.S.', Birmingham.

1825

£750-850 **BRI**

A George IV gold-mounted citrine vinaigrette.

c1825 *1¼in (3cm) wide*

£1,800-2,200 **L&T**

A silver 'castle-top' vinaigrette, depicting Balmoral, by Joseph Taylor and John Perry, Birmingham, date letter indistinct.

1¾in (4.5cm) long

£750-850 **SWO**

A Victorian silver handbag vinaigrette, by Gervase Wheeler, Birmingham.

1838

£300-400 **BRI**

A Victorian silver 'castle-top' vinaigrette, depicting Abbotsford, the reverse with engraved initials, maker's mark 'E.S.', Birmingham.

1841

£600-700 **BRI**

A George III silver patent slide-action vinaigrette, with a push button opening two eye holes, gilded interior, stamped 'Patent', by Daniel May, London.

1801 *1¼in (3cm) long ½oz*

£1,500-2,000 **WW**

A William IV silver-gilt vinaigrette, by Joseph Willmore, Birmingham.

1831 *3½in (9cm) high*

£1,000-1,400 **SWO**

ESSENTIAL REFERENCE – NATHANIEL MILLS

Nathaniel Mills (1746-1840) registered his first mark as a silversmith in 1803, as a partner of Mills and Langston. Soon afterwards he set up his own workshop in Caroline Street, Birmingham.

- **His son, also called Nathaniel Mills (1811-73) later took over the business.**
- **Both father and son were keen to incorporate new techniques into their work, such as stamping, casting and engine turning.**
- **The workshop made silver boxes, vinaigrettes, card cases and snuff boxes. It specialised in 'castle-top' pieces, which depicted architectural scenes. Obscure buildings, or rare views of well-known buildings, can attract high prices.**
- **These 'castle-top' boxes were sold as souvenirs and the business became very successful. Nathaniel Mills the younger died a rich man, leaving £30,000 in his will.**

A Victorian silver 'castle-top' vinaigrette, depicting Warwick Castle, by Nathaniel Mills, Birmingham.

1841

£800-900 **BRI**

An 18ct gold vinaigrette, by John Yapp and John Woodward, Birmingham.
1846 *1½in (3.5cm) long*
£2,000-2,500 **SWO**

A Victorian silver vinaigrette, depicting a watermill, by Nathaniel Mills, Birmingham.
1846
£500-600 **BRI**

A Victorian silver 'castle-top' vinaigrette, depicting Abbotsford House, by Nathaniel Mills, Birmingham.
1848 *1½in (4cm) long*
£650-750 **FLD**

An S. Mordan and Co. silver-gilt-mounted glass double scent bottle or vinaigrette, stamped 'S. Mordan & Co., Makers', with date mark.
1858
£500-600 **FLD**

A Victorian silver vinaigrette, with initials 'C.D.', by E. Smith, Birmingham.
1859
£250-300 **BRI**

A Victorian silver combination vinaigrette, modelled as barrel, by Henry William Dee, London, with associated silver bracelet.
1869 *1¼in (3cm) long 2⅛oz*
£1,200-1,600 **FELL**

A Victorian silver cornucopia-shaped combination vinaigrette and scent bottle, with suspension chain and amethyst coloured cabochon, by S. Mordan and Co., London.
1872 *4in (10cm) long 1¾oz*
£400-500 **GORL**

A Victorian silver thimble-shaped vinaigrette, of spider's web design, maker's mark 'A.D.', London.
1873
£600-700 **BRI**

A Victorian silver whistle vinaigrette, by George Unite, Birmingham.
1875 *2½in (6.5cm) long ¾oz*
£500-600 **WW**

A Victorian combined vinaigrette and scent bottle, maker's mark 'T.J.', London.
1877
£400-500 **BRI**

An Irish Georgian silver table snuff casket, the lids with a crest of a hand and monogram, by Benjamin Stokes, Dublin.

The sign of the hand dexter alludes to the Daly's kinship to the O'Neills of Ulster.

c1750 *3¾in (9.5cm) wide 7oz*

£5,500-6,500 **ADA**

A George II to George III Irish silver snuff box, with six compartments, an engraved crest and coat of arms, initialled 'EB', maker 'S', by Benjamin Stokes, Dublin.

c1760 *3in (7.5cm) diam 3½oz*

£3,500-4,000 **LC**

A George III silver-gilt and micromosaic snuff box, by Hockley and Bosworth, London.

1815 *3in (7.5cm) long*

£5,500-6,000 **WW**

An early Victorian 'castle-top' snuff box, depicting Warwick Castle, by Nathaniel Mills, Birmingham.

1838 *2½in (6.5cm) long 1½oz*

£850-950 **LC**

A silver 'castle-top' snuff box, depicting Kenilworth house, by Nathaniel Mills, Birmingham, some wear.

3in (7.5cm) wide 2½oz

£800-900 **PW**

CLOSER LOOK – SILVER SNUFF BOX

This is a fine example of a rare 'castle-top' snuff box.

The lid is engraved with a view of East Cliff Lodge, Ramsgate, after a watercolour by Turner, apparently painted when Turner visited the house in 1797.

The gilt interior is engraved with the Montefiore crest to the lid.

This was likely a one-off commission by Sir Moses Haim Montefiore (1784-1885), financier, philanthropist and President of the Board of Deputies of British Jews 1835-74. He purchased the house in 1830 and lived there with his wife until his death.

A Victorian silver snuff box, by Hilliard & Thomason, Birmingham.

1854 *3½in (9cm) long 6½oz*

£50,000-60,000 **MAB**

A George IV silver raised relief 'Pedlar' snuff box, engraved with two crests, by John Linnit, London.

The crests are those of Hervey-Bathurst, Baronets of Clarendon Park, Wiltshire.

1825 *4in (10cm) long 6¼oz*

£2,000-3,000 **WW**

An early Victorian silver table snuff box, by Nathaniel Mills, Birmingham.

1839 *3¼oz*

£550-650 **HAN**

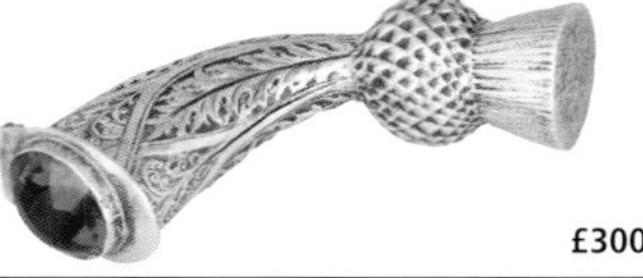

A Victorian Scottish silver thistle-form snuff box, with Cairngorm cover.

2½oz

£300-350 **WAD**

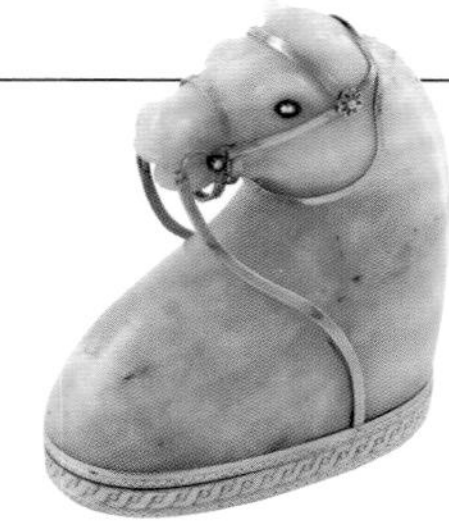

An 18thC diamond-set, carved quartz and gold-mounted horse's head snuff box, possibly by the widow of the jeweller Louis Buyrette, Berlin.

Similar stone selection, carving and eye mounts can be seen in a series of dudelsack (German bag pipe) boxes by the jeweller Louis Buyrette.

c1760 *3in (7.5cm) high*

£6,500-7,500 WW

A rare 18thC Channel Islands silver-mounted cowrie snuff box, maker's mark 'IH', Guernsey, engraved 'MSBK', some losses, some small dings to lid, lid hinge loose.

This is believed to be only the second piece of Channel Islands silver mounted with a cowrie shell. The other example is a cowrie shell spoon by Guillaume Henry of Guernsey.

3¼in (8.5cm) long

£1,800-2,200 MART

A French enamelled gold-mounted and tortoiseshell snuff box, maker's mark indistinct, discharge marks for Eloi Brichard (1756-62) and Paris date letter 'T', some cracks and paint loss.

1759-60 *3½in (9cm) wide*

£9,500-11,000 TEN

A German enamelled gold snuff box, maker's mark 'LC', with crowned 'K', Hanau, some losses.

c1780 *3¾in (9.5cm) wide 6⅛oz*

£23,000-26,000 ECGW

A Regency gold and enamel snuff box.

1¼in (3cm) wide

£700-800 HT

An early 19thC Swiss 18ct gold and enamelled snuff box, maker's mark 'S&D', Geneva, some chips and scratches.

c1820 *2¾in (7cm) long 1⅞oz*

£8,500-9,500 GORL

A 19thC Continental enamelled 20ct gold snuff box, in the manner of Jean Ducrollay, with panels after Francois Boucher, one panel probably a replacement, some wear.

A box of very similar design by Ducrollay, with en plein still life enamels, can be found in the Musee de Louvre, Paris.

3¼in (8cm) wide

£15,000-20,000 TEN

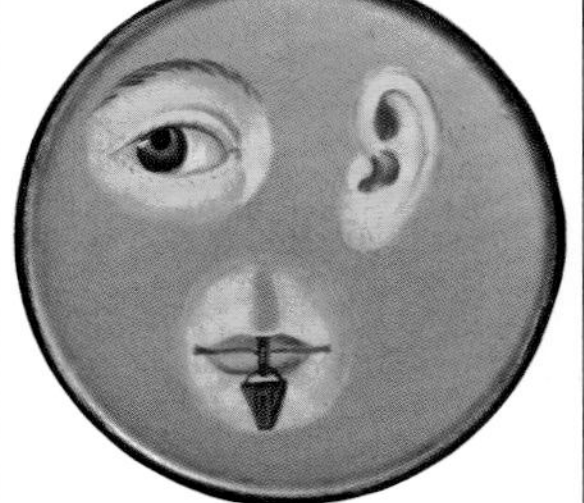

A mid-19thC lacquered papier mâché Freemasons' snuff box, painted with an eye, ear and padlocked lips alluding to the Freemasons' motto, 'Audi, Vide, Tace'.

The motto 'Audi, Vide and Tace' (Hear, See, Be Silent) relates to one of the symbols of Masonry that is most understood: secrecy.

4in (10cm) diam

£1,300-1,600 WW

A 19thC Italian micromosaic and tortoiseshell snuff box, depicting the falls at Tivoli, some cracking, lifting away from lid, base faded.

3in (7.5cm) diam

£4,500-5,000 GORL

An early 18thC Continental gold-mounted tortoiseshell box, set with three semi-precious stones and watercolours.

3½in (9cm) wide

£850-950 **CHOR**

A Georgian tortoiseshell étui, modelled as a saddle bag, with inlaid metal decoration.

3in (7.5cm) high

£700-800 **FELL**

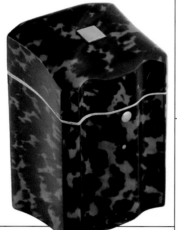

A Regency tortoiseshell nécessaire, with ivory banding, fitted a silver thimble and ivory cylindrical case.

4in (10cm) high

£400-500 **CHOR**

An early 19thC tortoiseshell needle packet box.

2½in (6.5cm) long

£220-280 **BLEA**

A tortoiseshell and mother-of-pearl étui, with needle card, silver scissors, silver pencil, tape measure, folding knife, scales, stiletto and thimble, some damages.

c1840 *4¼in (11cm) high*

£220-280 **BLEA**

A Victorian silver-mounted tortoiseshell playing cards box, by Saunders and Shepherd, Chester, with the playing card suits in silver, with a playing card under glass, the interior of set with two whist markers.

1897 *4in (10cm) long*

£400-500 **WW**

A George V silver and tortoiseshell ring box, by Kemp Brothers, Birmingham.

1918 *7in (18cm) wide*

£200-250 **TRI**

An early 20thC tortoiseshell piqué needle case.

£160-200 **FELL**

An inlaid tortoiseshell miniature box.

£400-500 **SWO**

A probably late 17thC silver quill case or toothpick case.

3¼in (8cm) long ¾oz

£300-400 **WW**

A George III velvet-lined gold-mounted tortoiseshell toothpick box, with a central carved ivory landscape scene, probably by Stephany and Dresch, in fitted case.

c1790 *4in (10cm) long*

£1,000-1,400 **WW**

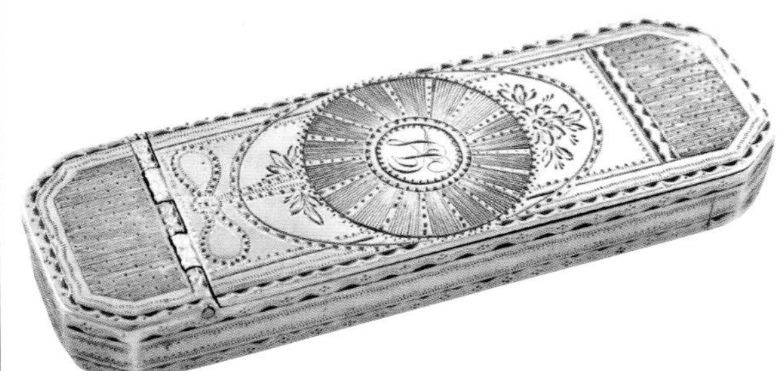

A George III silver toothpick box, the velvet-lined interior lacking mirror, by Samuel Pemberton, Birmingham.

1786 *3¼in (8.5cm) long 1⅛oz*

£1,100-1,400 **WW**

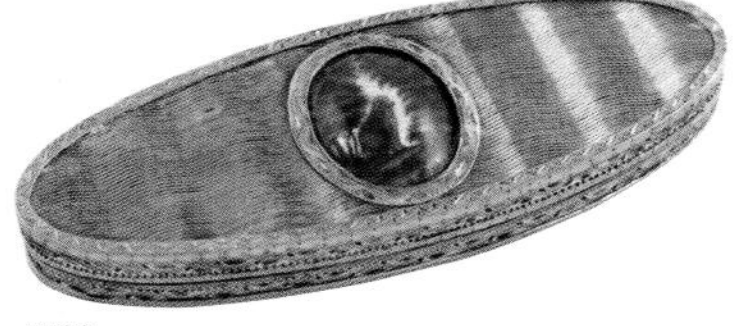

A George III gold-mounted silver toothpick box, set with an image of a dog.

c1790 *3½in (9cm) long 1¾oz*

£650-700 **WW**

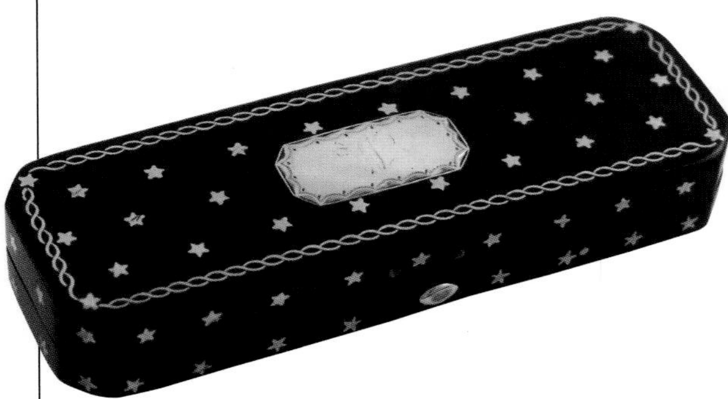

A George III gold-mounted tortoiseshell toothpick box, velvet-lined, with mirror.

c1800 *3½in (9cm) long*

£450-500 **WW**

A George III silver filigree toothpick box, velvet-lined, with mirror.

c1790-1800 *3¼in (8cm) long ⅞oz*

£350-400 **WW**

A George III silver-mounted shagreen toothpick box, velvet-lined, with mirror.

c1800 *4in (10cm) long*

£500-600 **WW**

A George III silver toothpick box, by Samuel Pemberton, Birmingham.

1800 *2¾in (7cm) long ¾oz*

£320-400 **WW**

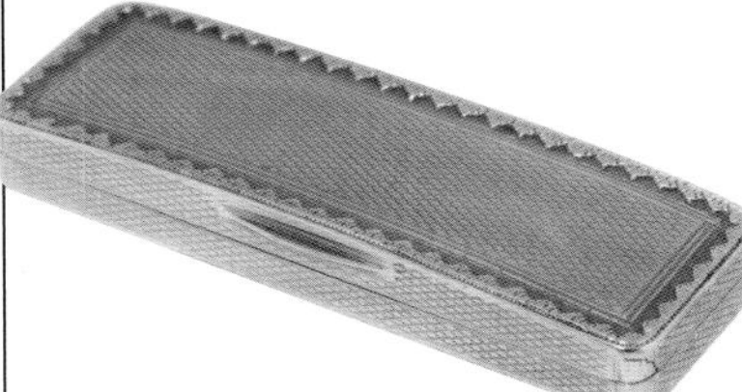

A George III 18ct gold toothpick box, by Alexander J. Strahan, London.

1805 *4oz*

£1,200-1,500 **SWO**

A 19thC gold-mounted rock crystal toothpick box, the coach door initialled 'WR'.

c1830-35 *2¾in (7cm) long*

£950-1,100 **WW**

A cast snail vesta case, by Thomas Johnson, London.

This is an unusual form, which accounts for the value. Animal vesta cases often attract a premium, and this particular example is especially appealing, being naturalistically modelled and life-size.

1884 *2¾in (7cm) long 1¼oz*

£3,500-4,000 **LC**

A silver horse's head vesta case, by 'HBS', Birmingham.

Vesta cases are small boxes designed to store matches and keep them dry.

1884 *2in (5cm) long ¾oz*

£950-1,100 **WW**

A silver cigar case vesta case, inscribed 'HAVANA', Chester.

1887 *1½in (4cm) long*

£350-400 **MOR**

An Edwardian silver vesta case, engraved with twenty-one Masonic symbols, engraved 'Wm Oliver no. 424', by John Gloster, Birmingham.

1904

£350-450 **HAN**

A silver 'The Man in The Moon' vesta case, with cabochon gem-set eyes, by S. Mordan and Co., London, possible repairs.

1899 *¾oz*

£600-700 **BELL**

A silver and enamel vesta case, depicting a racehorse and jockey, by Thomas Johnson II, London.

1886 *2in (5cm) long 1¾oz*

£700-800 **HAN**

A silver and enamel vesta case, of a coaching scene, the reverse engraved 'C.A.C-P Nov 14 1902', by John Millward Banks, Chester.

1899 *2¼in (5.5cm) long 1¾oz*

£450-550 **HAN**

A silver vesta case, enamelled with a racehorse and jockey, by Samuel Mordan, London.

1888 *2¼in (6cm) long 1⅛oz*

£800-900 **CAN**

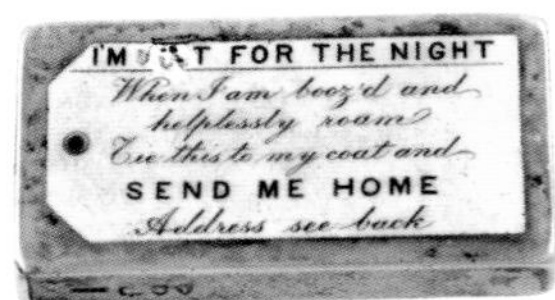

A silver and enamel vesta case, the front enamelled with a luggage label inscribed 'I'M OUT FOR THE NIGHT When I am boozed and helplessly roam tie this to my coat and SEND ME HOME Address see back', the reverse inscribed 'G.J. Merrit, 56 Cours La Reine, Paris', by S. Mordan and Co., London.

1894 *2¼in (6cm) long 1¼oz*

£550-650 **WW**

A silver vesta case, enamelled with a devil holding a trident, inscribed 'I am KING Who the [devil] are You?', by Horton & Allday, Birmingham.

1888 *⅞oz*

£450-550 **HAN**

A 9ct gold cigarette case, by Horace Woodward & Co., Birmingham.
1919 *3¼in (8.5cm) long 3½oz*
£1,300-1,600 **DN**

A 9ct gold engine-turned cigarette case, with sapphire-set push button.
4in (10cm) long 4¼oz
£1,600-2,000 **TRI**

A silver enamelled cigarette case, with a nude lady holding a pair of peaches, by George Heath, London.
c1883 *3¼in (8cm) long 2⅞oz*
£600-700 **WW**

A Continental silver enamelled cigarette case, depicting a nude lady by a lake.
£600-700 **JN**

An Alpaca silver enamelled cigarette case, depicting a nude lady painting her toenails.

Alpaca silver is a metal alloy of copper, nickel and sometimes zinc or iron.

£650-750 **JN**

An Edwardian silver and enamel cigarette case, the reverse inscribed 'F.F.E/ From Lonsdale' with crown, by Percy Edwards Ltd., London.

Hugh Cecil Lowther, 5th Earl of Lonsdale, KG, GCVO, succeeded his brother to the title in 1882.

1908 *3½in (9cm) long 3¾oz*
£600-700 **WW**

A Victorian wood-lined silver and enamelled table cigarette box, London.
1888 *5in (13cm) long*
£350-450 **BELL**

A Continental silver coloured and enamel cigarette case, depicting horses and dogs, stamped 'Sterling' and '935', probably Austro-Hungarian.
c1910 *4in (10cm) high 5oz*
£350-450 **DN**

An Edwardian silver cigarette case, embossed with a golfer, by Henry Matthews, Birmingham.

Please see page 423 for more golfing memorabilia.

1902 *3¼in (8.5cm) long*
£350-450 **DN**

An Edwardian Royal presentation silver and enamel cigarette case, with the signature of Edward VII in gold lettering, by Alfred Clark, London.

Provenance: Presented to John Savile Lumley-Savile, 2nd Baron Rufford by King Edward VII around 1905. John Savile Lumley-Savile inherited Rufford in 1896. King Edward VII regularly stayed at Rufford, Nottinghamshire, where he was entertained in grand style.

1904 *3¼in (8.5cm) long 3¾oz*
£3,500-4,000 **WW**

A rare London enamel snuff box, with the coat of arms for the Hippesley family, the sides with Meissen-style landscapes, with gilt-metal mounts.

The crest and the first quarter of the shield are those of Toby Ipsley of Hambleton in Rutland, granted in 1681.

c1740-45 *2½in (6.5cm) long*

£3,000-3,500 **WW**

A mid-to-late 18thC German enamel, painted with Meissen-style puce scenes, the interior lid with figures around a statue of Neptune.

3in (7.5cm) long

£3,000-3,500 **WW**

A Birmingham or South Staffordshire enamel gilt-metal-mounted lion snuff box, the lid with a hunter chasing a leopard.

c1760 *4¼in (11cm) long*

£3,500-4,000 **WW**

A Birmingham enamel snuff box, painted with figures, the interior with a portrait of the actress, Mrs Mary Brooks (nèe L'Hereux), with gilt-metal mounts.

The source for the portrait of Mrs Brooks is a mezzotint by Richard Houston, after Thomas Worlidge. Mary L'Hereux married the Irish engraver, John Brooks, in 1756. He was made bankrupt three years later. Mrs Brooks turned to acting in order to support herself and her three children.

1760-65 *3¼in (8cm) long*

£2,200-2,800 **WW**

A Birmingham enamel shoe snuff box.

c1760-70 *4in (10cm) long*

£800-900 **WW**

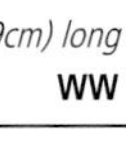

A Birmingham or South Staffordshire enamel snuff box, painted with a drunk and his bare-breasted companion, the base after a Robert Hancock print, with gilt-metal mounts.

c1765-70 *3½in (9cm) long*

£1,800-2,200 **WW**

CLOSER LOOK – BATTERSEA ENAMEL SNUFF BOX

Pictorial enamels emerged at a factory in Battersea in the mid-18thC and are highly collectable today.

The lid is printed in sepia with a scene of soldiers attacking the Trojan horse.

The sides and base have panels of shells and floral motifs on a diaper ground.

The lid's interior has a portrait of a Chancellor of the Exchequer. Given the date, and the similarly to a 1754 print by John Hinton, it seems likely that the portrait is of Henry Pelham. However, it also bears similarities to Sir Robert Walpole or Henry Boyle.

A Battersea enamel snuff box.

c1750-55 *3¼in (8.5cm) long*

£3,500-4,000 **WW**

Judith Picks

The Jacobites were the supporters of King James II, usurped by William and Mary in 1688 in the Glorious Revolution. Later it became a general term for those who favoured the restoration of the Stuart dynasty, including supporters of both James Francis Edward Stuart, James II's son, nicknamed the Old Pretender, and of his son Charles Edward Stuart, nicknamed Bonnie Prince Charlie or the Young Pretender. The portrait on this box of Bonnie Prince Charlie is after one by Sir Robert Strange. This box is unusual in its brazen display of the Prince's likeness. Such portraits would typically be concealed on the interior lid of a box, to protect its owner from accusations of treason.

A Birmingham enamel snuff box, of Jacobite interest, painted with a portrait of Bonnie Prince Charlie, reserved on ground of flags and other military motifs, the sides with Classical ruins and Italianate landscapes.

c1760 *3½in (9cm) long*

£900-1,200 **WW**

A Birmingham or South Staffordshire enamel bonbonnière, modelled as two dogs fighting over a game bird.
c1760-65 *3in (7.5cm) long*
£1,800-2,200 **WW**

A Birmingham or South Staffordshire enamel swan bonbonnière.
c1760-70 *3in (7.5cm) long*
£1,800-2,200 **WW**

A late 18thC Bilston enamel boxing match patch box, titled 'Set To'.
c1770 *1¾in (4.5cm) wide*
£1,200-1,500 **HAN**

An English enamel patch box, probably Bilston, inscribed 'God Bless the United States' to lid, paper label for 'D M & P Manheim, New York and London'.
c1770-80 *1¾in (4.5cm) wide*
£4,000-5,000 **WW**

A Bilston enamel patch box, inscribed 'Great Washington to Thee We owe our Liberty', with internal mirror, paper label for 'D M & P Manheim, New York and London'.
c1780 *1¾in (4.5cm) wide*
£2,500-3,000 **WW**

An early 19thC enamel patch box, probably South Staffordshire, printed with a portrait of Admiral Nelson, titled 'Nelson & Victory', with interior mirror.
2in (5cm) long
£1,500-2,000 **KEY**

A Battersea enamel portrait plaque, depicting Maria Gunning, Countess of Coventry, in a metal frame.

This image of Maria Gunning is copied from Jean-Etienne Liotard's 1749 painting of her in Turkish costume. Maria Gunning was a celebrated beauty of the 18thC, so much so that she was once mobbed in Hyde Park. Against her husband's advice, she wore heavy make up despite her young age, which contributed to her death at the age of 27 from lead and mercury poisoning.
c1760 *4¼in (10.5cm) high*
£2,200-2,800 **WW**

An oval enamel plaque, printed with a portrait of General Clinton.

General Clinton was British Commander-in-Chief in North America during the American War of Independence. Clinton laid siege to the city of Charleston in 1780, forcing the surrender of the city in May 1780.
c1780 *3in (7.5cm) long*
£1,800-2,200 **KEY**

A South Staffordshire enamel wine funnel, with gilt-metal mounts.
c1770 *4¼in (11cm) high*
£3,000-4,000 **WW**

A French Empire enamel perfume bottle and stopper, with silver cap and base.
2½in (6.5cm) high
£1,200-1,600 **JN**

ESSENTIAL REFERENCE – CARD CASES

From the late 18thC to the early 20thC, calling cards were used in polite society to announce the arrival of a visitor, to request a visit, or as a gesture in place of an actual social call.

- **On paying a first visit to a new acquaintance, it was good etiquette to leave a card with a servant and then depart. If a card was sent in return, a visit could be attempted next time.**
- **When visiting a friend, a lady or gentleman would present their card to the servant at the door. If the master or mistress of the house was 'at home' – here meaning not only in the house but at leisure to receive visitors – then the visitor would be invited in. If not, their card would be left to show that they had called.**
- **Both ladies and gentlemen would have carried cards with them when paying social calls. Young unmarried ladies sometimes held a joint card with their mothers, but husbands and wives typically had separate cards.**
- **Card cases were made from tortoiseshell, mother-of-pearl, ivory, silver and other metals.**
- **Silver 'castle-top' card cases, depicting buildings of note, often castles, cathedrals and country houses, are among the finest.**
- **Desirable makers of silver card cases include Edward Smith, Taylor & Perry, Joseph Wilmore and Nathaniel Mills.**

A William IV silver 'castle-top' card case, depicting Newstead Abbey, the reverse with a medallion of Lord Byron, by Taylor and Perry, Birmingham.
1836 *3¾in (9.5cm) long 2¼oz*
£1,000-1,400 **WW**

An early Victorian silver card case, by Joseph Willmore, Birmingham, William IV duty mark, cover loose.
1838 *3¾in (9.5cm) long*
£350-400 **DN**

A Victorian silver 'castle-top' card case, depicting Lincoln Cathedral and Windsor Castle, by Joseph Willmore, Birmingham.
1844 *4in (10cm) long 2¾oz*
£1,500-2,000 **WW**

A Victorian silver engraved 'castle-top' card case, depicting Bar Gate, Southampton, by Nathaniel Mills, Birmingham.
1843 *4in (10cm) long 2¼oz*
£3,000-3,500 **WW**

A Victorian silver-gilt 'castle-top' card case, with Melrose Abbey, by Nathaniel MIlls, Birmingham.
1845 *3½in (9cm) high 1¾oz*
£2,200-2,800 **HAN**

A rare Victorian silver 'castle-top' card case, depicting St Michael's Mount with the Royal yacht, 'The Victoria and Albert', by George Bower and Son, Birmingham.

Queen Victoria and Prince Albert visited St Michael's Mount on 6 September 1846.
1846 *4¼in (10.5cm) long 2¼oz*
£5,000-6,000 **WW**

A Victorian silver card case, engraved with the Scott monument, Edinburgh, minor dent, maker's mark 'FM', Birmingham.
1847 *4in (10cm) long*
£300-350 **CHOR**

A Victorian silver 'castle-top' card case, depicting St Paul's Cathedral, by Nathaniel Mills, Birmingham.
1844 *4in (10cm) long 2⅜oz*
£1,300-1,600 **WW**

A Victorian silver 'castle-top' card case, depicting Jenny Lind in Bellini's La Sonnambula, by Edward Smith, Birmingham.

Johanna Maria Lind (1820-87), better known as Jenny Lind, was a Swedish opera singer, often known as the 'Swedish Nightingale'. Lind gave her first performance in London on 4 May 1847.

1848 *4¼in (10.5cm) long 2⅜oz*

£900-1,100 **WW**

A Victorian silver 'castle-top' card case, depicting the Crystal Palace, by Nathaniel Mills, Birmingham.

1853 *4in (10cm) long 2⅛oz*

£1,800-2,200 **WW**

A Victorian silver 'castle-top' card case, depicting Balmoral, the reverse with similar decoration and inscribed 'F.Wright, 1893', by Alfred Taylor, Birmingham.

1861 *4in (10cm) long 2⅝oz*

£850-950 **WW**

A rare Victorian Irish silver 'castle-top' card case, depicting Dun Laoghaire harbour, the reverse with a crest and inscribed 'From Schriber and Sons 1864', by John Schriber, Dublin.

The cartouche is engraved with a viscount's coronet ensigning the crest of Menteith of Scotland and Hodge(s) and Hodgekins of England, but is absent from official Irish records.

1863 *4in (10cm) long 2¼oz*

£12,000-15,000 **WW**

A Victorian silver 'castle-top' card case, depicting Kensington Palace, by Nathaniel Mills, Birmingham.

1848 *3½in (9cm) long 1⅞oz*

£1,300-1,600 **WW**

A Victorian silver 'castle-top' card case, depicting King's College Cambridge, by Nathaniel Mills, Birmingham.

1853 *4in (10cm) long 2¼oz*

£1,800-2,200 **WW**

A mid-19thC Victorian gem painted tortoiseshell card case, depicting the Scott Monument, Edinburgh, with ivory edging.

4in (10cm) long

£130-160 **DN**

A Victorian pressed tortoiseshell and pewter strung card case, depicting York Minster to each side.

4in (10cm) long

£150-200 **DN**

A Victorian painted papier mâché card case, with ivory edging, hinge slightly loose, crazing crack.

4¼in (11cm) long

£150-200 **DN**

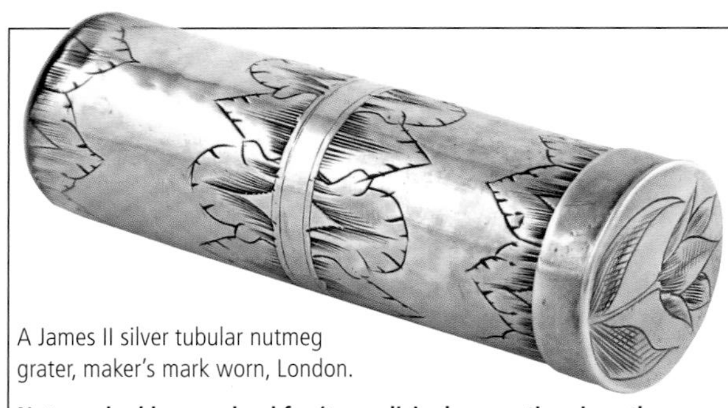

A James II silver tubular nutmeg grater, maker's mark worn, London.

Nutmeg had been valued for its medicinal properties since the Medieval Period. It gained popularity in the 18thC. After the Napoleonic Wars, when Britain gained control of Run Island, then the world's sole source of nutmeg, it became increasingly affordable.

1686 *2¼in (6cm) long ¾oz*

£1,500-2,000 WW

A William and Mary to William III silver tear-drop nutmeg grater, maker's mark 'I.A', London.

c1690-1700 1½in (4cm) long ¾oz

£1,800-2,200 WW

A William and Mary to William III silver nutmeg grater, the base cover opening to a compartment, by Thomas Kedden.

c1690-1700 *2¾in (7cm) long ⅞oz*

£1,000-1,400 WW

A Continental silver urn-shaped nutmeg grater, with pull-out grater.

c1740 *2in (5cm) high ¾oz*

£400-450 WW

A George III silver nutmeg grater, initialled 'A.H.', by Thomas Willmore, Birmingham.

1798

£400-450 BRI

A George III silver-gilt nutmeg grater, monogrammed, by Joseph Taylor, Birmingham.

1799 *1½in (4cm) high ⅝oz*

£500-550 WW

A George III silver novelty egg-shaped nutmeg grater, lacking interior, by Samuel Merriton II, London.

1810 *1½in (4cm) long*

£250-300 LSK

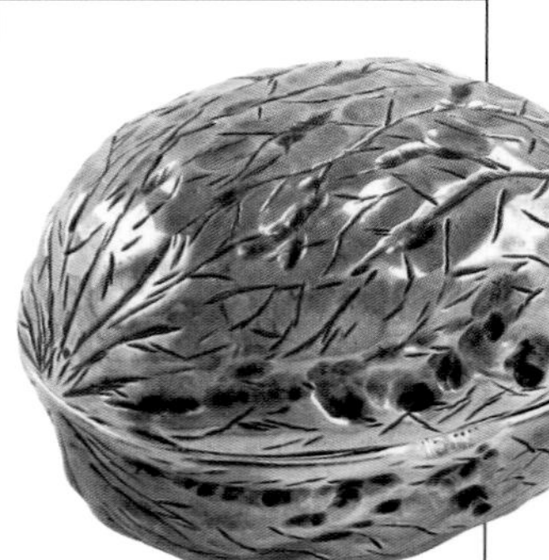

A Victorian silver walnut nutmeg grater, with silver-gilt interior, by Jane Brownett, London.

Jane Brownett was a smallworker, chiefly making silver vesta cases, boxes, tongs, purses and novelties. She took over her husband Abraham Brownett's silver workshop in London after his death in 1867. He had previously been half of the partnership Brownett & Rose formed c1858.

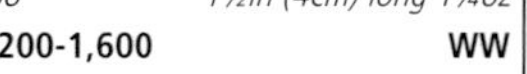

1886 *1½in (4cm) long 1¼oz*

£1,200-1,600 WW

A George IV silver nutmeg grater, with a crest, by Nathaniel Mills, Birmingham, lacking date letter.

c1825 *1⅛oz*

£400-450 HAN

A silver nutmeg grater, with initialled cartouche, by Hilliard & Thomason, Birmingham.

1855 *1½in (4cm) long ⅝oz*

£550-600 WW

A Victorian pear-form silver nutmeg grater, by Hilliard & Thomason, Birmingham.

1856 *1½in (4cm) long ¾oz*

£3,000-3,500 WW

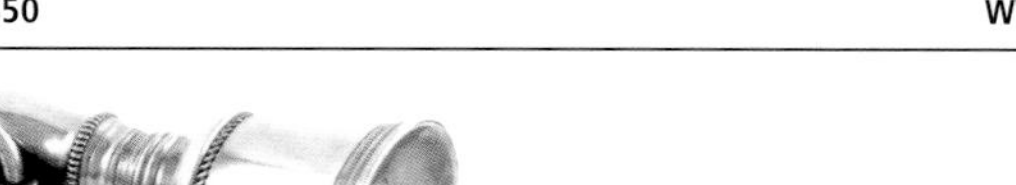

A Victorian 10ct gold pencil, modelled as a salmon, by S. Mordan and Co., retailed by Leuchars and Son.

Sampson Mordan (1790-1843) was a British silversmith. In 1822, along with his associate Joseph Isaac Hawkins, he patented the first mechanical pencil. The partnership dissolved in 1837, after which Mordan continued to sell his pencils and other metalware under the name S. Mordan and Co.

2¼in (6cm) long ¼oz

£750-850 WW

A Victorian silver 'super-size' propelling pencil, engraved 'Xmas 1881', by S. Mordan and Co., retailed by Jones of Paris and London.

1881 closed 5½in (14cm) long

£650-750 WW

A silver and gold four-stage telescopic pencil, with design registration number, by S. Mordan and Co. for Hamilton and Co., Calcutta.

designed 1881 1¼in (3cm) closed ½oz

£500-600 WW

A Victorian silver hand bell pencil.

closed 1½in (3.5cm) long ⅛oz

£700-800 WW

A silver watering can inkwell and pen, the pull-out telescopic spout forming the pen, by S. Mordan and Co., London.

1878 4¼in (10cm) high

£1,200-1,600 WW

A pair of silver menu card holders, by John Harris, London.

1853 2¼in (6cm) long 4¼oz

£450-550 WW

CLOSER LOOK – NOVELTY MUSTARD POT

This mustard pot and spoon is cast and chased in the form of a Hussars or Royal Artillery busby.

It is inscribed with the motto 'I Am Ready'.

It was manufactured by Elkington & Co., a metalware company founded by George Richard Elkington in Birmingham in 1801.

It is engraved with the Scottish family crest of Fraser and Maxwell.

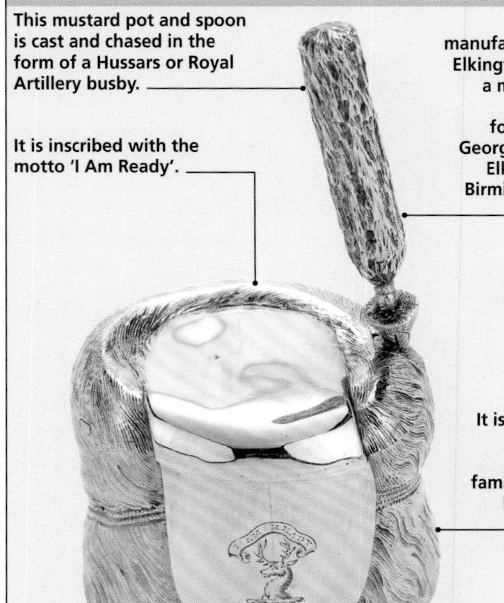

An Edwardian silver mustard pot and spoon, missing glass liner.

1910 4½in (11.5cm) high 6¼oz

£4,000-4,500 DN

A set of four Edwardian silver and enamel game bird menu card holders, by S. Mordan and Co., Chester, in retailer's case from Austin & William, Conduit Street, London, some scratches.

1908 1½in (3.5cm) high

£2,500-3,000 TEN

A Kate Greenaway napkin ring, showing a girl teaching children their alphabets, by Simpson, Hall, Miller & Co.

This is the only known figural napkin ring with three Kate Greenaway figures.

3½in (9cm) high

£1,800-2,200 MORP

A silver cat pepperette, by James Barclay Hennell, London, Design Registration mark for 1895.
1881 *3in (7.5cm) high 3¼oz*
£1,100-1,400 **DN**

A silver partridge pepper pot, by R.H.H., Sheffield.
1925 *3¾in (9.5cm) high 4⅜oz*
£750-850 **WW**

A Mappin & Webb silver-plated military-themed cruet set, raised on ball feet, one detached but present.
7in (18cm) wide
£350-400 **LOCK**

An engraved cast silver-gilt horn-form posy holder, with coat of arms and motto 'SIT PRUDENTIA' below 'WASHINGTON HIBBERT', by Samuel Rudduck and Jachariah Jennings, London.
1829 *4¼in (11cm) long 4oz*
£1,000-1,400 **LC**

An engraved posy holder, by George Unite, Birmingham.
1886 *4¾in (12cm) long 1¼oz*
£350-400 **LC**

A Victorian silver-mounted green hard stone scent bottle, the centre with a harp, the reverse with a shamrock, Queen's Duty head mark.
2¼in (5.5cm) long
£350-450 **WW**

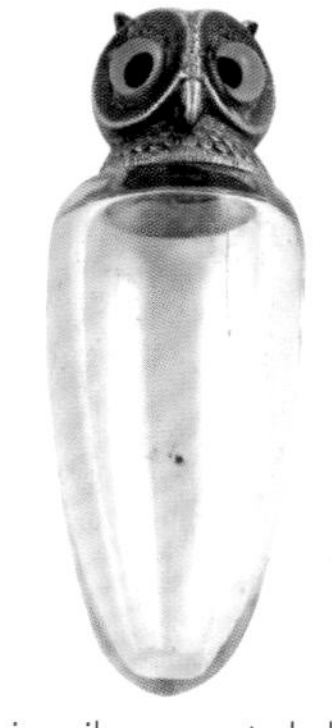

A Victorian silver-mounted glass owl scent bottle, with glass eyes, repaired scratch, by S. Mordan and Co., London.
1894 *3¼in (8cm) long*
£550-650 **WW**

A Dutch cast silver 'Lord Nelson' scent bottle, the head serving as the stopper.
2¼in (6cm) high
£1,200-1,600 **JN**

A silver amatory spice box, with 'MALGRE LAVIE', the base with a ho ho bird beneath 'A LA GUERRE ET A LA PAIS' ('at war and peace'), maker's mark 'T.T', London.
c1690 *1½in (4cm) long ⅞oz*
£2,500-3,000 **LC**

An 18thC silver spice box, later dot engraved 'PL 1781'.
3¼in (8cm) wide 3⅛oz
£550-650 **L&T**

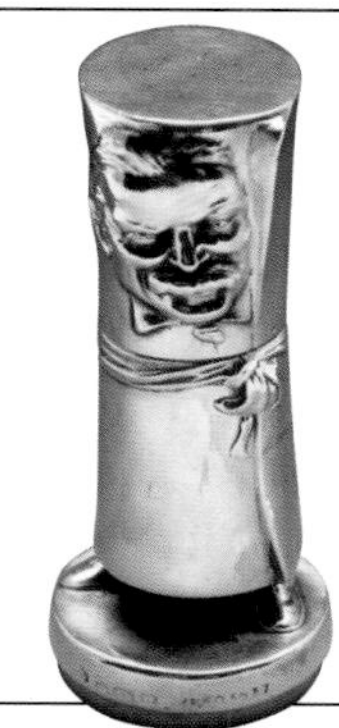

A silver stamp moistener, with the face of David Lloyd George, by William Hutton & Sons Ltd., Sheffield, some wear.
1912 *3in (7.5cm) high 2¾oz*
£300-350 **FELL**

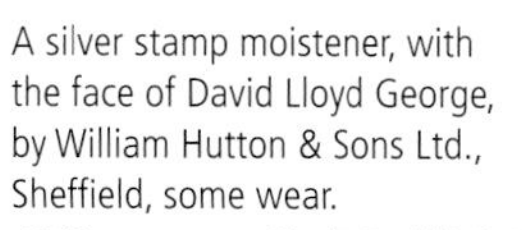

A silver apple corer, monogrammed, by Hampston, Prince and Cattles, York.
c1800 *6in (15cm) long 1¼oz*
£700-800 **WW**

A silver-gilt and gold filigree travelling mirror, with velvet lining.
c1680-90 *3½in (9cm) long*
£2,000-2,500 **WW**

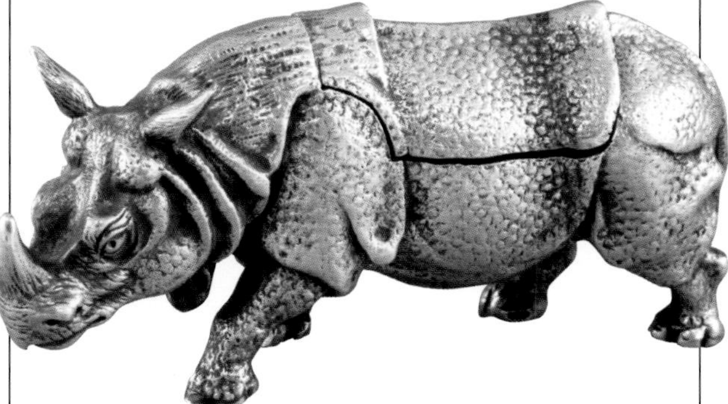

A rhinoceros silver box, by John Septimus Beresford, London.
1879 *4¼in (11cm) long 5½oz*
£3,000-3,500 **GORL**

A silver regimental-style dragon table cigar lighter, by Synyer & Beddoes, Birmingham, some dents.
1923 *5½in (14cm) long 6⅛oz*
£650-750 **DN**

A late 18thC Dutch silver pocket corkscrew, with later Dutch tax mark.
3¼in (8cm) long
£450-550 **WW**

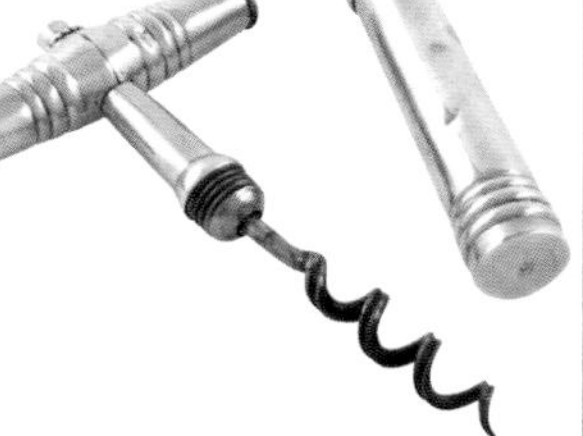

A George III silver pocket corkscrew, by Joseph Taylor, Birmingham.
c1800 *3½in (9cm) long*
£300-350 **WW**

A 19thC bone-handled steel twin-pillar rack and pinion corkscrew, in the manner of Lund, stamped 'Patent', lacks brush.
closed 6in (15cm) high
£650-700 **FLD**

ESSENTIAL REFERENCE – FANS

Folding fans were developed in China and Japan and came to Europe in the early 16thC. They were commonly used from the 17thC to early 20thC.

- **While some antique fans have struggled in recent years, the market is improving for rare fans in good condition.**
- **Chinese fans are often sought after. While chiefly associated with export trade, Chinese fans also had their place in the Qing court.**
- **Classic brisé fans are popular, as are European fans depicting scenes of great interest or by key designers, such as Frances Houghton or Jules Donzel.**

A George III engraved and hand-coloured imaginary map paper fan, the 'LAND OF MATRIMONY', with islands 'ENCHANTED', 'Coquet' and 'Divorce', with the 'OCEAN OF LOVE' and the 'Bay of Repentance', printed by T. Pike, King Street, Bloomsbury, with wooden guards and sticks.

1788 *9¼in (23.5cm) long*

£2,000-2,500 WW

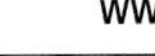

A French single paper leaf fan, by Jules Donzel, depicting a newly married couple departing a church, with mother-of-pearl sticks and guards, signed 'Donzel', in card box labelled 'F. Noble Jones'.

Donzel was one of the most fashionable 19thC fan painters, one of three members of the family whose designs were sought by the top Paris makers including Duvelleroy and Keys. This fan was carried by Queen Mary at the Wedding of Princess Victorian Louise of Prussia and Prince Ernest Augustus of Cumberland, Berlin, 24 May 1913.

c1880 *13in (33cm) wide*

£1,800-2,200 SAS

A late 19thC French ostrich feather fan, with tortoiseshell sticks and a rose-cut diamond-set monogram, in original silk covered box, retailed by Buissot.

£1,000-1,400 REEM

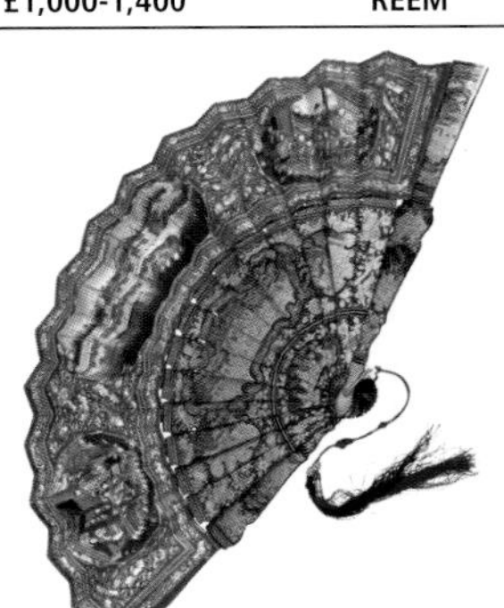

A Chinese harbour scene fan, the wooden sticks lacquered.

c1840-60 *guards 11in (28cm) long*

£2,500-3,000 TEN

A mid-19thC Chinese Canton tortoiseshell brisé fan.

9in (23cm) high

£1,400-2,000 MAB

A 19thC Chinese lacquer brisé fan, gilded and painted with equestrian figures and attendants.

7¾in (19.5cm) high

£1,300-1,600 MAB

A mid-19thC Chinese carved tortoiseshell Mandarin fan, the sticks and guards elaborately carved, in original box.

guards 10¾in (27cm) long

£4,500-5,000 TEN

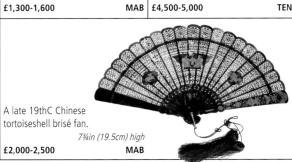

A late 19thC Chinese tortoiseshell brisé fan.

7¾in (19.5cm) high

£2,000-2,500 MAB

CLOSER LOOK – CHINESE REPUBLIC PERIOD FAN

This Chinese paper fan depicts a European girl and a hound in a garden.

It is in the style of Lang Shining, otherwise known as Giuseppe Castiglione (1688-1766). Castiglione was an 18thC Jesuit who took the name Lang Shining while in China.

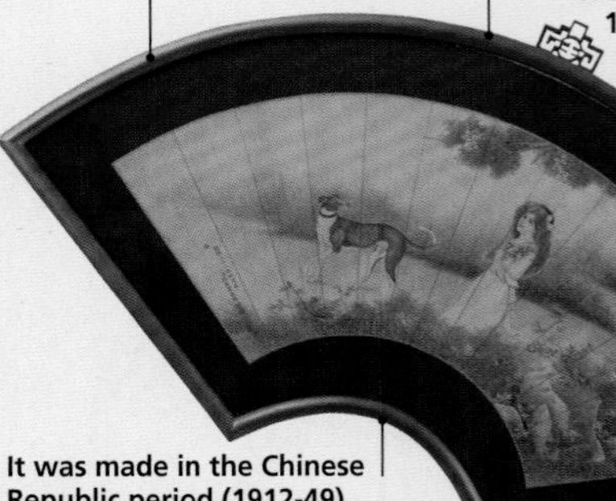

It was made in the Chinese Republic period (1912-49), but is apocryphally dated the 22nd year of Qianlong's reign, 1757, with a poem composed by Emperor Qianlong and signed 'Yu Minzhong' (1714-79).

The extreme fine quality of painting on this piece ensures its value.

An ink and colour on paper fan.

20¾in (52.5cm) wide

£11,000-15,000 L&T

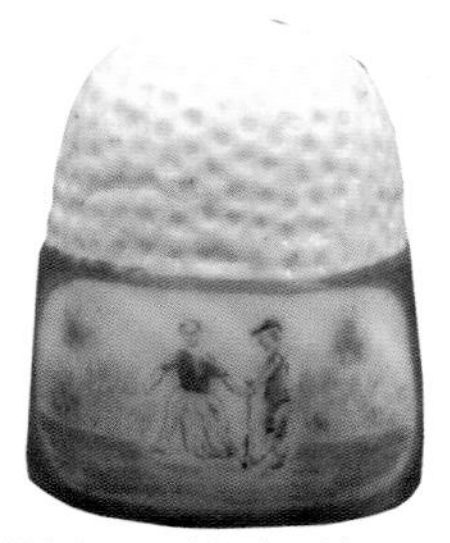
An 18thC porcelain thimble, probably French.
£350-400 **BLEA**

A 19thC gold thimble, with a band of coral and pearl-coloured stones.
£280-320 **BLEA**

A 19thC three-colour gold thimble, with various coloured stone flowerheads.
£500-600 **BLEA**

A gold thimble, set with a band of pearls, by Charles Horner.
1889
£400-450 **BLEA**

A late 19thC French silver thimble, probably by Vernon.
£300-350 **BLEA**

A 9ct gold thimble, by Charles Horner, Chester, minor surface scratches, in original case.
1905 *⅛oz*
£150-200 **BELL**

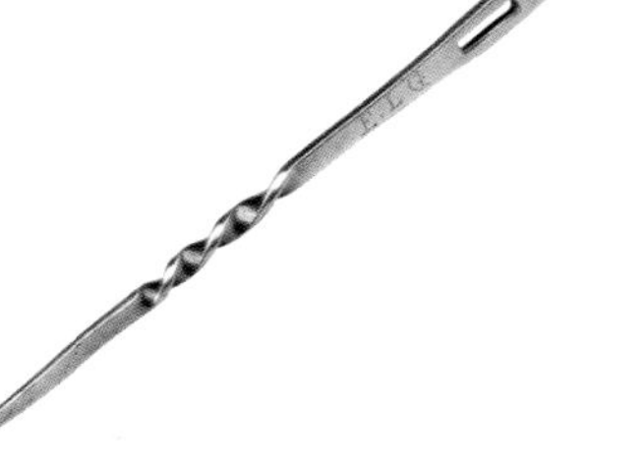
A rare George III Channel Islands silver bodkin, inscribed 'F.L.G', by George Hamon (fl.c1770-1830s), Jersey.
3¼in (8.5cm) long ⅛oz
£1,200-1,600 **MART**

A gilded metal and mother-of-pearl étui, attributed to Palais Royal, the interior with thimble, scissors, stiletto, needlecase and bodkin.
c1840 *5in (13cm) high*
£1,100-1,400 **BLEA**

A glass egg-form finger étui, attributed to Palais Royal, the interior with metal stiletto, needlecase, bodkin, scissors and thimble.
c1860 *3½in (9cm) high*
£900-1,000 **BLEA**

A French gilt-metal étui, with gilt-metal scissors, stiletto, bodkin, needlecase and matched thimble.
c1870 *5¼in (13.5cm) high*
£400-500 **BLEA**

A bodkin case, surface wear, possible repair to cover, stamped 'ET', and possibly 'GK'.

This bodkin case is not hallmarked gold, but tests between 11-14ct.

4½in (11.5cm) long ⅞oz
£750-850 **FELL**

An Edwardian silver coronation throne pin cushion, by William Comyns, London.

1902 *2¾in (7cm) high*

£400-450 **HT**

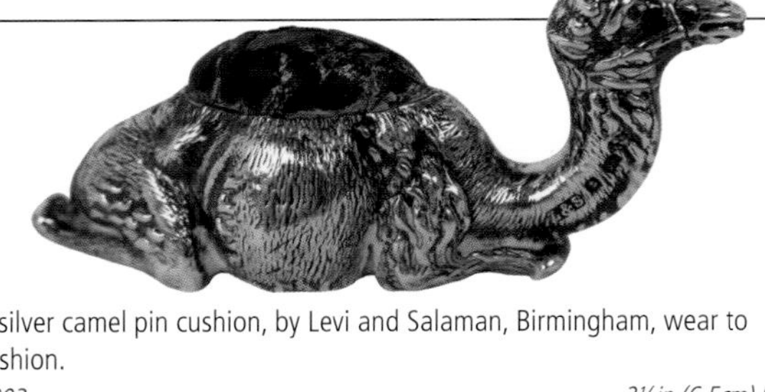

A silver camel pin cushion, by Levi and Salaman, Birmingham, wear to cushion.

1903 *2½in (6.5cm) long*

£2,500-3,000 **GWA**

An Edwardian silver cat pin cushion, by Adie & Lovekin, Birmingham.

1906 *3¼in (8cm) long*

£1,300-1,600 **WW**

An Edwardian silver polar bear pin cushion, by Charles and Cohen, Birmingham.

1906 *2¼in (5.5cm) long*

£1,500-2,000 **WW**

An Edwardian silver bulldog pin cushion, by Britton, Gould & Co., Birmingham.

1906 *2in (5cm) high*

£500-550 **WW**

An Edwardian silver emu pin cushion, with mother-of-pearl cart, by Robert Pringle and Sons, Birmingham.

1909 *5in (12.5cm) long*

£750-850 **WW**

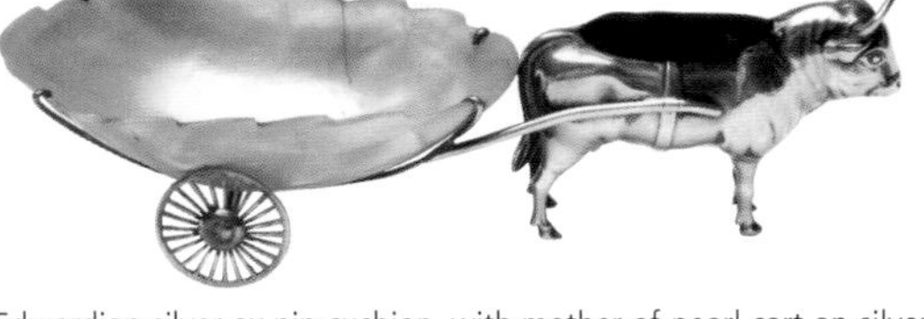

An Edwardian silver ox pin cushion, with mother-of-pearl cart on silver wheels, by Adie & Lovekin, Birmingham.

1908 *6in (15cm) long*

£800-900 **HT**

An Edwardian silver rhino pin cushion, by Levi and Salaman, Birmingham.

1908 *2¼in (5.5cm) long*

£1,400-1,800 **WW**

An Edwardian silver bear pin cushion, muzzled and chained, by H.V. Pithey and Co., Birmingham.

1909 *3¼in (8cm) high*

£1,200-1,500 **WW**

An Edwardian silver salamander pin cushion, by Crisford & Norris, Birmingham.

1909 *4¼in (11cm) long*

£800-900 **HT**

A silver tennis racket pin cushion, by Sydney & Co., Birmingham.

1913 *2½in (6.5cm) long*

£500-600 **WW**

A 19thC whalebone sailor's walking cane, the handle inset with abalone, the stem carved with diamond and spiral twist decoration.

37½in (95.5cm) long

£1,000-1,500 WW

A gold and malacca walking stick, possibly French, marks obscured, split at end of the stick, dated.

1781 36¾in (93.5cm) long

£700-800 DN

A 19thC Dresden porcelain and yellow-metal-mounted malacca cane, brass ferrule, some wear.

39¾in (101cm) long

£500-550 DN

CLOSER LOOK – WHALEBONE CANE

This rare scrimshaw whalebone walking cane is impressively decorated and clearly made by a master craftsman.

The shaft is unusual, carved with panels of spiralled, rope-twist and crosshatched patterns. The pommel is carved as a Turk's head knot.

This cane is particularly desirable because of its various tortoiseshell inlays to the handle.

Canes of this type were typically worked from the jawbone of a whale by American and European sailors and sold in the port cities.

A mid-19thC scrimshaw walking cane.

36¼in (92cm) long

£20,000-25,000 EBA

One of a pair of late 19thC Indian white metal choba staffs, with tiger head terminals, probably of Indian silver.

Provenance: formerly owned and brought back from India by Sir James Thompson (1948-29), Governor of Madras 1904.

23½in (60cm) long

£4,000-4,500 the pair BELL

A probably Viennese cased rock crystal and amethyst parasol or entoutcas handle, with gold and enamel mounts, in a fitted Vickery case, in the manner of Anton Wildhack, lacking original tips.

An entoutcas (French for 'in any case') is a combined parasol and umbrella. The firm of J.C. Vickery was founded around 1890 by John Collard Vickery. By 1913, Vickery was listed as a goldsmith, silversmith, jeweller, dressing case and fitted travelling bag manufacturer, watch and clock importer, with Royal Warrants from the King and Queen of the United Kingdom, the King of Spain, the King and Queen of Denmark, the Queen of Norway and the King of Sweden.

c1900 13½in (34.5cm) long

£2,000-2,500 BELL

A silver and Connemara marble mounted bog oak cane, by Bent and Parker, sponsor's mark B&P, Birmingham.

c1893 13in (33cm) long

£1,500-2,000 WHYT

A silver dog's head handle walking stick, with ebony tapered shaft, by 'W.S', London.

1887 35in (89cm) long

£350-400 SWO

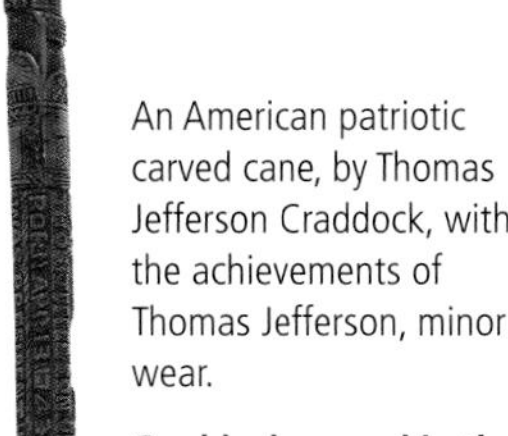

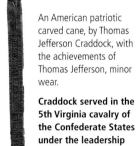

An American patriotic carved cane, by Thomas Jefferson Craddock, with the achievements of Thomas Jefferson, minor wear.

Craddock served in the 5th Virginia cavalry of the Confederate States under the leadership of Thomas L. Rosser.

c1890 36in (91.5cm) long

£650-750 POOK

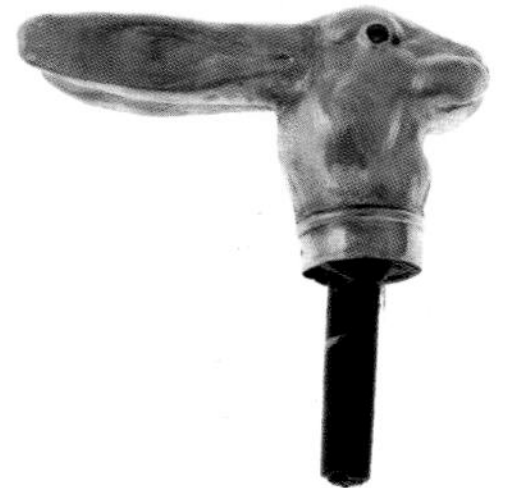

An early 20thC 18ct gold hare's head cane handle, with ruby eyes, French assay marks.

2¾in (7cm) long 1⅛oz

£3,000-3,500 FELL

An early to mid-20thC Dunhill Aquarium table lighter, reg. no.737418, maker's mark to base, decorated with fish amongst seaweed, with plated mounts.

4in (10cm) wide

£2,000-2,500 **ROS**

A Dunhill 'Aquarium' table lighter, with Perspex panels with tropical fish, with silvered mounts, stamped marks, 'Reg. No. 737418', some scuffing.

4in (10cm) wide

£3,500-4,000 **SWO**

A Dunhill Aquarium table lighter, by Ben Shillingford, reg. no.737418, the Perspex panels with tropical fish.

4in (10cm) wide

£3,000-3,500 **HAN**

An Art Deco silver-gilt Dunhill 'Unique' cigarette lighter, with a 15-jewel Swiss watch-movement, London import marks, numbered '1581', marked 'Pat No 143752', some wear, movement not working.

1926 *1¾in (4.5cm) high*

£1,000-1,400 **ECGW**

A Dunhill 9ct gold cigarette lighter, Birmingham.

1949 *2¼in (5.5cm) long*

£800-900 **FELL**

A 1950s Dunhill Aquarium table lighter, by Ben Shillingford, decorated with fish amongst seaweed, with gilt-metal fittings.

3¾in (9.5cm) wide

£4,000-4,500 **HAN**

A Dunhill 'Aquarium' table lighter, the Perspex panels with tropical fish amidst waterweed, with silvered metal fittings, stamped with patent number '143752'.

2¾in (7cm) high

£1,000-1,400 **SWO**

A 1950s Dunhill Aquarium table cigarette casket, by Ben Shillingford, the lid inset with a Perspex plaque with fish amongst seaweed, Dunhill label to the cedar-lined interior.

8¼in (21cm) wide

£4,000-4,500 **HAN**

A Dunhill lighter, stamped 'Dunhill U.S. Pat 2102108, Outer Jacket 14K Gold'.

2in (5cm) long

£250-300 **LOCK**

A Dunhill Namiki maki-e fountain pen, the black urushi ground with gold dust togidashi maki-e, with taka maki-e foliage, signed 'Namiki' in Kanji, with a red Kao, no.3 nib stamped '14ct', with lever filling system.
c1935
£6,500-7,000 **DN**

A Dunhill Namiki maki-e lacquer desk pen, fish and sea plants within a powder gilt ground, six character signature, nib marked 'Medium Dunhill Namiki 3 Made in Japan'.
c1930
£1,500-2,000 **HAN**

A limited edition Montblanc 'Skeleton Antoni Gaudi' fountain pen, no.109/128, with overlay reminiscent of the Casa Batllo, stamped 'Au750', the nib stamped '18K'.
£7,000-8,000 **DN**

A limited edition Montblanc 'Year Of The Golden Dragon' fountain pen, no.479/888, the Meissen porcelain handpainted with a dragon, the nib stamped '18K', with box and papers.
2000
£3,500-4,000 **DN**

A limited edition Montblanc 'Great Characters Mahatma Gandhi' fountain pen, no.199/241, stamped 'Au750', the nib stamped '18K', with box and papers.
2009
£9,000-10,000 **DN**

A limited edition Montblanc 'Skeleton Genghis Khan' fountain pen, no.20/35, with overlay resembling Mongol armour, stamped 'pt950', the nib stamped 'Au750'.
£16,000-20,000 **DN**

A Parker Duofold Giant 125th Anniversary gold and diamond fountain pen, limited edition no.4/125, the nib stamped '18K', in a Parker display box with a gold-plated pen holder and ink bottle.
issued 2013
£12,000-15,000 **DN**

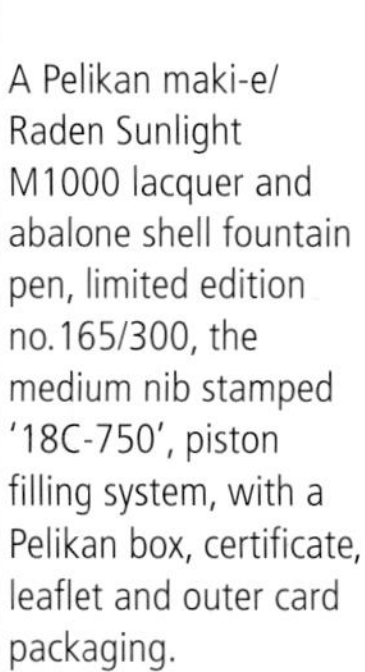

A Pelikan maki-e/ Raden Sunlight M1000 lacquer and abalone shell fountain pen, limited edition no.165/300, the medium nib stamped '18C-750', piston filling system, with a Pelikan box, certificate, leaflet and outer card packaging.
£4,500-5,000 **DN**

A Platinum Autumn maki-e fountain pen, by Rosui, the cap and barrel with togidashi and takamaki-e autumnal landscape, the nib stamped '14K', with a lever filling system, signed, with red kao mark.
c1930 *5½in (14cm) long*
£2,500-3,000 **DN**

A Waterman 452 fountain pen, BHR with silver overlay, engraved name.
c1920
£250-300 **HAN**

A George III Blue John Neo-classical -shape vase, on a Blue John and white marble pedestal on a slate plinth, lacking finial, some repairs.

Blue John is a semi-precious material found in Derbyshire, which was used in 18thC France and England to manufacture decorative urns and other objects.

c1780 *14¼in (36cm) high*

£4,500-5,000 DN

A George III Blue John campana urn, on a black marble plinth.

8¾in (22.5cm) high

£5,000-5,500 WW

A George III Blue John campana urn vase, on a black marble base.

11¾in (30cm) high

£3,500-4,000 HAN

A pair of late George III or Regency Blue John and fluorspar urns, the marble bases possibly replacements, one urn chipped, one urn glued.

9½in (24cm) high

£4,000-4,500 DN

A probably late 17thC German silver-gilt-mounted moss agate cup and cover, crack to cover.

4¼in (11cm) high

£6,500-7,000 BE

An 18thC gold-mounted green agate egg, French or English, inscribed 'DIEU VOUS BENIT' ('God bless you'), push button diamond opening.

2¼in (5.5cm) long

£3,000-3,500 WW

A late 18thC agate and gilt-metal-mounted nécessaire, with paste clasp, with scissors and pencil, metal mount loose, cover cracked.

4in (10cm) long

£650-700 CHEF

A 19thC gilt-metal-mounted porphyry urn vase, some scratches.

9¼in (23.5cm) high

£1,500-2,000 TEN

A French Mellerio dits Meller 18ct gold and enamel scent bottle, the cover set with a cabochon ruby and sapphire, engraved 'Mellerio R. Paix 9',in a Masis Joaillier box, wear to enamel.

c1880 *2¾in (7cm) high 2⅜oz*

£3,500-4,000 DN

A silver-gilt and enamel throne salt cellar, maker's mark of Savikov, unknown assay master, Moscow.

This is possibly not by Sazikov.

1895 *3¼in (8.5cm) high 4¼oz*

£1,500-2,000 **WW**

A silver-gilt and enamel box, set with coloured stones, by Feodor Ruckert, Moscow.

Feodor Ruckert was one of Fabergé's workmasters. He specialised in cloisonné enamel for the Moscow workshop and also worked independently for himself and for other retailers.

1908-17 *3½in (9cm) long 5⅞oz*

£10,000-12,000 **WW**

An Art Nouveau-style silver cloisonné pocket cigarette case, maker's mark, second Kokoshnik mark.

c1910 *4in (10cm) wide 7⅛oz*

£1,400-1,800 **HAN**

A silver and enamel kovsh, with date marks and French import marks.

A kovsh is a traditional oval-shaped drinking vessel or ladle, used to serve and drink mead from as early as the 10thC.

1896-1908 *5¼in (13.5cm) long*

£2,500-3,000 **WW**

A silver and enamel kovsh, with enamel landscape scene, with all-over enamel patterns and cabochon stones, mark head '88'.

9in (23cm) long 34oz

£8,500-9,500 **JN**

An enamel kovsh, with champlevé enamel and cabochon stones.

5in (12.5cm) long

£650-750 **JN**

A silver-gilt and enamel box, with eagle motif, cabochon, rubies and diamonds, stamped 'A.H.88', in leather fitted case.

3½in (9cm) long

£4,000-5,000 **JN**

A Fabergé-style enamel frame, set with seed pearls and cabochon sapphires.

4½in (11.5cm) high

£1,800-2,200 **JN**

ESSENTIAL REFERENCE – FABERGÉ

Fabergé was founded in St Petersburg in 1842 by Gustav Fabergé, a goldsmith of French extract. The business was later taken over by his two sons, Peter Carl and Agathon Fabergé.

- **It produced a wide range of items, including cigarette cases, boxes, mantel clocks, picture frames, animal sculptures, flower carvings and jewellery. It is best known for its jewelled enamel Easter eggs.**
- **Carl Fabergé attracted the attention of Tsar Alexander III in 1882 at the Pan-Russian Exhibition in Moscow. From 1885, the House of Fabergé held the title of 'Supplier to the Court of His Imperial Majesty'.**
- **Fabergé work was renowned for its innovation and beauty.**
- **At its height, Fabergé employed nearly five hundred people, including talented craftsmen such as Michael Perchin, Henrik Wigstrom, Feodor Ruckert and Erik Kollin.**
- **Fabergé was forced to close in Russia in 1918 following the Revolution.**

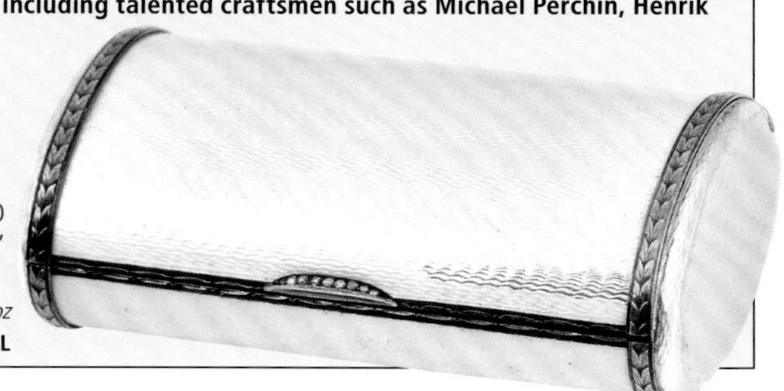

A Fabergé silver-gilt and enamel hinge-lidded cigarette box, engraved 'L.C.O March 1st 1936', by Albert Holmström (1876-1925), detailed '88', 'Fabergé' in Cyrillic, enamel losses throughout, with Cartier case.

3in (7.5cm) long 3oz

£4,500-5,500 **BELL**

An early 19thC silver pug dog snuff box, with later red eyes, unknown maker's mark, assay master Nikolay Dubrovin, Moscow.
c1830 *2¾in (7cm) long 1⅜oz*
£800-900 **WW**

A silver and silver-gilt cheroot case, the back depicting the Kremlin, maker's mark possibly for Fyedor Verkovsyev or Verkhovtsev, assay master 'A.C', Moscow, some wear.
1853 *5¼in (13.5cm) long 6⅛oz*
£1,300-1,600 **FELL**

A pair of silver beakers, maker's mark 'HJ', assay master Nicholai Bubrovin, Moscow, 84 zolotniki, some light scratches.

A zolotnik was a small Russian unit of weight, used from the 10thC to the 20thC. One zolotnik is equal to approximately ⅛ oz, or 4.27g.
1839 *3in (7.5cm) high 5⅞oz*
£950-1,100 **DN**

A silver and niello work cheroot case, with locking mechanism, the base with a view of the Kremlin, assay master Viktor Savinkov, Moscow.
1865 *4¼in (10.5cm) 4⅝oz*
£350-450 **WW**

A silver tankard, niello-decorated with four panels, depicting the Kremlin, with inscription, assay master Viktor Vasilyevich Savinsky, Moscow, some wear.
1862 *5in (13cm) high 16oz*
£2,500-3,000 **APAR**

A Fabergé silver snail, by Henrik Wigstrom, St Petersburg, import marks for London 1911, importer's mark of Charles Fabergé, 91 zolotnik.

This snail was probably modelled as the handle of a hardstone paperweight and is now lacking its stone base.
c1908 *4in (10cm) long 3⅞oz*
£5,000-6,000 **WW**

A Fabergé silver egg, with gold thumb-piece set with a sapphire, by Henrik Wigstrom, Fabergé.
2½in (6.5cm) long 2½oz
£5,000-6,000 **WW**

A Fabergé silver box, with a frieze of Imperial eagles, marked 'K Fabergé', Moscow.
6¾in (17cm) long 27oz
£7,000-8,000 **SWO**

A Fabergé silver paperknife, with rose quartz terminal, mounted with a cabochon garnet in gold collet, signed 'ÔÀÁÅĐÆÅ', maker's mark 'AR' for work master Anna Ringe, and 88 zolotnik with kokoshnik.
8¼in (21cm) long
£2,000-2,500 **WW**

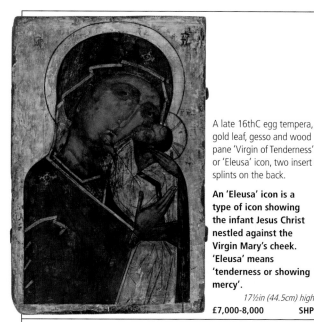

A late 16thC egg tempera, gold leaf, gesso and wood pane 'Virgin of Tenderness' or 'Eleusa' icon, two insert splints on the back.

An 'Eleusa' icon is a type of icon showing the infant Jesus Christ nestled against the Virgin Mary's cheek. 'Eleusa' means 'tenderness or showing mercy'.

17½in (44.5cm) high

£7,000-8,000 SHP

An 18thC triptych icon, polychrome and gold leaf iconography, wire hinges.

A triptych is a picture on three panels, typically hinged together and used as an altarpiece.

6¾in (17cm) high

£2,000-2,500 HAN

An 18thC Russian School painted and gilded quadripartite icon, of 'The Pokrov', 'The Procession of the Icon, Moscow', 'The Exaltation of the True Cross', and 'The Installation of the Girdle of the Mother of God'.

12½in (32cm) high

£1,500-2,000 WW

An early 19thC Moscow School egg tempera, gold leaf, gesso and wood portable iconostasis, consisting of 15 panels, the top row depicting Old Testament forefathers, the second depicting prophets paying homage to the Virgin of Znamenie, the third depicting feasts of the Orthodox church, the lowest row depicting Jesus Christ flanked by Mary, John the Baptist, archangels and several saints.

Provenance: Acquired through inheritance by the descendants of Alexander Ivanovich Nelidov (1835-1910), Russian Ambassador to Turkey, Italy and France.

extended 55in (139.5cm) wide

£12,000-15,000 SHP

A 19thC icon, 'The Mother and Child', with gilt-metal and silver oklad and walnut frame.

An oklad is a metal cover protecting an icon, usually made of gilt or silvered metal.

12¼in (31cm) high

£750-850 REEM

A mid-19thC icon, depicting Christ, with silver oklad, maker unknown, assay master 'AC', possibly A. Suyechin, Moscow, pre-Kokoshnik mark.

1868 *12¼in (31cm) high*

£550-650 GWA

A 'Madonna and Child' icon, with silver oklad, stamped marks, in later glazed case.

1883-84 *12¼in (31cm) high*

£800-900 SWO

An icon, depicting Christ Pantocrator.

14in (35.5cm) high

£1,300-1,600 CLAR

A travelling silver triptych icon, depicting St George and the Dragon, a King and Queen on either side, dated.

1889 *3¾in (9.5cm) long*

£1,200-1,600 JN

A pair of Imperial Porcelain Factory figures of Ottoman Janissaries, modelled after Meissen originals, blue cipher marks, some losses and chips, one hand re-glued.

The Imperial Porcelain Factory of St Petersburg was established in 1744, first under Dmitri Vinogradov and later under J.G. Müller. After the 1917 Revolution, the factory was taken over by the state.

c1770 *6¼in (16cm) high*

£4,000-4,500 **BELL**

A Gardner porcelain peasant street vendor, impressed mark, restored to neck, hat and basket.

In 1766, English entrepreneur Francis Gardner opened a porcelain factory in Verbilki, near Moscow, with the permission of Catherine the Great. The factory traded as Gardner until 1892, when it was acquired by M.S. Kusnetov and then known as Kusnetsov Brothers until its closure in 1917.

c1830 *7in (18cm) high*

£1,200-1,600 **DN**

A 19thC porcelain Kamchatka woman, possibly by Imperial Porcelain Factory, from the 'Peoples of Russia' series, titled in French and Cyrillic.

8¾in (22cm) high

£9,000-9,500 **GYM**

A Gardner porcelain berry picker, impressed '4', professional restoration.

c1830-40 *8¼in (21cm) high*

£2,500-3,000 **BE**

A 19thC porcelain Laplander, possibly by Imperial Porcelain Factory, from the 'Peoples of Russian' series, titled in French and Cyrillic.

£17,000-20,000 **GYM**

An Imperial Porcelain Factory figure of a masked lady, some chips and flaking.

c1840 *5in (13cm) high*

£3,500-4,000 **PW**

An early to mid-19thC Gardner porcelain desk stand, modelled as a kneeling peasant, the logs on his back forming an inkwell and pounce pot, impressed factory marks and '8', lacking cover.

5in (13cm) high

£4,500-5,000 **BE**

A 19thC porcelain Barbarian lady, possibly by Imperial Porcelain Factory, from the 'Peoples of Russia' series, titled 'Femme Barabien' in French and Cyrillic.

8¾in (22cm) high

£8,000-9,000 **GYM**

A mid-19thC Moscow biscuit porcelain figure, of a Russian peasant breaking a hole in the ice, impressed mark, some losses, glued repairs to arms.

9¾in (25cm) high

£1,200-1,600 **DN**

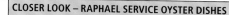

A late 19thC Imperial Porcelain Factory presentation Easter egg, with the cipher of Alexander III (1845-94).

4½in (11.5cm) high

£2,500-3,000 **WW**

A late 19thC to early 20thC Imperial Porcelain Factory presentation Easter egg, gilded with the monogram of Empress Maria Feodorovna (1847-1928).

Maria Feodorovna was born Princess Dagmar of Denmark. She had been engaged to the heir apparent, Nicholas Alexandrovich, at the time of his death from meningitis in 1865. She married the future Alexander III the following year. The couple were crowned in Moscow in 1883.

4¾in (12cm) high

£3,500-4,000 **WW**

CLOSER LOOK – RAPHAEL SERVICE OYSTER DISHES

These oyster dishes were made at the Imperial Porcelain Factory in St Petersburg and are part of the Raphael Service.

They are painted with Classical figures on a red ground, within radiating panels of Classical ornament, with heraldic devices painted to the handles.

The Raphael Service was commissioned by Alexander III in 1883 for the Tsarskoselsky Palace and was inspired by Raphael's frescos in the Loggias of the Vatican. The decoration was so extensive that the service was not completed until 1903.

The condition of these dishes is excellent. They have been carefully stowed in a cupboard for almost 90 years, having been acquired by an engineer from Blackburn in the 1920s while on a trade mission to Russia.

A set of three oyster dishes, dated.

1900-02 *5¾in (14.5cm) wide*

£22,000-28,000 **TEN**

An Imperial Porcelain Factory vase, painted with hazel tree branches, printed factory mark, impressed numeral '1', dated.

1909 *9½in (24cm) high*

£2,200-2,800 **BELL**

A 19thC carved cornelian bulldog's head cane handle, with tiger's eye eyes and a gold strap collar inset with a diamond, struck 'H.W', possibly for Henrik Wigstrom, with '56' control marks.

1¾oz

£1,500-2,000 **BE**

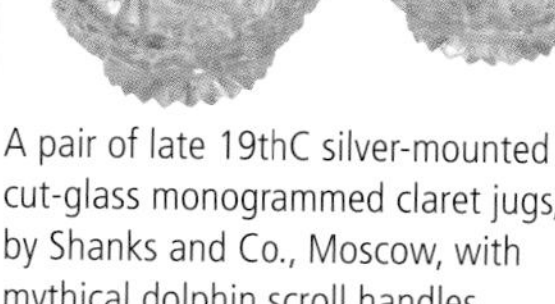

A pair of late 19thC silver-mounted cut-glass monogrammed claret jugs, by Shanks and Co., Moscow, with mythical dolphin scroll handles.

1890 *10¼in (26cm) high*

£3,500-4,000 **WW**

A Fabergé hardstone frame, the chalcedony frame with ten cabochon rubies set to the internal white enamel striated border, workmaster's initials 'A' for Karl Armfelt, 88 zolotnik, inventory no.14351, some cracks, in hollywood box, with Imperial eagle over the Fabergé mark.

3¼in (8cm) high

£30,000-35,000 **WW**

A Fabergé-style cut glass caviar bowl, with silver and enamel lid with sturgeon handle.

4½in (11.5cm) diam

£1,500-2,000 **JN**

A Fabergé-style green jade box and cover, with diamond-set gold initials.

2¾in (7cm) diam

£1,800-2,200 **JN**

A Queen Anne heavy baluster wine glass.
c1710 *6in (15cm) high*
£1,800-2,200 ROS

A teared balustroid stemmed wine glass.
c1720-30 *7¼in (18.5cm) high*
£700-800 WAD

CLOSER LOOK – JACOBITE WINE GLASS

The Jacobites were the supporters of King James II, usurped by William and Mary in 1688. Later it became a general term for those who favoured the restoration of the Stuart dynasty.

This glass is engraved with a rose, representing James Francis Edward Stuart, Prince of Wales, James II's son (nicknamed the Old Pretender); and with two rose buds, representing James' sons, Charles Edward Stuart (nicknamed Bonnie Prince Charlie or the Young Pretender) and Henry Benedict Stuart.

It is also engraved with an oak leaf, a symbol of the Stuart family.

It is inscribed with the Latin word 'Fiat', meaning 'let it come to pass'.

A Jacobite knopped airtwist-stemmed wine glass, tiny chips.
c1750 *6¾in (17cm) high*
£850-950 WAD

A George I baluster wine glass, with trumpet bowl, above ball knop and triple annulated knop, with teared hollow baluster knop.
c1725 *6in (15cm) high*
£1,200-1,600 ROS

A George II wine glass, with teared trumpet bowl, above triple angulated knop, true baluster and inverted baluster knop.
c1735 *7¾in (19.5cm) high*
£900-1,000 ROS

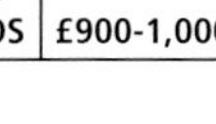

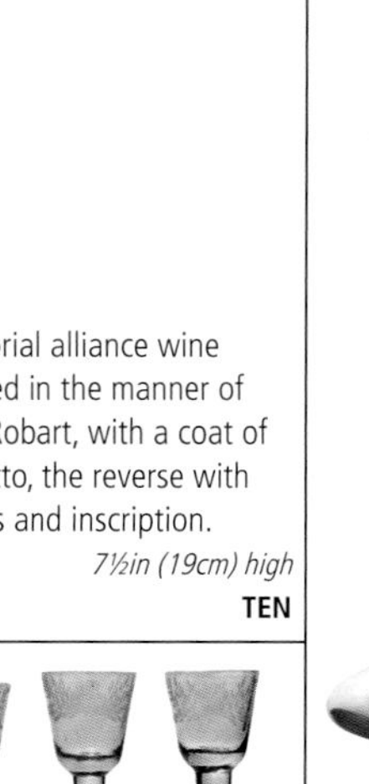

A Dutch armorial alliance wine glass, engraved in the manner of Willem Otto Robart, with a coat of arms and motto, the reverse with clasped hands and inscription.
c1740 *7½in (19cm) high*
£3,500-4,000 TEN

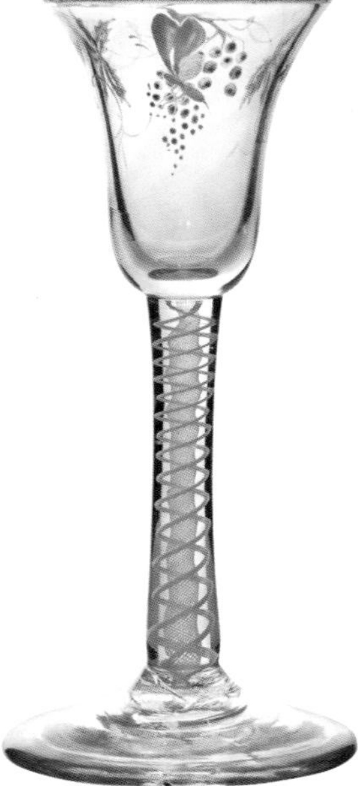

A George II Beilby wine glass, the bowl enamelled and gilded, above opaque double series twist stem, on conical foot.

The Beilby siblings, William, Richard and Mary, were all skilled glass decorators, working for various factories in the Newcastle area. Their glassware is characterised by its painted white and coloured enamel decoration, and was produced over a short period around 1760. Only a handful of pieces are signed, and many are attributed to the Beilby family on account of their style and quality.
c1750-60 *6in (15.5cm) high*
£5,000-5,500 ROS

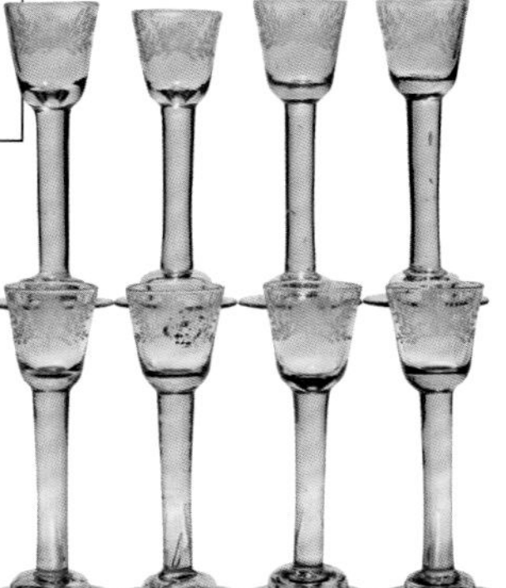

A set of eight mid-18thC plain stemmed engraved wine glasses.
7in (18cm) high
£3,500-4,000 WAD

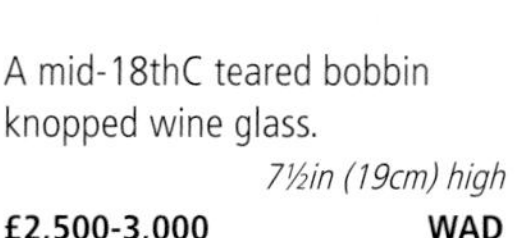

A mid-18thC teared bobbin knopped wine glass.
7½in (19cm) high
£2,500-3,000 WAD

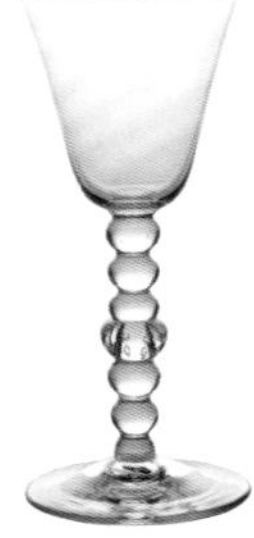

A mid-18thC teared knop airtwist composite stemmed wine glass.
7½in (19cm) high
£750-850 WAD

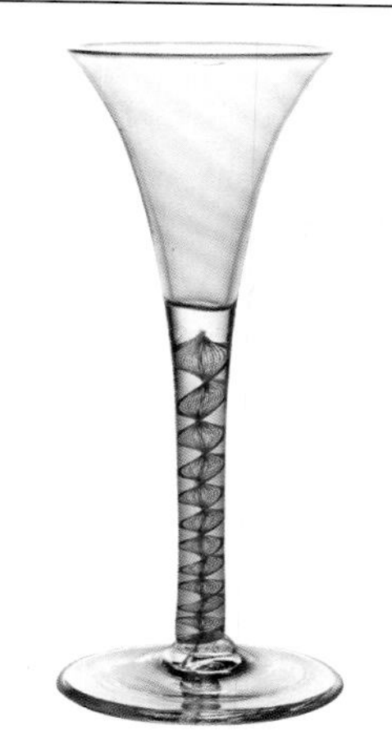

A rare blue twist wine glass, one small chip.
1760-70 6½in (16.5cm) high
£3,000-3,500 WAD

An engraved red colour twist-stemmed wine glass.
c1760-80 5¼in (13.5cm) high
£2,200-2,800 WAD

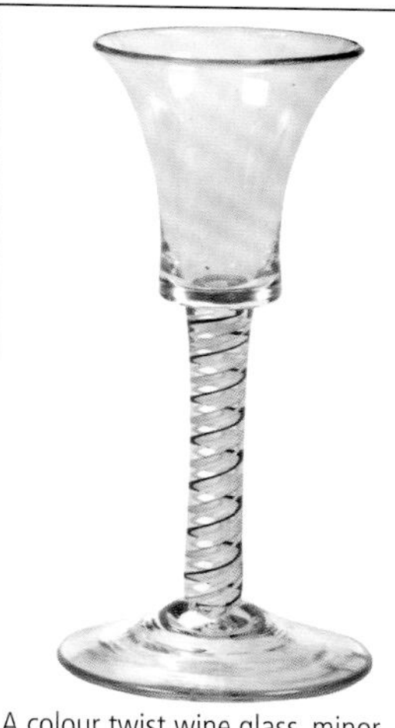

A colour twist wine glass, minor surface scratching.
c1765 6in (15cm) high
£1,200-1,500 TEN

An 18thC Continental friendship wine glass, engraved with two soldiers, inscribed 'AMITIE'.
6¾in (17cm) high
£3,000-3,500 DUK

A Georgian 'Britannia' engraved wine glass, on a facet cut stem and conical foot.
c1780 6in (15cm) high
£950-1,100 L&T

A Dutch armorial wine glass, engraved with arms of Delfland within a Dutch fence border on a beaded knop and baluster stem with air tear.

Delfland is the name of a Dutch water board. The use of a Dutch fence to encircle the armorial is also recorded on a large 18thC wall chart depicting numerous coats of arms of officials of the Delfland water board.
c1780 9¼in (23.5cm) high
£3,500-4,000 TEN

A mid-18thC knopped hollow inverted baluster stemmed sweetmeat or champagne glass.
6in (15.5cm) high
£600-700 WAD

An engraved airtwist-stemmed sweetmeat or champagne glass.
c1750-60 6in (15.5cm) high
£500-600 WAD

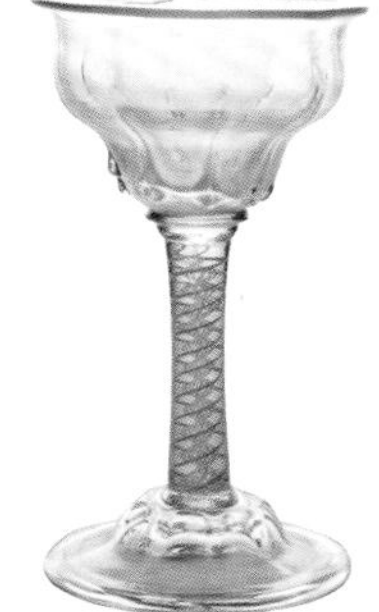

An opaque twist-stemmed sweetmeat or champagne glass.
c1760-70 7in (17.5cm) high
£500-600 WAD

GLASS

A teared heavy baluster-stemmed glass goblet.
c1710 *7¼in (18.5cm) high*
£3,000-3,500 WAD

A Queen Anne heavy baluster drinking glass, with conical bowl, knopped stem and spreading double foot.
c1710 *5¾in (14.5cm) high*
£800-900 ROS

A Queen Anne heavy baluster glass, with conical bowl above a teared angular knop, with a basal true baluster knop.
c1710 *7in (17.5cm) high*
£3,000-3,500 ROS

A teared balustroid stemmed glass goblet.
c1720-30 *7in (18cm) high*
£700-800 WAD

A mid-18thC enamelled ale glass, on a straight enamel twist stem, on a spreading foot.
7¼in (18.5cm) high
£450-550 L&T

A mid-18thC knopped airtwist-stemmed glass goblet, tiny chip.
7½in (19cm) high
£350-400 WAD

A rare red, white and blue colour twist-stemmed glass goblet.
c1760 *7¾in (20cm) high*
£10,000-12,000 WAD

A honeycomb-moulded opaque twist-stemmed glass goblet.
c1760-80 *7½in (19cm) high*
£400-500 WAD

A George III cordial glass, with funnel bowl above a double series opaque twist stem.
c1775 *7in (17.5cm) high*
£900-1,100 ROS

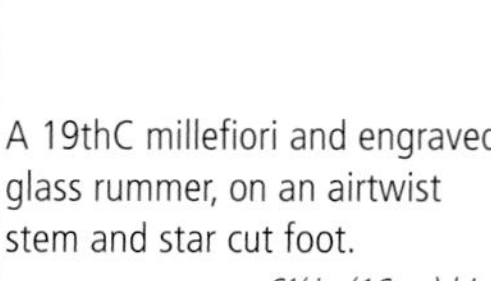

A 19thC millefiori and engraved glass rummer, on an airtwist stem and star cut foot.
6¼in (16cm) high
£3,500-4,000 DUK

A 17thC wine bottle, with applied stag's head seal, string rim.

The seal on this bottle was previously uncatalogued. It seems likely that the bottle has Cornish associations, perhaps with the Bolitho family. The surface of the glass shows signs of burial, and the family history suggests it was found by chance on the West Penwith moors.

c1665-70 *8¾in (22cm) high*

£10,000-14,000 **BKA**

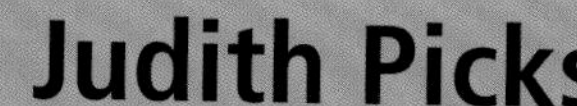

A Yorkshire collector bought this wine bottle for just £30 at Doncaster Antiques Fair early in 2018. Its exceptional condition led him to think it was a replica of an antique bottle, and it was only several days later that its true authenticity was established. It represents a late 17thC 'European' shaft and globe transitional form. Its most distinctive features are characteristic of the shaft and globe type, but it has a relatively squat shape and shorter neck, indicative of the emergence of the onion style of bottle dominant in the early 18thC. It is unusual in more than its shape, being green with a grey tinge in colour, with thick walls manufactured of high-quality glass.

A rare English transitional shaft and globe wine bottle, with 'GR' seal, dated.

1682 *6½in (16.5cm) high*

£20,000-25,000 **BBR**

A James II 'sack' onion bottle, label to reverse.

It is believed this bottle belonged to the famous pirate Samuel White who spent his time in Burma.

7½in (19cm) high

£1,200-1,600 **JN**

A late 17thC to early 18thC onion bottle, with an applied bladed lip, initialled 'WG'.

6in (15cm) high

£400-500 **FLD**

An early 18thC sealed onion mallet wine bottle, with kick-in base, the seal initialled 'P/HA'.

6¾in (17cm) high

£2,000-2,500 **WW**

An 18thC Alpine liquor bottle, with optical honeycomb decor and tin screw cap.

6in (15cm) high

£3,000-3,500 **FIS**

A 19thC Ricketts-style bottle, with 'RHC 1815' seal.

The seal refers to Richard Hall Clarke of Bridwell, Devon.

1815 *11in (28cm) high*

£140-180 **FLD**

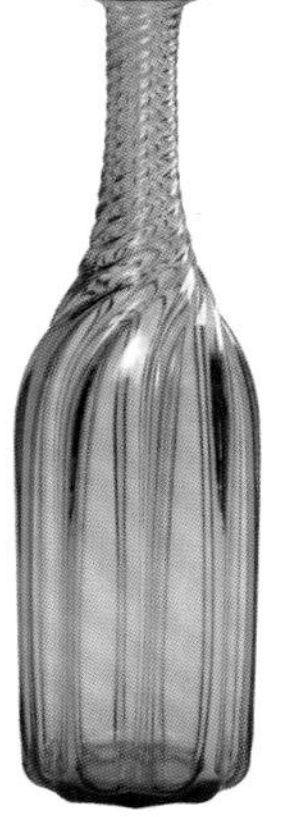

An English apple green glass wrythen bottle.

c1850 *10¼in (26cm) high*

£400-500 **DN**

A Victorian painted glass carboy, depicting the Cutty Sark and another clipper.

26¾in (68cm) high

£350-450 **L&T**

A Georgian decanter and stopper, with engraved crown and initials.

£150-200 **JN**

A pair of early 19thC Irish mould blown mallet-form decanters, one with rim chip.

11¾in (30cm) high

£700-800 **BE**

A pair of Anglo-Irish magnum decanters and stoppers, with mushroom stoppers, some chips.

£1,300-1,600 **CHEF**

A late 19thC plated claret jug, by William Hutton & Sons, the lid with two crossed golf clubs, above a strawberry-cut body, engraved with a golfer.

8¾in (22.5cm) high

£700-800 **L&T**

A silver-gilt-mounted glass claret jug, by Robert Garrard, London, the mounts with pierced decoration and lion mask motif.

1881 *10¾in (27.5cm) high*

£3,000-3,500 **WW**

A silver-mounted 'rock crystal' glass claret jug, the glass probably Stourbridge, the silver by Charles Edwards, London, the handle with griffin head terminal.

1892 *13in (33cm) high*

£2,000-2,500 **BE**

A silver-mounted Baccarat glass claret jug, mounts by J.G. & S, Birmingham, engraved 'TO H. WHITE. FROM H DE V.S./ DECR. 14TH 1886'.

1886 *8¾in (22cm) high*

£550-650 **L&T**

A silver and cut glass lemonade jug, with ice container, by The Goldsmiths & Silversmiths Co. Ltd., London.

1898 *11¼in (28.5cm) high*

£700-800 **DN**

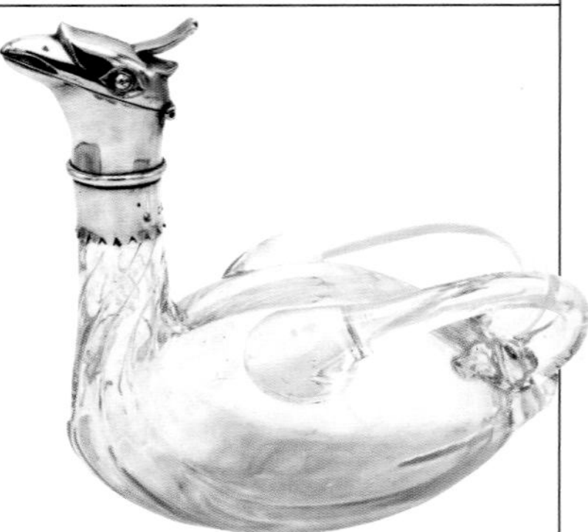

A silver-mounted glass eagle or griffin claret jug, by William Richard Corke, London, with 'wing' handles, tiny ding to crest above beak.

1899 *5¼in (13.5cm) long*

£1,100-1,400 **MART**

A 15thC German glass krautstrunk or beaker, with applied drops of glass.

4¼in (11cm) high

£16,000-20,000 **FIS**

A 16thC German marbled red glass mug, with spun sprawling foot.

4¼in (11cm) high

£2,000-2,500 **FIS**

An Austrian mug, by Anton Kothgasser, painted with a pair of birds, inscribed 'insèparable', the rim painted in gold.

c1820 *4¼in (10.5cm) high*

£1,800-2,200 **FIS**

A Czech Lithyalin cup, by Friedrich Egermann, with gilt medallions and Gothic panels, gold marks to base.

Lithyalin is a type of opaque glass made to resemble semiprecious stones. It was developed by Friedrich Egermann.

c1830 *4¼in (11cm) high*

£10,000-14,000 **FIS**

A mid-to-late 19thC Bohemian glass goblet and cover, engraved with deer in a forest, some chips, cover possibly associated.

21¾in (55.5cm) high

£2,000-2,500 **DN**

A pair of 19thC Bohemian glass and gilt candlestick lustres, with floral and portrait panels, lacking lustres, some losses.

11¾in (30cm) high

£1,300-1,600 **MART**

A pair of late 19thC Bohemian opaline glass vases.

14¾in (37.5cm) high

£2,000-2,500 **ROS**

A pair of late 19thC Bohemian or Beykoz glass enamelled bottles and stoppers, for the Eastern market, some chips.

16½in (42cm) high

£3,000-3,500 **DN**

A pair of late 19thC-style Bohemian campana urns, decorated with panels of foliate gilding.

14½in (36.5cm) high

£1,500-2,000 **ROS**

A pair of Regency cut glass urns and covers.

11¼in (28.5cm) high

£500-600 **L&T**

A pair of Irish glass lidded jars, some scattered chips.

11½in (29cm) high

£400-450 **CHOR**

An Irish glass navette-shaped pedestal bowl, some chips.

10½in (26.5cm) high

£500-600 **CHOR**

A pair of Irish lidded bowls, with diamond cuts, some chips.

11½in (29cm) high

£400-500 **CHOR**

A pair of early 19thC Roman micromosaic plaques, of the tomb of Caecilia Metella and of a ruined temple, possibly The Temple of Saturn, some running splits.

Micromosaics are a type of mosaic created from tiny fragments of glass, called tesserae.

2½in (6.5cm) diam

£7,500-8,500 **TEN**

A mid-19thC Italian micromosaic panel of the Roman Forum, in the manner of Domenico Moglia, some scuffing, some wear to frame.

14½in (37cm) wide

£7,500-8,500 **BELL**

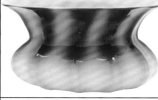

A 19thC New England Glass Company ruffled plated amberina glass bowl.

c1818-78 *2½in (6.5cm) high*

£1,500-2,000 **LHA**

A 19thC glass bell-shaped font/vessel, gilt highlighted.

This vessel is thought to be the base of an 18thC Mughal hookah pipe, which increases the interest and value.

7in (18cm) high

£4,000-4,500 **TRI**

A turquoise glass jewellery casket, possibly Palais Royal or Moser, minor losses.

5in (13cm) high

£700-800 **FELL**

A stained glass panel, some panels cracked, dated.

1536 *18¼in (46.5cm) high*

£850-950 **CHOR**

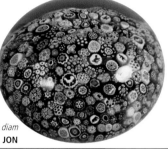

A Baccarat close-packed millefiori paperweight, inset with cane animals and birds, marked 'B', dated.
1847 *4¼in (11cm) diam*
£15,000-20,000 **JON**

A mid-19thC French millefiori paperweight, probably Clichy.
3¼in (8cm) diam
£1,200-1,600 **WW**

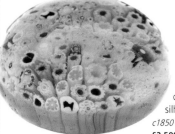

A George Bacchus close-packed glass paperweight, set with multicoloured canes and Queen Victoria silhouettes, top polished.
c1850 *3¼in (8cm) diam*
£2,500-3,000 **BE**

A rare 19thC Clichy millefleur double paperweight inkwell, minor bruising and chips.
4¼in (11cm) diam
£8,000-9,000 **GORL**

A Clichy swirl paperweight.
c1850 *2in (5cm) diam*
£600-700 **TEN**

A Millville yellow waterlily footed paperweight, by John Rhulander, New Jersey.
3½in (9cm) diam
£3,000-3,500 **POOK**

A St Louis paperweight, with a blue jasper ground.
c1850 *2¼in (6cm) diam*
£600-700 **TEN**

A St Louis mixed fruit paperweight, with a filigree ground.
c1850 *3¼in (8cm) diam*
£700-800 **TEN**

A pair of 19thC French millefleur glass paperweight pen holders/vases, some chips, loss of cable to one.
5½in (14cm) high
£11,000-13,000 **GORL**

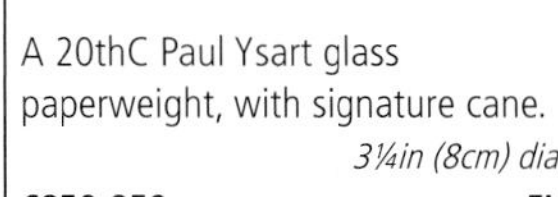

A 20thC Paul Ysart glass paperweight, with signature cane.
3¼in (8cm) diam
£850-950 **FLD**

A Rick Ayotte floral illusion faceted sculptural paperweight, signed 'Ayotte 2 of 3'.
4½in (11.5cm) wide
£2,500-3,000 **JDJ**

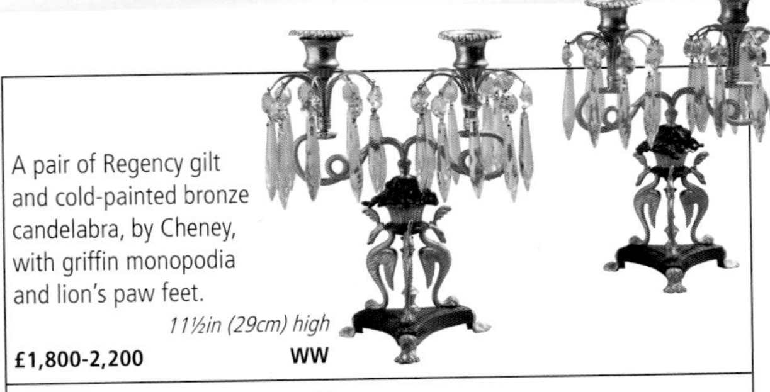

A pair of Regency gilt and cold-painted bronze candelabra, by Cheney, with griffin monopodia and lion's paw feet.

11½in (29cm) high

£1,800-2,200 **WW**

A pair of Napoleon III ormolu figural candelabra, attributed to Raingo Frères, inscribed 'Raingo 11 Vieux', stamped 'RG'.

The firm of Raingo Frères was founded by four brothers in Paris in 1813. It was initially known for its fine quality clocks, but by the 1840s also made bronzes and finely cast ormolu mounts. By 1860 they had carried out commissions for Napoleon III.

44in (112cm) high

£12,000-15,000 **WW**

A pair of French patinated bronze and gilt-bronze candelabra, by Henri Picard (1840-90), signed, stamped 'Victor Paillard'.

Henri Picard (1840-90) famously supplied works to Emperor Napoleon III of France.

38in (96.5cm) high

£13,000-16,000 **JN**

A pair of mid-19thC ormolu candelabra, with bronze putto support on white marble and gilt-metal base, both cherubs with holes, probably once for electrification.

42¼in (107cm) high

£20,000-25,000 **CHOR**

A pair of 19thC Empire-style gilt and patinated bronze candelabra, in the manner of Martin-Guillaume Biennais.

25¾in (65.5cm) high

£2,500-3,000 **WW**

A pair of 19thC six-light candelabra, supported by a bronze putto on a white marble column.

24½in (62cm) high

£1,600-2,000 **CHOR**

A pair of late 19thC ormolu and malachite four-light candelabra.

12¼in (31cm) high

£1,500-2,000 **WW**

A pair of 19thC gilt-metal nine-light candelabra, some rubbing.

34½in (87.5cm) high

£4,000-4,500 **CHOR**

A pair of early 20thC French gilt-metal and glass candelabra, attributed to Maison Bagues.

26½in (67cm) high

£4,500-5,000 **WW**

An 18thC Dutch brass twelve-light chandelier.
25¼in (64cm) wide
£1,400-1,800 WW

A 19thC French ormolu and cut glass Louis XVI-style twelve-branch chandelier.

By repute, originally owned by Princess Caroline Murat (1833-1902), Great Niece of Napoleon Bonaparte and granddaughter of Joachim Murat, King of Naples. She lived and died at Redisham Hall after marrying John Lewis Garden whose family owned it.
56in (142cm) high
£2,500-3,000 HALL

A 19thC French Sèvres porcelain ormolu-mounted six-light chandelier.
45in (114.5cm) high
£1,200-1,600 WAD

An early to mid-Victorian cut glass six-light waterfall chandelier, attributed to F. & C. Osler.
55in (140.5cm) high
£2,500-3,000 L&T

A 19thC Georgian-style brass hall lantern.
34¾in (88cm) high
£900-1,100 L&T

A 19thC gilt-metal framed hall lantern, with coloured glass panels.
£550-650 FLD

A 19thC brass lantern, lacking three glass panels.
35½in (90cm) high
£2,000-2,500 DN

A late 19thC ormolu hall lantern.
36¾in (93.5cm) high
£2,000-2,500 WW

A Louis XIV-style bronze hall lantern.
23½in (60cm) high
£5,000-6,000 CHOR

A Regency-style gilt and patinated brass hall lantern.
34¼in (87cm) high
£6,500-7,500 DN

A pair of Victorian patinated bronze figural gas lamps, by R.W. Winfield & Co., Birmingham, the supports cast as Native Americans, with Victorian lozenge marks, dated.

R.W. Winfield & Co. were prominent 19thC metalware producers. They exhibited at both the Great Exhibition of 1851, and again at the International Exhibition of 1862. The design registry at Kew holds the design and illustration for these lamps, confirming that they were produced by Winfield and registered in the summer of 1866.

1866 *21¾in (55cm) high*

£1,300-1,800 L&T

A 19thC Venetian carved, polychromed and gilt blackamoor torchère.

78¼in (199cm) high

£1,800-2,200 L&T

A late Victorian silver-plated Corinthian column pedestal oil lamp, by Walker & Hall.

35¼in (89.5cm) high

£400-500 LSK

An Edwardian silver Hinks Patent Corinthian column pedestal oil lamp, by Walker & Hall, base by Hawksworth, Eyre & Co., Sheffield.

1907 *26¾in (68cm) high*

£1,000-1,400 APAR

A pair of early 20thC Venetian polychrome-decorated carved pine blackamoor torchères.

74in (188cm) high

£4,000-5,000 WW

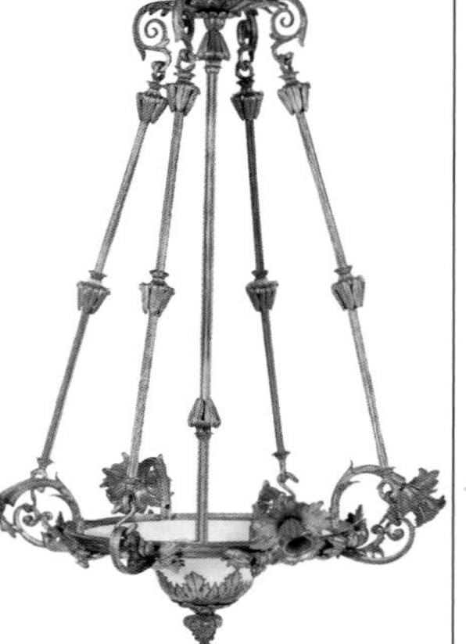

A Regency ormolu ceiling light, attributed to William Collins, previously fitted for gas, now for electricity.

36½in (93cm) high

£1,200-1,600 L&T

A French wrought iron, brass and glazed three-light electrolier.

c1900 *27½in (70cm) wide*

£1,300-1,600 DN

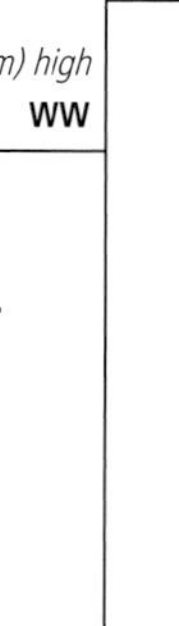

A set of four early 20thC Louis XV-style gilt-metal wall lights, wired for electricity.

19¼in (49cm) high

£900-1,100 L&T

A pair of 19thC glass and gilt-metal twin-branch table lights.

27½in (70cm) high

£4,000-4,500 BE

An 18thC silver-topped gold, diamond and polychrome enamel 'Carnival Mask' locket ring, with gold lettering reading 'SOVS LE MASQVE LA VERITE'.
⅛oz
£5,000-5,500 LHA

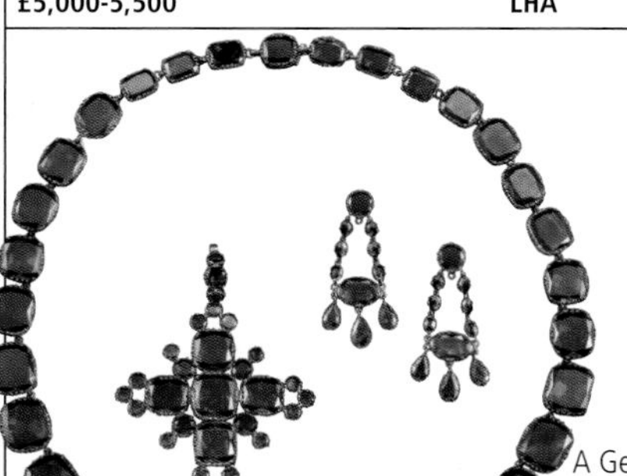

A George III garnet-set gold suite of jewellery, in fitted Payne & Son case.
necklace 16½in (42cm) long
£6,000-7,000 WW

A Georgian gold and garnet bracelet.
7½in (19cm) long
£1,800-2,200 LC

A Georgian diamond and blue enamelled marquise-shape brooch, one diamond lacking, damages to enamel.
c1800-20 *1in (2.5cm) long*
£1,800-2,200 HAN

A Regency gold brooch, set with a pearl, emerald, amethyst, chrysolite and emerald (PEACE), the reverse engraved 'Watier's 1 July 1814'.

This brooch was made to commemorate a victory of the Duke of Wellington over Napoleon in 1814. (In fact the war was far from over, and the Battle of Waterloo was fought the following year). John Watier was a favourite chef of the Prince Regent, and he was chosen to organise a masked ball held in Burlington House on 1 July 1814 in celebration. This brooch would have probably been presented to a lady guest to celebrate the occasion.
1814 *1¼in (3cm) wide*
£2,000-2,500 WW

A late Georgian gold mourning ring, comprising a white skeleton, on woven hair.
size O½ ⅛oz
£2,200-2,800 FELL

A rare 18ct gold enamel memorial ring, for Lord Byron, inscribed 'Byron', with 'In Memory Of' in gilt script, the inner band engraved 'Died 19 April 1824 Aged 36'.

There are believed to be only two other recorded examples of Lord Byron memorial rings of this type.
size O½
£12,000-15,000 TEN

CLOSER LOOK – FRENCH 1789 PENDANT

This pendant was made in May 1789 to commemorate Louis XVI's return to Paris from Versailles to summon the Estates General.

The Royal blue guilloché enamel is mounted with gold decoration and inscribed '1789' to the centre.

Around the outside, the pendant is inscribed 'Redeunt Saturnia Regna' ('the kingdom of Saturn returns'). The reverse is inscribed 'Rejouissons nous Le Roi nous est renou' ('We are pleased the King is returned').

This item's connection to the French Revolution adds to its interest and value.

An 18thC French pendant, on a 9ct gold neckchain.
2¼in (5.5cm) diam
£3,500-4,000 LC

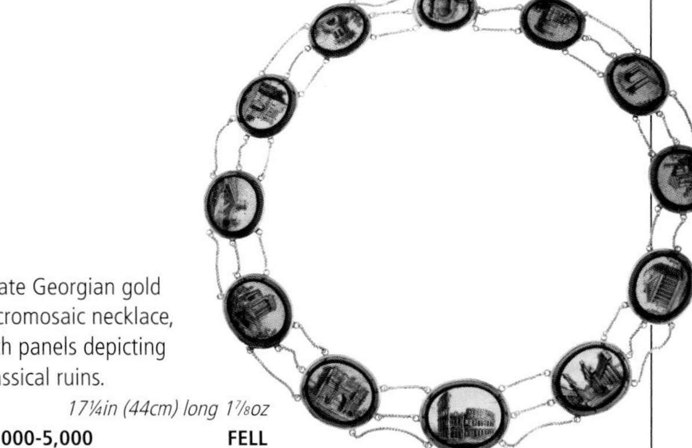

A late Georgian gold micromosaic necklace, with panels depicting Classical ruins.
17¼in (44cm) long 1⅞oz
£4,000-5,000 FELL

Judith Picks

Items linked to Lord Nelson are generally very desirable, and this ring is particularly special. It was given to Admiral Sir Benjamin Hallowell Carew by Admiral Lord Nelson. Hallowell was born near Boston in 1760 and was the only American member of Nelson's 'Band of Brothers'. His career spanned the American Revolutionary Wars, the French Revolutionary Wars and the Napoleonic Wars. This ring differs significantly in design from the well-known group of 58 enamelled rings made by John Salter in 1806 and given to every Admiral and post-captain who fought at the battle of Trafalgar. It is a unique piece, and its existence highlights the strong bond between Nelson and Hallowell.

The carved yellow gold memorial Nelson-Hallowell ring, containing a woven lock of Nelson's hair, engraved 'Lord Nelson OBT. 21st Oct. 1805 A47'.
¾in (2cm) diam
£25,000-30,000 DUK

A mid-19thC gold-filigree-mounted shell cameo pendant brooch, some chips and losses, later hinge and pin.
2½in (6.5cm) wide
£650-750 BELL

A Victorian 15ct gold-mounted shell cameo brooch, some scratches, needs re-setting.
2½in (6.5cm) high ¾oz
£500-600 PW

ESSENTIAL REFERENCE – MOURNING JEWELLERY

The Victorians took mourning etiquette very seriously.

- **Queen Victorian spent much of her reign in mourning for her husband, setting a trend for strict mourning amongst her subjects.**
- **Victorian mourning jewellery was typically dark in colour. It included gold and silver brooches enamelled in black, or pieces made of tortoiseshell or jet.**
- **Where Georgian mourning jewellery was often morbid in design, featuring grave-digging tools, skulls and skeletons (see page 353), Victorian mourning jewellery used softer imagery, such as angels, clouds and Classics motifs.**
- **Pieces of mourning jewellery often contain space to keep a lock of hair of the dead.**

A Victorian mourning carved hardstone cameo pendant brooch, with rose or pear cut 2.7ct diamonds, empty hair chamber to reverse.
3½in (9cm) long 1oz
£2,000-2,500 DRA

A 19thC gold-mounted sardonyx cameo brooch, probably Julius Caesar, some wear.
2in (5cm) long ⅝oz
£1,500-2,000 FELL

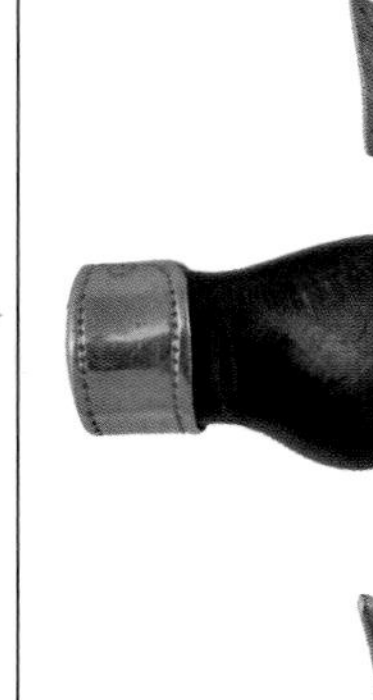

A Victorian gold and stained green tiger's eye brooch, later pin.
c1870 1in (2.5cm) long
£300-350 DN

A Victorian pearl and diamond crescent moon brooch.
1in (2.5cm) wide 0.6ct
£750-850 GWA

A Victorian diamond crescent and star brooch, one diamond missing, in original case.
1¼in (3cm) wide ¼oz
£1,800-2,200 BELL

A Victorian enamelled fox head handpainted brooch, with 18ct yellow gold bezel surround, the reverse inscribed 'W.B. Ford. 1871', hairline cracks.
1½in (4cm) wide
£450-550 HAN

A Victorian pearl and diamond-set 15ct gold star brooch.
1½in (4cm) diam
£600-700 PW

A Victorian enamel, seed pearl and diamond heart-shaped brooch or pendant, inscribed 'FP, 10th June 1897', in period leather case.
¾in (2cm) long
£1,000-1,400 CHEF

An early Victorian diamond brooch, the diamonds set in gold-backed silver.
c1840 2¼in (5.5cm) long ⅝oz 11.75ct
£7,000-8,000 DN

A mid-Victorian gold chimera brooch, French assay marks, surface scratches.
c1870 1in (2.5cm) diam ⅜oz
£700-800 FELL

A Victorian yellow metal, emerald and diamond set brooch, by Garrard & Co., in original box.
1½in (4cm) wide ¼oz
£450-550 LSK

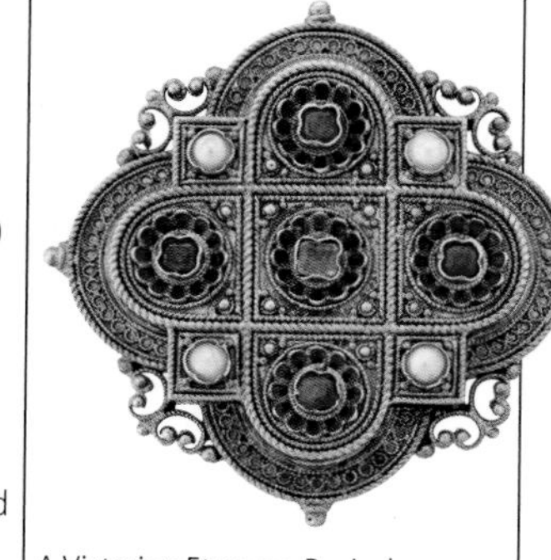

A Victorian Etruscan Revival gem-set yellow gold brooch, attributed to Marchesini, French import mark, with S.J. Shrubsole invoice and box.
c1875 1½in (4cm) wide ½oz
£1,100-1,400 DRA

A late Victorian turquoise and diamond flowerhead brooch, in silver and gold.
1¼in (3cm) diam
£1,800-2,200 WW

A late Victorian rose gold and 3ct diamond snowflake pendant/ brooch, containing 17 old European cut diamonds, stamp 'PAT.88'.
¼oz
£3,000-3,500 LHA

ESSENTIAL REFERENCE – GIULIANO FAMILY

Carlo Giuliano senior arrived in London c1860 and established a workshop in Frith St, initially making jewellery for other retailers.

- **In 1874 he opened his own outlet.**
- **He made jewellery in the Renaissance, Greek and Etruscan styles, always with a high level of craftsmanship.**
- **His sons, Carlo junior and Arthur, joined him in the business and continued after his death in 1895 until Arthur's death in 1914.**
- **Although this brooch is not signed, the design, execution and high quality of the piece are characteristic of the Giuliano workshop, and the Giuliano box was clearly made for this brooch.**

An enamel and diamond quatrefoil brooch, by Carlo and Arthur Giuliano, some losses to enamel, in original case.
1in (2.5cm) wide
£1,300-1,800 CHEF

A Victorian diamond arrow brooch, in silver and gold.
2¼in (6cm) long
£800-900 LC

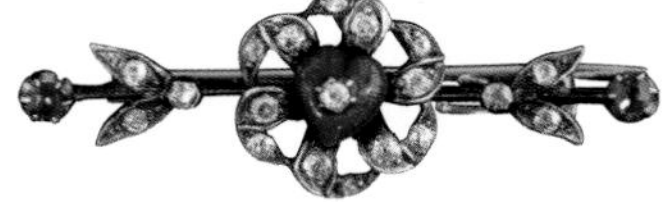

A Victorian diamond, ruby and enamel heart brooch, in silver and gold, numbered '1722'.
1¾in (4.5cm) long
£350-400 ECGW

A late Victorian Child & Child gold, enamel and 1.5ct diamond brooch, with maker's mark, some solder repairs, some chips to enamel.

Child & Child opened in Seville Street in Knightsbridge, London, in 1880. The firm closed in 1916.

2¼in (5.5cm) long ¼oz
£2,000-2,500 FELL

A Victorian 6ct diamond and 14ct gold crescent brooch, detachable hinged pin.
2¾in (7cm) long ½oz
£3,000-3,500 **HAN**

A 19thC gold, sapphire and diamond crescent brooch.
2½in (6.5cm) long ¼oz
£1,200-1,500 **BE**

An early Victorian gold turquoise sentimental brooch, minor dents and one chip, with case.
3¼in (8cm) long ⅜oz
£800-1,000 **FELL**

A Victorian ruby, pearl and diamond dragonfly brooch, with central 1.9ct diamond, in silver and gold.
2¾in (7cm) wide
£8,000-9,000 **WW**

A Victorian gold and topaz brooch.
2¼in (5.5cm) wide
£750-850 **LC**

A Victorian moonstone, ruby and diamond heart and bow brooch.
1in (2.5cm) long
£600-700 **HAN**

A Victorian diamond set garland-style drop bow brooch, in yellow gold-backed silver.
2¼in (6cm) long
£1,800-2,200 **HAN**

Judith Picks

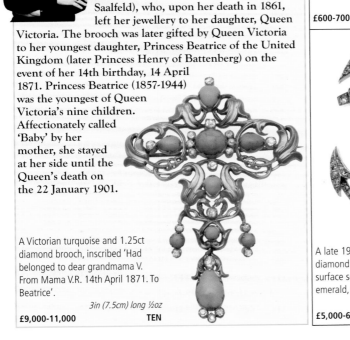

This brooch is believed to have belonged to Victoria, Duchess of Kent (formerly Princess Victoria of Saxe-Coburg-Saalfeld), who, upon her death in 1861, left her jewellery to her daughter, Queen Victoria. The brooch was later gifted by Queen Victoria to her youngest daughter, Princess Beatrice of the United Kingdom (later Princess Henry of Battenberg) on the event of her 14th birthday, 14 April 1871. Princess Beatrice (1857-1944) was the youngest of Queen Victoria's nine children. Affectionately called 'Baby' by her mother, she stayed at her side until the Queen's death on the 22 January 1901.

A Victorian turquoise and 1.25ct diamond brooch, inscribed 'Had belonged to dear grandmama V. From Mama V.R. 14th April 1871. To Beatrice'.
3in (7.5cm) long ½oz
£9,000-11,000 **TEN**

A late 19thC 0.81ct emerald and diamond anchor brooch, some surface scratches, some abrasion to emerald, with case.
2¼in (5.5cm) long ⅝oz
£5,000-6,000 **FELL**

A late Victorian sapphire and 5ct diamond openwork brooch, some replacement gems.
2¼in (5.5cm) high ½oz
£2,500-3,000 **FELL**

An early Victorian gold aquamarine cross pendant/brooch, with cannetille surrounds, with a late Victorian gold rope-twist chain.

pendant 2¾in (7cm) long ½oz

£2,500-3,000 **FELL**

A mid-Victorian 17ct diamond floral necklace, some wear, in Collingwood case.

6¼in (16cm) long 1¼oz

£14,000-18,000 **FELL**

A mid-Victorian 18ct gold, split pearl, enamel and gem-set snake necklace, some wear, small dent to snake head.

17¾in (45cm) long 1⅛oz

£3,000-3,500 **FELL**

A Victorian gem-set snake necklace, the snake's mouth forming the clasp and holding its own tail, in later snake print box.

Snake necklaces or chains, made of interlocking gold links to simulate scales were fashionable from the 1840s. Collectors aim to buy them in excellent condition, as they are difficult and expensive to repair.

14½in (37cm) long ¾oz

£2,500-3,000 **CHEF**

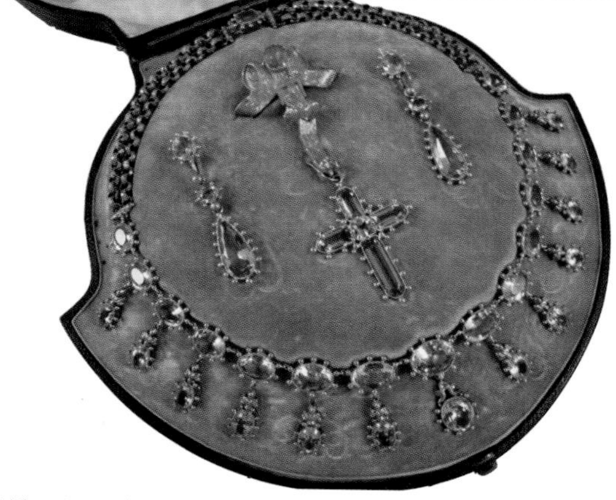

A Victorian pink topaz and gold parure, in Bright & Sons case.

necklace 15¾in (40cm) long

£18,000-22,000 **LC**

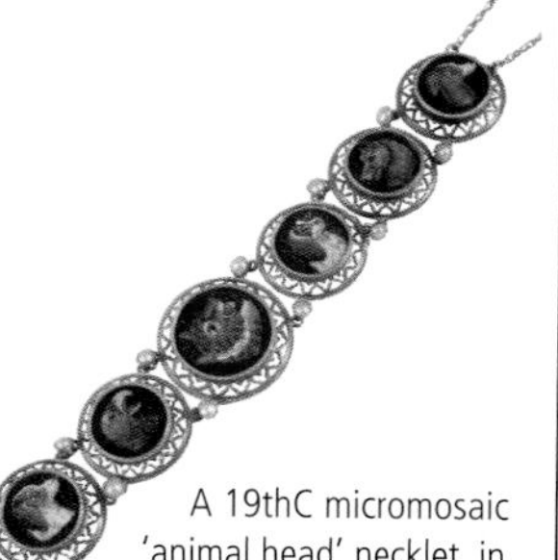

A 19thC micromosaic 'animal head' necklet, in gold openwork mounts.

15in (38cm) long

£2,500-3,000 **LC**

A Victorian Renaissance Revival ruby and emerald pendant, by John Brogden, in N. Bloom & Sons box.

c1880 *pendant 3¼in (8.5cm) long*

£4,000-4,500 **DN**

A Renaissance Revival yellow gold, sapphire, diamond and enamel pendant, by Edward Tessier, London, with fitted box signed 'EDWARD TESSIER 26. NEW BOND ST LONDON'.

This item is accompanied by an American Gemological Laboratories sapphire identification and origin certificate, no.1089852, dated 1 February 2018, stating Mineral Type: Natural Corundum, Variety: Sapphire, Origin: Ceylon (Sri Lanka).

2¼in (6cm) high ⅜oz

£18,000-22,000 **LHA**

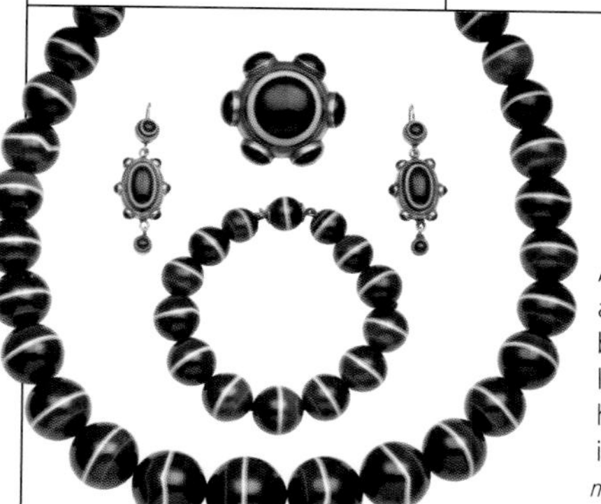

A Victorian banded agate suite, the brooch with a glazed locket back containing hairwork, some wear, in fitted case.

necklace 20in (51cm) long

£5,000-5,500 **TEN**

A late Victorian diamond and cultured pearl pendant necklace, with 'Savage, 41 High Street, Kensington W.' case.

£3,300-3,600 **BELL**

A late Victorian garnet, pearl and diamond pendant.

1¼in (3cm) diam

£1,800-2,200 **LC**

A Victorian bangle, with panels of Jupiter, Mars and Mercury, with pin clasp, light wear.

1½in (3.5cm) diam 1⅞oz

£5,000-5,500 TEN

A Victorian diamond, turquoise and gold bangle, with fitted box.

The stone section can be detached, allowing it to be worn as a brooch or pendant.

£4,500-5,000 LC

A Victorian gold and 18ct garnet slide bracelet, some rubbing.

c1880 *2¾in (7cm) long 1oz*

£2,000-2,500 ECGW

A late Victorian, gold, opal and diamond carved-head hinged bangle.

c1890 *2¼in (6cm) wide ⅝oz*

£1,800-2,200 SWO

A Victorian 18ct gold banded agate and black enamelled mourning ring, detailed 'In Memory Of' and 'James Dimond Obt 4th Septr 1845', London.

1845 *size J ¼oz*

£450-550 BELL

An early Victorian half pearl and emerald cluster ring, one claw missing, one replacement pearl.

c1850 *size R½*

£350-400 DN

A late Victorian diamond, ruby and 18ct gold ring, some wear.

c1890 *size N*

£600-650 DN

A gentleman's 18ct gold signet ring, set with a bloodstone engraved with a coat of arms, Chester.

1891 *size V*

£750-850 WW

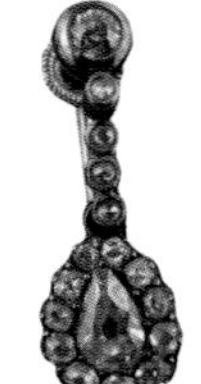

A pair of Victorian diamond ear pendants, with later screw fittings.

1in (2.5cm) long

£3,200-3,600 DN

ESSENTIAL REFERENCE – ETRUSCAN REVIVAL

The Etruscan civilisation resided in parts of ancient Italy from the 8thC BC to the 3rdC BC, when it was absorbed into the Roman Republic.

- **In the early 19thC, original Etruscan jewellery was unearthed in tombs outside Rome, including wrought golden earrings and necklaces.**
- **This led to a trend for Victorian Etruscan Revival jewellery, inspired by Etruscan designs.**
- **Etruscan Revival jewellery typically makes use of gold and some semi-precious stones, often with intricate filigree or granulation.**

A pair of Victorian Etruscan Revival pendant earrings.

2¾in (7cm) long ⅜oz

£1,200-1,600 TEN

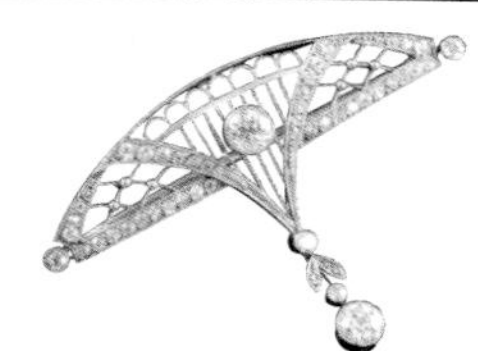

A Belle Époque gold, platinum and diamond set demi-lune drop brooch, stamped '18ct', maker's mark 'A', some chips.

The Belle Époque, of 'Beautiful Era', refers the period in European history between the end of the Franco-Prussian War and the start WWI. Belle Époche jewellery tends to cover Edwardian, Art Nouveau and Arts and Crafts styles.

1¾in (4.5cm) wide

£1,200-1,600 GORL

A gold and turquoise brooch, by James Cromar Watt with enamelled bands of iridescent green, with silver foiled backing.

James Cromar Watt (1862-1940) was born in Aberdeen. He worked in precious metals, developing skills in the ancient techniques of gold granulation and translucent foiled enamelling. Some of his pieces were influenced by the enamel work of Phoebe Traquair and some of it was designed in association with the painter and stained glass artist, Douglas Strachan.

c1905 *1¼in (3cm) wide*

£1,000-1,500 L&T

A Belle Époque 0.6ct diamond and enamel pendant necklace, with three guilloché enamel plaques, with fitted case and tool to change plaques.

pendant 2in (5cm) high

£4,000-4,500 TEN

An Edwardian amethyst, seed pearl and 15ct gold double drop pendant and chain, in original box.

amethyst ½in (1.5cm) long

£900-1,100 PW

An Edwardian 6.5ct diamond set pendant.

1¾in (4.5cm) long ⅜oz

£2,500-3,000 GWA

An Edwardian tourmaline, peridot and pearl-set pendant, on gold and platinum chain.

£1,300-1,600 LC

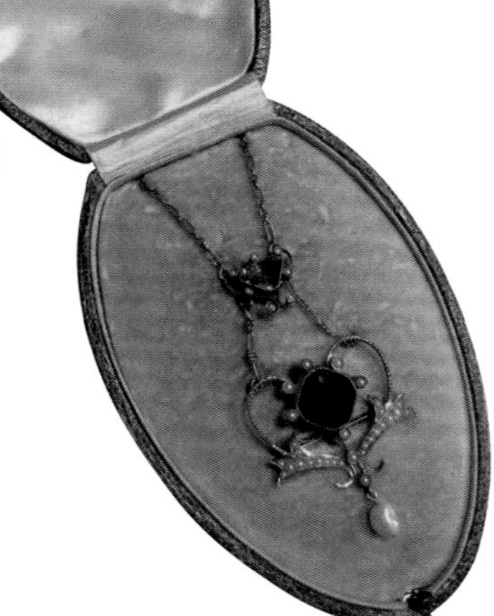

An Edwardian Suffragette peridot, amethyst and pearl necklace, in original case, some wear to case.

Emmeline Pethick-Lawrence, co-editor of 'Votes for Women', suggested a colour code in 1908 whereby the WSPU (Women's Social and Political Union) and associated Suffragettes could show their allegiance with flags, banners and rosettes, or by wearing clothes, tri-coloured ribbons or jewellery. The chosen colours were purple (for dignity), white (for purity) and green (for the fresh shoots of hope).

chain 17¼in (44cm) long

£1,200-1,600 CHEF

An Edwardian 12ct gold, turquoise and diamond pendant, surface scratches.

pendant 2½in (6.5cm) high ¼oz

£420-480 FELL

A gold and platinum 'cat and mouse' ring, by Tiffany & Co., with three mice, one in rose gold, each with platinum tail, signed in engraved capitals 'TIFFANY & CO'.

c1910 *size L½*

£7,000-8,000 ROS

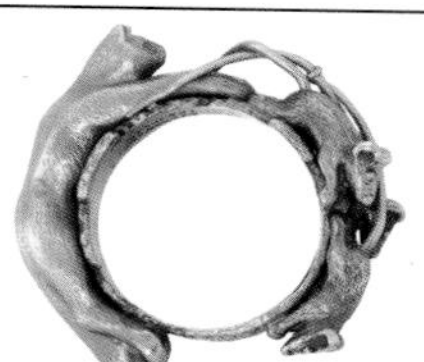

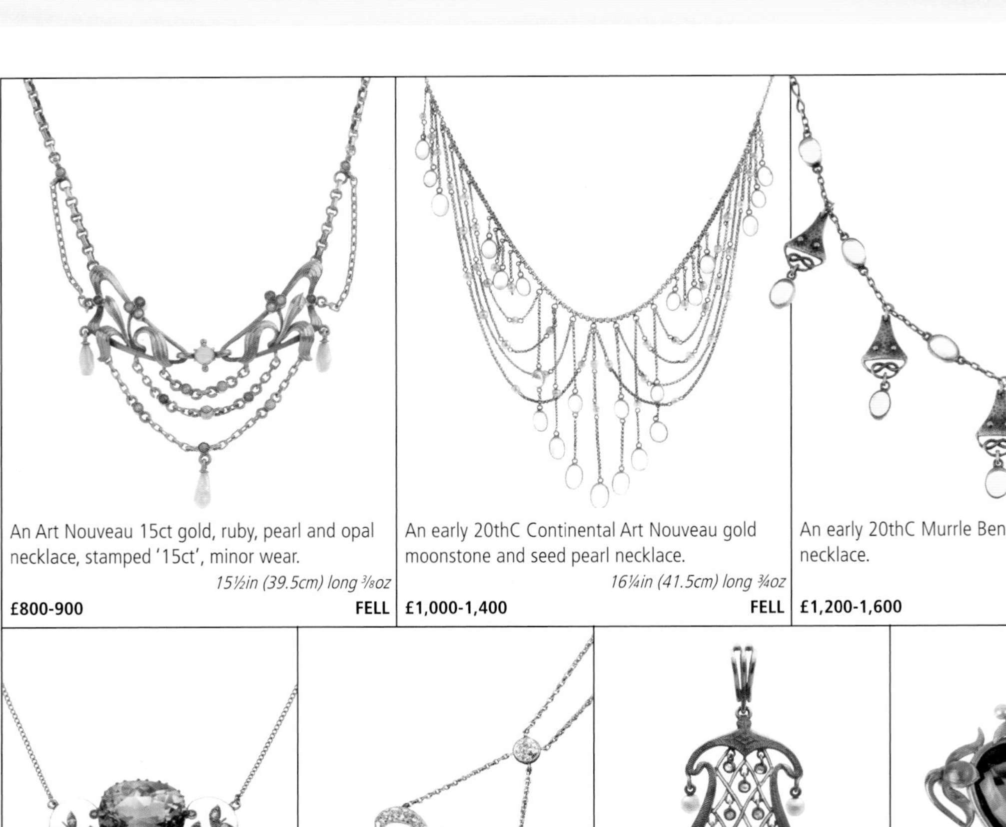

An Art Nouveau 15ct gold, ruby, pearl and opal necklace, stamped '15ct', minor wear.
15½in (39.5cm) long 3/8oz
£800-900 **FELL**

An early 20thC Continental Art Nouveau gold moonstone and seed pearl necklace.
16¼in (41.5cm) long ¾oz
£1,000-1,400 **FELL**

An early 20thC Murrle Bennett & Co. silver opal necklace.
17¾in (45cm) long ¼oz
£1,200-1,600 **FELL**

A Russian Art Nouveau amethyst and demantoid garnet pendant necklace, stamped '56 zolotnik gold' (14ct gold) with a Kazan regional mark.
pendant 2¼in (5.5cm) high ½oz
£1,400-2,000 **TEN**

An Art Nouveau garnet and diamond pendant, in platinum and gold.
pendant 1½in (4cm) long
£1,500-2,000 **WW**

An Art Nouveau enamel, diamond and pearl pendant, by Child & Child.
2¾in (7cm) high
£1,500-2,000 **TEN**

An Art Nouveau Krementz amethyst, diamond, freshwater pearl, enamel and 14ct yellow-gold pendant-brooch, marked, Newark, NJ.
1½in (4cm) high 3/8oz
£1,000-1,400 **CLAR**

A gold, diamond and red gem-set and plique-à-jour enamelled brooch.
2in (5cm) wide 3/8oz
£650-750 **BELL**

A late 19thC Art Nouveau plique-à-jour diamond, enamel, pearl and yellow-gold pendant brooch, some losses to enamel.
2½in (6.5cm) long
£1,800-2,200 **PW**

An Art Nouveau diamond scroll brooch, in silver on gold.
1½in (4cm) wide
£1,300-1,800 **WW**

A Riker Brothers Art Nouveau yellow gold bangle bracelet, with embossed pattern of dragons and Celtic scroll, with Riker cipher.
c1912 *7½in (19cm) diam 5/8oz*
£3,000-3,500 **DRA**

An Arts and Crafts white metal, moonstone and cabochon brooch, attributed to Sibyl Dunlop.
c1925 *2in (5cm) wide*
£400-500 L&T

An Arts and Crafts sterling silver and enamel pendant, by James Fenton, Birmingham, some chips.
1908 *1½in (4cm) long*
£300-400 SWO

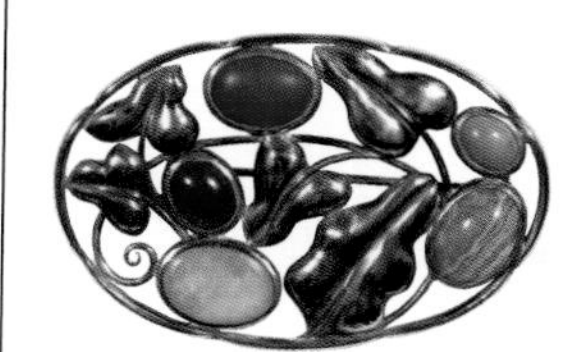

A Wiener Werkstätte silver and opal brooch, designed by Josef Hoffmann, marked 'JH' and 'WW'.

Wiener Werkstätte was an artistic community and organisation established by Koloman Moser and Josef Hoffmann in Vienna in 1903. It had much in common with the English Arts and Crafts movement.
1905-10 *2½in (6.5cm) wide*
£15,000-20,000 QU

A cabochon, sapphire, enamel and gem-set pendant, by H.G. Murphy, in pierced yellow gold setting, on a gold chain, in original box.

This pendant sold for a record price for the maker.
pendant 1½in (4cm) wide
£70,000-80,000 WW

An Arts and Crafts Murrle Bennett & Co. 'Tree of Life' silver and enamel pendant, on silver link chain, stamped 'MB' and '950'.
1¼in (3cm) wide
£700-800 DUK

An Arts and Crafts Murrle Bennett & Co. silver and enamel pendant, stamped 'MB' and '950'.
1½in (3.5cm) wide
£500-600 DUK

An Arts and Crafts silver, gold and opal necklace, attributed to Dorrie Nossiter, some surface wear, later brooch fittings.

Similarly designed pieces have also been attributed to Sybil Dunlop.
pendant 2¼in (6cm) high ½oz
£1,500-2,000 FELL

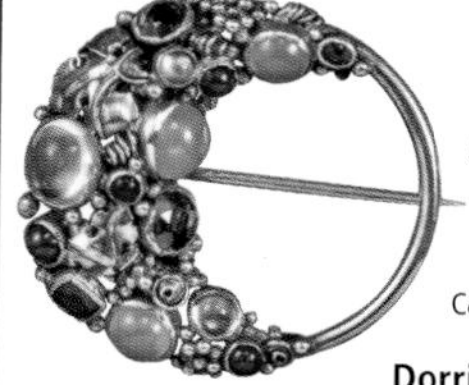

An Arts and Crafts gem-set silver brooch, attributed to Dorrie Nossiter, set with moonstone, lapis lazuli, chalcedony cabochons and circular-cut garnets.

Dorrie Nossiter (1893-1977) trained at the School of Art in Birmingham and went on to produce jewellery. Her work is rarely signed and is easily confused with that of her friend Sibyl Dunlop, who worked in a similar style.
1½in (3.5cm) long
£1,200-1,600 WW

CLOSER LOOK – PHOEBE ANNA TRAQUAIR BROOCH

This brooch is attributed to illustrator, painter and embroiderer Phoebe Anna Traquair (1852-1936), the first woman to be elected to the Royal Scottish Academy.

It depicts a slumbering figure attended by two angels, one playing an instrument.

It has a bead and cord border mount.

The enamel bears similarities to Traquair's enamel panel, 'The Dream' from 1909, and the frame bears similarities to her 'The Awakening' pendant from 1903.

An Arts and Crafts enamel and silver brooch, attributed to Phoebe Anna Traquair.
c1909 *2in (5cm) wide*
£6,500-7,000 GTH

A silver and chrysoprase pendant necklace, attributed to Omar Ramsden.
2¾in (7cm) long
£1,000-1,400 WW

A cloisonné enamel pendant necklace, by Harold Stabler.
1¾in (4.5cm) high
£850-950 WW

A gem-set Cartier 'Fruit Bowl' brooch, with black onyx, calibré-cut emeralds, sapphires and a ruby, inventory number to reverse '3577', in fitted case.

£18,000-22,000 **WW**

An Art Deco emerald and 3.6ct diamond bar brooch, some gaps between diamonds and settings.

3¼in (8cm) long ⅜oz

£2,000-2,500 **TEN**

An Art Deco jade and 0.15ct diamond brooch, one jade loose.

2¼in (5.5cm) long ¼oz

£900-1,200 **TEN**

An Art Deco platinum sapphire and diamond bow brooch.

2¾in (7cm) wide

£3,500-4,000 **FLD**

An Art Deco onyx and diamond bow brooch, with central old brilliant cut 0.4ct diamond.

c1920 *2in (5cm) long*

£350-450 **DN**

An Art Deco carved jadeite and brilliant cut diamond panel brooch, with platinum brooch fittings.

2¼in (5.5cm) long

£1,500-2,000 **PW**

An Art Deco diamond brooch.

2in (5cm) long

£1,800-2,200 **CHOR**

An Art Deco 3.25ct diamond double-clip brooch, set with round brilliant cut, eight-cut and baguette cut diamonds, one pin deficient.

2in (5cm) wide ½oz

£1,800-2,200 **TEN**

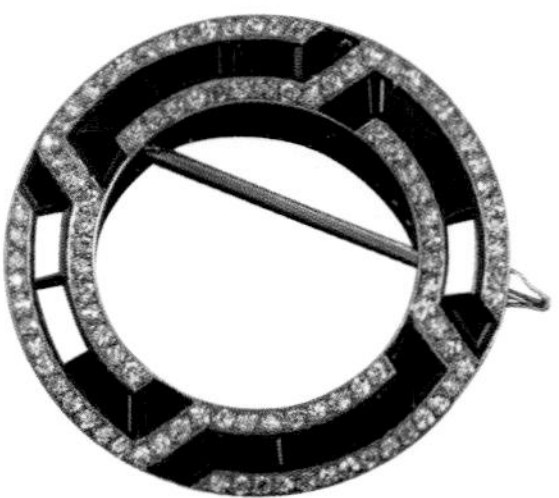

A French Art Deco brooch, set with carved black onyx and circular cut diamonds in white gold, French control marks, in fitted Bolin box.

1½in (4cm) wide

£4,000-4,500 **WW**

An Art Deco cultured pearl and diamond flowerhead cluster pendant/brooch, the platinum openwork setting with 114 round old-cut diamonds.

1½in (4cm) diam

£2,500-3,000 **HAN**

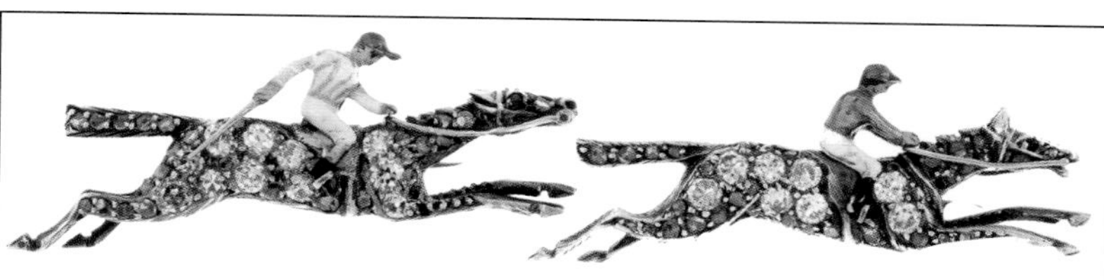

A pair of 1930s diamond and enamel horse and jockey brooches, depicting riders at the 1939 Northolt races, two diamonds deficient, with fitted case.

1½in (4cm) long ¼oz

£4,000-5,000 **FELL**

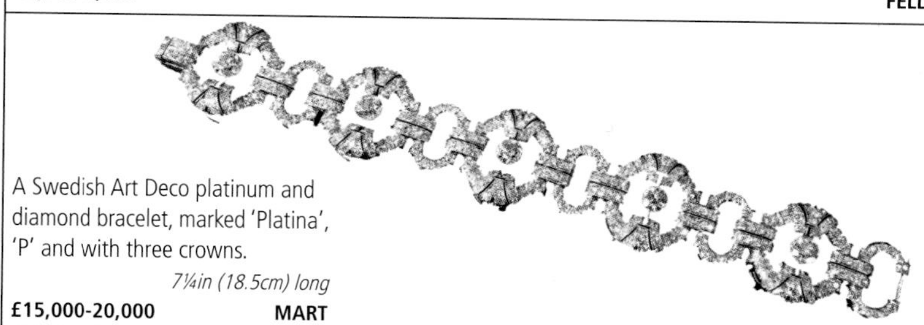

A Swedish Art Deco platinum and diamond bracelet, marked 'Platina', 'P' and with three crowns.

7¼in (18.5cm) long

£15,000-20,000 **MART**

An Art Deco 14ct yellow-gold, citrine and polychrome enamel lavalier necklace, stamped '14K'.

A lavalier is the type of pendant popularised in the late 17thC by the Duchess de la Valliere, a mistress of King Louis the XIV of France.

pendant ¾in (2cm) high 1oz

£1,800-2,200 **LHA**

An emerald, sapphire, ruby and 2.45ct diamond bracelet, signed twice 'Cartier London', some replacements.

6¾in (17cm) long 1⅜oz

£170,000-200,000 **TEN**

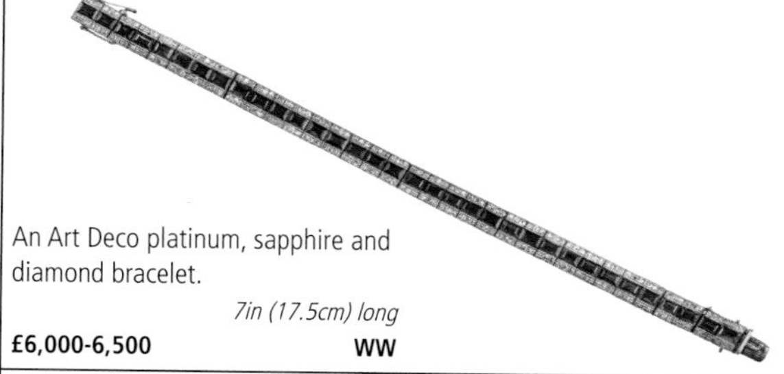

An Art Deco platinum, sapphire and diamond bracelet.

7in (17.5cm) long

£6,000-6,500 **WW**

A pair of diamond and sapphire scroll earrings, by Rubel Frères, French platinum control marks.

John Rubel and his brother Robert opened a workshop on Rue Vivienne in Paris in 1915. Their jewellery was soon known for its extremely high quality. The firm worked for several of the large jewellery houses, including Van Cleef & Arpels. On the outbreak of war in 1939, the brothers moved to New York.

c1935 *1½in (4cm) high 1oz*

£35,000-40,000 **WW**

A pair of Art Deco Cartier 3.2ct diamond and platinum ear clips, signed, in a Cartier case.

c1930 *1in (2.5cm) high*

£33,000-38,000 **BATE**

An Art Deco diamond solitaire platinum ring, some wear.

size N

£7,500-8,500 **HAN**

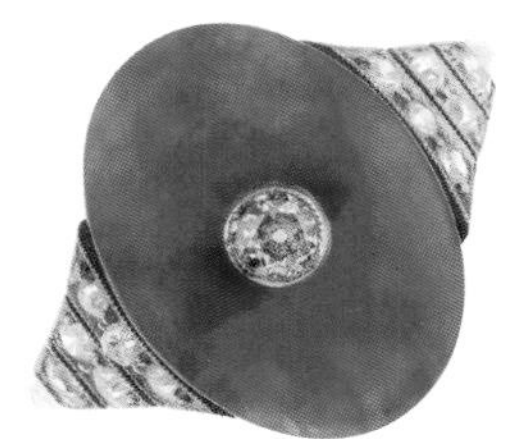

An Art Deco jade and 0.3ct diamond ring, stamped 'Pt', some replacement gems.

size N½ ⅛oz

£3,000-3,500 **FELL**

An Art Deco platinum and gold lapis lazuli Buddha and diamond set jabot pin, by La Cloche Frères.

2¼in (6cm) long

£2,800-3,200 **HAN**

A Chanel vintage gold-tone 'Matelassé' cuff bangle, signed, some hairlines and scratches.
c1981-85 *2¼in (6cm) diam*
£350-400 **FELL**

A Georg Jensen silver brooch, designed by Arno Malinowski, model no.318, stamped 'STERLING', 'DENMARK', '318', hallmarked 'GJLD', import mark for London, surface wear.
1964 *1½in (4cm) square ¾oz*
£800-900 **TEN**

A coral ring, by Gerda Flöckinger, set in yellow precious metal in the form of a crown, marked 'G F'.

Gerda Flöckinger is a pre-eminent mid-20thC jeweller. She was born in Austria in 1927 and moved to England as a child. She started her jewellery business in 1956 and, in 1971, became the first contemporary jeweller to have a solo exhibition at the V&A.

size L-M
£2,000-2,500 **CHEF**

A silver Georg Jensen 'Continuity' ring, designed by Vivianna Torun, model no.443, stamped '925S', '443', 'Torun', hallmarked 'GJLD', import mark for London, surface wear.
1969 *size O 1in (2.5cm) wide ¼oz*
£250-350 **TEN**

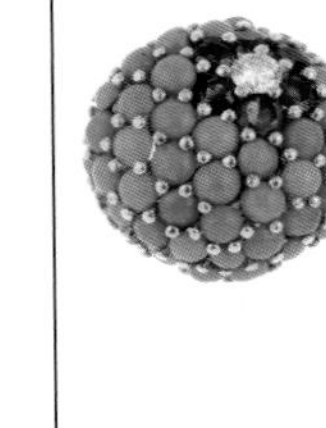

A pair of 1960s Kutchinsky 18ct gold 0.45ct diamond and turquoise earrings, signed, hallmarks for London, some wear.
1965 *¾in (2cm) diam ⅝oz*
£2,500-3,000 **FELL**

A 1950s Tiffany & Co. 14ct yellow gold, moonstone, ruby and diamond flower pin, in original box.
3in (7.5cm) long ⅝oz
£1,500-2,000 **POOK**

A 1970s Tiffany & Co. diamond, ruby, emerald and sapphire set clip, signed 'Tiffany & Co.', surface scratches, one gem deficient.
3in (7.5cm) long 1oz
£4,500-5,000 **FELL**

A mid-20thC 22-25ct diamond bracelet, French assay marks, surface scratches.
7¼in (18.5cm) long 2⅜oz
£16,000-20,000 **FELL**

A mid-20thC yellow gold, sapphire and diamond S-scroll brooch.
1½in (4cm) long
£600-700 **MART**

A 1950s 10ct diamond and 14ct white gold floral brooch, Austrian marks.
2¾in (7cm) high ½oz
£2,800-3,200 **ECGW**

An early 1970s 14ct gold retro tanzanite ring, with bark textured design in the style of Andrew Grima.

Tanzanite was discovered as a new gem in 1967.

size M ½oz
£1,400-1,800 **GWA**

A Jakob Bengal chrome-plated metal and red plastic necklace.
1932 *17in (43cm) long*
£450-550 **GRV**

A pair of 1960s Marcel Boucher gold-plated metal and enamel cuff bracelets.
2¼in (6cm) diam
£250-350 **GRV**

A 1980s Chanel gold-plated metal necklace.
16½in (42cm) long
£750-850 **GRV**

A pair of 1980s Chanel gold-plated metal earrings.
2¾in (7cm) long
£400-500 **GRV**

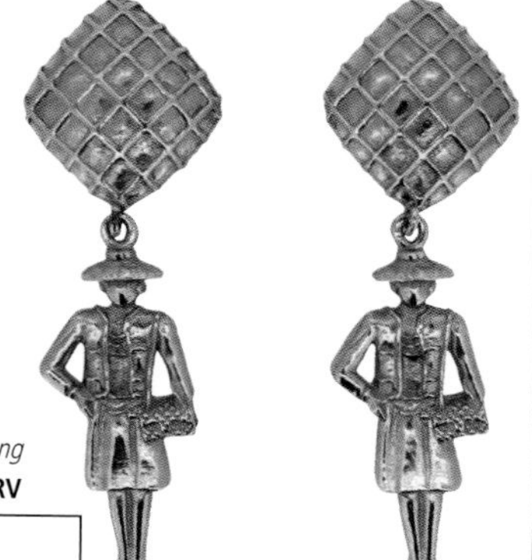

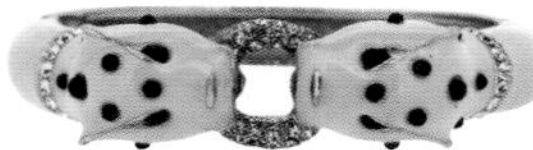

A 1970s Ciner gold-plated metal, rhinestone, glass and cream enamel bangle.
2¼in (6cm) diam
£200-250 **GRV**

A 1960s pair of Coppola e Toppo gold-tone metal and rhinestone earrings.
1½in (3.5cm) diam
£400-500 **GRV**

A 1950s Christian Dior gold vermeil plated and multicoloured rhinestone necklace, brooch and earrings set, designed by Mitchel Maer.
necklace 16½in (42cm) long
£1,000-1,500 **GRV**

A pair of Christian Dior rhodium-plated metal and rhinestone earrings.
1968 *1¾in (4.5cm) long*
£350-450 **GRV**

A 1930s Theodor Fahrner silver-gilt bracelet.
7½in (19cm) long
£550-650 **GRV**

A pair of 1960s Gripoix turquoise poured glass, rhinestone and gold-plated metal earrings.
1½in (4cm) diam
£550-600 **GRV**

A pair of 1950s Miriam Haskell gilt-metal, pink glass, faux pearl and rhinestone earrings.
2½in (6.5cm) long
£300-400 **GRV**

A 1960s Jomaz emerald green glass and rhinestone, rhodium-plated bracelet.
7¾in (19.5cm) long
£350-450 **GRV**

ESSENTIAL REFERENCE – JOSEFF OF HOLLYWOOD

Eugene Joseff (1905-48) was a prominent 1930s costume jewellery designer and the founder of Joseph of Hollywood.

- **He began his career in an advertising agency in Chicago, before moving to Los Angeles to train as a jewellery designer.**
- **From 1931, he made costume jewellery pieces for Hollywood films, renting his work to the studios to allow for potential re-hire. He worked in a huge range of styles, creating pieces for films such as 'The Wizard of Oz', 'Gone with the Wind' and 'Casablanca'.**
- **In 1935 he founded Joseff of Hollywood and opened a shop, Sunset Jewelry, where he sold replicas of cinema originals.**
- **His pieces were often large, to ensure they could be seen on screen. Another key feature was the use of semi-matt 'Russian gold' plating, which he developed to prevent reflections from studio lighting.**
- **Eugene Joseff died in a plane crash in 1948. The company was continued by his widow and is still family-run today.**

A 1940s Joseff of Hollywood Pinwheel necklace, bracelet and earring set, in 'Russian gold', necklace and bracelet signed 'Joseff Hollywood', earrings signed 'Joseff'.
necklace 10¾in (27.5cm) long fastened
£500-600 **PC**

A 1940s Joseff of Hollywood Egyptian Revival Scarab necklace, with three turquoise scarabs set on 'Russian gold' mounts and chain, signed 'Joseff Hollywood'.
9¾in (25cm) long
£550-650 **PC**

A 1950s Joseff of Hollywood 'Russian Gold Plate' necklace.
17¾in (45cm) long
£450-550 **GRV**

A 1950s Joseff of Hollywood 'Russian Gold Plate' and rhinestone bangle.
2¾in (7cm) diam
£400-500 **GRV**

A Knoll and Pregizer sterling silver, black enamel and rhinestone brooch.
2in (5cm) long
£500-600 **GRV**

A 1950s Matisse copper and enamel necklace and earrings set.
necklace 17¾in (45cm) long
£150-200 **GRV**

A 1920s Bohemian Egyptian Revival necklace, possibly by Max Neiger, with Jablonec bohemian green and red glass, unsigned.
8½in (21.5cm) long fastened
£150-200 **PC**

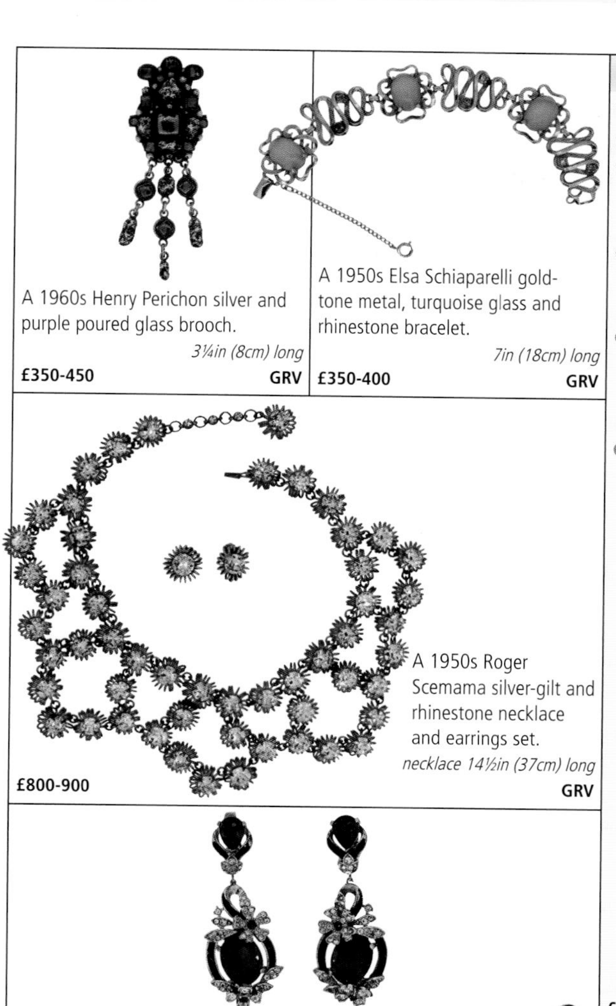

A 1960s Henry Perichon silver and purple poured glass brooch.

3¼in (8cm) long

£350-450 **GRV**

A 1950s Elsa Schiaparelli gold-tone metal, turquoise glass and rhinestone bracelet.

7in (18cm) long

£350-400 **GRV**

A 1950s Roger Scemama silver-gilt and rhinestone necklace and earrings set.

necklace 14½in (37cm) long

£800-900 **GRV**

A 1940s Trifari gold vermeil, sapphire rhinestone and enamel bracelet and earrings set.

bracelet 6¼in (16cm) long

£300-400 **GRV**

ESSENTIAL REFERENCE – TRIFARI

Trifari is probably the best-known costume jewellery manufacturer.

- **It was founded in New York in 1912 by Italian Gustavo Trifari (1883-1952), who was soon joined by Leo Krussman and Karl Fishel.**
- **Trifari produced a range of high-quality costume jewellery, supplying pieces to various Hollywood and Broadway productions.**
- **After Alfred Phillipe joined as head designer in 1930, it became the USA's second largest costume jewellery firm. Phillipe's designs were very popular in the 1930s-50s, especially his 'Crown' pins and 'Jelly Bellies'.**
- **Trifari was sold to Hallmark Jewelry Co. in 1975 and to Liz Claiborne, Inc. in 2000.**

A 1940s Trifari gold vermeil and rhinestone necklace.

15¾in (40cm) long

£350-400 **GRV**

A figural Peacock Trifari Moghul 'Jewels of India' brooch, designed by Alfred Philippe, with green melon carved 'Jello Mold' stone, signed crown 'Trifari Pat, Pend'.

designed 1949 *2in (5cm) long*

£300-400 **PC**

An early 1950s Trifari turquoise moulded glass necklace, in the shape of a chrysanthemum, signed 'Trifari'.

9½in (24cm) long

£250-300 **PC**

An early 1950s Trifari necklace and bracelet, signed 'Trifari Pat, Pend'.

necklace 8¾in (22cm) long

£250-350 **PC**

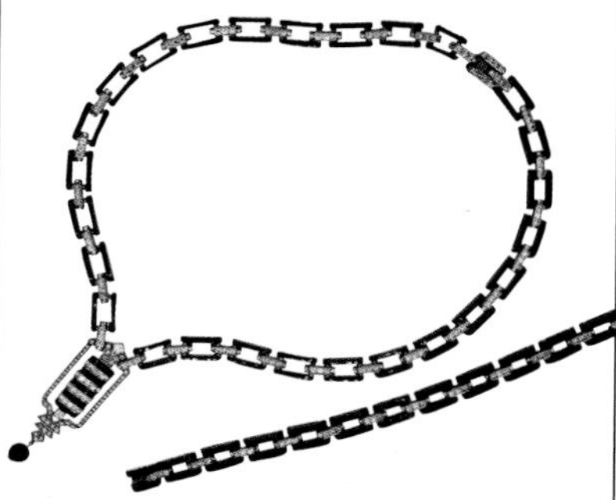

A 1930s German-patented (DRGM) black Bakelite, rhinestone and silver tone metal necklace and bracelet.

necklace 16¼in (41cm) long

£600-700 **GRV**

A mid-18thC and later carved giltwood chimney piece, in the manner of Matthias Locke, with statuary marble slips and plinths, jambs restored.

69in (175cm) wide

£12,000-15,000 **CHEF**

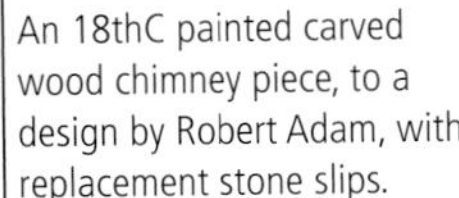

An 18thC painted carved wood chimney piece, to a design by Robert Adam, with replacement stone slips.

This chimney piece is comparable in design and size to two drawings of chimney pieces executed by Robert Adam for the Adelphi buildings in London, built 1768-72 and demolished in the early 1930s.

84½in (214.5cm) wide

£5,500-6,500 **CHEF**

A George III pine and gesso decorated chimney piece, with acanthus detail, the main frieze centred by a dancing putti.

c1790 *58¾in (149cm) high*

£900-1,200 **DN**

A late 18thC marble statuary chimney piece, the frieze depicting the Vestal Virgins, some losses.

The Vestal Virgins in ancient Rome were priestesses of Vesta, Goddess of the Hearth.

63¾in (162cm) wide

£20,000-25,000 **CHEF**

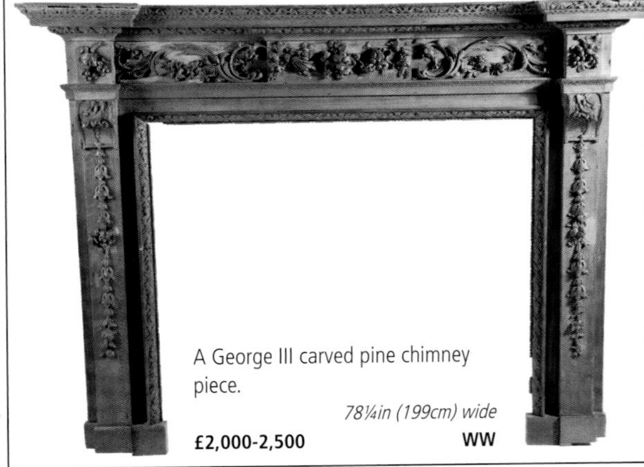

A George III carved pine chimney piece.

78¼in (199cm) wide

£2,000-2,500 **WW**

A George III carved and giltwood chimney piece, possibly by Thomas Johnson, with statuary marble slips.

64in (162.5cm) wide

£12,000-15,000 **CHEF**

A 19thC George II-style pine and gesso fire surround.

76¾in (195cm) wide

£1,800-2,200 **L&T**

A 19thC oak and burr oak fire surround, in the Palladian style.

90½in (230cm) wide

£900-1,200 **L&T**

A northern French Henri IV cast iron fireback, cast with Saint Hubertus, cast with the legend, 'Frilo.c. de Witri', dated.

Saint Hubertus or Hubert (c656-727) became Bishop of Liège in 708 AD. He was widely venerated during the Middle Ages, being patron saint of hunters, mathematicians, opticians and metalworkers, and was sometimes known as the Apostle of the Ardennes.

1570 *30¼in (77cm) wide*

£4,000-5,000 **DN**

An 18thC cast iron and steel serpentine fire grate, in the manner of Robert Adam.

30¾in (78cm) wide

£2,000-2,500 **CHEF**

A Regency cast iron fire grate, in the manner of George Bullock (1777-1818).

38¼in (97cm) wide

£1,500-2,000 **CHEF**

An early 19thC cast iron Sarcophagus fire grate, in the manner of George Bullock.

33in (84cm) wide

£2,500-3,000 **CHEF**

A Gothic Revival John Hardman & Co. wrought and cast iron fire basket and dogs, by A.W.N. Pugin (1812-52).

c1850 *51½in (131cm) wide*

£3,000-4,000 **L&T**

A 19thC cast iron fire grate, by Thomas Elsleyin, after a design by Thomas Chippendale.

35in (89cm) wide

£3,500-4,000 **CHEF**

A George III pierced steel fender.

48in (122cm) wide

£550-650 **SWO**

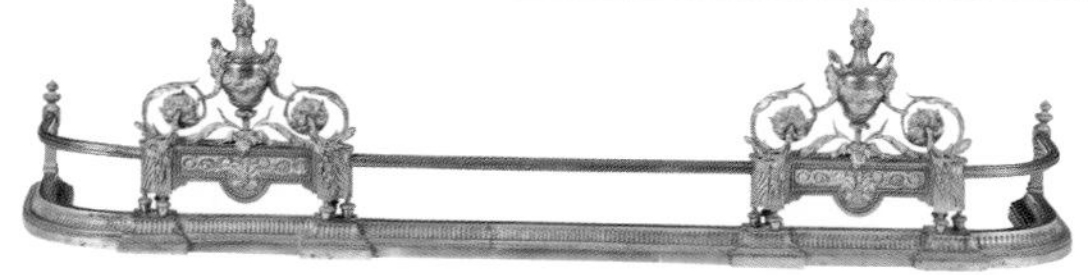

A Regency gilt-brass fender.

63¾in (162cm) wide

£1,500-2,000 **L&T**

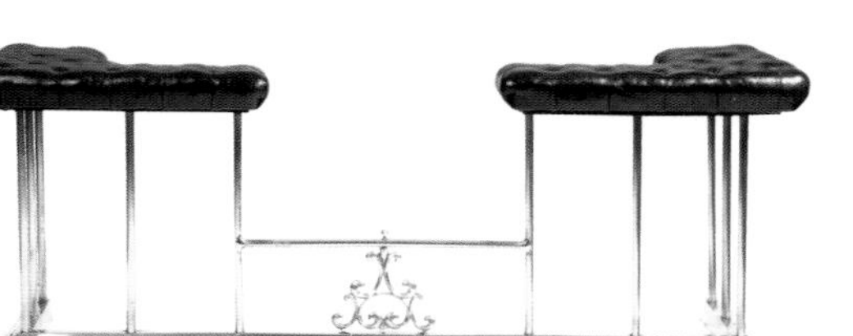

A late Victorian brass club fender.

54¾in (139cm) wide

£1,800-2,200 **WW**

A late 19thC to early 20thC brass fender, in late 18thC French taste, some wear, one sphinx wing restored.

63¾in (162cm) wide

£2,500-3,000 **DN**

A leather fire bucket, inscribed 'J. Fogg/No 3.', minor wear to paint, dated.

1823 *11in (28cm) high*

£2,000-2,500 **WHIT**

A painted leather fire bucket, by John Fenno, Boston, Massachusetts, inscribed 'NOBIS VICINISQUE/ JOHN HARBACH,' maker's mark 'I.FENNO', some scratches, dated.

1790 *12½in (32cm) high*

£2,200-2,800 **SK**

A 19thC navette-shaped mahogany and brass-mounted peat bucket.

14½in (37cm) high

£600-700 **WW**

A Victorian painted leather fire bucket, with the Royal coat of arms, with a later leather handle.

11½in (29cm) diam

£450-550 **L&T**

A pair of Philadelphia Chippendale brass andirons.

c1780 *19½in (49.5cm) high*

£8,000-9,000 **POOK**

A pair of 19thC Louis XV-style gilt and patinated bronze chenets.

21½in (54.5cm) high

£900-1,000 **WW**

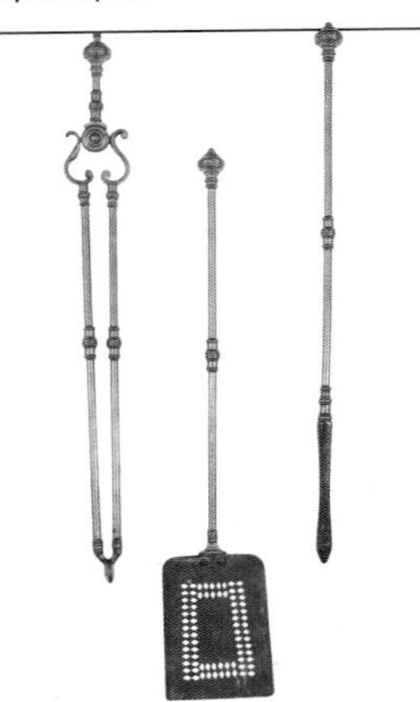

A set of early 19thC Georgian brass fire tools.

tongs 30¾in (78cm) long

£300-400 **L&T**

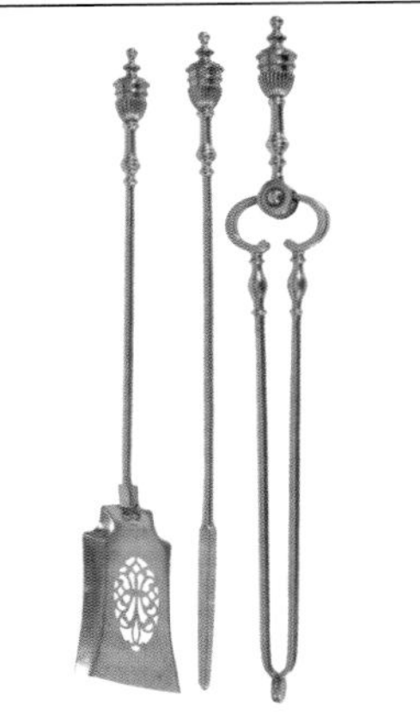

A set of early 19thC English steel fire irons, some wear.

28in (71cm) long

£1,500-2,000 **DN**

An 18thC carved and painted fire screen, designed as an Elizabethan woman, in-painting in breaks at the arm.

47in (119.5cm) high

£3,000-3,500 **SK**

A Victorian Coalbrookdale-type cast iron garden seat, with wooden slatted seat.

67¾in (172cm) long

£2,200-2,800 **BE**

A Victorian painted cast iron garden seat, with wooden splats.

68in (172.5cm) long

£1,200-1,600 **JN**

A Victorian painted cast iron 'oak, twigg and serpent' garden bench.

52in (132cm) long

£1,000-1,500 **L&T**

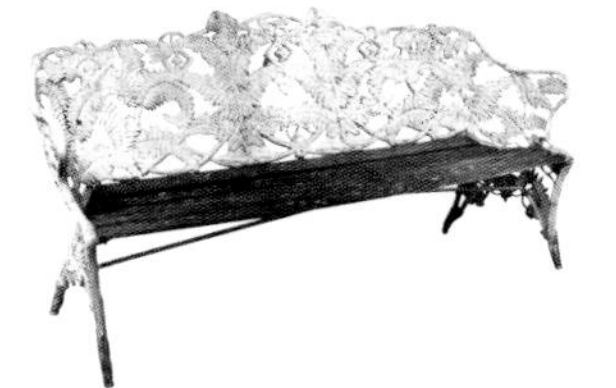

A Victorian Coalbrookdale fern-pattern garden bench.

71¾in (182cm) wide

£800-900 **CHEF**

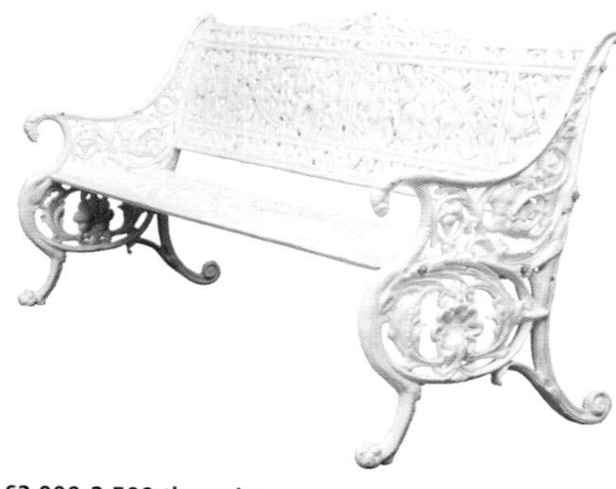

One of a pair of Coalbrookdale-style cast iron and pierced garden benches.

67in (170cm) wide

£2,000-2,500 the pair **MEA**

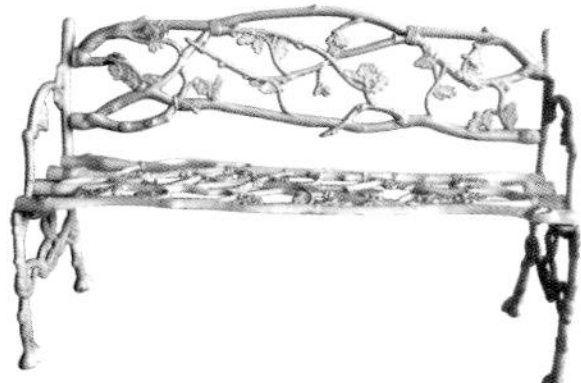

A 19thC botanical pattern rustic garden bench.

50in (127cm) wide

£1,100-1,400 **PW**

A late 19thC French cast iron garden seat, probably Val D'Osne foundry, with Gothic Revival decoration.

The design for this bench is illustrated in the 1858 Barbezat & Cie's Founderies du Val d'Osne catalogue, under 'Bancs de Jardin', plate 251. However, this pattern is also included in other publications as being of slightly earlier, English design; Himmelheber has it as being a production of James Yates at his Effingham Works in Rotherham, c1840. The later 19thC dating of this bench would suggest that the French foundry house is a more likely candidate.

48½in (123cm) wide

£5,000-6,000 **DN**

A late 19thC cast iron 'oak and ivy' pattern garden seat, attributed to Coalbrookdale, with slatted wood seat.

The original design, no.119253, was registered and patented by the Coalbrookdale Iron Foundry at the Public Record office on 8 March 1859, and is seat no.30 in their 1875 Castings Catalogue. It was designed by the sculptor John Bell, one of Coalbrookdale's principal designers.

59¾in (152cm) wide

£3,000-4,000 **DN**

A Victorian Coalbrookdale-type cast iron garden armchair, decorated with Gothic designs, with wooden slatted seat.

£250-300 **BE**

A pair of 19thC Scottish Garnkirk 'fireclay' urns on stands, one with script date '12/10/41'.

35½in (90cm) high

£1,500-2,000 **L&T**

A late 19thC pair of Scottish Garnkirk 'fireclay' garden urns and pedestals, stamped 'GARNKIRK'.

33¾in (86cm) high

£2,000-2,500 **L&T**

A pair of 20thC sculpted limestone garden urns, some scuffs.

48¾in (124cm) high

£20,000-25,000 **DN**

A pair of 20thC carved limestone garden urns.

54¼in (138cm) high

£7,500-8,500 **DN**

A pedestal horse trough, made to imitate white marble, some wear.

55in (139.5cm) long

£600-700 **JN**

A pair of lead garden urns, with cast cherub masks.

19in (48cm) high

£1,300-1,800 **BE**

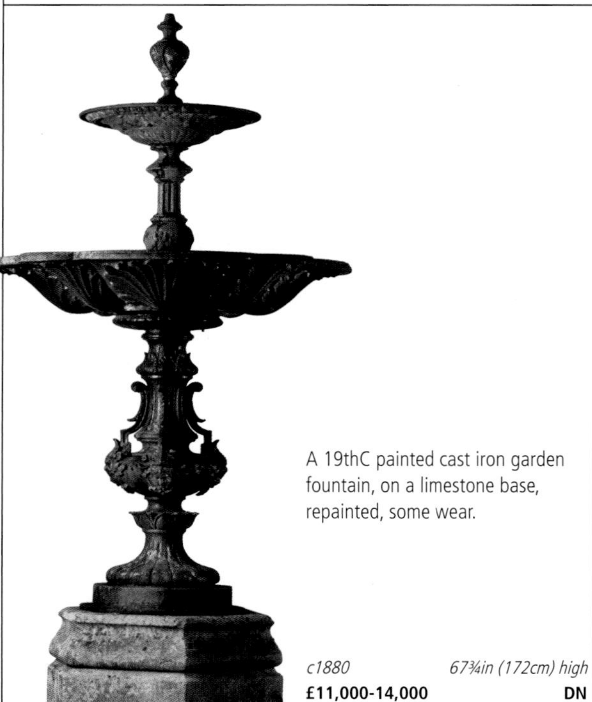

A 19thC painted cast iron garden fountain, on a limestone base, repainted, some wear.

c1880 *67¾in (172cm) high*

£11,000-14,000 **DN**

A bronze fountain of a cherub, seated on a dolphin playing a flute, signed 'A Rhind', dated.

The Rhinds were an important 19thC family of sculptors from Edinburgh, notably John, William Birnie and J Massey. A. Rhind is unrecorded, but believed to be a member of the family.

1926 *35in (89cm) high*

£2,500-3,000 **CHEF**

An early 20thC painted metal and carved limestone mounted armillary sphere, with internal copper register of Roman numerals, repainted, some wear, plinth associated.

66¼in (168cm) high

£3,200-3,800 **DN**

A late 17thC to early 18thC carved marble bust of a Classical lady, possibly Diana.

32¼in (82cm) high

£2,000-3,000 **WW**

Judith Picks

Robert of Baston was a Carmelite monk known for his verses and songs. It is said that he was taken by the Kings Edward I and Edward II on their military campaigns to Scotland, where he was captured by Robert the Bruce and forced to write and sing verses about the defeat of his own countrymen in return for his release. This is the event that is depicted in this sculpture.

The sculptor, Robert Forrest (1789-1852), was a successful stonemason from Carluke, Lanarkshire. His most famous work is the statue of Lord Melville that tops the column in St Andrew Square, Edinburgh. He often sculpted historical and literary figures.

A carved sandstone group, 'King Robert the Bruce and the Monk of Baston', by Robert Forrest of Carluke (1789-1852).

c1830 *118in (300cm) wide*

£8,500-9,500 **L&T**

A mid-19thC Scottish fireclay figure of Fidelity, by Grangemouth Coal Co., stamped.

The Grangemouth Coal Company was established in 1839 and by the mid-century they were operating the Grangemouth Brickworks, manufacturing fireclay bricks and ornamental pottery. They displayed at the Great Exhibition in 1851 and it is believed this model of 'Fidelity' was shown there. The company ceased trading in 1912.

49¼in (125cm) high

£4,000-5,000 **L&T**

A 19thC Scottish carved marble Classical figure, by Lawrence Macdonald (1799-1878), signed.

46¾in (119cm) high

£15,000-20,000 **HANN**

A life-size statue of Hebe.

84in (213.5cm) high

£1,000-1,500 **JN**

A marble figural group of 'The Three Graces'.

90½in (230cm) high

£4,000-4,500 **SWO**

A rare set of four early 20thC Bromsgrove Guild lead figures of 'The Seasons', modelled by Walter Gilbert, Winter with moulded mark.

The Bromsgrove Guild of Applied Arts was established in 1884 by Walter Gilbert, initially producing decorative ironwork but later producing bronze and lead work as well as wood and stone carvings. By 1908 they had established a retail outlet in Victoria Street, London as a result of their most famous commission, the iron and bronze gates outside Buckingham Palace.

42½in (108cm) high

£30,000-35,000 **TEN**

A bronzed metal garden fountain, modelled as a cherub supporting a shell, some dirt.

42¼in (107cm) high

£450-550 **CHOR**

A bronzed resin figure of Peter Pan, after the model in Kensington Gardens by George Frampton, incised 'EM'.

50½in (128cm) high

£2,000-2,500 **HALL**

A pair of 17thC to 18thC Scottish carved limestone lions.

37½in (95cm) high

£3,000-4,000 **L&T**

A pair of 19thC Scottish fire clay lions, by Brown's of Ferguslie Park, stamped 'R. Brown & Son/Ferguslie/Paisley'.

41¾in (106cm) long

£1,500-2,000 **L&T**

A 19thC stone figure of a lion.

41¼in (105cm) high

£3,000-4,000 **L&T**

A pair of early 20thC composition stone lion figures.

24in (61cm) wide

£500-600 **L&T**

A pair of 19thC Scottish cast iron lions, Carron Foundry, Falkirk.

44in (112cm) long

£3,000-4,000 **L&T**

A pair of 20thC sculpted limestone lions, in the manner of Antonio Canova (Venetian, 1757-1822).

The original lions upon which these are based were sculpted in marble by Canova in 1792 for the tomb of Pope Clement XIII in St Peter's in Rome. The lions were hugely admired, and therefore copied from the start. One well-known pair which was cast in bronze from Canova's original works in 1860 now adorns the front of the Corcoran Gallery of Art in Washington, D.C.

67¼in (171cm) long

£35,000-40,000 **DN**

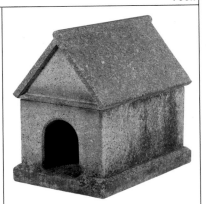

A pair of Philadelphia wood and perot cast iron Newfoundland dog garden figures.

These are the only pair known to exist and retain an excellent painted surface.

c1857-78 *65in (165cm) long*

£45,000-50,000 **POOK**

A pair of early 20thC stone figures of dogs, after a model by Henri Alfred Marie Jacquemart.

60¼in (153cm) high

£4,000-5,000 **L&T**

A late 19thC Continental stone composition model of an owl.

59in (150cm) high

£6,500-7,000 **DN**

A Victorian granite dog kennel.

26in (66cm) wide

£1,500-2,000 **L&T**

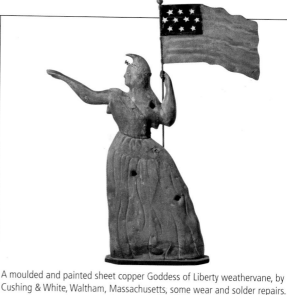

A 19thC Harris & Co. swell-bodied copper weathervane, of a Native American Indian, depicting Massasoit the great Wampanoag chief, retaining old yellow painted and verdigris surface.

35in (89cm) high

£18,000-22,000 **POOK**

A moulded and painted sheet copper Goddess of Liberty weathervane, by Cushing & White, Waltham, Massachusetts, some wear and solder repairs.

c1865-75 *38½in (98cm) high*

£20,000-25,000 **SK**

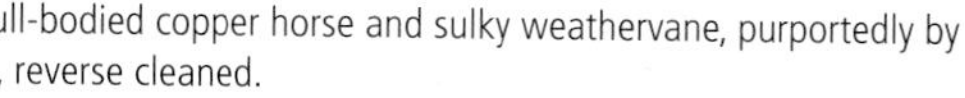

A 19thC full-bodied copper horse and sulky weathervane, purportedly by Dan Patch, reverse cleaned.

72in (183cm) wide

£13,000-18,000 **POOK**

A late 19thC moulded copper 'Smuggler' running horse weathervane.

31in (78.5cm) long

£3,000-4,000 **SK**

A swell-bodied leaping stag weathervane, attributed to L.D. Cushing & Co. Massachusetts, with old verdigris and gilt surface.

c1875 *27in (68.5cm) wide*

£15,000-20,000 **POOK**

A 19thC swell-bodied copper setter weathervane, with old gilt over verdigris surface.

31½in (80cm) wide

£4,000-4,500 **POOK**

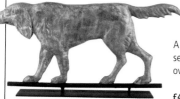

A 19thC swell-bodied copper rooster weathervane, with old yellow over verdigris surface, old repaired bullet hole.

28¼in (72cm) high

£3,500-4,000 **POOK**

A 19thC swell-bodied copper lamb weathervane, possibly Fiske, with cast zinc head retaining old verdigris surface, ears and bar replaced.

27½in (70cm) wide

£15,000-20,000 **POOK**

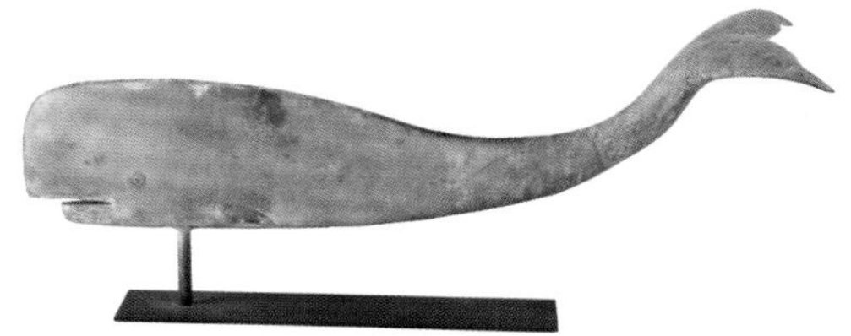

A 19thC swell-bodied copper whale weathervane, some repaired bullet holes.

36in (91.5cm) long

£25,000-30,000 **POOK**

A Bidjar handwoven wool palace-size oriental rug.

Bidjar is in North West Persia.

216in (548.5cm) long

£1,300-1,600 WHIT

A Bidjar carpet.

c1910 239¾in (609cm) long

£8,500-9,500 SWO

A Heriz 'Tree of Life' rug, some dirt and errors.

86¾in (220cm) long

£1,500-2,000 BELL

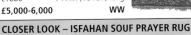

An early 20thC Heriz rug, the blue ground with herati field, some losses.

139in (353cm) long

£1,400-1,800 WES

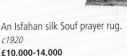

An early to mid-20thC Mamoury Isfahan carpet, signature to one end.

111in (282cm) long

£3,000-3,500 L&T

An Isfahan rug, with signature 'by order of Sadegh, Seirafian, Esfahan, Iran', some wear, one repair.

66¼in (168.5cm) long

£4,000-5,000 DN

A Bokhara carpet, the madder field decorated with foliate and geometric motifs.

Bokhara is in the North East of the Persian Empire.

149½in (380cm) long

£1,500-2,000 DN

A Heriz Tabriz silk pictorial rug, decorated with trees, animals, figures and portrait bust spandrels, heavy corrosion to the browns.

The weavers of Heriz, or Heris, in North West Persia, were famous for their large wool-piled carpets, made with strong dyes. In the late 19thC, fine silk carpets were also produced, on a cottage industry basis. Production had mainly ceased by 1900.

c1880 71¼in (181cm) long

£5,000-6,000 WW

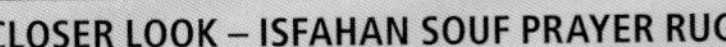

CLOSER LOOK – ISFAHAN SOUF PRAYER RUG

Isfahan, in Central Persia, was a centre for rug and carpet making in the 17thC. After two hundred years of decline, production was reintroduced by weavers brought in from Kashan in the 1920s.

The top of the rug depicts a mihrab, the niche in the wall of a mosque that shows the direction to Mecca.

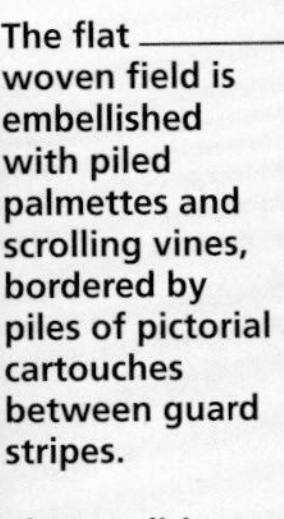

The flat woven field is embellished with piled palmettes and scrolling vines, bordered by piles of pictorial cartouches between guard stripes.

The condition is good and the colours vibrant.

An Isfahan silk Souf prayer rug.

c1920 76¾in (195cm) long

£10,000-14,000 LC

ESSENTIAL REFERENCE – KASHAN RUGS

Kashan, in Central Persia, was the centre of rug and carpet making in the 16thC and 17thC. Production declined in the 18thC, but the late 19thC saw a reintroduction of traditional craftsmanship.

- **Late 19thC and early 20thC Kashan weavings are typically of very high quality, woven using a cotton foundation with a Persian knot.**
- **Silk rugs were made alongside wool-piled ones. These were often of prayer format and made in large quantities in the 1920s.**
- **There are two terms loosely used to describe fine late 19thC to early 20thC Kashans: Kurk, referring to the quality of the wool, and Mohtasham, probably the name of a master weaver who owned workshops in the city.**

A wool Kashan Mohtasham rug.
c1880 *80in (203cm) long*
£12,000-15,000 FRE

A late 19thC to early 20thC Kashan Mohtasham carpet.
122in (310cm) long
£5,500-6,000 L&T

An antique Kirman scenic carpet.
92in (233.5cm) long
£3,500-4,000 CLAR

A Kashan carpet, the indigo field of scrolling vines around a cusped pole medallion.
c1930 *162¼in (412cm) long*
£3,000-4,000 TEN

A Khorassan carpet, some wear, losses and repairs.

The Khorassan province is in the North East of Persia.
161½in (410cm) long
£2,500-3,000 DN

An early 20thC Kashan silk souf carpet, frayed at borders, some staining.
125½in (319cm) long
£7,500-8,500 CHOR

A Kirman Laver carpet, the ivory field with a floral faceted medallion, some fading and dirt.

Kirman, or Kerman, carpets, are named after the city and province of Kirman in South East Persia. It has been a major centre for the production of carpets since the 15thC. The regional wool, Carmania wool, from which these carpets are made, is of very high quality.
111in (282cm) wide
£1,800-2,200 BELL

A Mahal carpet.

The term Mahal is used to describe rugs and carpets from a particular region in North West Persia. The name probably derives from the village of Mahallat.
141¾in (360cm) long
£5,000-5,500 DN

A Mahal carpet, the red ground with scrolling foliage.

c1900 *275½in (700cm) long*

£6,500-7,000 **SWO**

A late 19thC to early 20thC Meshed carpet, East Persia.

Meshed is in North East Persia.

164½in (418cm) long

£500-600 **L&T**

A Nain carpet, the ivory field of scrolling vines and palmettes around a sky blue pole medallion.

The town of Nain is in Central Persia.

c1970 *225½in (573cm) long*

£6,000-7,000 **TEN**

A Qum Erami silk carpet.

Qum, also Ghom or Kum, is in Central Persia.

£6,000-7,000 **DN**

A mid-20thC Qum Rug.

£1,500-2,000 **WAD**

A late 19thC to early 20thC Sarouk Fereghan rug.

Rugs and carpets were made in and around the village of Sarouk, in West Persia, in the second half of the 19thC and the early 20thC. Production was on a cottage industry basis, so designs and styles vary considerably. Central medallions framed by spandrels were a common motif.

78¾in (200cm) long

£1,000-1,400 **L&T**

An early 20thC Sarouk rug, some losses and alterations.

270in (686cm) long

£1,500-2,000 **WES**

A Serapi carpet, some wear and losses.

Serapi rugs were woven in the mountains of North West Persia, on a family and small workshop basis. They were woven almost exclusively by women. They are named after the town of Serab, from which these carpets were traded.

c1900 *144in (366cm) long*

£2,200-2,800 **POOK**

A Sultanabad carpet, some staining and light wear.

Sultanabad is in West Persia.

c1930 *141¾in (360cm) long*

£1,800-2,200 **TEN**

ESSENTIAL REFERENCE – TABRIZ CARPETS

Tabriz is an important weaving centre in North West Persia.

- **Tabriz was one of the world's major cities from the 11thC. In the 13thC it became capital of the Mongol Empire. It soon became an important weaving centre, and by the 16thC was one of the leading producers of carpets in the East.**
- **Weaving declined in the 18thC, but in the late 19thC was re-established on a workshop basis.**
- **Tabriz weavers often copied or adapted designs from other areas. They chiefly made room-size carpets, although smaller rugs were also produced.**
- **Their late 19thC to early 20thC pieces are typically soft red, cream and indigo.**

A late 19thC to early 20thC Tabriz 'Hadji Jalili' carpet.

137in (348cm) long

£1,200-1,600 L&T

An early 20thC Tabriz carpet, worn overall, some re-binding, fringes cut short.

128¼in (326cm) long

£1,400-1,800 DN

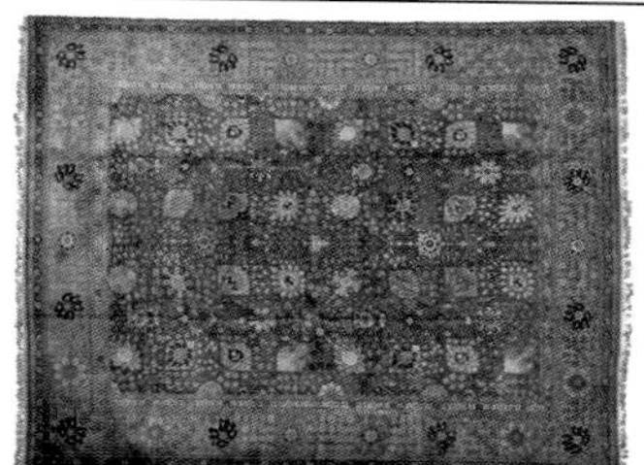

A 1940s Tabriz carpet, the sky blue field of Shah Abass design.

171¾in (436cm) long

£2,500-3,000 TEN

A Tabriz carpet, some wear, some replacement binding, losses to tassels.

152in (386cm) long

£5,000-6,000 DN

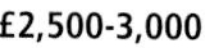

A part-silk Sino Tabriz carpet.

125in (317.5cm) long

£2,500-3,000 CLAR

A late 19thC Ziegler carpet.

Ziegler and Co., of Manchester, England, established a carpet manufactory in Sultanabad, West Persia, in 1883. The firm aimed to combine traditional 16thC and 17thC Persian carpet design with Western tastes, employing both major designers from Western department stores and local artisans in Sultanabad.

275½in (700cm) long

£5,500-6,000 L&T

A late 19thC Ziegler carpet.

151½in (385cm) long

£6,000-7,000 L&T

A Persian silk 'Tree of Life' rug, 'Ex Liberty'.

84in (213.5cm) long

£1,500-2,000 JN

A North West Persian runner, some repairs.

c1920

144in (366cm) long

£1,000-1,300 POOK

A mid-to-late 19thC Akstafa rug, South West Caucasus, with horse and riders with Akstafa peacocks.

102in (259cm) long

£4,000-5,000 WW

A late 19thC Kuba rug, East Caucasus.

62¼in (158cm) long

£750-850 MART

An early 20thC Lenkoran rug, South East Caucasus.

112½in (286cm) long

£400-500 WW

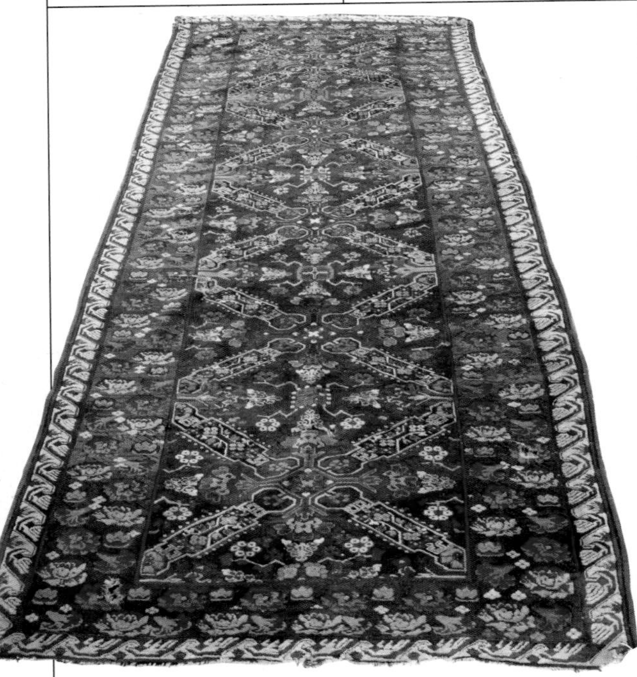

A late 19thC Seychour rug, East Caucasus, in a traditional Eastern design of stylised gul motifs within a Western-style floral border.

£6,000-7,000 PW

A Shirvan prayer rug, repairs to sides.

c1920 64in (162.5cm) long

£600-700 POOK

A late 19thC Soumac carpet.

157½in (400cm) long

£1,300-1,600 L&T

A late 19thC Caucasian runner, the indigo field surrounded by tribal and zoomorphic devices.

128in (325cm) long

£750-850 LC

A Caucasian carpet.

c1910 110in (279.5cm) long

£1,500-2,000 POOK

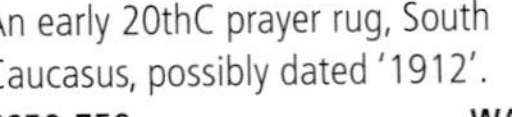

An early 20thC prayer rug, South Caucasus, possibly dated '1912'.

£650-750 WAD

A Mahal carpet.

179¼in (455cm) long

£3,000-4,000 **SWO**

An early 20thC Anatolian kelim.

119in (302cm) long

£700-800 **L&T**

A late 19thC Anatolian rug, in Gendje style.

62¼in (158cm) long

£500-600 **WW**

An Anatolian Kayseri rug.

c1920

£1,300-1,800 **WAD**

A Turkoman carpet.

c1910

132in (335.5cm) long

£1,300-1,800 **POOK**

A late 19thC Ushak carpet, West Anatolia, in two sections.

Ushak was a centre of carpet production in the 16thC and 17thC, best known for its 'star' and medallion carpets. In the late 19thC and early 20thC Ushak had a resurgence of carpet-making, often supplying pieces for export to Europe and North America.

169¼in (430cm) long

£1,000-1,500 **L&T**

An early 20thC Ushak runner, Anatolia, made from two runners.

270in (686cm) long

£2,500-3,000 **WW**

An Ushak carpet, the pale field decorated with geometric and stylised foliate motifs, losses to tassels, some areas of possible repair.

225¼in (572cm) long

£9,500-11,000 **DN**

An Ushak green ground carpet, damages and losses to borders.

145¾in (370cm) long

£3,500-4,500 **CHEF**

A 19thC French Savonnerie Empire-style carpet, with central fan medallion and a Classical twin griffin flaming athenienne.

193in (490cm) wide

£15,000-20,000 WW

A 19thC American hooked rug, minor fraying, old repairs, mounted.

75in (190.5cm) wide

£5,500-6,500 POOK

An Aubusson tapestry carpet, some fading, exterior border trimmed, later backing.

152in (386cm) long

£1,800-2,200 BELL

A pair of Agra runners, Central/North India.

c1880 267¾in (680cm) long

£22,000-28,000 LC

An Agra carpet, India.

c1930-50 191¼in (486cm) long

£4,000-5,000 WW

An Amritsar carpet, Punjab, North West India.

c1880 185in (470cm) long

£15,000-20,000 LC

A 1930s-40s Irish wool carpet, by Dun Emer Guild Ltd., Dublin.

144¾in (367.5cm) wide

£3,000-4,000 MEA

A Celtic 'hunting' wool carpet, designed by George Bain (1881-1968) for Quayle and Tranter Ltd., Kidderminster.

George Bain was born in Scrabster in Northern Scotland and single-handedly revived interest in Celtic and Insular art. His book, 'Celtic Art: The Methods of Construction', was published in 1951.

143¾in (365cm) wide

£2,500-3,500 SWO

A Spanish carpet, probably Madrid, inscribed 'MD', dated.

1954 136½in (347cm) long

£2,000-2,500 L&T

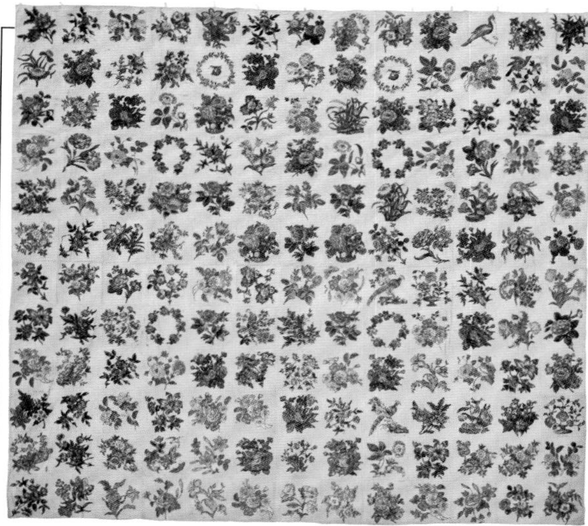

A New Jersey 'Broderie Perse' quilt, with 156 squares with chintz appliqués, inscribed 'Trenton N.J.', with names from the Vallette, Coleman, McNeely and Aitken families, some light staining, dated.

1843 *103in (261.5cm) wide*

£9,500-11,000 **POOK**

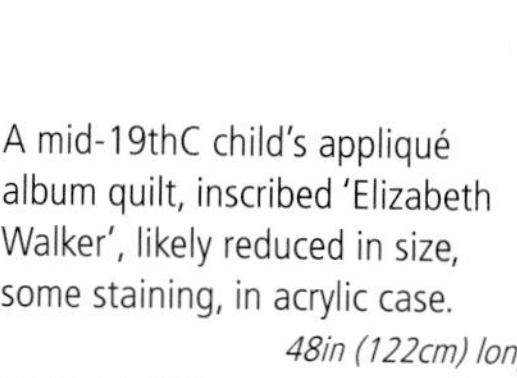

A mid-19thC child's appliqué album quilt, inscribed 'Elizabeth Walker', likely reduced in size, some staining, in acrylic case.

48in (122cm) long

£3,500-4,000 **POOK**

A mid-19thC appliqué 'Rose of Sharon' quilt.

78½in (199.5cm) wide

£1,600-2,000 **FRE**

A pieced and tied child's quilt, possibly New York State, with printed cotton and wool pieces, with appliqué figure of an African-American child, signed 'Ida Murphy'.

c1870 *53¾in (136.5cm) wide*

£2,500-3,500 **FRE**

An appliqué album quilt, signed 'Mrs. Catherine Tyson', scattered staining, dated.

1857 *84in (213.5cm) square*

£1,800-2,200 **POOK**

A 19thC pieced 'Bar and Star' quilt, probably Orange County, NY, with 18thC copperplate-printed linen and printed cotton patches.

The 18thC linen came from the wedding dress fabric of Abbie 'Nabby' Forsyth, who married Daniel Greenleaf, 3 October 1791, in Norwich, Connecticut.

87½in (222.5cm) wide

£1,200-1,600 **FRE**

A late 19thC appliqué 'Whig Rose' quilt, minor stains.

88in (223.5cm) wide

£400-500 **POOK**

A late 19thC pieced quilt, with potted tulips.

84in (213.5cm) wide

£400-450 **POOK**

A late 19thC Pennsylvania floral appliqué quilt, minor staining.

91in (231cm) long

£550-600 **POOK**

An early 20thC Hawaiian 'Ku'u Hae Aloha' or 'Flag' quilt, with Hawaiian flags and coat of arms, some stains and fading.

93in (236cm) long

£6,000-7,000 **SK**

This quilt, 'Scenes from American Life', was made by Mrs Cecil White, Hartford, Connecticut. It is incredibly detailed and is composed of fifty-five vignettes, depicting figures engaged in various pursuits, including a bartender serving his customers, a rodeo star, tennis players, golfers, baseball players, a billiards scene, farming scenes, a fiddle player, dancers, swimmers, weddings, men in uniform, a man getting his shoes shined, and many more scenes. The quilt is bordered by touring cars, pickup trucks and steam trains. The rich social history depicted on this quilt makes it an especially interesting piece.

A pieced and appliqué folk art quilt, 'Scenes of American Life'.

c1925-30 *77in (195.5cm) long*

£45,000-50,000 **SK**

An appliqué cockscomb quilt, minor staining.

c1900 *75in (190.5cm) long*

£450-550 **POOK**

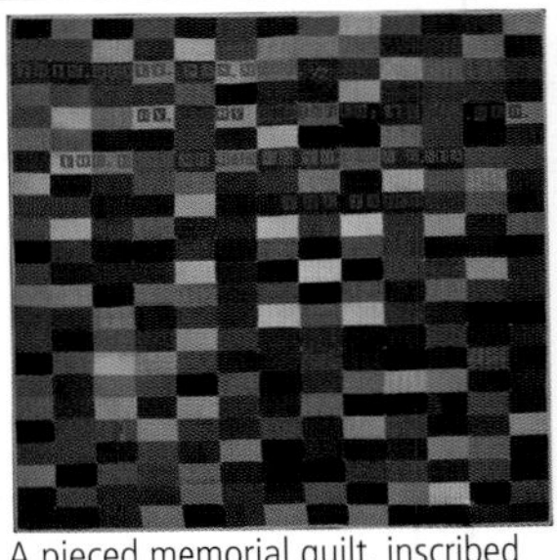

A pieced memorial quilt, inscribed 'This quilt was made 5/2 1907 by Mary R. Fisher 87 years old for remembrance to John R. Shaner the tailor', some staining.

1907 *80in (203cm) wide*

£800-900 **POOK**

A Tennessee State Fair First Prize quilt, silk and velvet star variant with triangle outer border, some losses and fraying.

1909 *83in (211cm) long*

£500-600 **POOK**

An early 20thC pieced alphabet quilt, mounted, light stains.

79in (200.5cm) long

£700-800 **POOK**

A 20thC Hawaiian floral quilt, with floral appliqué.

82in (208.5cm) long

£850-950 **SK**

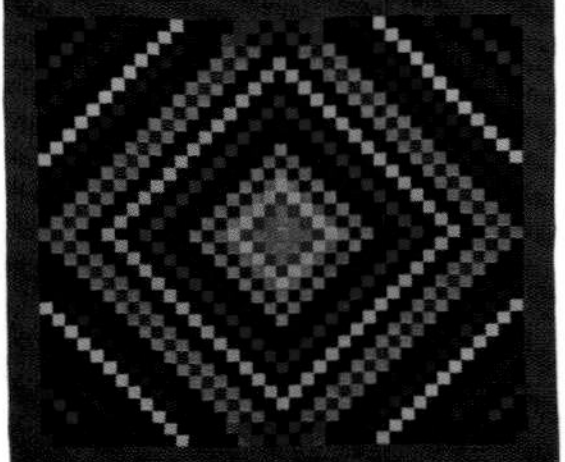

A Mennonite 'Trip Around the World, Sunshine and Shadow' quilt, Elmira, Waterloo County, Ontario.

c1940-50 *87in (221cm) wide*

£350-400 **SK**

CLOSER LOOK – BRUSSELS TAPESTRY

This important Brussels tapestry comes from the 'History of Venus' series. It depicts Venus disclosing to Diomedes the conduct of his wife Aegialia, with figures and trees to the foreground, the ocean and Cupid on an elephant behind.

It is probably after Bernard van Orley, and may be from the workshop of Guasparo di Bartolommeo Papini, after Alessandro Allori.

The scene is within a naturalistic border woven with animals, bunches of fruit, birds and flowers.

It is in good condition considering its age, with well-preserved colours.

A mid-16thC Brussels mythological tapestry, from the 'History of Venus' series.

256in (650cm) wide

£80,000-90,000 **SWO**

An 19thC Aubusson tapestry panel, some restoration, rebacked.

90in (228.5cm) high

£2,000-2,500 **CHEF**

A 17thC to 18thC Brussels verdure tapestry.

106in (269cm) wide

£7,500-8,500 **BRI**

A mid-16thC Brussels mythological tapestry, after Bernard van Orley, 'Venus saves Aeneas from the wrath of Diomedes', from the 'History of Venus' series.

154¼in (392cm) wide

£40,000-45,000 **SWO**

A mid-18thC Brussels Teniers tapestry, of the Kermesse, with groups of peasants making merry outside an inn, in picture frame border with the Brussels town mark in the selvedge.

This version of the Kermesse is attributed by H.C. Marillier in his 'Handbook to the Teniers Tapestries' to the Van der Borcht brothers, Pierre (fl.1712-63) and François (fl.1720-65).

213¾in (543cm) wide

£10,000-15,000 **SWO**

A late 17thC tapestry panel, emblematic of autumn, Mortlake or Hatton Garden, London, from the 'Mortlake Months' series woven with a vineyard scene.

The 'Mortlake Months' series was probably based on the Brussels suite of 'The Months', by Gilles de Leyniers.

109¾in (279cm) high

£18,000-22,000 **SWO**

A mid-18thC Brussels tapestry, in Rococo style, after Jean-Antoine Watteau's 'La Partie carrée'.

This tapestry in the fête galante style depicts figures in a stage-like setting in the manner of Jean-Antoine Watteau's celebrated painting 'La Partie carrée' of c1713. The figure of Pierrot is an almost exact copy.

56¼in (397cm) wide

£4,500-5,500 **WW**

A 16thC Flemish historical tapestry, 'The Story of Julius Caesar', depicting the 'Enthronement of Caesar and Cleopatra', from the 'Story of Julius Caesar and Cleopatra' series.

133½in (339cm) high

£20,000-25,000 **SWO**

A 17thC Franco-Flemish tapestry depicting soldiery in Roman-style armour and a horse, with later borders and rebacked.

62¼in (158cm) high

£6,000-7,000 **DN**

A mid-17thC Flemish tapestry, possibly depicting the story of Daphne 'from Ovid Metamorphoses'.

129½in (329cm) wide

£3,500-4,000 **GWA**

An early 17thC Florentine allegorical tapestry, emblematic of Winter, after Alessandro Allori.

161in (409cm) wide

£70,000-80,000 **SWO**

A late 17thC to early 18thC Flemish 'verdure' tapestry panel.

84¼in (214cm) high

£1,800-2,200 **DUK**

A late 17thC verdure tapestry, woven in wools, some fading and dirty, old repairs and possible alternations.

102¼in (260cm) high

£1,500-2,000 **BELL**

An early 17thC Florentine allegorical tapestry, emblematic of Spring, after Alessandro Allori.

192¼in (488cm) wide

£90,000-100,000 **SWO**

An 18thC verdure tapestry.

135¾in (345cm) high

£2,500-3,000 **WW**

A mid-17thC English embroidered panel, worked in silk and wool on a silk satin ground, framed and glazed.

15in (38cm) wide

£900-1,100 **HT**

A Charles II raised needlework portrait of a family, in later ebonised glazed frame.

20in (51cm) wide

£3,500-4,000 **SW**

A late 17thC Charles II embroidered beadwork panel, worked on white silk, in original japanned frame, some tears and stains to corners.

22¾in (58cm) wide

£7,000-8,000 **DN**

A silk and silver thread needlework picture, by Mary Sibley, depicting the Sibley sisters, the verso stating that 'all three were with child and that Mary was the daughter of Mr Cresnard of Earlscone (Earls Colne) Essex and married George Sibley gent of Westham, Essex, who was the son of Nathan Sibley, Deputy of Coleman Street ward of London', in later glazed frame.

The figures in this picture were directly taken from Wenceslaus Hollar's (1607-77) fashion plate etchings, 'Theatrum Mulierum'. The central figure is a direct copy of Mulier Generosa Anglica.

1670 *7in (18cm) wide*

£6,000-7,000 **WW**

A late 17thC English stump work picture, depicting Adam and Eve in the Garden of Eden, framed.

14½in (37cm) wide

£3,500-4,500 **SWO**

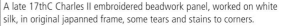

A late 17thC embroidered panel.

24½in (62cm) wide

£1,000-1,400 **SWO**

An 18thC early Georgian needlepoint wall hanging, worked in gros and petit point, some re-stitching.

102¼in (260cm) high

£4,500-5,000 **GORL**

An 18thC woolwork of a shepherd and shepherdess, framed, under glass.

4¼in (11cm) wide

£4,500-5,500 **CHEF**

A band sampler, with acorns above flowers, pairs of hands reaching for hearts and a thistle, all above 'Jane How... Her Sampler', with pine frame, some fading, dated.

1654 *32¾in (83cm) high*

£2,500-3,000 **CHEF**

A Charles II 'boxer' band needlework sampler, in later gilt frame.

32¾in (83.5cm) high

£1,000-1,400 **WW**

A Georgian sampler, by Frances Tydeman.

17in (43cm) high

£300-400 **LC**

A Regency needlework sampler, by M. Watt, inscribed 'M. WATT 1810', in later glazed ebonised frame.

8½in (21.5cm) high

£250-300 **WW**

A George IV needlework sampler, by Mary Simpson, worked with Adam and Eve, with a verse, inscribed, in later glazed mahogany frame, dated.

1828 *26in (66cm) wide*

£500-600 **WW**

An early 19thC Georgian silk and needlework sampler, with an alphabet above the names 'HENRY MACKENZIE' and 'PANUEL GRANT' and a verse, with the author's name 'MARGARET MACKENZIE', in an ebonised frame.

This sampler is thought to have been worked by the daughter of Henry Mackenzie (1745-1831), the author of the novel 'The Man of Feeling', and to have been bought from Cullen House previously.

15in (38cm) high

£7,500-8,500 **L&T**

A Pennsylvania silk-on-linen sampler, by Rose Abbott, allover toning, dated.

1829 *17in (43cm) high*

£2,000-2,500 **POOK**

A silk-on-linen house sampler, by Sarah Ann Rundell, minor staining, dated.

1828 *16½in (42cm) high*

£750-850 **POOK**

A Pennsylvania silk-on-linen sampler, by Elizabeth Cooper, a few tack holes and toning to edges, dated.

1831 *21¾in (55cm) high*

£1,000-1,400 **POOK**

CLOSER LOOK – 17THC VELVET JERKIN

The jerkin was a garment worn to protect the doublet worn below, and to provide extra warmth and protection.

This example is made of the finest Italian crimson velvet and must have belonged to a man of great wealth and importance.

It has silk to the shoulder wings and hem, adorned with gold and silver thread plaited braids. The collar is interlined with heavy buckram.

Few specimens of late 16thC or early 17thC costume survive, making this an especially rare find.

A short-waisted velvet jerkin, the shoulder interlined with linen, with silver-gilt wrapped acorn shaped buttons, with purpose-made mount.
c1610-25 *chest 40¼in (102cm) wide*
£75,000-80,000 **KT**

A French caraco bodice, of early 1760s brocade, woven with lacy ribbon trails, plumes and bouquets, with boned front closure.
c1780
£1,500-2,000 **KT**

A rare 1820s young man's brown wool double-breasted tailcoat, with stiffened collar, composition buttons, with short tails with pockets.
32in (81.5cm) chest
£5,000-6,000 **KT**

A Gabrielle Chanel couture crêpe romain 'little black dress', with sequinned fringes, the bolero edged with beaded and sequinned fronds, lacking shoulder fringes.

This design was illustrated in French and American Vogue between April and June 1926, notably worn by the Marquise de Jaucourt and modelled by Marion Morehouse.
1926 *34in (86.5cm) bust*
£8,000-9,000 **KT**

A striped silk gauze dress, with empire-line bodice and puffed sleeves, satin rouleaux edging and appliquéd flowers.
c1825 *30in (76cm) bust*
£4,000-5,000 **KT**

A Lucile Ltd. bridal gown, of silk and sheer chiffon, edged and trimmed with pearl beads and fringing, with small lace pouch, labelled '17 West 38th St, New York'.

Lucile traded from 17 West 36th Street between 1910-12. This was the wedding dress of Eugenie Ward Root Riley (1889-1974), granddaughter of multimillionaire landowner Andrew Ward, worn on her marriage to army officer James Wilson Riley of South Carolina.
1912 *32in (81cm) bust*
£4,500-5,000 **KT**

CLOSER LOOK – AVANT GARDE ROBE

This robe is an extraordinary example of British avant garde clothing made on the eve of World War I.

It was designed by Percy Wyndham Lewis (1882-1957), a writer, painter, critic and co-founder of the avant garde Vorticist movement in art.

It is decorated with stylised foxes, fish, swans and kneeling figures.

The fabric may have been among the textiles produced by the Bloomsbury Group's Omega Workshops, although another similar printed panel of this design was attributed to the Rebel Art Centre, a short-lived workshop set up in 1914 after Lewis and several Omega artists had quarrelled with the Bloomsbury set.

An embroidered and block-printed silk robe.
c1914 *52in (132cm) long*
£35,000-40,000 **MAL**

A Carven couture embroidered and beaded white organza dress.
1948-50 *20in (51cm) waist*
£25,000-30,000 **KT**

A Thea Porter muslin 'gypsy' dress, edged with gold braid, woven lily label.
1969-71 *size 10*
£6,500-7,500 **KT**

TEXTILES

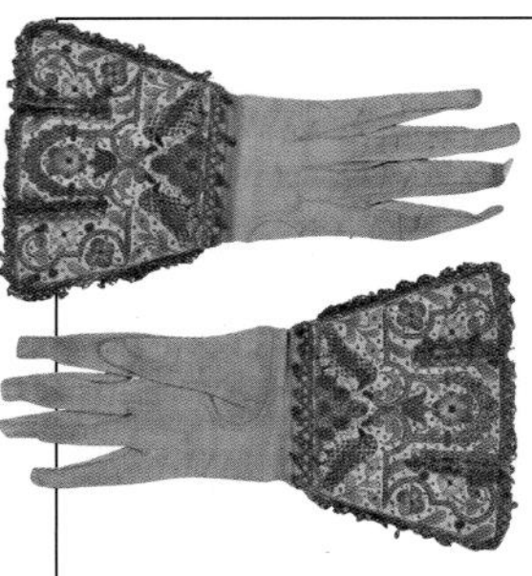

A pair of English doeskin gloves, with embroidered ivory satin gauntlets, edged in silver lace, lined in salmon pink silk, inked 'R.A.C Eshott, 1778'.

Provenance: Gifted to Rebecca Ann Colt of Eshott Hall, near Morpeth, Cumbria. In 1778 Rebecca's husband Thomas Carr was created High Sheriff of the county and for the inaugural procession he commissioned richly embroidered robes and saddle cloths and carried these 17thC gloves.

c1630-40 *11¾in (30cm) long*
£5,000-6,000 **KT**

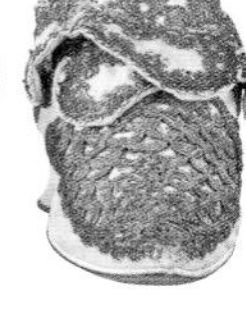

A pair of silver lace and ivory satin lady's shoes, adorned with silver bobbin lace and silver strip passementerie.

c1720-30 *10¼in (26cm) long*
£30,000-35,000 **KT**

A 1930s Jean Patou black wool felt hat, with two large cartwheels of monkey fur, colobus satanas, with central velvet coils, labelled.

22in (56cm) diam
£850-950 **KT**

Judith Picks

It is widely believed that the Votes for Women sash was first seen at the Women's Sunday demonstration held on 21 June 1908 in Hyde Park, London. The Editor of 'Votes for Woman' magazine, Emmeline Pethick-Lawrence, encouraged supporters to attend the demonstration dressed in their best white dress, to ensure the sash was clearly visible and show the world that they were respectable and to defuse fears of violence. The sash was created by the Women's Social and Political Union and is thought to have been designed by Sylvia Pankhurst, Emmeline Pankhurst's daughter.

It is likely that the sashes were sold at department stores. Selfridges certainly stocked a range of dresses, brooches, ribbons, hats and drapery in suffrage colours.

An early 20thC woven 'Votes for Women' sash, printed with black letters with green and purple stripes, the original hook and eye fastening stamped 'Nicklin's'.

£4,500-5,000 **FLD**

A Hermès 'Cosmos' scarf, designed by Philippe Ledoux, one pull to fabric.

issued 1964 *35½in (90cm) wide*
£400-500 **FELL**

A Hermès 'Wedgwood' scarf, designed by Philippe Ledoux, minor water marks.

designed 1974 *35¾in (91cm) wide*
£350-450 **FELL**

A Hermès 'Republique Francaise Liberte Egalite Fraternite' scarf, designed by Joachim Metz, signed, minor marks.

This scarf was designed to commemorate the bicentenary of the French Revolution.

issued 1989 *35½in (90cm) square*
£250-300 **FELL**

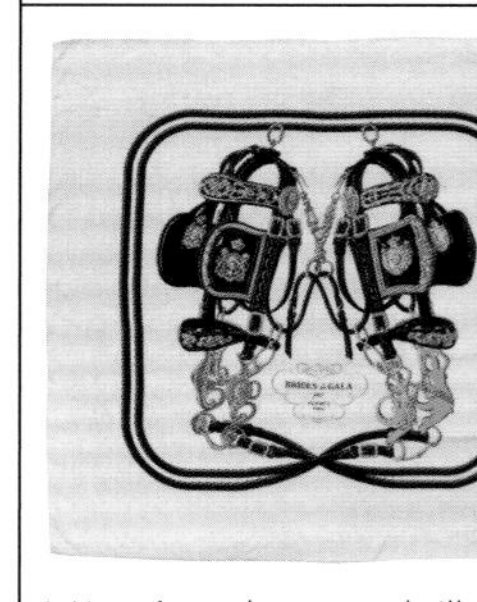

A Hermès cashmere and silk shawl, 'Brides de Gala' pattern, designed by Hugo Grygkar, some snags and pulls, some spots.

55in (140cm) square
£550-650 **LHA**

A Chanel silk and wool shawl, with the Chanel motif throughout, with label.

48½in (123cm) wide
£800-900 **DN**

An Aspinal of London pebble leather and calf 'Buffalo' cabin bag, with brass hardware, on two wheels, with dust bag.

18in (46cm) wide

£400-500 **DN**

An Asprey ostrich leather 'Darcy Belgravia' handbag, with alligator skin accents and silver-tone hardware.

14¾in (37.5cm) wide

£3,000-4,000 **FELL**

A Berluti alligator leather 'Deux Jours' briefcase, some wear, lacking shoulder strap.

15¾in (40cm) wide

£2,500-3,000 **FELL**

A Berluti 'Venezia' leather weekend bag, the zipped interior with two compartments and a zip compartment, blind stamped 'Berluti'.

13½in (34cm) wide

£650-700 **DN**

A Cartier vintage 'Happy Birthday Bordeaux' handbag, with dust bag and box.

11in (28cm) wide

£800-900 **FELL**

An early 1990s Cartier alligator skin 'Pantere' handbag and purse, with gold-tone hardware, with maker's dust bag.

11½in (29cm) wide

£1,000-1,500 **FELL**

A Céline 'Micro Luggage' leather handbag, with red leather trim, expandable side wings and red leather-lined interior.

10¼in (26cm) wide

£1,300-1,600 **FELL**

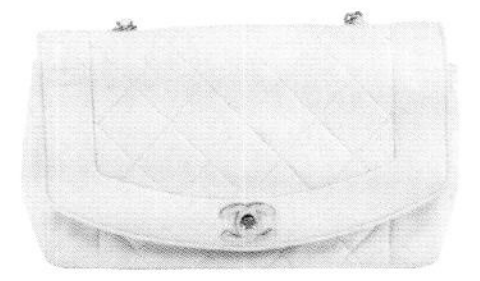

A Chanel vintage lambskin leather handbag, serial no.1708055, with gold-tone hardware and maker's signature CC turn-lock front fastening, minor wear.

Chanel was founded in France in 1910 by Coco Chanel, and today continues to create high-end clothing, jewellery and perfume.

c1989-91 *8¾in (22cm) wide*

£1,200-1,600 **FELL**

A vintage Chanel 'Maxi Classic Flap' quilted lambskin leather handbag, serial no.3061509, with gold-tone hardware and CC logo turn-lock fastening, some scuffs, hairlines to hardware.

c1994-96 *13¼in (33.5cm) wide*

£2,000-2,500 **FELL**

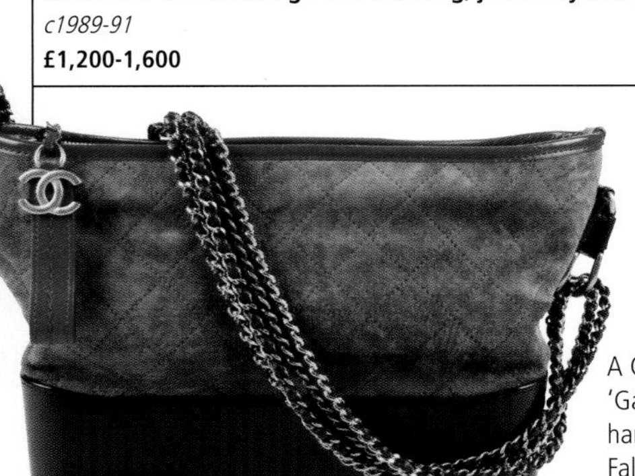

A Chanel tricolour 'Gabrielle Hobo' handbag, from the Fall/Winter 2017 Collection.

10¾in (27.5cm) wide

£2,200-2,800 **FELL**

A Chanel quilted leather shoulder bag, with gilt clasp and chain, stamped serial number, with original dust bag.

9¾in (25cm) wide

£800-900 **CHEF**

A Christian Dior 'Lady Dior' lizard skin handbag, with gold-tone hardware, some light scratches and scuffing, with maker's care guide, authenticity card, dust bag and associated box.

9½in (24cm) wide

£2,000-2,500 **FELL**

A Christian Dior 'Mini Micro-Cannage Diorama Flap' perforated calfskin leather exterior handbag, serial no.13.BO.0155, with silver-tone hardware, minor abrasion to base corners, with maker's dust bag.

27in (18cm) wide

£1,000-1,400 **FELL**

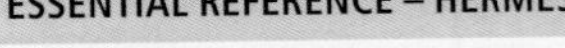

ESSENTIAL REFERENCE – HERMÈS

Hermès is one of the top brands of handbags.

- **It was founded in 1837 by Thierry Hermès. It originally specialised in horse saddles and carriage fittings. It produced its first handbags in 1922.**
- **Its famous bags include the 'Kelly', designed in the 1930s and later used by Grace Kelly, the 'Birkin', designed for actress Jane Birkin in 1984, and the 'Evelyne', designed for a casual everyday look.**
- **Vintage and new Hermès handbags are often sought after today. The world record for a Hermès bag was a Hermès Birkin which sold for £253,700 at Christie's in 2017. Another Hermès Birkin sold for £163,500 at Christie's in 2018.**
- **Condition has a significant effect on value, as does the material the bag is made of.**

A 1930s Hermès of Paris crocodile handbag, fully stamped 'Hermes Paris, 24FG St Honore', wear to metalwork, light rubbing, with a later Hermes slip case.

10½in (26.5cm) wide

£3,200-3,800 **GORL**

A Gucci 'Positano' hobo handbag, serial no.155563 200047, with maker's monogram canvas exterior and red leather trim, with twilly scarf woven through grommet holes, with maker's dust bag.

Gucci was founded by Guccio Gucci in Florence, Italy, in 1921. The firm originally specialised in leather riding gear and luggage and later added handbags and clothing to its list of products.

14¼in (26cm) wide

£250-300 **FELL**

A Gucci 'Soho' grained leather handbag, serial no.308983 520981, with gold-tone hardware, quilted interlocking 'GG' logo, light wear, with maker's dust bag and maintenance guide.

11in (28cm) wide

£600-700 **FELL**

A Hermès niloticus crocodile sellier 'Kelly' handbag, with gold-tone hardware, stamped 'Hermès', with 'H' blindstamp, some wear, with dustbag.

2004 *12½in (32cm) wide*

£8,000-9,000 **LHA**

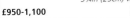

A Gucci 'GG Marmont' quilted leather handbag, with 'GG' snap closure, the interior with a zippered compartment.

9¾in (25cm) wide

£950-1,100 **DN**

An Hermès 'Chocolate Taurillon Clemence Jypsiere' bag, with palladium hardware, stamped 'Hermès, with 'N' blindstamp, with box and dustbag.

2010 *11in (28cm) wide*

£2,200-2,800 **LHA**

An Hermès 'Epsom Evelyne TPM' handbag, with silver and palladium hardware, stamped 'Hermès', with 'JO' blindstamp, with box and dustbag.

2011 *7in (18cm) high*

£1,500-2,000 **LHA**

A Hermès 'Birkin 35' ostrich leather handbag, gold-tone turn lock fastening, padlock, clochette and key, minor wear, with maker's dust bag, box and rain cover.

13¾in (35cm) wide

£9,500-11,000 **FELL**

A Hermès 'Blue Jean Birkin 35' pebbled leather handbag, with gold-tone turn lock fastening, feet scuffed, with maker's care guide, rain protector, dust bag and box.

13¾in (35cm) wide

£10,000-13,000 **FELL**

A Hèrmes Porosus Crocodile Kelly 35 handbag, with gold-tone hardware, with padlock and two keys.

14in (35.5cm) wide

£12,000-15,000 **FELL**

A limited edition Mulberry 'Beaded Bayswater' chocolate brown and oak Darwin leather handbag, serial no.063348, with antique brass hardware, oak leather handles and trim, and maker's signature postman's lock fastening, signs of use.

14¼in (36cm) wide

£500-600 **FELL**

A Mulberry Bayswater oak leather handbag, with brass clasp and padlock, with original retail tag.

14¼in (36cm) wide

£500-600 **CHEF**

A Prada 'Saffiano' leather handbag, the satin interior with two pockets and two zipped compartments, with Prada dust bag.

11¾in (30cm) wide

£450-550 **DN**

A Louis Vuitton 'Idylle Neverfull MM' handbag, serial no.CA0182.

The Monogram Idylle (previously Mini Lin) Canvas Collection is a newer line that sports a lighter canvas, made of 58% cotton, 24% linen and 18% polyamide.

18in (46cm) wide

£850-950 **FELL**

A Louis Vuitton 'Monogram Empreinte Artsy MM' monogram embossed calfskin leather handbag, serial no.CA0165, with gold-tone hardware, some scratches, with maker's dust bag.

15¼in (39cm) wide

£1,400-2,000 **FELL**

A Louis Vuitton 'Capucine MM' taurillon leather handbag, serial no.AH1105, with orange coated edges, maker's initials, with silver-tone hardware.

14¼in (36cm) wide

£2,200-2,800 **FELL**

A Louis Vuitton 'Monogram Carryall' coated canvas and leather soft multi-purpose bag, with two side pockets, a padlock and a name tag.

16½in (42cm) wide

£800-900 **DN**

A Louis Vuitton 'Monogram Vernis Alma BB' monogram embossed patent leather handbag, serial no.MI2110, some faint marks and hairlines.

c2010 *9in (23cm) wide*

£850-950 **FELL**

An early 20thC Maison Goyard fitted gown trunk, in black 'Goyardine' printed canvas, monogrammed 'M.A.K./PHILADELPHIA' with various shipping labels, labelled 'GOYARDAINE'.

43½in (110.5cm) wide

£7,000-8,000 **FRE**

An Edwardian leather travelling trunk, in hide with brass stud reinforced corners and strap banding, stencilled 'J.F. CHRISTIE', stamped 'LECKIE GRAHAM & CO./ MANUFACTURERS/GLASGOW'.

33in (84cm) wide

£700-800 **L&T**

A Hermès leather-bound canvas suitcase, with stamped brass furniture and bosses, opening to a void, cotton-lined interior with two leather straps.

c1935 *31¾in (80.5cm) wide*

£1,500-2,000 **L&T**

A Louis Vuitton Damier steamer trunk, serial no.N31640, stencilled 'E.B.K/Salem/Mass/u.s.a', locks stamped '0132', with brass handles, some wear.

c1890

£6,000-7,000 **WES**

A Louis Vuitton wardrobe steamer trunk, serial no.350391, retailed by Marshall Field & Company, Chicago, monogrammed and stencilled 'M.McC.', locks stamped '041545', tears, wear and abrasions.

c1914 *44½in (113cm) high*

£4,500-5,000 **WES**

Judith Picks

Louis Vuitton (1821-92) opened his first shop in 1854 and had his first great success with the 'Trianon' trunk in 1858. This trunk was waterproof, canvas-covered and airtight, meaning that, unlike previous trunks, it did not need to have a sloped top to allow water to run off it. Instead it was a more practical and stackable shape. To combat reproductions by rivals, Vuitton introduced beige and brown striped canvas in 1876, followed in 1888 by its chequered 'Damier' pattern and in 1896 by the 'LV' monogram fabric. From 1932 it also produced handbags, its first being the 'Noe' and the 'Speedy'.

Louis Vuitton trunks remain highly collectable today. The only problem with them is that, when full, you really need a servant to help you carry them! They are exceptionally heavy, and now usually used for decorative or storage purposes, not travel.

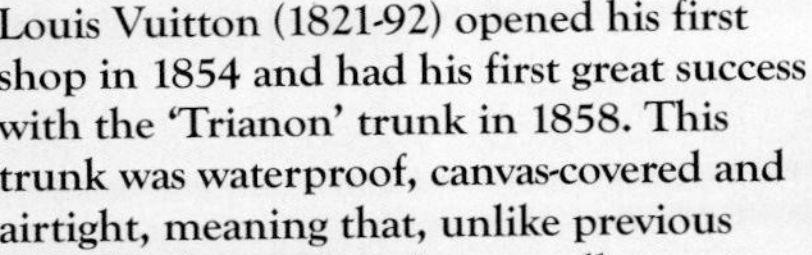

A Louis Vuitton travelling trunk, with brass mounts, wooded slats and 'LV' fabric, with interior label for '149 New Bond Street, London', stamped '192993', lacking internal tray.

43½in (110.5cm) wide

£5,500-6,000 **GORL**

A Louis Vuitton case, no.1074290, Paris, with brass corners, hinges and lock, no.290909, the interior with lift-out clothes holder, with outer cover.

29in (73.5cm) long

£3,000-3,500 **JN**

A 1990s Louis Vuitton monogrammed leather shoe trunk/ suitcase, with twelve interior compartments, labelled 'Ave. Marceau 78 Paris, Nice. 2 Ave de Suède', numbered '938217'.

23½in (60cm) long

£2,000-2,500 **KT**

A Louis Vuitton travelling jewellery case, with brass locks, no.1252027, opening to a velvet interior with lift out jewellery tray, serial no.1051049.

13½in (34cm) long

£4,000-5,000 **JN**

ESSENTIAL REFERENCE – JOSE DE ACOSTA

The 'Naturall and Morall Historie of the East and West Indies', originally 'Historia Natural y Moral', established Jose de Acosta's reputation as a keen observer capable of relating detailed and realistic descriptions of the New World. Acosta was a Spanish Jesuit who first travelled to the Americas in 1570. In addition to notes on the natural history of the places he visited, including Peru, Panama, and Mexico, he also describes Incan and Aztec customs and natural geographical features, such as tides, lakes, rivers, and mineral resources. He also established several universities in South America, where native languages were carefully studied and recorded, and was responsible for bringing a printing press to Peru in the 1570s.

Acosta, Jose de (1540-1600), 'Naturall and Morall Historie of the East and West Indies', first English edition, printed by Val Sims for Edward Blount and William Aspley, London, quarto, minor staining to leaves.
1604 *7¼in (18.5cm) high*
£13,000-16,000 **SK**

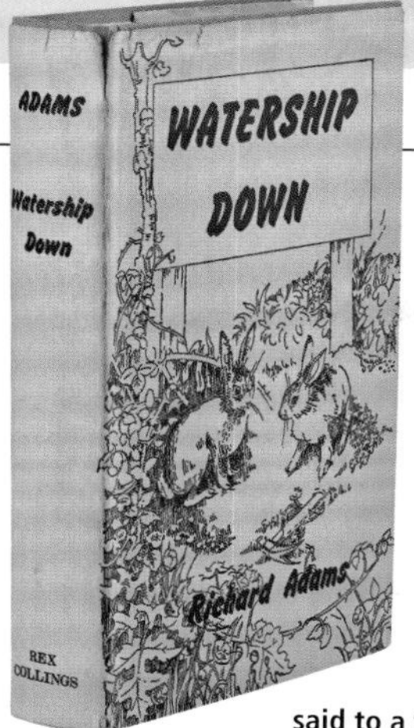

Adams, Richard, 'Watership Down', first edition, published by Rex Collings, London, 8vo, ownership signature to endpaper.

This copy contains a compliments slip from the Ministry of Agriculture, Fisheries and Food, where Adams worked at the time of writing. Rex Collings was a one-man publishing outfit who took on Watership Down in 1972, printing 2,500 copies. He said to a friend at the time, 'I've just taken on a novel about rabbits, one of them with extra-sensory perception. Do you think I'm mad?' The book was a success and was later republished by Penguin.
1972
£500-600 **L&T**

Barrie, J.M., 'Peter Pan in Kensington Gardens.', first edition, illustrated by Arthur Rackham, published by Hodder & Stoughton, London, small 4to, 50-colour plates, some rubbing and splitting.
1906
£500-600 **L&T**

Bemelmans, Ludwig, 'Madeline', first edition, illustrated by Bemelmans, published by Simon and Schuster, New York, 4to, some wear.
1939
£1,200-1,600 **SWA**

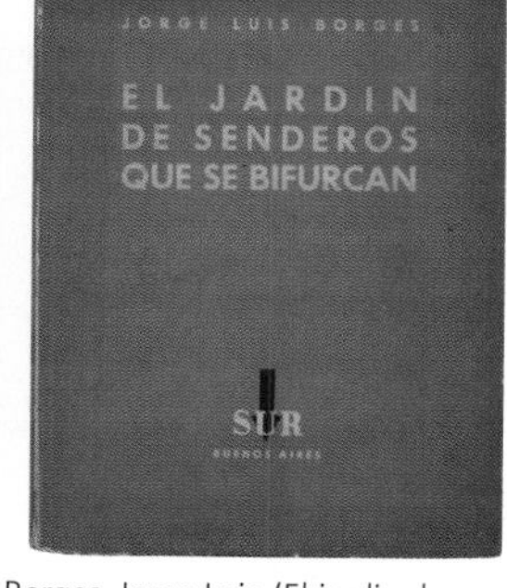

Borges, Jorge Luis, 'El jardin de senderos que se bifurcan' ('The Garden of Forking Paths'), first edition, published by Sur, Buenos Aires, 8vo, signed and dated to half title by Borges.
1942
£4,000-5,000 **FRE**

Bradbury, Ray, 'Fahrenheit 451', limited edition no.145/200, illustrated by Joe Muganini, published by Ballantine, New York, 8vo, signed by Bradbury, with first trade edition dust jacket with mild wear.

This limited edition of 'Fahrenheit 451' is bound in Johns-Manville Quinterra, an asbestos material that is very resistant to fire – the idea being that this book, unlike so many within the novel, cannot be burnt.
1953
£7,000-8,000 **SWA**

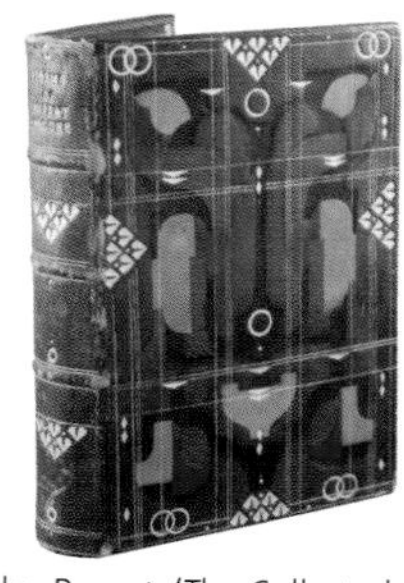

Brooke, Rupert, 'The Collected Poems', published by Sidgwick and Jackson, London, 8vo, binding by Sybil Pye, with her stamped monogram date for 1944.

Sybil Pye recorded her bindings, this being no.136 (See Marianne Tidcombe, 'Women Bookbinders 1880-1920').
1918
£2,200-2,800 **GORL**

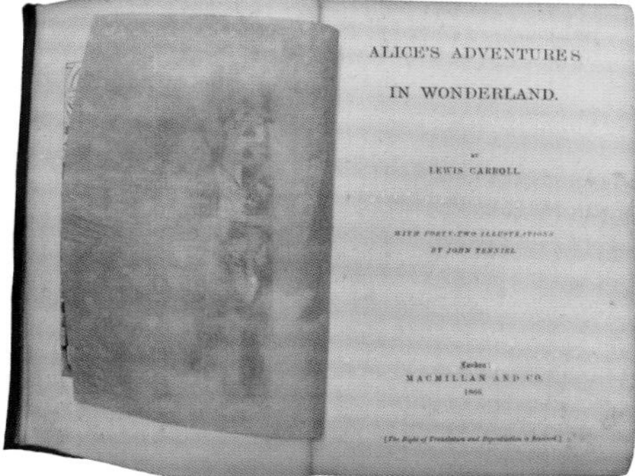

Carroll, Lewis, 'Alice's Adventures in Wonderland', illustrated by John Tenniel, second (first published) edition, published by Macmillan and Co., 8vo, spine torn, split, some losses, old ink signature 'Lizzie' to endmatter.

Owing to Tenniel's dissatisfaction with the printing of the illustrations, the original first edition was recalled before sale. This issue was the first published edition.
1866
£3,000-4,000 **BELL**

Cervantes, Saavedra, Miguel de (1547-1616) 'The History of the Most Renowned Don Quixote of Mancha: and his Trusty Squire Sancho Pancha', English translation by John Phillips (1631-1706), published by Thomas Hodgkin, London, some stains and tears.

1687 *12in (30.5cm) high*

£3,500-4,000 **SK**

Christie, Agatha, 'The Mysterious Affair at Styles', first edition, published by John Lane, The Bodley Head, London, in quarter morocco solander box.

Agatha Christie (1890-1976) was one of the best-loved and best-selling crime writers of the 20thC and remains incredibly popular today. 'The Mysterious Affair at Styles' was her first book and the debut of Hercule Poirot.

1921

£4,500-5,000 **KEY**

Collodi, Carlo, 'The Story of a Puppet or The Adventures of Pinocchio', first English edition, illustrated by Enrico Mazzanti, published by T. Fisher Unwin, made for The Children's Library.

1892

£2,000-2,500 **CHOR**

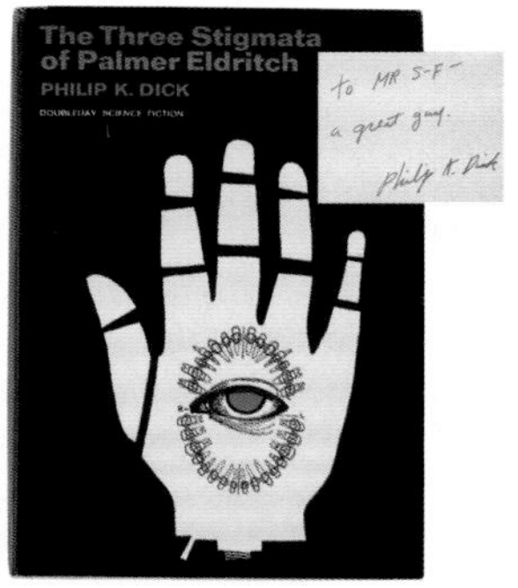

Dick, Philip K., 'The Three Stigmata of Palmer Eldritch', first edition, published by Doubleday & Company, Garden City, 8vo, inscribed by Dick 'To MR S-F-/a great guy/Philip K. Dick', some rubbing to spine.

1965

£13,000-16,000 **SWA**

Dickens, Charles, 'The Personal History of David Copperfield', first edition in original 19/20 parts, published by Bradbury & Evans, London, in a morocco backed box, with 40 engraved plates, some repairs.

1849-50 *8¾in (22cm) high*

£2,500-3,000 **DOY**

Dickinson, Emily, 'Poems Second Series', first edition, first issue (one of 960 copies), published by Roberts Brothers, Boston, edited by T.W. Higginson and Mabel Loomis Todd, some rubbing, spine darkened.

1891 *7in (18cm) high*

£1,500-2,000 **DOY**

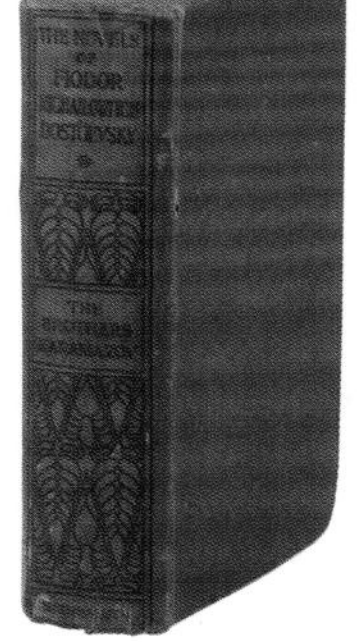

Donne, John (1572-1631), 'Pseudo-Martyr', first edition, printed by William Stansby for Walter Burre, London, quarto, in a custom phase box.

After Henry VIII led the British people into the protestant religion, his citizens struggled with Royal allegiances and religious conscience. In 'Pseudo-Martyr', Donne, himself a converted Catholic, advises British Roman Catholics to take the Oath of Allegiance to James I. This was Donne's first appearance in print; he later made his name as a poet.

1610 *8¾in (22cm) high*

£17,000-20,000 **SK**

Dostoevsky, Fyodor, 'The Brothers Karamazov', first English edition, translated by Constance Garnett, published by William Heinemann, London, 8vo, joints weak, some wear.

The original book was published in Russian in 1880.

1912

£5,000-6,000 **L&T**

Doyle, Sir Arthur Conan, 'The Hound of the Baskervilles', first edition, illustrated in 16 plates by Sidney Paget, 8vo, some rubbing.

1902

£900-1,100 **BLO**

Du Maurier, Daphne, 'Jamaica Inn', first edition, published by Victor Gollancz, 8vo, some chipping to spine.

1936

£3,000-3,500 CA

Fleming, Ian, 'Live and Let Die', first edition, first impression, published by Jonathan Cape, London, some chipping and tears, '2-4' in pencil to the lower wrapper.

1954

£4,500-5,000 L&T

CLOSER LOOK – FIRST EDITION FAULKNER

This is a first edition of Faulkner's first book, a poetry collection. Only about 500 copies of the first edition were printed.

It is signed and inscribed to Dorothy Wilcox from Faulkner and Phil Stone. Phil Stone was Faulkner's mentor in Oxford.

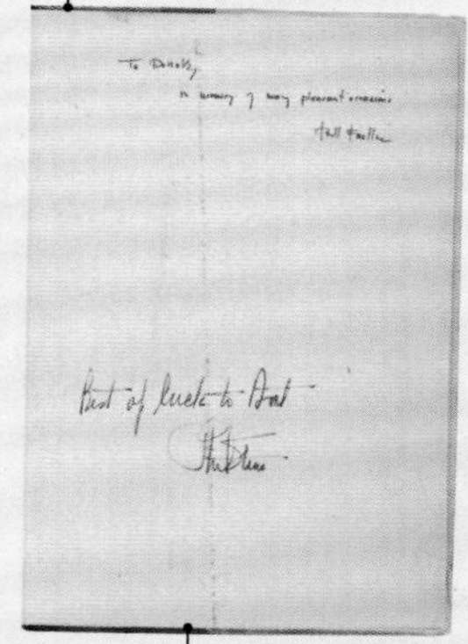

The history of this copy is documented in Joseph Blotner 'Faulkner: A Biography': 'One day when they went to Dot Wilcox's home for dinner, Faulkner brought along a copy of The Marble Faun... 'Dot,' Stone said, 'you keep this book. Someday this tramp will be famous."

Despite some wear, this remains a rare and valuable book. This edition is fairly fragile, and few copies have survived at all.

Faulkner, William, 'The Marble Faun', published by the Four Seas Company, Boston, 8vo.

1924

£18,000-22,000 SWA

Frank, Anne, 'Het Achterhuis: Dagboekbrieven van 12 Juni 1942-1 Augustus 1944' ('The House Behind: Diary Entries'/'Anne Frank's Diary'), first edition, first printing, published by Uitgeverij Contact, Amsterdam, original Dutch text, 8vo, contents showing usual browning.

This is one of only 1500 copies printed and, in its unrestored first issue dust jacket, is exceedingly rare. After its initial release, the book was translated and published in more than 60 languages. It remains one of the most widely read books in the world.

1947

£15,000-20,000 SWA

Garcia Marquez, Gabriel, 'Cien anos de soledad' ('One Hundred Years of Solitude'), first Spanish edition, first printing, published by Edhasa, Barcelona, 8vo, some creases.

1969

£1,000-1,500 FRE

Gosse, Philip Henry, 'Illustrations of the Birds of Jamaica', published by Jacob van Voorst, London, large 8vo, 52 hand-coloured lithographed plates, light stain, one plate (Himantopus nigricollis) with loss to image.

In 1844 Philip Henry Gosse travelled to Jamaica to collect exotic insects and other specimens on a commercial basis. He spent 18 months there, during which time he collected some 7,800 insects. He was also interested in birds, and published three books on the birds of Jamaica, including 'The Birds of Jamaica' (1847) and this, its accompanying plate volume, 'Illustrations of the Birds of Jamaica' (1849). The plate volume is the rarer of the two.

1849

£2,500-3,000 L&T

Hemmingway, Ernest, 'In Our Time', first edition, no.137/170, published by Three Mountains Press, Paris, tall 8vo, on Rives handmade paper, woodcut frontispiece portrait by Henry Strater, edges uncut, light rubbing.

1924

£18,000-22,000 CA

Hemingway, Ernest, 'The Old Man and the Sea', first edition, published by Scribner's, New York, with author's signature blind-stamped, small spotting, edges toned.

1952

£3,000-3,500 CA

Jardine, Sir William, and Selby, Prideaux John, 'Illustrations of Ornithology', first edition, published by W.H. Lizars, Edinburgh, and Longman, Rees and Co., London, 4vo, volumes 1-3, with 149 engraved plates, some hand-coloured.
1826-35
£3,500-4,000 L&T

Joyce, James, 'Haveth Childers Everywhere: Fragment from Work in Progress', first edition, no.38/100 (of 685 copies) published by Henry Babou and Jack Kahane and The Fountain Press, Paris and New York, 4to, signed in pencil by James Joyce, in box.

This is the second book instalment of Works in Progress, the gradually unfolding development of Finnegans Wake, which further unfolded into the revised text of the eventual full book publication in 1939.
1930
£5,000-6,000 FRE

Keith, George, 'Truth Advanced in the Correction of Many Gross & Hurtful Errors', published by William Bradford, New York, 4to, 18thC sewn wrappers over original wrapper, some worming causing losses.

This is one of the earliest books printed in New York.
1694
£25,000-30,000 FRE

Kerouac, Jack, 'On the Road', first edition, first printing, published by Viking, New York.
1957 *8¼in (21cm) high*
£1,400-1,800 DOY

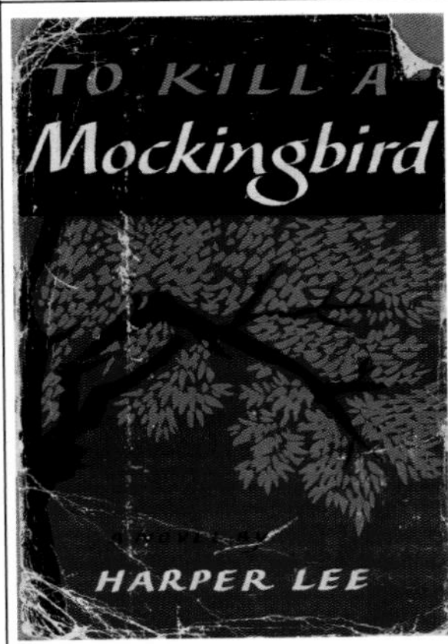

Lee, Harper, 'To Kill A Mockingbird', first edition, published by Lippincott, Philadelphia & New York, 8vo, with Jonathan Daniels blurb and Capote portrait of Harper Lee, dust jacket worn with damp-staining.
1960
£4,000-5,000 SWA

London, Jack, 'The Call of the Wild', first edition, first issue, illustrated by Philip R. Goodwin and Charles Livingston Bull, published by The Macmillan Company, New York, 8vo, inscribed by the author on the half-title 'Yours for the Revolution, Jack London, Glen Ellen, Feb. 22, 1911'.
1903
£3,000-3,500 SWA

McCarthy, Cormac, 'Blood Meridian: Or the Evening Redness in the West', first edition, first printing, published by Random House, New York.
1985
£1,300-1,600 DOY

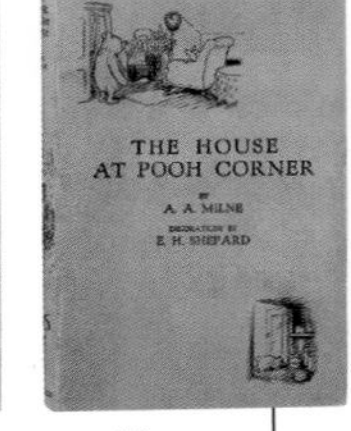

Milne, A.A., complete set of four 'Christopher Robin' first editions, illustrated by Ernest H. Shepard, published by Methuen, London, 8vo, all but the last title signed by Milne.
1924-28
£9,000-12,000 SWA

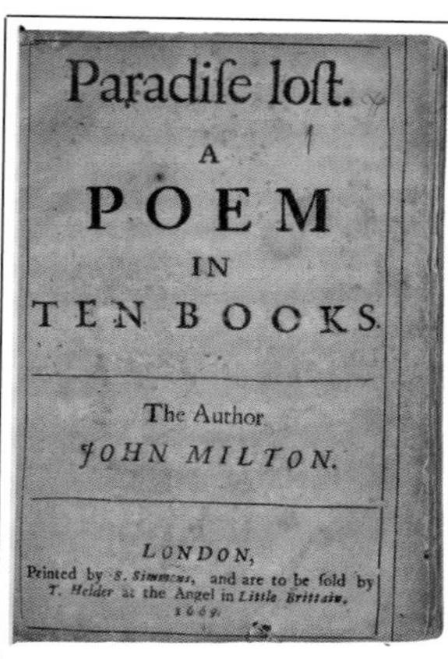

Milton, John (1608-74), 'Paradise Lost: A Poem in Ten Books', first edition, printed by S. Simmons, London, quarto, trimmed close, marginal loss to one text leaf, tooled in blind.

1669 *6¾in (17cm) high*

£11,000-14,000 **SK**

Montgomery, L.M., 'Anne of Green Gables', first edition, first impression, illustrated in eight plates by M.A. and W.A.J. Claus, published by L.C. Page & Company, Boston, 8vo, two owner's signatures at front.

1908

£3,000-4,000 **SWA**

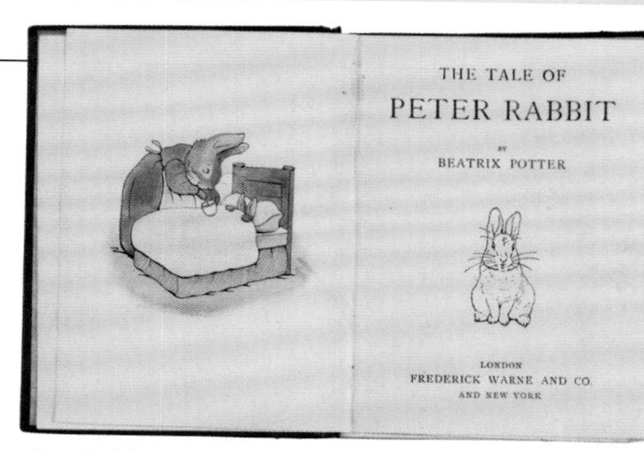

Potter, Beatrix, 'The Tale of Peter Rabbit', first trade edition, published by Frederick Warne, 16mo, colour frontispiece and 30 colour plates, some light rubbing and staining.

250 copies of 'The Tale of Peter Rabbit' were privately printed in 1901 by Strangeways. Owing to the book's success, it was then taken on by Frederick Warne, who printed 'The Tale of Peter Rabbit' in colour in 1902. The 1901 Strangeways edition is rarer than the 1902 trade edition, and therefore more valuable. See 'Miller's Antiques Handbook & Price Guide 2018-2019', page 397, for an example worth £20,000-25,000.

1902

£650-750 **BLO**

Steinbeck, John, 'Of Mice and Men', first edition, first issue, published by Covici-Friede, New York, 8vo.

1937

£1,200-1,600 **SWA**

Sharpe, R. Bowdler, 'Monograph of the Paradiseidae, or Birds of Paradise, and Ptilonorhynchidae, or Bower-Birds', first edition, published by H. Sotheran, London, 8 parts in 2 volumes, 79 hand-coloured lithographic plates by W. Hart after Hart, J. Gould and J.G. Keulemans.

1891-98

£28,000-32,000 **L&T**

Stanley, Henry M., 'How I Found Livingstone, Travels, Adventures and Discoveries in Central Africa', first edition, published by Sampson Low, London, 8vo, 5 maps and 28 plates.

1872

£750-850 **L&T**

Sendak, Maurice, 'Where the Wild Things Are', first issue with scarce original dust jacket, published by Harper & Row, New York, oblong 8vo, signed and inscribed by Sendak with an original early full-length drawing of Max.

Provenance: ex-collection playwright, choreographer, friend of Sendak and fellow children's book author and illustrator, William Archibald, with his ownership signature to the half-title.

1963

£11,000-15,000 **SWA**

Stoker, Bram, 'Dracula', first edition, first issue, published by Archibald Constable, Westminster, 8vo, spine darkened, scattered soiling, closed tear to title repaired.

1897

£10,000-14,000 **SWA**

Stowe, Harriet Beecher, 'Uncle Tom's Cabin, or, Negro Life in the Slave States of America', first English edition, published by C.H. Clarke, London, 8vo, 40 full-page illustrations, tissue guards, light spotting.

1852

£400-500 LC

Tolstoy, Leo, 'War and Peace', first edition, 8vo, Moscow, six parts in four vols, some wear and repair, with later morocco backed boards.

1868-69

£3,000-4,000 CHEF

Wells, H.G., 'The War In The Air', first edition, published by George Bell and Sons, with a story removed from 'The Strand' Magazine 1909 by H.G. Wells 'My First Aeroplane (Alauda Magna)', page ends foxed.

1908

£9,000-11,000 CUTW

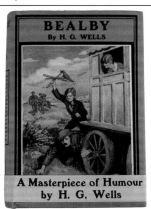

Tolkien, J.R.R. 'The Lord Of The Rings', first editions, published by Allen & Unwin, London, octavo, in three volumes, each volume with a map illustrated by the author, with Islip of paper inscribed 'If you would like a signature for 'The Lord of the Rings', you can stick this in with my good wishes. J.R.R.Tolkien 20/6/73'.

1954-55 *8¾in (22.5cm) high*

£6,500-7,500 WHYT

Twain, Mark, 'The Adventures of Huckleberry Finn', first edition, earliest available issue, published by Charles L. Webster, New York.

1885 *8½in (21.5cm) high*

£6,000-7,000 DOY

Wells, H.G., 'Bealby', first edition, published by Methuen & Co., printer's date '25/11/14', advert leaflets dated 'Spring 1915'.

1915

£1,500-2,000 CUTW

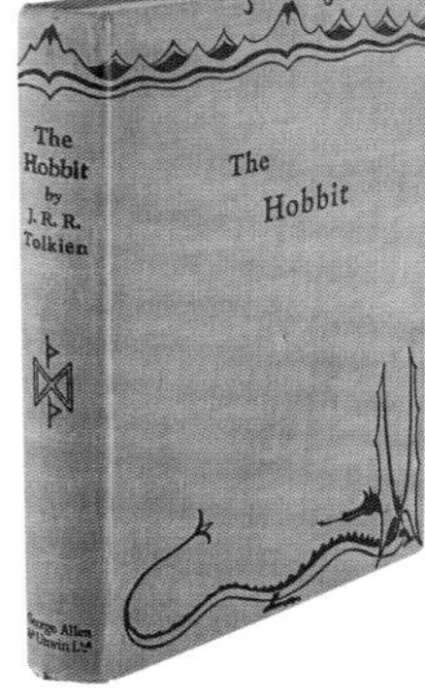

Tolkien, J.R.R., 'The Hobbit, or There and Back Again', second impression, published by George Alen & Unwin Ltd., London, 8vo.

1937

£1,800-2,200 L&T

Wells, H.G., 'Kipps: The Story Of A Simple Soul', first edition, first printing, published by Macmillan and Co., split inside spine, discolouration to jacket, creased end flap.

1905

£5,500-6,500 CUTW

Yeats, W.B., 'The Winding Stair And Other Poems', first edition, published by Macmillan and Co., London, 8vo, cloth to a design by Sturge Moore, some fading, book plate and early owner's inscription.

This edition differs considerably to the work of the same name published in New York in 1929.

1933

£550-650 L&T

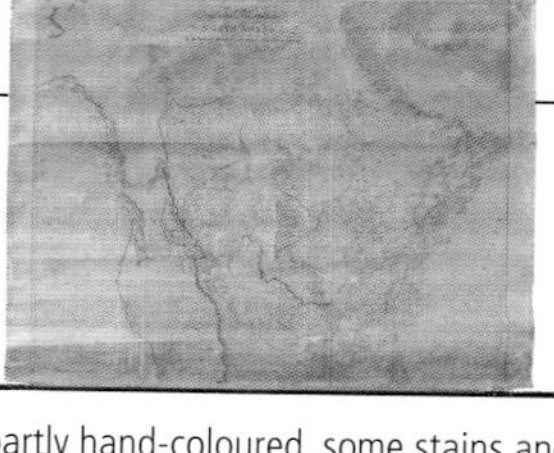

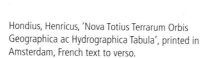

Arrowsmith, Aaron, 'Map Exhibiting all the New Discoveries in the Interior Parts of North America Inscribed by Permission to the Honourable Governor and Company of Adventurers of England Trading into Hudson's Bay', partly hand-coloured, some stains and wear, dated.
1795 *57¼in (145.5cm) wide*
£2,500-3,500 **L&T**

Clouet, Jean Baptiste Louis (c1730-90), 'Carte Generale de la Tierne ou Mappe Marde, Aue les Quatres Principaux Sisteries...', with hand-coloured detail, four sheets.
1787 *47¼in (120cm) wide*
£6,000-7,000 **SWO**

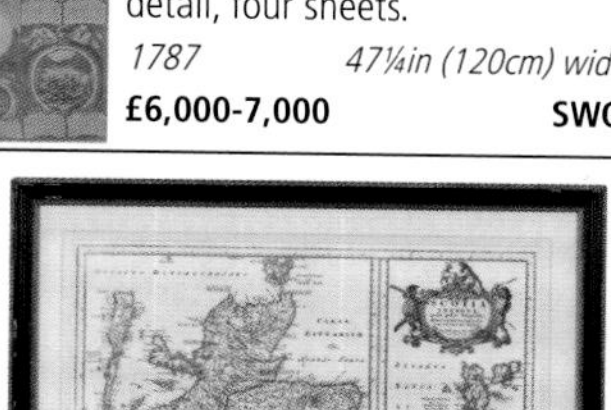

Gordon, Robert, 'Scotia Antiqua: Map Of Scotland', printed by Blaeu, Amsterdam, hand-coloured.
1653 *22in (56cm) wide*
£850-950 **L&T**

CLOSER LOOK – MAP OF NORTH AMERICA

This map is titled 'L'Amerique, divisee selon letendue de ses principales parties' ('America, divided according to the significance of its main parties').

The map is bordered by an engraved title banner and sheets of explanatory text.

Two important commercial elements of the New World are prominently represented: the Newfoundland cod fishery and the beaver fur trade.

The cartography shows a depiction of California as a very large island, and reflects contemporary Jesuit information of the Great Lakes and inland river systems.

De Fer, Nicolas, 'L'Amerique', printed in Paris, on four sheets, untrimmed deckle edges.
1716 *66in (167.5cm) wide*
£25,000-30,000 **SWA**

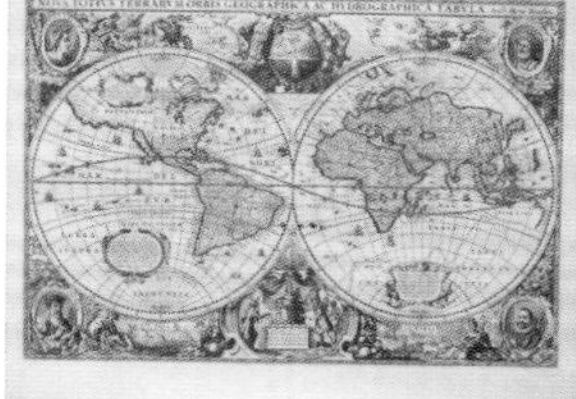

Hondius, Henricus, 'Nova Totius Terrarum Orbis Geographica ac Hydrographica Tabula', printed in Amsterdam, French text to verso.
1630 *22¾in (58cm) wide*
£4,000-5,000 **SWA**

Melish, John, 'Map of the United States with the Contiguous British & Spanish Possessions', printed in Philadelphia, engraved and hand-coloured, dissected in 40 sections, scattered staining, minor chipping, in original morocco-backed case.

This map is the first representation of the continental United States to be shown as an integrated landmass from the Atlantic Ocean to the Pacific, systematically incorporating the explorations and mappings of Lewis and Clark, Zebulon Pike, Aaron Arrowsmith, Alexander von Humboldt and others.
1816 *58in (147.5cm) wide*
£16,000-20,000 **SWA**

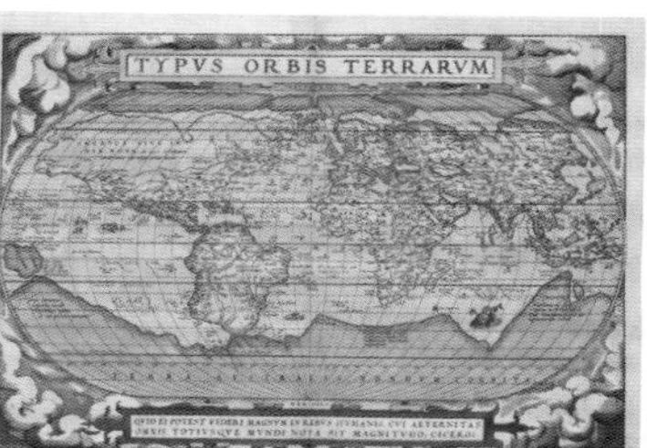

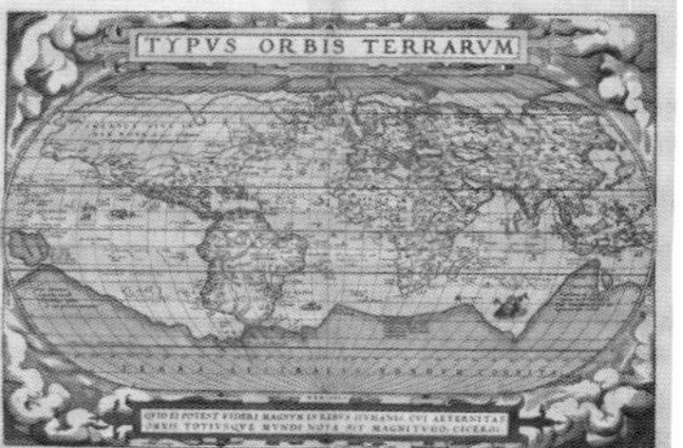

Ortelius, Abraham, 'Typus Orbis Terrarum', true first edition, printed in Antwerp, hand-coloured engraved world map, Latin text on verso.
1570 *20¼in (51.5cm) wide*
£8,500-9,500 **SWA**

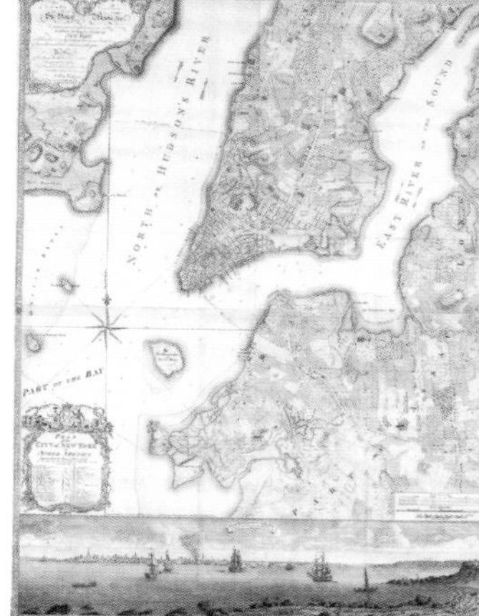

Ratzer, Bernard, 'Plan of the City of New York in North America, surveyed in the years 1766 & 1767', second issue, printed by Faden & Jeffreys, London, with view of New York from Governors Island, some repairs on verso to fold.

In 1765, Lieutenant Bernard Ratzer, a skilled surveyor and engineer in the Royal American Regiment, continued a survey of Manhattan begun by John Montressor in 1766. The following year he issued his highly accurate plan of Manhattan. The map was re-issued in 1776 as war became imminent, and was used by British officers. It is often encountered dissected and folded for easier use. It is considered one of the finest 18thC maps of an American city.
1776 *48½in (123cm) long*
£120,000-160,000 **DOY**

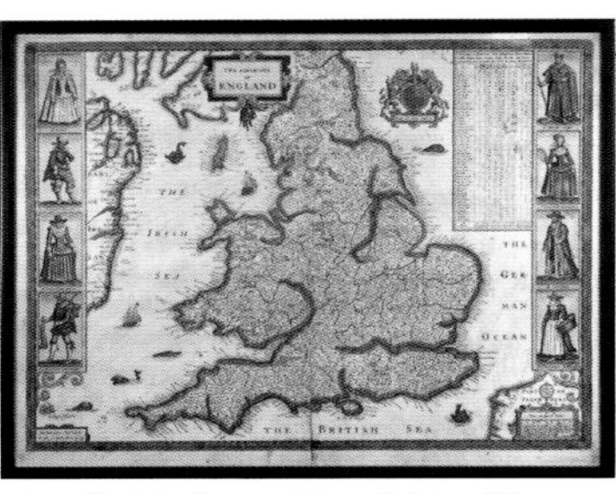

Saxton, Christopher and Speed, John, 'The Kingdome of England', hand-coloured, engraved by Abraham Goos for Bassett and Chiswell, inaccurately dated '1646'.
c1676 *21in (53.5cm) wide*
£450-550 **CHEF**

Sayer, Robert, 'North American Map', printed in London, hand-coloured in outline, signed 'Robert Sayer, Versailles, 20 Jan 1783', some tears.
1786 *47¼in (120cm) wide*
£1,400-1,800 **L&T**

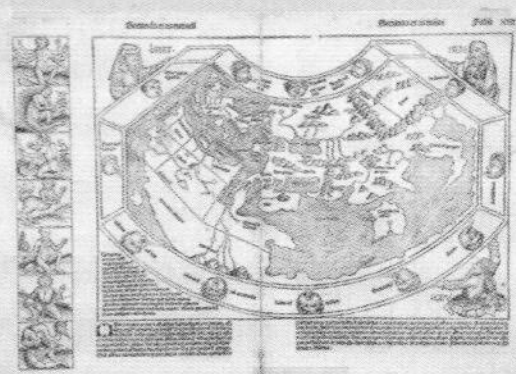

Schedel, Hartmann 'World map', extracted from the Liber Chronicaru, published by A. Koberger, Nuremberg, with Latin text, the reverse with 14 wood engravings, with some tape, small marginal losses, minor staining.

Based upon Ptolemy, and produced the year that Columbus announced his discovery of America, Schedel's map omits Scandinavia, southern Africa and the Far East. The Indian Ocean is depicted as a landlocked sea.
1493 *22¼in (56.5cm) wide*
£5,500-6,000 **DOY**

ESSENTIAL REFERENCE – JOHN SPEED

John Speed (c1552-1629) is arguably the most famous English cartographer. He was also a historian.

- **He was the son of a tailor, and was brought up to carry on the family trade, becoming a member of the Merchant Taylors' Company in 1580.**
- **Within the guild he came to the notice of Sir Fulk Greville, under whose patronage he was ultimately able to leave tailoring to pursue his history writing and map-making.**
- **In 1611, his first great work of history, 'The History of Great Britain under the Conquests of ye Romans, Saxons, Danes and Normans' was published.**

Speed, John, 'Map of the World', sold by George Humble, hand-coloured copper engraving, with allegorical figures representing the four elements, diagrams of 'Heavens and Elements', with illustrations of eclipses and celestial hemispheres, portraits of circumnavigators including Sir Francis Drake, framed.
22in (56cm) wide
£6,000-7,000 **HAN**

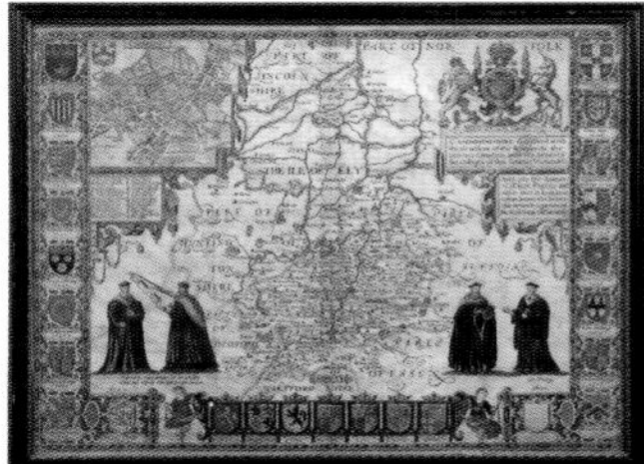

Speed, John, 'Cambridgeshire described with the devision of the hundreds', published by Sudbury and Humble, hand-coloured and engraved, some surface wear.

The shields around the edge are of Cambridge Colleges.
c1611 *20½in (52cm) wide*
£750-850 **CHEF**

Speed, John, 'The Invasions of England and Ireland', engraved by Cornelius Danckerts for George Humble.
c1627 *20¾in (53cm) wide*
£700-800 **CHEF**

Speed, John, 'Cornwall', published by Bassett & Chiswell, engraved by Jodocus Hondius, with hand-colouring, English text verso with woodcut initial by William Godbid.
1676 *15¼in (38.5cm) wide*
£850-950 **BLO**

Speed, John, 'Britain as it was devided in the tyme of the Englishe Saxons', published by Sudbury and Humble, hand-coloured copper engraving, English text to verso, framed and glazed.
20½in (52cm) wide
£1,400-1,800 **HAN**

Walton, Robert, 'A New and Accurat Map of the World Drawne According to ye Truest Descriptions Latest Discoveries & Best Observations yt Have Beene Made by English or Strangers', printed in London.

This is an exceptionally fine example of this scarce English world map, often mistaken for the very similar geography and design of John Speed.
1659 *22in (56cm) wide*
£5,000-6,000 **SWA**

CLOSER LOOK – 18THC WOODEN DOLL

This is a rare 18thC turned, carved and painted wooden doll.

She has a detailed face, with inset dark glass eyes, stitched brows, eyelashes and a wool wig.

She wears full formal evening dress, with wired skirt hoops, short shift, linen petticoat, knitted silk stockings, brocade shoes, and a cream silk brocade open robe, with a pearl choker around her neck.

She carries a glass bell and watch key, an enamelled watch set and silk gauze cap with pearls, artificial flowers and silk ribbons.

An English 18thC wooden doll, with stuffed cotton arms and white painted legs, slight wear to face, some fingers missing.

Provenance: purchased by Isabella Byne (1745-97), a reverend's daughter who married into the wealthy Carr family, probably as a gift for her daughters.

13in (33cm) high

£30,000-35,000 **SAS**

An 18thC turned and carved painted wooden doll, with stuffed wool wig, with stuffed cotton arms and wood hands, in original silk robe, missing one lower leg and two fingertips, some wear.

24in (61cm) high

£6,000-7,000 **SAS**

A George II wooden doll, 'Ursula', with painted gesso-covered face and remains of wig, in silk quilted dress, minor loss to gesso, lower leg loose.

It is written to the back of the torso that 'Ursula' belonged to Grace Marshall, London, 1752.

c1752 *28in (71cm) high*

£6,000-7,000 **C&T**

A carved and painted wooden doll, with gesso-covered head, with cloth and kid leather arms and legs, in a later silk gown, arms lacking stuffing, some repair to legs.

c1770 *29in (73.5cm) high*

£1,800-2,200 **C&T**

A late 18thC fully-jointed carved wooden doll, in early 19thC dress, some losses.

30in (76cm) high

£3,500-4,000 **WHP**

An Autoperipatetikos walking china-head doll, with concealed clockwork.

patented 1862 *9½in (24cm) high*

£750-850 **BE**

A late 18thC wooden doll, with gesso-covered and painted head and neck, with remnants of original wig.

Prices for these early dolls reached a zenith several decades ago which in general they rarely reach today; but exceptions such as this rare doll do occur.

21in (52cm) high

£15,000-20,000 **BER**

A German china shoulder-head doll, with glass eyes, on a cloth body with leather forearms and period clothing.

28in (72cm) high

£2,000-2,500 **BER**

ESSENTIAL REFERENCE – BRU JEUNE & CIE

Bru Jeune & Cie (1866-83) was founded in Paris by Léon Casimir Bru.

- **Bru dolls characteristically have fixed paperweight eyes and closed mouths.**
- **As well as fashion dolls, the firm made some novelties, including crying or laughing dolls and dolls with revolving heads.**
- **Dolls are typically marked 'Déposé' and 'Bru Jne & Cie' or 'Bru Jne'. Some dolls may also be marked with a letter (A-M) which relates to the doll's size.**

A Bru Bébé bisque shoulder-head doll, with paperweight eyes and old mohair wig, on a kid body with bisque forearms, paper label to body, bisque incised 'Bru Jne 6', fingers restored.

18in (45.5cm) high

£15,000-20,000 **BER**

A Bru Bébé bisque socket-head doll, with hand-blown glass eyes and human hair wig, on wood and composition jointed body, in original chemise, the head incised 'Bru Jne 5', some playwear, with extra clothes and accessories.

Provenance: originally owned by Ruth Colby (b.1893) of 74 Clinton Avenue, Montclair, New Jersey, USA. It is rare to find an all-original doll with clear provenance and documentation.

16in (40.5cm) high

£10,000-15,000 **MORP**

A fashion bisque socket-head doll, attributed to Bru, with glass eyes and 'Mona Lisa' smile, on a kid body, in a wool walking dress with lace trim, the head incised 'A'.

The 'A' model is the smallest known Bru doll; as the letters of the alphabet progress, the height of the model grows.

12in (30.5cm) high

£1,800-2,200 **MORP**

A 1890s French 'Eden Bébé' bisque head doll, with glass eyes and later wig, on original French jointed wood and composition body, incised 'Eden Bébé Paris'.

20in (51cm) high

£1,200-1,500 **MORP**

A shy-faced Gauthier Bébé, with glass eyes and replacement wig, on original French wood and composition body, re-costumed, the head incised 'F.G.8', some paint touch-ups.

20in (51cm) high

£1,600-2,000 **MORP**

ESSENTIAL REFERENCE – JUMEAU

Jumeau (1842-99) was founded at Montreuil-sur-Bois by Pierre François Jumeau.

- **The firm's dolls typically have large fixed paperweight eyes, swivel heads, pierced ears and closed mouths.**
- **Early Jumeau dolls are marked only with a number; later dolls, made after Pierre's son Emile Jumeau took over the company in 1875, are sometimes marked with a red tick on the head.**
- **Jumeau dolls are known for their elegant, fashionable outfits, and a surviving doll with its original wardrobe is very collectable.**
- **Jumeau remains one of the most sought-after doll makers internationally.**

A Jumeau bisque head doll, with fixed glass eyes and mohair wig, on composition jointed limbs and body, in silk dress, the body stamped with maker's name.

c1870 *15in (38cm) high*

£4,000-4,500 **HT**

A 1870s 'French fashion' bisque shoulder-head doll, probably by Gautlier, with glass eyes, swivel head and human hair wig, on leather body, with period clothing, head incised '4'.

15¼in (39cm) high

£900-1,200 **BER**

A French pressed bisque shoulder-head doll, probably Jumeau, with mohair wig, two fingers chipped, firing crack behind ear.

17¼in (44cm) high

£2,500-3,000 **SAS**

A Jumeau 'Triste' bisque socket-head doll, with distinctive 'longface' and mohair wig, on wood and composition body, head incised '14', body stamped 'Jemeau Medaille D'Or Paris', some paint wear.

29½in (75cm) high

£7,500-8,500 **MORP**

A Kammer & Reinhardt 117 'Mein Liebling' bisque head character doll, with glass eyes, on an articulated German wood and composition body, re-costumed, incised 'A&*R 117 58'.

The body, although German and of the same age as the doll, is not a style normally associated with a Kammer & Reinhardt doll.

23½in (59.5cm) high

£900-1,100 MORP

A Kammer & Reinhardt bisque head toddler doll, with glass flirty eyes and mohair wig, marked 'K & R SIMON & HALBIG 126'.

32in (81.5cm) high

£550-600 HT

A bisque socket-head 'AT' doll, attributed to Kestner, with glass sleep eyes and mohair wig, on a wood and composition Sonneberg-type body, in silk dress and later bonnet, impressed '9'.

This doll is believed to have been made by Kestner, and is referred to by collectors as the 'AT' Kestner, as it somewhat resembles the French doll marked 'AT'.

15in (38cm) high

£3,500-4,000 MORP

A Leopold Lambert automata, with Tete Jumeau bisque head, with original clothes and accessories, with gilt-metal lorgnette and composition legs, with key-wind and stop/start lever, head marked 'Depose Tete Jumeau', missing one fingertip.

c1890 *18in (45.5cm) high*

£2,500-3,000 C&T

An Armand Marseille Chinese bisque head boy doll, marked 'AM 350'.

17in (43cm) high

£400-500 HT

A Petit & DuMontier Bébé bisque socket-head doll, with paperweight eyes, on original French wood and composition jointed body with metal hands, incised 'P 5 D'.

26in (66cm) high

£3,000-4,000 MORP

A Schoenau & Hoffmeister bisque head doll, in original underclothes, later dress, marked 'S PB H 1906 No.15'.

36in (91.5cm) high

£600-700 HAN

An S.F.B.J. bisque head character boy doll, marked 'S.F.B.J. 226 PARIS'.

The Société Française de Fabrication de Bébés et Jouets, or S.F.B.J., was formed in the late 19thC and continued to make dolls until the early 1960s.

19in (48.5cm) high

£500-600 HT

A Simon & Halbig bisque head doll, with glass sleeping eyes, marked 'SH 1079 DEP 7'.

17½in (44.5cm) high

£600-700 HT

An 1890s Jules Steiner Bébé doll, on fully-jointed body, the head incised 'A. 25', backstamped 'Le Parisien FIre SGD.G 15', the body stamped 'Le Parisien Bébé Steiner Paris', retouching to fingers.

23in (58.5cm) high

£1,500-2,000 MORP

A Bliss paper lithograph on wood church, with 23 scripture blocks, some damage to turrets.

21¼in (54cm) high

£600-700 POOK

A G. & J. Lines No.33 dolls' house, with widow's walk, opening to four rooms and two hallways, repainted and re-papered.

c1909 32½in (82.5cm) high

£350-400 SAS

A wooden dolls' house, probably by G. & J. Lines, opening to six rooms, with fireplaces and a working elevator, refurbished, some replacements.

41in (104cm) high

£400-500 SAS

A mid-19thC Silber and Fleming-style painted and papered wood dolls' house, opening to four rooms.

25½in (65cm) high

£250-300 HT

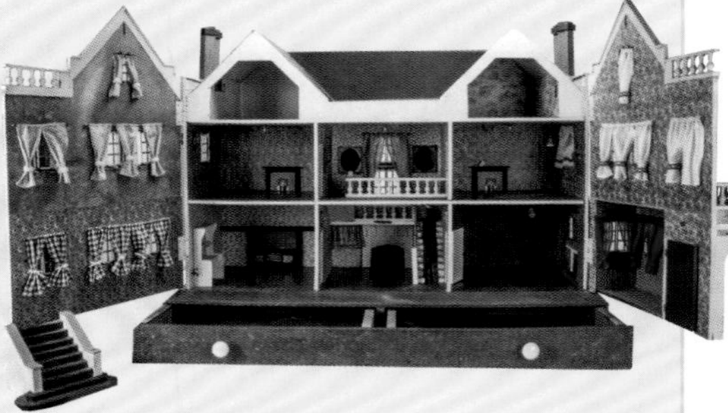

A Tri-ang wooden dolls' house, with tinplate windows and cardboard shutters, the rooms with original papers and fireplaces, electrically-lit.

42in (106.5cm) wide

£1,000-1,500 SAS

An 1870s Silber and Fleming box-back dolls' house, opening to four papered rooms with furniture, on later wood stand, some paint loss and cracks.

39¾in (101cm) high

£400-500 C&T

A Dutch wooden dolls' house.

43in (109cm) wide

£450-500 MORP

A Georgian-style dolls' house, opening to eight rooms, electrically-lit, fully furnished and with a family of dolls, signed and dated, with original 'deeds' or bill of sale.

This is an impressive dolls' house, with a high level of detail: some of the artworks on the wall are miniature reproductions of famous works; there are tiny black and white photographs situated around the house; and even some birds can be found nesting beneath the fascia.

1979 72in (183cm) high

£850-950 EBA

ESSENTIAL REFERENCE – STEIFF BEARS

Steiff is one of the best-known and most collectable makers of teddy bears and other soft toys.

- **Steiff was founded in 1880 by Margarete Steiff (1847-1909) in Giengen, south Germany.**
- **Her nephew Richard Steiff (1877-1939) joined the company in 1897. Together they created the first soft toy bear with jointed arms and legs, the 'Steiff Bär 55 PB'. This was an immediate success, and in 1903 alone Steiff sold over 12,000 bears.**
- **Early Steiff bears typically have long, curved arms, slim ankles, large oval feet and a hump at the top of their backs. Those made after 1904 have a button in one ear. Pre-World War I bears tend to have shoe-button eyes; later bears have glass eyes.**
- **Although the market has softened in recent years, early 20thC Steiff bears in good condition can sell for high prices.**

An early Steiff apricot mohair 'rod' teddy bear, with shoe-button eyes, with mohair loss, leather nose possibly replaced.
20in (51cm) high
£8,500-9,500 BER

An early Steiff gold plush mohair teddy bear, with mohair wear and loss, restorations to pads, wrists and ankles reinforced.
23½in (60cm) high
£5,500-6,000 BER

An early Steiff apricot mohair teddy bear, with swivel head and jointed limbs, with inoperative squeaker, blank ear button, some thinning.
c1906 *14in (35.5cm) high*
£2,500-3,000 SAS

A Steiff straw-stuffed centre-seam cinnamon mohair teddy bear, ear button, wear to mohair, repairs to pads.

Cinnamon-coloured Steiff bears are popular with collectors, but are rarely found in very good condition, as they age more rapidly owing to the dye used.
c1909 *24in (61cm) high*
£2,000-2,500 C&T

A Steiff mohair teddy bear, with inoperative growler and FF button, some thinning.
c1909 *16in (40.5cm) high*
£2,500-3,000 SAS

A Steiff straw-stuffed centre-seam mohair teddy bear, with swivel head, jointed at shoulders and hips, ear button, some wear.
c1909 *16in (41cm) high*
£1,600-2,000 C&T

A Steiff straw-filled plush teddy bear, with swivel joints, black button eyes and felt pads.
c1910 *12½in (32cm) high*
£800-900 HT

A Steiff mohair teddy bear, with swivel head and jointed limbs, inoperative growler, small hole to right pad.
c1910 *18¾in (47.5cm) high*
£3,200-3,800 SAS

An early Steiff blonde teddy bear, with shoe-button eyes and original paw pads, blank ear button, probably originally white.
12½in (32cm) high
£850-950 BER

A 1930s Chad Valley moon-eyed mohair teddy bear, 'Alexander', with inoperative squeaker, blue and white button in ear, some wear.

25½in (65cm) high

£500-600 SAS

A Chiltern mohair Hugmee teddy bear, 'Trevor', kapok and wood wool stuffed, with velveteen pads, cardboard backing to feet.

c1930 26in (66cm) high

£650-750 C&T

A 1920s Farnell mohair teddy bear, 'Compton', kapok and wood wool stuffed, some sparse areas.

24½in (62cm) high

£500-600 C&T

A Farnell mohair 'soldier' teddy bear, 'Lugless Douglas', with remains of pipe-cleaner ears, some wear.

3½in (9cm) high

£400-500 SAS

A Gabrielle Aunt Lucy bear, with original label, glasses.

Aunt Lucy is the aunt of Paddington Bear.

18in (46cm) high

£150-200 LOCK

A 1920s Omega mohair walking teddy bear, inoperative growler, some wear, repairs to pads.

When you hold this bear and walk him along, his weighted feet give him a walking motion.

18in (46cm) high

£1,800-2,200 SAS

A Strunz mohair teddy bear, with swivel head and jointed limbs, with card-lined feet pads, inoperative growler, some repairs.

c1910 22¾in (58cm) high

£3,000-3,500 SAS

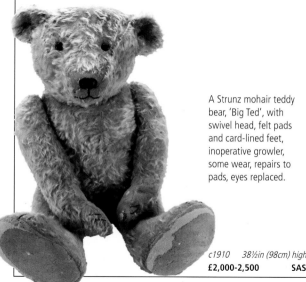

A Strunz mohair teddy bear, 'Big Ted', with swivel head, felt pads and card-lined feet, inoperative growler, some wear, repairs to pads, eyes replaced.

c1910 38½in (98cm) high

£2,000-2,500 SAS

An early German cinnamon mohair teddy bear, in the manner of Steiff, with shoe-button eyes and stitched face, dusty.

14in (35cm) high

£1,000-1,500 BER

A British mohair teddy bear, with unusual narrow-stitched nose and V-shaped mouth, inoperative growler, recovered pads, some wear and thinning.

1910-20 20½in (52cm) high

£550-650 SAS

An early 20thC Bing Werke tinplate open-top limousine, printed 'B W Made in Bavaria', some damages.

Bing was founded by brothers Ignatz and Adolf Bing in 1863. It made toy boats, cars and trains.

12½in (32cm) long

£900-1,000 FLD

A German Carette lithographed tin limousine, with rubber tires and seated chauffeur.

c1910 12½in (32cm) long

£2,500-3,000 BER

A Gunthermann tinplate clockwork car, modelled after 'Bluebird', in original box, with key.

Major Sir Malcolm Campbell MBE (1885-1948) was a British racing motorist and journalist, who gained the land speed record on land and water during the 1920s and 1930s using various vehicles called 'Bluebird.'

19¾in (50cm) long

£1,800-2,200 LC

A clockwork-driven Gunthermann 8-man racing scull, in lithographed tin, some touch-ups.

29in (73.5cm) long

£12,000-15,000 BER

A Märklin Jolanda painted tin clockwork river boat, with original rigging, anchor-wheeled cradle and American flag, some small touch-ups.

29in (73.5cm) long

£40,000-45,000 POOK

A Märklin handpainted tinplate revolving castle fort, some restoration.

Märklin was founded in Göppingen, Germany, in 1856 by Theodor Friedrich Wilhelm Märklin. It produced boats, trains, horse-drawn vehicles and more, and soon became a world leader in toy production.

21in (53.5cm) wide

£4,000-4,500 BER

A Rock & Graner tin toy omnibus, painted with destinations, 'Kew Gardens, Sloane St., Chelsea, Brompton', with a pair of carved and painted wooden horses, coachman and driver, incomplete, in a cardboard box with postage label.

Rock & Graner (1813-1904), Göppingen, Germany, were the premier toy maker of their time. They made a variety of omnibuses for different world cities. This model was made in the 1860s and posted in 1901 from a French lady in Manchester to a Miss J.B. Wright in Biggleswade, in a box inscribed 'Not to be opened'. Despite some damage, it is a remarkable survivor.

15¼in (39cm) long

£30,000-35,000 SWO

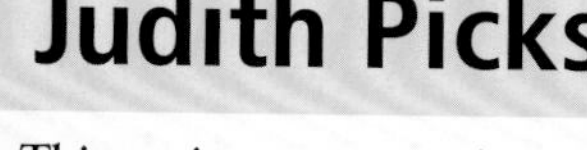

This toy is very rare, as it was only made as a gift for the best customers. It was one of the most complicated toys made in the 19thC. It features a lithographed tin clown sitting at an easel, sketching. The crank-operated mechanism is controlled by a double cam that can be changed to draw different designs. The cams or discs that come with the toy paint four alternative scenes: one man profile to left, two men profile to right, one with a top hat, one with a parrot.

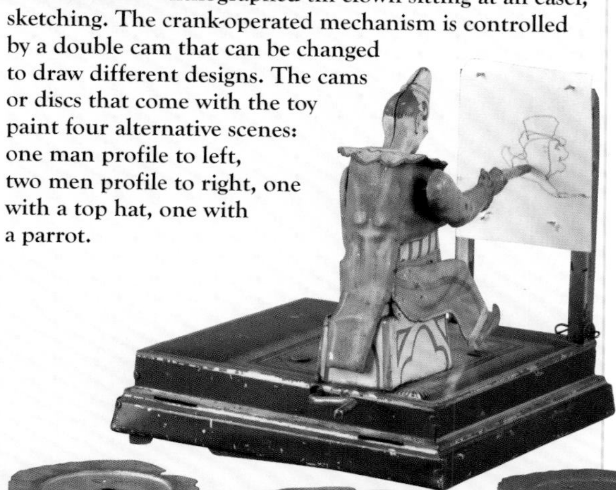

A mechanical toy, by Phillip Vielmetter Mechanische Werkstatten, Berlin.

1885 5in (13cm) wide

£5,500-6,000 BER

A near mint Japanese 'Tremendous Mike' lithographed tin clockwork robot, made by Aoshin Shoten, boxed.

9in (23cm) long

£11,000-14,000 BER

A near mint Corgi Toys 'The Riviera' Gift Set, no.31.

The Corgi Toys range of diecast models was launched by the Mettoy company in 1956.

£300-350 **W&W**

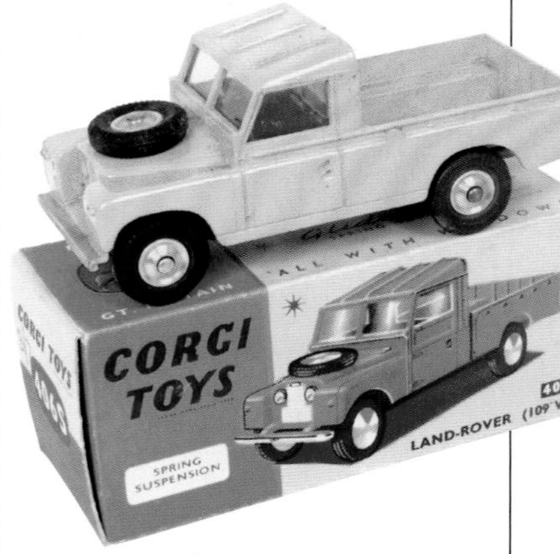

A yellow Corgi Toys No.406S LandRover 109WB, minor playwear, in original box.

£1,000-1,400 **LSK**

A near mint Corgi Toys No.490 Volkswagen breakdown truck, in original box.

£1,200-1,600 **LSK**

A Corgi Toys 'JAMES BOND'S ASTON MARTIN DB5', no.261, with one bandit figure and 'secret instructions' envelope.

£200-250 **LSK**

A near mint Corgi Toys Promotional Commer 'HAMMONDS' van, with 'HAMMONDS' paper label, in original box, numbered '462' in pen on end flaps.

£360-400 **LSK**

A mint Corgi Toys 'The Green Hornet's Black Beauty', no.268, in original box.

£300-400 **W&W**

A near mint Dinky Toys pre-war No.22B closed sports coupe, 'Hornby series' cast to underside.

£850-950 **LSK**

A near mint Dinky Toys No. 504 Foden 14-tonne tanker, in original box.

£850-950 **LSK**

A near mint Dinky Toys No.919 guy van, in original box.

£850-950 **LSK**

A French Dinky no.881 'Pinder' GMC circus lorry, with animals in the trailer, in original box with packing piece.

£500-600 **LSK**

An Austin 'Junior Forty Pathfinder' Grand Prix Racer pedal car.
c1950
£3,500-4,000 **CUTW**

A Gendron Buick pedal car, overpainted, windshield likely replaced.
56in (142cm) long
£12,000-15,000 **BER**

A clockwork-driven Hans Eberl Limousine.
c1910 *11in (28cm) long*
£2,200-2,800 **BER**

An Ives 'Flying Artillery' horse-drawn caisson.
22in (56cm) long
£6,000-6,500 **BER**

A cast iron William Shimer & Son police wagon, Freemansburg, PA, restored.
c1900 *21in (53.5cm) long*
£1,800-2,200 **MORP**

A pristine Structo motor dispatch truck.
9¼in (23.5cm) long
£3,000-3,500 **BER**

A 1920s American Nat'l Buick Juvenile Auto Line pedal car, some accessories replaced.
42in (106.5cm) long
£5,500-6,000 **BER**

An Arcade cast iron white removal van, sporadic paint loss.
13in (33cm) long
£1,500-2,000 **POOK**

A near mint Hubley HFD fire engine pumper, with original nickel-plated boiler, number plate '7292', with original decal at rear.
c1932 *21in (53.5cm) long*
£3,000-3,500 **BER**

A Citroen handpainted clockwork 'Au Louvre' delivery van, hand crank for starting the motor, windshield reattached to body, rear doors repainted.
15in (38cm) long
£40,000-45,000 **BER**

A Britains Set 60 1st Bombay Lancers Display, first issue, some paint chips, in 'Sons of Our Empire' label box.

This piece is fresh to the market, having been recently found in a loft. Vectis specialist Simon Clark has said, 'It is very rare to find a set of this age in 'untouched' condition still contained in its original box'.

1896

£14,000-18,000 VEC

An early Britains toy, 'The Walking Elephant', three wheels missing.

1885

£4,000-4,500 C&T

A Britains set no.1439, 'The Roundabout', driven by a spinning syroscopic wheel, in original box.

C&T Auction's expert James Opie described this roundabout as 'the most perfect example I have ever had the pleasure to twirl'.

1936

£7,000-8,000 C&T

A Doll Company handpainted electric lighthouse, the top section spinning, the base with 'Doll Co.' badge, some repainting.

13in (33cm) long

£5,500-6,000 BER

An Ives handpainted walking Santa figure, with original clothing.

9½in (24cm) high

£3,000-3,500 BER

A Marklin handpainted Churchbury Station.

13in (33cm) long

£30,000-35,000 BER

A Martin 'Bobby' English clockwork policeman, left hand replaced.

c1901 *7in (18cm) high*

£7,000-8,000 BER

CLOSER LOOK – MECHANICAL BANK

This rare cast iron mechanical bank is modelled as a barrel with a painted lead goat on top.

It was made by the firm of J. & E. Stevens & Co. and promotes the Germania Exchange Bank.

It is activated by placing a coin on the goat's tail and turning the faucet, allowing the figure to deposit the coin and seemingly present the depositor with a stein of beer.

It is in largely original unrestored condition and in scarcer painted barrel scheme colours.

An 1880s J. & E. Stevens & Co. mechanical bank, tin trap replaced.

£40,000-45,000 BER

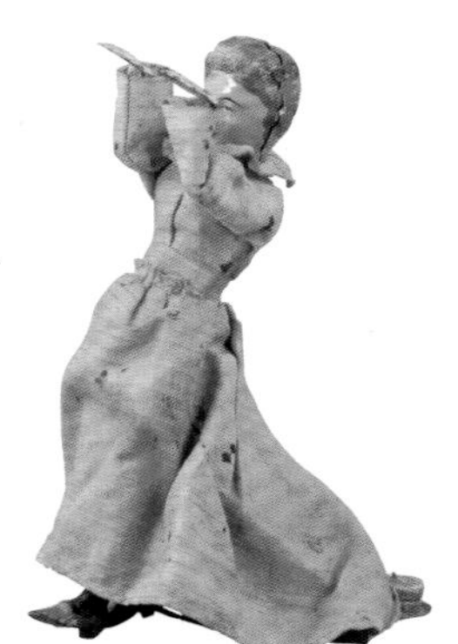

A Martin 'Le Cake-Walk!!!!', paint enhancement to face.

The winners of this dance competition won a cake – hence the name of the dance.

c1903 *8in (20.5cm) long*

£7,500-8,500 BER

A Martin model, 'Le Gymnaste', leaning back and forth when activated, working his way down the bars.

c1905 *14½in (37cm) long*

£14,000-18,000 BER

A 19thC boxed Jaques Staunton chess set, one king stamped 'Jaques London', labelled 'The Staunton Chess-Men, Two Prize Medals Awarded 1861, Jaques & Son, London', some losses and damages.

king 11½in (29cm) high

£2,500-3,000 **HAN**

A 20thC Venetian chess set, by Piero Benzoni, the onyx and marble top with a silvered-gilt border, the chess pieces of silver-plate and gold-plate.

£750-850 **CHOR**

A rosewood games compendium, with a Staunton pattern boxwood and ebonised chess set, draughts, dominoes, cribbage board, playing cards, a boxwood tumbler and dice.

1869 *13in (33cm) wide*

£700-800 **BE**

A Victorian walnut games compendium, with satin birch veneered interior, with ivory games boards and pieces for backgammon, chess, cribbage, draught, dominoes and whist, with dice, markers, counters and playing cards.

14½in (37cm) wide

£2,500-3,000 **WW**

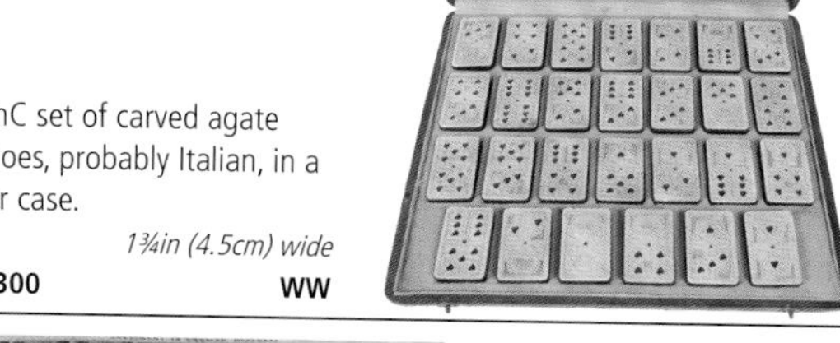

A 19thC set of carved agate dominoes, probably Italian, in a leather case.

1¾in (4.5cm) wide

£250-300 **WW**

A 19thC board game, 'Amusement in English History', by William Sallis, London, hand-coloured lithographs mounted on folding linen sheet, in publisher's cloth on boards.

Each lithograph depicts a monarch and an event during their reign up to the wedding of Queen Victoria. It is possible that this originally came with cards, although these are no longer present.

c1840 *25¼in (64cm) wide*

£250-300 **LSK**

A 19thC French Loysel's Patent Chivalric Game of Tournoy, with a roulette-type spinning wheel, scoring dial and two balls, with 24 pottery playing pieces, instruction booklet, in a walnut case.

£400-500 **LC**

A set of Charles Hodges 'Astronomical' playing cards, by Stopforth & Sons, London, with 52 hand-coloured engraved cards with duty card, rubbed at corners, lettering slightly faded, some foxing to cards, in a Morocco leather case with instruction book.

c1827

£5,000-6,000 **CHOR**

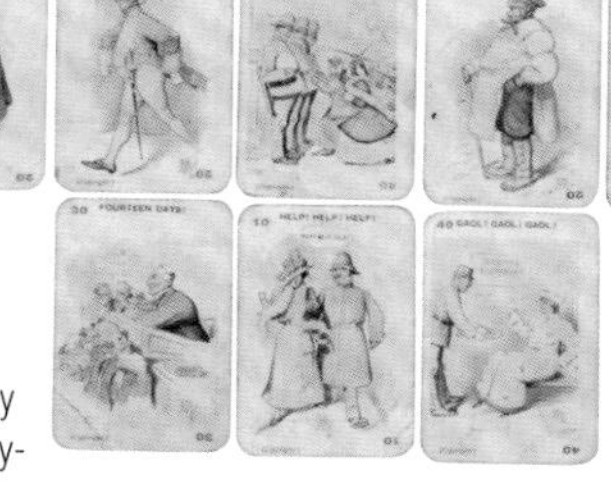

A part set of playing cards from the card game 'Panko or Votes for Women: The Great Card Game Suffragists v Anti-Suffragists', by Peter Gurney of London, comprising thirty-eight illustrated cards.

This game was sold by the Women's Social and Political Union at its shops, as well as through independent merchants, to raise funds for the cause. The cards show various scenes of Women's Suffrage, with one depicting Wallace Dunlop, one of the first hunger strikers, and another depicting Christabel Pankhurst holding a Votes for Women scroll.

c1910

£150-200 **FLD**

A Victorian-type safety rocking horse, by Ian Armstrong of Durham, of layered pine construction.

£350-400 **WHP**

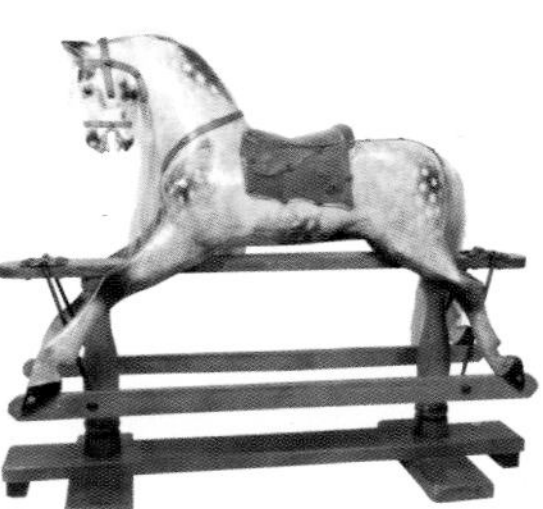

An F.H. Ayres carved and painted wooden trestle rocking horse, with original leather saddle and tack, horsehair tail and mane, with gold 'F.H. Ayres' transfer.

42¼in (107.5cm) wide

£500-600 **SAS**

A J. Collinson carved and painted wooden trestle rocking horse, remains of horsehair mane and tail, some paint lifting.

44¾in (113.5cm) long

£200-250 **SAS**

A Lines Bros. carved and painted wooden trestle rocking horse, cast 'LL & Bros' into metalwork, some wear.

44in (112cm) long

£350-400 **SAS**

A carved and painted wooden trestle rocking horse, No.2, for Selfridges, with original leather saddle and tack, with horsehair tail and mane, stencilled '2 SELFRIDGE', some wear.

32in (81.5cm) long

£550-600 **SAS**

A Stevenson Bros. rocking horse, with Elizabeth II hallmarked silver plaque, two replaced sections to upper right legs, cracks to left legs, minor chips to body.

45¾in (116cm) high

£700-800 **APAR**

A rocking horse, by H. Wakefield Boston, with walnut and mahogany turned stand, incised monogram and '44' to underside.

41¾in (106cm) high

£1,500-2,000 **PW**

An Edwardian rocking horse.

This rocking horse was on long-term loan to the National Trust for Scotland at Kellie Castle, Fife, where it was displayed in the children's nursery.

80in (203cm) long

£2,500-3,000 **L&T**

A late 19thC French Velocipede horse tricycle, with cast iron head, with hand-peddled chain mechanism causing the back wheels to turn, repainted.

32½in (82.5cm) long

£400-500 **SAS**

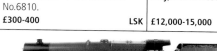

A Bassett-Lowke maroon LMS C/W 'Precurser' 4-4-2 tank loco No.6810.
£300-400 LSK

A near mint early German Bing handpainted stream-type 0-gauge engine and tender, with bell and stacks, marked 'GBN' and 'O/35'.

This was made for the American market. The cow-catcher at the front, to push objects on the tracks out of the way, resembles American trains rather than European.

engine 8½in (21.5cm) long
£12,000-15,000 MORP

A Hornby 'Princess Elizabeth' loco and tender 20V AC, some chips, light corrosion.
1938
£1,200-1,600 LSK

A mint Lee Marsh Model Company 0-gauge finescale 2-rail electric tender locomotive, British Railways Princess Royal Class 4-6-2 'Princess Beatrice' RN 46209, boxed with instruction manual.
£3,000-3,500 W&W

A Märklin 1-gauge handpainted clockwork outline locomotive, for the American market, cow catcher reattached, bell and smoke stack restored.
10in (25.5cm) long
£2,200-2,800 BER

A Märklin 0-gauge Schlitz Beer Car, with script advertising, 'Schlitz THE BEER THAT MADE MILWAUKEE FAMOUS', some discolouration.
6½in (16.5cm) long
£18,000-22,000 BER

A Märklin Gotthard 1-gauge handpainted electric locomotive, with dual motors and cast iron trucks, one hand rail missing, two steps bent.
16in (40.5cm) long
£1,800-2,200 BER

A Wrenn W2269X British Railways green Rebuilt Bulleid 4-6-2, no.34053, 'SIR KEITH PARK', no.61044, packer no.3.

Only 270 of this model were made.
£400-500 LSK

A Voltamp #2115 Interurban trolley, probably original first series, with factory-installed auto-reverse, with headlight bulb.
c1907-12
18in (45.5cm) long
£15,000-20,000 BER

A near mint limited edition Wrenn W2417 British Railways green Castle Class 4-6-0, no.5034, 'CORFE CASTLE', no.143 of a limited edition of 250, no.330892, packer no.2.
£500-600 LSK

An exhibition-quality model of a 7¼in-gauge Great Western Railway Grange Class 4-6-0 locomotive and tender, no.6860 'Aberporth Grange', built by David Aitken, with copper boiler.

100in (254cm) long

£75,000-85,000 **DN**

An exhibition-quality 5in-gauge model of the British Railways Standard Class 9F 2-10-0 tender locomotive No.92024, built by B.G. Aldred, to the Attilio Franco and Piero Crosti boiler design.

The British Railways BR Standard Class 9F 2-10-0 is a class of steam locomotive designed for British Railways by Robert Riddles. The Class 9F was the last in a series of standardised locomotive classes designed for British Railways during the 1950s, and was intended for use on fast, heavy freight trains over long distances. It was one of the most powerful steam locomotive types ever constructed in Britain.

70¾in (180cm) long

£25,000-30,000 **DN**

A 10¼in-gauge model of the London Midland Scottish No.6100 'Royal Scot' tender locomotive, built with Bassett Lowke castings.

The locomotive with the Royal Scot Train was exhibited at the Century of Progress Exposition, Chicago, 1933, and made a tour of Canada and the USA.

148¾in (378cm) long

£25,000-30,000 **DN**

A rare 7¼in-gauge model of a London and Northwestern Railway 4-4-0 tender locomotive No.2663, 'George the Fifth', with copper boiler no.87189 built by Swindon Boilers.

This model was built from Bassett Lowke castings c1912 and rebuilt by R. Fenwick in the 1980s to early 1990s.

84¼in (214cm) long

£20,000-25,000 **DN**

A live steam 7¼in gauge 2-6-4 Stainer class 4P boiler tank engine, with two outside cylinders, Walschaerts gear, 3 manometers marked 'BRUCE ENGINEERING', the loco mounted on a wheeled 'HANDY HEIGHT PRODUCTS' scissor jack.

£15,000-20,000 **LSK**

An exhibition-quality 5in-gauge model of a 4-4-0 Great Western Railway 'Armstrong' No.7 tender locomotive, based on the original design by William Dean, with copper boiler.

William Dean (1840-1905), designer of the original full size locomotive, was the second son of Henry Dean, manager of the Hawes soap factory in New Cross, London. William went on to become Chief Locomotive Engineer for the Great Western Railway from 1877 until his retirement in 1902.

81in (206cm) long

£9,000-11,000 **DN**

ESSENTIAL REFERENCE – CURLY LAWRENCE

The initials on the locomotive, LBSC, once stood for the London Brighton & South Coast railway, but in this case refer to the pen-name of the designer, Curly Lawrence (1883-1967), who worked for the LSBC company. He was born William Mathieson and changed his name to Lillian Lawrence in 1902. He was known to school chums as 'Dolly' and to friends as 'Curly'. He was a married man, an open cross-dresser and a skilled live-steam model engineer. He created some controversy over his view that scale locomotives should be powered like the real thing, with coal-fired multi fire-tube boilers, rather than spirit-fuelled water-tube boilers.

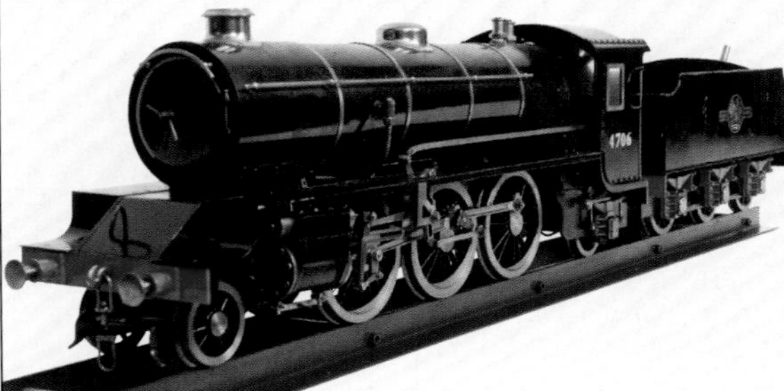

A 3½in live steam locomotive and tender, 'LBSC Betty', 2-6-2, constructed by T. Head, built to a design by Curly Lawrence.

47¼in (120cm) long

£22,000-26,000 **CHT**

An exhibition-quality 5in-gauge model of a Great Central Railway Robinson Class 11F 'Director' 4-4-0 tender locomotive No.505, 'Ypres', built by Steam Age, paintwork by Louis Raper of Failsworth.

1973 *62½in (159cm) long*

£10,000-14,000 **DN**

A 5in-gauge model of a LMS 2-6-0 Hughes Crab locomotive and tender, no.2874, built by Thomas Tegg of Reading.

Thomas Tedd won silver at the Model Engineer Exhibition in 2008. The LMS Hughes Crab or Horwich Mogul was a mixed class 2-6-0 designed by George Hughes and was built 1926-32. No.2874 was built at Crewe.

1994 *48in (122cm) long*

£16,000-20,000 **SHEF**

An exhibition-quality built 5in-gauge model of a Great Western Railway 4-4-0 'Bulldog' tender locomotive, no.3433, built by Bob Wilkinson, with copper boiler.

60¼in (153cm) long

£12,000-16,000 **DN**

A 19thC model steamboat, with boiler and steam plant, with brass fittings.

41¾in (106cm) long

£7,500-8,500 **WW**

A builder's model of the cargo vessel S.S. 'Knottingley'.

The steel screw cargo steamer 'Knottingley' was built by John Crown & Sons Ltd. at Sunderland and completed in June 1907. She sailed for the Wetherall Steamship Company, the Cambo Shipping Co., Davidson's of Aberdeen, the Antwerp Shipping & Bunkering Co., and the Brabo Steamship Co., before being torpedoed and sunk by a German E-boat on 26 July 1940.

1907 *70in (178cm) long*

£2,500-3,000 **CM**

A live steam-powered model launch, fitted with mahogany-lagged boiler to single cylinder engine, with flywheel.

c1910 *51in (129.5cm) long*

£1,100-1,500 **CM**

A builder's model of the S.S. 'Clan Malcolm', built by Craig, Taylor & Co., Stockton, for Clan line.

The 'Clan Malcolm' was completed in April 1917 and survived World War I. She was wrecked on passage from London to the Clyde on 25 September 1935.

1917 *88in (223.5cm) long*

£12,000-15,000 **CM**

A Marklin 'Battleship Sankt Georg' model, with replacement lifeboats and canes, some touching up, areas of masts reattached.

There is only one other known example of this model in existence.

1919-21 *28in (71cm) long*

£150,000-200,000 **BER**

A builder's model for the 'Suez Canal Radial Cutter Suction Dredger Kadruka', built by William Simons & Co. Ltd., Renfrew, for the Egyptian government.

1930 *65in (165cm) long*

£4,000-5,000 **CM**

A builder's model for the twin-screw motor yacht and 'little ship' 'Wilna' R.T.Y.C., latter H.M.S. 'Aisha', built by Cochrane & Sons Ltd., Selby, modelled by C. Crawford & Sons, Sunderland.

'Wilna' R.T.Y.C. was designed by Norman Hart and purchased by W.H. Collins in 1934 for £14,400. By 1939 he had ordered a larger replacement and 'Wilna' was sold to the Royal Navy, renamed H.M.S. 'Aisha' and deployed on harbour patrol and later in the rescue missions to Dunkirk.

1934 *32in (81.5cm) long*

£4,000-5,000 **CM**

A model of the Lowestoft steam drifter 'Diana' LT 593, built by Gordon Drew of Highnam Gloucestershire, fitted with gas-fired Cheddar Proteus live steam plant, the hull constructed from copper stakes with brass ribs and riveted copper plate.

58¼in (148cm) long

£3,500-4,000 **DN**

An exhibition-quality ramin, pine and mahogany model of a steam launch, 'Henry', built by Peter Arnott, with vertical live steam boiler designed by K.N. Harris, with Stuart Turner D10 steam engine.

54¼in (138cm) long

£5,000-6,000 **DN**

A Cliff Bastin red Arsenal 1930 FA Cup Final jersey, by Bukta, dated.

In 1930 Arsenal won the first major honour in their history with victory in the FA Cup Final, beating Huddersfield Town 2-0. Arsenal now have the most FA Cup wins of any team with a total of 13 victories.

£22,000-26,000 GBA

A Joe Mercer old gold Arsenal No.6 1950 FA Cup Final shirt, by Hope Brothers/Solus Sports, the badge dated.

As Arsenal and Liverpool both generally wore red, they had to change shirt colour for the 1950 FA Cup Final. Both teams' change shirt colours were white, so a decision was made by a coin toss. Liverpool played in white, and Arsenal in old gold. Arsenal continued to use the old gold as an alternative change kit throughout the 1950s.

1949-50

£12,000-16,000 GBA

CLOSER LOOK – 1909 FA CUP FINAL SHIRT

This shirt was worn during the 1909 FA Cup Final by Bob Hardy, Bristol City's inside-right.

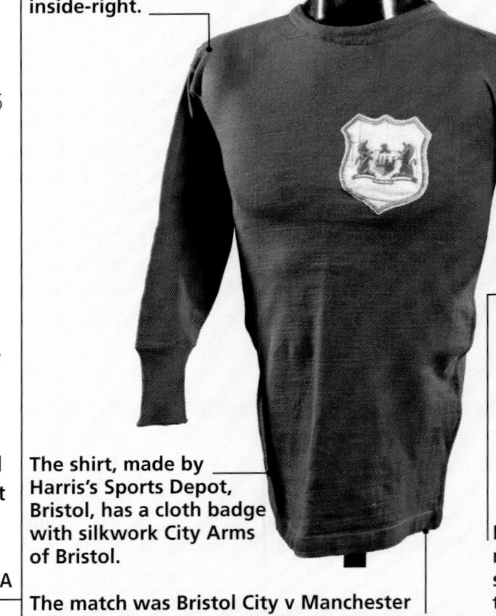

The shirt, made by Harris's Sports Depot, Bristol, has a cloth badge with silkwork City Arms of Bristol.

Both teams normally wore red shirts so, prior to the final, the FA issued orders for kit changes. United wore white shirts and City wore blue.

The match was Bristol City v Manchester United, at Crystal Palace. Manchester United, appearing in their first FA Cup Final, won the match 1-0. It was the only occasion that Bristol City has played in a FA Cup Final.

A Bristol City 1909 FA Cup Final shirt.

£15,000-20,000 GBA

A Bobby Moore England 1966 World Cup tracksuit, by Umbro, the reverse lettered 'ENGLAND', some mud marks, sold with certificate of authenticity.

1966

£8,500-9,500 GBA

A Terry Paine red England No.19 1966 World Cup Final jersey, by Umbro, with three lions badge.

Terry Paine would have worn this jersey in the 1966 World Cup Final had he been selected to play by manager Alf Ramsey. If he had been selected to play and had worn this shirt, it would be worth even more, roughly £40,000-60,000.

£14,000-18,000 GBA

A FIFA Centenary 1904-2004 jersey, signed by the top 125 players in the world as of 2004, limited edition no.8/10, sold with certificate of authentication.

£4,500-5,500 GBA

A Johnny Holt England international cap, awarded for four successive appearances v Scotland 1891-94, the purple cap inscribed '1891-2-3-4'.

Johnny Holt was born 10 April 1865 in Church, Lancashire. He joined Everton as a centre-half in the very first season of the Football League in 1888.

£3,000-3,500 GBA

A Thomas Low Scotland v England Junior international cap, inscribed 'S v E, 1896'.

This match was played at Perry Bar, Birmingham. Scotland won 4-1, though some reports have it at 4-0. The scorers were J. McGill and Low.

1896

£220-300 GBA

A Joe Mercer international cap, with 'F.A.' crest, inscribed 'ENGLAND v SCOTLAND', dated.

This was Mercer's second appearance for England, who beat Scotland 2-1 at Hampden Park.

1938-39

£2,200-2,600 GBA

A Roberto Carlos signed pair of Nike Zoom football boots, inscribed 'R. CARLOS', in display case.

15¾in (40cm) long

£350-450 GBA

A Billy Dunlop Football League Division One Championship 15ct gold and enamel medal, inscribed 'LIVERPOOL FOOTBALL CLUB', the reverse inscribed 'LEAGUE CHAMPIONSHIP, SEASON 1900-1901, W. DUNLOP, BACK'.

This was the first occasion that Liverpool FC won the Football League Division One Championship title. The Scottish left-back Billy Dunlop played for Liverpool FC 1894-1909.

1901

£9,500-11,000 **GBA**

A Blackburn Rovers 9ct gold and enamel football medal, inscribed 'BLACKBURN ROVERS FOOTBALL CLUB', hallmarked.

1905

£550-650 **GBA**

A Billy Wooldridge 15ct gold FA Cup winner's medal, inscribed 'THE FOOTBALL ASSOCIATION, WOLVERHAMPTON WANDERERS F.C., ENGLISH CUP, WINNERS, 1907-8, W.T. WOOLDRIDGE, CAPTAIN', cased.

The 1908 FA Cup Final was played at the Crystal Palace. Wolverhampton Wanderers defeated Newcastle United 3-1. The Cup was lifted by the Wolverhampton Wanderers's captain Billy Wooldridge.

1908

£9,500-11,000 **GBA**

A Patsy Gallacher Scottish Football League Championship 9ct gold and enamel winner's medal, inscribed 'SCOTTISH FOOTBALL LEAGUE, CHAMPIONSHIP, 1918-19, WON BY, CELTIC F.C., PAT, GALLACHER'.

Patrick 'Patsy' Gallacher (1891-1953) was an Irish footballer who played at inside-right for Celtic. In this season, Celtic won the Scottish Football League from their great rivals Rangers by just one point.

1919

£2,000-2,500 **GBA**

A Cliff Bastin Football League Division One Championship 9ct gold winner's medal, inscribed 'THE FOOTBALL LEAGUE, CHAMPIONS, DIVISION 1, ARSENAL F.C., C. BASTIN', dated, in fitted case.

Cliff Bastin was a winger for Arsenal, who won the 1932-33 Football League Division One Title with a total of 58 points, four clear of Aston Villa.

1932-33

£9,000-11,000 **GBA**

A Terry McDermott Liverpool FC 1977 UEFA European Cup yellow metal winner's medal, inscribed 'UEFA', the reverse inscribed 'COUPE DES CLUBS CHAMPIONS EUROPEENS'.

Liverpool beat Borussia Monchengladbach 3-1 in the 1977 European Cup Final played at the Olympic Stadium, Rome. Terry McDermott scored Liverpool's opening goal.

£15,000-20,000 **GBA**

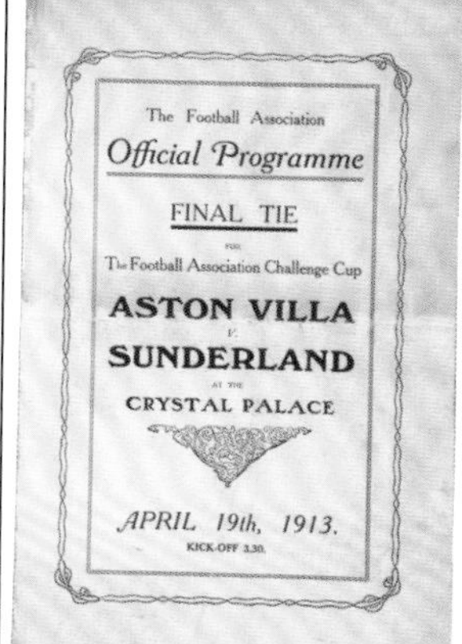
The Football Association
Official Programme
FINAL TIE
FOR
The Football Association Challenge Cup
ASTON VILLA
v.
SUNDERLAND
AT THE
CRYSTAL PALACE
APRIL 19th, 1913.
KICK-OFF 3.30.

An FA Cup Final Aston Villa v Sunderland programme, Crystal Palace 19 April 1913, heavy horizontal fold, splitting at the spine.

£5,000-6,000 **GBA**

A 1954 World Cup Korea v Turkey programme, with cigarette sticker and cigarette flyer.

This is the rarest programme issued at the 1954 World Cup, for the Korea v Turkey match, played in front of only 4,000 people in Lausanne on 20 June 1954.

£1,100-1,500 **GBA**

A Manchester United v West Bromwich Albion football programme, Div 1, 15 January 1921.

£1,100-1,400 **LOCK**

A Bradford Park Avenue v Grimsby Town football programme, 6 September 1924, Div 3 North.

£350-400 **LOCK**

A Derby County v Leeds United football programme, 26 December 1929, First Team.

£1,300-1,600 **LOCK**

An early 20thC Hardy Brothers Ltd. 'Perfect' trout reel, damage to foot.
3¼in (8.5cm) diam
£250-300 **CHEF**

A Hardy Brothers Ltd. 'Perfect Mk II' drum fly reel, in original box.
3¾in (9.5cm) diam
£500-600 **CHEF**

A Hardy Brothers Ltd. 'Perfect' reel.
c1960 *3¾in (9.5cm) diam*
£350-400 **CHEF**

An early 20thC Hardy Brothers Ltd. brass-faced 'Perfect' fly reel 4', with Turk's head locking screw and rod-in-hand trademark.
£1,200-1,500 **CHEF**

A Hardy Brothers Ltd. 'Perfect' fishing reel, with brass foot, rim tension adjuster and Bakelite winder, marked, in original box.
2¾in (7cm) diam
£400-500 **LC**

A Hardy Brothers Ltd. 'Perfect' fishing reel, with brass foot and rim tension adjuster, signs of use, with leather pouch, marked.
3¼in (8cm) diam
£250-300 **LC**

A carved wood and painted half-block model pike, by Charles Farlow & Co., mounted on a mahogany plaque, the verso with a handwritten label, 'Caught by J.M. Morgan, in the Oare? near the Maddocks?, Aldworth spinning with a afriat on crocodile tackle weight 19lbs, 1907, Yorkshire September', with Farlow stencil stamp.
49½in (125.5cm) wide
£7,000-8,000 **WW**

A George V carved and painted wood half-block trout, by Rowland Ward, mounted on oak, with ivory plaque inscribed '6 LBS 6 OZS, KILLED BY G.T. HAWKES IN SHERMAN'S LOCK AVINGTON, KENNET JUNE 6TH 1917', the verso with trade labels, numbered '1503'.
28in (71cm) long
£8,000-9,000 **WW**

A George V carved wood and painted half-block model trout, by Hardy Brothers Ltd., on an oak board, inscribed 'MOTE POOL, BLACKWATER, Co. MEATH. WEIGHT 6½ lbs, LENGTH 22½INS, GIRTH 15½'.
29in (73.5cm) wide
£3,500-4,500 **WW**

A Paris Olympic Games winner's medal plaque, designed by F. Vernon, inscribed 'CONCOURS DE TIR AUX PIGEONS', reverse inscribed 'REPUBLIQUE FRANCAISE, PARIS 1900, EXPOSITION UNIVERSELLE'.

1900

£950-1,100 **GBA**

A London 1908 Olympic Games silver prize medal, won by the Canadian athlete Garfield MacDonald for the Hop Step and Jump (Triple Jump).

£3,500-4,500 **GBA**

A rare St Moritz Winter Olympic Games gold prize winner's medal, designed by Arnold Hunerwadel, the reverse inscribed 'IL JEUX OLYMPIQUES D'HIVER, ST MORITZ, 1928', in original box.

The original recipient of this medal is unknown.

1928 *2in (5cm) diam*

£30,000-35,000 **GBA**

A Squaw Valley Winter Olympic Games bronze participant's medal.

1960 *2in (5cm) diam*

£500-600 **GBA**

A rare London 1908 Olympic Games Comite D'Honneur bronze and blue enamel badge, the reverse numbered '30'.

£9,000-10,000 **GBA**

An Antwerp Olympic Games gold prize winner's medal, designed by Josue Dupon, minted by Cossemans of Brussels.

The gold-plating on the Antwerp 1920 medals was very thin. The IOC later dictated that all gold winner's medals should have at least 6 grams of gold-plating to prevent the type of rubbing that occurred with the 1920 medal. The original recipient of this winner's medal is unknown.

1920

£12,000-15,000 **GBA**

An aluminium alloy London Olympic Games bearer's torch, designed by Ralph Lavers, inscribed 'XIVth OLYMPIAD, 1948, OLYMPIA TO LONDON, WITH THANKS TO THE BEARER'.

1948

£4,000-5,000 **GBA**

CLOSER LOOK – WINTER OLYMPICS GOLD MEDAL

The 'gold' medal is made of silver-gilt and was designed by Scott Given/Axiom Design.

The obverse has an organic shape, resembling Utah river rock, with an athlete holding a torch, breaking, over the Olympic Rings, inscribed 'OLYMPIC WINTER GAMES, LIGHT THE FIRE WITHIN'.

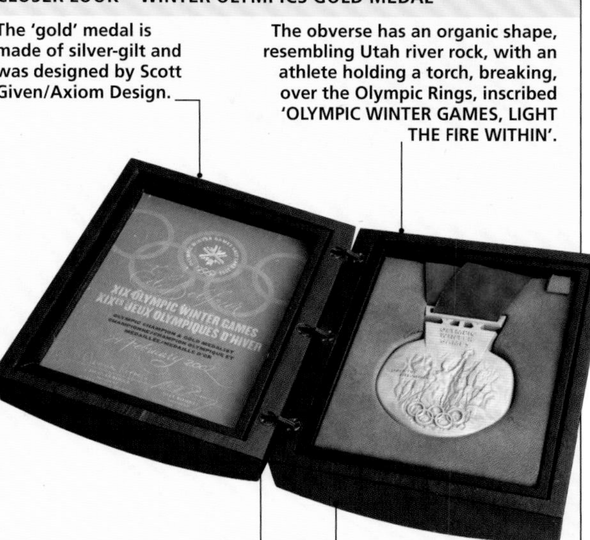

The reverse depicts the Greek Goddess Nike and an image of hockey, with the inscription 'SALT LAKE 2002, MEN'S ICE HOCKEY'.

The base of the ribbon loop has the Roman numeral XIX, signifying the 19th Winter Olympic Games.

A Salt Lake City Winter Olympic Games gold prize medal, awarded to a member of the Canadian men's ice hockey team, in original case.

The Canadian men's ice hockey team beat the USA 5-2 in the final.

2002 *3¼in (8.5cm) diam 18¼oz*

£80,000-90,000 **GBA**

A bronzed aluminium Rome 1960 Olympic Games bearer's torch, designed by Professor Maiure.

The design of this torch was based on drawings of torches on ancient Etruscan ceramics.

15½in (39.5cm) high

£3,000-4,000 **GBA**

A blackened aluminium alloy and stainless steel Tokyo Olympic Games bearer's torch, inscribed 'XVIII OLYMPIAD TOKYO 1964'.

25½in (65cm) high

£4,000-5,000 **GBA**

A Babe Ruth signed William Harridge American League baseball, with letters of authenticity from PSA/DNA, JSA and SGC.

This baseball was signed on 12 September 1947 at the Hotel Statler in Boston, where the Babe was a guest speaker. It was gifted to a guest at the American Legion Junior Baseball Scholarship banquet.

1947

£30,000-35,000 **MORP**

A Louisville Slugger baseball bat, made for President Gerald R. Ford, signed by the President and by forty members of the Baseball Hall of Fame.

1974-77

£2,500-3,000 **POOK**

A pair of 1950s Cassius Clay leather amateur training gloves, manufactured by Post, initialled 'C.C.' inside, stamped 'Columbia Gym' inside.

These were discovered in the attic of Cassius Clay's trainer Joe Martin. They were used during the time that Joe Martin was his trainer at the Columbia Gym.

£3,500-4,000 **MORP**

A 1958 Cassius Clay Louisville Golden Gloves Championship Medal.

1¾in (4.5cm) high

£2,000-3,000 **MORP**

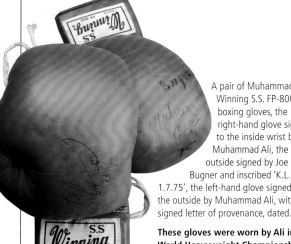

A pair of Muhammad Ali Winning S.S. FP-800 boxing gloves, the right-hand glove signed to the inside wrist by Muhammad Ali, the outside signed by Joe Bugner and inscribed 'K.L., 1.7.75', the left-hand glove signed to the outside by Muhammad Ali, with a signed letter of provenance, dated.

These gloves were worn by Ali in the World Heavyweight Championship bout v Joe Bugner in Kuala Lumpur, 30 June 1975.

1975 *10oz*

£55,000-65,000 **GBA**

A World Championship cricket bat, by Gray Nicholls, signed with team signatures of Australia, England, West Indies, New Zealand, India, Pakistan and Sri Lanka.

1985

£650-750 **MM**

A unique hand-built Graeme Obree bike frame, used by Obree during various time trials, built by Obree using Reynolds 653, silver soldered using cut down lugs and joining pieces for lightness.

Graeme Obree rode this at Donington Park motor racing circuit in 2009 at the BikerRader.

2006 *45⅞oz*

£4,500-5,000 **GWA**

A yellow-metal and enamel Hour Record medal, the obverse inscribed 'Record Du Monde De L'Heure, Graeme Obree', the reverse inscribed 'Bordeaux (Fra) 27 April 1994, 52km 713', in fitted case.

These are rare as sporting medals go. Only holders of the One Hour Record receive them.

£1,100-1,500 **GWA**

An unnamed featherie golf ball, some stitches partially undone.

£900-1,200 **MM**

A guttie golf ball hammer, with circular face and wide chisel, with leather sheepskin grip.

c1860 *9in (23cm) high*

£350-400 **MM**

An Osmond's patent automaton golf club caddie, with maker's brass plaque, original leather handles, some damages, leather belt strap needs replacing.

c1893 *12½in (32cm) long*

£350-400 **MM**

A rare 17thC to 18thC left-handed spur-toed golf club, the hand-forged iron head with dished face set on an ash shaft, some pitting and light rust.

Purchased in the 1950s for 10 shillings and purportedly purchased by the previous owner from a cellar clearance in Leven, Fife.

42½in (108cm) long

£32,000-38,000 GORL

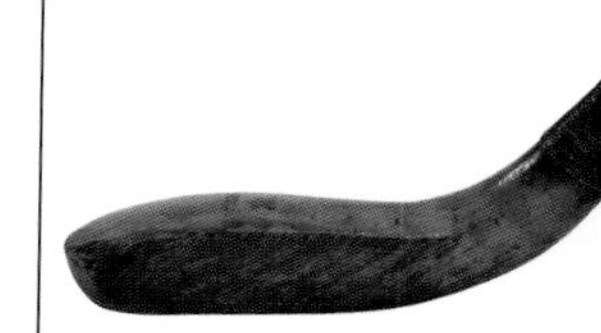

An early R. Forgan St Andrews golden thornwood play club, with Forgan block crown stamp mark and Prince of Wales Feathers to the head.

c1860 *head 5½in (14cm) long*

£2,000-2,500 MM

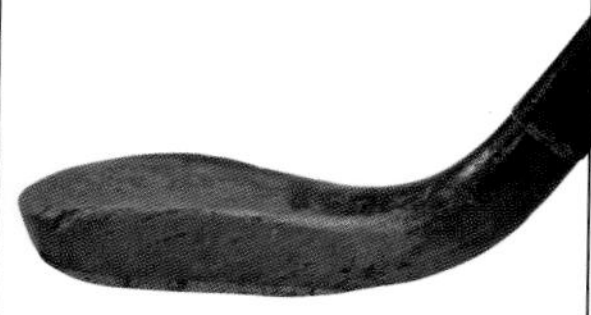

An R. Davidson Montrose stained beech wood putter, with most of the original hide grip.

Robert Davidson Montrose was a notable early club maker from 1825-70.

c1860 *head 5½in (14cm) long*

£1,100-1,400 MM

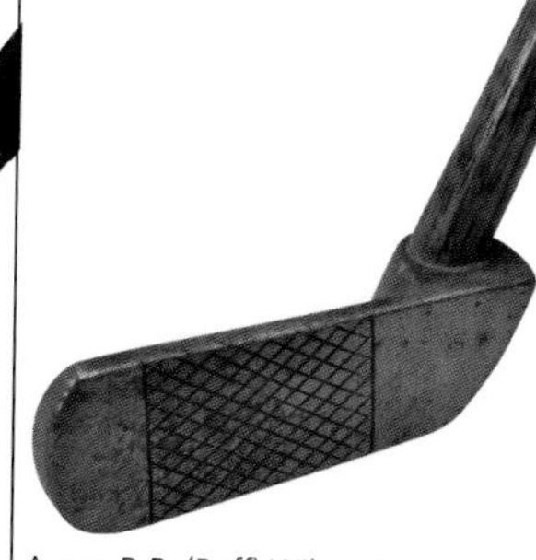

A rare R.B. (Buff) Wilson St Andrews A1 No Hosel Patent putting cleek.

c1900

£1,100-1,400 MM

A rare Browns patent perforated rake iron wry neck putter, lacking grip.

c1904

£900-1,200 MM

A Mika Hakkinen signed and worn late 1999 West McLaren-Mercedes Formula 1 racesuit, with Hakkinen's 'Flying Finn' signature, 'Hakkinen M, 07/10/99, Ref 037'.

In October 1999, Mika Hakkinen became only the seventh driver ever to win back-to-back F1 World Championships.

£6,000-7,000 GBA

A Ludo Stuart 1920s match-worn Scotland international rugby shirt.

Ludovic 'Ludo' Mair Stuart (1902-57) made his Scotland international debut v France at Inverleith on 20 January 1923. His final appearance was at Twickenham v England 15 March 1930.

£750-850 GBA

ESSENTIAL REFERENCE – REAL TENNIS

Real tennis, or courte paume, is the original indoor racket sport from which the modern game of lawn tennis is descended. Rackets and balls were typically made by the maître-paumiers, often professional players or proprietors of the 200-plus courts in and around Paris. As the best available, these were sold to English players. Tison, a well-known maître-palmier, was born in the 1740s and was still active, though elderly, in the 1820s.

A set of four lopsided real tennis rackets, by Tison, with ash frames and trebled gut stringing.

26½in (67cm) long

£17,000-22,000 SWO

A Kyran Bracken team-signed England No.20 shirt, from the Rugby World Cup match v Georgia, Perth 12 October 2003, inscribed 'KYRAN BRACKEN'.

2003

£1,100-1,400 GBA

A Roger Federer signed tennis racket.

£300-400 GBA

A Bamana wood mask, West Africa, with six horn crest, mounted.

30¼in (77cm) high

£1,100-1,400 **L&T**

A Royal Bamileke or Bamum carved wood head, Cameroon, with glass beads and cowry shells attached with mud cement, with buffalo horns and snarling leopard to crown.

Despite its size and weight, this head would have probably been worn during important ceremonies. The face probably represents the Fon or tribal chief. The buffalo horns represent power.

37½in (95cm) high

£850-950 **MART**

A Bushongo painted carved wood mask, Central Congo, with beads and shells, with fabric crown.

Collected c1898-1920 by Major Ian Kelsey. This mask would have been worn at secret military society rites.

7½in (19cm) high

£850-950 **WHYT**

An Ejagham hide-covered Janus helmet mask, Nigeria, with two faces, the lighter with symbols including unity and hatred.

The Ejagham, or Ekoi, people, come from southeast Nigeria and southwest Cameroon. They are best known for their impressive headdresses and masks.

17¾in (45cm) high

£5,500-6,500 **WW**

A Dan carved wood mask, Liberia/Côte d'Ivoire, with hinged jaw.

9½in (24cm) high

£2,300-2,800 **SK**

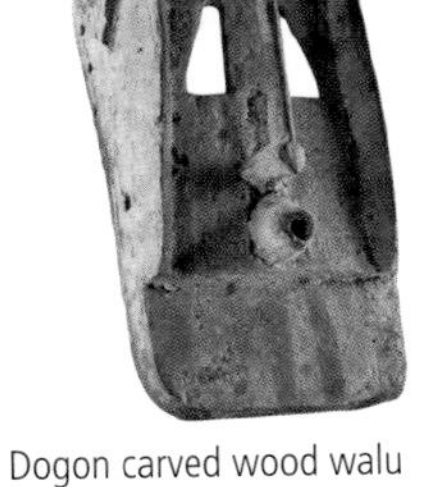

A Dogon carved wood walu antelope mask, Mali, encrustations throughout.

16½in (42cm) high

£2,500-3,000 **L&T**

A Kuba carved wood lion mask, Congo, with grass mane.

Collected c1898-1920 by Major Ian Kelsey.

13in (33cm) high

£650-750 **WHYT**

A Suku carved wood helmet mask, Democratic Republic of the Congo, with animal crest and geometric designs.

16½in (42cm) high

£2,000-2,500 **SK**

A Songye carved wood shield, Democratic Republic of the Congo, with relief-carved Kifwebe masks.

25in (63.5cm) high

£4,000-5,000 **SK**

A pair of male and female Yoruba Ibeji figures, Nigeria.

10¾in (27.5cm) high

£3,000-4,000 **WW**

A Duala carved wood stool, Cameroon, with a pierced frieze supported by figures.

21¾in (55.5cm) wide

£550-650 **WW**

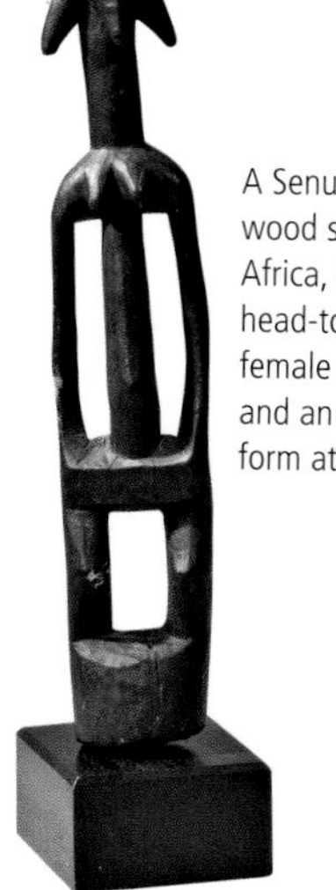

A Senufo carved wood staff, West Africa, with head-to-head female figures and an avian form at the top.

56in (142cm) high

£14,000-18,000 **SK**

A Jimma carved wood chair, Ethiopia.

38¾in (98.5cm) high

£700-800 **L&T**

A Songye carved wood headrest, Democratic Republic of the Congo, with beadwork and a face-mask.

5½in (14cm) high

£1,700-2,200 **L&T**

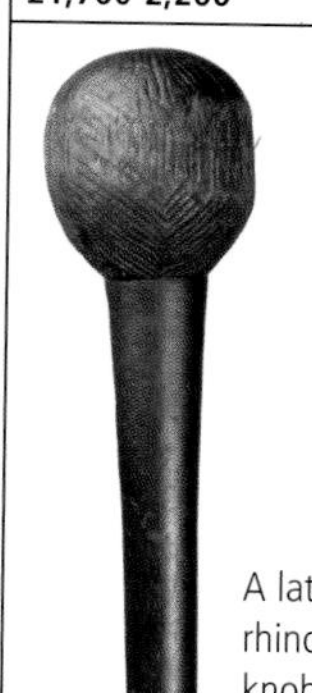

A late 19thC Zulu rhinoceros horn knobkerrie, South Africa.

22½in (57cm) long

£4,000-4,500 **WW**

A Benin bronze leopard, Nigeria, with dot and ring decoration, the head with barred teeth and raised whiskers.

19in (48cm) high

£18,000-22,000 **WW**

A mid-to-late 19thC North Nguni carved wood headrest, Southern Africa, in animal form.

This headrest is part of a wider group of items carved by Zulu speakers in the vicinity of Port Natal. The craftsmen created items both for elite African and western colonial clients. The majority of other pieces produced were vessels, making this headrest even more unique and valuable.

10¾in (27cm) long

£65,000-70,000 **L&T**

ESSENTIAL REFERENCE – FANTE ASAFO FLAGS

From the 17thC, the Fante groups which inhabited the south-west coast of modern-day Ghana formed military and political units known as 'asafo'.

- **The name derives from sa, meaning war, and fo, meaning people.**
- **Each unit developed elaborate traditions of visual art. Among the most striking are flags such as these.**
- **These flags comprised of bold naïve imagery appliquéd onto a cotton background, and commonly depict indigenous proverbs which relate closely to the commissioning Asafo group.**
- **With the British conquest of the region in 1856 many Asafo groups incorporated versions of the Union Jack into the flag to enhance the power of the imagery.**

An early 20thC Fante Asafo cotton appliqué flag, 'We can defend our sacred trees from all predators', Ghana, framed by John Jones.

Certain trees were considered sacred by the Fante and were protected as shrines.

70¾in (179.5cm) wide

£1,500-2,000 **L&T**

An early 20thC Fante Asafo cotton appliqué flag, 'If we can tame the leopard, what chance have you mere animals?', Ghana, framed by John Jones.

In this flag, an Asafo company is boasting of its military prowess and taunting a rival group. Some Asafo companies had a woman's auxiliary headed by female officers.

67½in (171.5cm) wide

£4,000-5,000 **L&T**

An Ipiutak walrus ivory carving of a bear, Point Hope, Northwest Alaska.
c600-800 *3½in (9cm) long*
£1,300-1,600 SK

An Eskimo Punuk period shaman's torso figure, St Lawrence Island, Alaska.
800-1400 *2¼in (5.5cm) high*
£800-900 SK

A mid-19thC Tsimshian carved wood shaman's rattle, with incised and painted thunderbirds, with two native repairs.

The Tsimshian are an indigenous people of the Pacific Northwest Coast. Their communities are mostly in coastal British Columbia and far southern Alaska.
12in (30.5cm) long
£20,000-25,000 SK

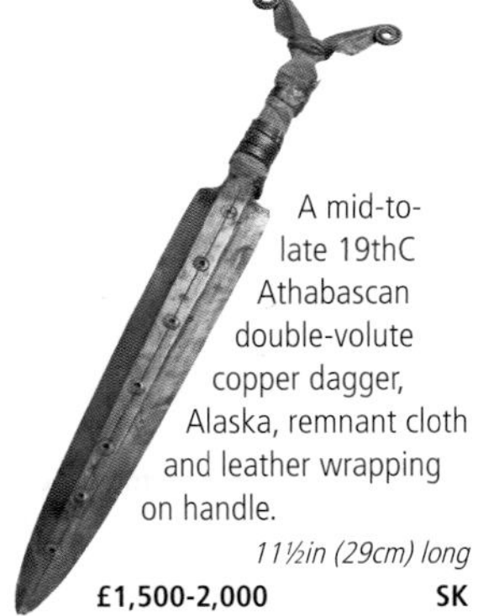

A mid-to-late 19thC Athabascan double-volute copper dagger, Alaska, remnant cloth and leather wrapping on handle.
11½in (29cm) long
£1,500-2,000 SK

A late 19thC Eskimo sheep horn spoon, with domestic and hunting scenes.
11in (28cm) long
£2,200-2,800 SK

An Eskimo mask, Point Hope, Alaska, with bone inlay eyes.

Collected in the 1920s in the Point Hope area.
c1900 *9½in (24cm) high*
£2,800-3,200 SK

A 19thC Eskimo Arctic walrus ivory bow drill, with incised decoration.
19in (48.5cm) long
£4,000-5,000 WW

An early 20thC Eskimo baleen lidded basket, carved walrus tusk handle.
2¾in (7cm) high
£600-700 SK

A 1890s Eskimo carved musk ox jawbone cribbage board, engraved with scenes of hunting and fishing.
13¾in (35cm) long
£900-1,100 SK

ESSENTIAL REFERENCE – ESKIMO AND INUIT

The term Inuit, meaning 'the people', refers to the indigenous groups residing in the Arctic regions of Alaska, Canada and Greenland. It replaced the term Eskimo from the mid-20thC; tribal art and antiques from pre-c1950 are therefore usually referred to as Eskimo, and those from post-c1950 are referred to as Inuit. The term Eskimo widely fell out of usage because it was considered offensive. However, the word Inuit is not a precise synonym, nor a fully accepted term. Many groups prefer to use their own tribal names, and several groups once called Eskimo, such as the Yupik people of Canada, are not Inuit and have no such word in their language.

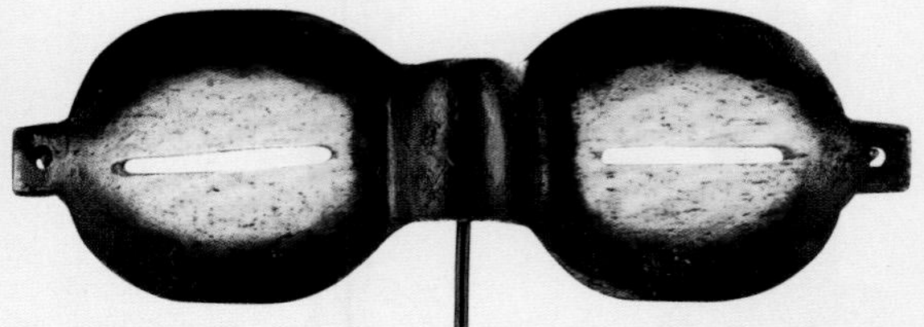

An Alaskan Inuit whalebone snow goggle, with carved eye slits and rounded nose bridge, mounted.
5½in (14cm) wide
£1,000-1,400 L&T

A stone and wood animal spirit umiak, by Abraham Apakark Anghik, Salt Spring Island, carried on the back of Sedna, the goddess of the sea.

An umiak is a type of boat used by the Yupik and Inuit peoples, chiefly for transport as opposed to hunting or fishing.

24in (61cm) wide

£16,000-20,000 **WAD**

A stone carving, 'Winged Shaman', by Barnabus Arnasungaaq (1924-2017), E2-213, Baker Lake/Qamani'tuaq.

Arnasungaaq was an important influence on the community of carvers in Baker Lake and one of the eldest from the original group in this region.

9½in (24cm) high

£2,000-3,000 **WAD**

A stone carving, 'Bird of Spring', by Abraham Etungat, R.C.A. (1911-99), E7-809, Cape Dorset/Kinngait, signed in syllabics.

Etungat's original small soapstone carving of 'Bird of Spring' was reproduced in a 7ft (2.1m) tall bronze for the Devonian Foundation. The bronze is now displayed in public areas in cities across Canada, including Halifax, Calgary, Vancouver and Toronto.

20in (51cm) high

£7,000-8,000 **WAD**

A stone carving, 'Composition', by Abraham Etungat, R.C.A. (1911-99), E7-809, Cape Dorset/Kinngait, signed in syllabics.

Etungat is most famous for his grand birds with raised wings. He started out working small scale, gradually building up to the larger works and incorporating humans and other animals.

23in (58.5cm) high

£3,500-4,000 **WAD**

CLOSER LOOK – SHAMAN WITH OPPOSING FACES

This was made by Karoo Ashevak, a talented Inuit artist who became highly popular c1972. He is considered one of the very best Inuit sculptors.

Ashevak died in a house fire in 1974 at the age of thirty-four, leaving behind him only about 250 works.

The rarity of his work, his originality and skill together increase the value of his work.

Shamans are thought to bridge the earthly and spiritual world, and the two sides of this sculpture represent this duality. With its intricate details and whimsical, distorted figure, this is a good example of Ashevak's characteristic style.

A bone, stone and ivory carving, 'Shaman With Opposing Faces', by Karoo Ashevak (1940-74), E4-196, Spence Bay/Taloyoak.

c1973 *15in (38cm) high*

£55,000-65,000 **WAD**

A stone falcon, by Kenojuak Ashevak, C.C., R.C.A. (1927-2013).

14½in (37cm) high

£2,200-2,800 **WAD**

A 1970s stone carving, 'Man With His Dog' by Osuitok Ipeelee, R.C.A. (1923-2005), E7-1154, Cape Dorset/Kinngait, signed in syllabics.

22½in (57cm) high

£3,000-4,000 **WAD**

A stone carving, 'Standing Figure', by John Kavik (1897-1993), E2-290, Rankin Inlet/Kangiqliniq, signed in syllabics.

19in (48.5cm) high

£8,500-9,500 **WAD**

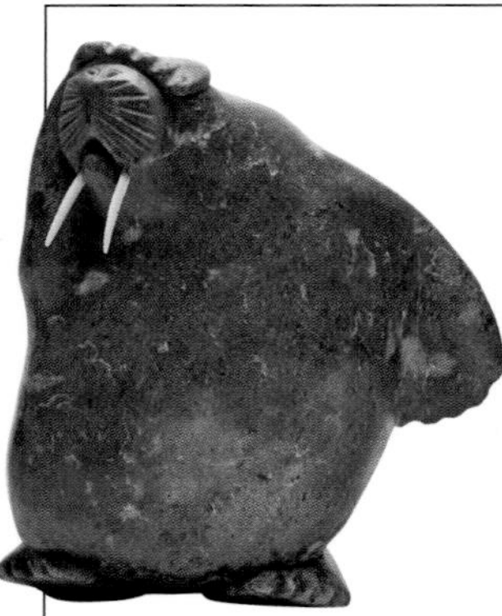

A stone carving, 'Bashful Walrus', by Kananginak Pootoogook, R.C.A. (1935-2010), E7-1168, Cape Dorset/Kinngait, signed in syllabics.

13in (33cm) high

£4,000-5,000 **WAD**

A stone carving, 'Strutting Polar Bear', by Pauta Saila, R.C.A. (1916-2009), E7-990, Cape Dorset/Kinngait, signed in Roman and syllabics.

Pauta Saila was one of the first Inuk artists to develop a distinctive, personally unique style. Although he worked on a wide variety of subjects, his dancing bears are particularly significant because polar bears are important shamanistic creatures, embodied spirit helpers of Inuit culture.

c1970 *10in (25.5cm) high*

£8,500-9,500 **WAD**

A stone carving, 'Mother Nursing Her Child', by Isa Aqiattusuk Smiler (1921-86), E9-706, Port Harrison/Inukjuak, signed in syllabics with disc number inscribed.

c1968 *8in (20.5cm) high*

£3,000-4,000 **WAD**

A stone carving, 'Dogs Defending Their Pack', by Qavaroak Tunnillie (1928-93).

23in (58.5cm) high

£2,000-2,500 **WAD**

A late 1980s stone, antler and musk ox horn carving, 'Shaman With Spirits', by Judas Ullulaq (1937-99), signed in syllabics, Gjoa Haven/Uqsuqtuuq.

Like his brothers, Charlie Ugyuk and Nelson Takkiruq, Judas Ullulaq's work offers a level of creativity and individuality. He worked expertly in stone and bone, and strongly influenced the next generation of artists in the region.

12in (30.5cm) high

£8,500-9,500 **WAD**

A sealskin stencil, 'Birds Over The Sun', by Kenojuak Ashevak, C.C., R.C.A. (1927-2013).

20in (51cm) wide

£2,000-2,500 **WAD**

A thread and embroidery floss stroud, by Essie Oonark, O.C., R.C.A. (1906-85), E2-384, Baker Lake/Qamani'tuaq, signed in syllabics.

Provenance: The York Downs Golf and Country Club Collection of Art, Unionville, ON. This work was displayed in the dining room from opening day in 1971 until c1990.

c1970 *60in (152.5cm) high*

£20,000-25,000 **WAD**

A framed stonecut picture, 'Bird Spirits' by Napatchie Pootoogook (1938-2002), E7-1104, Cape Dorset/Kinngait, no.22/50.

1960 *20½in (52cm) high*

£1,400-1,800 **WAD**

A framed stonecut picture, 'Animal Whalers II', by Pudlo Pudlat (1916-92).

20in (51cm) high

£2,500-3,000 **WAD**

A late 19thC Apache beaded hide doll with baby carrier, with tin cone and beaded detail.

11½in (29cm) high

£7,000-8,000 **SK**

Late 19thC Blackfeet beaded buffalo hide double saddlebags, with three brass bells.

112in (284.5cm) long

£3,200-3,800 **SK**

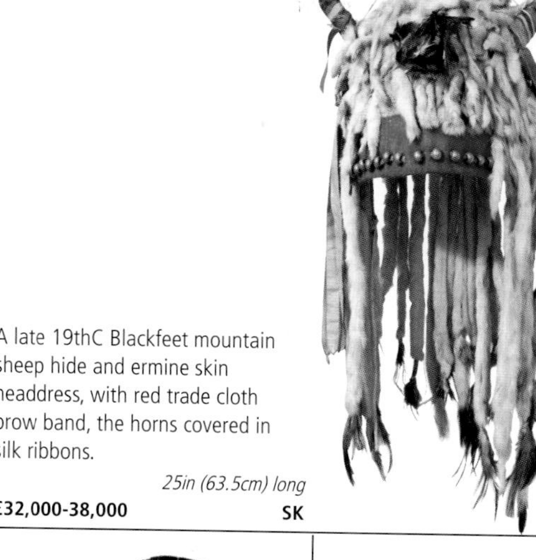

A late 19thC Blackfeet mountain sheep hide and ermine skin headdress, with red trade cloth brow band, the horns covered in silk ribbons.

25in (63.5cm) long

£32,000-38,000 **SK**

A late 19thC Blackfeet felt and ermine skin headdress, decorated with an animal tail, with carved wood horns.

28in (71cm) long

£18,000-22,000 **SK**

A Blackfeet buckskin, canvas, cloth and beaded rifle case, the inside edge inscribed 'BBI.73.PD'.

Collected in Montana, c1940.

40½in (103cm) long

£1,300-1,600 **WW**

1930s Cherokee beaded hide moccasins, black-dyed buckskin with velvet cuffs, remnant silk edging on the cuffs, heels restored.

9in (23cm) long

£10,000-14,000 **SK**

19thC Cheyenne hide moccasins, with buffalo rawhide soles, beaded with classic Cheyenne designs and a single thunderbird.

10in (25.5cm) long

£3,000-3,500 **SK**

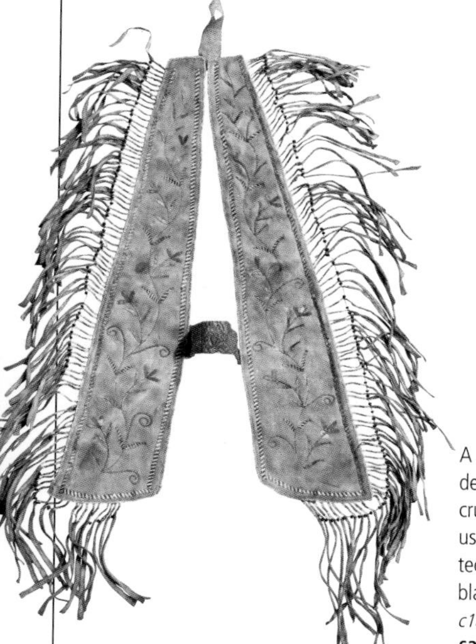

A rare Plains Cree quill-decorated hide horse crupper, buckskin decorated using six porcupine quill techniques, the fringe with black pony beads.

c1840 *24in (61cm) long*

£22,000-26,000 **SK**

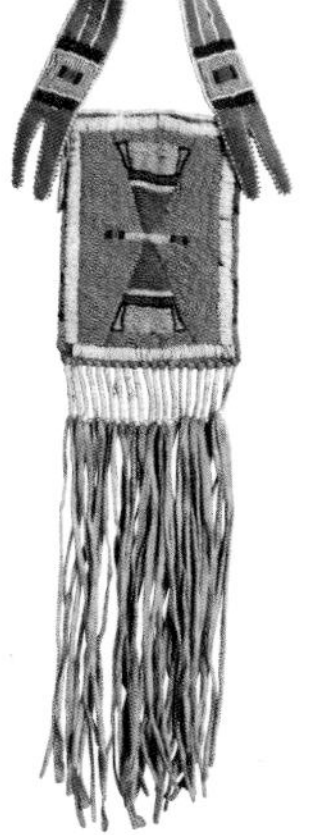

A 1870s Crow buffalo hide mirror bag, beaded with classic Crow designs, the fringe with white pony beads.

23in (58.5cm) long

£9,000-11,000 **SK**

A Hopi polychrome carved wood katsina, Shalako Mana.

A katsina, or kachina, is a spirit being in the religious reliefs of the Pueblo people, including the Hopi, Zuni, Hopi-Tewa and certain Keresan tribes.

6½in (16.5cm) high

£2,500-3,000 **SK**

A late 18thC Huron hide pouch, with porcupine quillwork, moose hair embroidery and a border of metal cones with tufts of deer hair.

9¼in (23.5cm) wide

£50,000-60,000 **SK**

A late 19thC Lakota beaded cloth and hide doll.

12in (30.5cm) high

£6,000-7,000 **SK**

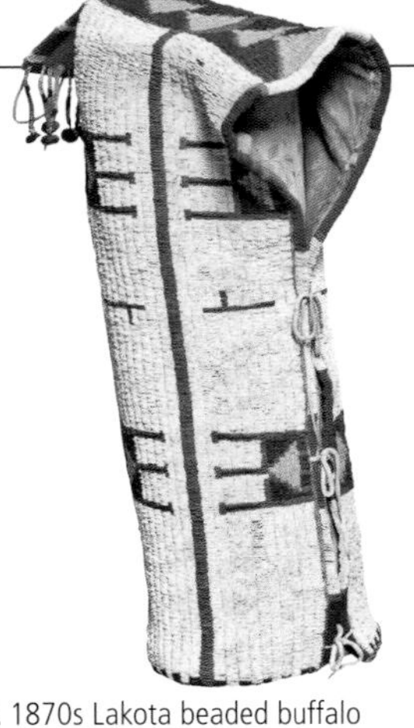

A 1870s Lakota beaded buffalo hide cradle, lined with printed cotton, the rawhide tab fringed with bugle beads and brass hawkbells.

24½in (62cm) high

£4,500-5,500 **SK**

1870s Lakota beaded buffalo hide moccasins.

10in (25.5cm) long

£2,000-2,500 **SK**

A Northeast beaded cloth bag, of Wabanaki type, possibly Mi'kmaa.

c1870 *6¼in (16cm) high*

£1,200-1,600 **SK**

A late 19thC Lakota parfleche box, with green trade cloth trim.

15in (38cm) long

£2,500-3,000 **SK**

ESSENTIAL REFERENCE – WINTER COUNT

A Winter Count is a pictorial record of events, kept by various North American peoples. This Count covers the years 1786-87 to 1876-77, and was made by Bo-i-de (the Flame, or the Blaze), a Dakota Sioux living 18 miles south of Fort Sully, Dakota Territory. An interpretation of the pictographs can be found in the fourth annual report of the Bureau of Ethnology, 1882-83. This particular Winter Count may have been obtained from Lieutenant H.T. Reed, who was stationed at Fort Sully in 1876. Reed was assisting Garrick Mallery in locating and interpreting Winter Counts. Mallery's studies were published in the fourth annual report of the Bureau of Ethnology, 1882-83.

A Navajo child's wearing blanket, woven on a three-ply wool warp, minor wool loss.

54in (137cm) long

£35,000-40,000 **SK**

An early 20thC Nez Perce beaded hide woman's dress, fringed with bugle beads and cowrie shells.

49in (124.5cm) long

£3,500-4,000 **SK**

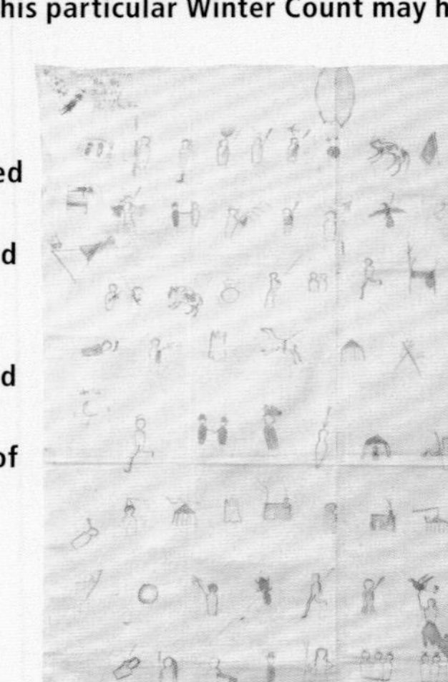

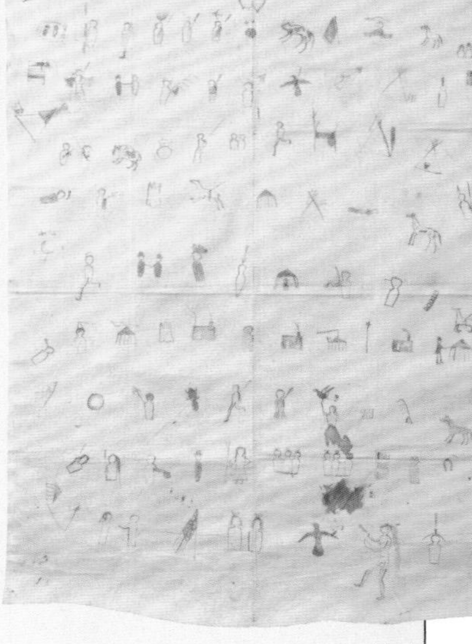

An 1870s Sioux Winter Count painted on muslin, by Bo-i-de.

43in (109cm) high

£20,000-25,000 **SK**

A late 19thC Sioux running horse effigy catlinite pipe bowl, rich patina of use.

10½in (26.5cm) long

£23,000-28,000 **SK**

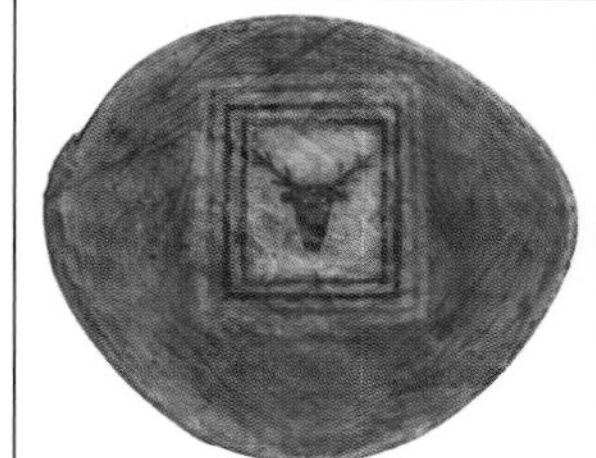

A late 19thC Sioux painted buffalo hide dance shield, painted with a deer head, pencilled 'Standing Rock Agency, Fort Yates, N.D. July 4, 1900'.

19in (48.5cm) diam

£14,000-18,000 **SK**

1870s Sioux beaded and quilled hide moccasins, the bifurcated tongues with tin cone and horsehair danglers, minor quill loss.

10½in (26.5cm) long

£2,000-2,500 **SK**

An 1870s Ute beaded hide tail bag, red ochre pigment overall.

8in (20.5cm) long

£2,500-3,000 **SK**

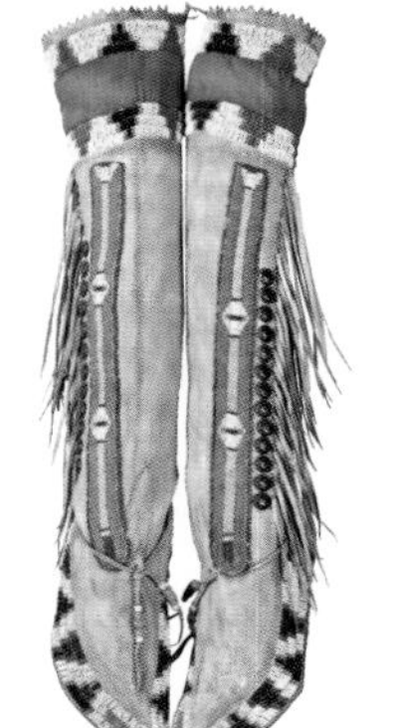

Late 19thC Ute beaded hide woman's high-top moccasins, fringed along the sides.

18½in (47cm) high

£4,500-5,000 **SK**

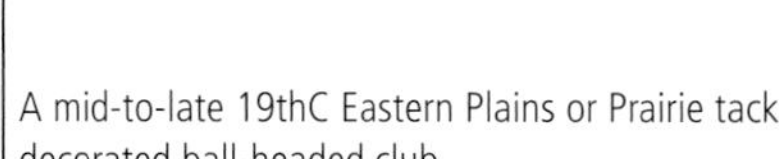

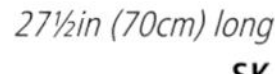

A mid-to-late 19thC Eastern Plains or Prairie tack-decorated ball-headed club.

27½in (70cm) long

£10,000-14,000 **SK**

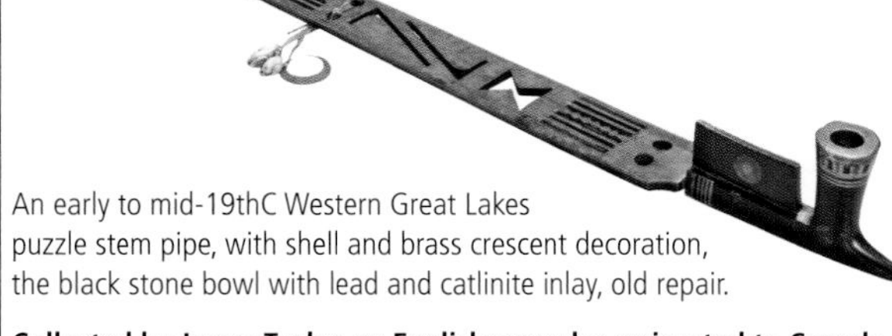

An early to mid-19thC Western Great Lakes puzzle stem pipe, with shell and brass crescent decoration, the black stone bowl with lead and catlinite inlay, old repair.

Collected by James Taylor, an Englishman who emigrated to Canada in 1852.

37½in (95.5cm) long

£11,000-14,000 **SK**

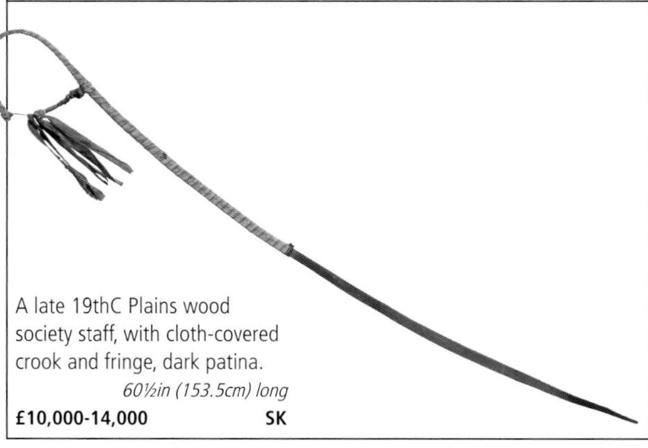

A late 19thC Plains wood society staff, with cloth-covered crook and fringe, dark patina.

60½in (153.5cm) long

£10,000-14,000 **SK**

A mid-to-late 19thC Plains or Prairie carved wood grass dance whistle, formed as a bird head.

22½in (57cm) long

£5,500-6,500 **SK**

A mid-to-late Plains grizzly bear claw necklace, buffalo hide wrapped, rich patina.

claws max 4in (10cm) long

£18,000-22,000 **SK**

A 19thC Micmac quilled birch bark box, minor quill loss.

The Micmac, or Mi'kmaq, people are indigenous to Canada's Atlantic Provinces, the Gaspé Peninsula of Quebec and the northeastern region of Maine.

5½in (14cm) diam

£750-850 SK

A Panamint coiled basketry bowl, eastern California, woven with geometric design.

c1900 *14½in (37cm) diam*

£3,200-3,800 SK

A Pima basketry olla, southern Arizona, with a vertical cross and ladder design, stitch loss.

16½in (42cm) high

£900-1,000 SK

A miniature Pomo basket, California, woven with geometric patterns and two figures, feather detail.

4½in (11.5cm) long

£950-1,100 SK

An early 20thC miniature Tlingit lidded basket, nick to rim.

The Tlingit people are indigenous to the Pacific Northwest Coast of North America.

2¼in (5.5cm) diam

£750-850 SK

A late 19thC to early 20thC Yokuts basketry olla, California, woven with a geometric design and 'rattlesnake' band.

14in (35.5cm) diam

£9,500-11,000 SK

A 1920s Acoma pottery jar, New Mexico.

13¾in (35cm) diam

£4,500-5,500 SK

An early 20thC Hopi pottery canteen, northeastern Arizona, with an avian pattern, some chips.

8½in (21.5cm) diam

£4,000-4,500 SK

A late 19thC Pueblo pottery bowl, flake to rim, surface abrasions.

The Pueblo people are indigenous to the Southwestern USA.

13in (33cm) diam

£650-750 POOK

A Zuni frog jar, with relief-moulded frogs and painted butterflies.

The Zuni people are indigenous to the Zuni River valley in New Mexico.

c1900 *12½in (32cm) diam*

£2,500-3,000 SK

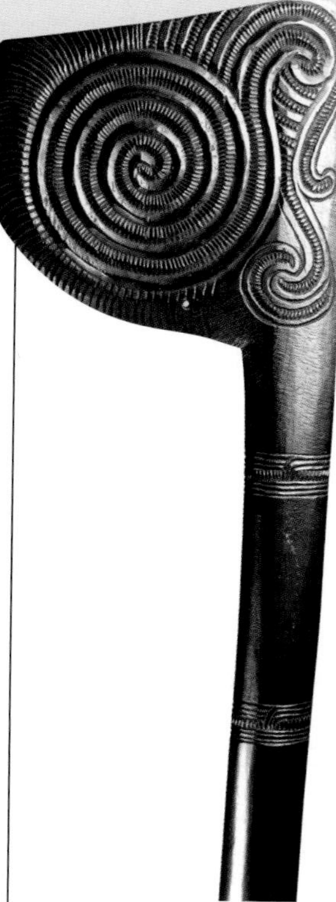

A mid-to-late 19thC Maori carved and notched wood tewhatewha fighting staff, attributed to Patoromu Tamatea.

Patoromu Tamatea was a prominent and prolific master carver around Lake Rotoiti in 1850-70 and carved various works including model canoes, paddles, house gable boards and wall slabs. He was also reported to have tattooed women.

59¼in (150.5cm) long

£6,000-7,000 WW

A late 19thC Maori carved wood and haliotis shell ceremonial paddle, the blade with three tiki figures, with a tiki head terminal.

61½in (156.5cm) long

£12,000-14,000 WW

An early 19thC Maori wood paddle hoe, with carved decoration.

Collected by Thomas Laslett (1811-87).

55¾in (141.5cm) long

£7,000-8,000 WW

A Maori carved wood and haliotis shell walking stick, with five tiki figures, the handle with a tiki terminal.

Presented to Joseph Manning in 1898 as recognition for his saving a Maori boy from drowning in the waters of Lake Rotoiti in the North Island of New Zealand.

35¼in (89.5cm) long

£2,500-3,000 WW

A Maori taiaha or staff, one eye socket inlaid with original paua shell, the others replaced with mother-of-pearl.

65½in (166.5cm) long

£2,500-3,000 BRI

A Maori cane, carved as a standing chief, with haliotis shell decoration and inset gold plaque to finial with motto 'Ready Aye Ready'.

33½in (85cm) long

£2,500-3,000 WW

A rare possibly 18thC Maori wooden hand club, carved with a face, the back with a sharp edge.

10¾in (27.5cm) long

£4,000-4,500 WW

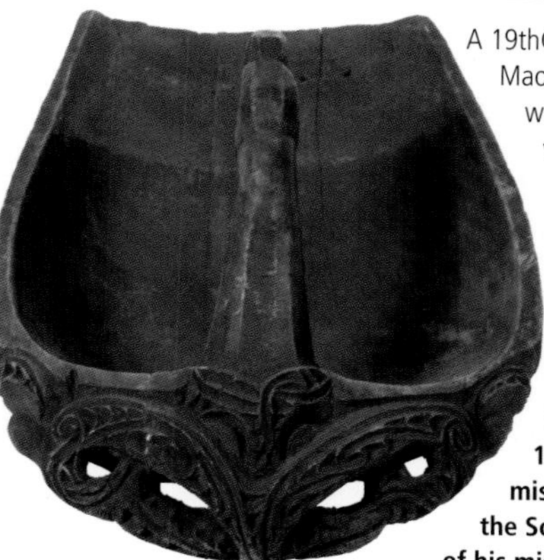

A 19thC or earlier wooden Maori canoe bailer, with low relief open work frontal crest representing an abstract face.

Provenance: By descent from the Family of John Williams. John Williams (1796-1839) was an English missionary, active in the South Pacific. Most of his missionary work was very successful, but in November 1839, while visiting the island of Erromango, Vanuatu, John Williams and fellow missionary James Harris were killed and eaten by cannibals. In December 2009 descendants of John and Mary Williams travelled to Erromango for a ceremony of reconciliation. To mark the occasion, Dillons Bay was renamed Williams Bay.

17¼in (44cm) high

£9,500-11,000 DUK

An early to mid-19thC Maori carved wood treasure box or 'Waku Huia', with projecting tiki heads.

19½in (49.5cm) long

£10,000-15,000 SK

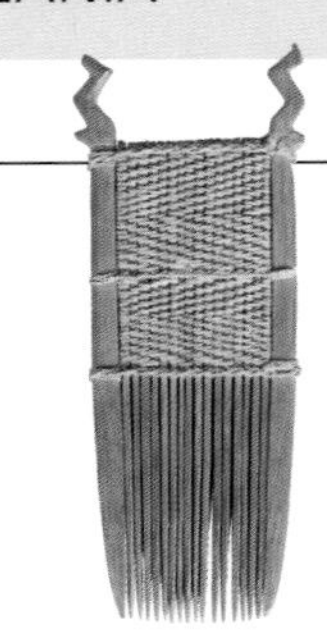

An early 19thC Maori heru mapara or small comb, the wooden teeth lashed together with flax fibre.

Maori men followed the Polynesian custom of wearing their hair long and tying it in a large topknot. Feathers were stuck into the topknot by their quills, the tail feathers of the huia, black with white tips, being regarded as the most valuable. Combs were also stuck in the hair for decoration.

6in (15cm) long

£1,500-2,000 JN

A pair of 19thC Maori carved horn scrimshaw powder flasks, one depicting and inscribed 'William King and his Wife', tattooed with Tâ moko and holding a war club and with mythical sea scenes, the other with scenes of Dancers.

Wiremu Kingi, also called Te Rangitake, or William King, was born in Manukorihi, New Zealand in 1795 and died in Kaingaru in 1882. He was a Maori chief whose opposition to the colonial government's purchase of tribal lands led to the First Taranaki War (1860-61). He inspired the Maoris' resistance throughout the 1860s to European colonisation of New Zealand's North Island.

12in (30.5cm) long

£4,500-5,000 JN

CLOSER LOOK – HEI-TIKI

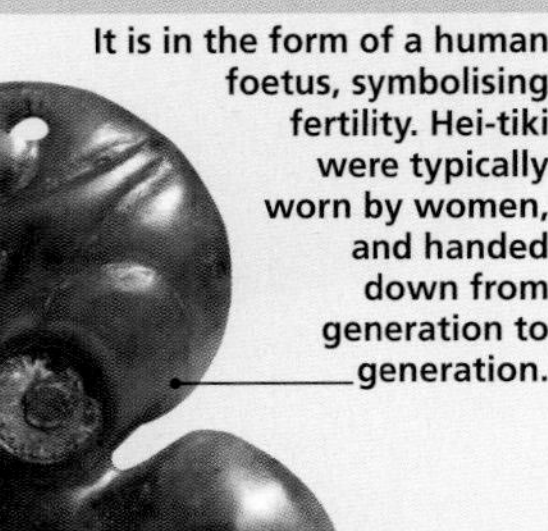

Hei-tiki are traditional pendants carved by the Maori.

It is in the form of a human foetus, symbolising fertility. Hei-tiki were typically worn by women, and handed down from generation to generation.

Like many hei-tiki, this example is made of green nephrite, with haliotis shell eyes. Nephrite is a very hard stone and would have been difficult to work.

Hei-tiki are greatly sought after by collectors today, and when in good condition can fetch high prices.

A 18thC to 19thC hei-tiki pendant, New Zealand.

5in (13cm) high

£35,000-40,000 WW

A Maori matau paua shell, bone, feather and fibre pä kahawai or fish hook.

Pä kahawai are trolling lures designed to attract and hook large surface-feeding fish, such as kahawai (sea trout). Adapted from Polynesian trolling lures, pä kahawai are composite lures typically constructed using a ground and shaped paua shell lure set in a wooden shank with a bone barb fixed at the base and bound tightly with muka (flax fibre) cord.

4½in (11.5cm) long

£1,000-1,400 JN

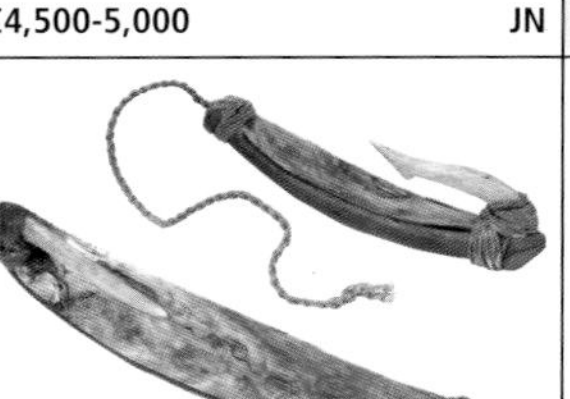

A pair of Maori wood, abalone shell and bone hei matau carvings or fish hooks.

Although these could be functional items, they were also worn as pendants for safekeeping, and were often treasured family heirlooms. They represented strength, good luck and safe travel across the water.

£2,000-2,500 HAN

A 19thC Maori hei-tiki pendant, nephrite with red sealing wax, the top with attachment piercing.

4in (10cm) high

£25,000-30,000 WW

A Fiji waseisei necklace, split sperm whale teeth, with thirty curved tusks with faceted tops, on a stand.

longest tusk 5in (12.5cm) long

£12,000-15,000 WW

A 19thC Fijian dui carved tribal club, the handle flaring in the shape of a fan, old knocks and scuffs.

The dui/fan club was used by warriors to deliver blows with a sharp edge.

32in (81.5cm) long

£2,200-2,800 MART

A 19thC Fijian wood ula or throwing club, inlaid in bone with a star and moon motifs.

The grip may possibly have been the work of a Maori carver working in Fiji.

17¼in (44cm) long

£4,000-5,000 DUK

A Fijian carved wood and fibre gunstock club, the name 'Sailósa' written near the base, mounted.

33¾in (86cm) high

£1,000-1,500 L&T

An Asmat ancestor figure, Buepis Village, Casuarinen Coast, Western Papua, Indonesia.

67in (170cm) high

£14,000-20,000 WW

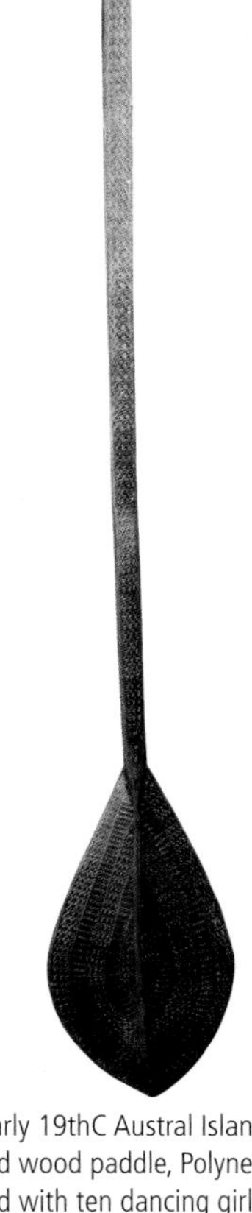

An early 19thC Austral Islands carved wood paddle, Polynesia, carved with ten dancing girls.

Collected by Thomas Laslett (1811-87).

46½in (118cm) long

£8,000-9,000 WW

An early 20thC South Sea Islands fighting staff, possibly Fijian.

39¾in (101cm) long

£2,000-2,500 HT

A Fijian pineapple or totokia club, with large toothed and spurred striking head.

34in (86.5cm) long

£3,000-3,500 BRI

A Kanak wood club, Vanuatu, with a root head.

26¾in (68cm) long

£1,800-2,200 WW

A Lake Sentani wood standing female figure, Papua New Guinea.

30in (76cm) high

£45,000-50,000 WW

A Lardil Aborigine cermonial dance headdress, Mornington Island, Queensland, bark wrapped in spun human hair, emu feather crest.

20in (51cm) high

£1,200-1,600 BRI

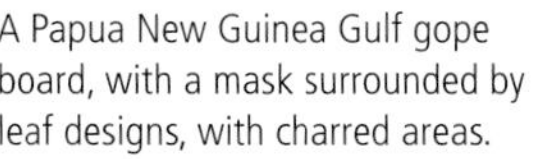

A Papua New Guinea Gulf gope board, with a mask surrounded by leaf designs, with charred areas.

61in (155cm) high

£4,000-5,000 WW

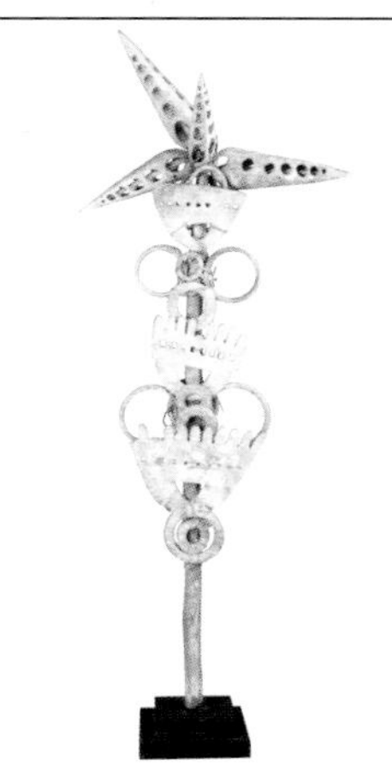

A Solomon Islands carved shell and wood barava funeral post, with fibre binding.

30½in (77.5cm) high

£4,000-5,000 WW

A Tikopia shell necklace, Solomon Islands, with a central double hook and twelve single hooks.

19in (48cm) long

£6,500-7,500 WW

An 19thC Aboriginal wood, resin and fibre woomera spearthrower, Western Australia, with remains of red ochre, with a textured back.

Collected by Arthur Allen (1874-1967).

The Indigenous population of Australia is composed of two groups, the mainland Aboriginal people and Torres Strait Islanders. The Torres Strait Islanders live in northern Queensland on the islands between Australia and Papua New Guinea. The Aboriginal people reside mostly in Queensland and New South Wales, along the Murray River. Aboriginal antiques are currently on the rise in value.

27¼in (69cm) long

£700-800 WW

A 19thC Aboriginal wood club, Murray River, South East Australia, with bands of 'peckwork' decoration, with incised hatching to the grip.

Collected by Arthur Allen (1874-1967).

28½in (72.5cm) long

£1,400-2,000 WW

A 19thC Aboriginal throwing club.

25in (63.5cm) long

£350-450 JN

A 19thC Aboriginal wood narrow shield, New South Wales, Australia, with possum tooth relief-carved wavy linear decoration with a line of lozenges with red ochre and with diaper filled lozenges.

Collected by Arthur Allen (1874-1967).

32¼in (82cm) long

£20,000-25,000 WW

An Aboriginal paddle-shaped club, decorated with panels of plain and wavy lines, some old repairs.

31in (79cm) long

£1,000-1,400 MOR

An Aboriginal nail club, Queensland, the head with band of metal flanked by clusters of horseshoe nails.

27¼in (69cm) long

£1,100-1,500 CHOR

An Aboriginal carved wood broad shield, decorated with rhythmical iterations of interlocking diamonds and waved lines.

43¾in (111cm) high

£6,500-7,000 L&T

An Aboriginal wood shield, decorated with stone carved zig-zag pattern, the reverse with an integral handle, mounted.

28¾in (73cm) high

£2,200-2,800 L&T

An Aboriginal bicornual basket, Jawun, Queensland, Australia, lawyer cane with traces of red ochre decoration.

13½in (34cm) high

£8,000-9,000 WW

A near pair of Saxon long wheel-lock holster pistols, by Hans Stockman, Dresden, stamped 'HS', with decorative marks.

These pistols are almost identical to other examples made for the Electoral Guard. They were almost certainly made for the Trabantenleibgarde of the Prince Elector Christian II. Hans Stockman is recorded working in Dresden from 1590 until his death in 1639. He became a master of the gunmaker's guild in 1603 and Burger of Dresden in 1605.

c1610 *barrel 19in (48cm) long*
£26,000-30,000 **TDM**

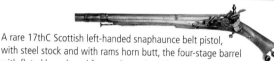

A rare 17thC Scottish left-handed snaphaunce belt pistol, with steel stock and with rams horn butt, the four-stage barrel with fluted breech and facetted muzzle with reeded sections dividing, dated.

1648 *19in (48cm) long*
£10,000-14,000 **L&T**

A pair of 30-bore silver-mounted flintlock duelling pistols, by John Manton, London, no.1921, with exceptionally elaborate silver mounts en rocaille, perhaps unfired, in original mahogany case.

These pistols belong to a group of only four known examples by John Manton with silver mounts made by Michael Barnett. They were probably made for Francis Ingram Seymour-Conway (1743-1822), 2nd Marquess of Hertford. What remains of the crest would reinforce this attribution, and they have been associated with a Marquess of Hertford since the early 20thC.

1790-91 *15in (38cm) long*
£62,000-70,000 **TDM**

ESSENTIAL REFERENCE – ROBERT WOGDON

Robert Wogdon (1737-1813) was a renowned Georgian gunmaker.

- **He was apprenticed in Lincolnshire to Irish gunmaker Edward Newton. He later moved to London, where he worked first on Cockspur Street and later at Haymarket.**
- **In 1794, he went into partnership with John Barton, forming Wogdon & Barton.**
- **Wogdon's duelling pistols were famous for their high quality and precision. He tuned his barrels to ensure they were accurate at twelve paces, resulting in more deaths from duels than previously.**
- **Wogdon pistols were used in the famous duel between prominent American politicians Aaron Burr and Alexander Hamilton in 1804. Wogdon pistols were so well known that duels were sometimes known as 'Wogdon affairs'.**

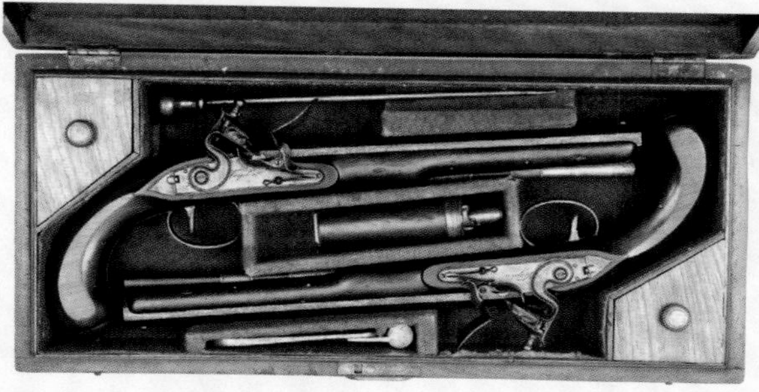

A cased pair of 22-bore flintlock duelling pistols, by Wogdon, single set triggers, some age splits to case.

c1785 *15in (38cm) long*
£14,000-20,000 **W&W**

A flintlock duelling pistol, by Wogdon & Barton, London, signed, the cock possibly replaced, crack to lock.

c1800
£850-950 **LOCK**

A 54-bore flintlock four-barrelled 'duck's foot' pistol, with four turn-off cannon barrels, false rifling, signed 'LAUGHER & SON', cleaned, not functional.

c1805
£4,500-5,000 **HOLT**

A Highland flintlock dress pistol, by Christie, signed lock, fitted with matching cock and sliding bolt safety, Tower Private proof marks, iron re-blued.

John Christie is recorded working in the Small Gun Office, the Tower of London 1794-1830.

c1820 *barrell 7¼in (18.5cm) long*
£7,500-8,500 **TDM**

An early 19thC flintlock pistol, by Harding, the barrel stamped 'J. Harding, Borough, London, No. 308', with proof marks, engraved 'For His Majesty's Mail Coaches'.

James Harding is recorded as 'Gunmaker to General Post Office', in Blackman Street, Borough between 1810-33.

14½in (37cm) long
£3,000-4,000 **SWO**

A double-barrelled 16-bore percussion holster pistol, by Westley Richards, the barrels engraved 'Westley Richards, 170 New Bond St, London', one hammer spur missing.

c1850 *12½in (32cm) long*
£1,400-1,800 **W&W**

ARMS & ARMOUR

A 9mm French model 1854 pin-fire rifled pistol, by Treuille de Beaulieu for the 'Cent Gardes' of Napoleon III.

The 'Cent Gardes' were an elite cavalry squadron created by Napoleon III. The contract for their firearms was awarded to Baron Antoine Hector Thésée Treuille de Beaulieu (1809-86), a French General and Captain Inspector of the Châtellerault manufactory.

c1854 *11½in (29cm) long*

£10,000-14,000 **TDM**

A DB side-by-side 38-bore percussion boxlock pistol, signed 'Steward, Yarmouth', B'ham proved.

9in (23cm) long

£750-850 **W&W**

A double-barrelled 28-bore percussion holster pistol.

13½in (34.5cm) long

£800-900 **W&W**

A Bergman no.5/1897 self-loading pistol, no.396, stamped 'Pistolet Bergman/Patent Brevete S.G.D.G.'.

The Bergman model 1897 underwent trials by both the Swiss and British military before being ultimately rejected. Around 800 pistols of this type are believed to have been made, most of which went to commercial customers.

barrel 3in (7.5cm) long

£14,000-18,000 **TDM**

A cased .41 rimfire over-under engraved derringer pistol, serial no.605, mother-of-pearl grips and spur trigger, in case.

c1888-1912 barrel 3in (7.5cm) long

£6,500-7,500 **HOLT**

A rare 7mm over-and-under 20-shot double-action pin-fire volley revolver, no.1226, by Lefaucheux, France, later chromed finish.

c1870 *5in (12.5cm) long*

£2,000-3,000 **TDM**

An American Smith and Wesson .44 calibre Russian model no.3.6 shot revolver, serial no.25,887, top barrel flat with patents and Springfield address.

1880 *barrel 5in (12.5cm) long*

£2,000-2,500 **LOCK**

CLOSER LOOK – US MODEL 1911A1 PISTOL

Only 500 of the US Model 1911A1 semi-automatic pistols were made, under Educational Order W-ORD-396. These were issued primarily to US Army Air Corps squadrons.

The pistol is stamped 'S. MFG. CO./ELIZABETH, N.J.,U.S.A.', 'UNITED STATES PROPERTY/ M1911 A1 U.S.ARMY' with serial number 'NoS800221'. It carries a 'JKC' inspection mark and 'P' proofmark.

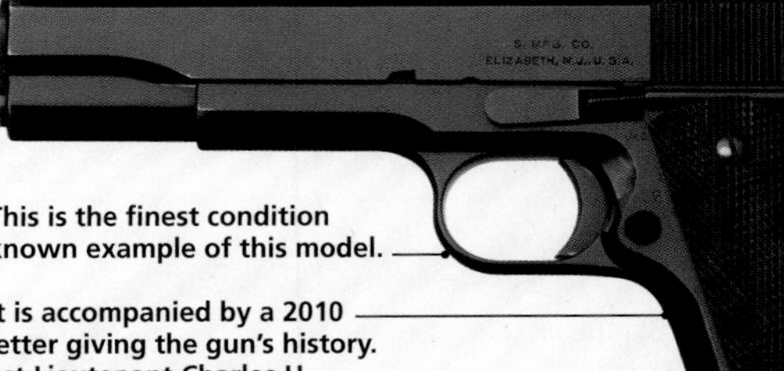

This is the finest condition known example of this model.

It is accompanied by a 2010 letter giving the gun's history. 1st Lieutenant Charles H. Clark of the Army Air Corps recovered it from a crash scene in 1943 when on a rescue mission.

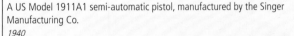

A US Model 1911A1 semi-automatic pistol, manufactured by the Singer Manufacturing Co.

1940

£250,000-300,000 **ROCK**

A cased 54 bore Irish six-shot percussion pepperbox revolver, by William & John Rigby, Dublin, no.10718, signed and inscribed 'Dublin', perhaps unfired, in original case.

1855 *barrel 3¾in (9.5cm) long*

£33,000-40,000 **TDM**

An early 5-shot 80-bore 1st type Kerr's Patent single-action percussion revolver, marked to the Sussex Artillery Volunteers, some scuffing.

£1,800-2,200 **W&W**

A late 18thC flintlock blunderbuss, the lock signed 'Bond', stamped 'EC' to stock, some scratches, locking mechanism not functional.

29in (73.5cm) long

£1,300-1,600 **GORL**

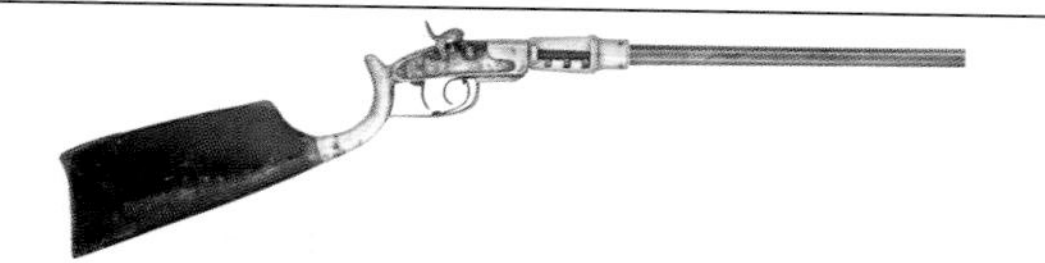

An American 40-bore Jennings pattern percussion rifle, converted from flintlock, barrel stamped '12', inscribed 'New York'.

Isaiah Jennings invented his all-metal breech-loading rifle in New York in 1818. Relatively few examples survive.

c1830 *32¾in (83cm) long*

£5,500-6,500 **TDM**

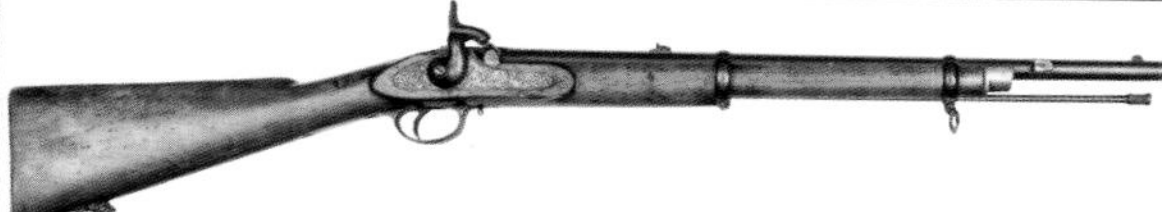

A 2nd Model 1853 percussion Artillery carbine, with two folding leaf rearsights and bayonet bar at the muzzle, the buttplate tang engraved 'V/ MxA3/ 411' (Middlesex Artillery Volunteers).

1853 *40in (101.5cm) long*

£800-1,000 **W&W**

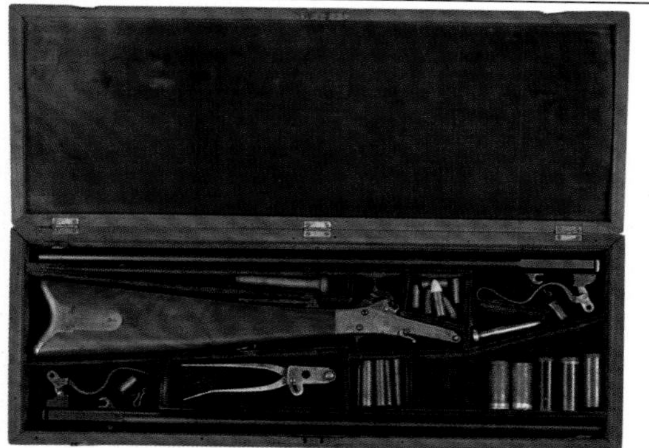

A presentation Maynard patent first model Saddle Ring Sporting single shot rifle/shotgun, with a .50 caliber rifled barrel and a .55 caliber smoothbore barrel, in case.

1857 *26in (66cm) long*

£5,500-6,500 **POOK**

A cased semi-smooth bore top lever hammerless boxlock ejector rook rifle, by Holland & Holland, no.21308.

42in (106.5cm) long

£3,200-3,800 **W&W**

CLOSER LOOK – JAMES PURDEY AND SONS RIFLE

This rifle is possibly unique, and may be the only best-quality 8-bore produced by James Purdey and Sons.

It has dovetailed fine 3-stripe Damascus barrels, made by A. Meers.

The metal is decorated with fine scroll and bouquet engraving, probably by J. Lucas, the head engraver at Purdey's.

It has bores with 17-groove Enfield-type rifling, and a marbled and figured full pistol grip Circassian walnut buttstock.

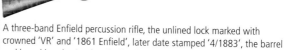

A James Purdey and Sons hammer underlever 8-bore rifle, engraved 'J. Purdey & Sons, Audley House, South Audley Street, London', stamped 'AM', refurbished, most likely by the factory, some minor pits, in oak and leather Purdey case, with steel bullet mould, striker keys, cleaning rod and other accessories.

barrels 24in (61cm) long

£55,000-65,000 **JDJ**

A three-band Enfield percussion rifle, the unlined lock marked with crowned 'VR' and '1861 Enfield', later date stamped '4/1883', the barrel and barrel bands pitted and refinished.

55in (139.5cm) long

£900-1,100 **W&W**

A WCF Winchester Model 1885 single shot falling block volunteer rifle, no.64136.

1893 *43½in (110.5cm) long*

£1,200-1,600 **W&W**

A Martini Henry Mark IV rifle, serial no.4884, the frame marked with crown over 'VR/Enfield/1886/IV/1', various Nepalese marks, some minor pitting and bruising, dated.

1908 *49½in (125.5cm) long*

£550-650 **W&W**

A New England cherry drop stock flint lock fowler.

60½in (153.5cm) long

£5,000-6,000 **NA**

A Brunswick State two-hand processional sword of the Guard of Julius, Duke of Brunswick and Lüneburg in Wolfenbüttel (1528-89), no.235, dated.

Provenance: The Brunswick Ducal Zeughaus, Wolfenbüttel. Duke Julius of Brunswick-Wolfenbüttel (1528-89) inherited the title following the death of his two older brothers in battle. The swords from his Ducal Guard are all numbered and may be divided into two series, one dated 1573 and the other 1574.

1573 *52¾in (134cm) long*

£17,000-20,000 TDM

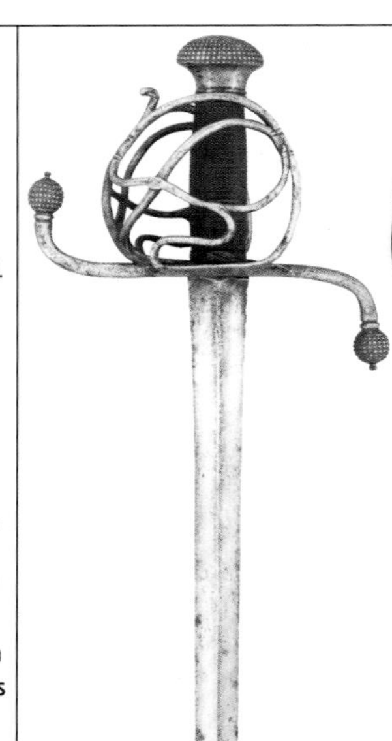

A late 16thC North European basket-hilted military backsword.

blade 33¼in (84.5cm) long

£5,000-6,000 TDM

Judith Picks

This sword tells an interesting story. The blade was made in the early 17thC, probably in Germany before being transported to Scotland to be hilted. The basket hilt is applied with silver mounts depicting Jacobite symbols and mottos. Some of these date from the early 17thC, some from c1707 around the time of the Act of Union. The mounts include Classical medallions, St Andrew on the cross and several thistles. The knuckle guard is inscribed, 'Prosperity to Schotland, No union, God save ye Kings James VIII'. The misspelling of Scotland can be seen on other swords of German manufacture. Together this suggests that this sword belonged to a Scottish family of high status who were very public in their support of the Jacobite cause. The sword's motto would have been clearly – and controversially – displayed when it was worn at the side or drawn in action.

An early 17thC silver-mounted Scottish basket-hilted sword.

c1620 *blade 40¼in (102cm) long*

£20,000-25,000 L&T

An 18thC and earlier Scottish basket hilted broadsword, The Cameron Family Sword, the basket of Stirling form, blade inscribed 'Yis Suerd was brukyt be Ht Cameron at ye Batttailly off Stirling Bryg MCCXCVII and Bannockburn MCCCXIIIII & Feili Melle', with further plaque engraved 'Yis Thrusande Claiffoff Metell gud aeft Tynt 3 hits Shynn in Saxonys Blud'.

The tradition of re-mounting historic family blades is well recorded, in part due to the early 19thC fashion for the Scottish revival fuelled by Sir Walter Scott. This blade unusually predates that fashion. Repute suggests that it was re-mounted in the early 18thC to be taken to Jacobite risings.

38½in (98cm) long

£9,000-10,000 L&T

A late 18thC French small-sword, with tapered German blade, with inscription 'Me Fecit Solingen' (Solingen made me), silver hilt close-plated with gold, face decorated in blue and white enamels, some dents, some enamel losses.

28¾in (73cm) long

£5,000-6,000 TDM

A 1796-pattern heavy cavalry trooper's sword, marked 'Osborn' and 'E/19', some wear.

blade 34½in (87.5cm) long

£2,500-3,000 W&W

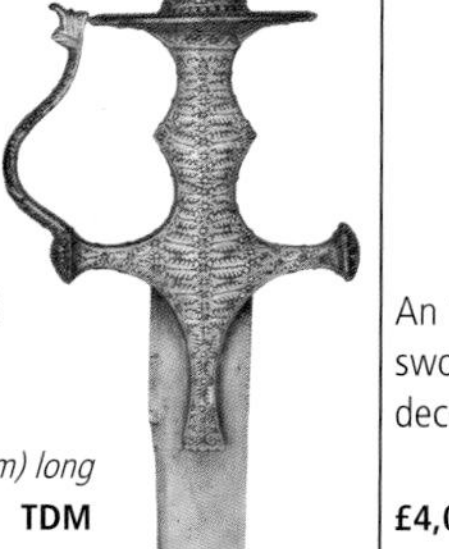

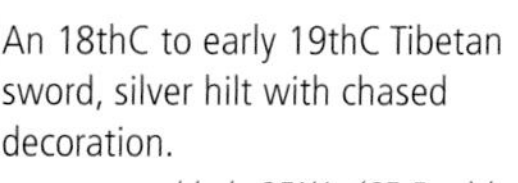

An 18thC to early 19thC Talwar or Indian sword, with iron hilt quillons and recurved knuckle-guard with monsterhead finial.

32in (81.5cm) long

£2,500-3,000 TDM

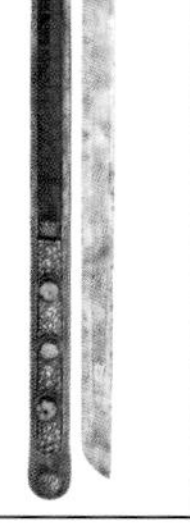

An 18thC to early 19thC Tibetan sword, silver hilt with chased decoration.

blade 25½in (65.5cm) long

£4,000-5,000 TDM

An early 19thC military officer's basket hilted sword, by Prosser, London, engraved 'Prosser'.

37½in (95cm) long

£1,400-1,800 L&T

A George IV presentation sword of the Honourable Artillery Company, of 1796 light cavalry style, inscribed 'Capt General, His Most Gracious Majesty Geo IVth. Colonel, HRH Prince Augustus Frederick, Duke of Sussex'.

blade 32in (81.5cm) long

£1,000-1,500 **W&W**

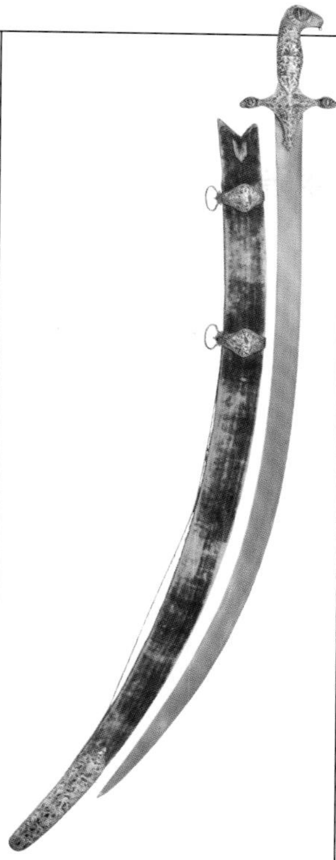

An early to mid-19thC Indian shamshir, with earlier Persian curved single-edged blade of watered steel, some wear.

32¼in (82cm) long

£8,500-9,500 **TDM**

An early 19thC French sidearm, with prominent cockerel's head pommel, hilt loose.

blade 23in (58.5cm) long

£350-400 **W&W**

A Japanese Shinto tachi, the blade decorated with a horimono of a dragon and a figure holding a tsurugi, marked 'Kato Tsunatoshi on orders of Fujiwara Teifuku/ On a day of the second month Tenpo eight [1837]', to the reserve, 'On the 27th day of the tenth month of the same year at Senju Yamakado Yazaemon [cut through] a head and into the earthenmound below'.

Kato Tsunatoshi (d.1863), real name Kato Hachiro, originally came from Dewa's Yonezawa and was a student of Suishinshi Masahide. He moved to Edo during the Bunsei era (1818-30). He also worked under the pseudonym Chojusai.

23½in (59.5cm) long

£5,000-6,000 **WHYT**

A 19thC Turkish yataghan sword.

31½in (80cm) long

£1,800-2,200 **HT**

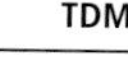

A Belgian French-style cavalry NCO's sword, marked 'Manufacture d'Armes de l'Etat à Liège' on backstrap, dated.

1844

36in (91.5cm) long

£300-400 **W&W**

A German Imperial Damascus honour sword, by A. Werth, Solingen, inscribed 'The Officers corps of the Hussars regiment No7 of the King To the Heir Prince Zu Bentheim as a friendly memory', stamped maker's marks.

41in (104cm) long

£6,000-7,000 **PSA**

A late 19thC Indian tulwar sword, the iron hilt with elephant's head pommel and tiger knucklebow, inlaid with gold and fitted with gems.

blade 30¼in (77cm) long

£8,500-9,500 **GORL**

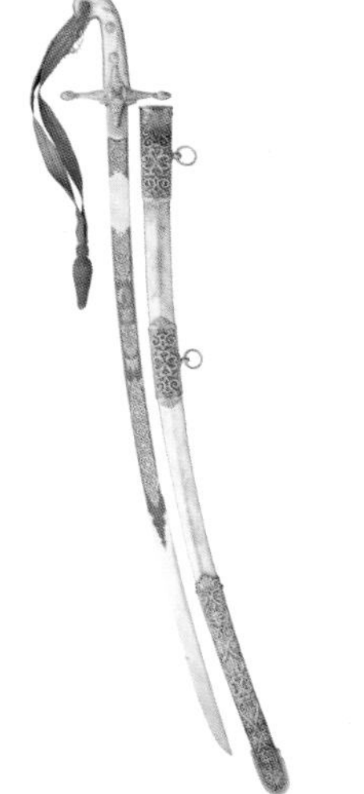

A George V 18th Hussars mameluke-hilted officer's sword.

blade 31¼in (79.5cm) long

£2,000-2,500 **TDM**

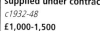

A Wilkinson 1822-pattern sword, as issued to the 'Blue Hussars'.

The Blue Hussars, officially called the Mounted Escort, were a ceremonial unit of the Irish Army established in 1932. It escorted the President of Ireland on state occasions, most famously to and from presidential inaugurations between 1938, when the first president took office, and 1948 when the Escort was disbanded. This sword lacks any serial number, signifying that it was supplied under contract.

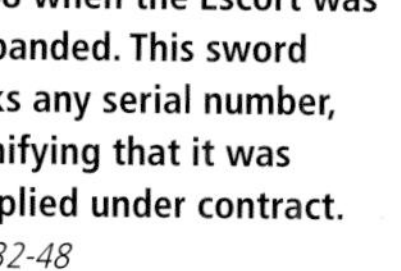

c1932-48

£1,000-1,500 **WHYT**

A medieval dagger, possibly Italian, in excavated condition.
c1470-90 *blade 12in (30.5cm) long*
£3,000-3,500 **TDM**

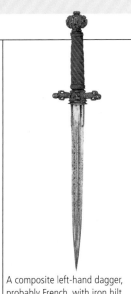

A composite left-hand dagger, probably French, with iron hilt decorated with cherubic figures and a Classical warrior, with later grip.
c1660 *10in (25.5cm) long*
£4,000-4,500 **TDM**

An English plug bayonet, stamped with a King's head mark, the mark of the London Cutler's Company and a copper-lined 'T' mark, inscribed 'God Save King William & Mary' and 'Nicholas Arnold 1690', dated.

Bayonets with inscriptions relating to King William and Queen Mary are notably rare. The mark is probably that of Gyles Lyndesy who became Free of the Cutler's Company in 1673.
1690 *11½in (29cm) long*
£9,000-11,000 **TDM**

An 18thC Indian katar or dagger.
9¾in (25cm) long
£2,000-2,500 **TDM**

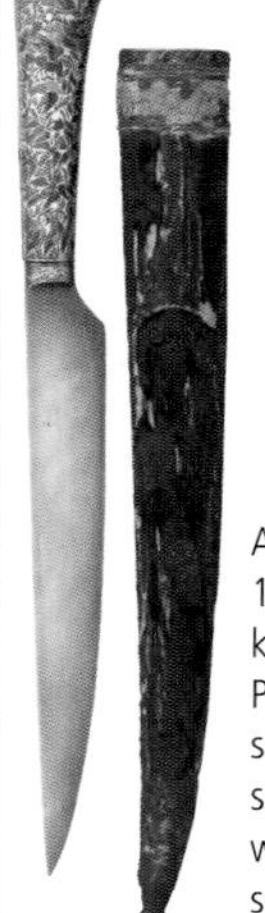

An early to mid-19thC Indian dagger kard, with earlier Persian watered single-edged blade, some losses, in its wooden silk-covered scabbard.
7½in (19cm) long
£5,000-6,000 **TDM**

A late 18thC Indian khanjar or dagger, with carved green jade hilt.
blade 8¾in (22cm) long
£11,000-15,000 **TDM**

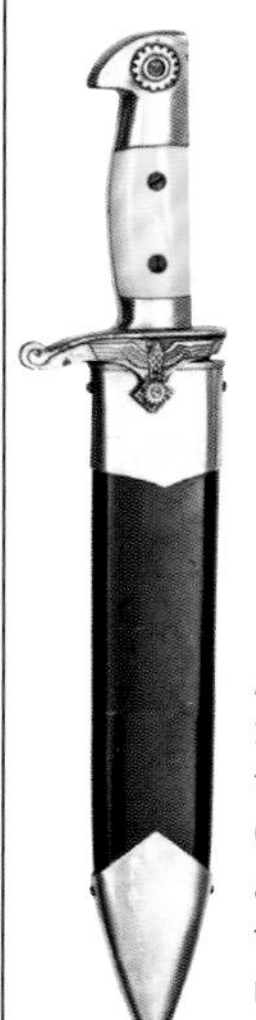

A Third Reich Teno Subordinate's hewer, the blade with Original Eickhorn and Teno marks, the throat mount numbered '2871'.
£1,300-1,800 **W&W**

A Japanese dagger or aikuchi, with kaku-mune blade, small copper tsuba.
9½in (24cm) long
£550-600 **TDM**

A Victorian dirk, Edinburgh, with bi-knife and fork.
1896 *17in (43cm) long*
£1,000-1,500 **L&T**

A Gordon Highlanders officer's dirk and sgian dubh, by R. & H.B. Kirkwood, Edinburgh.

A Scottish dirk is the ceremonial weapon of the Highland Cathairean (warrior), worn by officers, pipers and drummers of Scottish Highland regiments. A sgian-dubh is a small, single-edged knife worn on the leg as part of traditional Scottish Highland dress.
1906 *dirk 11¾in (30cm) long*
£5,500-6,500 **L&T**

A 1st Lanarkshire Militia officer's dirk, the handle with silver studs, mounted with crystal, the scabbard set with bi-knife (inscribed 'John Sellars') and fork.
17¼in (44cm) long
£2,000-2,500 **L&T**

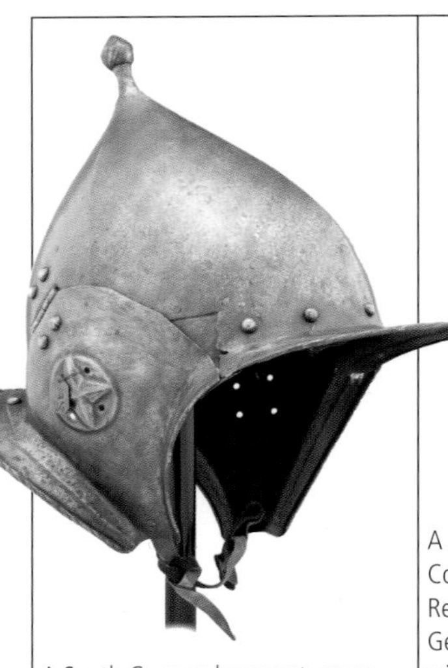

A South German burgonet, some pitting.
c1560-70 *9¼in (23.5cm) high*
£2,000-2,500 TDM

A mitre cap of the Grenadier Company, The Queen's Own Regiment of Foot, bearing a Georgian crown, 'GR' on Garter with motto, professionally restored, with related documents.
1727-43 *14in (35.5cm) high*
£1,500-2,000 W&W

An officer's white metal helmet of the Montgomeryshire Yeomanry Cavalry, back peak cracked, lining replaced.
£500-600 W&W

A Victorian 1847-pattern officer's 'Albert' helmet, of the 1st King's Dragoon Guards, some dents and rubbing, plume replaced.

The initials on the headband of this helmet appear to be those of Major Walter Clopton Wingfield, who served with the King's Dragoon Guards 1851-61, and is credited with the invention of Lawn Tennis.

£5,500-6,000 TDM

A 19thC mitre cap of the Prussian 1st Garde Regtiment, frontplate bearing the Prussian eagle and motto 'Pro Gloria et Patria' and 'FR', with owner's name 'Barthel' and '9. Ky 1. Garde-Regt.Z.F', some moth holes.
15in (38cm) high
£1,800-2,200 W&W

A Sussex Yeomanry officer's helmet, with star helmet plate inscribed 'Sussex Yeomanry'.
post-1902
£3,500-4,000 W&W

A Royal Irish Constabulary helmet, inscribed 'Con, Primrose' and 'JP 60943'.
1902
£1,500-2,000 WHYT

A Life Guards Other Ranks, lining leather damaged.
post-1902
£800-900 W&W

A World War I Brodie's Patent steel helmet.
£950-1,100 W&W

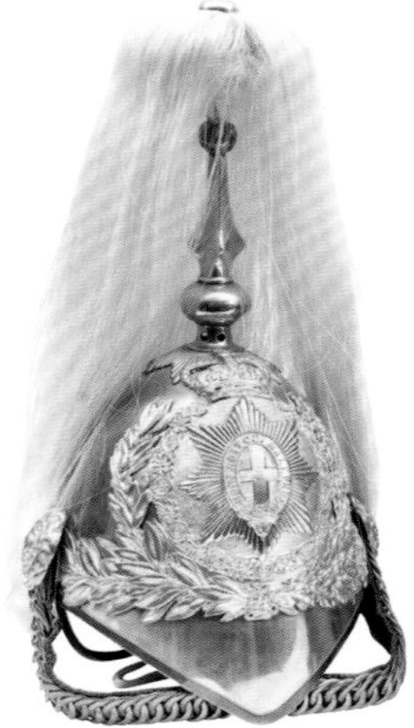

A Life Guards Other Ranks helmet, unissued.
post-1953
£1,100-1,500 W&W

An officer's tall blue cloth shako, of The Royal Dockyard Battalion, trade label of 'Wilkinson & Son London', small tar stain, in its tin case.
£4,500-5,500 W&W

A 2nd Edinburgh Rifles Volunteer Corps black cloth officer's helmet, inscribed 'Hill Bros military outfitters London'.
£1,700-2,000 L&T

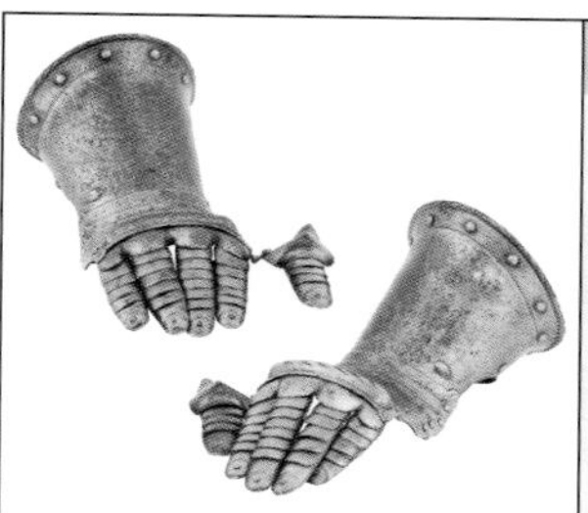

A pair of mid-16thC fingered gauntlets, probably German, with later leather finger linings.

11¾in (30cm) long

£2,000-3,000 **SWO**

A North European cuirassier's breastplate, in the late 'peascod' fashion, lightly patinated overall.

c1610 *14in (35.5cm) high*

£800-900 **TDM**

A set of 19thC cap-a-pie field armour, with etched decoration in the mid-to-late 16thC Italian style, mounted on a wood stand and accompanied by a sword.

£10,000-15,000 **TDM**

ESSENTIAL REFERENCE – JACKS OF PLATE

Jacks of plates, sometimes referred to as coats of plate, were a uniquely British piece of armour, especially common in North England and Scotland.

- **They ceased to be manufactured at the end of the 16thC, although they were used into the 17thC.**
- **Jacks of plate were once commonly used, but are also extremely fragile. Only sixteen known complete jacks of plates survive worldwide today.**
- **This one formed part of a collection assembled sometime after 1765 at Worden Hall, Lancashire, by Sir William Farington (c1704-81).**

An English jack of plate, the iron plates secured by stitches of crossbow twine, the outer fabric discoloured and worn.

c1580-90 *28¼in (72cm) high*

£8,000-9,000 **TDM**

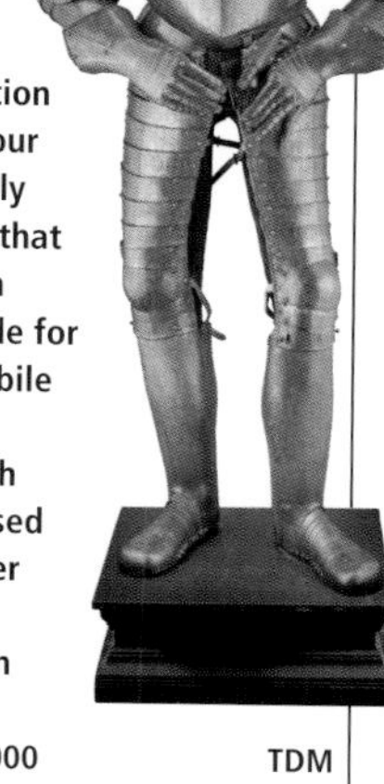

A set of composite 16thC and early 17thC cap-a-pie field armour, mainly Italian, with etched and gilt 19thC decoration.

The decoration of this armour was probably inspired by that of an Italian armour made for Count Annabile Capodilista c1620, which was purchased for the Tower of London Armouries in 1840.

£25,000-30,000 **TDM**

A Georgian Irish officer's gilt gorget, of the Royal Castlewellan Yeoman Infantry, engraved with crowned pre-1801 Royal Arms.

Castlewellan is in County Down, Northern Ireland. The unit was raised in October 1796, under Captain Commandant Richard, 2nd Earl of Annesley.

£2,800-3,200 **W&W**

An early 19thC silver officer's gorget, inscribed 'GIII Rex IX Regt.', soldered repair.

5½in (14cm) diam

£3,500-4,000 **MART**

A 19thC Turkish cavalry helmet, breast and backplate.

These were worn by someone of officer class in the Sudanese War.

£900-1,100 **W&W**

A Scots Guards Captain's tunic, with gilt bullion embroidery, with 24 gilt King's Crown regimental buttons by Robbins.

post-1902

£400-500 **W&W**

A World War I P/PH gas helmet, with two mica eyepieces, with exhaust valve with its metal tube and composite mouth piece.

This early gas mask was introduced in July 1915 to replace the 'Hypo' helmet. The flannel was dipped in sodium phenolate and glycerine. Later in October 1915 Hexamine was added for protection against phosgene. This altered the nomenclature to 'P.H. Helmet' (Phenate Hexamine).

£1,600-2,000 **LOCK**

A 17thC German signalling cannon, on wooden field-type carriage.

42in (106.5cm) long

£1,500-2,000 **W&W**

A George III painted hardwood truncheon, marked with crown, Royal cipher and 'Fauxhall'.

The land where Vauxhall, London, is now located was acquired in the 1230s by a Frenchman named Falkes de Breaute. Over time the area has been known as Faukeshall, Fauxhall, Fox Hall, Fulke's Hall, Fawkyhall, Faux Well and ultimately Vauxhall, when Vauxhall Gardens opened in 1785.

27½in (70cm) high

£400-500 **CHEF**

An 18thC stone bow, with red walnut frame and steel detail, inscribed 'H.W. Mortimer & Son, 89, Fleet St, London' and 'Gun Makers to His Majesty'.

28¾in (73cm) long

£4,000-5,000 **APAR**

A rare 1814-issue Georgian colour of No.15 Company, 2nd Battalion, the Coldstream Guards, with painted decoration of St Edward's Crown above the Company symbol (Carolingian crown), 'EGYPT', the Sphinx between laurel sprays, 'BARROSA', a bugle-horn, 'PENINSULA' and 'WATERLOO', further inscribed 'LINCELLES' and 'TALAVERA', 'XV' in the canton, restored.

This colour was recently discovered in near-relic condition and has been expertly restored to museum quality. The 1814-issue colour was used until the next issue in 1821.

c1814-21 *76½in (194.5cm) wide*

£16,000-20,000 **TDM**

A Civil War Era thirty-five star American flag.

1863-65 *54in (137cm) long*

£3,000-3,500 **NA**

A George V painted brass side drum of the 1st Battalion Coldstream Guards.

£400-500 **W&W**

An officer's gilt shoulder belt plate of the 13th 1st Somersetshire Prince Albert's Regiment of Light Infantry, some wear.

pre-1855

£850-950 **W&W**

A Victorian officer's full dress embroidered sabretache of the 21st Hussars, bearing crown, 'VR' cipher and '21/H' roundel, minor moth traces.

12in (30.5cm) high

£1,800-2,200 **W&W**

ESSENTIAL REFERENCE – NEMA CIPHER MACHINE

During World War II, the Swiss Army used a modified version of the German-made commercial Enigma model K machine.

- **Although Switzerland was neutral in WWII, many agents and diplomatic missions operated on Swiss soil, and both the allied forces and the Germans learned how to decode Swiss Enigma K traffic. After this, Switzerland started the development of their own improved machine, which they called Nema. The first machines entered service in 1947.**
- **A total of 640 were built by the Swiss manufacturer Zellweger AG. Three versions were in circulation, which can be discriminated by their serial numbers. TD100-199 were made for the Foreign Office, TD200-419 were training machines, and TD420-740 were operational machines.**
- **Operational machines differ from the training machines as they have two additional wheels stored inside the top lid and they can be recognised by the label on the outer case saying that it should only be released in case of war. As this is numbered TD610, it is an operational machine.**

A pair of German Third Reich Kriegsmarine U-boat binoculars, by Zeiss, stamped '7 x 50 48285 blc', some wear.

£750-850 **LSK**

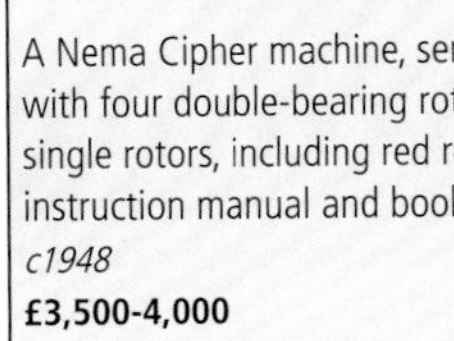

A Nema Cipher machine, serial no.TD610, with four double-bearing rotors and two single rotors, including red reflectors, with instruction manual and booklet.

c1948

£3,500-4,000 **CHEF**

An officer's gilt and silver-plated shako plate of the 98th Regiment.
1822-29
£1,200-1,600 **W&W**

A Naval General Service medal, marked 'Navarino'.
1848
£1,200-1,600 **W&W**

A Military General Service Medal, awarded to John Wilkinson 7th Foot, with bars for Toulouse, Orthes, Pyrenees, Vittoria, Salamanca, Badajoz, Albuhera and Talavera, replacement ribbon, wear to ribbon and clasp.
£2,500-3,000 **APAR**

An officer's silver glengarry badge of the Argyll & Sutherland Highlanders, marked 'Meyer & Mortimer. London', hallmarked 'HT', Edinburgh, brooch pin.
1914
£400-500 **W&W**

A World War I Other Ranks bronzed hat badge, of the 67th Bendigo Infantry, by Stokes & Sons Melbourne.
£400-450 **W&W**

An Easter Rising Medal, for Kathleen Clarke.

Kathleen Clarke (1878-1972) was one of the founding members of Cumann na mBan, an Irish republican women's paramilitary organisation founded in 1914. She was selected by the Irish Republican Brotherhood to be made acquainted with the plans for the 1916 Easter Rising, in case of the death or arrest of all its leaders. The day after the Rising ended, Kathleen founded what became the Irish Volunteers Dependants and National Aid Association, to provide support to families who had lost people in the Rising. She later became the first female Lord Mayor of Dublin.
1916
£13,000-16,000 **WHYT**

An East India Company silver medal for military service in the Third Mysore War.

The Third Anglo–Mysore War (1790–92) was a conflict in South India between the Kingdom of Mysore and the East India Company and its allies, including the Maratha Empire and the Nizam of Hyderabad. This medal was awarded to the higher ranks of native Indian troops, the Jemadars and Serangs.
1791-92 *1¾in (4.5cm) diam*
£2,500-3,000 **WHYT**

A Seringapatam Medal 1799 (Honourable East India Company), English version in silver.
2in (5cm) diam
£1,000-1,400 **LOCK**

A Canada General Service medal, with bars for Fenian Raids of 1866 and 1870, named '850 Pte W Piggott 1/RB', from Woolwich, Kent, with copy medal roll.
1899
£800-900 **LOCK**

A 1st pattern bronzed hat badge, of the Australia Commonwealth Horse.
£1,000-1,400 **W&W**

An Other Ranks white metal hat badge, of the 6th Australian Light Horse.
£350-400 **W&W**

An Imperial Russian officer's and silver-plated star helmet plate of the 3rd Regiment.
£400-450 **W&W**

An Egyptian Naqada II Period carved breccia stone bird vessel.
3500-3200 BC
£5,500-6,000 TL

An Egyptian 19th Dynasty Hapi canopic jar, New Kingdom, the lid with a human face representing the son of Horus Hapi, with hieroglyphic text, placing the vessel under the protection of Nephthys and Hapi.
1292-1189 BC 14in (35.5cm) high 346oz
£14,000-18,000 TL

An Egyptian Late Dynastic to Ptolemaic Period wood sarcophagus mask.
c700-30 BC 23in (58.5cm) high
£5,000-6,000 WW

An Egyptian Late Period moulded faience Shabti for Ankh-hor, with hieroglyphs for Ankh-hor, Governor of Upper Egypt.

A Shabti is a figure in the form of a mummy, placed in an ancient Eygptian tomb. It was believed that Shabtis would work for and assist those they were buried with in the afterlife.

640-570 BC 4in (10cm) high
£2,500-3,000 L&T

A 4th-3rdC BC bronze figure of Horus.
5in (13cm) high
£5,000-6,000 SWO

An Egyptian Ptolemaic Period cartonnage gilt mummy mask, depicting the Four Sons of Horus with mummifom bodies before Osiris, wearing Atef crown.
332-330 BC
£7,000-8,000 TL

A 4th-1stC BC Greek Hellenistic silver kantharos.
4¾in (12cm) wide 4oz
£3,500-4,000 TL

A 4th-3rdC BC Greek marble head of a youth, scuffed and worn, nose broken off.
4¼in (11cm) high
£2,000-2,500 DN

A 1stC BC Greek Hellenistic rock crystal flask.
1¾in (4.5cm) high
£2,500-3,000 TL

A 1stC BC-3rdC AD Romano-Egyptian gold coiled snake bracelet.
3½in (9cm) long 1½oz
£8,500-9,500 **TL**

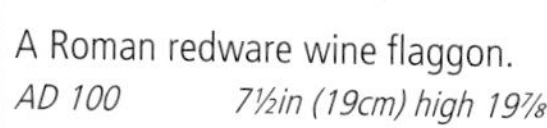

A Roman redware wine flaggon.
AD 100 *7½in (19cm) high 19⅞oz*
£160-200 **LOCK**

A 1stC AD Roman onion-form glass bottle, probably Alexandria.
5in (12.5cm) high
£450-550 **HALL**

A 3rd-4thC AD Roman 'Apotheosis of Hercules' mosaic centre panel, some reconstitution.

Hercules (Greek Herakles) was an important demi-god and hero in the Classical world, around whom a major cult developed during the Roman Empire. He was the son of Jupiter (Greek Zeus) and the mortal Alcmene, famous for his strength and guile. This mosaic depicts Hercules being taken to Mount Olympus to take up his place among the Immortals after his death.

4in (10cm) diam
£6,500-7,500 **TL**

A 5thC AD or later Roman oinochoe, body formed as the head of a boy, the neck with dolphins, handle with putto playing a syrinx.

In Etruria, bronze and terracotta wine jars, known as oinochoes, olpes and kantharoi, were often modelled as human heads. This vessel is a later Roman version and would have been used to serve guests at a symposium (Roman commissatio), the part of banquet after the meal dedicated to drinking, music, dancing, recitals and conversation, which was a key Hellenic – and later, Roman – social institution.

12¾in (32.5cm) high 7¾oz
£7,000-8,000 **TL**

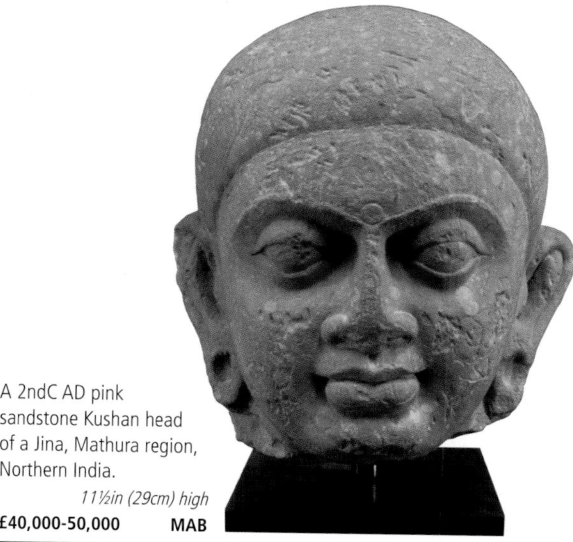

A 2ndC AD pink sandstone Kushan head of a Jina, Mathura region, Northern India.
11½in (29cm) high
£40,000-50,000 **MAB**

An Ancient Indus Valley terracotta painted zebu bull.
c3000-2200 BC
£500-600 **LOCK**

A Colima pottery dog.
c100 BC-AD 250 *11¾in (30cm) long*
£850-950 **SK**

A Pre-Columbian Olmec-style jade ceremonial celt, the blade form mimicking the early Mesoamerican agricultural axe, likely depicting a Yucatan chief.

A celt is a prehistoric tool, similar to an adze or an axe head, used for felling trees or shaping wood. Ceremonial celts were also made.

14in (35.5cm) high
£19,000-23,000 **CLAR**

A carved rosewood square piano, by Schomacker & Co., Philadelphia.

Provenance indicates, this piano was played by Swedish opera singer Jenny Lind.

patented 1848 *89½in (227.5cm) wide*

£25,000-30,000 FRE

A late 19thC satinwood grand piano, by F. Kaim & Sohn Kirchheim-Stuttgart, painted with Neo-classical scenes, in need of re-tuning.

71¾in (182cm) long

£6,500-7,500 BELL

A late 19thC to early 20thC double manual polychromed harpsichord.

82¼in (209cm) long

£2,500-3,000 L&T

An early 19thC violin, stamped 'PERRY, DUBLIN'.

14¼in (36cm) long

£4,000-5,000 SWO

A French violin, by Jean Baptiste Vuillaume, Paris, labelled 'Jean Baptiste Vuillaume a Paris, Rue Croix des Petits Champs', numbered '1660'.

Vuillaume's internal numbers '1660' are closer to the date 1845 rather than 1840, as quoted by W.E.Hill & Sons in 1917. It is possible that they did not have access to the full chronology of the Vuillaume numbers at that time.

c1845 *14¼in (36cm) long*

£110,000-140,000 BRO

A maple cello, by Johann Antes Bethlehem, Pennsylvania, top of scroll broken off, some damages, dated.

Johann Antes Bethlehem (1740–1811) is widely regarded as the first bowed string instrument maker in America. Very few examples of his work survive, including a violin at the Moravian Historical Society Nazareth and a viola in the Lititz Congregation Collection. This item may be the earliest American-made cello still in existence.

1763

£17,000-20,000 POOK

A harp, by Sebastian and Pierre Erard, London, engraved 'Sebastian and Pierre Erard Patent No. 5698, 18 Great Marlborough Street, London'.

Sebastian Erard (1752-1855) was born in Strasbourg and moved to Paris to work as a musical instrument maker. He was later joined in business by his nephew Pierre. Due to the turmoil of the French Revolution, he later moved to London. The firm was based at Great Marlborough Street c1790-1902.

£3,000-4,000 BRO

An Anglo Concertina, by Charles Jeffries, London, with thirty nickel keys, six-fold black bellows.

6in (15cm) diam

£4,000-5,000 BRO

A two-keyed boxwood oboe, by Thomas Cahusac, London, with silver keys.

c1785 *22½in (57cm) long*

£1,500-2,000 GHOU

An eight-keyed rosewood flute, by Rudall & Rose, London, with silver mounts and keys.

c1830 *22½in (57cm) long*

£3,000-4,000 GHOU

A French ten-string yew guitar, by Jean Henri Naderman (1734-99), restoration to inlay, some cracks, replacement pegs.
c1772 *17¼in (43.5cm) long*
£5,000-6,000 **BELL**

A 19thC parlour guitar, labelled 'Panormo 1827, 26 High Street, Bloomsbury, London, No 878', with ebony 18-fret finger board.
£4,000-5,000 **BRI**

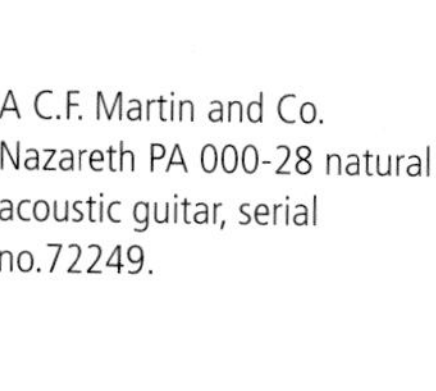

A C.F. Martin and Co. Nazareth PA 000-28 natural acoustic guitar, serial no.72249.
1939 *39in (99cm) high*
£15,000-20,000 **CLAR**

A Fender Stratocaster electric guitar, made in USA, serial no.9xxx9, with rosewood fretboard neck stamp 'JAN 63', pencil date '63', in soft case, with CITIES certificate.
1963
£15,000-20,000 **GHOU**

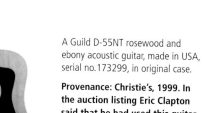

A Gibson ES-335 semi-hollow body electric guitar, made in USA, serial no.A2xxx0 FON T4xxx5, with rosewood fretboard, working electrics, some alterations made for Bigsby tailpiece since removed, with CITIES certificate.
1958
£16,000-20,000 **GHOU**

A Guild D-55NT rosewood and ebony acoustic guitar, made in USA, serial no.173299, in original case.

Provenance: Christie's, 1999. In the auction listing Eric Clapton said that he had used this guitar for writing and recording. Lee Dickson recalls that Clapton had owned this guitar since the late 1970s.
1978
£25,000-30,000 **GHOU**

A mid-1960s Wandre Blue Jeans electric guitar, made in Italy, in a vintage Stone Case Company case, with letter of provenance from Zoot Money.

Although Jimi Hendrix never used this guitar in a gig, it was in fact the first guitar he ever played in England. In September 1966, Jimi Hendrix arrived at Heathrow from New York with his manager Chas Chandler. They went to Zoot Money's flat in West London, where Chas asked if Zoot knew anyone with a left-handed guitar that Jimi could borrow for a gig. While discussing who to call, Jimi played around on this guitar.
£9,000-10,000 **GHOU**

A George Formby (1904-61) Gibson concert banjolele, serial no.132.
21¾in (55cm) long
£35,000-40,000 **HAN**

A Raffele Calace & Son of Naples mother-of-pearl and tortoiseshell-inlaid mandolin, labelled within, some splits.
24¾in (63cm) long
£700-800 **APAR**

DECORATIVE ARTS MARKET

Like many areas of collecting, Decorative Arts pieces have seen a rise in sales and prices of high-end items, and stagnation of mid- to low-end goods.

Many Doulton wares are quite simply now considered unfashionable. Demand for the Royal Doulton figures has fallen dramatically and only the prototypes, limited production and rare colourways are fetching good money. In addition, demand for works by the Barlows, Eliza Simmance and Frank Butler has been very sluggish. The opposite is true of the Doulton pieces with experimental glazes – especially anything unusual that is lustred or flambéd.

Martin Brothers continue to be strong sellers in the current marketplace. A rare Martin Brothers salt-glazed stoneware grinning grotesque crab, at Phillips Design sale in New York in December 2018 sold for $220,000 (£184,000, plus buyer's premium of 25%, see page 474). And that same month, Waddington's in Toronto had the most exciting sale of nearly 100 pieces of Martin Brothers work from a private collection – my friend Bill Kime drove across Canada to pick up this collection which included a small flock of Wally birds.

Moorcroft and Clarice Cliff will command high prices if the pattern and shape are rare, but the more common patterns are quite stagnant in the market. Wedgwood Fairyland lustre ceramics continue to be on a roll, particularly in the USA, Canada and Australia – rare patterns, unusual colourways and experimental or trial pieces are highly contested.

The Ohio school, meanwhile, including Rookwood and Roseville, has had a quiet year, with few exciting pieces coming onto the market. George Ohr continues to excite, but few exceptional pieces come on the market.

Silver from 20th century has continued to sell well, especially pieces by Charles Robert Ashbee and Omar Ramsden, as have rare and unusual Liberty pieces, particularly those designed by Archibald Knox.

In Art Nouveau glass, it is the big names that continue to sell: Lalique, Gallé, Tiffany, Loetz and Daum.

Bronze and ivory figures by Demêtre Chiparus, Bruno Zach and Ferdinand Preiss perform well if they are rare, iconic and exceptional. Even though bidders based in the US and Japan could not take part because of import restrictions on ivory, enough dealers and collectors from other countries are still collecting these figures.

As David Rago, of leading auction house Rago, says, 'As for decorative objects, such as ceramics and glass, we are seeing less fall-off on older work, and continued interest in pretty much all post-war glass, from 1950s Italian to high-end contemporary. One exception here has been the market for Tiffany glass and lighting which, in the past two years, has shown a resurgence. Oddly enough, early 20th century ceramics are drawing more attention than much of the post-war work, though that is a more recent trend and has yet to really play itself out.'

The sale of early 20th century furniture has been unremarkable, although when something fresh and with very good provenance appears on the market, so do the collectors – Charles Rennie Mackintosh continues to have a strong following.

Top Left: A Lenci figure, 'Primo Romanzo', by Helen Konig Scavini, restoration to hand, re-glued finger.

9¾in (25cm) high

£5,500-6,500 **WW**

Above: A bronze sculpture, 'The Rattlesnake', by Frederic S. Remington (1861-1909), inscribed 'Copyright Frederic Remington, ROMAN BRONZE WORKS INC. N-Y-' and 'No. 69', some dirt and surface wear.

24in (61cm) high EST:

£80,000-160,000 **LHA**

CLOSER LOOK – 'ANGLO-PERSIAN' VASE

This vase was painted by Leonard King with a Persian-inspired design. Leonard King is one of Burmantofts most sought-after decorators.

Each side is decorated with a varying design of a peacock amidst foliage.

It has been painted in an Iznik palette of blue, green, aubergine and yellow.

Its value is increased by its excellent condition.

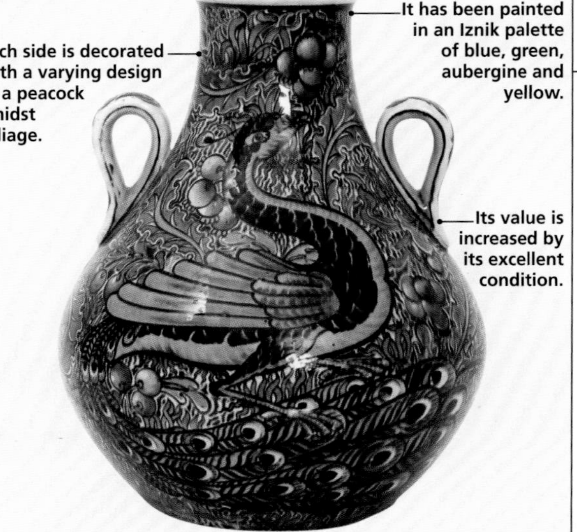

A Burmantofts Faience 'Anglo-Persian' vase, model no.DS9-94, impressed and painted marks.
14¼in (36cm) high
£9,000-11,000 **WW**

A Burmantofts Faience 'Anglo-Persian' Poseidon charger, by Leonard King, model no.606, impressed marks, painted marks, 'LK' monogram, minor firing faults and glaze crackling.
18¼in (46.5cm) diam
£5,500-6,000 **WW**

A Burmantofts Faience 'Anglo-Persian' floor vase, by Leonard King, model no.164.

Burmantofts Faience Pottery was founded by James Holroyd in 1881 as a side project to his company Wilcocks, and continued production until 1904. Its art pottery was strongly influenced by the Aesthetic Movement.
21in (53.5cm) high
£1,600-2,000 **WW**

A rare Burmantofts Faience wall charger, by Leonard King, painted with a fantastical beast, impressed maker's marks 'BURMANTOFTS/ FAIENCE' and with artist's monogram 'LK'.
c1880 *15½in (39.5cm) diam*
£2,500-3,500 **L&T**

A Burmantofts Faience charger, by William Neatby, impressed marks, painted 'Wm J Neatby', dated.
1887 *15½in (39.5cm) diam*
£4,000-5,000 **WW**

A Burmantofts Faience 'Partie-Colour' jardinière designed, by Joseph Walmsley, model no.2227, impressed and painted marks, minor glaze chips.
9¾in (24.5cm) high
£1,800-2,200 **WW**

A Burmantofts Faience 'Partie-Colour' jardinière and stand, model no.2115-2116, impressed marks, hairline crack, some chips.
37½in (95cm) high
£4,500-5,500 **WW**

A Burmantofts Faience 'Dragon' vase, model no.896, impressed marks.
13½in (34cm) high
£2,000-2,500 **WW**

A Burmantofts Faience seated dog, model no.1991, impressed marks, professional restoration to ears.
5½in (14cm) high
£400-500 **WW**

A Burmantofts Faience grotesque spoon-warmer, model no.1907, impressed marks, minor glaze frits.
6in (15cm) high
£650-750 **WW**

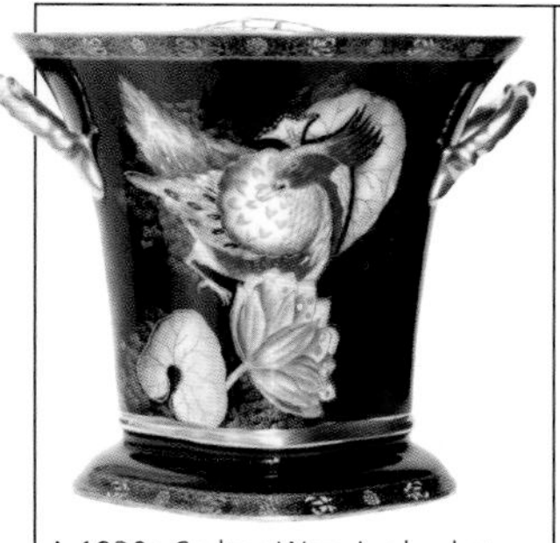

A 1930s Carlton Ware ice bucket, 'Crested Bird' and 'Water Lily' patterns, printed script mark.

8in (20.5cm) high

£220-280 **FLD**

A 1930s Carlton Ware pedestal gondola, 'Explosion' pattern, printed script mark.

13½in (34cm) long

£500-600 **FLD**

A 1930s Carlton Ware footed bowl, 'Melange' pattern, printed script mark.

12¼in (31cm) long

£250-300 **FLD**

A rare Carlton Ware coffee service, no.3765, 'Red Devil' pattern, with printed and painted marks.

c1933 *coffee pot 8in (20.5cm) high*

£3,500-4,000 **L&T**

A pair of 1920s Wiltshaw and Robinson Carlton Ware rouleau-shape vases, 'Tutankhamun' pattern, printed mark, Egyptian mark.

10¾in (27.5cm) high

£750-850 **FLD**

A 1930s Carlton Ware goblet-form vase, 'Wagon Wheels' pattern, printed script mark.

4½in (11.5cm) high

£250-300 **FLD**

A Carlton Ware 'Flower and Falling Leaf' charger, printed mark, numbered '1/1369' and '3948'.

12½in (32cm) diam

£350-400 **MOR**

A Carlton Ware Guinness toucan and pint glass wall appliqué, impressed 'GA2492'.

7in (18cm) high

£1,200-1,600 **GORL**

A Carlton Ware Guinness lamp base, printed around base, 'If he can say as you can Guinness is good for you How grand to be a Toucan Just think what Toucan do', printed mark, overall crazing.

9½in (24cm) high

£250-300 **PW**

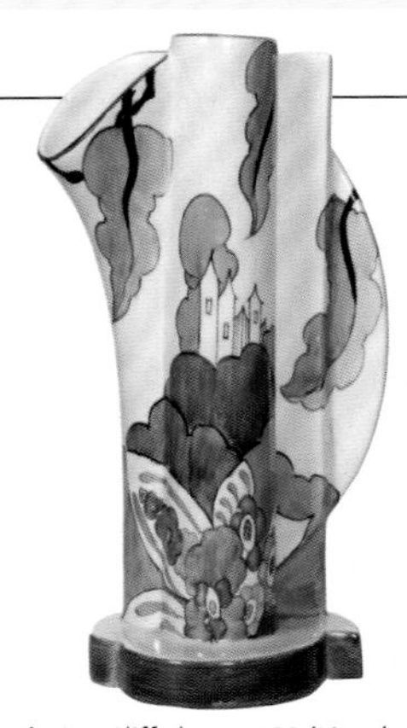

A Clarice Cliff shape 469 'Liner' vase, 'Brown Alton' pattern, 'Bizarre' mark.
c1933 *8¼in (21cm) high*
£1,800-2,200 FLD

A Clarice Cliff shape 356 vase, 'Applique Avignon' pattern, 'APPLIQUE' and 'Bizarre' marks.

This comes with original price label of 15/6 which calculates to £46.86 in today's money, when the average annual wage was the equivalent of £7,919.99.
c1930 *6¾in (17cm) high*
£2,200-3,000 FLD

ESSENTIAL REFERENCE – CLARICE CLIFF

Clarice Cliff (1899-1972) was an important Art Deco ceramics designer.

- **She started at A.J. Wilkinson in 1916 as an enameller, and by the mid-1920s Wilkinson had given her her own studio, Newport Pottery.**
- **Her 'Bizarre' range was launched in 1927 and her 'Fantasque' range followed shortly afterwards.**
- **Her tableware, vases and other items were covered with bold designs, handpainted in thickly applied bright colours. The designs were painted by a group of dedicated decorators, mostly women, who become known as the 'Bizarre Girls'.**
- **The demand for Clarice Cliff remains strong, with rare shapes, such as 'Yo-Yo' vases, and rare patterns, such as the 'Applique' range or 'May Avenue', being especially sought after.**

CLOSER LOOK – 'APPLIQUE BIRD OF PARADISE' WALL PLAQUE

This dish-form wall plaque is handpainted with the 'Applique Bird of Paradise' pattern.

Patterns in the 'Applique' range are rare and highly sought after.

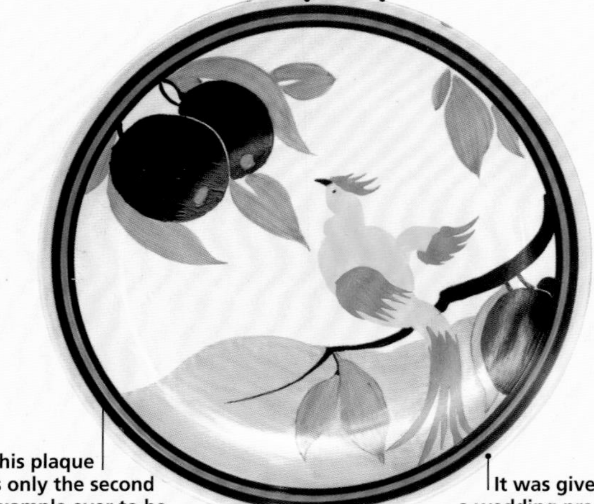

This plaque is only the second example ever to be discovered, being one of only four pieces known to exist in this pattern.

It was given as a wedding present in 1931 and has been handed down by family descent ever since.

A Clarice Cliff wall plaque, handpainted 'Applique' and 'Bizarre' marks.
c1931 *13½in (34cm) wide*
£10,000-14,000 FLD

A Clarice Cliff dish-form plate, 'Orange Applique Lucerne' pattern, 'APPLIQUE' and 'Bizarre' marks.
c1930 *9in (23cm) wide*
£2,500-3,000 FLD

A Clarice Cliff Bizarre 'Mei Ping' vase, 'Applique Red Tree' pattern, printed and painted marks.
6in (15.5cm) high
£3,000-3,500 WW

A Clarice Cliff shape 402 'Conical' biscuit box and cover, 'Blue Autumn' pattern, 'FANTASQUE' and 'Bizarre' marks.
c1930 *7¾in (20cm) high*
£3,000-3,500 FLD

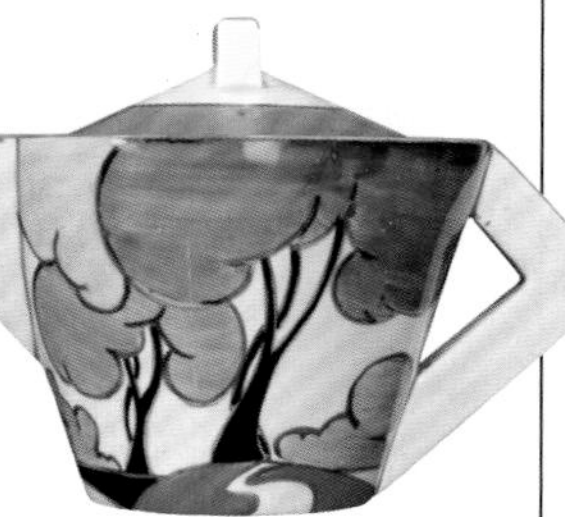

A Clarice Cliff 'Conical' teapot, 'Blue Autumn' pattern, 'FANTASQUE' and 'Bizarre' marks.
c1930 *5½in (14cm) high*
£1,400-1,800 FLD

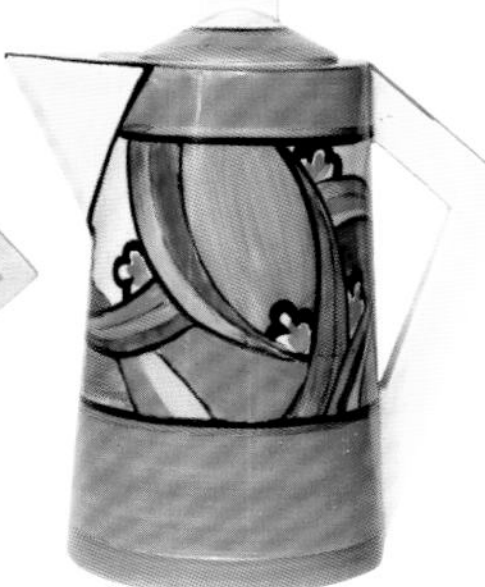

A Clarice Cliff 'Conical' coffee pot, 'Comets' pattern.
c1930 *7½in (19cm) high*
£1,000-1,400 FLD

A Clarice Cliff 'Mr Duck' egg cup set, 'Crocus' pattern, various marks.
c1930
£500-600 FLD

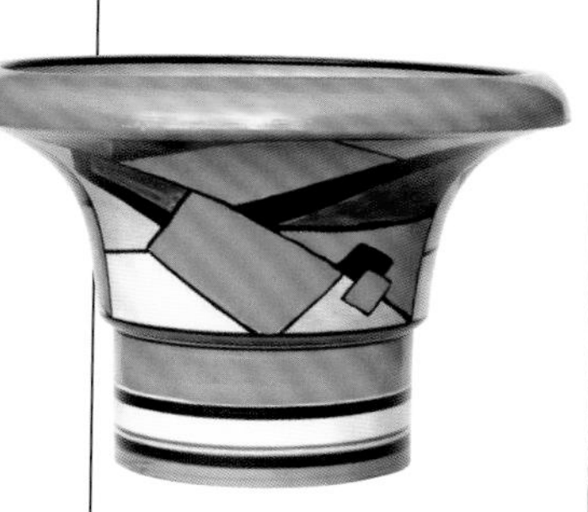

A Clarice Cliff 'Archaic' range vase, 'Cubist' pattern, 'Fantasque' mark, marked 'Replica. Temple of Luxor. Thebes. Capital of the large columns. 1250 BC'.
c1929 *7in (18cm) high*
£1,500-2,000 **FLD**

A Clarice Cliff 'Lotus' jug, 'Double V' pattern, 'Bizarre' mark.
c1929 *11¾in (30cm) high*
£2,000-2,500 **FLD**

A Clarice Cliff Bizarre shape 358 vase, 'Green Erin' pattern, printed factory marks.
8in (20.5cm) high
£1,200-1,600 **WW**

A Clarice Cliff Bizarre 'Isis' vase, 'Football' pattern, printed factory marks.
9¾in (24.5cm) high
£4,000-5,000 **WW**

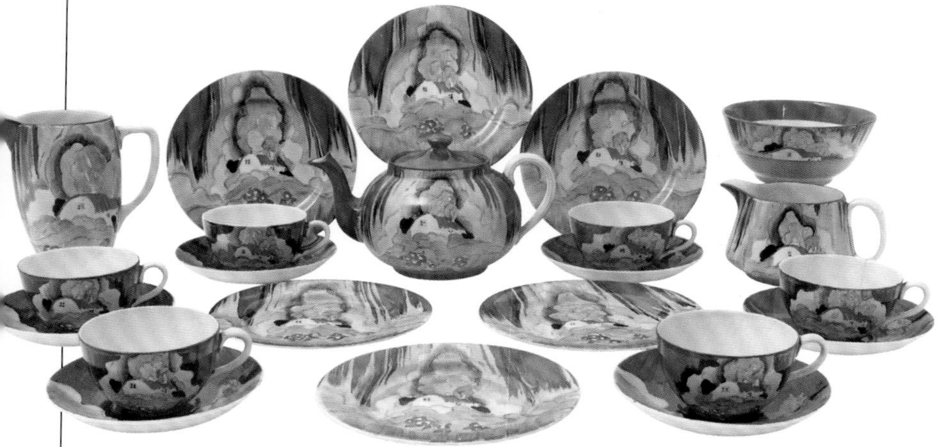

A Clarice Cliff 'Globe' tea set for six, 'Forest Glen' pattern, printed factory marks, hairlines to two cups, date mark.
1936 *teapot 5in (12.5cm) high*
£3,000-4,000 **WW**

A Clarice Cliff 'Lotus' jug, 'Honolulu' pattern, 'Bizarre' mark.
c1933 *11½in (29.5cm) high*
£2,200-2,800 **FLD**

A Clarice Cliff Fantasque Bizarre wall charger, 'House and Bridge' pattern, printed factory marks.
16½in (42cm) wide
£7,000-8,000 **WW**

A Clarice Cliff Bizarre shape 362 vase, 'House and Bridge' pattern, printed factory marks.
8¼in (21cm) high
£1,800-2,200 **WW**

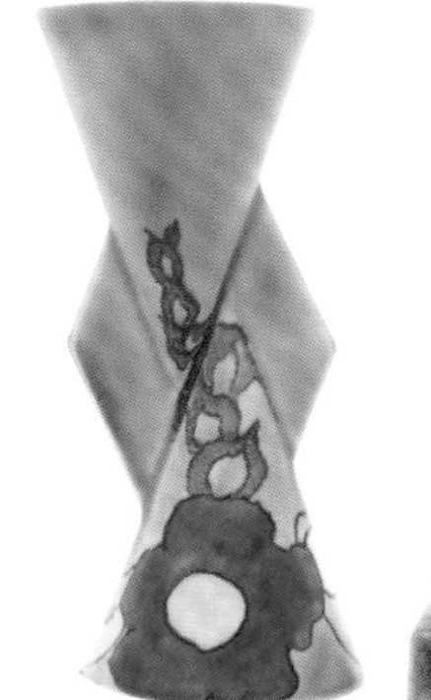

A Clarice Cliff shape 379 'Yo-Yo' vase, 'Inspiration Floral' or 'Daisy' pattern, 'Inspiration Bizarre' mark, restored.
c1930 *8¾in (22.5cm) high*
£2,000-2,500 **FLD**

A pair of Clarice Cliff novelty bird bookends, 'Inspiration L'Oiseau' pattern, 'INSPIRATION' and 'Bizarre' marks.
c1930 *7in (18cm) high*
£900-1,100 **FLD**

A Clarice Cliff shape 280 vase, 'Inspiration Persian', 'INSPIRATION' mark.
c1930 *6in (15.5cm) high*
£750-850 **FLD**

A Clarice Cliff shape 370 'Globe' vase, 'Jonquil' pattern, 'Bizarre' mark.
c1935 *6in (15cm) high*
£650-750 **FLD**

A Clarice Cliff 'Hereford' shape biscuit barrel, 'Latona Knight Errant' pattern, 'LATONA' and 'Bizarre' marks.
c1930 *6¼in (16cm) high*
£1,200-1,600 **FLD**

A Clarice Cliff shape 363 vase, 'Latona Orchid' pattern, 'LATONA' and 'Bizarre' marks.
c1929 *6¼in (16cm) high*
£1,800-2,200 **FLD**

A Clarice Cliff pedestal almond dish, 'Luxor' pattern, 'Bizarre' mark.
c1929 *3½in (9cm) wide*
£850-950 **FLD**

A Clarice Cliff Bizarre 'Daffodil' preserve pot and cover, 'May Avenue' pattern, printed marks.
5in (13cm) high
£2,500-3,000 **WW**

A Clarice Cliff Bizarre charger, 'Moonlight' pattern, printed marks.
18in (45.5cm) high
£4,000-4,500 **WW**

A Clarice Cliff Bizarre 'Isis' vase, 'Oranges & Lemons' pattern, printed marks.
9¾in (24.5cm) high
£1,800-2,200 **WW**

A Clarice Cliff 'Isis' vase, 'Poplars' pattern, printed marks, light scratching.
11¾in (30cm) high
£1,500-2,000 **CHEF**

A Clarice Cliff Bizarre 'Mei Ping' vase, 'Red Cafe' pattern, printed marks, 'Sevi Guatelli' paper label.
8¾in (22.5cm) high
£9,000-11,000 **WW**

A Clarice Cliff shape 370 'Globe' vase, 'Summerhouse' pattern, 'FANTASQUE' and 'Bizarre' marks.
c1931 *5½in (14cm) high*
£2,800-3,200 FLD

A pair of Clarice Cliff 'Teddy Bear' novelty bookends, 'Sunburst' pattern, 'Bizarre' mark.
c1930
£2,500-3,000 FLD

A Clarice Cliff Bizarre 'Lotus' jug, 'Sunray' pattern, printed marks.
11½in (29cm) high
£4,000-4,500 WW

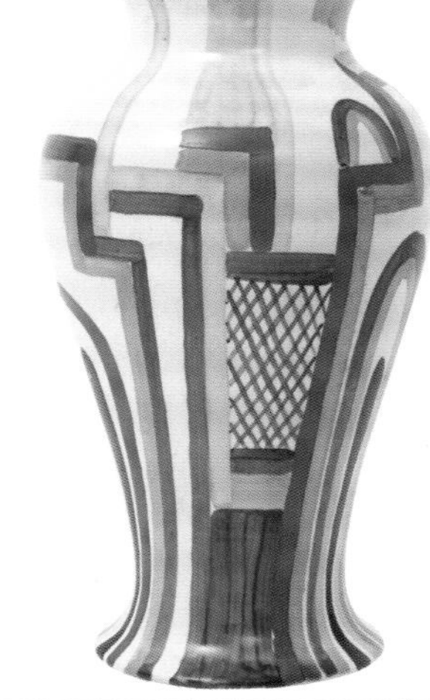

A Clarice Cliff Bizarre 'Mei Ping' vase, 'Tennis' pattern, printed mark, professional restoration the base rim.
12¼in (31cm) high
£4,000-5,000 WW

A Clarice Cliff 'Holborn' fruit bowl, 'Sunspots' pattern, 'Bizarre' mark.
c1931 *8¼in (21cm) wide*
£1,200-1,600 FLD

A rare full set of Wilkinson and Clarice Cliff 'Allied Commanders of the First World War' Toby jugs, designed by Sir F. Carruthers Gould, marked, some crazing, chips and minor wear.

These were issued in limited editions 1915-19.

£7,000-8,000 WM

A Clarice Cliff dish-form charger, 'Pastel/Seven Colour Trees & House' pattern, 'Fantasque' mark, restored.
c1930 *16½in (42cm) wide*
£3,000-4,000 FLD

A Clarice Cliff 'Tolphin' shape jug and wash bowl, 'Umbrellas & Rain' pattern, 'Fantasque' mark.
c1929
£2,200-2,800 FLD

A rare Clarice Cliff Bizarre 'Age of Jazz' table centrepiece, model no.434, printed marks.
8½in (21.5cm) diam
£19,000-22,000 WW

A rare Clarice Cliff Bizarre 'Grotesque Mask', designed by Ron Birks, in a 'Clouvre' glaze, printed marks, minor professional restoration.

Ron Birks was the son of Lawrence Birks, who worked for Minton. He studied modelling and handpainting as an apprentice of Clarice Cliff. It is likely that he modelled this and other 'Grotesque Masks' himself, under the supervision of Clarice Cliff.

11¼in (28.5cm) high
£5,000-5,500 WW

A framed William De Morgan four-tile panel.

William De Morgan (1839-1917) was an important English Arts and Crafts ceramic artist. He established his own pottery firm in Chelsea in 1872. In 1882 he relocated to new premises at Merton Abbey. In 1888 he moved to Sands End in Fulham, London.

frame 14¾in (37.5cm) square

£3,500-4,000 FLD

A William De Morgan 'Galleon' tile, impressed 'Sands End Pottery' mark.

6in (15cm) square

£3,000-3,500 SWO

A William De Morgan six-tile 'Persian Galleon' tile panel, Sands End Pottery, possibly designed by Halsey Ricardo, impressed marks, one tile restored.

18¼in (46.5cm) high

£6,500-7,500 WW

A William De Morgan ruby lustre charger.

c1880 *20½in (52cm) diam*

£11,000-14,000 K&O

A William De Morgan 'Galleon' charger.

17¼in (44cm) diam

£7,000-8,000 WW

A William De Morgan dish, by Charles Passenger, painted with an eagle, 'CP' monogram.

10in (25.5cm) diam

£6,000-7,000 WW

A William De Morgan lustre charger, painted with two snakes, bordered by lizards, scratch to well rim, heavy crazing, some firing faults.

16½in (42cm) diam

£3,000-3,500 TEN

A William De Morgan moonlit suite bowl, with an owl astride the moon, monogrammed 'F.P' for Fred Passenger.

5½in (14cm) diam

£5,500-6,500 K&O

A William De Morgan vase, by Joe Hersey, monogrammed 'JH' and impressed marks.

c1890 *4¼in (11cm) high*

£3,500-4,000 K&O

A William De Morgan tulip vase, by Edward Porter, painted 'E.P.', impressed 'WILLIAM DE MORGAN/MERTON ABBEY'.

c1880 *8in (20.5cm) high*

£1,500-2,500 L&T

ESSENTIAL REFERENCE – DOULTON

The Doulton Factory was founded in 1815 by John Doulton in Lambeth, London. It focused first on everyday stoneware and drainpipes, before turning to decorative wares from the early 1870s.

- **Key designers of late 19thC and early 20thC Doulton include the Tinworth brothers and the Barlow siblings. The company also worked closely with the Lambeth School of Art, and many of Doulton's Art Nouveau pieces were designed by students there.**
- **In 1901 Doulton received a Royal warrant. It later became known as Royal Doulton.**
- **Doulton began producing figurines in the 1880s, first under George Tinworth and later until Charles Noke. From 1912, all figurines were assigned an 'HN' number.**

A Doulton Lambeth stoneware two-tile panel, by Hannah Barlow, impressed mark, incised monogram, dated.
1874 *each 8¾in (22cm) square*
£1,200-1,600 WW

A Doulton Lambeth stoneware vase, by Hannah Barlow, impressed mark, unusual incised monogram, dated.
1878 *7¾in (19.5cm) high*
£1,500-2,000 WW

A Doulton Lambeth jug, by Hannah Barlow, with sgraffito decoration of polar bears, impressed marks, dated.
1882 *6¼in (16cm) high*
£4,000-5,000 K&O

A Doulton Lambeth jug, by Hannah Barlow, with sgraffito decoration of cats, with Lucy Barlow borders, dated.
1883 *7¾in (20cm) high*
£1,200-1,500 K&O

A pair of Doulton Lambeth ewers, by Hannah Barlow, with sgraffito decoration of cats.
c1895 *10½in (26.5cm) high*
£1,000-1,500 K&O

A Doulton Lambeth silver-mounted stoneware jug, by Hannah Barlow, impressed and incised marks.
9¼in (23.5cm) high
£600-700 CHEF

A Doulton Lambeth stoneware bowl, by Hannah and Lucy Barlow, impressed and incised marks, glazed chip to rim.
8¾in (22cm) wide
£1,200-1,600 CHEF

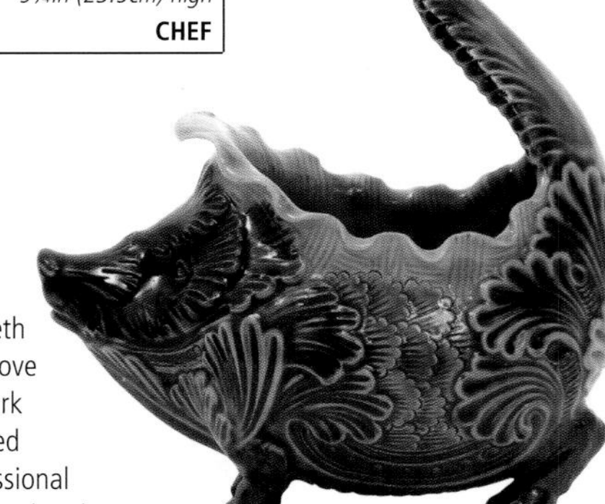

A Doulton Lambeth stoneware Borogove grotesque, by Mark V. Marshall, incised 'MVM 81', professional restoration to feet, dated.

The Borogove creature was inspired by Lewis Carroll's 'Alice Through the Looking Glass' published in 1871. This creature bears a stronger resemblance to the Mome Raths described by Humpty Dumpty as 'a sort of green pig'.
1881 *8¼in (21cm) high*
£1,500-2,000 WW

A Doulton Lambeth bird-shaped vase, by Mark V. Marshall, imprinted marks.
c1885 *5in (13cm) high*
£1,500-2,000 K&O

A Doulton Lambeth stoneware bear cruet set, the design attributed to Mark V. Marshall, with silver mounts by John Grinshell & Sons, impressed marks, stamped 'JG&S', Birmingham.

1899 *2¾in (7cm) high*

£700-800 **WW**

A Doulton Lambeth stoneware vase, by Elisa Simmance, impressed mark, incised artist's monogram.

19½in (49.5cm) high

£1,800-2,200 **WW**

A Doulton Lambeth stoneware 'Mouse Musician' menu holder, by George Tinworth, impressed mark and incised monogram, minor restoration, date mark.

George Tinworth (1843-1913) trained at Lambeth School of Art and began his career at Doulton's Lambeth factory in 1866. He became one of their more significant modellers and potters, known especially for his stoneware mouse figures, which predate the HN series by several decades.

1885 *3½in (9cm) high*

£1,800-2,200 **WW**

A possibly unique Doulton Lambeth figural group, by George Tinworth, artist's monogram, some firing cracks.

Provenance: Acquired by Margaret Bryan (1884-1977) who worked at the Lambeth factory. The piece has many similarities to Tinworth's model 'The Football Srimmage', modelled in 1876 and displayed at the Royal Academy in 1877 and the Paris Exhibition of 1878.

c1900 *6in (15.5cm) high*

£5,500-6,500 **CHEF**

A Doulton Lambeth 'School Board' group, by George Tinworth, signed 'GT' to the rear, impressed marks.

3½in (9cm) high

£2,500-3,000 **K&O**

A pair of Doulton Lambeth 'Seaweed' vases, by George Tinworth.

11in (28cm) high

£450-550 **WHP**

A pair of Doulton Burslem vases, by George White, with Classical scenes, one titled 'Spring', with backstamps, marked 'Luscian ware'.

In 1877, Doulton purchased an interest in a factory in Burslem, North Staffordshire. By 1882 it had fully acquired the factory. The Burslem works focused on bone china and porcelain, in contrast to the Lambeth works that chiefly produced stoneware.

36½in (93cm) wide

£10,000-12,000 **K&O**

A Doulton Burslem handpainted vase, by R. Holdcroft, printed marks.

c1920 *9¾in (25cm) high*

£2,200-2,800 **K&O**

A late Victorian Doulton Burslem Aesthetic Movement tea service, marks to base.

£500-600 **WM**

CLOSER LOOK – FISHERWOMEN

This is a rare and unusually large figural group, designed by Charles Noke.

It is decorated in a purple and red colourway, the central figure with a checked headscarf and polkadot shawl.

This piece was issued c1917, just four years after the release of the first HN series figure. Many of these early figures had a very short run and were produced, or even decorated, to order, making them especially rare.

Although the market for Royal Doulton figures is at a low ebb, rare figures such as this can fetch high prices.

A Royal Doulton group, 'Fisherwomen' or 'Waiting for the Boats' or 'Looking for the Boats', no.HN80, with maker's marks and designer's name.
c1917 *11¾in (30cm) high*
£8,500-9,500 **TEAR**

A Royal Doulton 'Double Jester' figurine, designed by Charles Noke, no.HN365, titled to base 'Two Heads Are Better Than One', some restoration to pillar.
issued 1920-38 *17in (43cm) high*
£7,500-8,500 **JN**

A Royal Doulton 'Butterfly' figure, designed by Leslie Harradine, no.HN720.
issued 1925-40 *6½in (16.5cm) high*
£500-600 **K&O**

A Royal Doulton 'Irish Colleen' figurine, designed by Leslie Harradine, no.HN767, marks, some damages.
issued 1925-36 *6½in (16.5cm) high*
£500-600 **FLD**

A Royal Doulton 'Lady Jester' figurine, designed by Leslie Harradine, no.HN1285, some restoration.
issued 1928-38
£700-800 **WM**

A Royal Doulton 'Two a Penny' figure, by Leslie Harradine, no.HN1359, restoration to neck.
£2,200-2,800 **PSA**

A Royal Doulton 'The Bather' figure, by Leslie Harradine, no.HN1708, hairlines to base and dress.
issued 1935-38 *7¾in (20cm) high*
£700-800 **WM**

A Royal Doulton prestige 'Jack Point' figure, designed Charles Noke, no.HN3925, from a limited edition of 85, printed marks, with certificate.
17in (43cm) high
£1,500-2,000 **K&O**

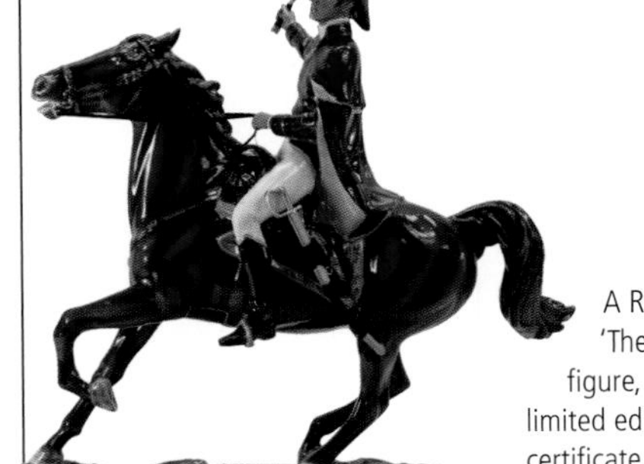

A Royal Doulton prestige 'The Duke Of Wellington' figure, no.HN5745, from a limited edition of 50, boxed with certificate signed by Michael Doulton.
£2,800-3,200 **PSA**

A 1950s Royal Doulton prototype cleaning maid figurine, designed by Mary Nichol, impressed '1865' to base.
8¼in (21cm) high
£1,800-2,200 **PSA**

A Royal Doulton prototype earthenware Viking figure, impressed '1513', marked 'Potted by Doulton & Co.', some restoration.
9¾in (25cm) high
£1,500-2,000 **PSA**

A Royal Doulton Titanian ware figure, 'Blighty', by E.W. Light, printed mark, impressed 'Blighty'.

Royal Doulton's Titanian glaze was developed in 1915 and was made with a titanium oxide, resulting in blue, grey and green colours. Examples of Titanian ware are rare and often unique.

11½in (29cm) high

£2,500-3,000 WW

A Royal Doulton Bunnykins 'Blue Band' set, comprising a drummer no.DB89, drum major no.DB90, cymbal no.DB88, trumpeter no.DB87 and sousaphone no.DB86, from a limited edition of 250.

£900-1,100 PSA

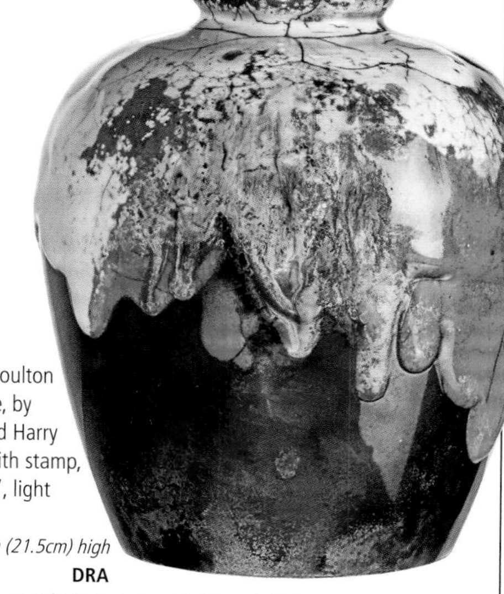

A 1920s Royal Doulton Chang ware vase, by Charles Noke and Harry Nixon, signed, with stamp, impressed '5229', light scratches.

8½in (21.5cm) high

£3,500-4,000 DRA

A Royal Doulton Chang flambé vase, by Charles Noke, with marks, light surface wear.

8¼in (21cm) high

£900-1,100 APAR

A Royal Doulton decanter box, with a Sung glaze plaque of 'The Alchemist' by Charles Noke, fixed for wall mounting, with two glass decanters.

15¾in (40cm) high

£7,000-8,000 K&O

A Royal Doulton miniature Sung moon flask vase, by Charles Noke and Harry Nixon, no.201, signed 'Sung'.

3¼in (8.5cm) high

£1,200-1,400 HAN

A Royal Doulton prototype 'The Fisherman' character jug, printed marks.

7in (18cm) high

£3,500-4,000 K&O

A large Royal Doulton prototype flambé character jug, 'Maori'.

£3,500-4,500 K&O

A Royal Doulton prototype 'Nelson Mandela' character jug, marked 'Pascoe & Co, prototype' to base.

£3,500-4,500 K&O

A Royal Doulton 'Jan Van Riebeek' loving cup, from a limited edition of 300.

10½in (26.5cm) high

£1,500-2,000 PSA

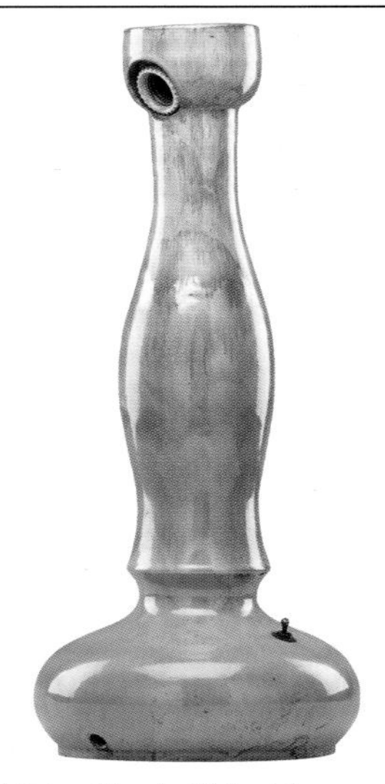

A Fulper 'Vasekraft' flambé earthenware lamp base, 'Vasekraft' stamp, 'PATENT PENDING U.S. AND CANADA', in need of rewiring.

Fulper was a pottery based in Flemington, NJ, USA. It moved from utilitarian stoneware to art pottery in the early 20thC.

c1908 *8¾in (22cm) high*

£700-800 **DRA**

A 1910s Fulper 'Cattail' vase, 'Verte Antique' glaze, vertical ink stamp, burst glaze bubble to rim, minor grinding chip to base.

12¾in (32.5cm) high

£4,000-4,500 **DRA**

A 1910s Fulper 'Vasekraft' vessel, 'Mission Matte' glaze, ink stamp, fleck to rim, grinding flakes to base.

12¼in (31cm) high

£5,000-6,000 **DRA**

A Fulper vase, with blue flambé over a matt purple glaze, raised racetrack mark, minor grinding chip, light scratches.

15in (38cm) high

£950-1,100 **DRA**

A 1910s Fulper 'Venetian Blue' vase, rectangular ink stamp, some scratches, minor grinding flakes.

12½in (32cm) high

£1,000-1,500 **DRA**

A 1910s-20s Fulper vase, 'Leopard Skin Crystalline' glaze, racetrack mark, grinding chips to base.

17in (43cm) high

£650-750 **DRA**

Judith Picks

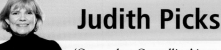

'Copperdust Crystalline' is arguably Fulper's best glaze. It was either only used on their best and rarest forms, or cost double the usual amount to put on a more common form. Pieces in the form of this vase are typically finished with the 'Copperdust Crystalline' glaze. This is a particularly strong example, with even and deep firing. It is in perfect condition, which further increases its value.

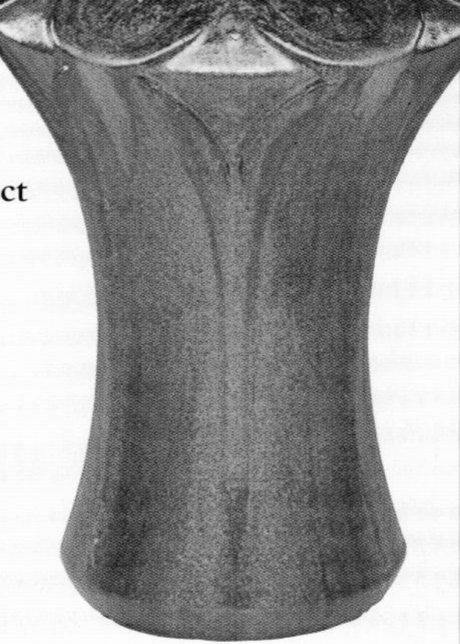

A rare Fulper vase, 'Copperdust Crystalline' glaze, vertical raised mark.

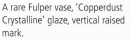

c1920 *11in (28cm) high*

£8,000-9,000 **DRA**

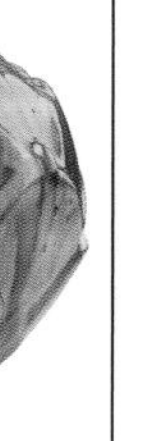

A Fulper 'Artichoke' vase, vertical incised mark, some burst glaze bubbles.

c1920 *8½in (21.5cm) high*

£1,200-1,600 **DRA**

A Fulper vase, 'Chinese Blue' and ivory flambé glaze, vertical incised mark, some burst glaze bubbles.

c1920 *6¼in (16cm) high*

£500-600 **DRA**

A Goldscheider terracotta figure, impressed 'FRIEDRICH GOLDSCHEIDER/ WIEN/REPRODUCTION RESERVEE/1890/10/19', signature 'HANIROFF'.
c1890 *11½in (29cm) high*
£2,500-3,000 **L&T**

A late 19thC Goldscheider earthenware figure, impressed marks.
38½in (98cm) high
£750-850 **HT**

A Goldscheider terracotta of a boy, signed 'Perigot', mark, numbered '3338 3 67'.
30in (76cm) high
£900-1,100 **JN**

A Goldscheider lady in a kimono, by Stephan Dakon, no.6071, fully marked.
15¾in (40cm) high
£2,800-3,200 **K&O**

A Goldscheider ballerina, by Stefan Dakon, no.6361, with facsimile signature, impressed '6361', overall crazing.
10¾in (27cm) wide
£450-550 **PW**

A Goldscheider dancer, by Stephan Dakon, no.6930, fully marked.
16½in (42cm) high
£1,800-2,200 **K&O**

A Goldscheider lady, by Stefan Dakon, no.8083, fully marked.
c1930 *13¼in (33.5cm) high*
£750-950 **L&T**

A Goldscheider dancer, possibly by Claire Herczeg, no.8399, with paper label, printed marks, impressed '8399/72/31', left hand restored.
c1930 *16¼in (41.5cm) high*
£1,200-1,500 **BELL**

A Goldscheider woman, by Claire Herczeg, no.8241, fully marked.
15in (38cm) high
£1,800-2,200 **K&O**

A Goldscheider figure, 'The Captured Bird', by Josef Lorenzl, no.5230, fully marked.
18¾in (47.5cm) high
£4,000-5,000 **K&O**

A Goldscheider lady, 'The Cabaret', by Josef Lorenzl, no.5523, fully marked.
12½in (32cm) high
£1,600-2,000 **K&O**

A Goldscheider 'Mephistopheles', by Josef Lorenzl, no.5537, fully marked.
14½in (37cm) high
£2,500-3,000 K&O

A Goldscheider 'Columbine', by Josef Lorenzl, no.5778, fully marked.
18in (46cm) high
£4,500-5,000 K&O

A Goldscheider woman in pyjamas, by Josef Lorenzl, no.5780, fully marked.
15in (38cm) high
£2,500-3,000 K&O

A Goldscheider 'Butterfly' dancer, by Josef Lorenzl, no.6022, fully marked, professional restoration to ankles and hem.
11in (28cm) high
£1,300-1,600 WW

A Goldscheider lady with a Pekinese, by Josef Lorenzl, no.6812, fully marked.
11½in (29cm) high
£1,400-1,800 K&O

A Goldscheider nude with a German Shepherd, by Josef Lorenzl, no.7041, fully marked.
14½in (37cm) high
£1,600-2,000 K&O

An early Goldscheider nude, 'Fascination', by Wihelm Thomasch, made by R. Spuller, no.5060, with eagle standard crest and artist's monogram, fully marked.
19in (48cm) high
£3,000-4,000 K&O

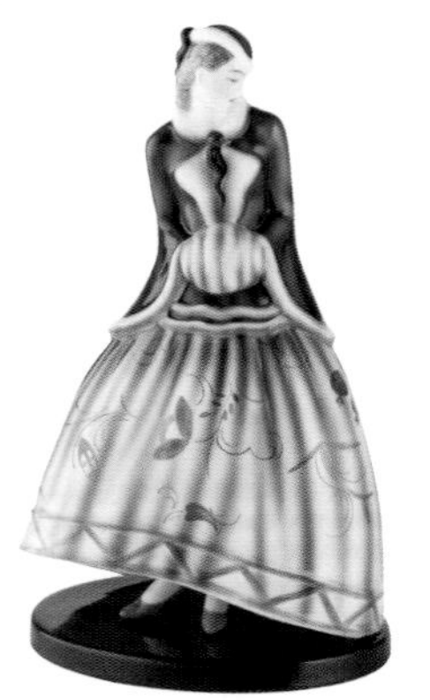

A Goldscheider girl, by Claire Weiss, no.6507, impressed signature, marked 'GOLDSCHEIDER/ WEIN/6507/52'.
c1920 *13in (33cm) high*
£650-750 L&T

A Goldscheider lady with borzoi, by Claire Weiss, no.7367, fully marked.
16¾in (42.5cm) high
£1,800-2,200 K&O

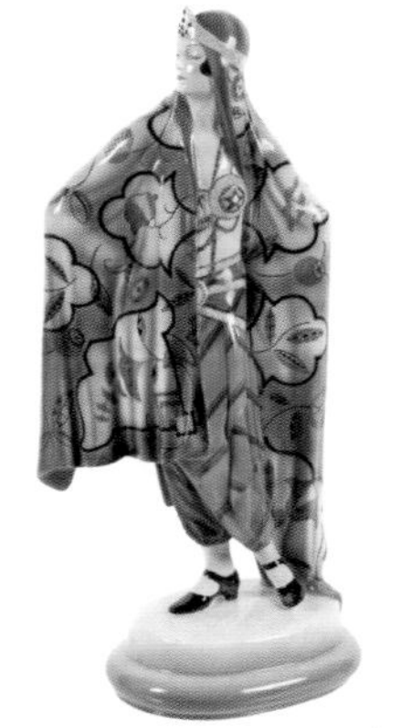

A Goldscheider earthenware figure, 'The Egyptian Dancer', no.5281, black printed mark, impressed '5281/905', some glaze bubbles.
18½in (47cm) high
£2,500-3,000 DN

A Goldscheider group of dancers, no.5975, possibly based on the Dolly Sisters, impressed '5975/401/19', marked 'Made in Austria', crazing to glaze.
15¾in (40cm) high
£4,500-5,500 GORL

A Goldscheider figure of a lady, no.8474, fully marked.
13in (33cm) high
£1,400-1,800 K&O

ESSENTIAL REFERENCE – GRUEBY FAIENCE COMPANY

The Grueby Faience Company was established in 1894 by William Henry Grueby in Revere, Massachusetts. It produced architectural tiles and art pottery.

- **Its art pottery was inspired by the matt glazes of French pottery and the simplicity of Japanese ceramics.**
- **Vessels were typically of organic forms, with stylised foliate designs. The majority of pieces were glazed in matt cucumber green.**
- **Grueby pottery and tiles were very popular in the late 19thC and early 20thC and partnered with Tiffany Studios to produce lamp bases.**
- **The firm began to struggle against increasing mass-market competition and declared bankruptcy in 1909, before finally closing in 1920.**

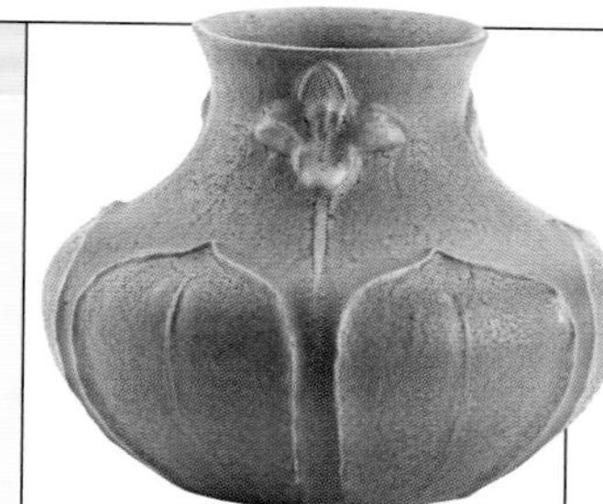

A Grueby vase, by Ruth Erickson, circular 'Pottery' stamp, incised 'RE', small bruises and flecks.
c1905 *5¾in (14.5cm) wide*
£2,500-3,000 DRA

A Grueby gourd-shaped vase, by George P. Kendrick, circular 'Pottery' stamp and '34'.
c1905 *12in (30.5cm) high*
£27,000-32,000 DRA

A Grueby vase or lamp base, by Wilhelmina Post, circular 'Faience' stamp and 'WP 4-18-', drilled for lamp.
c1900 *12½in (32cm) high*
£4,000-5,000 DRA

A Grueby five-handled vase, by Wilhelmina Post and Norma Pierce, circular 'Pottery' stamp, incised 'WP/145' with Pierce cipher, professionally repaired chips.
c1905 *8½in (21.5cm) high*
£6,000-7,000 DRA

A Grueby five-handled vase, by Wilhelmina Post, circular pottery stamp, incised 'WP', some chips.
c1905 *11in (28cm) high*
£4,500-5,500 DRA

A 1900s Grueby cuerda seca tile, framed, some chips to back, flecks to front.

In the cuerda seca ('dry cord' in Spanish) technique, thin bands of waxy resin are used to separate different coloured glazes during firing.

6¾in (17cm) wide
£2,000-2,500 DRA

A Grueby vase, circular 'Pottery' stamp, incised 'ER', some hairlines.
c1905 *10½in (26.5cm) high*
£3,500-4,000 DRA

A Grueby vase, with irises, the circular stamp partially glazed over, incised 'ER'.
c1905 *11¼in (28.5cm) high*
£5,000-6,000 DRA

A Grueby vase, with carved irises, circular 'Pottery' stamp, incised 'N', some small flecks and chips.
c1905 *12¼in (31cm) high*
£5,000-6,000 DRA

A framed 1910s Grueby cuerda seca ship tile.
6in (15cm) square
£2,200-2,800 DRA

ESSENTIAL REFERENCE – LENCI

The Lenci factory was founded in Turin, Italy, in 1919, by Helen (Elena) Konig Scavini (1886-1974) and her husband Enrico.

- **The name, 'Lenci', is thought to be a corruption of Helen Konig Scavini's nickname, 'Helenchen' or 'Lenchen'. It is also an acronym of the company's motto 'Ludus Est Nobis Constanter Industria' ('Play is Our Constant Work').**
- **The factory began as a maker of felt dolls, adding earthenware and ceramics figures to its range in 1928.**
- **Many of the figures were designed by Helen Konig Scavini herself, although Lenci also worked with designers such as Giovanni Grande (1887-1937), Abele Jacopi (1882-1957), Mario Sturani (1906-78) and Sandro Vacchetti (1889-1976).**
- **Konig Scavini's expressive figures perfectly capture the Art Deco style. Her designs were much admired, including by Walt Disney, who allegedly tried to persuade her to work for him.**
- **The company was taken over in 1937 and ceramic production ceased in 1964.**

A Lenci figure, 'Primo Romanzo', by Helen Konig Scavini, painted 'Lenci' marks and 'K' to base, restoration to hand, re-glued finger.

9¾in (25cm) high

£5,500-6,500 WW

A Lenci figure, 'Nella O Nasin' or 'Janetti', by Helen Konig Scavini, painted 'Lenci' marks, professional restorations.

15¼in (39cm) high

£9,000-11,000 WW

A 1930s Lenci glazed earthenware 'Sul Mondo' sculpture, Italy, by Mario Sturani and Helen Konig Scavini, signed 'Lenci MADE IN ITALY TORINO' with artists' initials, impressed '500', minor dark scuffs.

19in (48.5cm) high

£7,000-8,000 DRA

A Lenci ceramic group of a siren and infant riding a tortoise, by Helen Konig Scavini, signed 'Lenci Torino 3-1937 – XV MADE IN ITALY' and intialled 'K'.

1937 18in (45.5cm) diam

£3,500-4,000 DOY

A 1930s Lenci centre bowl, by Helen Konig Scavini, 'Nuda con Uccellino su Piatto', Italy, signed 'Lenci Made in Italy', professional restoration to bird.

16in (40.5cm) high

£1,200-1,600 DRA

A Lenci figure, 'Madonna del Vento', painted factory marks, minor chips.

16¼in (41cm) high

£1,100-1,500 WW

A Lenci figure of the Madonna, by Paola Bologna, painted marks and date.

1931 8¾in (22cm) high

£250-300 HAN

A Lenci wall mask, 'Maschera Con Nodo', by Helen Konig Scavini, painted marks, 'Lenci Torino Italy'.

c1930 10¾in (27.5cm) long

£2,000-2,500 K&O

A Lenci wall mask, 'Testa', by Helen Konig Scavini, painted marks, minor professional restoration to tip of scarf.

11½in (29cm) long

£400-500 WW

A mid-19thC Minton majolica 'Lychees' teapot and cover, impressed '1349/ MINTON' with indistinct date cipher.

Minton were the first English factory to produce majolica, inspired in part by Italian Renaissance maiolica (see page 56-57). Minton's majolica pieces impressed the public at the Great Exhibition of 1851 in London and went on to be very successful.

5in (12.5cm) high

£3,000-3,500 L&T

A Minton majolica game pie dish and cover, the cover moulded with dead game, with metal liner, impressed date marks, some chips.

c1870 13in (33cm) wide

£220-300 CHEF

A Minton majolica desk stand, with a hound, grotesque masks, two pen trays and spaces for an inkwell and pounce pot, impressed 'Mintons 1930', some small repairs, with date code.

1876

£2,000-2,500 BE

Judith Picks

Paul Comolera (1818-97) was a prominent French sculptor who travelled to work in Stoke-on-Trent in the 1870s to avoid political upheaval in France. He is recorded as working at Minton 1873-76, during which time he produced some of the factory's finest animal models. These were typically covered with a majolica glaze of rich bright colours inspired by the palette of Renaissance maiolica. Some of these, such as his heron and peacock, are well known. Others, like this stick stand, are very rarely seen. Despite many chips, the rarity of the stand makes it a valuable piece.

A Minton majolica stick stand, modelled by Paul Comolera, depicting a deer beside a tree trunk, the base impressed '2077' and 'P Comoler', severe chipping, back right leg missing, one ear detached.

33in (84cm) high

£20,000-25,000 DEN

A majolica oyster stand, in the manner of Minton, some damages throughout.

12in (30.5cm) high

£500-600 WHP

A George Jones majolica pitcher, in the Aesthetic manner, impressed mark, old repair to spout, minor frits.

c1870

£350-450 HAN

A George Jones majolica cheese dome and stand, with cow finial, impressed 'GJ' monogram, some restoration.

c1875 10¾in (27cm) high

£550-650 WW

A George Jones majolica teapot and cover, modelled as a cockerel, some restoration.

c1875 11in (28cm) wide

£3,000-4,000 WW

A George Jones & Son majolica teapot and cover, with monkey handle and floral finial, moulded registration diamond, restoration to spout.

c1875 9½in (24cm) wide

£500-600 WW

A late 19thC French HB & Co. Choisy Le Roi majolica jardinière, signed, some repairs.
24in (61cm) wide
£2,500-3,000 DRA

A Hugo Lonitz majolica mirror, double fish mark.
c1880 *21in (53.5cm) high*
£800-1,000 DRA

A Hugo Lonitz majolica four-light candelabrum, with a partridge and chicks below an oak tree, some damages.
c1880 *16½in (42cm) high*
£1,500-2,000 BE

A Lonitz majolica figurine group of partridges, with a vasaline glass flute, some minor nibbling to leaves.
13in (33cm) high
£180-220 PSA

A late 19thC to early 20thC Jérôme Massier majolica wishing well, modelled with musical frogs, painted 'JMF Vallauris' mark, minor damages.

Wells of this type are more commonly seen with songbirds in place of the frogs and are made in several sizes. This one is unusually large.
28¼in (71.5cm) high
£4,000-4,500 WW

A pair of late 19thC to early 20thC Swedish Rorstrand majolica pedestals, marks to base.
45¼in (115cm) high
£750-850 ROS

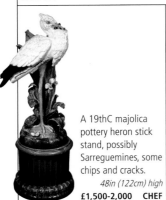

A 19thC majolica pottery heron stick stand, possibly Sarreguemines, some chips and cracks.
48in (122cm) high
£1,500-2,000 CHEF

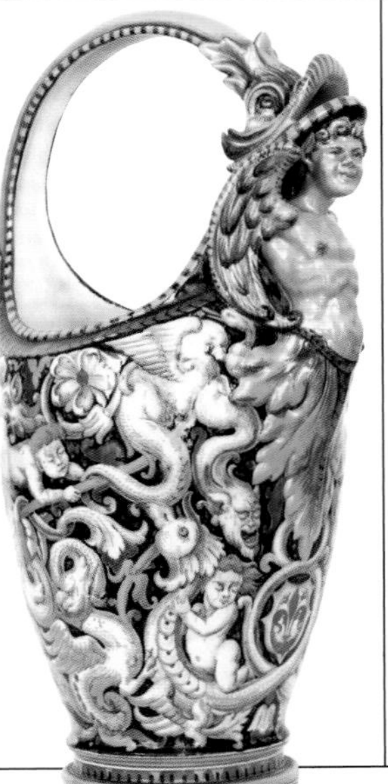

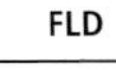

A early 20thC Cantagalli majolica pedestal basket vase, decorated with Renaissance-style cherubs, and a grotesque griffin, labelled 'The gift of her Majesty Queen Victoria to Susan, Duchess of Roxburghe'.
20in (51cm) high
£3,000-3,500 FLD

A French majolica group of a Turkish man and woman.
30in (76cm) high
£1,500-2,000 JN

A Martin Brothers stoneware bird tobacco jar, incised 'R.W. Martin/ London & Southall', restored, dated.

1880 *9in (23cm) high*

£18,000-22,000 WAD

A Martin Brothers stoneware bird jar and cover, by Robert Wallace Martin, incised 'R W Martin London' to tail feathers, 'R.W Martin London & Southall' to head, minor frit chips, dated.

1884 *13in (33cm) high*

£25,000-30,000 WW

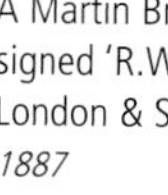

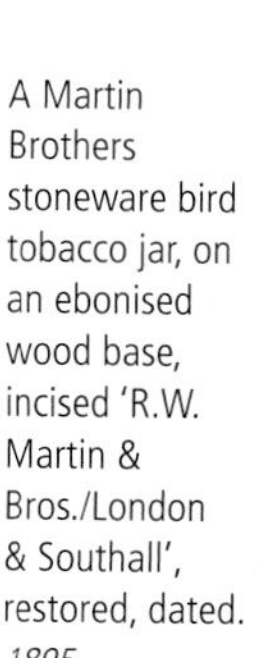

A Martin Brothers grotesque bird, signed 'R.W. Martin and Bros London & Southall', dated.

1887 *8¾in (22cm) high*

£14,000-20,000 K&O

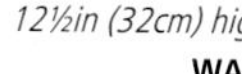

A Martin Brothers stoneware bird tobacco jar, on an ebonised wood base, incised 'R.W. Martin & Bros./London & Southall', restored, dated.

1895 *12½in (32cm) high*

£16,000-20,000 WAD

Judith Picks

Brothers Robert, Edwin, Charles and Walter Martin began making pottery at their family home in 1873, before setting up in a disused soap works in Southall in 1877. Production continued until 1923.

The brothers handcrafted unusual designs from salt-glazed stoneware. Each had a different role: Robert modelled the figures; Walter threw the pots; Edwin was the decorator, and Charles ran the shop in Holborn. He was known to hide his favourite pots under the floorboards to stop them being bought.

The creations of the Martin brothers are eccentric and unique, and this tobacco jar is no exception. It is formed as a highly characterised bird, with a large beak and spotted plumage. Waddington auctioneer Bill Kime drove for 10 days across Canada in order to bring this item and the collection it belonged to safely to the auction house for sale.

A Martin Brothers stoneware bird tobacco jar, with spotted plumage, incised 'R.W. Martin & Bros. London & Southall', dated.

1907 *8½in (21.5cm) high*

£30,000-35,000 WAD

A Martin Brothers salt-glazed stoneware bird tobacco jar, incised 'Martin Bros. London + Southall', dated.

1897 *10in (25.5cm) high*

£20,000-25,000 DRA

A Martin Brothers stoneware bird jar and cover, by Robert Wallace Martin, incised 'R W Martin & Bros London & Southall', dated.

1904 *10¼in (26cm) high*

£15,000-20,000 WW

A Martin Brothers stoneware bird tobacco jar and cover, by Robert Wallace Martin, incised 'R.W. Martin Bros, London, Southall', dated.

1907 *12½in (31.5cm) high*

£25,000-30,000 HALL

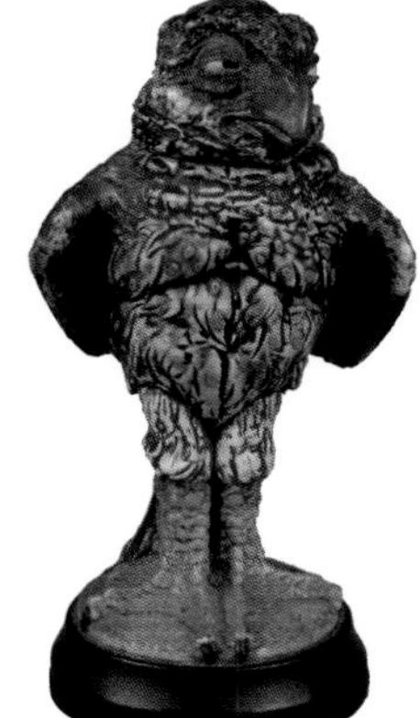

A Martin Brothers stoneware bird jar and cover, by Robert Wallace Martin, on later ebonised base, incised 'R W Martin & Bros Southall', dated.

1913 *7¼in (18.5cm) high*

£11,000-14,000 HALL

A Martin Brothers stoneware bird tobacco jar, on an ebonised wood base, incised 'R.W. Martin & Bros., London & Southall', dated.

1914 *9in (23cm) high*

£18,000-22,000 WAD

A Martin Brothers salt-glazed stoneware creature tobacco jar, by Robert W. Martin, incised 'R.W. Martin + Brothers London', some professional restoration, dated.

1888 *7½in (19cm) high*

£13,000-16,000 DRA

A Martin Brothers salt-glazed stoneware grinning grotesque crab, incised 'RW Martin + Brothers/ London/6.80 and RW MARTIN', dated.

This was a world record price for a piece of Martin Brothers.

1880 *8 1/8in (21cm) wide*

£250,000-300,000 PHI

A Martin Brothers stoneware face jug, with a smiling face on either side, incised 'R.W. Martin & Bros./ London & Southall', dated.

1897 *9½in (24cm) high*

£5,500-6,500 WAD

A Martin Brothers stoneware tobacco jar with cover, by Robert Wallace Martin, with a bemused man's face on each side, the cover formed as a nightcap, repairs, incised 'RWM, R.W. Martin & Bros./ London & Southall', dated.

1911 *7¼in (18.5cm) high*

£6,000-7,000 WAD

A Martin Brothers stoneware bat wall pocket, incised 'R.W. Martin/ Southall'.

c1880 *5in (12.5cm) high*

£2,500-3,000 WAD

A Martin Brothers stoneware figure of Will Childerhouse, 'The Norwich Bellman', inscribed 'THE NORWICH BELLMAN 1891', incised 'R.W. Martin & Bros. London & Southall', dated.

1900 *6½in (16.5cm) high*

£6,000-7,000 WAD

A Martin Brothers stoneware pawn chess piece, modelled as a bust of a soldier in armour, incised 'R.W. Martin & Bros., London & Southall', dated.

1902 *3¼in (8cm) high*

£2,500-3,000 WAD

A Martin Brothers stoneware jug, by Robert Wallace Martin, incised 'M16 RW Martin London', firing cracks, dated.
1875 *8¾in (22cm) high*
£850-950 **SWO**

A Martin Brothers stoneware 'Aquatic' bowl, by Robert Wallace Martin, incised 'R W Martin & Bros London & Southall', dated.
1886 *8¼in (21cm) diam*
£2,500-3,000 **WW**

A Martin Brothers stoneware loving cup, incised and painted with fish and eels, incised 'R.W. Martin & Bros./London & Southall', dated.
1888 *6½in (16.5cm) high*
£3,000-3,500 **WAD**

A Martin Brothers stoneware jardinière, decorated with snarling dragons, signed 'R.W. Martin & Brothers, London & Southall', dated.
1889 *11in (28cm) diam*
£3,500-4,000 **K&O**

A Martin Brothers stoneware vase, by Edwin and Walter Martin, painted with herons, incised 'Martin Bros London & Southall', dated.
1892 *10in (25.5cm) high*
£6,000-6,500 **WW**

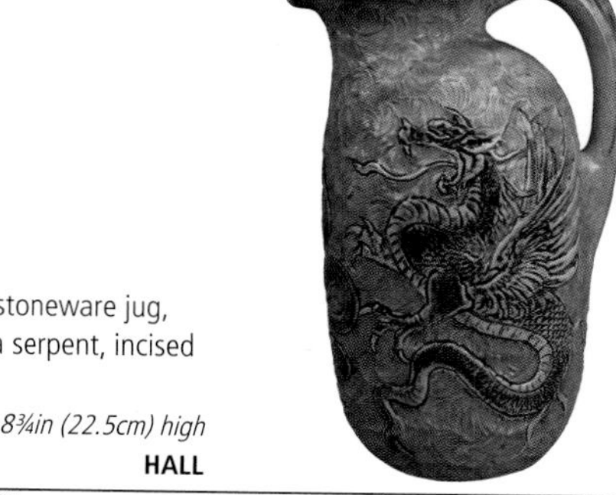

A Martin Brothers bowl, with grotesque fish, incised 'Martin Bros., London, Lambeth', dated.
1896 *7in (18cm) diam*
£2,000-2,500 **JN**

A Martin Brothers stoneware jug, with dragons and a serpent, incised marks, dated.
1903 *8¾in (22.5cm) high*
£2,000-2,500 **HALL**

A Martin Brothers stoneware 'Aquatic' vase, by Edwin and Walter Martin, incised 'Martin Bros London & Southall', dated.
1911 *8½in (21.5cm) high*
£2,500-3,000 **WW**

A pair of Martin Brothers stoneware 'Aquatic' vases by Edwin and Walter Martin, incised 'Martin Bros London & Southall', dated.
1909 *11½in (29cm) high*
£10,000-15,000 **WW**

A Martin Brothers Aquatic stoneware mug, incised and modelled with fish, the handle modelled as an eel, with the original paper receipt.

The original receipt from R.W. Martin & Brothers is dated 10 June 1929. It lists amongst other items two fish grotesque mugs priced at £6-6-0 to the purchaser R.W. Baxter.

3½in (9cm) high
£900-1,200 **WW**

A pair of late 19thC to early 20thC Minton pâte-sur-pâte vases, by Alboin Birks, on wood bases.

7¾in (19.5cm) high

£4,500-5,500 **PSA**

A late 19thC to early 20thC Minton pâte-sur-pâte vase and cover, on wood base.

Pâte-sur-pâte is a technique where a relief design is created on an unfired vessel by brushing on successive layers of white slip.

vase 9½in (24cm) high

£3,500-4,000 **PSA**

A pair of Minton pâte-sur-pâte pedestal vases, by Albion Birks.

10¾in (27cm) high

£1,200-1,500 **HAN**

A Minton Secessionist plate, with stylised flowering water lilies, printed and impressed marks, crazing, date code.

1910 *15in (38cm) diam*

£1,100-1,400 **SWO**

An Aesthetic Movement Minton art pottery charger, printed and impressed marks, painted 'LG 42'.

c1882 *17in (43cm) diam*

£250-300 **HAN**

A Mintons Aesthetic Movement tripod vase, in the Japonesque manner imitating bronze, impressed marks, date code.

1889 *7½in (19cm) high*

£300-400 **BE**

A Minton lidded box, with a Royal Persian turquoise glaze and dragon finial, with Chinese-style decoration, impressed marks, 'Minton 1625' and date code.

1872 *12in (30.5cm) high*

£1,300-1,600 **LC**

A set of four Minton's dust pressed tiles, designed by Christopher Dresser, impressed marks, repair to corner of one.

each 8in (20.5cm) square

£650-750 **WW**

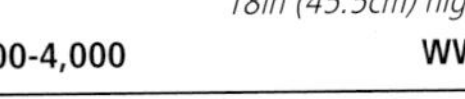

An Art Nouveau Minton's plaque, designed by Léon V. Solon, impressed marks and date code, minor chips to corners.

1898 *18in (45.5cm) high*

£3,500-4,000 **WW**

A set of four Minton Hollins & Co. two-tile panels, designed by Daniel Cottier, depicting Amor, Mars, Fama and Fortuna, impressed marks, some damages.

Provenance: Cairndhu House, Helensburgh, dining room fireplace. Cairndhu was built in 1871 to designs by William Leiper with the interior design of stained glass and decorative work designed by Daniel Cottier (1838-91).

16¼in (41cm) high

£7,500-8,500 **WW**

ESSENTIAL REFERENCE – MOORCROFT

Moorcroft was an important 20thC art pottery company.

- **William Moorcroft (1872-1945) began his career at James Macintyre & Co. in Staffordshire in 1897. He was soon running the Macintyre's art pottery studio.**
- **He founded W. Moorcroft Ltd. in 1913. The firm collaborated with Liberty of London and other major retailers. In 1928 William Moorcroft was appointed 'Potter to H.M. The Queen'.**
- **Moorcroft designs were produced through distinctive tube-lining, where outlines of a pattern were piped onto the surface, leaving a low relief outline design that was later filled with coloured glaze.**
- **On William Moorcroft's death, his son Walter took over the company. Today it continues to operate from the factory where it was founded over 100 years ago.**

A Moorcroft Macintyre 'Florian' ware plaque, 'Daffodil' pattern, printed mark and painted 'M909', painted 'W. Moorcroft/des', tiny glaze chip.
c1900
£700-800 WAD

A Moorcroft Macintyre miniature vase, 'Eighteenth Century' pattern, printed factory mark, painted green monogram.
2½in (6.5cm) high
£300-400 WW

A Moorcroft Macintyre 'Florian' ware vase, 'Lilac' pattern.
12in (30.5cm) high
£900-1,000 PSA

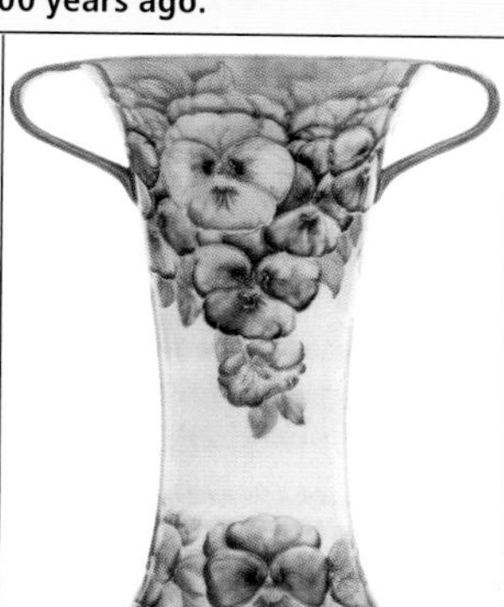

A Moorcroft Macintyre vase, 'Pansy' pattern, painted green signature and retailer's mark for Townsend & Co., Newcastle.
c1904-13 11½in (29cm) high
£3,500-4,000 BE

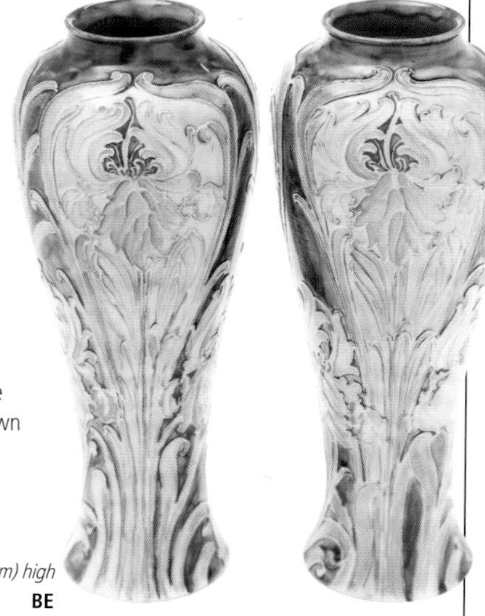

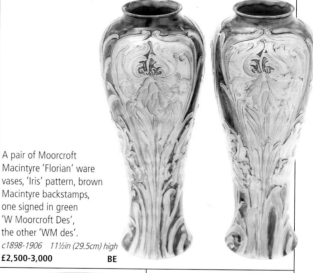

A pair of Moorcroft Macintyre 'Florian' ware vases, 'Iris' pattern, brown Macintyre backstamps, one signed in green 'W Moorcroft Des', the other 'WM des'.
c1898-1906 11½in (29.5cm) high
£2,500-3,000 BE

A Moorcroft Macintyre chamberstick, 'Poppy' pattern, printed 'Macintyre' mark, 'Rd. No. 401753' and retailer's mark for Stonier & Co., painted signature 'W. Moorcroft/des'.
c1904-13
£350-400 WAD

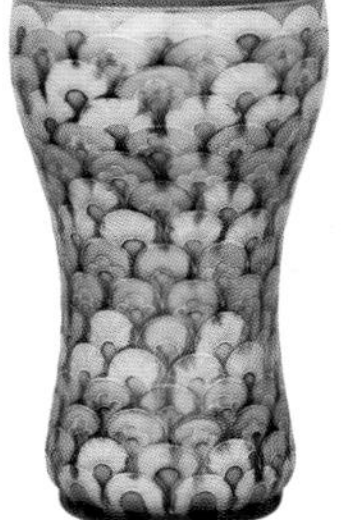

A Moorcroft Macintyre vase, 'Scale' pattern, painted marks 'W. Moorcroft/Liberty & Co./London-Paris' in green.
c1907 8in (20.5cm) high
£2,500-3,000 WAD

A Moorcroft Macintyre 'Florian' ware vase, 'Violets and Butterfies' pattern, printed 'Florian' mark in brown and painted signature 'W. Moorcroft/des'.
c1900 8¾in (22cm) high
£800-900 WAD

A Moorcroft Macintyre vase, 'Wisteria' pattern, printed factory mark, painted green signature, dated.
1913 8in (20.5cm) high
£3,000-3,500 WW

A Moorcroft Macintyre silver overlaid teapot, 'Claremont' pattern, printed 'Rd. No. 420081', painted signature and '8644', cover flange restored, minor loss.
c1905 6¾in (17cm) high
£1,500-2,000 WAD

A Moorcroft vase, 'Chrysanthemum' or 'Revived Cornflower' pattern, painted green signature.
10in (25.5cm) high
£1,500-2,000 WW

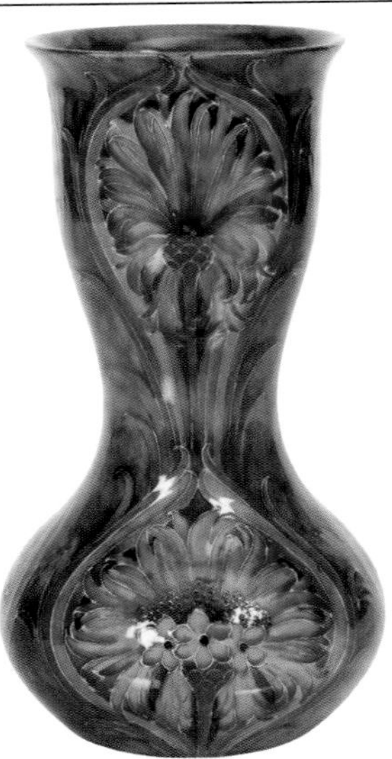

A Moorcroft vase, 'Chrysanthemum' or 'Revived Cornflower' pattern, painted green signature, impressed marks, fine stress line to rim.
10¾in (27.5cm) high
£1,800-2,200 WW

A Moorcroft vase, 'Flambé Claremont' pattern, impressed factory mark, painted signature.
7¾in (19.5cm) high
£2,000-2,500 WW

A Moorcroft flambé jar and cover, 'Claremont Toadstool' pattern, impressed factory marks and blue painted signature.
c1930 *11in (28cm) high*
£2,500-3,000 TEN

A Moorcroft trumpet-shaped vase, 'Dawn' pattern, with flambé lustre glaze, impressed mark and blue signature.
9in (23cm) high
£4,500-5,000 BRI

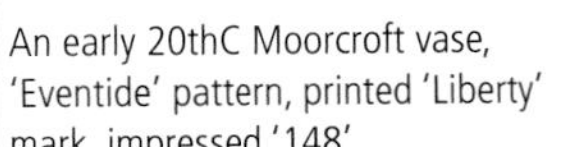

An early 20thC Moorcroft vase, 'Eventide' pattern, printed 'Liberty' mark, impressed '148'.
9in (23cm) high
£5,500-6,000 HT

A Moorcroft vase, 'Eventide' pattern, stamped 'MOORCROFT MADE IN ENGLAND with green signature', some scratches.
1918-26 *10½in (26.5cm) high*
£2,500-3,000 DRA

A Moorcroft matt salt glaze vase, 'Fish' pattern, underglaze blue signature.
c1928 *7¾in (20cm) high*
£2,200-3,000 HAN

A Moorcroft coffee service, 'Hazeldene' pattern, impressed Burslem marks, painted signature in green, minor crack to handle.
c1914-16 *9¾in (25cm) high*
£2,000-2,500 WAD

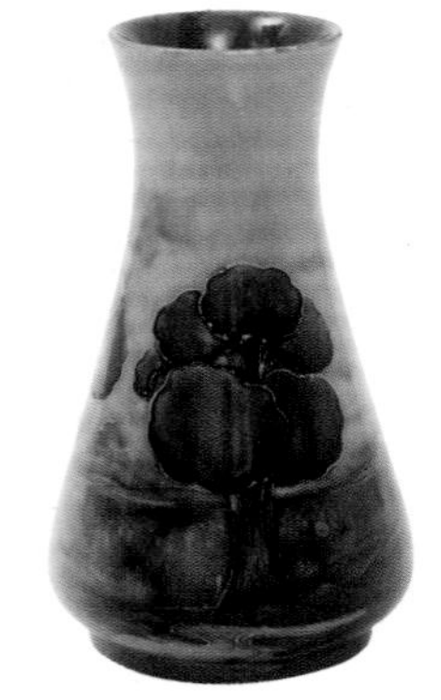

A Moorcroft vase, 'Hazledene' pattern, painted green signature, printed 'Liberty' mark.
6in (15.5cm) high
£2,000-2,500 WW

A Moorcroft vase, 'Moonlit Blue' pattern, impressed factory mark, painted green signature.

8½in (21.5cm) high

£2,200-3,000 **WW**

CLOSER LOOK – MOORCROFT TEA SET

This is an unusual Moorcroft tea set, created for Shreve and Company in San Francisco.

It is tube-lined with a green variation of the 'Peacock Feather' pattern.

Each piece is mounted with silver flowers, with silver handles and rims.

It is incised 'W Moorcroft Shreve & Company, San Francisco' to the teapot, and inscribed 'W Moorcroft' to the sucrier and the milk jug.

A Moorcroft tea set, some crazing, firing crack to teapot, chip to spout.

teapot 6½in (16.5cm) high

£7,000-8,000 **SWO**

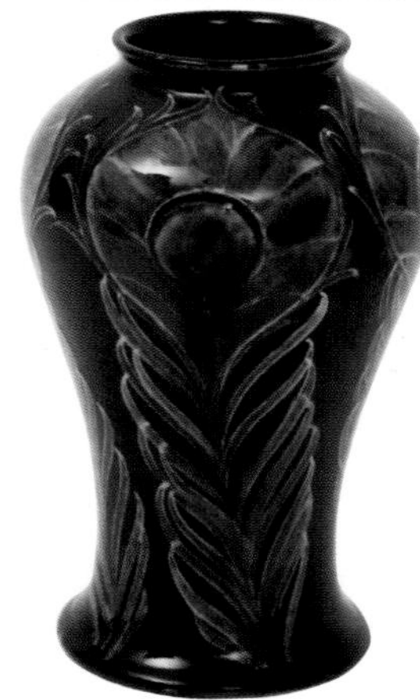

A Moorcroft vase, 'Black Peacock Feather' pattern, impressed factory marks, professional restoration to rim.

c1918 *6¼in (16cm) high*

£1,500-2,000 **WW**

A Moorcroft jardinière, 'Persian' pattern, impressed marks, painted green signature.

6½in (16.5cm) high

£2,000-2,500 **WW**

A Moorcroft squad vase, 'Pomegranate' pattern, impressed mark and underglaze green signature.

c1915-18 *7in (18cm) high*

£1,600-2,000 **HAN**

A Moorcroft 'Burslem' vase, 'Poppy' pattern.

13in (33cm) high

£4,000-5,000 **PSA**

A Moorcroft vase, 'Protea' pattern, impressed marks, painted blue signature.

8in (20.5cm) high

£6,000-6,500 **WW**

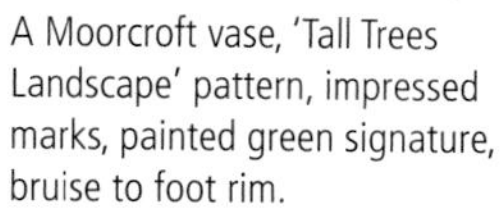

A Moorcroft vase, 'Tall Trees Landscape' pattern, impressed marks, painted green signature, bruise to foot rim.

9¼in (23.5cm) high

£1,300-1,600 **WW**

A Moorcroft footed bowl, 'Waratah' pattern, painted blue signature.

8¾in (22cm) diam

£8,000-9,000 **WW**

A Newcomb College vase, by Henrietta Bailey (1874-1950), with poppy pods, marked 'NC/BO19/HB/JM/Q', remnants of paper label, small fleck to base.

Newcombe College was a woman's art school founded in New Orleans in 1886. Under the tuition of their art professors, its students produced a range of impressive Arts and Crafts pottery until production ceased in 1940. Early pieces such as this one, from the 1900s, are rarer and typically more valuable than later 1920s-30s pieces.

1907 *9¼in (23.5cm) high*

£15,000-20,000 **DRA**

A Newcomb College bowl, by Mary W. Butler (1873-1937), marked 'NC/CD39/MWB/VS', remnants of original paper label, tight lines to rim, stilt pulls to foot.

1908 *10½in (26.5cm) wide*

£6,500-7,000 **DRA**

A Newcomb College vase, by Sadie Irvine (1887-1970), with poppies, marked 'NC/SI/OB96/JM', scuffs to body.

1924 *9in (23cm) high*

£2,000-2,500 **DRA**

A Newcomb College scenic vase, by Sadie Irvine, marked 'NC/JM/327/SL56/SI'.

1930 *5¾in (14.5cm) high*

£2,000-2,500 **DRA**

A Newcomb College vase, by Sara Bloom Levy, marked 'NC/BP45/SLB/Q/JM'.

1907 *4¾in (12cm) high*

£4,000-4,500 **DRA**

A Newcomb College Transitional vase, by Cynthia P. Littlejohn (d.1959), marked 'NC/FQ67/JM/CL/7', the stand with incised 'I' in circle.

1913 *8½in (21.5cm) high*

£3,000-3,500 **DRA**

A Newcomb College Transitional chamberstick, by Anna Frances Simpson (1880-1930), incised 'SILENTLY ONE BY ONE IN THE INFINITE MEADOWS OF HEAVEN BLOSSOMED THE LOVELY STARS THE FORGET-ME-NOTS OF THE ANGELS,' marked 'NC/AFS/DK87'.

1909 *5in (13cm) wide*

£1,600-2,000 **DRA**

A Newcomb College plate, by Anna Frances Simpson, marked 'NC/AFS/FZ81/JM/B', tight hairline and light wear.

1913 *8¾in (22cm) diam*

£1,000-1,400 **DRA**

A Newcomb College scenic vase, by Anna Frances Simpson, marked 'NC/150/JM/OC36/FS' with partial paper label.

1924 *10¾in (27.5cm) high*

£5,500-6,500 **DRA**

A Newcomb College lidded jar, by Anna Frances Simpson, marked 'NC/SG67/242/JH/AFS', bruise to foot.

1930 *6in (15cm) high*

£1,800-2,200 **DRA**

ESSENTIAL REFERENCE – GEORGE OHR

George Ohr (1857-1918) was an art potter, known for his eccentric behaviour and highly unusual pieces.

- **He was born in Biloxi, Mississippi, where he worked first as a blacksmith, then a file cutter, then a tinker and then a sailor. In 1879 his childhood friend Joseph Meyer invited him to New Orleans to learn pottery.**
- **Once back in Mississippi, Ohr dug his own clay from the banks of the Tchoutacabouffa River. With great skill he shaped, and then misshaped, his vessels, folding, denting, crumpling, twisting and squashing his pots into unique forms.**
- **Ohr did not confine his eccentricity to unconventional pottery. He called his pots 'mud babies' and his workshop the 'Pot-Ohr-E'. He referred to himself as George Ohr M.D. (mud dauber), George Ohr P.M. (pot maker), 'The Unequalled Variety Potter', the 'Pot-Ohr' and the 'Mad Potter of Biloxi'.**
- **The work of George Ohr is now celebrated and displayed at the Ohr-O'Keefe Museum of Art in Biloxi, designed by architect Frank Gehry.**

A George Ohr vase, with ruffled rim and in-body twist, stamped 'GEO. E. OHR BILOXI, MISS.', a few chips/flecks to ruffles.
1895-96 *4¼in (11cm) high*
£4,500-5,000 **DRA**

A George Ohr teapot, with ear handle, stamped 'G.E. OHR, Biloxi, Miss'.
1897-1900 *8in (20.5cm) wide*
£3,000-3,500 **DRA**

A George Ohr vase, with ribbon handles, raspberry, green and gunmetal glaze, stamped 'G.E. OHR, Biloxi, Miss'.
1897-1900 *7¾in (20cm) high*
£45,000-50,000 **DRA**

A George Ohr vase, with in-body twist, speckled and sponged-on ochre, brown, and green glaze, stamped 'GEO. E. OHR BILOXI MISS'.
1895-96 *6½in (16.5cm) high*
£8,500-9,500 **DRA**

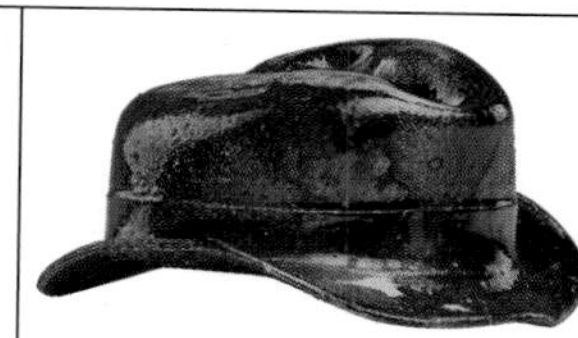

A George Ohr hat novelty, stamped 'G.E. OHR, BILOXI'.
1895-96 *4in (10cm) wide*
£6,500-7,000 **DRA**

An George Ohr pitcher, with ear handle, stamped 'G.E. OHR, Biloxi, Miss'.
1897-1900 *6¾in (17cm) high*
£13,000-16,000 **DRA**

A George Ohr vase, mahogany and gunmetal glaze, stamped 'G.E. OHR Biloxi, Miss.', some abrasions.
1897-1900 *6in (15cm) high*
£4,000-4,500 **DRA**

An George Ohr crumpled vase, stamped 'G.E. OHR Biloxi, Miss'.
1897-1900 *5in (12.5cm) high*
£9,500-11,000 **DRA**

A George Ohr vase, with folded rim, stamped 'G.E. OHR, Biloxi, Miss.'.
1897-1900 *5½in (14cm) high*
£3,500-4,000 **DRA**

A George Ohr mug, with ear-shaped handles, gunmetal glaze, glazed-over script signature.
1898-1910 *6in (15.5cm) high*
£5,500-6,000 **DRA**

A Pilkington's Lancastrian lustre vase, 'Apollo', by Gordon Forsyth (1879-1952), inscribed 'Apollo', with artist's cipher, impressed factory monogram, '2471/IX/ ENGLAND' and date cipher.

This impressive vase is one of the largest pieces ever produced by the factory in lustre glazes.

1909 *21¼in (54cm) high*

£45,000-50,000 L&T

A Pilkington's Lancastrian vase, by Gordon Forsyth, impressed marks, painted artist cipher, date code.

1909 *14½in (37cm) high*

£4,000-5,000 WW

A Pilkington's Lancastrian vase, by Gordon Forsyth, impressed factory mark, painted artist cipher, date code.

1911 *10¾in (27cm) high*

£3,500-4,000 WW

CLOSER LOOK – PILKINGTON'S LANCASTRIAN VASE

This vase was designed by Gordon Forsyth, a talented Scottish ceramic designer who worked at Pilkington's c1906-20.

The vase has interesting provenance, from Edward Fielden Pilkington and thence by descent. It was likely a gift from his father, Pilkington's founder Charles Pilkington.

It is an unusually large piece, possibly made for an exhibition.

It is painted with panels of young ladies walking in woodland landscapes.

A Pilkington's Lancastrian vase, impressed marks, painted artist cipher, date code.

1913 *19in (48cm) high*

£18,000-22,000 WW

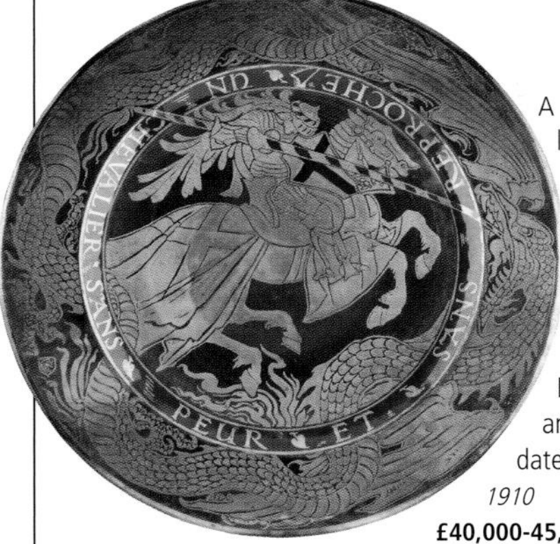

A Pilkington's Lancastrian lustre charger, 'St. George & The Dragon', designed by Walter Crane, decorated by Richard Joyce (1873-1931), inscribed 'CHEVALIER SANS PEUR ET SANS REPROCHE' (the fearless and blameless knight), with date cipher.

1910 *19in (48.5cm) diam*

£40,000-45,000 L&T

A Pilkington's Lancastrian lustre vase, by Richard Joyce, impressed and painted marks, some crazing, date marks.

1910 *11in (28cm) high*

£8,500-9,500 DN

A Pilkington's Lancastrian lustre vase, signed 'Richard Joyce', date cipher.

1910 *9in (23cm) high*

£3,000-3,500 K&O

A Pilkington's Lancastrian lustre vase, by Richard Joyce, no.3055, monogram and date cipher.

1913 *6½in (16.5cm) high*

£1,800-2,200 HAN

A Pilkington's Lancastrian vase, by William S. Mycock, impressed factory mark, painted artist cipher, date code.

1912 *4½in (11.5cm) high*

£1,800-2,200 WW

A Pilkington's Lancastrian dust-pressed 'Viking Ship' tile, designed by C.F.A. Voysey, impressed 'P' mark, minor glaze frits to edges.

6in (15.5cm) square

£2,200-2,800 WW

A Carter's Poole Pottery lustre vase, probably designed by Owen Carter, incised 'Carter's Poole', dated.
1904 *15in (38cm) high*
£1,800-2,200 WW

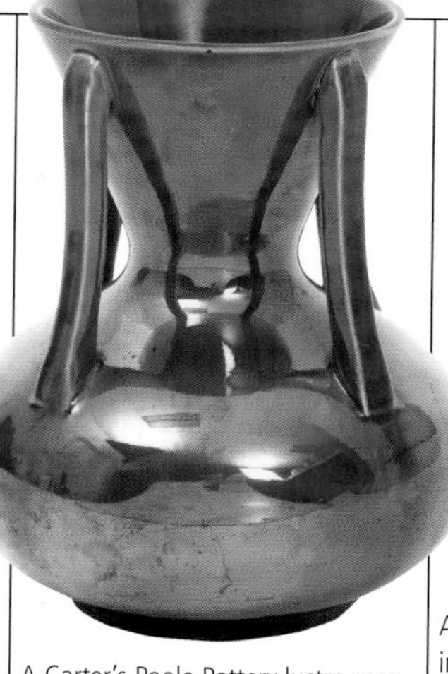

A Carter's Poole Pottery lustre vase, probably designed by Owen Carter, small chip to base rim.
7½in (19cm) high
£1,800-2,200 WW

A Carter & Company Poole Pottery lustre bowl, decorated by Lily Gilham, impressed 'Carter's Poole' mark.
10¾in (27cm) diam
£1,000-1,400 WW

A Carter Stabler & Adams Poole Pottery 'Persian Deer' vase, designed by Truda Adams, painted by Margaret Holder, shape no.911, pattern SK, impressed marks, painted marks and artist monogram.
8½in (21.5cm) high
£550-650 WW

A Carter Stabler and Adams Poole Pottery red earthenware shape number 621/NT vase, designed by Truda Adams, impressed and painted marks.
10½in (26.5cm) high
£150-200 SHEF

A Carter Stabler and Adams Poole Pottery red earthenware vase, painted by Truda Rivers, pattern ZA, with stylised leaves and flowers.
1922-32 *10¾in (27cm) high*
£150-200 SHEF

A Carter Stabler and Adams Poole Pottery red earthenware vase, painted by Ann Hatchard, pattern ZB, impressed and painted marks.
1918-36 *11¼in (28.5cm) high*
£550-600 SHEF

A Poole Pottery shape 966 vase, by Ruth Pavely, pattern BR, impressed and incised marks, painted artist cipher.
9¾in (24.5cm) high
£600-700 WW

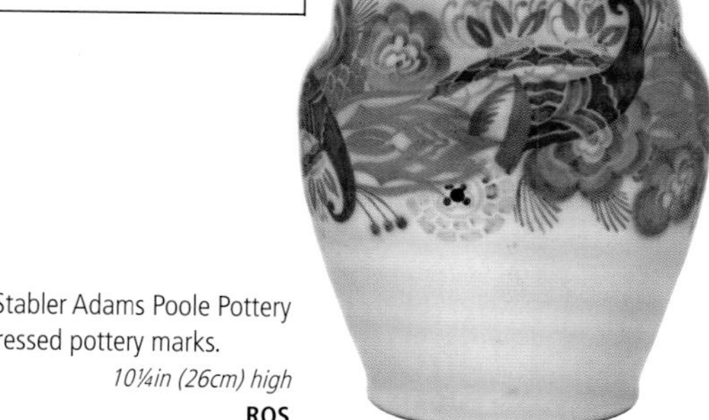

A Carter Stabler Adams Poole Pottery vase, impressed pottery marks.
1921-24 *10¼in (26cm) high*
£200-250 ROS

ESSENTIAL REFERENCE – ROOKWOOD

Rookwood was founded in 1880 in Cincinnati, OH, USA by Maria Longworth Nichols Storer. It began as a hobby, but soon became one of the most important art potteries in the USA.

- **Different glazes were used by Rookwood throughout their history. The 'Standard' glaze was introduced in 1884. The 'Iris', 'Sea Green' and 'Aerial Blue' glazes were introduced in 1894. The 'Vellum' glaze was introduced in 1904.**
- **Rookwood pieces are marked with a flame logo, and several numbers and letters, ciphers for the year of production, the piece's shape, its glaze and its artist.**
- **Rookwood suffered during the Depression. It filed for bankruptcy in 1941, and has changed ownership many times since.**

A Rookwood 'Banded Iris Glaze' vase, by Sallie Coyne, flame mark, 'X/907DD/SEC', some crazing.
1910 *10¼in (26cm) high*
£1,400-1,800 DRA

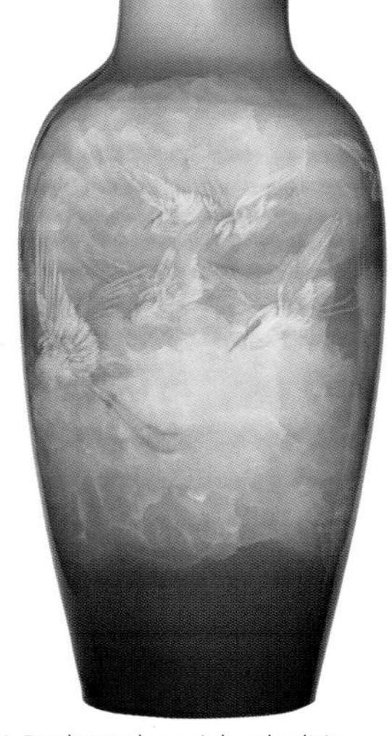

A Rookwood special-order 'Iris Glaze' vase, by Edward T. Hurley (1869-1950), flame mark, 'III/S1611A' artist's signature, minor underglaze imperfection.
1903 *19in (48.5cm) high*
£4,500-5,000 DRA

A Rookwood 'Vellum' vase, by Lenore Asbury (1866-1933), flame mark, 'XXX/904C/V/L.A.'.
1930 *12in (30.5cm) high*
£3,500-4,000 DRA

A Rookwood 'Green Vellum' vase, by Sallie Coyne (1876-1939), flame mark, 'VIII/904E/SEC/GV', fine crazing.
1908 *7¼in (18.5cm) high*
£1,300-1,600 DRA

A Rookwood 'Jewel Porcelain' vase, by Edward T. Hurley, flame mark, 'XXV/ETH/2818', missing lid, crazing, burst glaze bubbles.
1925 *17¼in (44cm) high*
£3,000-3,500 DRA

A Rookwood winter scenic 'Vellum' vase, by Edward T. Hurley, with flame mark and 'XV/1660A/V/ETH', fine crazing.
1915 *16½in (42cm) high*
£4,000-4,500 DRA

A Rookwood 'Black Iris' vase, by Sara Sax (1870-1949); flame mark, 'III/905BB/SX/W', minor crazing, some scratches.
1903 *13in (33cm) high*
£3,000-4,000 DRA

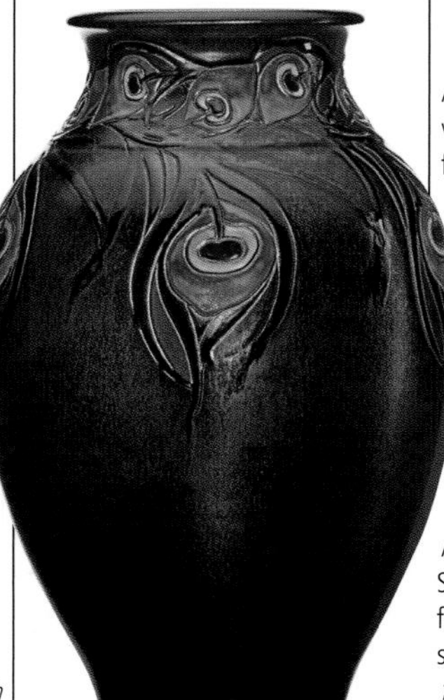

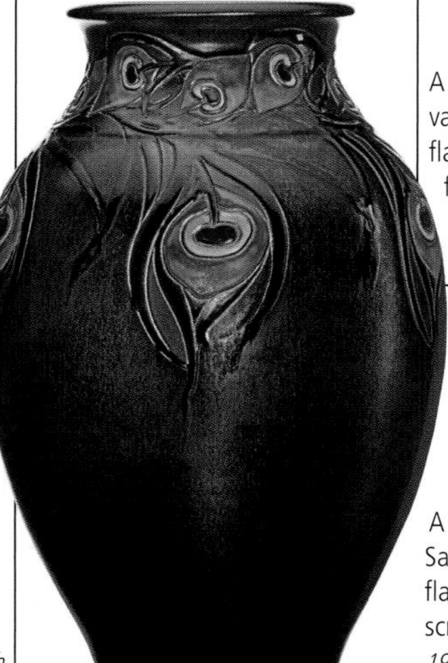

A Rookwood 'French Red' vase, by Sara Sax, with peacock feathers, flame mark, 'XXII/2247C/SX', minor scratches.
1922 *13½in (34cm) high*
£11,000-15,000 DRA

A Rookwood 'Ivory Jewel Porcelain' vase, by Sara Sax, flame mark, 'XXVII/927D/SX', scratches, one area of abrasions.
1927 *9in (23cm) high*
£900-1,100 DRA

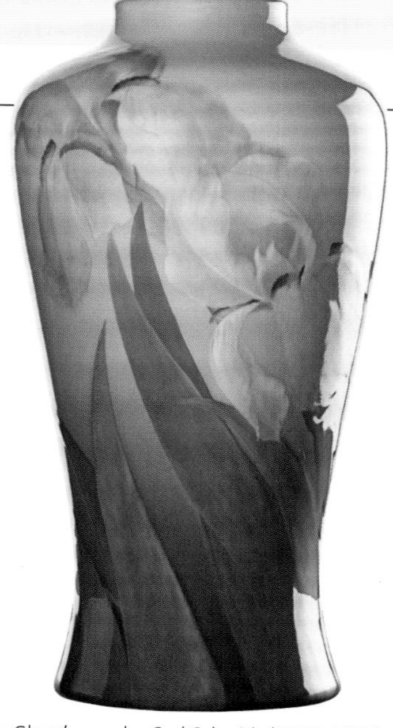

A Rookwood 'Iris Glaze' vase, by Carl Schmidt (1885-1969), flame mark, 'IIII/S1745/W' and artist's cipher.
1904 *3½in (34cm) high*
£5,500-6,000 **DRA**

A Rookwood 'Iris' glaze vase, by Carl Schmidt, flame mark, 'VII/905C/W/CS', some scratches.
1907 *10in (25.5cm) high*
£2,800-3,200 **DRA**

A Rookwood 'Iris Glaze' vase, by Carl Schmidt, flame mark, 'XI/CS/950D/W', some crazing, tiny burst glaze bubbles, faint scratches.
1911 *8in (20.5cm) high*
£3,500-4,000 **DRA**

A Rookwood 'Marine Scenic Vellum' vase, by Carl Schmidt, flame mark, 'XXIV/1358C/V', artist's cipher, some bubbles.
1924 *10¾in (27.5cm) high*
£2,000-2,500 **DRA**

A Rookwood 'Standard Glaze' American Indian portrait vase, 'Lone Elk Sioux', by Adeliza Sehon (d.1902), with flame mark, 'I/904D/ADS/Lone Elk Sioux', original retailer label, some crazing.
1901 *8in (20.5cm) high*
£3,500-4,000 **DRA**

A Rookwood 'Iris' glaze vase, by Kataro Shirayamadani (1865-1948), flame mark, 'VI/907D', artist's cipher, some crazing, some scratches.
1906 *10¼in (26cm) high*
£4,000-5,000 **DRA**

A Rookwood 'Double Vellum' vase, by Kataro Shirayamadani, flame mark, 'XXXIII/S', artist's cipher.
1933 *7½in (19cm) high*
£700-800 **DRA**

A Rookwood 'Iris' glaze vase, by Harriet Wilcox (1869-1943), flame mark, 'I/531E/HEW', some crazing.
1901 *5½in (14cm) high*
£550-650 **DRA**

A Rookwood carved matt production vase, flame mark, date and model, some glaze flecks.
1902 *10in (25.5cm) high*
£550-650 **DRA**

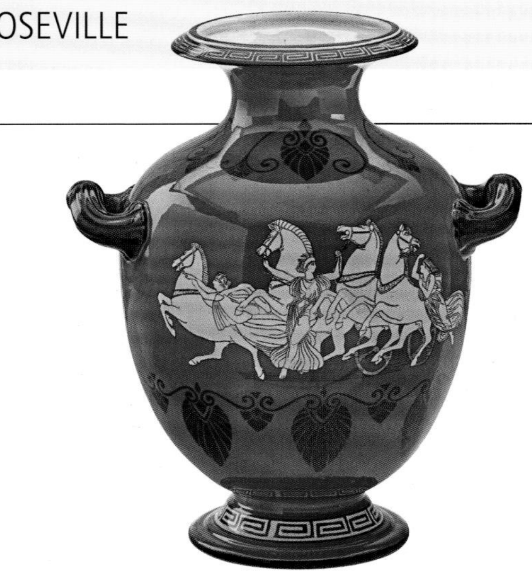

A rare Roseville 'Rozane Olympic' hydria, 'The Hours Taking the Horses from Juno's Car', marked 'ROZANE OLYMPIC POTTERY' with title.

Roseville was founded in Zanesville, OH, USA in 1890 and was closed in 1954.

c1910 *14in (35.5cm) high*

£4,000-4,500 DRA

A rare Roseville 'Della Robbia' volute krater, body incised 'G.B.', professional restoration to chip.

c1910 *17½in (44.5cm) high*

£4,500-5,000 DRA

A Roseville matt green jardinière and pedestal, two hairlines.

c1910 *12in (30.5cm) high*

£800-900 DRA

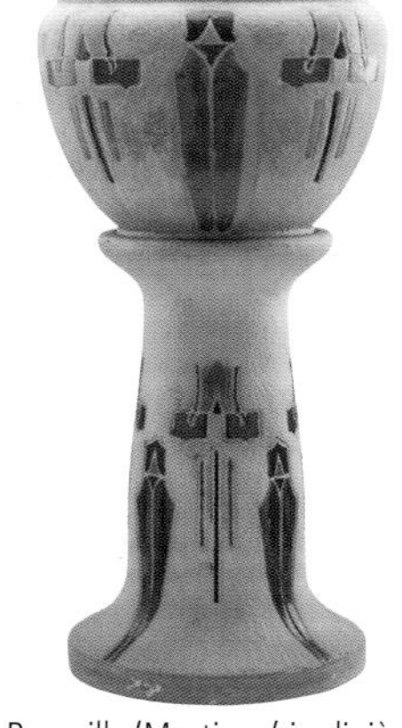

A Roseville 'Mostique' jardinière with pedestal.

1915 *10in (25.5cm) high*

£850-950 DRA

A Roseville 'Sunflower' jardinière and pedestal, bruise to interior rim.

1925 *10in (25.5cm) high*

£900-1,000 DRA

A Roseville 'Sunflower' vase.

1930 *10in (25.5cm) high*

£600-700 DRA

A 1930s Roseville experimental 'Nasturtium' vase, small chip and hairline to base.

8in (20.5cm) high

£500-600 DRA

A Roseville 'Pine Cone' jardinière and pedestal, stamped.

1935 *29in (73.5cm) high*

£650-750 DRA

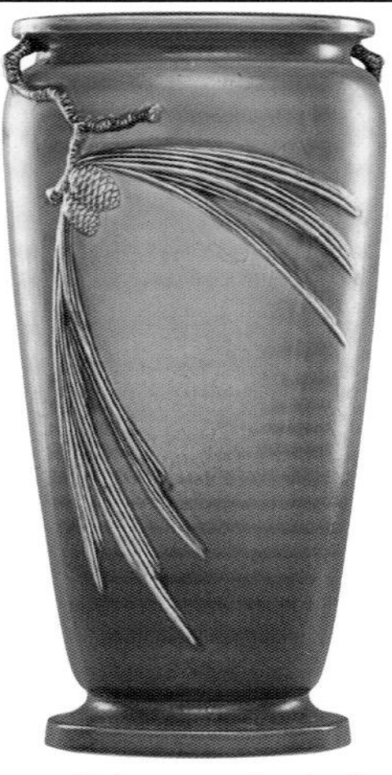

A Roseville 'Pine Cone' umbrella stand, raised mark.

1935 *20in (51cm) high*

£850-950 DRA

ESSENTIAL REFERENCE – RUSKIN

Ruskin pottery was founded in Birmingham in 1897-98 by Edward Richard Taylor and his son William Howson Taylor.

- **Howson Taylor experimented with a number of techniques, creating revolutionary glazes, including metallic lustre glazes and unusual sang-de-boeuf glazes. Some glazes were graduations of two colours, others textured multicoloured patterns. His glazes were leadless and the decoration handpainted.**
- **The factory struggled in the Depression, and finally closed in 1935. Before its closure, the formulae for every glaze was destroyed, to ensure that Howson Taylor's work could never be replicated.**
- **Ruskin pieces are currently on the rise in value, especially those with interesting glazes.**

A Ruskin Pottery high-fired stoneware vase, by William Howson Taylor, purple glaze with turquoise and mint spots, impressed marks, dated.
1906 *7¾in (20cm) high*
£3,000-3,500 WW

A Ruskin Pottery high-fired vase, in speckled sang-de-boeuf glaze, impressed marks, dated.
1906 *5in (13cm) high*
£650-750 K&O

An early 20thC Ruskin Pottery globe and shaft vase, with a mottled and streaked green soufflé glaze, impressed marks.
1911 *10¼in (26cm) high*
£850-950 FLD

A Ruskin Pottery vase, with a speckled blue soufflé glaze, impressed marks.
1916 *13¾in (35cm) high*
£400-500 FLD

A 1920s Ruskin Pottery vase, in mottled lavender over a sang-de-boeuf glaze, impressed 'Ruskin, England'.
13¾in (35cm) high
£4,500-5,000 HT

A Ruskin Pottery vase, in an iridescent kingfisher blue-type lustre glaze, impressed marks, dated.
1922 *6in (15cm) high*
£450-550 FLD

A Ruskin Pottery high-fired barrel vase, with a red and lavender glaze with copper green spotting, the rim and handles with sang-de-boeuf spotting, impressed marks, dated.
1933 *9¾in (25cm) high*
£1,200-1,500 FLD

A Ruskin Pottery high-fired vase, in sang-de-beouf with lavender sweeping and copper spotting glaze, impressed marks, incised 'W. Howson Taylor' and 'THIN'.
15¾in (40cm) high
£3,000-3,500 FLD

A Ruskin Pottery high-fired vase, shape no.1921, with a mottled purple glaze with the odd pale blue spot, impressed marks to base, minor firing imperfections.
8¾in (22.5cm) high
£1,000-1,400 PW

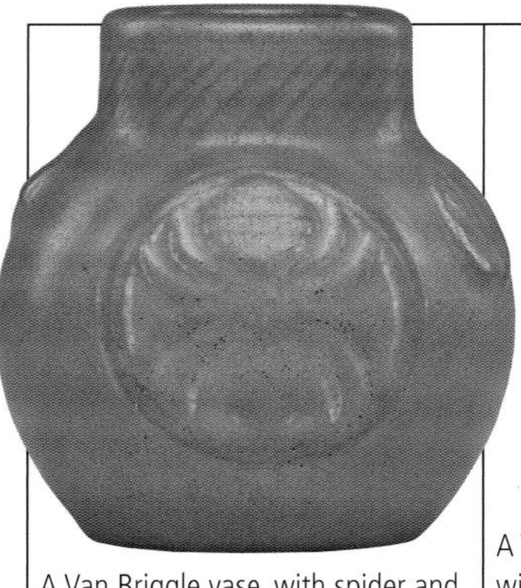

A Van Briggle vase, with spider and Native American symbols, incised 'AA VAN BRIGGLE 1902 III/15', glaze bubbles, minor scuffs.
1902 *5in (12.5cm) high*
£2,000-2,500 **DRA**

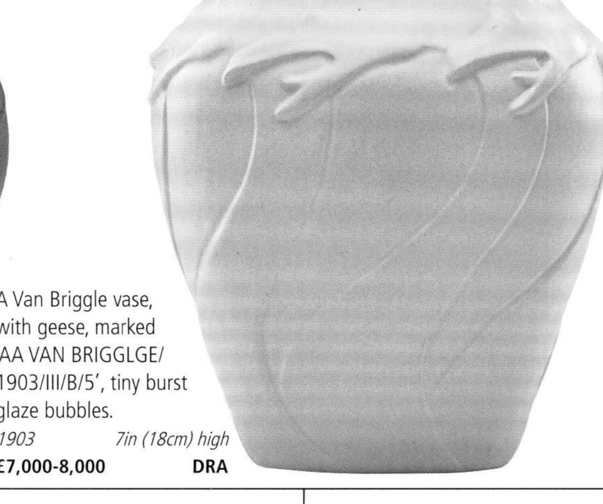

A Van Briggle vase, with geese, marked 'AA VAN BRIGGLGE/ 1903/III/B/5', tiny burst glaze bubbles.
1903 *7in (18cm) high*
£7,000-8,000 **DRA**

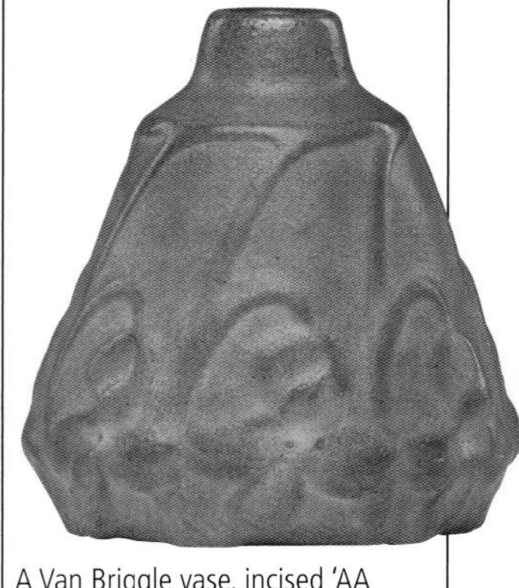

A Van Briggle vase, incised 'AA VAN BRIGGLE 1903 III/181', some peppering.
1903 *4¾in (12cm) high*
£1,800-2,200 **DRA**

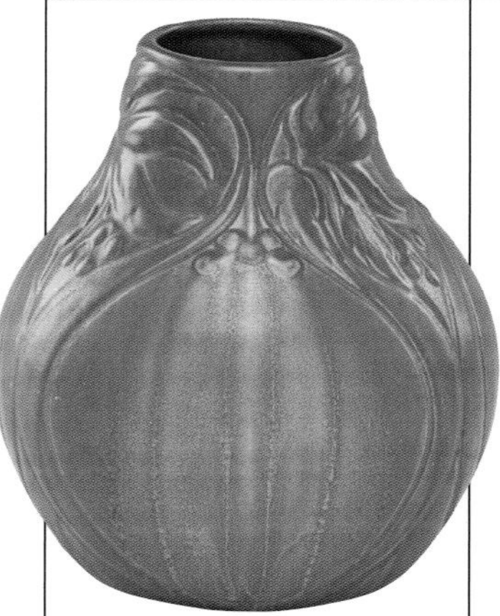

A Van Briggle vase, with Virginia creepers, marked 'AA Van Briggle/1904/V/164', scuffs and metal transfer marks.
1904 *8in (20.5cm) high*
£2,000-2,500 **DRA**

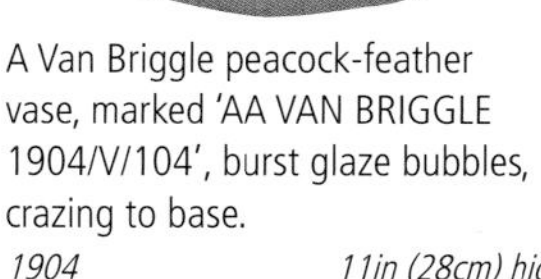

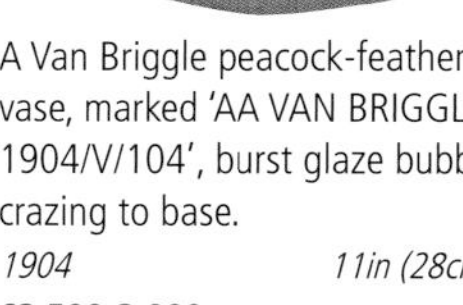

A Van Briggle peacock-feather vase, marked 'AA VAN BRIGGLE 1904/V/104', burst glaze bubbles, crazing to base.
1904 *11in (28cm) high*
£2,500-3,000 **DRA**

A Van Briggle vase, with tulips, marked 'AA VAN BRIGGLE', numbered '68', dated.
1905 *7½in (19cm) high*
£1,000-1,400 **DRA**

A Van Briggle bowl, marked 'AA Van Briggle/1905/387'.
1905 *11in (28cm) wide*
£1,200-1,600 **DRA**

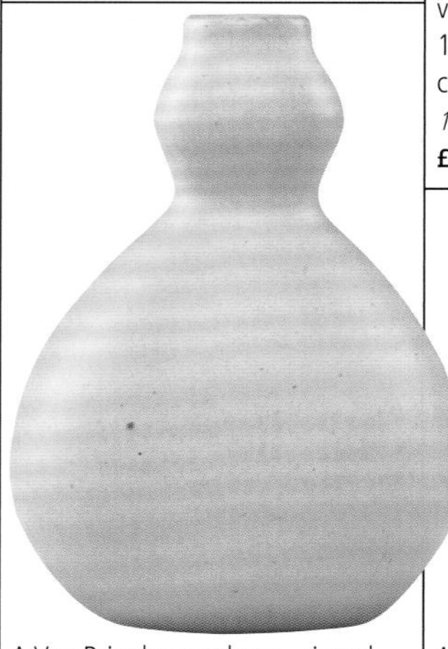

A Van Briggle gourd vase, signed 'AA VAN BRIGGLE/VX/1905/319'.
1905 *5in (13cm) high*
£550-650 **DRA**

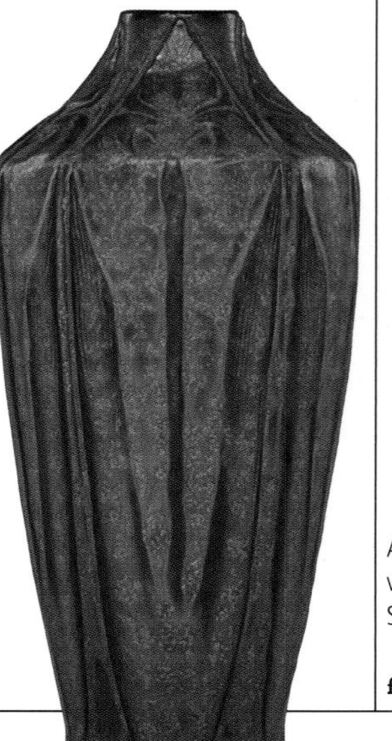

A Van Briggle vase, incised 'AA VAN BRIGGLE COLORADO SPRINGS'.
1908-11 *9¼in (23.5cm) high*
£3,000-3,500 **DRA**

A 1910s Van Briggle copper-clad vase, marked 'AA Van Briggle Colo Spgs 690'.
6¾in (17cm) high
£1,500-2,000 **DRA**

ESSENTIAL REFERENCE – FAIRYLAND LUSTRE

Wedgwood's distinctive Fairyland lustre range was designed by Daisy Makeig-Jones (1881-1945) from 1915-29.

- **Makeig-Jones studied at Torquay School of Art, before becoming a tableware painter and designer at Wedgwood in 1909.**
- **She decorated her Fairyland lustre series with colourful scenes of fantastical lands and magical kingdoms, featuring goblins, sprites, spirits and other supernatural beings.**
- **These wares were very popular during and just after WWI, but had fallen out of fashion by the late 1920s.**
- **Today they are valued by collectors, with the rarer patterns fetching high values.**

A pair of Wedgwood Fairyland lustre porcelain vases, 'Butterfly Woman' pattern, no.Z4968, with mythical creatures and winged maidens within trees.

9½in (24cm) high

£8,000-9,000 **HANN**

A Wedgwood 'Flame Daventry' lustre vase, pattern no.Z5413, gilt marks.

Provenance: Ann Makeing-Jones, direct descendant of Josiah Wedgwood I, niece of Daisy Makeing-Jones.

c1926 *7¾in (20cm) high*

£1,500-2,000 **HAN**

A 1930s Wedgwood Fairyland lustre bowl, 'Gargoyle' pattern to exterior, 'Bird in a Hoop, Rainbow Landscape' to interior, green mark, inscribed 'Z496F'.

7½in (19cm) wide

£3,000-3,500 **HT**

A 1920s Wedgwood Fairyland lustre bowl, 'Geisha' or 'Angels' pattern, no.Z4968, Portland Vase mark.

6½in (16.5cm) diam

£2,500-3,000 **FLD**

A Wedgwood Fairyland lustre Malfrey vase and cover, 'Ghostly Wood' pattern, with Portland vase in gold, incised 'Shape No. 2312', pattern no.Z4968.

This vase comes with its original receipt, dated 'January 27, 1926', which increases its value.

c1926 *13in (33cm) high*

£26,000-30,000 **SWO**

A Wedgwood Fairyland lustre shape 2046 vase, 'Ghostly Wood' pattern, printed gilt Portland Vase factory mark, painted 'Z4968/i', incised '2046', some firing faults.

15¼in (38.5cm) high

£7,500-8,500 **TEN**

A Wedgwood Fairyland lustre charger, 'Ghostly Wood' pattern, no.Z4968, printed 'Wedgwood' mark to base.

15¼in (38.5cm) diam

£18,000-25,000 **WW**

A Wedgwood Fairyland lustre vase, 'Goblin' pattern, with Portland Vase mark and 'Wedgwood Made in England'.

7in (18cm) high

£9,000-11,000 **JDJ**

A Wedgwood Fairyland lustre bowl, 'Jumping Faun' and 'Garden of Paradise' patterns, printed marks, some rubbing to gilt, some crazing.

8in (20.5cm) diam

£1,800-2,200 **PW**

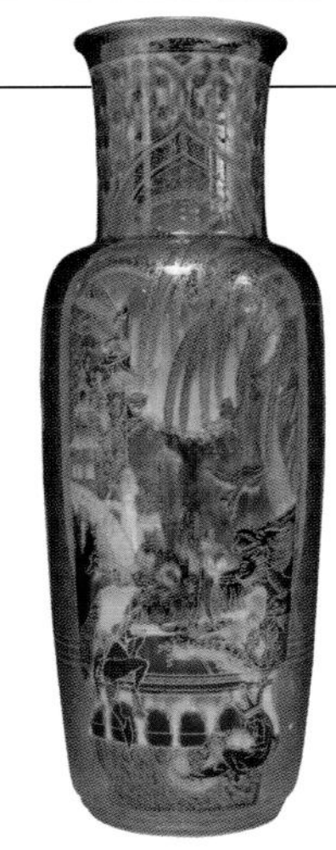

A Wedgwood Fairyland flame lustre vase, 'Pillars' pattern, printed marks.
c1925 *14¼in (36cm) high*
£4,500-5,500 **K&O**

A pair of Wedgwood Fairyland coral and bronze lustre vases with covers, 'Rainbow' pattern, no.Z5349, marked.
9in (23cm) high
£3,000-4,000 **HAN**

A Wedgwood Fairyland lustre vase, 'Sycamore Tree with Feng Hwang and Bridge' pattern, no.Z5360, gilt marks.
8in (20.5cm) high
£1,600-2,000 **HAN**

A Wedgwood Fairyland lustre plate, 'Thumbelina' pattern, with a 'Twyford' border, with Portland vase mark 'Wedgwood Made in England'.
10½in (26.5cm) diam
£5,000-6,000 **JDJ**

A pair of Wedgwood Fairyland lustre shape 3177 vases, 'Torches' pattern, the foot and rim interior with 'Flaming Wheel' pattern, gold Portland Vase mark and painted 'Z4968', one with glued sections on rim.
11½in (29cm) high
£5,000-6,000 **BE**

A pair of Wedgwood shape 3150 vases, 'Willow' pattern, no.Z5228, gold-printed marks, black enamelled pattern.
8in (20.5cm) high
£2,800-3,500 **GORL**

A Wedgwood Fairyland lustre 'K'ang Hsi' bowl, 'Woodland Bridge' pattern to exterior, 'Garden of Paradise' pattern to interior, highlighted in gilt, printed and painted marks.
7in (18cm) diam
£2,000-3,000 **WW**

A Wedgwood Fairyland lustre pedestal bowl, 'Woodland Bridge' pattern, no.Z4968, printed and painted marks.
7¾in (20cm) diam
£2,500-3,000 **DUK**

A 1920s Wedgwood Fairyland lustre bowl, 'Woodland Elves VII – Toadstool' pattern to exterior, 'Fairy in a Cage' pattern to interior, 'WEDGWOOD ENGLAND' gilt stamp, marked 'Z4968', fleck to foot ring, some scratches.
9½in (24cm) wide
£2,200-2,800 **DRA**

A set of Wedgwood Jasperware chess pieces, based on the figures from Macbeth, chip to the blue bishop.

Wedgwood chess sets can fetch high values as they have an appeal beyond pottery collectors. This set was first designed by John Flaxman in the late 18thC and reproduced from the original mould.

max 4¼in (11cm) high

£3,000-4,000 **PSA**

A Wedgwood 'Taurus Bull', by Arnold Machin.

designed c1957 *14¼in (36cm) long*

£160-200 **HAN**

A Wedgwood Pottery vase, by Keith Murray, model no.3820, covered in a 'Moonstone' matt white glaze, impressed, printed marks and facsimile signature.

6¾in (17cm) high

£400-500 **WW**

A Wedgwood matt green vase, by Keith Murray, 'KM' monogram.

9in (23cm) high

£240-300 **HAN**

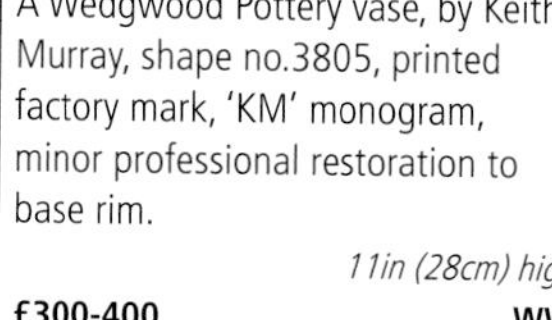

A Wedgwood Pottery vase, by Keith Murray, shape no.3805, printed factory mark, 'KM' monogram, minor professional restoration to base rim.

11in (28cm) high

£300-400 **WW**

A Wedgwood 'Boat Race' bowl, by Eric Ravilious, limited edition no.7/250, boxed with book on Ravilious's designs.

This bowl was originally designed in 1937, then re-issued 1986 to mark 50th anniversary of Ravilious's first employment by Wedgwood in 1936.

1986 *12in (30.5cm) diam*

£600-700 **CHOR**

A Wedgwood bachelor's nine-piece tea set, 'Afternoon Tea' pattern, by Eric Ravilious (1903-42), printed marks, minor scratches.

designed 1937 *teapot 6½in (16.5cm) wide*

£3,500-4,000 **GORL**

A Wedgwood King Edward VIII 1937 coronation mug, by Eric Ravilious, model no.CL.6203, printed and painted factory marks.

4¼in (10.5cm) high

£1,000-1,500 **WW**

A Wedgwood turquoise glazed bowl, by Norman Wilson, with moonstone glaze to exterior, impressed and printed 'NW'.

8¼in (21cm) diam

£120-160 **HAN**

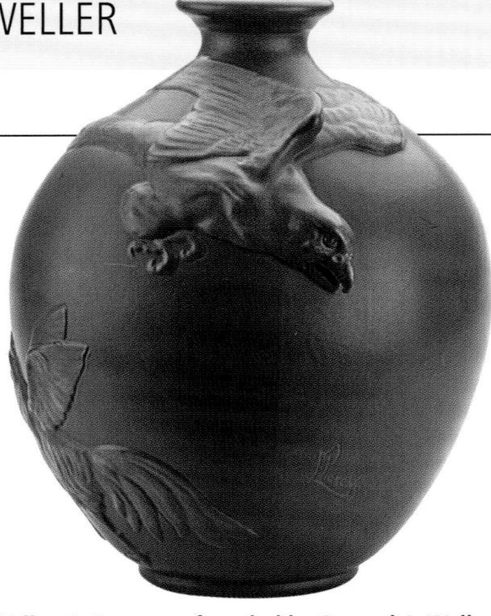

A Weller 'Fru-Russett' vase, with eagle, rooster and hen, signed 'Flickens', incised 'Weller', some chips and scuffs.

Weller Pottery was founded by Samuel A. Weller (1851-1925) in Fultonham, Ohio, in 1872. The company relocated to Zanesville in 1888. It originally produced tiles and plain pots, before launching its first art pottery line in 1893. Production continued until shortly after the end of World War II.

c1905 *6in (15cm) high*
£6,500-7,500 **DRA**

A Weller 'Fru-Russett' vase, with nude male and grapevines, body incised 'E. Pickens', the base incised 'Weller', chip under rim, minor efflorescence.

c1905 *18in (45.5cm) high*
£5,500-6,500 **DRA**

A Weller 'Dickensware' umbrella stand, by Edward Abel (1868-1937), stamped, etched signature, two chips to inner rim, some minor scratches.

26in (66cm) high
£650-750 **DRA**

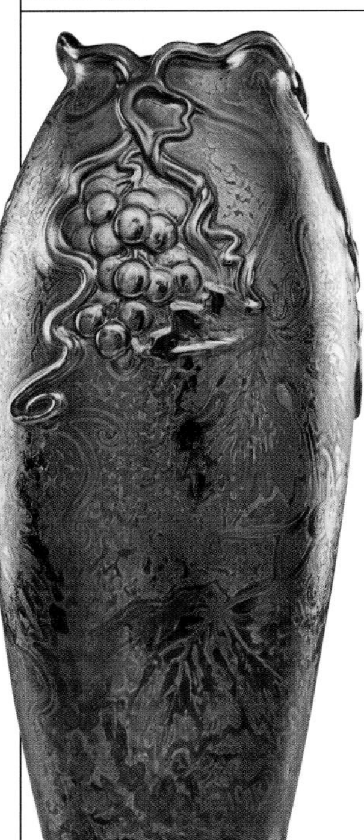

A Weller floor vase, by Jacques Sicard, signed, base stamped 'WELLER', minor abrasions.

1903-17 *23in (58.5cm) high*
£4,000-5,000 **DRA**

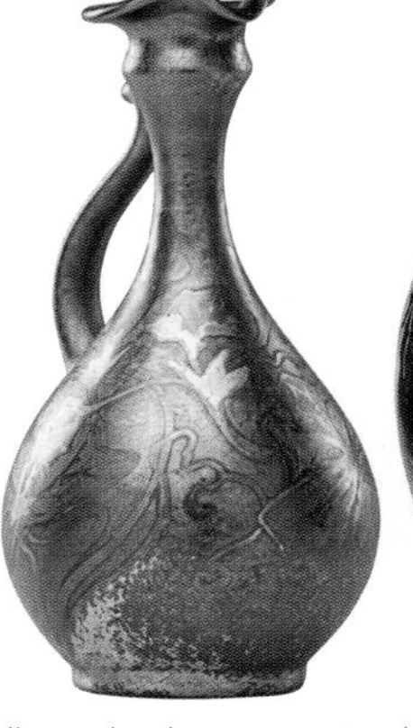

A Weller pitcher, by Jacques Sicard (1863-1925), glazed-over marks.

1903-17 *10in (25.5cm) high*
£1,600-2,000 **DRA**

A Weller vase, by Jacques Sicard, base signed 'WELLER SICARD'.

1903-17 *15in (38cm) high*
£1,600-2,000 **DRA**

A Weller pitcher, by Jacques Sicard, with maiden and grape clusters, signed 'Sicard Weller', minor glaze flakes.

1903-17 *22½in (57cm) high*
£2,500-3,000 **DRA**

A Weller Hudson floor vase, by Hester Pillsbury, signed, manufacturer stamp to base, some scuffs.

1917-34 *27in (68.5cm) high*
£4,000-5,000 **DRA**

A Weller Hudson floor vase, by Hester Pillsbury, signed, incised manufacturer mark to base, some glaze losses.

1917-34 *24½in (62cm) high*
£1,500-2,000 **DRA**

A rare Wemyss Ware lavender blue glazed pig.
c1900 *6in (15cm) long*
£5,000-6,000 **L&T**

A rare early 20thC Wemyss Ware sleeping pig, 'Thistles' pattern, impressed 'WEMYSS', minor restoration to ear.
6½in (16.5cm) long
£4,000-5,000 **L&T**

A rare Wemyss Ware cat, with inset glass eyes, impressed 'Wemyss Ware/R.H.&S.'.
c1900 *12¾in (32.5cm) high*
£5,000-6,000 **L&T**

A Wemyss Ware pottery cat, with cabbage roses, with inset glass eyes, painted 'Wemyss Ware J.N.' and 'Made in England'.
12¾in (32.5cm) high
£1,200-1,600 **BE**

A Wemyss Ware mug, 'Peacock' pattern, with impressed 'WEMYSS'.
c1900 *5½in (14cm) high*
£2,000-2,500 **L&T**

A Wemyss Ware Gordon dessert plate, 'Fuchsias' pattern, impressed 'WEMYSS' WARE/R.H.&S.', printed retailer's mark 'T. GOODE & CO.', restored.
c1900 *8¼in (21cm) diam*
£1,500-2,000 **L&T**

An early 20thC Wemyss Ware loving cup, 'Three Wise Monkeys' pattern, decorated by Karel Nekola, inscribed 'I HEAR NO EVIL./I SEE NO EVIL./I SPEAK NO EVIL.', impressed 'WEMYSS'.
5½in (14cm) high
£1,200-1,600 **L&T**

A pair of early 20thC Wemyss Ware vases, 'Cabbage Roses' pattern, decorated by Karel Nekola, with painted and impressed 'WEMYSS'.
11in (28cm) high
£2,200-3,000 **L&T**

An early 20thC Wemyss Ware 'Anemones' matchbox cover, decorated by Edwin Sandland, painted 'WEMYSS', retailer's mark 'T. GOODE & CO.'
3¼in (8cm) long
£2,200-3,000 **L&T**

An early 20thC Wemyss Ware biscuit barrel and cover, 'Violets' pattern, decorated by David Grinton, painted and impressed 'WEMYSS'.
5in (12.5cm) high
£450-550 **L&T**

ESSENTIAL REFERENCE – ZSOLNAY

The Zsolnay factory in Pecs, south west Hungary, was founded in 1853.

- **In 1885, it acquired the Fischer factory, which had been founded in 1867 and manufactured similar ceramics. Both companies looked to the Persian and Chinese for influence in their designs.**
- **From the 1890s, Zsolnay developed an eosin process to produce iridescent porcelain.**
- **They also manufactured frost resistant ceramics used for buildings, particularly popular during the Art Nouveau period – producing ornate roof tiles such as on St Matthais Church in Budapest.**
- **The company was nationalised under communism, but regained its independence in 1982 and continues to manufacture porcelain today.**

A Zsolnay ceramic vase, by Julia Zsolnay (1856-1950), with gilt detailing, printed underglaze blue spire mark, impressed '877'.
c1883 *16¼in (41cm) high*
£2,500-3,000 ROS

A Zsolnay eosin-glazed vessel, with lizards and cut-out rim, five churches mark, '6436/M', original paper price tag, some scratches.
c1900 *11½in (29cm) wide*
£25,000-30,000 DRA

A pair of 19thC Zsolnay vases, with painted and gilded arabesque designs, pattern no.1027, rubbing to gilding.
23½in (60cm) high
£12,000-16,000 B&H

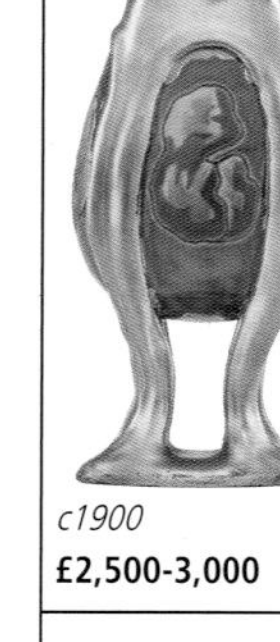

A Zsolnay eosin-glazed vase, with bird skulls, five churches mark, stamped '6157/26/36', professional restoration to one chip.
c1900 *7¾in (20cm) high*
£6,500-7,500 DRA

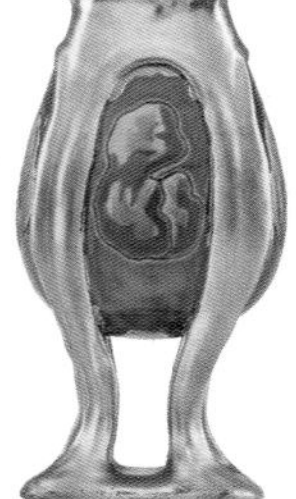

A Zsolnay eosin-glazed tulip-shaped vase, five churches mark, impressed '6174/M', small touch-ups and wear to foot.
c1900 *6¾in (17cm) high*
£2,500-3,000 DRA

A Zsolnay eosin-glazed vase, with waterlilies and reeds, five churches mark, impressed '6009/M/22', some scratches.
c1900 *11in (28cm) high*
£10,000-14,000 DRA

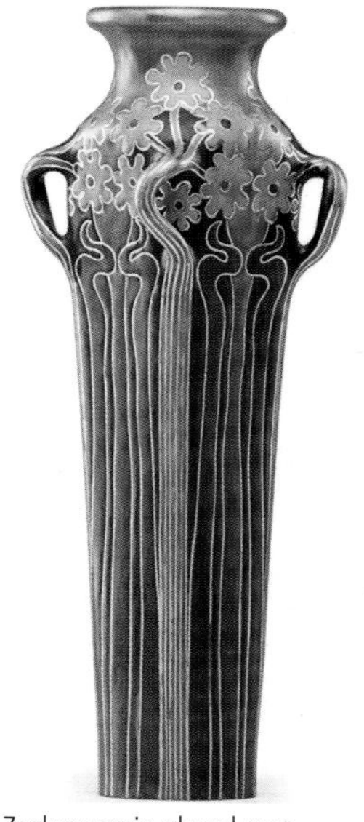

A Zsolnay eosin-glazed vase, five churches mark, impressed 'M/5994/23', some grinding flakes, short scratches.
c1900 *13in (33cm) high*
£12,000-16,000 DRA

A Zsolnay eosin-glazed vase, five churches mark, impressed '7300', professional restoration.
c1904 *19in (48.5cm) high*
£5,000-6,000 DRA

An early 20thC Zsolnay eosin-glazed vase, with a lobster and coral, five churches mark, impressed 'M 6177 23', some damages.

Despite the damage, the appearance and look of this vase assures its value. Fieldings' expert Will Farmer said of this vase: 'Collectors of different ceramics react differently to damage... the Hungarians put much less weight on the condition of Zsolnay than on the look and rarity of an object.'

9¾in (25cm) high
£6,000-7,000 FLD

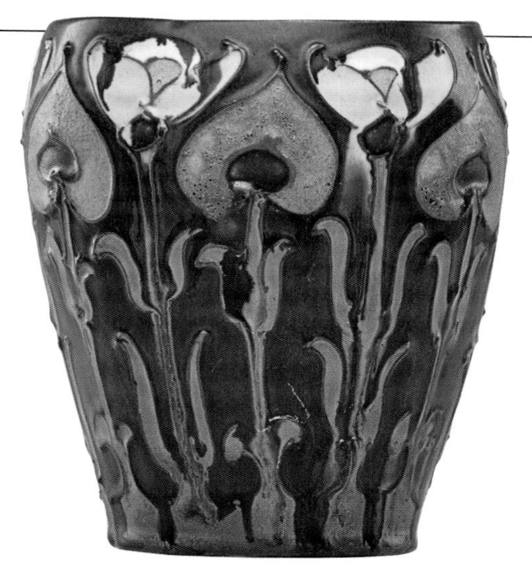

An Arequipa vase, by Frederick H. Rhead, blue pot under tree mark, marked 'AREQUIPA CALIFORNIA/1912/506A', grinding chip to base.
1912 *6¼in (16cm) high*
£75,000-85,000 **DRA**

CLOSER LOOK – RENÉ BUTHAUD VASE

This vase is the work of French Art Deco ceramicist René Buthaud (1886-1986).

He was heavily influenced by African tribal art, as is reflected in this vase.

One side is incised and glazed with a woman holding a bowl.

The reserve is decorated with a stylised crocodile and fish.

An Art Deco ceramic vase and cover, painted 'RB' monogram to base.
c1925 *23¾in (60.5cm) high*
£35,000-40,000 **ROS**

An Arequipa vase, by Frederick H. Rhead (1880-1942), blue pot under tree mark.
c1911-13 *5in (12.5cm) wide*
£25,000-30,000 **DRA**

An Ault vase, designed by Christopher Dresser, shape 319, feint impressed facsimile signature.
11½in (29cm) high
£280-340 **PW**

A Boch Frères Keramis urn, by Charles Catteau (1880-1966), with African farm scene, with 'Ch. Catteau' stamp, 'BOCH FRERES KERAMIS MADE IN BELGIUM' wolf stamp, impressed '1297', signed 'D.2299', minor scuffs to body.
designed 1937 *14½in (37cm) high*
£4,000-5,000 **DRA**

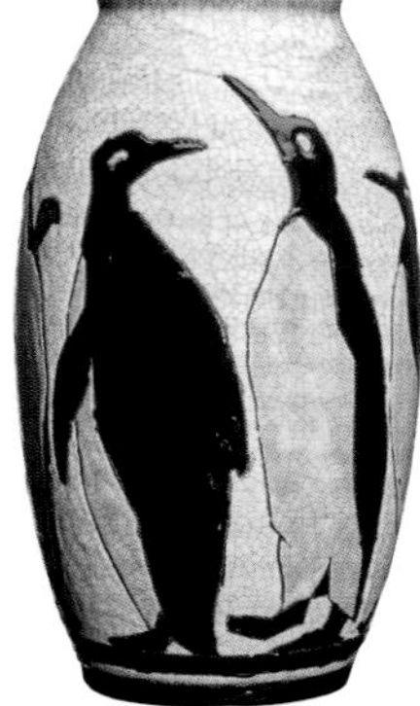

A Boch Frères Keramis glazed earthenware vase, decorated with penguins, circular black 'BOCH FRERES' stamp, signed 'D1104', minor scratches.
designed 1927 *11¾in (30cm) high*
£1,400-1,800 **DRA**

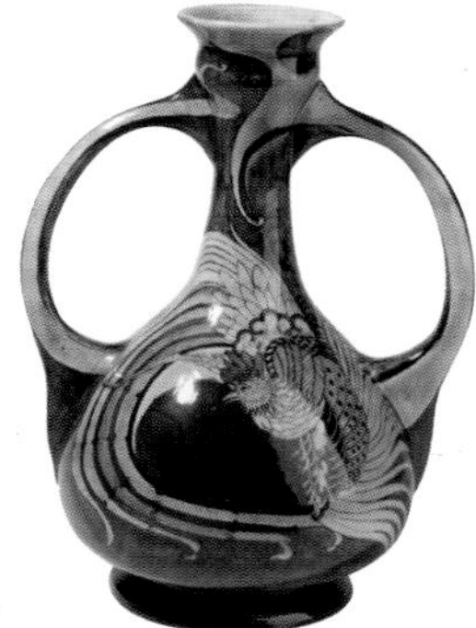

An Dutch Art Nouveau Brantjes Faience De Purmerend vase, no.1077, painted with a bird of prey, painted and signed marks.
14in (35.5cm) high
£1,200-1,600 **DUK**

A Cantagalli pottery Iznik charger, painted cockerel mark, minor glaze loss to rim.
15½in (39.5cm) diam
£2,800-3,200 **WW**

Judith Picks

The 'Jazz' series began in 1921 when Eleanor Roosevelt commissioned Cowan to make a punch bowl for her husband, Franklin D. Roosevelt, then governor of New York, later president of the USA. She liked the bowl so much that she immediately ordered two more. As the design was very much admired, Cowan produced a small series of similar bowls. Cowan's pieces epitomise American Art Deco style.

A Cowan glazed earthenware 'Jazz' bowl, by Viktor Schreckengost (1906-2008), artist's signature, base stamped 'COWAN', professional restoration to chips.

1931 *13¾in (35cm) diam*

£12,000-15,000 **DRA**

A Della Robbia two-tile panel, designed by Ford Madox Brown, by Emily Margaret Wood, incised and painted marks, 'EMW' monogram, incised '3/98'.

The panel has a paper label to the reverse stating that the figure is Archangel Michael, designed by Ford Madox Brown for Morris & Co. and made by his pupil Harold Rathbone at the Della Robbia Pottery. It is actually from Ford Madox Brown's design of Gideon for a stained glass window by Morris & Co. at St Martins on the Hill, Scarborough. The window depicts Joshua, St Michael and Gideon and was designed in 1862.

c1898 *panel 27½in (70cm) high*

£8,000-9,000 **WW**

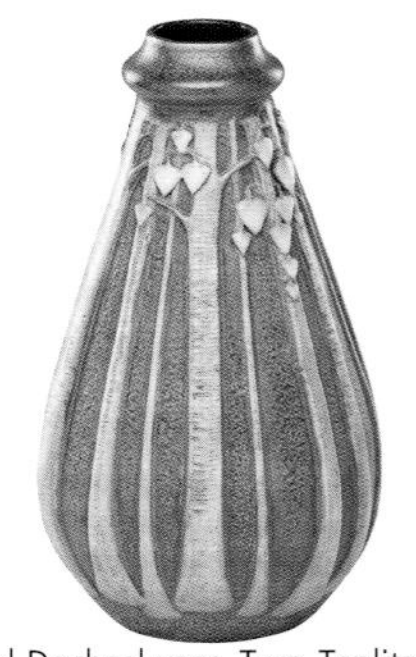

A Paul Dachsel vase, Turn-Teplitz, Bohemia, restored drill hole to base.

c1905 *15¾in (40cm) high*

£1,200-1,600 **DRA**

A French oxblood and turquoise glazed stoneware vase, by Pierre-Adrien Dalpayrat (1844-1910), signed, minor grinding chips.

c1900 *11½in (29cm) high*

£4,000-5,000 **DRA**

A glazed stoneware vase, by Pierre-Adrien Dalpayrat, with partial oxblood glaze, incised 'Dalpayrat', impressed '717', some touch-ups.

c1900 *10¾in (27.5cm) high*

£1,200-1,600 **DRA**

A Della Robbia bowl, by Annie Smith, inscribed 'Au Revoir', dated.

1896 *10½in (26.5cm) diam*

£550-650 **PW**

A Della Robbia Pottery candlestick, by Marian de Caluwe, painted 'DR', 'MdeC', and '5', incised '241', with X cipher.

14¾in (37.5cm) high

£9,000-11,000 **WW**

An Etling Art Deco group of children, by Marcel Guillard and Alexandre Kelety, marked, paper retail label, some crazing.

9¾in (24.5cm) high

£500-600 **BELL**

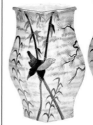

A pair of Gallé faience vases, inscribed 'E. Gallé a Nancy', some chips, wear to gilding.

c1900 *8¾in (22cm) high*

£350-450 **BELL**

An early 20thC Gallé faience pug, 'Monsieur le Comte', with inset glass eyes, signed 'Gallé Nancy', with St Clement backstamp.

11¾in (30cm) high

£1,800-2,200 **BE**

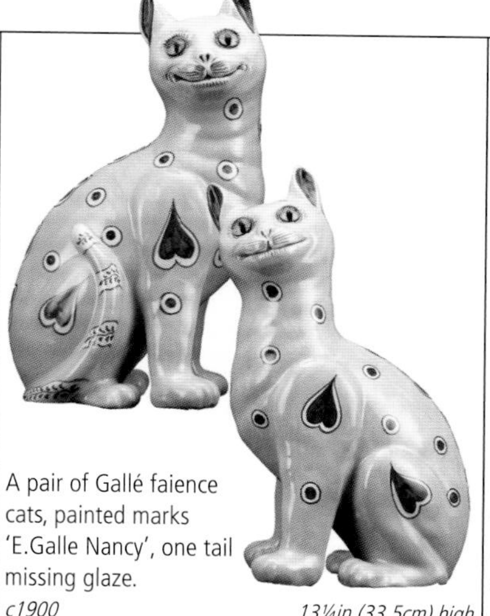

A pair of Gallé faience cats, painted marks 'E.Galle Nancy', one tail missing glaze.

c1900 *13¼in (33.5cm) high*

£3,500-4,500 **DN**

A 1930s Richard Ginori glazed earthenware lamp base, by Gio Ponti (1891-1979), 'RICHARD-GINORI S. CRISTOFORO' stamp, factory drill-hole, touch-ups to glaze flakes.

Gio Ponti was an architect, industrial designer, craftsman, writer and painter, and one of the most influential Italian designers of the 20thC. He designed for over 120 companies over his lifetime. **See also page 536.**

10in (25.5cm) high

£1,400-1,800 **DRA**

A 19thC Naples Giustiniani Egyptian Revival creamware part service.

£28,000-34,000 **WW**

A Hancock & Sons Morrisware vase, by George Cartlidge, no.C28-2, printed factory mark, painted facsimile signature.

14¼in (36.5cm) high

£500-600 **WW**

A Hancock & Sons Morrisware vase, by George Cartlidge, no.C27-28, printed and painted marks, facsimile signature.

12¼in (31cm) high

£400-500 **WW**

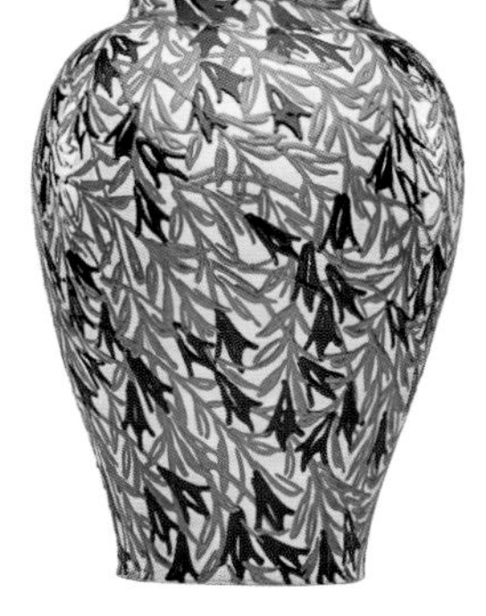

A German Karlsruhe enamel-decorated faience vase, by Max Laeuger (1864-1952), tube-lined with leaves, marks 'PROF. LAUGER' and 'Karlsruhe', deaccession number, tight interior hairline, chip to base.

post-1916 *13½in (34cm) high*

£1,600-2,000 **DRA**

A Langenzersdorfer Keramik earthenware model, 'Arrogance', by Eduard Klabena, signed 'EK, 114'.

c1913-14 *10¾in (27cm) high*

£6,000-7,000 **QU**

A glazed earthenware vase, by Émile Lenoble, with stamp mark, signed in red '1926.25'.

c1930 *11½in (29cm) high*

£3,000-4,000 **DOY**

A 1930s Longwy glazed earthenware 'Atlas' vase, by Maurice-Paul Chevallier (1892-1987), titled, with marks, flaw to inner rim in the making, crazing lines to interior.

15in (38cm) high

£3,500-4,000 **DRA**

A 1920s Marblehead vase, by Arthur Baggs (1886-1947) and Sarah Tutt (1859-1947), stamped ship mark 'MP', incised 'AB/T'.

4½in (11.5cm) wide

£1,500-2,000 **DRA**

CLOSER LOOK – MAW & CO. VASE

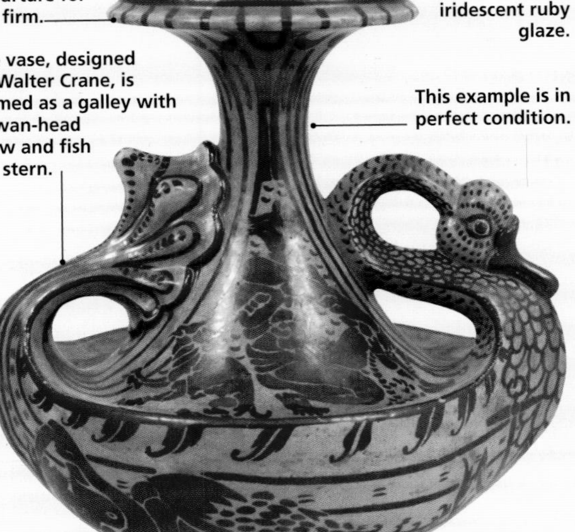

Maw & Co. of Jackfield, Shropshire, was best known for its mass production of earthenware tiles and architectural ceramics. Arts and Crafts pieces such as this vase were a real departure for the firm.

The vase, designed by Walter Crane, is formed as a galley with a swan-head prow and fish tail stern.

It is painted with dolphins and scenes from the Odyssey, and finished in a distinctive iridescent ruby glaze.

This example is in perfect condition.

A Maw & Co. vase, signed.

c1889 *9¼in (23.5cm) high*

£10,000-12,000 **K&O**

An early 20thC Marblehead vase, by Arthur Hennessey and Sarah Tutt, stamped ship mark 'MP', signed 'HT'.

3½in (9cm) high

£1,300-1,800 **DRA**

A Clement Massier vase, by M. Alexandy, marked and signed.

12½in (32cm) high

£1,500-2,000 **CHEF**

A Maw & Co. dust-pressed tile, by Walter Crane, 'Vesper', from the Times of the Day series, monogrammed 'WC'.

8in (20.5cm) square

£300-350 **FLD**

A French glazed and gilt stoneware vase, by Jean Mayodon (1893-1967), impressed 'MJ', 'Rouard' retailer paper label, minor rim chips, losses to gilding.

c1940 *14¼in (36cm) high*

£4,000-4,500 **DRA**

A Merrimac vase, some restoration, flecks to edges of feathers.

The Merrimac Pottery Company was founded in Newburyport, Massachusetts by Thomas Nickerson in 1902. The company made garden pottery, art pottery and reproductions of Roman pottery, and was known for its lustre, crackled and matt glazes. The pottery burned down in 1908.

c1905 *7¾in (20cm) high*

£3,000-3,500 **DRA**

A Merrimac vase, with crystalline glaze, incised 'M/III', some flakes.

c1905 *5in (12.5cm) high*

£2,500-3,000 **DRA**

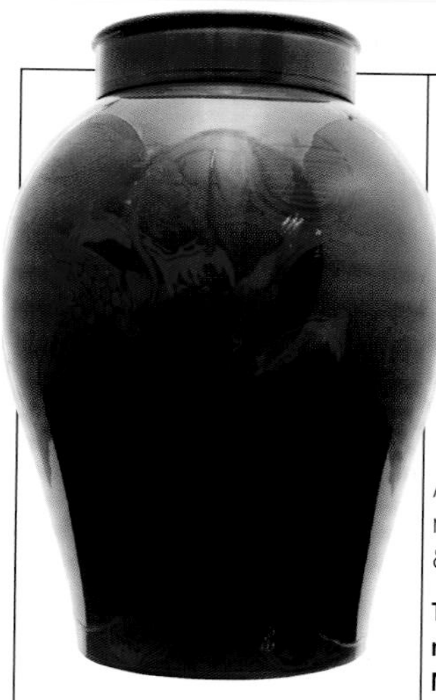

A Bernard Moore flambé temple jar and cover, the lid with Chinese symbol, signed and monogram 'HL'.

12½in (32cm) high

£2,200-2,800 HAN

A faience pottery pug, probably made by Mitterteich, Max Emanuel & Co., with glass eyes.

These dogs and cats are often referred to as Mosanic Pottery. Mosanic Pottery was a trade mark used by Max Emanuel & Co. for products made exclusively for the London store.

c1900 11¾in (30cm) high

£280-320 TEN

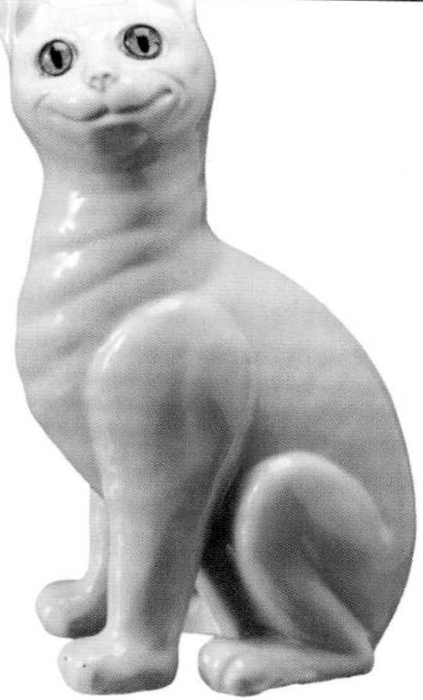

An early 20thC Gallé-style white pottery cat, probably by Mosanic/ Max Emanuel & Co., with glass eyes.

13in (33cm) high

£400-500 BE

A 1900s Norse Pottery vase, with modelled lizard, stamped 'Norse/25', some scuffs and scratches.

The Norse Pottery Works was based in Edgerton, Wisconsin. It operated c1903-13, run by Danish immigrant potters Louis Ipson and Thorwald Samson. They took inspiration from ancient Scandinavian artefacts.

12in (30.5cm) high

£1,100-1,500 DRA

A North Dakota School of Mines glazed earthenware vase, by Margaret Cable, blue 'NDSM' stamp, signed 'MKC 1917/#41'.

1917 8½in (21.5cm) high

£7,000-8,000 DRA

A North Dakota School of Mines vase, by Julia Mattson, Grand Forks, ND, blue 'NDSM' stamp, incised 'JM 466'.

1930 4½in (11.5cm) diam

£1,200-1,600 DRA

A rare Redlands Pottery burnished earthenware covered jar, with lizard, marked.

c1905 3in (7.5cm) wide

£8,000-9,000 DRA

A 1900s porcelain vase, by Adelaide Robineau (1865-1929), with crystalline glaze, carved 'AR 4 III/X'.

2½in (6.5cm) high

£4,000-5,000 DRA

A Rorstrand glazed earthenware floor vase, by Alf Wallander (1862-1914), triple crown mark, marked 'A. WALLANDER/99', minor scratches.

This was possibly an exhibition piece.

c1899 29½in (75cm) high

£4,000-5,000 DRA

An early 20thC Rosenthal figurine, marked 'Ferd Liebermann'.

14¼in (36cm) high

£1,000-1,400 **PSA**

A pair of Royal Dux Bohemia porcelain figures, by Edward Eichler, pink triangle, the male impressed '1183', the female '1184'.

max 31in (79cm) high

£400-500 **BE**

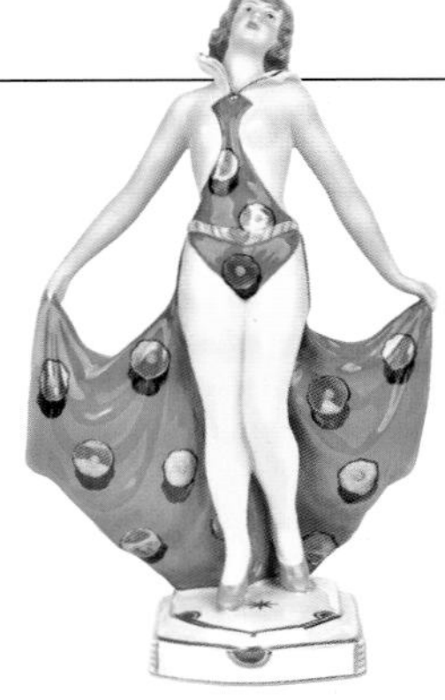

A Royal Dux dancing girl, by Elly Strobach, with pink triangle, impressed and printed marks.

c1925 *11¾in (30cm) high*

£600-700 **BELL**

A Royal Dux porcelain figure, pink triangle mark, impressed 'CZECHOSLOVAKIA/3268/2'.

c1930 *12¼in (31cm) high*

£1,000-1,500 **L&T**

An Art Deco Royal Dux group, no.3046, red triangle mark, impressed marks.

14½in (37cm) high

£500-600 **DUK**

A 1930s Royal Worcester figurine, 'Bubbles', by Freda Doughty, modelled as a young girl holding up a glass bubble with a basket of bubbles by her side, puce mark with date code, painted title.

1938 *7in (18cm) high*

£250-300 **FLD**

An Art Nouveau Rozenburg egg-shell porcelain vase, painted by S. Schellink, printed factory marks, painted marks and artist's cipher.

3¼in (8cm) high

£1,800-2,200 **WW**

An Art Nouveau Rozenburg egg-shell porcelain plate, painted by S. Schellink, printed factory mark, painted marks, artist's cipher.

6½in (16.5cm) diam

£2,000-2,500 **WW**

Judith Picks

Saturday Evening Girls pieces such as this sprung from a club founded in Boston in 1899 by librarian Edith Guerrier. Guerrier wanted to educate poor young women in the liberal arts and provide them with a safe and skilled way of earning a living. With the help of Helen Storrow and Edith Brown, by 1908 the Saturday Evening Club had become the Paul Revere Pottery Club.

The pieces made by the Saturday Evening Girls are, like this vase, simple and elegant in design, often making use of natural imagery. Patterns were applied with cuerda seca (Spanish for 'dry cord'), a method using thin lines of grease to prevent coloured glazes from running into one another.

A Saturday Evening Girls vase, Paul Revere stamp 'DECEMBER 1930 SR', marked 'BSE', some misses to glaze.

1930 *13½in (34.5cm) high*

£14,000-20,000 **DRA**

A Saturday Evening Girls vase, by Fannie Levine, signed and dated.
1921 *8¼in (21cm) high*
£5,500-6,500 **DRA**

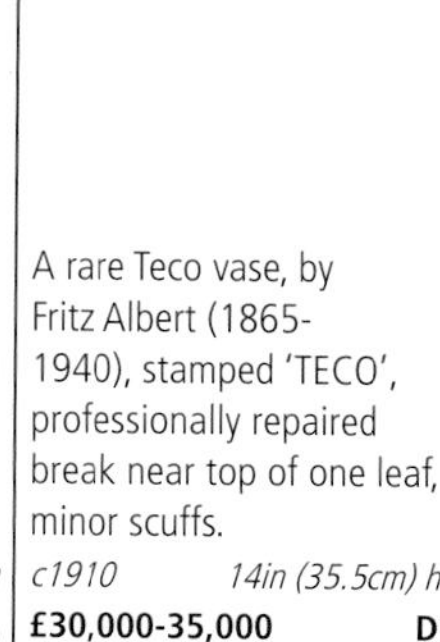

A Teco reticulated vase, stamped 'TECO'.

The American Terra Cotta Tile and Ceramic Company, or Teco, was founded in 1881 and based in Terra Cotta, Illinois.

c1905 *11¾in (30cm) high*
£4,500-5,500 **DRA**

A rare Teco vase, by Fritz Albert (1865-1940), stamped 'TECO', professionally repaired break near top of one leaf, minor scuffs.
c1910 *14in (35.5cm) high*
£30,000-35,000 **DRA**

A Teco vase, in a rare semi-matt green crystalline glaze, stamped 'TECO', restoration to one petal.
c1910 *12in (30.5cm) high*
£2,500-3,000 **DRA**

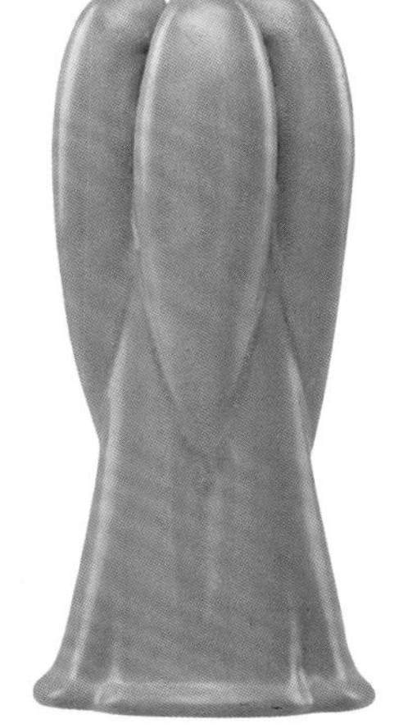

A Teco blue lobed vase, stamped 'TECO', glaze fleck, short line to rim.
c1910 *9in (23cm) high*
£800-900 **DRA**

A Tiffany Studios Favrile pottery vase, incised 'LCT', minor dark scuffs.
1904-19 *12¼in (31cm) high*
£7,500-8,500 **DRA**

A Charles Vyse model of a Pekingese dog, in tenmoku brown glaze, incised 'Charles Vyse Chelsea'.
6¾in (17cm) wide
£2,200-2,600 **WW**

A Chelsea pottery figure, 'The Tulip Woman', by Charles Vyse, initialled, marked 'Chelsea', some losses, the base stained, some crazing, dated.
1921 *10¾in (27.5cm) high*
£400-500 **CHEF**

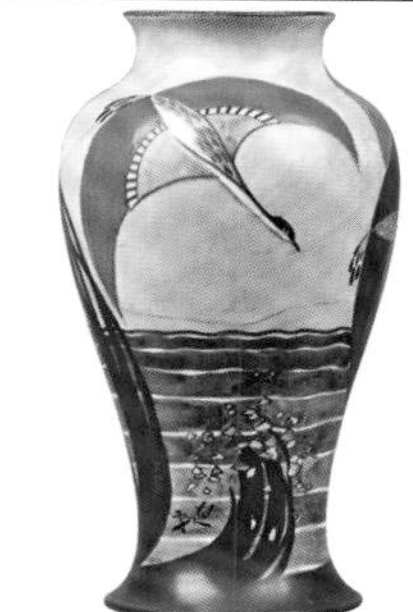

An Art Deco Wilkinson vase, by John Butler, 'Tahiti foam' pattern, signed, with painted and printed marks, some crazing.
14¼in (36cm) high
£300-400 **BELL**

A vessel, by Michael Cardew (1901-83), marks for Cardew and St Ives pottery.

This piece was made when Cardew was working with Bernard Leach.

c1922 *8¼in (21cm) high*

£1,300-1,600 CHOR

A tin-glazed Wenford Bridge pottery plate, by Michael Cardew, impressed seal marks.

9¾in (25cm) diam

£600-700 WW

A pair of Compton Pottery garden urns, designed by Archibald Knox (1864-1933), for Liberty & Co., mark, one missing a handle, large chips to rims.

c1900 *29½in (75cm) wide*

£2,200-2,800 GORL

A Compton Pottery terracotta jardinière, designed by Archibald Knox, for Liberty & Co.

c1905 *23¾in (60.5cm) high*

£900-1,100 ROS

The Compton Pottery was an Arts Guild founded in the village of Compton in 1900 by Mary Watts (1849-1938). Its work was stocked by Liberty & Co. After the death of its founder, the Guild continued until 1956.

A slab-built vase, by Shoji Hamada (1894-1978), wax-resist decorated in tenmoku over pale celadon.

7¾in (19.5cm) high

£4,000-5,000 WW

A St Ives Pottery stoneware 'Leaping Salmon' vase, by Bernard Leach (1887-1979), painted in tenmoku on a grey glaze, impressed seal marks.

11½in (29.5cm) high

£9,500-11,000 WW

A St Ives Pottery plate, by Bernard Leach, painted in blue and tenmoku on a celadon ground, with tenmoku rim, impressed seal mark and painted 'BL' monogram.

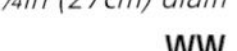

10¾in (27cm) diam

£2,000-3,000 WW

A St Ives Pottery stoneware slab vase, by Bernard Leach (1887-1979), with tenmoku glaze, impressed 'BL' and 'Leach Pottery' seals under foot.

7¾in (20cm) high

£2,200-2,800 L&T

A stoneware 'Aulos', by William Staite Murray (1881-1962), impressed seal mark, painted 'MA2', museum repair to one handle.

10¾in (27.5cm) high

£1,400-1,800 WW

A stoneware vase, by Katherine Pleydell-Bouverie (1895-1985), impressed seal mark.

8½in (21.5cm) high

£900-1,100 WW

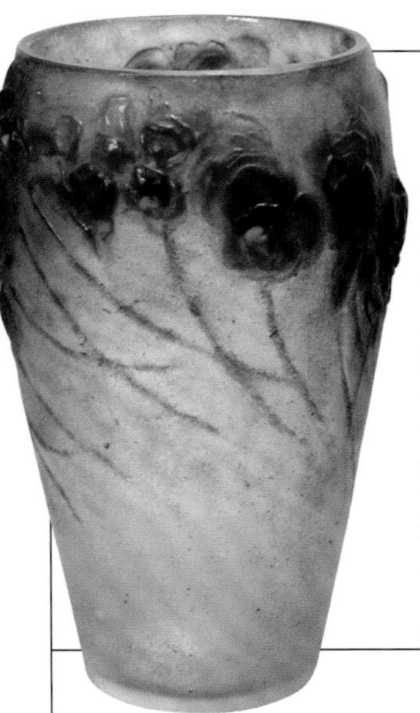

A pâte-de-verre glass 'Parma Violets' pattern vase, by Gabriel Argy-Rousseau, signed, 'FRANCE' to base.

Gabriel Argy-Rousseau (1885-1953) was a prominent glass artist and founder of the Société Anonyme des Pâtes de Verre d'Argy-Rousseau. The firm produced a range of Art Nouveau and Art Deco pieces, many using the technique of pâte-de-verre.

introduced 1918 *6in (15cm) high*

£5,000-6,000 CHEF

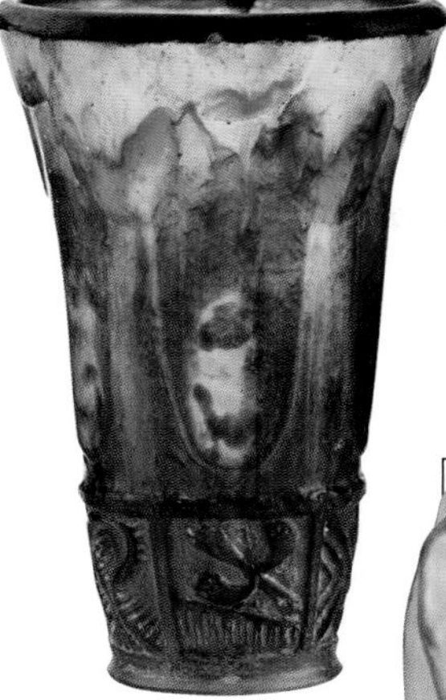

A pâte-de-verre glass vase, by Gabriel Argy-Rousseau, moulded mark 'G. ARGY-ROUSSEAU'.

c1920 *7¾in (19.5cm) high*

£1,800-2,200 L&T

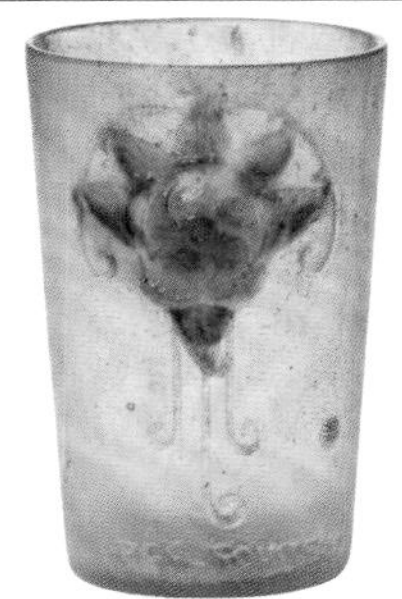

A liqueur glass, by Gabriel Argy-Rousseau, signed 'Argy-Rousseau'.

1922 *2¼in (5.5cm) high*

£750-800 ROS

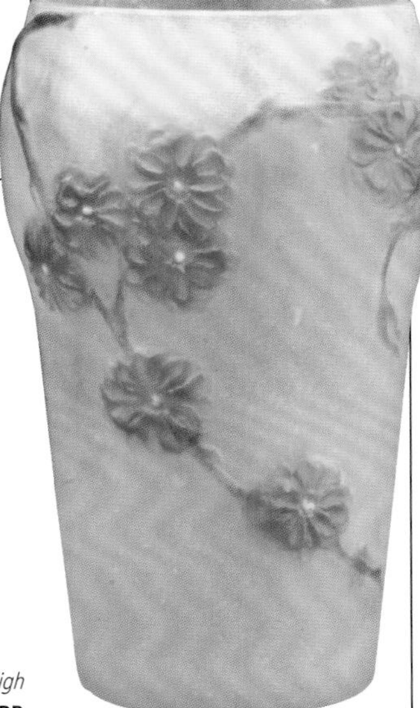

A pâte-de-verre vase, by Gabriel Argy-Rousseau, with moulded prunus blossoms, signed 'G. Argy-Rousseau' and '5487'.

6½in (16.5cm) high

£4,500-5,000 MORP

A small pâte-de-cristal 'Blackberries' bowl, by Gabriel Argy-Rousseau, signed 'G Argy-Rousseau'.

c1914 *4in (10cm) diam*

£650-750 ROS

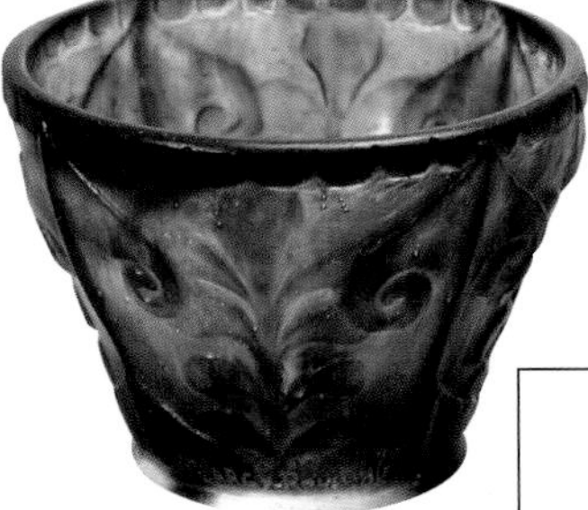

A pâte-de-verre glass bowl, by Gabriel Argy-Rousseau, signed in the mould.

introduced 1925 *4in (10cm) wide*

£1,200-1,600 CHEF

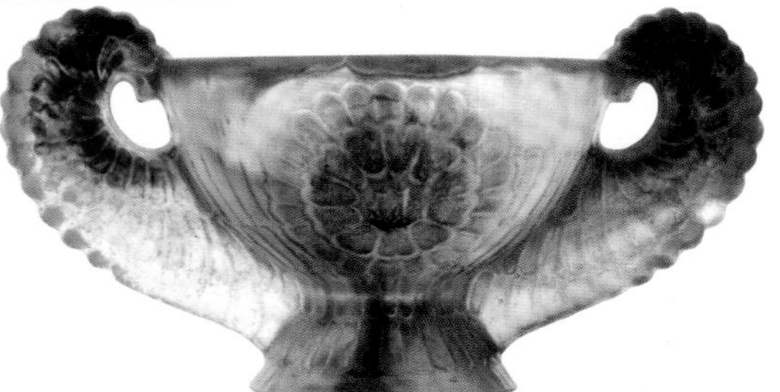

A pâte-de-verre glass bowl, by Gabriel Argy-Rousseau, signed, some damages.

c1927 *8¼in (21cm) wide*

£1,300-1,600 FLD

An enamelled glass bowl, by Gabriel Argy Rousseau, decorated with deer, gilt signature, some scratches and wear.

7¾in (19.5cm) wide

£1,100-1,500 CHEF

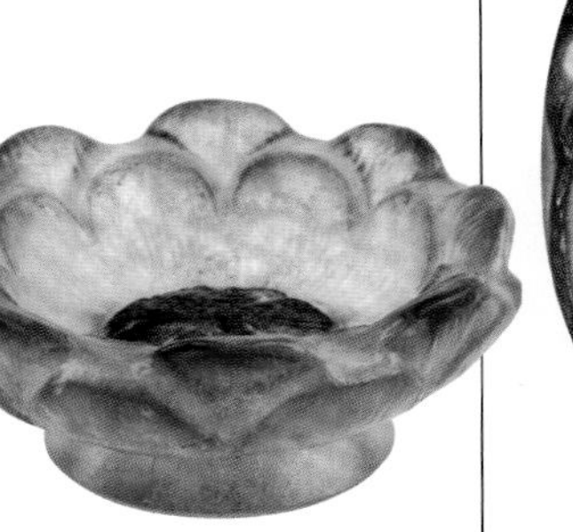

A pâte-de-verre 'fleur ouverte' ashtray, by Gabriel Argy-Rousseau, with dark grey fusions, signed 'G. ARGY-ROUSSEAU'.

1924 *3¾in (9.5cm) diam*

£1,500-2,000 QU

A pâte-de-verre 'Edelweiss' pendant, by Gabriel Argy-Rousseau, marked 'G.A.R', with three holes for cord and tassel.

1924 *2¾in (7cm) high*

£1,200-1,600 QU

ESSENTIAL REFERENCE – DAUM

The Daum glassworks was founded in 1878 in Nancy, France, by Jean Daum. His sons Auguste and Antonin Daum took over the factory in 1890s. Daum is still active today.

- **The brothers focused on art glass, introducing their cameo glass wares at the Chicago World Fair in 1893. Cameo glass is a technique where multiple layers of glass are carved to achieve a design in low relief.**
- **Alongside cameo glass, the Daum brothers used a range of techniques, including acid-etching, wheel-turning, pâte-de-verre (where crushed glass is packed into moulds and fused in a kiln) and 'intercalaire' (where powdered glass is sealed between layers of glass).**
- **The Daum brothers were inspired by the Art Nouveau and later Art Deco movements, and combined these influences with natural imagery and Asian and Far Eastern inspiration. They were also greatly influenced by the work of Émile Gallé.**

A Daum 'Pluviose' or 'Une pluie' vase, by Henri Bergé, etched with birches in the rain, signed 'DAUM NANCY' with Cross of Lorraine.
1900 *3¼in (8.5cm) high*
£3,500-4,000 QU

A Daum enamelled glass vase, with winter landscape, signed.
c1905 *4¾in (12cm) high*
£1,800-2,200 K&O

A Daum 'Winter Scene' vase, with a cameo and enamel scene, signed 'Daum Nancy' with Cross of Lorraine.
14½in (37cm) high
£6,500-7,500 JDJ

A Daum 'Neige, Corbeaux' vase, with a winter landscape with ravens, signed 'Daum Nancy' with Cross of Lorraine.
1905 *4½in (11.5cm) high*
£5,500-6,500 QU

A Daum 'Iris et Papillon' vase, with silver mounts, signed 'Daum Nancy' with Cross of Lorraine, with Head of Minerva and maker's mark.
1893 *8½in (21.5cm) high*
£2,500-3,000 QU

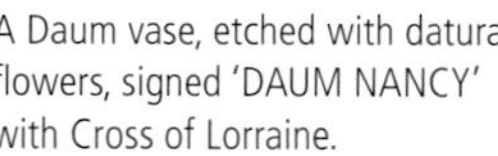

A Daum vase, etched with datura flowers, signed 'DAUM NANCY' with Cross of Lorraine.
c1900 *15¾in (40cm) high*
£7,000-8,000 FIS

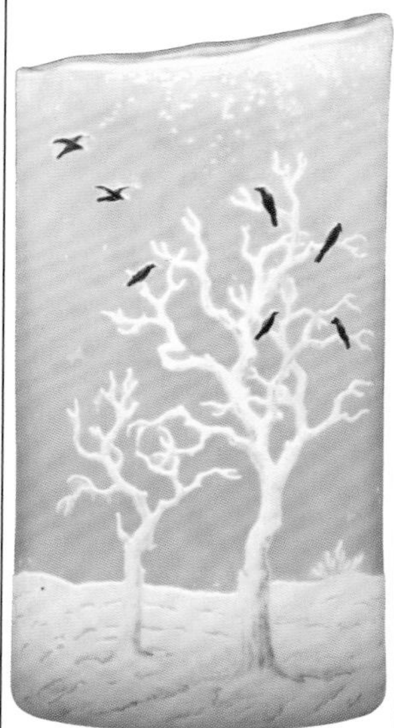

A Daum cameo and enamelled 'Blackbird' vase, etched 'Daum Nancy' with Cross of Lorraine.
6¼in (16cm) high
£9,500-11,000 MORP

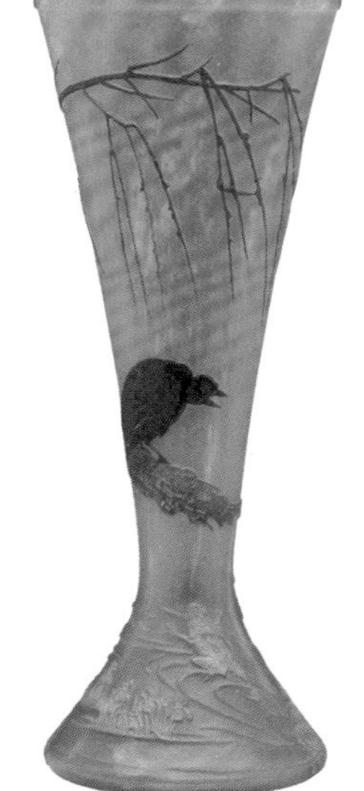

A rare Daum 'Corbeau et Grenouille' (raven and frog) cameo vase, signed 'Daum Nancy' with Cross of Lorraine.
14in (35.5cm) high
£12,000-15,000 JDJ

A Daum vase, with lady's slipper orchids, spiderwebs and bees, acid-etched 'DAUM NANCY' with Cross of Lorraine, minor losses to gilding, one fleck to rim.
c1900 *21in (53.5cm) high*
£6,500-7,000 DRA

An early 20thC Daum cameo vase, with dogwood blossoms, signed in cameo, some bubbles.
7¾in (20cm) high
£850-950 DRA

An early 20thC Daum acid-etched vase, wheel-carved signature, chip to inner rim.

7in (18cm) high

£6,000-7,000 **DRA**

A Daum vase, etched in relief, signed 'DAUM NANCY FRANCE' with Cross of Lorraine.

c1910 *19in (48cm) high*

£5,000-6,000 **FIS**

CLOSER LOOK – DAUM 'CROCUS' VASE

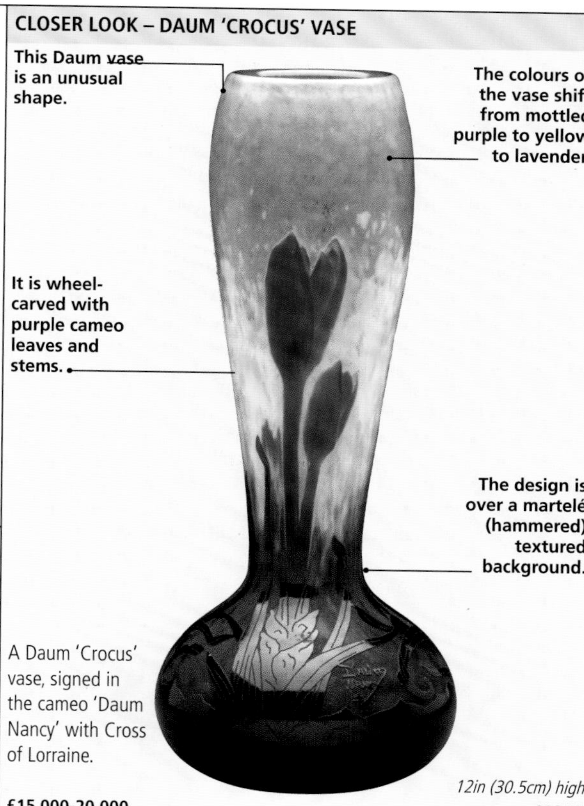

This Daum vase is an unusual shape.

The colours of the vase shift from mottled purple to yellow to lavender.

It is wheel-carved with purple cameo leaves and stems.

The design is over a martelé (hammered) textured background.

A Daum 'Crocus' vase, signed in the cameo 'Daum Nancy' with Cross of Lorraine.

12in (30.5cm) high

£15,000-20,000 **MORP**

An early 20thC Daum acid-etched cameo vase, signed in cameo.

3in (7.5cm) high

£1,000-1,400 **DRA**

A Daum vase, etched in flat relief with primroses, etched 'DAUM NANCY FRANCE' with Cross of Lorraine.

c1910-15 *11in (28cm) high*

£5,500-6,500 **FIS**

A Daum vase, etched with tobacco plants, signed 'DAUM NANCY' with Cross of Lorraine, etched '73'.

c1914 *12½in (32cm) high*

£3,500-4,500 **FIS**

A Daum cameo glass 'Geranium' vase, etched signature 'Daum/ Nancy' with the Cross of Lorraine.

8in (20.5cm) high

£4,000-5,000 **CLAR**

A Daum 'Libellules et Renoncules Jaunes' vase, by Henri Bergé and Ernest Schneider, signed 'DAUM NANCY' with Cross of Lorraine.

c1904 *7¾in (20cm) high*

£8,000-9,000 **QU**

A late 19thC Daum pitcher, acid-etched, gilded and enamelled internally with nightshade, gilt signature, minor losses to gilding.

5½in (14cm) high

£3,000-3,500 **DRA**

A Daum acid-etched cameo glass 'Mushroom' pitcher, etched with maker's mark.

c1900 *5¼in (13.5cm) high*

£6,000-6,500 **CA**

ESSENTIAL REFERENCE – ÉMILE GALLÉ

Émile Gallé (1846-1904) was an important Art Nouveau glass designer.

- **He was born in Nancy, France, and studied botany, chemistry, philosophy, art and glass-making before joining his father's factory.**
- **He founded his own studio in 1873. Early works were usually clear glass with gilded or enamelled decoration.**
- **In 1878 Gallé visited the International Exhibition in Paris, and was impressed by the cameo glass of English makers Joseph Locke and John Northwood. He switched his own focus to cameo glass, with great success.**
- **His factory continued after his death in 1904, run by his widow and son-in-law until 1936.**

A Gallé 'Indien' vase, signed 'E. Gallé Nancy'.
c1875 *7½in (19cm) diam*
£4,500-5,500 QU

A Gallé 'Cerfeuil hérisse' vase, with etched, painted and enamelled decoration, signed 'E. Gallé Nancy'.
c1889-95 *5in (12.5cm) high*
£4,000-5,000 QU

A late 19thC Gallé vase, enamelled with purple irises, enamel signature.
c1890 *8in (20.5cm) high*
£2,500-3,000 FLD

A pair of late 19thC Gallé Japonesque bottles, enamelled and gilded, foot of one reduced, minor flecks to stoppers.
8¾in (22cm) high
£20,000-25,000 DRA

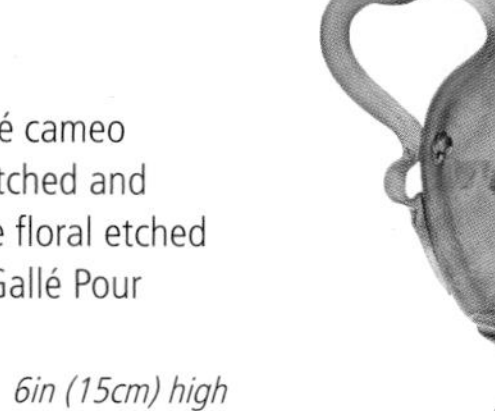

A late 19thC Gallé cameo glass vase, acid-etched and enamelled, ornate floral etched signature 'Émile Gallé Pour bonheur'.
6in (15cm) high
£8,500-9,500 DRA

A Gallé vase, marbled in brown, black and violet, with algae, shells and sea life engraved in relief.
c1895 *11in (28cm) high*
£35,000-40,000 FIS

A late 19thC to early 20thC Gallé cameo vase, acid-etched and fire-polished with an aquatic scene, signed in cameo, tiny flecks to rim.
9½in (24cm) high
£7,500-8,500 DRA

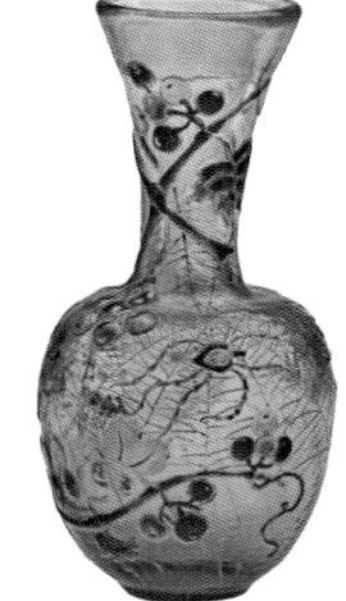

A late 19thC Gallé bud vase, acid-etched, enamelled and martelé-decorated, etched signature.
5½in (14cm) high
£3,500-4,000 DRA

A Gallé vase, inscribed 'LES ARBRES SE PARLENT TOUT BAS', signed 'Gallé'.

The quote is from Victor Hugo's poem 'Aux Arbres' and translates as 'the trees speak to each other'.
c1900 *18in (46cm) high*
£4,500-5,500 QU

An early 20thC Gallé cameo vase, acid-etched with poppies, signed in cameo, some scuffs.

24¾in (63cm) high

£9,000-10,000 **DRA**

A Gallé vase, with marquetry crocus flowers and stems, with etched Asian-style signature 'Gallé' and 'Etude', some stress lines.

8½in (21.5cm) high

£9,000-10,000 **MORP**

An early 20thC Gallé cameo vase, acid-etched with roses, signed in cameo.

14½in (37cm) high

£1,100-1,500 **DRA**

An early 20thC Gallé oleander acid-etched cameo vase, signed in cameo, minor scuffs, metal transfer marks.

18in (45.5cm) high

£4,000-5,000 **DRA**

A 1920s Gallé 'Le Lac de Côme le Soir' (Lake Como at Night) vase, signed 'Gallé'.

14in (35.5cm) high

£20,000-25,000 **QU**

A 1920s Gallé lemon-yellow soufflé vase, with plums and leafy branches, signed.

12½in (32cm) high

£7,000-8,000 **FIS**

A Gallé cameo Japanese cherry blossom vase, signed with ornate Asian-style signature 'Gallé'.

15in (38cm) high

£4,500-5,500 **JDJ**

A Gallé boat-shaped cameo vase, signed 'Gallé'.

7½in (19cm) long

£2,000-2,500 **JDJ**

A Gallé tulip-shaped bowl, acid-etched, fire-polished and gilded, gilt signature to base, some losses to gilding.

c1900 *8¼in (21cm) wide*

£6,500-7,500 **DRA**

A Lalique clear and frosted electric blue glass 'Perruches' vase, no.876, etched 'R. Lalique France', some flecks.

designed 1919 *10in (25.5cm) high*

£11,000-14,000 **DRA**

A Lalique cased glass 'Poissons' vase, moulded 'R. LALIQUE', etched 'R. Lalique FRANCE', minor bubbles, some flecks and chips.

designed 1921 *10in (25.5cm) wide*

£10,000-14,000 **DRA**

A Lalique clear and frosted glass 'Acanthes' vase, etched 'R. Lalique France', some bubbles.

designed 1921 *11¼in (28.5cm) high*

£9,500-11,000 **DRA**

A Lalique cased glass 'Druide' vase, etched 'R. Lalique France No.937', rim uneven, residue to interior.

designed 1924 *7¾in (20cm) wide*

£3,500-4,000 **DRA**

CLOSER LOOK – 'MARTIN-PÊCHEURS'

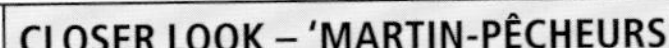

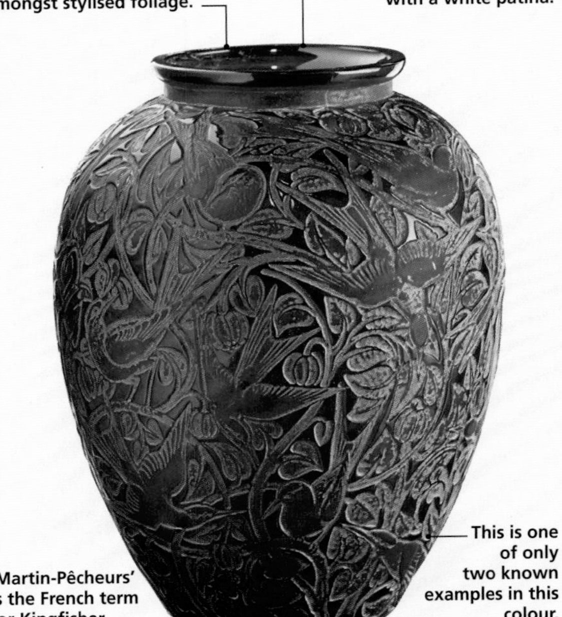

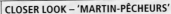

This vase is moulded with birds amongst stylised foliage.

It is made of blue-violet glass, with a white patina.

'Martin-Pêcheurs' is the French term for Kingfisher.

This is one of only two known examples in this colour.

A Lalique glass 'Martin-Pêcheurs' vase, no.920, moulded 'R. LALIQUE', some nicks.

designed 1923 *9½in (24cm) high*

£20,000-25,000 **DRA**

A Lalique amber glass 'Sophorai' vase, with white patina, etched 'R. Lalique France No.977', some burst bubbles.

designed 1926 *9½in (24cm) high*

£9,000-11,000 **DRA**

A rare Lalique Alexandrite glass 'Tortues' vase, no.966, moulded 'R. Lalique', stencilled 'R. LALIQUE FRANCE', flecks to base.

designed 1926 *10½in (26.5cm) high*

£25,000-30,000 **DRA**

A Lalique 'Salmonides' vase, with blue-grey patina, acid-stamped 'R. LALIQUE FRANCE'.

designed 1928 *11½in (29cm) high*

£15,000-20,000 **DRA**

A Lalique glass 'Milan' vase, acid-stamped 'R. LALIQUE', some scratches near base.

designed 1929 11¼in (28.5cm) high

£11,000-15,000 **DRA**

A Lalique cased glass 'Espalion' vase, etched 'R. Lalique mark' and numbered '996'.

7in (18cm) high

£5,000-6,000 **CHEF**

A Lalique frosted glass 'Dahlias' vase, no.938, with black enamel accents, stamped 'R. LALIQUE FRANCE'.
c1923 *7in (17.5cm) wide*
£1,100-1,500 **CLAR**

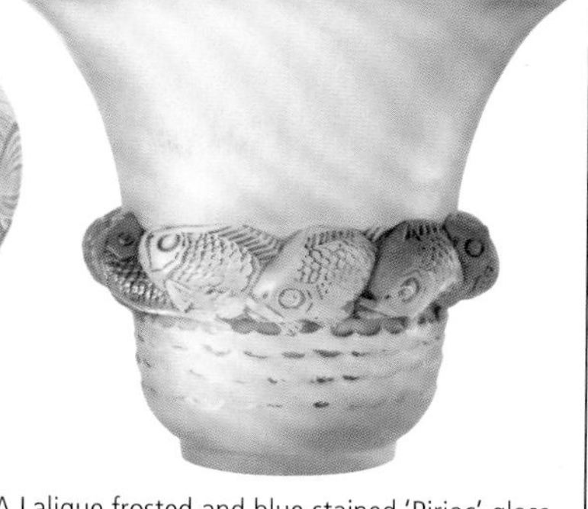

A Lalique frosted and blue stained 'Piriac' glass vase, no.1043, wheel cut 'R LALIQUE FRANCE'.
designed 1930 *7in (18cm) high*
£1,100-1,500 **TEN**

A Lalique 'Silènes' vase, etched 'R. Lalique France', paint transfer to edge of base.
designed 1938 *8in (20.5cm) high*
£2,000-2,500 **DRA**

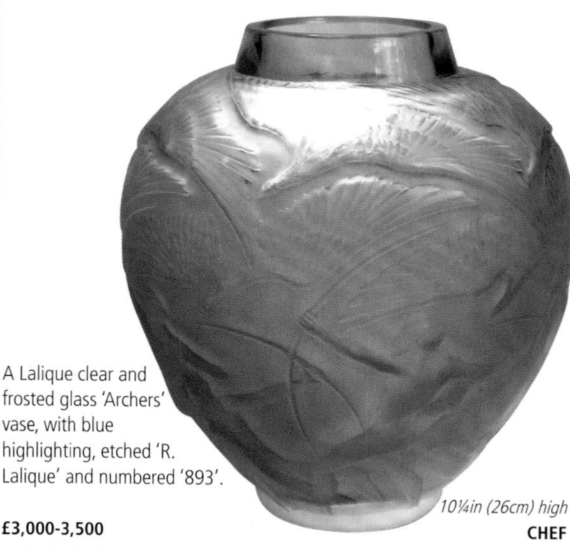

A Lalique clear and frosted glass 'Archers' vase, with blue highlighting, etched 'R. Lalique' and numbered '893'.
10¼in (26cm) high
£3,000-3,500 **CHEF**

A Lalique opalescent glass 'Formose' vase, engraved mark 'R. Lalique France No. 934', one surface chip.
7in (17.5cm) high
£1,800-2,200 **GORL**

A Lalique opalescent glass 'Davos' vase, wheel-engraved mark, some scratches.
11in (28cm) high
£2,200-3,000 **DN**

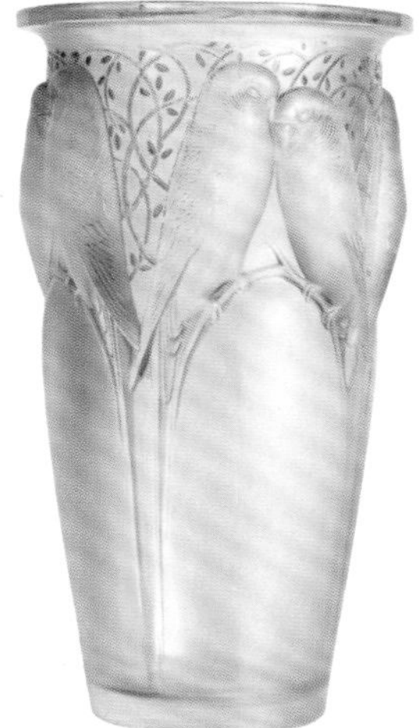

A Lalique opalescent, stained and frosted 'Ceylan' glass vase, no.905, wheel cut mark 'R LALIQUE FRANCE', etched '905'.
9¾in (25cm) high
£4,000-5,000 **TEN**

A Lalique frosted glass 'Bacchantes' vase, engraved 'Lalique, France'.
9½in (24cm) high
£1,500-2,000 **JN**

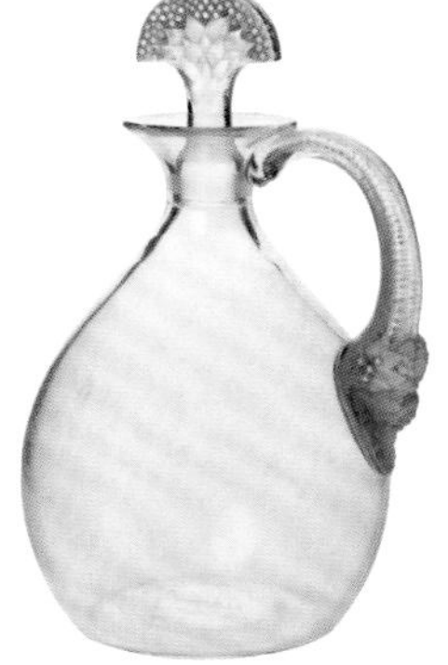

A Lalique decanter and stopper, 'Satyre', no.3167, with sepia staining, stencil acid mark 'R. Lalique'.
designed 1923 *9¾in (25cm) high*
£800-900 **ROS**

A Lalique clear and frosted glass car mascot, 'St Christopher', no.1142, remains of sepia staining, intaglio 'R. Lalique France'.
4¾in (12cm) high
£1,000-1,400 **WW**

ESSENTIAL REFERENCE – LOETZ

Loetz was a significant 19thC and early 20thC Bohemian glass manufacturer.

- **In 1852 a glassworks factory in Klostermühle, Bohemia, was acquired by Susanne Loetz, widow of the glassmaker Johann Loetz. The factory became known as Loetz Witwe (Loetz Widow) and later just as Loetz.**
- **In 1879 it was taken over by Max Ritter von Spaun, whose innovative ideas and strong team of designers made Loetz one of Central Europe's largest glassmakers by the turn of the century.**
- **Many Loetz pieces use iridescence and Art Nouveau decoration.**
- **The factory closed in 1947.**

A Loetz red to cream vase, enamelled with blooming dogwood, enameller's marks to base.
c1888 *9in (23cm) high*
£450-550 **M&DM**

A pair of early Loetz blue opal pieced top vases, with floral enamel and gilding.
c1890 *9in (23cm) high*
£600-700 **M&DM**

A pair of Loetz 'Octopus' vase, 'Federzeichnung' pattern with gilded tracery, inscribed 'Patent' to base, losses to gilding.
c1887 *6¼in (16cm) high*
£2,000-2,500 **POOK**

A Loetz 'Rubin Phaenomen Gre 8100' vase, with iridescence, engraved to base 'Loetz Austria'.
1899 *6¾in (17cm) high*
£8,500-9,500 **FIS**

A Loetz blown glass vase, with silver floral overlay, some burst bubbles.
c1900 *7½in (19cm) high*
£4,500-5,500 **DRA**

A Loetz 'Papillon' (butterfly wing) vase, made for Max Emanuel, London, after a design by Christopher Dresser.
c1900 *6in (15cm) high*
£300-400 **M&DM**

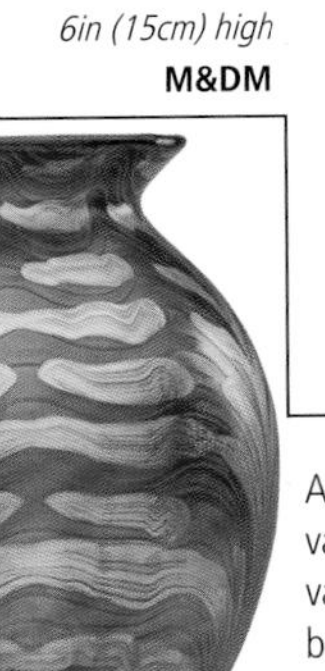

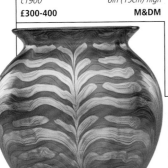

A Loetz 'Phaenomen Gre 2/450' vase, in rare pink or 'rosalin' colour variant, etched 'Loetz Austria' to base, tiny burst bubble.
c1900 *7in (18cm) high*
£4,000-5,000 **DRA**

A Loetz candia (gold-green) 'Phaenomen' vase, no.7506, signed 'Loetz Austria'.
c1900 *7½in (19cm) high*
£1,800-2,200 **M&DM**

A Loetz 'Phaenomen' vase, with iridescent decoration, signed 'Loetz Austria'.
9½in (24cm) high
£10,000-12,000 **MORP**

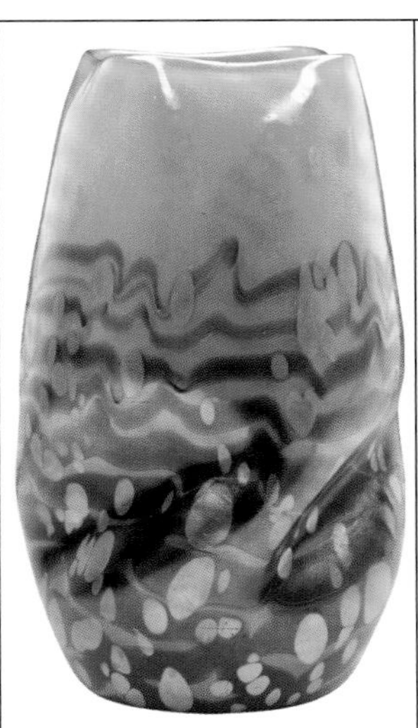

A Loetz 'Cytisus' vase, with wavy band pattern and iridescent oil spots, unsigned.
c1902 *7¾in (20cm) high*
£3,500-4,000 **JDJ**

A Loetz 'Cytisus' green, pink and red iridescent vase.
1902 *14¼in (36.5cm) high*
£2,000-2,500 **FIS**

An early 20thC Loetz iridescent glass vase, etched 'Loetz Austria'.
8¾in (22cm) high
£550-650 **LSK**

A Loetz 'Titania' vase, with green metallic threads between two layers of glass, fleabite to rim.
c1907 *7½in (19cm) high*
£1,500-2,000 **MORP**

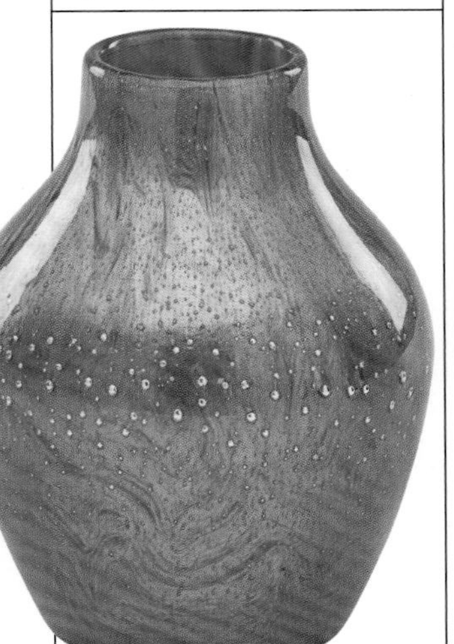

A Loetz 'Titania Perl' vase, attributed to Otto Prutscher (1880-1949).
c1908 *7in (18cm) high*
£4,000-5,000 **DRA**

A Loetz vase, designed by Josef Hoffmann, overlaid etched violet floral decoration on a blue opal ground.
c1911 *8in (20.5cm) high*
£23,000-30,000 **FIS**

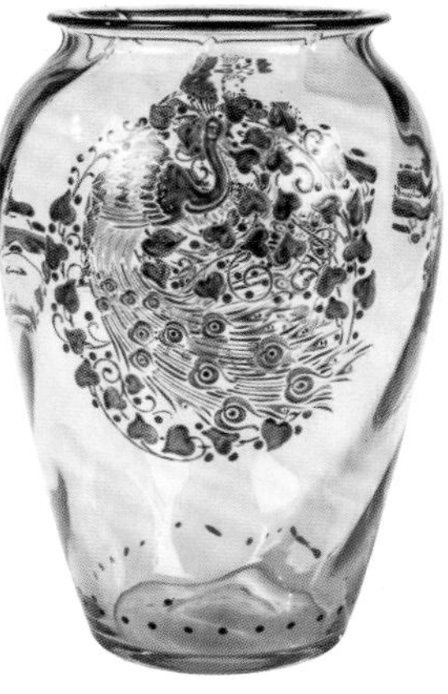

A Loetz vase, designed by Adolf Beckert, painted by Franz Wilms, enamelled with a peacock design.
1911 *11in (28cm) high*
£4,000-5,000 **FIS**

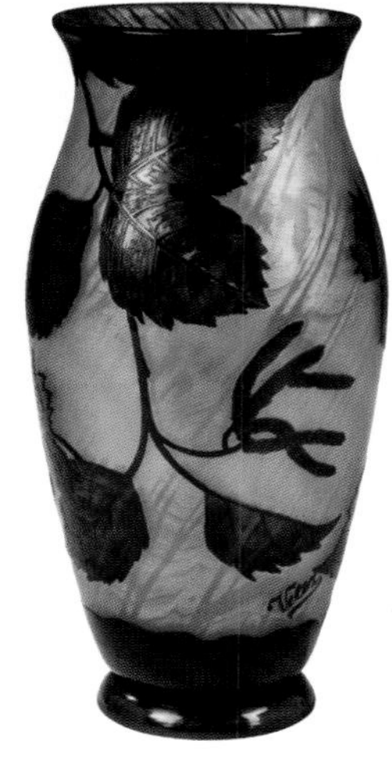

A Loetz vase, etched with a hazelnut branch, etched 'Velez'.
c1925 *8¾in (22.5cm) high*
£1,300-1,800 **FIS**

A Loetz red on uranium green cameo panel rose vase.
c1925 *7in (18cm) high*
£1,200-1,500 **M&DM**

A pair of Loetz 'Blau an Kamelienrot' vases.

This is a newly discovered Loetz design.
c1925 *11in (28cm) high*
£2,250-2,750 **M&DM**

A Monart 'Paisley Shawl' glass vase, shape C, with slight iridescence, remains of paper label 'V.C.55'.

8¾in (22.5cm) high

£800-900 **ROS**

A Monart cased 'Cloisonné' glass vase, shape C.

7¼in (18.5cm) high

£500-600 **ROS**

A Monart vase, shape GA, size VI.

c1935 *6in (15cm) high*

£300-400 **M&DM**

A Monart glass vase, with mottled green graduating to blue with purple whorls and aventurine inclusions.

9¾in (25cm) high

£400-500 **WW**

A Monart vase, shape N, size VI.

c1935 *9in (23cm) high*

£400-500 **M&DM**

A Monart vase, shape OE, size VI.

c1935 *9in (23cm) high*

£350-450 **M&DM**

A 1930s Monart glass vase, in red and blue mottled glass with bubble inclusions, with maker's label and label for the 'Parkington Collection/427/Christie's'.

10¼in (26cm) high

£1,100-1,500 **L&T**

A Monart 'Paisley Shawl' bowl, shape MC, size III.

c1935 *13in (33cm) diam*

£800-900 **M&DM**

A 1930s Monart glass vase, 'Stoneware' pattern, with a lustre sheen, with a label for 'The Parkington Collection/429/Christie's'.

9¾in (24.5cm) high

£650-750 **L&T**

A Monart glass decanter with stopper and five glasses, printed 'Monart' label, all marked 'QC-XI'.

decanter 11¼in (28.5cm) high

£850-950 **ROS**

A Moser green to clear 'cut out' intaglio cut vase, with poppies and irises.

c1905 *13in (33cm) high*

£1,800-2,200 **M&DM**

An early 20thC Moser marquetry vase, wheel-carved cameo glass, etched manufacturer and artist marks, some flecks and chips.

6½in (16.5cm) high

£800-900 **DRA**

A 1920s Moser glass vase, with a gilt Oroplastic band of Classical figures, etched mark, scratches to base.

10½in (26.5cm) high

£220-300 **DN**

A Moser 'Alexandrit' vase, designed by Heinrich Hussmann, signed 'Moser Alexandrit'.

c1929 *13in (33cm) high*

£500-600 **M&DM**

A Moser 'Lion Hunt' vase, by Gustav Moser-Millot, signed 'Moser', with original 'Moser-Millot' shop label.

This vase was designed for the Paris 1937 Exhibition and available after exclusively from the Paris Moser shop.

c1937 *10in (25.5cm) high*

£800-1,000 **M&DM**

A Moser 'Alexandrit' decanter and stopper, signed 'Moser Alexandrit'

Alexandrit is a type of glass used by Moser where the colour changes depending on light, shifting from purple to blue.

c1929

£500-600 **M&DM**

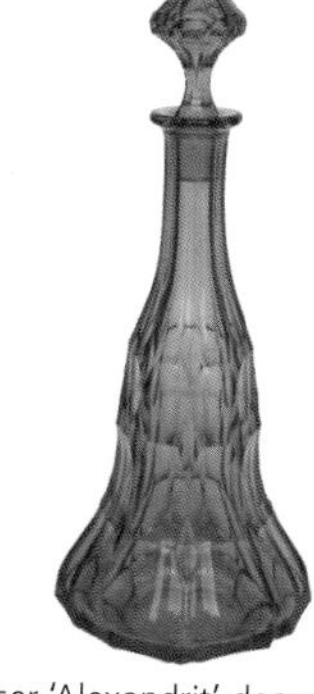

A Moser 'Alexandrit' decanter and stopper, designed by Heinrich Hussmann, signed 'Moser Alexandrit'.

c1929 *14in (35.5cm) high*

£500-600 **M&DM**

A 1930s Moser glass decanter, with a facet-cut spire stopper, acid-marked.

17¾in (45cm) high

£250-300 **FLD**

A set of eight Moser green to clear wine glasses, enamelled and applied jewels.

1897 *5in (12.5cm) high*

£1,000-1,200 **M&DM**

ESSENTIAL REFERENCE – ERCOLE BAROVIER

Ercole Barovier (1889-1974) joined his father's company, Artisti Barovier, in 1919 at the age of thirty, giving up a career as a doctor to focus on art glass.

- **He became artistic director of the firm in 1926 and took over management in 1936. After the company's merger with Ferro-Toso in 1942, he remained artistic director until 1972.**
- **Over his career, he experimented with original and innovative methods, inventing new formulas and dies and perfecting new techniques to create impressive works of art glass.**
- **His memorable pieces included murine vessels, his 1929 'Primavera' series, his 1930s 'Crepuscolo' and 'Marina Gemmata' series, and his 1940s organic textured shapes in thick-walled glass.**

An Artisti Barovier 'Murrine Applicate' vase, cristallo sfumato glass with applied polychrome murrine, signed 'AB' with murrine.
c1918-19 *11¾in (30cm) high*
£50,000-60,000 **WRI**

An Artisti Barovier 'Murrine Floreali' vase, internally-decorated glass with rose and leaf murrine and polychrome threads.
c1920 *11½in (29cm) high*
£25,000-30,000 **WRI**

A Ferro Toso Barovier 'Crepuscolo' glass vase, by Ercole Barovier, with iron wool inclusions.
1935-36 *14in (35.5cm) high*
£7,000-8,000 **QU**

A Ferro Toso Barovier 'Medusa' vase, by Ercole Barovier, of iridised glass with applications.
1938 *18in (46cm) high*
£19,000-24,000 **WRI**

A Barovier & Toso 'Oriente' vase, by Ercole Barovier, cased glass with fused coloured ribbons and dark purple on burst gold foil.
c1940 *11in (28cm) high*
£11,000-15,000 **QU**

A Barovier, Toso & Co. 'Lenti' vase, by Ercole Barovier, with semi-spherical applications and gold leaf.
1940 *9¾in (25cm) wide*
£12,000-16,000 **WRI**

A Vetreria Artistica Barovier & C. 'Crepuscolo' vase, by Ercole Barovier, model no. 14038, with metal inclusions.
c1940 *11½in (29cm) high*
£5,000-6,000 **PHI**

A Barovier & Toso 'A Stelle' vase, by Ercole Barovier.
1942 *14¾in (37.5cm) high*
£4,500-5,500 **QU**

A Barovier Seguso Ferro 'Incamiciato' vase, with applied collar and foot with gold leaf.
c1938 *14¼in (36cm) high*
£14,000-18,000 **WRI**

A Fratelli Toso vase, with multicoloured melted murrins, the surface stained with acid.

c1910 *7in (18cm) high*

£300-400 **FIS**

A monumental incamiciato vase, by C. Maschio, with applied silver-leaf and ribbed pasta di vetro handle.

1932 *16¼in (41cm) high*

£13,000-16,000 **WRI**

A Venini & C. 'Laguna' glass bowl, by Tomaso Buzzi.

1932-33 *9½in (24cm) diam*

£12,000-16,000 **WRI**

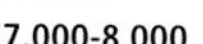

A Venini & C. 'Soffiato' vase, by Napoleone Martinuzzi, model 3044, acid-stamped 'Venini Murano', and 'C.V.M.' with a crown.

c1925-26 *8½in (21.5cm) diam*

£7,000-8,000 **WRI**

A Venini & C. bubbly 'Pulegoso' vase, by Napoleone Martinuzzi, acid-stamped 'venini murano'.

c1930 *14¾in (37.5cm) high*

£6,500-7,500 **QU**

ESSENTIAL REFERENCE – VENINI & C.

Venini & C. was an important Murano glassworks throughout the 20thC. Today it is owned by the Damiani Group.

- **It was founded in 1921 as Cappellin Venini & C. by Milanese lawyer Paolo Venini and antiques dealer Cappellin. Cappellin left the company a few years later.**
- **After much success in the 1920s-30s, Venini & C. went on to become one of the leading post-war Italian glassworks.**
- **Its important designers included Vittorio Zecchin (1878-1947), Gio Ponti (1891-1979), Naopoleone Martnuzzi (1892-1977), Tomaso Buzzi (1900-81) and Carlo Scarpa (1906-78).**

A Venini & C. ribbed pink and clear glass 'Diamante' vase, by Paolo Venini, acid-stamped 'venini murano MADE IN ITALY'.

1934-36 *5in (12.5cm) high*

£700-800 **QU**

A Fratelli Toso 'Rosso e Nero' vase, incamiciato glass with silver-leaf.

c1930 *7¼in (18.5cm) high*

£6,000-7,000 **WRI**

A Venini & C. 'Sommerso a Bollicine' vase, by Carlo Scarpa, with burst gold foil and air bubbles, acid-stamped 'venini murano'.

c1934-36 *6in (15cm) wide*

£3,500-4,500 **QU**

A Venini & C. 'A Bolle' bowl, by Carlo Scarpa, acid-stamped 'venini murano'.

c1934 *14½in (37cm) wide*

£450-550 **QU**

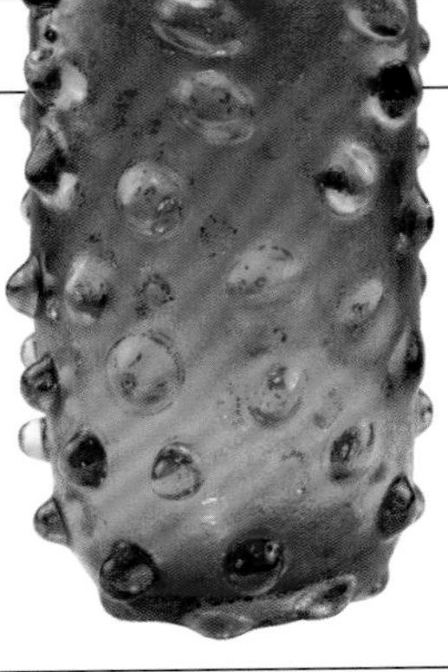

A Venini & C. 'Corroso' cased glass vase, by Carlo Scarpa, acid-stamped 'venini murano'.
c1936 *11½in (29cm) high*
£12,000-16,000 **QU**

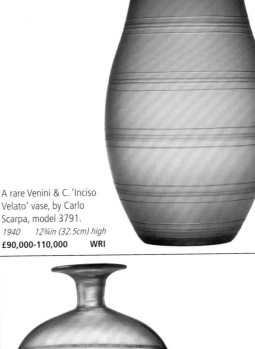

A rare Venini & C. 'Inciso Velato' vase, by Carlo Scarpa, model 3791.
1940 *12¾in (32.5cm) high*
£90,000-110,000 **WRI**

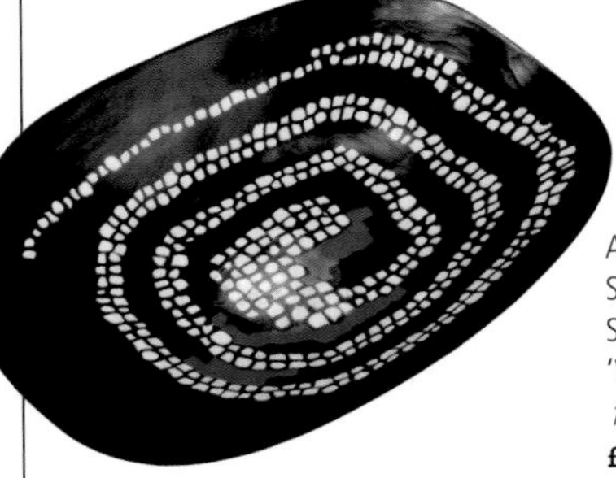

A Venini & C. 'Murrina del Serpente' bowl, by Carlo Scarpa, maker's decal 'VENINI S.A. MURANO'.
1940 *13in (33cm) long*
£9,000-11,000 **QU**

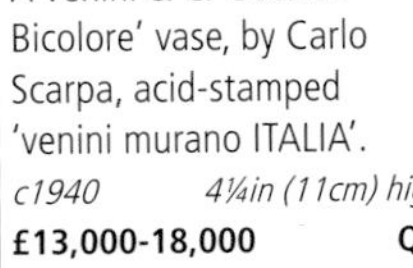

A Venini & C. 'Battuto Bicolore' vase, by Carlo Scarpa, acid-stamped 'venini murano ITALIA'.
c1940 *4¼in (11cm) high*
£13,000-18,000 **QU**

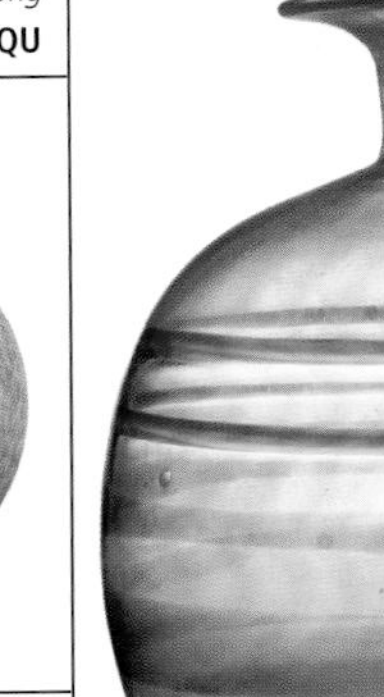

A Venini & C. 'A Fili' vase, by Carlo Scarpa, model no.4540, with a fili and a fasce decoration, light iridisation, acid-etched 'venini/murano/ITALIA'.
c1942 *7in (18cm) high*
£40,000-50,000 **PHI**

A Venini & C. 'A Macchie' bowl, by Carlo Scarpa, acid-stamped 'venini murano ITALIA'.
c1942 *11in (28cm) long*
£5,000-6,000 **QU**

A Venini & C. 'Soffiato' vase, by Vittorio Zecchin, model 1998.
c1925-26 *13in (33cm) high*
£10,000-14,000 **WRI**

A Venini & C. 'Amethyst Soffiato' vase, by Vittorio Zecchin, model 1867, signed 'Venini Murano'.
c1928 *16¼in (41.5cm) high*
£19,000-22,000 **WRI**

A Zecchin-Martinuzzi 'Rosso e Nero' vase, by Napoleone Martinuzzi.
c1932 *11¾in (30cm) high*
£8,500-9,500 **WRI**

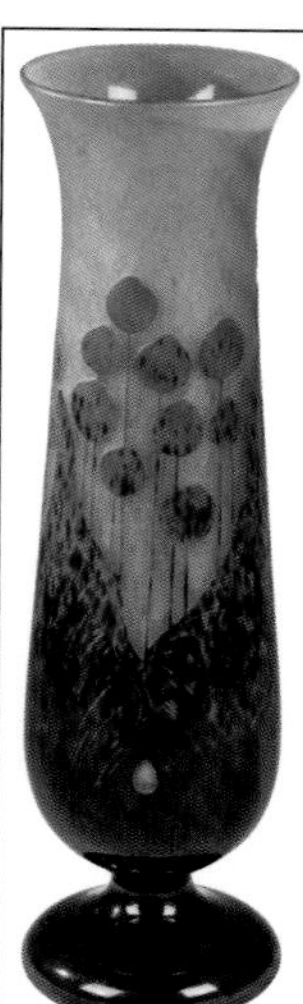

A Charles Schneider 'Cherries' vase, etched in relief.

Charles Schneider (1881-1953) and his brother Ernest (1877-1937) were raised in Nancy, France. Both brothers worked for Daum, before founding the Schneider Glassworks in 1917 in Epinay-sur-Seine.

1918-21 *18in (45.5cm) high*

£1,200-1,600 **FIS**

A Charles Schneider vase, in cased mottled glass with applied jade glass decoration, etched signature with amphora mark.

1918-25 *6in (15cm) diam*

£400-500 **DRA**

A Charles Schneider glass floor vase, etched signature and paper label, some light scratches.

1918-30 *18¾in (47.5cm) high*

£500-600 **DRA**

A Charles Schneider amphora vase, Epinay-Sur-Seine, signed, light scratches.

1918-30 *12in (30.5cm) high*

£500-600 **DRA**

An Art Deco Schneider glass and wrought iron vase, internally decorated, acid-stamped 'SCHNEIDER' to glass, metal etched 'FRANCE', small bruise.

18in (45.5cm) wide

£700-800 **DRA**

A 1920s Charles Schneider marbled glass shouldered vase, Epinay-Sur-Seine, signed.

12¼in (31cm) high

£400-500 **DRA**

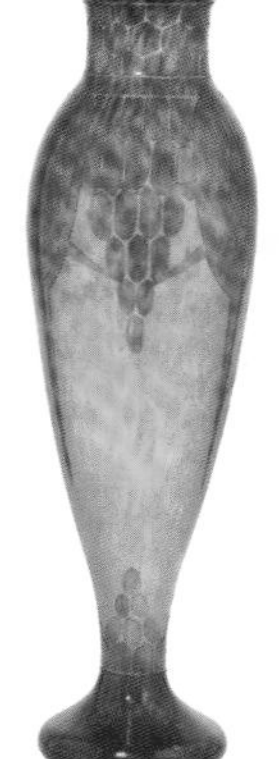

A Schneider 'Le Verre Français' cameo glass vase, acid-etched, inset with maker's candy-cane mark.

'Le Verre Français' was a line of art glass made by Schneider Glassworks c1918-32.

c1925 *19½in (49.5cm) high*

£600-700 **ROS**

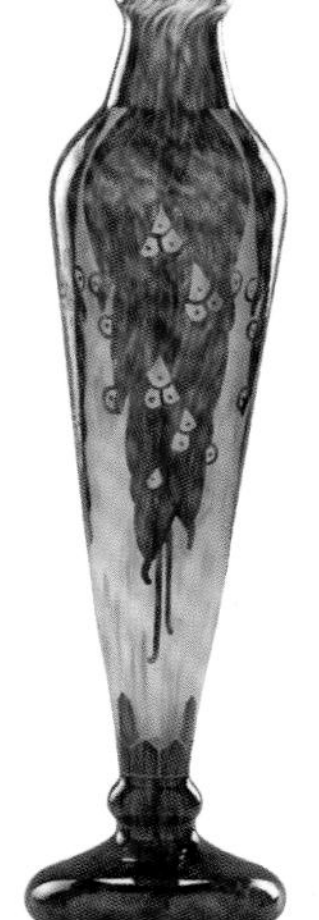

A Schneider 'Le Verre Français' cameo glass vase, acid-etched with 'Lauriers' motif, signed, small filled hole near base.

c1930 *19in (48.5cm) high*

£400-500 **DRA**

A Schneider 'Le Verre Français' cameo glass vase, overlaid and acid-etched, signed.

c1930 *25½in (65cm) high*

£800-900 **ROS**

A Schneider 'Le Verre Français' 'Poissons' vase, with cameo fish and aquatic plants, on acid-textured frosted background, with internal controlled bubbles, signed 'Charder Le Verre Francais'.

5½in (14cm) high

£10,000-14,000 **JDJ**

A late 19thC Stevens & Williams cameo glass vase, cut with convolvulus and a butterfly.

Stevens & Williams was established in Stourbridge in 1847. In the early 1880s, under manager John Northwood and designer Frederick Carder, Stevens & Williams created new art glass ranges. It received a Royal Warrant in 1919 and changed its name to Royal Brierley. The firm closed in the 1990s. This item was a wedding gift from the management of Stevens & Williams to Marion Jenkins, who was a designer at the factory.

7¼in (18.5cm) high

£2,200-2,800 FLD

A late 19thC Stevens & Williams Rockingham crystal glass bottle vase, with internal gold aventurine flecked decoration.

13¾in (35cm) high

£750-850 FLD

A late 19thC Stevens & Williams 'Verre De Soie' glass vase.

8¾in (22.5cm) high

£400-500 FLD

A late 19thC Stevens & Williams 'Osiris' glass vase, acid-marked 'PATENT'.

6in (15cm) high

£1,200-1,600 FLD

A 1930s Stevens & Williams crystal glass vase, pattern no.65332.

12¼in (31cm) high

£400-450 FLD

An early 20thC Stevens & Williams glass claret jug, intaglio-cut with arched motifs, with silver-plated mounts.

9¾in (25cm) high

£400-500 FLD

An early 20thC Stevens & Williams sleeve-form decanter, crystal-cut 'Whisky'.

8¼in (21cm) high

£300-400 FLD

An early 20thC Stevens & Williams liqueur glass, intaglio-cut with a floral band in a matt and polished finish.

4in (10cm) high

£300-400 FLD

A 1920s Stevens & Williams hock glass, pattern no.53008, intaglio-cut with fruiting grapevines.

8¼in (21cm) high

£750-850 FLD

A late 19thC Thomas Webb & Sons gem cameo glass vase, by George Woodall, impressed mark, chip to foot rim.

Thomas Webb & Sons was founded in 1837 in Stourbridge by Thomas Webb. On his death it was taken over by his son. Thomas Webb & Sons was known for its rock crystal-style glass and cameo pieces. The firm was bought by Crown House Ltd. in 1964 and later became part of the Coloroll group. The factory closed in 1990.

8¼in (21cm) high

£20,000-25,000 **DRA**

A Thomas Webb cameo glass vase, cut with flowering plants.

c1880-90 *3½in (9cm) high*

£1,500-2,000 **WW**

A Thomas Webb & Sons cameo glass vase, wheel-carved with ferns.

c1890 *6½in (16.5cm) high*

£650-750 **DUK**

A Thomas Webb & Sons cameo glass vase, wheel-carved with flowers and insects, white opaque interior.

c1890 *12in (30.5cm) high*

£2,000-2,500 **DUK**

A Thomas Webb & Sons cameo glass vase, wheel-carved with tree blossoms and butterflies, acid-etched crescent mark to base.

c1890 *11in (28cm) high*

£1,300-1,600 **DUK**

A Thomas Webb & Sons cameo glass vase, wheel-carved with jasmine blossoms and butterflies, acid-etched mark to base.

c1890 *8¾in (22.5cm) high*

£850-950 **DUK**

A Thomas Webb & Sons cameo glass vase, wheel-carved with flowers and insects.

c1890 *8¾in (22cm) high*

£1,200-1,600 **DUK**

A late 19thC Thomas Webb and Sons miniature ewer, intaglio-cut with ferns and insects.

5¼in (13.5cm) high

£950-1,100 **FLD**

A Thomas Webb cameo pink and white scent bottle, with flowers and butterfly, with silver top hallmarked for Birmingham.

1888 *2½in (6.5cm) high*

£1,500-2,000 **JN**

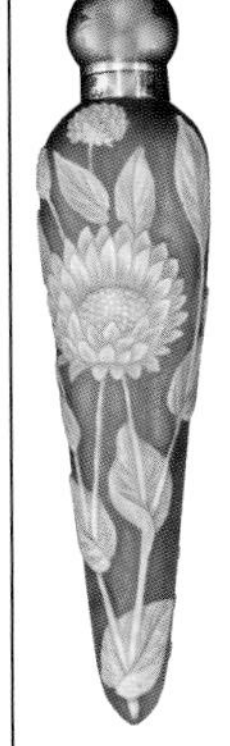

A Thomas Webb & Co. cameo yellow glass scent bottle, with silver cover hallmarked for London.

1884 *6in (15cm) long*

£950-1,100 **SWO**

An early 20thC Thomas Webb & Sons hock glass, acid-marked.

7¼in (18.5cm) high

£150-200 **FLD**

A late 19thC Tiffany Studios Favrile glass vase, etched 'TGC', one burst bubble to rim, residue to interior.

4in (10cm) wide

£2,000-3,000 DRA

A Tiffany Favrile presentation vase, with gold and blue iridescent finish, engraved 'G Y Tiffany Feby 15th 1898 Lewis C Tiffany'.

7¾in (20cm) high

£5,500-6,500 MORP

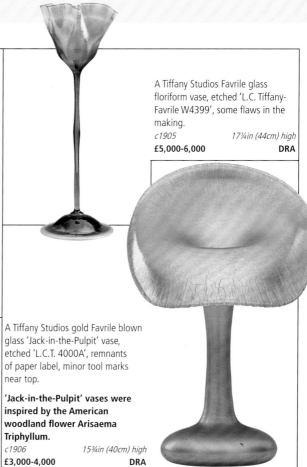

A Tiffany Studios Favrile glass floriform vase, etched 'L.C. Tiffany-Favrile W4399', some flaws in the making.

c1905 17¼in (44cm) high

£5,000-6,000 DRA

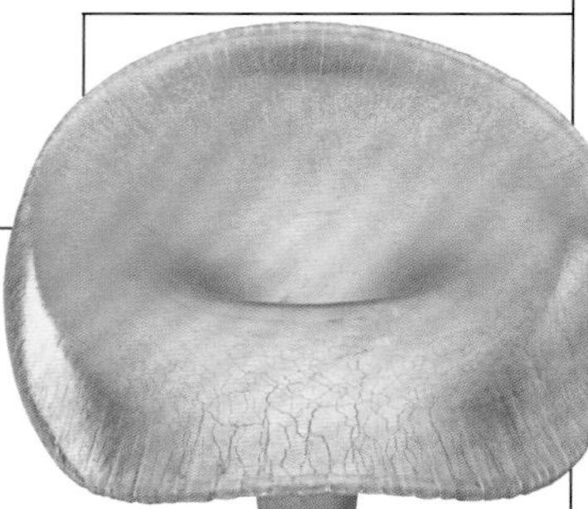

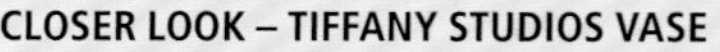

A Tiffany Studios gold Favrile blown glass 'Jack-in-the-Pulpit' vase, etched 'L.C.T. 4000A', remnants of paper label, minor tool marks near top.

'Jack-in-the-Pulpit' vases were inspired by the American woodland flower Arisaema Triphyllum.

c1906 15¾in (40cm) high

£3,000-4,000 DRA

A Tiffany Studios floriform vase, etched 'L.C.T. 521A', some bubbles.

c1906 9½in (24cm) high

£2,000-2,500 DRA

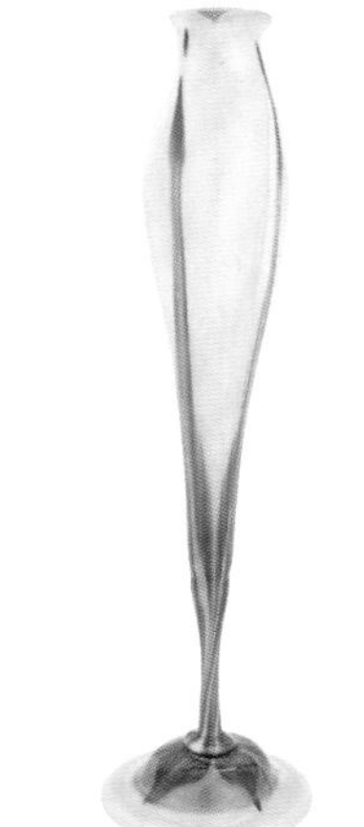

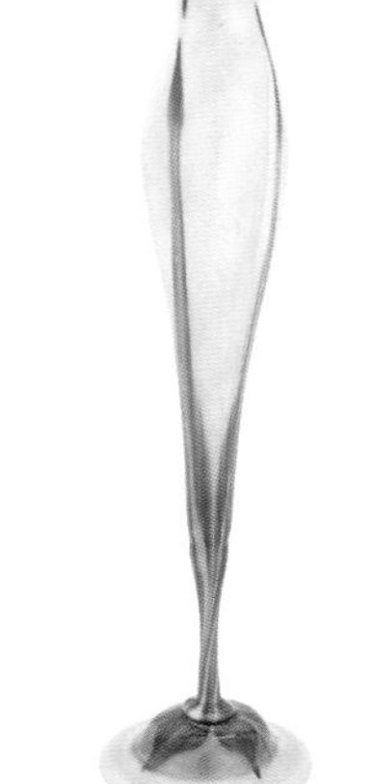

A Tiffany Favrile glass calyx floriform vase, engraved 'L.C.T. Y7779'.

c1905 19½in (49.5cm) high

£2,000-3,000 DOY

A pair of early 20thC Tiffany Studios Favrile glass vases, marked, some bubbles in making of, light wear to bases.

13½in (34.5cm) high

£1,300-1,800 DRA

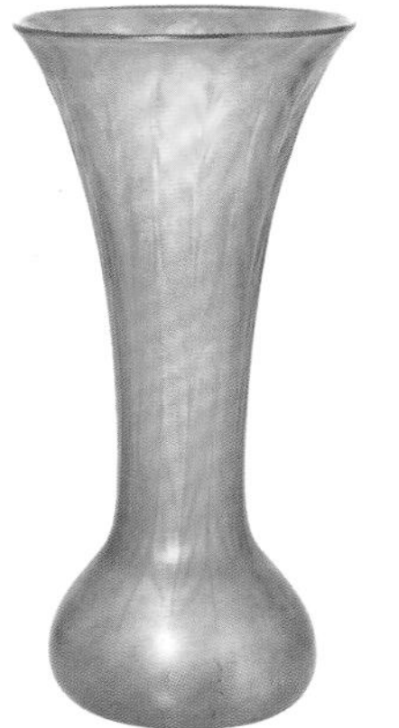

A Tiffany Favrile iridescent glass vase, signed 'L.C Tiffany Favrile 1811'.

c1910 10½in (26.5cm) high

£400-500 ROS

CLOSER LOOK – TIFFANY STUDIOS VASE

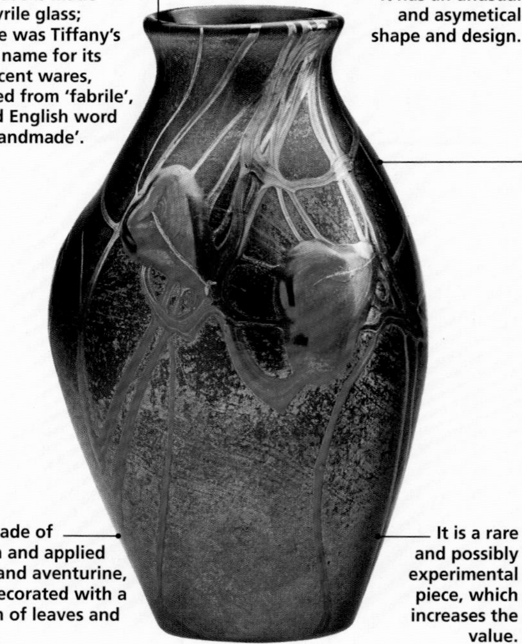

This vase is made of Favrile glass; Favrile was Tiffany's trade name for its iridescent wares, derived from 'fabrile', an old English word for 'handmade'.

It has an unusual and asymetical shape and design.

It is made of blown and applied glass and aventurine, and decorated with a design of leaves and vines.

It is a rare and possibly experimental piece, which increases the value.

A Tiffany Studios vase, etched 'L.C. Tiffany Favrile 4570E'.

c1910 6½in (16.5cm) high

£8,500-9,500 DRA

A Tiffany green Favrile vase, with applied gold iridescent collar, signed 'L.C. Tiffany – Favrile 163 G'.

10in (25.5cm) high

£3,200-3,800 MORP

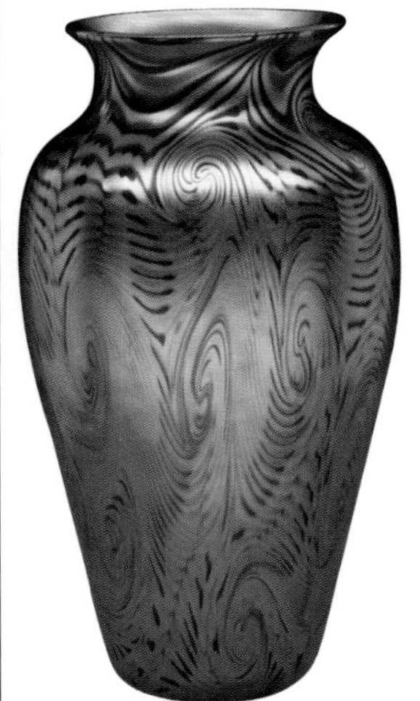

A Tiffany Favrile vase, with iridescent swirl decoration, signed 'L.C. Tiffany – Favrile E8432'.

8¾in (22cm) high

£3,000-4,000 MORP

An early 20thC Tiffany Studios acid-etched blown glass Favrile bud vase, on gilt bronze base, base stamped 'TIFFANY STUDIOS NEW YORK 711'.

14in (35.5cm) high

£1,400-1,800 DRA

An early 20thC Tiffany Studios special-order blown glass Favrile vase, etched 'LCT o8787', small burst bubble.

7in (18cm) high

£1,300-1,800 DRA

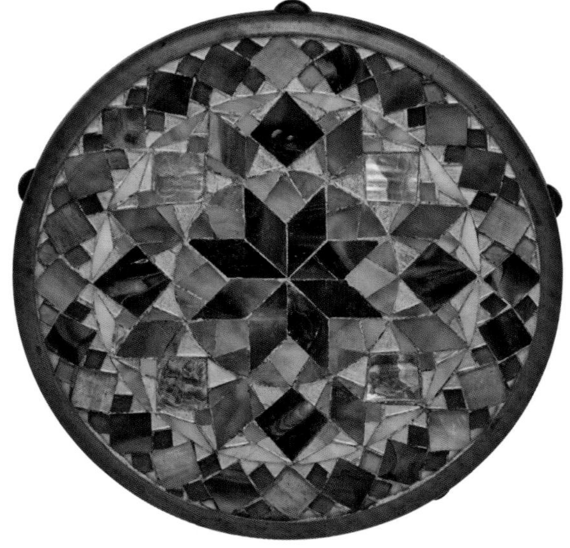

An early 20thC Tiffany Studios patinated bronze, Favrile glass and mother-of-pearl Mosaic trivet.

7½in (19cm) diam

£13,000-18,000 DRA

A Tiffany Studios Favrile ruffled compote, etched '1529-1259M L.C. Tiffany-Favrile'.

c1918 6in (15cm) wide

£1,500-2,000 DRA

A Tiffany Studios blown glass 'Cypriote' vase, etched '4989N L.C. Tiffany-Inc. Favrile'.

c1919 4in (10cm) high

£8,500-9,500 DRA

A Tiffany Studios paperweight vase, internally decorated with crocuses, etched '964V L.C.T. Favrile'.

c1927 4in (10cm) high

£7,500-8,500 DRA

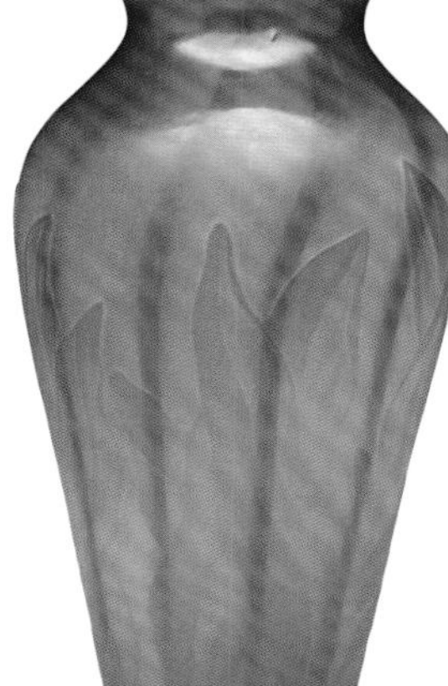

A Tiffany cameo vase, with cameo leaves and gold iridescent glass insert, vase signed 'L.C.T. 1014B', insert signed 'L.C.T. Y6406'.

8½in (21.5cm) high

£6,000-7,000 JDJ

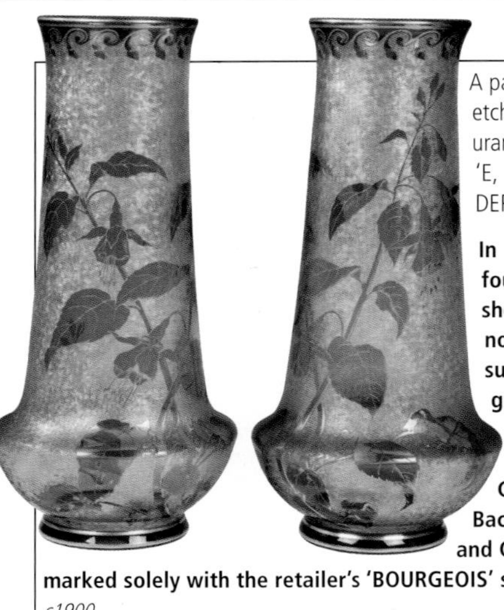

A pair of Baccarat vases, etched with fuchsias on a uranium glass base, signed 'E, BOURGEOIS PARIS DEPOSÈ'.

In 1862, Émile Bourgeois founded a glassware shop in Paris. He did not allow those who supplied him with glassware to sell it under their own names in his shop. Glass exists from Baccarat, Muller Frères and Caranza that is marked solely with the retailer's 'BOURGEOIS' signature.

c1900 *13¾in (35cm) high*

£3,000-3,500 FIS

A Baccarat polychrome enamel acid-cut vase.

c1895 *8in (20.5cm) high*

£900-1,100 M&DM

A James Couper & Sons 'Clutha' glass vase, designed by Christopher Dresser (1834-1904).

c1880 *7½in (19cm) high*

£500-600 L&T

A pair of James Couper & Sons 'Clutha' glass bottle vases, with aventurine and milky trailed inclusions.

c1900 *5in (13cm) high*

£650-750 L&T

A Bergun & Schverer cameo vase, with wheel-carved and Martele-carved decoration, signed 'Verrerie D'Art De Lorraine B S& Co. Depose'.

8½in (21.5cm) high

£4,500-5,500 MORP

A D'Argental cameo vase, by Paul Nicolas, signed 'D'Argental', with Cross of Lorraine.

St Louis launched its D'Argental cameo range in c1918, inspired by the success of firms like Gallé and Daum. Its main designer was Paul Nicolas (1875-1952), a former protégé of Émile Gallé. The range continued until the mid-1920s.

12in (30.5cm) high

£2,000-2,500 M&DM

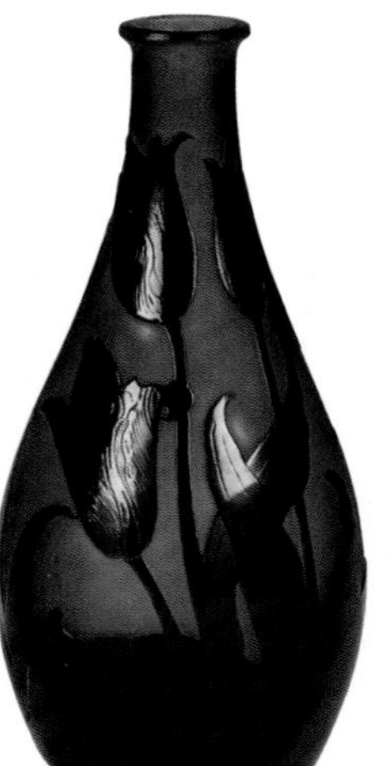

A D'Argental vase, by Paul Nicolas, etched 'd'Argental'.

c1919-25 *6in (15.5cm) high*

£700-800 FIS

A D'Argental vase, decorated with a Lake Como-like scene, signed 'D'Argental'.

21½in (54.5cm) high

£1,500-2,000 JDJ

A 1920s Degue cameo glass vase, sandblasted glass, signed in cameo, etched 'Made in France'.

15in (38cm) high

£1,200-1,600 DRA

An early 20thC Durand threaded glass vase, some losses to threading.

Durand glass was produced at the Vineland Glass Co. in Vineland, NJ, and was funded by French-born glassmaker Victor Durand Jr. (1870-1931). After Durand's death, Vineland merged with the Kimble Glass Co. and art glass production ceased.

8½in (21.5cm) high

£250-350 DRA

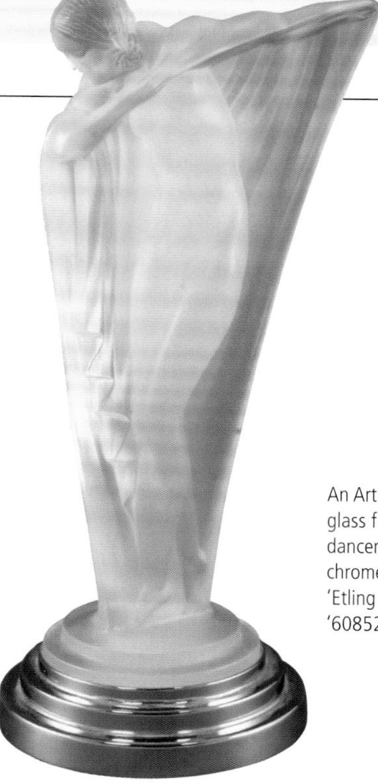

An Art Deco Etling opalescent glass figure of a semi-nude dancer, model no.50, on chrome plinth, moulded mark 'Etling France 50', etched '60852', nick to base.

8¾in (22cm) high

£1,400-1,800 **GORL**

A Harrach Japonaise vase, enamelled with Asian cartouche.

The Harrach family took over a glassworks in Harrochow, Bohemia, in the early 18thC. By 1900 the firm had become a pioneer for Art Nouveau glass. The Harrach glassworks are still in production today.

c1890 *14in (35.5cm) high*

£600-700 **M&DM**

A Harrarch iridised and enamelled 'Rubinglaser' vase.

This design was first shown at the Paris 1900 exhibition.

c1900 *12in (30.5cm) wide*

£1,200-1,500 **M&DM**

A Harrach gilded vase, depicting branches and birds.

c1900 *5in (13cm) wide*

£300-400 **M&DM**

A set of six Harrach tango cocktail glasses.

c1925 *7in (18cm) high*

£600-700 **M&DM**

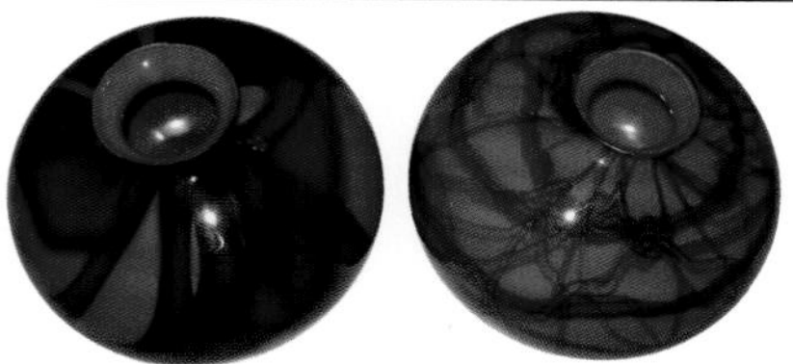

A pair of Kralik ball vases, marked in silver 'Made in Czechoslovakia'.

These were made for the American market. Wilhelm Kralik Söhne was an important Bohemian art glass producer active in the late 19thC and early 20thC.

c1930 *8in (20.5cm) high*

£900-1,100 **M&DM**

A pair of Kralik ball vases.

c1930 *8in (20.5cm) high*

£900-1,100 **M&DM**

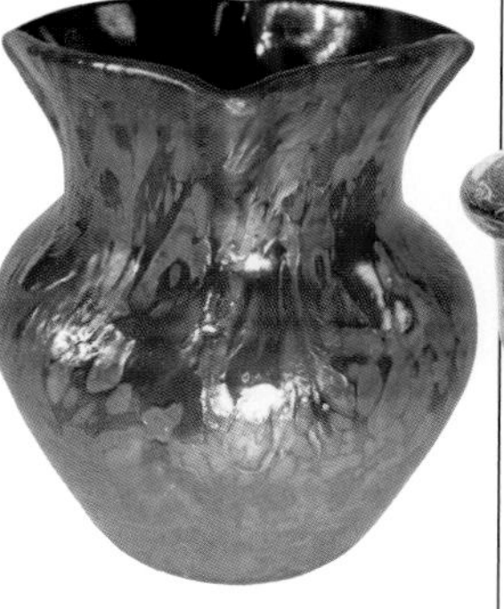

A Fritz Heckert purple on brick brown iridised vase, designed by Otto Thamm.

c1900 *5in (12.5cm) high*

£300-400 **M&DM**

A Joh, Oertel & Co. covered glass box, designed by the Haida school, enamelled with vases and flowers.

c1915 *7in (17.5cm) high*

£1,000-1,500 **FIS**

A Kralik cameo vase, with a landscape scene.

c1935 *11in (28cm) high*

£600-750 **M&DM**

A Kralik cameo vase, with a landscape scene.

c1935 *6in (15cm) wide*

£400-600 **M&DM**

A Lamartine cameo landscape vase, made by ex-Daum workers in French Algeria, signed.
c1920 *3in (7.5cm) high*
£1,200-1,500 **M&DM**

An early 20thC French Legras scenic acid-etched cameo glass vase, signed in cameo, burst bubble to one tree, handles uneven.
10¼in (26cm) high
£500-600 **DRA**

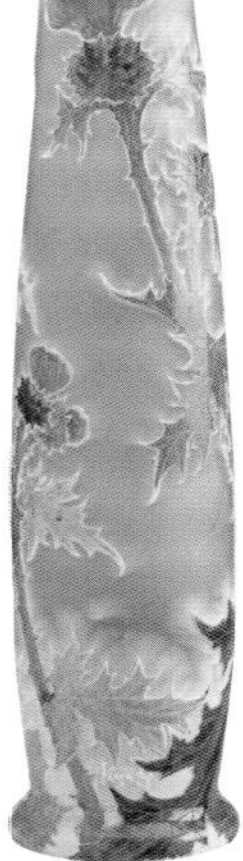

An early 20thC French Legras vase, acid-etched and enamelled with thistles, signed in cameo, minor roughness to rim, small bubbles throughout.
18¼in (46.5cm) high
£1,600-2,000 **DRA**

A cased glass flacon, by Maurice Marinot (1882-1960), internally decorated with black and rust-red flecks, signed 'Marinot', lacking stopper, some trapped bubbles.
c1930 *5¼in (13.5cm) high*
£5,500-6,500 **ROS**

A glass goblet, designed by Karl Massanetz, made by Oskar Strnad.
c1914 *6¾in (17cm) high*
£2,800-3,200 **FIS**

A Meyr's Neffe glass, by Otto Prutscher, with green enamel sunflower decoration.

Meyr's Neffe was founded in 1815 and was later taken over by Wilhelm Kralik. After his death in 1877, two of his sons continued to trade as Meyr's Neffe and two others formed Wilhelm Kralik Söhne. In 1922 Meyr's Neffe merged with Moser.
c1910 *8¼in (21cm) high*
£3,000-4,000 **FIS**

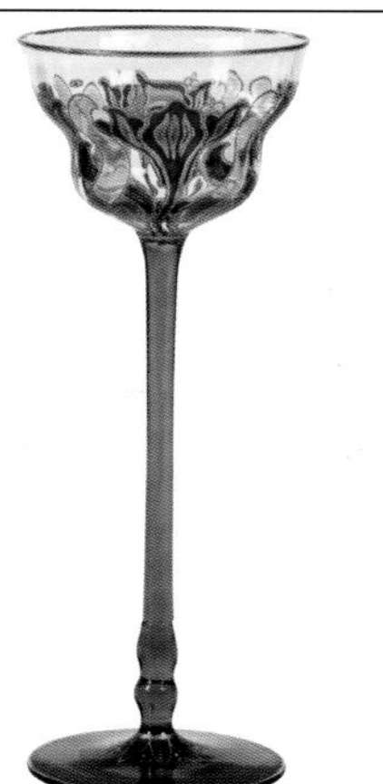

A Meyr's Neffe green and colourless wine glass, base marked '547'.
c1910 *7¾in (20cm) high*
£500-600 **FIS**

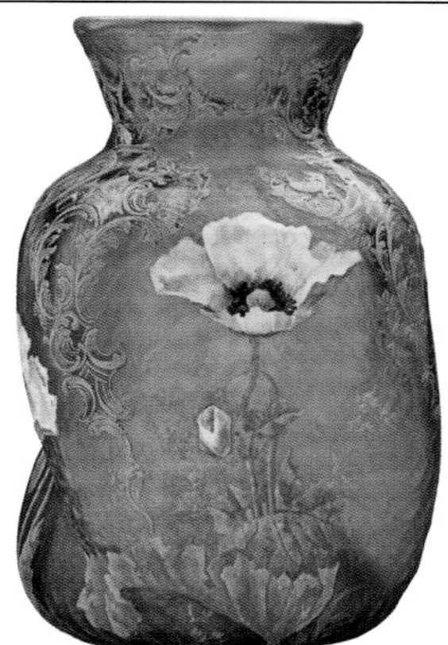

An early 20thC Mont Joye twisting vase, gilt glass, enamelled and acid-etched with poppies.
11¼in (28.5cm) high
£450-550 **DRA**

A Muller Croismare acid-etched glass 'Fluogravure' vase, signed 'Muller Croismare'.
c1910 *6¾in (17cm) high*
£500-600 **ROS**

An early 20thC Muller Frères cameo glass vase, acid-etched internally with poppies, signed in cameo, polished chip to inner rim, some metal transfer marks.
5¾in (14.5cm) high
£400-500 **DRA**

An early 20thC Muller Frères acid-etched cameo vase, with boar hunting scene, signed 'Muller Frès Lunéville' in cameo, some minor flecks.

10¾in (27.5cm) high

£2,500-3,000 **DRA**

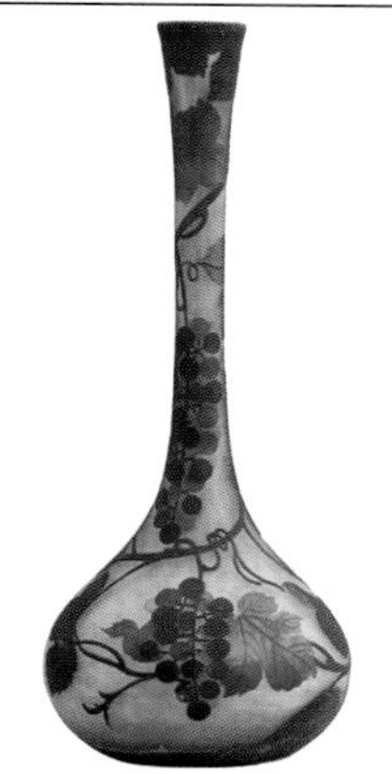

An early 20thC Muller Frères acid-etched cameo glass vase, signed.

16in (40.5cm) high

£600-700 **DRA**

A rare Phoenix Consolidated Cubist 'Ruba Rombic' vase, in topaz, designed by Reubin Haley.

c1928-32 *7in (18cm) high*

£1,200-1,500 **M&DM**

A Portieux Vallerysthal vase, etched with chestnut leaves and flowers, etched 'Vallerysthal'.

c1895-1900 *13¾in (35cm) high*

£5,000-5,500 **FIS**

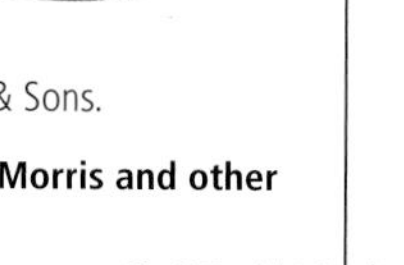

A set of eight drinking glasses, by Thomas Graham Jackson (1835-1924), for James Powell & Sons.

Laurence W. Hodson, who owned these, was an art collector and a patron of William Morris and other leading artists of the English Arts and Crafts movement.

c1870 *6in (15cm) high*

£550-650 **L&T**

An early 20thC Quezal glass vase, etched 'QUEZAL II'.

Quezal was founded in 1901 by former Tiffany employees Thomas Johnson and Martin Bach. It ceased production in 1925.

11in (28cm) high

£1,500-2,000 **DRA**

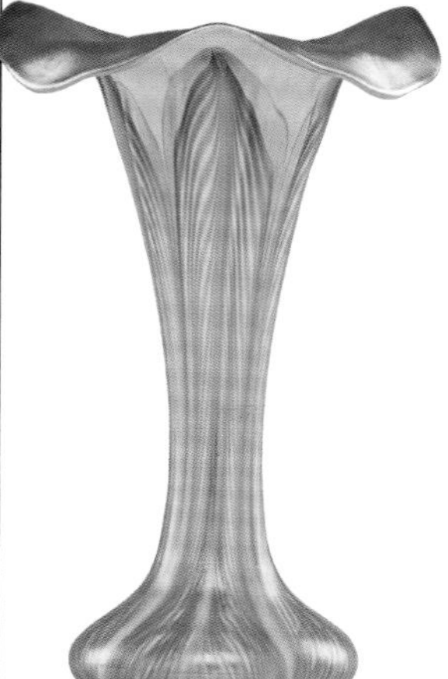

An early 20thC Quezal glass pulled-feather vase, etched 'QUEZAL 1000', some imperfections to the rim.

7½in (19cm) high

£700-800 **DRA**

A Verrerie De Sèvres acid-etched and fire-polished cameo glass vase, with silver-plated mounts, etched 'VS' to base, dent to rim, wear to mounts.

c1900 *8in (20.5cm) high*

£900-1,100 **DRA**

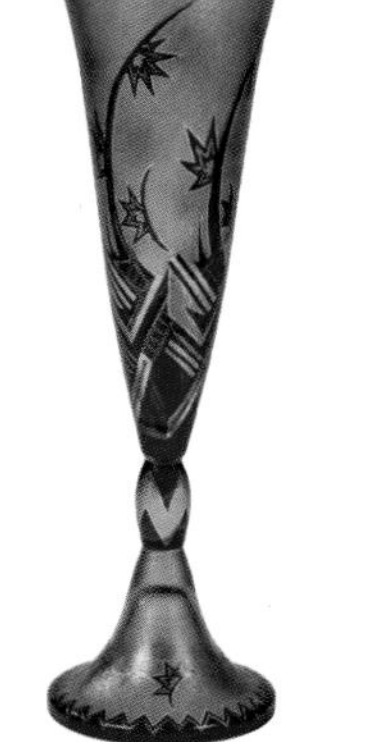

A Fachschule Steinschönau vase.

This vase was made for the 1925 Paris World Fair.

1925 *11½in (29cm) high*

£5,500-6,000 **FIS**

A 1920s Steuben 'Plum Jade' acid-etched cased glass vase, with lotus flowers, minor polishing near base.

6¾in (17cm) wide

£1,800-2,200 **DRA**

An early 20thC Steuben blue blown glass 'Aurene' vase, etched 'Aurene 2683', some scratches.

12in (30.5cm) high

£2,200-2,800 DRA

An early 20thC Steuben gold blown glass 'Aurene' vase, on wood stand, etched 'AURENE 2412', scuffs and scratches.

8in (20.5cm) high

£400-500 DRA

A Val St Lambert red over clear 'Seurat' vase, shallow foot rim chip.

Val St Lambert was founded in 1826 in Belgium and is still operational today.

c1930 12in (30.5cm) high

£1,800-2,200 DN

A Val St Lambert vase, inscribed 'VSL'.

c1906-07 23½in (60cm) high

£3,000-3,500 FIS

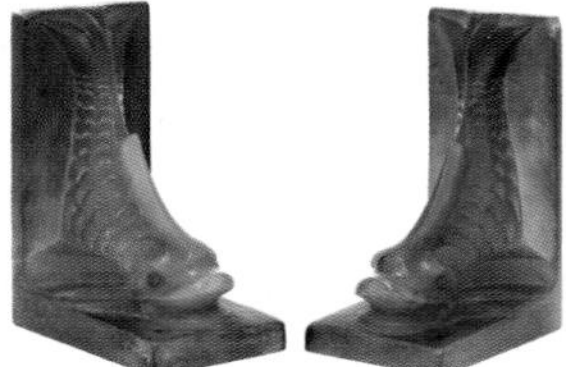

A pair of Amalric Walter relief-moulded glass dolphin bookends, by Auguste Houillon (1885-1954), signed in mould 'A Walter, Nancy, A Houillon', some chips, pencil marks to back, '400', '£2-10-0 Pair'.

£1,800-2,200 SWO

A Val St Lambert cut glass vase, in 'Topaz' and 'Bleu Francais', acid-etched mark.

c1930 6in (15cm) high

£1,800-2,200 DN

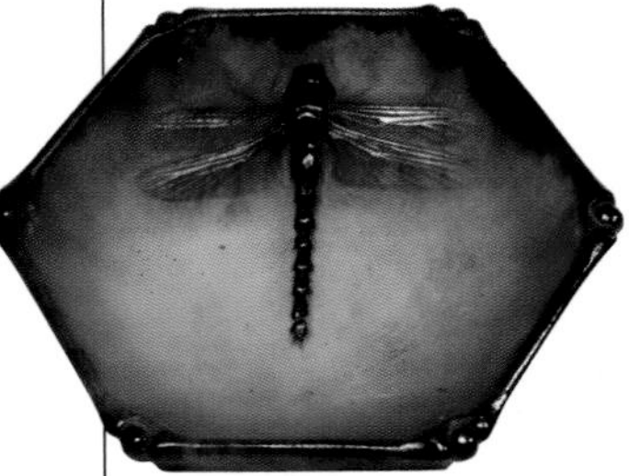

A 1920s Amalric Walter 'Libellule' pâte-de-verre 'vide poches' or 'empty pocket', by Henri Bergé, signed 'AWALTER NANCY', 'HBergé'.

6¾in (17cm) long

£2,800-3,200 QU

An enamelled glass jug, by Hannah Walton, painted with a mermaid, signed with initials 'HW'.

Hannah Walton (1863-1940) trained at the Glasgow School of Art and exhibited at the 1888 Glasgow International Exhibition. She shared a studio with her sisters Helen and Constance; all three worked painting and enamelling ceramics and glass.

c1900 6in (15.5cm) high

£1,200-1,600 L&T

CLOSER LOOK – 'APHRODITE RISING FROM THE WAVES'

The cameo glass plaque is cased in opal over blue over red.

This design is bordered with a triple line, with six arched panels with a seashell motif.

It is carved with the nude figure of Aphrodite rising from crashing waves, her legs submerged in the water, surrounded by seagulls. Aphrodite was a favoured subject for Woodall, featuring in variations across a number of plaques and vases.

It was made by George Woodall in c1920, though he had first designed the plaque when working for Thomas Webb & Sons in the 1870s.

A cameo glass plaque, 'Aphrodite Rising from the Waves', by George Woodall, signed.

c1920 8¼in (21cm) diam

£11,000-14,000 FLD

A Victorian Aesthetic breakfront oak side cabinet, possibly designed by Charles Bevan for Marsh Jones & Cribb.

Charles Bevan (fl.1865-83) was a furniture designer and manufacturer based in London. He made several designs for Marsh & Jones of Leeds, including a suite of furniture for Titus Salt. He took his son George Alfred into partnership from 1872.

71in (180.5cm) high

£1,000-1,400 HT

An Aesthetic Movement Collinson & Lock ebonised and painted side cabinet, by Thomas Edward Collcutt.

Thomas Edward Collcutt (1840-1924) was an architect and furniture designer, who gained international acclaim for his black ebonised furniture designs for the firm Collinson & Lock. He also designed Wakefield Town Hall, the Imperial Institute in South Kensington and Lloyd's Register building.

c1871 94½in (240cm) high

£5,500-6,500 DN

CLOSER LOOK – AESTHETIC MOVEMENT CHAIR

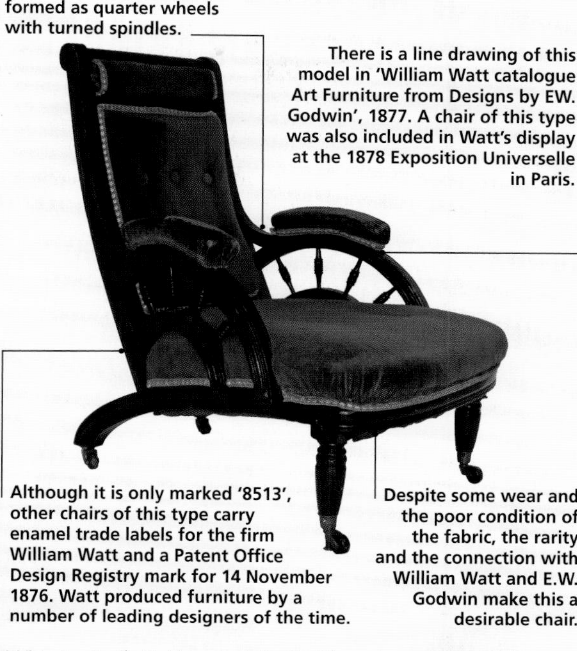

This chair has swept arms formed as quarter wheels with turned spindles.

There is a line drawing of this model in 'William Watt catalogue Art Furniture from Designs by EW. Godwin', 1877. A chair of this type was also included in Watt's display at the 1878 Exposition Universelle in Paris.

Although it is only marked '8513', other chairs of this type carry enamel trade labels for the firm William Watt and a Patent Office Design Registry mark for 14 November 1876. Watt produced furniture by a number of leading designers of the time.

Despite some wear and the poor condition of the fabric, the rarity and the connection with William Watt and E.W. Godwin make this a desirable chair.

A Victorian Aesthetic Movement ebonised framed armchair, by William Watt, after the original design by Edward William Godwin (1833-86).

c1877

£55,000-60,000 MAI

An Aesthetic Lamb of Manchester inlaid coromandel and rosewood occasional table, by Charles Edward Hoston, the top with copper, brass and shell inlaid foliate design, stamped 'J. Lamb Manchester 51600', minor fire damage, split to one lobe.

26in (66cm) high

£12,000-16,000 GORL

A late 19thC Anglo-Japanese carved hardwood padouk cabinet, with Aesthetic-style floral, lunette and medallion decoration in the manner of Thomas Jeckyll, old shippers label of 'Crews & Son, Exmouth' to rear.

60¼in (153cm) high

£3,000-3,500 FELL

A stained wood, copper, bone and inlaid metal throne chair, by Carlo Bugatti (1856-1940), with a vellum circular back and seat.

c1900 57in (145cm) high

£6,000-7,000 SWO

An ebonised, walnut inlaid and brass and pewter mounted corner chair, by Carlo Bugatti, some damage, later upholstery.

£1,200-1,500 BE

A Gallé carved nutwood writing desk, with inlaid wood design, signed.

1905-15 46¼in (117.5cm) high

£17,000-20,000 QU

An oak settee, by Sidney Barnsley.

Sidney Barnsley (1865-1926) was an important Arts and Crafts architect and furniture maker. In the workshop he shared with his brother Ernest and friend Ernest Gimson, he made chests, cabinets, tables and other pieces, combining rural carpentry techniques with sophisticated design.

86in (218cm) wide

£40,000-50,000 **LC**

A walnut dressing table, by Edward Barnsley, with ebonised wood handles.

59in (150cm) high

£1,800-2,200 **WW**

A Heal's oak sideboard or compactum, ivorine disc to one door, one shrinkage crack, some wear and scratches.

Heal's opened their first store in 1810. By the end of the 19thC, it was one of the best-known furniture suppliers in London, and it is still operational today.

c1910 *51¼in (130cm) wide*

£2,000-2,500 **CHEF**

A pair of Heal's oak settles, ivorine plaques to reverse, previous repairs.

The chequered motif of inlaid pewter and ebony on this piece was used by Heals in their furniture exhibited at the 1900 Paris Exhibition.

c1900-10 *40¼in (102cm) high*

£1,500-2,000 **CHEF**

A J.S. Henry mahogany and inlaid secrétaire, by George Montague Ellwood (1875-1955), the slatted back with two cupboards enclosing a marquetry-inlaid fall.

c1900 *73½in (187cm) high*

£3,500-4,500 **L&T**

A Liberty & Co. oak corner cupboard, with patinated metal, applied ivorine label.

77½in (197cm) high

£850-950 **WW**

A Liberty & Co. walnut 'Thebes' stool.

c1900 *13½in (34.5cm) wide*

£800-900 **CHEF**

A pair of beech and elm laboratory stools, attributed to Charles Rennie Mackintosh (1868-1928) for Queen Margaret Medical College, Glasgow.

Queen Margaret Medical College was the sole women's-only college of its type in the UK at the time.

1894 *27¼in (69cm) high*

£4,000-5,000 **TEN**

Judith Picks

This armchair was designed for the men's Billiards and Smoking Rooms at Miss Cranston's Argyle Street Tea Rooms in Glasgow. In 1898, early in his career, Scottish architect Charles Rennie Mackintosh (1868-1928) was commissioned by entrepreneur Catherine Cranston to furnish her new tearooms. Designer George Walton worked with him, designing the interiors while Mackintosh was in charge of the furnishings.

Mackintosh's designs are bold, simple and distinctive, combining strong Scottish vernacular design with English Arts & Crafts. He produced three types of seating for the Billiards and Smoking Rooms of the tearoom: a prominent ladder-back armchair, a stool, and this chair, a cube-shaped tub armchair. Its construction is traditional, but its form is unusual; it has broad panels of sawn timber stripped of decoration, a solid box shape and curved aprons and subtle detailing under the arms and back.

The Argyle Tea Rooms closed in 1920, and much of the furniture was dispersed. This armchair came into the possession of established Glasgow restaurateur William Smith, whose daughter passed it to a friend as a gift.

A Glasgow stained oak armchair, by Charles Rennie Mackintosh.

1898 *33in (84cm) high*

£113,000-118,000 **L&T**

A Morris & Co. oak sideboard, stamped 'MORRIS & Co/449 OXFORD St' and 'no.693', some wear.

79½in (202cm) wide

£4,500-5,500 **DN**

A Morris & Co. walnut refectory table, by George Washington Jack (1855-1931).

c1890 *90¼in (229cm) long*

£13,000-16,000 **L&T**

A Morris & Co. mahogany table, by George Washington Jack, stamped 'MORRIS & CO./449 OXFORD ST/W/1000'.

c1895 *30in (76cm) diam*

£12,000-16,000 **L&T**

A Thompson of Kilburn 'Mouseman' oak panel-back armchair, carved in relief with a mouse.

c1940

£4,000-5,000 **MOR**

ROBERT 'MOUSEMAN' THOMPSON

Robert Thompson (1876-1955) was a Yorkshire cabinetmaker and important figure in the Arts and Crafts movement.

- **His distinctive furniture was made from plain English oak, then shaped with an adze to give the wood a rippled surface.**
- **Each piece was embellished with a carved mouse. The mouse signature supposedly came from Thompson's description of himself in his early career as being 'as poor as a church mouse' and led to him and his furniture being referred to as 'Mouseman'.**
- **Several of the craftsman who trained under Thompson went on to set up on their own, using similar carved animals to sign their work. These included Peter 'Rabbitman' Heap and Graham 'Swanman' Duncalf.**
- **The firm Mouseman continues to make handmade furniture today.**

A Robert 'Mouseman' Thompson oak tallboy, with iron disc hinges and latch, carved with a mouse.

c1928 *48½in (123cm) high*

£13,000-16,000 **MOR**

Judith Picks

This armchair was made by Morris & Co., the decorative arts and furnishings company founded by William Morris in 1861. It was designed by Philip Webb (1831-1915), a close friend of Morris's and the designer of his home, Red House.

Morris & Co.'s reclining armchair was one of the firm's popular designs and was available both in this black finish and in mahogany. The c1912 Morris & Co. illustrated catalogue shows that loose covers could be supplied either in 'Utrecht Velvet' or in chintz (printed cotton). The commercial success of the design encouraged other firms, notably Liberty & Co. of London and Gustav Stickley in the USA, to produce their own versions.

A Morris & Co. ebonised walnut ladderback open reclining armchair, by Philip Webb, with five adjustable settings.

26½in (67cm) wide

£7,500-8,500 **LSK**

A Robert 'Mouseman' Thompson oak dresser, the central carcass carved 'H' and '1930', the sides with 'mouse' signatures.

The Robert Thompson ledger for 1930 notes 'Lieut. Col. A.J. Horlick c/o Horlicks Ltd., Slough Buckinghamshire Dresser as sketch submitted 6'0 long x 7' high app. £45- -'.

83in (211cm) high

£45,000-55,000 **SWO**

A Robert 'Mouseman' Thompson monk's armchair, centred with a carved 'H' for Horlick, mouse signature to front right leg.

The Robert Thompson ledger for 1939 '1939, Dec 12, 'One Monks chair' £8/8/.'

£5,500-6,500 **SWO**

A Robert 'Mouseman' Thompson oak refectory table, carved inscription 'D.D JOAN 1921-1926, MARY, DIANA, ANGELA, HELEN AND BRIDGET WESTMACOTT 1947-1964', with carved mouse.

72in (183cm) long

£1,500-2,000 **TEN**

A Peter 'Rabbitman' Heap oak sideboard, some sun staining to top.

72in (183cm) wide

£1,700-2,000 **PW**

An oak hay rake dining table, by Gordon Russell, stamped 'Gordon Russell Ltd'.

c1930 *66¼in (168cm) wide*

£4,000-5,000 **DN**

A high-back oak armchair, by Mackay Hugh Baillie Scott (1865-1945).

c1895 *47¼in (120cm) high*

£1,800-2,200 **L&T**

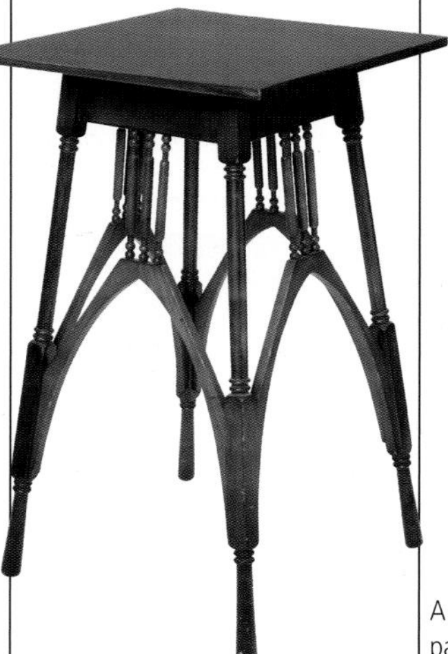

A walnut table, by Mackay Hugh Baillie Scott.

1898 *27in (68.5cm) high*

£3,000-4,000 **ROS**

A Shapland & Petter oak bookcase cabinet, the door with a stencilled panel inscribed 'MY LADIES GARDEN'.

Shapland & Petter was a cabinetmaking firm based in Barnstaple, Devon, founded in 1854. The firm continued into the 20thC and was taken over by the LS Group in 1999.

c1900 *87½in (222cm) wide*

£5,000-6,000 **L&T**

A Shapland & Petter inlaid mahogany cabinet, with marquetry decoration in specimen woods and mother-of-pearl, the locks stamped 'S&P/B'.

c1900 *51¾in (131.5cm) high*

£5,500-6,500 **L&T**

A Shapland & Petter oak settle, the back with inset copper panel, 'Welcome ever Smiles'.

The inscription 'Welcome Ever Smiles' is taken from Shakespeare's 'Troilus and Cressida'.

42¼in (107cm) long

£6,500-7,500 **BE**

A Shapland & Petter oak stand, designed by William Cowie.

c1905 *80¼in (204cm) high*

£1,500-2,000 **TDG**

An Arts and Crafts oak bookcase, with Art Nouveau-style script motto 'IT'S GUID TO BE MERRY AND WISE', with repoussé copper and leaded glass.

The motto is a quote of Robert Burns, from 'Here's a Health to Them That's Awa'. This style of furniture is often associated with Liberty & Co., who may have retailed this piece.

c1905 *78in (198cm) high*

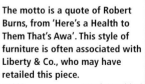

£3,000-3,500 **TDG**

ESSENTIAL REFERENCE – GUSTAV STICKLEY

Gustav Stickley (1858-1942) was a designer and furniture maker, and one of the leading figures of the American Arts and Crafts movement.

- **He learnt furniture-making from his uncle, the owner of a Pennsylvania chair factory. After leaving his uncle's factory, he founded the Stickley Brothers Chair Co. with his brothers Albert and Charles in 1883. It became the largest manufacturer in the state during the 1890s.**
- **Gustav Stickley founded his own company in 1898, after leaving Stickley Brothers.**
- **He was strongly influenced by William Morris, but while the English Arts and Crafts Movement focused on hand-crafting, Gustav Stickley used machines to create his new and original designs. His work was a radical departure from 19thC American furniture.**
- **The firm was a great success in the first decade of the 20thC, but by 1915 it was overstretched and Gustav Stickley filed for bankruptcy.**

A rare early Gustav Stickley mitered-mullion bookcase, with red decal, lightly cleaned, minor sun-fading.
c1901 *56in (142cm) high*
£7,500-8,500 **DRA**

A Gustav Stickley bride's chest, with iron hardware, large red decal, some chips, some wear.
c1940 *40½in (103cm) wide*
£8,500-9,500 **DRA**

A Gustav Stickley high-back spindle bench, with red decal, old overcoat to original finish, later artificial rush to seat.
c1905 *48½in (123cm) high*
£5,000-6,000 **DRA**

A Gustav Stickley and Harvey Ellis bookcase/cabinet, with large red decal, minor staining and fading, one glass crack.

Harvey Ellis (1852-1904) was an architect and painter. He spent the last months of his life working as an architect and designer for Gustav Stickley.
c1903 *68½in (174cm) wide*
£40,000-50,000 **DRA**

A Gustav Stickley and Harvey Ellis bookcase, remnants of paper label, red decal, some staining, missing metal keyhole liners.
c1910 *54in (137cm) wide*
£5,500-6,500 **DRA**

A 1910s Gustav Stickley sideboard, branded, refinished, some filled chips, veneer repairs to doors.
56in (142cm) wide
£3,000-4,000 **DRA**

A Gustav Stickley bow-arm Morris chair, with early red decal, light wear and minor stains, possible burn to front.
c1901 *38½in (98cm) high*
£7,000-8,000 **DRA**

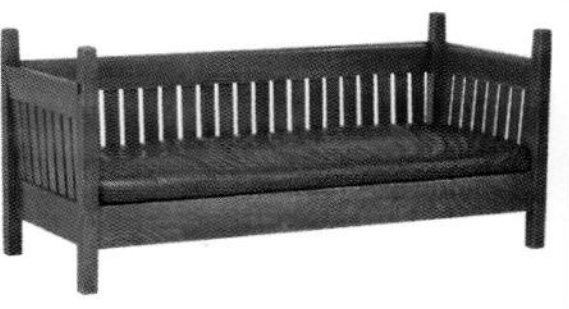

An early 20thC Gustav Stickley settle, no.222, red decal, some edge wear, some wear to cushion and pillows.
80in (203cm) wide
£5,000-6,000 **DRA**

A Gustav Stickley spindled loveseat, red decal, original spring cushion, minor edge wear.
c1910 *50in (127cm) long*
£5,000-6,000 **DRA**

A Gustav Stickley leather-top hexagonal library table, with red decal, remnants of paper label, some wear to leather, two metal brackets stabilising the top.
c1903 *55in (139.5cm) wide*
£14,000-18,000 **DRA**

An L. & J.G. Stickley bookcase, with handcraft decal, one darkened gouge to front left side, minor wear.

Leopold and John George Stickley, brothers of Gustav Stickley, established a new furniture business in Fayetteville in 1902. They initially used the trademark 'Onondaga Shops'. L. & J.G. Stickley continued after Leopold's and John George's death; it was acquired by Alfred Audi in the 1970s and continues to make furniture today as Stickley, Audi & Co.
c1908 *55¼in (140.5cm) high*
£2,500-3,500 **DRA**

A Gustav Stickley and Grueby twelve-tile table, with paper label, crack to one tile, minor edge wear.
c1905 *26in (66cm) high*
£11,000-14,000 **DRA**

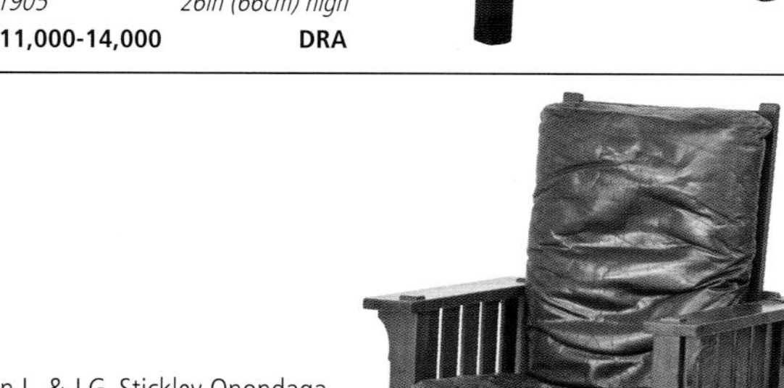

An L. & J.G. Stickley Onondaga Shops flat-arm Morris chair, some dints and wear, crazing to original leather.
c1902-07 *42in (106.5cm) high*
£2,000-3,000 **DRA**

An L.& J.G. Stickley quartersawn oak rocking Morris chair.
38in (96.5cm) high
£2,200-2,800 **CLAR**

An L. & J.G. Stickley Onondaga Shops settle, minor edge wear.
c1902-07 *76in (193cm) wide*
£3,000-4,000 **DRA**

An L. & J.G. Stickley copper-top drink stand, with 'The Work Of…' decal, some fading, some chips.
c1912 *28½in (72.5cm) high*
£1,100-1,400 **DRA**

An L. & J.G. Stickley server, branded, some wear.
c1920 *44in (112cm) wide*
£1,600-2,000 **DRA**

An L. & J.G. Stickley twin bed, handcraft decal, side rails replaced.
c1905 *79in (200.5cm) long*
£1,000-1,400 **DRA**

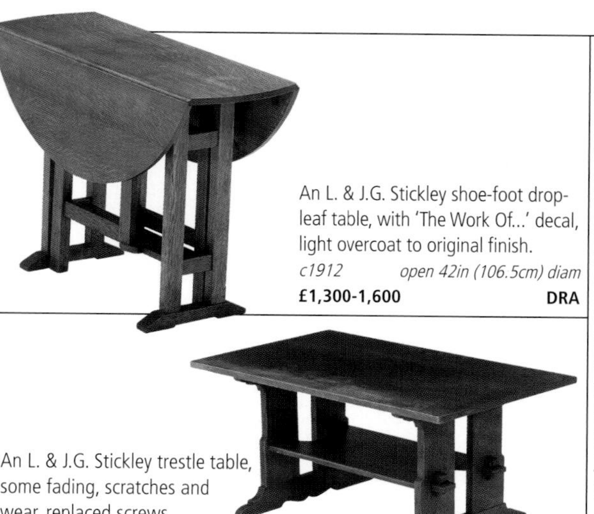

An L. & J.G. Stickley shoe-foot drop-leaf table, with 'The Work Of...' decal, light overcoat to original finish.
c1912 *open 42in (106.5cm) diam*
£1,300-1,600 **DRA**

An L. & J.G. Stickley trestle table, some fading, scratches and wear, replaced screws.
c1912-18 *60in (152.5cm) long*
£1,800-2,200 **DRA**

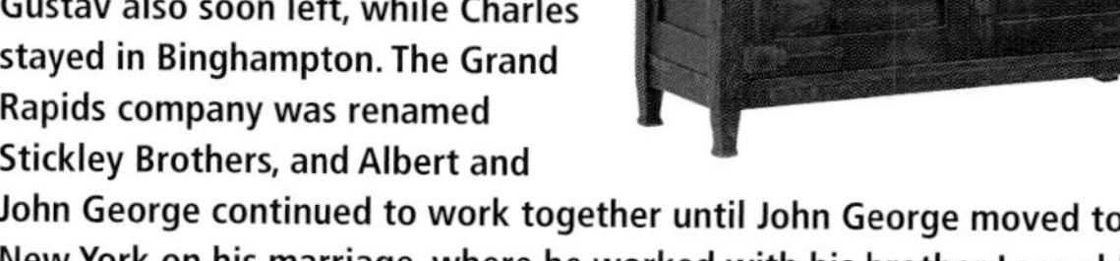

A 1910s Stickley Brothers china cabinet, 'Quaint' metal label, some darkened damage to front right foot.

The Stickley family consisted of five brothers, all of whom worked as furniture makers. In 1883, Albert, Gustav and Charles Stickley founded the Stickley Brothers Chair Company in Binghampton, New York. In 1891, Albert moved to Grand Rapids to work with his brother John George; Gustav also soon left, while Charles stayed in Binghampton. The Grand Rapids company was renamed Stickley Brothers, and Albert and John George continued to work together until John George moved to New York on his marriage, where he worked with his brother Leopold as L. & J.G. Stickley.

68¼in (173.5cm) high
£3,500-4,000 **DRA**

A Stickley Brothers china cabinet, no.8446, with original hammered hardware, with adjustable shelves.
55½in (141cm) high
£1,300-1,600 **CLAR**

A Stickley Brothers quartersawn oak single-drawer server, with 'Quaint' metal tag, some seam separations.

Some Stickley Brothers pieces were marked with a metal tag reading 'Quaint' or 'Quaint Furniture'. The brothers used this term to define and describe their furniture, and as a way to uniquely brand their work to distinguish it from their brother Gustav Stickley's.

c1910 *34in (86.5cm) wide*
£550-650 **DRA**

A Stickley Brothers sideboard, branded, 'Quaint' decal, stencilled numbers, some wear.
c1910-15 *50in (127cm) wide*
£750-850 **DRA**

An early 20thC Stickley Brothers server, with copper strap hardware, some replaced pull, some filled chips, damage to veneer, some losses.
54in (137cm) wide
£7,000-8,000 **DRA**

A Stickley Brothers Mission oak 'Morris' armchair, with leather cushions.
c1910 *37in (94cm) high*
£1,500-2,000 **L&T**

A Stickley Brothers side table, with 'Quaint' metal label, some wear to partial overcoat over original finish.
c1910 *28in (71cm) high*
£2,500-3,000 **DRA**

A Grand Rapids Furniture Co. quartersawn oak library table, with integrated book shelves, dark stains to top.

38in (96.5cm) wide

£450-500 **DRA**

A Jamestown Furniture Co. stained oak hall chair, in the style of Charles Rohlfs, with polychrome pyrography, chip to one front leg.

c1915 *56in (142cm) high*

£800-1,200 **DRA**

A Limbert sideboard, metal label, dent to centre door, seam separations to left side.

c1910 *57in (145cm) wide*

£3,500-4,000 **DRA**

A Limbert dining table, no.403, some edge wear, extensive wear to top.

Limbert Furniture was founded in 1894 in Grand Rapids, Michigan, by Charles P. Limbert. The factory produced furniture until its closure in 1944.

c1903 *50in (127cm) wide*

£4,000-5,000 **DRA**

A 1900s Charles Rohlfs tall-back chairs, 'R' cipher to each, loose joinery, wear to replaced seats, repair to one chair.

Charles Rohlfs (1853-1936) was an important designer and furniture-maker working in Buffalo, New York. He was influenced by the Art Nouveau and Aesthetic Movements.

53in (134.5cm) high

£5,000-6,000 **DRA**

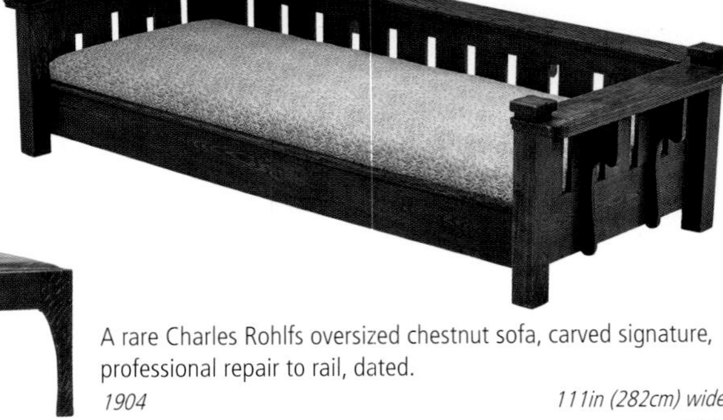

A rare Charles Rohlfs oversized chestnut sofa, carved signature, professional repair to rail, dated.

1904 *111in (282cm) wide*

£23,000-30,000 **DRA**

A Charles Rohlfs carved library table, with carved signature and date, some sun fading.

1900 *48in (122cm) wide*

£10,000-14,000 **DRA**

A Roycroft quartersawn oak and leather tall chair, with brass tacks.

Roycroft was a community of artists and craftsmen based near Buffalo, New York, in the late 19thC and early 20thC.

c1915 *41in (104cm) high*

£700-800 **DRA**

An early 20thC Shop of the Crafters inlaid cabinet, water damage to base, straps replaced.

The Shop of the Crafters was owned by Oscar Onken and specialised in Mission furniture in the Arts and Craft style. It was in business 1904-20 and was based in Cincinnati, Ohio.

63¼in (160.5cm) high

£1,800-2,200 **DRA**

A Bath Cabinet Makers Ltd. walnut and coromandel wood chest, by Charles A. Richter (1876-1945), marked 'BCM/1928/C.A. RICHTER', stamped '19826/9769/2'.
1928 *55in (140cm) high*
£5,500-6,500 **L&T**

A pair of leather, fabric and bronze-covered wood armchairs, by Paul Dupré-Lafon, with certificate of authenticity.
c1929 *37½in (95.5cm) wide*
£90,000-120,000 **PHI**

A 1930s-50s Epstein Brothers console sideboard, in maple and burr maple veneers, with original twin-tone handles.
58¾in (149cm) wide
£3,000-3,500 **TDG**

A 1930s Epstein six-seater dining suite, with bird's eye maple veneers, restored and re-upholstered in faux suede.
table 72in (183cm) long
£7,500-8,500 **TDG**

An Heal's Art Deco demi-lune walnut desk, with a central locking mechanism, ivorine label.
57in (144.5cm) wide
£4,000-5,000 **SWO**

CLOSER LOOK – ART DECO DRESSING TABLE

This dressing table was designed by George Betjemann and Sons Macassar and retailed by Asprey.

It is made of ebony, with ivory and chrome details.

The hinged top has a triptych fold-out mirror, and the base has two swivel compartments.

It comes with a fitted glass, shagreen and ivory-mounted toilet set, including hallmarked brushes and scent bottles.

An ebony fitted dressing table, marked 'Asprey' and 'GB&S London'.
1928-29 *closed 33¾in (86cm) wide*
£12,000-15,000 **WW**

A 1930s Epstein Brothers lounge suite, in cloud, with wrap-around figured walnut veneers, re-upholstered in faux suede.
sofa 70in (178cm) wide
£13,000-15,000 **TDG**

A 1930s Art Deco burr walnut sideboard, with macassar ebony banding, labelled 'A H Holden, Hammersmith School of Arts and Crafts'.
54¼in (138cm) wide
£2,500-3,000 **TDG**

A 1930s French amboyna, mahogany and silk upholstery club chair, by Jules Leleu (1883-1961), impressed 'LELEU PARIS', refinished, re-upholstered.

28½in (72.5cm) high

£2,000-2,500 **DRA**

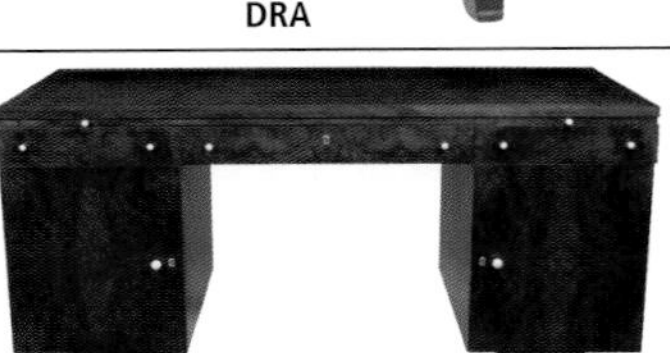

An Art Deco figured walnut pedestal desk, in the manner of Jules Leleu, with ivory handles and escutcheon plates, with bronze sledge feet.

63¼in (160.5cm) wide

£3,500-4,000 **CHOR**

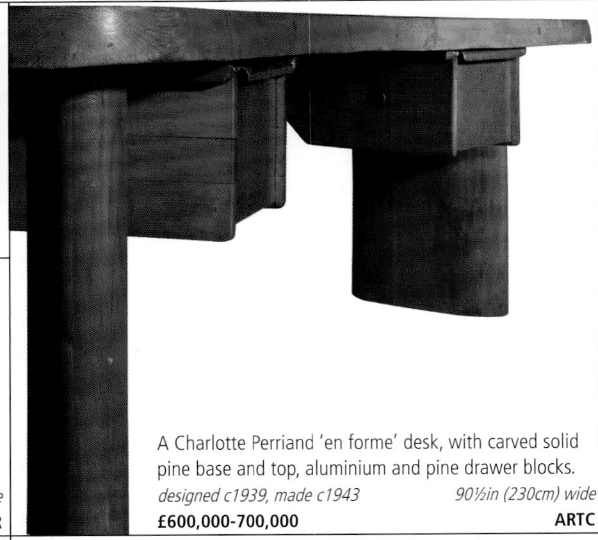

A Charlotte Perriand 'en forme' desk, with carved solid pine base and top, aluminium and pine drawer blocks.

designed c1939, made c1943 *90½in (230cm) wide*

£600,000-700,000 **ARTC**

A rare coffee table, designed by Gio Ponti, made from East Indian rosewood-veneered wood, walnut-veneered wood, walnut, brass and glass, with a certificate of expertise from the Gio Ponti Archives.

c1940 *33½in (85cm) long*

£40,000-45,000 **PHI**

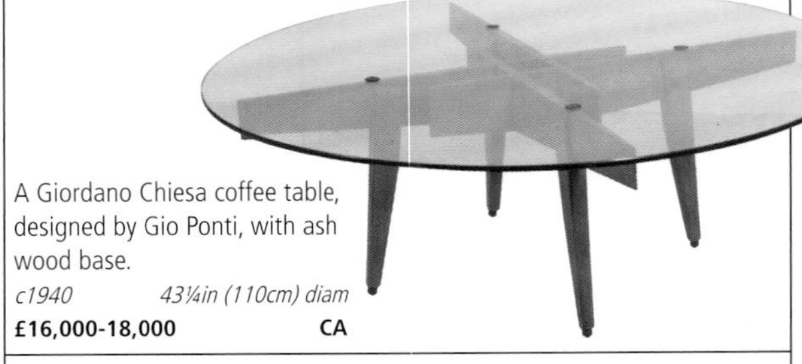

A Giordano Chiesa coffee table, designed by Gio Ponti, with ash wood base.

c1940 *43¼in (110cm) diam*

£16,000-18,000 **CA**

A Isokon painted plywood 'Penguin Donkey' bookcase, designed by Egon Riss (1901-64).

23¼in (59cm) wide

£1,800-2,200 **SWO**

A 1930s Art Deco rosewood and upholstery club chair, by Eugene Schoen, USA/England, impressed 'Hungate Schmieg and Kotzian' mark, refinished and re-upholstered.

29in (73.5cm) wide

£1,000-1,500 **DRA**

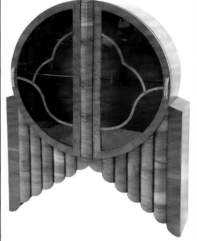

An Art Deco walnut rocket-form display cabinet.

40¼in (102cm) wide

£800-900 **SWO**

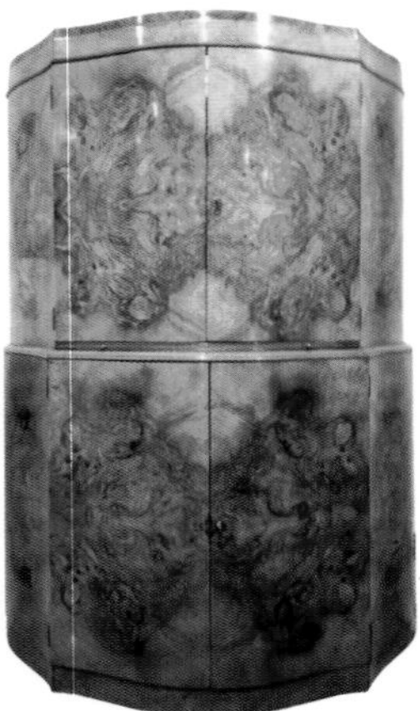

A 1930s Art Deco cocktail cabinet, in figured walnut veneers, the interior fitted and mirrored with light.

61½in (156cm) high

£3,500-4,500 **TDG**

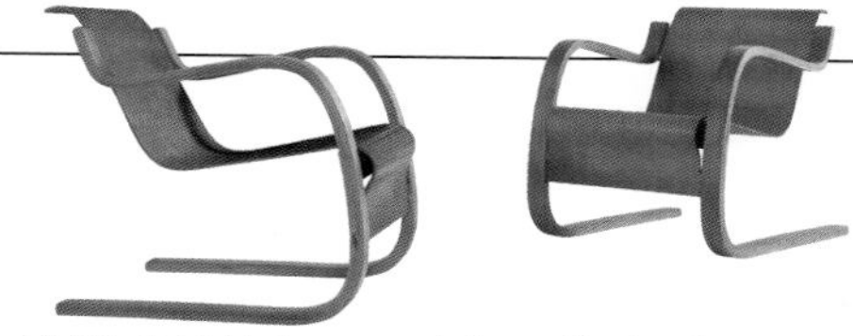

A pair of 1950s Artek birch-veneered plywood 'Paimio' armchairs, designed by Alvar Aalto, Finland, model no.41.
designed 1931-32 *26in (66cm) high*
£12,000-16,000 **PHI**

A set of four pine and steel garden chairs, by Alvar Aalto (1898-1976), Finland, unmarked, some scuffs and scratches.
c1938 *35½in (90cm) high*
£8,000-9,000 **DRA**

A rare pair of walnut, cane and fabric armchairs, by Paolo Buffa, with a certificate of expertise from the Paolo Buffa Archive.
c1940 *30¼in (77cm) wide*
£70,000-80,000 **PHI**

A rare 1940s Johnson Furniture Co. teak, birch, leather and brass ameoba desk, by Paul Frankl (1886-1958), refinished, some veneer sanded through.

The chest-of-drawers and desk can be used separately or together.

66in (167.5cm) long
£4,000-5,000 **DRA**

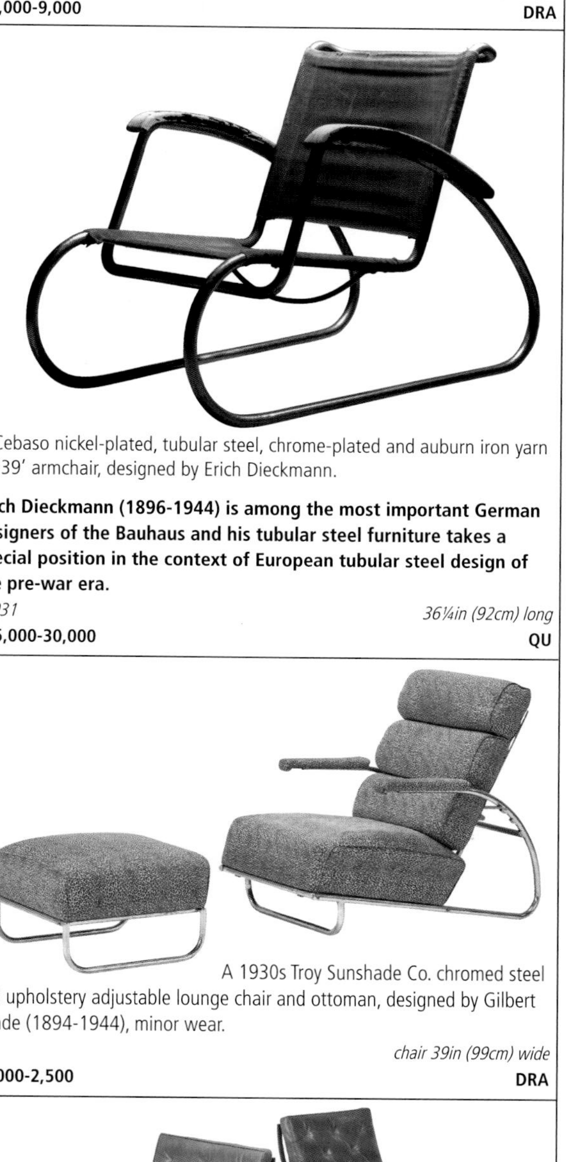

A Cebaso nickel-plated, tubular steel, chrome-plated and auburn iron yarn '8239' armchair, designed by Erich Dieckmann.

Erich Dieckmann (1896-1944) is among the most important German designers of the Bauhaus and his tubular steel furniture takes a special position in the context of European tubular steel design of the pre-war era.

c1931 *36¼in (92cm) long*
£25,000-30,000 **QU**

A pair of 1940s model H-269 bentwood and upholstery armchairs, by Jindrich Halabala (1903-78), Czechoslovakia.
28½in (72.5cm) high
£2,500-3,000 **ROS**

A 1930s Troy Sunshade Co. chromed steel and upholstery adjustable lounge chair and ottoman, designed by Gilbert Rohde (1894-1944), minor wear.
chair 39in (99cm) wide
£2,000-2,500 **DRA**

A pair of 1930s Troy Sunshade chromed steel and vinyl lounge chairs, by Gilbert Rohde, sticker label to one.
29½in (75cm) high
£6,000-7,000 **DRA**

A pair of 1980s Knoll International bronze and leather 'Barcelona' chairs, designed by Ludwig Mies Van Der Rohe (1886-1969).
designed 1929 *31in (78.5cm) high*
£4,500-5,500 **DRA**

Two embroidered panels, by Walter Crane (1845-1915), with period frames.

These panels, with their complex composition inspired by historical design, was probably exhibited as part of the Royal School of Art Needlework's section at the Philadelphia Exposition of 1876.

c1876 *max 56¾in (144cm) high*

£4,000-5,000 **L&T**

A pair of Morris & Co. 'Bird' pattern wool curtains, by William Morris (1834-96), jacquard-woven woollen double cloth, lined with Morris & Co. 'Cray' pattern block-printed cotton fabric.

designed c1884, made c1890

141in (358cm) long

£5,000-6,000 **L&T**

An Alexander Morton & Co. Donegal carpet, by Gavin Morton and G.K. Robertson.

Donegal carpets are a kind of wool carpets produced in Killybegs, a town in County Donegal, Ireland. Alexander Morton (1844-1923) opened several carpet factories in Donegal in the late 1890s.

c1900 *273¼in (694cm) long*

£7,500-8,500 **L&T**

Judith Picks

John Henry Dearle (1859-1932) began his career with Morris & Co. in 1878 as a shop assistant. Morris recognised his potential, and by 1890 he was Head Designer. Under the guidance of May Morris, William Morris's daughter and a skilled embroiderer, Dearle produced a series of portières featuring some of his most recognisable designs. While much of Morris's early embroidery work features repeating patterns, in 'Acanthus', Dearle used a central motif which grounds the piece, surrounded by interlocking vines and swirls of coloured flowers.

A Morris & Co. 'Acanthus', embroidered portière, designed by John Henry Dearle, silk embroidery on linen with green cotton backing, labelled 'MORRIS & COMPANY/449 OXFORD STREET/LONDON. W.'.

c1890 *94½in (240cm) high*

£30,000-35,000 **L&T**

A Morris & Co. Arts and Crafts embroidered panel, later framed and glazed.

This is a previously unrecorded design for Morris & Co. Worked with their silks and with the same techniques, the design demonstrates the characteristic sophisticated style of the company.

c1895 *47¼in (120cm) high*

£3,500-4,000 **L&T**

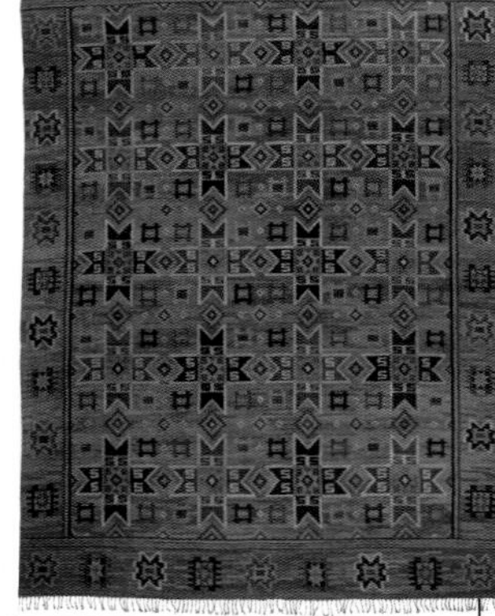

An early 'Stjärnor på rödt' ('Stars on red') rug, by Märta Måås-Fjetterström, handwoven wool on a linen warp, hand-stitched at a later date with designer's intials 'MMF'.

1913-19 *161½in (410cm) long*

£25,000-30,000 **PHI**

A blue marine rug, by Eileen Gray, cleaned.

designed 1920s-30s *137½in (349.5cm) wide*

£1,500-2,000 **DRA**

An Art Deco hand-knotted wool carpet.

c1930 *118in (300cm) diam*

£3,000-3,500 **ROS**

A brass mantel clock, by W.A.S. Benson, with French drum movement.

This rare design is depicted in Ian Hamerton's 'W.A.S. Benson', Antiques Collectors' Club, page 102.

10in (25.5cm) high

£6,500-7,000 SWO

A Martin Brothers stoneware clock case, of architectural form, supported by two dragons, numbered '27', inscribed 'R.W. Martin/London', dated.

See pages 473-475 for more Martin Brothers.

1875 *10½in (26.5cm) high*

£2,000-3,000 WAD

A Burmantoft Faience mantel clock, model no.1429, modelled in relief with a lioness and cubs, impressed 'W.A.', minor glaze loss and frits.

See page 454 for more Burmantofts.

10¼in (26cm) high

£1,200-1,500 WW

A Moorcroft mantel timepiece, with 'Made for Liberty & Co' mark and green 'W. Moorcroft' signature, some crazing, brass bezel tarnished.

See pages 477-479 for more Moorcroft.

c1910 *5½in (14cm) high*

£1,500-2,000 GORL

An Art Nouveau James Fenton & Co. silver and enamel mantel clock, with arched oak case, stamped maker's mark, hallmarked Birmingham.

1906 *6¼in (16cm) high*

£500-600 L&T

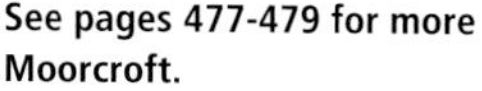

A Liberty & Co. silver 'Cymric' mantle clock, designed by Archibald Knox (1864-1933), hallmarked 'L&CO', Birmingam.

See page 549 for more Liberty & Co.

1902 *3¾in (9.5cm) high*

£8,000-9,000 LOCK

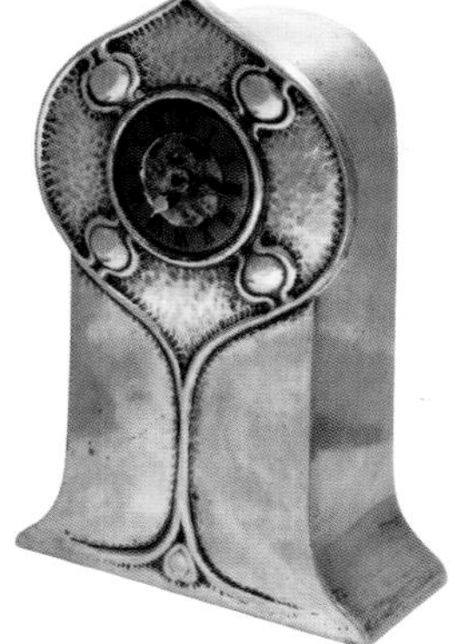

A Liberty & Co. pewter, enamel, copper and glass 'Tudric' clock, by Archibald Knox, stamped 'TUDRIC MADE IN ENGLAND 0629', minor dents.

c1903-14 *7¼in (18.5cm) high*

£3,500-4,000 DRA

A Liberty & Co. pewter and enamelled 'Tudric' mantel timepiece, in Art Nouveau style, within a planished and cast stylised tree, numbered '0557'.

7½in (19cm) high

£3,500-4,000 HAN

A Robert 'Mouseman' Thompson English oak mantel clock, with spring-driven movement, the stepped case simulating bricks, with two carved mice, movement not working, small re-glued chip to one corner, some water marks.

See page 529 for more Mouseman.

12in (30.5cm) wide

£2,800-3,200 TEN

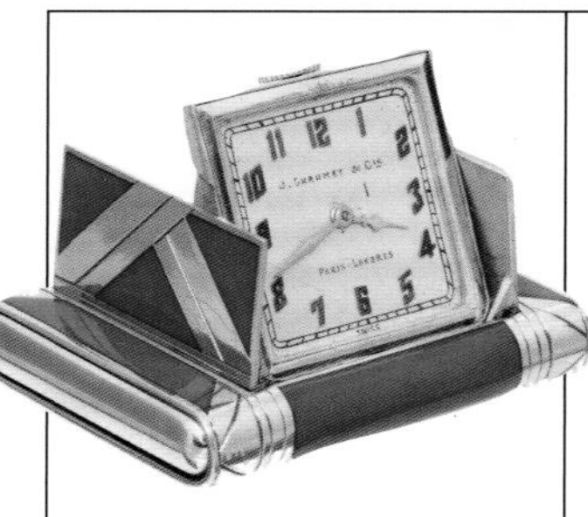

A 1920s Art Deco J. Chaumet & Cie 18ct red enamelled yellow-gold retractable purse timepiece, movement by Vacheron Constantin, stamped indistinctly 'Bte S.G.B.G 12045', dial marked 'J. Chaumet & Cie Paris Londres', enamel restored to reverse.

1½in (4cm) wide

£2,500-3,000 HAN

A Lalique 'Le Jour et La Nuit' clock, in smoky topaz glass and enamelled metal, acid-stamped 'R. LALIQUE', re-enamelled metal base.

designed 1926 *15¾in (40cm) high*

£25,000-30,000 DRA

A 1920s Art Deco E. Mathey-Tissot silver and enamel travel clock, eleven-jewel movement striking on a gong, with lapis lazuli feet and button, the case marked 'Sterling' and 'No.12179', in original case.

Provenance: This piece was given by the Duke and Duchess of Windsor to their butler, Alan Fisher (1930-2006). Fisher worked for the Windsors from 1954 at their French retreat Le Moulin de la Tuilerie at Gif-sur-Yvette and their Parisian home in the Bois de Boulogne.

3½in (9cm) high

£8,000-9,000 HAN

A Stevenson Manufacturing Bakelite, glass and printed paper clock and kitchen timer, by Isamu Noguchi (1904-88), La Porte, IN, some scuffs and scratches.

c1932 *6in (15cm) high*

£500-600 DRA

A French silver clock compendium, retailed by Tiffany and Co., Paris, with ivory numbering, barometer and thermometer, later inscribed to base.

c1920 *2¼in (6cm) high*

£1,500-2,000 WW

A 1940s Art Deco Vitascope Industries Ltd. Bakelite clock, the Odeon-style case with a viewing window with three masted sailing ship automaton.

13in (33cm) high

£500-600 FLD

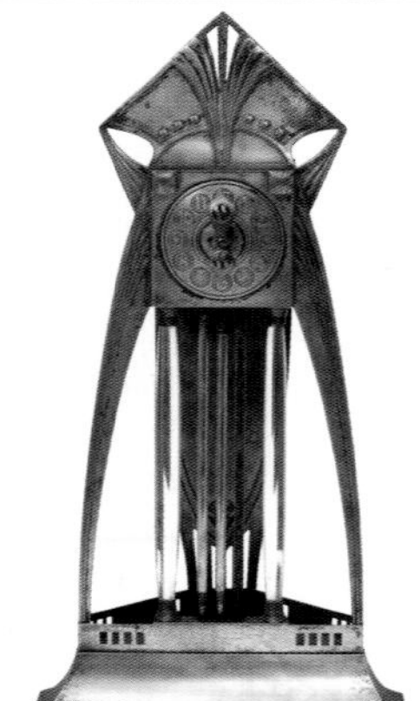

A Continental Secessionist silvered metal mantel clock, in the style of W.M.F.

17½in (44.5cm) high

£1,500-2,000 WW

An early 20thC French Art Deco onyx and marble mantel clock, with eight-day time and strike movement, gilt bronze trim.

26in (66cm) wide

£400-500 DRA

An early 20thC French Art Deco onyx and marble mantel clock.

21in (53.5cm) wide

£300-400 DRA

An Art Deco chinoiserie walnut-cased mantel clock.

c1930 *14in (35.5cm) wide*

£450-550 L&T

A Philippe-Joseph Brocard enamelled glass mosque lamp, with naskh inscription, signed 'Brocard'.

Philippe-Joseph Brocard was initially a glass restorer and later created his own pieces. He is credited with rediscovering the techniques of glass enamelling which would inspire Art Nouveau designers such as Émile Gallé and Daum. Brocard's mosque lamps were shown at the International Exhibition in London in 1871.

7in (17.5cm) long

£2,000-3,000 WW

A Loetz chandelier, with an iridescent blown shade, on brass chains and ceiling cap, shallow flake on fitter.

40in (101.5cm) high

£2,500-3,000 JDJ

An Arts and Crafts glass and patinated brass five-light hanging fixture, with Loetz-style shades, fixture marked 'UNO', some chips.

17¾in (45cm) diam

£800-900 DRA

A pair of 20thC coloured glass and repoussé brass dish lights, one pane cracked.

53¼in (135cm) diam

£2,000-2,500 SWO

An Arts and Crafts ironwork lamp, in the manner of Edward Spencer for Artificers Guild, with Monart glass bowl, no.VIII of 70a, paper label.

50¾in (129cm) high

£700-800 DUK

A Siot-Decauville gilded bronze table light, 'La danse, la Loïe Fuller', by Larche Raoul, made for the Paris World Fair, signed, foundry mark 'SIOT-DECAUVILLE FONDEUR'.

1900 18in (45.5cm) high

£30,000-35,000 QU

An Art Nouveau patinated bronze table lamp, 'La Voie Lactee' (The Milky Way), by Leo Laporte-Blairsy (1865-1923), with a cased blue glass shade probably made by Daum, signed.

An example of this spectacular bronze lamp was exhibited at the Salon of the Societe des Artistes Francais in 1904.

16¼in (41.5cm) high

£30,000-35,000 WW

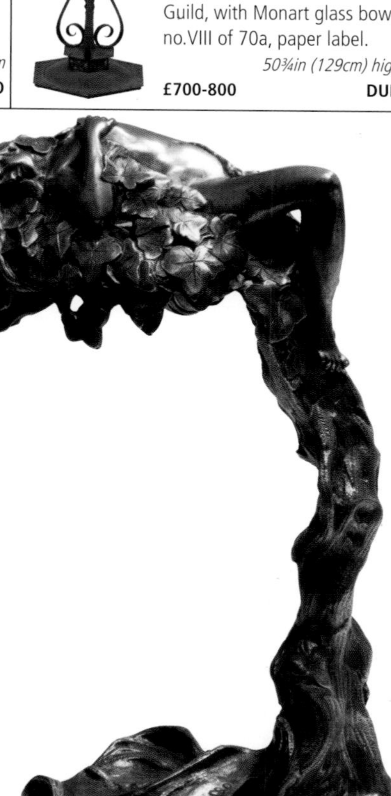

A bronze 'Daphne' table light, by Emil Thomasson, signed, re-electrified.

c1902 11½in (29cm) high

£2,000-2,500 QU

A Daum cameo grapevine table lamp, with hammered iron collar and three-armed spider, signed, base signed 'DNF' with Cross of Lorraine, rewired.

14½in (37cm) high

£5,000-5,500 **JDJ**

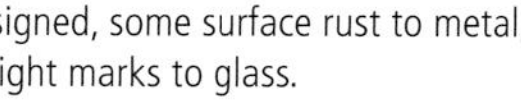

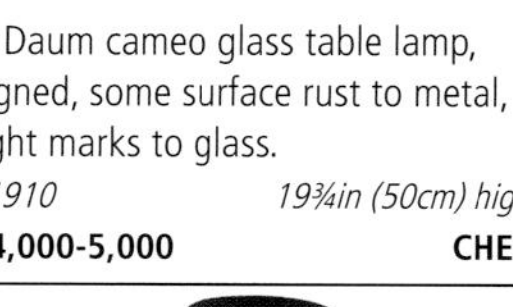

A Daum cameo glass table lamp, signed, some surface rust to metal, light marks to glass.

c1910 *19¾in (50cm) high*

£4,000-5,000 **CHEF**

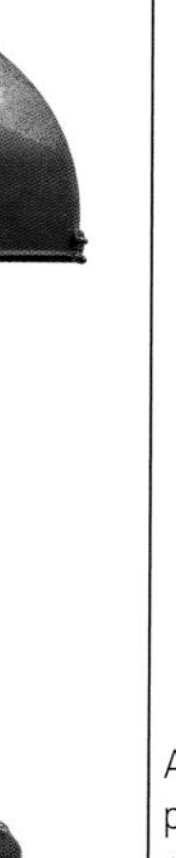

A Daum 'Verre de Jade' table light, on wrought-iron foot.

1918-25 *19¾in (50cm) high*

£3,000-3,500 **QU**

A 1930s Daum and Edgar Brandt patinated wrought iron and glass chandelier, metal stamped 'FRANCE E. BRANDT', shades signed 'DAUM NANCY FRANCE' with Cross of Lorraine.

35in (89cm) high

£5,500-6,000 **DRA**

CLOSER LOOK – GALLÉ 'CLEMATIS' LAMP

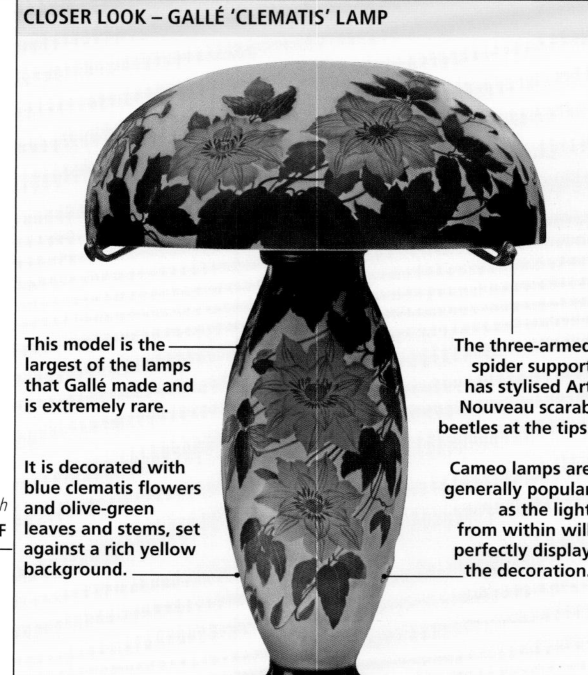

This model is the largest of the lamps that Gallé made and is extremely rare.

It is decorated with blue clematis flowers and olive-green leaves and stems, set against a rich yellow background.

The three-armed spider support has stylised Art Nouveau scarab beetles at the tips.

Cameo lamps are generally popular as the light from within will perfectly display the decoration.

A Gallé cameo glass 'Clematis' lamp, signed 'Galle' in cameo.

31in (78.5cm) high

£150,000-200,000 **MORP**

An early 20thC Gallé painted metal and acid-etched cameo glass clematis plafonnier, signed, some bubbles around rim, replacement metal components.

24in (61cm) high

£4,500-5,500 **DRA**

An early 20thC Gallé cameo lamp, acid-etched with flowers, signed, some scuffs to base.

17¼in (44cm) high

£4,500-5,000 **DRA**

A Le Verre Francais cameo glass table lamp, signed, some dimpling to surface in the making.

17in (43cm) high

£3,500-4,000 **JDJ**

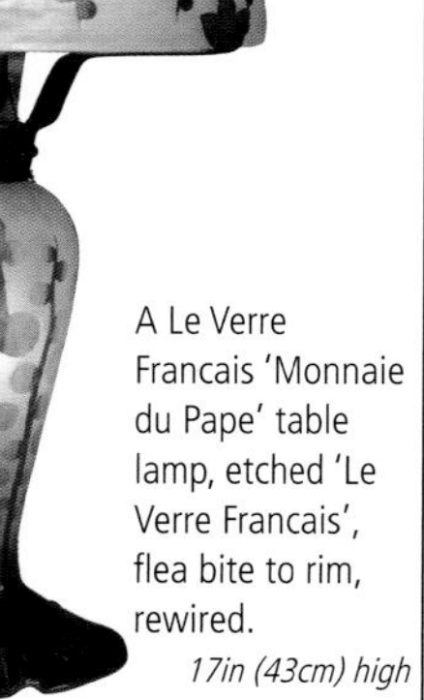

A Le Verre Francais 'Monnaie du Pape' table lamp, etched 'Le Verre Francais', flea bite to rim, rewired.

17in (43cm) high

£3,000-3,500 **JDJ**

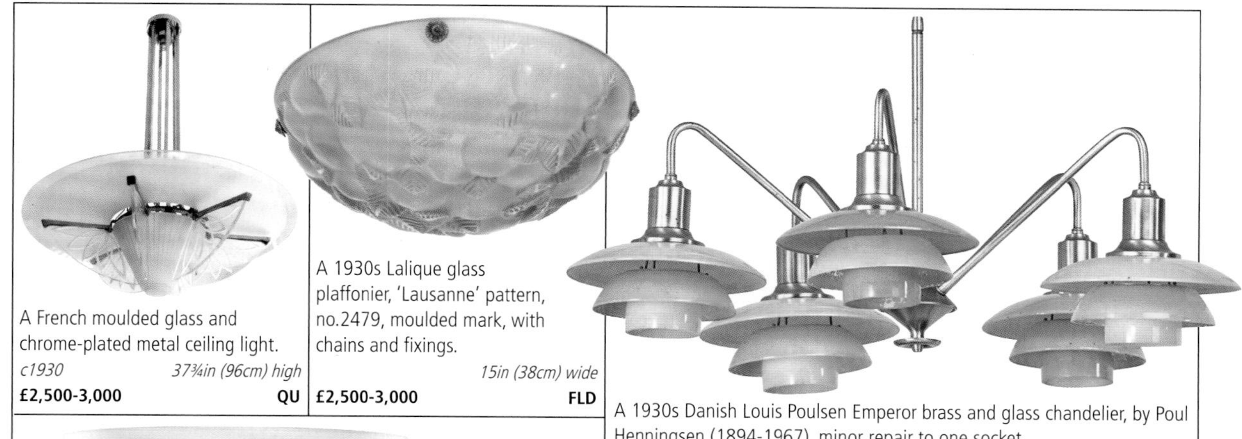

A French moulded glass and chrome-plated metal ceiling light.
c1930 *37¾in (96cm) high*
£2,500-3,000 **QU**

A 1930s Lalique glass plaffonier, 'Lausanne' pattern, no.2479, moulded mark, with chains and fixings.
15in (38cm) wide
£2,500-3,000 **FLD**

A 1930s Danish Louis Poulsen Emperor brass and glass chandelier, by Poul Henningsen (1894-1967), minor repair to one socket.
24in (61cm) diam
£4,000-4,500 **DRA**

An early-to-mid 20thC French glazed earthenware and patinated metal table lamp, by Jean Besnard (1889-1958), signed, rewired, with new paper shade.
27in (68.5cm) high
£5,500-6,000 **DRA**

A pair of 1930s-50s Art Deco chrome dome table lamps, re-wired and PAT tested.
21in (53.5cm) high
£2,200-2,600 **TDG**

An Art Deco carved alabaster and bronze mounted table lamp, on a cold-painted bronze base, with later shade.
c1925 *base 10½in (26.5cm) high*
£850-950 **ROS**

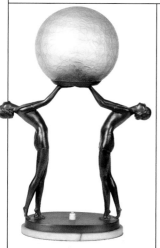

An Art Deco gilt patinated spelter figural lamp, stamped 'Foreign', on onyx base, cracks to shade, in need of re-wiring.
20in (51cm) high
£1,200-1,600 **TEN**

An Art Deco bronzed metal lamp, with opaque glass ball shade.
25½in (65cm) high
£550-600 **BE**

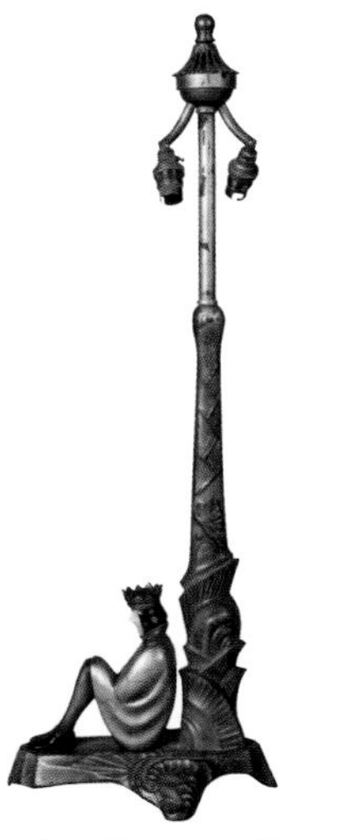

A cold-painted bronze and ivory figural table lamp, by Roland Paris and C. Morin, signed 'C. Morin'.
c1930 *22½in (57cm) high*
£2,000-2,500 **ROS**

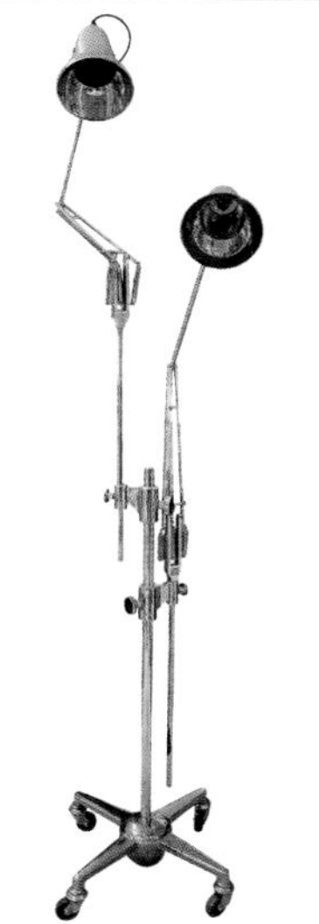

A Herbert Terry Anglepoise trolley lamp, model no.1227.
c1935-55 *73in (185.5cm) high*
£1,200-1,500 **TDG**

ESSENTIAL REFERENCE – TIFFANY LAMPS

Tiffany Studios began as Tiffany Glass Company in 1885.

- **It was founded by Louis Comfort Tiffany (1848-1933), the son of one of the founders of Tiffany & Co. He had trained as a painter in New York and Paris, later specialising in stained glass.**
- **In 1893 Louis Comfort Tiffany created and trademarked Favrile glass (see also pages 520-521).**
- **In 1895 the firm made its first Tiffany lamp. This was not designed by Louis Comfort Tiffany himself but by Clara Driscoll, one of the company's designers.**
- **Typically in the Art Nouveau style, Tiffany lamps usually consist of a leaded slag glass shade and a patinated metal base. The shades were produced by fusing hundreds of pieces of coloured glass together.**
- **Tiffany lamps became incredibly popular and are still prized by collectors today, often fetching very high prices.**

An early 20thC Tiffany Studios leaded slag glass 'Arrowroot' shade, on associated reproduction patinated metal base, metal 'TIFFANY STUDIOS NEW YORK' tag to shade, some cracks to glass, loss of one piece.

26¼in (66.5cm) high

£42,000-50,000 **DRA**

A Tiffany Studios 'Dogwood' table lamp, on bronze library base, the shade with 'Tiffany Studios New York' tag, base signed, some hairlines.

26in (66cm) high

£46,000-50,000 **MORP**

CLOSER LOOK – TIFFANY 'DRAGONFLY' TABLE LAMP

The leaded glass shade is decorated with dragonflies, each with striated red and cream wings, deep red bodies and blue eyes.

These are set against a heavily texture, striated green and amber background, embellished with oval green glass cabochons.

The leading and etched bronze wing overlays are finished in a rich brown patina.

The shade rests on a Tiffany Studios faux turtleback bronze base, finished in a two-tone patina of dark brown and gold dore.

A Tiffany Studios 'Dragonfly' table lamp, fully signed, some tight hairlines, rewired.

23in (58.5cm) high

£50,000-60,000 **JDJ**

A Tiffany Studios 'Linenfold' table lamp, shade signed 'Tiffany Studios New York 1927 PAT, APPL'D FOR', base signed, some small cracks, some discolouration to base.

24in (61cm) high

£14,000-18,000 **JDJ**

An early 20thC Tiffany Studios 'Lotus' table lamp, metal 'TIFFANY STUDIOS NEW YORK' tag to shade, base stamped, some cracks.

26½in (67.5cm) high

£55,000-60,000 **DRA**

A Tiffany Studios 'Shell' table lamp, base stamped 'TIFFANY STUDIOS NEW YORK 9936', metal tag 'TIFFANY STUDIOS NEW YORK', some cracks to glass.

c1900 *21in (53.5cm) high*

£11,000-14,000 **DRA**

A Tiffany Studios 'Woodbine' table lamp, shade with applied labels stamped 'TIFFANY STUDIOS/ NEW YORK', base impressed 'TIFFANY STUDIOS/ NEW YORK' and numbered '333', some heat cracks.

c1910 *19¾in (50cm) high*

£15,000-20,000 **WES**

A Tiffany Studios banded floral table lamp, on a bronze base, signed to shade 'Tiffany Studios New York', base signed 'Tiffany Studios New York 21667' with Tiffany logo.

23in (58.5cm) high

£35,000-40,000 **JDJ**

A 1920s Tiffany Studios table lamp, blue wave-pattern Favrile glass shade on acid-etched gilt bronze base, shade etched 'L.C.T. Favrile', base stamped, rewired, replaced socket and paddle switch.

17¾in (45cm) high

£23,000-30,000 **DRA**

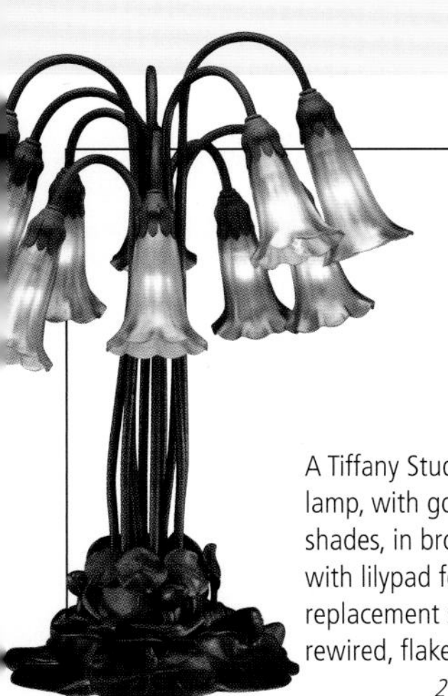

A Tiffany Studios ten-light lamp, with gold Favrile lily shades, in bronze fixture with lilypad foot, signed, replacement switch, rewired, flakes and chips.

21in (53.5cm) high

£15,000-20,000 **JDJ**

A pair of Tiffany Studios 'Jewelled' bronze and blue Favrile ribbed glass candlesticks, engraved 'L.C.T. 4846' and '4849', bases signed.

c1910 *23¼in (59cm) high*

£11,000-15,000 **DOY**

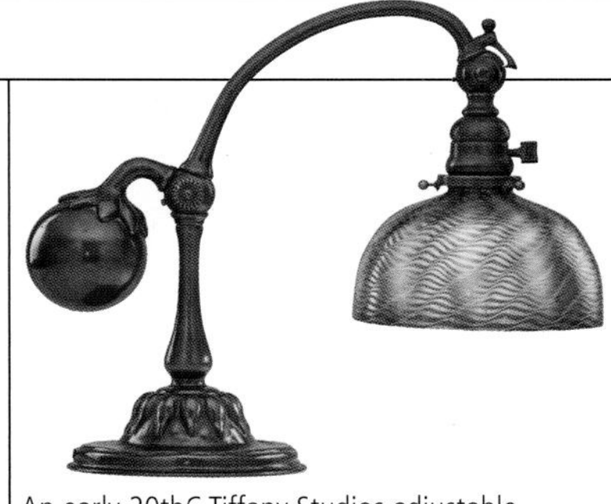

An early 20thC Tiffany Studios adjustable counterbalance desk lamp, 'Wave' pattern shade, base stamped, shade etched 'L.C.T. Favrile', some flecks to glass, one bubble.

14in (35.5cm) high

£6,000-8,000 **DRA**

An early 20thC Tiffany Studios floor lamp, with Favrile glass wave pattern shade, base stamped, shade etched 'L.C. Tiffany-Favrile', some chips.

56in (142cm) high

£5,000-6,000 **DRA**

A 1920s Tiffany Studios glass 'Linenfold' table lamp, stamped 'TIFFANY STUDIOS NEW YORK 590', baseplate replaced, broken pullchain, some oxidation to base.

19in (48.5cm) high

£3,500-4,000 **DRA**

An early 20thC Tiffany Studios leaded slag glass hanging shade, with metal tag, with modern reproduction hardware and chains, some cracks.

62in (157.5cm) high

£10,000-12,000 **DRA**

A early 20thC Tiffany Studios 'Acorn' hanging shade, with metal 'TIFFANY STUDIOS NEW YORK' tag, minor cracks, installed associated wheel for use as a chandelier.

20in (51cm) wide

£7,500-8,500 **DRA**

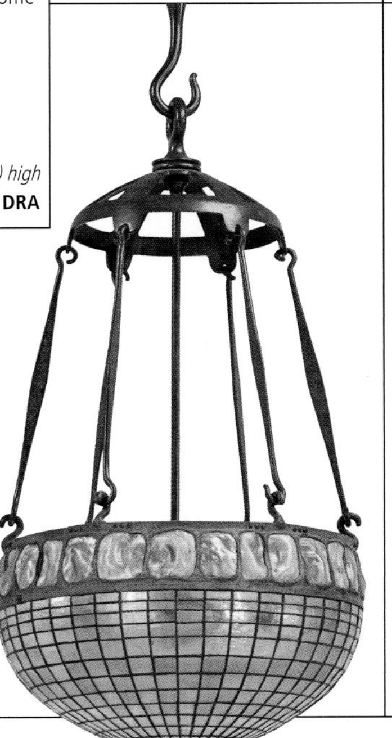

An early 20thC Tiffany Studios 'Turtleback' chandelier, leaded slag glass with Favrile glass tiles, metal tag to shade, some cracks to glass.

55in (139.5cm) high

£22,000-26,000 **DRA**

A Tiffany Studios 'Turtleback' lantern, with iridescent turtleback tiles and bronze wire coins.

28in (71cm) high

£55,000-60,000 **MORP**

DECORATIVE ARTS

A Handel 'Hawaii' opal glass table light, signed 'HANDEL', with bronze foot.

Philip J. Handel and Adolph Eydam founded Eydam and Handel in 1885 in Meriden, Connecticut. By 1903 Handel had bought out his partner and the firm became the Handel Company. The firm was best known for its distinctive reverse-painted glass lampshades.

c1910 *23½in (60cm) high*

£2,500-3,000 **QU**

CLOSER LOOK – HANDEL 'AQUARIUM' LAMP

The finial topping of the lamp is formed as a trident.
This Handel lamp is decorated with reverse-painted panels of underwater scenes, showing fish swimming amongst aquatic plants.
Each panel is finished on the exterior with chipped ice.
The original Handel two-armed base is decorated with fish and aquatic plants, and finished in a rich brown patina with green highlights.

A Handel 'Aquarium' lamp, numbered and signed 'Handel', re-wired with plastic cord.

14½in (37cm) wide

£50,000-55,000 **JDJ**

A Handel 'Wisteria' table lamp, the tree trunk base with leaded branches and openwork top, signed to shade, signed to base 'Handel', some hairlines and oxidation.

31in (78.5cm) high

£11,000-14,000 **MORP**

A 1910s Handel Art and Crafts-style table lamp, with obverse-painted acid-etched glass shade, shade signed, some chips to shade, resoldering to shade ring.

19½in (49.5cm) high

£1,800-2,200 **DRA**

A Handel table lamp, reverse-painted shade acid-etched with birds of paradise and roses, fully signed, sockets replaced, scratches to heat cap, finial possibly associated.

designed c1924 *24in (61cm) high*

£5,000-6,000 **DRA**

A Handel 'Birds of Paradise' table lamp, signed, artist signed 'Broggi', base signed 'Handel', minor wear.

23½in (59.5cm) high

£4,000-5,000 **MORP**

A Handel patinated metal and iridised glass globe pendant, reverse and obverse-painted, shade signed 'HANDEL 6996', minor flecks to glass, associated ceiling cap.

designed c1922 *28in (71cm) high*

£2,000-2,500 **DRA**

A Handel cast metal and glass torchière, reverse-painted with stylised daisies, fully signed.

15½in (39.5cm) high

£1,100-1,400 **MORP**

A Handel patinated metal and glass floor lamp, reverse-painted acid-etched shade, fully signed, rewired.

designed 1921 *61in (155cm) high*

£6,000-7,000 **DRA**

An early 20thC hammered copper and blown glass chandelier, attributed to Benedict Studios, Syracuse, NY, some scratches.

28in (71cm) high

£2,500-3,000 **DRA**

An early 20thC Classique table lamp, Chicago, IL, reverse-painted and acid-etched, fabric label to base, rewired, socket guts replaced, some scratches.

22½in (57cm) high

£1,800-2,200 **DRA**

A Duffner and Kimberly 'Waterlillies' table lamp, three sockets marked 'HUBBELL'.

1906-11 *22½in (57cm) high*

£6,000-7,000 **NA**

A Duffner and Kimberly hanging leaded glass light fixture, with metal tag.

c1910 *28in (71cm) wide*

£1,800-2,200 **CLAR**

CLOSER LOOK – FULPER VASEKRAFT LAMP

This lamp was made by Fulper, a pottery firm based in Flemington, New Jersey (see page 466).
The shade is made of earthenware and leaded slag glass.
The base is made of earthenware, finished with a 'Leopard Skin Crystalline' glaze.
Fulper Arts and Crafts 'Vasekraft' lamps were made c1911-18 and are distinctively shaped. This is a very rare and fine example.

A 1910s Fulper 'Vasekraft' lamp, vertical rectangular ink stamps, some grinding chips.

17¾in (45cm) high

£20,000-25,000 **DRA**

A Fulper 'Vasekraft' glazed earthenware and slag glass hanging shade, ink stamp, some chips, restoration to rim.

c1915 *15in (38cm) diam*

£5,000-6,000 **DRA**

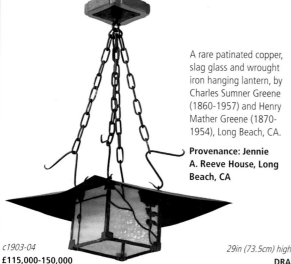

A rare patinated copper, slag glass and wrought iron hanging lantern, by Charles Sumner Greene (1860-1957) and Henry Mather Greene (1870-1954), Long Beach, CA.

Provenance: Jennie A. Reeve House, Long Beach, CA

c1903-04 *29in (73.5cm) high*

£115,000-150,000 **DRA**

An early 20thC Frederick Lueders patinated copper and conch shell floriform lamp, signed 'DESIGNED & EXECUTED BY F.H.W. LUEDERS PASADENA CA.', rewired, some wear.

19in (48.5cm) high

£4,500-5,500 **DRA**

A John Morgan & Sons table lamp, with leaded glass shade with pansies, with enamelled detail, on bronze base, some tight hairlines.

23in (58.5cm) high

£18,000-22,000 **JDJ**

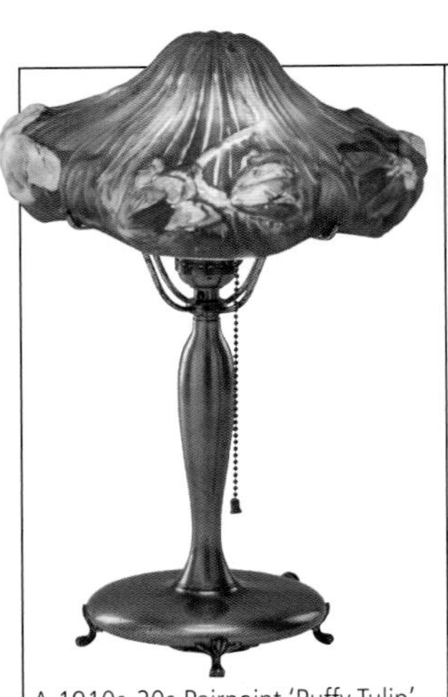

A 1910s-20s Pairpoint 'Puffy Tulip' patinated metal and frosted glass boudoir lamp, base stamped, three chips to shade, losses to gold paint.

14¾in (37.5cm) high

£1,500-2,000 **DRA**

A Pittsburg 'Native American' table lamp, reverse-painted, the base with textured glass body painted with Native American tapestries, two socket cluster, rewired.

16½in (42cm) wide

£3,000-4,000 **MORP**

A rare Gustav Stickley hammered copper and leaded slag glass lantern, with stylised flowers.

c1905 *12¼in (31cm) high*

£55,000-60,000 **DRA**

An early 20thC Gustav Stickley hammered copper and glass newel post lantern.

19½in (49.5cm) high

£3,500-4,000 **DRA**

An early 20thC Unique 'Cherry Blossom' table lamp, Brooklyn, NY, some splits and cracks, rewired.

29½in (75cm) high

£1,200-1,600 **DRA**

A Dirk Van Erp (1860-1933) hammered copper and mica table lamp, open-box windmill stamp, base resoldered, some scratches to shade, rewired.

c1915 *20½in (52cm) high*

£4,000-5,000 **DRA**

A Dirk Van Erp hammered copper and mica 'Bean Pot' table lamp, open-box windmill mark, some scratches.

c1913-15 *10½in (26.5cm) high*

£4,500-5,500 **WES**

One of a pair of early 20thC Arts and Crafts hammered iron and patinated metal chandeliers, with slag glass lanterns, some cracks, both needing rewiring.

33in (84cm) high

£650-750 the pair **DRA**

An Arts and Crafts leaded glass table lamp, with patinated floral-decorated three socket standard.

c1920 *25in (63.5cm) high*

£1,400-2,000 **CLAR**

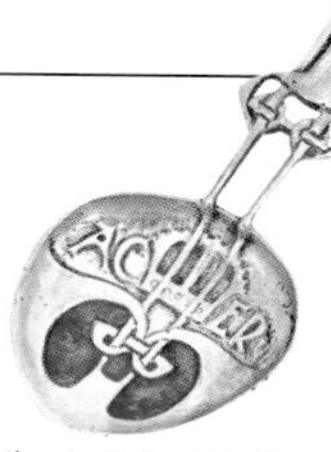

A Liberty & Co. Art Nouveau silver and enamelled spoon, commemorating King Edward VII and Queen Alexandra, the bowl detailed 'AC ERVII', detailed 'CYMRIC Rd391475', small chips to enamel.

The department store Liberty & Co. opened in London in 1875 as a furniture and drapery shop, known as East India House. It expanded in the late 19thC, commissioning and creating carpets, ceramics, clothing, furniture and silver. It registered its own silver hallmark in 1894; the majority of its silver was made in Birmingham.

1901 *4¾in (12cm) high ¾oz*
£1,500-2,000 **BELL**

A Liberty & Co. silver Cymric Coronation Spoon, by Archibald Knox (1864-1933), inscribed 'AC ER VII', stamped 'L&C Cymric', Birmingham.

1902 *6¼in (16cm) long*
£400-500 **LSK**

A set of six Liberty & Co., London 'Cymric' silver and enamel coffee spoons, by Archibald Knox, stamped maker's marks 'L&Co', hallmarked Birmingham.

1929 *4¼in (11cm) long*
£650-750 **L&T**

A Liberty & Co. Art Nouveau silver vase, stamped maker's marks 'L&Co', hallmarked Birmingham.

This piece was designed by Oliver Baker for the 'Cymric' range; the original design for 1900 indicated the collar should be enamelled. Only one example dated 1901 is known. It is more commonly found in pewter.

1900 *5½in (14cm) high 32⅞oz*
£3,000-3,500 **L&T**

A Liberty & Co. Arts and Crafts silver and enamel napkin 'Cymric' ring.

1904 *2in (5cm) diam 1¼oz*
£400-500 **APAR**

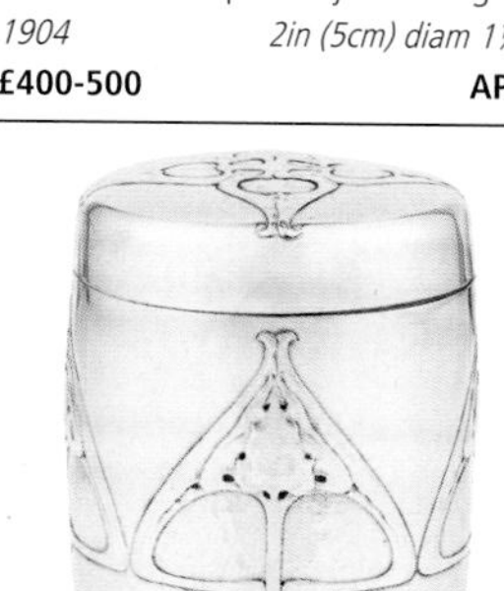

A Liberty & Co. Art Nouveau 'Cymric' silver box and cover, stamped maker's marks 'CYMRIC/ L&Co', hallmarked London.

1902 *5¼in (13.5cm) high 15¼oz*
£950-1,100 **L&T**

A Liberty & Co. Art Nouveau silver and enamel menu card holder, with registration number.

1906 *1½in (4cm) long ¼oz*
£400-500 **WW**

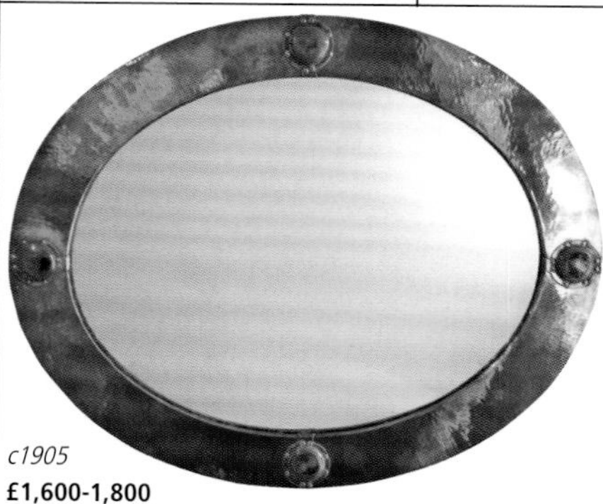

A Liberty & Co. copper-framed mirror with ceramic cabochons, with 'Liberty' label.

c1905 *24¾in (63cm) wide*
£1,600-1,800 **TDG**

A Liberty & Co. pewter 'Tudric' rose bowl, by David Veazey, with inscription 'THE MUSK OF THE ROSE IS BLOWN AND THE WOODBINE SPICES ARE WAFTED ABROAD', stamped '011'.

c1900 *12¼in (31cm) wide*
£300-400 **L&T**

A Liberty & Co. pewter 'Tudric' flower vase and liner, by Archibald Knox, stamped 'MADE IN ENGLAND/TUDRIC/0957'.

c1900 *8¾in (22cm) high*
£400-500 **L&T**

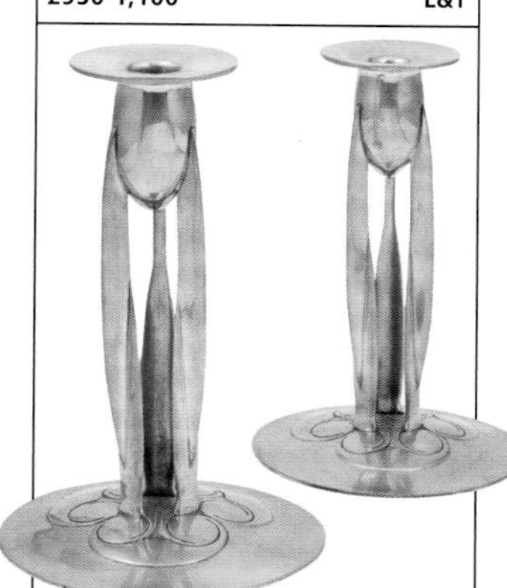

A pair of Liberty & Co. pewter 'Tudric' candlesticks, by Archibald Knox, stamped 'MADE IN ENGLAND/ENGLISH PEWTER/0223'.

c1905 *9¼in (23.5cm) high*
£700-800 **L&T**

A Tiffany & Co. mokume and silver cup and saucer, marked '5044/900', French import marks.

Mokume is a Japanese metalworking technique which produces a mixed-metal laminate of layered patterns, imitating wood grain. Tiffany & Co. design director Edward C. Moore owned several examples of Japanese mokume, and in the late 1870s his firm mastered the technique.

c1878 *saucer 4in (10cm) wide*

£6,500-7,500 DRA

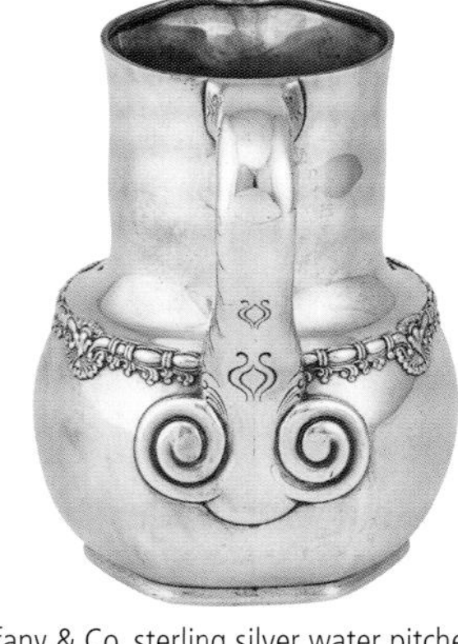

A Tiffany & Co. sterling silver water pitcher, marked '7097/4523'.

1882-91 *8in (20.5cm) high 34⅝oz*

£2,000-2,500 DRA

A 20thC Tiffany & Co. bronze floor vase, stamped 'Tiffany & Co. 19039D', light scratches.

18in (45.5cm) high

£1,100-1,500 DRA

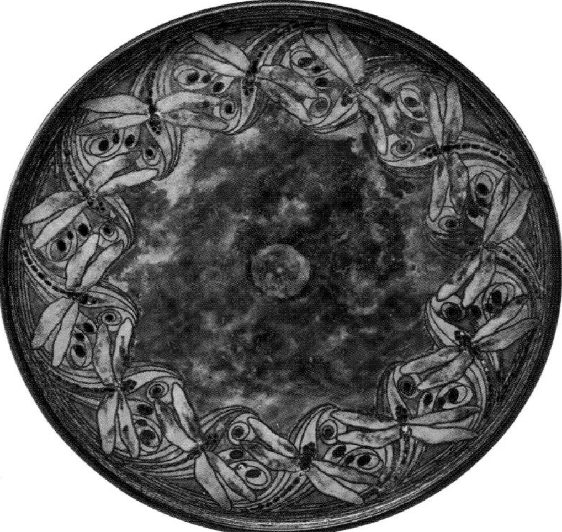

A Tiffany Studios enamelled copper dragonfly tray, stamped 'TGDCO. TIFFANY STUDIOS NEW YORK 2/9064', small losses to enamel.

This design is closely related to the 'Swirling Dragonfly' leaded shade.

c1900 *14¾in (37.5cm) diam*

£30,000-35,000 DRA

A Tiffany Studios bronze and glass scarab inkwell, stamped 'TGDCO. TIFFANY STUDIOS NEW YORK 25056', with dark overcoat.

c1900 *4¼in (11cm) high*

£4,500-5,500 DRA

A Tiffany Studios picture frame, marked 'Tiffany Studios New York 949', inscribed '1858 A.F-HMc A. 1908'.

The glass backing of red, purple, blue and green, gives the effect of a sunset when back lit.

7in (17.5cm) high

£900-1,000 JDJ

A 1920s Tiffany Studios cedar and gilt and enamelled bronze cigar box, no.134, stamped 'LOUIS C. TIFFANY FURNACES INC FAVRILE 134', minor wear to gilding.

7in (18cm) wide

£1,600-2,000 DRA

A 1920s Tiffany Studios acid-etched gilt bronze and glass 'Zodiac' picture frame, stamped 'TIFFANY STUDIOS NEW YORK 920', some wear.

14in (35.5cm) high

£2,000-2,500 DRA

A Tiffany Studios Chinese-style bronze inkwell, with original glass insert, signed 'Tiffany Studios New York 1753', some wear to patina.

6in (15cm) wide

£1,300-1,600 JDJ

ESSENTIAL REFERENCE – GEORG JENSEN

Georg Jensen (1866-1935) was the son of a Danish knife grinder. He was apprenticed as a goldsmith and also worked as a modeller in a porcelain factory.

- **He opened a pottery workshop in 1898, but soon gave this up to work as a silversmith and designer. In 1904 he founded his own silversmith shop, the Georg Jensen Co.**
- **He took inspiration from the Arts and Crafts and Art Nouveau Movements to create his distinctive style. He is known for his hollowware and jewellery (see page 364).**
- **He encouraged his designers to work in their own styles, and worked with many talented people, including Gundorph Albertus (1887-1969), Henning Koppel (1918-81), Harald Nielsen (1892-1977), Johan Rohde (1865-1935) and Vivianna Torun Bülow-Hübe (1927-2004).**
- **George Jensen died in 1935. Georg Jensen Co. is still operational today.**

A Georg Jensen sterling silver and wood tea caddy, model no.136.
c1915-30 *5¼in (13.5cm) high*
£5,000-5,500 **DOY**

A Georg Jensen sterling silver centerpiece bowl, model no.252.
c1915-30 *10¼in (26cm) diam 42oz*
£7,500-8,500 **DOY**

A Georg Jensen sterling silver compote, 'Grape' pattern, model no.265A.
designed 1918 *11in (28cm) high 38¼oz*
£4,500-5,500 **FRE**

A Georg Jensen sterling silver beaker, no.338, with a band of rosettes and garnet cabochons, marked, some wear.
1925-32 *4½in (11.5cm) high 7⅛oz*
£3,500-4,000 **DRA**

A Georg Jensen sterling silver footed bowl, 'Louvre' pattern, no.19A, marked.
1925-32 *8in (20.5cm) diam*
£2,200-3,000 **DRA**

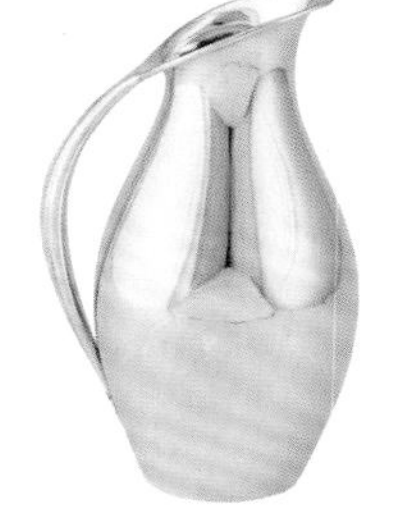

A Georg Jensen sterling silver water pitcher, designed by Johan Rohde, no.432A, marked.
1933-44 *9in (23cm) high 17¼oz*
£2,500-3,000 **DRA**

A Georg Jensen sterling silver toast rack, designed by Oscar Gundlach Pedersen, no.510, marked, light scratches.
1933-44 *6in (15cm) long 7⅜oz*
£3,500-4,000 **DRA**

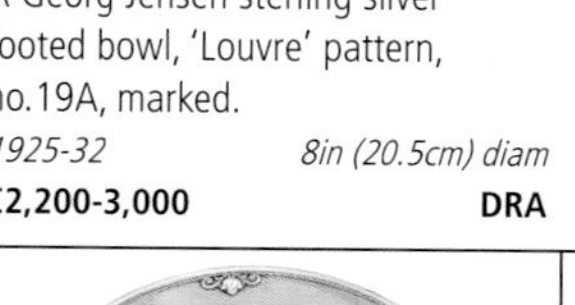

A Georg Jensen sterling silver serving platter, 'Acorn' pattern, designed by Gundorph Albertus, no.642S, marked, minor scratches.
1945-77 *16¾in (42.5cm) diam 44⅞oz*
£3,500-4,000 **DRA**

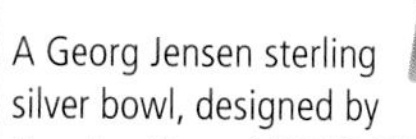

A Georg Jensen sterling silver bowl, designed by Henning Koppel (1918-81), with artist's monogram and maker's marks 'A11/HK/GEORG JENSEN/ STERLING/DENMARK/925S/980A'.

This asymmetrical bowl was designed in 1948 and received the gold medal at the 1951 Milan Triennale. An example of this model is kept in the collection at Goldsmiths' Hall, London.
designed 1948 *15¾in (40cm) wide 124¾oz*
£9,500-11,000 **L&T**

A Georg Jensen silver 'blossom' pattern oval tray, post-1945 mark, marked 'DENMARK,' 'GEORG JENSEN', 'STERLING' and '2E'.
22¼in (56.5cm) long 53oz
£7,000-8,000 **NA**

A pair of Edwardian J. Aitkin & Son silver-mounted photograph frames, later cold enamel accents, Birmingham, refurbished, some surface scratches.

1909 *7¼in (18.5cm) high*

£800-1,000 **FELL**

A set of four early 20thC Japanese Art Nouveau silver and jade cups, impressed with the marks of the English-owned Arthur & Bond Company of Yokohama and with a 'Sterling' mark.

4¼in (11cm) diam silver 9⅜oz

£750-850 **JN**

An Artificers Guild Arts and Crafts silver powder pot and cover, with chrysoprase finial and punch borders, London.

1919 *4½in (11.5cm) diam 12oz*

£3,000-3,500 **WW**

An early 20thC J.E. Caldwell & Co. sterling silver 'Chrysanthemum' vase, Philadelphia, fully marked, numbered '3975', some dents and abrasions.

17½in (44.5cm) high 49½oz

£1,500-2,000 **WES**

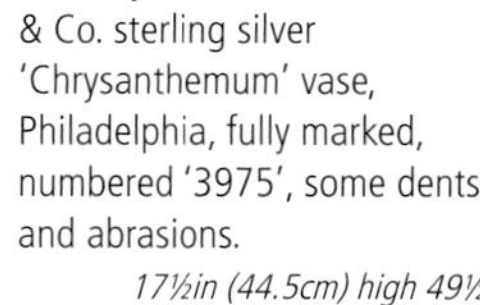

A pair of James Dixon & Son Arts and Crafts silver candlesticks, probably designed by Jan Eisenloeffel (1876-1957), Sheffield, some dings, filled.

1919 *8¾in (22cm) high*

£1,800-2,200 **TEN**

An Elkington & Co. silver tea and coffee set, pattern no.16644, with engraved Japanese-style decoration, Birmingham.

1891 *60¼oz*

£2,000-2,500 **PW**

A Gieves Ltd. Art Deco silver tea and coffee set, with Bakelite handles, Birmingham.

Provenance: With original Thurlow Champness & Son of Abbegate Street, Bury St Edmunds, purchase receipt dated 6 April 1968, for a total of £105.

1933 *coffee pot 7in (17.5cm) high 57oz*

£1,200-1,600 **LSK**

ESSENTIAL REFERENCE – CHRISTOPHER DRESSER

Christopher Dresser (1834-1904) was Britain's first professional and independent industrial designer.

- **Dresser embraced new production techniques in colour, pattern, material and ornamentation, and worked with innumerable manufacturers.**
- **His aim was to make high-quality and beautifully-designed products available to the widest possible audience. His work looks astoundingly 'modern' even today.**
- **He combined new Victorian technology with traditions from a range of cultures, influenced by his study of botany and his travels in Japan in the 1870s.**
- **This rare teapot is one of a group of remarkable designs produced by Dresser for James Dixon & Sons of Sheffield from 1879-83. He produced approximately 80 designs for the firm.**

A James Dixon & Son silver teapot, designed by Christopher Dresser, with ebony handle, with engraved presentation, Sheffield, with Victorian lozenge marks, stamped serial numbers '2278/N27/14-11'.

1882 *5½in (14cm) high*

£15,000-18,000 **L&T**

A pair of Goldsmiths & Silversmiths Co. Art Deco silver candelabra, London, some dings.

1937 *9¾in (24.5cm) high 34oz*

£1,800-2,200 **TEN**

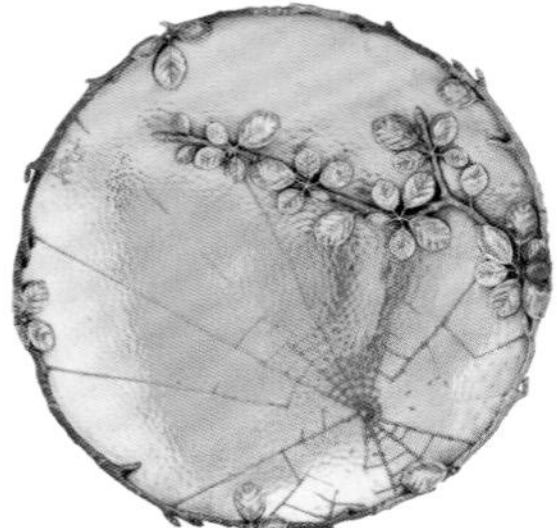

A late 19thC Gorham sterling silver tazza, with silver-gilt and copper accents, for Theodore B. Starr, New York, engraved to underside 'Emma Paige Eells Oct. 11th 1880', some losses.

12½in (32cm) diam 35oz

£2,500-3,000 **DRA**

A Guild of Handicraft silver and enamel box, the inset cover painted by William Mark (1868-1956), signed, maker's mark 'GofH Ltd', London, scratched number '4196', bent cover, deep mark to base, some other wear.

1902 *5in (12.5cm) long*

£6,000-7,000 **TEN**

A rare Guild of Handicraft Arts and Crafts silver dish, liner and spoon, by Charles Robert Ashbee (1863-1942), London, with handle set with a green chrysoprase cabochon, minor scratches and wear.

1903 *7in (17.5cm) wide*

£10,000-12,000 **CHEF**

A pair of William Hutton & Sons Art Nouveau silver and enamel photograph frames, London.

1903 *8in (20.5cm) high*

£2,000-2,500 **ROS**

A George Lawrence Connell Ltd. hammered silver rocket bowl, London.

1909 *10½in (26.5cm) diam 52oz*

£2,500-3,000 **LSK**

A Chase Brothers of Sheffield Glasgow School teaspoon, designed by Charles Rennie Mackintosh for Cranston's tea rooms.

This was a minor part of Mackintosh's commission to furnish Miss Cranston's Willow Tea Rooms in Glasgow, which included Makintosh's iconic chairs. The original Willow Tea Rooms, dating from 1903, opened again to the public in 2018, following a £10m restoration. The tearooms are now called Mackintosh at the Willow and there is a visitors' centre next door.

£300-400 **HAN**

A Danish Anton Michelsen sterling silver pitcher, designed by Kay Fisker (1893-65), fully marked, some scratches.

1947 *9in (23cm) high 19oz*

£1,100-1,600 **DRA**

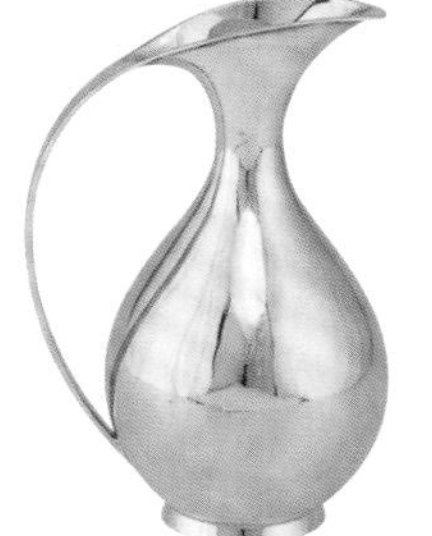

ESSENTIAL REFERENCE – H.G. MURPHY

H.G. Murphy (1884-1939) was an influential Arts and Crafts and Art Deco designer of jewellery and silverware.

- **He was born in Birchington-on-Sea in Kent and grew up in London.**
- **After an apprenticeship to Arts and Crafts designer Henry Wilson, he established retail premises in Marylebone in 1928, called the Falcon Studio.**
- **By the early 1930s, Murphy's success was established. He received silver commissions from city institutions, churches and schools, as well as making jewellery in silver and gold.**
- **In 1938 Murphy received the award of Royal Designer for Industry (RDI) from The Duke of Gloucester and Harry was appointed the Faculty's First Master.**
- **In the late 1930s, Murphy's health began to deteriorate. He died on 10 July 1939.**

A Falcon Studio Art Deco silver tea pot, in the French manner, by H.G. Murphy, carved ivory handle and finial, with Falcon Studio mark.

1930 *8½in (21.5cm) long 23¾oz*

£8,500-9,500 **WW**

A Falcon Studio matched three-piece silver café-au-lait set, by H.G. Murphy, with Falcon Studio mark.

1931/37 *max 12¼in (31cm) high 79oz*

£8,000-9,000 **WW**

A silver bishop's crozier, by Ramsden and Carr, London, engraved 'OMAR RAMSDEN ET ALWYN CARR ME FECERUNT'.

1908 *69½in (176.5cm) high 12oz*

£3,000-4,000 **WW**

A silver caddy spoon, by Omar Ramsden, the handle set with three chrysoprase.

1917 *3¼in (8.5cm) long 1⅜oz*

£2,000-2,500 **DUK**

A Reed & Barton sterling silver tea and coffee service.
tray 27¾in (70.5cm) wide 302oz
£4,500-5,500 POOK

A Walker & Tolhurst Arts and Crafts silver bowl, probably designed by Gilbert Marks, stamped maker's mark 'WWBT', London.
1894 9in (23cm) diam 24oz
£3,000-3,500 WW

A Christofle & Cie electroplated metal teapot, modelled as a zoomorphic creature, with ivory spacers, stamped marks, designed by Emile Reiber, dated.

This design is based on an antique Japanese bronze in the Henry Cernuschi collection. This is listed by the Musee d'Orsay as being prepared for the 1878 Exposition Universelle.
1878 9in (23cm) wide
£2,500-3,000 WW

A silver-plated soup ladle, by Christopher Dresser, with ebonised wood handle, with date lozenge mark.
1880 11½in (29cm) long
£1,800-2,200 L&T

A Guild of Handicrafts silver-plated dish and cover, by Charles Robert Ashbee (1863-1942), the cover set with moonstone cabochon, stamped 'GofHLtd'.
c1901 9¼in (23.5cm) wide
£2,000-2,500 L&T

A silver tea service, by Robert Scott, Sheffield and Glasgow.
1921-25 169¼oz
£1,800-2,200 WAD

A Tuttle Silversmiths silver cocktail shaker, Boston, in the form of a milk churn, initialled 'W'.
c1923-29 12¼in (31cm) high 41½oz
£2,000-2,500 TEN

A John T. Vansant & Co., sterling silver water pitcher, Philadelphia, marked 'English Sterling 925', nicks to rim.
c1880 8½in (21.5cm) high 27½oz
£2,000-2,500 DRA

A Hukin & Heath silver-plated tureen, cover and ladle, with ebony handles, designed by Christopher Dresser (1834-1904), stamped 'Designed By Dr C Dresser' and 'H & H 2123'.
12¼in (31cm) wide
£5,000-6,000 BE

A W.M.F. Art Nouveau electroplated 'Echo' strut mirror, stamped marks.
c1905 14¼in (36cm) high
£500-600 L&T

A pair of Neo-Grec parcel gilt and patinated bronze vases, by Ferdinand Barbedienne and Ferdinand Levillain, inscribed 'F. BARBEDIENNE' to base and 'F. LEVILLAIN' to body.

Ferdinand Levillain (1837-1905) began his career as a master bronze artist as an apprentice in the studio of sculptor Francois Jouffroy. By 1861, while still in his early twenties, Levillain was already exhibiting at the Paris Salon. He won a silver medal at the 1889 Paris Exposition Universelle. These vases exemplify the sculptor's fruitful collaboration with bronzier Ferdinand Barbedienne 1871-c1890.

c1875 *19in (48cm) high*

£7,000-8,000 **DN**

A copper vase, by John Pearson, struck 'J.P. 1908' and numbered '2772'.

6in (15cm) high

£500-600 **SWO**

A Roycroft hammered copper and enamel vase, after a design by Walter Jennings, with Italian enamel decoration.

c1910-15 *7in (18cm) high*

£3,500-4,000 **WES**

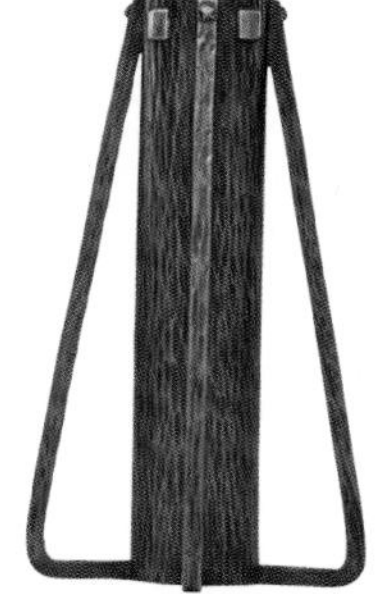

A 1910s Roycroft nickel silver and hammered and wrought copper buttressed vase, by Karl Kipp (1881-1954), orb and cross mark, some wear.

8¼in (21cm) high

£3,500-4,000 **DRA**

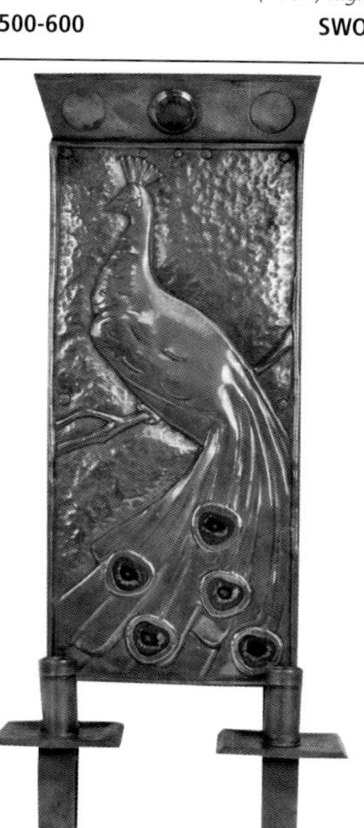

An Arts and Crafts copper and enamel decorated wall sconce, small dent to corner.

24¾in (63cm) high

£2,500-3,000 **APAR**

A Stickley Brothers hammered copper jardinière, impressed '241'.

c1910 *15in (38cm) wide*

£2,000-2,500 **CLAR**

A William Hutton & Sons Art Nouveau pewter butter dish, attributed to Kate Harris, Sheffield, with lid and glass liner.

c1910 *8¾in (22cm) wide*

£500-600 **TDG**

ESSENTIAL REFERENCE – FREDERIC SHIELDS

Frederic Shields was an illustrator, designer, mural decorator, stained glass designer and enamellist.

- **He was born in Hartlepool and brought up in extreme poverty. As a young man he worked as a commercial engraver, studying at evening classes in London and later Manchester.**
- **His illustrations for Defoe's 'History of the Plague' (1862) and 'Bunyan's Pilgrim's Progress' (1864) brought him to the attention of John Ruskin and Dante Gabriel Rossetti, who invited him to visit them in London.**
- **In 1876 he settled in London. Rossetti offered him space in his own studio and helped and encouraged him with his work.**

An Arts and Crafts copper and enamel casket, by Frederic James Shields (1833-1911), stamped monogram to lid and clasp.

c1890 *6¼in (16cm) wide*

£4,500-5,500 **L&T**

A pair of W.M.F. Art Nouveau pewter and brass figural candelabra, model no.269 and no.269A, faint stamped maker's marks.

c1906 *10½in (26.5cm) high*

£1,500-2,000 **ROS**

ESSENTIAL REFERENCE – FRANZ BERGMAN

Franz Bergman and his son, also named Franz Bergman, were important Austrian bronze manufacturers.

- **Franz Bergman senior (1838-94) was born in Bohemia and worked as a metalwork finisher. In 1860 he founded a bronze factory in Vienna.**
- **Franz Bergman junior (1861-1939) took over the factory after his father's death. Bergman was not a sculptor himself, but directed his factory in the production of a range of cold-painted and patinated bronze sculptures.**
- **Animal figures were common, as were sculptures inspired by Asian and Arabian people.**
- **Bergman also made erotic figures. These are sometimes stamped 'Namgreb' – Bergman in reverse.**

A late 19thC Franz Bergman cold-painted bronze figure, cast as an Arab scribe reading the Koran, stamped marks, on matched hardwood stand.

5½in (14cm) wide

£1,600-2,000 **HT**

An early 20thC Franz Bergman cold-painted bronze Arab horseman, stamped 'B' within urn and numbered.

9in (23cm) high

£2,500-3,000 **DN**

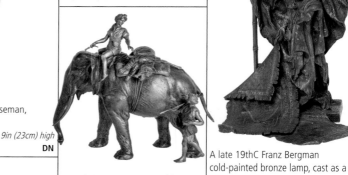

A Franz Bergman cold-painted bronze Arab trader shrouding a female nude, marked 'Nam Greb' and 'B' within urn.

9¾in (25cm) wide

£2,000-2,500 **HAN**

A 19thC Franz Bergman cold-painted bronze elephant, carrying two hunters and a fallen lion.

9¾in (25cm) high

£2,000-2,500 **HANN**

A late 19thC Franz Bergman cold-painted bronze lamp, cast as a Middle Eastern carpet seller, marked 'B' within urn and 'GESCH', wired for electricity.

18½in (47cm) high

£5,000-6,000 **ROS**

An Austrian cold-painted bronze lamp base of chess players, in the style of Franz Bergman, base stamped 'AUSTRIA'.

17¼in (44cm) high

£2,500-3,000 **BRI**

A Franz Bergman cold-painted bronze porcupine, indistinct stamp number and 'GESCHUTZT', some losses, spraining to quills.

6in (15cm) long

£2,500-3,000 **TEN**

A late 19thC Franz Bergman cold-painted bronze figure of a lion, urn mark.

7in (18cm) long

£800-900 **L&T**

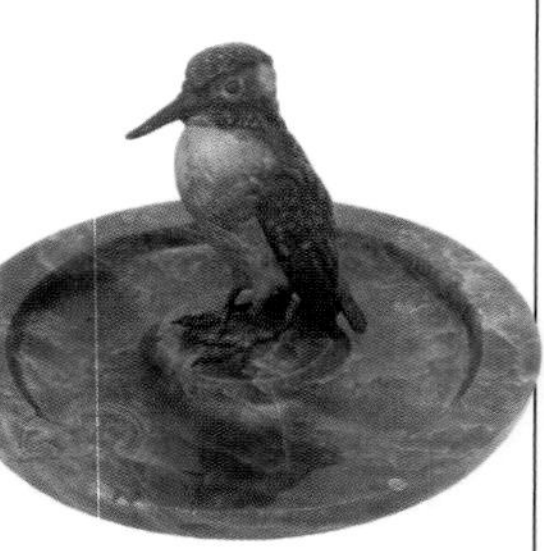

A Franz Bergman cold-painted bronze kingfisher, on veined marble dish, broken at ankles.

4¾in (12cm) long

£350-450 **WW**

An Austrian cold-painted bronze model of a game bird, stamped 'B' within urn, for the Bergman manufactory.

c1900 *10½in (26.5cm) high*

£2,500-3,000 **DN**

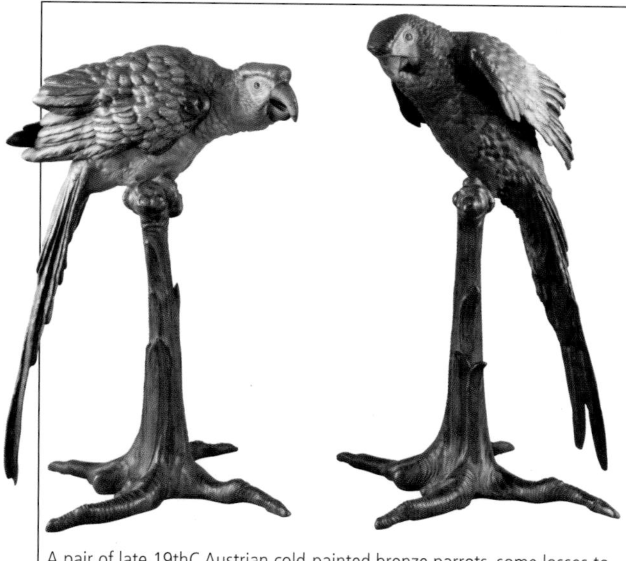

A pair of late 19thC Austrian cold-painted bronze parrots, some losses to painted finish, some rubbing.

11¾in (30cm) high

£4,500-5,500 **GORL**

A cold-painted bronze table lamp, by Anton Chotka (1881-1955), in the form of an Arabian scene, signed, on a marble plinth.

13¾in (35cm) high

£3,500-4,000 **HAN**

A 1920s Austrian gilt bronze of a young Turkish girl, by E. Wante, signed, on onyx base.

10½in (26.5cm) high

£850-950 **JN**

A late 19thC to early 20thC Austrian cold-painted bronze model of an owl, in the manner of Bergman, on a marble plinth.

6in (15cm) high

£500-600 **WW**

A late 19thC Austrian cold-painted bronze cockerel, on slate base.

7½in (19cm) high

£450-550 **REEM**

A late 19thC cold-painted bronze bulldog, paint finish dirty.

7¼in (18.5cm) long

£650-750 **GORL**

A late 19thC Austrian cold-painted bronze puppy, stamped 'Depose' twice, with kite registration mark, wear to paint.

7½in (19cm) long

£550-650 **REEM**

A late 19thC Austrian cold-painted bronze puppy, 'Depose' mark and kite registration mark, wear to muzzle.

6¾in (17cm) long

£850-950 **REEM**

A late 19thC to early 20thC Austrian cold-painted cast bronze basset hound, stamped 'Geschutzt'.

5¾in (14.5cm) long

£400-500 **TOV**

A late 19thC to early 20thC Austrian cold-painted bronze lizard.

7¼in (18.5cm) long

£750-850 **WW**

A French bronze figure of a bear, 'Ours Dans Son Auge', by Antoine-Louis Barye (1796-1875), signed 'BARYE', inscribed 'F BARBEDIENNE FONDEUR'.

5¼in (13.5cm) long

£12,000-16,000 **TEN**

A bronze figure, 'The Glint Of The Sea', by Chester Beach (1881-1956), signed 'BEACH' with foundry stamp 'KUNST FOUNDRY NY', on marble plinth.

9¾in (25cm) high

£600-700 **L&T**

A Spanish bronze group, 'Dancing Ladies', by Joachin Bilbao Martinez (1864-1934), signed, stamped 'CODINO INOS/ MADRID'.

16¾in (42.5cm) high

£1,000-1,500 **L&T**

A French bronze bull, by Isidore Jules Bonheur (1827-1901), signed 'I BONHEUR' and stamped 'PEYROL EDITEUR'.

Bonheur was a regular Paris Salon exhibitor and the bull was one of his most popular subjects. This bronze was cast by his brother-in-law, Hippolyte Peyrol.

21½in (54.5cm) long

£6,000-7,000 **WW**

A French bronze bull, by Rosa Bonheur (1822-99), signed 'ROSA B' to base.

7in (17.5cm) high

£1,200-1,600 **L&T**

A patinated bronze 'Verliebtes Mädchen' or 'Girl in Love' model, by Arno Breker (1900-91), Germany, signed, with Venturi Arte foundry stamp and '195/300'.

11½in (29cm) high

£2,200-3,000 **CHEF**

A bronze figure of a worker, by Aimé-Jules Dalou, signed, with 'Susse' Freres foundry stamp and indistinct inscription 'SUSSE FRES EDTS PARIS'.

Dalou was a founder of the Société Nationale des Beaux-Arts, and a commander of the Legion of Honour known for his realistic and unpretentious depiction of the human form. Dalou openly sympathised with the working classes, and his alignment with the Paris Commune in 1871 resulted in his exile to London until 1879. Despite this, his works were commissioned in Paris – from the monumental sculpture at the Place de la Nation to numerous decorative sculptures lining the new boulevards of the city.

7¾in (20cm) high

£2,000-3,000 **L&T**

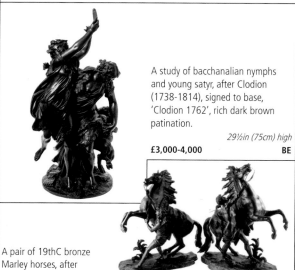

A study of bacchanalian nymphs and young satyr, after Clodion (1738-1814), signed to base, 'Clodion 1762', rich dark brown patination.

29½in (75cm) high

£3,000-4,000 **BE**

A pair of 19thC bronze Marley horses, after Guillaume Coustou.

21¼in (54cm) high

£1,200-1,600 **PW**

A bronze figure, 'Le Grand Paysan', by Aimé-Jules Dalou (1838-1902), signed and inscribed, with foundry stamp.

17in (43cm) high

£4,500-5,000 **L&T**

A French 'Pro Patria' Classical bronze of a winged angel and young man, by Edouard Drouot (1859-1945), signed and inscribed.

23½in (59.5cm) high

£1,200-1,600 JN

A late 19thC French patinated bronze model of a standing geisha, by Vincent Desiré Faure de Broussé.

Vincent Desiré Faure de Broussé (c1876-1908) was born in Paris and apprenticed to the renowned portrait sculptor Jean-Jules Salmson. He is recorded to have exhibited at the Salon from 1876, and was known for creating figural sculpture influenced by examples from the Florentine Renaissance. Though this statue depicts a Japanese-inspired subject, the contrapposto pose of the figure, her serene facial features and naturalistically, heavily draped garment still recall Faure de Broussé's interest in Renaissance sculpture.

32¼in (82cm) high

£3,000-4,000 DN

A French gilt bronze figural group, 'Orpheus and Eurydice', by Paul Jean Baptiste Gasq (1860-1944), with an applied plaque.

32in (81cm) high

£5,000-6,000 DN

Judith Picks

This charming bronze is based on the original statue of Peter Pan, which still stands in Kensington Gardens, London. Both were designed by Sir George Frampton, who was commissioned to make the larger statue by J.M.Barrie in 1911. Frampton (1860-1928) was a central figure of the New Sculpture movement, and produced many public monuments, including a number of statues of Queen Victoria. His original sculpture of Peter Pan is perhaps his most famous. The statue was placed in Kensington Gardens on April 1912, overnight and without permission, so that it might seem to the local children that it had appeared by magic.

A patinated bronze model of Peter Pan, by Sir George James Frampton RA, monogrammed 'GF' and inscribed 'PP' within a circle in the maquette, on a Connemara marble socle, dated.

1921 *20in (51cm) high*

£13,000-16,000 DN

A French patinated bronze model of a maiden, 'Retour des Hirondelles' ('Return of the Swallows'), by Adrien Étienne Gaudez (1845-1902).

Gaudez studied under Francois Jouffroy at the Ecole des Beaux-Arts in Paris, making his debut at the Paris Salon in 1864. He worked almost exclusively in bronze and produced a wide array of sculpture, ranging from genre subjects to military and patriotic themes. His earlier work was Classical, but some of his later pieces, such as this model, can be categorised as Art Nouveau.

c1900 *38¼in (97cm) high*

£4,000-5,000 DN

A bronze figure of a donkey, by August Gaul (1861-1921), on marble base, signed 'A. GAUL/AG', with foundry mark 'H. NOACK/BERLIN/ FRIEDENAU', on marble plinth.

Gaul was a noted sculptor and lithographer with a keen interest in depicting animals. He was one of the founding members of the Berlin Secession in 1898. This sculpture of a walking donkey forms part of a series of six sculptures entitled 'Eselei' ('folly') studying the various movements of a donkey.

5¾in (14.5cm) long

£5,000-6,000 L&T

A bronze figure, 'Perseus Arming', by Sir Alfred Gilbert R.A. (1854-1934), on a verde antico marble plinth.

Alfred Gilbert was born in London and joined the Royal Academy in 1873 before going on to study at the École des Beaux-Arts, Paris, and becoming one of the most influential sculptors of his generation and the New English Sculpture movement.

15¾in (40cm) high

£40,000-50,000 L&T

A bronze figure, 'Comedy and Tragedy: Sic Vita', by Sir Alfred Gilbert R.A., on a ebonised wood plinth.

15¼in (39cm) high

£25,000-30,000 L&T

A patinated bronze nude, 'Message of Love', cast from a model by Pierre Le Faguays, on veined marble base, signed in the cast to base rim 'Le Faguays' and foundry mark.

22½in (57cm) high

£1,800-2,200 WW

A French Classical bronze faun, by Eugene Lequesne (1815-87), signed 'E. LEQUESNE, SUISSE STAMP'.

20in (51cm) high

£1,300-1,800 **JN**

A 19thC bronze study of two rutting stags, by Clovis Edmond Masson (1838-1913), on a marble base, signed.

21¾in (55cm) long

£1,500-2,000 **FLD**

A bronze horse, 'French Cheval A La Barriere', by Pierre Jules Mene (1810-77), the horse named 'Djinn', signed 'P. J. MENE'.

14½in (37cm) long

£1,800-2,200 **JN**

A French bronze Arab on horseback, by Ferdinand Pautrot (1832-74), signed, lacking musket.

19¾in (50cm) high

£2,000-2,500 **WHP**

A Joan of Arc bronze, after Henri Honore Ple (1853-1922), signed 'Henri Ple', stamped 'Elkington & Co', on a marble base.

37¾in (96cm) high

£3,000-3,500 **BE**

A bronze figure of a woman tying her sandal, 'La Toilette d'Atalante', by Jean Jacques Pradier (1790-1852), signed, with Susse foundry stamp, minor wear.

12¾in (32.5cm) high

£3,500-4,000 **TEN**

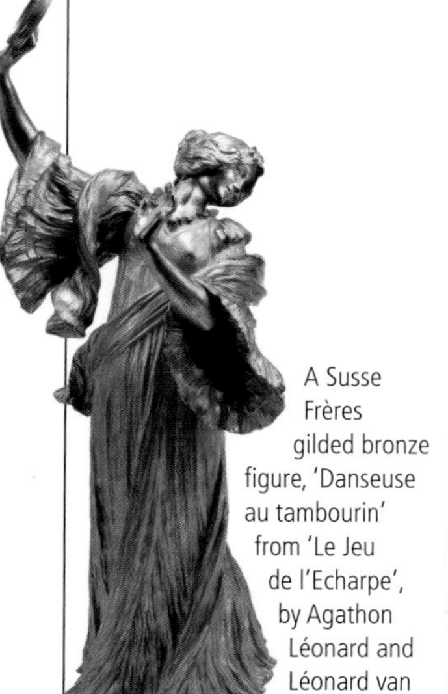

A Susse Frères gilded bronze figure, 'Danseuse au tambourin' from 'Le Jeu de l'Echarpe', by Agathon Léonard and Léonard van Weydeveldt, Paris, marked 'ALeonard Sculp, SUSSE FRES EDITEURS PARIS'.

c1901 *21¾in (55.5cm) high*

£20,000-25,000 **QU**

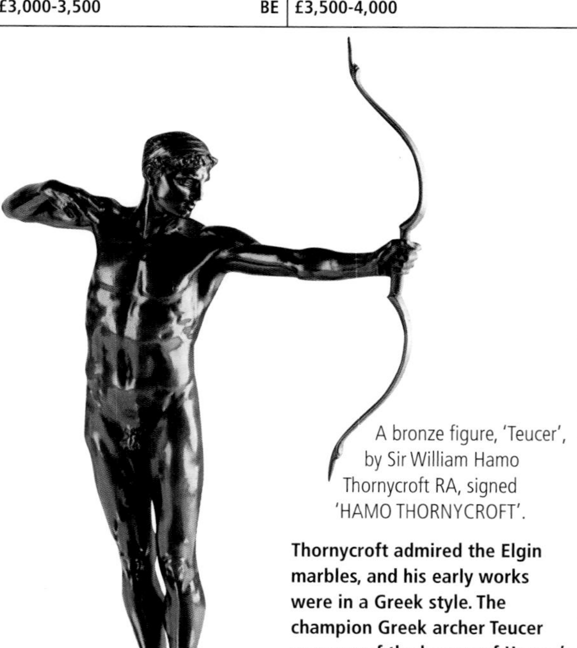

A bronze figure, 'Teucer', by Sir William Hamo Thornycroft RA, signed 'HAMO THORNYCROFT'.

Thornycroft admired the Elgin marbles, and his early works were in a Greek style. The champion Greek archer Teucer was one of the heroes of Homer's story of the Trojan War.

16¾in (42.5cm) high

£22,000-30,000 **L&T**

A standing bronze, by Sir William Hamo Thornycroft RA (1850-1925), depicting a member of 129th Duke of Connaught's Own Baluchis, signed and inscribed.

14½in (37cm) high

£7,000-8,000 **JN**

ESSENTIAL REFERENCE – DEMETRE H. CHIPARUS

Demetre H. Chiparus (1886-1947) was born in Romania and later moved to Paris.

- **In Paris he studied at the Ecole des Beaux Arts, before working for Etling and the Les Neveau de J. Lehmann foundry, chiefly as a designer and sculptor.**
- **He mostly worked in chryselephantine (bronze and ivory), depicting stylised exotic women, often dancers, sometimes figures taken from the Russian Ballet, French theatre or early film.**
- **His figures are generally very detailed, with impressive decorative effects.**

A gilt and patinated bronze and ivory figure, 'Ayouta', by Demetre H. Chiparus, on onyx base, signed 'D Chiparus'.

Ivory was commonly used in Art Deco figures. With new laws on the trade of ivory, figures with over 10% ivory are likely to be banned. Figures such as this one, with under 10% ivory, may remain on the market, but the prices are struggling in the uncertainty of legal status. Art Deco figures without any ivory content are on the rise in comparison.

c1925 *11½in (29cm) high*

£8,500-9,500 TEN

A gilt-bronze and marble sculpture, 'Accident de Chasse' ('The Hunting Accident'), by Demetre H. Chiparus, signed, some chips and wear.

16½in (42cm) wide

£2,000-2,500 DRA

A patinated ormolu figure, 'The Dancer of Lebanon', by Demetre H. Chiparus, on onyx base, signed.

15in (38cm) high

£6,500-7,500 BE

A bronze sculpture, 'Dancer of Olynthus', by Demetre H. Chiparus, on a veined onyx base with light fitting, etched 'Chiparus' to base, cast number to her foot.

13in (33cm) high

£6,500-7,500 WW

A silvered-bronze and ivory figure 'Leaving the Opera', by Dimitri H. Chiparus, on onyx base, signed 'D.H. Chiparus, Etling Paris'.

c1930 *9in (23cm) high*

£4,000-5,000 ROS

Judith Picks

This impressive figure by Demetre H. Chiparus is entitled 'Antinea'. In Greek and Roman mythology, Queen Antinea was the grand-daughter of Neptune and Clito, the last Kings of Atlantis, and through Cleopatra Selene, also a descendent of the Ptolemies of Egypt. Antinea was said to keep an underground mausoleum of red marble with 120 alcoves where she housed the numbered and labelled bodies of her former lovers, lost soldiers and explorers. This detailed bronze and ivory figure has been in the same family for the last 40 years.

A cold-painted and patinated bronze and ivory figure, 'Antinea', by Demetre H. Chiparus, the base marked 'Etling Paris', signed 'D H Chiparus' in the marble, some chips to marble.

c1928 *26½in (67.5cm) high*

£50,000-60,000 ECGW

A large cold-painted bronze and ivory figure, 'Les Amis de Toujours' ('Friends Forever'), by Demetre H. Chiparus, on veined marble base, signed 'Chiparus'.

26in (66cm) wide

£40,000-50,000 WW

ESSENTIAL REFERENCE – JOSEF LORENZL

Josef Lorenzl (1892-1950) was a significant Art Deco designer and sculptor.

- **He worked for several Austrian manufacturers, including Vienna Arsenal and Goldscheider (see page 467-468).**
- **He worked in ceramics and metal, and produced small sculptures in bronze, ivory and sometimes chryselephantine. The figures often have a patinated silver or gilt finish, and stand on an onyx or marble base.**
- **Lorenzl's sculptures are generally of women, and reflect the fashions of the 1920s-30s.**

An ivory and cold-painted bronze figure, by Josef Lorenzl, on onyx base, signed in the cast 'LORENZL'.
c1925 *10¼in (26cm) high*
£2,200-2,800 TEN

A silvered and cold-painted bronze figure, 'Allegory of Victory', by Josef Lorenzl, on onyx base, signed.

The same model was sold from the former sample stock of the Bergman factory, Vienna.
c1925 *11¾in (30cm) high*
£1,800-2,200 TEN

A bronze figure, by Josef Lorenzl, on onyx plinth, stamped 'Lorenzl, real Bronze, Made in Austria'.
c1930 *12½in (32cm) high*
£1,500-2,000 ROS

A cold-painted bronze figure, by Josef Lorenzl, on onyx base, signed 'R.Lor Austria'.
c1930 *13½in (34cm) high*
£2,500-3,000 ROS

A figurine, 'Bridgitte', by Josef Lorenzl.
c1930 *13½in (34cm) high*
£3,000-3,500 TDG

A patinated gilt bronze dancer, by Josef Lorenzl, on onyx base, signed, fracture to wrist, chip to base.
11½in (29cm) high
£1,500-2,000 CHEF

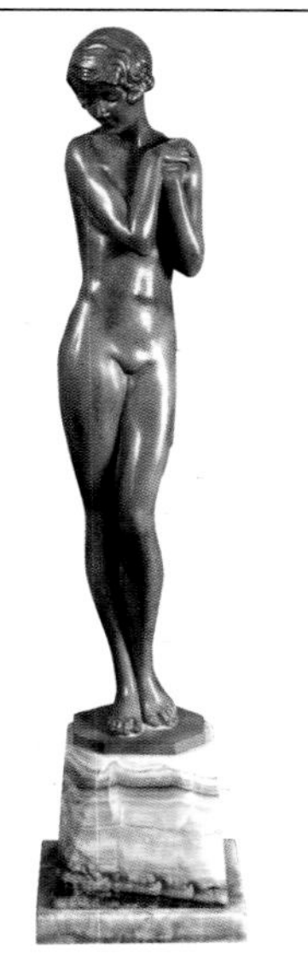

A green patinated bronze nude maiden, by Josef Lorenzl, on onyx base, signed, some wear.
23in (58.5cm) high
£3,000-3,500 CHEF

A cold-painted bronze dancer, by Josef Lorenzl, on onyx base, signed, chip to base, discolouration around eye, wear to legs.
9¾in (25cm) high
£2,300-2,800 TEN

A gilt-bronze and ivory Classical maiden, cast from a model by Leonie Boehm-Henes, marble base, signed, one finger missing.

13¾in (35cm) high

£2,000-2,500 **WW**

A bronze figure, 'Girl with Hoop', by Marcel-André Bouraine (1886-1948), on a marble base, signed 'a Bouraine'.

c1925 *12in (30.5cm) high*

£4,500-5,000 **TEN**

A patinated bronze dancer, by Marcel-André Bouraine, on a marble plinth, signed 'M. Bouraine', stamped 'Bronze', chips to extremities.

19¼in (49cm) high

£1,500-2,000 **GORL**

A patinated metal sculpture, 'Woman with Dogs', by A. Delatour, on marble base with onyx, signed 'A Delatour'.

33¼in (84.5cm) wide

£1,000-1,400 **WW**

A bronze sculpture, 'The Call' by Charles Charles, Patrouilleau foundry, signed 'C. Charles'.

c1930 *22½in (57cm) long*

£4,000-4,300 **TDG**

Judith Picks

Erté's career was an unusual one. Born Romain de Tirtoff in St Petersburg in 1892, he moved to Paris in 1910, disobeying his family's wishes for him to become a naval officer. To avoid the embarrassment of his family, he took on the pseudonym 'Erté' (after his initials, R.T.). In Paris he achieved great success as a designer and fashion illustrator.

Erté's Art Deco sculptures unusually date not from the 1920s and 1930s but from the later half of the 20thC. At the age of 75, during the Art Deco revival of the 1960s, Erté was encouraged to embark on a new career, recreating the designs of his younger days. He began to create elegant bronze sculptures like this one, and was still working just two years before his death in 1990.

An Art Deco bronze sculpture, 'Elegance', by Erté (1892-1990), signed and numbered '116/250', lacking dog's leash, some wear, dated.

1980 *15½in (39.5cm) high*

£1,800-2,200 **DRA**

An Art Deco bronze sculpture, 'Chinese Legend', by Erté, signed and numbered '238/500', some abrasions, dated.

1988 *22½in (57cm) high*

£1,800-2,200 **DRA**

A spelter figural group, 'Seduction', by Pierre Le Faguay (1892-1962), on a marble plinth, signed 'FAYRAL'.

Fayral was the pseudonym of Pierre Le Faguay.

c1925 *25½in (65cm) wide*

£2,000-2,500 **L&T**

A cold-painted bronze figure, 'Dancer with Thyrsus', by Pierre Le Faguays, on a marble base, signed 'Le Faguays', 'Etling Paris' on base.

c1930 *10¾in (27.5cm) high*

£2,500-3,000 **ROS**

A bronze figure of a dancer, by Georges Flamand (1895-1925), on onyx socle, signed, chips to base.

11¾in (30cm) high

£850-950 **GORL**

A patinated cold-painted bronze and ivory figure, 'Temple Dancer', by Gerda Iro (Gerdago), on onyx base, signed, with foundry mark.

19in (48cm) high

£20,000-25,000 **WW**

A gilt and patinated bronze and ivory figure, 'Sleep of the Pierrot', by A. Gilbert (1884-1961), on marble base, stamped, signed 'A Gilbert'.

c1925 *12¼in (31cm) wide*

£4,000-5,000 **TEN**

A patinated bronze and ivory figure, 'Dance of the Harlequinade', cast from a model by A. Gilbert.

22in (56cm) high

£5,500-6,000 **WW**

A cold-painted bronze, by Godard, mounted on a slate base, signed.

c1930 *25½in (65cm) wide*

£2,500-3,000 **ROS**

A silvered bronze model, 'Thyrse Dancer', by J.D. Guirande, on marble base, signed.

26½in (67cm) high

£2,500-3,000 **WW**

A cold-painted bronze figure, 'Stella', by Maurice Guiraud-Riviere (1881-1947), on marble base, signed.

c1930 *11in (28cm) high*

£4,000-5,000 **ROS**

A Hagenauer silver-plated and ebonised model of a dancer, stamped 'Hagenauer Wien Made in Austria', figure detached from base.

c1930 *12½in (31.5cm) high*

£1,300-1,800 **BELL**

A cold-painted and gilt patinated bronze and ivory figure, by Samuel Lipchytz (1880-1943), on a marble base, signed.

c1925 *8½in (21.5cm) high*

£1,200-1,600 **TEN**

A cold-painted and gilt patinated bronze figure, 'Hoop Girl', by Franz Mazura, on marble base, signed.
c1925 *15¾in (40cm) high*
£3,000-4,000 **TEN**

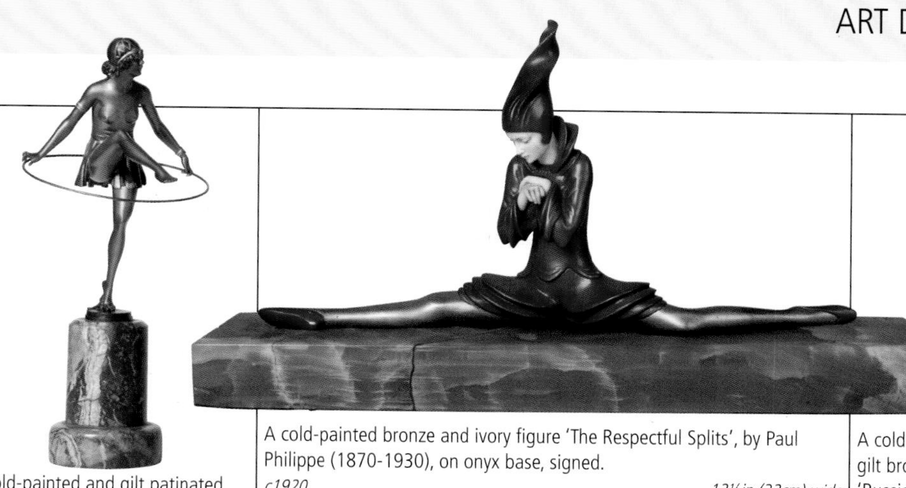

A cold-painted bronze and ivory figure 'The Respectful Splits', by Paul Philippe (1870-1930), on onyx base, signed.
c1920 *12½in (32cm) wide*
£6,000-7,000 **ROS**

A cold-painted and gilt bronze figure, 'Russian Dancer', by Paul Philippe, stamped to foot '144', on onyx base, signed.
c1925 *16¾in (42.5cm) high*
£4,000-4,500 **TEN**

A silvered and cold-painted bronze and ivory figure, 'Pierrette', by Paul Philippe, on onyx base, signed 'Philippe' and 'R.u.M' (Rosenthal und Maeder).
c1925 *8¼in (21cm) high*
£3,500-4,000 **TEN**

A patinated bronze figure, 'Dancer with Cymbals', by Charles d'Orville Pilkington-Jackson (1887-1973), on slate, signed and dated.
1922 *31½in (80cm) high*
£10,000-14,000 **WW**

A cold-painted bronze and ivory figure 'Snake Dancer', by Professor Otto Poertzel (1876-1963), on bronze base cast with two snakes, on onyx plinth, signed.
c1930 *10¾in (27.5cm) high*
£5,000-6,000 **ROS**

A gilt and patinated bronze and ivory figure, 'Lieselotte', by Johann Philipp Ferdinand Preiss, model no.3754, on a marble base, signed.

Ferdinand Preiss (1882-1943) was a German sculptor. He specialised in ivory and chryselephantine (bronze and ivory) figures.

c1925 *7in (17.5cm) high*
£3,000-3,500 **TEN**

A cold-painted bronze and ivory figure, 'Girl Fencer', by Ferdinand Preiss, on marble base, signed.
c1930 *7in (18cm) high*
£5,000-6,000 **ROS**

A cold-painted and gilt patinated group of ballet dancers, by Bruno Zach, signed, on onyx marble base, some wear and filler, visible arm join, possibly repainted.

Bruno Zach (1891-1945) was born in the Ukraine. He studied at the Vienna Academy and produced sculpture in Art Nouveau, Art Deco and Asian styles. His work often features sparsely clad women in stockings and garters.

c1920 *17in (43cm) high*
£3,000-3,500 **TEN**

MODERN MARKET

Where other areas have faltered financially, interest in, and prices for, outstanding post-World War II design has, in many cases, quadrupled. The market is fed by the quantity of items available. Design in this period was completely international and, with the added impetus of the internet, so is the collecting market. Moreover, many pieces are found in large numbers and are consequently relatively affordable, making this area accessible to younger buyers; the styles are also in tune with a younger taste.

While the seeds of mid-century modern lay in the Scandinavian 'Soft Modernism' of the 1930s, the designers who started working during and after World War II were excited by the possibilities of new materials and the demands of an enthusiastic consumer class. Designers such as Charles and Ray Eames in America said their mission was 'getting the most of the best to the greatest number of people for the least amount of money'. Of course, many of the Eames' original designs can no longer be purchased for 'the least amount of money' as they are now highly-prized icons of design. But these designs have been copied over the years, and although the replicas won't make the prices of anything like the originals, you can still get 'the look'.

As David Rago, of leading auction house Rago, says, 'We're still seeing less strength in mid-century 'factory' furniture (Knoll, Eames, etc), though it still does quite well. Instead, I'm watching prices rise for studio work by Nakashima, Powell, Evans, Castle and so on. Wharton Esherick is perhaps the temporary victim of too little production and strong prices realized in the past. His work seems among the bargains in the market at this time.'

The Modern movement is by its very nature diverse – it covers everything from the great studio craftsmen, including potters such as the Natzlers and Peter Voulkos, to 1960s plastic and Postmodern pieces by designers such as Joe Colombo and Ettore Sottsass. There is something in this area to suit all tastes and pockets, for example, Stuart Devlin, the noted Australian/British silversmith and goldsmith, designed some highly individual furniture in the 1970s, as well as award-winning silver and gold.

Glass from the 20th century greats – the designers and factories of Scandinavia and Murano – continues to sell well, and buyers like the vibrant colours and modern forms. Big names are another plus factor, and prices for the work of luminaries, such as Murano-trained American designer Dale Chihuly, have quadrupled in recent years. However, there is a great deal of glass on the market that is in the style of 'the greats' and appeals to a younger market. A particular favourite of mine are the whimsical 'pulcinos' (little chicks) designed by Alessandro Pianon for Vetreria Vistosi in 1962 (see page 580).

As I mentioned in the previous edition of *Miller's Antiques Handbook and Price Guide*, there is growing interest in a newcomer to the growing 20th century glass stable in the form of Post-War Czech glass, triumphed by my friend and colleague Mark Hill in his book *Hi Sklo Lo Sklo* (2008). Currently, the low end of the market (£50–500) is the most popular, and as people become more comfortable with the unusual names of the designers, this market seems only set to rise.

Top Left: A sculptural studio pottery vase, by John Ward, with artist's seal.

c1993 *9¾in (25cm) high*

£10,000-12,000 **CA**

Above A Nakashima Studio walnut and hickory lounge chair with arm, by George Nakashima, signed with client name.

1960 *33½in (85cm) high*

£8,000-9,000 **DRA**

A French Edition Rougier steel, bamboo and rattanwork wicker chair and ottoman, attributed to Janine Abraham and Dirk Jan Rol.
c1955 *36½in (92.5cm) high*
£1,500-2,000 **QU**

A 1970s Stendig 'Nonstop' leather and felt sofa in fourteen sections, designed by Ueli Berger, Eleanora Peduzzi-Riva and Heinz Ulrich, Switzerland, with fabric label.
154in (391cm) long
£4,500-5,000 **DRA**

A pair of 2000s Italian Cappellini teak stools/ side tables, designed by Barber & Osgerby.
29½in (75cm) wide
£2,500-3,000 **DRA**

A pair of 1950s Italian Tecno P32 enamelled steel, brass and upholstery lounge chairs, by Osvaldo Borsani (1911-85), with manufacturer labels, some stains and fading.
33in (84cm) high
£3,500-4,000 **DRA**

A 2000s Erda Favela pine and birch plywood chair, by Fernando Campana (b.1961) and Umberto Campana (b.1953), Brazil/Italy.
30½in (77.5cm) high
£4,500-5,000 **DRA**

A sculpted walnut and leather 'Crescent Rocker', designed by Wendell Castle (1932-2018), Scottsville, NY, signed and dated.
1980 *40in (101.5cm) long*
£14,000-18,000 **DRA**

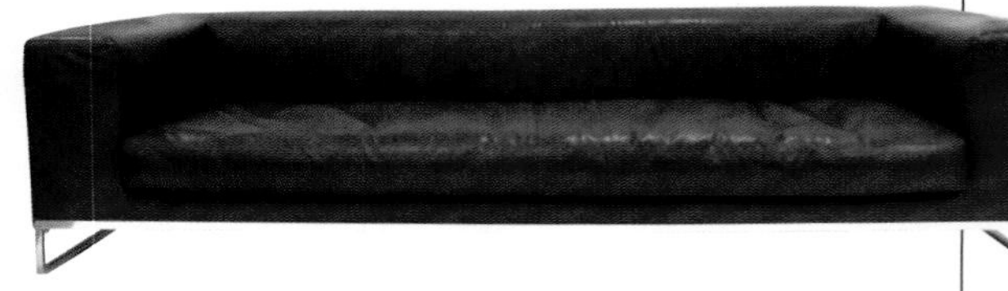

A B&B Italia 'Dadone' leather three-seater sofa, by Antonio Citterio, on chromed frame.
£1,200-1,600 **WHP**

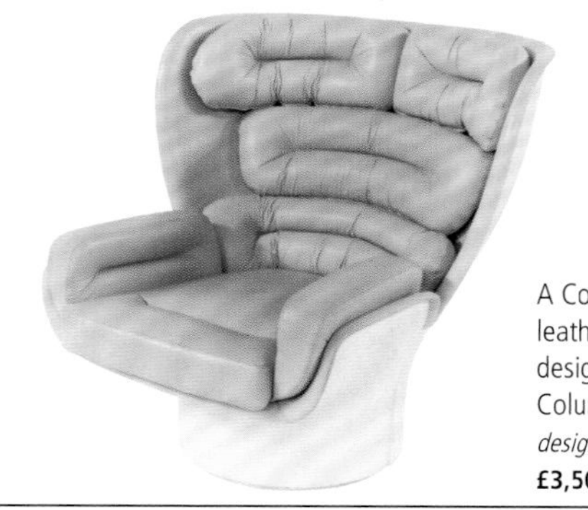

A Comfort cream leather 'Elda' chair, designed by Joe Columbo.
designed 1963
£3,500-4,000 **SWO**

An early 1960s Hille club armchair, designed by Robin Day (1915-2010), leather upholstery on a teak underframe.
designed 1962 *31½in (80cm) wide*
£550-650 **L&T**

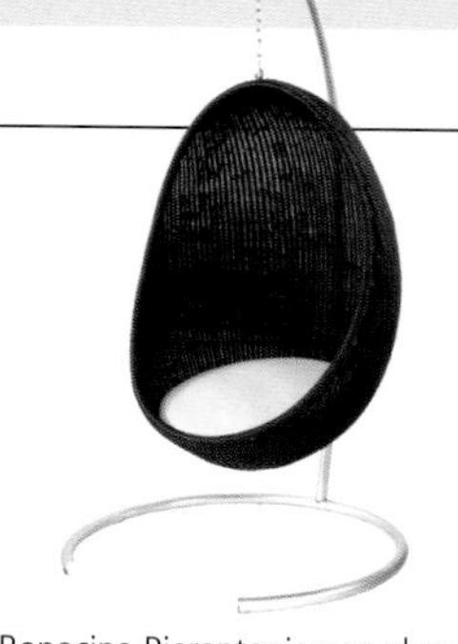

A Bonacina Pierantonio egg-shaped rattan hanging chair, designed by Nanna Ditzel, fitted with a chain and stand.

1957

£750-850 SWO

An 'S' Chair variant, designed by Tom Dixon.

40¼in (102cm) high

£1,500-2,000 SWO

A Herman Miller laminated rosewood and leather lounge chair and ottoman, designed by Charles and Ray Eames.

designed 1956

£7,000-8,000 ECGW

A Swedese bentwood and woolen upholstery 'Lamino' chair, by Yngve Ekstrom, stamped mark.

c1965

£600-700 WHP

ESSENTIAL REFERENCE – CHARLES AND RAY EAMES

Charles and Ray Eames were two of the most important 20thC American designers.

- **Charles Eames (1907-78) was born in St Louis, Missouri. He studied architecture at Washington University for two years, before being expelled for his advocacy of the radical architect Frank Lloyd Wright.**
- **Eames established his own architectural studio in 1930 with Charles Gray.**
- **In 1938, Eames received a fellowship to the Cranbrook Academy of Art in Bloomfield Hills, Michigan. Here he met his future wife, design student Ray Kaiser (1912-88).**
- **They married in 1941 and together experimented with moulded plywood. They were commissioned by the research and development division of the US Navy, for whom they created various moulded forms of splints, stretchers, and gliders for use by the Allies during WWII.**
- **After the war, Charles and Ray Eames turned to domestic furniture, developing designs for moulded plywood and fiberglass chairs as well as the iconic Eames Lounge Chair, desks, storage units, sofas, tables and more.**

A Herman Miller birch plywood, laminated plywood, enamelled masonite, fiberglass and enamelled steel first edition ESU-400, by Charles Eames and Ray Eames, some dents and finish loss, re-glued handles, one leg bent.

c1951-52 *59in (150cm) high*

£30,000-35,000 DRA

ESSENTIAL REFERENCE – PAUL EVANS

Paul Evans (1931-87) was an important 20thC studio furniture maker.

- **He trained as a silversmith at the Cranbook Academy of Art in Bloomfield Hills, Michigan.**
- **In 1955 he moved to New Hope, Pennsylvania, where he met fellow craftsman Phillip Lloyd Powell. He and Powell shared a showroom for the next ten years. Together they produced unique pieces, often fusing together materials like stone, wood, glass and metal.**
- **Evans's background in welding, metalwork and jewellery design strongly influenced his furniture designs.**
- **In 1966, he relocated to Plumsteadville, Pennsylvania, and set up his own studio.**
- **Evans also designed pieces for the furniture company Directional.**
- **He retired to Massachusetts in 1987 and died later that year.**

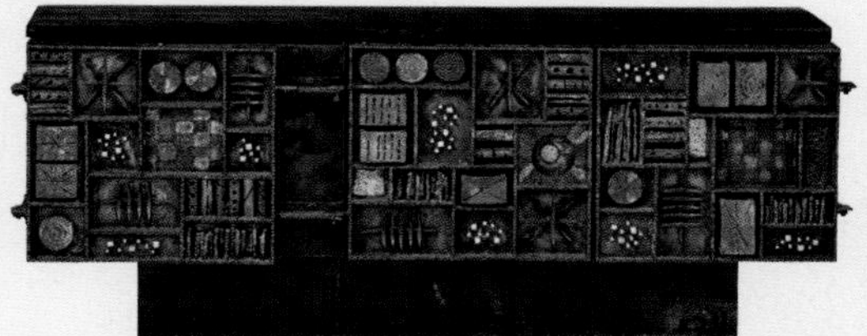

A sculpture-front steel cabinet, by Paul Evans, with 23ct gold leaf, painted wood, cleft slate and felt decoration, welded 'Paul Evans 68 D.R.', some scuffs, and oxidation.

1968 *75in (190.5cm) long*

£110,000-150,000 DRA

An Ercol settee or daybed, with a detachable back, some scuffing, split to left arm, recent cushions.

82in (208cm) wide

£850-950 SWO

A sculptured welded and patinated steel and bronze glass-topped dining table, no.PE21, by Paul Evans, oxidation to base, scratches.

1969 *95½in (242.5cm) long*

£18,000-22,000 DRA

A lithographic transfer-printed and lacquered four-leaf screen on casters, by Piero Fornasetti (1913-88), printed to one side with 'Battaglia Navale' pattern and to the other side with 'Lesene' pattern.

c1954 *57in (145cm) wide*

£6,000-7,000 ROS

A pair of 2000s German Vitra corrugated cardboard and masonate 'Wiggle' chairs, by Frank Gehry (b.1929), manufacturer labels.

34in (86.5cm) high

£2,500-3,000 DRA

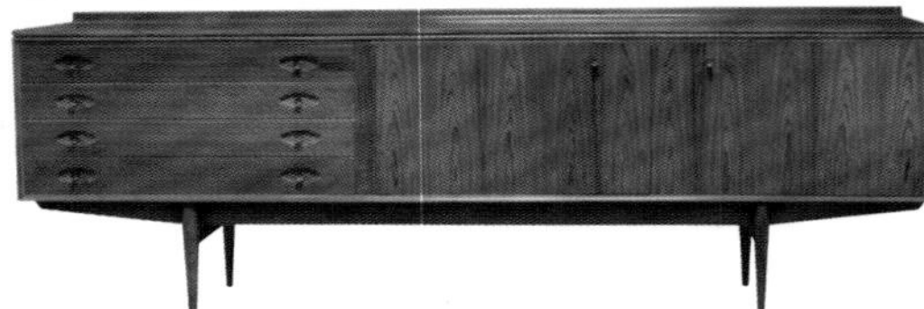

An Archie Shine LTD 'Hamilton' rosewood sideboard, by Robert Heritage, on tapered legs.

c1958 90¼in (229cm) wide

£1,500-2,000 ROS

A 1960s Danish Mogens Kold rosewood and crossbanded sideboard, by Arne Hovmand Olsen, with 'sled'-type base, minor stains.

94½in (240cm) long

£2,000-2,500 WHP

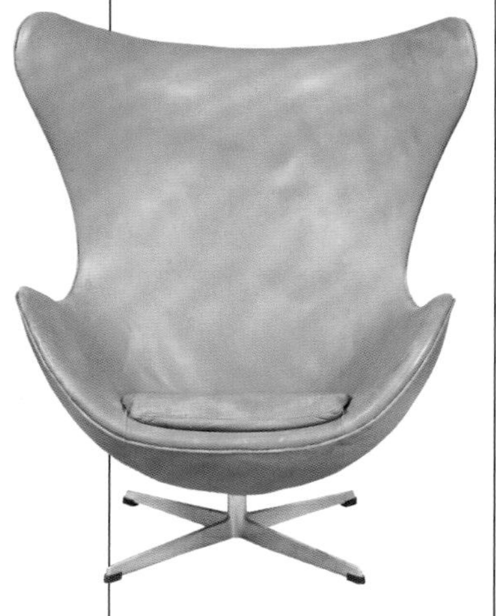

A leather upholstered egg chair, by Arne Jacobsen (1902-71).

42in (106.5cm) high

£900-1,100 DOY

A pair of 1950s handmade teak and upholstery armchairs, by Pierre Jeanneret (1896-1967), from Punjab University, Chandigarh, India/France, new upholstery and stuffing.

Literature: 'Le Corbusier Pierre Jeanneret: The Indian Adventure, Design-Art-Architecture', Touchaleaume E., Moreau G. & Vigo M.

34½in (87.5cm) high

£16,000-20,000 DRA

A pair of 1960s Danish Selig teak and upholstery lounge chairs, by Poul Jensen (1905-90), manufacturer labels, some scuffs.

33½in (85cm) high

£5,500-6,000 DRA

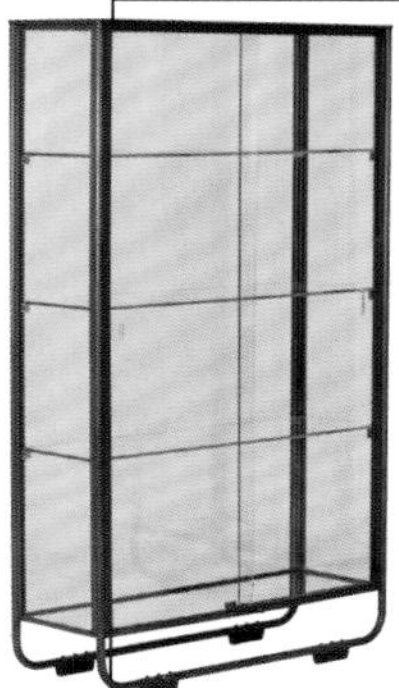

A pair of mid-20thC Belgian bronze and glass industrial display cabinets, with mirror bottoms and rubber feet, metal 'DE JONCKHEERE-ANDRES, PLACE DU SAMEDI-BRUXELLES' label, some scratches and chips, some oxidation.

71in (180.5cm) high

£8,500-9,500 DRA

A 'Judas' rosewood dining table, designed by Finn Juhl (1912-89), with two leaves, with inlaid silver buttons, marked 'Illums Bohligus'.

c1950 55in (139.5cm) long

£26,000-30,000 CLAR

A set of eight Niels Vodder Egyptian rosewood chairs, designed by Finn Juhl, branded 'Niels Vodder Cabinetmaker Copenhagen Denmark Design Finn Juhl', one lacking mark.

36in (91.5cm) high

£60,000-70,000 CLAR

ESSENTIAL REFERENCE – VLADIMIR KAGAN

Vladimir Kagan (1927-2016) was an important mid-century furniture designer.

- **He was born in Germany. His family were Jewish and left the country to escape Nazisim in 1937, moving first to France and later to the United States.**
- **Kagan took architecture courses at Columbia University, but did not graduate. In 1947 he went to work for his father, who was a cabinetmaker.**
- **He took his first major commission in 1947 and opened an independent shop in New York City in 1948. From 1950, he parterned with Hugo Dreyfuss, forming Kagan-Dreyfuss.**
- **Kagan's designs mixed the simplicity of Danish Modern masters such as Finn Juhl and Hans Wegner with the organic shapes of designers like Isamu Noguchi. He wanted to create furniture that was suitable for everyday living.**
- **The market for Kagan's designs remains very strong and notable collectors today include Brad Pitt, Demi Moore, Uma Thurman and Tom Cruise.**

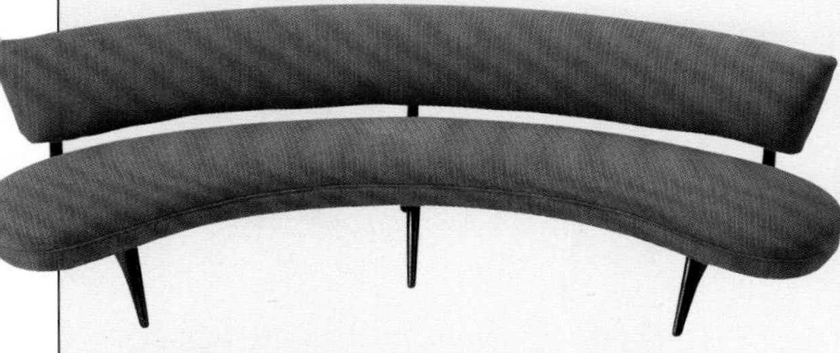

A 1950s Kagan-Dreyfuss sculpted walnut and upholstery 'Floating Seat and Back' sofa, designed by Vladimir Kagan (1927-2016), one repair, some fraying.

94in (239cm) wide

£14,000-20,000 **DRA**

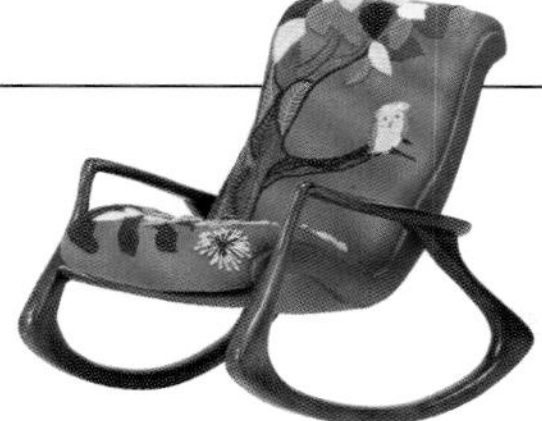

A 1980s Vladimir Kagan Designs embroidered wool, leather and sculpted walnut rocking chair, designed by Vladimir Kagan and after Erica Wilson, New York, refinished frame.

Erica Wilson, wife of Vladimir Kagan, operated a Manhattan needlepoint shop until 2005. This fabric was created after one of her designs.

designed 1950s *38½in (98cm) high*

£10,000-14,000 **DRA**

An pair of early 1960s Karpen Furniture Co. turned wood, brushed aluminium and upholstery lounge chairs, with labels, minor sun-fading and wear.

35½in (90cm) wide

£4,500-5,000 **DRA**

CLOSER LOOK – WRITING DESK

This writing desk is made of chrome-plated steel and oak, with a rosewood veneer.

The desk is part of a furniture series designed by Bodil Kjaer (b.1932), a Danish architect and designer, for E. Pedersen & Son.

It was in high demand in the early 1960s, and starred prominently in two James Bond movies, 'From Russia with Love' and 'You Only Live Twice'.

The actor Michael Caine and Prince Philip, Duke of Edinburgh, are said to have been some of the first customers who purchased this model.

A writing desk.

c1959 *78¾in (200cm) wide*

£14,000-18,000 **QU**

A pair of 1950s Danish E. Kold Christiansen chromed steel and leather 'PK22' lounge chairs, designed by Poul Kjaerholm, extensive oxidation, some stains and tears.

28in (71cm) high

£1,800-2,200 **DRA**

A 1960s Knoll Associates walnut, enamelled wood, birch and chromed steel cabinet, designed by Florence Knoll (b.1917), no.541, some scratches.

75½in (192cm) long

£4,000-5,000 **DRA**

A Memphis 'Kyoto' table, designed by Shiro Kuramata, manufactured by Ishimaru Co. Ltd., Tokyo, Japan, made of 'Star Piece' terrazzo and chromium-plated steel, stencilled 'SHIRO KURAMATA/FOR MEMPHIS MILANO'.

c1983 *28¾in (73cm) high*

£8,500-9,500 **PHI**

A 1960s Brazilian rosewood and leather sofa, by Percival Lafer, with upholstery labels, some scratches.

90in (228.5cm) wide

£3,500-4,000 **DRA**

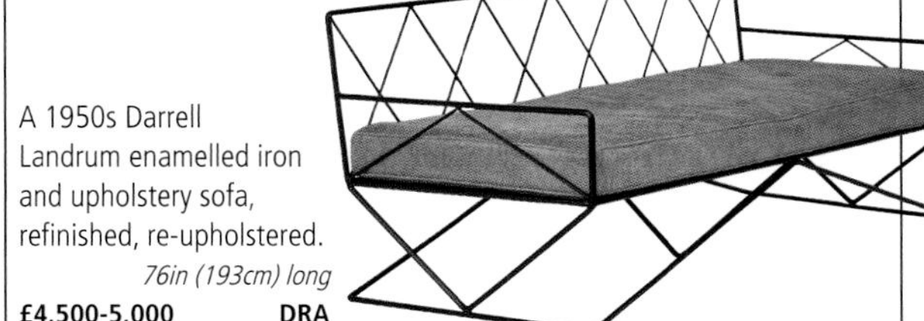

A 1950s Darrell Landrum enamelled iron and upholstery sofa, refinished, re-upholstered.

76in (193cm) long

£4,500-5,000 **DRA**

A pair of G-Plan 'Housemaster' armchairs, designed by Ib Kofod Larsen, with black leather cushions.

32¼in (82cm) high

£1,500-2,000 **SWO**

A 1980s Belgian Georges Mathias polished and etched brass, agate and enamelled steel coffee table, light scuffs, and finish loss.

45¾in (116cm) long

£5,000-5,500 **DRA**

ESSENTIAL REFERENCE – GEORGE NAKASHIMA

George Nakashima (1905-90) was one of the most talented 20thC studio furniture makers.

- **He was born in Washington and studied architecture at the University of Washington, MIT and L'Ecole Americaine des Beaux Arts in France.**
- **His work for the architect Antonin Raymond sent him to Pondicherry, India, where he began his second career as a furniture maker.**
- **Confined at the Japanese-American internment camp in Minidoka, ID, during World War II, Nakashima, his wife and daughter were released through the sponsorship of Raymond and settled in Bucks County, PA, where Nakashima was able to work on his furniture designs.**
- **His work incorporated Japanese design and practices, Modernist ideas and high-level craftsmanship. His interest in the natural quality and form of different woods can be seen in his furniture. His work was quite unique.**

A Nakashima Studio figured walnut single pedestal turned-leg desk, by George Nakashima, unmarked, some fading and some chips to top.

1955 *72in (183cm) long*

£10,000-14,000 **DRA**

One of a pair of 1940s Danish Fredericia rosewood bookcases, designed by Borge Mogensen (1914-72), stamped, refinished.

63in (160cm) high

£3,500-4,000 the pair **DRA**

A Jordan Mozer Studios LLC carved and kevlar-reinforced resin and leather prototype 'Frankie' chair, designed by Jordan Mozer (b.1958), Chicago, IL, signed.

2007 *46in (117cm) high*

£10,000-15,000 **DRA**

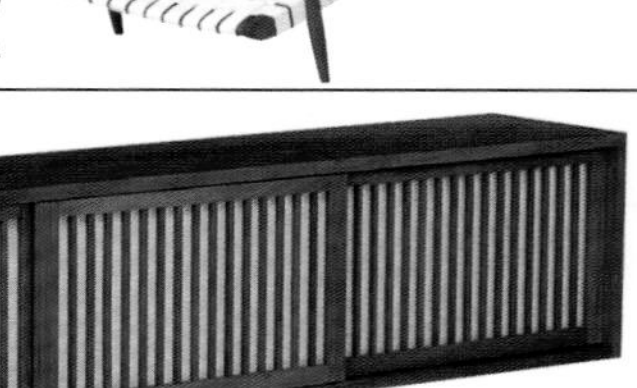

A Nakashima Studio cherry wood and webbing long chair with arm rest, by George Nakashima, unmarked, refinished, re-webbed.

1958 *66in (167.5cm) long*

£30,000-35,000 **DRA**

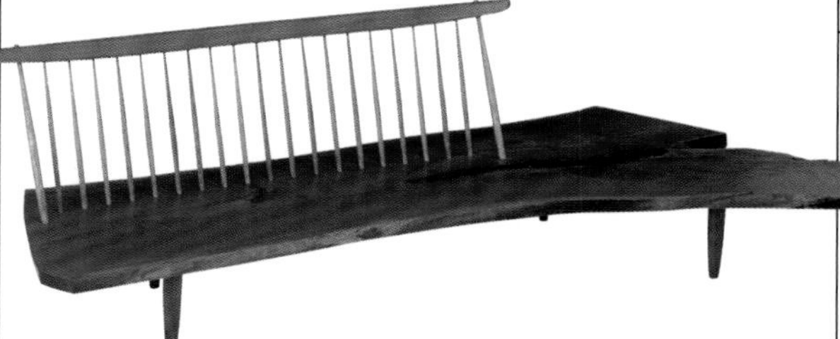

A Nakashima Studio figured walnut, hickory and rosewood 'Conoid' bench, by George Nakashima.

Provenance: Originally made for Toby Royston (1913-2009), who lived in Folly Cottage in Exton, PA. The cottage is a Frank Lloyd Wright-designed home built in the 1960s by Wright's protégé, John Howe, and Wright's son-in-law, William Wesley Peters, of Taliesin Associated Architects. It was ultimately dubbed 'Folly' due to the length and unexpected expense of the project. Royston commissioned exceptional pieces of furniture from George Nakashima to decorate the home.

100in (254cm) long

£40,000-50,000 **DRA**

A George Nakashima walnut and pandanus cloth hanging wall case, by George Nakashima, signed with client name, some scuffs, scratches and stains.

1963 *84in (213.5cm) long*

£35,000-40,000 **DRA**

A pair of 1950s Herman Miller rosewood, plastic-coated metal and aluminium 'Thin Edge' cabinets, designed by George Nelson (1908-86).

34in (86.5cm) wide

£3,000-4,000 **DRA**

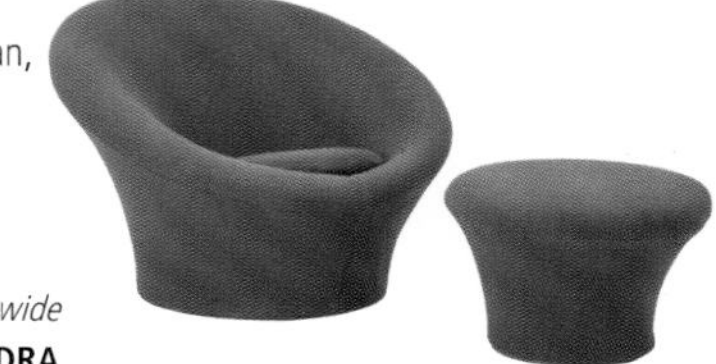

A 1970s Artifort 'Mushroom' model 560 chair and ottoman, designed by Pierre Paulin, France/Netherlands, with manufacturer's labels, some fading.

chair 36in (91.5cm) wide

£3,500-4,000 **DRA**

A Charlotte Perriand 'Shadow' chair, of 'Shuiro' coloured moulded plywood, made by Tendo Mokko.

This chair comes from a private order of six copies in this shade made in 1975.

designed 1954 24¾in (63cm) high

£55,000-65,000 **ARTC**

A late 20thC Isa rosewood, leather and vinyl 'Sheriff' chair and ottoman, designed by Sergio Rodrigues (1927-2014), replaced straps.

chair 45in (114.5cm) long

£2,000-2,500 **DRA**

ESSENTIAL REFERENCE – CHARLOTTE PERRIAND

Charlotte Perriand (1903-99) was an influential furniture designer and key figure in the Modernist movement.

- **She was born and raised in Paris, and studied at the École de l'Union Centrale des Arts Décoratifs.**
- **She worked for the designer and architect Le Corbusier from 1927 and from 1937 collaborated with the industrial designer Jean Prouvé, with whom she later designed furnishings for student accommodation at the Cité Internationale Universitaire in Paris.**
- **Throughout her life, she worked with a range of designers and architects. Her work has been displayed at numerous exhibitions.**
- **She is known for her bold designs, blunt geometric forms and versatile approach to different materials, from wood and moulded ply to anodised aluminium and melamine.**

A rare Charlotte Perriand 'House of Mexique' bookcase, of lacquered aluminium and solid wood, with lacquered 'pointe de diamant' aluminium sliding doors.

1952 72½in (184cm) wide

£85,000-95,000 **ARTC**

Judith Picks

The 'Allegro' dining suite was a landmark in post-war British furniture design. It was designed in collaboration between Neil Morris of Morris of Glasgow and Sir Basil Spence. It was awarded a diploma by the Council of Industrial Design in January 1949, and exhibited at Glasgow Today and Tomorrow and the Scottish Industries Exhibition later that year. Its manufacture process was inspired by wartime innovation. During World War II, the Southampton-based helicopter manufacturers, Cierva Autogiro, had developed techniques of laminating and shaping wood to make strong and light helicopter blades – these blades were supplied by Morris of Glasgow by 1946, and the same technology was used in creating the 'Allegro' suite. It was an incredibly expensive process. In 1950 a single chair was advertised at £31 18s 3d; the average British annual income was then just £101. As such, the furniture went into a very limited production and surviving examples are rare.

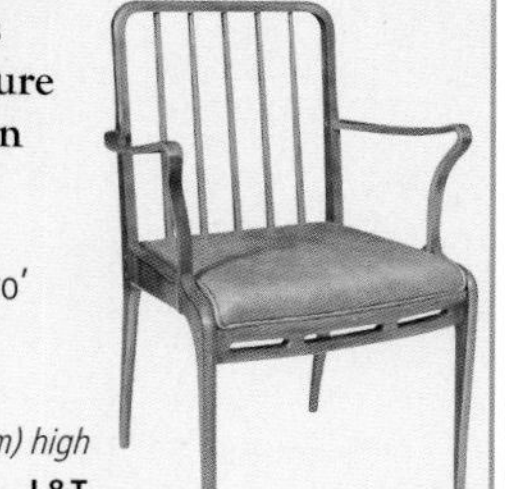

An H. Morris & Co. laminated wood 'Allegro' armchair, by Sir Basil Spence (1907-76), Glasgow, labelled.

designed 1947-48 33½in (85cm) high

£12,000-15,000 **L&T**

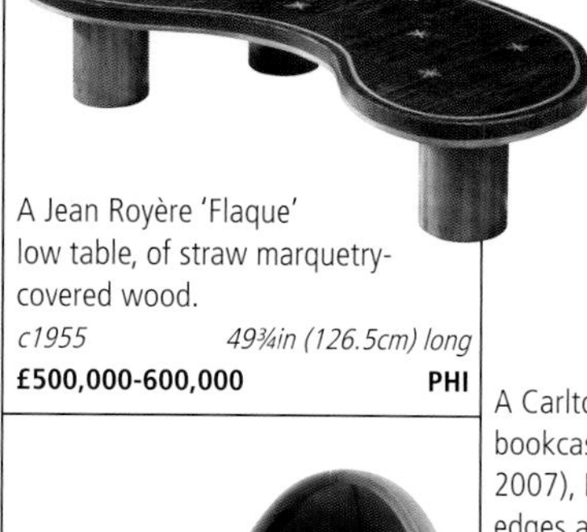

A Jean Royère 'Flaque' low table, of straw marquetry-covered wood.

c1955 49¾in (126.5cm) long

£500,000-600,000 **PHI**

A Carlton laminated wood bookcase, by Ettore Sottsass (1917-2007), Memphis, Italy, nicks to edges and corners.

1981 77¾in (197.5cm) high

£20,000-25,000 **DRA**

An 'Ovalia' fibreglass and aluminium easy chair and stool, by Henrik Thor-Larsen for Torlan, with built-in loudspeakers.

1968 chair 52in (132cm) high

£4,000-5,000 **QU**

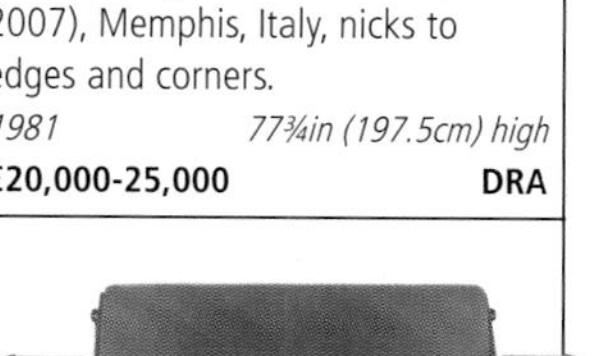

A late 1950s to early 1960s 'Wentworth' afromosia teak day bed, by Toothill, retailed by Heals, with copper piping and supports.

£2,000-2,500 **WHP**

CLOSER LOOK – 'RACKET' CHAIR

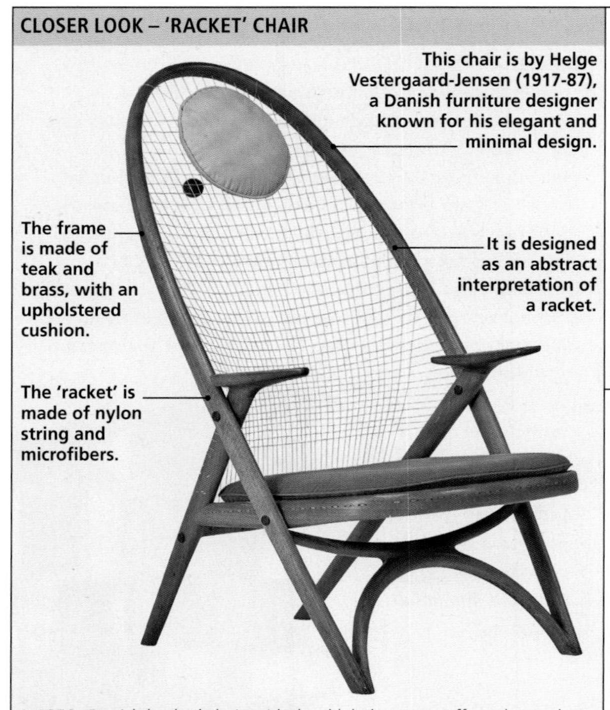

This chair is by Helge Vestergaard-Jensen (1917-87), a Danish furniture designer known for his elegant and minimal design.

The frame is made of teak and brass, with an upholstered cushion.

It is designed as an abstract interpretation of a racket.

The 'racket' is made of nylon string and microfibers.

A 1950s Danish 'racket' chair, with decal label, some scuffs and scratches, some repairs.

46in (117cm) high

£9,500-11,000 **DRA**

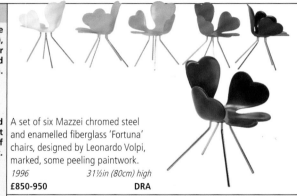

A set of six Mazzei chromed steel and enamelled fiberglass 'Fortuna' chairs, designed by Leonardo Volpi, marked, some peeling paintwork.

1996 *31½in (80cm) high*

£850-950 **DRA**

A 1960s Danish Johannes Hansen teak, chromed steel and aluminium desk, by Hans Wegner, some wear and marks.

Hans Wegner was a 20thC Danish Modernist designer. He learned woodworking as a boy, studied design in Copenhagen and worked for Erik Møller and Arne Jacobsen before establishing his own furniture studio in the early 1940s. From the late 1940s until the 1960s, he collaborated with Johannes Hansen to realise his designs.

69in (175.5cm) wide

£1,100-1,500 **DRA**

A 1960s Danish Ry Mobler teak and matt-chromed steel four-bay wall unit, designed by Hans Wegner (1914-2007), from the RY 100 series.

162½in (413cm) wide

£3,000-4,000 **DRA**

A 1960s Danish A.P. Stolen teak and upholstery 'Papa Bear' chair and ottoman, by Hans Wegner (1914-2007), minor stains.

chair 39in (99cm) high

£7,000-8,000 **DRA**

A N. Eilersen rosewood and leather 'Model No. 4' armchair, designed by Illum Wikkelso.

£350-450 **WHP**

A 1950s Danish two-door rosewood cabinet, attributed to Kai Winding, one small filled chip.

45¾in (116cm) wide

£1,000-1,500 **DRA**

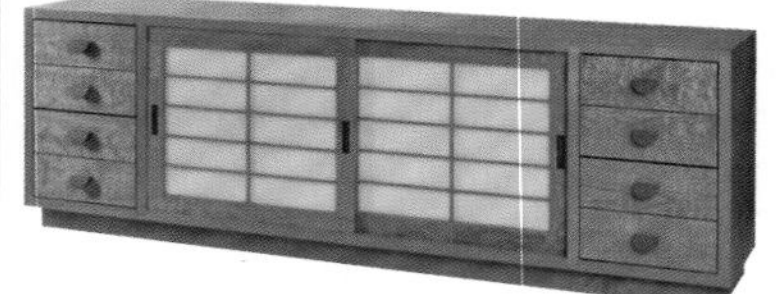

A figured maple credenza, by Craig Yamamoto, with Shoji doors.

84in (213.5cm) wide

£750-850 **POOK**

A L'Atelier 'Jacaranda' desk, designed by Jorge Zalszupin, with rosewood patchwork design.

c1960 *74¾in (190cm) wide*

£3,000-3,500 **CHOR**

A 1960s Galerie Beyeler wool and cotton tapestry, after Alexander Calder, made for Beyeler Gallery, Basle, marked 'Calder'.

80in (203cm) high

£8,500-9,500 **QU**

A Pinton Studios 'Many Triangles' wool rug, signed, by Alexander Calder (1898-1976).

81in (205.5cm) wide

£14,000-18,000 **DRA**

A 'Trilli' wool carpet, by Aappo Härkönen for Mattokutomo Oy.

1960 *93in (236cm) wide*

£1,000-1,500 **QU**

A Larsen Design Studio cotton, vinyl, nylon and polyester magnum fabric, designed by Jack Lenor Larsen (b.1927), USA.

Originally designed for the Phoenix Civic Plaza Symphony Hall curtain, this design's popularity kept it in production until 1992.

designed 1970 *193in (490cm) wide*

£1,200-1,800 **DRA**

A 1960s Danish 'Geometri' upholstery fabric, by Verner Panton (1926-98), unmarked.

£200-300 **DRA**

A Hammer Prints Ltd. 'Barkcloth' textile panel, by Nigel Henderson (1917-85) and Sir Eduardo Paolozzi (1924-2005), hand screenprinted on cotton twill, stretched on a frame.

After his return to London from Paris in 1949, Paolozzi started teaching in the textile design department of the Central School of Art and Design. He produced screenprints that were often inspired by organic forms, and paper collages that reveal his interest in abstract expressionism. In 1954 he and the artist Nigel Henderson set up Hammer Prints Ltd. to publish screenprinted textiles, ceramics and wallpapers.

c1954 *74¾in (190cm) long*

£3,000-3,500 **L&T**

A hand-tufted floor rug, by Barbara Rae RA (b.1943), depicting an Australian scene, woven by the Edinburgh Tapestry Company, Dovecot Studios, Edinburgh, signed and labelled.

c1995-97 *65in (165cm) wide*

£3,500-4,000 **SWO**

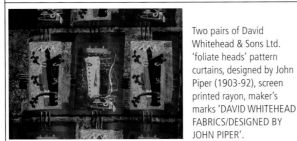

Two pairs of David Whitehead & Sons Ltd. 'foliate heads' pattern curtains, designed by John Piper (1903-92), screen printed rayon, maker's marks 'DAVID WHITEHEAD FABRICS/DESIGNED BY JOHN PIPER'.

Piper's original painting for this textile was exhibited in 'Painting into Textiles' in 1953. Foliate Heads were a favoured theme for Piper, who used them in scarf, rug and tapestry design throughout his career.

c1954 *118in (300cm) long*

£2,500-3,000 **L&T**

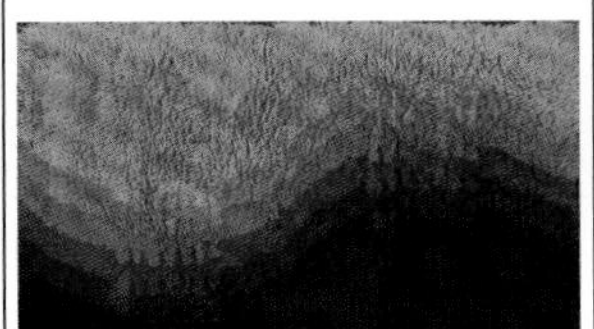

A 1960s-70s Finish Rya wool rug, with wave pattern in warm tones.

64in (162.5cm) wide

£300-350 **DRA**

A 1950s wool tapestry panel, by Marc Saint-Saëns (1903-73), depicting a cellist, signed in the tapestry 'MARC SAINT-SAËNS'.

80in (203cm) high

£600-700 **L&T**

ESSENTIAL REFERENCE – LUCIE RIE

Lucie Rie (1902-95) was one of the most important studio potters of the 20thC.

- **She was born in Vienna and studied at the Vienna Kunstgewerbeschule before setting up her own pottery in 1925.**
- **After being forced to flee Austria in 1938, she came to Britain, where she established a pottery workshop in London. She made buttons at first, later shifting focus to a range of crafted hollowware.**
- **From 1946 to 1958, the German ceramist Hans Coper (1920-81) worked alongside her. He, like her, was a refugee. He left in 1958 to set up his own studio, but the pair remained friends all their lives.**
- **She received recognition during her lifetime, being awarded the CBE in 1981 and being made a dame in 1991; but it is only recently, since 2014, that her pottery has reached the heights of price it sees today.**

A porcelain footed bowl, by Dame Lucie Rie, the rim with fluxing and running bronze glaze, impressed seal mark, flea bite to rim, overall crazing.
7in (17.5cm) diam
£40,000-50,000 **WW**

A 1970s porcelain conical bowl, by Dame Lucie Rie, with a golden manganese glaze, with sgraffito on the exterior, impressed with artist's seal.
9¼in (23.5cm) diam
£80,000-90,000 **PHI**

A stoneware bowl, by Dame Lucie Rie, raised monogram to base.
10in (25.5cm) diam
£30,000-35,000 **MJB**

A stoneware footed bowl, by Dame Lucie Rie, with yellow glaze and bronzed manganese rim, with artist's seal, faint crazing and pitting.
7in (17.5cm) diam
£25,000-30,000 **CHOR**

A porcelain bottle vase with flaring rim, by Dame Lucie Rie, incised with two bands and radiating sgraffito lines, impressed seal mark.
6in (15.5cm) high
£30,000-35,000 **WW**

A porcelain footed bowl, by Dame Lucie Rie, in a golden bronze glaze with radiating sgraffito lines, impressed seal mark.
7¾in (19.5cm) diam
£35,000-40,000 **WW**

A 'Poppy Head' stoneware vase, by Hans Coper, impressed seal mark.
11¾in (30cm) high
£50,000-60,000 **WW**

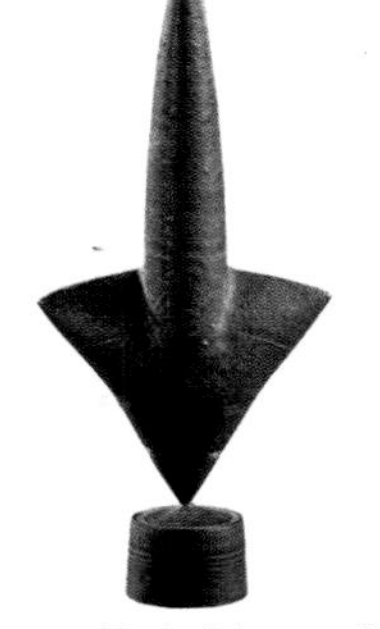

A stoneware 'Cycladic' arrow-form vase, by Hans Coper, with a black glaze, impressed with artist's seal.
1970 *9¼in (23.5cm) high*
£100,000-150,000 **PHI**

CLOSER LOOK – 'CYCLADIC' ARROWHEAD VASE

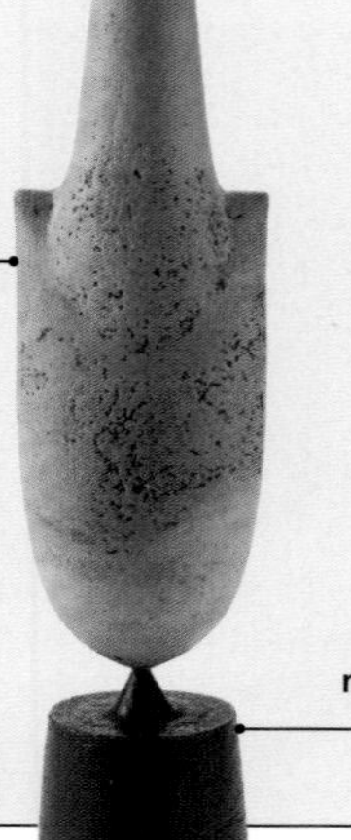

The 'Cycladic' series was made in Frome in the mid-1970s, and represents the last and most critically acclaimed of Coper's work.

Coper's 'Cycladic' arrowhead-form vases are very rare, with only four or five examples of each variation.

This vase is in the form of an arrowhead. It would have been fired in two pieces and joined later by a short metal pin.

The vase is set on a manganese base with an incised spiral.

A stoneware 'Cycladic' vase, by Hans Coper, impressed seal to underside.
12in (30.5cm) high
£400,000-500,000 **BE**

An asymmetric coil-built stoneware vase, by Jennifer Lee (b.1956), 'JL' monogram, 'Galerie Besson' label.

7in (18cm) high

£20,000-30,000 **WW**

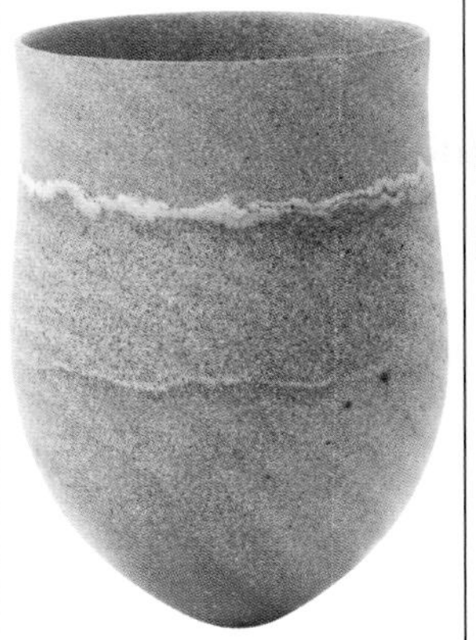

A coil-built stoneware vase, by Jennifer Lee (b.1956), 'JL' monogram, 'Galerie Besson' label.

6in (15cm) high

£10,000-14,000 **WW**

A 'Suffolk Marshes with Black Bird' vessel, by John Maltby (b.1936), signed.

14¼in (36cm) high

£4,000-5,000 **MAL**

An American lidded stoneware vessel, by Peter Voulkos (1924-2002), incised 'Voulkos'.

c1953 *16¼in (41.5cm) high*

£9,000-10,000 **DRA**

A Poole Pottery Studio vase, designed by Robert Jefferson, thrown by Guy Sydenham, printed 'Poole Studio TV' mark.

12¼in (31cm) high

£650-750 **WW**

A stoneware vase 'Winter Grasses-Opus 202', by James Tower RA (1919-88), incised 'James Tower 86', paper label 'James Tower 202'.

1986 *17¾in (45cm) high*

£30,000-35,000 **WW**

A sculptural studio pottery vase, by John Ward, with artist's seal.

c1993 *15¾in (40cm) high*

£15,000-20,000 **CA**

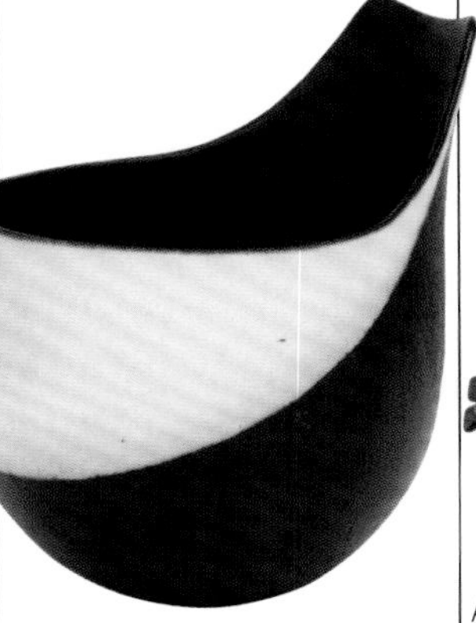

A black and white tailed stoneware bowl, by John Ward (b.1938), impressed seal mark to base.

8¼in (21cm) high

£4,000-5,000 **WW**

A Bjorn Wiinblad Studio candleabra, modelled as a horseman with three candle holders, model no.L5, the base with Wiinblad shop mark.

15in (38cm) high

£700-750 **LYN**

An Aldermaston Pottery tin-glazed charger, by Alan Caiger-Smith MBE (b.1930), painted monogram, painted date mark.
1980 *17¼in (43.5cm) diam*
£1,300-1,600 **WW**

A Jean Cocteau pottery charger, enamelled with a bull, signed 'Jean Cocteau 1957' and 'Villefranche', marked 'Edition Originale de Jean Cocteau Atelier Madeline-Jolly 3/25', with certificate of authenticity.
12¾in (32.5cm) diam
£3,000-3,500 **JDJ**

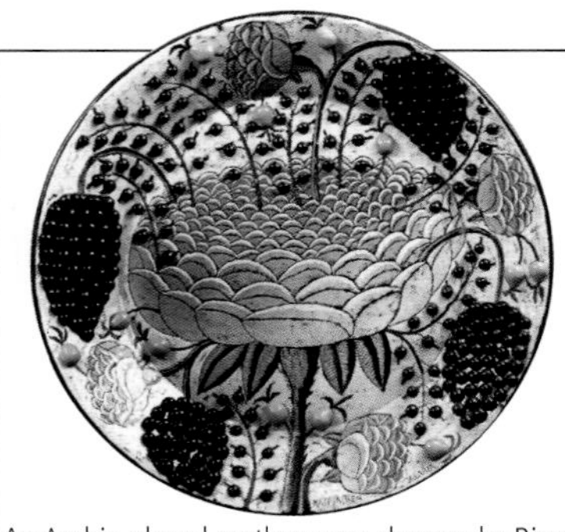

An Arabia glazed earthenware charger, by Birger Kaipiainen (1915-88), Helsinki, Finland, applied with fruit and berries, painted 'KAIPIAINEN ARABIA' mark, some crazing.
25in (63.5cm) wide
£6,500-7,500 **CHEF**

A Madoura mottled fish ('Poisson Chiné') partially glazed earthenware plate, by Pablo Picasso (1881-1973), from a limited edition of 200, impressed 'MADOURA PLEIN FEU EMPREINTE ORIGINALE DE PICASSO'.
designed 1952 *17in (43cm) wide*
£15,000-20,000 **DRA**

A Madoura 'Visages Et Hibou' ceramic pitcher, by Pablo Picasso (1881-1973), impressed marks 'Edition Picasso', 'Madoura Plein Feu'.
11in (28cm) high
£7,500-8,500 **DUK**

A Richard Parkinson Pottery model of a golfer, designed by Susan Parkinson, impressed and printed marks.
15¼in (39cm) high
£700-800 **WW**

A 1950s Poole Pottery 'Freeform' shape 698 vase, designed by Alfred Read, 'PGS' pattern, printed and painted marks.
15¼in (39cm) high
£300-350 **FLD**

A Royal Copenhagen pillow-form earthenware vase, designed by Grette Helland Hansen, design no.441, shape no.3121, with factory marks and designer's mark.
7¾in (20cm) high
£110-130 **LYN**

A rare Troika Pottery pillar vase, painted marks, artist's monogram 'AD' to base.
21½in (54.5cm) high
£2,000-2,500 **WW**

A Wedgwood 'Vorticist' vase, by Norman Wilson, shape no.4669, printed and impressed marks, impressed 'NW' monogram.
15¼in (39cm) high
£1,800-2,200 **WW**

A rare Aureliano Toso 'Frammentato' vase, designed by Dino Martens.
c1955 *7¾in (19.5cm) high*
£2,000-2,500 **FIS**

An Aureliano Toso 'Oriente' vase, by Dino Martens, with burst gold foil.
c1955 *13½in (34.5cm) high*
£4,000-5,000 **QU**

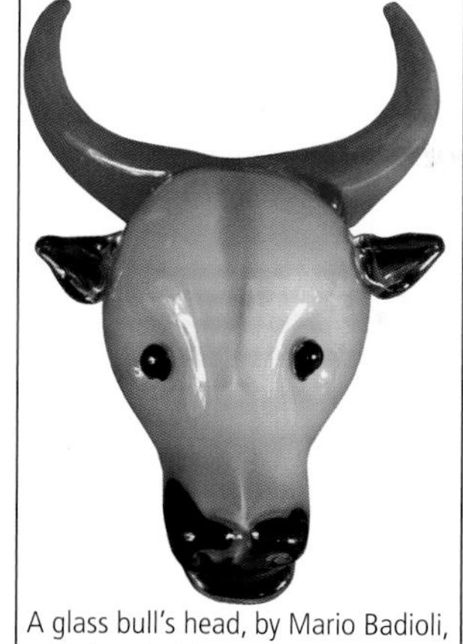

A glass bull's head, by Mario Badioli, with detachable wall bracket.
c1980 *15in (38cm) high*
£800-900 **CHEF**

A Barovier & Toso 'Tessere ambra' vase, by Ercole Barovier.
1957 *15¾in (40cm) high*
£11,000-15,000 **QU**

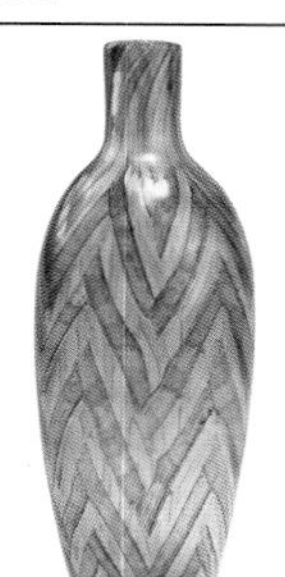

A Barovier & Toso 'A Spina' vase, by Ercole Barovier, engraved 'barovier & toso murano'.
1958 *12½in (31.5cm) high*
£8,000-9,000 **QU**

A Barovier & Toso. 'Intarsio' vase, by Ercole Barovier.
1961-63 *14in (35.5cm) high*
£9,000-11,000 **QU**

An Effetre International blown glass egg, by Lino Tagliapietra (b.1934), signed and dated.
1987 *10in (25.5cm) high*
£1,500-2,000 **DRA**

A Fratelli Toso 'Cathedral' vase, designed by Pollio Perelda, original factory label.
c1955-60 *13¾in (35cm) high*
£3,500-4,500 **FIS**

A Fucina degli Angeli dove, designed by Pablo Picasso, made by Ermanno Nason, marked 'P.Picasso-E, Costantini Fucina Angeli-PA PA 1956', with original adhesive label 'IVR MAZZEGA MURANO'.

From 1954-57, master glassblower Ermanno Nason collaborated with the Fucina degli Angeli, Murano, run by Egidio Costantini. Nason modelled designs by several artists, including Georges Braque, Marc Chagall, Pablo Picasso and Jean Cocteau.
1954 *15in (38cm) high*
£8,000-9,000 **FIS**

A Nastri blown glass vase, designed by Yoichi Ohira (b.1946), executed by Maestro Livio Serena and Maestro Giacomo Barbini, etched 'Yoichi Ohira Mo. L. Serena Mo. G. Barbini 1/1 unico Friday 4 February 2000 murano'.

Yoichi Ohira was born in Japan in 1946. He attended Tokyo's Kuwasawa Design School and graduated in 1969, then worked in Japanese glass factories before moving to Venice to study sculpture. He began working with glass in Murano in 1973 and went on to become the artistic director at Murano's de Majo Glassworks, then an independent artist and glass designer.
2000 *6½in (16.5cm) high*
£7,000-8,000 **DRA**

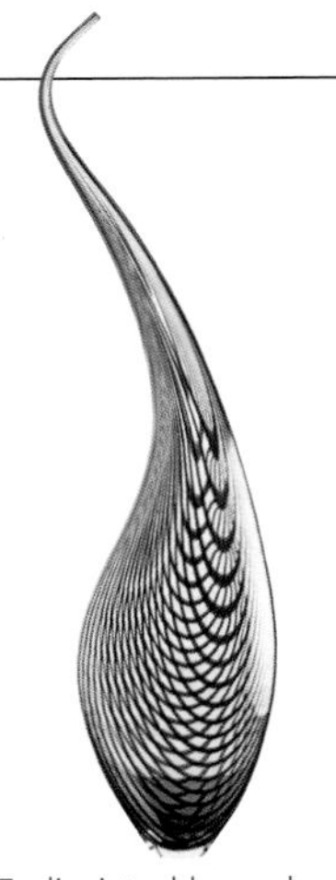

A Lino Tagliapietra blown glass dinosaur sculpture, signed and dated.

2000 *41in (104cm) high*

£15,000-20,000 DRA

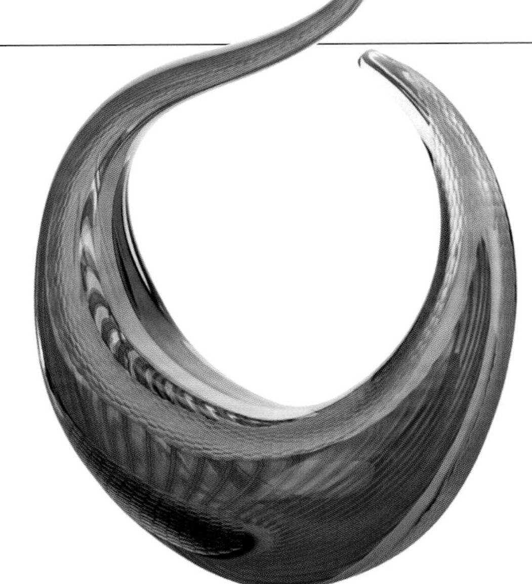

A Lino Tagliapietra blown and battuto glass sculpture, 'Fenice' (Phoenix), signed, one minor scratch, dated.

Lino Tagliapietra was born in 1934 in Murano, Italy. He was apprenticed to glass maestro Archimede Seguso at the age of twelve and by the age of 25 had been awarded the rank of maestro. Over his career, Tagliapietra has worked with many key Murano glass manufactures, such as La Murrina, Vetreria Galliano Ferro and Effetre International. From the late 1980s, he increasingly focused on studio art glass.

2005 *17in (43cm) high*

£20,000-30,000 DRA

A Venini & C. 'Pezzato' vase, by Fulvio Bianconi, acid-stamped 'venini murano ITALIA'.

c1951 *9¾in (24.5cm) high*

£6,000-7,000 QU

A Vetreria Vistosi 'Pulcino' sculpture, by Alessandro Pianon, with copper legs.

c1962 *8¼in (21cm) high*

£9,500-11,000 FLD

A Vetreria Vistosi 'Pulcino' sculpture, by Alessandro Pianon, model no.S193.

c1962 *8¾in (22.5cm) high*

£4,000-5,000 SAV

A Vetreria Vistosi 'Pulcino' sculpture, by Alessandro Pianon.

c1962 *6¾in (17cm) high*

£9,500-11,000 FLD

A Venini & C. vase, by Gianni Versace, with fused murrhines, engraved 'Venini 2000 Gianni Versace'.

c1995 *10¼in (26cm) high*

£2,500-3,000 QU

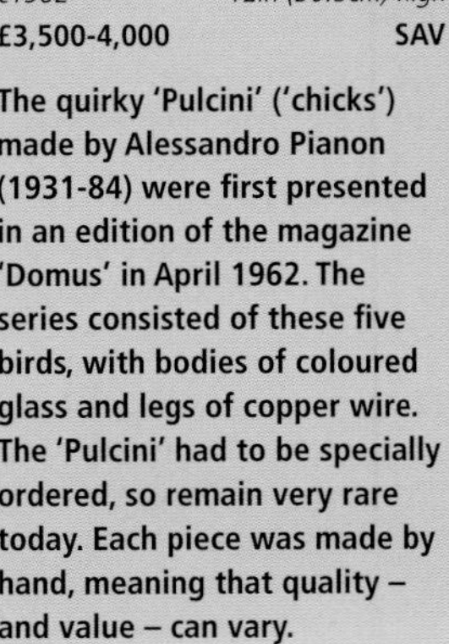

A Vetreria Vistosi 'Pulcino' sculpture, by Alessandro Pianon.

c1962 *9½in (24cm) high*

£4,000-6,000 SAV

A Vetreria Vistosi 'Pulcino' sculpture, by Alessandro Pianon, model no.S189, labelled 'VISTOSI'.

c1962 *12in (30.5cm) high*

£3,500-4,000 SAV

The quirky 'Pulcini' ('chicks') made by Alessandro Pianon (1931-84) were first presented in an edition of the magazine 'Domus' in April 1962. The series consisted of these five birds, with bodies of coloured glass and legs of copper wire. The 'Pulcini' had to be specially ordered, so remain very rare today. Each piece was made by hand, meaning that quality – and value – can vary.

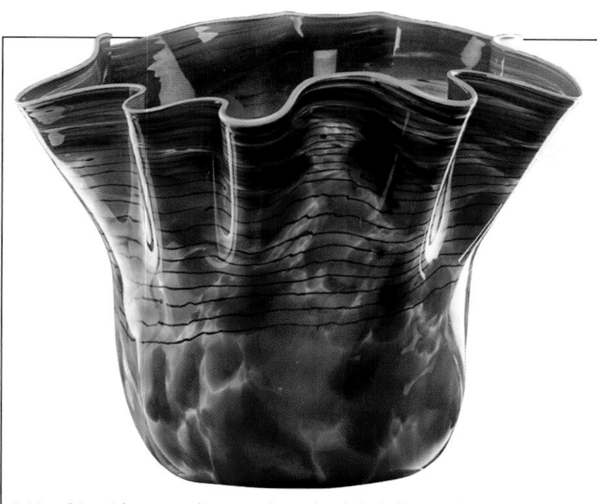

A Macchia with orange lip wrap, by Dale Chihuly (b.1941), Seattle, WA, signed and dated.

1989 *21½in (54.5cm) high*

£8,500-9,500 **DRA**

A Loco Glass sculptural glass vase, by Samuel J. Herman, signed.

Provenance: from The Private Collection Of Samuel J. Herman.

14¼in (36.5cm) high

£2,000-2,500 **DAWS**

A Lots Road sculptural attenuated bottle, by Samuel J. Herman, with applied chips, trails and silver chloride side wings, signed.

Provenance: from The Private Collection Of Samuel J. Herman. This bottle is from a series of six or seven unique bottles devised by Herman in response to his curiosity about how the glass would flow, and what the resulting form would be, if he allowed gravity to take over, in addition to hotworking the molten fluid glass in his usual manner.

c1982 *25¾in (65.5cm) high*

£1,200-1,600 **DAWS**

A Kosta 'Autumn' cased glass vase, by Vicke Lindstrand, acid mark to base, engraved 'LU 2011'.

c1954 *6½in (16.5cm) high*

£1,500-2,000 **FLD**

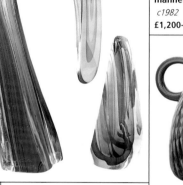

A glass sculpture, 'Blue Sliced Descending Form', by Harvey Littleton (1922-2013), signed, numbered '9-1987-2', some roughness and flakes, dated.

1987 *larger 17in (43cm) high*

£20,000-25,000 **DRA**

A blown glass 'Crazy Quilt Teapot', by Richard Marquid (b.1945), Washington State, signed, copyrighted and numbered, dated.

1979 *5½in (14cm) high*

£2,500-3,000 **DRA**

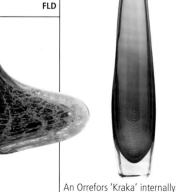

A late 1960s Mdina glass 'Crizzle Stone' vase, by Michael Harris, signed.

10¾in (27cm) wide

£3,500-4,000 **FLD**

An Orrefors 'Kraka' internally decorated glass vase, by Sven Palmquist (1906-84), signed, engraved 'S.G.A 1956 1 Pris'.

1956 *13¾in (35cm) high*

£900-1,100 **ROS**

A Whitefriars 'Textured' range prototype 'Banjo' vase lamp base, by Geoffrey Baxter, in kingfisher blue, original label.

This is a variation of the pattern 9681 vase. The piece was made as a prototype in the factory and never made it to the production stage.

13¾in (35cm) high

£1,600-2,000 **FLD**

A filet-de-verre fused and thermoformed glass thread vessel, 'Veloce', by Toots Zynsky (b.1951), Providence, RI, signed 'Z'.

2016 *10½in (26.5cm) wide*

£8,000-9,000 **DRA**

A Studio BBPR patinated brass ceiling light, designed by Gian Luigi Banfi, Ludovico Belgiojoso, Enrico Peressutti and Ernesto Nathan Rogers.
c1952 *24in (61cm) high*
£30,000-40,000 **PHI**

A 1990s welded and patinated steel chandelier, by Tom Dixon (b.1959), with three sockets.
34in (86.5cm) diam
£3,000-3,500 **DRA**

A pair of Danish Louis Poulsen enamelled aluminium PH 4/3 ceiling pendants, by Poul Henningsen, with affixed labels.
designed 1966 *10in (25.5cm) high*
£800-900 the pair **DOY**

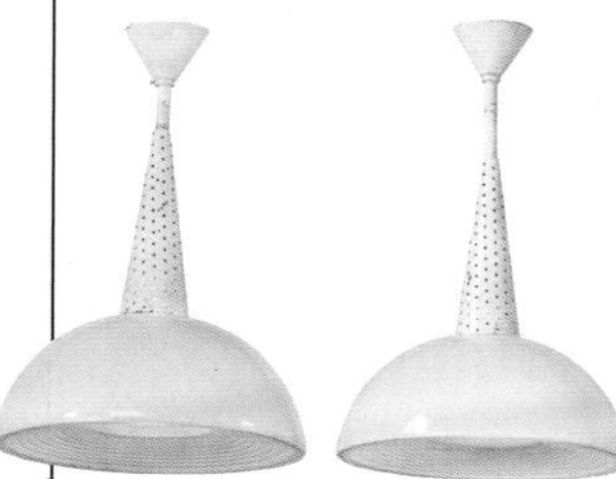

A near pair of 1950s French Holophane enamelled perforated metal and milk glass pendant lamps, by Mathieu Mategot (1910-2001), marked 'HOLOPHANE FRANCE', losses to enamel, some chips and flecks.
max 25in (63.5cm) high
£3,000-3,500 **DRA**

A 1970s Italian polished aluminium and acrylic pendant light fixture, by Gaetano Sciolari (1927-94), light oxidation.
23in (58.5cm) diam
£2,500-3,000 **DRA**

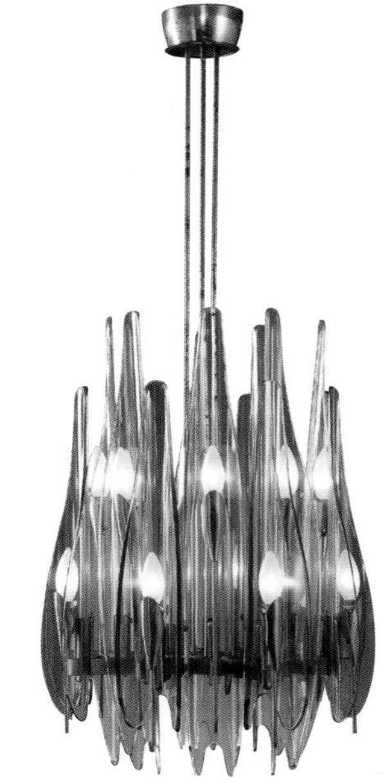

A Fontana Arte glass, brass and aluminium 'Dahlia' ceiling light, by Max Ingrand.
c1955 *18in (45.5cm) diam*
£12,000-16,000 **PHI**

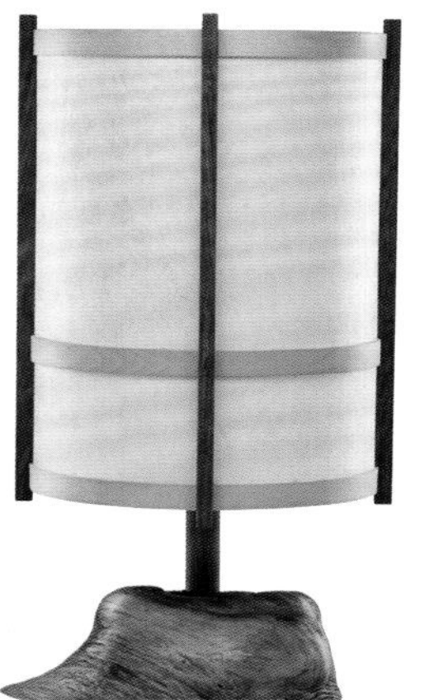

A Nakashima Studio walnut, holly and fiberglass table lamp, by George Nakashima, signed with client name, replaced shade.
1973 *29½in (75cm) high*
£11,000-15,000 **DRA**

A Lightolier tripod table lamp, by Gerald Thurston, with walnut, brass, plastic and enamelled metal base and linen shade, some stains.
c1950 *24in (61cm) high*
£850-950 **DRA**

A 1940s Finish Taito Oy brass table lamp, by Paavo Tynell (1890-1973), base stamped 'MADE IN FINLAND TAITO TT 546', with later shade, some wear.
22in (56cm) high
£2,500-3,000 **DRA**

A 1990s Italian chromed and enamelled metal and fabric floor lamp, by Mariano Fortuny Y. Madrazo (1871-1949), bulb socket and wiring missing.

78in (198cm) high

£2,500-3,000 DRA

A 1960s Swedish Luxus teak, oak, linen and brass floor lamp, by Uno Kristiansson (b.1925) and Osten Kristiansson (1927-2003), one replaced screw, replaced shade.

50in (127cm) high

£1,000-1,400 DRA

An Arredoluce nickelled brass, enamelled steel, aluminium and leather triennale floor lamp, by Angelo Lelii (1911-79), stamped 'MADE IN ITALY', some scuffs.

c1960 59½in (151cm) high

£4,500-5,000 DRA

An Arredoluce Monza brass 'Calla' floor lamp, by Angelo Lelli.

c1955 78in (198cm) high

£3,000-3,500 QU

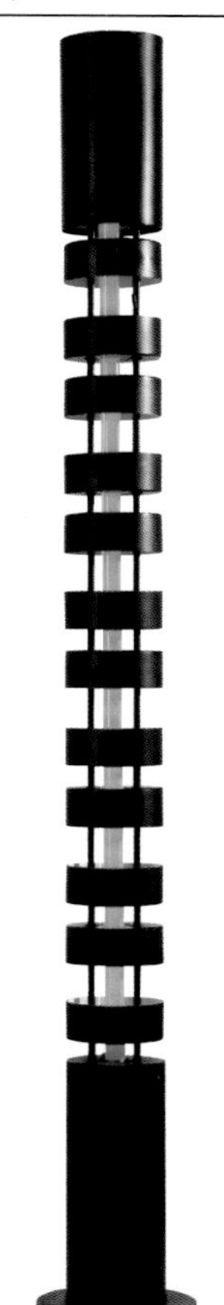

A French Société de Création de Modèles painted steel, painted aluminium and walnut 'Grand Totem' floor lamp, by Serge Mouille.

c1962 67¼in (170.5cm) high

£75,000-85,000 PHI

A set of three patinated bronze floor lamps, by Andrew Lord (b.1950), with tea-dyed papier mâché shades, signed, dated and numbered '4/10', armatures detached, wiring fraying, shades with tears.

1988 72in (183cm) high

£25,000-30,000 DRA

A French 1950s-60s carved and stained wood and enamelled iron floor lamp, in the style of Jean Rispal, some wear.

74½in (189cm) high

£1,600-2,000 DRA

A pair of 2000s enamelled metal and brass industrial-style adjustable floor lamps, with marble bases, some chips to marble.

60in (152.5cm) high

£900-1,100 DRA

A Nakashima Studio walnut and fiberglass floor lamp, by George Nakashima, some yellowing to shade.

1962 60in (152.5cm) high

£14,000-18,000 DRA

ESSENTIAL REFERENCE – STUART DEVLIN

Stuart Devlin (1931-2018) was a significant and influential modern goldsmith and silversmith.

- **He was born in Geelong, Victoria, Australia. He was the son of a painter and decorator. He studied gold and silversmithing at the Royal Melbourne Technical College and later at the Royal College of Art and Columbia University, New York.**
- **In 1963 he won a competition to design the first decimal coinage for Australia.**
- **In 1965 he opened a small workshop in Clerkenwell, London.**
- **He was awarded a CMG in 1980, granted a Royal warrant in 1982 and served as prime warden of the Goldsmiths' Company 1996-97.**
- **Rejecting the prevailing taste for Scandinavian design, Devlin focused on romanticism and ornate pieces. The Duke of Edinburgh described him as 'probably the most original and creative goldsmith and silversmith of his time.'**

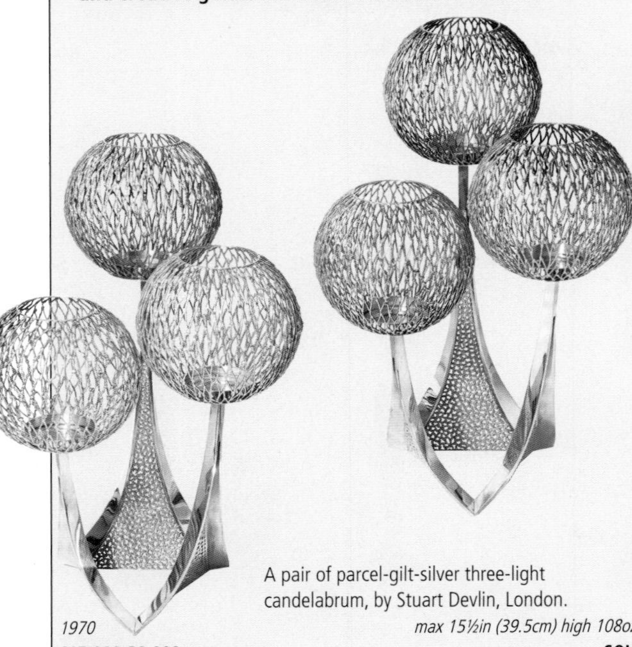

A pair of parcel-gilt-silver three-light candelabrum, by Stuart Devlin, London.
1970 *max 15½in (39.5cm) high 108oz*
£15,000-20,000 **SOU**

A parcel-gilt silver ice bucket, by Stuart Devlin, London, the lift-off cover with textured ball finial, with liner, some dings and discolouration.
1972 *6¾in (17cm) high 52¼oz*
£2,000-2,500 **TEN**

A silver-gilt 'Flower Surprise Egg', by Stuart Devlin, opening to reveal five enamelled petal flowers with leaves.
1972 *3¼in (8.5cm) high 4oz*
£450-550 **SOU**

A parcel-gilt silver rose bowl centrepiece, by Stuart Devlin, London, mounted with a silver-gilt-mounted amethyst finial.
1974 *8¾in (22.5cm) high 22oz*
£3,000-3,500 **WW**

A parcel-gilt-silver cased cylinder music box, by Stuart Devlin, the rosewood interior with a Swiss Reuge Ste Croix cylinder movement playing Tchaikovsky's Piano Concerto No.1 on a single comb.
1976 *7½in (19cm) long 43oz*
£4,000-5,000 **SOU**

A pair of Swid Powell plated 'Skyscraper' candlesticks, by Richard Meier (b.1934), stamped maker's marks 'SWID POWELL/SILVER PLATED'.
designed 1983 *9½in (24cm) high*
£400-500 **L&T**

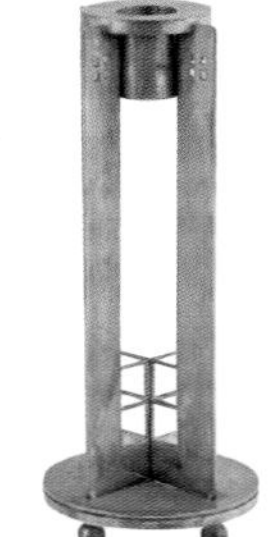

A Walker & Hall matched silver 'Pride' tea service, by David Mellor (1930-2009), Sheffield.
1959-60 teapot 5½in (14cm) high 74oz
£3,000-3,500 **L&T**

A silver and vase, by Fred Rich (b.1954), London, enamelled with four frogs amongst reeds, signed 'Fred Rich 94'.
1994 *6¼in (16cm) high 25oz*
£14,000-18,000 **WW**

A Christofle 'Como' silver-plate coffee and tea service, by Lino Sabattini (b.1925), with impressed maker's marks 'GALLIA/FRANCE/PROD. CHRISTOFLE'.
designed 1956 teapot 12in (30.5cm) high
£4,000-4,500 **L&T**

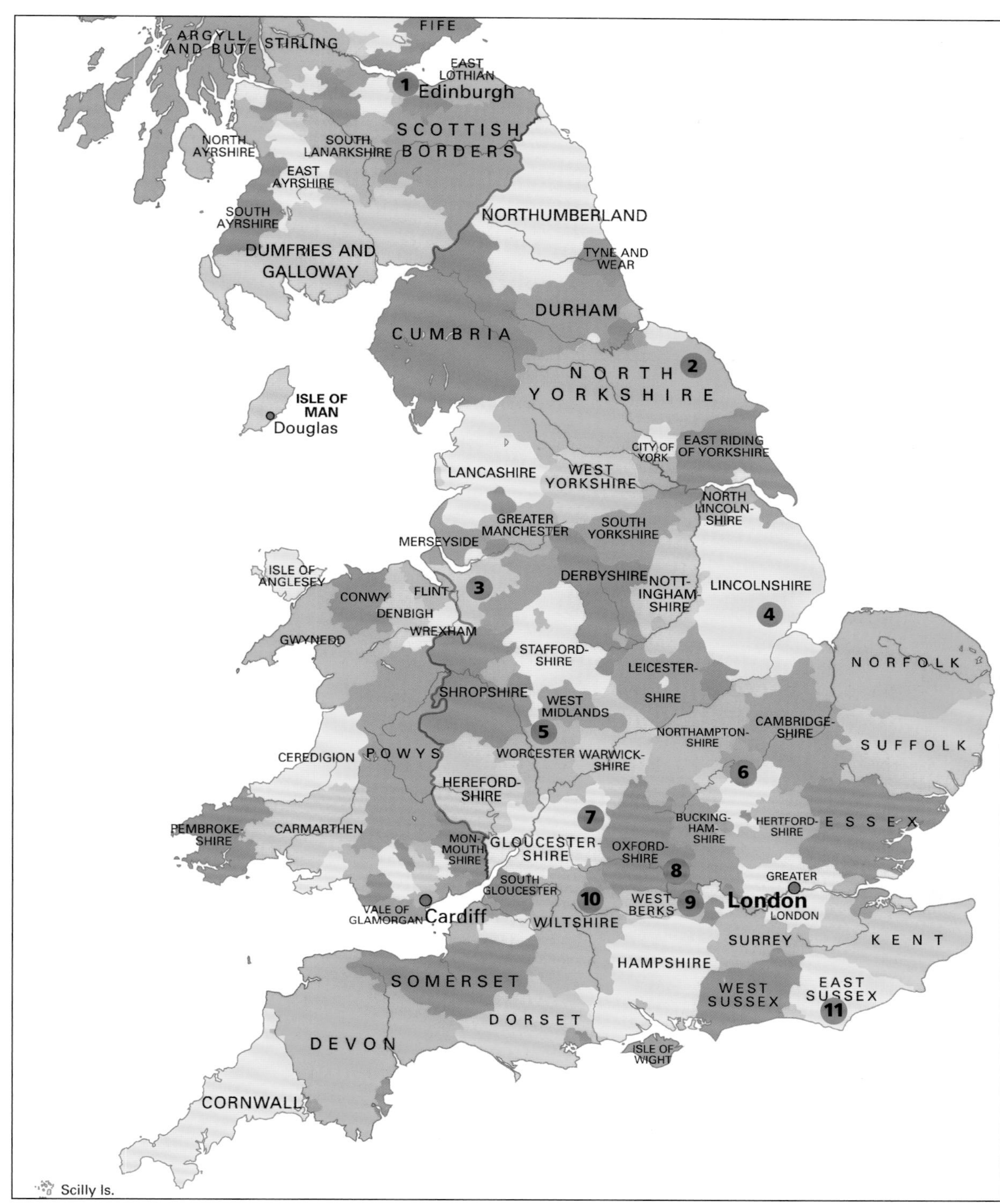

1 Lyon & Turnball, see page 116

2 Tennants, see page 586

3 Wright Marshall's, see page 586

4 Bateman's, see page 586

5 Fieldings, see page 458

6 W & H Peacock, see page 587

7 British Bespoke Auctions, see page 587

8 Jones & Jacob, see page 587

9 Dreweatts, see page 182

10 Woolley & Wallis, see page 20

11 Waddington's, see page 443

6

W&H PEACOCK
AUCTIONEERS & VALUERS
Auction Centre & Café
OPEN TO THE PUBLIC SIX DAYS A WEEK
The Auction Centre provides five spacious auction rooms, reception area, offices, meeting rooms, gallery display areas and a fully serviced restaurant, open six days a week. To further enhance the customer experience the Auction Centre has wifi and modern audio visual systems, over 200 parking spaces, excellent loading facilities and is set in landscaped surroundings.
Bedford Auction Centre
Eastcotts Park, Wallis Way, Bedford, MK42 0PE
01234 266 366 | info@peacockauction.co.uk
www.peacockauction.co.uk

7

British Bespoke
AUCTIONS
WWW.BESPOKEAUCTIONS.CO.UK

8

Jones & Jacob Ltd
Fine Art Auctioneers and Valuers
The Watcombe Manor Saleroom, Ingham Lane, Watlington, Oxfordshire
Tel: 01491 612810
Fax: 01491 614564
www.jonesandjacob.com
saleroom@jonesandjacob.com
AUCTIONEERS & VALUERS OF
ANTIQUES, FINE ART & CHATTELS

Every antique illustrated has a letter code, which identifies the dealer or auction house that sold it. The list below is a key to these codes. In the list, auction houses are shown by the letter A and dealers by the letter D.

Inclusion in this book in no way constitutes or implies a contract or a binding offer on the part of any of our contributors to supply or sell the goods illustrated, or similar items, at the prices stated.

ADA Ⓐ
ADAM'S
www.adams.ie

APAR Ⓐ
ADAM PARTRIDGE
www.adampartridge.co.uk

ARTC Ⓐ
ARTCURIAL
www.artcurial.com

AST Ⓐ
ASTON'S
www.astonsauctioneers.co.uk

B&H Ⓐ
BURSTOW & HEWETT
www.burstowandhewett.co.uk

BAM Ⓐ
BAMFORDS
www.bamfords-auctions.co.uk

BATE Ⓐ
BATEMANS
www.batemans.com

BBR Ⓐ
BBR AUCTIONS
www.onlinebbr.com

BE Ⓐ
BEARNES, HAMPTON & LITTLEWOOD
www.bhandl.co.uk

BELL Ⓐ
BELLMANS
www.bellmans.co.uk

BER Ⓐ
BERTOIA AUCTIONS
www.bertoiaauctions.com

BKA Ⓐ
BARBARA KIRK AUCTIONS
www.barbarakirkauctions.co.uk

BLEA Ⓐ
BLEASDALES
www.bleasdalesltd.co.uk

BLO Ⓐ
DREWEATTS & BLOOMSBURY
www.bloomsburyauctions.com

BOUR Ⓐ
BOURNE END AUCTION ROOMS
www.bourneendauctionrooms.co.uk

BRI Ⓐ
BRIGHTWELLS
www.brightwells.com

BRO Ⓐ
BROMPTON'S
www.bromptons.co

C&T Ⓐ
C&T AUCTIONEERS & VALUERS
www.candtauctions.co.uk

CA Ⓐ
CHISWICK AUCTIONS
www.chiswickauctions.co.uk

CAN Ⓐ
THE CANTERBURY AUCTION GALLERIES
www.thecanterburyauctiongalleries.com

CAPE Ⓐ
CAPES DUNN
www.capesdunn.com

CHEF Ⓐ
CHEFFINS
www.cheffins.co.uk

CHIL Ⓐ
CHILCOTTS
www.chilcottsauctioneers.co.uk

CHOR Ⓐ
CHORLEY'S
www.chorleys.com

CHT Ⓐ
CHARTERHOUSE
www.charterhouse-auction.com

CLAR Ⓐ
CLARS
www.clars.com

CM Ⓐ
CHARLES MILLER LTD.
www.charlesmillerltd.com

CUTW Ⓐ
CUTTLESTONES
www.cuttlestones.co.uk

DAWS Ⓐ
DAWSON'S
www.dawsonsauctions.co.uk

DEN Ⓐ
DENHAMS
www.denhams.com

DN Ⓐ
DREWEATTS & BLOOMSBURY
www.dreweatts.com

DOY Ⓐ
DOYLE
www.doyle.com

DRA Ⓐ
RAGO ARTS
www.ragoarts.com

DUK Ⓐ
DUKE'S
www.dukes-auctions.com

EBA Ⓐ
EAST BRISTOL AUCTIONS
www.eastbristol.co.uk

ECGW Ⓐ
EWBANK'S
www.ewbankauctions.co.uk

FELL Ⓐ
FELLOWS
www.fellows.co.uk

FIS Ⓐ
AUKTIONHAUS DR FISCHER
www.auctions-fischer.de

FLD Ⓐ
FIELDINGS
www.fieldingsauctioneers.co.uk

FLIN Ⓐ
FLINTS
www.flintsauctions.com

FRE Ⓐ
FREEMAN'S
www.freemansauction.com

GBA Ⓐ
GRAHAM BUDD
www.grahambuddauctions.co.uk

GHOU Ⓐ
GARDINER HOULGATE
www.gardinerhoulgate.co.uk

GKID Ⓐ
GEORGE KIDNER
www.georgekidner.co.uk

GORL Ⓐ
GORRINGE'S
www.gorringes.co.uk

GRV D
GEMMA REDMOND VINTAGE
www.gemmaredmondvintage.co.uk

GTH Ⓐ
GREENSLADE TAYLOR HUNT
www.gth.net

GWA Ⓐ
GREAT WESTERN AUCTIONS
www.greatwesternauctions.com

GYM Ⓐ
GOLDING YOUNG & MAWER
www.goldingyoung.com

H&C Ⓐ
HISTORICAL & COLLECTABLE
www.historicalandcollectable.com

HALL Ⓐ
HALLS
www.hallsgb.com/fine-art

HAN Ⓐ
HANSONS
www.hansonsauctioneers.co.uk

HANN Ⓐ
HANNAM'S
www.hannamsauctioneers.com

HOLT Ⓐ
HOLTS
www.holtsauctioneers.com
Photography: Andrew Orr

HT Ⓐ
HARTLEY'S
www.hartleysauctions.co.uk

HW Ⓐ
HOLLOWAY'S
www.hollowaysauctioneers.co.uk

JDJ Ⓐ
JAMES D. JULIA INC.
(now part of Morphy Auctions)
www.morphyauctions.com

JN Ⓐ
JOHN NICHOLSON'S
www.johnnicholsons.com

JON Ⓐ
ROGERS JONES & CO.
www.rogersjones.co.uk

K&O Ⓐ
KINGHAM & ORME
www.kinghamandorme.com

KEY Ⓐ
KEYS
www.keysauctions.co.uk

KT Ⓐ
KERRY TAYLOR AUCTIONS
www.kerrytaylorauctions.com

L&T Ⓐ
LYON & TURNBULL
www.lyonandturnbull.com

LC Ⓐ
LAWRENCES AUCTIONEERS (CREWKERNE)
www.lawrences.co.uk

LHA Ⓐ
LESLIE HINDMAN
www.lesliehindman.com

LOC Ⓐ
LOCKE & ENGLAND
www.leauction.co.uk

LOCK Ⓐ
LOCKDALES
www.lockdales.com

LOW Ⓐ
LOWESTOFT PORCELAIN AUCTIONS
www.lowestoftchina.co.uk

LSK Ⓐ
LACY SCOTT & KNIGHT
www.lsk.co.uk

LYN Ⓓ
LYNWAYS
www.lynways.com

M&DM Ⓓ
M&D MOIR
www.manddmoir.co.uk

MAB Ⓐ
MATTHEW BARTON LTD
www.matthewbartonltd.com

MAI Ⓐ
MOORE ALLEN & INNOCENT
www.mooreallen.co.uk

MAL Ⓐ
MALLAMS
www.mallams.co.uk

MART Ⓐ
MARTEL MAIDES AUCTIONS
www.martelmaidesauctions.com

MEA Ⓐ
MEALY'S (NO LONGER TRADING)
www.mealys.ie

MJB Ⓐ
MICHAEL J. BOWMAN
www.michaeljbowman.co.uk

MM Ⓐ
MULLOCK'S
www.mullocksauctions.co.uk

MOR Ⓐ
MORPHETS
www.morphets.co.uk

MORP Ⓐ
MORPHY
www.morphyauctions.com

MTZ Ⓐ
AUKTIONSHAUS METZ
www.metz-auktion.de

NA Ⓐ
NORTHEAST AUCTIONS
northeastauctions.com

PBE Ⓐ
PAUL BEIGHTON
www.pbauctioneers.co.uk

PC
PRIVATE COLLECTION

PFR Ⓐ
PETER FRANCIS
www.peterfrancis.co.uk

PHI Ⓐ
PHILLIPS
www.phillips.com

POOK Ⓐ
POOK & POOK
www.pookandpook.com

PSA Ⓐ
POTTERIES AUCTIONS
www.potteriesauctions.com

PW Ⓐ
PETER WILSON
www.peterwilson.co.uk

QU Ⓐ
QUITTENBAUM
www.quittenbaum.de

REEM Ⓐ
REEMAN DANSIE
www.reemandansie.com

RMA Ⓐ
ROB MICHIELS AUCTIONS
www.rm-auctions.com

ROCK Ⓐ
ROCK ISLAND AUCTION COMPANY
www.rockislandauction.com

ROS Ⓐ
ROSEBERYS
www.roseberys.co.uk

SAS Ⓐ
SPECIAL AUCTION SERVICES
www.specialauctionservices.com

SAV Ⓐ
STOCKHOLMS AUKTIONSVERK
www.auktionsverket.se

SHAP Ⓐ
SHAPES
www.shapesedinburgh.co.uk

SHEF Ⓐ
SHEFFIELD AUCTION GALLERY
www.sheffieldauctiongallery.com

SHP Ⓐ
SHAPIRO AUCTIONS
www.shapiroauctions.com

SK Ⓐ
SKINNER INC.
www.skinnerinc.com

SOU Ⓐ
CATHERINE SOUTHON
www.catherinesouthon.co.uk

STA Ⓐ
STACEY'S
www.staceyauction.com

SW Ⓐ
SILVERWOODS OF LANCASHIRE

SWA Ⓐ
SWANN GALLERIES
www.swanngalleries.com

SWO Ⓐ
SWORDERS
www.sworder.co.uk

T&F Ⓐ
TAYLER & FLETCHER
www.taylerandfletcher.co.uk

TDG D
THE DESIGN GALLERY
www.designgallery.co.uk

TDM Ⓐ
THOMAS DEL MAR LTD.
www.thomasdelmar.com

TEAR Ⓐ
MCTEAR'S
www.mctears.co.uk
Photography: Ken McArthur Photography

TEN Ⓐ
TENNANTS
www.tennants.co.uk

TL Ⓐ
TIMELINE AUCTIONS
www.timelineauctions.com

TOV Ⓐ
TOOVEY'S
www.tooveys.com

TRI Ⓐ
TRING MARKET AUCTIONS
www.tringmarketauctions.co.uk

TW Ⓐ
THOMAS WATSON
www.thomaswatson.com

UNI Ⓐ
UNIQUE AUCTIONS
www.unique-auctions.com

VEC Ⓐ
VECTIS
www.vectis.co.uk

W&W Ⓐ
WALLIS & WALLIS
www.wallisandwallis.co.uk

WAD Ⓐ
WADDINGTON'S, TORONTO
www.waddingtons.ca

WES Ⓐ
WESCHLER'S
www.weschlers.com

WHIT Ⓐ
WHITE'S
www.whitesauctions.com

WHP Ⓐ
W&H PEACOCK
www.peacockauction.co.uk

WHYT Ⓐ
WHYTE'S
www.whytes.ie

WM Ⓐ
WRIGHT MARSHALL
www.wrightmarshall.co.uk

WRI Ⓐ
WRIGHT
www.wright20.com

WW Ⓐ
WOOLLEY & WALLIS
www.woolleyandwallis.co.uk

This is a list of auctioneers that conduct regular sales. Auction houses that would like to be included in the next edition should email us at: info@millersguides.com

ENGLAND
LONDON
Bainbridges
www.bainbridges.auction

Baldwin's
www.baldwin.co.uk

Barnes Auctions
www.barnesauctions.com

Matthew Barton Ltd
www.matthewbartonltd.com

Bonhams
www.bonhams.com

Bromley Fine Art
www.bromleyfinearts.com

Graham Budd
www.grahambuddauctions.co.uk

The Cabinet Rooms
www.thecabinetrooms.com

Chiswick Auctions
www.chiswickauctions.co.uk

Christie's
www.christies.com

Criterion
www.criterionauctioneers.com

Dawson's
www.dawsonsauctions.co.uk

Thomas Del Mar Ltd.
www.thomasdelmar.com

Dix Noonan Webb
www.dnw.co.uk

Dreweatts & Bloomsbury
www.bloomsburyauctions.com

Fellows
www.fellows.co.uk

Forum Auctions
www.forumauctions.co.uk

Greenwich Auctions
www.greenwichauctions.co.uk

Holts
www.holtsauctioneers.com

Ingles & Hayday
www.ingleshayday.com

James Auctioneers
www.jamesauctioneers.co.uk

London Auctions
www.londonauctions.co

Lots Road Auctions
www.lotsroad.com

Charles Miller Ltd.
www.charlesmillerltd.com

Phillips
www.phillips.com

Roseberys
www.roseberys.co.uk

Sotheby's
www.sothebys.com

Southgate Auction Rooms
www.southgateauctionrooms.com

Spink
www.spink.com

Kerry Taylor Auctions
www.kerrytaylorauctions.com

Watches of Knightsbridge
www.watchesofknightsbridge.com

BEDFORDSHIRE
W&H Peacock
www.peacockauction.co.uk

Charles Ross Auctioneers
www.charles-ross.co.uk

BERKSHIRE
Berkshire Auction Rooms
www.berkshireauctionrooms.co.uk

Dawson's
www.dawsonsauctions.co.uk

Dreweatts & Bloomsbury
www.dreweatts.com

Flints
www.flintsauctions.com

Historical & Collectable
www.historicalandcollectable.com

Loddon Auctions Ltd.
www.loddonauctions.co.uk

Manor House Auctions
www.manorhouseauctions.co.uk

Martin & Pole
www.martinpole.co.uk

Special Auction Services
www.specialauctionservices.com

Thimbleby & Shorland
www.tsauction.co.uk

Windsor Auctions
www.windsorauctions.co.uk

Wokingham Auctions
www.wokinghamauctions.com

BRISTOL
Bristol Auction Rooms
www.bristolauctionrooms.co.uk

East Bristol Auctions
www.eastbristol.co.uk

Priory Auctions
www.prioryauctions.co.uk

BUCKINGHAMSHIRE
Amersham Auction Rooms
www.amershamauctionrooms.co.uk

Bourne End Auction Rooms
www.bourneendauctionrooms.co.uk

Dickins Auctioneers
www.dickinsauctioneers.com

Kings Auction Amersham
www.kingsauctionamersham.co.uk

CAMBRIDGESHIRE
Cheffins
www.cheffins.co.uk

Clifford Cross Auctions Ltd.
www.cliffordcrossauctions.co.uk

Harrison Auction Centre
www.harrisonsauctions.co.uk

Hyperion Auctions
www.hyperion-auctions.co.uk

Rowley's
www.rowleyfineart.com

Willingham Auctions
www.willinghamauctions.com

CHANNEL ISLANDS
Channel Islands Auctions
www.channelislandsauctions.com

Martel Maides Auctions
www.martelmaidesauctions.com

CHESHIRE
Adam Partridge Auctioneers & Valuers
www.adampartridge.co.uk

The Auction Centre
www.theauctioncentre.co.uk

British Toy Auctions
www.britishtoyauctions.co.uk

Byrne's
www.byrnesauctioneers.co.uk

Andrew Hilditch & Son Ltd.
www.andrewhilditchauctioneers.co.uk

Maxwells
www.maxwells-auctioneers.co.uk

Omega Auctions
www.omegaauctions.co.uk

Ashley Waller Auctioneers
www.ashleywaller.co.uk

Warrington Auction
www.warringtonauctions.co.uk

Whittaker & Biggs
www.whittakerandbiggs.co.uk

Peter Wilson
www.peterwilson.co.uk

Wright Marshall
www.wrightmarshall.co.uk

CORNWALL
Clarks Auction Rooms
www.clarksauctionrooms.com

Jefferys
www.jefferys.uk.com

Barbara Kirk Auctions
www.barbarakirkauctions.co.uk

L&M Auction House
www.landmauctions.co.uk

W.H. Lane & Son
www.whlane.auction

David Lay FRICS
www.davidlay.co.uk

Lodge & Thomas
www.lodgeandthomas.co.uk

Truro Auction Centre
www.cornwallauction.co.uk

CUMBRIA
Eighteen Eighteen Auctioneers
www.1818auctioneers.co.uk

H&H Auction Rooms
www.hhauctionrooms.co.uk

Laidlaw Auctioneers & Valuers
www.laidlawauctioneers.co.uk

Mitchells
www.mitchellsantiques.co.uk

Penrith Farmers' & Kidd's
www.pfkauctions.co.uk

Thomson Roddick Auctioneers & Valuers
www.thomsonroddick.com

DERBYSHIRE
Albion Auctions
www.albionauctions.com

Bamfords
www.bamfords-auctions.co.uk

Hansons
www.hansonsauctioneers.co.uk

DEVON
Bearnes Hampton & Littlewood
www.bhandl.co.uk

Chilcotts
www.chilcottsauctioneers.co.uk

Drake's Auctions
www.drakesauctions.co.uk

Eldreds Auctioneers & Valuers
www.eldreds.net

Kivells
www.kivells.com

Lyme Bay Auctions
www.lymebayauctions.co.uk

Michael J. Bowman
www.michaeljbowman.co.uk

Okehampton Auctions
www.okehamptonauctions.co.uk

Ottery Auction Rooms
www.otteryauctionrooms.co.uk

Piers Motley Auctions
www.piersmotleyauctions.co.uk

Pilton Auctions
www.piltonauctions.co.uk

Plymouth Auction Rooms Ltd.
www.plymouthauctions.co.uk

Potburys
www.potburysauctions.co.uk

Pyle's Auctions
www.pylesauctions.co.uk

Queens Road Auctions
www.queensroadauctions.com

Rendells
www.rendells.co.uk

West of England Auctions
www.westofenglandauctions.co.uk

Whitton & Laing Auctioneers
www.whittonandlaing auctioneers.co.uk

Whittons Auctioneers & Valuers
www.whittonsauctions.co.uk

DORSET
Bridport Auctions
www.bridportauctionhouse.com

Bulstrodes
www.bulstrodes.co.uk

Busby
www.busby.co.uk

Charterhouse
www.clarkesauctions.co.uk

Clarke's Auctioneers & Valuers
www.clarkes-auctions.co.uk

Cottees
www.cottees.co.uk

Dalkeith Auctions
www.dalkeithcatalogue.com

Duke's
www.dukes-auctions.com

Elliotts UK
www.elliottsuk.co.uk

House & Son
www.houseandson.com

Onslows
www.onslows.co.uk

Semley Auctioneers
www.semleyauctioneers.com

DURHAM
Vectis
www.vectis.co.uk

Thomas Watson
www.thomaswatson.com

ESSEX
Boningtons
www.boningtons.com

Chalkwell Auctions
www.chalkwellauctions.co.uk

Chelsford Auction Rooms
www.chelmsfordauctionrooms.co.uk

Reeman Dansie
www.reemandansie.com

Stacey's
www.staceyauction.com

Sworders
www.sworder.co.uk

TimeLine Auctions
www.timelineauctions.com

GLOUCESTERSHIRE
British Bespoke Auctions
www.bespokeauctions.co.uk

Chorley's
www.chorleys.com

The Cotswold Auction Company
www.cotswoldauction.co.uk

David Hancock & Co.
www.davidhancock-co.co.uk

Mallams
www.mallams.co.uk

Moore, Allen & Innocent
www.mooreallen.co.uk

Smiths of Newent
www.smithsnewentauctions.co.uk

Stroud Auction Rooms
www.stroudauctions.com

Tayler & Fletcher
www.taylerandfletcher.co.uk/fine-art

Dominic Winter Auctioneers
www.dominicwinter.co.uk

Wotton Auction Rooms Ltd.
www.wottonauctionrooms.co.uk

HAMPSHIRE
Angling Auctions
www.angling-auctions.co.uk

Andrew Smith & Son
www.andrewsmithandson.com

Bellmans
www.bellmans.co.uk

Hannam's
www.hannamsauctioneers.com

George Kidner
www.georgekidner.co.uk

Jacobs & Hunt
www.jacobsandhunt.com

Nesbits
www.nesbits.co.uk

Pump House Auctions
www.pumphouseauctions.co.uk

Ringwood Auctions
www.ringwoodauctions.co.uk

Toogood & May
www.mayauctioneers.co.uk

HEREFORDSHIRE
Brightwells
www.brightwells.com

John Goodwin
www.johngoodwin.co.uk

Nigel Ward & Co.
www.nigel-ward.co.uk

R.G. & R.B. Williams
www.rgandrbwilliams.co.uk

HERTFORDSHIRE
Acorn Antiques
www.acornantiques-collectables.co.uk

The Pedestal
www.thepedestal.com

Sworders
www.sworder.co.uk

Tring Market Auctions
www.tringmarketauctions.co.uk

Bushey Auctions
www.busheyauctions.com

ISLE OF MAN
Murray's
www.murrays.im

ISLE OF WIGHT
HRD Auction Rooms
www.hrdauctionrooms.co.uk

KENT
Frederick Andrews Ltd.
www.frederickandrews.uk

Bentley's Fine Art Auctioneers
www.bentleysfineartauctioneers.co.uk

C&T Auctioneers & Valuers
www.candtauctions.co.uk

The Canterbury Auction Galleries
www.thecanterburyauctiongalleries.com

Chaucer
www.chaucercollectables.co.uk

Gordon Day & Partners
www.gordondayauctions.com

Gorringe's
www.gorringes.co.uk

Grand Auctions
www.grandauctions.co.uk

Ibbet Mosely
www.ibbettmosely.co.uk

Kent Auction Galleries Ltd.
www.kentauctiongalleriesltd.co.uk

Pettmans
www.pettmans.com

Catherine Southon
www.catherinesouthon.co.uk

Sidcup Auction Rooms
www.sidcupauctions.co.uk

J. Stuart Watson
www.jstuartwatson.com

Watermans Auction Rooms
www.watermansauctionrooms.co.uk

Westenhanger Auctioneers
www.westenhangerauctioneers.com

LANCASHIRE

Bank Hall Auctions
www.bank-hall-auctions.co.uk

Capes Dunn
www.capesdunn.com

Gerrards Auction Rooms
www.gerrardsauctionrooms.com

Heliers Auctions
www.heliers.co.uk

Silverwoods of Lancashire
www.silverwoods.co.uk

Smythes Fine Art
www.smythes.net

Walton's
www.waltonandwalton.co.uk

Warren & Wignall
www.warrenandwignall.co.uk

LEICESTERSHIRE

Churchgate Auctions
www.churchgateauctions.co.uk

Gildings Auctioneers
www.gildings.co.uk

Shouler & Son
www.shoulers.co.uk

David Stanley Auctions
www.davidstanley.com

Sutton Hill Farm Country Auctions
www.suttonhillfarmcountryauctions.com

LINCOLNSHIRE

Batemans
www.batemans.com

Eddisons CJM
www.cjmasset.com

Golding Young & Mawer
www.goldingyoung.com

Jackson, Green & Preston
www.jacksongreenpreston.co.uk

Longstaff
www.longstaff.com

Perkins George Mawer & Co.
www.perkinsgeorgemawer.co.uk

Stamford Auction Rooms Ltd.
www.stamfordauctionrooms.com

John Taylors
www.johntaylors.com

Unique Auctions
www.unique-auctions.com

MANCHESTER

Bolton Auction Rooms
www.boltonauction.co.uk

Capes Dunn
www.capesdunn.com

MERSEYSIDE

Adam Partridge Auctioneers & Valuers
www.adampartridge.co.uk

Cato Crane Auctioneers
www.cato-crane.co.uk

Turner & Sons
www.turnersauctions.co

NORFOLK

Barry Hawkins
www.barryhawkins.co.uk

James Beck Auctions
www.jamesbeckauctions.co.uk

Blyths Auctioneers & Valuers
www.blyths.com

TW Gaze
www.twgaze.com

Holts
www.holtandcompany.co.uk

Horners Valuers & Auctioneers
www.horners.co.uk

James & Sons Auctioneers
www.jamesandsonsauctioneers.com

Keys
www.keysauctions.co.uk

Knights Sporting Auctions
www.knights.co.uk

Landles Auctioneers 1856 Ltd.
www.landlesauctioneers1856.co.uk

Townsend Auction Galleries
www.townsend-auctions.co.uk

NORTHAMPTONSHIRE

J.P. Humbert Auctioneers
www.jphumbert.com

Antiques 2 Go
www.antiques2go.co.uk

NORTHUMBERLAND

Alnwick Auctions
www.alnwickauctions.co.uk

Railtons
www.jimrailton.com

NOTTINGHAMSHIRE

Tim Davidson Auctions
www.timdavidsonauctions.co.uk

Arthur Johnson & Sons
www.arthurjohnson.co.uk

Mellors & Kirk
www.mellorsandkirk.com

Northgate Auction Rooms
www.northgateauctionroomsnewark.co.uk

John Pye & Sons
www.johnpye.co.uk

Scotarms
www.scotarms.co.uk

OXFORDSHIRE

Duchy Auctioneers
www.duchyauctions.com

Holloway's
www.hollowaysauctioneers.co.uk

Jones & Jacob
www.jonesandjacob.com

J.S. Auctions
www.jsauctions.co.uk

Mallams
www.mallams.co.uk

RUTLAND

Oakham Auction Centre
www.oakhamauctioncentre.co.uk

SHROPSHIRE

Brettells Auctioneers & Valuers
www.brettells.com

Halls Fine Art
www.hallsgb.com/fine-art/

Hendersons Auctions
www.hendersonsauctions.co.uk

Mullock's
www.mullocksauctions.co.uk

Nock Deighton
www.nockdeighton.co.uk/auctions

Perry & Phillips
www.perryandphillips.co.uk

Trevanion & Dean
www.trevanionanddean.com

SOMERSET

Aldridges of Bath Ltd.
www.aldridgesofbath.com

Bath Auctioneers
www.bathauctioneers.com

Clevedon Salerooms
www.clevedon-salerooms.com

Dore & Rees
www.doreandrees.co.uk

Greenslade Taylor Hunt
www.gth.net/auctions/antiques

Lawrences Auctioneers (Crewkerne)
www.lawrences.co.uk

McCubbing & Redfern
www.mccubbingandredfern.co.uk

Mendip Auction Rooms
www.mendipauctionrooms.co.uk

Tamlyns
www.tamlynsprofessional.co.uk

STAFFORDSHIRE

Bury & Hilton
www.buryandhilton.co.uk

Cuttlestones
www.cuttlestones.co.uk

Potteries Auctions
www.potteriesauctions.com

Louis Taylor Auctioneers
www.louistaylorfineart.co.uk

Richard Winterton Auctioneers Ltd.
www.richardwinterton.co.uk

SUFFOLK

Nick Barber Auctions
www.nickbarberauctions.com

Bishop & Miller
www.bishopandmillerauctions.co.uk

Clarke & Simpson
www.clarkeandsimpson.co.uk

Diamond Mills & Co.
www.diamondmills.com

Durrants
www.durrants.com

Lacy Scott & Knight
www.lskauctioncentre.co.uk

Lockdales
www.lockdales.com

Lowestoft Auction Rooms
www.lowestoftauctionrooms.com

Lowestoft Porcelain Auctions
www.lowestoftchina.co.uk

Mander
www.manderauctions.co.uk

Tony Murland Antique Tools
www.antiquetools.co.uk

SURREY

Crow's Auction Gallery
www.crowsauctions.co.uk

Ewbank's
www.ewbankauctions.co.uk

John Nicholson's
www.johnnicholsons.com

Lawrences Auctioneers Ltd.
www.lawrencesbletchingley.co.uk

Catherine Southon
www.catherinesouthon.co.uk

Sterling Vault Auctioneers
www.sterlingvault.co.uk

Wellers of Guildford
www.wellersofguildford.com

P.F. Windibank
www.windibank.co.uk

Young's Auction
www.youngsauctions.co.uk

EAST SUSSEX

Brighton General Auctions
www.brightongeneralauctions.co.uk

Burstow & Hewett
www.burstowandhewett.co.uk

Pippa Deeley Auctions
www.pippadeeley.com

Eastbourne Auctions
www.eastbourneauction.com

Falmer Auctions
www.falmerauctions.co.uk

Gorringe's
www.gorringes.co.uk

Inmans
www.inmansauctioneers.co.uk

Rosan Reeves Auctions
www.rosanreevesauctions.co.uk

Rye Auction Galleries Ltd.
www.ryeauctiongalleries.com

Tunbridge Wells Auctions Ltd.
www.tandtauctions.com

Wallis & Wallis
www.wallisandwallis.co.uk

Watsons Auctioneers
www.watsonsauctioneers.co.uk

WEST SUSSEX

Henry Adams
www.henryadamsfineart.co.uk

Bellmans
www.bellmans.co.uk

Campbells
www.campbellsauctions.co.uk

Denhams
www.denhams.com

Mid Sussex Auctions
www.mid-sussex-auctions.com

Stride & Son
www.stridesauctions.com

Summers Place Auctions
www.summersplaceauctions.com

Toovey's
www.tooveys.com

TYNE AND WEAR

Anderson & Garland
www.andersonandgarland.com

Boldon Auction Galleries
www.boldonauctions.co.uk

Corbitts
www.corbitts.com

Featonby's Auctioneers & Valuers
www.featonbys.co.uk

Jarrow Auction Rooms
www.jarrowauctions.co.uk

Thomas N. Miller
www.millersauctioneers.co.uk

WARWICKSHIRE

Bleasdales
www.bleasdalesltd.co.uk

Bigwood Fine Art Auctioneers
www.bigwoodauctioneers.co.uk

Locke & England
www.leauction.co.uk

Warwick & Warwick
www.warwickandwarwick.com

WEST MIDLANDS

Aston's Auctioneers & Valuers
www.astonsauctioneers.co.uk

Biddle & Webb
www.biddleandwebb.com

Cuttlestones
www.cuttlestones.co.uk

Fellows
www.fellows.co.uk

Fieldings
www.fieldingsauctioneers.co.uk

Sporting Memorys
www.sportingmemorys.com

Warwick Auctions of Coventry
www.warwickauctions.co.uk

WILTSHIRE

Henry Aldridge & Son
www.henry-aldridge.co.uk

Chippenham Auction Rooms
www.chippenhamauctionrooms.co.uk

Richard Edmonds Auctions Ltd
www.richardedmondsauctions.com

Harrison Auctions Ltd.
www.jubileeauctions.com

Gardiner Houlgate
www.gardinerhoulgate.co.uk

Kidson-Trigg
www.kidsontrigg.co.uk

Marlborough Auction Rooms
www.marlboroughauctionrooms.org

Netherhampton Salerooms
www.salisburyauctioncentre.co.uk

Wessex Auction Rooms
www.wessexauctionrooms.co.uk

Woolley & Wallis
www.woolleyandwallis.co.uk

WORCESTERSHIRE

GW Railwayana Auctions
www.gwra.co.uk

John Goodwin
www.johngoodwin.co.uk

Kingham & Orme
www.kinghamandorme.com

Littleton Auctions
www.littletonauctions.com

Philip Serrell
www.serrell.com

EAST YORKSHIRE

Clubleys
www.clubleys.com

Dee Atkinson & Harrison
www.dee-atkinson-harrison.co.uk

Gilbert Baitson
www.gilbert-baitson.co.uk

Hawley's Auctioneers
www.hawleys.info

NORTH YORKSHIRE

Boulton & Cooper
www.boultoncooper.co.uk

M.W. Darwin & Sons
www.darwin-homes.co.uk

David Duggleby Auctioneers & Valuers
www.davidduggleby.com

Harrogate Auction Centre
www.harrogateauctioncentre.co.uk

Hutchinson-Scott
www.hutchinsonscott.co.uk

Lithgow Sons & Partner
www.lithgowsauctions.com

Morphets
www.morphets.co.uk

Richardson & Smith
www.richardsonandsmith.co.uk

Ryedale Auctioneers
www.ryedaleauctioneers.com

Summersgills
www.summersgills.com

Tennants
www.tennants.co.uk

Thompson's Auctioneers
www.thompsonsauctioneers.com

Wombell's
www.wombells.co.uk

SOUTH YORKSHIRE

BBR Auctions
www.onlinebbr.com

Paul Beighton Auctioneers
www.pbauctioneers.co.uk

Sheffield Auction Gallery
www.sheffieldauctiongallery.com

Sheffield Railwayana Auctions
www.sheffieldrailwayana.co.uk

Wilby's
www.wilbys.net

Wilkinson's Auctioneers
www.wilkinsons-auctioneers.co.uk

WEST YORKSHIRE

Calder Valley Auctioneers
www.caldervalleyauctioneers.com

Gary Don
www.garydon.co.uk

Hartley's
www.hartleysauctions.co.uk

KLM Auctions
www.klmauctioneers.com

Shelby Auctioneers
www.shelbysauctioneers.net

SCOTLAND
Border Auctions Ltd
www.borderauctions.co.uk

Lindsay Burns
www.lindsayburns.co.uk

Thomas R. Callan
www.trcallan.com

Cluny Auctions
www.clunyauctions.co.uk

Curr & Dewar Auctioneers
www.curranddewar.com

Huntly Auctions
www.huntlyauctions.co.uk

Morris Leslie
www.morrisleslie.com

D.J. Manning Auctioneers
www.djmanning.co.uk

John Milne
www.johnmilne-auctioneers.com

Peebles Auction House
www.peeblesauctionhouse.co.uk

Robertsons of Kinbuck
www.kinbuckauctions.co.uk

L.S. Smellie & Sons Ltd.
www.hamiltonauctionmarket.com

Taylors Auction Rooms
www.taylors-auctions.com

EDINBURGH
Bonhams
www.bonhams.com

Franklin Browns
www.franklinbrowns.co.uk

Ramsay Cornish Auctioneers & Valuers
www.ramsaycornish.com

Lyon & Turnbull
www.lyonandturnbull.com

Thomson Roddick Auctioneers & Valuers
www.thomsonroddick.com

Shapes
www.shapesedinburgh.co.uk

GLASGOW
Great Western Auctions
www.greatwesternauctions.com

McTear's
www.mctears.co.uk

Mulberry Bank Auctions
www.mulberrybankauctions.com

WALES
Anthemion Auctions
www.anthemionauction.com

Cardiff City Auctions
www.cardiffcityauctions.com

McCartneys
www.mccartneys.co.uk

Morgan Evans
www.morganevans.com

Peter Francis
www.peterfrancis.co.uk

Rogers Jones & Co.
www.rogersjones.co.uk

R.W.G. Auctions
www.rwgauctions.co.uk

J. Straker Chadwick & Sons
www.jschadwick.co.uk

Wingetts
www.wingetts.co.uk

NORTHERN IRELAND
Bangor Auctions
www.bangorauctions.co.uk

Belfast Auctions
www.belfastauctions.com

Bloomfield Auctions
www.bloomfieldauctions.co.uk

McAfee Auctions
www.mcafeeauctions.com

North Coast Auction Rooms
www.northcoastauctionrooms.com

Ross's
www.rosss.com

IRELAND
Cobwebs
www.cobwebs.ie

Sean Eacrett Antiques
www.seaneacrettantiques.ie

Fonsie Mealy Auctioneers
www.fonsiemealy.ie

Lynes & Lynes
www.lynesandlynes.com

Matthews Auction Rooms
www.matthewsauctionrooms.com

Mitchell's
www.victormitchell.com

Mullen's
www.mullenslaurelpark.com

Larry O'Keeffe Auctioneers
www.larryokeeffeauctions.com

Purcell Auctioneers
www.purcellauctioneers.ie

Sheppard's
www.sheppards.ie

DUBLIN
Adam's
www.adams.ie

Danker Antiques
www.dankerantiques.com

De Veres Art Auctions
www.deveres.ie

O'Reilly's Auction Rooms 1948 Ltd.
www.oreillysfineart.com

John Weldon Auctioneers
www.jwa.ie

Whyte's
www.whytes.ie

AUSTRALIA
Bonhams & Goodman
www.bonhams.com/locations/MEL

Menzies
www.menziesartbrands.com

Leonard Joel
www.leonardjoel.com.au

Lawsons
www.lawsons.com.au

Shapiro
www.shapiroauctioneers.com.au

NEW ZEALAND
Dunbar Sloane
www.dunbarsloane.co.nz

Webb's
www.webbs.co.nz

Specialists and dealers who would like to be listed in the next edition, or have a new address or telephone number, should email us at: info@millersguides.com. Readers should contact dealers before visiting to avoid a wasted journey.

GENERAL
Alfies Antique Market
www.alfiesantiques.com

Grays Antiques Markets
www.graysantiques.com

Heritage
www.atheritage.co.uk

Otford Antiques & Collectors Centre
www.otfordantiques.co.uk

The Swan at Tetsworth
www.theswan.co.uk

ANTIQUITIES
Ancient Art
www.antiquities.co.uk

Finch & Co.
www.finch-and-co.co.uk

TimeLine Auctions
www.timelineauctions.com

ARCHITECTURAL
Nigel Bartlett
www.nigelbartlett.co.uk

Joanna Booth
www.joannabooth.co.uk

Nicholas Gifford-Mead
www.nicholasgiffordmead.co.uk

Lassco
www.lassco.co.uk

Robert Mills Ltd.
www.rmills.co.uk

Wharton Antiques
www.whartonantiques.com

ARMS & MILITARIA
Jim Bullock Militaria
www.jimbullockmilitaria.com

Thomas Del Mar Ltd.
www.thomasdelmar.com

The Old Brigade
www.theoldbrigade.co.uk

Q&C Militaria
www.qcmilitaria.com

Scotarms
www.scotarms.co.uk

Garth Vincent
www.garthvincent.com

West Street Antiques
www.antiquearmsandarmour.com

ASIAN
Laura Bordignon
laurabordignon.co.uk

Roger Bradbury
www.onlinegalleries.com/dealers/g/roger-bradbury-antiques/46036

Philip Carrol Antiques
www.philipcarrol.com

John Eskenazi Ltd.
www.john-eskenazi.com

Guest & Gray
www.chinese-porcelain-art.com

Catherine Hunt
www.cathy-hunt.co.uk

Robert McPherson Antiques
www.orientalceramics.com

Kevin Page
www.antiques-oriental.co.uk

Steve Sly
www.steveslyjapaneseart.com

S&J Stodel
www.chinesesilver.com

Van Halm & Van Halm
www.vanhalmandvanhalm.co.uk

BOOKS & MAPS
Albion Auctions
www.albionauctions.com

Altea Maps
www.alteagallery.com

George Bayntun
www.georgebayntun.com

Barter Books
www.barterbooks.co.uk

Dreweatts & Bloomsbury
www.bloomsburyauctions.com

Forum Auctions
www.forumauctions.co.uk

Dominic Winter Auctioneers
www.dominicwinter.co.uk

BOXES & TREEN
Bleasdales
www.bleasdalesltd.co.uk

J. Collins & Sons
www.collinsantiques.co.uk

Mostly Boxes
www.mostlyboxesantiques.com

CARPETS & RUGS
David Adam Lindfield Galleries
www.davidadam.co.uk

James Cohen Antique Carpets
www.jamescohencarpets.com

John Eskenazi Ltd.
www.john-eskenazi.com

Farnham Antique Carpets
www.farnhamantiquecarpets.com

Esther Fitzgerald Rare Textiles
www.estherfitzgerald.co.uk

Gideon Hatch
www.gideonhatch.co.uk

Joshua Lumley Ltd.
www.joshualumley.com

Rare Rugs
www.rarerugs.co.uk

Gallery Yacou
www.galleryyacou.com

CERAMICS
Serhat Ahmnet
www.serhatahmet.com

Alexandra Alfandary
www.finemeissen.com

Albert Amor Ltd.
www.albertamor.co.uk

Garry Atkins
www.englishpottery.com

Roy W. Bunn Antiques
www.roywbunnantiques.co.uk

Philip Carrol Antiques
www.philipcarrol.com

China Search
www.chinasearch.co.uk

Andrew Dando
www.andrewdando.co.uk

Davies Antiques
www.antique-meissen.com

Historical & Collectable
www.historicalandcollectable.com

Tony Horsley
www.tonyhorsley.co.uk

John Howard
www.antiquepottery.co.uk

Roderick Jellicoe
www.englishporcelain.com

Lynways
www.lynways.com

E & H Manners
www.europeanporcelain.com

Valerie Main
www.valeriemain.co.uk

Sue Norman
www.blueandwhitepottery
suenormanlondon.co.uk

Retroselect
www.retroselect.com

Adrian Sassoon
www.adriansassoon.com

Steppes Hill Farm Antiques
www.steppeshillfarm.com

Stockspring Ceramics Consultants
www.stockspringconsultants.co.uk

Clive Payne
www.clivepayne.co.uk

Mary Wise & Grosvenor Antiques
www.wiseantiques.com

CLOCKS, WATCHES & BAROMETERS
Campbell & Archard Ltd.
www.qualityantiqueclocks.com

Coppelia Antiques
www.coppeliaantiques.co.uk

The Clock Work Shop
www.hampshireantiqueclocks.co.uk

The Clock Clinic
www.clockclinic.co.uk

A.W. Firth Antique Restorations
www.awf-restorations.co.uk

Horological Workshops
www.horologicalworkshops.com

Kembery Antique Clocks Ltd.
www.kdclocks.co.uk

Northern Clocks
www.northernclocks.co.uk

P.A. Oxley
www.british-antiqueclocks.com

Pendulum of Mayfair
www.pendulumofmayfair.co.uk

Raffety
www.raffetyclocks.com

Somlo Antiques
www.somlo.com

Styles Antique Clocks
www.stylesantiqueclocks.co.uk

Timewise Vintage Watches
www.timewisevintagewatches.com

Richard Twort
www.barographsforsale.co.uk

Alan Walker
www.alanwalker-barometers.com

Watches of Knightsbridge
www.watchesofknightsbridge.com

Anthony Woodburn
www.anthonywoodburn.com

DECORATIVE ARTS
Beth Adams, Alfies Antiques Market
www.alfiesantiques.com

AD Antiques
www.adantiques.com

Artius Glass
www.artiusglass.co.uk

Nigel Benson
www.20thcentury-glass.org.uk

Bowman Sculpture
www.bowmansculpture.com

Vincenzo Caffarella
www.vinca.co.uk

Rupert Cavendish
www.rupertcavendish.co.uk

Central Collectables
www.centralcollectables.com

Cornishware.biz
www.cornishware.biz

The Design Gallery
www.designgallery.co.uk

Dorian Antiques
www.dorian-antiques.com

Richard Gardner Antiques
www.richardgardnerantiques.co.uk

Garret & Hurst Sculpture
www.garretandhurst.co.uk

Glass Etc.
www.decanterman.com

Halcyon Days
www.halcyondays.co.uk

Hall-Bakker
www.hall-bakker.com

Hazelhurst Antiques
www.hazlehurstantiques.com

Hickmet Fine Arts
www.hickmet.com

Richard Hoppé Antiques
www.richardhoppe.co.uk

KCS Ceramics
www.kcsceramics.co.uk

Jeroen Markies Art Deco
www.jeroenmarkies.co.uk

Francesca Martire
www.francescamartire.com

Mike & Debby Moir
www.manddmoir.co.uk

Andrew Muir
www.andrew-muir.com

Newsum Antiques
www.newsumantiques.co.uk

Red House Antiques
www.redhouseyork.co.uk

Robinson Antiques
www.robinsonantiques.co.uk

Rogers de Rin
www.rogersderin.co.uk

Rumours Decorative Arts
www.rumoursdecorativearts.co.uk

Spencer Swaffer Antiques
www.spencerswaffer.co.uk

Morgan Strickland Decorative Arts
www.morganstricklandantiques.com

Style Gallery
www.styleantiques.co.uk

Titus Omega
www.titusomega.com

Van Den Bosch
www.vandenbosch.co.uk

Mike Weedon
www.mikeweedonantiques.com

FURNITURE

Adam Antiques
www.adams-antiques.com

Anthemion
www.anthemionantiques.co.uk

Antique Oak
www.antiqueoak.co.uk

The Antiques Warehouse
www.theantiqueswarehouse.com

Baggott Church Street Ltd.
www.baggottantiques.com

David Bedale
www.davidbedale.com

John Bird Antiques
www.johnbirdantiques.com

Blanchard Collective
www.blanchardcollective.com

John Bly
www.johnbly.com

Christopher Buck Antiques
www.christopherbuck.co.uk

Mark Buckley Antiques
www.markbuckleyantiques.co.uk

Peter Bunting
www.countryoak.co.uk

Lennox Cato Antiques
www.lennoxcato.com

Thomas Coulborn & Sons
www.coulborn.com

Country Oak Antiques
www.countryoakantiques.co.uk

Cross Hayes Antiques
www.crosshayes.co.uk

Guy Dennler
www.guydennler.com

Denzil Grant
www.denzilgrant.com

Drennan & Sturrock Antiques
www.drennan-sturrock.com

Gallery 1930, Alfies Antique Market
www.alfiesantiques.com

Georgian Antiques
www.georgianantiques.net

D.J. Green Antiques
www.djgreenantiques.co.uk

W.R. Harvey & Co Ltd.
www.wrharvey.com

Keith Hockin Antiques
www.keithhockin.com

Owen Humble Antiques
www.owenhumble.co.uk/antiques.htm

Lucy Johnson
www.lucy-johnson.com

Mike Melody Antiques
www.mikemelodyantiques.com

R.N. Myers & Son Ltd.
www.myersantiques.co.uk

On-Reflection Mirrors
www.antiquemirrors.co.uk

Elaine Phillips Antiques
www.elainephillipsantiques.co.uk

W.A. Pinn & Sons
www.pinnantiques.com

Puckhaber
www.puckhaberdecorativeantiques.com

Pugh's Antiques
www.pughsantiques.com

Reindeer Antiques Ltd.
www.reindeerantiques.co.uk

Patrick Sandberg Antiques
www.antiquefurniture.net

Tim Saltwell
www.timsaltwell.co.uk

Streett Marburg
www.streettmarburg.co.uk

S&S Timms
www.timmsantiques.com

Wakelin & Linfield
www.wakelin-linfield.com

Witney Antiques
www.witneyantiques.com

Youlls Antiques
www.youllsantiques.co.uk

Robert Young Antiques
www.robertyoungantiques.com

GLASS

Adamson Antiques
www.adamsonantiques.com

Alexia Amato Antiques
www.alexiaamatoantiques.com

Bonnon's Antique Glass
www.bonnonsantiqueglass.co.uk

Delomosne & Son Ltd.
www.delomosne.co.uk

Jeanette Hayhurst Fine Glass
www.jeanettehayhurst.net

Andrew Lineham Fine Glass
www.antiquecolouredglass.com

Marris Antiques
www.marrisantiqueglass.com

Timothy Mills Antique Glass
www.antiqueglass.org.uk

JEWELLERY

Anderson Jones
www.andersonjonesltd.co.uk

N. Bloom & Son
www.nbloom.com

Cristobal, Alfies Antiques Market
www.alfiesantiques.com

Didier Antiques
www.didierltd.com

Eclectica
www.eclectica.biz

Gemma Redmond Vintage
www.gemmaredmondvintage.co.uk

Goodwins
www.goodwinsantiques.com

T. Robert
www.t-robert.com

Payne & Son
www.goldandsilverjewellery.co.uk

Plaza
www.plazajewellery.com

Scarab Antiques
www.scarabantiques.com

Shapiro & Co.
www.shapiroandco.co.uk

William Wain
www.williamwain.com

LIGHTING

Antique Textiles and Lighting
www.antiquesofbath.com

Exeter Antique Lighting Company
www.antiquelightingcompany.com

Jones Antique Lighting
www.jonesantiquelighting.com

Norfolk Decorative Antiques
www.antiquelighting.co.uk

MODERN

20th Century Marks
www.20thcenturymarks.co.uk

Ed Butcher
www.edbutcher.com

The Cabinet Rooms
www.thecabinetrooms.com

Fragile Design
www.fragiledesign.com

Francesca Martire
www.francescamartire.com

Rennies Seaside Modern
www.rennart.co.uk

The Modern Warehouse
www.themodernwarehouse.com

MUSIC

Gardiner Houlgate
www.gardinerhoulgate.co.uk

Ingles & Hayday
www.ingleshayday.com

Stephen T. P. Kember Ltd.
www.antique-musicboxes.co.uk

Turner Violins
www.turnerviolins.co.uk

POSTERS

At The Movies
www.atthemovies.co.uk

Dodo Posters
www.dodoposters.com

Limelight Movie Art
www.limelightmovieart.com

The Reel Poster Gallery
www.reelposter.com

Rennies Seaside Modern
www.rennart.co.uk

Barclay Samson Ltd.
www.barclaysamson.com

Twentieth Century Posters
www.twentiethcenturyposters.com

SCIENTIFIC INSTRUMENTS

Flints
www.flintsauctions.com

Charles Miller Ltd.
www.charlesmillerltd.com

SILVER & METALWARE

Beau Nash Bath
www.beaunashbath.com

Paul Bennett Antique Silver
www.paulbennettonline.com

Daniel Bexfield Antiques
www.bexfield.co.uk

John Bull Antiques
www.antique-silver.co.uk

Peter Cameron Antique Silver
www.petercameronantiquesilver.com

Mary Cooke Antiques Ltd.
www.marycooke.co.uk

Eastdale Antiques
www.eastdaleantiques.com

Thomas Glover
www.trivette.co.uk

Goodwins
www.goodwinsantiques.com

Highland Antiques
www.highlandantiques.com

Keith Hockin Antiques
www.keithhockin.com

Sanda Lipton
www.antique-silver.com

S&A Marsh
www.marshantiquesilver.com

Payne & Son
www.goldandsilverjewellery.co.uk

Silverman
www.silverman-london.com

Smith & Robinson
www.smithandrobinson.com

Steppes Hill Farm Antiques
www.steppeshillfarm.com

S&J Stodel
www.chinesesilver.com

Peter Szuhay
www.peterszuhay.com

Wakelin & Linfield
www.wakelin-linfield.com

William Walter Antique Silver
www.williamwalter.co.uk

SPORTING

Graham Budd
www.grahambuddauctions.co.uk

Knights Sporting Auctions
www.knights.co.uk

Loddon Auctions Ltd.
www.loddonauctions.co.uk

Manfred Schotten Antiques
www.sportantiques.co.uk

Mullock's
www.mullocksauctions.co.uk

Sporting Antiques
www.sportingantiques.co.uk

Sporting Memorys
www.sportingmemorys.com

TEXTILES

Antique Textiles and Lighting
www.antiquesofbath.com

Beyond Retro
www.beyondretro.com

Esther Fitzgerald Rare Textiles
www.estherfitzgerald.co.uk

Hiscock & Shepherd
www.ernahiscockantiques.com

Sally Hoban
www.sallyhoban.com

Modes & More
www.modesandmore.com

Rellick
www.relliklondon.co.uk

Rokit
www.rokit.co.uk

Kerry Taylor Auctions
www.kerrytaylorauctions.com

Vintage to Vogue
www.vintagetovoguebath.co.uk

Deborah Woolf
www.deborahwoolf.com

TOYS & DOLLS

Bébés et Jouets
Tel: 01289304802
Email: bebesetjouets@tiscali.co.uk

British Toy Auctions
www.britishtoyauctions.co.uk

British Doll Showcase
www.britishdollshowcase.co.uk

C&T Auctioneers & Valuers
www.candtauctions.co.uk

Collectors Old Toy Shop
www.collectorsoldtoyshop.com

Mike Delaney
www.vintagehornby.co.uk

Donay Games
www.donaygames.com

The House of Automata
www.thehouseofautomata.com

Metropolis Vintage Toys
www.metropolistoys.co.uk

Special Auction Services
www.specialauctionservices.com

Teddy Bears of Witney
www.teddybears.co.uk

Vectis
www.vectis.co.uk

Wallis & Wallis
www.wallisandwallis.co.uk

TRIBAL ART

Entwistle
www.entwistlegallery.com

Handbury Tribal Art
www.ancestorgallery.co.uk

David Malík African Art
www.davidmalikarts.com

Bryan Reeves
www.tribalgatheringlondon.com

Tribal Art Antiques
www.tribalartantiques.com

Page numbers in **bold** refer to pages with special features

INDEX